Lecture Notes in Computer Science 6876

Commenced Publication in 1973
Founding and Former Series Editors:
Gerhard Goos, Juris Hartmanis, and Jan van Leeuwen

Editorial Board

David Hutchison
  Lancaster University, UK
Takeo Kanade
  Carnegie Mellon University, Pittsburgh, PA, USA
Josef Kittler
  University of Surrey, Guildford, UK
Jon M. Kleinberg
  Cornell University, Ithaca, NY, USA
Alfred Kobsa
  University of California, Irvine, CA, USA
Friedemann Mattern
  ETH Zurich, Switzerland
John C. Mitchell
  Stanford University, CA, USA
Moni Naor
  Weizmann Institute of Science, Rehovot, Israel
Oscar Nierstrasz
  University of Bern, Switzerland
C. Pandu Rangan
  Indian Institute of Technology, Madras, India
Bernhard Steffen
  TU Dortmund University, Germany
Madhu Sudan
  Microsoft Research, Cambridge, MA, USA
Demetri Terzopoulos
  University of California, Los Angeles, CA, USA
Doug Tygar
  University of California, Berkeley, CA, USA
Gerhard Weikum
  Max Planck Institute for Informatics, Saarbruecken, Germany

Jimmy Lee (Ed.)

Principles and Practice of Constraint Programming – CP 2011

17th International Conference, CP 2011
Perugia, Italy, September 12-16, 2011
Proceedings

 Springer

Volume Editor

Jimmy Lee
The Chinese University of Hong Kong
Department of Computer Science and Engineering
Shatin, N.T., Hong Kong, China
E-mail: jlee@cse.cuhk.edu.hk

ISSN 0302-9743   e-ISSN 1611-3349
ISBN 978-3-642-23785-0   e-ISBN 978-3-642-23786-7
DOI 10.1007/978-3-642-23786-7
Springer Heidelberg Dordrecht London New York

Library of Congress Control Number: Applied for

CR Subject Classification (1998): F.4.1, F.2, F.3, G.2, F.1, E.1

LNCS Sublibrary: SL 2 – Programming and Software Engineering

Typesetting: Camera-ready by author, data conversion by Scientific Publishing Services, Chennai, India

Printed on acid-free paper

Springer is part of Springer Science+Business Media (www.springer.com)

Preface

This volume contains the proceedings of the 17th International Conference on Principles and Practice of Constraint Programming (CP 2011), held in Perugia, Italy, during September 12-16, 2011. Detailed information about the 2011 conference can be found on the conference website (http://www.dmi.unipg.it /cp2011/). We would like to thank our sponsors for their generous support in various forms for this event. Held annually, the CP conference is the premier international forum on constraint programming. The conference is concerned with all aspects of computing with constraints, including: theory, algorithms, environments, languages, models and systems, applications such as decision making, resource allocation, and agreement technologies. CP 2011 was organized by the Università degli Studi di Perugia and Dipartimento di Matematica e Informatica on behalf of the Association for Constraint Programming (ACP). Information about ACP can be found at http://www.a4cp.org/ and that of the conferences in the series can be found at http://www.a4cp.org/events/cp-conference-series.

CP 2011 included two calls for contributions: one for research papers, describing fundamental innovations in the field, and one for application papers, describing uses of constraint technology in real-life scenarios. We received a total of 159 submissions (139 to the Research Track and 20 to the Application Track). We did not differentiate between long and short submissions. They were both evaluated to the same high standard in terms of quality. In particular, no long submissions were accepted as short papers. Every paper received at least three reviews. An author rebuttal process was implemented, allowing authors to provide responses to the initial reviews of their papers. In many cases, several rounds of intense discussions among the Program Committee members in charge of the papers were carried out before final decisions were made. Where necessary, additional reviews were solicited for individual papers. There were separate Research Track and Application Track Program Committees. Eventually, 51 (37%) research papers (7 short) and 7 (35%) application papers were accepted. All papers, long and short, were presented at the main conference.

The conference program featured three invited talks by distinguished scientists: Leonardo de Moura, Laurent Perron and Jean-Charles Régin. The abstracts of the talks are included in these proceedings. Winners of the 2011 ACP Research Excellence and Doctoral Research Awards presented their award talks. In addition to regular paper presentations, the conference encompassed pre-conference workshops, tutorials, a panel and social activities.

CP 2011 continued the tradition of the CP Doctoral Program, in which PhD students presented their work, attended tutorials and discussed their work with senior researchers via a mentoring scheme. This year, the Doctoral Program received 39 submissions and selected 30 of them for financial support (2 of whom were supported in the form of an AI*IA scholarship).

The conference management system, EasyChair, made our life a lot easier from paper submission to reviewing to discussions and to producing the proceedings. We are grateful to Andrei Voronkov for providing such a nice platform to the community for free.

A successful conference is the result of hard work by many people. I thank Stefano Bistarelli, the Conference Chair, who had the huge task of planning the whole event. He and his team put in much time and effort in budgeting, logistical planning, booking, maintaining the conference website, and essentially making everything work. I thank Helmut Simonis, the Application Track Chair, for assembling the Program Committee and taking care of papers of the application track. I thank Christian Schulte, the Workshop and Tutorial Chair, for soliciting and putting together an interesting workshop and tutorial program. I thank Christopher Jefferson and Guido Tack, the Doctoral Program Chairs, for composing a fantastic program for our future generation. My applause to Ian Miguel, the Sponsorship Chair, for his relentless pursuit of various sponsorship possibilities. As usual, Helmut Simonis took great photos of the conference for our fond memories.

The conference would not have been possible without the high-quality and interesting submissions from authors, who made the decision process so challenging. I must thank all Program Committee (PC) members for their dedication over the past months. They all reviewed papers in a timely and professional manner. Of course, we could not leave out the additional reviewers recruited by our PC members. Together, these wonderful colleagues helped to assemble an excellent conference program. Pedro Meseguer was kind enough to oversee submissions from CUHK, assign PC members and make final decisions. I am also indebted to many of my "secret agents" (who should remain anonymous for obvious reasons) who offered last-minute help with additional reviews and arbitration. I would like to salute my mentors: Peter Stuckey, Ian Gent and David Cohen, who were the Program Chairs of CP 2008, 2009 and 2010, respectively. They were always good sources of advice and inspiration. Barry O'Sullivan was always there to answer my many questions.

I also acknowledge local assistance from Ivy Chau, Jingying Li, Lirong Liu, Terrence Mak, Irwin Shum, Charles Siu, May Woo and Yi Wu.

Last but not least, I would like to thank members of the Executive Committee of the Association for Constraint Programming for entrusting me with the responsibility of being the Program Chair, thus giving me an opportunity for a thriving and rewarding experience. I hope I met at least some of their expectations for CP 2011.

July 2011   Jimmy Lee

Distinguished Papers

Separate small subcommittees were formed to help decide on the papers deserving recognition as the highest standard of those submitted for each submission category.

Best Application Track Paper

"The Design of Cryptographic Substitution Boxes Using CSPs," by Venkatesh Ramamoorthy, Marius Silaghi, Toshihiro Matsui, Katsutoshi Hirayama and Makoto Yokoo

Runner-Up

"Optimal Carpet Cutting," by Andreas Schutt, Peter J. Stuckey and Andrew R. Verden

Best Research Track Paper

"On Minimal Constraint Networks," by Georg Gottlob

Best Student Paper[1]

"Octagonal Domains for Continuous Constraints," by Marie Pelleau, Charlotte Truchet and Frédéric Benhamou

---

[1] Student papers were those papers declared by the authors to be mainly the work (both in research and writing) of PhD or other students.

Workshops and Tutorials

Workshops

A range of workshops affiliated with the conference took place the day before the main conference on September 11, 2011. The accepted workshops were as follows.

- Preferences and Soft Constraints (Soft 2011)
- Local Search Techniques in Constraint Satisfaction (LSCS 2011)
- Constraint-Based Methods for Bioinformatics (WCB 2011)
- Logics for Component Configuration (Lococo 2011)
- Symmetry in Constraint Satisfaction Problems (SymCon 2011)
- Constraint Modelling and Reformulation (ModRef 2011)
- Parallel Methods for Constraint Solving (PMCS 2011)
- MiniZinc (MZN 2011)

Tutorials

Three tutorial presentations were given during the main program of the conference as follows.

- *Automatic Solver Configuration and Solver Portfolios*, by Meinolf Sellmann (IBM, USA)
- *Integer Programming for Constraint Programmers*, by Chris Beck (University of Toronto, Canada), Timo Berdhold, Ambros Gleixner, Stefan Heinz, Kati Wolter (Zuse Institute Berlin, Germany)
- *Machine Learning and Data Mining: Challenges and Opportunities for Constraint Programming*, by Luc De Raedt, Siegfried Nijssen (Katholieke Universiteit Leuven, Belgium)

Conference Organization

Program Chair

Jimmy Lee   The Chinese University of Hong Kong

Conference Chair

Stefano Bistarelli   University of Perugia, Italy

Application Track Chair

Helmut Simonis   4C, University College Cork, Ireland

Tutorial and Workshop Chair

Christian Schulte   KTH - Royal Institute of Technology in
                                             Stockholm, Sweden

Doctoral Program Chairs

Christopher Jefferson   University of St. Andrews, UK
Guido Tack   Katholieke Universiteit Leuven, Belgium

Sponsorship Chair

Ian Miguel   University of St. Andrews, UK

Organizing Committee

Marco Bottalico (Publicity)
Dario Campagna
Paola Campli (Webmaster and Graphic Design)
Alessandro Costantini
Andrea Formisano
Eleonora Gentili
Raffaella Gentilini
Massimo Giulietti
Laura Marozzi
Fernanda Panbianco
Francesco Santini (Local Sponsorship)

Sponsors

Agreement Technologies (COST Action IC0801)
Artificial Intelligence Journal
Association for Constraint Programming (ACP)
Associazione Italiana per l'Intelligenza Artificiale (AI*IA)
Comune di Assisi
Comune di Perugia
Conservatorio di Musica di Perugia Istituto di Alta Cultura
Cork Constraint Computation Centre (4C)
European Association for Theoretical Computer Science (EATCS)
Fondazione Cassa di risparmio di Perugia
IBM
Institute for Computational Sustainability (ICS)
IOS Press
Ministero degli Affari Esteri
Ministero per i beni e le attività culturali
NICTA - National Information and Communications Technology Australia
Perugina
Provincia di Perugia
PSI
Regione Umbria
Swedish Institute of Computer Science (SICS)
Springer

Program Committee (Application Track)

Laurent Michel	University of Connecticut, USA
Michela Milano	DEIS Universitá di Bologna, Italy
Barry O'Sullivan	4C, University College Cork, Ireland
Christian Schulte	KTH - Royal Institute of Technology, Sweden
Paul Shaw	IBM, France
Peter Stuckey	University of Melbourne, Australia
Mark Wallace	Monash University, Australia
Roland Yap	National University of Singapore

Program Committee (Research Track)

Fahiem Bacchus	University of Toronto, Canada
Peter van Beek	University of Waterloo, Canada
Nicolas Beldiceanu	EMN, France
Frédéric Benhamou	Nantes Atlantic Universities, France
Christian Bessiere	University of Montpellier, CNRS, France
Stefano Bistarelli	Università di Perugia, Italy
Lucas Bordeaux	Microsoft Research, Cambridge, UK

Hubie Chen — Universitat Pompeu Fabra, Spain
Dave Cohen — Royal Holloway, University of London, UK
Martin Cooper — IRIT - Université Paul Sabatier, France
Pierre Flener — Uppsala University, Sweden
Alan Frisch — University of York, UK
Simon de Givry — INRA Biometrics and Artificial Intelligence, France

Carla Gomes — Cornell University, USA
Emmanuel Hebrard — 4C, University College Cork, Ireland
Christopher Jefferson — University of St. Andrews, UK
George Katsirelos — CRIL/CNRS UMR8188, France
Zeynep Kiziltan — Università di Bologna, Italy
Arnaud Lallouet — GREYC, University of Caen, France
Javier Larrossa — Technical University of Catalonia, Spain
Yat-Chiu Law — The Chinese University of Hong Kong
Joao Marques-Silva — University College Dublin, Ireland
Pedro Meseguer — IIIA-CSIC, Spain
Laurent Michel — University of Connecticut, USA
Ian Miguel — University of St. Andrews, UK
Michela Milano — DEIS Università di Bologna, Italy
Peter Nightingale — University of St. Andrews, UK
Barry O'Sullivan — 4C, University College Cork, Ireland
Gilles Pesant — Ecole Polytechnique de Montreal, Canada
Karen Petrie — University of Dundee, Scotland
Claude-Guy Quimper — Université Laval, Canada
Emma Rollon — Technical University of Catalonia, Spain
Francesca Rossi — University of Padova, Italy
Ashish Sabharwal — IBM, USA
Thomas Schiex — INRA - UBIA, France
Christian Schulte — KTH - Royal Institute of Technology, Sweden
Meinolf Sellmann — IBM, USA
Helmut Simonis — 4C, University College Cork, Ireland
Kostas Stergiou — The University of Western Macedonia, Greece
Peter Stuckey — University of Melbourne, Australia
Guido Tack — Katholieke Universiteit Leuven, Belgium
Michael Trick — Carnegie Mellon University, USA
Pascal Van Hentenryck — Brown University, USA
Mark Wallace — Monash University, Australia
Toby Walsh — NICTA and UNSW, Australia
Roland Yap — National University of Singapore
Standa Zivny — University of Oxford, UK

Additional Reviewers

Magnus Ågren
Ozgur Akgun
Carlos Ansótegui
Alejandro Arbelaez
Gilles Audemard
Thanasis Balafoutis
Pedro Barahona
Nicolas Barnier
Anton Belov
Brandon Bennett
Thierry Benoist
Timo Berthold
Christian Blum
Manuel Bodirsky
Alessio Bonfietti
Simone Bova
Edwin Brady
Sebastian Brand
Ken Brown
Hadrien Cambazard
Paola Campli
Mats Carlsson
Roberto Castañeda
   Lozano
Martine Ceberio
Gilles Chabert
Federico Chesani
Carleton Coffrin
Remi Coletta
Jean-Francois Condotta
Paidi Creed
Victor Dalmau
Thi-Bich-Hanh Dao
Jessica Davies
Leslie De Koninck
Romuald Debruyne
Rina Dechter
Erin Delisle
Luca Di Gaspero
Ivan Dotu
Conrad Drescher
Renaud Dumeur
Ozan Erdem

Boi Faltings
Thibaut Feydy
Ian Gent
Alexandre Goldsztejn
Giorgio Gosti
Arnaud Gotlieb
Georg Gottlob
Alexandra Goultiaeva
Gianluigi Greco
Diarmuid Grimes
Patricia Gutierrez
Tarik Hadzic
Steven Halim
Martin Henz
Federico Heras
Willem-Jan van Hoeve
Mikoláš Janota
Tim Januschowski
Peter Jeavons
Serdar Kadioglu
Kalev Kask
Tom Kelsey
Frederic Koriche
Konstantinos Kotis
Lars Kotthoff
Michael Krajecki
Lukas Kroc
Philippe Laborie
Mikael Zayenz
   Lagerkvist
Katherine Lai
Ronan Le Bras
Christophe Lecoutre
Olivier Lhomme
Chavalit
   Likitvivatanavong
Michele Lombardi
Ines Lynce
Florent Madelaine
Michael Maher
Yuri Malitsky
Toni Mancini
Felip Manya

Radu Marinescu
Chris Mears
Deepak Mehta
Guillaume Melquiond
Jrme Mengin
Eric Monfroy
Marco Montali
Neil Moore
Moritz Mueller
Jean-Philippe Métivier
Nina Narodytska
Peter Nightingale
Gustav Nordh
Eoin O'Mahony
Albert Oliveras
Dario Pacino
Chris Pal
Alexandre Papadopoulos
Justin Pearson
Justyna Petke
Maria Silvia Pini
Vlad Pisanov
Cdric Pralet
Steven Prestwich
Marc Pujol-Gonzalez
Luca Pulina
Luis Quesada
Raghuram Ramanujan
Igor Razgon
Andrea Rendl
Enric Rodrguez-
   Carbonell
Jerome Rogerie
Andrea Roli
Louis-Martin Rousseau
Tyrel Russell
Pierre Régnier
Régis Sabbadin
Lakhdar Saïs
Abdelilah Sakti
Loudni Samir
Horst Samulowitz
Francesco Santini

Frdric Saubion
Pierre Schaus
Andreas Schutt
Andrew See
Laurent Simon
Charles Fai Keung Siu
Davide Sottara
David Stynes
Pavel Surynek
Stefan Szeider

Johan Thapper
Evgenij Thorstensen
Marc Thurley
Gilles Trombettoni
Charlotte Truchet
Jeremie Vautard
Nadarajen Veerapen
Gérard Verfaillie
Petr Vilím
Meritxell Vinyals

Nic Wilson
Christoph M.
    Wintersteiger
Hiu Chun Woo
Michal Wrona
Pieter Wuille
Justin Yip
Roie Zivan

Association for Constraint Programming

The Association for Constraint Programming (ACP) aims at promoting constraint programming in every aspect of the scientific world, by encouraging its theoretical and practical developments, its teaching in academic institutions, its adoption in the industrial world, and its use in applications. The ACP is a non-profit association, which uses the surplus of the organized events to support future events or activities.

The ACP is led by an Executive Committee (EC), which takes all the decisions necessary to achieve the goals of the association. In particular, the ACP EC organizes a summer school in CP and the ACP Research Excellence Award and the ACP Doctoral Research Award. The ACP EC also organizes an annual international conference on constraint programming, and decides the venue of the conference, as well as its program and conference chairs.

The ACP EC maintains a website (http://www.a4cp.org/) about all aspects of CP, and publishes a quarterly newsletter about CP events.

Executive Committee

President: Barry O'Sullivan, Ireland
Secretary: Jimmy Lee, Hong Kong
Treasurer: Thomas Schiex, France
Other Members:

- Yves Deville, Belgium
- John Hooker, USA
- Helmut Simonis, Ireland
- Peter Stuckey, Australia
- Roland Yap, Singapore

Also supporting the EC is Pedro Meseguer, Spain, acting as Conference Coordinator.

Table of Contents

Invited Talks

Application Track Papers

Research Track Papers

Orchestrating Satisfiability Engines

Leonardo de Moura

Microsoft Research, One Microsoft Way, Redmond, WA 98052, USA
leonardo@microsoft.com

Abstract. Constraint satisfaction problems arise in many diverse areas including software and hardware verification, type inference, static program analysis, test-case generation, scheduling, planning and graph problems. These areas share a common trait, they include a core component using logical formulas for describing states and transformations between them. The most well-known constraint satisfaction problem is *propositional satisfiability*, SAT, where the goal is to decide whether a formula over Boolean variables, formed using logical connectives can be made *true* by choosing *true/false* values for its variables. Some problems are more naturally described using richer languages, such as arithmetic. A supporting *theory* (of arithmetic) is then required to capture the meaning of these formulas. Solvers for such formulations are commonly called *Satisfiability Modulo Theories* (SMT) solvers.

Software analysis and model-based tools are increasingly complex and multi-faceted software systems. However, at their core is invariably a component using logical formulas for describing states and transformations between system states. In a nutshell, symbolic logic is *the calculus* of computation. The state-of-the art SMT solver, Z3, developed at Microsoft Research, can be used to check the satisfiability of logical formulas over one or more theories. SMT solvers offer a compelling match for software tools, since several common software constructs map directly into supported theories.

Z3 comprises of a collection of symbolic reasoning engines. These engines are combined to address the requirements of each application domain. In this talk, we describe the main challenges in orchestrating the different engines, and the main application domains within Microsoft.

J. Lee (Ed.): CP 2011, LNCS 6876, p. 1, 2011.
© Springer-Verlag Berlin Heidelberg 2011

Operations Research and Constraint Programming at Google

Laurent Perron

Google SA,
38 avenue de l'opéra,
75002 Paris, France

Abstract. The Operations Research and Optimization team at Google develops both general purpose optimization tools and solutions for internal optimization problems. We will describe the tools – most of which are available at http://code.google.com/p/or-tools – and present a few applications, for example in the area of assigning jobs to machines. Furthermore, we will discuss our usage of Constraint Programming in greater detail, and how it fits into the general usage of Operations Research at Google. Finally, we will also share our future plans.

J. Lee (Ed.): CP 2011, LNCS 6876, p. 2, 2011.

Solving Problems with CP: Four Common Pitfalls to Avoid

Jean-Charles Régin

Université de Nice-Sophia Antipolis, I3S UMR 6070, CNRS, France
jcregin@gmail.com

Abstract. Constraint Programming (CP) is a general technique for solving combinatorial optimization problems. Real world problems are quite complex and solving them requires to divide work into different parts. Mainly, there are: the abstraction of interesting and relevant subparts, the definition of benchmarks and design of a global model and the application of a particular search strategy. We propose to identify for each of these parts some common pitfalls and to discuss them. We will successively consider undivided model, rigid search, biased benchmarking and wrong abstraction.

1 Introduction

The resolution of real world complex problems is hard for several reasons: the size of the problem, the intrinsic difficulty of some subparts and the combination of subparts. Therefore, it requires the implementation of a complex procedure divided into several steps. We can identify four of them. First, the user has to try to abstract some parts of the problem in order to focus his attention on difficult and relevant parts, or on combinations of these parts. Then, a benchmarking process must be defined in order to be able to work on smaller instances than the whole problem. This process is needed for ensuring that the previous step abstraction and the obtained results with small problems will be generally applicable. Next, a global model must be defined. Here, we mean the method that will be used for solving the whole problem and not each part. That is, for instance, the successive resolution of each part and their combination. At last, a search strategy is defined for the most important parts.

All these different aspects are well known. However, it appears that we tend to repeat the same mistakes. Hence, we propose to try to identify some pitfalls. We will show the benefit that we can obtain by avoiding them. For each step of the resolution process, we identify one strong pitfall and try to give it a pertinent name:

- undivided model
- rigid search
- biased benchmarking
- wrong abstraction

J. Lee (Ed.): CP 2011, LNCS 6876, pp. 3–11, 2011.

The undivided model pitfall means that the global model for solving the whole problem is too much general, in other words, we could certainly improve the resolution if we split the resolution into different parts.

The rigid search expresses the idea of a search strategy which is too much linked to a depth first search procedure. We should benefit from the recent research about random restart and avoid waiting too long in a wrong part of the search tree before leaving it.

The biased benchmarking corresponds to a process which cannot be globally applicable. In other words, the obtained results for the smaller problems that are considered could not be used to derive some global rules or ideas for solving the whole problem.

The wrong abstraction defines a wrong identification of a relevant subpart of the whole problem. For instance, the subpart may not include an important constraint and be easy to solve in this context, whereas in the whole problem the introduction of the missing constraint will totally change the difficulty.

We propose to detail these fours aspects

2   Undivided Model

Complex problems usually involve the combination of some other complex problems. Thus, we have two possibilities: either we deal with the whole problem in one step, that is we integrate all the constraints and we try to solve the obtained problem, or we split the problem into different parts and then we solve the parts independently and we try to combine them. Note that the independent resolutions of the subparts may be relative. Classical MIP formulations and resolutions have nice examples of decompositions. The most well known are certainly column generation and Bender's decomposition.

We propose to emphasize this point on a well known example in CP the sports scheduling problem of the MIPLIB which is described in [10]. A more recent and nice example of decomposition can be found in [8], where a load balancing problem must be solved.

The problem consists of scheduling games between n teams over $n-1$ weeks. In addition, each week is divided into $n/2$ periods. The goal is to schedule a game for each period of every week so that the following constraints are satisfied:

1. Every team plays against every other team;
2. A team plays exactly once a week;
3. A team plays at most twice in the same period over the course of the season.

The first two constraints just define a round robin. The third one complexifies the problem.

A solution to this problem for 8 teams is shown in Figure 1. The problem can be made more uniform by adding a "dummy" final week and requesting that all teams play exactly twice in each period.

With the dummy column, the most efficient model seems to be the following one:

	Week 1	Week 2	Week 3	Week 4	Week 5	Week 6	Week 7
period 1	0 vs 1	0 vs 2	4 vs 7	3 vs 6	3 vs 7	1 vs 5	2 vs 4
period 2	2 vs 3	1 vs 7	0 vs 3	5 vs 7	1 vs 4	0 vs 6	5 vs 6
period 3	4 vs 5	3 vs 5	1 vs 6	0 vs 4	2 vs 6	2 vs 7	0 vs 7
period 4	6 vs 7	4 vs 6	2 vs 5	1 vs 2	0 vs 5	3 vs 4	1 vs 3

Fig. 1. A solution to the Sports-Scheduling Application with 8 teams

We use two classes of variables:
- team variables specifying the team playing on a given week, period and slot;
- game variables specifying which game is played on a given week and period.

The use of game variables makes it simple to state the constraint that every team must play against each other team. Since games are uniquely identified by their two teams, there are $n * (n - 1)/2$ possible values for the game variables, and by defining an alldiff constraint on the game variables we ensure that the first constraint is satisfied. Team variables and game variables are simply linked by ternary table constraints given in extension. For each slot i, a table constraint involves the variables g_i, th_i, ta_i where g_i is the game variable, th_i and ta_i the team variables of this slot. For 8 teams, it is defined by the list of tuples $< 1, 1, 2 >, < 2, 1, 3 >, ..., < 56, 7, 8 >$ where a combination $< g, t_1, t_2 >$ means that the game number g corresponds to the game t_1 vs t_2. For each week, the constraint on the week (constraint 2) is represented by an alldiff constraint involving the team variables of the week. For each period, the constraint on the period (constraint 3) is represented by a global cardinality constraint involving the team variable of the period.

We add an additional constraint for breaking symmetry: the game 0 vs w appears in week w. In addition, the search strategy is defined as follows. Teams are instantiated (that is value of team variables). We select the team which is the most instantiated and we select the team variable having this value in its domain and the smallest domain size and we assign this variable to this team value. Here are the results we obtain:

#teams	#fails	time (s)
8	32	0.08
10	417	0.8
12	41	0.2
14	3,514	9.2
16	1,112	4.2
18	8,756	36
20	72,095	338
24	6,391,470	12h

This model is a global one and it involves only one step: all the constraints are defined and we try to find a solution. The results are good but we can really improve them if we try to decompose the model. For instance, the link between rows and columns is an issue. In addition, this problem can be seen in a different way: we have to find a round robin which satisfies the period constraint. Thus, instead of trying to find a round robin and at the same time to satisfy the period constraint, we could try to decompose the problem into its two natural parts:

1. We compute a round robin, which is an easy task (i.e. a polynomial algorithm is available). This means that we satisfy the alldiff constraint on game variables and we satisfy all the constraints on team variables for each week.
2. Then, we try to rearrange the elements of each column such that the period constraint is satisfied.

In this model, symmetries are broken by setting 0 vs 1 as the first game of the dummy column. Then, rows and columns are successively instantiated. The major risk of this decomposition is that there may be no way to satisfy the period constraints for the computed round robin. In this case, another round robin should be computed and so on... Fortunately, this is not the case, as shown by the obtained results given in Figure 2.

First Model		
#teams	#fails	time (s)
8	32	0.08
10	417	0.8
12	41	0.2
14	3,514	9.2
16	1,112	4.2
18	8,756	36
20	72,095	338
24	6,391,470	12h

Second Model		
#teams	#fails	time (s)
8	10	0.01
10	24	0.6
12	58	0.2
14	21	0.2
16	182	0.6
18	263	0.9
20	226	1.2
24	2,702	10.5
26	5,683	26.4
30	11,895	138
40	2,834,754	6h

Fig. 2. The results obtained with two different models for solving sports scheduling problems

This example clearly shows that decomposition may lead to huge improvements. Note that the method we use is quite general: we precompute a solution for a part of the problem and we try to rearrange it in order to satisfy some additional constraints.

3   Rigid Search

At the beginning of CP, mainly static search strategies were considered. This means that the set of variables is ordered a priori, that is before starting the search. Then, the next assigned variable is selected w.r.t this order: the first

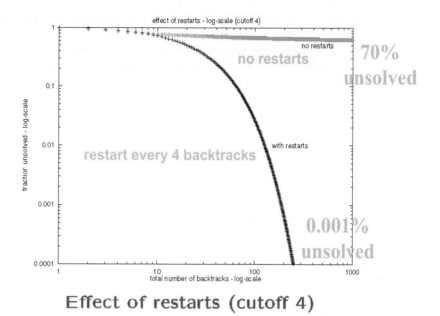

Effect of restarts (cutoff 4)

Fig. 3. Impact of restarts (published with the courtesy of C. Gomes)

non assigned variable is selected and a value is assigned to it. Then, dynamic orderings have been introduced. With dynamic orderings, the next variable to assign is computed. Generally, a criteria is defined and recomputed for each variable when a selection has to be made. The variable having the best value for this criteria is chosen as the next variable to assign. A lot of studies have been made and several orders have been proposed.

In addition, the search space is usually traversed by a depth first search.

These methods work well for a lot of problems, however they have in general a huge drawback as it has been shown by C. Gomes et al [4] who emphasized heavy tails phenomena in quasigroup completion problem.

Heavy tails phenomena have been observed by Pareto in the 1920's. A standard distribution has an exponential decay, whereas a heavy tail distribution has a power law decay. This phenomena arises in a lot of problems and in constraint programming. For instance, while trying to solve some instances of the latin square completion problem, Gomes et al. discovered that there is no ordering which is able to solve all the instances in a short period of time. About 18% of the instances remain unsolvable even with 100, 000 backtracks. Then, they proved theoretically that heavy tail phenomena may be eliminated by using a strategy for selecting the next assignment which involves some randomness and by restarting the search when the solver begins to backtrack. The idea is very nice and quite simple. Roughly, the idea can be described as follows: when selecting a variable instead of taking the one having the best score in regards to some criteria, consider the 10% best variables and randomly select one among them. This is the selection method. Now, after a certain number of backtracks, we restart the search for a solution from scratch: this is the restart method. Figure 3 shows the effect of this method.

This method performs very well in practice and has been intensively used in commercial solvers like ILOG CP. It is also used by some MIP solvers. It encourages us to be careful with too much rigid search and to accept to be less deterministic.

4 Biased Benchmarking

Identifying an interesting problem is a first step but not the only one. It is also quite important to design some benchmarks from which we could expect to derive general considerations. This part is not enough studied and may cause some problems because we have to make sure that the deduction may be still valid in general and not only for the particular instances we studied. Biased benchmarking represents the fact that the result obtained from a benchmark can be not representative of the whole problem. Biased benchmarking will prevent us from generalizing our results.

In other words, it means that benchmarks should not be too much focused on a very specific part of a more general problem. Unfortunately, this is not always the case. For instance, for the bin packing problem[1], it appears that most of the instances proposed in the literature have some major drawbacks. Gent [3] criticized the well known Falkenauer's benchmarks [2]. He closed five benchmark problems left open by cpu-intensive methods using a genetic algorithm and an exhaustive search method by using a very simple heuristic method requiring only some seconds of cpu time and hours of manual work. He questioned the underlying hardness of test data sets. One reason of the problem is the kind of data sets: most of the time, bins are filled in with only 3 items or less. Unfortunately, the same kind of data sets have been proposed by others [9,6,5]. Korf took it right up to explicitly consider triplets instances.

The issue here is not only the type of the data. It changes the kind of problem which is solved. With such data sets, we can only conclude about problems involving only few items per bins and not for the bin packing problem in general. In fact, if there are few items per bin, then the capacity constraints dominate the problems, whereas it is not the case when there are more items per bin. We can prove this by considering the set of solution of the Diophantine equation $ax + by = c$. If we consider the case where the greatest common divisor (gcd) is 1, then this equation has always a solution when $ab \geq c$ and a solution in half of the cases when $ab < c$ (from Paoli's theorem). If we consider now the equation $ax + by + cz = d$ then we have less chance to have a gcd greater than 1 and the equation is equivalent to the system $ax+by = d-c$ or $ax+by = d-2c$ or ... This means that the density of solutions increases. So, if several variables are involved, then the equation will have more chances to be satisfied. Since this equation corresponds to the sum constraint involved for each bin, this means that we

---

[1] From Wikipedia: objects of different volumes must be packed into a finite number of bins of capacity V in a way that minimizes the number of bins used.

have less and less chance to be able to filter the domains of the variables when the number of variables increases. Therefore, benchmarks for the bin packing problems should consider different types of data depending on the number of items per bin.

5   Wrong Abstraction

In general, it is difficult to identify the relevant subparts of a problem, that is the part that deserves a particular study. The wrong abstraction pitfall corresponds to the identification of a subproblem which is not relevant for the resolution of the whole problem whereas it looks interesting. This problematic has been considered by Bessiere and Régin who proposed to test first the advantage of having a constraint by using the solver before designing a new specific filtering algorithm [1]. We propose to study another example.

Consider that we have a problem in which a counting constraint, like the alldiff, is combined with arithmetic constraints. In this case, we could look at the literature, like the CSPLIB, and try to find some problems having the same type of combination. We can identify two problems: the Golomb Ruler problem and the All Interval series. At first glance, these problems look very similar.

All interval series is described as prob007 in the CSPLIB. It can be expressed as follows. Find a permutation $(x_1, ..., x_n)$ of $\{0, 1, ..., n-1\}$ such that the list $|x_2 - x_1|, |x_3 - x_2|, ..., |x_n - x_{n-1}|$ is a permutation of $\{1, 2, ..., n-1\}$.

The Golomb Ruler is the problem prob006 in the CSPLIB. It may be defined as a set of m integers $0 = a_1 < a_2 < ... < a_m$ such that the $m(m-1)/2$ differences $a_j - a_i, 1 <= i < j <= m$ are distinct. Such a ruler is said to contain m marks and is of length a_m. The objective is to find optimal (minimum length) or near optimal rulers.

As shown in [7], the All interval series may be easily solved for large values of n. For instance, the first two solutions can be found without any fail for $n = 2000$ and the $9,912$ solutions for $n = 14$ may be found with $670,000$ fails in $600s$. On the other hand, the Golomb Ruler is hard to solve for $n = 13$ where more than 20 millions of backtracks are required (see the CSPLIB comments).

In fact, these problems have a strong difference. The integration of arithmetic constraints into the alldiff constraint which models the permutation are quite different. For the All Interval series the combination is weak because arithmetic constraints involve only successive variables whereas in the Golomb Ruler all the $n(n-1)/2$ differences between variables are implied.

Therefore, if you select the wrong problem that is if you make the wrong abstraction, then you will miss the interesting part. On the other hand, if you select the right abstraction you could better understand the weakness of your CP model. For instance, the model for solving the Golomb Ruler clearly shows the weakness of the combination of symbolic (or counting) and arithmetic constraints. Figure 4 shows a part of the solution of the alldiff constraint. We can clearly see that the combination of arithmetic and counting constraints is not really taken into account. It is not consistent to assign at the same time the

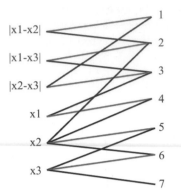

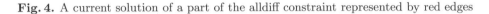

Fig. 4. A current solution of a part of the alldiff constraint represented by red edges

variables x_2 to 5, x_3 to 6 and the absolute difference $|x_2 - x_3|$ to 3. Unfortunately, we do not know any model which prevents such bad assignments. Thus, it is quite important to figure out which kind of combination is implied in your problem, that is to make the right abstraction.

6   Conclusion

In this paper, we showed and detailed four common pitfalls when solving real world problems with CP. Our goal has been to recall some principles that are usually worthwhile in practice. First, we should avoid undivided models because the decomposition of a model into different subproblems, their resolution and their recombination give often good results in practice. Second, even if we have clever strategies we should not forget that there is no ideal strategy and that we have to avoid some parts of the search quickly when there are not successful and apply principles like the random-restart mechanism. Then, we have to be careful with benchmarking and ensure that we will be able to extrapolate the results we obtained for some restricted version of the whole problem. At last, the identification of relevant subparts of the problem on which we should focus our attention is not an easy task and we should try to make the right abstraction.

References

1. Bessière, C., Régin, J.-C.: Enforcing arc consistency on global constraints by solving subproblems on the fly. In: Jaffar, J. (ed.) CP 1999. LNCS, vol. 1713, pp. 103–117. Springer, Heidelberg (1999)
2. Falkenauer, E.: A hybrid grouping genetic algorithm for bin packing. Journal of Heuristics 2, 5–30 (1996)
3. Gent, I.: Heuristic solution of open bin packing problems. Journal of Heuristics 3, 299–304 (1998)

4. Gomes, C., Selman, B., Crato, N., Kautz, H.: Heavy-tailed phenomena in satisfiability and constraint satisfaction problems. Journal of Automated Reasoning 24(1/2), 67–100 (2000)
5. Korf, R.: An improved algorithm for optimal bin packing. In: Proc. IJCAI 2003, pp. 1252–1258 (2003)
6. Martello, S., Toth, P.: Knapsack Problems. John Wiley and Sons Inc., Chichester (1990)
7. Puget, J.-F., Régin, J.-C.: Solving the all interval problem. In: Hnich, B., Miguel, I. (eds.) CSP Lib. (2001)
8. Schaus, P., Régin, J.-C., Van Hentenryck, P.: Scalable load balancing in nurse to patient assignment problems. In: CP-AI-OR 2009, pp. 233–247 (2009)
9. Scholl, A., Klein, R., Jürgens, C.: Bison: a fast hybrid procedure for exactly solving the one-dimensional bin packing problem. Computers & Operations Research 24, 627–645 (1997)
10. Van Hentenryck, P., Michel, L., Perron, L., Régin, J.-C.: Constraint programming in opl. In: Nadathur, G. (ed.) PPDP 1999. LNCS, vol. 1702, pp. 98–116. Springer, Heidelberg (1999)

A Constraint Seeker: Finding and Ranking Global Constraints from Examples

Nicolas Beldiceanu[1] and Helmut Simonis[2],[*]

[1] TASC team (INRIA/CNRS), Mines de Nantes, France
Nicolas.Beldiceanu@mines-nantes.fr
[2] Cork Constraint Computation Centre,
Department of Computer Science, University College Cork, Ireland
h.simonis@4c.ucc.ie

Abstract. In this paper we describe a Constraint Seeker application which provides a web interface to search for global constraints in the global constraint catalog, given positive and negative, fully instantiated (ground) examples. Based on the given instances the tool returns a ranked list of matching constraints, the rank indicating whether the constraint is likely to be the intended constraint of the user. We give some examples of use cases and generated output, describe the different elements of the search and ranking process, discuss the role of constraint programming in the different tools used, and provide evaluation results over the complete global constraint catalog. The Constraint Seeker is an example for the use of generic meta-data provided in the catalog to solve a specific problem.

1 Motivation

The global constraint catalog [4] provides a valuable repository of global constraint information for both researchers in the constraint field and application developers searching for the right modelling abstraction. The catalog currently describes over 350 constraints on more than 2800 pages. This wealth of information is also its main weakness. For a novice (and even for an experienced) user it can be quite challenging to find a particular constraint, unless the name in the catalog is known. As a consistent naming scheme (like the naming scheme for chemical compounds http://en.wikipedia.org/wiki/IUPAC_nomenclature, for example) does not exist in the constraint field, and different constraint systems often use incompatible names and argument orders for their constraints, there is no easy way to deduce the name of a constraint and the way its arguments are organized from its properties. The catalog already provides search by name, or by keywords, and provides extensive cross-references between constraints, as well as a classification by the required argument type. All of these access methods can be helpful, but are of limited use if one does not know too much about the constraint one is looking for.

---

[*] The second author is supported by Science Foundation Ireland (Grant Numbers 05/IN/I886 and 10/IN.1/I3032). Part of this work was created while the second author visited Nantes in 2010 sponsored by CNRS (INS2I).

J. Lee (Ed.): CP 2011, LNCS 6876, pp. 12–26, 2011.

The Constraint Seeker (http://seeker.mines-nantes.fr) provides another way of finding constraint candidates, sorted by potential relevance, in the catalog. The user provides positive and/or negative ground instances for a constraint, and the tool provides a ranked list of possible candidates which match the given examples.

The paper is structured as follows: Section 2 describes related work, Section 3 shows the use of the Constraint Seeker on an example query. Section 4 describes how candidate explanations are created, the next section discusses the ranking of candidates, followed by a discussion of instance generation. In Section 7 we show the different constraint solvers in the system, before evaluating the Seeker in section 8. We close with a summary and description of future work, which discusses the role of meta-data for this work.

2 Related Work

Our Constraint Seeker is related to a number of other systems, and, more fundamentally, to a strand of research in constraints.

2.1 Integer Sequences

A key motivation for developing the Constraint Seeker was the example of an interactive website http://oeis.org/Seis.html for Integer Sequences [22]. In this tool, the user can enter a sequence of integer values, and the search tool will return a list of those integer sequences in its library which seem to match that sequence, either as a prefix, or as a subset of the values. Candidates are ranked by similarity to the example given, for example a prefix is considered more similar than a subset matching.

2.2 Constraint Taxonomy

Taxonomies (structure/sub-structure relations) are often used to give access to large collections of information, and form the basis of many on-line information retrieval systems. Unfortunately, there has been rather little work on providing a taxonomy of different constraints. A taxonomy considering only difference and equality is proposed in [15], while a taxonomy of the global constraints in the CHIP system was given in [21].

2.3 Library Seeker

Library search tools for programming languages typically allow search by name and by a taxonomy of intended function. A search tool for CamlLight [26] at http://www.dicosmo.org/TESTS/ENGLISH/CamlSearchCGI.english.html also provides lookup by type. One can enter a type specification for a library function, and the system should return all library functions with isomorphic types.[1]

Using the signature of the constraint is an important element of our Constraint Seeker, as it allows to restrict the search to a relatively small subset of the complete catalog, while at the same time not requiring to guess the complete signature of the constraint.

---

[1] The system seems to be no longer operational.

2.4   Electronic Symbol Catalog

The interactive **Electrical What** catalog http://electricalwhat.com/ gives another example of a search tool, where just searching by name is not sufficient. The catalog lists images of electronic symbols, and the user can search by category (transistor, diode, etc), but also by structural properties of the symbol (how many connections, major symbol a circle, a rectangle or a triangle, etc). This is required by a use case where a novice sees a new symbol, but does not know what it stands for. This is quite similar to our use case of encountering a constraint, and describing its properties, instead of searching for it by name.

2.5   Constraint Acquisition

Constraint Acquisition [17] is the process of finding a constraint network from a training set of positive and negative examples. The learning process operates on a library of allowed constraints, and a resulting solution is a conjunction of constraints from that library, each constraint ranging over a subset of the variables.

This area of research has attracted a fair bit of work over the last ten years [8,24,6,16,5,14,7,13,18,20,19]. A key idea for solving this problem is the use of version space learning from AI, which considers the set of all possible constraint networks which accept the training set.

In an interactive setting, the training set is not fixed, but will be derived incrementally. If the target model has not been identified, the system may suggest new training instances, which the user has to classify as either positive or negative. Ideally, these new examples are chosen to maximally reduce the version space that needs to be considered.

One of the challenges of constraint acquisition for a library of global constraints is that many global constraints have additional parameters which might not occur in the examples given, which only list the main decision variables describing the problem. The values of these parameters must be learned from the examples as well, this is considered in [9,10].

Another issue is that in constraint acquisition we don't know over which subset of the decision variables a constraint will be expressed. When we consider only binary constraints, this does not matter, we can explore all binary combinations of variables in quadratic time. For a global constraint with k variables which ranges over a subset of n decision variables, we are faced with a combinatorial explosion, especially if the order of the variables in the constraint matters.

Our problem of the Constraint Seeker is closely related to the constraint acquisition problem, but subtly different. We are not looking for a model of a complete constraint problem, we are searching for a single constraint in the global constraint catalog. It means that we know the variables over which the constraint ranges, as well as their order in a collection, and we assume that most (but not necessarily all) additional parameters are given as well. This makes it possible to search over the complete catalog of 350+ constraints without a combinatorial explosion.

3   User Experience

We now show the behaviour of the Constraint Seeker on a simple example. The user interacts with the system through a simple web form, where he must give at least one positive example for the constraint. Suppose the user enters the query

   p(2 , [4,2,4,5] , 4)

where *p* stands for positive example. The colors for the arguments are applied by the Seeker to help visualize changes in the argument order in the output.

3.1   Seeker Matches

Figure 1 shows the output of the Constraint Seeker for the sample query, formatted for pdf output.

   In the output the candidate explanations are listed by relevance, i.e. for the given example the first entry, the `exactly` constraint, is the best explanation. It has rank 0, a numerical value computed from structural information about the candidate. The density value (3125) shows how many solutions were counted for a small instance of the constraint, constraints with few solutions are more likely candidate explanations than constraints with many solutions. The `exactly` constraint has 9 links, i.e. its description refers to nine other constraints in the catalog. Constraints with many links are typically more common and useful, e.g. `alldifferent` has 72 links. The `exactly` constraint is also marked as having a functional dependency. One of the arguments (the first) is determined by the values for the other arguments, as we are counting in the first argument how often a particular value (the third argument) occurs in a list of values (the

Constraint	Rank	Density	Links	UnTyp	ArgOrder	Crisp	Func	Tr
exactly	0	3125	9	0	0	n/a	graph	-
Pattern: exactly(2 , [[var-4],[var-2],[var-4],[var-5]] , 4)								
Relations: exactly implies atmost / exactly implies atleast								
atleast	5	5625	11	0	0	0	n/a	-
Pattern: atleast(2 , [[var-4],[var-2],[var-4],[var-5]] , 4)								
Relations: atleast implied by exactly								
atmost	5	9188	12	0	0	0	n/a	-
Pattern: atmost(2 , [[var-4],[var-2],[var-4],[var-5]] , 4)								
Relations: atmost implied by exactly								
minimum_greater_than	30	2146	10	0	3	n/a	n/a	-
Pattern: minimum_greater_than(4 , 2 , [[var-4],[var-2],[var-4],[var-5]])								
int_value_precede	30	7060	11	0	3	n/a	n/a	-
Pattern: int_value_precede(4 , 2 , [[var-4],[var-2],[var-4],[var-5]])								
atmost	30	9188	12	1	2	3	n/a	-
Pattern: atmost(4 , [[var-4],[var-2],[var-4],[var-5]] , 2)								
Relations: atmost implied by exactly								

Fig. 1. Example Output of Constraint Seeker for Query p(2 , [4,2,4,5] , 4)

second argument). Constraints with functional dependencies are considered good candidate explanations, therefore the rank value for the `exactly` constraint is very low. The functional dependency is derived from the graph description [1] of the constraint in the catalog, i.e. it was not specified manually. For other constraints this property can be deduced from the specification of the constraint as an automaton [2], but for some of the constraints (mostly numerical constraints) we had to define this property manually as meta-data in the catalog.

The second line of the `exactly` constraint shows the actual call pattern that must be used, in this case the user input is used without any transformation. The Constraint Seeker does allow for permutations of the arguments, and even within list arguments, since it is not reasonable to require that a user knows the particular argument order used in the catalog. The third line shows relations between the `exactly` constraint and other candidates found. The `exactly` constraint implies both the `atleast` and the `atmost` constraint, it is therefore a better (more specific) candidate explanation and ranked above the other candidates.

The second candidate shown is the `atleast` constraint, with a rank of 5 and a density of 5625. Its rank must be greater than that of the `exactly` constraint, as `atleast` is implied by `exactly`, but it is also influenced by what we call *crispness* of its first argument. In the `atleast` constraint, the first argument is not a functional dependency of the other arguments, but it is monotonic. If the constraint is satisfied for some value k in the first argument, it is also satisfied for all values smaller than k. The crispness of the constraint (column *Crisp*) is the difference between the maximal value for the argument that satisfies the constraint and the value that occurs in the user given pattern. Candidates with small crispness values are considered good explanations.

The third candidate is `atmost`, which also has a rank of 5, but a density value of 9188, and which therefore is ranked lower than `atleast`.[2]

The next two candidates `minimum_greater_than` and `int_value_precede` require a permutation of their arguments to match the example instance given by the user, and have neither a functional dependency nor a monotonic argument. This leads to a relatively bad ranking value. The number of arguments that need to be permuted is given in the column *ArgOrder*.

The last candidate is another variation of the `atmost` constraint. Instead of stating that atmost 2 values in the collection have value 4, this candidate explanation says that atmost 4 variables in the collection have value 2. This requires two argument swaps (*ArgOrder*=2), but also shows a crispness value of 3. In the instance given only one variable has value 2, so the first argument with its value 4 is three steps off the crisp value. This candidate also shows another issue, one of the typical restrictions for `atmost` is violated. The typical restrictions state conditions which hold in normal use of a constraint. For the `atmost(N,Variables,Value)` constraint, these restrictions are given in the catalog:

1. $N > 0$
2. $N < |VARIABLES|$

---

[2] This difference in solutions counted will become clear when, in Section 5.2, we describe the method for computing the density.

3. $|VARIABLES| > 1$
4. atleast(1, $VARIABLES$, $VALUE$)

Restriction 2 is not satisfied, as the collection contains only four variables, and the first argument N is also set to 4. Candidates which violate typical restrictions are considered weak explanations, and are therefore down-ranked.

Wider Matches. The candidates above were found by looking for explanations with the same compressed type as the example given, i.e. where the arguments were permutations of the user example. The Seeker can find more general examples, where the user input must be transformed in a more complex way to find the explanation. Typical cases are optional arguments which may or may not be present, reorganization of the arguments (a matrix for example may be given as a matrix, or as a collection describing the rows, or as a collection describing the columns). The two wider matches in the output in Figure 2 show explanations based on such transformations: In the first case, we find a match for element, based on a shift of an index argument. The global constraint catalog assumes that indices are counted from 1. Some constraint systems (like Choco or Gecode) instead follow their host language and count indices from 0. To match examples intended for such systems, we try to add one to index arguments. If we change the first argument from 2 to 3, then the instance matches an element constraint. This is the same as considering the constraint with the index in the first argument being counted from 0. The second candidate, count, is obtained by adding an additional argument with the equality operator. The user may not have considered parametrizing his example with such an operator, we therefore try to add this argument and try out all possible operator values, but only keep the strongest (most restrictive) of the possible choices.

Note that the ranking for element would place it at the top of the list if both result lists are combined. This is due to the functional dependency in the element constraint (the third argument is determined by the index and the list of values), and the small number of solutions it admits. The column *Func* indicates the functional dependency as manual, i.e. this is specified explicitly in the description of the constraint. Also note how the modified value in the first argument of element is highlighted, as well as the added argument in the count constraint. This matching of the arguments against the original example instance is done by a small constraint program, which also deals with new or modified arguments.

Constraint	Rank	Density	Links	UnTyp	ArgOrder	Crisp	Func	Tr
element	0	2500	35	0	0	n/a	manual	T11
Pattern:	element(3 , [[value-4],[value-2],[value-4],[value-5]] , 4)							
count	30	3125	16	0	3	n/a	n/a	T1
Pattern:	count(4 , [[var-4],[var-2],[var-4],[var-5]] , = , 2)							

Fig. 2. Extended Search Results

4   Generating Candidates

Given a set of positive and negative examples, we first have to find candidate explanations, constraints that match these examples. This requires the following steps:

- We first construct a type signature from the examples, using the following ground types (page 6-8 of [4]) in the given lexicographical order:

$$\text{atom} \prec \text{int} \prec \text{real} \prec \text{list} \prec \text{collection}$$

- We sort the arguments and collections in lexicographical order to generate a normalized type.
- If we partition the constraints in the catalog by their normalized type signature, we find 97 distinct types, with the largest equivalence class containing 40 constraints (see page 109 of [4]).
- For each constraint in the selected equivalence class we have to evaluate it against all positive and negative examples. In order to do this, we have to permute the examples given to create the call pattern matching the argument order of each constraint. There can be multiple ways to do this, for example if a constraint has multiple arguments of the same type, and we have to explore each of those possibilities. Fortunately, the number of permutations to be considered is often quite limited, there are only 15 constraints in the catalog for which we have to consider more than 72 permutations.
- Different permutations can lead to the same call pattern, if for example multiple arguments have the same value. In other cases, the catalog explicitly provides the information that some arguments in the constraint are interchangeable (page 19 in [4]), i.e. there are symmetries which we don't have to present multiple times. We can filter such duplicates before (or sometimes only after) the ranking of the candidate list.
- In many cases we want to consider more than just a strict matching of the argument types. The user may present the arguments in a different form, e.g. use a matrix rather than a collection of collections. He might also have ignored or added some arguments, or optional parameters. We deal with these possibilities by using a rule-based transformation system which, based on pre- and post conditions, can modify the argument structure of the examples given. At the moment we use 13 such rules in the system (http://seeker.mines-nantes.fr/transformations.htm).

The process above results in a set of call pattern in the correct format for every constraint with the correct compressed type. In order to evaluate these pattern, we need some code that can check if these ground instances satisfy the constraint. In principle, we only need a constraint checker, which operates on a ground instance, and returns true or false. But the catalog descriptions may contain stronger implementations:

built-in. The Seeker code is executed in SICStus Prolog [12], which contains a finite domain solver that implements a number of global constraints. We can call these built-ins to execute the constraint, after some syntactic transformation.

reformulation. The constraint can be evaluated by executing a Prolog program which calls other global constraints and possibly some general Prolog code to transform arguments. Obviously, the call tree must not be cyclic, i.e. any constraints called may not use a reformulation which calls the initial constraint.

automaton. The constraint can be evaluated by an automaton with counters [3]. These can be executed directly in SICStus Prolog.

logic. An evaluator is provided as a logic based formula in the rule language extending the geost constraint described in [11]. An evaluator for the rule language is available in SICStus Prolog.

checker. A small number of complex constraints (e.g. `cycle`) are described only with a constraint checker, which can evaluate ground instances only. While this is sufficient for the candidate generation, this will not be enough for other elements of the overall Seeker application.

none. No evaluator for the constraint is given in the catalog.

For some constraints, multiple evaluators are given. Table 1 shows the current state of evaluators for the global constraint catalog. 274 of 354 (77.4%) can be evaluated. Most of the missing constraints use finite set variables or are graph constraints, which are not provided in the SICStus Prolog constraint engine. The finite set constraints could be added through a basic set solver, adding the graph constraints would require more extensive work on either evaluating the graph description in the catalog algorithmically, or implementing some of the constraints in SICStus Prolog.

Table 1. Evaluators for Global Constraints

Evaluator	Nr Constraints
reformulation	137
automaton	49
reformulation + automaton	40
builtin	26
logic	9
builtin + automaton	8
checker	3
reformulation + reformulation	1
builtin + reformulation	1
none	80
Total	354

5   Ranking

Not all candidate explanations are equally useful to the user. We use three criteria to order the candidates, the rank being the most important, and the number of links the least important tie breaker:

rank. The rank of the constraint indicates how specific it is. The relative rank value is determined on-line by a constraint program which compares all candidates with each other.

density. We compute a solution density for each constraint by enumerating all solutions for small problem instances. Constraints with few solutions are considered better explanations. The solution density is pre-computed by another constraint program.

links. The number of cross references between constraints in the catalog gives an indication of their popularity.

5.1 Rank Computation Solver

The rank computation solver is run on-line for each query to produce a relative position for each candidate. The rank for each candidate is represented by a domain variable, small values are better than large ones.

We use unary and binary constraints in this model. Unary constraints affect the lower bound of the domain variable based on a combination of:

functional dependency. If one or multiple arguments of a constraint depend on other arguments, it is quite unlikely that a user did pick the correct value by chance. Candidates with functional dependencies are good explanations.

crispness. Slightly weaker than functional dependencies, the crispness is derived from monotonic arguments. If the constraint holds for some value k of such an argument, it must also hold for all values larger (smaller) than k. We call the minimal (maximal) value for which the constraint holds, its *crisp* value. The smaller the difference between the crisp value and the value given in the example, the better is the candidate explanation.

typical restriction violations. For each constraint, the catalog describes restrictions which apply to a typical use of the constraint. If a candidate violates these typical restrictions, it should not be considered a good explanation, and it should be down ranked.

argument reordering. If the user has given the arguments of the constraint in the correct order, so that no re-ordering is required, we consider the constraint a better candidate than one where all arguments must be permuted. This is a rather weak criterion, as it is based on convention rather than structure.

The exact formula on how these criteria are combined to affect the lower bound is based on a heuristic evaluation of different parameter choices.

Binary constraints are imposed between candidate constraints for which semantic links (page 84 of [4]) are given in the catalog. As we had seen in our example in Section 3, the `exactly` constraint implies both `atleast` and `atmost` constraints. It is therefore a better candidate, and we impose inequality constraints between all candidates for which such semantic links exist. At the moment we only use the *implies* and *implied by* links, the links *generalization* and *soft variant* do not seem to work as well, typically relying on added parameters which change the constraint signature.

We search for a solution which minimizes the sum of all rank variables, this solution can be found by assigning the variables by increasing lower bound and fixing the smallest value in each domain. No backtracking is required. As a constraint problem this is not very difficult, the main advantage that CP gives is the flexibility with which different scenarios can be explored without much effort.

5.2 Density Solver

The solution density of each constraint is estimated off-line by two constraint models, and stored result values are then used in the on-line queries. Unfortunately, closed form formulas for solution counting are known for very few constraints [27], and thus can not be used in the general case. Instead, we create small problem instances only: For a given size parameter n, we enumerate all argument pattern where all collections have n or fewer entries. For many constraints, the length of the collections is constrained by restrictions provided in the catalog, so that these choices can not be made arbitrarily. A small constraint program considers all these restrictions, by enumeration we find all combinations which are allowed. Having fixed the size of the collections in the first model the second model creates domains ranging from 0 to n, calls the constraint and enumerates all solutions with a timeout. The value 0 is included in the domain, as it often plays a special role in the constraint definition. In our experiments we restrict n to 4 or 5. Note that by imposing the "typical" restrictions in our models, we can also count how many typical solutions exist for a given constraint.

6 Instance Generation

The two models of the density solver can be used for another purpose. We can also generate positive instances for the constraints. In this variant, we change the domain limits from $-2n$ to $2n$, allow larger values for n, and use a more complex search routine, which tries to sample the complete solution space. The search routine first tries to assign some regular instances pattern, like setting each collection to all zero values, or enforcing monotonicity in some argument. In a second step, we try to set randomly selected arguments to random values. In a last step, we try to find instances for missing values. If in the previous phase some value has not been chosen for some argument, we try to force that value, in order to increase variety in the solution set. All phases are linked to time outs, set to finish the complete catalog overnight. We can again impose the typical restrictions in order to find typical examples.

We will use these randomly generated instances in our evaluation to compare against the manually chosen examples in the catalog.

7 Constraint Solving Inside the Seeker

We have seen that the complete Constraint Seeker tool uses constraint models for multiple roles:

1. Check positive and negative examples for satisfaction (on-line)
2. Rank candidate lists by estimated relevance (on-line)
3. Determine the argument order used for output coloring (on-line)
4. Compute all call patterns up to given size (off-line)
5. Count all (typical) solutions for small problem sizes (off-line)
6. Sample solution space to generate positive (typical) instances (off-line)

Each of these models is quite small, sometimes only involving the constraint under test. In other cases, various other constraints, from the typical restrictions for example, will be added. The search complexity ranges from trivial (ranking solver without backtracking), to quite complex (instance generator). Note that all of these models are generated automatically from the meta-data given in the catalog description. This means in particular that we generate typical and non-typical test cases for many global constraints solely from the abstract description in the catalog.

8   Evaluation

We have tested the Constraint Seeker against different example datasets:

Catalog Examples. The first set uses the examples which are given for each constraint in the catalog. For the vast majority of constraints, only a single positive instance is given, which was manually designed as part of the constraint description. We either use all tests for which an evaluator exists (Column *all*), only those for which we were able to also generate tests (Column *restricted*), or (Column *first*) only the first example given in the restricted set.

Generated. The second set uses the generated examples described in section 6. The order of the instances for each constraint is randomized. Instances can normally only be generated if an efficient evaluator for the constraint is available.

Representatives. We try to reduce the number of examples for each constraint, while maintaining some variety. Many generated examples produce the same candidate set. In this set we only use one representative from each such group.

Single. We pick a single, best test from the generated examples, i.e. one which minimizes the number of candidates and which has the highest ranking for the intended constraint.

Combined. We also pick a single best test, but this time from both the hand-crafted and the generated examples.

In a first test we only check how many candidates are generated when running over all provided instances, and ignore the ranking. This should show if either the candidate list is so short that ranking is not required, or an unmanageable number of candidates is produced. The numbers indicated in row k of table 2 state for how many constraints the Seeker found k candidates. The examples from the catalog produce up to 14 candidates, while for the generated examples and for the representative set up to nine candidates are produced. We can also see that the generated examples are much more selective. For 155 constraints, there is only one candidate left. This drops to 140 constraints, if we only consider representatives, but that is still more than twice the number of examples with a single candidate when using the hand-crafted examples from the catalog. If we only consider a single test example, the generated examples do not fare quite as well, but still better than the hand-crafted examples. Combining both sets brings further improvements, showing that the hand-crafted examples are not always worse than the generated ones. Overall, we can see that the number of candidates is not excessive in any of the test scenarios, but that it is clearly not enough to just produce the candidate list.

Table 2. Number of Candidates Generated

Nr	Catalog Examples		Generated	Representative	Single	Combined
	all	restricted	first	Examples	Examples		
1	66	63	63	155	140	96	107
2	35	28	28	48	60	59	45
3	27	25	20	23	24	33	29
4	32	31	28	11	13	22	27
5	26	24	22	8	9	11	11
6	30	30	32	6	5	12	11
7	15	15	16	1	2	7	10
8	11	9	9	2	2	7	7
9	12	12	12	1	-	4	3
10	7	7	7	-	-	2	3
11	7	7	7	-	-	-	-
12	2	2	2	-	-	-	-
13	2	2	2	-	-	-	-
14	-	-	7	-	-	2	2

Table 3. Quality of Ranking

Nr	Catalog Examples		Generated	Representative	Single	Combined
	all	restricted	first	Examples	Examples		
only	66	63	63	155	140	96	107
first	149	142	135	89	99	124	121
second	33	27	31	10	14	25	17
third	12	11	13	0	0	6	6
other	13	12	13	1	2	5	4
total	273	255	255	255	255	255	255

We now consider how good the ranking is at identifying the intended constraint. Table 3 shows in row *only* for how many constraints we get a single candidate which identifies the constraint. In that case the ranking is irrelevant. The next rows (*first, second, third*) indicate for how many constraint the ranking puts the correct constraint in first, second or third place. The next line (*other*) indicates that the intended constraint was not in the top three entries. The last row gives the total number of constraints identified for each dataset. The candidate selection together with the ranking produces rather strong results for the generated examples. For 244 of 255 constraints do we find the intended constraint in first position, in only 11 of 255 (4.3%) case do we not find the intended constraint at the top of the candidate list, and in only one case it is not in the top three. This increases to 16 of 255 (6.2 %) cases for the representative set, and to 35 of 255 (13.7%) if we pick only one example. The hand-crafted examples are somewhat weaker, in 58 of 273 cases (21.2 %) do we not find the intended constraint in first position. Picking a single, best example from both generated and hand-crafted examples leaves us with 27 of 255 cases not identified in first position (10.6 %), but only 4 cases (1.6 %) not in the top three.

We can also provide some analysis at the system level. The Constraint Seeker is written in SICStus Prolog, integrated with an Apache web server. Nearly all of the HTML output is generated, the rest is fairly simple forms and CSS data. The Prolog code is just over 6,400 lines, developed over a period of 3 months by one of the authors. The six constraint models in the Seeker make up 2,000 lines, roughly one third of the code. This line count does not include the 50,000 lines of Prolog describing the constraints themselves. This description is not specific to the Seeker, instead it provides the meta data that systematically document the various aspects of the global constraints, while its first use was to generate the textual form of the catalog itself.

9   Summary and Future Work

Besides introducing the Constraint Seeker, the key contribution of the paper is to illustrate the power of meta data and meta programming in the context of future constraints platforms. Constraint platforms today typically provide some or all of the following features:

1. The core engine dealing with domains, variables and propagation.
2. A set of built-in constraints with their filtering algorithms.
3. Some generic way to define new constraints (e.g. table, MDD, automata).
4. A low level API to define new constraints and their filtering algorithms.
5. A modelling language which may also allow to express reformulation.

However, it is well known that a lot of specific knowledge is required for achieving automatically various tasks such as validating constraints in a systematic way, breaking symmetries, or producing implied constraints. To deal with this aspect we suggest a complementary approach where we use meta data for explicitly describing different aspects of global constraints such as *argument types*, *restrictions on the arguments*, *typical use of a constraint*, *symmetries w.r.t. the arguments of a constraint*, *links between constraints* (e.g. implication, generalisation). The electronic version of the global constraint catalog provides such information in a systematic way for the different global constraints. The Constraint Seeker presented in this paper illustrates the fact that the same meta data can be used for different purposes (unlike ad-hoc code in a procedural language which is designed for a specific (and unique) usage and a single system). In fact to build our Constraint Seeker we have systematically used the meta data describing the constraints for solving a number of dedicated problems such as:

– Estimating the solution density of a constraint, which was needed for the ranking.
– Extracting structural information about a constraint from meta data (e.g. functional dependency between the arguments of a constraint) used for the ranking.
– Generating discriminating examples for all constraints, as well as typical examples with some degree of diversity for systematically evaluating our Constraint Seeker.
– Using the symmetry information for automatically filtering out symmetrical answers of the Constraint Seeker.

Beside these problems, the meta data is also used for generating the catalog. It is worth noting that it could also be used for simulating the effect of various consistencies, getting interesting examples of missing propagation, and providing certificates for testing constraints for all constraints of the catalog. The key point to keep in mind is that with this approach it is possible to design a variety of tools that don't need to be updated when new constraints are added (i.e., we only need to provide meta data for the new constraint as well as an evaluator). This contrasts with today's approach where constraint libraries need to modify a number of things as soon as a new constraint is added (e.g. update the manual, write specific code for testing the parameters of the constraint, generate meaningful examples, update the test cases, …).

The current version of the Constraint Seeker has been deployed on the web (`http://seeker.mines-nantes.fr`), future work will study queries given by the users to identify further improvements of the user experience.

References

1. Beldiceanu, N.: Global constraints as graph properties on a structured network of elementary constraints of the same type. In: Dechter, R. (ed.) CP 2000. LNCS, vol. 1894, pp. 52–66. Springer, Heidelberg (2000)
2. Beldiceanu, N., Carlsson, M., Debruyne, R., Petit, T.: Reformulation of global constraints based on constraint checkers. Constraints 10(3) (2005)
3. Beldiceanu, N., Carlsson, M., Petit, T.: Deriving filtering algorithms from constraint checkers. In: Wallace (ed.) [25], pp. 107–122
4. Beldiceanu, N., Carlsson, M., Rampon, J.: Global constraint catalog, 2nd edn. Technical Report T2010:07, SICS (2010)
5. Bessière, C., Coletta, R., Freuder, E.C., O'Sullivan, B.: Leveraging the learning power of examples in automated constraint acquisition. In: Wallace (ed.) [25], pp. 123–137
6. Bessière, C., Coletta, R., Koriche, F., O'Sullivan, B.: A SAT-based version space algorithm for acquiring constraint satisfaction problems. In: Gama, J., Camacho, R., Brazdil, P.B., Jorge, A.M., Torgo, L. (eds.) ECML 2005. LNCS (LNAI), vol. 3720, pp. 23–34. Springer, Heidelberg (2005)
7. Bessière, C., Coletta, R., Koriche, F., O'Sullivan, B.: Acquiring constraint networks using a SAT-based version space algorithm. In: AAAI. AAAI Press, Menlo Park (2006)
8. Bessière, C., Coletta, R., O'Sullivan, B., Paulin, M.: Query-driven constraint acquisition. In: Veloso (ed.) [23], pp. 50–55
9. Bessière, C., Coletta, R., Petit, T.: Acquiring parameters of implied global constraints. In: van Beek, P. (ed.) CP 2005. LNCS, vol. 3709, pp. 747–751. Springer, Heidelberg (2005)
10. Bessière, C., Coletta, R., Petit, T.: Learning implied global constraints. In: Veloso (ed.) [23], pp. 44–49
11. Carlsson, M., Beldiceanu, N., Martin, J.: A geometric constraint over k-dimensional objects and shapes subject to business rules. In: Stuckey, P.J. (ed.) CP 2008. LNCS, vol. 5202, pp. 220–234. Springer, Heidelberg (2008)
12. Carlsson, M., et al.: SICStus Prolog User's Manual. Swedish Institute of Computer Science, release 4 edn. (2007) ISBN 91-630-3648-7
13. Charnley, J., Colton, S., Miguel, I.: Automatic generation of implied constraints. In: Brewka, G., Coradeschi, S., Perini, A., Traverso, P. (eds.) ECAI. Frontiers in Artificial Intelligence and Applications, vol. 141, pp. 73–77. IOS Press, Amsterdam (2006)
14. Coletta, R., Bessière, C., O'Sullivan, B., Freuder, E.C., O'Connell, S., Quinqueton, J.: Semi-automatic modeling by constraint acquisition. In: Rossi, F. (ed.) CP 2003. LNCS, vol. 2833, pp. 812–816. Springer, Heidelberg (2003)

15. Hebrard, E., Marx, D., O'Sullivan, B., Razgon, I.: Constraints of difference and equality: A complete taxonomic characterisation. In: Gent, I.P. (ed.) CP 2009. LNCS, vol. 5732, pp. 424–438. Springer, Heidelberg (2009)

16. O'Connell, S., O'Sullivan, B., Freuder, E.C.: Timid acquisition of constraint satisfaction problems. In: Haddad, H., Liebrock, L.M., Omicini, A., Wainwright, R.L. (eds.) SAC, pp. 404–408. ACM, New York (2005)

17. O'Sullivan, B.: Automated modelling and solving in constraint programming. In: AAAI. AAAI Press, Menlo Park (2010)

18. Quinqueton, J., Raymond, G., Bessiere, C.: An agent for constraint acquisition and emergence. In: Negru, V., Jebelean, T., Petcu, D., Zaharie, D. (eds.) SYNASC, pp. 229–234. IEEE Computer Society, Los Alamitos (2007)

19. Rossi, F., Sperduti, A.: Acquiring both constraint and solution preferences in interactive constraint systems. Constraints 9(4), 311–332 (2004)

20. Shchekotykhin, K.M., Friedrich, G.: Argumentation based constraint acquisition. In: Wang, W., Kargupta, H., Ranka, S., Yu, P.S., Wu, X. (eds.) ICDM, pp. 476–482. IEEE Computer Society, Los Alamitos (2009)

21. Simonis, H.: Building industrial applications with constraint programming. In: Comon, H., Marché, C., Treinen, R. (eds.) CCL 1999. LNCS, vol. 2002, pp. 271–309. Springer, Heidelberg (2001)

22. Sloane, N.J.A., Plouffe, S.: The Encyclopedia of Integer Sequences. Academic Press, San Diego (1995)

23. Veloso, M.M. (ed.): Proceedings of the 20th International Joint Conference on Artificial Intelligence, IJCAI 2007, Hyderabad, India, January 6-12 (2007)

24. Vu, X., O'Sullivan, B.: Generalized constraint acquisition. In: Miguel, I., Ruml, W. (eds.) SARA 2007. LNCS (LNAI), vol. 4612, pp. 411–412. Springer, Heidelberg (2007)

25. Wallace, M. (ed.): CP 2004. LNCS, vol. 3258. Springer, Heidelberg (2004)

26. Weis, P., Leroy, X.: Le langage Caml. InterEditions (1993) (in French)

27. Zanarini, A., Pesant, G.: Solution counting algorithms for constraint-centered search heuristics. Constraints 14(3), 392–413 (2009)

Bin Repacking Scheduling in Virtualized Datacenters

Fabien Hermenier[1], Sophie Demassey[2], and Xavier Lorca[2]

[1] University of Utah, School of Computing
fhermeni@cs.utah.edu
[2] TASC project, Mines Nantes-INRIA, LINA CNRS UMR 6241
firstname.lastname@mines-nantes.fr

Abstract. A datacenter can be viewed as a dynamic bin packing system where servers host applications with varying resource requirements and varying relative placement constraints. When those needs are no longer satisfied, the system has to be reconfigured. Virtualization allows to distribute applications into Virtual Machines (VMs) to ease their manipulation. In particular, a VM can be freely migrated without disrupting its service, temporarily consuming resources both on its origin and destination.

We introduce the Bin Repacking Scheduling Problem in this context. This problem is to find a final packing and to schedule the transitions from a given initial packing, accordingly to new resource and placement requirements, while minimizing the average transition completion time. Our CP-based approach is implemented into Entropy, an autonomous VM manager which detects reconfiguration needs, generates and solves the CP model, then applies the computed decision. CP provides the awaited flexibility to handle heterogeneous placement constraints and the ability to manage large datacenters with up to 2,000 servers and 10,000 VMs.

1 Introduction

A datacenter is a hosting platform of hundreds of interconnected servers. To make this infrastructure costly effective, it should be able to host simultaneously a large range of client applications. Virtualization eases the deployment of the applications. An application is distributed into Virtual Machines (VMs) which can be colocated on any servers, and dynamically manipulated under different kinds of actions, including live migration between hosts.

The deployment of the applications is constrained by the finite capacity of the servers in shared resources like CPU and memory. In addition, clients and system administrators have specific expectations with regards to the relative placement of the VMs on the servers. For instance, a client may require the replicas of his application to be continuously hosted on distinct servers to ensure fault tolerance, or an administrator may require to isolate a group of servers for maintenance purpose.

J. Lee (Ed.): CP 2011, LNCS 6876, pp. 27–41, 2011.
© Springer-Verlag Berlin Heidelberg 2011

A system *configuration* is an assignment of the VMs to the servers which satisfies both the resource and placement requirements. Over time, the system evolves: placement requirements vary, servers are intentionally or unexpectedly halted or restarted, VMs are launched or killed and their resource requirements change. When the current configuration is no longer viable, a new configuration has to be computed, and the transition actions to apply to reach the new configuration have to be planned to ensure their feasibility.

The *reconfiguration problem* is then made of a packing and a scheduling subproblems, both being subject to resource and placement constraints. The problem may have no solution, either because no feasible final configuration exists, or because reaching such a configuration induces an unsolvable cycle of transitions. Furthermore, a reconfiguration has an impact on the running applications. Thus the objective is to get a reconfiguration plan with minimum average transition completion time. Although this objective affects the scheduling part only, it is also conditioned by the packing to reach.

The reconfiguration problem is clearly intractable in theory. In practice, the automated VM manager of the datacenter needs to periodically solve online large-sized instances. For scalability reasons, incomplete optimization is then required and a tradeoff has to be made between the computation time of the reconfiguration plan and its execution time. In a previous work [6] on a reconfiguration problem without side constraints, we shown that despite a fast computation time, a standard greedy algorithm tends to compute reconfiguration plans with large execution durations. On the opposite, our solution, partially based on CP, computed faster plans in an extra time that was drastically lesser than the execution duration gain. In this paper, we follow this viewpoint: VM managers would benefit from embedding smarter reconfiguration decision modules. By smarter, we mean able to compute high-quality decisions even if an additional, still acceptable, solving time is required. We mean also flexible and generic enough to handle the various user requirements, which are traditionally not considered. For these reasons, we first adopt a centralized solution approach, by contrast to cheaper distributed approaches which only apply local changes. Although the problem induces a natural decomposition into two subproblems, we solve them conjointly as they both contribute to get a reliable and fast reconfiguration plan. Finally, we rely on Constraint Programming to easily handle the problem as a whole, including any combinations of user requirements.

In this paper, we first formalize the general reconfiguration problem and discuss its complexity (Section 2). We describe the specifications of the practical problem of automated VM management and show how CP fulfills them (Section 3). We then present the CP model, the search strategy, and the two resolution modes we developed for this problem (Section 4). All these elements are pre-implemented into the autonomous VM manager Entropy [6]. Experiments on realistic workloads show that our implementation solves problems involving 10,000 VMs on 2,000 servers with 900 side constraints in less than 5 minutes (Section 5). Last, we review the literature on process and data migration, and

show how our general model fits many of these related problems (Section 6).
Our conclusions and perspectives are provided in Section 7.

2   Core Problem Statement

Without side constraints, a configuration is a standard packing of items with arbitrary heights (VMs) to multidimensional bins with arbitrary capacities (servers).
A reconfiguration plan is a schedule of the transition actions applied to the VMs,
subject to the same resource limitations. The specificity of this scheduling problem comes from the occupation of the resources by each VM: on its initial host
before and during the transition, and on its final host during and after the transition. The reconfiguration problem can be dissociated from the context of VM
management. To our knowledge, no such formalization has formerly been proposed. Hereafter it is referred to as the BIN REPACKING SCHEDULING PROBLEM.

2.1   The Repacking and Scheduling Problem

Consider a 2-states (initial/final) dynamic system which consists of a set $\mathcal{R}$ of
p-dimensional bins with static capacities $B_r \in \mathbb{N}^p$, for all $r \in \mathcal{R}$, and a set $\mathcal{J}$ of
items with dynamic initial $b_j^o \in \mathbb{N}^p$ and final $b_j^f \in \mathbb{N}^p$ heights, for all $j \in \mathcal{J}$. The
initial state of the system is known and defined as an assignment $s_o : \mathcal{J} \to \mathcal{R}$
satisfying $\sum_{j \in s_o^{-1}(r)} b_j^o \leq B_r$ for each bin $r \in \mathcal{R}$.[1] The system state changes by
applying a transition action to each item $j \in \mathcal{J}$. The restricted set of allowed
transitions is given as a table $\Delta_j \subset \mathcal{T} \times \mathcal{R}$, where each element $\delta = (\tau, r)$ indicates
that a transition of type $\tau \in \mathcal{T}$ can be applied to item $j \in \mathcal{J}$ to reassign it from
bin $s_o(j)$ to bin r. With any transition $\delta \in \Delta_j$ are associated a duration $d_\delta \in \mathbb{N}$
and a weight $w_\delta \in \mathbb{N}$.

Definition 1. *The* BIN REPACKING SCHEDULING PROBLEM (BRSP) *is to as-
sociate with each item $j \in \mathcal{J}$, a transition $\delta(j) = (\tau(j), s_f(j)) \in \Delta_j$ and a time
$t_j \in \mathbb{N}$ to start this transition, such that the bin capacities are satisfied at any
time*

$$\sum_{\substack{j \in s_o^{-1}(r) \\ t < t_j + d_{\delta(j)}}} b_j^o + \sum_{\substack{j \in s_f^{-1}(r) \\ t \geq t_j}} b_j^f \leq B_r, \quad \forall r \in \mathcal{R}, \forall t \geq 0, \tag{1}$$

and the weighted sum of the completion times is minimized

$$\sum_{j \in \mathcal{J}} w_{\delta(j)} (t_j + d_{\delta(j)}), \tag{2}$$

or to prove that no such feasible packing or scheduling exists.

We deliberately present a first conceptual model as the notion of allowed transition action is context-dependent. In the context of VM management, we consider
3 groups of items: items $j \in \mathcal{J}_S$ have to be suspended ($b_j^o > 0$, $b_j^f = 0$), items

---

[1] $s^{-1}(r) \subseteq \mathcal{J}$ denotes the preimage of $\{r\} \subset \mathcal{R}$ under function s from $\mathcal{J}$ to $\mathcal{R}$.

$j \in \mathcal{J}_L$ have to be launched ($b_j^o = 0$, $b_j^f > 0$), items $j \in \mathcal{J}_A$ have to be let active ($b_j^o > 0$, $b_j^f > 0$). To each group corresponds one transition table:

$$\Delta_j = \begin{cases} \{(S,r) \mid r \in \mathcal{R}\} & \forall j \in \mathcal{J}_S \\ \{(L,r) \mid r \in \mathcal{R}\} & \forall j \in \mathcal{J}_L \\ \{(F, s_o(j))\} \cup \{(M,r) \mid r \in \mathcal{R} \setminus \{s_o(j)\}\} & \forall j \in \mathcal{J}_A. \end{cases}$$

The transition types $\mathcal{T} = \{S, L, M, U\}$ stand for *Suspend, Launch, Migrate, Unmoved*, respectively. The duration and the weight of a transition are 0 if it is of type U, and the duration is positive and the weight is 1 otherwise. Let VM REPACKING SCHEDULING PROBLEM (VRSP) refer to this instance of the BRSP. This model totally fits our application: VMs can be suspended (S) or resumed (L), either on their current server or on another, incurring different costs in these two cases. Running VMs can also either stay on their origin server (U) or migrate live to another server (M). In the first case, the transition is immediate ($d_U = 0$), even if the VM resource requirements change, and it does not alter the VM service ($w_U = 0$). Finally, the action of turning a server off or on can be modeled by introducing a dummy VM, respectively to be launched or suspended, statically assigned to the server, and occupying its entire resources.

In the VRSP, the transition typecast is determined by the item j itself, its origin $s_o(j)$ and destination $s_f(j)$ bins. Hence, determining a set of transitions δ_j comes to compute a MULTIDIMENSIONAL BIN PACKING. This problem is NP-complete in the strong sense [5] even in the one-dimensional case ($p = 1$). In turn, determining the times t_j yields to a particular scheduling problem.

2.2   The Scheduling Subproblem

Definition 2. *Given a final packing $s_f : \mathcal{J} \to \mathcal{R}$ such that $\sum_{j \in s_f^{-1}(r)} b_j^f \leq B_r$, $\forall r \in \mathcal{R}$, and a transition $\delta(j) \in \Delta_j$ for each item $j \in \mathcal{J}$, the* REPACKING TRANSITION SCHEDULING PROBLEM (RTSP) *is to schedule all the transitions such that the resource constraints* (1) *are satisfied and the weighted sum of the completion times* (2) *is minimized, or to prove that no such schedule exists.*

This can be viewed as a RESOURCE CONSTRAINED SCHEDULING PROBLEM [5] with no-wait, variable durations and consumer/producer tasks : to each item $j \in \mathcal{J}$ correspond two operations, O_j occupying b_j^o resource units on $s_o(j)$ in time interval $[0, t_j + d_j)$ and F_j occupying b_j^f resource units on $s_f(j)$ in $[t_j, \bar{H})$, where $\bar{H}$ denotes any large enough scheduling horizon. A decision variant of this problem, with unit durations $d_j = 1$ and constant requirements $b_j^o = b_j^f$, has previously been studied by Sirdey et al. [8] and referred to as ZERO-IMPACT PROCESS MOVE PROGRAM. It asks whether a total order exists over the set of transitions. As durations are unit, this is equivalent to find a timed schedule. In [8], this problem is proved to be NP-hard in the strong sense. We give below a sketch of the proof.

Proposition 1. *The decision variant of* RTSP *is NP-hard in the strong sense, even with 2 one-dimensional bins, unit durations and constant requirements.*

Proof. Consider an instance of 3-PARTITION [5], made of a bound $W \in \mathbb{N}$ and a set A of $3m$ elements of sizes $W/4 < w_a < W/2$ for all $a \in A$ such that $\sum_{a \in A} w_a = mW$. This reduces to an instance of RTSP with two one-dimensional bins $\mathcal{R} = \{r_1, r_2\}$ each of capacity mW and two sets of items: $\mathcal{J}_1$ composed of $3m$ items of height w_j migrating from r_1 to r_2, and $\mathcal{J}_2$ composed of $k-1$ items of height W and migrating from r_2 to r_1. Then finding a partition of A in m sets, each of size W, is equivalent to find a migration plan transferring a height W of resource, alternatively from r_1 to r_2 and from r_2 to r_1.   □

3   An Automated VM Manager Relying on CP

The VRSP models a reconfiguration problem centered on the resource requirements. In practice, a VM manager should also deal with user placement requirements. This section first presents, as a proof of concept, 4 typical placement constraints. It then describes the concrete specifications of a VM manager and why CP is suitable. It finally presents the VM manager Entropy that relies on CP for modeling and solving, on-the-fly, instances of a specialized VRSP.

3.1   Side Placement Constraints

A side placement constraint restricts the assignment of given VMs to given servers, or the relative assignments of sets of VMs. Some restrictions are required by the system administrators for management purposes; others are required by the clients for the good execution of their applications. The 4 examples below are representative of concrete standard requirements.

Ban. To perform a hardware or a software maintenance on a server, a system administrator has first to migrate the hosted VMs to other servers. More generally, administrators and clients may want to disallow a given set of VMs to be hosted by a given set of servers. We refer to this constraint as *ban*.

Spread. Highly-available applications use replication to achieve tolerance to hardware failures. To be fully effective, the VMs running the replicas must, at any time, be hosted on distinct servers. We refer to this constraint as *spread*. Figure 1 depicts an instance of VRSP with two VMs subject to a *spread* constraint. As its resource requirements increase, VM1 has to migrate to server N2. *Spread* enforces to delay this action after the migration of VM2 to N3 is completed.

Lonely. Using a denial-of-service, a VM may over-use the CPU and memory resources of its host and then impact the colocated VMs or crash the host. A solution is to make critical application VMs to be hosted on servers on their own. Typically, a system administrator separates the service VMs that manage the datacenter from the client VMs. We refer to this constraint as *lonely*.

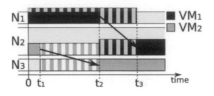

Fig. 1. spread enforces VM1 and VM2 to always be hosted on distinct servers

Capacity. A system administrator controls how shared resources are distributed among the VMs. For instance, each VM reachable from outside the datacenter requires a public IP address. As the pool of public IPs is limited, the number of simultaneous running VMs is restricted to the size of this pool. We refer to as *capacity* the constraint that limits the maximum number of VMs colocated on a given set of servers.

3.2   Constraint Programming for VM Management

The Autonomous VM Manager of a datacenter relies on a periodic or event-driven control loop composed of four modules: *monitoring* retrieves the current system configuration, *provisioning* predicts the future requirements, *plan* computes the reconfiguration plan, and *execution* performs the physical reconfiguration. The plan module gathers the informations of the monitoring and provisioning modules, adapts the solution algorithm, and runs it. The specifications for an efficient plan module are as follows. First, the algorithm should scale up to the size of the datacenter. Second, as the applications run in degraded mode until the configuration becomes viable, computing a solution should be fast and the reconfiguration durations of the applications should be short. Third the algorithm does not need to ensure optimality, but it is strongly required to be flexible. Indeed, it must be dynamically adaptable to handle different types of side constraints and to deal with any combinations of them. Last, virtualized datacenters exist for a short while, but they spread rapidly and new needs emerge with new usages. As a consequence, a VM manager should be extensible to take into consideration future needs.

Constraint Programming is known as a suitable solution for packing and scheduling problems. We claim that CP actually offers unique capabilities to deal with the practical reconfiguration problem considered here. First, modeling with global constraints eases the specification of new side placement constraints. Second, the propagation engine ensures the automatic composability needed to handle the packing and scheduling problems together with extra placement constraints. Finally, the framework of tree search can easily be specialized in most CP solvers with pre-implemented or ad-hoc variable and value ordering heuristics. Such framework is thus convenient to quickly develop and test complete or local search strategies. The search strategy matches the optimization objective, while the CP propagation engine enforces the feasibility part of the problem.

The statement of the lonely constraint illustrates well the flexibility of our approach. This constraint was specified after Amazon EC2 described this new feature in march 2011.[2] Its whole implementation in Entropy, from the selection of the appropriate global constraint to the tests, has taken only 3 hours, and its model, relying on a global constraint already available in the CP solver Choco (see next Section), is about 50 lines of code. We did not have to modify our heuristics to take this new constraint into account. The same holds true for the 3 other placement constraints described above. Obviously, the expressivity and flexibility of CP have their limits, yet we have not reached them in our current application.

Entropy is an open-source autonomous VM manager.[3] The specificity of Entropy lies in its plan module based on the CP Solver Choco[4] and in its configuration script language for its specialization. The scripts allow administrators and clients to each describe a datacenter and an application, respectively, while focusing on their primary concerns: the administrator manages its servers without any knowledge of the hosted applications, while a client specifies its placement requirements without knowledge of the infrastructure or the other hosted applications. Listing 2a illustrates the description of a 3-tiers highly-available application. A tier ($T1, $T2, or $T3) is composed of several VMs, each running a replica of a same service. For fault tolerance, a *spread* constraint enforces all the VMs of each tier to be placed on distinct servers. To improve the application isolation, a *lonely* constraint enforces all the VMs to be placed on servers on their own. Listing 2b illustrates administrator needs. It describes a datacenter made of 3 racks ($R1, $R2, $R3) of 50 servers each. A maximum of 100 hosted VMs per rack is enforced by 3 *capacity* constraints. Last, all VMs are disallowed to be placed on server N101 in order to prepare a maintenance.

```
1 $T1 = VM[1..5];
2 $T2 = VM[6..15];
3 $T3 = {VM17, VM21, VM22};
4 for $t in $T[1..3] {
5     spread($t);
6 }
7 lonely($T1 + $T2 + $T3);
```

```
1 $R1=N[1..50];
2 $R2=N[51..100];
3 $R3=N[101..150];
4 for $r in $R[1..3] {
5     capacity($r, 100);
6 }
7 ban($ALL_VMS, N101);
```

(a) Description of a 3-tiers HA application.   (b) Description of a datacenter.

Fig. 2. Sample configuration scripts provided by clients or administrators

Given the current configuration retrieved by the monitoring module and the future resource requirements estimated by the provisioning module, the plan module first generates a Choco model of the corresponding VRSP instance.

---

[2] https://aws.amazon.com/dedicated-instances/
[3] http://entropy.gforge.inria.fr
[4] http://choco.emn.fr

The configuration scripts are then interpreted and the placement constraints are added in turn to the model. If the current configuration is consistent with this model, then Entropy restarts the control loop. Otherwise, the model is optimized for a limited time and the best solution found, if exists, is sent to the execution module in charge to apply the reconfiguration plan.

4   Elements of Solution

This section presents the CP model including the four examples of placement constraints, the search strategy dedicated to incomplete optimization and the two modes of resolution currently implemented in Entropy. The model relies on several standard constraints mentioned in the Global Constraint Catalog [2]; details on these constraints can be found in this reference.

4.1   Modeling the Core Problem

The end of the schedule is the first time the final configuration is reached. In our model, it is represented by a domain variable H, defined on the integer interval $[0, \bar{H}]$, $\bar{H}$ being the given horizon. In order to properly represent a schedule, we first introduce the notion of task variable:

Definition 3. *A* task variable *is a compound object made of integer variables* $T = \langle T^s, T^e, T^r, T^{b1}, T^{b2}, \ldots, T^{bp} \rangle$ *denoting respectively:* T^s *and* T^e *the starting and the ending times of the task,* T^r *the resource the task is assigned to, and* $T^{b1}, \ldots, T^{bp}$ *the heights of the task in the p dimensions.*

Producer/consumer tasks. Each VM $j \in \mathcal{J}$ is modeled by two multidimensional task variables representing the occupation of the initial server (O_j) and of the final server (F_j). Such a representation is a variant of the producer-consumer model [7] with no negative stock: O_j *produces* resources at the transition completion time, while F_j *consumes* resources from the transition start time. The two task variables associated with each VM $j \in \mathcal{J}$ are formally defined by:

- $O_j = \langle 0, O_j^e, s_o(j), b_j^{o1}, \ldots, b_j^{op} \rangle$ where only O_j^e is a variable defined on $[0, \bar{H}]$. It means j occupies heights b_j^o on initial server $s_o(j)$ from time 0 to O_j^e.
- $F_j = \langle F_j^s, H, F_j^r, b_j^{f1}, \ldots, b_j^{fp} \rangle$, where F_j^s is a variable defined on $[0, \bar{H}]$, and F_j^r is a discrete variable defined on $\mathcal{R}$. It means j occupies heights b_j^f on final server F_j^r from time F_j^s to the end of the schedule H.

Transition types and no-wait. The tasks associated with a VM $j \in \mathcal{J}$ are subject to a *precedence relation with no-wait*, $O_j^e - F_j^s = d_{\delta(j)}$, which depends on the applied transition action $\delta(j)$. In order to model transition $\delta(j)$, we consider a variable X_j defined on $\mathcal{T}$ denoting the transition type, and a variable W_j, defined on $\mathbb{N}$ denoting the transition weight. Then, the different variables associated with a VM can be related by one table constraint:

$$(X_j, F_j^r, O_j^e - F_j^s, W_j) \in \{(\tau, r, d_\delta, w_\delta) \mid \delta = (\tau, r) \in \Delta_j\}, \quad \forall j \in \mathcal{J}.$$

Resource constraints. The resource constraints can be modeled on each dimension by one `cumulatives` constraint as follows:

$$\texttt{cumulatives}(\langle O_j, F_j \mid j \in \mathcal{J}\rangle, \mathcal{R}, \leq, k), \quad \forall k \in \{1, \ldots, p\}.$$

This signature is slightly different from the original one, as it specifies the dimension k to constrain. The filtering of `cumulatives` runs in $O(|\mathcal{R}|.|\mathcal{J}|^2)$. Actually, as this constraint was not available in Choco, we developed our own version specialized to producer/consumer tasks, running with the same time complexity.

Redundant constraints. A transition typed as *Unmoved* has no duration and no cost. It can then be scheduled at any time freeing maximum resources. Formally, for each solution of VRSP, there exists a solution of equal or least cost where an *Unmoved* transition is scheduled at time 0, if the VM requirements decrease, or at time H, if they increase. The property remains true when adding any side placement constraints, as those considered VMs keep precisely the same placement. The property only applies to VMs which requirements vary uniformly in all dimensions, which is usually the case in practice.

$$X_j = U \;\Rightarrow\; O_j^e = F_j^s = 0, \qquad\qquad \forall j \in \mathcal{J}_A \mid b_j^o \geq b_j^f,$$
$$X_j = U \;\Rightarrow\; O_j^e = F_j^s = H, \qquad\qquad \forall j \in \mathcal{J}_A \mid b_j^o < b_j^f.$$

4.2   Modeling the Side Constraints

Ban. The model of *ban* is straightforward as it relies on a simple domain reduction of the final assignment variables. For any subset of VMs $J \subseteq \mathcal{J}$, and any subset of servers $R \subseteq \mathcal{R}$, constraint *ban*(J, R) is modeled by:

$$F_j^r \neq r, \quad \forall j \in J, \forall r \in R.$$

Spread. Despite appearances, the model of *spread* cannot rely on `disjunctives` constraints as the specified VMs are possibly hosted by a same server in the initial configuration. An alternative is to ensure that the VMs are on distinct servers in the final configuration; then, on each server, to ensure that the arrival of a VM is delayed after all other involved VMs left. For any subset of VMs $J \subseteq \mathcal{J}$, constraint *spread*(J) is modeled by:

$$\begin{cases} \texttt{allDifferent}(\langle F_j^r \mid j \in J\rangle), \\ F_i^r = s_o(j) \;\Rightarrow\; O_i^e \leq F_j^s, \quad \forall i, j \in J, i \neq j. \end{cases}$$

Lonely. The model of *lonely* relies on one *disjoint* constraint enforcing the set of servers hosting the specified VMs to be disjoint from the set of servers hosting the remaining VMs. For any subset of VMs $J \subseteq \mathcal{J}$, *lonely*(J) is modeled by:

$$\texttt{disjoint}(\langle F_j^r \mid j \in J\rangle, \langle F_j^r \mid j \notin J\rangle).$$

Capacity. The model of *capacity* relies on a redundant set model for the VRSP. A set variable, associated with each server, indicates the hosted VMs. The constraint bounds the sum of the set cardinalities over the specified servers. For any subset of servers $R \subseteq \mathcal{R}$ and value $n \in \mathbb{N}$, $capacity(R, n)$ is modeled by:

$$\begin{cases} \sum_{r \in R} \texttt{card}(V_r) \leq n, \\ j \in V_r \iff F_j^r = r, \quad \forall r \in \mathcal{R}, \ \forall j \in \mathcal{J}, \\ V_r \subseteq \mathcal{J}, \qquad\qquad \forall r \in \mathcal{R}. \end{cases}$$

4.3 Solving the VRSP

Dedicated Search Strategy. Entropy solves the CP model using a time-truncated branch-and-bound. The search strategy is conceived to descend quickly towards a local optimum, by following the natural decomposition of the problem. First, it focuses on the final packing and instantiates the assignment variables $\langle F_j^r \rangle_{j \in \mathcal{J}}$. Starting with the VMs whose placement in the initial configuration violates a resource or a placement constraint, the heuristic selects the VMs in order of decreasing memory requirements and attempts at placing them to their initial host first, then to another server selected in a worst-fit fashion. Once the final packing is instantiated, the tasks $\langle F_j \rangle_{j \in \mathcal{J}}$ are started as early as possible, in turn, starting from the tasks which are entering a server with no leaving transition.

A Repair Approach. We experimented two modes of resolution: either starting from scratch or from a partial solution. In the *rebuild mode*, all VMs are allowed to migrate, contrary to the *repair mode* where some candidates are *a priori* fixed to their current location. The repair mode may drastically reduce the size of the model – and then speed and scale up the solution process – if a maximum number of candidates is fixed. On the other hand, the pre-packing should be loose enough to ensure a solution to exist. The issue here is to build a feasible and reasonable-sized partial solution. For this, we compute the intersection of the candidate sets returned by simple heuristics that come with each resource and side constraint.

5 Evaluation

In this section, we evaluate the solving abilities of Entropy on realistic workloads. The critical parameters we evaluate are the consolidation ratio, the size of the datacenter, and the side constraints.

For these experiments, we simulate a datacenter composed of racks with 50 servers each. Each server provides 80 GB RAM and 150 uCPU (an abstract unit to establish the computing capacity of a server). This infrastructure hosts 3-tiers applications, each composed of 20 VMs. The VMs are sized according to the standards defined by Amazon EC2[5]. The first and the second tiers are

---

[5] http://aws.amazon.com/ec2

composed of 5 and 10 VMs, respectively. Each VM uses 7.5 GB RAM and at most 4 uCPU (*large instances* in the EC2 terminology). The third tier is composed of 5 VMs, each using 17.1 GB RAM and at most 6.5 uCPU (*high-memory extra-large instances*). The initial configuration is generated randomly. To simulate a load spike, the uCPU demand is asked to grow for half the applications. To simulate transitions, 4% of the VMs have to be launched or resumed, 2% of the running VMs will be stopped or suspended, and 1% of the servers are being taken off-line. The estimated duration of each transition is: 1 second to launch a VM, 2 seconds to stop a VM, 4 to suspend, 5 to resume on the current server and 6 on another one. Finally, the migration of a VM lasts 1 second per gigabyte of RAM. For each instance, 10 minutes have been given to the plan module to compute one first solution on an Intel Xeon E5520 at 2.27 GHz running Linux 2.6.26-2-amd64 and Sun JVM 1.6u21 with 8 GB RAM allocated to the heap.

The tables hereafter display the average computational results by sets of 100 instances each: *solved* is the number of solved instances (failures are due to timeout), *obj* the average sum of the completion times in seconds, *nodes* the average number of nodes open in the search tree, *fails* the average number of fails, *time* the average solution time in seconds.

The consolidation ratio is the average number of VMs hosted per server. For this experiment, we simulated 5 ratio values by fixing the number of servers to 1,000 and varying the number of VMs from 2,000 to 6,000.

Table 1. Impact of the consolidation ratio on the solving process.

Ratio	Rebuild Mode					Repair Mode				
	solved	obj	nodes	fails	time	solved	obj	nodes	fails	time
2:1	100	452	2034	352	42.2	100	381	163	0	3.5
3:1	94	1264	3119	3645	75.2	100	749	394	0	8.4
4:1	65	3213	4574	11476	129.3	100	1349	836	0	18.7
5:1	10	7475	6878	47590	241.2	100	2312	1585	44	37.7
6:1	0	-	-	-	-	86	4092	2884	2863	71.5

Table 1 shows the impact of the consolidation ratio on the solving process in rebuild and repair modes. Increasing the consolidation ratio naturally makes the problem harder: the number of VMs to place rises up, making the packing tighter. The cost of the computed reconfiguration plan also grows as the migrations on the overloaded servers have to be more precisely orchestrated. The repair mode outperforms significantly the rebuild mode as it tackles, for a same ratio value, much smaller models. The results show that our policy for fixing VMs *a priori* in the repair mode is correctly balanced as it reduces well the model size without making the problem unsolvable, even for a consolidation ratio of 5:1. Such a ratio implies an average CPU demand of 72% of the datacenter capacity. This utilization rate is considered as ideal by system administrators as it provides an efficient tradeoff between a high resource usage and the ability to absorb the temporary load spikes.

The datacenter size. For this experiment, we generated 4 sets of instances using a fixed consolidation ratio of 5:1 and a variable datacenter size, from 500 servers and 2,500 VMs to 2,000 servers and 10,000 VMs.

Table 2. Impact of the datacenter size on the solving process (repair mode)

Set	#servers	#VMs	solved	obj	nodes	fails	time
x1	500	2,500	100	1160	805	13	7.0
x2	1,000	5,000	99	2321	1594	17	36.2
x3	1,500	7,500	99	3476	2374	43	105.5
x4	2,000	10,000	100	4635	3171	15	217.0

Table 2 shows the impact of the datacenter size on the computation in repair mode. We observe that the solving time grows non-linearly with the datacenter size, accordingly to the temporal complexity of the VRSP. The solver is however able to compute at least one solution for almost all the instances. Finally, the slow objective value growth and the few number of fails indicate the reliability of our search heuristics to guide the solver to solutions of high quality. These results show the ability of Entropy to handle large representative datacenter sizes. Indeed, the current trend in datacenter architecture consists in acquiring servers per shipping container. Each container is almost autonomous and contains between 500 and 2,500 servers[6]. While it is possible to aggregate several containers, *i.e.* several physical partitions, in one logical partition, the technical limitations of the platform software may prevent migrations between them. Entropy is then dimensioned to manage each partition individually.

The side constraints are now experimented in the context of Highly Available applications. For this experiment, one `spread` constraint is specified for each application tier to provide fault tolerance. One application asks for dedicated servers using a `lonely` constraint. Using `capacity` constraints, the hosted capacity of each rack is limited to 300 VMs. Maintenance are prepared using `ban` constraints on 0.5% of the running servers.

Table 3. Impact of the side constraints on the solving process (repair mode)

variable consolidation ratios					variable datacenter sizes				
Set	solved	obj	nodes	fails	time / Set	solved	obj	nodes	fails	time

Set	solved	obj	nodes	fails	time	Set	solved	obj	nodes	fails	time
2:1	100	381	163	0	3.7	x1	97	1255	1156	3518	12.2
3:1	100	751	394	0	9	x2	93	2511	1872	3018	47.1
4:1	100	1376	841	31	19.2	x3	88	3778	2477	1670	120.2
5:1	95	2491	2007	7053	53.2	x4	91	4980	3271	957	238.7
6:1	35	4512	3603	9661	110.1						

Table 3 shows the impact of the side constraints on the instances with a variable consolidation ratio (left) and with a variable datacenter size (right).

[6] http://www.datacentermap.com/blog/datacenter-container-55.html

For the highest consolidation ratio, the solver becomes unable to compute a solution. The packing is already tight and hard to solve, and the additional side constraints only exacerbate the situation. For lower ratios, the impact of the side constraints on the solving time and on the solution cost is quite acceptable. Until ratio 4:1, the difference is not significant. With ratio 5:1, the solver takes only 15 additional seconds to compute a solution subject to 750 `spread` constraints, 20 `capacity` constraints, 5 `ban` constraints, and one `lonely` constraint, while the cost of the reconfiguration plan is increased by 13%. When the datacenter size varies, the impact of the side constraints appears again to be limited. With fixed ratio 5:1, the solver is always able to compute a solution for more than 88% of the instances. For the largest problems, the solving time is only 9% greater than for the core VRSP, while the cost of the solutions is only 7% higher.

These experiments show that the impact of the side constraints is significant only when the core VRSP is itself already hard. In a well-designed datacenter, the primary bottleneck is the limited capacity of its servers. The side placement constraints should remain only tools provided to the administrators and clients to express their preferences. When they become preponderant, then the dimension of the datacenter should be rethought.

6   Related Works

Dynamic reconfiguration arises in real-time computing systems with two dominant applications: reallocation of storage devices to data and reallocation of processors to processes. In both cases, the goal is to improve the efficiency of the service as the system evolves, but the main concerns differ.

One key issue in *data migration* is when to schedule, given a final configuration and the limited capacity of the network, the transfer of data blocks to involve the least impact on the service. In the core problem, the reconfiguration time should be minimized, and each transfer occupies, simultaneously during one unit time, the unique ports of its sender and receiver devices. Such a *port constraint* is similar to the concurrent resource constraint of the RTSP. It is however simpler since it is a disjunctive resource constraint, uncorrelated with the storage capacity of the devices which is usually assumed to be unlimited during migration. In the DATA MIGRATION WITH SPACE CONSTRAINTS [1] variant, both port and storage constraints have to be satisfied during the reconfiguration, but data blocks are assumed to be identical and the devices never full.

The key issue in *process migration* is rather where to redispatch the processes, given the limited capacities of the processors. Most former works, actually, only consider migrations by service disruption and thus are not subject to scheduling problems. CP-based approaches were proposed for two opposite objectives: LOAD REBALANCING [4] aims at finding a more balanced configuration while minimizing the number of migrations; SERVICE CONSOLIDATION [3,6] aims at gathering the load in order to switch off the maximum number of unused processors.

Live process migration induces a scheduling problem with concurrent resource requirements during the reconfiguration. To our knowledge, this problem has previously only been studied in [6,8]. Sirdey et al. [8] presented the PROCESS MOVE

PROGRAM, a variant of the RTSP oriented to load balancing, with two transition types: unit-time live migration and migration by disruption. The resource requirements are constant and the final configuration is given. The problem is to minimize the number of disruptions and to order the live migrations of the remaining processes for solving the resource conflicts. The ZIPMP problem, evoked in Section 2, is the decision variant where no disruption is allowed. The authors provided a branch-and-bound and several metaheuristics solutions. In a previous implementation of Entropy oriented to consolidation [6], a fast schedule is searched in a greedy way, using a CP model to enforce the resource constraints to be satisfied at any time. The considered problem is an extension of the RTSP as it allows to migrate VMs on bypass servers to avoid cycles.

It turns out that, in former works, the packing and the scheduling parts of the reconfiguration problem have never been handled at once. Such a decomposition allows to deal with a quality criterion on the final configuration, namely load balancing or consolidation, but it hinders the objective to get fast reconfiguration plans. In the VRSP, consolidation and load balancing criteria could also be enforced as extra soft constraints or within the search heuristic.

The aforementioned reconfiguration problems match the exact resource constraints (1) of the BRSP, or a natural extension of them:

$$\sum_{\substack{j \in s_o^{-1}(r) \\ t < t_j}} b_j^o + \sum_{\substack{j \in s_o^{-1}(r) \\ t_j \le t < t_j + d_{\delta(j)}}} b_{\delta(j)}^o + \sum_{\substack{j \in s_f^{-1}(r) \\ t_j \le t < t_j + d_{\delta(j)}}} b_{\delta(j)}^f + \sum_{\substack{j \in s_f^{-1}(r) \\ t_j + d_{\delta(j)} \le t}} b_j^f \le B_r, \quad \forall r \in \mathcal{R}, \forall t \ge 0.$$

This extension allows the requirements to differ as the transitions are performed. Thus it allows to model disruptions $(b_{\delta(j)}^o = b_{\delta(j)}^f = 0)$ as in PROCESS MOVE PROGRAM or port constraints $(b_{\delta(j)}^o = b_{\delta(j)}^f = 1$ and $b_j^o = b_j^f = 0)$ as in DATA MIGRATION. Furthermore our CP model can be extended to handle these constraints, using 4 task variables for each transition instead of 2. As a consequence, this model, with different objectives, fits most of the problems above described, at one notable exception: it cannot deal with bypass as in [1,6].

Regarding now the flexibility and the scalability of our approach, a dozen of relative placement constraints are currently implemented in Entropy. In the same context of datacenter resource management, Dhyani et al. [3] also advocated the power of CP technologies to handle some of these constraints. As previously said, they perform only consolidation, not reconfiguration, and experiment on instances with up to 30 servers with 4 resources each, and 250 VMs. Commercial VM managers propose also more and more services to their clients to express their needs in terms of placement. For example, the DRS [9] manager by VMWare performs consolidation and provides 3 affinity rules to customize the VM placement. These rules match the constraints, called in Entropy: spread, ban and its opposite, fence. A cluster managed by DRS can not exceed 32 nodes and 1280 VMs. The technology behind DRS is concealed.

7   Conclusion

Virtualized datacenters host and manage large ranges of applications, each application being distributed in VMs. The resource requirements of the VMs change over time. In addition, clients and system administrators have specific expectations regarding the relative placement of the VMs on the servers. Automatic reconfiguration is needed each time the current placement is no longer viable. Considering both the resource requirements and the placement constraints, the problem is to determine a new placement of the VMs and to schedule the transitions so as to provide a fast and reliable reconfiguration.

In this paper, we presented a general formalization of this problem, called Bin Repacking Scheduling Problem, and a model of Constraint Programming providing the flexibility needed to dynamically inject side placement constraints. Our model is implemented and integrated into the autonomous VM manager Entropy. Experiments with realistic simulated workloads show the ability of Entropy to solve problems involving up to 10,000 VMs on 2,000 servers with 900 side constraints in less than 5 minutes.

In future works, we want to enrich Entropy with more placement constraints, including constraints on the network topology, which could make our model drastically harder to solve. We aim also at providing side constraints with violation penalties, as clients prefer a controlled degradation of the service to any non-viable configurations. In addition, we want Entropy to be able to help a system administrator to locate issues, such as resource bottleneck CP provides, through soft constraints and explanations, the elements to address these needs. Their development will contribute to improve the usability of datacenters.

References

1. Anderson, E., Hall, J., Hartline, J., Hobbes, M., Karlin, A., Saia, J., Swaminathan, R., Wilkes, J.: Algorithms for data migration. Algorithmica 57(2), 349–380 (2010)
2. Beldiceanu, N., Carlsson, M., Rampon, J.: Global constraint catalog. Tech. Rep. 2007, SICS (2010), http://www.emn.fr/z-info/sdemasse/gccat/
3. Dhyani, K., Gualandi, S., Cremonesi, P.: A constraint programming approach for the service consolidation problem. In: Lodi, A., Milano, M., Toth, P. (eds.) CPAIOR 2010. LNCS, vol. 6140, pp. 97–101. Springer, Heidelberg (2010)
4. Fukunaga, A.: Search spaces for min-perturbation repair. In: Gent, I.P. (ed.) CP 2009. LNCS, vol. 5732, pp. 383–390. Springer, Heidelberg (2009)
5. Garey, M., Johnson, D.: Computers and Intractability: A Guide to the Theory of NP-completeness. WH Freeman & Co., New York (1979)
6. Hermenier, F., Lorca, X., Menaud, J.M., Muller, G., Lawall, J.: Entropy: a consolidation manager for clusters. In: VEE 2009, pp. 41–50. ACM, New York (2009)
7. Simonis, H., Cornelissens, T.: Modelling producer/consumer constraints. In: Montanari, U., Rossi, F. (eds.) CP 1995. LNCS, vol. 976, pp. 449–462. Springer, Heidelberg (1995)
8. Sirdey, R., Carlier, J., Kerivin, H., Nace, D.: On a resource-constrained scheduling problem with application to distributed systems reconfiguration. European Journal of Operational Research 183(2), 546–563 (2007)
9. VMWare: Resource Management with VMWare DRS. Tech. rep. (2006)

Route Finder: Efficiently Finding k Shortest Paths Using Constraint Programming

Michel P. Lefebvre[1], Jean-François Puget[2], and Petr Vilím[3]

[1] IBM. 21 chemin de la Sauvegarde, 69130 Ecully, France
[2] IBM, 350 Avenue de Boulouris, 83700 Saint Raphael, France
[3] IBM, V Parku 2294/4, 148 00 Praha 4 - Chodov, Czech Republic
{mlefebvre,j-f.puget}@fr.ibm.com, petr_vilim@cz.ibm.com

Abstract. In this paper, we describe a Constraint Programming (CP) route finding application for a container transportation company. Mathematically, this amounts to finding the k shortest paths in a directed graph. However the nature of the business constraints rule out known algorithms such as Dijkstra's. Indeed, one cannot unfold all constraints into a directed graph as the resulting graph would be too large. Given an origin and destination (two places), the problem is to decide which ships should be used (routes), and when and where the containers should be loaded from one ship to another (connections), while satisfying many business rules specified by the transportation company. The CP model described in this paper is quite simple, it doesn't use any specialized constraints, but it is surprisingly effective. Queries for the best route are answered in a matter of a second or fraction of a second, although the problem is very large: around 900 places, 2,300 routes, 22,000 connections and 4,200 business rules. The system gracefully handles 100,000 requests a day on a single server.

Keywords: Transportation, Shortest Path, Routing.

1   Problem Description

One of the major container carrier companies has contacted IBM about a route finding (RF) application they needed to rewrite. The RF application is part of the system that supports the commercial operations of that company. Basically, the problem is about rapidly finding feasible ways to ship goods from one place to another place, worldwide. The system response must be fast enough to be used during a phone call where a company representative negotiates with a potential customer. In order to support the commercial negotiation the RF system must propose several alternative ways for shipping goods. The fastest way does not have to be necessarily the cheapest, the company needs a system able to propose several different paths so that the customer can make a choice. The RF system is also used by various IT applications as a subroutine. All in all, RF system must answer about 100,000 requests a day.

In the following we concentrate on transportation by container ships but the definitions can be extended to other transportation means such as trains or

J. Lee (Ed.): CP 2011, LNCS 6876, pp. 42–53, 2011.

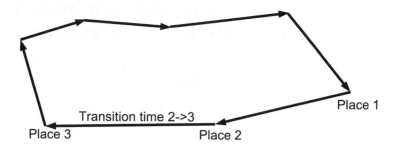

Fig. 1. Example of a route

barges. Therefore, in data description, we will use generic terms such as place, connection and so on. This section gives a quick overview of the problem, terminology and notation.

Container ships usually operate on fairly regular schedules which are known in advance and do not change a lot. Typically, a ship follows a circular path called *route* (see Figure 1). A route doesn't have any particular start or end, containers can be loaded or unloaded at each stop. Transition times between places on the route are known in advance. A route is therefore a closed loop that visits a series of *places* (harbors usually) in a predefined order. A ship following a given route visits all places on the route according to their (route specific) sequence number. The same place can appear several times on a route with different sequence numbers.

An operation of unloading a container from one ship and loading it on another ship is called *transhipment*. In order to make a transhipment, both ships must make a stop at the same port, but not necessarily at the same time: the container can be stored at the port for a short period of time. However, even if the two ships make a stop at the same port, it still may be impossible to make the transhipment: some ports are very large and transportation from one part of the port to another may be costly or not allowed at all. Therefore, possible connections are specified by a set of tuples of the form [place, from-route, to-route]. Note that connections are not symmetrical – from-route and to-route cannot be exchanged. See Figure 2.

The task is to find k shortest paths (in terms of duration) from Place Of Load (POL) to Place Of Discharge (POD), see Figure 3.

The path must fulfill the following conditions:

- Maximum number of transhipments is 5.
- All business rules are satisfied (will be explained later).

To simplify the problem, we solve it in two phases. In the first phase, we concentrate only on finding the best routes, without assigning the schedule. In another words, we ignore limitations such as:

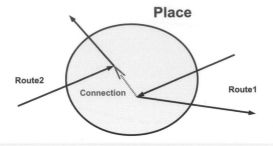

Fig. 2. Example of a connection at Place1 from Route1 to Route2

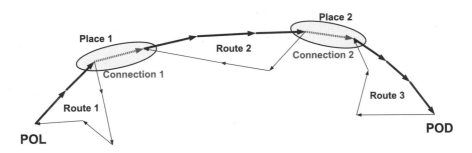

Fig. 3. Example of a path from POL to POD. The path starts by Route1, at Place1 it changes to Route2 using Connection1 etc. until it reaches POD.

- **Exact ship schedules:** We take into account the time it usually takes for a ship to travel from place A to place B, but we ignore the fact that the particular trip takes 1 more day (for example, due to planned repairs).
- **Exact transhipment times:** We precompute the usual time necessary for each allowed connection. Then we use these values instead of real connection times which depend on real ship schedules.
- **Ship capacity etc.:** We assume that the ship can always transport the cargo. For example, there are no capacity constraints or type constraints.

In the second phase (post processing) we use real ship schedules to compute the real length of the path. The second phase is pretty straightforward, it doesn't use CP, and therefore we do not describe it in this paper.

Note that post processing can change duration of routes found by CP, in extreme case some solutions found by CP can be even found infeasible during post processing. This is one of the reasons why it is necessary to find k shortest paths instead of only the best one during the first phase. There is no guarantee that (after the post processing) one of the k shortest paths is the optimal one, however we didn't see such a case in practice. Note also that the current solution developed by the customer also split the problem in this way and it was a requirement of the customer to keep it this way.

1.1 Business Rules

Aside of the path constraints, the solution must satisfy a set of approximately 4,200 business rules. These rules have the following form:

```
IF
  applicabilityPart and
  (IF1 or IF2 or ... or IFn)
THEN [NOT]
  (TH1 or TH2 or ... or THn)
```

Where

- `applicabilityPart` specifies when the rule is active in terms of POL and POD. For example, it is possible to specify that a rule is active only for paths from Europe to China. But it is also possible to specify a rule which is always active.
- IFi and THi are if/then literals. They could be, for example, one of the following conditions:
  - Place P is on the path.
  - Route R is on the path.
  - Place P1 is directly followed by place P2.
  - Route R1 is directly followed by route R2.
- If `NOT` is present then the THEN part may be empty (no THi). In this case all of the IFi conditions must be false in order to satisfy the rule.

Here are two examples of the business rules:

1. If POL is New York and POD is in France (`applicabilityPart`) and route R1 or route R2 is used (two IF literals) then place P must be on the path (one TH literal).
2. If POL is in Brazil and POD in Germany (`applicabilityPart`) then route R cannot be used (one IF literal for route R, NOT is present, no TH literal).

Note that the possible connections at a place may depend on the origin (POL) and destination (POD) of the request, the rules are not local. This is what makes the problem not solvable by classical methods as we shall see in the next section.

2 Why CP?

Shortest path problems are *very* easy to solve, and one could wonder why we did not consider using classical algorithms such as Dijkstra's. The issue is that a fundamental property required by Dijkstra and all dynamic programming approaches is that any sub path of an optimal path is also optimal. Indeed, there are business rules that make a perfectly optimal sub path not extensible into an optimal path.

For instance, while looking for a path from A to C, reaching the intermediate point B from A within 10 days does not mean we can ignore ways to reach B in more than 10 days. Indeed, the allowed path from B to C may depend on how (which route) B is reached. One way to solve this could be to construct a derived graph where the unconstrained shortest paths are the shortest constrained path in the original graph. For this one needs to duplicate place nodes so that business rules are replaced by possible arcs. Business rules depend on the origin, destination, place of transhipment, and also on incoming and outgoing routes to the place of transhipment. Therefore we need to create one node per origin/destination/place/route tuple. In our case this means about 10^{12} nodes, which is not manageable with the time and space constraints we have for finding routes. Refinement of this brute force approach is certainly possible, but we decided to keep the graph implicit and treat the business rules as constraints.

The shipping company had developed a system that was searching for constrained paths as outlined above. That system was poorly designed as it grew over time with ad hoc coding of business rules into the control flow. It was difficult to maintain as it was made of:

- several heterogeneous and interdependent modules (500,000 lines of hand made code, written in Forte)
- with additional technical features to compensate for the low performance (frequent request caching, graph reduction)
- and many similar and redundant concepts coexisting.

It was therefore decided to:

- keep the business-specific part of the system i.e., the routing rules and the authorized connections,
- to replace the complex procedural code by a declarative CP model, based on those constraints and solved by a generic solver (IBM ILOG CP Optimizer [5]),
- to isolate the static graph set-up, in order to avoid useless data reloading and graph set-up for each routing request.

2.1   Related Work

Problem of finding shortest paths using CP was already studied by several authors, see for example [11, 3, 8]. The recommended approach is to use a dedicated constraint for propagation.

In our case, the maximum number of transhipments is 5 what simplifies the problem a lot. Therefore we tried first to model the problem using only standard constraints available our CP solver. In the end, performance of this model is so good that it is not necessary to implement a dedicated constraint. Moreover, the customer already experienced how hard it is to maintain existing RF system. Therefore it was very appreciated that implementation of a new constraint is not necessary and CP could be used as a kind of black-box solver.

3   CP Model

3.1   Development

The RF application has been developed with IBM CPLEX Optimization Studio [1]. This product contains several components among which the modeling language OPL[1], and the Constraint Programming system CP Optimizer (CPO) [5]. At the beginning, we started the development in OPL. Thanks to the OPL we were able to connect to the customer database, read the data, and quickly experiment with different models until we found the best one.

In case of the routing application, every fraction of a second matters as the target is to solve thousands of requests per hour. Therefore once the model was stabilized, we converted it from OPL to the C++ API of CPO in order to eliminate overhead of model building (although the overhead was only a few percents in speed).

3.2   General Framework

CP is a great tool for solving optimization problems. However, it should be used to solve only the core part of the problem and leave remaining work to preprocessing and post processing. Therefore we use the following framework:

```
GlobalPreprocessing();
while (WaitForQuery()) do begin
  LocalPreprocessing();
  SolveCPModel();
  Postprocessing();
end;
```

Where:

- GlobalPreprocessing does preprocessing independent of POL and POD. For example, it computes usual transhipment times for all allowed connections. At the end of this phase, all necessary data are loaded into memory in order to avoid disc access during following phases.
- LocalPreprocessing does preprocessing dependent on POL and POD. For example, it filters applicable rules and adds StopPlace into the graph (will be described later).
- PostProcessing assigns schedules to found paths, resorts the solutions according to real duration or according to any other business criteria.

In the following, we will concentrate on the SolveCPModel part.

---

[1] The OPL language has significantly evolved since its original design by Pascal Van Hentenryck, Irv Lustig, Laurent Michel, and Jean-François Puget [4]. The current version documentation can be found at
http://publib.boulder.ibm.com/infocenter/cosinfoc/v12r2/index.jsp

3.3   Decision Variables

As usual with real problems, there are many ways to represent them as a constrained optimization problem. For instance one could create one decision variable per place whose value would be the next place. One issue with this model is to deal with the places that won't be visited for a given request. One would need to both introduce dummy values for such nodes and extend constraints to ignore those dummy values. A seemingly better model would be to create an array of decision variables, one decision variable per visited place. For instance, the fourth variable would denote the fourth visited place. This model still requires dummy values as we do not know the number of places that the shortest path will visit. The dummy values would be used for the variables whose indices are larger than the index of the one valued with the destination.

A much better model leverages two facts. First of all, if no transhipment takes place at a place, then the container stays on the same ship before and after visiting that place. The only *real* decisions to be made are where transhipments occur, that is, which connections are used. Therefore, a solution to the problem is a chain of routes, places and connections. For each of them we create a decision variable (see Figure 4):

- route[i]: i-th route on the path.
- duration[i]: duration of the transportation using route[i].
- place[i]: i-th place on the path.
- connex[i]: connection used at place[i].
- trTime[i]: usual time spent by connex[i].

The second fact is that the number of transhipments is limited to 5, which limits the number of decision variables we need to consider.

The number of transhipments is not known in advance, it can range from 0 to 5. In order to deal with it we add a new place in the graph – StopPlace – which is reachable only from POD using ToStop connection and ToStop route, see Figure 5. Once StopPlace is reached the only way to continue the path is to use an artificial StopRoute back to StopPlace. This way, instead of looking for

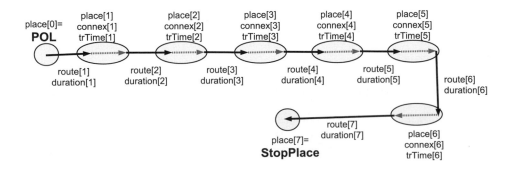

Fig. 4. Decision variables of the problem

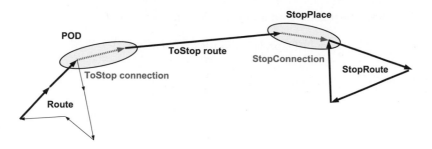

Fig. 5. Addition of StopPlace into the graph

a path from POL to POD with maximum 5 transhipments, we are looking for a
path from POL to StopPlace with exactly 6 transhipments (including artificial
transhipments at StopPlace). That's why there are 6 connections in Figure 4
and `place[0]` is set to POL and `place[7]` is set to StopPlace.

3.4   Constraints for Path

The variables described above are connected using the `allowedAssignment` constraint of CPO (also known as table constraint [6]). Using OPL syntax:

```
forall(i in 1..6)
  allowedAssignments(allowedConnections,
                     place[i], connex[i],
                     route[i], route[i+1], trTime[i]);
forall(i in 1..7)
  allowedAssignments(distances,
                     route[i], place[i-1], place[i], duration[i]);
```

Where `allowedConnections` is a set of tuples [place, connection, from-route, to-
route, transhipment-time] and `distances` is a set of tuples [route, from-place,
to-place, duration].

Of course, no place (aside from StopPlace) can appear on the path more
than once. This could be modeled using the `count` expression in CPO (note
that these expressions are automatically aggregated into a global cardinality
constraint [10]):

```
forall(p in places)
  count(place, p) <= 1;
```

3.5   Business Rules

The constraints for applicable business rules are built on the fly. First we create
integer expressions for all `IF`i and `TH`i literals: the expression has value 1 if the
literal is true, 0 otherwise. Then, if `NOT` is not present in the rule then we add
the following constraint:

$$\max_i \left\{\text{IfExpr}_i\right\} \leq \max_i \left\{\text{ThenExpr}_i\right\}$$

Otherwise (if NOT is present) we add the following constraint:

$$\max_i \big\{ \text{IfExpr}_i \big\} \le 1 - \max_i \big\{ \text{ThenExpr}_i \big\}$$

If there is no THi literal then we define:

$$\max_i \big\{ \text{ThenExpr}_i \big\} = 1$$

In Section 1.1 we gave two examples of business rules. Assuming that they are applicable (considering the current POL and POD), they will generate the following constraints:

1. If POL is New York and POD is in France (applicabilityPart) and route R1 or route R2 is used (two IF literals) then place P must be on the path (one TH literal):

   ```
   max( count(route, R1), count(route, R2) ) <= count(place, P)
   ```

2. If POL is in Brazil and POD in Germany (applicabilityPart) then route R cannot be used (one IF literal for route R, NOT is present, no TH literal):

   ```
   count(route, R) <= 1 - 1
   ```

3.6   The Search

We started the development by looking for a single shortest path using default search of CPO. The results were very good, however for this particular model the default search was "too clever". Thanks to strong propagation, CPO was able to find solutions almost without any backtrack. However, the impact measurement used in its default search [9] slowed it down. Therefore we switched to simple DepthFirst search focusing on the place variables first as these variables have the biggest impact. This could be done using CPO high level search statements called *search phases*. The net result was a speedup of around 20%, even though there was more backtracking.

The customer was not interested in only one best path, the request was to find best k paths. Currently, there is no public API for this kind of output in CPO. Therefore we designed a workaround in the following way:

1. Start the search for all solutions, without supplying any objective function.
2. Iterate over solutions and remember k best solutions found so far. If there are more than 1,000 solutions then continue by 3, otherwise return best k solutions found.
3. Add constraint saying that we are interested only in solutions strictly better than the worst one from the k stored solutions. Forget all stored solutions with exception of the worst one. Restart the search and continue by 2.

Usually, one restart was enough. In rare cases it was necessary to restart the search twice. Note that without restarting we could end up by enumeration millions of solutions which would require minutes instead of a fraction of a second.

4   Added Value of CP

The CP based route finder code is quite small compared to the previous system, as it is about 2,000 lines of C++ code instead of about 50,000 lines of code for the search part of the previous system. Moreover, the declarative nature of the CP code enables consistency checking and review by humans whereas it is almost impossible to check the logic embedded in the old system. This alone has been seen as a tremendous progress by the shipping company team. A nice side effect of this is that the system is much easier to maintain and to evolve.

The CP based system prototype has been developed in less than two months in elapsed time, and four man months in total. This is much smaller than the time required to develop the original system.

Having a nice small piece of code is a desirable property, but what matters the most is the quality of the routes found, their adequateness with the business operations, and the speed at which these routes have been found, for any possible request.

The quality of the routes has been evaluated the following way. On a significant sample of 9,127 requests the two systems have been run. On 92.8% of the requests, the best route found by the old system is also found by the CP based system. Conversely, the best route found by the new system is also found by the old one in 73.2% of the requests. This shows that the quality of the new system routes is better on average. The fact that CP did not found the best stored solution in 100% of the cases can be explained by the nature of the procedural code of the old system. All business rules and constraints are coded as part of the procedural code that searches for routes, and it is probable that some mistakes have been made in these encodings. On the contrary, the declarative nature of the CP based system enables easy code review.

The adequateness of the routes found with the business needs has been evaluated the following way. A sample of routes for which the best route has been validated by a human operator has been provided to us. This is a by product of an attempt to speed up the old system. With the old system, each time a request is answered its result is cached to speed up the next query with the same (origin, destination) pair. The most frequent ones are then looked up by a human operator and stored as a routing instructions (RI). We were provided a sample of 839 routing instructions. For each of them we ran our route finder with the (origin, destination) pair and we compared with the best route stored with the one computed by CP. Our system found the stored answer in 815 of the cases, i.e. 97.1%. For the remaining few cases where CP did not find the stored solutions, CP found a better route, or some constraints were not met by the stored solution.

The speed of the new system has been evaluated against the speed of the old system using a 998 request sample. In a first experiment the requests were handled sequentially. The new system response time was about 1 second on average against 9.4 seconds for the old system. However the new system does not implement some post processing done by the old system (computing the exact schedule of the trip once a route is found). In order to make the comparison fair we take into account the time to do this post processing, and it is estimated to take 1 extra second. Therefore the new system would take about 2 seconds on average against 9.4 seconds for th old one. We then did a second experiment where requests are triggered concurrently, at the rate in which they arrive in reality (about one per second). Then the response time of the new system is unchanged, at about 1 second without post processing, whereas the old system response time goes up to 47 seconds on average. The response time of the new system is therefore about 24 times better than the old one.

The experiments above show that the new system finds better routes on average and that it finds them much faster than the old system. The new system is also easier to evolve given the declarative code used. One very interesting evolution was to use a small variant of the CP model to provide explanations using the original business rules. We introduced this as a way to debug our encoding of the business rules as follows.

Sometimes the problem didn't have any solution and we wanted to know why. Therefore, instead of applying the rules all the time we added 0/1 decision variable controlling whether the rule is turned on or not. This is straightforward to implement in CP Optimizer using conditional constraints. Then, by minimizing the sum of these additional variables we are able to identify which rule(s) make the problem infeasible (and that again in a matter of a second). This possibility became quickly very popular and due to the demand, we also added a possibility to choose which rules cannot be relaxed and to check why a particular solution is not possible.

Given the dramatic speedup and route quality improvements the shipping company has decided to integrate the CP based route finder application within its overall IT system and to deploy it. This is currently underway.

Note that the customer team did not had to understand the CP technology as we only used straightforward modeling constructs. They are able to read the C++ code that translates their business rules into CPO constraints.

Our use of CP for this project was focused on modeling. We did not write fancy search algorithms nor new constraint propagators. The resulting code is quite declarative and it can be seen as an instance of the *model and run* paradigm for CP advocated in [7]. This is one of the lessons learned from using CPO on this project. It is very important to have a code that business users can check and understand, which is key to build confidence into the system. The ability to provide explanations in terms of the original business rules was also key to build confidence.

The old system, beside its poor performance, was a gigantic black box that no one could understand at the shipping company. They had to rely on a costly third party consulting firm for any change to the system. The new one is much more maintainable and ready for evolution.

The CP approach developed for this customer is original as far as we know. There is little literature on finding constrained shortest path, with or without CP. One can cite [12] who solve a constrained shortest path problem in telecom networks. However, their problem had significant difference from the one we discussed in this paper. For instance, their graph is such that each arc (A, B) has a corresponding arc (B, A), whereas in our case arcs and connections do not necessarily have a symmetric counterpart. Another attempt at using CP for shortest path is given in [2]. This paper explores constrained variants of shortest path problems, but these variants do not cover constraints we generate from business rules.

As a summary, we have presented a quite effective use of CP for solving a complex business problem, namely how to route goods from one place to the other in the shortest possible time. A rather simple CP model requiring 2,000 lines of code yields much better performance than a system made of 500,000 lines of procedural code. The results of the application are so good that the shipping company has decided to deploy the CP based application. This is a remarkable endorsement since *all* the business of the shipping company depends on the quality of the proposed routes.

References

[1] IBM ILOG CPLEX Optimization Studio, http://www-01.ibm.com/software/integration/optimization/cplex-optimization-studio/
[2] Bistarelli, S., Montanari, U.: Soft constraint logic programming and generalized shortest path problems. Journal of Heuristics 8(1), 25–41 (2002)
[3] Dooms, G., Deville, Y., Dupont, P.: CP(Graph): Introducing a graph computation domain in constraint programming. In: van Beek, P. (ed.) CP 2005. LNCS, vol. 3709, pp. 211–225. Springer, Heidelberg (2005)
[4] Van Hentenryck, P., Lustig, I., Michel, L., Puget, J.-F.: The OPL optimization programming language. MIT Press, Cambridge (1999)
[5] IBM. IBM ILOG CPLEX Optimization Studio documentation. volume 8:1. IBM (2010), http://publib.boulder.ibm.com/infocenter/cosinfoc/v12r2/index.jsp
[6] Lhomme, O., Régin, J.-C.: A fast arc consistency algorithm for n-ary constraints. In: AAAI 2005 (2005)
[7] Puget, J.-F.: Constraint programming next challenge: Simplicity of use. In: Wallace, M. (ed.) CP 2004. LNCS, vol. 3258, pp. 5–8. Springer, Heidelberg (2004)
[8] Quesada, L., Roy, P.V., Deville, Y., Collet, R.: Using dominators for solving constrained path problems. In: PADL, pp. 73–87 (2006)
[9] Refalo, P.: Impact-based search strategies for constraint programming. In: Wallace, M. (ed.) CP 2004. LNCS, vol. 3258, pp. 557–571. Springer, Heidelberg (2004)
[10] Régin, J.-C.: Generalized arc consistency for global cardinality constraint. In: Proceedings of the 13th National Conference on AI (AAAI/IAAI 1996), vol. 1, pp. 209–215. AAAI Press / The MIT Press (1996)
[11] Sellmann, M.: Cost-based filtering for shorter path constraints. In: Rossi, F. (ed.) CP 2003. LNCS, vol. 2833, pp. 694–708. Springer, Heidelberg (2003)
[12] Wallander, M.P., Szymanek, R., Kuchcinski, K.: CP-LP hybrid method for unique shortest path routing optimization. In: Proceedings of the International Network Optimization Conference (2007)

The Design of Cryptographic S-Boxes Using CSPs

Venkatesh Ramamoorthy[1], Marius C. Silaghi[1], Toshihiro Matsui[2],
Katsutoshi Hirayama[3], and Makoto Yokoo[4]

[1] Florida Institute of Technology, Melbourne, FL 32901, United States of America
vramamoo@my.fit.edu, msilaghi@cs.fit.edu
[2] Nagoya Institute of Technology, Nagoya, Aichi, 466-8555, Japan
matsui.t@nitech.ac.jp
[3] Kobe University, Kobe, 657-8501, Japan
hirayama@maritime.kobe-u.ac.jp
[4] Kyushu University, Hakozaki 6-10-1, Higashi-ku, Fukuoka, 812-8581, Japan
yokoo@is.kyushu-u.ac.jp

Abstract. We use the Constraint Satisfaction Problem (CSP) framework to
model and solve the problem of designing substitution functions for substitution-
permutation (SP) networks as proposed by Shannon for the architecture of ciphers. Many ciphers are designed using the SP pattern, and differ mainly by two
parametrized functions: substitution and permutation. The most difficult of the
two is the substitution function, which has to be nonlinear (a requirement that was
difficult to define and quantify). Over time, researchers such as Nyberg, Pieprzyk
and Matsui have proposed various metrics of nonlinearity that make the function robust to modern attacks. Before us, people have attempted various ways to
design functions that respect these metrics. In the past people hand-picked substitution tables (S-boxes) by trying various values. Recently they use difficult to
analyze constructs (such as Bent functions, spectral inversion, inverses in Galois
fields) whose outputs are tested for nonlinearity. While efficient, such techniques
are neither exhaustive (optimal), nor did they manage to generate better substitutions than the ones hand-picked in the past.

We show that Matsui's nonlinearity requirement can be naturally modelled
using CSPs. Based on a combination of existing CSP techniques and some new
filtering operators that we designed specially for the new types of constraints,
we manage to obtain better S-boxes than any previously published ones. The
simplicity of the CSP framework and availability of general CSP solvers like
ours, makes it easy for more people to design their own ciphers with easy to
understand security parameters. Here we report on this new application of CSPs.

Keywords: CSP Model, S-Boxes, DES, 3DES, Nonlinearity, Linear Cryptanalysis, Differential Cryptanalysis.

1 The Cipher Design Problem

We discuss an application of the Constraint Satisfaction Problem (CSP) framework to
the design of Substitution Boxes (S-Boxes) used extensively in cryptographic algorithms to secure data for confidentiality purposes.

J. Lee (Ed.): CP 2011, LNCS 6876, pp. 54–68, 2011.

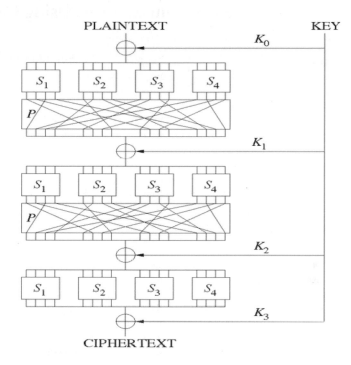

Fig. 1. Shannon's Substitution Permutation (SP) Network

Claude Shannon proposed the Substitution Permutation (SP) network, considered to be the heart of modern cryptography [22]. To transform (encrypt or decrypt) bits of data to ensure confidentiality, an SP network such as the one shown in Fig. 1, performs three steps. First, a function of the transformation key, called a *subkey*, is exclusively-ORed into the input data bits.

The second step is the one we are interested in. A substitution function $S_i : \mathbb{Z}_{2^n} \rightarrow \mathbb{Z}_{2^n}$ ($i = 1, \ldots, 4$ in Fig. 1) replaces n bits of data by another set of n bits to introduce *confusion* into the data. By $\mathbb{Z}_k$ we denote the set of residues $\{0, 1, ..., k - 1\}$ modulo-k. The replacement is performed using lookup tables called Substitution Boxes, or S-Boxes.

In the third step, a permutation function P shuffles the bits to cause *diffusion* within the data. Shannon's SP network requires that each of the S-functions be invertible. The three steps constitute a *round* of the SP network and are repeated several times. Each round other than the first acts on the output of a previous round. Fig. 1 constitutes a three-round SP network, with subkeys $K_0, \ldots, K_3$ derived from the transforming key.

One of the most productive contributions to modern cryptography is Feistel's architecture [8], also referred to as the *Feistel network* in the literature. It offers a simple

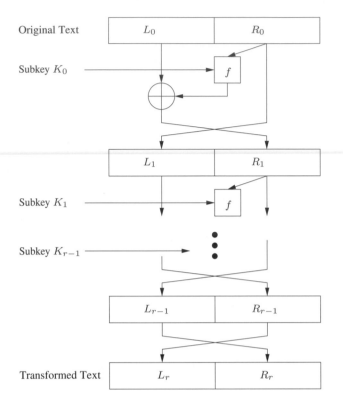

Original Text

Subkey K_0

Subkey K_1

Subkey K_{r-1}

Transformed Text

Fig. 2. Rounds of encryption / decryption in a typical Feistel Cipher

mechanism for generating countless sound[1] encryption schemes. The Feistel network, first designed by Horst Feistel and depicted in Fig. 2, is a product cipher. Each block of data being transformed is divided into two halves, a left and right half. Input bits being transformed are permuted to introduce *diffusion* into the bits.

Next, a function f applies the S-Boxes on these permuted bits to further introduce *confusion* into the data being transformed. These substitution-permutation steps form a *round* of transformation, and are repeated several times. In addition, f mixes a function of the transformation key called *subkey*, precomputed from the transformation key using a *key schedule*. Each round uses a subkey different from the others.

New sound encryption schemes on $2mk$ bits are obtained[2] for any choice of k $n \times m$ S-Boxes for any desired m and n. Feistel's cipher architecture is a variant of Shannon's substitution-permutation (SP) network [22]. When compared with Shannon's network, the soundness requirement imposes no constraint on the Feistel's substitution boxes (i.e., on the S function)[3].

---

[1] An encryption scheme is sound if decryption always returns the original plaintext.
[2] One for each key schedule.
[3] Shannon required that S-Boxes be invertible.

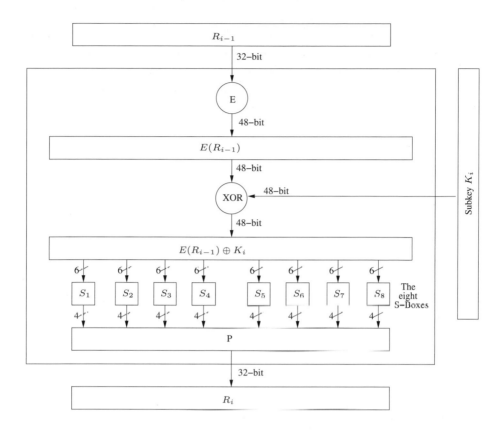

Fig. 3. One Round of encryption / decryption in 3DES using the S-Boxes

1.1   Examples of SP Networks

Blowfish, Twofish, Camellia, RC5, IBM's Data Encryption Standard (DES) [15], and the widely used *Triple*-DES (3DES), are examples of Feistel ciphers. Note that 3DES is one of the main ciphers used in protocols such as Secure Sockets Layer (SSL) and the newer Transport Layer Security (TLS). It is also employed in the Secure Shell (SSH) protocol used in applications such as `sftp` and `ssh`. Non-Feistel architectures abound in the literature such as, for example, the International Data Encryption Algorithm (IDEA) [11] and Rijndael, the current Advanced Encryption Standard (AES) [7], that employ the SP architecture.

A round of 3DES employs eight 6×4 S-Boxes numbered $S_1, S_2, \ldots, S_8$ as depicted in Fig. 3 with S_1 shown in Fig. 4. An S-box substitution of 4 bits for a 6-bit input i is obtained by indexing into the row number formed by the first and last bits of i, and the column number formed by the middle bits of i. For example, input of $45 (= 101101_2)$ to S-Box S_1 yields 1, obtained by reading the entry in row 3 $(= 11_2)$, column 6 $(= 0110_2)$ of Fig. 4.

S_1	\multicolumn{16}{c}{$y_1y_2y_3y_4$}
y_0y_5	0 1 2 3 4 5 6 7 8 9 10 11 12 13 14 15
0	14 4 13 1 2 15 11 8 3 10 6 12 5 9 0 7
1	0 15 7 4 14 2 13 1 10 6 12 11 9 5 3 8
2	4 1 14 8 13 6 2 11 15 12 9 7 3 10 5 0
3	15 12 8 2 4 9 1 7 5 11 3 14 10 0 6 13

Fig. 4. S-box S_1 used in 3DES

Table 1. The S-box criteria used by IBM for designing 3DES [6]

S-1 Each S-box has six bits of input and four bits of output.

S-2 No output bit of an S-box should be too close to a linear function of the input bits. (That is, if we select any output bit position and any subset of the six input bit positions, the fraction of inputs for which this output bit equals the exclusive-OR of these input bits should not be close to 0 or 1, but rather should be near $\frac{1}{2}$).

S-3 If we fix the leftmost and rightmost input bits of the S-box and vary the four middle bits, each possible 4-bit output is attained exactly once as the middle four input bits range over their 16 possibilities.

S-4 If two inputs to an S-box differ in exactly one bit, the outputs must differ in at least two bits.

S-5 If two inputs to an S-box differ in the two middle bits exactly, the outputs must differ in at least two bits.

S-6 If two inputs to an S-box differ in their first two bits and are identical in their last two bits, the two outputs must not be the same.

S-7 For any nonzero 6-bit difference between inputs $\Delta I_{i,j}$, no more than eight of the 32 pairs of inputs exhibiting $\Delta I_{i,j}$ may result in the same output difference $\Delta O_{i,j}$.

1.2 The Security Requirements of S-Boxes

The only part of the Feistel network that is highly nonlinear and therefore difficult to cryptanalyze, consists of the S-Boxes in the function f of Fig. 2. Thus, the security of the S-Boxes is highly important. The numbers in Fig. 4 are obtained due to S-box design. The design requirements have evolved through years of research by the cryptographic community.

For example, the S-Boxes of 3DES are so designed to satisfy the security criteria numbered **S-1**, **S-2**, and so on [6], which are listed in Table 1. These criteria were classified and eventually, revealed [6] only after reporting of results of differential cryptanalysis by Biham, et. al [4] and linear cryptanalysis by Matsui [13].

Subsequently, security requirements such as maximum nonlinearity, minimum autocorrelation, the strict avalanche criterion (SAC), the bit independence criterion (BIC), highest dynamic distance, and several others, have found their way into the design principles to enhance S-box security [18,14].

2   Rationale of the CSP Approach to S-Box Design

The first S-Boxes for Feistel ciphers were designed by hand. Early security attacks have propelled the research for guidelines (i.e., requirements) that avoid known vulnerabilities. These requirements prove to be so difficult to achieve, to the point where it is said [15] that the 3DES designing team dropped guards when hand-picking their last S-box (given the fact that their last S-box is susceptible to attacks from differential cryptanalysis [4]). Some subsequent proposals build keyed one-time usage S-Boxes dynamically. This avoids the need of hand-building them, but results in expensive start-up times at encryption and decryption (e.g., Blowfish, Twofish [21]).

Some of the criteria used for design of static S-Boxes (such as maximum nonlinearity and minimum autocorrelation) are defined using numerical satisfaction functions where the absolute satisfaction appears unreachable[4]. Therefore the design process becomes an *optimization* procedure where the satisfaction of the criteria is maximized.

The approach on which we build here, is to automatically generate the needed S-Boxes based on the relevant security criteria. S-box generation approaches can be classified as: random generation of S-Boxes, random generation-and-testing of S-Boxes, human-made S-Boxes, and math-made S-Boxes [23].

An exhaustive generation of all possible S-Boxes followed by validating them using security criteria known at that time has been tested for 4×4 S-Boxes as reported in [1]. Among the existing math-made S-box generation schemes, a number of approaches pre-load bent functions, often constructing them bit by bit, into an S-box entry, and testing the entry against design criteria. For example Mister, et.al [14] loads a bent function bit-by-bit into an S-box entry and tests for its nonlinearity and highest dynamic distance. Adams, et.al [2] test combinations of the bits of a 4×4 S-box entry against design criteria such as nonlinearity, strict avalanche and output bit independence. O'Connor [16] combinatorially analyzes the bit-by-bit approach and shows that there are practical limits up to which this scheme can generate S-boxes efficiently. Pieprzyk, et.al construct $n \times n$ bijective S-Boxes by focussing only on nonlinearity requirements [18]. Gupta, et.al [9] construct $n \times m$ S-Boxes in two ways – one, by modifying a technique by Zhang and Zheng and the other, by using a sharpened version of Maiorana-McFarland technique to construct nonlinear resilient functions.

Recently, evolutionary approaches using local search have been applied to obtain S-Boxes satisfying security requirements [12]. The approaches employ hill climbing, simulated annealing and spectral inversion. A typical approach generates a fully-filled S-box that is "approximate" in that not all criteria are satisfied, and entries in the S-box are adjusted to guide the search towards criteria satisfaction. None of these approaches has the elegance of a CSP model. They did not manage to produce S-Boxes of a higher quality than the hand-made ones. Neither can they be so simply extended with new constraints, nor do their efficiency benefit immediately from advances in general computing techniques. In contrast, in our work, we employ *automatic generation* of S-Boxes using CSPs.

---

[4] This observation of unreachability is supported by our experiments, as well as by the existing S-box selections of various ciphers.

3   The CSP Approach

Our model of the problem is based on the following definition of a CSP:

Definition 1. *A Constraint Satisfaction Problem (CSP) is a tuple $(X, D, \mathcal{C})$ where X is a set of variables, D, a set of domains of each variable in X, and $\mathcal{C}$ is a set of constraints between variables in X, all of which are required to be satisfied.*

3.1   Notations

For a number x, we use $|x|$ to denote its absolute value. If S is a set, then $|S|$ represents its cardinality (number of elements in S). Whenever a set is written with braces, its cardinality is written with a $\#$ preceding the set itself, such as $\#\{a_0, a_1, a_2, \ldots a_{k-1}\}$. The symbols $\cdot$ and $\oplus$ represent, respectively, the bit-wise AND and exclusive-OR (XOR) operations on two identical-sized bit patterns. Bit pattern $\bar{x}$ denotes the one's-complement of x. A linear combination of Boolean variables $x_0, x_1, x_2, \ldots, x_{k-1}$, is given by the expression

$$\bigoplus_{i=0}^{k-1} a_i \cdot x_i = a_0 \cdot x_0 \oplus \ldots \oplus a_{k-1} \cdot x_{k-1} \tag{1}$$

where the a_i's are Boolean coefficients. A linear Boolean function $L_\omega(x)$ on an n-bit input $x = x_0 \ldots x_{n-1}$ defined by an n-bit selector $\omega = \omega_0 \ldots \omega_{n-1}$ is computed [5] as:

$$L_\omega(x) = \omega_0 \cdot x_0 \oplus \ldots \oplus \omega_{n-1} \cdot x_{n-1} = \bigoplus_{i=0}^{n-1} \omega_i \cdot x_i \tag{2}$$

1 The *parity* $P(x)$ of an n-bit pattern $x = x_0 x_1 \ldots x_{n-1}$ is equal to the exclusive-OR of the bits in x, that is, $P(x) = x_0 \oplus x_1 \oplus \ldots \oplus x_{n-1}$. Using these facts, we derive the following property of $L_\omega(x)$:

Property 1. $L_\omega(\bar{x}) = L_\omega(x) \oplus P(\omega)$

Some existing criteria are based on the concepts of *Hamming weight* and *Hamming Distance*. The Hamming weight of a given bit-pattern u, denoted by $wt(u)$, is defined as the number of 1's in u. Two n-bit numbers x and y *differ* by an amount equal to $x \oplus y$. The Hamming Distance between x and y is the minimum number of changes to be made to x to obtain y, and is equal to $wt(x \oplus y)$.

y_0y_5	$y_1y_2y_3y_4$							
	0	1	2	3	...	13	14	15
0	x_0	x_2	x_4	x_6	...	x_{26}	x_{28}	x_{30}
1	x_1	x_3	x_5	x_7	...	x_{27}	x_{29}	x_{31}
2	x_{32}	x_{34}	x_{36}	x_{38}	...	x_{58}	x_{60}	x_{62}
3	x_{33}	x_{35}	x_{37}	x_{39}	...	x_{59}	x_{61}	x_{63}

Fig. 5. The relation between the selected variables and a 6×4 S-box

Each security criteria is now implemented by a set of corresponding constraints, taking IBM's criteria (Table 1) applied to $n \times m$ S-box design as an example. IBM's Criterion **S-1** is implicit in the choice of variables. Criteria **S-4** through **S-6** are formulated as binary constraints. Criteria **S-2** and **S-7** have to be implemented using n-ary constraints and **S-3** generates `Alldiff` constraints. The constraints for **S-2** are the most involved and are first presented (Sec. 3.3).

3.2 Variables and Domains for an $n \times m$ S-Box

To model, using constraints, an $n \times m$ S-box (i.e., on n-bit inputs), we propose to use 2^n variables. The ith variable will be denoted x_i, $0 \le i < 2^n$. Each x_i specifies the output of the S-box for input i. The set of variables for the CSP is the set $X = \{x_0, x_1, \ldots, x_{2^n-1}\}$. Since the output of an S-box is m bits long, the domain of each variable x_i is defined as $x_i \in \{0, 1, \ldots, 2^m - 1\}, 0 \le i < 2^n$.

In the example for 3DES, where $n = 6$ and $m = 4$, there are 64 different S-box input values. Let the corresponding 64 output values be represented by variables $x_0, x_1, \ldots x_{63}$. Since each output is 4 bits, the domains are defined by $x_i \in \{x : 0 \le x \le 15\}$, $0 \le i \le 63$. Using these variables, a 6×4 S-box such as the one for 3DES is organized as shown in Fig. 5, as addressed by incrementing the input. In Fig. 5, 6-bit inputs $i, 0 \le i \le 63$ are represented as bit-patterns $y_0 y_1 y_2 y_3 y_4 y_5$ for clarity.

3.3 The Nonlinearity Constraint S-2

The rationale behind IBM's criterion **S-2** (see Table 1) is to ensure that an S-box is highly nonlinear. Matsui's work on linear cryptanalysis [13] uses a table called the Linear Approximation Table that records the counts of linear combinations of all subsets of input and output bits, for a particular S-box. Consider an $n \times m$ S-box, i.e., that for any n-bit input $i = i_0 \ldots i_{n-1}$ yields the m-bit output $x_i = x_{i_0} \ldots x_{i_{m-1}}$. The linear combinations to be checked for equality are obtained by selecting bits in i and x_i using selectors a and b respectively, where $0 \le a < 2^n$ and $0 \le b < 2^m$. For a given S-box Φ with all variables in X, let us define $N_X^\Phi(a, b)$ as follows:

$$N_X^\Phi(a, b) = \#\{i : L_a(i) = L_b(x_i); a, i \in \mathbb{Z}_{2^n}; b, x_i \in \mathbb{Z}_{2^m}\} \tag{3}$$

where $L_\omega(x)$ is defined in (2). The minimum value of $N_X^\Phi(a, b)$ is zero and the maximum value is 2^n. Matsui [13] considered the general case when b is not a power of 2, corresponding to a criterion **S-2'** that is stricter than **S-2**.

Given an $n \times m$ S-box Φ' and $X' \subseteq X$, let us define $N_{X'}^{\Phi'}(a, b)$ as follows:

$$N_{X'}^{\Phi'}(a, b) = \#\{i : L_a(i) = L_b(x_i); x_i \in X'; a \in \mathbb{Z}_{2^n}; b, x_i \in \mathbb{Z}_{2^m}\}$$

A Measure of Nonlinearity. For selectors a and b defined as above, let $p(a, b)$ denote the fraction of cases when $L_a(i) = L_b(x_i)$, computed as:

$$p(a, b) = \frac{N_X^\Phi(a, b)}{2^n} \tag{4}$$

If $p(a, b)$ is equal to 1, this indicates that the linear combination of the output bits selected by b equals a linear combination of the input bits selected by a, i.e., $\forall i, L_a(i) = L_b(x_i)$. If $p(a, b)$ is equal to zero, then the linear combination of the output bits selected by b is never equal to the linear combination of input bits selected by a. **S-2** stipulates that $p(a, b)$ should be near $\frac{1}{2}$, i.e. $|N_X^\Phi(a, b) - \frac{|X|}{2}|$ should be as close to zero as possible.

The Score of an S-box. The ideal case where $N_X^\Phi(a, b) - \frac{|X|}{2}$ is zero for all selector-pairs (a, b), has so far not been attained in the literature for common cryptosystems. The most effective linear approximation of a 3DES S-box is obtained if, for some a and b, $|N_X^\Phi(a, b) - \frac{|X|}{2}|$ is maximal. To reduce the weakest point of the S-box, we use the so called *effectiveness* of linearization [17] of an S-box Φ as its score:

$$\sigma_X(\Phi) = max\{|N_X^\Phi(a, b) - \frac{|X|}{2}| : 1 \le a < |X|; 1 \le b < |D|\} \qquad (5)$$

An S-box with a smaller score is considered better. For our search heuristics we proved and use the following property:

Property 2. The score $\sigma_X(\Phi)$ of a complete assignment Φ does not change if all of its assigned values are replaced by their one's-complements, into an assignment $\bar{\Phi}$.

The score $\sigma_{X'}, X' \subseteq X$, of a partially-filled $n \times m$ S-box Φ' is defined as follows:

$$\sigma_{X'}(\Phi') = max\{|N_{X'}^{\Phi'}(a, b) - \frac{|X|}{2}| : 1 \le a < \frac{|X|}{2}; 1 \le b < |D|\} \qquad (6)$$

The Constraint for S-2. The criteria **S-2** leads to a soft constraint that minimizes $\sigma_X(\Phi)$. When implemented as a hard constraint for a threshold τ, it has the form:

$$\sigma_X(\Phi) \le \tau \qquad (7)$$

The maximum value of $\sigma_X(\Phi)$ is equal to $\frac{|X|}{2}$, which is attained when the S-box output bits are given by a linear combination of its input bits.

This constraint is not implemented using an extensional representation. Rather, a specialized function is added to the solver that works with a 2^{n+m} size storage, replicated at each level in the search tree. This results in a total space requirement of 2^{2n+m} bytes. For 3DES-size boxes the constraint requires $64kB$. This heuristic will be referred to as $H_S^{\Phi,\tau}$.

An Incomplete, Incremental Heuristic for S-2 using Partial Assignments. The incomplete constructive search heuristic $H_I^{\phi,\tau}$ is based on abandoning partial assignments larger than ϕ variables, with score exceeding a threshold τ. For example, for 6×4 S-box generation with $H_I^{48,16}$, partial S-Boxes having 48 instantiated variables will be rejected if they do not have entries with $N_{X'}^{\Phi'}(a, b)$ of at least 16. The $H_I^{48,16}$ heuristic with MAC yielded a large number of S-Boxes having score 8, (better than those in 3DES) whose retrieval using other search techniques required a lot of computation time.

Projections of n-ary constraints to partial assignments. The following property of a partial assignment allows for projection of (Eq. 7) into lower-arity constraints.

Property 3 (Projections). A partial assignment Φ' with values for variables in X', $X' \subseteq X$, cannot be extended to a solution with score better than a threshold τ if the following inequality is not satisfied:

$$|X'| - \tau - \frac{|X|}{2} \le \max_{a,b} N_{X'}^{\Phi'}(a,b) \le \frac{|X|}{2} + \tau \tag{8}$$

A *complete, incremental heuristic* that uses this property will be referred to as $H_C^{\phi,\tau}$.

S-3 (see Table 1). Fixing the leftmost and rightmost input bits $y_0 y_5$ to any of the possible four combinations, selects one of four subsets of the variables. To formulate constraints for **S-3**, all we require is that no two output variables, in each subset, should be equal. The inequations are directly expressible as Alldiff constraints [19], [10]:

$$\text{Alldiff}(x_0, x_2, x_4, ..., x_{30})$$
$$\text{Alldiff}(x_1, x_3, x_5, ..., x_{31})$$
$$\text{Alldiff}(x_{32}, x_{34}, x_{36}, ..., x_{62})$$
$$\text{Alldiff}(x_{33}, x_{35}, x_{37}, ..., x_{63})$$

3.4 Constraints for Criteria S-4 to S-6

For criteria **S-4**, **S-5** and **S-6**, consider any two n-bit inputs i and j and their corresponding m-bit outputs $x_i, x_j \in D$, of a 3DES S-box S.

S-4 *"If two inputs to an S-box differ in exactly one bit, the outputs must differ in at least two bits."* This requirement is expressible in First-Order Logic as:

$$(\forall i)(\forall j)(0 \le i < j < 2^n) \wedge wt(i \oplus j) = 1 \Rightarrow wt(x_i \oplus x_j) \ge 2 \tag{9}$$

For 3DES, each variable will participate in exactly 6 such binary constraints (one for each bit), generating 192 binary constraints. For an $n \times m$ S-box, the number of binary constraints for criterion **S-4** is equal to $n \times 2^{n-1}$.

S-5 *"If two inputs to an S-box differ in the two middle bits exactly, the outputs must differ in at least two bits."* The fact that n-bit inputs i and j differ in the two middle bits implies that the 6-bit difference is exactly equal to $3 \cdot 2^{\frac{n}{2}-1}$ when n is even. **S-5** is expressible in First-Order Logic as:

$$(\forall i)(\forall j)(0 \le i, j < 2^n) \wedge (i \ne j) \wedge (i \oplus j = 3 \cdot 2^{\frac{n}{2}-1} \Rightarrow wt(x_i \oplus x_j) \ge 2 \tag{10}$$

For 3DES, this results in 32 binary constraints, each input (S-box entry) participating in exactly one such binary constraint. For an $n \times m$ S-box, the number of binary constraints for criterion **S-5** is equal to 2^{n-1} when n is even.

S-6 *"If two inputs to an S-box differ in their first two bits and are identical in their last two bits, the two outputs must not be the same."* The fact that n-bit inputs i and j differ in their first two bits and are identical in their last two bits, implies that the input-difference $(i \oplus j) \wedge 3(2^{n-2} + 1)$ is exactly equal to $3 \cdot 2^{n-1}$ when $n \geq 4$. **S-6** is expressible in First-Order Logic as:

$$(\forall i)(\forall j)(0 \leq i < j < 2^n), [(i \oplus j) \wedge 3(2^{n-2} + 1)] = 3 \times 2^{n-2} \Rightarrow x_i \neq x_j \quad (11)$$

For 3DES, each variable is involved in 4 such binary constraints (one for each possible combination of the two middle input bits), resulting in a total of 128 new binary constraints. For an $n \times m$ S-box, the number of binary constraints for criterion **S-6** is equal to 2^{2n-5} when $n \geq 4$.

Total Number of Binary Constraints. For the $n \times m$ S-box design problem using this framework, the total number of binary constraints, obtained by adding the three results for **S-4**, **S-5** and **S-6**, is equal to $2^{n-1}(2n - 1)$ when $n \geq 4$. One can observe the independence of the total number of constraints on m. For 3DES, this works out to 352 constraints. Also, no binary constraints are observed to contain the same two variables.

3.5 The Global Constraint S-7

S-7: *"For any nonzero 6-bit difference between inputs $\Delta I_{i,j}$, no more than eight of the 32 pairs of inputs exhibiting $\Delta I_{i,j}$ may result in the same output difference $\Delta O_{i,j}$."*

Let $O_7 = \{(x_i, x_{2^n-1-i}) : 0 \leq i < 2^{n-1}\}$ be the set of pairs of variables corresponding to pairs of subscripts $(i, 2^n - 1 - i)$ of those n-bit inputs to an $n \times m$ S-box that differ by all n bits with $|O_7| = 2^{n-1}$. **S-7** applies to m-bit differences $d = x_i \oplus x_{2^n-1-i}$.

Let $f : \mathbb{Z}_{2^m} \to \mathbb{Z}_{2^{n-1}}$ denote a *count* function, where $f(d)$ is the *frequency of occurrence* of an m-bit number $d = x_i \oplus x_{2^n-1-i}$ where $(x_i, x_{2^n-1-i}) \in O_7, 0 \leq i < 2^{n-1}$, and $0 \leq d < 2^m$. Note that $\Sigma_{i=0}^{2^{n-1}-1} f(x_i \oplus x_{2^n-1-i}) = 2^{n-1}$.

According to **S-7**, at most eight elements in O_7 should evaluate to the same m-bit difference d. **S-7** is modeled as a global, n-ary, Boolean constraint in the following way:

$$\bigwedge_{i=0}^{2^{n-1}-1} (f(x_i \oplus x_{2^n-i-1}) \leq 8) \quad (12)$$

This n-ary global constraint is not straightforwardly decomposable into smaller arity constraints. After assigning x_i, if the count of a given AND-term in Eq. 12 equals 8, values from domains of not yet assigned variables that would further increase this count are removed (as they violate Eq. 12).

4 The Advantages of the CSP Approach

The CSP solver helped us find S-Boxes of quality better (with respect to the standard 3DES security metrics) than that of any other published S-box.

The solver we use is an implementation of Maintenance of Arc Consistency (MAC) [20] with AC2001 [3], as discussed in Section 3. The CSP solution was built starting

Table 2. Statistics of 4×2 S-Boxes generated by our CSP framework to satisfy combinations of 3DES criteria

Constraint Combinations	Time (seconds)	# of S-Boxes	Score-wise breakup			
			Score 8	Score 6	Score 4	Score 2
No constraints	136228.906250	4294967296	3931260	517882560	3496729600	276422720
S-3 only	35.029600	331776	11904	153600	166272	0
S-4 only	0.000089	4	4	0	0	0
S-5 only	6.410940	65536	7936	45056	12544	0
S-6 only	13214.516602	429981696	2103616	91728896	323934912	12214272
S-3, S-5	0.433693	4096	384	2048	1664	0
S-3, S-6	5.224500	46656	6240	22272	18144	0
S-5, S-6	2.085620	20736	4160	13312	3264	0
S-3, S-5, S-6	0.165739	1600	224	768	608	0

from an existing generic C++ implementation, to which we have added modules for dynamically checking and propagating the decompositions of the global constraints.

The generation of the constraints and the development of the related theory and involved filtering operators are the main topic of the PhD thesis of the first author, and took approximately 2 to 3 years to refine.

Experiments are being run with the final version for approximately one year. Users of the system that solely plan to design ciphers using the standard security criteria in Table 1 do not need to thoroughly understand the workings of CP solvers. Most extensions with additional constraints could also be performed with little CP knowledge, except if new filtering operators for those constraints are desired.

We have used the system to generate S-Boxes of different sizes, such as 4×2, 5×3 and 6×4 that resemble those used in 3DES. We have tuned the solver by trying various heuristics for criteria **S-2** and **S-7**. One of these heuristics instantly generated 6×4 S-Boxes that are of quality better than those published so far, with respect to Matsui's nonlinearity metric.

4×2 *S-box Generation:* The smallest S-Boxes we have encountered in the literature is an educational example of 4×2 [23]. Not all criteria in Table 1 apply to S-Boxes that are not of size 6×4. In the 4×2 case, our solver has proven that it is even impossible to generate S-Boxes that respect the criteria that apply. The CSP approach generated 4×2 S-Boxes when some of the conditions are relaxed. Table 2 displays the results on combinations of satisfied criteria.

5×3 *S-box Generation:* The complete CSP solver is able to explore the entire search space for generating 5×3 S-Boxes (32 variables, each with domain $\{0, 1, \ldots, 7\}$). Criteria **S-5** and **S-6** had to be relaxed since the original version did not apply to this size. Table 3 shows generation times and number of S-Boxes for various scores, with a total of 32,640 S-Boxes generated. The optimum score possible for 5×3 S-Boxes is 8.

6×4 *S-box Generation:* We have used the three heuristics $H_S^{\phi,\tau}$, $H_I^{\phi,\tau}$ and $H_C^{\phi,\tau}$ for generation of S-Boxes of this size. For $H_I^{\phi,\tau}$, we have fixed thresholds $\tau = 16, 10$ and

Table 3. The scores of obtained 5×3 S-Boxes, with criteria **S-5** and **S-6** relaxed

Total time (seconds)	Total number of S-Boxes	Score-wise breakup		
		Score 16	Score 12	Score 8
14.2659	32,640	25728	3456	3456

Table 4. Solver Performance Using Complete Heuristics, with S-box threshold $\tau = 16$

Time (hrs)	Non-incremental		Incremental	
	$r^{(6\times4)} \times 10^{49}$	S-box Count	$r^{(6\times4)} \times 10^{49}$	S-box Count
1	1.198	4	206,990	38,124
2	21.725	14	978,520	54,725
3	42.091	15	999,560	93,523
4	42.091	26	1,083,100	104,904
5	61.340	40	1,342,900	127,111

```
0   3   5   6   9 10 15 12 7   4 14 13   2   1   8 11
3   0   6   5 10   9 12 15 4   7 13 14   1   2 11   8
3 15   0 12   5   9 10   6 4   8 11   7 14   2   1 13
9   5 15   3 12   0   6 10 7 11   8   4   2 14 13   1
```

Fig. 6. A 6×4 S-box with score 8, generated by our CSP solver

for the other two heuristics, $\tau = 16$. In a 5-hour run, we observed that $H_C^{64,16}$ proceeds approximately 20–200 times faster than $H_S^{64,16}$. 3DES S-box S_7 has the maximum nonlinearity score equal to 18 while the minimum of 10 is possessed by S_4. *Heuristic $H_I^{64,10}$ is observed to yield 6×4 S-Boxes having a score of 8, which is far better than the "best" published 3DES S-Boxes.* 3,600 such 6×4 S-Boxes were generated in the first hour and this number went up to more than 13,500 in the 5-hour run. Fig. 6 shows one such S-box generated by our CSP solver employing heuristic $H_I^{64,10}$.

A New Metric: Percentage of the Search Space Explored. Although our techniques have found S-Boxes with the "best" score so far, we do not know if they are optimal. To know whether we have found optimal-quality S-Boxes we have to exhaust the whole search space. If the search space is too large to be exhausted with available techniques, we would like to at least know what fraction of this search space we have managed to explore, as a measure of the probability that the optimal solution could have been found.

We therefore quantify the size of the search space, as the total number of potential $n \times m$ S-Boxes. Assuming that the solver is systematic, each node of the search tree defines a traversed distance (explored search space):

$$S_p^{(n\times m)} = \sum_{i=0}^{|X'|-1} x_i \cdot (2^m)^{|X'|-i-1} \tag{13}$$

For 6×4 S-Boxes, $S_p^{(6 \times 4)}$ evaluates to 78-digit base-10 numbers. Given the large size of this search space, distances typically covered by the MAC solver in reasonable time differed only in their last few assignments (78-digit numbers differed in approximately the last 15 digits). Sometimes, certain constraints rule out much larger areas of the search space. To conveniently report this, we define a *search offset* metric S-box $S_{p_1}^{(n \times m)}$:

$$r^{(n \times m)} = \frac{S_p^{(n \times m)} - S_{p_1}^{(n \times m)}}{2^{n \times 2^m}} \tag{14}$$

Here, $S_{p_1}^{(n \times m)}$ denotes the value for $S_p^{(n \times m)}$ (determined from Eq. 13) for the first S-box obtained by the solver. The solver has yielded $S_{p_1}^{(6 \times 4)} \approx \text{0x033} \times 16^{60}$. The difference between $S_{p_1}^{(6 \times 4)}$ for the incomplete and complete heuristics is $\approx 3 \times 16^{52}$ even when they use the same value for τ (graphs not shown due to lack of space). Table 4 reports the (scaled) search offsets of the solver using complete heuristics.

Developments. One can now extend the CSP model with constraints for various special security requirements. We would like to post the obtained constraints as benchmarks for the CSP community. Once the CSP model is available, it can be easily used to generate SAT models and test SAT techniques. The obtained S-Boxes can be used to strengthen protocols such as SSL (where 3DES is now one of the main ciphers). In this direction, the first author moved to one of the main US-based providers of SSL technologies.

5 Conclusion

We conclude that CP is a powerful formalism, able to model accurately such complex criteria as the 3DES security constraints, and in particular the nonlinearity requirement. The fact that generic solvers can then address such complex problems efficiently and improve over all existing results is a testimony to the importance of this tool.

References

1. Adams, C.M., Tavares, S.E.: Good S-boxes are easy to find. In: Brassard, G. (ed.) CRYPTO 1989. LNCS, vol. 435, pp. 612–615. Springer, Heidelberg (1990)
2. Adams, C., Tavares, S.: Generating and counting binary bent sequences. IEEE Transactions on Information Theory 36(5), 1170–1173 (1990)
3. Bessière, C., Régin, J.C.: Refining the basic constraint propagation algorithm. In: Nebel, B. (ed.) IJCAI, pp. 309–315. Morgan Kaufmann, San Francisco (2001)
4. Biham, E., Shamir, A.: Differential cryptanalysis of the data encryption standard. Springer, Heidelberg (1993)
5. Clark, J., Jacob, J., Maitra, S., Stanica, P.: Almost boolean functions: the design of boolean functions by spectral inversion. Evolutionary Computation 3, 2173–2180 (2003)
6. Coppersmith, D.: The data encryption standard (des) and its strength against attacks. IBM J. Res. Dev. 38(3), 243–250 (1994)
7. Daemen, J., Rijmen, V.: Aes proposal: Rijndael (September 1999),
   http://csrc.nist.gov/archive/aes/rijndael/
   Rijndael-ammended.pdf

8. Feistel, H.: Cryptography and computer privacy. Scientific American 228, 15–23 (1973)
9. Gupta, K.C., Sarkar, P.: Construction of high degree resilient S-boxes with improved nonlinearity. Inf. Process. Lett. 95(3), 413–417 (2005)
10. Hoeve, W.V.: The alldifferent constraint: A survey. In: Proceedings of the Sixth Annual Workshop of the ERCIM Working Group on Constraints (2001)
11. Lai, X., Massey, J.L.: A proposal for a new block encryption standard. In: Damgård, I.B. (ed.) EUROCRYPT 1990. LNCS, vol. 473, pp. 389–404. Springer, Heidelberg (1991)
12. Laskari, E.C., Meletiou, G.C., Vrahatis, M.N.: Utilizing evolutionary computation methods for the design of S-boxes. In: Proceedings of the International Conference on Computational Intelligence and Security 2006 (CIS 2006), China (2006) (in press)
13. Matsui, M.: Linear cryptanalysis method for des cipher. In: Helleseth, T. (ed.) EUROCRYPT 1993. LNCS, vol. 765, pp. 386–397. Springer, Heidelberg (1994)
14. Mister, S., Adams, C.: Practical S-Box design (1996)
15. NIST: Data encryption standard (DES). Federal Information Processing Standard (FIPS) 46-2 (January 1988)
16. O'Connor, L.: An analysis of a class of algorithms for s-box construction. J. Cryptology 7(3), 133–151 (1994)
17. O'Connor, L.: Properties of linear approximation tables. In: Preneel, B. (ed.) FSE 1994. LNCS, vol. 1008, pp. 134–136. Springer, Heidelberg (1995)
18. Pieprzyk, J., Finkelstein, G.: Towards effective nonlinear cryptosystem design. IEE Proceedings Computers and Digital Techniques 135(6), 325–335 (1988)
19. Puget, J.-F.: A fast algorithm for the bound consistency of alldiff constraints. In: AAAI 1998, pp. 359–366 (1998)
20. Sabin, D., Freuder, E.C.: Contradicting conventional wisdom in constraint satisfaction. In: PPCP 1994. LNCS, vol. 874, pp. 10–20. Springer, Heidelberg (1994)
21. Schneier, B.: Applied cryptography — protocols, algorithms, and source code in c. In: Textbook, ch. 12, pp. 265–301 (2002)
22. Shannon, C.E.: A mathematical theory of communication. Bell System Technical Journal 27, 379–423, 623–656 (1948)
23. Stallings, W.: Cryptography and network security - principles and practices. In: Textbook, ch. 3, pp. 86–90 (2003), http://www.prenhall.com/stallings

Optimal Carpet Cutting

Andreas Schutt[1], Peter J. Stuckey[1], and Andrew R. Verden[2]

[1] National ICT Australia, Department of Computer Science & Software Engineering,
The University of Melbourne, Victoria 3010, Australia
{aschutt,pjs}@csse.unimelb.edu.au
[2] National ICT Australia, School of Computer Science and Engineering,
University of New South Wales, UNSW Sydney, NSW 2052, Australia
andrew.verden@nicta.com.au

Abstract. In this paper we present a model for the carpet cutting problem in which carpet shapes are cut from a rectangular carpet roll with a fixed width and sufficiently long length. Our exact solution approaches decompose the problem into smaller parts and minimise the needed carpet roll length for each part separately. The customers requirements are to produce a cutting solution of the carpet within 3 minutes, in order to be usable during the quotation process for estimating the amount of carpet required. Our system can find and prove the optimal solution for 106 of the 150 real-world instances provided by the customer, and find high quality solutions to the remainder within this time limit. In contrast the existing solution developed some years ago finds (but does not prove) optimal solutions for 30 instances. Our solutions reduce the wastage by more than 35% on average compared to the existing approach.

1 Introduction

The carpet cutting problem is a two-dimensional cutting and packing problem in which carpet shapes (also called items or objects) are cut from a rectangular carpet roll with a fixed roll width and a sufficiently long roll length. The goal is to find a non-overlapping placement of all carpet shapes on the carpet roll, so that the waste is minimised or in other words the utilisation of used carpet material is maximised while meeting all additional constraints. In our case the objective is to minimise the carpet roll length.

In this paper the carpet shapes are rectilinear polygons of up to 12 sides that can be made up of non-overlapping rectangles, that must be placed orthogonal on the carpet roll, i.e., their edges must be parallel to the borders of the roll. Before the placement of a carpet shape a rotation may be allowed by 90°, 180°, or 270°, i.e., it can be put onto the roll in one of four cardinal directions 0°, 90°, 180°, or 270°. But depending on the pile direction of the carpet there may be restrictions on the which cardinal directions can be used: perhaps only 0°, 180° or perhaps fixed to 0°.

Normally, a carpet shape is cut as a single piece from the carpet roll, but carpet shapes for covering stairs or filling up the remainder of a room are allowed to be cut in several pieces provided that the partition of these carpet shapes satisfy

J. Lee (Ed.): CP 2011, LNCS 6876, pp. 69–84, 2011.
© Springer-Verlag Berlin Heidelberg 2011

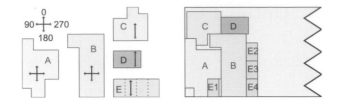

Fig. 1. Example of a carpet cutting instance

additional constraints which are described later. The joint of carpets for stairs that is then introduced between two adjacent pieces can be hidden between the tread and the riser of the stairs once they are laid. The resulting seams of carpets filling up a room are hidden at the edge of a room. Moreover, these carpet shapes are simple rectangles.

Another complexity of the problem is that carpets have a *pile direction* that may constrain the orientations of some carpet shapes to be dependent on one or another. Clients may also prefer to have the pile direction fixed to ensure an even colour of the carpet when laid relative to a window. Where two carpets join, e.g. at a door way, the pile direction becomes visible if the two pieces are not laid with a similar pile direction. Therefore, all carpet shapes that are joined together must be arranged pile aligned in the plan. Carpet shapes for stairs must be pile aligned with the pile direction being up the stairs, for safety reasons this ensures that it is less easy to slip down the stairs.

Example 1. Figure 1 shows an example of a carpet cutting instance. On the left side the five carpet shapes A, B, C, D, and E are shown and on the right side their placement on the carpet roll (gray area). The roll is laid out from the left to the right, *i.e.*, its width is the vertical edge and its length the horizontal one.

On the left-hand side each object contains arrows displaying in which direction the object can be placed where an arrow pointing to the top, left, bottom, or right stands for the direction 0°, 90°, 180°, and 270° respectively. As shown the object A, and B can placed in any direction, but not the objects C, D, and E which must be pile aligned. Moreover, the object E is a carpet for covering four stair steps. The vertical dotted line shows the edge between the tread and riser of two steps. The object E can be split at those edges.

In the placement shown on the right-hand side the objects A and B are placed in the 0° direction whereas the other objects are rotated by 180°. The object E is partitioned in four parts in order to minimise the needed roll length.

The carpet retailer uses a solution as a base of an on-site cost estimation and ordering process, to submit an offer to customers. The offer should be made in a timely manner and a three-minutes runtime limit is given to the cut-plan optimisation process.

The carpet cutting problem can be characterised as an extension of a two-dimensional orthogonal strip packing (OSP) problem (referred to as a two-dimensional orthogonal open dimension problem by [22]) with additional constraints in which a packing of rectangles with minimal waste is sought. The extensions are the placement constraints between rectangles belonging to the same carpet shape and the partition constraints for carpet shapes covering stairs. The side effect of the first constraints is that for those carpet shapes a rotation by 180° and 270° may be not symmetric to a rotation by 0° and 90° respectively.

For OSP and related cutting and packing problems different methods have been applied, a survey can be found in [9]. The different methods can be roughly categorised in these groups: (1) positional placement/reasoning and (2) relational placement/reasoning. The first category includes methods such as the bottom-left rule [7,11] and the discretisation of the large rectangle [3]. The second category includes methods that determines the relations (above, under, left, and right) of each pair of rectangles [16] and the graph-theoretical models [5]. Our approach includes features of both categories.

A two-dimensional cutting and packing problem can be relaxed into two scheduled problems, once the problem is projected on the length-axis of the large rectangle and the other on the width-axis of the large rectangle. These relaxations are used in order to infer more about possible positions of the items to be laid on the large rectangle and detect infeasibility of partial solution earlier.

Constraint programming methods include the global constraints `cumulative` [1] that models a cumulative scheduling problem, the sweep pruning technique for k-dimensional objects [3] and the geost constraint [2] (modelling k-dimensional objects that can take different shapes). Moreover, special pruning algorithms exists for the `cumulative` constraint in the case of non-overlapping rectangles [4]. The sweep algorithm and the geost constraint are specifically designed to model non-overlapping object with at least 2-dimensions. These algorithms demonstrate very good results if the *slack* (the unused space) is small. If the slack is not small then the additional computational effort may not rewarded by the reduction of the search space.

The existing fielded solution [14,15] uses a combination of heuristic search and dynamic programming in a series of optimisation steps. The algorithm incrementally selects carpet shapes that are placed across the roll considering all alternatives and reduces the overall length of material in a branch-and-bound backtracking search. The algorithm is complex and can be subject to reduced performance when certain rare combinations of heuristic choice lead to inefficiencies of placement. It is not exact and often uses the full 3 minutes of runtime but considerably less for smaller problems. It was designed to run on 100MHz tablet PCs with considerably less computing power available than today's processors.

We define two new exact approaches to the carpet cutting problems. The first approach decomposes the problem into multiple instances where all the carpets have fixed dimension and orientation. These subproblems are solved sequentially maintaining the best solution found overall. Since all dimensions are fixed the constraint propagation is strong. But a disadvantage is there may be many instances for a single problem. The second approach models the orientation of the carpet as a variable and hence reduces the number of instances required for each problem. It can handle problems that the first approach cannot.

The subproblems are solved by the lazy clause generation (LCG) [13] which is a hybrid of a Boolean satisfiability (SAT) solving and finite domain (FD) solving. The LCG lazily transforms an FD problem into an SAT problem during the progress of a search where the conflict analysis only takes the SAT part into account. At the moment LCG is one of the best exact solution approaches for tackling the basic resource-constrained project scheduling problem [19] and its extension with minimal and maximal time lags [18] in which an optimal schedule minimising the project duration is demanded. These problems involve an explaining version of the global constraint `cumulative` in their model which is also used to solve carpet cutting.

2   The Carpet Cutting Problem

In the carpet cutting problem there are three different types of carpet shapes: (*i*) *room carpets* that cover rooms which are made up of a number of rectangular pieces which are constrained to align; (*ii*) *stair carpets* that cover stairs which can be cut into regular pieces and are always rectangular; (*iii*) *edge filler carpets* that cover the remainder of a room that is only slightly wider than the width of the carpet. The remainder of the room is covered with multiple narrow pieces cut at any point providing each piece is of a minimum length.

A room carpet is characterised by its set of (possible) orientations and offsets from its origin to the origin of its rectangles for each orientation. The origin of a room carpet is the bottom left corner of the smallest rectangle that encloses all its rectangles in each orientation. Each rectangle has a width and a length which are given for the 0° orientation. The carpet *origin* is the bottom left corner in each orientation. Where a room is larger in both directions than the width of the carpet, a choice of where the full roll width is aligned is made by the user in advance of the placement optimisation.

Example 2. Figure 2a shows the room carpet laid out in each orientation. Its smallest enclosing rectangle is displayed with a red-dotted line. The small black squares in each rectangle indicates the origin for the carpet and its rectangles. These pictures show how the offsets from the origin differ for each orientation.

Stair and edge filler carpets are characterised by their width and length. Each of them may be allowed to be cut in several pieces. Stair carpets are cut with regular breaks between the tread and the riser of two or more steps hence each single piece must cover an integral number of steps.

Edge filler pieces may be cut arbitrarily with irregular length breaks. These shapes can be divided at any position so long as their length is not smaller than a minimal given length. The resulting seam(s) is hidden at the edge of a room. Significant savings in material wastage occur for certain single room carpet orders using this approach. For both kinds of breaks a maximal number of pieces and minimal length of sub-pieces can be given.

Example 3. Figure 2b shows a stair carpet with 4 pieces and possible partitions, with a maximum of three pieces allowed. Figure 2c shows possible partitions for

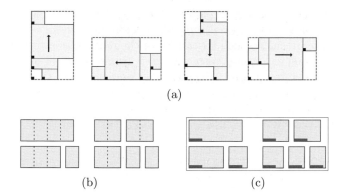

(a)

(b)   (c)

Fig. 2. The origin of a room carpet and its rectangles in each orientation (a). Possible partitions for a stair carpet (b) and an edge filler carpet (c).

Fig. 3. A solution (split into two parts) for CC instance with 34 room carpets (involving 74 rectangles) and 2 stair carpets (involving 7 rectangles). The roll length is about 93m to a granularity of 1cm.

an edge filler carpet with length 200 units, with a minimal length of 50 units (indicated by the bar in the bottom left corner) and a maximum of two cuts.

A formal specification of an instance I of the carpet cutting problem is defined as follows. We are given 3 sets of disjoint objects: (*i*) *Room* is a set of room carpets. Each $c \in Room$ is defined by a set of rectangles $c.rect$. For each rectangle $r \in c.rect$ we have a length $r.len$ and width $r.wid$ (in the $0°$ orientation) together with an offset $(r.ox, r.oy)$ from the origin of the room carpet (in the $0°$ orientation). Moreover, each $c \in Room$ is also given a set of allowable orientations $c.ori \subseteq \{0°, 90°, 180°, 270°\}$. (*ii*) *Str* is a set of stair carpets. For each $c \in Str$ we have a width $c.wid$, step length $c.step$ and number of steps $c.n$ as well as a maximum number of pieces $c.pcs$ and minimum steps per piece length $c.min$. (*iii*) *Edg* is a set of edge filler carpets. For each $c \in Edg$ we have a width $c.wid$, length $c.len$ as well as a maximum number of pieces $c.pcs$ and minimum length per piece length $c.min$. The remaining part of the model is a set $Pile \subseteq Room$ which determines which carpets must be pile aligned, *i.e.*, $c.ori = \{0°, 180°\}$ for each $c \in Pile$, and a roll width RW. Hence, $I = (Room, Str, Edg, Pile, RW)$. Note that all stair and edge filler carpets must be pile aligned, but this constraint can be neglected, since the pile orientations are symmetrical for rectangles as it is for parts of these carpets.

The aim is to find an allowable partitioning $c.part$ of each carpet $c \in Str \cup Edg$ into rectangles, and position (x, y) and allowed orientation for each rectangle r appearing in a room carpet such that: none of the rectangles overlap; each of the rectangles in a room carpet are correctly offset from the origin of the carpet; all pile aligned carpets are aligned in the same orientation, and the roll length RL is minimised.

Figure 3 shows the best solution found by our method for a large instance. It reduces the wastage by about 33% in comparison to the current method.

3   Static Model

The first model we present, the *static* model, splits the original problem into instances where the orientations and dimensions of each of the rectangular pieces are fixed in advance (*statically known*). This is achieved by fixing rotations of room carpets and fixing the partitions for stair carpets. The advantage of the static model is that it reduces the number of variables required to specify the problem, and gives stronger initial propagation. It reduces the requirements of the global constraints needed to model non-overlap, since dimensions are fixed. It also improves the strength of preprocessing. The obvious disadvantage of the static model is that the number of instances required to specify one original problem may become prohibitive.

To apply the static model we wish to fix the orientation and dimensions of all the rectangles in the problem. To do so we have to split the problem into multiple instances. For many problems in the customer data the number of instances required is not too large since they are often reasonably constrained.

3.1   Dealing with Orientations

Every carpet $c \in Room \setminus Pile$ has an allowable set of orientations in $\{0°, 90°, 180°, 270°\}$. We can split an instance I to remove possibilities of different orientations for a carpet c by creating the set of instances $I_o, o \in c.ori$ that are each identical to I except that $c.ori = \{o\}$, and for room carpets we swap the length $r.len$ and width $r.wid$ of the component rectangles if $o \in \{90°, 270°\}$, and update the offsets $(r.ox, r.oy)$ to reflect them from the new origin in this orientation.

If pile aligned carpets are involved in an instance then the instance is split in two instances. In one instance all pile aligned carpets c are fixed to the orientation $0°$ and in the other to $180°$.

Note that before doing this we preprocess instances for reducing the possible orientations of carpets: (***i***) For room carpets consisting of one rectangle the orientations $0°$ and $180°$ ($90°$ and $270°$) are symmetric. If both orientations are given then one of them is removed. For square carpets the orientation is fixed to $0°$. (***ii***) Some room carpets are too wide for the carpet roll if they are placed in a certain orientations. All those orientations are removed. (***iii***) Finally, if all room carpets in one instance that are made of more than one rectangle must be pile aligned then the pile-aligned constraint is removed from all of them and their orientation is fixed to $0°$, since each solution for the direction $0°$ is a solution for the direction $180°$ by rotating the carpet roll and all the placed objects by $180°$.

3.2   Stair Carpets

Carpets for stairs play an important role for the difficulty of a problem because they can be partitioned in many combinations and introduce symmetries if two parts in the partition have the same length. We can reduce the difficulty of stair carpets by avoiding considering all possible partitions by determining "dominated" partitions.

Example 4. Suppose a stair carpet covers 15 steps and can be cut into an unlimited number of pieces where each part must consists of at least two steps. Possible partitions are $\{10, 5\}$, $\{10, 3, 2\}$, $\{5, 4, 3, 3\}$, etc. where each multiset represents a partition and the elements express the size in steps of each piece. The total number of possible partitions (incl. the partition $\{15\}$) is 41.

The partition problem is well studied in number theory. The (generating) function that counts the number of different partitions for a sum n is called the *partition function* [6]. This function grows exponentially as the value n increases. For stair carpets an important simplification of the problem arises when we realise that not all partitions need to be considered because some parts of a partition can be broken into smaller pieces which can be laid out in a way identical to the original coarser pieces.

Example 5. Consider a stair carpet with the possible partitions $\{10, 5\}$ and $\{10, 3, 2\}$. Given a layout for the first partition, the piece of length 5 steps in the first partition can be split into two parts in which one part covers three steps and the other one two steps, thus giving a layout for the second partition. Hence we need not consider laying out the first partition, the partition $\{10, 5\}$ is *dominated* by the partition $\{10, 3, 2\}$.

Definition 1. Let P_1 and P_2 be two different partitions of n (*i.e.,* $\sum P_1 = \sum P_2 = n$). We say $P_2 = \{p_{21} \ldots, p_{2k}\}$ is *dominated* by $P_1 = \{p_{11}, \ldots, p_{1m}\}$ iff a mapping $\sigma : 1..m \rightarrow 1..k$ exists such that $\forall i \in 1..k : p_{2i} = \sum_{j \in 1..m \text{ where } \sigma(j)=i} p_{1j}$. That is we can further partition P_2 to obtain P_1. Given a set of partitions $\mathbf{P}$ we say $P \in \mathbf{P}$ is *dominating* if it is not dominated by any $P' \in \mathbf{P} - \{P\}$.

We note that [10] use a more general dominance criterion for one-dimensional bin-packing problems, which is defined in the opposite sense.

It follows that only dominating partitions must be considered during the solution process. We now construct a recursive definition of the number $nd(n, p, k)$ of dominating partitions for a stair carpet of length n steps with maximum number of pieces p and minimal step length k as follows:

$$nd(n, p, k) = nd(n, p, k, k)$$

$$nd(n, p, l, k) = \begin{cases} 0 & \text{if } 0 < n \wedge n < l \text{ or } 0 \wedge p > 0 \wedge l \geq 2k \\ 1 & \text{if } n = 0 \wedge p = 0 \text{ or } n = 0 \wedge p > 0 \wedge l < 2k \\ \sum_{l \leq i \leq n} nd(n-i, p-1, i, k) & \text{otherwise.} \end{cases}$$

Table 1. All dominating partitions for various lengths n where the minimal step length k is 2, and maximal pieces is n (so effectively no limit on pieces)

n partitions	n partitions	n partitions	n partitions
2 $\{2\}$	8 $\{3,3,2\}$, $\{2,2,2,2\}$	12 $\{3,3,3,3\}$,	14 $\{3,3,3,3,2\}$,
3 $\{3\}$	9 $\{3,3,3\}$, $\{3,2,2,2\}$	$\{3,3,2,2,2\}$,	$\{3,3,2,2,2,2\}$,
4 $\{2,2\}$	10 $\{3,3,2,2\}$,	$\{2,2,2,2,2,2\}$	$\{2,2,2,2,2,2,2\}$
5 $\{3,2\}$	$\{2,2,2,2,2\}$	13 $\{3,3,3,2,2\}$,	15 $\{3,3,3,3,3\}$,
6 $\{3,3\}$, $\{2,2,2\}$	11 $\{3,3,3,2\}$,	$\{3,2,2,2,2,2\}$	$\{3,3,3,2,2,2\}$,
7 $\{3,2,2\}$	$\{3,2,2,2,2\}$		$\{3,2,2,2,2,2,2\}$

The function $nd(n,p,l,k)$ returns the number of dominating partitions for a carpet of length n, maximal pieces p, minimum length l and minimum original length k. The definition captures the following reasoning. The first case is where there is carpet left but it is smaller that the minimal required length, or there is no carpet left but there are pieces remaining and one of the earlier pieces (which is at least size l) could be split in two. The second case is where there is no carpet and no pieces left, or there is no carpet left, and more pieces possible but the longest piece is not big enough to split. The recursive case adds up the possibilities of selecting a piece of size i in the range l to n from a carpet of size n, and determine how many ways to partition the remaining carpet. The remaining subproblem is for a carpet of length $n-i$, with one less piece possible, and a minimum length of i (so we pick pieces in increasing order of length). The function can be easily modified to return the dominating partitions.

In the customer data the parameter k is either 1 or 2 and the number of steps n in a stair carpet ranges from 1 to 18 and 2 to 15 for $k=1$ and $k=2$ respectively. For most of the customer data the number of cuts constraint is not constraining ($\geq n$ when $k=1$ and $\geq \lfloor n/2 \rfloor$ when $k=2$), and the total number of dominating partitions is small. This means we can separate the problem into different instances with different fixed (dominating) partitions. Table 1 shows the dominating partitions for stair carpets up to 15 steps for $k=2$. If $k=1$ then the partition with n parts "1", i.e., $\{1,\dots,1\}$ is the only dominating partition for stair carpets covering n steps.

We can split a carpet cutting instance I involving a stair carpet c as follows. For a stair carpet c we determine the set of dominating partitions $\mathbf{P}$ of c and create a new instance $I_P, P \in \mathbf{P}$ where $P = \{p_1,\dots,p_m\}$ which is identical to I except that the partition function for carpet c is fixed so that $c.part = \{r_1,\dots,r_m\}$ and the rectangular pieces r_i are constrained as follows: $r_i.wid = c.wid$, $r_i.len = p_i \times c.step$.

Too many dominating partitions. For some cases in the customer data, for example $n=18$, $k=1$ and $p=7$, there are 49 dominating partitions. Splitting into different instances becomes prohibitive when we have to consider other reasons for splitting such as multiple stair carpets, and different room carpet orientations.

When the number of dominating partitions is too large, we modify the partitioning as follows. We consider the partitioning problem with no limit on the number of pieces (or equivalently limit n). For the customer data, the maximal number of dominating partitions that arise with this weakening is 3 (as illustrated by Tab. 1). We split into instances using these dominating partitions. This model of course can create a carpet cutting with too many carpet pieces for a regular carpet c. For each rectangle $r \in c.part$ we add a Boolean variable $r.last$ to the model.

We constrain $r.last$ to hold if the rectangle does not have another rectangle $r' \in c.part$ directly to the right (1) and ensure that there are at most $c.pcs$ last parts (2). These constraints are posted for all carpets $c \in Str$:

$$\forall r \in c.part : \quad r.last \leftrightarrow (\forall r' \in c.part \setminus \{r\} : r.x + r.len \neq r'.x \vee r.y \neq r'.y) \quad (1)$$

$$\sum_{r \in c.part} r.last \leq c.pcs \ . \quad (2)$$

3.3 The Model

After handling rotations and stair carpets our original instance I is transformed into a set of *static instances* $\mathbf{I}$ in which all rectangles are fixed in orientation and length and width. If the splitting process created too many instances $\mathbf{I}$ or involved edge filler carpets then we will have to handle the original problem using the dynamic model defined in the next section.

We can now model each static instance $I' \in \mathbf{I}$ reasonably straightforwardly. Let a variable tuple $(r.x, r.y)$ be defined for each rectangle in the instance $Rect = (\bigcup_{c \in Str} c.part) \cup (\bigcup_{c \in Room} c.rect)$ which gives the position of the rectangle on the roll, and variable tuples $(c.x, c.y)$ for each room carpet $c \in Room$. We introduce variable RL to hold the roll length. The constraints of the model are (1–2) if required, together with:
Each rectangle must be on the roll

$$\forall r \in Rect : 0 \leq r.x \wedge r.x + r.len \leq RL \wedge 0 \leq r.y \wedge r.y + r.wid \leq RW \ . \quad (3)$$

Each rectangle in a room carpet must be placed correctly relative to the carpet

$$\forall c \in Room, \forall r \in c.rect : r.x = c.x + r.ox \wedge r.y = c.y + r.oy \ . \quad (4)$$

No rectangles overlap.

$$\texttt{diff2}([r.x \mid r \in Rect], [r.y \mid r \in Rect], [r.len \mid r \in Rect], [r.wid \mid r \in Rect]) \quad (5)$$

For the solver we make use of there is no global definition of $\texttt{diff2}$, instead it is decomposed into a disjunction of possibilities where $\prec$ is simply an arbitrary total order imposed on the rectangles.

$$\forall r_1, r_2 \in Rect \text{ s.t. } r_1 \prec r_2 : r_1.x + r_1.len \leq r_2.x \vee r_2.x + r_2.len \leq r_1.x$$
$$\vee r_1.y + r_1.wid \leq r_2.y \vee r_2.y + r_2.wid \leq r_1.y \ . \quad (6)$$

This decomposition is very weak, and only propagates if three inequalities are unsatisfiable and the remaining one undecided. In order to get a stronger propagation on the involved variables two global `cumulative` constraints are used, *i.e.*, one for the roll length and the other one for the roll width. We hence enhance the model with the redundant constraints

$$\texttt{cumulative}([r.x \mid r \in Rect], [r.len \mid r \in Rect], [r.wid \mid r \in Rect], RW) , \quad (7)$$

$$\texttt{cumulative}([r.y \mid r \in Rect], [r.wid \mid r \in Rect], [r.len \mid r \in Rect], RL) . \quad (8)$$

The `cumulative` constraints are implemented as global constraints with explanation [19]. They provide much stronger propagation than the decomposed `diff2`. Equation (8) also provides strong lower bound reasoning on the objective RL.

In order to find the optimal solution to an original problem instance I using the static model we must find the minimal roll length solution for any of the instances **I** it was split into.

4 Dynamic Model

The static model splits the problem into multiple instances to fix the dimensions of the rectangles. But this can be prohibitive when an original problem splits into very many instances, and it does not give an approach to edge filler carpets. The dynamic model models the problem more directly.

Orientation. For each room carpet c we model its orientation with variable $c.vori$ which takes a value in $c.ori$. We introduce two Boolean variables $c.0or180$ which is true if the carpet is oriented at $0°$ or $180°$, and similarly $c.0or90$.

For each rectangle r we introduce a variable $r.vlen$ to hold its length (after orientation), and similarly a variable to hold its width $r.vwid$, and x offset $r.vox$ and y offset $r.voy$ from the carpet origin. For each carpet c and rectangle $r \in c.rect$ we precalculate two arrays of offsets of r from the carpet origin and each orientation $o \in \{0°, 90°, 180°, 270°\}$ given by $ox_{c,r}[o]$, and $oy_{c,r}[o]$.

The model includes the following constraints for each carpet $c \in Room$: Enforcing agreement of the orientation and Boolean variables

$$c.0or180 = (c.vori \in \{0°, 180°\}) \ \wedge \ c.0or90 = (c.vori \in \{0°, 90°\}) . \quad (9)$$

Setting length, width and offsets of each rectangle depending on orientation

$$\forall r \in c.rect: \quad r.vox = ox_{c,r}[c.vori] \ \wedge \ r.voy = oy_{c,r}[c.vori]$$
$$\wedge \quad r.vwid = r.len + (r.wid - r.len) \times c.0or180 \quad (10)$$
$$\wedge \quad r.vlen = r.wid + (r.len - r.wid) \times c.0or180 . \quad (11)$$

Note that the offset calculation constraints are examples of `element` constraints.

Edge filler carpets. Given an edge filler carpet $c \in Edg$ we model this with a set of $c.pcs$ different rectangles $c.part$ (so $|c.part| = c.pcs$). We have to ensure that these pieces either 0 length (and hence only really pseudo pieces) or reach the minimal length.

$$\forall c \in Edg, \forall r \in c.part : r.vwid = c.wid \land (r.vlen = 0 \lor r.vlen \geq c.min) \quad (12)$$

And the sum of the lengths must equal the irregular break length

$$\forall c \in Edg : \sum_{r \in c.part} r.vlen = c.len \ . \quad (13)$$

We can also reason about dominating partitions for irregular breaks. Any partition with a piece r where $r.vlen \geq 2c.min$ and one piece of zero length will be dominated by a partition where r is broken in two. Hence we can add

$$\forall c \in Edg : \ (\exists r \in c.part : r.vlen = 0) \rightarrow (\forall r \in c.part : r.vlen < 2c.min) \ . \ (14)$$

If $c.len \geq 2(c.pcs - 1) \times c.min$ then there can be no zero length pieces since the right hand side of the implication in (14) cannot be satisfied at the same time as (13), hence in this case we can simplify (12).

The Model. The set of rectangles is $Rect = \bigcup_{c \in Room} r.rect \cup \bigcup_{c \in Str \cup Edg} c.part$. We assume that for each stair piece $r.vlen = r.len$ and $r.vwid = r.wid$. The constraints of the model are: (1–2) if required, (3–8) with $r.len$ replaced by $r.vlen$ and $r.wid$ replaced with $r.vwid$, (9–11) and (12–14) if required.

5   Refining the Models

The basic model can be further enhanced in order to improve the propagation, reduce the model size, and strengthen the reasoning and the conflict-driven search in the LCG solver.

Variable views. Variable views [17] are a form of variable aliasing. Suppose $y = ax + c$ where a and c are constants, then rather than creating a new variable for y use a view to compute information about the (view) variable y from the real variable x. This refinement (views) is particularly useful for LCG solvers since it improves learning. For a fixed orientation room carpet c we can replace the variables $r.x$ and $r.y$ by views on $c.x$ and $c.y$ for all $r \in c.rect$ using (4). For non-fixed orientation carpets c we can use views to define $r.vlen$ and $r.vwid$ for $r \in c.rect$ using (10) and (11).

Disjunction and Better diff2 decomposition. In all carpet cutting problems the roll width is narrow in comparison to some carpets, so that no other carpet can be positioned below or above to those carpets. We say these carpets are *in disjunction*. Carpets that are in disjunction with all others can be placed at the beginning of the roll. We denote this as the disj refinement.

We can use disjunction to improve the diff2 decomposition (diff2). Assume function $not\_par(r_1, r_2)$ holds if r_1 and r_2 cannot overlap horizontally on the role. For pairs r_1, r_2 with this holds we replace the body of (6) by $r_1.x + r_1.len \leq r_2.x \ \lor \ r_2.x + r_2.len \leq r_1.x$. The simplest definition of not_par just $r_1.wid + r_2.wid > RW$, but it can be improved by considering the compulsory parts [8] and possible y coordinates of r_1 and r_2 to determine if there is insufficient space for them to overlap.

Symmetry breaking constraints. In the model symmetries can occur between rectangles that have the same size, *i.e.*, length and width. The most common case for symmetries occurs for pieces of stair carpets. We assume a function $same(r, r')$ which (statically) tests if two rectangles have the same dimensions, are not rotatable and are not part of a room carpet with more than one rectangle. For refinement sym we add a lexicographic ordering on $(r.y, r.x)$ for rectangles that are the same. Symmetry breaking can also considerably simplify the definition of $r.last$ for stair carpets $c \in Str$ since we only need to consider the lexicographically least member of each symmetric group that appears in the partition $c.part$. Finally we can enforce that the pieces of an edge filler carpet are ordered in length.

Forbidden gaps. *Forbidden gaps* [20] are areas between a rectangle and a long edge (either from another rectangle or a boundary) that are too small to accommodate any part of other rectangles. In this paper, we forbid these gaps between rectangles that have fixed orientation and do not belong to room carpets with multiple rectangles, and the borders of the carpet roll as follows.

Let gap be the minimal width of any rectangle. In the y direction (fbg y) We consider how many rectangles (multiples of gap) might fit between the considered object edge and the border of the carpet roll: (*i*) none, (*ii*) one, and (*iii*) two or more. In case (*i*) the y coordinate is set to 0. In case (*ii*) the object is aligned with either the top or the bottom. In case (*iii*) constraints are added to forbid placements of the object that creates a smaller gap than gap with either the top or bottom of the roll. Similarly, we impose forbidden gaps (fbg x) for the left and right border of the roll.

6   Search

To solve a carpet cutting problem instance I in our approaches we need to solve a series of instances **I** determined by splitting. The generic algorithm first attempts to find a good solution for each $I' \in \mathbf{I}$ and then uses the best solution found as an upper bound on roll length, and searches for an optimal solution of each $I' \in \mathbf{I}$ in the order of how good a first solution we found for them. During this process the upper bound is always the best solution found so far.

The two phase approach has two benefits. First it means that domain sizes of variables in the optimisation search are much smaller. Because lazy clause generation generates a Boolean representation of the size of the initial domain size this makes the optimisation search much more efficient. Second the first phase ranks the split instances on likelihood of finding good solutions, so usually later instances in the optimisation phase are quickly found to be unable to lead to a better solution.

First solution generation. The goal of the first search is to quickly generate a first solution that gives a good upper bound on the carpet roll length. We examine each split instance in **I** in turn. We order the split instances by the partitions of regular stair carpets examining partitions with fewer pieces before partitions with more pieces, and otherwise breaking ties arbitrarily.

We use a simple sequential search on each split instance. We treat the room carpets first, in decreasing order of total area. First we assign a horizontal or vertical orientation for all room carpets by fixing the $c.0or180$, which fixes the dimensions of each rectangle. Then we fix the orientation by fixing $c.0or90$. We then fix the lengths of edge filler carpets. We next determine $c.x$ for all room carpets c, and then determine each $c.y$ again in decreasing area order. Finally we place each stair carpet rectangles by fixing $r.x$ and then $r.y$ treating each rectangle in input order.

Minimisation. A hybrid sequential/activity based search is used to find optimal solutions. We first fix the orientations of each room carpet as we did in the first-solution search. Then we switch to the activity-based search (a variant of VSIDS [12]) which concentrates on variables which are involved in lots of recent failures. Activity-based search is tightly tied to the learning solver we use, but is acknowledged from the SAT community to be very effective.

For the activity-based search, we use a geometric restart policy on the number of node failures in order to make the search more robust. The restart base and factor are 128 failures and 2.0, respectively.

7   Experiments

The experiments were carried out on a 64-bit machine with Intel(R) Pentium(R) D processing with 3.4 GHz clock and Ubuntu 9.04. For each original problem instance I an overall 3 minutes runtime limit was imposed for calculating carpets that are in disjunction with all other carpets if the refinement disj is used, finding a first solution and minimising the roll length for all split instances **I**.

The G12/FDX solver from the G12 Constraint Programming Platform [21] was used as the LCG solver. We also experimented with the G12 FD solver using search more suitable for FD (placement of the biggest carpets at first). It could only optimally solve 7 instances compared to 76 for LCG using the same search. This shows that LCG is vital for solving the problem to prune substantial parts of the search space.

Dynamic versus static model. Table 2 compares the static and dynamic model as well as the current solution approach on the instances which the static model can handle (126 of 150). It shows the number of instances solved optimally ("opt."), the sum of the best first solutions found for each instance ("init. ΣRL"), the sum of the best solutions found for each instance ("ΣRL") and the area of wastage ("wast."), *i.e.*, for one instance $RL \times RW - \sum_{c \in Rect} c.len \times c.wid$, relatively to the wastage created by the current method as well as the total runtime to solve all instances ("Σrt."). The static approach solves one more problem and its first solutions are better than for the dynamic approach. In total, a better first solution was generated for 55 instances. Where applicable the static approach is preferable.

The existing method finds, but does not prove, 27 optimal solutions. It was tested by IF Computer GmbH on a Dell Latitude D820 with a Intel(R) Core(TM)

Table 2. Comparison between dynamic and static approach

approach	opt.	init. ΣRL	ΣRL	wast.	Σrt.
dynamic	92/126	171,645	160,536	66.5%	6,247s
static	93/126	168,270	160,399	65.9%	6,946s
Current method	27/126	-	167,668	100%	7,450s†

Table 3. Results of different refinements

disj	views	diff2	sym	fbg x	fbg y	opt.	init. ΣRL	ΣRL	wast.	Σrt.
						86/150	232,181	221,542	67.9%	12,721s
×						88/150	232,075	221,521	67.8%	12,360s
	×					89/150	232,181	221,248	66.9%	11,999s
		×				89/150	232,181	221,240	66.9%	11,980s
			×			99/150	232,181	221,344	67.2%	9,933s
				×		88/150	232,181	221,596	68.1%	12,295s
					×	88/150	232,181	221,399	67.4%	12,302s
				×	×	89/150	232,181	221,060	66.3%	12,385s
×	×	×	×	×	×	**106/150**	232,075	**220,775**	**65.2%**	**9,290s**
Current method						30/150	-	230,795	100%	8,988s†

Duo processor T2400 processing with 1.86 Ghz clock. The times marked (†) for the existing approach are the sum of times when the best solution was found. Since it cannot prove optimality for the majority of instances the method uses the whole 3 minutes. The new approach reduces the wastage of over 33%.

Refinements. Table 3 presents the impact of different refinements on the dynamic models. The entry × means that the refinement was used. We compare the different refinements with the same features as before.

The change in number of optimally solved instances clearly illustrates the important of symmetry breaking for proving optimality. Variable views and forbidden gaps have a minor impact on proving optimality.

We can see a tradeoff in the refinements. Most make it harder to find solutions, but reduce the search space required to prove optimality. When applying all refinements we solve the most instances, and generate solutions with minimal total length, since the new optimal solutions make up for unsolved problems where we found worse solutions.

8 Conclusion

We have created an approach to carpet cutting that can find and prove the optimal solution for typical problems instances within 3 minutes. The power of the approach comes from the combination of careful modelling of the stair breaking constraints to eliminate symmetries and dominated solutions, and the use of lazy clause generation to drastically reduce the time to prove optimality.

Acknowledgements. We are indebted to IF Computer GmbH for providing us not only real world data, but also sharing their knowledge and results with us. NICTA is funded by the Australian Government as represented by the Department of Broadband, Communications and the Digital Economy and the Australian Research Council through the ICT Centre of Excellence program.

References

1. Aggoun, A., Beldiceanu, N.: Extending CHIP in order to solve complex scheduling and placement problems. Math. Comput. Model. 17(7), 57–73 (1993)
2. Beldiceanu, N., Carlsson, M., Poder, E., Sadek, R., Truchet, C.: A generic geometrical constraint kernel in space and time for handling polymorphic k-dimensional objects. In: Bessière, C. (ed.) CP 2007. LNCS, vol. 4741, pp. 180–194. Springer, Heidelberg (2007)
3. Beldiceanu, N., Carlsson, M.: Sweep as a generic pruning technique applied to the non-overlapping rectangles constraint. In: Walsh, T. (ed.) CP 2001. LNCS, vol. 2239, pp. 377–391. Springer, Heidelberg (2001)
4. Beldiceanu, N., Carlsson, M., Poder, E.: New filtering for the cumulative constraint in the context of non-overlapping rectangles. In: Trick, M.A. (ed.) CPAIOR 2008. LNCS, vol. 5015, pp. 21–35. Springer, Heidelberg (2008)
5. Fekete, S.P., Schepers, J., van der Veen, J.C.: An exact algorithm for higher-dimensional orthogonal packing. Oper. Res. 55(3), 569–587 (2007)
6. George, A.E.: The Theory of Partitions. Cambridge University Press, Cambridge (1998)
7. Hadjiconstantinou, E., Christofides, N.: An exact algorithm for general, orthogonal, two-dimensional knapsack problems. Eur. J. Oper. Res. 83(1), 39–56 (1995)
8. Lahrichi, A.: Scheduling: the notions of hump, compulsory parts and their use in cumulative problems. C. R. Acad. Sci., Paris, Sér. I, Math. 294(2), 209–211 (1982)
9. Lodi, A., Martello, S., Monaci, M.: Two-dimensional packing problems: A survey. Eur. J. Oper. Res. 141(2), 241–252 (2002)
10. Martello, S., Toth, P.: Lower bounds and reduction procedures for the bin packing problem. Discrete Appl. Math. 28(1), 59–70 (1990)
11. Martello, S., Vigo, D.: Exact solution of the two-dimensional finite bin packing problem. Manage. Sci. 44(3), 388–399 (1998)
12. Moskewicz, M.W., Madigan, C.F., Zhao, Y., Zhang, L., Malik, S.: Chaff: Engineering an efficient SAT solver. In: DAC 2001, pp. 530–535 (2001)
13. Ohrimenko, O., Stuckey, P.J., Codish, M.: Propagation via lazy clause generation. Constraints 14(3), 357–391 (2009)
14. Pearson, C., Birtwistle, M., Verden, A.R.: Reducing material wastage in the carpet industry. In: PAP 1998, pp. 101–112 (1998)
15. Pearson, C., Birtwistle, M., Verden, A.R.: Reducing material wastage in the carpet industry. In: INAP 1998, pp. 88–99 (1998)
16. Pisinger, D., Sigurd, M.: Using decomposition techniques and constraint programming for solving the two-dimensional bin-packing problem. INFORMS J. Comput. 19(1), 36–51 (2007)
17. Schulte, C., Tack, G.: Views iterators for generic constraint implementations. In: van Beek, P. (ed.) CP 2005. LNCS, vol. 3709, pp. 817–821. Springer, Heidelberg (2005), doi:10.1007/11564751_71

18. Schutt, A., Feydy, T., Stuckey, P.J., Wallace, M.G.: Solving the resource constrained project scheduling problem with generalized precedences by lazy clause generation (September 2010), http://arxiv.org/abs/1009.0347
19. Schutt, A., Feydy, T., Stuckey, P.J., Wallace, M.G.: Explaining the cumulative propagator. Constraints 16(3), 250–282 (2011)
20. Simonis, H., O'Sullivan, B.: Search strategies for rectangle packing. In: Stuckey, P.J. (ed.) CP 2008. LNCS, vol. 5202, pp. 52–66. Springer, Heidelberg (2008)
21. Stuckey, P.J., de la Banda, M.G., Maher, M.J., Marriott, K., Slaney, J.K., Somogyi, Z., Wallace, M., Walsh, T.: The G12 project: Mapping solver independent models to efficient solutions. In: Gabbrielli, M., Gupta, G. (eds.) ICLP 2005. LNCS, vol. 3668, pp. 9–13. Springer, Heidelberg (2005)
22. Wäscher, G., Haußner, H., Schumann, H.: An improved typology of cutting and packing problems. Eur. J. Oper. Res. 183, 1109–1130 (2007)

A Hybrid Approach for Solving Real-World Nurse Rostering Problems

Martin Stølevik, Tomas Eric Nordlander, Atle Riise, and Helle Frøyseth*

SINTEF ICT, Department of Applied Mathematics,
P.O. Box 124 Blindern, NO-0314 Oslo, Norway
{Martin.Stolevik,Tomas.Nordlander,Atle.Riise}@sintef.no
hellef@gmail.com
http://www.SINTEF.no

Abstract. Nurse rostering is the process of creating a plan for nurse working hours over a given time horizon. This problem, most variants of which are NP-hard, has been studied extensively for many years. Still, practical nurse rostering is mostly done manually, often by highly qualified health care personnel. This underlines the need to address the challenges of realistic, applied nurse rostering, and the implementation of advanced rostering methods in commercial software.

In this paper, we present an industrial case study of a nurse rostering software currently used in several hospitals and other health care institutions in Norway and Sweden. The presented problem model has a rich set of hard and soft constraints, as required by Norwegian hospitals. Our solution approach is a hybrid: An Iterated Local Search framework that uses Constraint Programming for initial solution construction and diversification, and a Variable Neighborhood Descent for iterative improvement. The search method shows good results in terms of solution quality and computation time on a set of real world instances. We make these test instances available on-line.

Keywords: Nurse rostering, Iterated Local Search, Constraint Programming, Variable Neighborhood Descent, Hybrid optimization, Real-world test cases, Industrial case study.

1 Introduction

Nurse rostering is the process of creating a work schedule for hospital nurses by matching employees to shifts over a given planning horizon, while considering skills, competence, fairness, and laws and regulations. The output is a roster of the working hours for the nurses that also provides an overview of staff utilization and associated costs.

Producing a nurse roster is a complex task: The hospital typically has a continuous demand for personnel, and this demand varies over time. In addition, the roster must follow labor laws, union regulations, as well as hospital policy. Also,

---

* Corresponding author.

J. Lee (Ed.): CP 2011, LNCS 6876, pp. 85–99, 2011.
© Springer-Verlag Berlin Heidelberg 2011

the problem involves multiple stakeholders (employer, employees, and patients), whose preferences must be taken into consideration. The main focus of the employer might be efficient resource utilization at minimum cost, while an employee would like to have a fair distribution of work load and the option to influence the planning of his or her days off. For the patients, short waiting time and treatment by personnel with the right competence could be the main concern.

Currently, nurse rostering is usually conducted manually, often by highly qualified health care personnel. There are important advantages to be gained by automating the construction and maintenance of rosters. Not only can the added computation power lead to better rosters, it also drastically reduces the time used in this task. Thus, time is freed up for the involved health care personnel — time that can be better spent on clinical tasks and care.

The presented work was done in a R&D project for Gatsoft AS, a developer of personnel management software that currently serves 80 % of the Norwegian Hospital market. The solution approach showed very good results and was implemented in their personnel management system already in 2005. Today, the module is used by several hospitals and other health care institutions in Norway and Sweden, and has also attracted interest from food production and transportation companies.

In this paper we present the developed problem model and solution approach. These were developed to meet performance requirements and functional specifications from Norwegian hospitals. The solution approach is a hybrid between Constraint Programming, Iterated Local Search [20] and Variable Neighborhood Descent [13], and will be presented in the following. The test results (section 5) show that this search method can solve large, realistic instances within reasonable time. All test instances are from real world rostering applications, and are available online [25].

The paper is organized as follows: Section 2 provides background information on related research. In section 3, we describe the problem, while the solution method is presented in section 4. Experimental results are given in section 5. We conclude and highlight possible directions for future research in section 6.

2   Background

Nurse rostering problems (NRPs) are combinatorial optimization problems that in most cases are NP-hard [17]. There is a large literature on different solution methods applied on NRPs. However, according to [8] and [18], only a few methods have been tested on real world instances and even fewer have been implemented and used in hospitals: For a more comprehensive overview of the nurse rostering literature, see [8].

2.1   Related Work

Both complete and incomplete solution methods have been applied to the NRP. Examples of complete methods are: Mathematical Programming [3], Goal Programming [11], and Constraint Programming [14,29]. Examples of incomplete methods includes: Variable Neighborhood Search [7], Simulated Annealing [5], Genetic Algorithm [23], Tabu Search [6,12], and Multi-Objective Optimization with Variable Neighborhood Search [9].

Our approach is a hybrid, combining Constraint Programming (CP) with Iterated Local Search (ILS) and Variable Neighborhood Descent (VND). Similar hybrid approaches include [19], who combine CP with Tabu Search. However, while they formulate a weighted Constraint Satisfaction Problem, we differentiate between hard and soft constraints in a manner similar to that of CP's constraint hierarchy [4]. There is also a difference in CP heuristics: [19] involve only some of the nurses in their CP model, while our CP search constructs complete solutions for all nurses. Also, while they use Tabu Search for improving their partial solution, we use ILS to improve on our complete solution. [28] present an early and interesting hybrid approach: They use a simplified Integer Linear Programming (ILP) formulation of the complete model to produce an initial solution. Tabu Search is used in a second stage to repair and improve on the solution found by ILP. Another relevant approach is [15], where Large Neighborhood Search is used as the algorithmic framework. Here, fragments of low quality in the solution are destroyed, and CP assists by rebuilding the solution. [7] has the approach most similar to ours. They use an iterative process of Variable Neighborhood Search (VNS), then destroy (un-assign) shifts for the most penalized nurses. However, their re-construction is done by a heuristic construction method rather than a CP search, and the solutions so constructed are allowed to be infeasible. These infeasibilities are subsequently removed by the next application of VNS.

There are few systems implemented and used in hospitals. For example, Gymnaste [22], Interdip [1], and Orbis:Dienstplan [2], which all use CP as their solution method. In addition, we have ORTEC's rostering software Harmony [23], which use Genetic Algorithm as its solution method. The only hybrid we have found is Plane [6], which combine simple Tabu Search with problem solving heuristics (diversification and greedy shuttling).

3   Problem Description

Based on extensive dialog with Norwegian hospitals, we believe that the proposed model includes all important constraints for Norwegian nurse rostering. In the following, E is the set of all employees, while D is the set of all days in the roster. Table 1 lists the hard and soft constraints of the model.

Each shift is a member of one and only one *shift category*, which is a "collection" of shifts that are concurrent (day shifts, evening shifts and night shift). A *manpower plan* (cover requirement) is a table summarizing how many employees that are needed for each shift on the different weekdays. The inclusion and parametrization of individual constraints will vary between problem instances. A feasible solution must satisfy all included hard constraints. The objective function of the problem, f, is a weighted sum of the penalties derived from violating the soft constraints. For an exact mathematical definition of the problem, please see [26].

Table 1. Hard and soft constraints

Hard constraints	Soft constraints
HC1: Maximum one shift is assigned on each day to each employee.	**SC1:** Avoid too many consecutive working days with the same shift category.
HC2: The manpower plan must be covered exactly on each day ('cover requirement').	**SC2:** Avoid too many consecutive working days.
HC3: The sum of working hours for each employee must not deviate too much with respect to the employee's contracted hours (typical for Norway). Note that within the hard limits of HC3, the deviation is minimized by soft constraint SC6.	**SC3:** Avoid too few consecutive working days with the same shift category.
	SC4: Avoid too few consecutive working days.
	SC5: Minimize deviation from minimum and maximum number of shifts in each category.
HC4: Employees can only work shifts for which they have the required competence.	**SC6:** Minimize deviation from the employee's contracted hours. While HC3 provide a minimum and maximum limit for the sum working hours, this constraint tries to minimize the distance to the contracted number of working hours within those limits.
HC5: There must be a minimum time between shifts on consecutive working days.	
HC6: Every week must have a minimum continuous free period.	
HC7: The maximum weekly working time must not be violated.	**SC7:** Cluster days off as much as possible.
	SC8: Maximize wanted shift patterns.
	SC9: Minimize unwanted shift patterns.

4   Solution Method

We employ a hybrid solution approach combining Constraint Programming (CP) and Variable Neighborhood Descent (VND) in an Iterated Local Search (ILS) framework. All parts of this hybrid algorithm were implemented using SINTEF's in-house optimization library, SCOOP.

```
    keywordstyle
1  IteratedLocalSearch
2      x* ← x ← CPBuild(x₀)
3      repeat
4          x ← VariableNeighborhoodDescent(x)
5          x* ← Accept(x, x*)
6          repeat // Diversification
7              x' ← DestroyPartsOfSolution(x)
8              x' ← CPBuild(x')
9          until x' is a legal solution
10         x ← x'
11     until some termination condition is met
12     return x*
```

Listing 1.1. The iterated local search scheme

Listing 1.1 shows a high level pseudo-code of the algorithm. The search is initiated in line 2 where CP is used to create an initial feasible solution. This becomes
the starting point of the improvement phase in the ILS algorithm. More details
on the procedure *CPBuild* can be found in Section 4.1. In line 4, VND is run
to improve the current solution **x**. For more details about the VND algorithm,
see Section 4.2. The VND can get stuck in local optima and the purpose of
the diversification step in lines 7 and 8 is to escape these. We employ a ruin
(*DestroyPartsOfSolution*) and recreate (*CPBuild*) methodology for this diversification; see section 4.3 for a detailed description. The procedure *Accept* (line 5)
simply accepts **x** as the new best solution if it improves the objective value. The
search terminates when a pre-set time limit is reached, when a solution with
zero penalty is found, or upon manual interruption by the user. Throughout the
search we only store the best found solution ($\mathbf{x}^*$) at any time. Inferior solutions
found during the search are discarded.

4.1   Initial Solution Construction

The procedure *CPBuild* applies CP search on a Constraint Satisfaction Problem (CSP) involving only the hard constraints. In line 2 in Listing 1.1, *CP-
Build* constructs a complete feasible initial solution from scratch. We will later
(in section 4.3) describe how *CPBuild* is used in the diversification step of the
algorithm, to complete partial solutions where only some of the variables are
instantiated.

The CSP model has a set of variables $X = \{X_{ed}\}$, where $e \in E$ and $d \in D$
indicates the corresponding employee and day, respectively. Each variable has a
finite domain of discrete shift code values. A set of hard constraints restrict the
domain values that any subset of variables can take simultaneously. A feasible
solution contains an assignment of a shift code value to every variable X_{ed} in such
a way that all the hard constraints are satisfied, and the procedure terminates
as soon as as such a solution is found. If the procedure cannot find a feasible
solution within an allocated time limit it will return a solution satisfying as many
of the hard constraints as possible. This is ensured by first finding a solution
that satisfy the two hard constraints, HC2 and HC3 (and HC1 implicitly by
modelling). For our test cases, finding such "basic solution" is always possible
and in general fast, if the rostering problem is set up with the right amount
of personnel (which it typically true since this is used in hospitals where the
cover / manpower plan is adjusted to the amount of available personnel). Next
we try to find a solution where all the hard constraints in the problem are
satisfied, if that works, this solution becomes the initial solution. If not; different
combinations of the constraints are tried, in a pre-defined order. When the time
limit is reached, the solution involving the most important / highest ranked
constraint combination is returned.

The hard constraints HC1 and HC2 in Table 1 are always required to be satisfied and to ensure this, the time limit can be exceeded. Those hard constraints
that are not satisfied are relaxed and added to the set of soft constraints that
form the basis for the objective function used in the subsequent local search.

Note that this happens very rarely, and did not happen in any of our tests. Therefore, in the following discussion we assume that *CPBuild* always returns a feasible solution, satisfying all hard constraints.

We use a MAC CP search algorithm (from our SCOOP library) that establish arc consistency before and search and maintain it during search. The algorithm uses a depth first search with dynamic variable and value orderings. A standard CP search algorithm usually first selects a variable to instantiate, and then a value (or vice versa). In our CP search algorithm the variable and value selection is interconnected: The algorithm first partially orders variables by day, then orders shift values by criticality, and finally orders the variables by employees. The details of this selection procedure are as follows:

1. **Select days, most critical first.** The first variables to consider are those concerning weekend days. This is because the model requires that "weekends off" for the employees are specified as problem input. Thereafter the weekday variables are ordered in sequence of the last Friday to the first Monday of the plan.

2. **Select shift, most critical shift category first.** The shift categories are first ordered by descending value of the ratio p_{dc}/n_{dc} where p_{dc} is the required number of shifts of category c left to assign on day d and n_{dc} is the number of employees with shifts of category c in its domain on day d in the current solution.

   For example, assume that there are five night shifts and two day shifts left to assign on day d. Eight employees have night shifts ($c=1$) and four employees have day shifts ($c=2$) in their domain on day d. By looking at the ratios $p_{d1}/n_{d1} = 5/8 > p_{d2}/n_{d2} = 2/4$, we see that the next shift to assign will be a shift from the night shift category. We use a lexicographical ordering of shift codes within each shift category.

3. **Select employee for the shift according to employee's 'need'.** The selected shift is assigned to the variable on the selected day that correspond to the employee that 'needs' this shift the most. We define m_{ec} as the desired number of shifts of category c for employee e. Initially, m_{ec} is computed by adding all shifts required from the manpower plan for all days and all employees over the planning horizon and computing employee e's share according to his/her contract. This number is updated during the search, as shifts are assigned to the employee. Following the previous partial ordering described above, the variables are now ordered by descending m_{ec} value for the corresponding employees. If we continue with the previous example, then for day d, the next shift to assign is from the night shift category ($c=2$). We assign it to the employee e with the highest m_{e2}.

4.2   Variable Neighborhood Descent

When the construction algorithm *CPBuild* has created a feasible solution, either as an initial solution (line 2) or as part of the diversification step (line 8), VND is applied to locally refine the solution. The basic VND algorithm is described in [13].

Our implementation cycles through a set of basic neighborhoods, performing a first-improvement Descent local search for each of them. The search terminates when no improving neighbors can be found in any basic neighborhood (i.e. in a local optimum), or when the total improvement over a certain number of iterations is less than a set fraction of the best found objective value ('flattening'). We use the following three basic neighborhoods:

1. **2-Exchange**: This neighborhood consists of all moves where two shifts are swapped on the same day between two different employees, as illustrated in Thursday's column in Figure 1.
2. **3-Exchange**: All moves where three shifts are swapped on the same day between three different employees, as illustrated in Monday's column in Figure 1.
3. **Double 2-Exchange**: All moves that swap shifts between two employees on two days. Such moves are made up of two 2-Exchange moves on different days for the same two employees. Note that the two days are not necessarily consecutive. The two shifts that are moved must belong to the same shift category. This move is illustrated in Saturday's and Sunday's columns in Figure 1.

Before we added the Double 2-Exchange neighborhood, we experienced that the hard constraint concerning working hours for employees (HC3) often prevented the removing or adding of a free-shift to a roster using 2-Exchange. The Double 2-Exchange operator makes it easier to preserve the working hours when moving a free-shifts because exchanging a working shift with a free shift on one day, will be coupled with a free shift being exchanged with a working shift on the other day in the move. This preserves the number of shifts of different categories for both employees, thus improving the likelihood of an improving move.

The above neighborhoods are used in many local search applications for the nurse rostering problem. The most basic move operator in nurse rostering is the replace move [21] which corresponds to (in our model) moving a shift from one employee to another. The 2-Exchange move can be viewed as a combination of two opposite replace moves.

	Mon	Tue	Wed	Thu	Fri	Sat	Sun
Employee 1	E	D	N		E		E
Employee 2			D	E	N		D
Employee 3	D	N		D			
Employee 4	N	E				E	
Employee 5			E		D	N	N

Fig. 1. Example of 2-Exchange (Thursday) and 3-Exchange (Monday), and Double 2-Exchange (Saturday+Sunday) neighborhoods. All blank cells are free shifts.

Note that soft constraint SC8 is challenging for local search methods: The obvious objective function to use is the number of complete wanted patterns in the solution. However, such a function is lacking because its value is only reduced when a new complete pattern is found. This motivates keeping patterns that are already found, but there is no explicit mechanism that actually drives the local search in the direction of completing patterns. To introduce such a driving mechanism in our method, we use a modified penalty function [26] which decreases the penalty as we get closer to completing a wanted pattern. For instance, let D,D,D,E be a wanted pattern: When evaluating part of a roster with D,D,F,E (3 out of 4 shifts correct) against one with N,D,F,E (2 out of 4 shifts correct) the first combination (D,D,F,E) receives the lowest penalty. We use a fixed number from which we subtract the squared (normalized) Hamming distance. This is then a function with the property that a pattern with two wrong shifts are penalized harder than two patterns each with one wrong shift.

4.3   Neighborhood Reduction

The neighborhoods, described in Section 4.2, are rather large. For example, the 2-Exchange neighborhood has a size of order $|E|^2|D|$. We use *focal points* to significantly reduce the size of the neighborhoods. A focal point identifies features in the solution which is expected to be critical to further improvement of the objective value. We create one focal point for each variable that is involved in a violation of one or more of the soft constraints. During the VND search, each neighborhood is reduced to those moves that somehow involve one or more focal points. When a move is performed, the list of focal points is updated. This is comparable to the "Cost-based Neighborhood" idea presented by [10] in which the authors focus the search effort on the part of the problem which has the greatest effect on the objective. In that work, however, more effort was done in evaluating several candidate improvements, in contrast to our first-improvement strategy. Analogous ideas exists in the project scheduling literature, where local search neighborhoods can be focused on critical paths in the project graph. Also, the Fast Local Search algorithm of [27] is similar.

4.4   Diversification

The purpose of the diversification step (line 7 and 8 in Listing 1.1) is to escape local optima and areas of the search space where little improvement is found ('flattening'). We do this by making a major change to the current solution by ruin-and-recreate [24]. The "ruin" mechanism removes the shift assignments for a subset (E') of the employees. A partial CSP solution is created, based on the partially ruined solution $(\mathbf{x'})$, where some of the variables are instantiated while those variables involved in the above "ruin" process get their full, initial domains. This partial solution becomes the input to *CPBuild* which then constructs a new feasible solution.

The number of rosters to ruin is picked randomly between 2 % and 30 % of the total number of rosters. Half of the rosters to ruin are randomly selected, while the other half are those that produce the highest penalties. We focus partly on the parts of the solution that have the largest potential for improvement — similar to the focal points of the VND, but also include some randomly chosen rosters to avoid recreating the same, high penalty solution, and intensify the diversification.

If a feasible solution is not found by *CPBuild* within a given time limit, the algorithm retries *DestroyPartsOfSolution* with a different selection of randomly chosen rosters. The time limit is equal to the time used when creating the initial solution. Our experience is that this happens very rarely.

5   Computational Experiments

5.1   Test Cases

The presented problem model and solution method were designed for integration in the leading nurse rostering system in the Norwegian market. The aim in this context was to develop a robust solution method that could solve a wide range of realistic problem instances as they occur in the hospitals. The model has a very similar structure to those found in common academic benchmark problems such as those at http://www.cs.nott.ac.uk/~tec/NRP/. There are, however, some differences. For example, most benchmark problems involve time limited "horizontal" constraints (constraints for one employee) while our horizontal constraints spans over the complete planning horizon (except for HC7). Furthermore, we assume the assignment of free weekends to be part of the problem input, which is not common in benchmark problems. Also, our functional requirement demanded that the manpower plan (cover requirement) must be covered exactly — it is a hard constraint that we implicitly handle by algorithm design. In the literature, some flexibility in the coverage is normally allowed, often modeled as a soft constraint.

Table 2 describe our seven test cases (OpTur1 – OpTur7). The first four rows provide general information for each case (e.g. number of employees to schedule, number of hours for the complete scheduling period, etc.). The following rows provide the parameterization for the constraints (see Table 1 in section 4 for more information about the individual constraints). In Table 2, the shift categories "Day", "Evening", and "Night" are represented by "D", "E", and "N". For example: For the case OpTur2, the hard constraint "HC5: N → E" forces the minimum time between consecutive shifts in the night category (N) and the evening category (E) to be at least 8 hours. An empty cell signifies that the corresponding constraint is not used in the test case. The notation '10/8' in for instance OpTur6's three HC5 constraints, sets this minimum time to 10 and 8 for weekends and weekdays, respectively. The symbol '-' means that the constraint parameter is not set (e.g. SC1 in OpTur2 has no specific maximum limit for day shift (D) while it only allows 4 consecutive evening shifts (E) and night shifts (N).

Each of our seven test cases contain a mix of employee contracts. E.g. most of the 51 employees in OpTur1 are on standard Norwegian nursing contracts with an

Table 2. Overview of the seven test cases; characteristics and parameterization of the constraints used

	OpTur1	OpTur2	OpTur3	OpTur4	OpTur5	OpTur6	OpTur7
General information:							
# of employees	51	83	29	30	20	54	15
# of hours to schedule	19170	12819	4159.5	17352	2280	18978	2209.5
# days to schedule	84	42	42	168	28	84	42
# of shifts in use	9	9	8	8	9	5	6
Hard constraints:							
HC1	Yes	Yes	Yes	Yes	Yes	Yes	Yes
HC2	Yes	Yes	Yes	Yes	Yes	Yes	Yes
HC3	Yes	Yes	Yes	Yes	Yes	Yes	Yes
HC4	Yes						Yes
HC5: $(N \rightarrow E)$	8	8	11	11	11	10/8	11
HC5: $(E \rightarrow D)$	8	9	11	9	8	10/8	11
HC5: $(D \rightarrow N)$	8	8	11	11	11	10/8	11
HC6:	32	32	32	32	32	32	32
HC7:	54	50	48	48	48	54	48
Soft constraints:							
SC1: (D,E,N)	6,3,4	-,4,4	5,2,4	4,3,4	3,2,3	-,-,3	-,-,4
SC2:	6	6	12	7	5		6
SC3: (D,E,N)		-,-,2	2,2,2	-,-,2	2,-,2		-,-,2
SC4:			(Not used in any of the test cases)				
SC5: D			0/10				
SC5: E			0/10		0/5		
SC5: N			3/10		2/6		
SC6:	Yes	Yes	Yes	Yes	Yes	Yes	Yes
SC7:		Yes	Yes	Yes	Yes	Yes	Yes
SC8:	1 p.		1 p.				3 ps.
SC9:			(Not used in any of the test cases)				

average 35.5 hours working time is s. The same test case also involves contracts with an average of 26.6, 17.7, 8.9 and even 4.4 hours/week. Other important aspects of each test case concerns skills, nurse contracts, shifts, manpower plans patterns, etc. A complete description of all test cases can be found in [25].

5.2   Experimental Results

We have conducted the experiments described in this paper on a PC (Intel Core2 Duo CPU at 2.53 GHz with 4 GB RAM) running 64-bits Windows 7. Through extensive testing we have determined the values for the different parameters of the algorithm. The most important of these are: first-improvement (rather than best-improvement) in the VND, the number of rosters to destroy in the diversification step (random number between 2 % and 30 %), and the "flat" criterion in VND (less than 5 % change in the objective value over the last n iterations, where $n = 50\sqrt{|D||E|}$).

The algorithm contains random elements in the neighborhood generation for VND and in the ruin part of diversification (see Listing 1.1, Section 4). Therefore, to statistically verify our results, we have run every test case 66 times (the exact number was determined by our experimental setup), terminating each run after 1200 seconds. Table 3 presents some statistics of the results, taken over all runs. Line 2 shows the number of backtracks in the CP search used to compute an initial solution. The following rows present time spent (Mean, standard deviation, and coefficient of variation) on each of the following parts of the iterated local search: Generate Initial Solution (line 2), VND (line 4) and Diversification (line 7 | 8). The row "Initial Obj val" shows the objective value after the initial solution generation. The five last rows show statistics for the objective values found after 1200 seconds.

Table 3. Results for the seven test cases: Number of backtracks. Time spent on the initial solution generation, variable neighborhood search, and diversify parts of the algorithm, Last rows provide information concerning the objective value. All cases were run 66 times and for 1200 seconds.

	OpTur1	OpTur2	OpTur3	OpTur4	OpTur5	OpTur6	OpTur7
# backtracks	199106	3994	160100	52133	294	1274	0
Initial solution							
Mean (sec)	59.0	1.87	33.8	17.2	0.131	0.818	0.0694
StDev (sec)	6.25	0.0162	0.184	0.164	0.00594	0.0124	0.00713
CV (%)	10.6	0.866	0.546	0.954	4.54	1.52	10.3
VND							
Mean (sec)	1141	1188	1144	1181	1104	1199	883
StDev (sec)	6.88	6.86	8.21	1.08	9.59	2.16	27.8
CV (%)	0.603	0.578	0.717	0.0914	0.869	0.180	3.15
Diversification							
Mean (sec)	0.472	10.3	22.4	2.00	96.3	1.19	317
StDev (sec)	1.79	6.88	8.27	1.02	9.53	2.15	27.8
CV (%)	379	66.6	36.9	50.9	9.90	181	8.76
Initial Obj val	428	162	253	203	253	48.0	378
Final Obj val							
Mean	17.0	3.09	81.7	2.48	8.34	1.83	156
StDev	6.95	0.190	1.79	0.503	1.99	0.0759	0.303
CV (%)	40.8	6.16	2.20	20.2	23.8	4.16	0.194
Min	13.1	2.82	78.1	1.56	4.48	1.66	156
Max	42.3	3.53	86.1	3.78	12.9	1.97	157

Finding a solution with an objective value of zero on these over-constrained instances is very unlikely, as is the case in most real-world problems. Several of the soft constraints are easily parameterized in such way that violation of some soft constraints cannot be avoided. The results show that there are differences in how difficult it is to compute the initial solution. The number of backtracks (and thus time spent) during initial solution construction varies from almost nothing for OpTur5 and OpTur7, to several hundred thousand for OpTur1 and OpTur4. This is partly connected to the problem size and how constrained the problem is. But also because the diversification step is run many times, and the number of times differ between the cases. (The number depends on how often the variable neighborhood descent will end up in a local optimum or on a "flat" plateau.) If the diversification step is run a large number of times, the time spent on diversification will increase compared to the initial solution construction which is a one-time action. The most important observation to make, however, is that the time used to generate a feasible initial solution is very fast (less than a minute on average for all cases) compared to manual rostering, in which one typically use days to set up a feasible roster. In this sense, the performance of the construction algorithm is more than adequate.

After 1200 seconds, the objective value of the initial solution was drastically improved by the ILS algorithm, in most cases by more than 96 %. This is not surprising, since the initial solution was constructed without considering soft constraints. The exceptions are the cases OpTur7 (378 → 156) and OpTur3 (253 → 81.7), for which the improvements were 58.7 % and 67.7 %, respectively. Both OpTur 3 and OpTur7 contains wanted patterns (SC8) for the weekends.

To assess how the algorithm improves the objective value over time, one can consider the run-time distributions for each test case [chap. 4.2] [16]. Figure 2 shows such distributions for the case OpTur6, each curve representing the observed cumulative fraction of all runs reaching the corresponding objective value threshold as a function of computation time. Note that since we do not know the optimal value, solution quality thresholds are given in terms of percentual deviation from the best found value in any run. Observe that all runs achieved an objective value of 24 % deviation from the best known value, or better, in the first 162 seconds. After 1200 seconds, 10.6 % of the runs had passed the 3 % deviation threshold, while 25.8 % of the runs resulted in an objective value of less than 6 % above the best known objective value.

For some cases there is substantial variation in the objective value across runs, especially for OpTur1 (cv = 40.8 %), OpTur4 (cv = 20.2 %), and OpTur6 (cv = 23.8 %). For OpTur1, this seems to happen because the best found value for each run ends up in one of three objective value ranges; 13.1 – 14.1, 18.2 – 19.8 or above 36.3. This may indicate that there are some distinct valleys or plateaus in the objective function surface of this problem instance. For the two other test cases, however, the observed objective values at the time of run termination are more or less evenly distributed between the minimum and the maximum values.

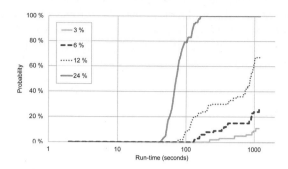

Fig. 2. Qualified Run-Time Distribution of OpTur6 for solution quality levels of 3 %, 6 %, 12 % and 24 % of the best found objective value, across all runs

6   Conclusions and Future Work

The case study presented here concerns a nurse rostering module that was developed for the software company Gatsoft AS and implemented in their personnel management system in 2005. Today, the module is used by several hospitals and other health care institutions in Norway and Sweden. The module applies a hybrid solution approach: An Iterated Local Search framework that uses Constraint Programming for initial solution construction and diversification, and a Variable Neighborhood Descent in the iterative improvement phase. The requirements and specifications for the model and the algorithm evolved from regular meetings and workshops with health care personnel. We believe it includes all the important constraints that are applied in Norwegian hospitals. In this paper, we show that the module can solve large real-world instances within reasonable time.

Further research involves adapting the model to handle a rigorous testing on the standard academic benchmarks. To further improve performance, we aim to develop massively parallel algorithms that exploit the computation power of emerging heterogeneous hardware platforms, where graphical processing units and multiple CPUs can be used together to produce high performance search methods.

It is also important to extend the research context to encompass related and practical extensions of the problem. For example, by introducing flexibility in the model's shifts by allowing their length, start, and end time to be dynamically adjusted: A small changes in start or end times may allow for plans that violate fewer soft constraints without affecting patient quality or increasing personnel costs.

Also, nurse rosters are typically static, while the daily situations at a hospital is very dynamic — employees get sick, take days off on a short notice, or the staff demand temporarily increases. In Norway, the resulting personnel shortages are normally filled through temporary work agencies, which is not only very expensive but quite inefficient. This opens up interesting research directions, such as robust nurse scheduling to minimize the impact due to dynamic events. A related problem is the dynamic re-scheduling of nurses across departments to minimize the impact of unexpected events while maximizing the competence build-up to obtain a more robust future personnel structure.

Acknowledgment. This work is supported by the Research Council of Norway (grant no. 182610/I40) and Gatsoft AS. We wish to thank Morten Smedsrud for assisting us with coding and reading the manuscript.

References

1. Abdennadher, S., Schlenker, H.: Nurse scheduling using constraint logic programming. In: Proceedings of the Sixteenth National Conference on Artificial Intelligence and the Eleventh Innovative Applications of Artificial Intelligence Conference Innovative Applications of Artificial Intelligence, AAAI 1999/IAAI 1999, pp. 838–843. American Association for Artificial Intelligence, Menlo Park (1999)
2. Meyer, H., Meyer auf'm Hofe, H.: Conplan/siedaplan: Personnel assignment as a problem of hierarchical constraint satisfaction. In: Proceedings on the 3rd International Conference on Practical Applications of Constraint Technologies, pp. 257–272. Practical Application Company Ltd. (1997)
3. Beaumont, N.: Scheduling staff using mixed integer programming. European Journal of Operational Research 98(3), 473–484 (1997)
4. Borning, A., Freeman-Benson, B., Wilson, M.: Constraint hierarchies. LISP and Symbolic Computation 5(3), 223–270 (1992), 10.1007/BF01807506
5. Brusco, M.J., Jacobs, L.W.: Cost analysis of alternative formulations for personnel scheduling in continuously operating organizations. European Journal of Operational Research 86(2), 249–261 (1995)
6. Burke, E.K., De Causmaecker, P., Berghe, G.V.: A hybrid tabu search algorithm for the nurse rostering problem. In: McKay, B., Yao, X., Newton, C.S., Kim, J.-H., Furuhashi, T. (eds.) SEAL 1998. LNCS (LNAI), vol. 1585, pp. 187–194. Springer, Heidelberg (1999)
7. Burke, E.K., Curtois, T., Post, G., Qu, R., Veltman, B.: A hybrid heuristic ordering and variable neighbourhood search for the nurse rostering problem. European Journal of Operational Research 188(2), 330–341 (2008)
8. Burke, E.K., De Causmaecker, P., Berghe, G.V., Van Landeghem, H.: The state of the art of nurse rostering. Journal of Scheduling 7(6), 441–499 (2004)
9. Burke, E.K., Li, J., Qu, R.: A hybrid model of integer programming and variable neighbourhood search for highly-constrained nurse rostering problems. European Journal of Operational Research 203(2), 484–493 (2010)
10. Carchrae, T., Beck, J.C.: Cost-based large neighborhood search. In: Workshop on Combination of Metaheuristic and Local Search with Constraint Programming Techniques, pp. 28–29 (2005)
11. Chen, J.-G., Yeung, T.: Hybrid expert system approach to nurse scheduling. Computers in Nursing, 183–192 (1993)
12. Dowsland, K.A.: Nurse scheduling with tabu search and strategic oscillation. European Journal of Operational Research 106(2-3), 393–407 (1998)
13. Hansen, P., Mladenovic, N.: Variable neighborhood search. In: Burke, E.K., Kendall, G. (eds.) Search Methodologies - Introductory Tutorials in Optimization and Decision Support Techniques, pp. 211–238. Springer, Heidelberg (2005)

14. Hattori, H., Ito, T., Ozono, T., Shintani, T.: A nurse scheduling system based on dynamic constraint satisfaction problem. In: Ali, M., Esposito, F. (eds.) IEA/AIE 2005. LNCS (LNAI), vol. 3533, pp. 799–808. Springer, Heidelberg (2005)
15. He, F., Qu, R.: A constraint-directed local search approach to nurse rostering problems. In: Deville, Y., Solnon, C. (eds.) Proceedings 6th International Workshop on Local Search Techniques in Constraint Satisfaction, pp. 69–80 (2009)
16. Hoos, H.H., Stützle, T.: Stochastic Local Search: Foundations & Applications. Morgan Kaufmann Publishers Inc., San Francisco (2004)
17. Karp, R.M.: Reducibility among combinatorial problems. In: Miller, R.E., Thatcher, J.W. (eds.) Complexity of Computer Computations, pp. 85–103. Plenum Press, New York (1972)
18. Kellogg, D.L., Walczak, S.: Nurse Scheduling: From Academia to Implementation or Not? INTERFACES 37(4), 355–369 (2007)
19. Li, H., Lim, A., Rodrigues, B.: A hybrid ai approach for nurse rostering problem. In: Proceedings of the 2003 ACM Symposium on Applied Computing, SAC 2003, pp. 730–735. ACM, New York (2003)
20. Lourenço, H.R., Martin, O.C., Stützle, T.: Iterated Local Search, pp. 321–353. Kluwer Academic Publishers, Dordrecht (2003)
21. Meisels, A., Schaerf, A.: Modelling and solving employee timetabling problems. Annals of Mathematics and Artificial Intelligence 39(1), 41–59 (2003)
22. Heus, K., Chan, G.W.P.: Nurse scheduling with global constraints in chip: Gymnaste. In: Practical Applications of Constraint Technology, PACT (1998)
23. Post, G., Veltman, B.: Harmonious personnel scheduling. In: Burke, E.K., Trick, M.A. (eds.) PATAT 2004. LNCS, vol. 3616, pp. 557–559. Springer, Heidelberg (2005)
24. Schrimpf, G., Schneider, J., Stamm-Wilbrandt, H., Dueck, G.: Record breaking optimization results using the ruin and recreate principle. Journal of Computational Physics 159(2), 139–171 (2000)
25. Stølevik, M., Nordlander, T.E., Riise, A.: SINTEF ICT: Nurse rostering data (2010), http://www.comihc.org/index.php/Test-Beds/sintef-ict-nurse-rostering-data.html (accessed October 13, 2010)
26. Stølevik, M., Nordlander, T.E., Riise, A.: A mathematical model for the nurse rostering problem. SINTEF Technical Report A19133 (2011), http://www.comihc.org/index.php/Models/sintef-ict-nurse-rostering-model.html (accessed April 08, 2011)
27. Tsang, E., Voudouris, C.: Fast local search and guided local search and their application to british telecom's workforce scheduling problem. Operations Research Letters 20(3), 119–127 (1997)
28. Valouxis, C., Housos, E.: Hybrid optimization techniques for the workshift and rest assignment of nursing personnel. Artificial Intelligence in Medicine 20(2), 155–175 (2000); Planning and Scheduling in the Hospital
29. Wong, G.Y.C., Chun, H.W.: Nurse rostering using constraint programming and meta-level reasoning. In: Chung, P.W.H., Hinde, C.J., Ali, M. (eds.) IEA/AIE 2003. LNCS, vol. 2718, pp. 712–721. Springer, Heidelberg (2003)

Constraint Programming for Controller Synthesis

Gérard Verfaillie and Cédric Pralet

ONERA - The French Aerospace Lab,
F-31055, Toulouse, France
{Gerard.Verfaillie,Cedric.Pralet}@onera.fr

Abstract. In this paper, we show how the problem of synthesis of a controller for a dynamic system that must satisfy some safety properties, possibly in a non deterministic and partially observable setting, can be modeled as a pure constraint satisfaction problem, by replacing the reachability property by a so-called weak reachability property. We show, first on a toy illustrative example, then on a real-world example of control of a satellite subsystem, how standard constraint programming tools can be used to model and solve the controller synthesis problem. Finally, we conclude with the strengths and weaknesses of the proposed approach.

1 The Controller Synthesis Problem

1.1 An Informal View

In this paper, we are interested in the closed loop control of dynamic systems (see Fig. 1). More precisely, we are interested in software controllers that are implemented on digital computers (most of the modern controllers) and that do not act continuously on the systems they control, but in a discrete way, by successive steps.

At each step, the controller collects information on the system it controls (observations) and makes reactively a control decision (commands) as a function of the collected information. Observations may come from the system itself, from other systems with which the system interacts, or from human operators. They may contain synthetic information on past observations or commands (controller

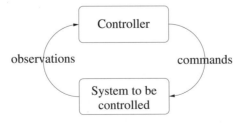

Fig. 1. Closed loop control of a dynamic system

J. Lee (Ed.): CP 2011, LNCS 6876, pp. 100–114, 2011.

memory). In the opposite direction, commands are sent to the system itself, to other systems, or to operators.

We assume that the system evolution that follows a command (system transition) is not deterministic and Markovian: several transitions are possible from the current state and command; the actual transition depends only on the current state and command; it does not depend on previous ones. However, we do not assume the existence of probability distributions on the set of possible transitions: only possible and impossible transitions are distinguished. Moreover, we do not assume that the actual state of the system is known at each step by the controller: only observations are available. We assume that the set of possible system states, the set of possible observations, and the set of possible commands are all discrete and finite.

We are interested in safety properties, that is in properties that must be satisfied by any transition of the controlled system. In such a setting, the controller synthesis problem consists in building off-line, before bringing the system into service, what is called a policy, that is a function which associates with each observation a command and which guarantees that, in spite of non deterministic transitions, every transition satisfies the safety properties.

Sect. 1 introduces the controller synthesis problem. Sect. 2 presents a CSP formulation of this problem, based on the notion of weak reachability. Sect. 3 shows how the proposed approach can be applied to the problem of control of a satellite subsystem. Sect. 4 concludes with the strengths and weaknesses of the proposed approach.

1.2 A Formal Definition

The controller synthesis problem can be formally defined as follows.

Problem data is:

- a finite sequence S of state variables;
- a sub-sequence $O \subseteq S$ of observable state variables;
- a finite sequence C of command variables;
- a set $I \subseteq \mathbf{d}(S)$ of possible initial states, assumed not to be empty;
- a set $T \subseteq \mathbf{d}(S) \times \mathbf{d}(C) \times \mathbf{d}(S)$ of possible transitions;
- a set $P \subseteq \mathbf{d}(S) \times \mathbf{d}(C) \times \mathbf{d}(S)$ of acceptable transitions.

Each state or command variable is assumed to have a finite domain of value[1]. Sets I, T, and P can be implicitly defined by finite sets of constraints[2].

A policy π is a partial function from $\mathbf{d}(O)$ to $\mathbf{d}(C)$. Let $df_\pi \subseteq \mathbf{d}(O)$ be the domain of definition of π.

---

[1] If x is a variable, $\mathbf{d}(x)$ denotes its domain. If X is a sequence of variables, $\mathbf{d}(X)$ denotes the Cartesian product of the domains of the variables in X. If X is a sequence of variables and Y a sub-sequence of X and if A is an assignment of X, $A_{\downarrow Y}$ denotes the assignment of Y (projection).

[2] We use the same notation for a set and its characteristic function: If S is a set and $SS \subseteq S$, for all $e \in S$, $SS(e)$ is true if and only if $e \in SS$.

Given a policy π, the set r_π of the states that are reachable from an initial state by following π can be defined as follows. If $r_{\pi,k}$ is the set of states that are reachable in less than k steps from an initial state, we have:

$$\forall s \in \mathbf{d}(S), r_{\pi,0}(s) = I(s) \tag{1}$$

$$\forall k, 1 \le k \le |\mathbf{d}(S)| - 1, r_{\pi,k}(s) = r_{\pi,k-1}(s) \vee \tag{2}$$
$$(\exists s' \in \mathbf{d}(S), r_{\pi,k-1}(s') \wedge df_\pi(s'_{\downarrow O}) \wedge T(s', \pi(s'_{\downarrow O}), s))$$

$$r_\pi(s) = \max_{0 \le k \le |\mathbf{d}(S)|-1} r_{\pi,k}(s) \tag{3}$$

Eq. 1 expresses that a state is reachable in 0 step if and only if it is a possible initial state. Eq. 2 expresses that a state is reachable in less than k steps if and only if it is reachable in less than $k - 1$ steps or if a transition is possible from a state that is is reachable in less than $k - 1$ steps. Finally, Eq. 3 says that a state is reachable if and only if it is reachable in less than k steps, with $0 \le k \le |\mathbf{d}(S)| - 1$. Indeed, for any state $s \in S$, either it is not reachable, or it is in at most $|\mathbf{d}(S)| - 1$ steps. It must be stressed that, according to this definition, the set of reachable states depends on the chosen policy π.

Requirements on policy are the following:

$$\forall s \in \mathbf{d}(S), r_\pi(s) \rightarrow df_\pi(s_{\downarrow O}) \tag{4}$$

$$r_\pi(s) \rightarrow (\exists s' \in \mathbf{d}(S), T(s, \pi(s_{\downarrow O}), s')) \tag{5}$$

$$r_\pi(s) \rightarrow (\forall s' \in \mathbf{d}(S), T(s, \pi(s_{\downarrow O}), s') \rightarrow P(s, \pi(s_{\downarrow O}), s')) \tag{6}$$

Eq. 4 specifies that the policy shall be defined for all the reachable states. Eq. 5 specifies that the policy shall not lead to dead ends: for each reachable state, by following the policy, there is a possible transition. Finally, Eq. 6 enforces that the policy be "acceptable": for each reachable state, by following the policy, every possible transition is acceptable. It must be stressed that these requirements shall be satisfied, not on all the possible states, but only on those that are reachable from an initial state by following the chosen policy π.

A policy is valid if and only if it satisfies requirements 4, 5, and 6. The objective of controller synthesis is to produce a valid policy or to prove that such a policy does not exist.

1.3   A Toy Example

As an example, let us consider the toy example used in [16]. We consider a robot that is able to move on the grid of Fig. 2 where walls are shown in bold. Initially, the robot is on one of the places of x-coordinate 2. At each step, it is on a place p that it does not know directly. It only observes the walls immediately around p. At each step, it moves north, south, east, or west. It cannot stay where it is. Because of the presence of walls, some moves are not feasible. The robot shall avoid the place marked X ($x = 3, y = 1$) that is considered to be dangerous.

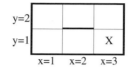

Fig. 2. Robot control problem on a grid

To model this problem, we consider six state variables: $S = \{x, y, w_N, w_S, w_E, w_W\}$. x and y represent the robot position, with $\mathbf{d}(x) = [1..3]$ and $\mathbf{d}(y) = [1..2]$. w_N, w_S, w_E, and w_W are Boolean variables that represent the presence or the absence of a wall at north, south, east, and west of the current place. Only state variables w_N, w_S, w_E, and w_W are observable by the robot: $O = \{w_N, w_S, w_E, w_W\}$. We consider only one command variable m which represents the robot move, with $\mathbf{d}(m) = \{m_N, m_S, m_E, m_W\}$ (four possible moves).

The set I of the possible initial states is defined by the following five unary constraints: $x = 2$, w_N, w_S, $\neg w_E$, and $\neg w_W$.

The set T of the possible transitions is defined by the following constraints:

$$w_N \rightarrow (m \neq m_N),\ w_S \rightarrow (m \neq m_S),\ w_E \rightarrow (m \neq m_E),\ w_W \rightarrow (m \neq m_W)$$

$$x' = x + (m = m_E) - (m = m_W),\ y' = y + (m = m_N) - (m = m_S)$$

$$w'_N - (y' = 2 \vee (y' = 1 \wedge x' = 2)),\ w'_S = (y' = 1 \vee (y' = 2 \wedge x' = 2))$$
$$w'_E = (x' = 3),\ w'_W = (x' = 1)$$

The first four constraints (first line) express the feasible moves, taking into account the possible presence of walls. The following two (second line) express the possible transitions which, in this case, are all deterministic. For each state variable z, z' represents its value at the next step. We assume that a constraint returns value 1 if it is satisfied and value 0 otherwise. The last four constraints (last two lines) result from the available knowledge of the grid topology.

The set P of the acceptable transitions is defined by the binary constraint $\neg((x' = 3) \wedge (y' = 1))$.

1.4 Existing Methods

The method that is by far the most used to build a controller consists in specifying it using any general or specific purpose programming language, for example one of the family of the synchronous languages [9]. Once the controller programmed, its properties can be checked, either experimentally by simulation, or formally by using proof or model-checking tools [4].

Controller synthesis is an alternative approach which aims at building a controller automatically from the properties of the system to be controlled and from the requirements on the controlled system. The resulting controller is valid by construction and no further check is theoretically necessary on it.

The first works on controller synthesis are based on automata and language theory [18]. Then, many works use automata to model the physical system and temporal logics to specify requirements [14] (see for example the ANZU et RATSY tools [11,19], which both assume complete state observability). The MBP tool (Model-Based Planner) uses symbolic model-checking techniques, based on BDDs (Binary Decision Diagrams) to synthesize controllers that guarantee a goal to be reached in spite of non determinism and partial observability [2,13]. Generic search algorithms for the synthesis of finite memory controllers are proposed in [3,16], with the same assumptions of non determinism and partial observability (but with some restrictions in [3]).

The proximity between the controller synthesis problem and (PO)MDP ((Partially Observable) Markov Decision Processes [17]) must be emphasized. Dynamic programming algorithms are the most used to solve (PO)MDP. The first difference between both problems is that, in (PO)MDP, conditional probability distributions on the states resulting from a transition and on the observations resulting from a state are assumed to be available. The second one is that requirements take in (PO)MDP the form of an additive global criterion to be optimized.

The difference between the controller synthesis problem and the planning problem in Artificial Intelligence [8] must be emphasized too. In planning, we are interested in reachability properties: a goal state must be reached and the control is assumed to be stopped once the goal reached. In controller synthesis, we are interested in safety properties which must be satisfied along the whole system trajectory and the control is assumed to never stop.

2   Formulation as a Constraint Satisfaction Problem

2.1   First Formulation

Let us associate with each observation $o \in \mathbf{d}(O)$ a variable $\pi(o)$ of domain $\mathbf{d}(C) \cup \{\bot\}$ which represents the command to be applied when o is observed. Value $\bot$ represents the absence of command. Let us associate with each state $s \in \mathbf{d}(S)$ the following variables:

- a Boolean variable $r_\pi(s)$ which represents the fact that s is reachable or not;
- for each $k, 0 \leq k \leq |\mathbf{d}(S)| - 1$, a Boolean variable $r_{\pi,k}(s)$ which represents the fact that s is reachable or not in less than k steps.

If we replace $df_\pi(o)$ by $\pi(o) \neq \perp$, Eqs. 1 to 6 define a constraint satisfaction problem P (CSP [20]) which models exactly the controller synthesis problem. Unfortunately, the number of variables of P is prohibitive, mainly due to variables $r_{\pi,k}(s)$: for each $s \in \mathbf{d}(S)$, we have $|\mathbf{d}(S)|$ such variables. As a result, the number of variables $r_{\pi,k}(s)$ is equal to $|\mathbf{d}(S)|^2$. To get round this difficulty, we are going to use a relaxation of the reachability property we will refer to as weak reachability.

2.2   Reachability and Weak Reachability

We use the following definition of weak reachability: a relation wr_π is a weak reachability relation associated with a policy π if and only if it satisfies the following two equations:

$$\forall s \in \mathbf{d}(S), \quad I(s) \rightarrow wr_\pi(s) \tag{7}$$

$$\forall s, s' \in \mathbf{d}(S), (wr_\pi(s) \wedge df_\pi(s_{\downarrow O}) \wedge T(s, \pi(s_{\downarrow O}), s')) \rightarrow wr_\pi(s') \tag{8}$$

Eq. 7 expresses that, if a state is a possible initial state, it is weakly reachable. Eq. 7 expresses that, if a state s is weakly reachable and if a transition is possible from state s to another state s', state s' is weakly reachable too. From this definition of weak reachability, the following four properties can be established.

Property 1. *Let π be a policy. The associated reachability relation r_π is unique. On the contrary, several associated weak reachability relations wr_π may exist.*

The reachability relation is unique because it is defined by Eqs. 1 to 3 which are all equality equations. The possible existence of several weak reachability relations is shown in the example of Fig 3 where the reachability graph associated with a policy is displayed. In this graph, nodes represent states and arcs represent possible transitions.

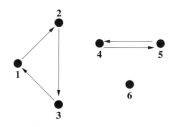

Fig. 3. Example of reachability graph associated with a policy

On this example, if 1 is the only possible initial state, reachability relation r is defined by the set of states $\{1, 2, 3\}$. However, the four relations defined by the set of states $\{1, 2, 3\}$, $\{1, 2, 3, 4, 5\}$, $\{1, 2, 3, 6\}$, and $\{1, 2, 3, 4, 5, 6\}$ all satisfy Eqs. 7 and 8 and thus are all weak reachability relations.

Property 2. *Let π be a policy, r_π be the associated reachability relation, and wr_π be any associated weak reachability relation. r_π is a subset of wr_π.*

To establish this property, let us prove that $\forall s' \in \mathbf{d}(S), r_\pi(s') \rightarrow wr_\pi(s')$.

If $r_\pi(s')$, there exists k, $0 \le k \le |\mathbf{d}(S)| - 1$ such that $r_{\pi,k}(s')$ (according to Eq. 3). Let us prove by recurrence on k that $\forall k \ge 0, \forall s' \in \mathbf{d}(S), r_{\pi,k}(s') \rightarrow wr_\pi(s')$.

For $k = 0$, if $r_{\pi,0}(s')$, we have $I(s')$ (according to Eq. 1) and thus $wr_\pi(s')$ (according to Eq. 7).

For $k > 0$, let us assume that $\forall s' \in \mathbf{d}(S), r_{\pi,k-1}(s') \rightarrow wr_\pi(s')$. If $r_{\pi,k}(s')$, we have (according to Eq. 2), either $r_{\pi,k-1}(s')$ and thus $wr_\pi(s')$ (according to the recurrence assumption), or $\exists s \in \mathbf{d}(S)$, $r_{\pi,k-1}(s) \wedge df_\pi(s_{\downarrow O}) \wedge T(s, \pi(s_{\downarrow O}), s')$ and thus $\exists s \in \mathbf{d}(S)$, $wr_\pi(s) \wedge df_\pi(s_{\downarrow O}) \wedge T(s, \pi(s_{\downarrow O}), s')$ (still according to the recurrence assumption) and finally $wr_\pi(s')$ (according to Eq. 8). From that, we can deduce that $\forall s' \in \mathbf{d}(S), r_{\pi,k}(s') \rightarrow wr_\pi(s')$.

As a consequence, $\forall s' \in \mathbf{d}(S), r_\pi(s') \rightarrow wr_\pi(s')$.

Property 3. *Let π be a policy. The associated reachability relation r_π is an associated weak reachability relation.*

To establish it, it suffices to prove that r_π satisfies Eqs. 7 and 8 which define weak reachability. r_π satisfies them due to the definition of reachability (Eqs. 1 to 3).

Property 4. *Let π be a policy. The associated reachability relation r_π is the unique smallest weak reachability relation associated with π (smallest with regard to inclusion and thus to cardinality).*

This property is the immediate consequence of properties 1, 2, and 3.

2.3   Second Formulation

By using the notion of weak reachability, we propose the following formulation of the controller synthesis problem.

This formulation uses two sets of variables:

- for each observation $o \in \mathbf{d}(O)$, a variable $\pi(o)$ of domain $\mathbf{d}(C) \cup \{\bot\}$ which represents the command to be applied when o is observed;
- for each state $s \in \mathbf{d}(S)$, a Boolean variable $wr_\pi(s)$ which represents the fact that s is weakly reachable or not.

The constraints to be satisfied are defined by the following equations:

$$\forall s \in \mathbf{d}(S), \quad I(s) \rightarrow wr_\pi(s) \tag{9}$$

$$\forall s, s' \in \mathbf{d}(S), (wr_\pi(s) \wedge T(s, \pi(s_{\downarrow O}), s')) \rightarrow wr_\pi(s') \tag{10}$$

$$\forall s \in \mathbf{d}(S), \, wr_\pi(s) \rightarrow (\pi(s_{\downarrow O}) \neq \perp) \tag{11}$$

$$wr_\pi(s) \rightarrow (\exists s' \in \mathbf{d}(S), \, T(s, \pi(s_{\downarrow O}), s')) \tag{12}$$

$$wr_\pi(s) \rightarrow (\forall s' \in \mathbf{d}(S), \, T(s, \pi(s_{\downarrow O}), s') \rightarrow P(s, \pi(s_{\downarrow O}), s')) \tag{13}$$

Eqs. 9 and 10 are copies of Eqs. 7 and 8 which define weak reachability. Eqs. 11 to 13 are copies of Eqs. 4 to 6 which define requirements on policy, where r_π is replaced by wr_π. In Eq. 11, $df_\pi(o)$ is replaced by the equivalent formulation $(\pi(o) \neq \perp)$. Eq. 10 is finally simplified to take into account Eq. 11.

Whereas the previous CSP P (see Sect. 2.1) involved $|\mathbf{d}(O)| + |\mathbf{d}(S)| + |\mathbf{d}(S)|^2$ variables, this CSP P' involves only $|\mathbf{d}(O)| + |\mathbf{d}(S)|$ variables.

We are going to show that, as P does, P' models exactly the controller synthesis problem, that is that solving P' in order to solve the controller synthesis problem is correct, complete, and possibly optimal. Correctness means that, if P' has a solution Sol, the projection of Sol on policy variables π is a solution of the controller synthesis problem. Completeness means that, if the controller synthesis problem has a solution, P' has a solution too. Optimality means that the produced policy is defined only for reachable observations (associated with at least one reachable state).

2.4   Correctness, Completeness, and Optimality

Correctness results from Prop. 2. Let us indeed assume that P' has a solution, made of a policy π and of a relation wr_π. According to Eqs. 9 and 10, relation wr_π is a weak reachability relation. Let r_π be the reachability relation associated with π. According to Prop. 2, we have : $\forall s \in \mathbf{d}(S), r_\pi(s) \rightarrow wr_\pi(s)$. Hence, relation r_π satisfies the requirements associated with Eqs. 11 to 13. As a consequence, π is a solution of the controller synthesis problem.

As for completeness, it results from Prop. 3. Let us indeed assume that the controller synthesis problem has a solution, made of a policy π and of the associated reachability relation r_π. According to Prop. 3, r_π is a weak reachability relation. Hence, π and r_π make up together a solution of P'. P' is thus consistent and a complete constraint solver is able to produce a solution.

It remains that, if P' is consistent, the produced policy π may be defined for unreachable observations (associated with no reachable states). Practically, there is no issue because these observations will never be reached by following π. However if, for the sake of readability or compactness, we prefer a policy π that is defined only for reachable observations, it suffices to replace $wr_\pi(s) \rightarrow (\pi(s_{\downarrow O}) \neq \perp)$ by $wr_\pi(s) \leftrightarrow (\pi(s_{\downarrow O}) \neq \perp)$ in Eq. 11 and to transform the resulting constraint satisfaction problem into a constraint optimization problem where the criterion to be minimized is the number of weakly reachable states ($\sum_{s \in \mathbf{d}(S)} wr_\pi(s)$). If we get an optimal solution with optimality proof, we have, according to Prop. 4, the guarantee that the produced relation wr_π is the reachability relation r_π and that the produced policy π is defined only for reachable observations.

2.5   OPL Model

We used the OPL language [10] to express the constraint satisfaction (optimization) model associated with any given controller synthesis problem. Any other constraint programming language could have been used. These models are optimized in order to limit as much as possible the number of resulting CSP constraints. For the moment, these models are built manually, what is a potential source of errors. The automatic construction of an OPL model from the sets of variables S, O, and C and from the sets of constraints that define relations I, T, and P could be however considered.

On the toy example of Sect. 1.3, this model generates 112 variables and 980 constraints. It is solved by the CP Optimizer tool associated with OPL in less than $1/100$ second. The policy produced is the following one:

$$w_N \wedge w_S \wedge \neg w_E \wedge \neg w_W : m = m_W$$
$$w_N \wedge \neg w_S \wedge \neg w_E \wedge w_W : m = m_S$$
$$\neg w_N \wedge w_S \wedge \neg w_E \wedge w_W : m = m_N$$

Each line is associated with a weakly reachable observation. On each line, the observation appears before the colon and the associated command after. For example, the first line specifies that, if walls are observed at north and south and not at east and west, the robot shall move west. This policy consists in moving west and then in alternating north and south moves. In this case, the policy produced without optimization (no optimization criterion) is luckily "optimal": it is defined for only reachable observations.

3   A Real-World Example

To validate the proposed approach, we made use of it on a real-world problem of control of a satellite subsystem, previously introduced in [15].

The context is an Earth watching satellite whose mission is to detect and to observe hot spots at the Earth surface, due to forest fires or volcanic eruptions [5]. It is equipped with a wide swath detection instrument and with a narrow swath observation one. In case of detection of a hot spot, an alarm must be sent to the ground using a geostationary relay satellite and observations of the ground area must be performed. Observation data is then downloaded towards ground stations during visibility windows. In such a context, we are interested in an equipment referred to as DSP (Digital Signal Processor) in charge of the analysis of the images produced by the detection instrument and of the detection of hot spots in these images. The DSP is made of three elements:

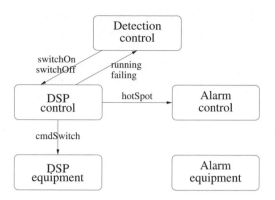

Fig. 4. Inputs and outputs of the module in charge of controlling the DSP

- an analyser in charge of image analysis itself;
- a circuit which supplies the analyser with the necessary current;
- a switch which allows the circuit to be open or not and thus tension to be present or not at the ends of the circuit.

The DSP control module receives ON or OFF requests from the detection control module. At each step, it produces several outputs (see Fig. 4):

- a command to the DSP switch;
- signals towards the detection control module, giving information about the correct or incorrect behavior of the DSP;
- a signal towards the alarm control module, giving information about the detection or not of hot spots.

Each of the three elements that make the DSP may fail. When the analyser does not fail and receives current, hot spot detection is assumed to run correctly. When the analyser fails or does not receive current, hot spot detection does not run. When the circuit fails, the analyser does not receive current. When the switch fails, tension in the circuit may be inconsistent with the switch command.

Informally speaking, the highest level safety properties that must be satisfied at each step are the following: when the DSP is ON and no element fails, detection shall be correct (hot spot detection signal in case of hot spot; no detection signal, otherwise); when the DSP is OFF, it shall detect nothing.

To model this problem, we use the following state variables (set S):

- $switchOn \in \{0,1\}$: presence or not of an ON request: 1 for presence;
- $switchOff \in \{0,1\}$: presence or not of an OFF request: 1 for presence;
- $switched \in \{0,1\}$: last ON or OFF request received by the controller (controller memory): 1 for ON and 0 for OFF;
- $tension \in \{0,1\}$: presence or not of tension at the ends of the circuit: 1 for presence;

- $current \in \{0,1\}$: presence or not of current in the circuit: 1 for presence;
- $faultAnalyser \in \{0,1\}$: analyser failure or not: 1 for failure;
- $faultCircuit \in \{0,1\}$: circuit failure or not: 1 for failure;
- $faultSwitch \in \{0,1\}$: switch failure or not: 1 for failure;
- $inputIm \in \{NOIM, NORM, HOT\}$: type of the analyser input image: $NOIM$ in case of absence of image, $NORM$ in case of an image without hot spot, HOT in case of an image with hot spot; to control the DSP, we are not interested in the precise content of images, for example, the geographical position of hot spots; we are only interested in the presence or not of hot spots;
- $resultAnal \in \{NOIM, NORM, HOT\}$: result of analysis.

Among these variables, only variables $switchOn$, $switchOff$, $switched$, $tension$, $current$, and $resultAnal$ are observable by the controller (set O). Failures, as well as the type of the analyser input image, are not known by the controller.

We use the following command variables (set C):

- $cmdSwitch \in \{0,1\}$: command to the switch: 1 for ON and 0 for OFF;
- $cmdMemory \in \{0,1\}$: updating of the controller memory: 1 for ON and 0 for OFF;
- $running \in \{0,1\}$: information about the correct behaviour of the DSP: 1 for correct;
- $failing \in \{0,1\}$: information about the incorrect behaviour of the DSP: 1 for incorrect;
- $hotSpot \in \{0,1\}$: information about hot spot detection: 1 for detection.

To structure model writing (relations I, T, and P), it may be useful to build the graph that represents dependencies between state and command variables. Fig. 5 shows this graph in a modeling framework that is close to the graphical language associated with the SCADE tool [7]. Boxes labelled with "pre" allow access to the previous value of a state variable to be represented. We can see for example that the current tension depends on the previous one, on the command to the DSP switch, and on the switch state (failure or not).

Possible initial states (relation I) are defined by the following constraints on state variables: $\neg switchOn$, $\neg switchOff$, $\neg switched$, $\neg current$, $\neg tension$, $(resultAnal = NOIM)$, $(inputIm = NOIM)$. Failures are thus possible in the initial state.

Possible transitions (relation T) are defined by the following constraints on state and command variables:

Constraints on higher level modules:

$\neg(switchOn \wedge switchOff)$

Constraints on controller memory:

$switched' = cmdMemory$

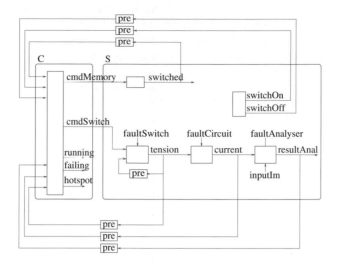

Fig. 5. Dependency graph between state and command variables

Constraints on switch:

$\neg tension \wedge \neg cmdSwitch \rightarrow \neg tension'$

$tension \wedge cmdSwitch \rightarrow tension'$

$\neg faultSwitch \rightarrow (tension' = cmdSwitch)$

Constraints on circuit:

$current = (tension \wedge \neg faultCircuit)$

Constraints on analyser:

$(\neg current \vee faultAnalyser) \rightarrow (resultAnal = NOIM)$

$(current \wedge \neg faultAnalyser) \rightarrow (resultAnal = inputIm)$

Let us recall that, for each state variable x, x' represents its value at the next step. Constraints on higher level modules express that an ON request and an OFF request cannot be emitted simultaneously. Constraints on controller memory express that the controller memory is always correctly updated. Constraints on the switch express that, when the switch does not fail, tension is consistent with the command to the switch. Those on the circuit express that there is current if and only if there is tension and no circuit failure. Finally, those on the analyser express that, when the analyser does not fail, the result of analysis is consistent with the type of the input image.

Acceptable transitions (set P) are defined by the following constraints on state and command variables:

Requirements on controller memory updating:

$switchOn \rightarrow cmdMemory$

$switchOff \rightarrow \neg cmdMemory$

$(\neg switchOn \wedge \neg switchOff) \rightarrow (cmdMemory = switched)$

Requirements on hot spot detection:

$hotSpot = (running \wedge (resultAnal = HOT))$

Requirements on failure detection:

$running = (switched \wedge (resultAnal \neq NOIM))$

$failing = (switched \wedge (resultAnal = NOIM)) \vee$

$\quad (tension \neq switched)) \vee (current \neq tension))$

$\neg(running \wedge failing)$

$switched \rightarrow (running \vee failing)$

Highest level requirements:

$((inputIm = HOT) \wedge running) \rightarrow hotSpot$

$hotSpot \rightarrow (inputIm = HOT)$

$(\neg faultSwitch \wedge \neg faultCircuit' \wedge \neg faultAnalyser' \wedge switched')$

$\quad \rightarrow (resultAnal' = inputIm')$

$(\neg faultSwitch \wedge \neg switched') \rightarrow (resultAnal' = NOIM)$

For example, constraints on hot spot detection enforce that a detection signal is emitted if and only if the DSP runs correctly and a hot spot is detected in the input image. Constraints on failure detection enforce that the DSP controller cannot say simultaneously that the DSP is running correctly and that it is failing and that, when the DSP is ON, the DSP controller must say whether or not the DSP runs correctly. Highest level requirements enforce that, when a hot spot is detected in the input image and the DSP runs correctly, a detection signal is emitted. Conversely, they enforce that, when a detection signal is emitted, a hot spot is present in the input image. Moreover, they enforce that, when no failure occurs and the DSP is ON, the result of analysis is consistent with the type of the input image. On the contrary, they enforce that, when the DSP is OFF and the switch does not fail, there is no analysis result.

The associated OPL model generates 2356 variables and 512175 constraints (information given by the OPL interface). It is solved by CP Optimizer in 3.39 seconds seconds thanks to initial constraint propagation which assigns 2338 variables (results obtained on a Ultra 45 SUN workstation running under Unix and using a 1.6 GHz processor and 1 GB of RAM). As with the toy example of Sect. 1.3, the policy produced without optimization is luckily "optimal": it is defined for only reachable observations.

4 Strengths and Weaknesses of the Proposed Approach

In this paper, we proposed a formulation of the problem of synthesis of a controller for a dynamic system that must satisfy some safety properties as a pure constraint satisfaction (optimization) problem. As far as we know, this the first time that such a formulation has been proposed. The constraint-based approach proposed in [12] is correct, but incomplete: it may fail to find a valid policy, even if such a policy exists. Beyond classical planning and scheduling applications of constraint programming, this opens a large new domain of application of constraint programming techniques to the control of discrete event dynamic systems. It must be moreover stressed that the proposed formulation can be used either to synthesize or to check controllers: checking is simpler than synthesis because the policy is known in case of checking, whereas it is unknown in case of synthesis. It must be also stressed that, using the same approach, ILP (Integer Linear Programming) or SAT (Boolean Satisfiability) modeling frameworks can be used instead of CP, depending on the nature of variables, domains, and constraints.

The proposed approach can be compared with the formulation of the problem of synthesis of an optimal policy for an MDP (Markov Decision Process [17]) as a pure linear programming problem [6]. Indeed, in this formulation, a variable is associated with each state s, representing the optimal gain it is possible to get from s. Bellman optimality equations [1] take the form of linear constraints: one constraint per state-command pair. The criterion to be optimized is the sum of the variables. However, reachability is not taken into account: all states are assumed to be reachable at any step. The approach we proposed can be seen as the "logical" counterpart of this MDP solving approach.

The main advantage of the proposed approach is that it allows us to rely entirely on existing generic constraint programming tools for solving. When constraint programming models will be automatically built from the problem definition (sets of variables S, O, and C, and sets of constraints that define relations I, T, and P), only problem definition shall be changed from a dynamic system to another.

Its main drawback is the huge number of resulting CSP variables and constraints: at least one variable per state and one constraint per pair of states. Because the number of possible states is an exponential function of the number of state variables (not to be mistaken for CSP variables), this approach can be used only on problems that involve a small number of state variables: in the order of ten as in the DSP example of Sect. 3.

The number of CSP variables and constraints has an impact on efficiency: as an example, on the DSP example of Sect. 3, whereas CP Optimizer takes 3.39 seconds to produce a valid policy, the Dyncode tool [16], which implements search algorithms dedicated to controller synthesis, takes only 0.12 second.

As a consequence, other approaches, still based on constraint programming, but less consuming in terms of variables and constraints, should be explored.

Acknowledgments. This work has been performed in the context of the French CNES-ONERA AGATA project (Autonomy Generic Architecture: Tests and Applications; see `http://www.agata.fr`) whose aim is to develop techniques allowing space system autonomy to be improved. We would like to thank Michel Lemaître for his valuable contribution.

References

1. Bellman, R.: Dynamic Programming. Princeton University Press, Princeton (1957)
2. Bertoli, P., Cimatti, A., Roveri, M., Traverso, P.: Planning in Nondeterministic Domains under Partial Observability via Symbolic Model Checking. In: Proc. of IJCAI 2001, pp. 473–478 (2001)
3. Bonet, B., Palacios, H., Geffner, H.: Automatic Derivation of Memoryless Policies and Finite-State Controllers Using Classical Planners. In: Proc. of ICAPS 2009 (2009)
4. Clarke, E., Grumberg, O., Peled, D.: Model Checking. MIT Press, Cambridge (1999)
5. Damiani, S., Verfaillie, G., Charmeau, M.C.: An Earth Watching Satellite Constellation: How to Manage a Team of Watching Agents with Limited Communications. In: Proc. of AAMAS 2005, pp. 455–462 (2005)
6. Dantzig, G.: Linear Programming and Extensions. Princeton University Press, Princeton (1963)
7. Esterel Technologies: SCADE, `http://www.esterel-technologies.com/`
8. Ghallab, M., Nau, D., Traverso, P.: Automated Planning: Theory and Practice. Morgan Kaufmann, San Francisco (2004)
9. Halbwachs, N.: Synchronous Programming of Reactive Systems. Kluwer, Dordrecht (1993)
10. IBM ILOG: Cplex optimization studio,
    `http://www-01.ibm.com/software/integration/optimization/`
    `cplex-optimization-studio/`
11. Jobstmann, B., Galler, S., Weiglhofer, M., Bloem, R.: Anzu: A Tool for Property Synthesis. In: Damm, W., Hermanns, H. (eds.) CAV 2007. LNCS, vol. 4590, pp. 258–262. Springer, Heidelberg (2007)
12. Lemaître, M., Verfaillie, G., Pralet, C., Infantes, G.: Synthèse de contrôleur simplement valide dans le cadre de la programmation par contraintes. In: Actes de JFPDA 2010 (2010)
13. MBP Team: Model Based Planner, `http://sra.itc.it/tools/mbp/`
14. Pnueli, A., Rosner, R.: On the Synthesis of a Reactive Module. In: Proc. of POPL 1989, pp. 179–190 (1989)
15. Pralet, C., Lemaître, M., Verfaillie, G., Infantes, G.: Synthesizing Controllers for Autonomous Systems: A Constraint-based Approach. In: Proc. of iSAIRAS 2010 (2010)
16. Pralet, C., Verfaillie, G., Lemaître, M., Infantes, G.: Constraint-based Controller Synthesis in Non-deterministic and Partially Observable Domains. In: Proc. of ECAI 2010, pp. 681–686 (2010)
17. Puterman, M.: Markov Decision Processes, Discrete Stochastic Dynamic Programming. John Wiley & Sons, Chichester (1994)
18. Ramadge, P., Wonham, W.: The Control of Discrete Event Systems. Proc. of the IEEE 77(1), 81–98 (1989)
19. RATSY Team: RATSY: Requirements Analysis Tool with Synthesis, `http://rat.fbk.eu/ratsy/`
20. Rossi, F., Beek, P.V., Walsh, T. (eds.): Handbook of Constraint Programming. Elsevier, Amsterdam (2006)

Neuron Constraints to Model Complex Real-World Problems

Andrea Bartolini, Michele Lombardi, Michela Milano, and Luca Benini

DEIS, University of Bologna
{a.bartolini,michele.lombardi2,michela.milano,luca.benini}@unibo.it

Abstract. The benefits of combinatorial optimization techniques for the solution of real-world industrial problems are an acknowledged evidence; yet, the application of those approaches to many practical domains still encounters active resistance by practitioners, in large part due to the difficulty to come up with accurate declarative representations. We propose a simple and effective technique to bring hard-to-describe systems within the reach of Constraint Optimization methods; the goal is achieved by embedding into a combinatorial model a soft-computing paradigm, namely Neural Networks, properly trained before their insertion. The approach is flexible and easy to implement on top of available Constraint Solvers. To provide evidence for the viability of the proposed method, we tackle a thermal aware task allocation problem for a multi-core computing platform.

Keywords: Constraint Programming, Neural Network, Thermal aware allocation and scheduling.

1 Introduction

The benefits of combinatorial optimization for the solution of real-world industrial problems are a widely acknowledged evidence, sitting of an ever-growing collection of success stories [11,12,20]. Yet, the application of optimization approaches to many practical domains still encounters active resistance by practitioners. A considerable part of the issue stems from difficulties in devising an accurate representation for the target domain. As matter of fact, many optimization approaches assume the availability of a declarative description of the system, usually obtained by introducing some degree of approximation; the resulting accuracy is critical for the optimization effectiveness: an over-simplified model may threat the successful application of the most advanced combinatorial method. Coming up with an accurate model may be very challenging whenever there are elements admitting no obvious numerical description, or the system behavior results from the interaction of a very large number of actors.

In this work, we propose a simple and effective technique to bring hard-to-describe systems within the reach of optimization methods; the goal is achieved by embedding a properly trained Neural Network into a combinatorial model. The Neural Network basically learns how to link decision variables either with a corresponding metric or with observable variables or with other decision variables.

J. Lee (Ed.): CP 2011, LNCS 6876, pp. 115–129, 2011.

Such a hybridization with a soft-computing paradigm allows the model to accurately represent complex interactions and to handle difficult-to-measure metrics.

As a host technology, Constraint Programming (CP) represents an ideal candidate, thanks to the ability to deal with non-linear functions and the modularity of constraint based models. Specifically, we introduce a novel class of global Neuron Constraints to capture the behavior of a single Neural Network node. The ability to incorporate soft-computing system representations marks a distinguishing advantage of CP over competitor techniques (namely those based on linear models), increasing its appeal for the solution of industrial problems.

To showcase the proposed approach, we consider a temperature aware workload allocation problem over a Multi-Processor Systems on Chip (MPSoC) with Dynamic Voltage and Frequency Scaling (DVFS) capabilities. DVFS allows the programmer to slow the pace of one or more processors, to let the system cool down and become ready to accept more demanding tasks later on. The thermal behavior of a MPSoC device is the result of the interaction of many concurrent factors (including heat conduction, processor workload, chip layout). Despite the dynamic of the single phenomena is known, the complexity of the overall system makes it very hard to devise a declarative thermal model. In such a context, a Neural Network can be designed and trained to approximate the system thermal behavior. The resulting network can then be embedded in a combinatorial model and used to produce an optimized workload allocation, avoiding resource overheating as well as over-usage. We tested the approach obtaining consistently better result compared to a load balancing strategy guided by a temperature aware heuristic; moreover, we even improve the results of a very well-performing surrogate temperature measure.

2   Neural Networks: Background and Definitions

An artificial Neural Network (NN) is a computational system emulating the operation of a *biological* neural network; NNs are capable to perform non-linear computations and can be deployed to perform different tasks by proper *training*. NNs are parallel systems, consisting of o set of many interconnected computing elements; the basic computation block is called *artificial neuron* and mimics the behavior of a neural cell, processing multiple electrical input from neighboring cells to produce a single electrical output. The first simplified neuron models date back to the 40' [13]: basically, an artificial neuron is a non-linear function with vector input $\overline{x}$ and scalar output y; in detail:

$$y = \phi \left(b + \sum_i w_i x_i \right) \tag{1}$$

where x_i denotes a single component in $\overline{x}$, the argument of ϕ is known as neuron *activity*, b is a *bias* and ϕ is called *activation function*; ϕ is a monotonic nondecreasing function, so that inhibitory/excitatory connections between biological neurons can be respectively modeled as negative/positive weights w_i. Artificial neurons differ by the type of activation function and can be broadly classified into *threshold, linear/piecewise-linear* and *sigmoid* neurons; for example:

$$\phi(a) = \begin{cases} 1 \text{ if } a \geq 0 \\ 0 \text{ if } a < 0 \end{cases} \quad (2) \qquad \phi(a) = a \quad (3) \qquad \phi(a) = \frac{2}{1+e^{-2a}} - 1 \quad (4)$$

the function in Equation (2) corresponds to a threshold neuron (the classical *perceptron* from [19]), Equation (3) corresponds to a linear neuron and Equation (4) is a sigmoid neuron (hyperbolic tangent). In many cases ϕ acts as a squashing function, restricting the output to be in the interval $[0,1]$ or $[-1,1]$.

A Neural Network is a system with vector input/output (say $\overline{x}, \overline{y}$) and composed of one or more artificial neurons; each neuron receives input from neighbors (or from the outside the network, i.e. $\overline{x}$) and computes an output signal which is propagated to other neurons; designated neurons provide the network output $\overline{y}$. A NN can be represented as a directed graph and is said *feed-forward* in case the graph is cycle-free, *recurrent* if at least a loop is present. Feed-forward networks are usually organized into *layers*; in this case neurons/nodes in level 0 accept the input $\overline{x}$, neurons in the last layer provide the output $\overline{y}$, while each neuron in the remaining layers (*hidden*) is connected to all nodes in the previous and in the next layer; there is no connection between nodes in the same layer.

Weights of a NN are usually decided in a learning stage to match input/output pairs in a *training set*; this can be done (e.g.) by means of the back-propagation process [6,17]. Depending on the neuron types and the training set, the network acts as a classifier or performs regression analysis; the network ability to treat previously unseen input patters (i.e. generalization) depends to a large extent on the chosen training set. Single layer networks can only match linearly separable training sets [14]; conversely, multi-layer networks have no such limitation and can model any $\mathbb{R}^n \to \mathbb{R}^m$ function with finitely many discontinuities [8], provided the hidden layers have a non-linear activation function and the network is sufficiently large.

3   Neuron Constraints

The main appeal of Neural Networks stems from their ability to learn the approximate behavior of opaque or very complex systems, without requiring detailed knowledge of their components and interactions. User intervention is required in the preparation of the training set, but not in the actual definition of weights. Once the training stage is over, the network *is intrinsically declarative* and can therefore be embedded into a classical combinatorial model. In detail, we proceed by introducing a novel and simple class of (global) *Neuron Constraints*, modeling a single artificial neuron with a specific activation function. Real valued variables are associated to the output and to each component of the input vector; hence a Neuron Constraint has the following signature:

$$\text{actfunction}(\text{Y}, \overline{\text{X}}, \overline{w}, b)$$

where 'actfunction' denotes the activation function type — i.e. function ϕ in Equation (1) —, Y is the output variable, $\overline{\text{X}}$ is the vector of input variables, $\overline{w}$ is the vector of weights and b is the bias. The integration of a trained NN into a CP model is as straightforward as introducing a Neuron Constraint for each node, connecting input/outputs variables and setting arc weights. Using a global constraint for each single neuron rather than for a whole network provides a fine grained modeling approach, allowing complex networks (even recurrent ones) to be defined with a limited number of basic components, i.e. a constraint for each type of activation function. In particular, we have implemented the activation functions from Equations (2),(3) and (4), corresponding to the Neuron Constraints 'hardlim', 'purelin' and 'tansig'[1].

3.1   Filtering for Neuron Constraints

Filtering in a Neuron Constraint can be done by separately tackling the activity expression and the activation function; namely, Equation (1) can be decomposed so that we have:

$$A = b + \sum_i X_i w_i \qquad (5) \qquad\qquad Y = \phi(A) \qquad (6)$$

where A is an artificially introduced *activity variable*. Equation (5) is linear and poses no issue; function ϕ is monotonic non-decreasing, so that bound consistency can be enforced by means of the following rules:

$$\max(A) \text{ updated } \Rightarrow \qquad \max(Y) \leftarrow \max\{y' \mid \phi(\max(A)) = y'\} \qquad (7)$$
$$\max(Y) \text{ updated } \Rightarrow \qquad \max(A) \leftarrow \max\{a' \mid \max(Y) = \phi(a')\} \qquad (8)$$

Rules for "min" are analogous. Observe that, from a mathematical standpoint, the set $\{y' \mid \phi(\max(A)) = y'\}$ is a singleton and only contains the value $\phi(\max(A))$, similarly the set $\{a' \mid \max(Y) = \phi(a')\}$ is in fact $\{\phi^{-1}(\max(Y))\}$ and so on. The distinction becomes however relevant when finite computing precision is taken into account. As an example, the filtering rules for the upper bound with *tansig* function are:

$$\max(A) \text{ upd. } \Rightarrow \qquad \max(Y) \leftarrow tansig(\max(A))$$

$$\max(Y) \text{ upd. } \Rightarrow \qquad \max(A) \leftarrow \begin{cases} tansig^{-1}(\max(Y)) & \text{if } \max(Y) \in]-1,1[\quad (A) \\ \max\{a' \mid tansig(a) = 1\} & \text{if } \max(Y) = 1 \quad (B) \\ \max\{a' \mid tansig(a) = -1\} & \text{if } \max(Y) = -1 \quad (C) \end{cases}$$

where $tansig(a)$ is as from Equation (4) and $tansig^{-1}(y) = 0.5 \times \ln((1-y)/(1+y))$. The expressions from case (B) and (C) are implementation dependent *constants*. The rules for lower bound filtering are analogous. As an important consequence of precision issues, an A variable may be unbound even if the corresponding Y variable is bound; forcing A to be bound would result in an incorrect behavior; hence the uncertainty due to precision errors should be eventually carried on in the problem solution. As one can see, aside from precision issues the filtering rules are simple, making the implementation of the approach fairly easy on off-the-shelf available solvers.

---

[1] The naming convention comes from the MATLAB Neural Network Toolbox.

4   A Use Case: Thermal Aware Workload Allocation

Providing evidence of the method effectiveness requires a problem with non-trivial modeling issues; specifically, in this paper we tackle a thermal-aware workload allocation problem on Multi Core Systems on Chip (MPSoC); due to the inherent complexity, the description of the problem and the solution approach takes an extensive portion of the paper.

4.1   Context and Motivation

Temperature management in MPSoCs is receiving growing research interest in recent years, pushed by the awareness that the development of modern multi-core platforms is about to hit a thermal wall. A larger number of cores packed on a single silicon die lead to an impressing heat generation rate; this is the source of a number of issues [5] such as (1) the cost of the cooling system; (2) reduced reliability and lifetime; (3) reduced performance.

Classical approaches include changing the operating frequency, task migration or core shutdown, triggered when a specified threshold temperature is reached. This reactive method avoids chip overheating, but may have a relevant impact on the performance. Hence several works have investigated thermal-aware workload allocation, making use of mechanisms as DVFS to prevent the activation of more drastic cooling measures. Those approaches include: (1) on-line optimization policies [4,5,2,22], based on predictive models and taking advantage of run-time temperatures read from hardware sensors; (2) off-line allocation and scheduling approaches [18,15], usually embedding a simplified thermal model of the target platform [16]; (3) off-line iterative methods [1,21], performing chip temperature assessment via a simulator (e.g. the HotSpot system [10]).

Capturing the thermal behavior of an MPSoC platform is a tricky task; the temperature depends on the workload, the position of the heat sinks, thermal interactions between neighboring cores. This is why off-line approaches rely on simplified models and often disregard either non-homogeneities due to the floorplan or heat transfer between neighboring cores. Iterative approaches overcome the issue by performing thermal simulation after each iteration, but this prevents information on the temperature behavior to be directly used in the optimization procedure. Despite the dynamic of the single elements concurring to system temperature is known, the complexity of the overall system makes it very hard to devise a declarative model: in such a context, however, a Neural Network can still be designed and trained to approximate the system thermal behavior.

4.2   The Target Problem

Specifically, we address a workload allocation problem on a multi-core system consisting of a set P of Processing Elements p_j (PE); the operating frequency of each element can be dynamically changed between a minimum and maximum value (say f_{min}, f_{max}) with a fixed step[2]; the workload is specified as a set T of independent[3] tasks t_i. As a target system we designed a framework (implemented in MATLAB) for accurate emulation of the temperature evolution of a multicore platform when executing a sequence of tasks. The optimization problem consists in the assignment of a PE and an operating frequency to each task, so that the full workload is executed within a specified deadline and the final peak temperature is minimized. Higher operating frequencies result in lower durations, but also higher power consumption and heat generation; PEs are non-homogeneous from a thermal point of view; custom starting temperatures (say $Tstart_j$) can be specified for each PE to take into account the case of an already running system.

4.3 Simulation Framework

The simulation framework has been developed to simulate system evolution, with specific regard for the thermal transient;, but we also take into account the dependency of execution time and power consumption on the frequency and the task properties [3].

Task Duration: We assume task execution time to be frequency dependent, with cpu-bounded tasks being more sensitive to frequency changes than memory-bounded tasks; the Clock per Instruction (CPI) metric is a simple and widely adopted [2] way to estimate the degree of memory boundedness of a task. For an in-order CPU[4], the execution time D_i of t_i can be expressed as follow:

$$D_i = \frac{1}{f_{max}} \cdot NI_i \cdot \left(\frac{f_{max}}{f_i} + CPI_i - 1 \right)$$

where NI_i is the total number of instruction composing the task; f_i is the PE frequency during the execution of t_i and CPI_i is the average task CPI when running at maximum frequency. According to this model, each task is therefore characterized by an NI_i, CPI_i pair. The use of cycle accurate simulation would provide a more detailed duration model, but the corresponding computational burden is prohibitive with the time resolution needed to identify thermal transients. We assume a constant operating frequency for each task, even if in principle it is possible to switch the frequency during execution, since the overhead induced by recording this information at run-time would be too high.

Power Consumption: We use a model to estimate the power consumption of a Processing Element, accounting for the dependency on the frequency and the CPI of the task currently in execution; this is in line with several approaches, showing how to extract a power model directly from an MPSoC by combining

---

[2] This is in line with the real HW DVFS capabilities of today and future MPSoC [9] that allow frequency to change by steps of hundreds of MHz.

[3] Independent tasks are common in many scenarios, such as real time OS, web servers, high performance computing...

[4] Recent trends in many-core often witness the use of a simple, in-order cores as basic blocks for the parallel architecture [9].

power and performance measurements with data regression techniques [7]. In detail, our power model has been empirically extracted from measurements performed on an Intel® server system S7000FC4UR based on the quad-core Xeon® X7350 processor, with a maximal frequency of 2.93GHz (see [3]). The resulting model for a task t_i is reported in the following equation, together with the value of each constant; the static power consumption $Wstat$ is 3 Watt:

$$Wdyn = k_A \cdot f_{PE}{}^{k_B} + k_C + (k_D + k_E \cdot f_{PE}) \cdot CPI_i{}^{k_F} + Wstat \qquad (9)$$

with:

$$k_A = 3.87 \cdot 10^{-8} \qquad k_B = 2.41 \qquad k_C = 1.10$$
$$k_D = -4.14 \qquad k_E = 5.1 \cdot 10^{-3} \qquad k_f = -3.02 \cdot 10^{-1}$$

Thermal Behavior: We use a state-of-the-art thermal simulator to emulate the system temperature evolution in time and space under different power stimuli [16,10]. State-of-the-art simulators start from a representation of the platform and allocate the input PE power, dissipated in each thermal simulation time interval over the floorplan. Then the entire surface of the die is spatially discretized in a two dimensional grid. Each spatial block models a heat source and is characterized by an intrinsic temperature. This models the bottom surface and the injection of heat in the target multicore package. In addition, the package volume is partitioned in cells. Each cell is modeled with the equivalent thermal capacitance and resistance and connected with the adjacent ones. At each simulation step the R, C thermal-equivalent differential problem is solved providing the new temperature value for each cell as output. We embed in our set-up the HotSpot simulator [10], since it is a de-facto standard in MPSoC thermal simulation. Each time a new task is scheduled the power consumption of each core is estimated by using the power model and fed to the simulator.

5   Workload Allocation as an Optimization Problem

5.1   Modeling the Thermal Behavior via a Neural Network

The use of a thermal simulator to model temperature dynamics allows our framework to accurately emulate the behavior of a real-world MPSoC system; as a main drawback, the resulting thermal model is not declarative and cannot be directly handled via CP. Hence, *devising a declarative thermal model is a necessary step if Constraint Optimization is to be applied* and Neuron Constraints provide us an effective tool to deal with the issue.

In detailed we are interested in predicting the temperature after the system has been running some workload for a specific time span Δ; this depends non-linearly on the the initial temperature $Tstart_j$ and the power consumption P_j of every PE in the platform, plus the environment temperature $Tenv$:

$$T_j = f(\overline{Tstart}, \overline{P}, Tenv, \Delta)$$

where $\overline{Tstart}$ is the vector of initial temperatures and $\overline{P}$ is the vector with the average power consumption of each core. The network used to learn such a non-linear relationship must ideally be as simple as possible to reduce the computational burden of the optimization problem. We evaluated different topologies and input configurations: the best trade-off between NN complexity and accuracy is obtained by using a feed-forward two-layer neural network for each PE, with 'tansig' neurons in the hidden layer and a single 'purelin' one in the output layer. In detail, the network for PE p_j models the function:

$$\|T_j\| = g(\|\overline{Tstart}\|, \|\overline{P}\|, \|\overline{P} \cdot \Delta\|, \|\Delta\|)$$

all network inputs are normalized (see the $\|\cdot\|$ notation) and $\overline{P} \cdot \Delta$ represents the average consumed energy (i.e. the product between the consumption vector and the interval duration). Overall, each network has 13 inputs for a 4 core platform; the hidden layer size is 3/4 of the input number, i.e. 10 neurons in this case. The network output is the (normalized) predicted temperature for PE p_j.

The training and test set consist each of N randomly generated tuples, containing values for the inputs $\overline{Tstart}, \overline{P}, \Delta, T_{env}$. We then use HotSpot to simulate the final temperatures T_j corresponding to each tuple. Network training is performed via back-propagation, adjusting weights and bias according to Levenberg-Marquardt. Figure 1 shows the prediction error for a training and test set of $N = 5000$ random elements. One can observe from the plot that the selected Neural Network provides an estimation error below 0.1^oC for more than the 90% of the validation patterns; moreover, the error prediction is always within $\pm 1^oC$.

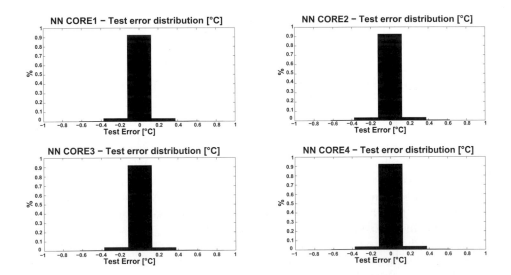

Fig. 1. Neural Network Test Error histogram

5.2   Combinatorial Model and Solution Process

Now, the workload allocation over a single time interval can modeled as a Constraint Optimization Problem, featuring two decision variable arrays P and F (respectively representing the chosen frequency and processing element for each task). In detail, let D_{max} be the global deadline value, W_{max} the maximum power consumption, let $Tenv$ be the environmental temperature and T_{max} the maximum allowed temperature; let $Tstart_j$ denote the initial temperature of p_j and T_j be the final one; then the problem can be formulated as:

$$\min_{p_j \in P} \quad \max \; \mathtt{T_j}$$

$$\text{s.t.:} \quad \mathtt{D_i} = \frac{1}{f_{max}} NI_i \left(\frac{f_{max}}{\mathtt{F_i}} + CPI_i - 1 \right) \qquad \forall t_i \in T \qquad (10)$$

$$\sum_{t_i \in T} \mathtt{D_i} \cdot (\mathtt{P_i} = j) \leq D_{max} \qquad \forall p_j \in P \qquad (11)$$

$$\mathtt{WT_i} = (k_A \cdot \mathtt{F_i}^{k_B} + k_C) + (k_D + k_E \cdot \mathtt{F_i}) \cdot cpi_i^{k_F} + Wstat \qquad \forall t_i \in T \qquad (12)$$

$$\mathtt{W_j} = \frac{1}{D_{max}} \sum_{t_i \in T} \mathtt{D_i} \cdot \mathtt{WT_i} \cdot (\mathtt{P_i} = j) \qquad \forall p_j \in P \qquad (13)$$

for the Neural Network:

$$\mathtt{NW_j} = \mathtt{W_j}/W_{max}, \mathtt{ND_j} = D_{max}, \mathtt{NWD_j} = \mathtt{NW_j} \qquad \forall p_j \in P \qquad (14)$$

$$\mathtt{NTI_j} = (Tstart_j - Tenv)/(T_{max} - Tenv) \qquad \forall p_j \in P \qquad (15)$$

$$\mathtt{NTO_j} = (\mathtt{T_j} - Tenv)/(T_{max} - Tenv) \qquad \forall p_j \in P \qquad (16)$$

Neuron Csts between $\mathtt{NW_j}, \mathtt{ND_j}, \mathtt{NWD_j}, \mathtt{NTI_j}$ and $\mathtt{NTO_j}$ $\qquad (17)$

with:

$$\mathtt{P_i} \in \{0, |P| - 1\} \qquad \forall t_i \in T$$

$$\mathtt{F_i} \in \{f_{min}..f_{max}, \text{ multiple of 100 MHz}\} \qquad \forall t_i \in T$$

$$\mathtt{D_i} \in [0, D_{max}], \mathtt{T_i} \in [T_{env}, T_{max}], \mathtt{WT_i} \in [0, W_{max}] \qquad \forall t_i \subset T$$

$$\mathtt{W_j} \in [0, D_{max}], \mathtt{NW_j}, \mathtt{ND_j}, \mathtt{NWD_j}, \mathtt{NTI_j}, \mathtt{NTO_j} \in [0, 1] \qquad \forall p_j \in P$$

Basically, real variables $\mathtt{D_i}$ model task durations; $\mathtt{WT_i}$ and $\mathtt{W_j}$ respectively represent the power consumption for each task and the average power consumption for each processor as from Section 4.3; $\mathtt{NW_j}$, $\mathtt{ND_j}$, $\mathtt{NWD_j}$, $\mathtt{NTI_j}$ are the normalized inputs to the neural network and correspond to power consumption, duration, energy and input temperature; $\mathtt{NTO_j}$ are the normalized network outputs and $\mathtt{T_j}$ are the final temperature variables. Constraints (10) and (12) respectively correspond to the duration and power model in the simulation framework; Constraints (11) and Constraints (13) are the deadline restrictions and average power computation. Constraints (14) to (16) are normalization formulas. Finally, the model contains Neuron Constraints matching the structure of the network from Section 5.1.

Observe all variable except for the decision ones (i.e. P_i and F_i) are real valued. Our current implementation is based on Comet 2.1.1, which lacks real variables support in the CP module; therefore, we use integer variables with a fixed precision factor and all constraints are formulated so as to avoid rounding errors. As a consequence, there may be (bounded) imprecision on the final temperature values forecast by the networks: in this case we assume a conservative approach and pick the worst possible value given the rounding error bound.

5.3 Solution Process

The constraint model has been implemented in Comet 2.1.1 using the CP (rather than the local search) module and solved by alternating restarts and Large Neighborhood Search (LNS). In both cases, the base approach is tree search, with a relatively simple two-stage strategy; in detail:

– *Stage 1, PE allocation:* search is performed on the P_i variables, by opening binary choice points:
  • the branching variable is selected uniformly at random among those of the 15% tasks with the smallest number of instructions NI_i;
  • the value to be assigned on the left-branch is the index of the PE p_j with smallest lower bound for the expression: $\sum_{t_i \in T} D_i \cdot (P_i = j)$ (see Constraints (11) in the model); on the right branch $P_i \neq j$ is posted.
– *Stage 2, frequency assignment:* once all P_i variables are bound, search is performed on the F_i variables by domain splitting:
  • the branching variable is chosen with the same criterion as in Stage 1;
  • let F_i be the selected variable and f^* be the middle value in its current domain; search is performed by opening a binary choice point and respectively posting $F_i \leq f^*$ and $F_i > f^*$ on the left/right branch.

The main underlying idea is to assign a PE and a frequency to tasks with low NI_i value early in search. The solution initially performs tree search with restarts; each attempt is capped at 800 fails and the limit grows by 7.5% if no solution is found. Whenever a solution is reached the LNS loop begins; at each LNS iteration the incumbent solution is partially relaxed; in detail, tasks are ranked by decreasing value of the expression $NI_i \cdot r$ (with r a random number in $[0, 1]$), the first 60% tasks in the ranking are selected and the corresponding P_i, F_i variables de-assigned. The the problem is re-optimized with the described tree search method. Each LNS iteration is capped at 800 fails and the value is increased by 7.5% in case the limit is reached (same as for restarts). Every 3 iterations with no solution improvement, the process switches back to restarts and so on.

6 Experimental Results

In principle, the embedded neural network should provide the solver with a powerful model of the system behavior, taking into account the diversity of the thermal dynamics of each core and the effect of non-homogeneous starting temperatures; on the other side, the network complexity may lead to poor propagation and slow down the solution process. To assess the effectiveness of the proposed approach, we performed an experimental evaluation: our method was compared to two different variants, making use of simpler (arguably less accurate) thermal cost functions.

Considered Problem Variants: Due to the tight connection between temperature and power consumption, in the first considered variant we replaced the temperature minimization from Section 5.2 with a *power balancing* objective; namely, we minimize:

$$\max_{p_j \in P} W_j \tag{18}$$

in the following, we refer to the original approach as NN and as PP to this first variant. The resulting combinatorial model is much simpler, as it contains no neural network; moreover, this surrogate thermal objective performs usually very well, due to the strong dependency of temperature on power consumption. However, this approach does not account for non-homogeneous thermal behaviors (e.g. due to the core location) and still requires an accurate power model with a well defined structure, which may not be available in many practical situations. In this case, a Neural Network can still be trained to approximate the thermal behavior, while Equation (18) can no longer be used. Therefore, we considered a second problem variant with a *load balancing* objective; namely, we maximize the smallest cumulative duration among the processors:

$$\min_{p_j \in P} \sum_{t_i \in T} D_i \cdot (P_i = j) \tag{19}$$

we refer to this second variant as HH. In this case, the search strategy is modified to incorporate some knowledge of the thermal behavior; in particular, the left and right branches in the frequency assignment stage are *inverted* depending on the task CPI. In detail, the solver prefers high frequency values if $CPI_i \leq 10$, while low frequencies are given priority if $CPI_i > 10$. The reason is that the duration of a low CPI task has a strong dependence on the operating frequency, allowing the heat contribution from static power consumption to be minimized by reducing the execution time; conversely, high CPI tasks have less elastic behavior and are best tackled by reducing the dynamic power consumption with a low frequency assignment. This modification proved very effective for the HH method behavior.

Input Workload and Target System: we synthesized 40 random workload instances, counting around 50 tasks each. Task durations (in seconds) and CPI were generated according to a mixed Gaussian distribution, representative of a mostly computation intensive workload, with a minor portion of memory-bounded tasks. The NI_i values were synthesized so as to keep the system 80% busy at maximal frequency. We considered two quad core platform, with a 1x4 (linear) and 2x2 (square) floorplan; frequencies range between 1600 and 2900 MHz and the global deadline D_{max} is 10 seconds. The choices are representative of a server system, regularly accepting a typical workload to be dispatched before the next arrival.

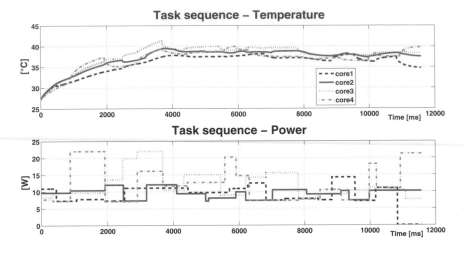

Fig. 2. Temperature and power dynamics on a single experiment

We computed optimized workload allocation and frequency assignments for both the target platforms, by running each approach for 90 seconds on an Intel Core 2 T7200, 2GHz; the resulting solutions were *executed on the simulation framework*, with all cores starting from a room temperature of 26.5°C. Since all considered variants make use of approximated thermal model, there is no theoretical guarantee for the dominance of one approach over another: the use of simulation to evaluate the results ensures a fair comparison and a reliable effectiveness assessment. Moreover, since the optimized solution are evaluated via simulation, the results are unaffected by any numerical issue in the models.

The typical thermal behavior exhibited by the NN approach solutions is depicted in Figure 2, showing both temperature and power dynamics for a single experiment; each line in the graphs corresponds to a PE: as one can see, after an initial transient behavior the temperature becomes pretty stable, thanks to the thermal aware allocation.

Next, we compared the final (simulated) peak temperature obtained by each of the considered approaches; the results are shown in Figure 3, depicting for the 40 instances the distribution (histogram) of the difference $T_{HH} - T_{NN}$ (in dark grey) and $T_{PP} - T_{NN}$ (in light grey). For the considered configuration, discrepancies of around 1-2°C were found to be already significant; as one can see, the network based approach is consistently better than the HH one and even improves (on average) the PP approach, which is known to use a very good temperature proxy measure.

In order to investigate the effect of non-homogeneity, we performed a second evaluation after having asymmetrically pre-heated the target platforms; in this case the starting temperature for each core are 31.05°C, 33.55°C, 35.75°C, 36.48°C. The resulting differences in the final peak temperature are shown in Figure 4; as one can see the advantage of the NN approach becomes more relevant, due to the inability of the surrogate objective functions to capture the initial asymmetry.

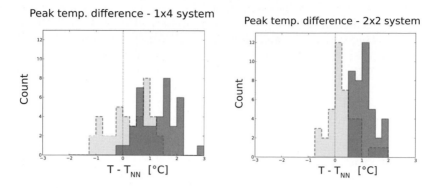

Fig. 3. Difference from NN in final peak temperature for the HH (dark grey) and the PP (light grey) approach

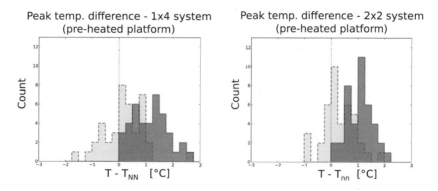

Fig. 4. Difference from NN in final peak temperature for the HH (dark grey) and the PP (light grey) approach – pre-heated platform

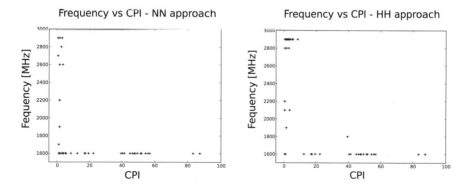

Fig. 5. (Frequency, CPI) values for each task in sample solution, for the NN and the HH approach

Finally, Figure 5 is a scatter plot representing, for a sample workload instance, the assigned operating frequency and the CPI of each task in the NN and the HH solution; as one can see, the two plot are very similar, with low CPI tasks receiving high operating frequencies and high CPI ones usually running at 1600 MHz: as discussed earlier, this is a reasonable choice. However, while such information was *fed* to the HH approach by customization of the search strategy, the same relation has been *learned* by the Neural Network and *enforced via propagation*; by generalization of this reasoning, we conjecture a properly designed network has the chance of greatly reducing the effort in search strategy tuning.

7   Conclusions

We have introduced the idea of hybridizing Constraint Programming with a soft-computing paradigm, namely Neural Networks, to model complex real world problems; the novel Neuron (global) Constraint class provide a simple and yet effective tool to incorporate a trained network into a declarative CP model. As an important consequence training and designing the network becomes part of the modeling process; this involves deciding the parts of the target system to be represented via soft-computing and those to be tackled by more traditional means. To provide some evidence of the approach viability, we tackled a realistic thermal-aware workload allocation problem, with promising results.

Future research directions include experimentation with different real world problems, to investigate the applicability and effectiveness of the Neural Network integration approach to a broader set of target domains. Moreover, we are interested in improving the use of the Network provided information, e.g. search heuristics based on weight and connection structures could be designed. Finally, we plan to investigate the generalization of the approach to different soft-computing paradigms.

References

1. Bao, M., Andrei, A., Eles, P., Peng, Z.: On-line thermal aware dynamic voltage scaling for energy optimization with frequency/temperature dependency consideration. In: Proc. of DAC 2009, pp. 490–495. IEEE, Los Alamitos (2009)
2. Bartolini, A., Cacciari, M., Tilli, A., Benini, L.: A Distributed and Self-Calibrating Model-Predictive Controller for Energy and Thermal management of High-Performance Multicores. Accepted for publication at DATE 2011 (2011)
3. Bartolini, A., Cacciari, M., Tilli, A., Benini, L., Gries, M.: A virtual platform environment for exploring power, thermal and reliability management control strategies in high-performance multicores. In: Proc. of the 20th Great Lakes Symposium on VLSI, pp. 311–316. ACM, New York (2010)
4. Coskun, A.K., Rosing, T.S., Gross, K.C.: Utilizing predictors for efficient thermal management in multiprocessor SoCs. IEEE Transactions on Computer-Aided Design of Integrated Circuits and Systems 28(10), 1503–1516 (2009)
5. Coskun, A.K., Rosing, T.S., Whisnant, K.: Temperature aware task scheduling in MPSoCs. In: Proc. of DATE 2007, pp. 1659–1664. EDA Consortium (2007)

6. Fausett, L.V.: Fundamentals of neural networks: architectures, algorithms, and applications. Prentice-Hall, Englewood Cliffs (1994)
7. Goel, B., et al.: Portable, scalable, per-core power estimation for intelligent resource management. IEEE, Los Alamitos (2010)
8. Hecht-Nielsen, R.: Theory of the backpropagation neural network. Neural Networks (1988)
9. Howard, J., et al.: A 48-Core IA-32 message-passing processor with DVFS in 45nm CMOS. IEEE, Los Alamitos (2010)
10. Huang, W., Ghosh, S., Velusamy, S.: HotSpot: A compact thermal modeling methodology for early-stage VLSI design. IEEE Transactions on VLSI 14(5), 501–513 (2006)
11. IBM Press Release. Netherlands Railways Realizes Savings of 20 Million Euros a Year With ILOG Optimization Technology (2009),
http://www-03.ibm.com/press/us/en/pressrelease/27076.wss#release
12. INFORMS. Operations Research Success Stories (2011),
http://www.scienceofbetter.org/can_do/success_alpha.php
13. McCulloch, W.S., Pitts, W.: A Logical Calculus of the Ideas Immanent in Nervous Activity. Bulletin of Mathematical Biophysics 5, 115–133 (1943)
14. Minsky, M.L., Papert, S.: Perceptrons: An introduction to computational geometry. MIT Press, Cambridge (1969)
15. Murali, S., Mutapcic, A., Atienza, D., Gupta, R., Boyd, S., Benini, L., De Micheli, G.: Temperature Control of High-Performance Multi-core Platforms Using Convex Optimization. In: Proc. of DATE 2008, pp. 110–115. IEEE, Los Alamitos (2008)
16. Paci, G., Marchal, P., Poletti, F., Benini, L.: Exploring temperature-aware design in low-power MPSoCs. In: Proc. of DATE 2006, vol. 3(1/2), pp. 836–841 (2006)
17. Patterson, D.: Artificial Neural Networks. Theory and Applications. Prentice Hall, Singapore (1996)
18. Puschini, D., Clermidy, F., Benoit, P., Sassatelli, G., Torres, L.: Temperature-aware distributed run-time optimization on MP-SoC using game theory. In: Proc. of ISVLSI 2008, pp. 375–380. IEEE, Los Alamitos (2008)
19. Rosenblatt, F.: The perceptron: a perceiving and recognizing automaton (Technical Report 85-460-1) (1957)
20. Simonis, H.: Constraint Application Blog (2011),
http://hsimonis.wordpress.com/
21. Xie, Y., Hung, W.L.: Temperature-aware task allocation and scheduling for embedded multiprocessor systems-on-chip (MPSoC) design. The Journal of VLSI Signal Processing 45(3), 177–189 (2006)
22. Zanini, F., Atienza, D., Benini, L., De Micheli, G.: Multicore thermal management with model predictive control. In: Proc. of ECCTD 2009, pp. 711–714. IEEE, Los Alamitos (2009)

A Constraint Based Approach to Cyclic RCPSP

Alessio Bonfietti, Michele Lombardi, Luca Benini, and Michela Milano

DEIS, University of Bologna,
Viale del Risorgimento 2, 40136 Bologna, Italy
{alessio.bonfietti,michele.lombardi2,michela.milano,luca.benini}@unibo.it

Abstract. A cyclic scheduling problem is specified by a set of activities that are executed an infinite number of times subject to precedence and resource constraints. The cyclic scheduling problem has many applications in manufacturing, production systems, embedded systems, compiler design and chemical systems. This paper proposes a Constraint Programming approach based on Modular Arithmetic, taking into account temporal resource constraints. In particular, we propose an original modular precedence constraint along with its filtering algorithm. Classical "modular" approaches fix the modulus and solve an integer linear sub-problem in a generate-and-test fashion. Conversely, our technique is based on a non-linear model that faces the problem as a whole: the modulus domain bounds are inferred from the activity-related and iteration-related variables. The method has been extensively tested on a number of non-trivial synthetic instances and on a set of realistic industrial instances. Both the time to compute a solution and its quality have been assessed. The method is extremely fast to find close to optimal solutions in a very short time also for large instances. In addition, we have found a solution for one instance that was previously unsolved and improved the bound of another of a factor of 11.5%.

Keywords: Constraint Resource Constrained Cyclic Scheduling.

1 Introduction

The cyclic scheduling problem concerns setting times for a set of activities, to be indefinitely repeated, subject to precedence and resource constraints. It can be found in many application areas. For instance, it arises in compiler design implementing loops on parallel architecture, and on data-flow computations in embedded applications. Moreover, cyclic scheduling can be found in mass production, such as cyclic shop or Hoist scheduling problems.

In cyclic scheduling often the notion of optimality is related to the period of the schedule. A minimal period corresponds to the highest number of activities carried out on average over a large time window.

Optimal cyclic schedulers are lately in great demand, as streaming paradigms are gaining momentum across a wide spectrum of computing platforms, ranging from multi-media encoding and decoding in mobile and consumer devices, to advanced packet processing in network appliances, to high-quality rendering in

J. Lee (Ed.): CP 2011, LNCS 6876, pp. 130–144, 2011.

game consoles. In stream computing, an application can be abstracted as a set of tasks that have to be performed on incoming items (frames) of a data stream. A typical example is video decoding, where a compressed video stream has to be expanded and rendered. As video compression exploits temporal correlation between successive frames, decoding is not pure process-and-forward and computation on the current frame depends on the previously decoded frame. These dependencies must be taken into account in the scheduling model. In embedded computing contexts, resource constraints (computational units and buffer storage) imposed by the underlying hardware platforms are of great importance. In addition, the computational effort which can be spent to compute an optimal schedule is often limited by cost and time-to-market considerations.

In this paper we introduce a Constraint Programming approach based on modular arithmetic for computing minimum-period resource-constrained cyclic schedules. Our main contribution is an original modular precedence constraint and its filtering algorithm. The solver has several interesting characteristics: it deals effectively with temporal and resource constraints, it computes very high quality solutions in a short time, but it can also be pushed to run complete search. An extensive experimental evaluation on a number of non-trivial synthetic instances and on a set of realistic industrial instances gave promising results compared with a state-of-the art ILP-based (Integer Linear Programming) scheduler and the Swing Modulo Scheduling (SMS) heuristic technique.

2   The Problem

The cyclic scheduling problem is defined on a directed graph $G(V, A)$ with n ($|V| = n$) nodes that represent activities with fixed durations d_i, and m ($|A| = m$) arcs representing dependencies between pair of activities.

As the problem is periodic (it is executed an infinite number of times) we have an infinite number of repetitions of the same task. We call $start(i, \omega)$ the starting time of activity i at repetition ω. An edge (i, j) in this setting is interpreted as a precedence constraint such that: $start(j, \omega) \geq start(i, \omega) + d_i$. Moreover, a dependency edge from activity i to activity j might be associated with a minimal time lag $\theta_{(i,j)}$ and a repetition distance $\delta_{(i,j)}$. Every edge of the graph can be formally represented as:

$$start(j, \omega) \geq start(i, \omega - \delta_{(i,j)}) + d_i + \theta_{(i,j)} \tag{1}$$

In other words, the start time of j at iteration ω must be higher than the sum of the time lag θ and the end time of i at ω shifted by the repetition distance δ of the arc. For a periodic schedule, the start times follow a static pattern, repeated over iterations: $start(i, \omega) = start(i, 0) + \omega \cdot \lambda$, where $\lambda > 0$ is the duration of an iteration (i.e. the iteration period, or *modulus*) and $start(i, 0)$ is the start time of the first execution. Hence, we can deduce that scheduling a periodic task-set implies finding feasible assignments for $start(i, 0)$ and a feasible modulus λ.

Observe that, since the schedule is repeated every λ time units, resource requirement at a time instant t may be caused by activities from different schedule repetitions (i.e. with different ω values). From this point of view, the schedule execution exhibits an initial, finite length, transient phase and then enters a fully periodic behaviour (i.e. the resource usage profile becomes periodic as well).

Therefore it is convenient to focus on an arbitrary λ length time span in the periodic phase; the relative start time of an activity i within such an interval can be obtained by applying $start(i,0) = \mathsf{s}_i + \mathsf{k}_i \cdot \lambda$, where s_i is the start time *within the modulus* ($0 \leq \mathsf{s}_i \leq \lambda - \mathsf{d}_i$) and k_i, called iteration number, refers to the number of full periods elapsed before $start(i,0)$ is scheduled. Note that, any schedule start time can be formally represented as: $start(i, \omega) = \mathsf{s}_i + \mathsf{k}_i \cdot \lambda + \omega \cdot \lambda$.

The key step of our approach is the generalization of equation (1) that enables activities to be assigned to arbitrary iterations (i.e. by taking into account inter-iteration overlappings). Hence, for every (i, j), we have a *modular* precedence constraint:

$$\mathsf{s}_j + \mathsf{k}_j \cdot \lambda \geq \mathsf{s}_i + d_i + \theta_{(i,j)} + (\mathsf{k}_i - \delta_{(i,j)}) \cdot \lambda \tag{2}$$

where k_i and k_j denote the iteration numbers to which activities i and j belong. Note that, by definition $\mathsf{k}_j \geq \mathsf{k}_i - \delta_{(i,j)}$. The modular precedence relation can be satisfied either by modification of the start times s_i, or by moving the involved activities across iterations.

Finally, each activity i requires a certain amount req_{i,r_k} of one or more renewable resources r_k with capacity cap_{r_k}.

The problem consists in finding a schedule (that is, an assignment of start times s and iteration values k to activities), such that no resource capacity is exceed at any point of time and the modulus λ of the schedule (that is the makespan) is minimized.

In the context of chemical processes, the problem described above is described via Petri net's (see [23]), where δ is the number of markers over the places. In embedded system design this model is equivalent to scheduling homogeneous synchronous data-flow graphs (see [18]), where δ is the number of initial tokens in the buffer of the edges.

Fig. 1 presents a simple instance with 5 activities with different execution times and resource consumption. Assuming a total resource capacity of 3, the schedule depicted in Fig. 1 and labeled as *solution* is the optimal schedule. The activity coloured in light grey are scheduled at iteration 0 while the darkest at iteration 1. The execution of the schedule is plotted in Fig. 1 labeled as *execution*.

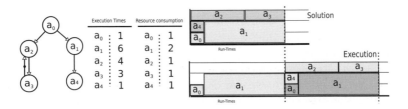

Fig. 1. Example instance and schedule

3   Constraint-Based Approach

We propose a complete constraint-based approach for the cyclic scheduling problem. The model is based on modular arithmetic. The solving algorithm interleaves propagation and search. We have implemented a modular precedence constraint taking into account propagation on iteration variables, start time and the modulus variable. The search strategy interleaves the instantiation of start and iteration variables.

3.1   Model

The model we devised is based on three classes of variables: activity starting time within the modulus, iterations and the modulus. The starting time of each activity has a domain $[0..\texttt{MAX\_TIME} - d]$, the iterations have the domain $[-|V|.. + |V|]$ and the modulus $]0..\texttt{MAX\_TIME}]$, where $|V|$ is the number of nodes and $\texttt{MAX\_TIME}$ represents the sum of the execution times of the activities and the sum of the time lags of the edges. These variables are subject to temporal, resource (including buffers) and symmetry breaking constraints.

Temporal constraints. The time model we devised is an extension of the Simple Temporal Network Model (STNM, see [8]). Each node i of the graph is represented with a pair of time points s_i, e_i with associated time windows, connected by a directional binary constraints of the form:

$$s_i \xrightarrow{[d_i]} e_i$$

where d_i (the execution time of activity i) is the distance between the activity starting point s_i and the activity endpoint e_i, meaning that $e_i = s_i + d_i$.

We extend the STNM with a new precedence edge formulation: each edge (i, j) of the graph, described by (2), is represented as:

$$e_i \xrightarrow{[\theta_{(i,j)}, \texttt{k}_i, \texttt{k}_j, \delta_{(i,j)}]} s_j$$

where $\theta_{(i,j)}$ is the minimal time lag between the end of i (e_i) and the start of j (s_j). The construct also takes in account the iteration numbers $\texttt{k}_i, \texttt{k}_j$ and their minimal iteration distance $\delta_{(i,j)}$. This precedence is modeled through a dedicated *Modular Precedence Constraint* whose signature is as follows. Let $e = (i, j) \in \mathbf{A}$ be an edge of the graph.

$$\texttt{ModPCst}([\texttt{e}_\texttt{i}], [\texttt{s}_\texttt{j}], [\texttt{k}_\texttt{i}], [\texttt{k}_\texttt{j}], [\lambda], \theta, \delta)$$

where $[\texttt{e}_\texttt{i}], [\texttt{s}_\texttt{j}], [\texttt{k}_\texttt{i}], [\texttt{k}_\texttt{j}], [\lambda]$ are the variables representing respectively the end time of activity i, the start time of activity j, their respective iterations and the modulus, and $\theta_{(i,j)} = \theta$, $\delta_{(i,j)} = \delta$ are constant values. The filtering for a single precedence relation constraint achieves GAC and runs in constant time.

Resource constraints (including buffers). Unary and discrete resources in cyclic scheduling are modeled via traditional resource constraints. In fact, having starting time within a modulus, we can reuse the results achieved in constraint-based scheduling. In addition, in real contexts, a precedence constraint often implies an exchange of intermediate step products between activities that should be stored in buffers. For example, in the embedded system context activities may exchange data packets that should be stored in memory buffers.

Every time the activity i ends, its *product* is accumulated in a *buffer* and whenever the activity j starts, it consumes a *product* from it. It is common to have size limits for each *buffer*. We model this limit through the following constraint:

$$\mathbf{k}_j - \mathbf{k}_i + (e_i \leq s_j) \leq \mathbf{B}_{(i,j)} - \delta_{(i,j)} \tag{3}$$

where $\mathbf{B}_{(i,j)}$ is the size limit of the *buffer* and the reified constraint $(e_i \leq s_j)$ equals one if the condition is satisfied. Obviously $\mathbf{B}_{(i,j)} \geq \delta_{(i,j)}$, otherwise the problem is unsolvable. In fact, the value $\delta_{(i,j)}$ counts the number of *products* already accumulated in the *buffer* (i,j) as initial condition. Inequality (3) limits the number of executions of activity i (*the producer*) before the first execution of j (*the consumer*).

Symmetry Breaking constraints. One important observation is that the assignment of different iteration values to communicating tasks allows one to assign apparently infeasible values to activities starting times.

Suppose there exists a precedence constraint between activities (i,j) and suppose we decide to overlap their executions, such that $\mathbf{s}_j \leq \mathbf{s}_i + d_i$ and that $\theta_{(i,j)} = \delta_{(i,j)} = 0$. From (2) we derive:

$$\mathbf{k}_j \geq \mathbf{k}_i + \left\lceil \frac{\mathbf{s}_i + d_i - \mathbf{s}_j}{\lambda} \right\rceil \tag{4}$$

Observe that the precedence relation does indeed hold, but appears to be violated on the modular time horizon. The minimum iteration difference that enables such an apparent order swap to occur is with $\mathbf{k}_j = \mathbf{k}_i + 1$, and any larger number obtains the same effect.

Therefore the iteration value of the activity j should be at most one unit greater than all the predecessors iteration values: the following constraint is used to remove symmetries and narrow the search space on $\mathbf{k}$ variables:

$$\mathbf{k}_j \leq \max_{i \in \mathbf{P}_j} \left(\mathbf{k}_i - \delta_{(i,j)} + \left\lceil \frac{\mathbf{s}_i + d_i - \mathbf{s}_j + \theta_{(i,j)}}{\lambda} \right\rceil\right) + 1 \tag{5}$$

where $\mathbf{P}_j : \{i \in \mathbf{P}_j | (i,j) \in \mathbf{A}\}$ is the set of the predecessors of j.

3.2   Constraint Propagation

The filtering on buffer and symmetry breaking constraints is the one embedded in mathematical constraints. In the same way, traditional resource constraints are propagated as usual. What is original in this paper is the filtering algorithm for the modular precedence constraint.

Modular Precedence Constraint. The filtering algorithm of the Modular Precedence Constraint has three fundamental components:

- Filtering on the iteration variables k: the goal of this component is to maintain a proper distance between iteration variables.
- Filtering on the start time variables s: the aim of this part is to modify the start times of the involved variables to avoid infeasible overlapping of activities.
- Filtering on the modulus variable λ: this phase computes and sets a lower bound for the modulus.

The algorithm is executed whenever the domain of any variable involved changes.

Referring to the temporal model proposed in section 3.1 we can rewrite the inequality (2) as:

$$s_j + k_j \cdot \lambda \geq e_i + \theta + (k_i - \delta) \cdot \lambda \qquad (6)$$

Filtering on iteration variables Starting from the equation above, we have

$$k_i \quad k_j \quad \delta \leq \frac{s_j - e_i - \theta}{\lambda} \qquad (7)$$

with $-\lambda \leq s_j - e_i \leq \lambda$ and $\theta \geq 0$.

In the following we refer to $\overline{x}$ and $\underline{x}$ as the highest and the lowest values of the domain of a generic variable x.

Then, we can identify the highest integer value of the right part of the inequality: $\left\lfloor \frac{\overline{s_j} - e_i - \theta}{\lambda} \right\rfloor$ that is upper-bounded to 1 if $d_j = d_i = 0$, $\theta = 0$ and $\overline{s_j} = \overline{\lambda}$, $\underline{e_i} = 0$.

Hence, we can define two expressions computing bounds over the k variables:

$$k_i \leq \overline{k_j} + \delta + \left\lfloor \frac{\overline{s_j} - e_i - \theta}{\lambda} \right\rfloor \qquad k_j \geq \underline{k_i} - \delta - \left\lfloor \frac{\overline{s_j} - e_i - \theta}{\overline{\lambda}} \right\rfloor \qquad (8)$$

As an example, suppose during search two activities i and j connected with a precedence (i,j) temporally overlap and that $s_j = 0, e_i = 3, \delta = 0, \theta = 0$: then the inequality (8) appears as follows:

$$k_j \geq \underline{k_i} - \left\lfloor \frac{-3}{\overline{\lambda}} \right\rfloor \qquad (9)$$

that implies that $k_j > k_i$; in fact, two *connected* activities can overlap iff their iteration values differ: in particular $k_{sinkNode} > k_{sourceNode}$.

Filtering on starting variables Let now $\Delta_k = k_i - k_j - \delta$ and $\underline{\Delta_k} = \underline{k_i} - \overline{k_j} - \delta$, the constraint (6) could be written as:

$$s_j - e_i - \theta \geq \Delta_k \cdot \lambda \qquad (10)$$

It is trivial to prove that $\Delta_k \leq 0$: in fact $\Delta_k > 0$ implies that $k_j < k_i - \delta$ which is, by definition, impossible.

If $\Delta_k \leq 0$, we can deduce two inequalities and their relative bound:

$$s_j \geq e_i + \theta + \Delta_k \cdot \lambda \geq \underline{e_i} + \theta + \Delta_k \cdot \overline{\lambda} \tag{11}$$

$$e_i \leq s_j - \theta - \Delta_k \cdot \lambda \leq \overline{s_j} - \theta - \Delta_k \cdot \overline{\lambda} \tag{12}$$

Note that, if $\Delta_k = 0$, the modular constraint is turned into a simple time constraint: $s_j \geq e_i + \theta$. In fact, two *connected* activities with the same iteration value cannot overlap and the inequality (11) *pushes* the destination activity j after the end time of i plus the arc time lag θ.

Filtering on the modulus The filtering on the modulus variable can be obtained only in one case, namely when $\Delta_k < 0$: in fact, we can derive from formula (10) the following inequality, that computes a lower bound on the modulus variable:

$$\lambda \geq \frac{e_i - s_j + \theta}{-\Delta_k} = \left\lceil \frac{\underline{e_i} - \overline{s_j} + \theta}{\overline{k_j} - \underline{k_i} + \delta} \right\rceil \tag{13}$$

3.3   Search

The solver is based on *tree search* adopting a *schedule or postpone* approach (described in[17]).

The main idea underlying the search strategy is the following: since the schedule is periodic, the starting time values of each activity can be positioned with respect to an arbitrarily chosen reference; we select one activity as reference and assign its starting time to zero. The choice is guided by a simple heuristics; in particular, the candidates to become the reference node should have no in-going arc with a strictly positive δ. Formally, for node i to be a candidate, it must hold $\nexists (j, i) \in \mathbf{A}$ such that $\delta_{(j,i)} > 0$. Then we accord preference to nodes with a high number of outgoing arcs. The rationale behind this choice is that it seems to ease propagation of symmetry breaking constraints. Hence, the reference node assumes standard values: $s_{src} = 0, k_{src} = 0$. Note that fixing the start time of one activity to 0 does not compromise completeness as the iteration variables $k \in \mathbb{Z}$ can assume negative values: therefore optimality is guaranteed.

At each search step a new node is selected among the activities connected with the already considered nodes. Two activities are connected if there exists al least an edge between them. This method improves the efficiency of the propagation of symmetry breaking constraints. Other variable selection strategies radically worsen the performance of the solver.

The search interleaves the assignment of start times and iteration values. The algorithm assigns to an activity its earliest start time. In backtracking, the decision is postponed until its earliest start time has been removed. This removal can occur as a result of a combination of search decisions and constraints propagation. Hence, the algorithm, considering the same activity, assigns to it an iteration value. Note that the iteration assigned is always the lowest absolute value in the variable domain. In case of failure, the value is removed from the domain and a higher number is assigned. In fact, if a solution results infeasible with $k_i = \phi$, it is trivial to prove that it is infeasible for any value $\phi' \leq \phi$ (remember that $k_{sinkNode} \geq k_{sourceNode} - \delta$).

4   Experimental Results

The main purpose of the experimental evaluation is to show our approach to cyclic scheduling is viable; in particular, the focus is to assess the effectiveness on practically significant benchmarks.

In this work we show four groups of experimental results: the first (1) considers an industrial set of 36 instruction scheduling instances for the ST200 processor by STmicroelectronics [2]. The second (2) group considers a set of synthetic instances and compares the best solution obtained within 300 seconds and the (ideal) lower bound of the instance. The third (3) set of experiments considers a set of a synthetic instances and compares the solution quality of our *modulo* approach with a classic *blocked* approach on cyclic scheduling (see [3]). Finally, the fourth (4) group of results is used to assess the efficiency of the combined propagation of the buffer constraints and the symmetry breaking constraints.

The system described so far was implemented on top of ILOG Solver 6.7; all tests were run on a 2.8GHz Core2Duo machine with 4GB of RAM. The synthetic instances were built by means of a internally developed task-graph generator, designed to produce graphs with realistic structure and parameters. Designing the generator itself was a non-trivial task, but it is out of the scope of this paper.

4.1   Industrial Instances

The first set of 36 instances refers to compilers for VLIW architectures. These instances belong to compilers when optimizing inner loops at instruction level for very-long instruction word (VLIW) parallel processors. Since the resource consumption is always unary, to obtain a more challenging set, in [2] the authors replaced the original resource consumption with a random integer number bounded by the resource capacity. Nodes represent operations and their execution time is unary: the smallest instance features 10 nodes and 42 arcs, while the largest one features 214 nodes and 1063 arcs. In [2] the authors present two ILP formulations for the resource-constrained modulo scheduling problem (RCMSP), which is equivalent to a cyclic RCPSP. As described in [2], both ILP approaches adopt a *dual* process by iteratively increasing an infeasible lower bound; as a consequence, the method does not provide any feasible solution before the optimum is reached. Given a large time limit (604800 seconds) their solvers found the optimal solution for almost all the instances: our experiments compare the optimal value and the solution found by our method within a 300 sec. time limit. In addition, to empathize the quality of our solutions, we compare also with a state of the art heuristic approach: the *Swing Modulo Scheduling (SMS)*, presented in [20], used by the gcc compiler [13].

The set of instances is composed by two subsets: the easiest one containing industrial instances and the more difficult one generated with random resource consumptions. Tab. 1 reports a summary of the experiments results: the first three columns describe the instances (name, number of nodes and arcs), the third shows the run-times of the fastest ILP approach (in [2]), the fourth reports the quality of our solutions achieved within a second and 300 seconds and the fifth presents the quality of the solutions computed with the *SMS* heuristic approach. The remaining three columns report the same figures referred to the modified set of instances. For the *easiest* set, our method computes the optimal value within one second for all but one instance (adpcm-st231.2) whose optimal gap is 2.44%. We also found a solution for the gsm-st231.18 instance that was previously unsolved; clearly, we cannot evaluate its quality as the optimal solution has never been found.

We also compared our approach with the *SMS* heuristic that presents an average optimality gap of 14.58%. Its average solution time is lower than ten seconds; the highest computation time refers to instance gsm-st231.18 and is 58 seconds.

The last three columns of Tab. 1 report the experimental results on the *modified* set of instances. Again, time refers to the fastest ILP approach, while gap(%) and SMS(%) report the optimality gap of our approach and the *SMS* heuristic respectively. Within a second we found the optimal value of 89% of the instances and the average gap is 0.813%. Within 300 seconds its value improves to 0.61%. *Swing Modulo Schedule* solves all the instances with an average gap of 3.03% within few tens of seconds.

Finally, referring to instances gsm-st231.25 and gsm-st231.33, the authors of [2] claim to compute two sub-optimal solutions in 604800 seconds (though no details are given on how the dual process they propose converges to sub-optimal solutions). For instance gsm-st231.25 both the modular and the SMS approaches find the same solution as the bound computed in the original paper. Instead, in gsm-st231.33, the solution proposed in [2] has value 52. While the heuristic solver finds the same solution, the modular method finds in one second a solution with value 47 and within 56 seconds a solution of value 46.

Note that, within the time limit we prove optimality in 12.5% of the instances: we are currently investigating how to improve the efficiency of the proof of optimality, even though the optimality gap is so narrow to reduce the significance of finding (and proving) the optimal solution.

4.2   Evaluating the Solution Quality on Synthetic Benchmarks

The second set of experiments targets a task scheduling problem over a multi-processor platform; this set contains 1200 synthetic instances with 20 to 100 activities: each instance corresponds to a cyclic graph with a high concurrency between the activities. This form has been empirically proven to be the hardest structure for the solver developed. The generated instances contain a single cumulative resource with capacity 6 and activities have a unary consumption.

Table 1. Run-Times/Gaps of Industrial/Modified instances

Instances	nodes	arcs	Industrial			Modified		
			time(sec)	**Gap(%)**	SMS(%)	time(sec)	**Gap(%)**	SMS(%)
adpcm-st231.1	86	405	14400	0%	19.23%	X	X	X
adpcm-st231.2	142	722	582362	2.44/2.44%	0%	X	X	X
gsm-st231.1	30	190	0.05	0%	0%	250	10.7/10.7%	10.7%
gsm-st231.2	101	462	79362	0%	0%	X	X	X
gsm-st231.5	44	192	0.05	0%	13.33%	280	0%	5.26%
gsm-st231.6	30	130	17	0%	31.25%	152	0%	0%
gsm-st231.7	44	192	0.05	0%	41.66%	92	0%	2.38%
gsm-st231.8	14	66	0.05	0%	31.25%	0.27	0%	0%
gsm-st231.9	34	154	0.05	0%	0%	0.56	5.88/0%	8.57%
gsm-st231.10	10	42	0.05	0%	0%	0.1	0%	0%
gsm-st231.11	26	137	0.05	0%	0%	0.37	0%	0%
gsm-st231.12	15	70	0.05	0%	0%	12.65	0%	0%
gsm-st231.13	46	210	1856	0%	0%	985.03	0%	0%
gsm-st231.14	39	176	301.25	0%	17.39%	220	2.94/2.94%	0%
gsm-st231.15	15	70	0.05	0%	28.57%	12.36	0%	8.33%
gsm-st231.16	65	323	7520	0%	0%	X	X	X
gsm-st231.17	38	173	0.05	0%	23.81%	90	0%	0%
gsm-st231.18	214	1063	X	0%	30.76%	X	X	X
gsm-st231.19	19	86	0.05	0%	0%	38.23	0%	6.25%
gsm-st231.20	23	102	0.05	0%	0%	123	3.23/3.23%	4.76%
gsm-st231.21	33	154	0.05	0%	45.45%	42.06	0%	3.24%
gsm-st231.22	31	146	0.05	0%	0%	80.36	0%	0%
gsm-st231.25	60	273	3652	0%	0%	(604800)	0%	1.75%
gsm-st231.29	44	192	12.6	0%	23.81%	210	0%	0%
gsm-st231.30	30	130	12	0%	0%	58	0%	3.84%
gsm-st231.31	44	192	47	0%	41.67%	142	0%	2.5%
gsm-st231.32	32	138	0.05	0%	31.25%	0.25	0	0%
gsm-st231.33	59	266	2365	0%	11.76%	(604800)	0%	0%
gsm-st231.34	10	42	0.05	0%	6.25%	5.05	0%	0%
gsm-st231.35	18	80	0.05	0%	0%	52	0%	0%
gsm-st231.36	31	143	27	0%	14.29%	230	0%	7.69%
gsm-st231.39	26	118	0.05	0%	0%	95	0%	4.55%
gsm-st231.40	21	103	0.05	0%	0%	15	0%	5.56%
gsm-st231.41	60	315	2356	0%	0%	X	X	X
gsm-st231.42	23	102	0.05	0%	0%	12	0%	14.29%
gsm-st231.43	26	115	0.05	0%	21.73%	15	0%	9.1%

Table 2. Solution quality

time(s)	avg(%)	best(%)	worst(%)
1	3.706%	2.28%	5.18%
2	3.68%	2.105%	5.04%
5	3.51%	1.81%	5.015%
10	3.37%	1.538%	4.98%
60	3.14%	1.102%	4.83%
300	2.9%	0.518%	4.73%

Tests run with a time limit of 300 seconds: Tab. 2 shows the average, best and worst gap between the best solution found within a time limit (reported in the first column) and the ideal lower bound of the instance.

The lower bound is the following:

$$lb = \left\lceil \max \left(ib, \frac{\sum_{i \in V} d_i}{cap} \right) \right\rceil,$$

that is the maximum between the intrinsic iteration bound[1] *ib* of the graph and the ratio between the sum of the execution times and the total capacity.

The first row of the table reports that within one second run-time the solver finds a solution which is about 3.7% distant from the ideal optimal value; at the end of the time limit the gap is decreased to 2.9%. Fig. 2 depicts a zoom of the progress of the gap values.

From the results of these experiments, we can conclude that our approach converges very quickly close to a value that is an ideal optimal. The optimal value lies somewhere in-between the two values and therefore is even closer to the solution found within 300 seconds.

4.3   Modulo vs. Unfolding Scheduling

The aim of this third experimentation is to investigate the impact of the overlapped schedule (namely a schedule explicitly designed such that successive iterations in the application overlap) w.r.t. the so called *blocked* classic approach that considers only one iteration. Since the problem is periodic, and the schedule is iterated essentially infinitely, the latter method pays a penalty in the quality of the schedule obtained. A technique often used to exploit inter-iteration parallelism is **unfolding** (see [22]). The unfolding strategy schedules u iterations of the application, where u is called the blocking factor. Unfolding often leads to improved blocked schedules, but it also implies an increased size of the instance.

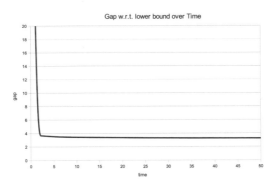

Fig. 2. Graphical representation of the optimality gap

The third set of instances contains 220 instances with an activity number from 14 to 65. We have divided these instances into three classes: small instances featuring 14 to 24 nodes, medium-size instances (25 to 44 activities) and big instances with 45 to 65 activities. Also we have considered eight solver configurations: the *blocked* one (scheduling only one iteration) and seven configurations called *UnfoldX* where X is the number of iteration scheduled. Tab. 3 shows the average gap

---

[1] The iteration bound of the graph is in relation with the cycles, in particular with the maximum cycle mean; details in [7,12].

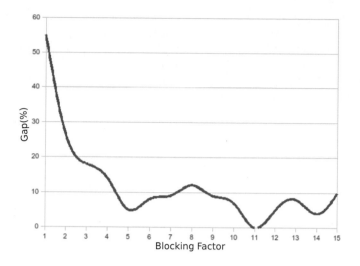

Fig. 3. Optimality gap over blocking factor

between the above mentioned configurations and our approach. Obviously, the worst gap is relative to the blocked schedule, while the unfolded ones tend to have an oscillatory behaviour. Fig. 3 depicts the relation between the gap (Y axes) and the blocking factor (X axes) of a selected instance with 30 nodes. The figure highlights the waveform of the gap. With unfolding factor $u = 11$ the solver found a solution equivalent to the overlapped one, with the difference that the unfolded problem consists of 330 activities. The last column presents the average optimality gap over the whole experimental set.

Note that for the instance analysed in Fig. 3 there exists a blocking factor that enables to find the optimal solution. However, Parhi and Messerschmitt in [22] widely studied the unfolding techniques and provide an example of an application for which no blocked schedule can be found, even allowing unfolding.

4.4 Buffer-Size Constraints Tests

The last set of tests contains 400 instances with 20 nodes; for each instance, the resource free optimal solution has buffer request from 3 to 6. This property was obtained via careful tuning of the instance generation problem.

The purpose of this experimental section is to highlight the efficiency of the buffer and symmetry breaking propagation. The results show that reasonable limits on the buffer size do not compromise solution quality, while providing a tremendous boost to the search time. All instances were solved with five different buffer sizes (1,2,3,6,9). Tab. 4 reports the average and median running time. The first two rows refer to tightly constrained instances, while the last one refers to loosely constrained instances.

The second and the third columns show respectively the average and the median run times in seconds to find the optimal solution. Note that the propagation drastically impacts the run time of the search.

Table 3. Unfolding set results

Solver	Solution Gap (%)			
	[14-20]	[25-40]	[45-65]	AVG
Blocked	108.16%	65.45%	38.83%	**55.32%**
Unfold2	55.92%	26.06%	19.89%	**26.23%**
Unfold3	33.31%	16.15%	9.99%	**18.6%**
Unfold4	29.41%	14.27%	6.278	**14.13%**
Unfold5	21.35%	5.33%	8.76%	**5.67%**
Unfold6	39.06%	8.67%	4.39%	**8.67%**
Unfold8	78.31%	10.71%	7.65%	**12.44%**
Unfold10	16.95%	10.21%	10.03%	**8.65%**

Table 4. Buffer set results

buffesSize	avg(s)	median(s)	gap%
1	1.1423	0.05	4.925%
2	52.1894	0.1	0.052%
3	157.4673	0.31	0%
6	599.9671	1.215	0%
9	791.5552	1.83	0%

Another interesting aspect to observe is that since value 6 is the intrinsic buffer size of the instances, a solution with that buffer limit is considered as the *reference* solution. The last column presents the gap between the optimal found and the *reference*. The interesting aspect is that the trade-off between the run-time speed-up and the optimality loss is not linear: in fact, despite the tests with buffer limit 2 run over 10 times faster, the solution, remains close to the *reference* one.

5   Related Work

The static cyclic scheduling literature arises from two main contexts: the industrial and the computing contexts. The former includes mass production (i.e. [15],[9]), chemical (i.e. [19]), robot flow-shop (i.e. [6]) and hoist scheduling problems(i.e. [5]), the latter includes parallel processing(i.e. [21],[14]), software pipelining(i.e. [24]) and the emerging embedded system data-flow problems (i.e. [16]).

There is a considerable body of work on the problem available in the OR literature, while from the AI community, the problem has not received much focus.

An important subset of cyclic scheduling problems is the modulo scheduling: here, start times and modulus are required to assume integer values; as stated in section 2 we make the same assumption.

Several heuristic and complete approaches have been proposed since many years to solve this problem. An heuristic approach is described in [24], wherein the algorithm, called *iterative modulo scheduling*, generates near-optimal schedules. Another interesting heuristic approach, called *SCAN* and in part based on the previous one, is presented in [4]. The latter method is based on an ILP model. A state of the art incomplete method is *Swing Modulo Scheduling* approach, described in [20], [21], and currently adopted in the GCC compiler [13].

Heuristic approaches compute a schedule for a single iteration of the application: the schedule is characterized by the value of the makespan (the *horizon*) and by an *initiation interval* which defines the real throughput. However, the *horizon* makespan could be extremely large, with implications on the size of the model. Our model, instead, is compact, since both *horizon* and *initiation* makespan coincide in the modulus value.

Advanced complete formulations were proposed in [11,10], both report ILP models; the first comprises both binary and integer variables while the latter includes only binary variables. In [2] the authors report an excellent overview of the state-of-the-art formulations (including Eichenberger and Dupont de Dinechin models) and present a new formulation issued from Danzig-Wolfe Decomposition. Finally, good overviews of complete methods can be found in [14,1].

To the best of our knowledge the state-of-the-art complete approaches are based on iteratively solving the problem with a fixed modulus. Modeling the modulus as a decision variable yields non-linear mathematical programs; on the other hand, with a fixed value, the resulting problem is a linear mathematical program. Hence, fixing the modulus and iteratively solving an ILP model is a common formulation for solving cyclic RCPSP.

Our methodology is constraint-based and tackles the non-linear problem as a whole: the modulus value is inferred from the others variables avoiding the iterative solving procedure thus increasing efficiency.

6   Conclusions

We propose a constraint formulation based on modular arithmetic solving the cyclic resource-constraint project scheduling problem. Keys of the efficiency are three different set of constraints: the buffer, the symmetry breaking and the modular precedence constraints. In particular, for the latter we devise an original filtering algorithm.

The experiments highlight a good performance and a solution quality that converges close to the optimal very quickly. In particular, the solver is extremely effective in finding a solution with a negligible optimality loss in terms of a few seconds; conversely, the optimality proof takes much longer to complete.

As a natural extension, future works will focus on allowing an activity to be scheduled across different iterations. Consequently a new cumulative filtering algorithm should be studied.

References

1. Artigues, C., Demassey, S., Néron, E.: Resource-constrained project scheduling - Models, Algorithms, Extensions and Applications. Wiley, Chichester (2008)
2. Ayala, M., Artigues, C.: On integer linear programming formulations for the resource-constrained modulo scheduling problem (2010),
   http://hal.archives-ouvertes.fr/docs/00/53/88/21/PDF/
   ArticuloChristianMaria.pdf
3. Bhattacharyya, S.S., Sriram, S.: Embedded Multiprocessors - Scheduling and Synchronization (Signal Processing and Communications), 2nd edn. CRC Press, Boca Raton (2009)

4. Blachot, F., de Dinechin, B.D., Huard, G.: SCAN: A Heuristic for Near-Optimal Software Pipelining. In: Nagel, W.E., Walter, W.V., Lehner, W. (eds.) Euro-Par 2006. LNCS, vol. 4128, pp. 289–298. Springer, Heidelberg (2006)
5. Chen, H., Chu, C., Proth, J.-M.: Cyclic scheduling of a hoist with time window constraints. IEEE Transactions on Robotics and Automation 14(1), 144–152 (1998)
6. Crama, Y., Kats, V., van de Klundert, J., Levner, E.: Cyclic scheduling in robotic flowshops. Annals of Operations Research 96, 97–124 (2000), 10.1023/A:1018995317468
7. Dasdan, A.: Experimental analysis of the fastest optimum cycle ratio and mean algorithms. ACM Transactions on Design Automation of Electronic Systems (TODAES) 9(4), 385–418 (2004)
8. Dechter, R.: Temporal constraint networks. Artificial Intelligence 49, 61–95 (1991)
9. Draper, D.L., Jonsson, A.K., Clements, D.P., Joslin, D.E.: Cyclic scheduling. In: Proc. of IJCAI, pp. 1016–1021. Morgan Kaufmann Publishers Inc., San Francisco (1999)
10. de Dinechin, B.D.: From Machine Scheduling to VLIW Instruction Scheduling (2004), http://www.cri.ensmp.fr/classement/doc/A-352.ps
11. Eichenberger, A.E., Davidson, E.S.: Efficient formulation for optimal modulo schedulers. ACM SIGPLAN Notices 32(5), 194–205 (1997)
12. Georgiadis, L., Goldberg, A.V., Tarjan, R.E., Werneck, R.F.: An experimental study of minimum mean cycle algorithms. In: Proc. of ALENEX, p. 13 (2009)
13. Hagog, M., Zaks, A.: Swing modulo scheduling for gcc (2004)
14. Hanen, C., Munier, A.: Cyclic scheduling on parallel processors: an overview, pp. 193–226. John Wiley & Sons Ltd., Chichester (1994)
15. Hanen, C.: Study of a np-hard cyclic scheduling problem: The recurrent job-shop. European Journal of Operational Research 72(1), 82–101 (1994)
16. Kudlur, M., Mahlke, S.: Orchestrating the execution of stream programs on multicore platforms. In: Proc. of PLDI, vol. 43, pp. 114–124 (May 2008)
17. Le Pape, C., Couronné, P.: Time-versus-capacity compromises in project scheduling. In: Proc. of the 13th Workshop of the UK Planning Special Interest Group (1994)
18. Lee, E.A., Messerschmitt, D.G.: Synchronous Data Flow. Proceedings of the IEEE 75(9), 1235–1245 (1987)
19. Li, Z., Ierapetritou, M.: Process scheduling under uncertainty: Review and challenges. Computers and Chemical Engineering 32(4-5), 715–727 (2008); Festschrift devoted to Rex Reklaitis on his 65th Birthday
20. Llosa, J., Gonzalez, A., Ayguade, E., Valero, M.: Swing Modulo Scheduling: A Lifetime-Sensitive Approach. In: PACT 1996, pp. 80–87 (1996)
21. Llosa, J., Gonzalez, A., Ayguade, E., Valero, M., Eckhardt, J.: Lifetime-sensitive modulo scheduling in a production environment. IEEE Trans. on Comps. 50(3), 234–249 (2001)
22. Parhi, K.K., Messerschmitt, D.G.: Static rate-optimal scheduling of iterative dataflow programs via optimum unfolding. IEEE Transactions on Computers 40(2), 178–195 (1991)
23. Peterson, J.L.: Petri Net Theory and the Modeling of Systems. Prentice Hall PTR, Englewood Cliffs (1981)
24. Rau, R.B.: Iterative modulo scheduling: An algorithm for software pipelining loops. In: Proc. of MICRO-27, pp. 63–74. ACM, New York (1994)

An Efficient Light Solver for Querying the Semantic Web

Vianney le Clément de Saint-Marcq[1,2], Yves Deville[1], and Christine Solnon[2]

[1] ICTEAM Research Institute,
Université catholique de Louvain,
Place Sainte-Barbe 2, 1348 Louvain-la-Neuve, Belgium
{vianney.leclement,yves.deville}@uclouvain.be
[2] Université de Lyon,
Université Lyon 1, LIRIS, CNRS UMR5205,
69622 Villeurbanne, France
christine.solnon@liris.cnrs.fr

Abstract. The Semantic Web aims at building cross-domain and distributed databases across the Internet. SPARQL is a standard query language for such databases. Evaluating such queries is however NP-hard. We model SPARQL queries in a declarative way, by means of CSPs. A CP operational semantics is proposed. It can be used for a direct implementation in existing CP solvers. To handle large databases, we introduce a specialized and efficient light solver, Castor. Benchmarks show the feasibility and efficiency of the approach.

1 Introduction

The Internet has become the privileged means of looking for information in everyday's life. While the information abundantly available on the Web is increasingly accessible for human users, computers still have trouble making sense out of it. Developers have to rely on fuzzy machine learning techniques [5] or site-specific APIs (e.g., Google APIs), or resort to writing a specialized parser that has to be updated on every site layout change.

The Semantic Web is an initiative of the World Wide Web Consortium (W3C) to enable sites to publish computer-readable data aside of the human-readable documents. Merging all published Semantic Web data results in one large global database. The global nature of the Semantic Web implies a much looser structure than traditional relational databases. A loose structure provides the needed flexibility to store unrelated data, but makes querying the database harder. SPARQL [16] is a query language for the Semantic Web that has been standardized by the W3C. Evaluating SPARQL queries is known to be NP-hard [15].

The execution model of current SPARQL engines (e.g., Sesame [4], 4store [10] or Virtuoso [7]) is based on relational algebra. A query is subdivided in many small parts that are computed separately. The answer sets are then joined together. User-specified filters are often processed after such join operations. Constraint Programming (CP), on the other hand, is able to exploit filters as constraints during the search. A constraint-based query engine is thus well suited for the Semantic Web.

J. Lee (Ed.): CP 2011, LNCS 6876, pp. 145–159, 2011.

Contributions. Our first contribution is a declarative model based on CSPs and an operational semantics based on CP for solving SPARQL queries. Existing CP solvers however are not designed to handle the huge domains linked with the Semantic Web datasets. The second contribution of this work is a specialized lightweight solver, called Castor, for executing SPARQL queries. On standard benchmarks, Castor is competitive with existing engines and improves on complex queries.

Outline. The next section explains how data is represented in the Semantic Web and how to query the data. Section 3 and 4 show respectively the declarative model and the operational semantics to solve queries. Section 5 presents our lightweight solver implementing the operational semantics. Section 6 evaluates the feasibility and efficiency of the approach through a standard benchmark.

2   The Semantic Web and the SPARQL Query Language

The Resource Description Framework (RDF) [11] allows one to model knowledge as a set of triples (subject, predicate, object). Such triples express relations, described by predicates, between subjects and objects. The three elements of a triple can be arbitrary resources identified by Uniform Resource Identifiers (URIs)[1]. Objects may also be literal values, such as strings, numbers, dates or custom data. An RDF dataset can be represented by a labeled directed multigraph as shown in Fig. 1.

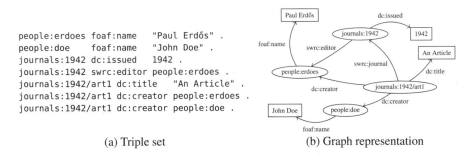

```
people:erdoes foaf:name    "Paul Erdős" .
people:doe    foaf:name    "John Doe" .
journals:1942 dc:issued    1942 .
journals:1942 swrc:editor people:erdoes .
journals:1942/art1 dc:title    "An Article" .
journals:1942/art1 dc:creator people:erdoes .
journals:1942/art1 dc:creator people:doe .
```

(a) Triple set   (b) Graph representation

Fig. 1. Example RDF dataset representing a fictive journal edited by Paul Erdős and an article of the journal written by Erdős and Doe. Here, people:erdoes and foaf:name are URIs whereas "Paul Erdős" is a literal.

SPARQL [16] is a query language for RDF. A basic query is a set of triple patterns, i.e., triples where elements may be replaced by variables. Basic queries can be assembled in compound queries with composition, optional or alternative parts. Filters add

---

[1] More precisely, RDF makes use of URI References, but the differences are not relevant to this paper. The specification also allows subjects and objects to be blank nodes, i.e., resources without an identifier. Without loss of generality, blank nodes will be considered as regular URIs for the purpose of this paper.

constraints on the variables. A solution of a query is an assignment of variables to URIs or literals appearing in the dataset. Substituting the variables in the query by their assigned values in the solution gives a subset of the dataset. A SPARQL query may also define a subset of variables to return, a sort order, etc., but those are not relevant for this paper and are omitted.

More formally, let U, L and V be pairwise disjoint infinite sets representing URIs, literals, and variables, respectively. A SPARQL problem instance is defined by a pair (S, Q) such that $S \subset U \times U \times (U \cup L)$ is a finite set of triples corresponding to the dataset, and Q is a query. The syntax of queries is recursively defined as follows[2]. The semantics will be defined in the next section.

- A basic query is a set of triple patterns (s, p, o) such that $s, p \in U \cup V$ and $o \in U \cup L \cup V$. The difference with RDF datasets is that we can have variables in place of URIs and literals.
- Let Q_1 and Q_2 be queries. $Q_1 . Q_2$, Q_1 OPTIONAL Q_2 and Q_1 UNION Q_2 are compound queries.
- Let Q be a query and c be a constraint such that every variable of c occurs at least once in Q. Q FILTER c is a constrained query. The SPARQL constraint expression language used to define c includes arithmetic operators, boolean operators, comparisons, regular expressions for string literals and some RDF-specific operators.

Given a dataset S, we respectively denote U_S and L_S the set of URIs and literals that occur in S. Given a query Q, we denote vars(Q) the set of variables appearing in Q.

3   A CSP Declarative Modeling of SPARQL Queries

A solution to a SPARQL problem instance (S, Q) is an assignment σ of variables of Q to values from $U_S \cup L_S$, i.e., a set of variable/value pairs. Given a solution σ and a query Q, we denote $\sigma(Q)$ the query obtained by replacing every occurrence of a variable assigned in σ by its value. The goal is to find all solutions. We denote sol(S, Q) the set of all solutions to (S, Q).

Contrarily to classical CSPs, a solution σ does not have to cover all the variables occurring in Q. For example, if a variable x appears only in an optional part that is not found in a solution σ, x will not appear in the solution σ. Such variables are said to be unbound.

In this section, we define the set of solutions of a SPARQL problem instance by means of CSPs, thus giving a denotational semantics of SPARQL queries. Note that, while doing so, we transform a declarative language, SPARQL, into another one based on CSPs which may be solved by existing solvers.

3.1   Basic Queries

A basic query BQ is a set of triple patterns (s, p, o). In this simple form, an assignment σ is a solution if $\sigma(BQ) \subseteq S$.

---

[2] To keep things clear, we make some simplifications to the language. These assumptions do not alter the expressive power of SPARQL.

The SPARQL problem (S,BQ) may be viewed as a graph matching problem from a query graph associated with BQ to a target graph associated with S [3], as illustrated in Fig. 2. However, even the simple basic form of query is more general than classical graph matching, such as graph homomorphism or subgraph isomorphism. Variables on the edges (the predicates) can impose additional relationships between different edges. This problem is thus already NP-hard.

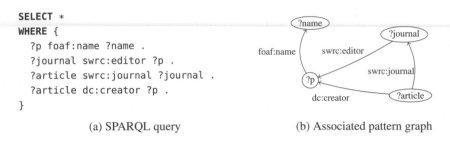

```
SELECT *
WHERE {
    ?p foaf:name ?name .
    ?journal swrc:editor ?p .
    ?article swrc:journal ?journal .
    ?article dc:creator ?p .
}
```

(a) SPARQL query   (b) Associated pattern graph

Fig. 2. Example of a basic query searching for journal editors having published an article in the same journal. Variables are prefixed by a question mark, e.g., ?name. Executing the query on the dataset of Fig. 1 results in the unique solution $\{(p, \text{people:erdoes}), (name, \text{"Paul Erdős"}), (journal, \text{journals:1942}), (article, \text{journals:1942/art1})\}$.

We formally define the set $\text{sol}(S, BQ)$ as the solutions of the CSP (X, D, C) such that

– $X = \text{vars}(BQ)$,
– all variables have the same domain, containing all URIs and literals of S, i.e., $\forall x \in X, D(x) = U_S \cup L_S$,
– constraints ensure that every triple of the query belongs to the dataset, i.e.,

$$C = \{ \text{Member}((s, p, o), S) \mid (s, p, o) \in BQ \} \ ,$$

where Member is the set membership constraint.

3.2 Compound Queries

More advanced queries, e.g., queries with optional parts, cannot directly be translated into CSPs. Indeed some queries rely on the non-satisfiability of a subquery, which is coNP-hard. CSPs can only model NP problems.

$Q_1 . Q_2$. Two patterns can be concatenated with the join or concatenation symbol (.). The solution set of a concatenation is the cartesian product of the solution sets of both queries. Such cartesian product is obtained by merging every pair of solutions assigning the same values to the common variables. Note that the operator is commutative, i.e., $Q_1 . Q_2$ is equivalent to $Q_2 . Q_1$. The set of solutions is defined as follows:

$$\mathrm{sol}(S, Q_1 \cdot Q_2) =$$
$$\{\sigma_1 \cup \sigma_2 \mid \sigma_1 \in \mathrm{sol}(S, Q_1),$$
$$\sigma_2 \in \mathrm{sol}(S, \sigma_1(Q_2))\} \ .$$

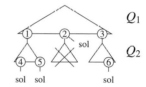

The figure on the right depicts an example. A triangle represents the search tree of a subquery. Circles at the bottom of a triangle are the solutions of the subquery. Circles 1, 2 and 3 represent $\mathrm{sol}(S, Q_1)$. Solution 1 is extended into the solutions 4 and 5 in the search tree of $\mathrm{sol}(S, \sigma_1(Q_2))$. Solutions 4, 5 and 6 are the solutions of the concatenation. If Q_1 and Q_2 are both basic queries, we can compute the concatenation more efficiently by merging both sets of triple patterns and solve the resulting basic query as shown in Section 3.1.

Q_1 *OPTIONAL* Q_2. The OPTIONAL operator solves its left-hand side subquery Q_1 and *tries* to solve its right-hand side subquery Q_2. If a solution of Q_1 cannot be extended into a solution of $Q_1 \cdot Q_2$, then that solution of Q_1 becomes a solution of the query too. More formally,

$$\mathrm{sol}(S, Q_1 \text{ OPTIONAL } Q_2) =$$
$$\mathrm{sol}(S, Q_1 \cdot Q_2) \cup$$
$$\{\sigma \in \mathrm{sol}(S, Q_1) \mid \mathrm{sol}(S, \sigma(Q_2)) = \varnothing\} \ .$$

Compared to the example for the concatenation operator, circle 2 in the figure becomes a solution of the compound query. The inconsistency check makes the search difficult. Indeed, in the simple case, Q_2 is a basic query and is thus solved by a CSP. However, as checking the consistency of a CSP is NP-hard, checking its inconsistency is coNP-hard. To ensure the semantics are compositional, we impose that if Q_1 OPTIONAL Q_2 is a subquery of a query Q, then variables occurring in Q_2 but not in Q_1 (vars$(Q_2)\setminus$ vars(Q_1)) do not appear elsewhere in Q. Such condition does not alter the expressive power of the language [1].

Q_1 *UNION* Q_2. Disjunctions are introduced by the UNION operator. The solution set of the union of two queries is the union of the solution sets of both queries. The solutions of the two queries are computed separately:

$$\mathrm{sol}(S, Q_1 \text{ UNION } Q_2) = \mathrm{sol}(S, Q_1) \cup \mathrm{sol}(S, Q_2) \ .$$

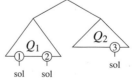

3.3   Filters

The FILTER operator removes solutions of Q not satisfying the constraint c, i.e.,

$$\mathrm{sol}(S, Q \text{ FILTER } c) = \{\sigma \in \mathrm{sol}(S, Q) \mid c(\sigma)\} \ ,$$

where $c(\sigma)$ is true if c is satisfied by σ. The SPARQL reference [16] defines the semantics of the constraints, also in the event of unbound variables.

The FILTER operator may be used a posteriori, to remove solutions which do not satisfy some constraints. This is usually done by existing SPARQL engines. However, such constraints may also be used during the search process in order to prune the search tree. A goal of this paper is to investigate the benefit of using CP, which actively exploits constraints to prune the search space, for solving SPARQL queries.

When the FILTER operator is directly applied to a basic query BQ, the constraints may be simply added to the set of member constraints associated with the query, i.e., $sol(S, BQ\,\text{FILTER}\,c)$ is equal to the set of solutions of the CSP $(X, D, C \cup \{c\})$, where (X, D, C) is the CSP associated with (S, BQ). Of course, finding all solutions to the CSP $(X, D, C \cup c)$ is usually more quickly achieved than finding all solutions to (X, D, C) and then removing those which do not satisfy c.

Filters applied on compound queries can sometimes be *pushed* down onto subqueries [18]. For example $(Q_1\,\text{UNION}\,Q_2)\,\text{FILTER}\,c$ can be rewritten as $(Q_1\,\text{FILTER}\,c)$ UNION $(Q_2\,\text{FILTER}\,c)$. Such query optimization is common in database engines.

4   A CP Operational Modeling of SPARQL Queries

The denotational semantics of SPARQL can be turned into an operational semantics using conventional CP solvers provided they allow posting constraints during the search. Examples of such solvers are Comet [6] or Gecode [8]. We detail the operational semantics of SPARQL queries, i.e., how the set $sol(S, Q)$ is computed. This model can be used for a direct implementation in existing solvers.

To run a query Q in a dataset S, we define a global array of CP variables $X = vars(Q)$. The initial domain of each variable $x \in X$ is $D(x) = U_S \cup L_S$. The set of constraints C is initially empty. To explain the posting of constraints and the search, we use Comet as a notation. The following code solves the query Q.

```
solveall<cp> {
} using {
  sol(Q);
  output();  // print the solution
}
```

The first (empty) block posts the constraints, the second describes the search. The $sol(Q)$ function will be defined for every query type. It posts constraints and introduces choice points. Choice points are either explicit with the try keyword or implicit when labeling variables with label. When a failure is encountered, either explicitly with cp.fail() or implicitly during the propagation of a constraint, the search backtracks to the latest choice point and resumes the execution on the other branch. A backtrack also occurs after outputting a solution at the end of the using block to search for other solutions. We assume a depth-first search expanding branches from left to right.

As we do not label all variables in every branch, the domain of some variables may still be untouched when outputting a solution. Such variables are considered unbound and are not included in the solution. Indeed, we always label all variables of a basic query. Unbound variables do not appear in the basic queries along one branch, due to disjunctions introduced by UNION or inconsistent optional subqueries. No constraints are posted on such variables. Their domains are not reduced.

Figure 3a shows the sol function for a basic query with a filter. The filter is posted with the triples constraints and prunes the search tree from the beginning. In some cases, specific propagators can be used, e.g., for the comparison or arithmetic operators. In all cases we can fall back on an off-the-shelf SPARQL expression evaluator to propagate the condition with forward checking consistency, i.e., when all but one variables are assigned, propagation is realized on the domain of the uninstantiated variable.

Filters on compound queries however can only be checked after each solution of the subquery as shown in Fig. 3b. Note that the condition c is not posted as there may be unbound variables that need to be handled according to the SPARQL specification.

```
function sol(BQ FILTER c) {
  forall((s,p,o) in BQ)
    cp.post(Member((s,p,o),S));
  cp.post(c);
  label(vars(BQ));
}
```

```
function sol(Q FILTER c) {
  sol(Q);
  if( ! c )
    cp.fail();
}
```

(a) Basic query with filter

(b) Compound query with filter

Fig. 3. Filters applied on basic queries are posted as constraints. In all other cases, they are checked after solving the subquery.

Concatenations are computed sequentially as shown in Fig. 4a. The OPTIONAL operator is similar to the concatenation and is shown in Fig. 4b. First, $sol(Q_1)$ is computed. Before executing the second subquery Q_2, a choice point is introduced. The left branch computes $sol(Q_2)$, hence providing solutions to $Q_1 . Q_2$. If it succeeds, the right branch is pruned. Otherwise, the right branch is empty and therefor $sol(Q_1)$ is returned as a solution. Note that this only works with depth first search exploring the left branch first. Finally, for the UNION operator the two subqueries are solved in two separate branches as shown in Fig. 4c.

It is clear that this operational semantics of SPARQL queries computes the set of solutions defined by the declarative modeling.

5 Castor: A Lightweight Solver for the Semantic Web

We now present Castor, a lightweight solver designed to compute SPARQL queries. A query does not involve many variables and constraints. The main challenge is to handle the huge domains associated with the variables. Existing CP solvers do not scale well in this context as shown in the experimental section. The key idea of Castor is to avoid maintaining and backtracking data structures that are proportional to the domain sizes. On the one hand we do not use advanced propagation techniques that need such

```
function
sol(Q₁ . Q₂) {
    sol(Q₁);
    sol(Q₂);
}
```

```
function
sol(Q₁ OPTIONAL Q₂) {
    sol(Q₁);
    Boolean cons(false);
    try<cp> {
        sol(Q₂);
        cons := true;
    }|{
        if(cons)
            cp.fail();
    }
}
```

```
function
sol(Q₁ UNION Q₂) {
    try<cp> {
        sol(Q₁);
    }|{
        sol(Q₂);
    }
}
```

(a) Concatenation   (b) Optional   (c) Union

Fig. 4. Compound queries are solved recursively

expensive structures. On the other hand backtracking is a cheap operation allowing us to explore large trees fast enough to compensate for the loss of propagation.

In this section, we first present the database schema we use to store an RDF dataset. Then, we explain the three major components of the solver: the variables and the representation of their domains, the constraints and their propagators, and the search techniques used to explore the tree.

5.1 Database Schema

To run a query on a dataset, we need data structures to represent the dataset. We settled on an SQLite database. Such a relational database provides efficient lookups through the use of indexes. We use a standard schema designed for RDF applications [9]. It mainly consists of two tables.

- One table contains the set of all values occurring in the dataset, i.e., $U_S \cup L_S$. The values are numbered sequentially starting from 1.
- Another table contains the triples. The table has three columns containing only the identifier number of the value. Indexes are created on all column combinations to allow fast lookups in the table.

We only consider the value identifiers in the solver. We thus loose information about what the values represent. To get such information back quickly, e.g., for evaluating an expression, we load the table of values in memory before starting the search. We estimate a value to take on average 80 bytes. Large datasets contain around 10^8 values, taking 8 GB of memory. Having such amount of memory available is not uncommon in today's servers.

5.2 Variables and Domains Representation

Variables in Castor are integers taking values from 1 up to the number of values in the dataset. There is no direct relation between two numbers. As such, the ordering of the values in the domain of a variable does not matter if bound consistency is not considered. We exploit this property in the data structures of the domains. When backtracking, we only need to restore the sizes of each domain. Such structures are also used in the code computing subgraph isomorphisms presented in [20].

We represent the finite domain $D(x)$ of a variable x by its size and two arrays dom and map. The size first values of dom are in the domain of the variable, the others have been removed (see Fig. 5). The map array maps values to their position in the dom array.

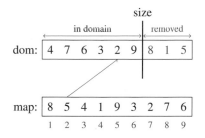

Fig. 5. Example representation of the domain $\{2,3,4,6,7,9\}$, such that size $=6$, when the initial domain is $\{1,\ldots,9\}$. The size first values in dom belong to the domain; the last values are those which have been removed. The map array maps values to their position in dom. For example, value 2 has index 5 in the dom array. In such representation, only the size needs to be restored on backtrack.

The following invariants are enforced.

- Arrays dom and map are coherent, i.e., map$[v] = i \Leftrightarrow$ dom$[i] = v$.
- The domain $D(x)$ is the set of the first size values of dom, i.e.,
  $D(x) = \{$ dom$[i] \mid i \in \{1,\ldots,\text{size}\}\}$.
- Any reduction of the domain does not modify the previously removed values (i.e., the values from size $+ 1$ up to the end of the dom array).

The last invariant allows us to restore only size when backtracking. Indeed, the partition between removed values and values left in the domain will be the same. The order of the values before size may have changed however. The last invariant is respected when using depth-first search, since we keep removing values along one branch before backtracking.

The basic operations on the domain all have a constant time complexity. Checking if a value is still in the domain can be done with the property $v \in D(x) \Leftrightarrow$ map$[v] \le$ size. To remove a value, we swap it with the latest value in the domain and decrease size. For example, to remove value 3 in Fig. 5, we swap the values 3 and 9 in dom, update map accordingly and decrease size by one.

To restrict the domain to a set of values, we *mark* each values to keep, i.e., we swap the value with the left-most non-marked value in dom and increase the count of marked values. We then set the domain size to the count of marked values. The complete operation has a linear time complexity w.r.t. the number of values kept.

5.3 Constraints and Propagators

There are two kinds of constraints in SPARQL queries: triple patterns and filters. Filters on compound queries are only checked after assigning all their variables. Filters on basic queries and triple patterns are posted and exploited during the search. As for domain representation, the goal is to minimize trailable structures that need to be backtracked. In the current prototype of Castor, no such structures exist for constraints.

A constraint in Castor is an object that implements two methods: propagate and restore. When the constraint is created, it registers to events of the variables. The propagate method is called when one of the registered events occurs. The restore method is called when the search backtracks. Currently, each variable has two events: bind, occurring when the domain becomes a singleton, and change, occurring when the domain has changed. To know which values have been removed from a variable since the last execution of the propagator, we store (locally to the constraint) the size of the domain at the end of the propagate method. Removed values are between the new and the old size in the dom array at the next call of the method. The restore method is used to reset the stored sizes after a backtrack. Propagators are called until the fix-point is reached.

Triple patterns. A triple pattern is a table constraint. It reacts on the bind event of the variables. When a variable is bound, we fetch all the consistent triples from the SQLite database and restrict the domains of the remaining unbound variables.

Filters. Checking filters on compound queries is done by an expression evaluator following SPARQL specifications. The evaluator considers all variables with a domain size larger than 1 as unbound. Filters on basic queries are posted together with the triple patterns. The propagator achieves forward checking consistency. As soon as all variables but one are bound, we iterate over the values in the domain of the unbound variable, keeping only values making the expression true.

Some filters can be propagated more efficiently with specialized algorithms. The propagator for $x \neq y$ waits for a value to be assigned to one of the two variables and removes it from the domain of the other variable. There is no need to iterate over all values in the domain. The constraint $x = y$ achieves arc consistency by removing from $D(y)$ the values that have been removed from $D(x)$ and vice versa, reacting to the change event.

5.4 Search

The search tree is defined by using a labeling strategy. At each node, a variable is chosen and a child node is created for each of the values in the domain of the variable. The standard smallest domain heuristic is used for choosing the variable. The order of the values is defined by their current order in the dom array representation.

The search tree is explored with a depth-first search algorithm. Such exploration is required for efficient backtracking of the domains (Section 5.2) and efficient inconsistency check of optional subqueries (Section 4).

To enable posting constraints during the search, we introduce *subtrees*. A subtree has a set of constraints and a set of variables to label. It iterates over all assignments of the variables satisfying the constraints, embedding the backtrack trail. At each assignment, Castor can create a new subtree or output the solution, depending on the query. When a subtree has been completely explored, the domains of the variables are restored to their state when the subtree was created and the constraints are removed. The search can then continue in the previous subtree.

6   Experimental Results

To assess the feasibility and the performances of our approach, we have run queries from the SPARQL Performance Benchmark (SP^{2}Bench) [17]. SP^{2}Bench consists of a deterministic program generating an RDF dataset of configurable size, and 12 representative queries. The datasets represent relationships between fictive academic papers and their authors, following the model of academic publications in the DBLP database. The benchmark includes both basic and compound queries, but only makes use of simple comparison filters. We removed unsupported solution modifiers like DISTINCT and ORDER BY from the queries. We focus on the queries identified as difficult by the SP^{2}Bench authors (q4, q5, q6 and q7) as well as one simpler query (q2) and two queries involving the UNION operator (q8 and q9). We thus consider 8 queries as q5 comes in two flavors.

We compare the performances of three engines: the state-of-the-art SPARQL engine Sesame [4], the lightweight solver Castor described in Section 5 and a direct implementation of the operational semantics in Comet [6]. The Comet implementation loads the whole dataset in memory. It uses the built-in table constraint for the triple patterns and built-in expressions for the filters. Sesame was run both using an on-disk store and an in-memory store.

We have generated 6 datasets of 10k, 25k, 250k, 1M and 5M triples. We have performed three cold runs of each query over all the generated datasets, i.e., the engines were restarted and the databases cleared between two runs. Such setting corresponds to the one used by the authors of SP^{2}Bench. All experiments were conducted on an Intel Pentium 4 2.40 GHz computer running Ubuntu Linux 10.10 with 2 GB of DDR-400 RAM and a 160 GB Maxtor 6Y160P0 ATA/133 disk. We report the time spent to solve the queries, not including the time needed to load the datasets. We checked that all engines find the exact same set of solutions.

Figure 6 shows the execution time of the considered queries. Note that both axes have logarithmic scales. We now discuss the results for each query.

Simple query. Query q2 has the form BQ_1 OPTIONALBQ_2. BQ_1 is a basic query with 9 variables and 9 triple patterns. The optional part BQ_2 has a single triple pattern with only one variable not appearing in BQ_1. Executing subquery BQ_2 can thus be done by one access to the database. Sesame and Castor perform equally well. Comet however suffers from the heavy data structures.

Filters. Queries q4 and q5a are similar. Both are basic queries with one filter. Query q4 has 7 variables, 8 triple patterns and a filter $x_1 < x_2$ on two variables x_1 and x_2. Query

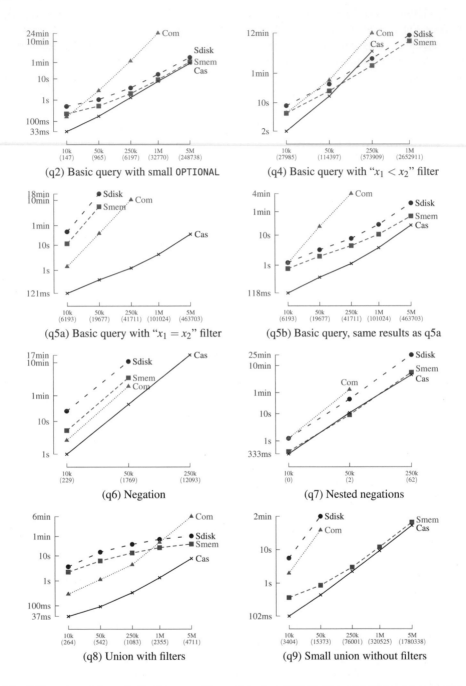

Fig. 6. Experimental results for Sesame with on-disk store (Sdisk), Sesame with in-memory store (Smem), Comet (Com) and Castor (Cas). The x-axis represents the dataset size in terms of number of triples. The y-axis is the query execution time. Both axes have a logarithmic scale. The number of solutions is written in parentheses.

q5a has 6 variables, 6 triple patterns and a filter $x_1 = x_2$. The CP engines are able to outperform Sesame on q5a thanks to their efficient propagation of the equality constraint. We suspect this constraint to be post-processed in Sesame. Query q4 however shows the opposite situation. It has many more solutions than q5a ($2.65 \cdot 10^6$ versus $1.01 \cdot 10^5$ for the dataset with 1M triples). As such, filtering is not the bottleneck anymore. Solving the query mostly involves pure database access.

The two flavors of q5, q5a and q5b, compute exactly the same set of solutions. The latter encodes the equality constraint into its 5 triple patterns using 4 variables. Unsurprisingly, the CP engines perform similarly on both queries as they exploit the filters early-on during the search. Sesame handles the filter-less query much better than q5a. This shows the relevance of our approach, especially considering filters are present in about half of the real-world queries [2].

Negations. A negation in SPARQL is a compound query that has the form (Q_1 OPTIONAL Q_2) FILTER (!bound(x)), where x is a variable appearing only in Q_2. The filter removes all solutions assigning a value to x, i.e., we keep only solutions of Q_1 that cannot be extended into solutions of $Q_1 . Q_2$. Query q6 is one such negation with additional filters inside Q_2. Query q7 has no additional filters, but Q_2 is itself a nested negation. Counter-intuitively, q6 is actually more difficult than q7. Possible reasons are given in [17]. Castor has better results than Sesame for the former query and behaves similarly to Sesame on the latter.

Unions. The compound queries q8 and q9 use the UNION operator. The former adds inequality filters in both its subqueries. The subqueries of the latter contain only two triple patterns each. Yet, q9 generates many solutions. Neither Comet with its heavy structures nor Sesame with its on-disk store are able to go beyond 50k triples. Castor and Sesame with in-memory store are close to each other. In query q8, the two alternative subqueries have some duplicate triple patterns. Exploiting such property might explain the relative flatness of Sesame's execution time compared to Castor.

Conclusion. Table 1 shows the relative speed of Castor w.r.t. Sesame using an in-memory store. The goal of Castor is to use CP to solve very constrained queries, i.e., queries where filters eliminate many solutions. Such queries (e.g., q5a and q6) are handled much more efficiently by Castor than by Sesame. On queries relying more on database access (e.g., q2 and q9), the CP approach is still competitive.

Table 1. Speedup of Castor w.r.t. Sesame with in-memory store. The letter 'C' (resp. 'S') means only Castor (resp. Sesame) was able to solve the instance within the time limit.

	q2	q4	q5a	q5b	q6	q7	q8	q9
10k	6.75	2.95	94.15	6.51	5.13	1.21	61.52	3.60
50k	3.03	1.38	799.26	5.01	6.38	0.84	68.91	1.94
250k	1.54	0.41	C	3.93	C	1.24	39.32	1.34
1M	1.19	S	C	2.79	—	—	15.99	1.29
5M	1.19	—	C	2.00	—	—	3.81	1.24

7 Discussion

We proposed a declarative modeling and operational semantics for solving SPARQL queries using the Constraint Programming framework. We introduced a specialized lightweight solver implementing the semantics. We showed that the approach outperforms the state of the art on very constrained queries, and is competitive on most other queries.

Related work. Mamoulis and Stergiou have used CSPs to solve complex XPath queries over XML documents [13]. XML documents can be viewed as graphs, like RDF data[3], but with an underlying tree structure. Such structure is used by the authors to design specific propagators. However, they cannot be used for SPARQL queries.

Mouhoub and Feng applied constraint programming to solve combinatorial queries in relational databases [14]. Such queries involve joining multiple tables subject to relatively complex arithmetic constraints. The problem is similar to SPARQL. However, the authors do not deal with large datasets. Their experiments are limited to tables with 800 rows. Such size is not realistic for RDF data.

Other work aims at extending the standard SQL query language to support explicit constraint satisfaction expressions [12,19]. This allows to solve CSPs within relational databases.

Future work. Two paths are possible. On the one hand, we can create a full-in-memory engine, getting rid of the SQLite database. More advanced propagators for the table constraint could then be used. While such engine would not scale well, it could still be of interest for very complex queries on small to medium-sized datasets. On the other hand, we can make a heavier database usage, eliminating the need to load all values in memory. The current propagators for triple patterns and equality constraints already do not need to know the meaning of a value. The query can also be preprocessed to reduce the initial domain before the variables are created to further reduce the memory consumption.

In both cases, specialized propagators need to be written for the various SPARQL expressions. Other consistency levels, e.g., bound consistency, may be considered for such tasks. Different variable selection heuristics can be investigated. More comprehensive benchmarks with other engines also needs to be done.

Acknowledgments. The authors want to thank the anonymous reviewers for their insightful comments. The first author is supported as a Research Assistant by the Belgian FNRS (National Fund for Scientific Research). This research is also partially supported by the Interuniversity Attraction Poles Programme (Belgian State, Belgian Science Policy) and the FRFC project 2.4504.10 of the Belgian FNRS. This work was done in the context of project SATTIC (ANR grant Blanc07-1 184534).

References

1. Angles, R., Gutierrez, C.: The expressive power of SPARQL. In: Sheth, A.P., Staab, S., Dean, M., Paolucci, M., Maynard, D., Finin, T., Thirunarayan, K. (eds.) ISWC 2008. LNCS, vol. 5318, pp. 114–129. Springer, Heidelberg (2008)

---

[3] XML is in fact one of the syntaxes of RDF.

2. Arias, M., Fernández, J.D., Martínez-Prieto, M.A., de la Fuente, P.: An empirical study of real-world SPARQL queries. In: 1st International Workshop on Usage Analysis and the Web of Data (USEWOD 2011), in Conjunction with WWW 2011 (2011)
3. Baget, J.F.: RDF entailment as a graph homomorphism. In: Gil, Y., Motta, E., Benjamins, V.R., Musen, M.A. (eds.) ISWC 2005. LNCS, vol. 3729, pp. 82–96. Springer, Heidelberg (2005)
4. Broekstra, J., Kampman, A., van Harmelen, F.: Sesame: A generic architecture for storing and querying RDF and RDF Schema. In: Horrocks, I., Hendler, J. (eds.) ISWC 2002. LNCS, vol. 2342, pp. 54–68. Springer, Heidelberg (2002)
5. Cafarella, M.J., Halevy, A., Madhavan, J.: Structured data on the web. Commun. ACM 54, 72–79 (2011)
6. Dynamic Decision Technologies Inc.: Comet (2010), http://www.dynadec.com
7. Erling, O., Mikhailov, I.: RDF support in the Virtuoso DBMS. In: Networked Knowledge – Networked Media. SCI, vol. 221, pp. 7–24. Springer, Heidelberg (2009)
8. Gecode Team: Gecode: Generic constraint development environment (2006), http://www.gecode.org
9. Harris, S., Shadbolt, N.: SPARQL query processing with conventional relational database systems. In: Dean, M., Guo, Y., Jun, W., Kaschek, R., Krishnaswamy, S., Pan, Z., Sheng, Q.Z. (eds.) WISE 2005 Workshops. LNCS, vol. 3807, pp. 235–244. Springer, Heidelberg (2005)
10. Harris, S., Lamb, N., Shadbolt, N.: 4store: The design and implementation of a clustered RDF store. In: 5th International Workshop on Scalable Semantic Web Knowledge Base Systems (SSWS 2009), at ISWC 2009 (2009)
11. Klyne, G., Carroll, J.J., McBride, B.: Resource description framework (RDF): Concepts and abstract syntax (2004), http://www.w3.org/TR/2004/REC-rdf-concepts-20040210/
12. Lohfert, R., Lu, J., Zhao, D.: Solving SQL constraints by incremental translation to SAT. In: Nguyen, N.T., Borzemski, L., Grzech, A., Ali, M. (eds.) IEA/AIE 2008. LNCS (LNAI), vol. 5027, pp. 669–676. Springer, Heidelberg (2008)
13. Mamoulis, N., Stergiou, K.: Constraint satisfaction in semi-structured data graphs. In: Wallace, M. (ed.) CP 2004. LNCS, vol. 3258, pp. 393–407. Springer, Heidelberg (2004)
14. Mouhoub, M., Feng, C.: CSP techniques for solving combinatorial queries within relational databases. In: Nguyen, N.T., Szczerbicki, E. (eds.) Intelligent Systems for Knowledge Management. SCI, vol. 252, pp. 131–151. Springer, Heidelberg (2009)
15. Pérez, J., Arenas, M., Gutierrez, C.: Semantics and complexity of SPARQL. ACM Trans. Database Syst. 34, 16:1–16:45 (2009)
16. Prud'hommeaux, E., Seaborne, A.: SPARQL query language for RDF (January 2008), http://www.w3.org/TR/2008/REC-rdf-sparql-query-20080115/
17. Schmidt, M., Hornung, T., Lausen, G., Pinkel, C.: SP^{2}Bench: A SPARQL performance benchmark. In: Proc. IEEE 25th Int. Conf. Data Engineering, ICDE 2009, pp. 222–233 (2009)
18. Schmidt, M., Meier, M., Lausen, G.: Foundations of SPARQL query optimization. In: Proceedings of the 13th International Conference on Database Theory, ICDT 2010, pp. 4–33. ACM, New York (2010)
19. Siva, S., Wang, L.: A SQL database system for solving constraints. In: Proceeding of the 2nd PhD Workshop on Information and Knowledge Management, PIKM 2008, pp. 1–8. ACM, New York (2008)
20. Solnon, C.: Alldifferent-based filtering for subgraph isomorphism. Artificial Intelligence 174(12-13), 850–864 (2010)

On Guaranteeing Polynomially Bounded
Search Tree Size

David A. Cohen[1], Martin C. Cooper[2,*],
Martin J. Green[1], and Dániel Marx[3,**]

[1] Dept. of Computer Science, Royal Holloway, University of London, UK
[2] IRIT, University of Toulouse III, 31062 Toulouse, France
[3] Institut für Informatik, Humboldt-Universität zu Berlin, Germany

Abstract. Much work has been done on describing tractable classes of
constraint networks. Most of the known tractable examples are described
by either restricting the structure of the networks, or their language. Indeed, for both structural or language restrictions very strong dichotomy
results have been proven and in both cases it is likely that all practical
examples have already been discovered.

As such it is timely to consider tractability which cannot be described
by language or structural restrictions. This is the focus of the work here.

In this paper we investigate a novel reason for tractability: having at
least one variable ordering for which the number of partial solutions to
the first n variables is bounded by a polynomial in n.

We show that the presence of sufficient functional constraints can
guarantee this property and we investigate the complexity of finding
good variable orderings based on different notions of functionality.

What is more we identify a completely novel reason for tractability
based on so called Turan sets.

Keywords: Constraint satisfaction, satisfiability, hybrid tractability,
functional constraints, Turan tractability, variable ordering.

1 Introduction

A *constraint network* consists of a collection of *variables*, each of which must take
its value from a specified *domain*. Some subsets of these variables have a further
limitation, called a *constraint*, on the values they may simultaneously take. Thus
a constraint has two components: a list of variables called its *scope*, and a set of
allowed valuations that this list may be assigned, called its *relation* [10].

The set of relations occurring in a particular constraint network is often called
the *language* of the network. The scopes of a constraint network, abstracted as
sets of variables, are called the *structure* of the network.

It is natural to define tractable classes of constraint networks by restricting
the language or the structure. It is conjectured that there is a dichotomy for all

---

* Martin Cooper is supported by ANR Project ANR-10-BLAN-0210.
** Dániel Marx is supported by the Alexander von Humboldt Foundation.

constraint languages: they are either tractable or NP-hard [7]. This dichotomy has been made explicit by Bulatov [2]. Since much work has been done in this area we have a growing base of evidence for this conjecture.

On the other hand, the work on structural tractability is even further advanced. Grohe [8] showed that a set of structures is tractable if and only if the tree-width of their cores is bounded.

In this paper we extend the classical theory of constraint network tractability beyond the artificial distinction between language and structure. Such *hybrid* tractability is just beginning to be systematically studied [3,11,13].

We will exhibit two novel polytime-testable hybrid properties of constraint networks which guarantee a polynomial-size search tree as well as a polynomial number of solutions. Classes defined by such properties are clearly tractable. Indeed, in such cases, polytime solvability is preserved even after the addition of any number of arbitrary constraints and/or the addition of any polytime objective function, since it suffices to test the extra constraints and/or evaluate the objective function for each of the polynomial number of solutions.

We say that a constraint is *functional* [6] on one of its variables if the value of this variable is uniquely determined by an assignment to the rest of the variables of the scope. Examples include functional dependencies in databases, or mathematical constraints of the form $X_i = f(X_{i_1}, \ldots, X_{i_r})$. In particular, linear constraints are functional in all variables. A constraint network with sufficient functional constraints has the property for which we are looking.

In the second case we use a structure from combinatorial mathematics called a Turan set. By making sure that constraints with sufficiently tight relations have scopes which form a Turan set we can find a polynomial bound on the number of partial solutions to any subset of the variables.

We show that the constraints required by the Turan example generalise functional constraints and so there is an overlap between these two classes. However, the classes are incomparable as the first guarantees at most one solution whilst the second allows for more general global constraint types.

The paper is structured as follows. In Sect. 2 we introduce the necessary basic definitions and give a motivating example. Section 3 is a study of different forms of functional constraint networks. Section 4 presents a novel tractable class which guarantees a polynomial bound on the number of solutions, but which is not based on any form of functionality.

2   Background

We first define the problem we are trying to solve.

Definition 1. *A **constraint network** is a triple $\langle V, D, C \rangle$ where:*

- *V is a finite set of variables;*
- *D is a finite domain;*
- *C is a set of constraints. Each **constraint** $c \in C$ consists of a pair $c = \langle \sigma(c), \rho(c) \rangle$ where $\sigma(c) \in V^*$, the constraint **scope**, is a list of variables and $\rho(c) \subseteq D^{|\sigma(c)|}$, is the constraint **relation**.*

A **solution** to $P = \langle V, D, C \rangle$ is a mapping $s : V \to D$ which satisfies each constraint. That is, for each $\langle \sigma, \rho \rangle \in C$, $s(\sigma) \in \rho$.

For any set of variables $X \subseteq V$ we have the standard notion of the **induced network** $P[X] = \langle X, D, C' \rangle$ on X, where, for every $c \in C$ whose scope includes at least one variable of X there is a corresponding induced constraint $c[X] \in C'$. The scope of $c[X]$ is the sublist of variables of σ that occur in X and the relation of $c[X]$ consists of those tuples of values that extend to tuples in ρ.

We assume that constraint relations are explicitly stored and so $|\langle V, D, C \rangle| = \sum_{\langle \sigma, \rho \rangle \in C} \log(|D|)|\sigma||\rho| + \log(|V|)|\sigma|$.

2.1 Ordered Polynomial Tractability

We are interested in constraint networks for which we only ever generate a polynomial number of partial solutions during complete backtrack search. As such we are interested in networks which have particularly well behaved variable orderings.

Definition 2. *A class of constraint networks is **ordered polynomial** if there is some polynomial p such that, for any such instance P, there is some ordering $x_1 < x_2 < \ldots < x_n$ of the variables of P where, for each $i = 1, \ldots, n$ the induced network $P[\{x_1, \ldots, x_i\}]$ has at most $p(|P[\{x_1, \ldots, x_i\}]|)$ solutions.*

Example 1. This example describes the tractable class of constraint networks with fractional edge cover number at most k discovered by Grohe and Marx [9].

For any constraint network $P = \langle V, D, C \rangle$ we define the structure of P to be the hypergraph $H(P)$ with vertex set V and a hyperedge for each constraint scope (abstracted as a set of variables).

A fractional edge cover of the hypergraph $\langle V, E \rangle$ is a mapping $\psi : E \to \mathbb{Q}^+$ such that, for every $v \in V$, $\sum_{e \in E, v \in e} \psi(e) \geq 1$. The weight of ψ is $\sum_{e \in E} \psi(e)$ and the fractional weight, $\rho^* H$, of H is the minimum weight of all fractional edge covers of H.

Grohe and Marx [9] proved that the number of solutions to any constraint network P is at most $|P|^{\rho^*(H(P))}$.

Since the fractional edge cover number of any induced network is at most that of the original network it follows that the class of constraint networks with fractional edge cover number at most k is ordered polynomial.

Grohe and Marx proved that enumerating all solutions can be done in time $|I|^{\rho^*(H(I))+O(1)}$. We generalise this result to arbitrary ordered polynomial classes.

Proposition 1. *Let $P = \langle V, D, C \rangle$ be any constraint network with variable ordering $x_1 < x_2 < \ldots < x_n$ such that the induced network $P[\{x_1, \ldots, x_i\}]$ can be solved in time $p(|P[\{x_1, \ldots, x_i\}]|)$. All solutions to P can be enumerated in time $p(|P|).|P|^2$.*

Proof. For $i = 1, \ldots, |V|$ the algorithm generates a list L_i of solutions to $P[\{x_1, \ldots, x_i\}]$. The list L_1 contains at most $|D|$ solutions. Since every solution in L_{i+1} induces a solution in L_i by projection, to find L_{i+1} we have only to find those solutions in L_i which extend to a solution of $P[\{x_1, \ldots, x_{i+1}\}]$. Clearly this extension can be done in time $|L_i|.|D|.|P[\{x_1, \ldots, x_{i+1}\}]|$.

Now since $|P[\{x_1, \ldots, x_{i+1}\}]| \geq |P[\{x_1, \ldots, x_i\}]|$ we can bound the total running time by $|V|.|D|.p(|P|).|P| \leq p(|P|).|P|^2$.

3   Functional Constraint Networks

In this section, we begin by studying the class of constraint networks which have sufficient functional constraints to guarantee backtrack free search.

Functional constraints have been extensively studied in the case of *binary* networks [6,4,5]. We extend previous studies to the case of functional constraints of arbitrary arity and generalise to the case of incrementally-functional networks.

Definition 3. *A constraint $\langle \sigma, \rho \rangle$ is **functional** on variable $i \in \sigma$ if ρ contains no two tuples differing only at variable i.*

*A constraint network P is **functional** if there exists a variable ordering $x_1 < x_2 < \ldots < x_n$ such that, for all $i \in \{1, \ldots, n\}$, there is some constraint of $P[\{x_1, \ldots, x_i\}]$ that is functional on x_i.*

Example 2. Consider the following constraint network with variables $\{x_1, \ldots, x_4\}$ and domain the integers modulo 7: $\{0, \ldots, 6\}$.

We have four constraints: $x_1 = 4, 2x_1 + x_2 = 5, 3x_1 + 4x_2 + x_3 = 2$ and $x_1 + x_2 + x_3 + x_4 = 0$.

With respect to the ordering $x_1 < x_2 < x_3 < x_4$ this is a functional network. The unique solution is: $x_1 = 4, x_2 = 4, x_3 = 2, x_4 = 4$.

Any functional network always has at most one solution. Furthermore, functional networks form a tractable class: they are both identifiable and solvable in polynomial time. We will, in fact, prove this for the much larger class defined below.

Definition 4. *A constraint network P is **incrementally functional** if there is an ordering $x_1 < x_2 < \ldots < x_n$ of its variables such that for all $i \in \{1, \ldots, n-1\}$, each solution to $P[\{x_1, \ldots, x_i\}]$ extends to at most one solution to $P[\{x_1, \ldots, x_{i+1}\}]$.*

An incrementally functional constraint network has at most one solution.

Proposition 2. *The number of nodes in the backtracking search tree of an incrementally functional constraint network is $O(n)$ when the variables are instantiated according to the correct ordering.*

It is possible to determine in polynomial time whether a network P is incrementally functional. This is a corollary of the following result which says that we can determine in polynomial time the maximum-cardinality subset $M \subseteq \{1, \ldots, n\}$ such that $P[M]$ is incrementally functional. This provides us with a simple variable-ordering heuristic: if the variables in M are instantiated in the order that makes $P[M]$ incrementally functional, then, in the backtracking search tree, there is no branching at any of the variables of M.

Proposition 3. *Given a constraint network $P = \langle V, D, C \rangle$, it is possible to find in polynomial time the maximum-cardinality set $M \subseteq V$ such that $P[M]$ is incrementally functional.*

Proof. We initialize M to the empty set and a_M to the empty tuple. We then use a greedy algorithm to repeatedly add variables i to M if there is *at most* one value a_i for i which is consistent with the partial assignment a_M. If such an a_i exists then a_M is extended to include the assignment of a_i to i. If a_M has no consistent extension to variables $M \cup \{i\}$, then we halt, returning V (since, in this case, the conditions of Definition 4 are satisfied on i and so trivially on all variables not in $M \cup \{i\}$).

Consider the set M returned by this greedy algorithm. Suppose that $P[M']$ is incrementally functional where $|M'| > |M|$. Without loss of generality, we can assume that $M' = \{1, \dots, t\}$ and that the variable ordering which makes P incrementally functional on M' is the usual ordering of the integers. Let $i = \min(M' \setminus M)$ and let $X = \{j \in M' : j < i\}$. Since $i \in M'$, all consistent assignments to the variables P can be extended to at most one consistent assignment to the variables $X \cup \{i\}$. But, by choice of i, $X \subseteq M$, and hence all consistent assignments to the variables M can be extended to at most one consistent assignment to the variables $M \cup \{i\}$. Thus, i would have been added to M by our greedy algorithm. This contradiction completes the proof.

Corollary 1. *It is possible to determine in polynomial time whether a constraint network is incrementally functional.*

For the constraint network $P = \langle V, D, C \rangle$, if the induced network $P[M]$ is incrementally functional, then after instantiating the variables in $V - M$, P becomes incrementally functional. The converse is not necessarily true, in the sense that P may be incrementally functional on all remaining variables after instantiation of the variables in a proper subset of $V - M$. This leads us to notions which are related to strong backdoor sets.

In a SAT instance, given a polynomial-time algorithm A (such as unit-propagation), a set X of variables is a **strong backdoor set** with respect to A if, for any assignment to the variables in X, the algorithm A determines whether or not this assignment can be extended to a complete solution. The set of problem instances having a strong backdoor set of size $O(\log n)$ is a hybrid tractable class [17], but does not provide a polynomial bound on the number of solutions. Szeider [15] showed that when the SAT algorithm A is unit propagation, pure literal elimination or a combination of both of these, the detection of a strong backdoor set (with respect to A) of size bounded by a fixed integer k is W[P]-complete. This means that it is highly unlikely that smallest backdoor sets can be found more efficiently than by exhaustive search.

The remainder of this section is devoted to types of backdoor sets, called *root sets*, defined in terms of simple forms of functionality.

Definition 5. *In a constraint network $P = \langle V, D, C \rangle$, a **root set** is a subset Q of the variables for which there exists a variable ordering $x_1 < x_2 < \dots < x_n$*

such that, for all $i \in V - Q$, there is some constraint of $P[\{x_1, \ldots, x_i\}]$ that is functional on x_i.

The existence of a root set Q means that the constraint network I will become functional after instantiation of all variables in Q. It is therefore of interest to find a minimum-cardinality root set. David [5] showed that this can be achieved in polynomial time in the case of binary CSPs. Unfortunately, if I contains ternary functional constraints, then finding the minimum-cardinality root set is NP-hard, as we now show.

Theorem 1. *The problem of finding a minimum-cardinality root set in a ternary constraint network is NP-hard, for all $d \geq 2$ (where d is the maximum domain size).*

Proof. We demonstrate a polynomial reduction from MAX CLIQUE (which is known to be NP-complete [12]). Let G be a graph with n vertices $1, \ldots, n$ and m edges. For simplicity of presentation, we identify a clique C in G with its vertex set. We will construct a ternary constraint network P_G such that $\{X_i : i \notin C\} \cup \{X_0\}$ is a minimum-cardinality root set of P_G if and only if C is a maximum clique in G.

We first give an example of a ternary functional constraint which is functional on only one of its variables. Let R_3 denote the relation $\{\langle 0, 0, 0 \rangle, \langle 0, 1, 0 \rangle, \langle 1, 0, 0 \rangle, \langle 1, 1, 1 \rangle\}$. It is straightforward to verify that R_3 is functional only on its third variable.

The constraint network P_G has a "dummy" variable X_0 (which, by construction, must appear in every root set) as well as a variable X_i corresponding to each of the n vertices of G. Apart from these variables X_i $(i = 0, \ldots, n)$, P_G has two other types of variables: non-edge variables denoted by Y_i $(1 \leq i \leq M$ where $M = \frac{n}{2}(n-1) - m)$ and cascade variables Z_j^i $(i = 1, \ldots, n; 1 \leq j \leq N)$. For each pair of distinct vertices $j, k \in \{1, \ldots, n\}$ which are not connected by an edge in G, there is a corresponding non-edge variable Y_i in P_G together with two ternary functional constraints: $\langle \langle X_0, X_j, Y_i \rangle, R_3 \rangle$ and $\langle \langle X_0, X_k, Y_i \rangle, R_3 \rangle$. These constraints are both functional on Y_i and are the only constraints of P_G which are functional on Y_i.

For each of the X_i variables, there is a cascade of ternary functional constraints from the set of *all* the non-edge variables Y_j $(1 \leq j \leq M)$ to X_i. This is illustrated in Fig. 1 which shows a cascade from the variables $Y_1, \ldots, Y_8$ to the variable X_i via the cascade variables $Z_1^i, \ldots, Z_6^i$. Each two-tailed arrow represents a ternary functional constraint from the two tail variables to the head variable: if U, V are the tail variables and W the head variable, then there is the constraint $\langle \langle U, V, W \rangle, R_3 \rangle$ in P_G. We require a total of $N = n(2^{\lceil \log_2 M \rceil} - 2) = O(n^3)$ cascade variables.

For any subset $C \subseteq \{1, \ldots, n\}$ of the vertices of G, denote by R_C the set $\{X_i : i \notin C\} \cup \{X_0\}$. C is a clique if and only if R_C contains one of X_j, X_k for each non-edge $\{j, k\}$ in G. We claim that, by construction of P_G, this is a necessary and sufficient condition for R_C to be a root set of P_G. For each non-edge $\{j, k\}$ with corresponding variable Y_i in P_G, the only functional constraints

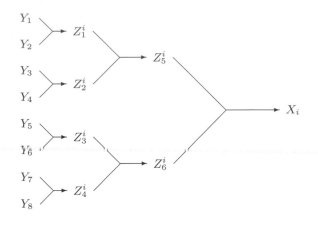

Fig. 1. Example of a cascade of variables from the variables $Y_1, \ldots, Y_8$ to variable X_i

on Y_i are $\langle\langle X_0, X_j, Y_i\rangle, R_3\rangle$ and $\langle\langle X_0, X_k, Y_i\rangle, R_3\rangle$; hence R_C is a root set only if it contains one of X_j, X_k. If R_C contains one of X_j, X_k for each non-edge $\{j, k\}$ in G, then any ordering which places the variables in R_C first, then the variables $\{Y_i : 1 \leq i \leq M\}$, then the variables $\{Z_j^i : 1 \leq i \leq n, \ 1 \leq j \leq N\}$ and finally the variables $\{X_i : i \leq i \leq n\} - R_C$ satisfies the conditions of Definition 5.

It is possible to replace some number of the X_i variables $(1 \leq i \leq n)$ in the root set R_C by some number of the Y_j and Z_k^i variables (for example, X_i in Fig. 1 could be replaced by Z_5^i, Z_6^i), but, by our construction, this never reduces the cardinality of the root set. We can conclude that R_C is a minimum-cardinality root set of P_G if and only if C is a maximum clique in G. This reduction from MAX CLIQUE is clearly polynomial.

4   Turan Sets

In this section, we study conditions which guarantee the existence of only a polynomial number of solutions, but which are not so restrictive as to guarantee the existence of at most one solution. Very little work appears to have been done in this area.

We will define a class of constraint networks, the k-Turan networks, with this property, which have many constraints with small scopes that each satisfy a weak tightness condition. This contrasts with networks of bounded fractional edge cover number [9] which require quite large scopes. Many of the well-known global constraints [1] satisfy the k-Turan tightness restriction, but we have only space to give the (simple) proofs for functional constraints (Proposition 4) and Boolean clauses (Corollary 3).

To simplify our proofs we define a technical device: the *domain pair arity function* (DPAF). For any particular DPAF, α, we can then capture the class of constraint networks which are α-*restrictive*, which we prove to have a polynomial bound on the number of solutions. The k-Turan networks are α-restrictive for a *constant* DPAF, α, but a direct proof of the polynomial bound (Theorem 3) is simplified by first proving the general result, Theorem 2, using an induction on the weight of a general DPAF.

Definition 6. *U^* is the set of all lists of elements of U and $[a,b]^{|\sigma|}$ is the set of length $|\sigma|$ tuples consisting of just a's and b's.*

*For any domain D we define a **domain pair arity function (DPAF)** to be a symmetric mapping $\alpha : D^2 \to \mathbb{N}^+$.*

*The **weight** of α is then defined as $\mathrm{wt}(\alpha) = \sum_{\{a,b\} \subseteq D} \alpha(a,b)$.*

*For any DPAF α we say that constraint network $P = \langle V, D, C \rangle$ is α-**restrictive** if*

$$\forall \{a,b\} \subseteq D, U \subseteq V, |U| = \alpha(a,b), \exists \langle \sigma, \rho \rangle \in C, \sigma \in U^* \text{ and } [a,b]^{|\sigma|} \not\subseteq \rho .$$

Let $F(n, D, \alpha)$ be the maximum number of solutions to any α-restrictive constraint network with domain D and n variables.

Theorem 2. $F(n, D, \alpha) \leq n^{\mathrm{wt}(\alpha)}$.

Proof. Let D be any domain and α be any DPAF. Choose an n variable α-restrictive constraint network $P = \langle V, D, C \rangle$ with $F(n, D, \alpha)$ solutions.

Choose any variable $x \in V$. We say that a pair of solutions to P are an $\{a,b\}$-pair at x if they differ only in their value for variable x: one having value a, the other value b.

Let $S_{\{a,b\}}$ be the solutions to P which are in $\{a,b\}$-pairs. Let S_1 be the solutions to P that are in no $\{a,b\}$-pair for any $\{a,b\} \subseteq D$.

We get an upper bound on the number of solutions to P, $F(n, D, \alpha)$, by counting the size of these sets.

First, for any $\{a,b\}$ where $\alpha(a,b) > 1$, consider the set $S_{\{a,b\}}$.

Choose any $U \subseteq V$ with $x \in U$ and $|U| = \alpha(a,b)$.

Since P is α-restrictive there is a constraint $\langle \sigma, \rho \rangle \in C$ for which $\sigma \subseteq U^*$ and $[a,b]^{|\sigma|} \not\subseteq \rho$. Hence the restriction of $S_{\{a,b\}}$ to $U - \{x\}$ cannot contain $[a,b]^{|U|-1}$.

So, for each such U, we can build a constraint with scope $U - \{x\}$ that allows all solutions in $S_{\{a,b\}}$, but whose relation does not contain $[a,b]^{|U|-1}$.

Add all such constraints to the induced network $P[V - \{x\}]$ to obtain the $\alpha^{\{a,b\}-}$-restrictive network $P(a,b)$. By construction, every solution in $S_{\{a,b\}}$ restricted to $V - \{x\}$ is a solution to $P(a,b)$. Since every element of $S_{\{a,b\}}$ has value either a or b at x we know that the number of solutions to $P(a,b)$ is at least half of the size of $S_{\{a,b\}}$.

Now consider the set S_1. Each solution to $P[V - \{x\}]$ extends to at most one element of S_1, so the α-restrictive network $P[V - \{x\}]$ has precisely $|S_1|$ solutions that extend to an element of S_1.

Finally, observe that if $\alpha(a,b) = 1$ then $S_{\{a,b\}}$ is empty since there is a constraint with scope $\langle x \rangle$ whose relation does not contain $[a,b]$.

Defining

$$\alpha^{\{a,b\}-}(x,y) = \begin{cases} \alpha(x,y) - 1 & \text{if } \{x,y\} = \{a,b\}, \\ \alpha(x,y) & \text{otherwise.} \end{cases}$$

we have shown that:

$$F(n, D, \alpha) \leq \left(\sum_{\{a,b\} \subseteq D, \alpha(a,b) > 1} 2F(n-1, D, \alpha^{\{a,b\}-}) \right) + F(n-1, D, \alpha) \ . \quad (1)$$

We now prove the theorem by induction on the weight of α.

The base case is when α is identically 1. Here $F(n, D, \alpha) = 1$ since in the solution set to any α-restrictive constraint network we can have, for each variable, at most one of each pair of domain values.

For the inductive step we can assume that $F(n, D, \alpha') \leq n^{\mathrm{wt}(\alpha')}$ whenever $\mathrm{wt}(\alpha') < \mathrm{wt}(\alpha)$. Using inequality (1) we now obtain

$$F(n, D, \alpha) \leq \binom{D}{2}(n-1)^{\mathrm{wt}(\alpha)-1} + (n-1)^{\mathrm{wt}(\alpha)} \ .$$

It therefore remains to show that

$$n^{\mathrm{wt}(\alpha)} \geq \binom{D}{2}(n-1)^{\mathrm{wt}(\alpha)-1} + (n-1)^{\mathrm{wt}(\alpha)}.$$

We can rewrite this inequality as:

$$\left(1 + \frac{1}{n-1}\right)^{\mathrm{wt}(\alpha)} \geq \frac{\binom{D}{2}}{(n-1)} + 1 \ .$$

This equality must hold since $\mathrm{wt}(\alpha) \geq \binom{D}{2}$.

Given an arbitrary DPAF α it is clear that if P is α-restrictive then so is every network induced by P on a subset of its variables. It follows immediately from Theorem 2 and Proposition 1 that the class of α-restrictive constraint networks is polynomially solvable for any fixed domain size.

Corollary 2. *For any fixed domain D and DPAF α the class of α-good constraint networks over domain D is polynomial time solvable.*

Now we will need the notion of a Turan set in order to define classes of α-restrictive networks for a constant function α. This will allow us not only to give some concrete examples of tractable classes but also to estimate the minimum number of constraints in an α-restrictive constraint network.

Definition 7. *We say that a subset of variables σ **represents** another set τ if σ is contained in τ.*

*An (n, k)-**Turan system** is a pair $\langle \chi, \mathcal{B} \rangle$ where $\mathcal{B}$ is a collection of subsets of the n-element set χ such that every k-element subset of χ is represented by some set in $\mathcal{B}$. The size of the system $\langle \chi, \mathcal{B} \rangle$ is the number of subsets in $\mathcal{B}$.*

The restricted notion of a Turan system where every member is required to have precisely $r < k$ elements has been well-studied in the mathematics community and, for many set of parameters, minimal size examples are known [14,16].

Definition 8. *An n-variable constraint network over domain D is said to be k-**Turan** if the scopes of the constraints $\langle \sigma, \rho \rangle$ for which:*

$$\forall a, b \in D, [a, b]^{|\sigma|} \not\subseteq \rho$$

are an (n, k)-Turan system.

Example 3. For any $k > 2$ we can construct a binary k-Turan network with variables $\{1, \ldots, n\}$ and domain $\{1, \ldots, d\}$ as follows. The scopes are all pairs of variables of the same parity, like $\langle 4, 12 \rangle$ and $\langle 3, 7 \rangle$. Each binary constraint has the same constraint relation that disallows only $d - 1$ tuples: $\langle 2, 2 \rangle, \ldots, \langle d, d \rangle$.

Every k-set of variables contains (at least) two variables with the same parity and so is represented by the scope of some constraint. Hence the scopes form an (n, k)-Turan system. Furthermore, for any pair of domain values $a < b$ each constraint relation disallows the tuple $\langle b, b \rangle$ and so does not contain $[a, b]^2$.

Theorem 3. *For any domain D and fixed k, the class of k-Turan constraint networks is tractable.*

Proof. Let P be any k-Turan constraint network over domain D.

Since every k-set of variables contains the scope $\langle \sigma, \rho \rangle$ of a constraint for which:

$$\forall a, b \in D, [a, b]^{|\sigma|} \not\subseteq \rho \ .$$

We immediately get that P is α-restrictive for the constant DPAF $\alpha(a, b) = k$, and so the class is polynomially solvable.

To see that such a class is polynomially recognisable observe that there are polynomially many subsets of variables of size k and, for each of these sets we have only to check the relations of constraints whose scope they contain. That is, one check is required for each pair of domain elements, for each constraint and for each subset of size k giving time complexity $O(|D|^2 |P|^{k+1})$.

It is worth observing that the restriction:

$$\forall a, b \in D, [a, b]^{|\sigma|} \not\subseteq \rho$$

is not very strong. For instance every clause (seen as a constraint over a Boolean domain) satisfies the restriction. There is just one domain pair $0, 1$ and so we only require there to be at least one disallowed tuple.

Hence, a direct consequence of Theorem 3 is for the case of k-SAT (boolean domains, where each constraint is a clause on k-variables).

Corollary 3. *The class of k-SAT instances where every k-tuple is restricted by a k-clause is tractable.*

What is more, every functional constraint satisfies this property.

Proposition 4. *Let $\langle \sigma, \tau \rangle$ be any functional constraint. We have that:*

$$\forall a, b \in D, [a, b]^{|\sigma|} \not\subseteq \rho \ .$$

Proof. Suppose that $\langle \sigma, \tau \rangle$ is functional at x. Choose arbitrary domain elements a and b. We know that any assignment of values from $\{a, b\}$ to the variables of σ other than x extends to at most one value at x. So we are done.

The result of David's [4] is another corollary of Theorem 3.

Corollary 4. *[4] If a constraint network P has all arity-q constraints and each of these constraints is functional then we can solve I in polynomial time*

5 Conclusion

We have defined different classes of constraint networks whose tractability stems from the fact that each network has only a polynomial number of solutions. This means that we can list or count all solutions or find all optimal solutions (according to any polytime objective function) in polynomial time.

Incrementally functional constraint networks have a single solution and a forward-checking search tree is linear when a dynamic smallest-domain first variable-ordering is used. Finding a maximum-cardinality subset of the variables on which a network is incrementally functional is polynomial-time. Finding a maximum-cardinality root set (a set of variables on which all others are functionally dependent) would appear to be NP-hard except in the case that each variable is functionally dependent on a single previous variable.

We have also presented novel tractable classes of constraint networks with *no* functional constraints which have a polynomial bound on the number of solutions. These k-Turan networks require many constraints with small scopes but put only a very weak restriction on the relations of these constraints. As such this is an interesting contrast with the (structural) class of networks with small fractional edge cover number.

An interesting open question is whether there exist other conditions guaranteeing a polynomial number of solutions.

References

1. Beldiceanu, N., Carlsson, M., Rampon, J.-X.: Global constraint catalog. 2nd edition. Technical Report T2010:07, Swedish Institute of Computer Science, SICS, Isafjordsgatan 22, Box 1263, SE-164 29 Kista, Sweden (November 2010)
2. Bulatov, A.A.: A dichotomy theorem for constraints on a three-element set. In: Proceedings 43rd IEEE Symposium on Foundations of Computer Science, FOCS 2002, pp. 649–658. IEEE Computer Society, Los Alamitos (2002)
3. Cooper, M.C., Jeavons, P.G., Salamon, A.Z.: Generalizing constraint satisfaction on trees: Hybrid tractability and variable elimination. Artif. Intell. 174(9-10), 570–584 (2010)
4. David, P.: Prise en compte de la sémantique dans les probl 'emes de satisfaction de contraintes: étude des contraintes fonctionnelles. PhD thesis, LIRMM, Université Montpellier II (1994)
5. David, P.: Using pivot consistency to decompose and solve functional csps. J. Artif. Intell. Res. (JAIR) 2, 447–474 (1995)

6. Deville, Y., Van Hentenryck, P.: An efficient arc consistency algorithm for a class of csp problems. In: Proceedings of the 12th International Joint Conference on Artificial Intelligence, vol. 1, pp. 325–330. Morgan Kaufmann Publishers Inc., San Francisco (1991)

7. Feder, T., Vardi, M.Y.: The computational structure of monotone monadic SNP and constraint satisfaction: A study through Datalog and group theory. SIAM Journal of Computing 28(1), 57–104 (1998)

8. Grohe, M.: The structure of tractable constraint satisfaction problems. In: Královič, R., Urzyczyn, P. (eds.) MFCS 2006. LNCS, vol. 4162, pp. 58–72. Springer, Heidelberg (2006)

9. Grohe, M., Marx, D.: Constraint solving via fractional edge covers. In: SODA, pp. 289–298. ACM Press, New York (2006)

10. Jeavons, P.G., Cohen, D.A., Gyssens, M.: A test for tractability. In: Freuder, E.C. (ed.) CP 1996. LNCS, vol. 1118, pp. 267–281. Springer, Heidelberg (1996)

11. Jegou, P.: Decomposition of domains based on the micro-structure of finite constraint-satisfaction problems. In: Proceedings of the 11th National Conference on Artificial Intelligence, pp. 731–736. AAAI Press, Menlo Park (1993)

12. Karp, R.M.: Reducibility Among Combinatorial Problems. In: Miller, R.E., Thatcher, J.W. (eds.) Complexity of Computer Computations, pp. 85–103. Plenum Press, New York (1972)

13. Salamon, A.Z., Jeavons, P.G.: Perfect constraints are tractable. In: Stuckey, P.J. (ed.) CP 2008. LNCS, vol. 5202, pp. 524–528. Springer, Heidelberg (2008)

14. Sidorenko, A.F.: Precise values of turan numbers. Mathematical Notes 42, 913–918 (1987), 10.1007/BF01137440

15. Szeider, S.: Backdoor sets for dll subsolvers. J. Autom. Reasoning 35(1-3), 73–88 (2005)

16. Turan, P.: Research problems. Publ. Hung. Acad. Sci. 6, 417–423 (1961)

17. Williams, R., Gomes, C.P., Selman, B.: Backdoors to typical case complexity. In: Gottlob, G., Walsh, T. (eds.) IJCAI, pp. 1173–1178. Morgan Kaufmann, San Francisco (2003)

A Framework for Decision-Based Consistencies

Jean-François Condotta and Christophe Lecoutre

CRIL - CNRS, UMR 8188,
Univ Lille Nord de France, Artois
F-62307 Lens, France
{condotta,lecoutre}@cril.fr

Abstract. Consistencies are properties of constraint networks that can be enforced by appropriate algorithms to reduce the size of the search space to be explored. Recently, many consistencies built upon taking decisions (most often, variable assignments) and stronger than (generalized) arc consistency have been introduced. In this paper, our ambition is to present a clear picture of decision-based consistencies. We identify four general classes (or levels) of decision-based consistencies, denoted by S_Δ^ϕ, E_Δ^ϕ, B_Δ^ϕ and D_Δ^ϕ, study their relationships, and show that known consistencies are particular cases of these classes. Interestingly, this general framework provides us with a better insight into decision-based consistencies, and allows us to derive many new consistencies that can be directly integrated and compared with other ones.

1   Introduction

Consistencies are properties of constraint networks that can be used to make inferences. Such inferences are useful to filter the search space of problem instances. Most of the current constraint solvers interleave inference and search. Typically, they enforce generalized arc consistency (GAC), or one of its partial form, during the search of a solution. One avenue to make solvers more robust is to enforce strong consistencies, i.e., consistencies stronger than GAC. Whereas GAC corresponds to the strongest form of local reasoning when constraints are treated separately, strong consistencies necessarily involve several constraints (e.g., path inverse consistency [12], max-restricted path consistency [8] and their adaptations [20] to non-binary constraints) or even the entire constraint network (e.g., singleton arc consistency [9]).

A trend that emerges from recent works on strong consistencies is the resort to taking decisions before enforcing a well-known consistency (typically, GAC) and making some deductions. Among such decision-based consistencies, we find SAC (singleton arc consistency), partition-k-AC [2], weak-k-SAC [22], BiSAC [4], and DC (dual consistency) [15]. Besides, a partial form of SAC, better known as shaving, has been introduced for a long time [6,18] and is still an active subject of research [17,21]; when shaving systematically concerns the bounds of each variable domain, it is called BoundSAC [16]. What makes decision-based consistencies particularly attractive is that they are (usually) easy to define and

J. Lee (Ed.): CP 2011, LNCS 6876, pp. 172–186, 2011.

understand, and easy to implement since they are mainly based on two concepts (decision, propagation) already handled by constraint solvers. The increased interest perceived in the community for decision-based consistencies has motivated our study.

In this paper, our ambition is to present a clear picture of decision-based consistencies that can derive nogoods of size up to 2; i.e., inconsistent values or inconsistent pairs of values. The only restriction we impose is that decisions correspond to unary constraints. The four classes (or levels) of consistencies, denoted by S_Δ^ϕ, E_Δ^ϕ, B_Δ^ϕ and D_Δ^ϕ, that we introduce are built on top of a consistency ϕ and a so-called decision mapping Δ. These are quite general because:

1. Δ allows us to introduce a specific set of decisions for every variable x and every possible (sub)domain of x,
2. decisions are membership decisions (of the form $x \in D_x$ where D_x is a set of values taken from the initial domain of x) that generalize both variable assignments (of the form $x = a$) and value refutations (of the form $x \neq a$),
3. decisions may ignore some variables and/or values, and decisions may overlap each other,
4. ϕ is any well-behaved nogood-identifying consistency.

We study the relationships existing between them, including the case where Δ covers every variable and every value. We also show that SAC, partition-k-AC, BiSAC and DC are particular cases of S_Δ^ϕ, $S_\Delta^\phi + E_\Delta^\phi$ (the two consistencies combined), B_Δ^ϕ and D_Δ^ϕ, respectively. BoundSAC, and many other forms of shaving, are also elements of the class S_Δ^ϕ. The general framework we depict provides a better insight into decision-based consistencies while allowing many new combinations and comparisons of such consistencies. For example, the class of consistencies S_Δ^ϕ induces a complete lattice where the partial order denotes the relative strength of every two consistencies.

2   Technical Background

This section provides technical background about constraint networks and consistencies, mainly taken from [1,11,3,13].

Constraint Networks. A *constraint network* (CN) P is composed of a finite set of n variables, denoted by $vars(P)$, and a finite set of e constraints, denoted by $cons(P)$. Each variable x has a domain which is the finite set of values that can be assigned to x. Each constraint c involves an ordered set of variables, called the *scope* of c and denoted by $scp(c)$, and is defined by a relation which is the set of tuples allowed for the variables involved in c. The initial domain of a variable x is denoted by $dom^{init}(x)$ whereas the current domain of x (in the context of P) is denoted by $dom^P(x)$, or more simply $dom(x)$. Assuming that the initial domain of each variable is totally ordered, $min(x)$ and $max(x)$ will denote the smallest and greatest values in $dom(x)$. The initial and current relations of a constraint c are denoted by $rel^{init}(c)$ and $rel(c)$, respectively.

A constraint is *universal* iff $rel^{init}(c) = \Pi_{x \in scp(c)}dom^{init}(x)$. For simplicity, a pair (x, a) with $x \in vars(P)$ and $a \in dom(x)$ is called a *value* of P, which is denoted by $(x, a) \in P$. A *unary* (resp., *binary*) constraint involves 1 (resp., 2) variable(s), and a *non-binary* one strictly more than 2 variables. Without any loss of generality, we only consider CNs that do not involve unary constraints, universal constraints and constraints of similar scope. The set of such CNs is denoted by $\mathscr{P}$. An *instantiation* I of a set $X = \{x_1, \ldots, x_k\}$ of variables is a set $\{(x_1, a_1), \ldots, (x_k, a_k)\}$ such that $\forall i \in 1..k, a_i \in dom^{init}(x_i)$; X is denoted by $vars(I)$ and each a_i is denoted by $I[x_i]$. An instantiation I *on* a CN P is an instantiation of a set $X \subseteq vars(P)$; it is *complete* if $vars(I) = vars(P)$. I is *valid* on P iff $\forall(x, a) \in I, a \in dom(x)$. I *covers* a constraint c iff $scp(c) \subseteq vars(I)$, and I *satisfies* a constraint c with $scp(c) = \{x_1, \ldots, x_r\}$ iff (i) I covers c and (ii) the tuple $(I[x_1], \ldots, I[x_r]) \in rel(c)$. An instantiation I on a CN P is *locally consistent* iff (i) I is valid on P and (ii) every constraint of P covered by I is satisfied by I. A *solution* of P is a complete locally consistent instantiation on P; $sols(P)$ denotes the set of solutions of P. An instantiation I on a CN P is *globally inconsistent*, or a *nogood*, iff it cannot be extended to a solution of P. Two CNs P and P' are *equivalent* iff $vars(P) = vars(P')$ and $sols(P) = sols(P')$.

The *nogood representation* of a CN is a set of nogoods, one for every value removed from the initial domain of a variable and one for every tuple forbidden by a constraint. More precisely, the nogood representation $\widetilde{x}$ of a variable x is the set $\{\{(x, a)\} \mid a \in \overline{dom}(x)\}$ with $\overline{dom}(x) = dom^{init}(x) \setminus dom(x)$. The nogood representation $\widetilde{c}$ of a constraint c is $\{\{(x_1, a_1), \ldots, (x_r, a_r)\} \mid (a_1, \ldots, a_r) \in \overline{rel}(c)\}$, with $scp(c) = \{x_1, \ldots, x_r\}$ and $\overline{rel}(c) = \Pi_{x \in scp(c)}dom^{init}(x) \setminus rel(c)$. The nogood representation $\widetilde{P}$ of a CN P is $(\cup_{x \in vars(P)}\widetilde{x}) \cup (\cup_{c \in cons(P)}\widetilde{c})$. Based on nogood representations, a general partial order can be introduced to relate CNs. Let P and P' be two CNs such that $vars(P) = vars(P')$, we have $P' \preceq P$ iff $\widetilde{P'} \supseteq \widetilde{P}$ and we have $P' \prec P$ iff $\widetilde{P'} \supsetneq \widetilde{P}$. $(\mathscr{P}, \preceq)$ is the partially ordered set (poset) considered in this paper. The search space of a CN can be reduced by a filtering process (called constraint propagation) based on some properties (called consistencies) that allow us to identify and record explicit nogoods in CNs; e.g., identified nogoods of size 1 correspond to inconsistent values that can be safely removed from variable domains. In $\mathscr{P}$, there is only one manner to discard an instantiation from a given CN, or equivalently to "record" a new explicit nogood. Given a CN P in $\mathscr{P}$, and an instantiation I on P, $P \setminus I$ denotes the CN P' in $\mathscr{P}$ such that $vars(P') = vars(P)$ and $\widetilde{P'} = \widetilde{P} \cup \{I\}$. $P \setminus I$ is an operation that retracts I from P and builds a new CN. If $I = \{(x, a)\}$, we remove a from $dom(x)$. If I corresponds to a tuple allowed by a constraint c of P, we remove this tuple from $rel(c)$. Otherwise, we introduce a new constraint allowing all possible tuples (from initial domains) except the one that corresponds to I.

Consistencies. A consistency is a property defined on CNs. When a consistency ϕ holds on a CN P, we say that P is ϕ-*consistent*; if ψ is another consistency, P is $\phi + \psi$-*consistent* iff P is both ϕ-consistent and ψ-consistent. A consistency ϕ is *nogood-identifying* iff the reason why a CN P is not ϕ-consistent is that some instantiations, which are not in $\widetilde{P}$, are identified as globally inconsistent by ϕ; such instantiations are said to be ϕ-*inconsistent*. A *kth-order consistency* is a nogood-identifying consistency that allows the identification of nogoods of size k. A *domain-filtering consistency* [10,5] is a first-order consistency. A nogood-identifying consistency is *well-behaved* when for any CN P, the set $\{P' \in \mathscr{P} \mid P'$ is ϕ-consistent and $P' \preceq P\}$ admits a greatest element, denoted by $\phi(P)$, equivalent to P. Enforcing ϕ on a CN P means computing $\phi(P)$. Any well-behaved consistency ϕ is *monotonic*: for any two CNs P and P', we have: $P' \preceq P \Rightarrow \phi(P') \preceq \phi(P)$. To compare the pruning capability of consistencies, we use a preorder. A consistency ϕ is *stronger* than (or equal to) a consistency ψ, denoted by $\phi \trianglerighteq \psi$, iff whenever ϕ holds on a CN P, ψ also holds on P. ϕ is *strictly stronger* than ψ, denoted by $\phi \triangleright \psi$, iff $\phi \trianglerighteq \psi$ and there is at least a CN P such that ψ holds on P but not ϕ. ϕ and ψ are *equivalent*, denoted by $\phi \approx \psi$, iff both $\phi \trianglerighteq \psi$ and $\psi \trianglerighteq \phi$.

Now we introduce some concrete consistencies, starting with GAC (Generalized Arc Consistency). A value (x, a) of P is *GAC-consistent* iff for each constraint c of P involving x there exists a valid instantiation I of $scp(c)$ such that I satisfies c and $I[x] = a$. P is GAC-consistent iff every value of P is GAC-consistent. For binary constraints, GAC is often referred to as AC (Arc Consistency). Now, we introduce known consistencies based on decisions. When the domain of a variable of P is empty, P is unsatisfiable (i.e., $sols(P) = \emptyset$), which is denoted by $P = \bot$; to simplify, we consider that no value is present in a CN P such that $P = \bot$. The CN $P|_{x=a}$ is obtained from P by removing every value $b \neq a$ from $dom(x)$. A value (x, a) of P is *SAC-consistent* iff $GAC(P|_{x=a}) \neq \bot$ [9]. A value (x, a) of P is *1-AC-consistent* iff (x, a) is SAC-consistent and $\forall y \in vars(P) \setminus \{x\}, \exists b \in dom(y) \mid (x, a) \in GAC(P|_{y=b})$ [2]. A value (x, a) of P is *BiSAC-consistent* iff $GAC(P^{ia}|_{x=a}) \neq \bot$ where P^{ia} is the CN obtained after removing every value (y, b) of P such that $y \neq x$ and $(x, a) \notin GAC(P|_{y=b})$ [4]. P is SAC-consistent (resp., 1-AC-consistent, BiSAC-consistent) iff every value of P is SAC-consistent (resp., 1-AC-consistent, BiSAC-consistent). P is BoundSAC-consistent iff for every variable x, $min(x)$ and $max(x)$ are SAC-consistent [16]. A decision-based second-order consistency is dual consistency (DC) defined as follows. A locally consistent instantiation $\{(x, a), (y, b)\}$ on P, with $y \neq x$, is DC-consistent iff $(y, b) \in GAC(P|_{x=a})$ and $(x, a) \in GAC(P|_{y=b})$ [14]. P is *DC-consistent* iff every locally consistent instantiation $\{(x, a), (y, b)\}$ on P is DC-consistent. P is *sDC-consistent* (strong DC-consistent) iff P is GAC+DC-consistent, i.e. both GAC-consistent and DC-consistent. All consistencies mentioned above are well-behaved. Also, we know that sDC $\triangleright$ BiSAC $\triangleright$ 1-GAC $\triangleright$ SAC $\triangleright$ BoundSAC $\triangleright$ GAC.

3 Decision-Based Consistencies

In this section, we introduce decisions before presenting general classes of consistencies.

3.1   Decisions

A *positive decision* δ is a restriction on a variable x of the form $x = a$ whereas a *negative decision* is a restriction of the form $x \neq a$, with $a \in dom^{init}(x)$. A *membership decision* is a decision of the form $x \in D_x$, where x is a variable and $D_x \subseteq dom^{init}(x)$ is a non-empty set of values; note that D_x is not necessarily $dom(x)$, the current domain of x. Membership decisions generalize both positive and negative decisions as a positive (resp., negative) decision $x = a$ (resp., $x \neq a$) is equivalent to the membership decision $x \in \{a\}$ (resp., $x \in dom^{init}(x) \setminus \{a\}$). The variable involved in a decision δ is denoted by $var(\delta)$.

For a membership decision δ, we define $P|_\delta$ to be the CN obtained (derived) from P such that, if δ denotes $x \in D_x$ and if x is a variable of P then each value $b \in dom^P(x)$ with $b \notin D_x$ is removed from $dom^P(x)$. If Γ is a set of decisions, $P|_\Gamma$ is obtained by restricting P by means of all decisions in Γ, and $vars(\Gamma)$ denotes the set of variables occurring in Γ. Enforcing a given well-behaved consistency ϕ after taking a decision δ on a CN P may be quite informative. As seen later, analyzing the CN $\phi(P|_\delta)$ allows us to identify nogoods. Computing $\phi(P|_\delta)$ in order to make such inferences is called a decision-based ϕ-check on P from δ, or more simply a *decision-based check*. For SAC, a decision-based check from a pair (x, a), usually called a singleton check, aims at comparing $GAC(P|_{x=a})$ with $\bot$.

From now on, Δ will denote a mapping, called *decision mapping*, that associates with every variable x and every possible domain $dom_x \subseteq dom^{init}(x)$, a (possibly empty) set $\Delta(x, dom_x)$ of membership decisions on x such that for every decision $x \in D_x$ in $\Delta(x, dom_x)$, we have $D_x \subseteq dom_x$. For example, an illustrative decision mapping Δ^{ex} may be such that $\Delta^{ex}(x, \{a, b, c, d\}) = \{x \in \{a, b\}, x \in \{d\}\}$. For the current domain of x, i.e., the domain of x in the context of a current CN P, $\Delta(x, dom(x)) = \Delta(x, dom^P(x))$ will be simplified into $\Delta(x)$ when this is unambiguous. To simplify, we shall also refer to Δ as the set of all "current" decisions w.r.t. P, i.e., Δ will be considered as $\cup_{x \in vars(P)} \Delta(x)$. This quite general definition of decision mapping will be considered as our basis to perform decision-based checks. Sometimes, we need to restrict sets of decisions in order to have each value occurring at least once in a decision. A set of decisions Γ on a variable x is said to be a *cover* of $\cup_{(x \in D_x) \in \Gamma} D_x$. For example, $\Delta^{ex}(x, \{a, b, c, d\})$, as defined above, is a cover of $\{a, b, d\}$. Δ is a *cover* for (x, dom_x), where $dom_x \subseteq dom^{init}(x)$, iff $\Delta(x, dom_x)$ is a cover of dom_x. For example, Δ^{ex} is not a cover for $(x, \{a, b, c, d\})$. Δ is a *cover* for x iff for every $dom_x \subseteq dom^{init}(x)$, Δ is a *cover* for (x, dom_x). Δ is *covering* iff for every variable x, Δ is a *cover* for x.

As examples of decision mappings, we have for every variable x:

- $\Delta^{id}(x)$ containing only $x \in dom(x)$;
- $\Delta^=(x)$ containing $x = a$, $\forall a \in dom(x)$;
- $\Delta^{\neq}(x)$ containing $x \neq a$, $\forall a \in dom(x)$;
- $\Delta^{bnd}(x)$ containing $x = min(x)$ and $x = max(x)$;
- $\Delta^{P_2}(x)$ containing $x \in D_x^1$ and $x \in D_x^2$ where D_x^1 and D_x^2 resp. contain the first and last $|dom(x)|/2$ values of $dom(x)$.

For example, if P is a CN such that $vars(P) = \{x, y\}$ with $dom(x) = dom^P(x) = \{a, b, c\}$ and $dom(y) = dom^P(y) = \{a, b\}$ then:

- $\Delta^{id}(x) = \{x \in \{a, b, c\}\}$ and $\Delta^{id}(y) = \{y \in \{a, b\}\}$;
- $\Delta^=(x) = \{x = a, x = b, x = c\}$ and $\Delta^=(y) = \{y = a, y = b\}$;
- $\Delta^{\neq}(x) = \{x \neq a, x \neq b, x \neq c\}$ and $\Delta^{\neq}(y) = \{y \neq a, y \neq b\}$;
- $\Delta^{bnd}(x) = \{x = a, x = c\}$ and $\Delta^{bnd}(y) = \{y = a, y = b\}$;
- $\Delta^{P_2}(x) = \{x \in \{a, b\}, x = c\}$ and $\Delta^{P_2}(y) = \{y = a, y = b\}$.

Note that, except for Δ^{bnd}, all these decision mappings are covering. Also, the reader should be aware of the dynamic nature of decision mappings. For example, if P' is obtained from P after removing a from $dom^P(x)$ then we have $\Delta^{bnd}(x, dom^{P'}(x)) = \{x = b, x = c\}$.

3.2   Two Classes of First-Order Consistencies

Informally, a decision-based consistency is a property defined from the outcome of decision-based checks. From now on, we consider given a well-behaved nogood-identifying consistency ϕ and a decision mapping Δ. A first kind of inferences is made possible by considering the effect of a decision-based check on the domain initially reduced by the decision that has been taken.

Definition 1 (Consistency S_Δ^ϕ). *A value (x, a) of a CN P is S_Δ^ϕ-consistent iff for every membership decision $x \in D_x$ in $\Delta(x)$ such that $a \in D_x$, we have $(x, a) \in \phi(P|_{x \in D_x})$.*

The following result can be seen as a generalization of Property 1 in [2].

Proposition 1. *Any S_Δ^ϕ-inconsistent value is globally inconsistent.*

Proof. If (x, a) is an S_Δ^ϕ-inconsistent value, then we know that there exists a decision $x \in D_x$ in $\Delta(x)$ such that $a \in D_x$ and $(x, a) \notin \phi(P|_{x \in D_x})$. We deduce that $x \in D_x \wedge x = a$ cannot lead to a solution because ϕ is nogood-identifying. This simplifies into $x = a$ being a nogood because $a \in D_x$. $\square$

SAC is equivalent to $S_{\Delta^=}^{GAC}$ (because no value belongs to $\bot$), and BoundSAC[1] is equivalent to $S_{\Delta^{bnd}}^{GAC}$. Note also that GAC is equivalent to $S_{\Delta^{id}}^{GAC}$. As a simple illustration of S_Δ^ϕ, let us consider the five binary CNs depicted in Figure 1; each vertex denotes a value, each edge denotes an allowed tuple and each dotted vertex (resp., edge) means that the value (resp., tuple) is removed (resp., no more relevant). P_1, P_2, P_3 and P_4 are obtained from P by removing values that are S_Δ^{AC}-inconsistent when Δ is set to Δ^{id}, Δ^{P_2}, Δ^{bnd} and $\Delta^=$, respectively. For example, for Δ^{P_2}, we find that $(y, c) \notin AC(P|_{y \in \{c, d\}})$. Note that the CN P_4 is also obtained when setting Δ to $\Delta^{\neq}$.

---

[1] Another related consistency is Existential SAC [16], which guarantees that some value in the domain of each variable is SAC-consistent. However, there is no guarantee about the network obtained after checking Existential SAC due to the non-deterministic nature of this consistency. Existential SAC is not an element of S_Δ^ϕ.

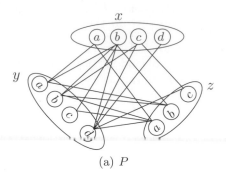

(a) P

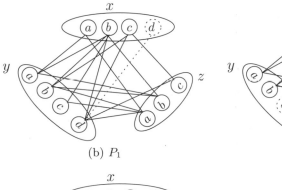

(b) P_1 (c) P_2

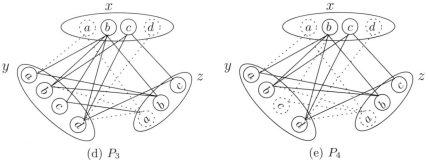

(d) P_3 (e) P_4

Fig. 1. Illustration of S_Δ^{GAC}

In [2], it is also shown that inferences regarding values may be obtained by considering the result of several decision-based checks. This is generalized below. The idea is that a value (x, a) of P can be safely removed when there exist a variable y and a cover $\Gamma \subseteq \Delta(y)$ of $dom(y)$ such that every decision-based check, performed from a decision in Γ, eliminates (x, a).

Definition 2 (Consistency E_Δ^ϕ). *A value (x, a) of a CN P is E_Δ^ϕ-consistent w.r.t. a variable $y \neq x$ of P iff for every cover Γ of $dom(y)$ such that $\Gamma \subseteq \Delta(y)$, there exists a decision $y \in D_y$ in Γ such that $(x, a) \in \phi(P|_{y \in D_y})$. (x, a) is E_Δ^ϕ-consistent iff (x, a) is E_Δ^ϕ-consistent w.r.t. every variable $y \neq x$ of P.*

Proposition 2. *Any E_Δ^ϕ-inconsistent value is globally inconsistent.*

Proof. If (x, a) is an E_Δ^ϕ-inconsistent value, then we know that there exists a variable $y \neq x$ of P and a set $\Gamma \subseteq \Delta(y)$ such that (i) $dom^P(y) = \cup_{(y \in D_y) \in \Gamma} D_y$ and (ii) every decision $y \in D_y$ in Γ entails $(x, a) \notin \phi(P|_{y \in D_y})$. As Γ is a cover of $dom(y)$, we infer that $sols(P) = \cup_{(y \in D_y) \in \Gamma} sols(P|_{y \in D_y})$. Because ϕ preserves solutions, we have $sols(P) = \cup_{(y \in D_y) \in \Gamma} sols(\phi(P|_{y \in D_y}))$. For every $y \in D_y$ in Γ, we know that $(x, a) \notin \phi(P|_{y \in D_y})$. We deduce that (x, a) cannot be involved in any solution. $\qquad\square$

As an illustration, let us consider the CN of Figure 1(a) and $\Delta(x) = \{x \in \{a, c\}, x \in \{b, d\}\}$. We can show that (z, a) is E_Δ^{GAC}-inconsistent because $(z, a) \notin AC(P|_{x \in \{a,c\}})$ and $(z, a) \notin AC(P|_{x \in \{b,d\}})$. The consistency P-k-AC, introduced in [2], corresponds to $S_\Delta^\phi + E_\Delta^\phi$ where $\phi = AC$ and Δ necessarily corresponds to a partition of each domain into pieces of size at most k.

3.3 Classes Related to Nogoods of Size 2

Decision-based consistencies introduced above are clearly domain-filtering: they allow us to identify inconsistent values. However, decision-based consistencies are also naturally orientated towards identifying nogoods of size 2. $NG2(P)_\Delta^\phi$ denotes the set of nogoods of size 2 that can be directly derived from checks on P based on the consistency ϕ and the decision mapping Δ. From this set, together with a decision $x \in D_x$, we obtain a set $ND1(P, x \in D_x)_\Delta^\phi$ of negative decisions that can be used to make further inferences.

Definition 3. *Let P be a CN and $x \in D_x$ be a membership decision in $\Delta(x)$.*

- $NG2(P)_{x \in D_x}^\phi$ *denotes the set of locally consistent instantiations $\{(x, a), (y, b)\}$ on P such that $a \in D_x$ and $(y, b) \notin \phi(P|_{x \in D_x})$.*
- $NG2(P)_\Delta^\phi$ *denotes the set $\cup_{\delta \in \Delta} NG2(P)_\delta^\phi$.*
- $ND1(P, x \in D_x)_\Delta^\phi$ *denotes the set of negative decisions $y \neq b$ such that every value $a \in D_x$ is such that $\{(x, a), (y, b)\} \in \widetilde{P}$ or $\{(x, a), (y, b)\} \in NG2(P)_{\Delta \setminus \{\tau \in D_x\}}^\phi$.*

From *ND1* sets, we can define a new class B_Δ^ϕ of consistencies.

Definition 4 (Consistency B_Δ^ϕ). *A value (x, a) of a CN P is B_Δ^ϕ-consistent iff for every membership decision $x \in D_x$ in $\Delta(x)$ such that $a \in D_x$, we have $(x, a) \in \phi(P|_{\{x \in D_x\} \cup ND1(P, x \in D_x)_\Delta^\phi})$.*

Proposition 3. *Any B_Δ^ϕ-inconsistent value is globally inconsistent.*

Proof. The proof is similar to that of Proposition 1. The only difference is that the network P is made smaller by removing some additional values by means of negative decisions. However, in the context of a decision $x \in D_x$ taken on P, the inferred negative decisions correspond to inconsistent values because they are derived from nogoods of size 2 (showing that elements of $NG2(P)_\Delta^\phi$ are nogoods is immediate). $\qquad\square$

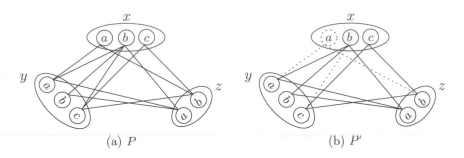

$$(a)\ P \qquad\qquad (b)\ P'$$

Fig. 2. Illustration of B_Δ^{GAC} and D_Δ^{GAC}

As an illustration of B_Δ^ϕ, let us consider the binary CN P in Figure 2(a). For $\phi = AC$ and $\Delta = \Delta^{P_2} = \{x \in \{a,b\}, x = c, y \in \{a,b\}, y = c, z = a, z = b\}$ we obtain $NG2(P)_\Delta^\phi = \{\{(x,a),(y,a)\}, \{(x,a),(z,b)\}, \{(x,b),(y,c)\}\}$ since for example $(x,a) \notin AC(P|_{y \in \{a,b\}})$. Because $\{(x,b),(z,b)\} \in \widetilde{P}$ and $\{(x,a),(z,b)\} \in NG2(P)_\Delta^\phi$, $ND1(P, x \in \{a,b\})_\Delta^\phi = \{z \neq b\}$, and (x,a) is B_Δ^ϕ-inconsistent as $(x,a) \notin AC(P|_{x \in \{a,b\} \cup \{z \neq b\}})$. Here, P is S_Δ^ϕ-consistent, but not B_Δ^ϕ-consistent.

Note that BiSAC [4] is equivalent to $B_{\Delta=}^{GAC}$. On the other hand, there is a 2-order consistency that can be naturally defined as follows.

Definition 5 (Consistency D_Δ^ϕ). *A locally consistent instantiation $\{(x,a), (y,b)\}$ on a CN P is D_Δ^ϕ-consistent iff for every membership decision $x \in D_x$ in $\Delta(x)$ such that $a \in D_x$, $(y,b) \in \phi(P|_{x \in D_x})$ and for every membership decision $y \in D_y$ in $\Delta(y)$ such that $b \in D_y$, $(x,a) \in \phi(P|_{y \in D_y})$.*

Proposition 4. *Any D_Δ^ϕ-inconsistent instantiation is globally inconsistent.*

Proof. D_Δ^ϕ-inconsistent instantiations are exactly those in $NG2(P)_\Delta^\phi$, which are nogoods. □

Note that DC [15] is equivalent to $D_{\Delta=}^{GAC}$, and recall that DC is equivalent to PC (Path Consistency) for binary CNs. D_Δ^ϕ (being 2-order) is obviously incomparable with previously introduced domain-filtering consistencies. However, a natural practical approach is to benefit from decision-based checks to record both S_Δ^ϕ-inconsistent values and D_Δ^ϕ-inconsistent instantiations. This corresponds to the combined consistency $S_\Delta^\phi + D_\Delta^\phi$.

As an illustration of D_Δ^ϕ, let us consider again Figure 2. For $\phi = AC$ and $\Delta = \Delta^{P_2} = \{x \in \{a,b\}, x = c, y \in \{a,b\}, y = c, z = a, z = b\}$, we have that P is S_Δ^ϕ-consistent, not B_Δ^ϕ-consistent and not D_Δ^ϕ-consistent. Enforcing $S_\Delta^\phi + D_\Delta^\phi$ on P yields the CN P', which is also the strong DC-closure (here, AC+PC-closure) of P.

4   Qualitative Study

In this section, we study the relationships between the different classes of consistencies (as well as some of their combinations), and discuss refinements and well-behavedness of consistencies.

4.1   Relationships between Consistencies

From Definitions 1 and 4, it is immediate that any S_Δ^ϕ-inconsistent value is necessarily B_Δ^ϕ-inconsistent.

Proposition 5. $B_\Delta^\phi \trianglerighteq S_\Delta^\phi$.

In order to relate B_Δ^ϕ with E_Δ^ϕ, we need to consider covering sets of decisions.

Proposition 6. *If Δ is covering, $B_\Delta^\phi \trianglerighteq E_\Delta^\phi$.*

Proof. We show that every E_Δ^ϕ-inconsistent value in a CN P is necessarily B_Δ^ϕ-inconsistent. Assume that (x, a) is a E_Δ^ϕ-inconsistent value. It means that there exists a variable $y \neq x$ of P and $\Gamma \subseteq \Delta(y)$ such that $dom^P(y) = \cup_{(y \in D_y) \in \Gamma} D_y$ and every decision $y \in D_y$ in Γ is such that $(x, a) \notin \phi(P|_{y \in D_y})$. We deduce that for every value $b \in dom^P(y)$, we have $\{(x, a), (y, b)\}$ in $NG2(P)_\Delta^\phi$. On the other hand, we know that there exists a decision $x \in D_x$ in Δ such that $a \in D_x$ (since Δ is covering). Hence, $ND1(P, x \in D_x)_\Delta^\phi$ contains a negative decision $y \neq b$ for each value in $dom^P(y)$. It follows that $\phi(P|_{\{x \in D_x\} \cup ND1(P, x \in D_x)_\Delta^\phi}) = \bot$, and (x, a) is B_Δ^ϕ-inconsistent. $\square$

As a corollary, we have $B_\Delta^\phi \trianglerighteq S_\Delta^\phi + E_\Delta^\phi$ when Δ is covering. Note that there exist consistencies ϕ and decision mappings Δ such that B_Δ^ϕ is strictly stronger ($\triangleright$) than S_Δ^ϕ and E_Δ^ϕ (and also $S_\Delta^\phi + E_\Delta^\phi$). For example, when $\phi = AC$ and $\Delta = \Delta^=$, we have $B_\Delta^\phi = BiSAC$, $S_\Delta^\phi = SAC$ and $S_\Delta^\phi + E_\Delta^\phi = 1\text{-}AC$, and we know that $BiSAC \triangleright 1\text{-}AC$ [4], and $1\text{-}AC \triangleright SAC$ [2].

Because D_Δ^ϕ captures all 2-sized nogoods while S_Δ^ϕ can eliminate inconsistent values, it follows that the joint use of these two consistencies is stronger than B_Δ^ϕ.

Proposition 7. $S_\Delta^\phi + D_\Delta^\phi \trianglerighteq B_\Delta^\phi$.

Proof. Let P be a CN that is $S_\Delta^\phi + D_\Delta^\phi$-consistent. As P is S_Δ^ϕ-consistent, for every decision $x \in D_x$ in Δ and every $a \in D_x$, we have $(x, a) \in \phi(P|_{x \in D_x})$. But $\phi(P|_{x \in D_x}) = \phi(P|_{\{x \in D_x\} \cup ND1(P, x \in D_x)_\Delta^\phi})$ since P being D_Δ^ϕ-consistent entails $NG2(P)_\Delta^\phi = \emptyset$ and $ND1(P, x \in D_x)_\Delta^\phi = \emptyset$. We deduce that P is B_Δ^ϕ-consistent. $\square$

One may expect that $S_\Delta^\phi \trianglerighteq \phi$. However, to guarantee this, we need both ϕ to be domain-filtering and Δ to be covering, For example, $S_\Delta^{AC} \trianglerighteq AC$ does not hold if for every $dom_x \subseteq dom^{init}(x)$, we have $\Delta(x, dom_x) = \emptyset$: it suffices to build a CN P with a value (x, a) being arc-inconsistent.

Proposition 8. *If ϕ is domain-filtering and Δ is covering, $S_\Delta^\phi \trianglerighteq \phi$.*

Proof. Assume that (x, a) is a ϕ-inconsistent value of a CN P. This means that $(x, a) \notin \phi(P)$. As Δ is covering, there exists a decision $x \in D_x$ in Δ with $a \in D_x$. We know that $P|_{x \in D_x} \preceq P$. By monotonicity of ϕ, $\phi(P|_{x \in D_x}) \preceq \phi(P)$. Since $(x, a) \notin \phi(P)$, we deduce that $(x, a) \notin \phi(P|_{x \in D_x})$. So, (x, a) is S_Δ^ϕ-inconsistent, and S_Δ^ϕ is stronger than ϕ.   □

Figure 3 shows the relationships between the different classes of consistencies introduced so far. There are many ways to instantiate these classes because the choice of Δ and ϕ is left open. If we consider binary CNs, and choose $\phi = AC$ and $\Delta = \Delta^=$, we obtain known consistencies. We directly benefit from the relationships of Figure 3, and have just to prove strictness when it holds. Figure 4 shows this where an arrow denotes now $\triangleright$ (instead of $\trianglerighteq$). An extreme instantiation case is when $\Delta = \Delta^{id}$ and ϕ is domain-filtering. In this case, all consistencies collapse: we have $S_{\Delta^{id}}^\phi = E_{\Delta^{id}}^\phi = B_{\Delta^{id}}^\phi = D_{\Delta^{id}}^\phi = \phi$. This means that our framework of decision-based consistencies is general enough to encompass all classical local consistencies. Although this is appealing for theoretical reasons (e.g., see Proposition 11 later), the main objective of decision-based consistencies remains to learn relevant nogoods from nontrivial decision-based checks.

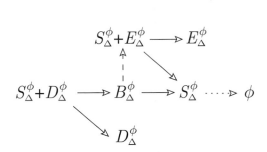

Fig. 3. Summary of the relationships between (classes of) consistencies. An arrow from φ to ψ means that $\varphi \trianglerighteq \psi$. A dashed (resp., dotted) arrow means that the relationship is guaranteed provided that Δ is covering (resp., Δ is covering and ϕ is domain-filtering).

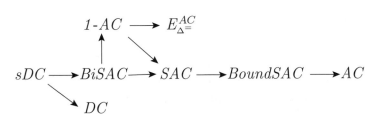

Fig. 4. Relationships between consistencies when $\phi = AC$ and $\Delta = \Delta^=$ (except for BoundSAC which is derived from Δ^{bnd}). An arrow from φ to ψ means that $\varphi \triangleright \psi$.

4.2   Refinements

Now, we show that two consistencies of the same class can be naturally compared when a refinement connection exists between their decision mappings.

Definition 6. *A decision mapping Δ' is a refinement of a decision mapping Δ iff for each decision $x \in D_x$ in Δ there exists a subset $\Gamma \subseteq \Delta'(x)$ that is a cover of D_x.*

For example, $\{x \in \{a,b\}, x = c\}$ is a refinement of $\{x \in \{a,b,c\}\}$, and $\{x \in \{a,b\}, x = c, y = a, y = b, y = c\}$ is a refinement of $\{x \in \{a,b,c\}, y \in \{a,b\}, y \in \{b,c\}\}$. Unsurprisingly, using refined sets of decisions improves inference capability as shown by the following proposition.

Proposition 9. *If Δ and Δ' are two decision mappings such that Δ' is a refinement of Δ, then $X_{\Delta'}^\phi \trianglerighteq X_\Delta^\phi$ where $X \in \{S, E, B, D\}$.*

Proof. Due to lack of space, we only show that $S_{\Delta'}^\phi \trianglerighteq S_\Delta^\phi$. Assume that (x,a) is an S_Δ^ϕ-inconsistent value of a CN P. This means that there exists a decision $x \in D_x$ in $\Delta(x)$ such that $a \in D_x$ and $(x,a) \notin \phi(P|_{x \in D_x})$. We know, by hypothesis, that there exists a subset $\Gamma \subseteq \Delta'(x)$ such that $D_x = \cup_{(x \in D'_x) \in \Gamma} D'_x$. Hence, there exists (at least) a decision $x \in D'_x$ in Γ such that $a \in D'_x$ and $D'_x \subseteq D_x$. As $D'_x \subseteq D_x$, we have $P|_{x \in D'_x} \preceq P|_{x \in D_x}$, and by monotonicity of ϕ, $\phi(P|_{x \in D'_x}) \preceq \phi(P|_{x \in D_x})$. Consequently, $(x,a) \notin \phi(P|_{x \in D_x})$ implies $(x,a) \notin \phi(P|_{x \in D'_x})$. We deduce that there exists a decision $x \in D'_x$ in $\Delta'(x)$ such that $a \in D'_x$ and $(x,a) \notin \phi(P|_{x \in D''_x})$. Then (x,a) is $S_{\Delta'}^\phi$-inconsistent. We conclude that $S_{\Delta'}^\phi \trianglerighteq S_\Delta^\phi$. ⌐

As a corollary, for any decision mapping Δ, we have: $X_{\Delta^=}^\phi \trianglerighteq X_\Delta^\phi \trianglerighteq X_{\Delta^{id}}^\phi$ where $X \in \{S, E, B, D\}$. In particular, if $\phi = GAC$, we have $SAC = S_{\Delta^=}^{GAC} \trianglerighteq S_\Delta^{GAC} \trianglerighteq S_{\Delta^{id}}^{GAC} = GAC$.

Because, consistencies S_Δ^ϕ identify inconsistent values on the basis of a single decision, we obtain the two following results. In the spirit of our set view of decision mappings, for any two decision mappings Δ_1 and Δ_2, $\Delta_1 \cup \Delta_2$ is the decision mapping such that for every variable x and every $dom_x \subseteq dom^{init}(x)$, $(\Delta_1 \cup \Delta_2)(x, dom_x) = \Delta_1(x, dom_x) + \Delta_2(x, dom_x)$.

Proposition 10. *Let Δ_1 and Δ_2 be two decision mappings. We have $S_{\Delta_1}^\phi + S_{\Delta_2}^\phi = S_{\Delta_1 \cup \Delta_2}^\phi$.*

Proof. Let P be a CN and (x,a) be a value of P. (x,a) is $S_{\Delta_1 \cup \Delta_2}^\phi$-inconsistent $\Leftrightarrow$ there exists a decision $x \in D_x$ in $\Delta_1 \cup \Delta_2$ such that $(x,a) \notin \phi(P|_{x \in D_x}) \Leftrightarrow (x,a)$ is $S_{\Delta_1}^\phi$-inconsistent or (x,a) is $S_{\Delta_2}^\phi$-inconsistent $\Leftrightarrow (x,a)$ is $S_{\Delta_1}^\phi + S_{\Delta_2}^\phi$-inconsistent. □

$\mathscr{S}^\phi$ denotes the set of equivalence classes modulo $\approx$ of the consistencies S_Δ^ϕ that can be built from ϕ and all possible decision mappings Δ. It forms a complete lattice, in a similar way to what has been shown for qualitative constraint networks [7].

Proposition 11. $(\mathscr{S}^\phi, \trianglerighteq)$ *is a complete lattice with* $S^\phi_{\Delta^=}$ *as greatest element and* $S^\phi_{\Delta^{id}}$ *as least element.*

Proof. Let $S^\phi_{\Delta_1}$ and $S^\phi_{\Delta_2}$ be two consistencies in $\mathscr{S}^\phi$.

(Existence of binary joins) From Proposition 10, we can infer that $S^\phi_{\Delta_1 \cup \Delta_2}$ is the least upper bound of $S^\phi_{\Delta_1}$ and $S^\phi_{\Delta_2}$.

(Existence of binary meets) Let us define the set E as $E = \{S^\phi_\Delta \in \mathscr{S}^\phi : S^\phi_\Delta \trianglelefteq S^\phi_{\Delta_1}$ and $S^\phi_\Delta \trianglelefteq S^\phi_{\Delta_2}\}$. Note that $E \neq \emptyset$ since $S^\phi_{\Delta^{id}} \in E$. Next, let us define $S^\phi_{\Delta^E}$ such that $\Delta^E = \bigcup_{S^\phi_{\Delta_i} \in E} \Delta_i$. For every $S^\phi_{\Delta_i} \in E$, Δ^E is a refinement Δ_i, and so, from Proposition 9, we know that $S^\phi_{\Delta^E}$ is an upper bound of E. We now prove by contradiction that $S^\phi_{\Delta^E} \trianglelefteq S^\phi_{\Delta_1}$. Suppose that there is a value (x, a) of a CN P that is $S^\phi_{\Delta^E}$-inconsistent and $S^\phi_{\Delta_1}$-consistent. This means that there exists a decision $x \in D_x$ in $\Delta(x)$ such that $(x, a) \notin \phi(P|_{x \in D_x})$. From construction of Δ, we know that there exists a decision mapping Δ_i such that $S^\phi_{\Delta_i} \in E$ and $x \in D_x$ is in Δ_i. By definition of E, we know that $S^\phi_{\Delta_i} \trianglelefteq S^\phi_{\Delta_1}$. Consequently, (x, a) is $S^\phi_{\Delta_i}$-consistent and $(x, a) \in \phi(P|_{x \in D_x})$. This is a contradiction, so $S^\phi_\Delta \trianglelefteq S^\phi_{\Delta_1}$. Similarly, we have $S^\phi_\Delta \trianglelefteq S^\phi_{\Delta_2}$. Then S^ϕ_Δ is the greatest lower bound of $S^\phi_{\Delta_1}$ and $S^\phi_{\Delta_2}$. $\qquad\square$

4.3 Well-Behavedness

Finally, we are interested in well-behavedness of consistencies. Actually, in the general case, the consistencies S^ϕ_Δ, E^ϕ_Δ, B^ϕ_Δ and D^ϕ_Δ are not necessarily well-behaved for $(\mathscr{P}, \preceq)$. Consider as an illustration three CNs P, P_1 and P_2 which differ only by the domain of the variable x: $dom^P(x) = \{a, b, c, d\}$, $dom^{P_1}(x) = \{a, b, c\}$ and $dom^{P_2}(x) = \{d\}$. Now, consider a decision mapping Δ defined for the variable x and the domains $\{a, b, c, d\}$, $\{a, b, c\}$ and $\{d\}$ by: $\Delta(x, \{a, b, c, d\}) = \{x \in \{a\}\}$, $\Delta(x, \{a, b, c\}) = \{x \in \{a, b, c\}\}$ and $\Delta(x, \{d\}) = \{x \in \{d\}\}$. Despite the fact that $dom^P(x) = dom^{P_1}(x) \cup dom^{P_2}(x)$, one can see that the value (x, a) could be S^ϕ_Δ-consistent in P_1 and P_2, whereas S^ϕ_Δ-inconsistent in P. With such a Δ, S^ϕ_Δ is not guaranteed to be well-behaved.

Nevertheless, there exist decision mappings for which consistencies are guaranteed to be well-behaved, at least those of the class S^ϕ_Δ. Informally, a relevant decision mapping is a decision mapping that keeps its precision (in terms of decisions) when domains are restricted.

Definition 7. *A decision mapping* Δ *is said to be* relevant *if and only if for any variable* x, *any two sets of values* dom_x *and* dom'_x *such that* $dom'_x \subsetneq dom_x \subseteq dom^{init}(x)$ *and any decision* $x \in D_x$ *in* $\Delta(x, dom_x)$, *we have:*

$$D_x \cap dom'_x \neq \emptyset \Rightarrow \exists \Gamma \subseteq \Delta(x, dom'_x) \mid D_x \cap dom'_x = \cup_{(x \in D'_x) \in \Gamma} D'_x.$$

We can notice that Δ^{id}, $\Delta^=$, $\Delta^{\neq}$, Δ^{bnd} are relevant decision mappings. For our proposition, we need some additional definitions. A CN P' is a sub-CN of a

CN P if P' can be obtained from P by simply removing certain values. If P_1 and P_2 are two CNs that only differ by the domains of their variables, then $P = P_1 \cup P_2$ is the CN such that P_1 and P_2 are sub-CNs of P and for every variable x, $dom^P(x) = dom^{P_1}(x) \cup dom^{P_2}(x)$.

Proposition 12. *Let Δ be a relevant decision mapping and let P, P_1, and P_2 be three CNs such that $P = P_1 \cup P_2$. If P_1 and P_2 are S_Δ^ϕ-consistent then P is S_Δ^ϕ-consistent.*

Proof. Let (x, a) be a value of $P = P_1 \cup P_2$. Let us show that this value is S_Δ^ϕ-consistent. Consider a membership decision $x \in D_x$ in $\Delta(x, dom^P(x))$ such that $a \in D_x$. We have to show that $(x, a) \in \phi(P|_{x \in D_x})$. We know that $dom^P(x) = dom^{P_1}(x) \cup dom^{P_2}(x)$. Hence, $a \in dom^{P_1}(x)$ or $x \in dom^{P_2}(x)$. Assume that $a \in dom^{P_1}(x)$ (the case $a \in dom^{P_2}(x)$ can be handled in a similar way). Since Δ is a relevant decision mapping, there exists $\Gamma \subseteq \Delta(x, dom^{P_1}(x))$ such that $D_x \cap dom^{P_1}(x) = \cup_{(x \in D'_x) \in \Gamma} D'_x$. It follows that there exists a decision $x \in D_x^1$ in $\Delta(x, dom^{P_1}(x))$ such that $a \in D_x^1$ and $D_x^1 \subseteq D_x$. From the fact that P_1 is S_Δ^ϕ-consistent we know that $(x, a) \in \phi(P_1|_{x \in D_x^1})$. Since $a \in D_x^1$, $D_x^1 \subseteq D_x$ and P_1 is a sub-CN of P we can assert that $(x, a) \in \phi(P|_{x \in D_x})$. We conclude that (x, a) is a S_Δ^ϕ-consistent value of P. □

Corollary 1. *If Δ is a relevant decision mapping then S_Δ^ϕ is well-behaved.*

Indeed, to obtain the closure of a CN P, it suffices to take the union of all sub-CNs of P which are S_Δ^ϕ-consistent. Hence, the consistency S_Δ^ϕ for which Δ is a relevant decision mapping is well-behaved for $(\mathscr{P}, \preceq)$.

5   Conclusion

In this paper, our aim was to give a precise picture of decision-based consistencies by developing a hierarchy of general classes. This general framework offers the user a vast range of new consistencies. Several issues have now to be addressed. First, we must determine the conditions under which overlapping between decisions may be beneficial. Overlapping allows us to cover domains while considering weak decisions (e.g., decisions in $\Delta^{\neq}$) that are quick to propagate, and might also be useful to tractability procedures (e.g., in situations where only some decisions lead to known tractable networks). Second, we must seek to elaborate dynamic procedures (heuristics) so as automatically select the right decision-based consistency (set of membership decisions) at each step of a backtrack search as in [19]; many new combinations are permitted. Finally, bound consistencies and especially singleton checks on bounds may be revisited by checking several values at once (using intervals at bounds with the mechanism of detecting X_Δ^ϕ-inconsistent values), so as to speed up the inference process in shaving procedures. These are some of the main perspectives.

Acknowledgments. We would like to thank the anonymous reviewers for their valuable comments and suggestions. This work was supported by OSEO (project ISI PAJERO).

References

1. Apt, K.R.: Principles of Constraint Programming. Cambridge University Press, Cambridge (2003)
2. Bennaceur, H., Affane, M.S.: Partition-k-AC: An efficient filtering technique combining domain partition and arc consistency. In: Walsh, T. (ed.) CP 2001. LNCS, vol. 2239, pp. 560–564. Springer, Heidelberg (2001)
3. Bessiere, C.: Constraint propagation. In: Handbook of Constraint Programming, ch. 3. Elsevier, Amsterdam (2006)
4. Bessiere, C., Debruyne, R.: Theoretical analysis of singleton arc consistency and its extensions. Artificial Intelligence 172(1), 29–41 (2008)
5. Bessiere, C., Stergiou, K., Walsh, T.: Domain filtering consistencies for non-binary constraints. Artificial Intelligence 72(6-7), 800–822 (2008)
6. Carlier, J., Pinson, E.: Adjustments of heads and tails for the job-shop problem. European Journal of Operational Research 78, 146–161 (1994)
7. Condotta, J.-F., Lecoutre, C.: A class of df-consistencies for qualitative constraint networks. In: Proceedings of KR 2010, pp. 319–328 (2010)
8. Debruyne, R., Bessiere, C.: From restricted path consistency to max-restricted path consistency. In: Smolka, G. (ed.) CP 1997. LNCS, vol. 1330, pp. 312–326. Springer, Heidelberg (1997)
9. Debruyne, R., Bessiere, C.: Some practical filtering techniques for the constraint satisfaction problem. In: Proceedings of IJCAI 1997, pp. 412–417 (1997)
10. Debruyne, R., Bessiere, C.: Domain filtering consistencies. Journal of Artificial Intelligence Research 14, 205–230 (2001)
11. Dechter, R.: Constraint processing. Morgan Kaufmann, San Francisco (2003)
12. Freuder, E.C., Elfe, C.: Neighborhood inverse consistency preprocessing. In: Proceedings of AAAI 1996, pp. 202–208 (1996)
13. Lecoutre, C.: Constraint networks: techniques and algorithms. ISTE/Wiley (2009)
14. Lecoutre, C., Cardon, S., Vion, J.: Conservative dual consistency. In: Proceedings of AAAI 2007, pp. 237–242 (2007)
15. Lecoutre, C., Cardon, S., Vion, J.: Second-order consistencies. Journal of Artificial Intelligence Research (JAIR) 40, 175–219 (2011)
16. Lecoutre, C., Prosser, P.: Maintaining singleton arc consistency. In: Proceedings of CPAI 2006 Workshop held with CP 2006, pp. 47–61 (2006)
17. Lhomme, O.: Quick shaving. In: Proceedings of AAAI 2005, pp. 411–415 (2005)
18. Martin, P., Shmoys, D.B.: A new approach to computing optimal schedules for the job-shop scheduling problem. In: Cunningham, W.H., Queyranne, M., McCormick, S.T. (eds.) IPCO 1996. LNCS, vol. 1084, pp. 389–403. Springer, Heidelberg (1996)
19. Stergiou, K.: Heuristics for dynamically adapting propagation. In: Proceedings of ECAI 2008, pp. 485–489 (2008)
20. Stergiou, K., Walsh, T.: Inverse consistencies for non-binary constraints. In: Proceedings of ECAI 2006, pp. 153–157 (2006)
21. Szymanek, R., Lecoutre, C.: Constraint-level advice for shaving. In: Garcia de la Banda, M., Pontelli, E. (eds.) ICLP 2008. LNCS, vol. 5366, pp. 636–650. Springer, Heidelberg (2008)
22. van Dongen, M.R.C.: Beyond singleton arc consistency. In: Proceedings of ECAI 2006, pp. 163–167 (2006)

Hierarchically Nested Convex VCSP*

Martin C. Cooper[1] and Stanislav Živný[2]

[1] IRIT, University of Toulouse III, 31062 Toulouse, France
[2] University College, University of Oxford, UK
cooper@irit.fr   standa.zivny@cs.ox.ac.uk

Abstract. We introduce tractable classes of VCSP instances based on convex cost functions. Firstly, we show that the class of VCSP instances satisfying the *hierarchically nested convexity property* is tractable. This class generalises our recent results on VCSP instances satisfying the *non-overlapping convexity property* by dropping the assumption that the input functions are non-decreasing [3]. Not only do we generalise the tractable class from [3], but also our algorithm has better running time compared to the algorithm from [3]. We present several examples of applications including soft hierarchical global cardinality constraints, useful in rostering problems. We go on to show that, over Boolean domains, it is possible to determine in polynomial time whether there exists some subset of the constraints such that the VCSP satisfies the hierarchically nested convexity property after renaming the variables in these constraints.

1   Preliminaries

VCSPs As usual, we denote by $\mathbb{N}$ the set of positive integers with zero, and by $\mathbb{Q}$ set of all rational numbers. We denote $\overline{\mathbb{Q}} - \mathbb{Q} \cup \{\infty\}$ with the standard addition operation extended so that for all $\alpha \in \mathbb{Q}$, $\alpha + \infty = \infty$.

In a VCSP (Valued Constraint Satisfaction Problem) the objective function to be minimised is the sum of cost functions whose arguments are subsets of arbitrary size of the variables $v_1, \ldots, v_n$ where the domain of v_i is D_i. For notational convenience, we interpret a solution x (i.e. an assignment to the variables $v_1, \ldots, v_n$) as the set of $\langle$variable,value$\rangle$ assignments $\{\langle v_i, x_i \rangle : i = 1, \ldots, n\}$. The range of all cost functions is $\overline{\mathbb{Q}}$.

Network flows. Here we review some basics on flows in graphs. We refer the reader to the standard textbook [1] for more details. We present only the notions and results needed for our purposes. In particular, we deal with only integral flows. Let $G = (V, A)$ be a directed graph with vertex set V and arc set A. To each arc $a \in A$ we assign a *demand/capacity* function $[d(a), c(a)]$ and a *weight*

* Martin Cooper is supported by ANR Projects ANR-10-BLAN-0210 and ANR-10-BLAN-0214. Stanislav Živný is supported by a Junior Research Fellowship at University College, Oxford.

(or cost) function $w(a)$, where $d(a), c(a) \in \mathbb{N}$ and $w(a) \in \mathbb{Q}$. Let $s, t \in V$. A function $f : A \to \mathbb{N}$ is called an $s - t$ *flow* (or just a flow) if for all $v \in V \setminus \{s, t\}$,

$$\sum_{a=(u,v)\in A} f(a) = \sum_{a=(v,u)\in A} f(a) \qquad \text{(flow conservation)}.$$

We say that a flow is *feasible* if $d(a) \leq f(a) \leq c(a)$ for each $a \in A$. We define the *value* of flow f as $val(f) = \sum_{a=(s,v)\in A} f(a) - \sum_{a=(v,s)\in A} f(a)$. We define the *cost* of flow f as $\sum_{a\in A} w(a)f(a)$. A *minimum-cost flow* is a feasible flow with minimum cost.

Algorithms for finding the minimum-cost flow of a given value are well known [1]. We consider a generalisation of the minimum-cost flow problem. To each arc $a \in A$ we assign a convex weight function w_a. In particular, we consider the model in which the weight functions w_a ($a \in A$) are convex piecewise linear and given by the breakpoints (which covers the case of convex functions over the integers). We define the *cost* of flow f as $\sum_{a\in A} w_a(f(a))$. The corresponding problem of finding a minimum-cost integral flow is known as the *minimum convex cost flow* problem. In a network with n vertices and m edges with capacities at most U, the minimum convex cost flow problem can be solved in time $O((m \log U)SP(n, m))$, where $SP(n, m)$ is the time to compute a shortest directed path in the network [1].

2   Hierarchically Nested Convex

A discrete function $g : \{0, \ldots, s\} \to \overline{\mathbb{Q}}$ is called *convex on the interval* $[l, u]$ if g is finite-valued on the interval $[l, u]$ and the derivative of g is non-decreasing on $[l, u]$, i.e. if $g(m + 2) - g(m + 1) \geq g(m + 1) - g(m)$ for all $m = l, \ldots, u - 2$. For brevity, we will often say that g is *convex* if it is convex on some interval $[l, u] \subseteq [0, s]$ and infinite elsewhere (i.e. on $[0, l - 1] \cup [u + 1, s]$).

Two sets A_1, A_2 are said to be *non-overlapping* if they are either disjoint or one is a subset of the other (i.e. $A_1 \cap A_2 = \emptyset$, $A_1 \subseteq A_2$ or $A_2 \subseteq A_1$). Sets $A_1, \ldots, A_r$ are called *hierarchically nested* if for any $1 \leq i, j \leq r$, A_i and A_j are non-overlapping. If A_i is a set of $\langle$variable,value$\rangle$ assignments of a VCSP instance $\mathcal{P}$ and x a solution to $\mathcal{P}$, then we use the notation $|x \cap A_i|$ to represent the number of $\langle$variable,value$\rangle$ assignments in the solution x which lie in A_i.

Definition 1. *Let $\mathcal{P}$ be a VCSP instance. Let $A_1, \ldots, A_r$ be hierarchically nested sets of $\langle$variable,value$\rangle$ assignments of $\mathcal{P}$. Let s_i be the number of distinct variables occurring in the set of $\langle$variable,value$\rangle$ assignments A_i. Instance $\mathcal{P}$ satisfies the hierarchically nested convexity property if the objective function of $\mathcal{P}$ can be written as $g(x) = g_1(|x \cap A_1|) + \ldots + g_r(|x \cap A_r|)$ where each $g_i : [0, s_i] \to \overline{\mathbb{Q}}$ ($i = 1, \ldots, r$) is convex on an interval $[l_i, u_i] \subseteq [0, s_i]$ and $g_i(z) = \infty$ for $z \in [0, l_i - 1] \cup [u_i + 1, s_i]$.*

Theorem 1. *Any VCSP instance $\mathcal{P}$ satisfying the hierarchically nested convexity property can be solved in polynomial time.*

In our previous paper [3], we proved a special case of Theorem 1 where all functions g_i $(i = 1, \ldots, r)$ are non-decreasing. We give an algorithm to solve VCSPs satisfying the hierarchically nested convexity property in Section 2.1 and a proof of polynomial-time complexity of this algorithm in Section 2.2.

Observe that the addition of any unary cost function cannot destroy the hierarchically nested convexity property. This is because for each $\langle$variable,value$\rangle$ assignment $\langle v_j, a \rangle$ we can add the singleton $A_i = \{\langle v_j, a \rangle\}$ which is necessarily either disjoint or a subset of any other set A_k (and furthermore the corresponding function $g_i : \{0, 1\} \to \overline{\mathbb{Q}}$ is trivially convex).

Example 1 (Value-based soft GCC). The GLOBAL CARDINALITY CONSTRAINT (GCC), introduced by Régin [8], is a generalisation of the ALLDIFFERENT constraint. Given a set of n variables, the GCC specifies for each domain value d a lower bound l_d and an upper bound u_d on the number of variables that are assigned value d. The ALLDIFFERENT constraint is the special case of GCC with $l_d = 0$ and $u_d = 1$ for every d. Soft versions of the GCC have been considered by van Hoeve et al. [6].

The value-based soft GCC minimises the number of values below or above the given bound. We show that the value-based soft GCC satisfies the hierarchically nested convexity property.

For every domain value $d \in D$, let $A_d = \{\langle v_i, d \rangle : i = 1, \ldots, n\}$. Clearly, $A_1, \ldots, A_s$ are disjoint, where $s = |D|$. For every d, let

$$g_d(m) = \begin{cases} l_d - m & \text{if } m < l_d \\ 0 & \text{if } l_d \leq m \leq u_d \\ m - u_d & \text{if } m > u_d \end{cases}$$

From the definition of g_d, $g_d(m+1) - g_d(m)$ for $m = 0, \ldots, n-1$ is the sequence $-1, \ldots, -1, 0, \ldots, 0, 1, \ldots, 1$. Therefore, for every d, g_d has a non-decreasing derivative and hence is convex.

Example 2 (Nurse Rostering). In a nurse rostering problem, we have to assign several nurses to each shift [2]. There may be strict lower and upper bounds l_i, u_i on the number of nurses assigned to shift i. For example, assigning zero nurses to a shift is no doubt unacceptable. There is also a penalty if we assign too few or too many nurses to the same shift. The cost function is not necessarily symmetric. For example, being short-staffed is potentially dangerous (and hence worse) than being over-staffed which just costs more money. The cost function for shift i could, for example, be $g(z) = \frac{l_i}{z} - 1$ for $0 \leq z < l_i$, $g(z) = 0$ for $z \in [l_i, u_i]$ and $g(z) = z - u_i$ for $z > u_i$. It is easily verified that this function is convex.

Example 3 (Hierarchically nested value-based soft GCC). Being able to nest GCC constraints is useful in many staff assignment problems where there is a hierarchy (e.g. senior manager-manager-personnel, foreman-worker, senior nurse-nurse) [9]. We might want to impose soft convex constraints such as each day we prefer that there are between 10 and 15 people at work, of which at least 5 are managers among whom there is exactly 1 senior manger, with convex penalties if these constraints do not hold.

Suppose that the constraints of a VCSP instance consist of soft GCC constraints on pairwise non-overlapping sets of variables $S_1, \ldots, S_t$. Let $A_{id} = \{\langle x, d \rangle : x \in S_i\}$. Clearly, the sets of assignments A_{id} are hierarchically nested and, as shown in Example 1, the cost functions corresponding to each GCC constraint are convex.

2.1 Algorithm

Our algorithm is similar to the algorithm presented in [3] based on finding a minimum-cost flow in a network. We use a similar network, with the difference that we only require a single arc between any pair of nodes and the corresponding cost function g_i is now an arbitrary convex function (which is not necessarily non-decreasing). Somewhat surprisingly, this small generalisation allows us to solve many more problems, as we have demonstrated in Section 2 since all these examples involve cost functions g_i which are not monotone non-decreasing.

We call the sets A_i ($i = 1, \ldots, r$) assignment-sets. We assume that the assignment-sets A_i are distinct, since if $A_i = A_j$ then these two sets can be merged by replacing the two functions g_i, g_j by their sum (which is necessarily also convex). Note that the assignment-set consisting of all variable-value assignments, if present in $\mathcal{P}$, can be ignored since it is just a constant. We say that assignment-set A_k is the *father* of assignment-set A_i if it is the minimal assignment-set which properly contains A_i, i.e. $A_i \subset A_k$ and $\nexists A_j$ such that $A_i \subset A_j \subset A_k$. It follows from the definition of hierarchically nested convexity that A_k is unique and hence that the father relation defines a tree. Moreover, again from the definition of hierarchically nested convexity, for every variable v_i of $\mathcal{P}$ and every $a \in D_i$, there is a unique minimal assignment-set containing $\langle v_i, a \rangle$. Indeed, we can assume without loss of generality that this is precisely $\{\langle v_i, a \rangle\}$.

We construct a directed graph $G_{\mathcal{P}}$ whose minimum-cost integral flows of value n are in one-to-one correspondence with the solutions to $\mathcal{P}$. $G_{\mathcal{P}}$ has the following nodes:

1. the source node s;
2. a variable node v_i ($i = 1, \ldots, n$) for each variable of $\mathcal{P}$;
3. an assignment node $\langle v_i, d \rangle$ ($d \in D_i$, $i = 1, \ldots, n$) for each possible variable-value assignment in $\mathcal{P}$;
4. an assignment-set node A_i ($i = 1, \ldots, r$) for each assignment-set in $\mathcal{P}$;
5. the sink node t.

$G_{\mathcal{P}}$ has the following arcs:

1. $a = (s, v_i)$ for each variable v_i of $\mathcal{P}$; $d(a) = c(a) = 1$ (this forces a flow of exactly 1 through each variable node v_i); $w(a) = 0$;
2. $a = (v_i, \langle v_i, d \rangle)$ for all variables v_i and for each $d \in D_i$; $d(a) = 0$; $c(a) = 1$; $w(a) = 0$;

3. $a = (\langle v_i, d \rangle, A_j)$ for all variables v_i and for each $d \in D_i$, where A_j is the minimal assignment-set containing $\langle v_i, d \rangle$; $d(a) = 0$; $c(a) = 1$; $w(a) = 0$;

4. for each assignment-set A_i with father A_j, there is an arc a from A_i to A_j with cost function g_i, demand $d(a) = l_i$ and capacity $c(a) = u_i$.

Clearly, $G_{\mathcal{P}}$ can be constructed from $\mathcal{P}$ in polynomial time. We now prove that minimum-cost flows f of value n in $G_{\mathcal{P}}$ are in one-to-one correspondence with assignments in $\mathcal{P}$ and, furthermore, that the cost of f is equal to the cost in $\mathcal{P}$ of the corresponding assignment.

All feasible flows have value n since all n arcs (s, v_i) leaving the source have both demand and capacity equal to 1. Flows in $G_{\mathcal{P}}$ necessarily correspond to the assignment of a unique value x_i to each variable v_i since the flow of 1 through node v_i must traverse a node $\langle v_i, x_i \rangle$ for some unique $x_i \in D_i$. It remains to show that for every assignment $x = \{\langle v_1, x_1 \rangle, \ldots, \langle v_n, x_n \rangle\}$ which is feasible (i.e. whose cost in $\mathcal{P}$ is finite), there is a corresponding minimum-cost feasible flow f in $G_{\mathcal{P}}$ of cost $g(x) = g_1(|x \cap A_1|) + \ldots + g_r(|x \cap A_r|)$.

For each arc a which is incoming to or outgoing from $\langle v_i, d \rangle$ in $G_{\mathcal{P}}$, let $f(a) = 1$ if $d = x_i$ and 0 otherwise. By construction, each assignment-set node A_i in $G_{\mathcal{P}}$ only has outgoing arcs to its father assignment-set. The flow f_a in arc a from A_i to its father assignment-set A_j is uniquely determined by the assignment of values to variables in the solution x. Trivially this is therefore a minimum-cost flow corresponding to the assignment x. The cost of flow f is clearly $\sum_i g_i(|x \cap A_i|)$ which corresponds precisely to the cost of the assignment x.

We remark that since our construction is projection-safe [7], it can be used for Soft Global Arc Consistency for hierarchically nested convex constraints.

2.2   Complexity

Let $\mathcal{P}$ be a VCSP instance with n variables, each with a domain of size at most d, and r assignment-sets A_i. The maximum number of distinct non-overlapping sets A_i is $2nd - 1$ since the sets of assignments A_i form a tree with at most nd leaves (corresponding to single $\langle$variable,value$\rangle$ assignments) and in which all non-leaf nodes have at least two sons. Thus $r = O(nd)$. The network $G_{\mathcal{P}}$ has $n' = O(n + nd + r) = O(nd)$ vertices and arcs. $G_{\mathcal{P}}$ can be built in $O((nd)^2)$ time in a top-down manner, by adding assignment-sets in inverse order of size (which ensures that an assignment-set is always inserted after its father) and using a table $T[\langle v, a \rangle]$=smallest assignment set (in the tree being built) containing $\langle v, a \rangle$.

In a network with n' vertices and m' arcs with capacities at most U, the minimum convex cost flow problem can be solved in time $O((m \log U)SP(n', m'))$, where $SP(n', m')$ is the time to compute a shortest directed path in the network with n' vertices and m' edges [1]. Using Fibonacci heaps [4], $SP(n', m') = O(m' + n' \log n') = O(nd \log(nd))$, since the number of vertices n' and arcs m' are both $O(nd)$. The maximum capacity U in the network $G_{\mathcal{P}}$ is at most n. Hence an optimal solution to a hierarchically nested convex VCSP can be determined in $O((nd \log n)(nd \log(nd))) = O((nd)^2 (\log n)(\log n + \log d))$ time.

The running time of our algorithm is better than the running time of the algorithm from [3], which is $O(n^3 d^2)$. The improvement is mostly due to the fact that the new construction involves only $O(nd)$ arcs as opposed to $O((nd)^2)$ arcs in [3]. Moreover, our algorithm solves a bigger class of problems compared to [3]. Overall, we solve more and faster!

3   Renamable Boolean Hierarchically Nested Convex VCSP

In this section we extend the class of hierarchically nested convex VCSPs to allow renaming of certain variables in the case of Boolean domains.

We begin by illustrating the notion of renaming by means of an example. First, we require some notation.

Cost function $\text{ATMOST}_r(A)$ returns 0 if x contains at most r assignments from the set of assignments A, and $\text{ATMOST}_r(A)$ returns 1 otherwise. Similarly, cost function $\text{ATLEAST}_r(A)$ returns 0 if x contains at least r assignments from the set of assignments A, and $\text{ATLEAST}_r(A)$ returns 1 otherwise. Note that cost functions ATLEAST_1 and ATMOST_r, where $r = |A| - 1$, are both convex on $[0, |A|]$. In the remainder of this section we will consider only Boolean VCSPs.

Example 4. Let $\mathcal{P}$ be a Max-SAT instance given in CNF form by the following clauses:

$$(a \vee b \vee c), \quad (c \vee d), \quad (\neg c \vee \neg d \vee e), \quad (\neg a \vee \neg e).$$

Clearly, a clause with literals A can be written as $\text{ATLEAST}_1(A)$. Notice that, in this example, the first two clauses are overlapping. However, we can replace the second clause by the equivalent constraint $\text{ATMOST}_1(\{\neg c, \neg d\})$. This gives us an equivalent problem with the following constraints:

$$(a \vee b \vee c), \quad \text{ATMOST}_1(\{\neg c, \neg d\}), \quad (\neg c \vee \neg d \vee e), \quad (\neg a \vee \neg e).$$

Now $\mathcal{P}$ is expressed as an instance satisfying the hierarchically nested convexity property on the hierarchically nested sets of assignments $\{a, b, c\}$, $\{\neg c, \neg d\}$, $\{\neg c, \neg d, e\}$, $\{\neg a, \neg e\}$.

Example 4 leads to the following definitions:

Definition 2. *Given a valued constraint in the form of the cost function $g(|x \cap A|)$, where A is a set of Boolean assignments (i.e. literals) of size m, we define the* renaming *of this valued constraint, on the set of Boolean assignments denoted by* $rename(A) = \bar{A}$, *as the valued constraint $g'(|x \cap \bar{A}|) = g(m - |x \cap \bar{A}|) = g(|x \cap A|)$, where $\bar{A} = \{\neg x \mid x \in A\}$.*

The function $g'(z) = g(m - z)$ is clearly convex if and only if g is convex.

Definition 3. *A Boolean VCSP instance $\mathcal{P}$ with the objective function $g_1(|x \cap A_1|) + \ldots + g_r(|x \cap A_r|)$ is* renamable hierarchically nested convex *if there is a subset of the constraints of $\mathcal{P}$ whose renaming results in an equivalent VCSP instance $\mathcal{P}'$ which is hierarchically nested convex.*

Theorem 2. *The class of renamable hierarchically nested convex VCSPs is recognisable and solvable in polynomial time.*

Proof. We show that recognition is polynomial-time by a simple reduction to 2-SAT, a well-known problem solvable in polynomial time [5]. Let $\mathcal{P}$ be a Boolean VCSP instance with r constraints such that the ith constraint ($i = 1, \ldots, r$) is $g_i(|x \cap A_i|)$ for a convex function g_i. For each constraint in $\mathcal{P}$, there is a Boolean variable ren_i indicating whether or not the ith constraint is renamed. For each pair of distinct $i, j \in \{1, \ldots, r\}$, we add clauses of length 2 as follows:

1. if A_i and A_j overlap then add constraint $ren_i \Leftrightarrow \neg ren_j$ (since we must rename just one of the two constraints);
2. if $rename(A_i)$ and A_j overlap then add constraint $ren_i \Leftrightarrow ren_j$ (to avoid introducing an overlap by a renaming).

It is easy to see that solutions to the constructed 2-SAT instance correspond to valid renamings of $\mathcal{P}$ which give rise to an equivalent VCSP instance satisfying the hierarchically nested convexity property. Tractability of solving the resulting instance follows directly from Theorem 1. $\qquad\square$

4   Maximality of Hierarchically Nested Convex

This section shows that relaxing either convexity or hierarchical nestedness leads to intractability.

Proposition 1. *The class of VCSP instances whose objective function is of the form $g(x) = g_1(|x \cap A_1|) + \ldots + g_r(|x \cap A_r|)$ where the functions g_i are convex, but the sets of assignments A_i may overlap, is NP-hard, even if $|A_i| \leq 2$ for all $i \in \{1, \ldots, r\}$ and all variables are Boolean.*

Proof. It suffices to demonstrate a polynomial-time reduction from the well-known NP-hard problem Max-2SAT [5]. We have seen in Section 3 that any Max-2SAT clause $l_1 \vee l_2$ (where l_1, l_2 are literals) is equivalent to the $\{0, 1\}$-valued convex cost function $\textsc{AtLeast}_1(|x \cap \{l_1, l_2\}|)$. It is therefore possible to code any instance of Max-2SAT using convex cost functions (on possibly overlapping sets of assignments). $\qquad\square$

Proposition 2. *The class of VCSP instances whose objective function is of the form $g(x) = g_1(|x \cap A_1|) + \ldots + g_r(|x \cap A_r|)$ where the sets of assignments A_i are hierarchically nested, but the functions g_i are not necessarily convex, is NP-hard even if $|A_i| \leq 3$ for all $i \in \{1, \ldots, r\}$ and all variables are Boolean.*

Proof. We give a polynomial-time reduction from the well-known NP-complete problem 3SAT [5]. Let I_{3SAT} be an instance of 3SAT with m clauses. The constraint $\textsc{AllEqual}(l_1, l_2, l_3)$ (where l_1, l_2, l_3 are literals) is equivalent to the (non-convex) cost function $g(|x \cap \{l_1, l_2, l_3\}|)$ where $g(0) = g(3) = 0$ and $g(1) = g(2) = \infty$. For each variable v in I_{3SAT}, we use the following gadget G_v based on non-overlapping AllEqual constraints to produce multiple copies $v_1, \ldots, v_m$ of the variable v and multiple copies $w_1, \ldots, w_m$ of its negation $\overline{v}$: G_v consists of the constraints AllEqual$(\overline{u_i}, \overline{v_i}, \overline{y_i})$ ($i \in \{1, \ldots, m\}$), AllEqual$(y_i, \overline{w_i}, u_{i+1})$ ($i \in \{1, \ldots, m-1\}$), and AllEqual$(y_m, \overline{w_m}, u_1)$, where the variables u_i, y_i only occur in the gadget G_v. It is easy to verify that G_v imposes $v_1 = \ldots = v_m = \overline{w_1} = \ldots = \overline{w_m}$. Furthermore, the variables v_i, w_i only occur negatively in G_v. We now replace the ith clause of I_{3SAT} by a clause in which each positive variable v is replaced by its ith copy v_i and each negative variable $\overline{v}$ is replaced by the ith copy w_i of $\overline{v}$. This produces a hierarchically nested VCSP instance which is equivalent to I_{3SAT} (but whose cost functions are not all convex).   □

5   Conclusions

The complexity of the recognition problem for hierarchically nested convex VCSPs is an open problem if the functions g_i are not explicitly given. The complexity of hierarchically nested non-convex VCSPs where all assignment-sets are of size at most 2 is open as well. (Note that the NP-hardness reduction in the proof of Proposition 2 requires assignment-sets of size up to three.)

Acknowledgments. We are grateful to Jean-Philippe Métivier for pointing out the utility of soft hierarchically nested GCC in nurse rostering.

References

1. Ahuja, R., Magnanti, T., Orlin, J.: Network Flows: Theory, Algorithms, and Applications. Prentice Hall/Pearson (2005)
2. Burke, E.K., Causmaecker, P.D., Berghe, G.V., Landeghem, H.V.: The state of the art of nurse rostering. Journal of Scheduling 7(6), 441–499 (2004)
3. Cooper, M.C., Živný, S.: Hybrid tractability of valued constraint problems. Artificial Intelligence 175(9-10), 1555–1569 (2011)
4. Fredman, M.L., Tarjan, R.E.: Fibonacci heaps and their uses in improved network optimization algorithms. Journal of the ACM 34(3), 596–615 (1987)
5. Garey, M., Johnson, D.: Computers and Intractability: A Guide to the Theory of NP-Completeness. W.H. Freeman, New York (1979)
6. van Hoeve, W.J., Pesant, G., Rousseau, L.M.: On global warming: Flow-based soft global constraints. Journal of Heuristics 12(4-5), 347–373 (2006)
7. Lee, J.H.M., Leung, K.L.: Towards efficient consistency enforcement for global constraints in weighted constraint satisfaction. In: Proceedings of the 21st International Joint Conference on Artificial Intelligence (IJCAI 2009), pp. 559–565 (2009)
8. Régin, J.C.: Generalized Arc Consistency for Global Cardinality Constraint. In: Proceedings of the 13th National Conference on AI (AAAI 1996), vol. 1, pp. 209–215 (1996)
9. Zanarini, A., Pesant, G.: Generalizations of the global cardinality constraint for hierarchical resources. In: Van Hentenryck, P., Wolsey, L.A. (eds.) CPAIOR 2007. LNCS, vol. 4510, pp. 361–375. Springer, Heidelberg (2007)

Tractable Triangles⋆

Martin C. Cooper[1] and Stanislav Živný[2]

[1] IRIT, University of Toulouse III, 31062 Toulouse, France
[2] University College, University of Oxford, UK
cooper@irit.fr standa.zivny@cs.ox.ac.uk

Abstract. We study the computational complexity of binary valued constraint satisfaction problems (VCSP) given by allowing only certain types of costs in every triangle of variable-value assignments to three distinct variables. We show that for several computational problems, including CSP, Max-CSP, finite-valued VCSP, and general-valued VCSP, the only non-trivial tractable classes are the well known maximum matching problem and the recently discovered joint-winner property [9].

1 Introduction

1.1 Background

An instance of the constraint satisfaction problem (CSP) consists of a collection of variables which must be assigned values subject to specified constraints. Each CSP instance has an underlying undirected graph, known as its *constraint network*, whose vertices are the variables of the instance, and two vertices are adjacent if corresponding variables are related by some constraint. Such a graph is also known as the *structure* of the instance.

An important line of research on the CSP is to identify all tractable cases which are recognisable in polynomial time. Most of this work has been focused on one of the two general approaches: either identifying forms of constraint which are sufficiently restrictive to ensure tractability no matter how they are combined [3,16], or else identifying structural properties of constraint networks which ensure tractability no matter what forms of constraint are imposed [13].

The first approach has led to identifying certain algebraic properties known as polymorphisms [20] which are necessary for a set of constraint types to ensure tractability. A set of constraint types with this property is called a tractable *constraint language*. The second approach has been used to characterise all tractable cases of bounded-arity CSPs (such as binary CSPs): the *only* class of structures which ensures tractability (subject to certain complexity theory assumptions) are structures of *bounded tree-width* [19].

In practice, constraint satisfaction problems usually do not possess a sufficiently restricted structure or use a sufficiently restricted constraint language to

⋆ Martin Cooper is supported by ANR Projects ANR-10-BLAN-0210 and ANR-10-BLAN-0214. Stanislav Živný is supported by a Junior Research Fellowship at University College, Oxford.

J. Lee (Ed.): CP 2011, LNCS 6876, pp. 195–209, 2011.

fall into any of these tractable classes. Nevertheless, they may still have properties which ensure they can be solved efficiently, but these properties concern both the structure and the form of the constraints. Such properties have sometimes been called *hybrid* reasons for tractability [12,7,6,8].

Since in practice many constraint satisfaction problems are over-constrained, and hence have no solution, *soft* constraint satisfaction problems have been studied [12]. In an instance of the soft CSP, every constraint is associated with a function (rather than a relation as in the CSP) which represents preferences among different partial assignments, and the goal is to find the best assignment. Several very general soft CSP frameworks have been proposed in the literature [29,2]. In this paper we focus on one of the very general frameworks, the *valued* constraint satisfaction problem (VCSP) [29].

Similarly to the CSP, an important line of research on the VCSP is to identify tractable cases which are recognisable in polynomial time. Is is well known that structural reasons for tractability generalise to the VCSP [1,12]. In the case of language restrictions, only a few conditions are known to guarantee tractability of a given set of valued constraints [5,4,21,22].

1.2   Contributions

In this paper, we study hybrid tractability of binary VCSPs for various valuation structures that correspond to the CSP, CSP with soft unary constraints, Max-CSP, finite-valued VCSP and general-valued VCSP.

We focus on classes of instances defined by allowed combinations of binary costs in every assignment to 3 different variables (called a *triangle*). Our motivation for this investigation is that one such restriction, the so-called joint-winner property has recently been shown to define a tractable class with several practical applications [9].

The JWP (joint-winner property) states that for any triangle of variable-value assignments $\{\langle v_i, a \rangle, \langle v_j, b \rangle, \langle v_k, c \rangle\}$, no one of the binary costs $c_{ij}(a,b)$, $c_{jk}(b,c)$, $c_{ik}(a,c)$ is strictly less than the other two. This holds, for example, if there is a (soft) not-equal constraint between each pair of variables (v_i, v_j), (v_j, v_k), (v_i, v_k), by transitivity of equality. In [9] we gave several applications of the JWP in CSPs and VCSPs. For example, the class of CSP instances satisfying the JWP generalises the AllDifferent constraint with arbitrary unary constraints, since its binary constraints are equivalent to allowing at most one assignment from each of a set of disjoint sets of (variable,value) assignments. We also showed how to code a set of non-overlapping SoftAllDifferent constraints with either graph- or variable-based costs as a VCSP satisfying the JWP. As another example, a job-shop scheduling problem in which the aim is to minimise the sum, over all jobs, of their time until completion can be coded as a VCSP satisfying the JWP [9]. The JWP has also been generalised to VCSPs in which the objective function is the sum of hierarchically nested arbitrary convex cost functions [10]: applications include soft hierarchical global cardinality constraints, useful in rostering problems.

For finite valuation structures (corresponding to the CSP and Max-CSP), there are only finitely many possibilities of multi-sets of binary costs in a triangle. For example, in Max-CSP there are only four possible multi-sets of costs, namely $\{0,0,0\}, \{0,0,1\}, \{0,1,1\}$ and $\{1,1,1\}$. However, for infinite valuation structures (corresponding to the finite-valued CSP and general-valued VCSP) there are infinitely many combinations. Obviously, we cannot consider them all, and hence we consider an equivalence relation based on the total order on the valuation structure. There are 4 equivalence classes, thus giving 4 types of combinations of the three binary costs α, β, γ given by $\alpha = \beta = \gamma$, $\alpha = \beta < \gamma$, $\alpha = \beta > \gamma$, $\alpha < \beta < \gamma$.

For all valuation structures we consider, we prove a dichotomy theorem, thus identifying all tractable cases with respect to the equivalence relation on the combinations of costs. It turns out that there are only two non-trivial tractable cases: the well-known maximum weighted matching problem [15], and the recently discovered joint-winner property [9].

The study of the tractability of classes of instances defined by properties on triangles of costs can be seen as a first step on the long road towards the characterisation of tractable classes of VCSPs based on so-called hybrid properties which are not captured by restrictions on the language of cost functions or the structure of the constraint graph. The intractability results in this paper provide initial guidelines for such a research program.

Paper organisation. The rest of this paper is organised as follows. We start, in Section 2, with defining valuation structures, binary valued constraint satisfaction problems and cost types. In Section 3, we present our results on the CSP, followed up with results on the CSP with soft unary constraints. In Section 4, we present our results on the Max-CSP, followed by the results on the finite-valued and general-valued VCSP in Section 5. Finally, we conclude in Section 6.

2   Preliminaries

A *valuation structure*, Ω, is a totally ordered set, with a minimum and a maximum element (denoted 0 and ∞), together with a commutative, associative binary aggregation operator (denoted $\oplus$), such that for all $\alpha, \beta, \gamma \in \Omega$, $\alpha \oplus 0 = \alpha$, and $\alpha \oplus \gamma \geq \beta \oplus \gamma$ whenever $\alpha \geq \beta$. Members of Ω are called *costs*.

An instance of the binary *Valued Constraint Satisfaction Problem* (VCSP) is given by n variables $v_1, \ldots, v_n$ over finite domains $D_1, \ldots, D_n$ of values, unary cost functions $c_i : D_i \to \Omega$, and binary cost functions $c_{ij} : D_i \times D_j \to \Omega$ [29]. (If the domains of all the variables are the same, we denote it by D.) The goal is to find an assignment of values from the domains to the variables which minimises the total cost given by

$$\bigoplus_{i=1}^{n} c_i(v_i) \ \oplus \ \bigoplus_{1 \leq i < j \leq n} c_{ij}(v_i, v_j) .$$

Note that we assume that all binary cost functions c_{ij} exist. The absence of any constraint between variables v_i, v_j is modelled by a cost function c_{ij} which is uniformly zero.

We shall denote by $\mathbb{Q}_+$ the set of all non-negative rational numbers. We define $\overline{\mathbb{Q}}_+ = \mathbb{Q}_+ \cup \{\infty\}$. In this paper, we consider the following valuation structures: $\{0, \infty\}$, $\{0, 1\}$, $\mathbb{Q}_+$ and $\overline{\mathbb{Q}}_+$, where in all cases the aggregation operation is the standard addition operation on rationals, $+$, extended so that $a + \infty = \infty$ for all $a \in \overline{\mathbb{Q}}_+$. These valuation structures correspond to CSP, Max-CSP, finite-valued VCSP and general-valued VCSP, respectively.

Given an infinite valuation structure, such as $\mathbb{Q}_+$ or $\overline{\mathbb{Q}}_+$, there is an infinite number of possible sets of triples of costs. Obviously, we cannot consider all such sets. Therefore, we only consider the cases defined by the total order on Ω. We use curly brackets $\{\}$ for multi-sets. The following table defines possible cost types of 3 costs.

Symbol	Costs	Remark
$\triangle$	$\{\alpha, \beta, \gamma\}$	$\alpha, \beta, \gamma \in \Omega,\ \alpha \neq \beta \neq \gamma \neq \alpha$
$<$	$\{\alpha, \alpha, \beta\}$	$\alpha, \beta \in \Omega,\ \alpha < \beta$
$>$	$\{\alpha, \alpha, \beta\}$	$\alpha, \beta \in \Omega,\ \alpha > \beta$
$=$	$\{\alpha, \alpha, \alpha\}$	$\alpha \in \Omega$

We use the word *triangle* for any set of assignments $\{\langle v_i, a\rangle, \langle v_j, b\rangle, \langle v_k, c\rangle\}$, where v_i, v_j, v_k are distinct variables and $a \in D_i, b \in D_j, c \in D_k$ are domain values. The multi-set of costs in such a triangle is $\{c_{ij}(a, b), c_{ik}(a, c), c_{jk}(b, c)\}$.

We denote by $\mathfrak{D} = \{\triangle, <, >, =\}$ the set of all possible cost types. Let Ω be a fixed valuation structure. For any set $S \subseteq \mathfrak{D}$, we denote by $\mathcal{A}_\Omega(S)$ ($\mathcal{A}$ for allowed) the set of binary VCSP instances with the valuation structure Ω where for every triangle the multi-set of costs in the triangle is of a type from S.

For instance, if $\Omega = \mathbb{Q}_+$ and $S = \{\triangle\}$, then $\mathcal{A}_\Omega(S)$ is the set of binary finite-valued VCSP instances where for every triangle $\{\langle v_i, a\rangle, \langle v_j, b\rangle, \langle v_k, c\rangle\}$ the multi-set of costs in the triangle $\{c_{ij}(a, b), c_{ik}(a, c), c_{jk}(b, c)\}$ contains exactly three distinct costs.

Our goal is to classify the complexity of $\mathcal{A}_\Omega(S)$ for every $S \subseteq \mathfrak{D}$.

Proposition 1. *Let Ω be an arbitrary valuation structure and $S \subseteq \mathfrak{D}$.*

1. *If $\mathcal{A}_\Omega(S)$ is tractable and $S' \subseteq S$, then $\mathcal{A}_\Omega(S')$ is tractable.*
2. *If $\mathcal{A}_\Omega(S)$ is intractable and $S' \supseteq S$, then $\mathcal{A}_\Omega(S')$ is intractable.*

A triangle $\{\langle v_i, a\rangle, \langle v_j, b\rangle, \langle v_k, c\rangle\}$, where $a \in D_i, b \in D_j, c \in D_k$, satisfies the *joint-winner property* (JWP) if either all three $c_{ij}(a, b)$, $c_{ik}(a, c)$, $c_{jk}(b, c)$ are the same, or two of them are equal and the third one is bigger. A VCSP instance satisfies the joint-winner property if every triangle satisfies the joint-winner property.

Theorem 1 ([9]). *The class of VCSP instances satisfying JWP is tractable.*

In [9], we also showed that the class defined by the joint-winner property is maximal – allowing a single extra triple of costs that violates the joint-winner property renders the class NP-hard.

Theorem 2 ([9]). *Let $\alpha < \beta \leq \gamma$, where $\alpha \in \mathbb{Q}_+$ and $\beta, \gamma \in \overline{\mathbb{Q}}_+$, be a multi-set of (not necessarily distinct) costs that do not satisfy the joint-winner property. The class of instances where the costs in each triangle either satisfy the joint-winner property or are $\{\alpha, \beta, \gamma\}$ is NP-hard*

In this paper we consider a much broader question, whether allowing any arbitrary set S of triples of costs in triangles, where S does not necessarily include all triples allowed by the JWP, defines a tractable class of VCSP instances.

Remark 1. We implicitly allow all unary cost functions. In fact, all our tractability results work with unary cost functions, and our NP-hardness results do no require any unary cost functions.

Remark 2. We consider problems with unbounded domains; that is, the domain sizes are part of the input. However, all our NP-hardness results are obtained for problems with a fixed domain size.[1] In the case of CSPs, we need domains of size 3 to prove NP-hardness, and in all other cases domains of size 2 are sufficient to prove NP-hardness. Since binary CSPs are known to be tractable on Boolean domains, and any VCSP is trivially tractable over domains of size 1, all our NP-hardness results are tight.

Remark 3. Binary finite-valued/general-valued VCSPs have also been studied under the name of pair-wise MinSum or pair-wise Markov Random Field (MRF). Consequently, our results readily apply to these frameworks, and other graphical models equivalent to the VCSP.

3 CSP

In this section, we will focus on the valuation structure $\Omega = \{0, \infty\}$; that is, the Constraint Satisfaction Problem (CSP). It is clear that the $\triangle$ cost type cannot occur. Since there are only 2 possible costs, we split the cost type $=$ into two:

Symbol	Costs
0	$\{0, 0, 0\}$
∞	$\{\infty, \infty, \infty\}$

The set of possible cost types is then $\mathfrak{D} = \{<, >, 0, \infty\}$. Indeed, these four cost types correspond precisely to the four possible multi-sets of costs: $\{0, 0, 0\}$, $\{0, 0, \infty\}$, $\{0, \infty, \infty\}$ and $\{\infty, \infty, \infty\}$. The dichotomy presented in this section therefore represents a complete characterisation of the complexity of CSPs defined by placing restrictions on triples of costs in triangles.

---

[1] In other words, the considered problems are not fixed-parameter tractable [14] in the domain size.

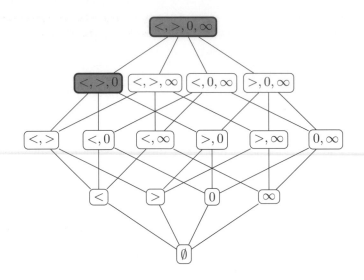

Fig. 1. Complexity of CSPs $\mathcal{A}_{\{0,\infty\}}(S), S \subseteq \{<, >, 0, \infty\}$

As $\mathcal{A}_{\{0,\infty\}}(\mathfrak{D})$ allows all binary CSPs, $\mathcal{A}_{\{0,\infty\}}(\mathfrak{D})$ is intractable [26] unless the domain is of size at most 2, which is equivalent to 2-SAT, and a well-known tractable class [28].

Proposition 2. $\mathcal{A}_{\{0,\infty\}}(\mathfrak{D})$ *is intractable unless* $|D| \leq 2$.

The joint-winner property for CSPs gives

Corollary 1 (of Theorem 1). $\mathcal{A}_{\{0,\infty\}}(\{<, 0, \infty\})$ *is tractable.*

Proposition 3. $\mathcal{A}_{\{0,\infty\}}(\{>, 0, \infty\})$ *is tractable.*

Proof. Since $<$ is forbidden, if two binary costs in a triangle are zero then the third binary cost must also be zero. In other words, if the assignment $\langle v_1, a_1 \rangle$ is consistent with $\langle v_i, a_i \rangle$ for each $i \in \{2, \ldots, n\}$, then for all $i, j \in \{1, \ldots, n\}$ such that $i \neq j$, $\langle v_i, a_i \rangle$ is consistent with $\langle v_j, a_j \rangle$. Thus Singleton Arc Consistency, which is a procedure enforcing Arc Consistency for every variable-value pair [27], solves $\mathcal{A}_{\{0,\infty\}}(\{>, 0, \infty\})$.   □

Proposition 4. $\mathcal{A}_{\{0,\infty\}}(\{<, >, \infty\})$ *is tractable.*

Proof. This class is trivial: instances with at least three variables have no solution, since the triple of costs $\{0, 0, 0\}$ is not allowed.   □

Proposition 5. $\mathcal{A}_{\{0,\infty\}}(\{<, >, 0\})$ *is intractable unless* $|D| \leq 2$.

Proof. It is straightforward to encode the 3-colouring problem as a binary CSP. The result then follows from the fact that 3-colouring is NP-hard for triangle-free graphs, which can be derived from two results from [24]. (Indeed, 3-colouring is

NP-hard even for triangle-free graphs of degree at most 4 [25].) The triple of costs $\{\infty, \infty, \infty\}$ cannot occur in the CSP encoding of the colouring of a triangle-free graph.   □

Results from this section, together with Proposition 1, complete the complexity classification, as depicted in Figure 1: white nodes represent tractable cases and shaded nodes represent intractable cases.

Theorem 3. *For $|D| \geq 3$ a class of binary CSP instances defined as $\mathcal{A}_{\{0,\infty\}}(S)$, where $S \subseteq \{<, >, 0, \infty\}$, is intractable if and only if $\{<, >, 0\} \subseteq S$.*

A simple way to convert classical CSP into an optimisation problem is to allow soft unary constraints. It turns out that the dichotomy given in Theorem 3 remains valid even if soft unary constraints are allowed. We use the notation $\mathcal{A}_{\{0,\infty\}}^{\overline{\mathbb{Q}}_+}(S)$ to represent the set of VCSP instances with binary costs from $\{0, \infty\}$, unary costs from $\overline{\mathbb{Q}}_+$ and whose triples of costs in triangles belong to S. In other words, we now consider VCSPs with crisp binary constraints and soft unary constraints.

Theorem 4. *For $|D| \geq 3$ a class of binary CSP instances defined as $\mathcal{A}_{\{0,\infty\}}^{\overline{\mathbb{Q}}_+}(S)$, where $S \subseteq \{<, >, 0, \infty\}$, is intractable if and only if $\{<, >, 0\} \subseteq S$.*

Proof. It suffices to show tractability when S is $\{<, >, \infty\}$, $\{<, 0, \infty\}$ or $\{>, 0, \infty\}$, the three maximal tractable sets in the case of CSP shown in Figure 1, since sets S which are intractable for CSPs clearly remain intractable when soft unary constraints are allowed.

The tractability of $\mathcal{A}_{\{0,\infty\}}^{\overline{\mathbb{Q}}_+}(\{<, 0, \infty\})$ is again a corollary of Theorem 1 since the joint-winner property allows any unary soft constraints.

To solve $\mathcal{A}_{\{0,\infty\}}^{\overline{\mathbb{Q}}_+}(\{>, 0, \infty\})$ in polynomial time, we establish Singleton Arc Consistency in the CSP corresponding to the binary constraints and then loop over all assignments to the first variable. For each assignment a_1 to variable v_1, we can determine the optimal global assignment which is an extension of $\langle v_1, a_1 \rangle$ by simply choosing the assignment a_i for each variable v_i with the least unary cost $c_i(a_i)$ among those assignments $\langle v_i, a_i \rangle$ that are consistent with $\langle v_1, a_1 \rangle$.

As in the proof of Proposition 4, any instance of $\mathcal{A}_{\{0,\infty\}}^{\overline{\mathbb{Q}}_+}(\{<, >, \infty\})$ is tractable, since instances with at least three variables have no solution.   □

4   Max-CSP

In this section, we will focus on the valuation structure $\Omega = \{0, 1\}$. It is well known that the VCSP with the valuation structure $\{0, 1\}$ is polynomial-time equivalent to unweighted Max-CSP (no repetition of constraints allowed) [27]. It is clear that the $\triangle$ cost type cannot occur. Since there are only 2 possible costs, we split the cost type $=$ into two:

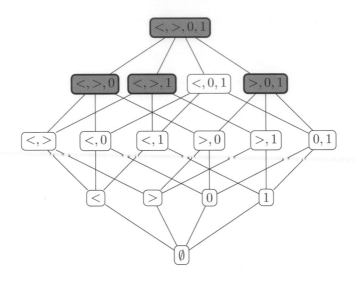

Fig. 2. Complexity of Max-CSPs $\mathcal{A}_{\{0,1\}}(S), S \subseteq \{<,>,0,1\}$

Symbol	Costs
0	$\{0,0,0\}$
1	$\{1,1,1\}$

The set of possible cost types is then $\mathfrak{D} = \{<,>,0,1\}$. Again, these four costs types correspond precisely to the four possible multi-sets of costs: $\{0,0,0\}$, $\{0,0,1\}$, $\{0,1,1\}$, and $\{1,1,1\}$. As for CSP, our dichotomy result for Max-CSP represents a complete characterisation of the complexity of classes of instances defined by placing restrictions on allowed costs in triangles.

As $\mathcal{A}_{\{0,1\}}(\mathfrak{D})$ allows all binary Max-CSPs, $\mathcal{A}_{\{0,1\}}(\mathfrak{D})$ is intractable [17,26] unless the domain is of size 1.

Proposition 6. $\mathcal{A}_{\{0,1\}}(\mathfrak{D})$ *is intractable unless* $|D| \leq 1$.

The joint-winner property [9] for Max-CSPs gives

Corollary 2 (of Theorem 1). $\mathcal{A}_{\{0,1\}}(\{<,0,1\})$ *is tractable.*

Proposition 7. $\mathcal{A}_{\{0,1\}}(\{<,>\})$ *is tractable.*

Proof. We show that $\mathcal{A}_{\{0,1\}}(\{<,>\})$ contains instances on at most 5 variables, thus showing that $\mathcal{A}_{\{0,1\}}(\{<,>\})$ is trivially tractable. Consider an instance of $\mathcal{A}_{\{0,1\}}(\{<,>\})$ on 6 or more variables. Choose 6 arbitrary variables $v_1,\ldots,v_6$ and 6 domain values $d_i \in D_{v_i}$, $1 \leq i \leq 6$. Every cost is either 0 or 1. It is well known [18] and not difficult to show[2] that for every 2-colouring of edges of K_6 (the complete graph on 6 vertices) there is a monochromatic triangle. Therefore, there is a triangle with costs either $\{0,0,0\}$ or $\{1,1,1\}$. But this is a contradiction with the fact that only cost types $<$ (i.e. $\{0,0,1\}$) and $>$ (i.e. $\{1,1,0\}$) are allowed. □

Remark 4. Both $\mathcal{A}_\Omega(\{>\})$ and $\mathcal{A}_\Omega(\{<,>\})$ are tractable over any finite valuation structure Ω due to a similar Ramsey type of argument: given $\Omega = \{0,1,\ldots,K-1\}$, there is $n_0 \in \mathbb{N}$ such that for every graph G on n vertices, where $n \geq n_0$, and every colouring of the edges of G with K colours, there is a monochromatic triangle or an independent set of size 3. Hence there are only finitely many instances, which can be stored in a look-up table. However, once the valuation structure is infinite (e.g. $\mathbb{Q}_+$), both classes become intractable, as shown in the next section.

Proposition 8. $\mathcal{A}_{\{0,1\}}(\{>,0,1\})$ *is intractable unless* $|D| \leq 1$.

Proof. Given an instance of the Max-2SAT problem, we show how to reduce it to a $\{0,1\}$-valued VCSP instance from $\mathcal{A}_{\{0,1\}}(\{>,0,1\})$. The result then follows from the well known fact that Max-2SAT is NP-hard [17,26]. Recall that an instance of Max-2SAT is given by a set of m clauses of length 2 over n variables $x_1,\ldots,x_n$ and the goal is to find an assignment that maximises the number of clauses that have at least one true literal.

In order to simplify notation, rather than constructing a VCSP instance from $\mathcal{A}_{\{0,1\}}(\{>,0,1\})$ with the goal to minimise the total cost, we construct an instance from $\mathcal{A}_{\{0,1\}}(\{<,0,1\})$ with the goal to maximise the total cost. This implies that the allowed multi-sets of costs in triangles are $\{0,0,1\}$, $\{0,0,0\}$, and $\{1,1,1\}$. Clearly, these two problems are polynomial-time equivalent.

For each variable x_i, we create a large number M of copies x_i^j of x_i with domain $\{0,1\}$, $1 \leq i \leq n$ and $1 \leq j < M$. For each variable x_i, the new copies of x_i are pairwise joined by an equality-encouraging cost function h, where $h(x,y) = 1$ if $x = y$ and $h(x,y) = 0$ otherwise. By choosing M very large, we can assume from now on that all copies of x_i will be assigned the same value in all optimal solutions. We can effectively ignore the contribution of these cost functions, which is $K = n\binom{M}{2}$, to the total cost. It is straightforward to check that all triangles involving the new copies of the variables have the allowed costs.

For each clause $(l_1 \vee l_2)$, where l_1 and l_2 are literals, we create a variable z_i with domain $\{l_1,l_2\}$, $1 \leq i \leq m$. For each literal l in the domain of z_k: if l is a positive literal $l = x_i$, we introduce cost function g between z_k and each copy x_i^j of x_i, where $g(l,1) = 1$ and $g(.,.) = 0$ otherwise; if l is a negative literal

---

[2] Take an arbitrary vertex v in K_6 where every edge is coloured either blue or red. By the pigeonhole principle, v is incident to at least 3 blue or at lest 3 red edges. Without loss of generality, we consider the former case. Let v_1, v_2 and v_3 be the three vertices incident to three blue edges incident to v. If an any of the edges $\{v_1,v_2\}$, $\{v_1,v_3\}$, $\{v_2,v_3\}$ is blue, we have a blue triangle. If all three edges are red, we have a red triangle.

$l = \neg x_i$, we introduce cost function g' between z_k and each copy x_i^j of x_i, where $g'(l,0) = 1$ and $g'(.,.) = 0$ otherwise.

To make sure that the only multi-sets of costs in all triangles are $\{0,0,1\}$, $\{0,0,0\}$, and $\{1,1,1\}$, we also add cost functions f between the different clause variables z_k and $z_{k'}$ involving the same literal l, where $f(l,l) = 1$ and $f(.,.) = 0$ otherwise. The contribution of all the cost functions between z_k and $z_{k'}$, $1 \leq k \neq k' \leq m$, is less than M and hence of no importance for M very large.

Answering the question of whether the resulting VCSP instance has a solution with a cost $\geq K + pM$ is equivalent to determining whether the original Max-2SAT instance has a solution satisfying at least p clauses. This is because each clause variable z_k can only add a score $\geq M$ if we assign value l to z_k for some literal l which is assigned true. □

Proposition 9. *Both $\mathcal{A}_{\{0,1\}}(\{<,>,0\})$ and $\mathcal{A}_{\{0,1\}}(\{<,>,1\})$ are intractable unless $|D| \leq 1$.*

Proof. We present a reduction from Max-Cut, a well-known NP-hard problem [17], which is NP-hard even on triangle-free graphs [23]. An instance of Max-Cut can easily be modelled as a Boolean $\{0,1\}$-valued VCSP instance: every vertex of the graph is represented by a variable with the Boolean domain $\{0,1\}$, and every edge yields cost function f, where $f(x,y) = 1$ if $x = y$ and $f(x,y) = 0$ if $x \neq y$. Observe that since the original graph is triangle-free, there cannot be a triangle with costs $\{1,1,1\}$. Therefore, the constructed instance belongs to $\mathcal{A}_{\{0,1\}}(\{<,>,0\})$.

For the $\mathcal{A}_{\{0,1\}}(\{<,>,1\})$ case, instead of minimising the total cost, we maximise the total cost for instances from $\mathcal{A}_{\{0,1\}}(\{<,>,0\})$. Again, we model an instance of the Max-Cut problem using Boolean variables, and every edge yields a cost function g, where $g(x,y) = 0$ if $x = y$ and $g(x,y) = 1$ if $x \neq y$ (where in this case the aim is to maximise the total cost). The constructed instance belongs to $\mathcal{A}_{\{0,1\}}(\{<,>,0\})$ when the original graph is triangle-free. The result then follows from the fact that Max-Cut is NP-complete on triangle-free graphs [23]. □

Proposition 10. *$\mathcal{A}_{\{0,1\}}(\{>,0\})$ is tractable.*

Proof. Let I be an instance from $\mathcal{A}_{\{0,1\}}(\{>,0\})$. The algorithm loops through all possible assignments $\{\langle v_1, a_1 \rangle, \langle v_2, a_2 \rangle\}$ to the first two variables. Suppose that $c_{12}(a_1, a_2) = 1$ (the case $c_{12}(a_1, a_2) = 0$ is similar). Observe that the possible variable-value assignments to other variables $\{\langle v_i, b \rangle \mid 3 \leq i \leq n, b \in D_i\}$ can be uniquely split in two sets L and R such that: (1) for every $\langle v_i, b \rangle \in L$, $c_{1i}(a_1, b) = 1$ and $c_{2i}(a_2, b) = 0$; for every $\langle v_i, b \rangle, \langle v_j, c \rangle \in L$, $c_{ij}(b, c) = 0$; (2) for every $\langle v_i, b \rangle \in R$, $c_{1i}(a_1, b) = 0$ and $c_{2i}(a_2, b) = 1$; for every $\langle v_i, b \rangle, \langle v_j, c \rangle \in R$, $c_{ij}(b, c) = 0$; (3) for every $\langle v_i, b \rangle \in L$ and $\langle v_j, c \rangle \in R$, $c_{ij}(b, c) = 1$. Ignoring unary cost functions for a moment, to find an optimal assignment to the remaining $n-2$ variables, one has to decide how many variables v_i, $3 \leq i \leq n$, will be assigned a value $b \in D_i$ such that $\langle v_i, b \rangle \in L$. The cost of a global assignment involving k variable-value assignments from L is $1 + k + (n - 2 - k) + k(n - 2 - k) = n - 1 + k(n - 2 - k)$. For some variables v_i it could happen that $\langle v_i, b \rangle \in L$ for all $b \in D_i$ or $\langle v_i, c \rangle \in R$ for all $c \in D_i$. If this is the case, then we choose an arbitrary value b for x_i with minimum unary cost $c_i(b)$. This is an optimal choice whatever the assignments to the variables x_j ($j \in \{3, \ldots, i-1, i+1, \ldots, n\}$).

Assuming that all such variables have been eliminated and now taking into account unary cost functions, the function to minimise is given by the objective function (in which we drop the constant term $n - 1$):

$$\left(\sum x_i\right)\left(n - 2 - \sum x_i\right) + \sum w_i^L x_i + \sum w_i^R (1 - x_i)$$

(each sum being over $i \in \{3, \ldots, n\}$), where $x_i \in \{0, 1\}$ indicates whether v_i is assigned a value from R or L, $w_i^L = \min\{c_i(b) : b \in D_i \wedge \langle v_i, b \rangle \in L\}$, and similarly $w_i^R = \min\{c_i(c) : c \in D_i \wedge \langle v_i, c \rangle \in R\}$. The objective function is thus equal to $k(n - 2 - k) + \sum w_i^L x_i + \sum w_i^R (1 - x_i)$, where, as above, $k = \sum x_i$ is the number of assignments from L. This objective function is minimised either when $k = 0$ or when $k = n - 2$. This follows from the fact that the contribution of unary cost functions to the objective function is $\sum w_i^L x_i + \sum w_i^R (1 - x_i)$ which is at most $n - 2$ (since in Max-CSP all unary costs belong to $\{0, 1\}$). This is no greater than the value of the quadratic term $k(n - 2 - k)$ for all values of k in $\{1, \ldots, n - 3\}$, i.e. not equal to 0 or $n - 2$.

The optimal assignment which involves $k = 0$ (respectively $k = n - 2$) assignments from L is obtained by simply choosing each value a_i (for $i > 2$) with minimum unary cost among all assignments $\langle v_i, a_i \rangle \in R$ (respectively L).

In the case that $c_{12}(a_1, a_2) = 0$, a similar argument shows that the quadratic term in the objective function is now $2(n-2-k) + k(n-2-k) = (k+2)(n-2-k)$. This is always minimised by setting $k = n - 2$ and again the sum of the unary costs is no greater than the value of the quadratic term for other values of $k \neq n - 2$. The optimal assignment which involves all $k = n - 2$ assignments from L is obtained by simply choosing each value a_i (for $i > 2$) with minimum unary cost among all assignments $\langle v_i, a_i \rangle \in L$. $\qquad \square$

Proposition 11. $\mathcal{A}_{\{0,1\}}(\{>, 1\})$ *is tractable.*

Proof. Let I be an instance from $\mathcal{A}_{\{0,1\}}(\{>, 1\})$ without any unary constraints; i.e. all constraints are binary. Observe that every variable-value assignment $\langle v_i, a \rangle$, where $a \in D_i$, is included in zero-cost assignment-pairs involving at most one other variable; i.e. there is at most one variable v_j, such that $c_{ij}(a, b) = 0$ for some $b \in D_j$. In order to minimise the total cost, we have to maximise the number of zero-cost assignment-pairs. In a global assignment, no two zero-cost assignment-pairs can involve the same variable, which means that this can be achieved by a reduction to the maximum matching problem, a problem solvable in polynomial time [15]. We build a graph with vertices given by the variables of I, and there is an edge $\{v_i, v_j\}$ if and only if there is $a \in D_i$ and $b \in D_j$ such that $c_{ij}(a, b) = 0$.

To complete the proof, we show that unary constraints do not make the problem more difficult to solve; it suffices to perform a preprocessing step before the reduction to maximum matching. Let v_i be an arbitrary variable of I. If $c_i(a) = 1$ for all $a \in D_i$, then we can effectively ignore the unary cost function c_i since it simply adds a cost of 1 to any solution. Otherwise, we show that all $a \in D_i$ such that $c_i(a) = 1$ can be ignored. Take an arbitrary assignment s to all variables such that $s(v_i) = a$, where $c_i(a) = 1$. Now take any $b \in D_i$ such that $c_i(b) = 0$. We claim that assignment s' defined by $s'(v_i) = b$ and $s'(v_j) = s(v_j)$ for every $j \neq i$ does not increase the total cost compared with s. Since the assignment $\langle v_i, a \rangle$ can occur in at most one zero-cost assignment-pair, there are two cases to consider: (1) if there is no $\langle v_j, c \rangle$ with $s(v_j) = c$ such that $c_{ij}(a, c) = 0$, then the claim holds since $c_i(a) = 1$ and $c_i(b) = 0$, so the overall cost can only decrease if we replace a by b; (2) if there is exactly one $j \neq i$ such that $c_{ij}(a, c) = 0$ and $s(v_j) = c$, then again the cost of s' cannot increase because the possible increase of cost by 1 in assigning b to v_i is compensated by the unary cost function c_i. Therefore, before using the reduction to maximal matching, we can remove all $a \in D_i$ such that $c_i(a) = 1$ and keep only those $a \in D_i$ such that $c_i(a) = 0$.   □

Results from this section, together with Proposition 1, complete the complexity classification, as depicted in Figure 2: white nodes represent tractable cases and shaded nodes represent intractable cases.

Theorem 5. *For $|D| \geq 2$ a class of binary unweighted Max-CSP instances defined as $\mathcal{A}_{\{0,1\}}(S)$, where $S \subseteq \{<, >, 0, 1\}$, is intractable if and only if either $\{<, >, 0\} \subseteq S$, $\{<, >, 1\} \subseteq S$, or $\{>, 0, 1\} \subseteq S$.*

5   VCSP

In this section, we will focus on finite-valued and general-valued VCSP. First, we focus on the valuation structure $\Omega = \mathbb{Q}_+$; that is, the finite-valued VCSP.

The set of possible cost types is $\mathfrak{D} = \{\triangle, <, >, =\}$. As $\mathcal{A}_{\mathbb{Q}_+}(\mathfrak{D})$ allows all finite-valued VCSPs, $\mathcal{A}_{\mathbb{Q}_+}(\mathfrak{D})$ is intractable [5] as it includes the Max-SAT problem for the exclusive or predicate [11].

Proposition 12. $\mathcal{A}_{\mathbb{Q}_+}(\mathfrak{D})$ *is intractable unless $|D| \leq 1$.*

The joint-winner property [9] for finite-valued VCSPs gives

Corollary 3 (of Theorem 1). $\mathcal{A}_{\mathbb{Q}_+}(\{<, =\})$ *is tractable.*

Proposition 13. $\mathcal{A}_{\mathbb{Q}_+}(\{\triangle\})$ *is intractable unless $|D| \leq 1$.*

Proof. We show a reduction from Max-Cut, a well-known NP-hard problem [17]. An instance of Max-Cut can be easily modelled as a Boolean finite-valued VCSP instance: every vertex of the graph is represented by a variable with the Boolean domain $\{0, 1\}$, and every edge yields cost function f, where $f(x, y) = 1$ if $x = y$ and $f(x, y) = 0$ if $x \neq y$. However, the constructed instance does not belong to $\mathcal{A}_{\mathbb{Q}_+}(\{\triangle\})$. Nevertheless, we can amend the VCSP instance by infinitesimal perturbations: all occurrences of the cost 0 are replaced by different numbers that are very close to 0, and all occurrences of the cost 1 are replaced by different numbers very close to 1. Now since all the cost are different, clearly the instance belongs to $\mathcal{A}_{\mathbb{Q}_+}(\{\triangle\})$.   □

Proposition 14. $\mathcal{A}_{\mathbb{Q}_+}(\{>\})$ *is intractable unless* $|D| \le 1$.

Proof. We prove this by a perturbation of the construction in the proof of Proposition 8, which shows intractability of $\mathcal{A}_{\mathbb{Q}_+}(\{>,=\})$. In order to simplify the proof, similarly to the proof of Proposition 8, we prove that maximising the total cost in the class $\mathcal{A}_{\mathbb{Q}_+}(\{<\})$ is NP-hard.

In the construction in the proof of Proposition 8 we add $i\epsilon$ to each binary cost $c_{ij}(a,b)$, where $i < j$, if $c_{ij}(a,b)$ was equal to 1. We assume that ϵ is very small ($n\epsilon < 1$). This simply ensures that each triple of costs $\{1,1,1\}$ in a triangle of assignments is now perturbed to become $\{1+i\epsilon, 1+i\epsilon, 1+j\epsilon\}$.

In the reduction from Max-2SAT, for each literal l, let C_l be the set of all variable-value assignments corresponding to l (in both the x_i^j and the z_k variables). Recall that all binary costs for pairs of the assignments within C_l were 1 and all binary costs for pairs of the assignments from distinct $C_l, C_{l'}$ were all 0 in the VCSP encoding of the Max-2SAT instance. We place an arbitrary ordering on the literals $l_1 < l_2 < \cdots < l_r$. We then add $i\epsilon$ to each binary cost between two variable-value assignments whenever these assignments correspond to literals l_i, l_j with $i < j$. This simply ensures that each triple of costs $\{0,0,0\}$ in a triangle of assignments is now perturbed to become $\{0+i\epsilon, 0+i\epsilon, 0+j\epsilon\}$.

The resulting VCSP instance is in $\mathcal{A}_{\mathbb{Q}_+}(\{>\})$ and correctly codes the original Max-2SAT instance for sufficiently small ϵ. ☐

Results from this section, together with Proposition 1, complete the complexity classification, as depicted in Figure 3: white nodes represent tractable cases and shaded nodes represent intractable cases.

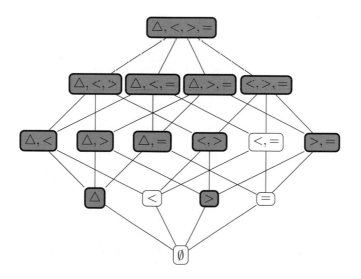

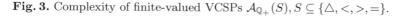

Fig. 3. Complexity of finite-valued VCSPs $\mathcal{A}_{\mathbb{Q}_+}(S), S \subseteq \{\triangle, <, >, =\}$.

Theorem 6. *For $|D| \geq 2$ a class of binary finite-valued VCSP instances defined as $\mathcal{A}_{\mathbb{Q}_+}(S)$, where $S \subseteq \{\triangle, <, >, =\}$, is tractable if and only if $S \subseteq \{<, =\}$.*

We now consider the case of general-valued VCSPs. In other words, we consider the valuation structure $\Omega = \overline{\mathbb{Q}}_+$. Theorem 6 applies to this valuation structure as well. Indeed, the hard cases remain intractable when we allow more triangles (involving infinite costs), and the only tractable case, $\mathcal{A}_{\mathbb{Q}_+}(\{<, =\})$, remains tractable: $\mathcal{A}_{\overline{\mathbb{Q}}_+}(\{<, =\})$ is tractable by Theorem 1.

Theorem 7. *For $|D| \geq 2$ a class of binary general-valued VCSP instances defined as $\mathcal{A}_{\overline{\mathbb{Q}}_+}(S)$, where $S \subseteq \{\triangle, <, >, =\}$, is tractable if and only if $S \subseteq \{<, =\}$.*

6   Conclusions

In the CSP and Max-CSP case, we have obtained a complete dichotomy concerning the tractability of problems defined by placing restrictions on the possible combinations of binary costs in triangles of variable-value assignments. In the case of finite-valued and general-valued VCSP, we have obtained a complete dichotomy with respect to the equivalence classes which naturally follow from the total order on the valuation structure. In particular, we have shown that the joint-winner property is the only tractable class for finite-valued and general-valued VCSPs.

References

1. Bertelé, U., Brioshi, F.: Nonserial dynamic programming. Academic Press, London (1972)
2. Bistarelli, S., Montanari, U., Rossi, F.: Semiring-based Constraint Satisfaction and Optimisation. Journal of the ACM 44(2), 201–236 (1997)
3. Bulatov, A., Krokhin, A., Jeavons, P.: Classifying the Complexity of Constraints using Finite Algebras. SIAM Journal on Computing 34(3), 720–742 (2005)
4. Cohen, D.A., Cooper, M.C., Jeavons, P.G.: Generalising submodularity and Horn clauses: Tractable optimization problems defined by tournament pair multimorphisms. Theoretical Computer Science 401(1-3), 36–51 (2008)
5. Cohen, D.A., Cooper, M.C., Jeavons, P.G., Krokhin, A.A.: The Complexity of Soft Constraint Satisfaction. Artificial Intelligence 170(11), 983–1016 (2006)
6. Cohen, D., Jeavons, P.: The complexity of constraint languages. In: Rossi, F., van Beek, P., Walsh, T. (eds.) The Handbook of Constraint Programming. Elsevier, Amsterdam (2006)
7. Cohen, D.A.: A New Class of Binary CSPs for which Arc-Consistency Is a Decision Procedure. In: Rossi, F. (ed.) CP 2003. LNCS, vol. 2833, pp. 807–811. Springer, Heidelberg (2003)
8. Cooper, M.C., Jeavons, P.G., Salamon, A.Z.: Generalizing constraint satisfaction on trees: hybrid tractability and variable elimination. Artificial Intelligence 174(9-10), 570–584 (2010)
9. Cooper, M.C., Živný, S.: Hybrid tractability of valued constraint problems. Artificial Intelligence 175(9-10), 1555–1569 (2011)

10. Cooper, M.C., Živný, S.: Hierarchically nested convex VCSP. In: Lee, J. (ed.) CP 2011. LNCS, vol. 6876, pp. 187–194. Springer, Heidelberg (2011)
11. Creignou, N., Khanna, S., Sudan, M.: Complexity Classification of Boolean Constraint Satisfaction Problems. SIAM Monographs on Discrete Mathematics and Applications, vol. 7. SIAM, Philadelphia (2001)
12. Dechter, R.: Constraint Processing. Morgan Kaufmann, San Francisco (2003)
13. Dechter, R., Pearl, J.: Network-based Heuristics for Constraint Satisfaction Problems. Artificial Intelligence 34(1), 1–38 (1988)
14. Downey, R., Fellows, M.: Parametrized Complexity. Springer, Heidelberg (1999)
15. Edmonds, J.: Paths, trees, and flowers. Canadian Journal of Mathematics 17, 449–467 (1965)
16. Feder, T., Vardi, M.: The Computational Structure of Monotone Monadic SNP and Constraint Satisfaction: A Study through Datalog and Group Theory. SIAM Journal on Computing 28(1), 57–104 (1998)
17. Garey, M., Johnson, D.: Computers and Intractability: A Guide to the Theory of NP-Completeness. W.H. Freeman, New York (1979)
18. Goodman, A.W.: On Sets of Acquaintances and Strangers at any Party. The American Mathematical Monthly 66(9), 778–783 (1959)
19. Grohe, M.: The complexity of homomorphism and constraint satisfaction problems seen from the other side. Journal of the ACM 54(1), 1–24 (2007)
20. Jeavons, P.: On the Algebraic Structure of Combinatorial Problems. Theoretical Computer Science 200(1-2), 185–204 (1998)
21. Kolmogorov, V., Živný, S.: Generalising tractable VCSPs defined by symmetric tournament pair multimorphisms. Tech. rep. (August 2010)
22. Kolmogorov, V., Živný, S.: The complexity of conservative VCSPs (submitted for publication, 2011)
23. Lewis, J.M., Yannakakis, M.: The node-deletion problem for hereditary properties is NP-complete. Journal of Computer System Sciences 20(2), 219–230 (1980)
24. Lovász, L.: Coverings and colorings of hypergraphs. In: Proceedings of the 4th Southeastern Conference on Combinatorics, Graph Theory and Computing, pp. 3–12 (1973)
25. Maffray, F., Preissmann, M.: On the NP-completeness of the k-colorability problem for triangle-free graphs. Discrete Mathematics 162(1-3), 313–317 (1996)
26. Papadimitriou, C.: Computational Complexity. Addison-Wesley, Reading (1994)
27. Rossi, F., van Beek, P., Walsh, T. (eds.): The Handbook of Constraint Programming. Elsevier, Amsterdam (2006)
28. Schaefer, T.: The Complexity of Satisfiability Problems. In: Proceedings of the 10th Annual ACM Symposium on Theory of Computing (STOC 1978), pp. 216–226 (1978)
29. Schiex, T., Fargier, H., Verfaillie, G.: Valued Constraint Satisfaction Problems: Hard and Easy Problems. In: Proceedings of the 14th International Joint Conference on Artificial Intelligence, IJCAI 1995 (1995)

On Minimal Weighted Clones*

Páidí Creed[1] and Stanislav Živný[2]

[1] Department of Computer Science, Royal Holloway, University of London, UK
[2] University College, University of Oxford, UK
paidi@rhul.ac.uk standa.zivny@cs.ox.ac.uk

Abstract. The connection between the complexity of constraint languages and clone theory, discovered by Cohen and Jeavons in a series of papers, has been a fruitful line of research on the complexity of CSPs. In a recent result, Cohen et al. [14] have established a Galois connection between the complexity of valued constraint languages and so-called weighted clones. In this paper, we initiate the study of weighted clones. Firstly, we prove an analogue of Rosenberg's classification of minimal clones for weighted clones. Secondly, we show minimality of several weighted clones whose support clone is generated by a single minimal operation. Finally, we classify all Boolean weighted clones. This classification implies a complexity classification of Boolean valued constraint languages obtained by Cohen et al. [13]

1 Introduction

The general constraint satisfaction problem (CSP) is NP-hard, and so is unlikely to have a polynomial-time algorithm. However, there has been much success in finding tractable fragments of the CSP by restricting the types of relation allowed in the constraints. A set of allowed relations has been called a *constraint language* [20]. For some constraint languages the associated constraint satisfaction problems with constraints chosen from that language are solvable in polynomial-time, whilst for other constraint languages this class of problems is NP-hard [21,20,19]; these are referred to as *tractable languages* and *NP-hard languages*, respectively. Dichotomy theorems, which classify each possible constraint language as either tractable or NP-hard, have been established for constraint languages over 2-element domains [27], 3-element domains [8], for conservative constraint languages [10,3], and maximal constraint languages [6,7].

The general *valued* constraint satisfaction problem (VCSP) is also NP-hard, but again we can try to identify tractable fragments by restricting the types of allowed *cost functions* that can be used to define the valued constraints. A set of allowed cost functions has been called a *valued constraint language* [13]. Much less is known about the complexity of the optimisation problems associated with different valued constraint languages, although some results have been obtained for certain special cases. In particular, a complete characterisation of complexity

* This research was supported by EPSRC grant EP/F01161X/1. Stanislav Živný is supported by a Junior Research Fellowship at University College, Oxford.

has been obtained for valued constraint languages over a 2-element domain with real-valued or infinite costs [13]. This result generalises a number of earlier results for particular optimisation problems such as MAX-SAT [15] and MIN-ONES [16]. Recently, the complete classification of conservative valued languages has been obtained for finite-valued [22] and general-valued languages [23].

In the classical CSP framework it has been shown that the complexity of any constraint language over any finite domain is determined by certain algebraic properties known as *polymorphisms* [21,20]. This result has reduced the problem of the identification of tractable constraint languages to that of the identification of suitable sets of polymorphisms. The set of polymorphisms of a constraint language forms a *clone of operations* and a tight (one to one) correspondence has been shown to exist between clones and constraint languages (closed under expressibility). In other words, we can study properties of constraint languages by studying properties of clones. This algebraic approach has been laid out in detail in [9] and has already proved fruitful in classifying the complexity of constraint languages over finite domains of arbitrary size [19,9,2,4,1,5]. In particular, by considering the set of *minimal clones*, it has been possible to classify the complexity of all *maximal constraint languages* on a finite domain D [6,7] (these are the constraint languages which can express all relations over D if we add a single new type of constraint).

Recently, it has been shown that the complexity of valued constraint languages can be determined by studying properties known as *weighted polymorphisms*[1] [11,14]. The set of weighted polymorphisms of any valued constraint language form an object called a *weighted clone* and is has been shown that there exists a tight (one to one) connection between weighted clones and valued constraint languages (closed under expressibility) [14]. Previously, a special type of weighted polymorphism, called a *multimorphism*, has been used to analyse the complexity of certain valued constraint languages [13]. In particular, multimorphisms have been used to show that there are precisely eight maximal tractable valued constraint languages over a 2-element domain with real-valued or infinite costs, and each of these is characterised by having a particular form of multimorphism [13]. Furthermore, it was shown that many known maximal tractable valued constraint languages over larger finite domains are precisely characterised by a single multimorphism and that key NP-hard examples have (essentially) no multimorphisms [13,12].

Contributions. In this paper, we initiate the study of weighted clones. In particular, we focus on *minimal* weighted clones, which define maximal valued constraint languages. As the main contribution, we demonstrate that the theory developed by Cohen et al. [14] can be used for answering non-trivial questions concerning the complexity of valued constraint languages. We see this paper as a first step towards using the theory of weighted clones in the study of the complexity of valued constraint languages. We believe that the techniques from this paper can be used for other problems as well.

---

[1] In [11] these were called *fractional polymorphisms*.

On the technical side, we prove a Rosenberg-type classification for minimal weighted clones. Furthermore, we prove minimality of several interesting weighted clones, which correspond to well-studied maximal valued constraint languages. Finally, for Boolean domains, we provide a complete classification of weighted clones. This implies a complexity classification of Boolean valued constraint languages.

Paper organisation. The rest of the paper is organised as follows. In Section 2, we define valued constraint satisfaction problems (VCSPs), the notion of expressibility, weighted operations and weighted clones. In Section 3 we prove an analogue of Rosenberg's Classification Theorem [26] for weighted clones, which establishes certain properties minimal weighted clones must satisfy. Then, in Section 4 we give several examples of minimal weighted clones. Finally, in Section 5 we show how the results of the preceding sections can be used to obtain the Boolean classification of [13]. Although this paper does not identify any novel tractable valued constraint languages, we believe the tools described herein will prove invaluable in future efforts to identify the tractable cases of the VCSP.

2   Preliminaries

2.1   VCSP

We will use $[k]$ to denote the set $\{1, \ldots, k\}$ for any positive integer k. We shall denote by $\mathbb{Q}_+$ the set of all non-negative rational numbers. We define $\overline{\mathbb{Q}}_+ = \mathbb{Q}_+ \cup \{\infty\}$ with the standard addition operation extended so that for all $a \in \mathbb{Q}_+$, $a + \infty = \infty$. Members of $\overline{\mathbb{Q}}_+$ are called *costs*. Throughout the paper, we denote by D any fixed finite set, called a *domain*, consisting of *values*.

A function ϕ from D^r to $\overline{\mathbb{Q}}_+$ will be called a *cost function* on D of *arity* r. If the range of ϕ lies entirely within $\mathbb{Q}_+$, then ϕ is called a *finite-valued* cost function. If the range of ϕ is $\{0, \infty\}$, then ϕ is called a *crisp* cost function. A *language* is a set of cost functions with the same domain D. Language Γ is called finite-valued (crisp) if all cost functions in Γ are finite-valued (crisp). A language Γ is *Boolean* if $|D| = 2$.

Definition 1. *An instance of the **valued constraint satisfaction problem**, (**VCSP**), is a 3-tuple $\mathcal{P} = \langle V, D, C \rangle$ where V is a finite set of **variables**; D is a set of possible **values**; C is a multi-set of **constraints**. Each element of C is a pair $c = \langle \sigma, \phi \rangle$ where σ is a tuple of variables called the **scope** of c, and $\phi : D^{|\sigma|} \to \overline{\mathbb{Q}}_+$ is a $|\sigma|$-ary cost function on D. An **assignment** for $\mathcal{P}$ is a mapping $s : V \to D$. The **cost** of an assignment s, denoted $Cost_{\mathcal{P}}(s)$, is given by the sum of the costs for the restrictions of s onto each constraint scope, that is,*

$$Cost_{\mathcal{P}}(s) \stackrel{\text{def}}{=} \sum_{\langle \langle v_1, v_2, \ldots, v_m \rangle, \phi \rangle \in C} \phi(s(v_1), s(v_2), \ldots, s(v_m)).$$

*A **solution** to $\mathcal{P}$ is an assignment with minimal cost, and the question is to find a solution.*

We define VCSP(Γ) to be the set of all VCSP instances in which all cost functions belong to Γ. A valued constraint language Γ is called **tractable** if, for every finite subset $\Gamma_f \subseteq \Gamma$, there exists an algorithm solving any instance $\mathcal{P} \in$ VCSP(Γ_f) in polynomial time. Conversely, Γ is called **NP-hard** if there is some finite subset $\Gamma_f \subseteq \Gamma$ for which VCSP(Γ_f) is NP-hard.

2.2   Weighted Relational Clones

We denote by $\mathbf{\Phi}_D$ the set of cost functions on D taking values in $\overline{\mathbb{Q}}_+$ and by $\mathbf{\Phi}_D^{(r)}$ the r-ary cost functions in $\mathbf{\Phi}_D$. Any cost function $\phi : D^r \to \overline{\mathbb{Q}}_+$ has an associated cost function which takes only the values 0 and ∞, known as its **feasibility relation**, denoted Feas(ϕ), which is defined as Feas(ϕ)$(x_1, \ldots, x_r) = 0$ if $\phi(x_1, \ldots, x_r) < \infty$, and Feas($\phi$)$(x_1, \ldots, x_r) = \infty$ otherwise.

We say $\phi, \phi' \in \mathbf{\Phi}_D$ are **cost-equivalent**, denoted by $\phi \sim \phi'$, if there exist $\alpha, \beta \in \mathbb{Q}_+$ with $\alpha > 0$ such that $\phi = \alpha \phi' + \beta$. We denote by $\Gamma_\sim$ the smallest set of cost functions containing Γ which is closed under cost-equivalence.

We now define a closure operator on cost functions, which adds to a set of cost functions all other cost functions which can be obtained from that set by minimising over a subset of variables:

Definition 2. *For any VCSP instance $\mathcal{P} = \langle V, D, C \rangle$, and any list $L = \langle v_1, \ldots, v_r \rangle$ of variables of $\mathcal{P}$, the **projection** of $\mathcal{P}$ onto L, denoted $\pi_L(\mathcal{P})$, is the r-ary cost function defined as follows:*

$$\pi_L(\mathcal{P})(x_1, \ldots, x_r) \overset{\text{def}}{=} \min_{\{s:V\to D \;|\; \langle s(v_1),\ldots,s(v_r)\rangle=\langle x_1,\ldots,x_r\rangle\}} Cost_\mathcal{P}(s).$$

*We say that a cost function ϕ is **expressible** over a constraint language Γ if there exists a VCSP instance $\mathcal{P} \in$ VCSP(Γ) and a list L of variables of $\mathcal{P}$ such that $\pi_L(\mathcal{P}) = \phi$. We define Express($\Gamma$) to be the **expressive power** of Γ; that is, the set of all cost functions expressible over Γ.*

Note that the list of variables L may contain repeated entries, and we define the minimum over an empty set of costs to be ∞.

Example 1. Let $\mathcal{P}$ be the VCSP instance with a single variable v and no constraints, and let $L = \langle v, v \rangle$. Then, by Definition 2,

$$\pi_L(\mathcal{P})(x, y) = \begin{cases} 0 & \text{if } x = y \\ \infty & \text{otherwise} \end{cases}.$$

Hence for any valued constraint language Γ, over any set D, Express(Γ) contains this binary cost function, which will be called the **equality** cost function.

Definition 3. *We say a set $\Gamma \subseteq \mathbf{\Phi}_D$ is a **weighted relational clone** if it contains the equality cost function and is closed under cost-equivalence and feasibility, rearrangement of arguments, addition of cost functions, and expressibility. For each $\Gamma \subseteq \mathbf{\Phi}_D$ we define wRelClone(Γ) to be the smallest weighted relational clone containing Γ.*

It is known that for any $\Gamma \subseteq \mathbf{\Phi}_D$, $\mathrm{Express}(\Gamma \cup \mathrm{Feas}(\Gamma))_\sim = \mathrm{wRelClone}(\Gamma)$ [14]. Moreover, it follows from [11] that Γ is tractable if and only if $\mathrm{wRelClone}(\Gamma)$ is tractable. Hence, the search for tractable valued constraint languages corresponds to a search for suitable weighted relational clones.

2.3 Weighted Clones

First we recall some basic terminology from clone theory [18]. A function $f : D^k \to D$ is called a k-ary **operation** on D. We denote by $\mathbf{O}_D$ the set of all finitary operations on D and by $\mathbf{O}_D^{(k)}$ the k-ary operations in $\mathbf{O}_D$. The k-ary **projections** on D, defined for $i = 1, \ldots, k$, are the operations $e_i^{(k)}(a_1, \ldots, a_k) = a_i$. (We drop the superscript (k) if it is clear from the context.) Let $f \in \mathbf{O}_D^{(k)}$ and $g_1, \ldots, g_k \in \mathbf{O}_D^{(l)}$. The **superposition** of f and $g_1, \ldots, g_k$ is the l-ary operation $f[g_1, \ldots, g_k](x_1, \ldots, x_l) = f(g_1(x_1, \ldots, x_l), \ldots, g_k(x_1 \ldots, x_l))$.

A set $F \subseteq \mathbf{O}_D$ is called a **clone** of operations if it contains all the projections on D and is closed under superposition.

For each $F \subseteq \mathbf{O}_D$ we define $\mathrm{Clone}(F)$ to be the smallest clone containing F. For any clone C, we use $C^{(k)}$ to denote the k-ary terms in C. We say a clone C is **minimal** if any non-trivial operation in C generates C, i.e. for all $f \in C$ other than the projections, we have $C = \mathrm{Clone}(\{f\})$. An operation f in a minimal clone C is called **minimal** if f has smallest arity among the non-trivial operations in C.

It has been shown [21] that crisp constraint languages are in one to one correspondence with clones. Recently, Cohen et al. [14] have shown that a similar correspondence exists between valued constraint languages and objects called **weighted clones**. We will now briefly describe their results.

Definition 4. *We define a k-ary **weighted operation** on a set D to be a function $\omega : \mathbf{O}_D^{(k)} \to \mathbb{Q}$ such that $\omega(f) < 0$ only if f is a projection and*

$$\sum_{f \in \mathbf{dom}(\omega)} \omega(f) = 0 \,.$$

*The **domain** of ω, denoted $\mathbf{dom}(\omega)$, is the subset of $\mathbf{O}_D^{(k)}$ on which ω is defined. We denote by $ar(\omega) = k$ the arity of ω.*

We denote by $\mathbf{W}_D$ the finitary weighted operations on D and by $\mathbf{W}_D^{(k)}$ the k-ary weighted operations in $\mathbf{W}_D$.

Definition 5. *Let C be a clone of operations on D. We define the k-ary **zero weighted operation** supported by C to be the k-ary weighted operation which satisfies $\omega(f) = 0$ for all $f \in C^{(k)}$.*

Definition 6. *Let C be a clone of operations on D. A **weighted clone supported** by C is a set of weighted operations that contains all zero-weighted operations whose domains are subsets of C and is closed under:*

proper translation. *Given a k-ary weighted operation $\omega : C^{(k)} \to \mathbb{Q}$ and $\mathbf{t} = \langle g_1, \ldots, g_k \rangle$, where $g_1, \ldots, g_k \in C^{(\ell)}$, we define the **translation** of ω by $g_1, \ldots, g_k$, denoted as $\omega[g_1, \ldots, g_k]$ or simply $\omega[\mathbf{t}]$, to be the function $\omega' : C^{(\ell)} \to \mathbb{Q}$ satisfying*

$$\omega'(f') = \sum_{f \in C^{(k)} : f' = f[g_1, \ldots, g_k]} \omega(f),$$

*for each $f' \in C^{(\ell)}$. A translation is called a **proper translation** if ω' is a weighted operation.*

addition. *Given a pair of k-ary weighted operations $\omega_1, \omega_2 : C^{(k)} \to \mathbb{Q}$, we define the **addition** $\omega_1 + \omega_2$ to be the weighted operation ω' satisfying*

$$\omega'(f) = \omega_1(f) + \omega_2(f),$$

for each $f \in C^{(k)}$.

scaling. *Let ω be a k-ary weighted operation supported by C and let $\alpha > 0$. We define the α-scaling of ω, $\alpha\omega$, to be the weighted operation ω' satisfying*

$$\omega'(f) = \alpha\omega(f),$$

for each $f \in C^{(k)}$.

Example 2. Let ω be the 4-ary weighted operation on D given by

$$\omega(f) = \begin{cases} -1 & \text{if } f \text{ is a projection} \\ +1 & \text{if } f \in \{\max(x_1, x_2), \min(x_1, x_2), \max(x_3, x_4), \min(x_3, x_4)\} \end{cases},$$

and let

$$\langle g_1, g_2, g_3, g_4 \rangle = \left\langle e_1^{(3)}, e_2^{(3)}, e_3^{(3)}, \max(x_1, x_2) \right\rangle.$$

Then, by Definition 6, the translation of ω by $\langle g_1, g_2, g_2, g_3 \rangle$ is:

$$\omega[g_1, g_2, g_3, g_4](f) = \begin{cases} -1 & \text{if } f \text{ is a projection} \\ +1 & \text{if } f \in \{\max(x_1, x_2, x_3), \min(x_1, x_2), \min(x_3, \max(x_1, x_2))\} \\ 0 & \text{if } f = \max(x_1, x_2) \end{cases}.$$

Note that $\omega[g_1, g_2, g_3, g_4]$ satisfies the conditions of Definition 4 and hence is a weighted operation. Hence the translation is proper.

For each $W \subseteq \mathbf{W}_D$ we define wClone(W) to be the smallest weighted clone containing W. In particular, we write wClone(ω) for the smallest weighted clone containing weighted operation ω. Note that the support of wClone(W) is the clone generated by the domains of the elements of W; i.e. the support of wClone(W) is given by Clone($\cup_{\omega \in W} \mathbf{dom}(\omega)$). The following is a direct consequence of the definition of weighted clones.

Proposition 1. *Let ω be a weighted operation supported by a clone C. Then every k-ary element of* wClone(ω) *can be obtained as a weighted sum of translations of ω by tuples of terms from $C^{(k)}$.*

Proposition 1 can be used to decide whether $\mu \in \text{wClone}(\omega)$, where $\mu \in \mathbf{W}_D^{(\ell)}$ and $\omega \in \mathbf{W}_D^{(k)}$ are weighted operations. We define the **translation matrix** of ω to be the matrix A_ω whose columns correspond to the translations of ω by $g_1, \ldots, g_k$ where $g_1, \ldots, g_k \in C^{(\ell)}$. By Proposition 1, $\mu \in \text{wClone}(\omega)$ if and only if we can find a non-negative solution to the system of equations $A_\omega x = \mu$.

Definition 7. *Let $\phi \in \mathbf{\Phi}_D^{(r)}$ and let $\omega \in \mathbf{W}_D^{(k)}$. We say that ω is a **weighted polymorphism** of ϕ if, for any $x_1, x_2, \ldots, x_k \in D^r$ such that $\phi(x_i) < \infty$ for $i = 1, \ldots, k$, we have*

$$\sum_{f \in \mathbf{dom}(\omega)} \omega(f)\phi(f(x_1, x_2, \ldots, x_k)) \leq 0. \tag{1}$$

*If ω is a weighted polymorphism of ϕ we say ϕ is **improved** by ω.*

Note that, because $a\infty = \infty$ for any value $a \in \mathbb{Q}_+$ (in particular, $0\infty = \infty$), if inequality (1) holds we must have $\phi(f(x_1, \ldots, x_k)) < \infty$, for all $f \in \mathbf{dom}(\omega)$, i.e., each $f \in \mathbf{dom}(\omega)$ is a polymorphism of ϕ [14].

Example 3. Consider the class of submodular set functions [24]. These are precisely the cost functions on $\{0, 1\}$ satisfying

$$\phi(\min(x_1, x_2)) + \phi(\max(x_1, x_2)) - \phi(x) - \phi(y) \leq 0.$$

In other words, the set of submodular functions are defined as the set of cost functions on $\{0, 1\}$ with the 2-ary weighted polymorphism

$$\omega(f) = \begin{cases} -1 & \text{if } f \in \{e_1^{(2)}, e_2^{(2)}\} \\ +1 & \text{if } f \in \{\min(x_1, x_2), \max(x_1, x_2)\} \end{cases}.$$

This shows that weighted polymorphisms capture an important class of submodular functions, which have been studied within various contexts in computer science [29].

3   Weighted Rosenberg

Rosenberg's Classification Theorem [26], given below, gives certain conditions that minimal clones must satisfy. This has been a major tool in the efforts to identify all tractable maximal constraint languages [6,7] and, furthermore, in efforts to classify all tractable constraint languages [8,10].

For a unary operation we define $f^1 = f$ and $f^i(x) = f(f^{i-1}(x))$. A unary operation f is a **retraction** if $f^2(x) = f(x)$ for all $x \in D$, and a cyclic permutation of prime order if $f^p(x) = x$ for some prime p and all $x \in D$.

An operation f is **idempotent** if $f(x, \ldots, x) = x$ for all $x \in D$. A k-ary, $k \geq 3$, operation f is a **semiprojection** if there is $1 \leq i \leq k$ such that $f(x_1, \ldots, x_k) = e_i^{(k)} = x_i$ for all $x_1, \ldots, x_k \in D$ such that $x_1, \ldots, x_k$ are not pairwise distinct. A ternary operation f is a **majority** operation (denoted by Mjrty) if $f(x, x, y) =$

$f(x, y, x) = f(y, x, x) = x$ for all $x, y \in D$. A ternary operation f is a **minority** operation (denoted by Mnrty) if $f(x, x, y) = f(x, y, x) = f(y, x, x) = y$ for all $x, y \in D$. A ternary operation f is a **Pixley** operation if $f(y, y, x) = f(x, y, x) = f(y, x, x) = y$ for all $x, y \in D$ (up to permutations of inputs). We say a k-ary operation f is **sharp** if f is not a projection but the operation obtained by equating any two inputs in f is a projection. The following lemma shows that the only sharp operations of arity $k \geq 4$ are semiprojections.

Lemma 1 (Świerczkowski's Lemma [30]). *Given an operation of arity ≥ 4, if every operation arising from the identification of two variables is a projection, then these projections coincide.*

Świerczkowski's Lemma can be used to prove Rosenberg's Classification Theorem [26], stated below.

Theorem 1 (Rosenberg). *If C is a minimal clone on D, then C must contain an operation f satisfying one of the following conditions:*

1. *f is a retraction or a cyclic permutation of prime order.*
2. *f is binary and idempotent.*
3. *f is a ternary minority operation of the form $f(x, y, z) = x - y + z$, where addition is over some elementary 2-group[2].*
4. *f is a ternary majority operation.*
5. *f is a n-ary semiprojection, $n \geq 3$.*

In this section, we define minimal weighted clones, and give some necessary conditions for a weighted operation to generate a minimal weighted clone. These results can be viewed as an analogue to Rosenberg's Classification Theorem for weighted clones.

Definition 8. *Let W be a weighted clone. We say W is **minimal** if every non-zero $\omega \in W$ generates W, i.e., for all non-zero $\omega \in W$, $W = \mathrm{wClone}(\omega)$.*

*For a minimal weighted clone W, we say $\omega \in W$ is a **minimal weighted operation** if ω has smallest arity amongst non-zero elements of W and ω assigns weight -1 to each projection.*

The following lemma shows that every minimal weighted clone is generated by a minimal weighted operation.

Lemma 2. *Let ω be a non-zero weighted operation. There exists some $\omega' \in \mathrm{wClone}(\omega)$ of equal arity which assigns weight -1 to each projection.*

Proof. Suppose ω a is non-zero weighted operation of arity k. Let $Cycle(k)$ denote the set of cyclic permutations of $[k]$. For each permutation $\sigma \in Cycle(k)$, let $\mathbf{t}_\sigma = \left\langle e^{(k)}_{\sigma(1)}, \ldots, e^{(k)}_{\sigma(k)} \right\rangle$. Then, the weighted operation $\sum_{\sigma \in Cycle(k)} \omega[\mathbf{t}_\sigma]$ assigns equal weight to each projection. Thus, by a suitable scaling we can obtain a k-ary weighted operation $\omega' \in \mathrm{wClone}(\omega)$ satisfying $\omega'(e^{(k)}_i) = -1$ for each $i \in [k]$.   □

---

[2] An elementary 2-group is an Abelian group of order 2, i.e. for every element x of the group, $x + x = 0$.

We will use the following shorthand for candidate minimal weighted operations (weighted operations which assign weight -1 to each projection):

$$\{(\omega(f), f) : \omega(f) > 0\}.$$

We can now give our classification theorem for minimal weighted operations. The format, and indeed the proof, follow directly from Rosenberg [26], see also [17]. Our result is slightly weaker, because we cannot rule out the possibility of sharp, but non-minimal, operations occurring with negative weight in a minimal weighted operation.

Theorem 2. *The set of operations assigned positive weight by a minimal weighted operation is one of the following four types:*

1. *A set of unary operations.*
2. *A set of binary idempotent operations.*
3. *A set consisting of sharp ternary operations, i.e. majority operations, minority operations, Pixley operations and semiprojections.*
4. *A set of k-ary semiprojections $(k > 3)$.*

Proof. Suppose ω is a minimal weighted operation of arity at least two. Then, every f with $\omega(f) > 0$ must be idempotent since otherwise translating by $\langle e_1, \ldots, e_1 \rangle$ would yield a non-zero unary weighted operation μ. If wClone$(\mu) =$ wClone(ω), then since ω has bigger arity than μ we get a contradiction with ω being a minimal weighted operation; if wClone$(\mu) \neq$ wClone(ω), then wClone(ω) is not a minimal weighted clone.

Next, suppose that ω is a ternary minimal weighted operation. We cannot have any f with $\omega(f) > 0$ for which identifying two variables gives a non-projection operation, since otherwise ω would generate a minimal binary weighted operation. There are precisely 8 types of sharp ternary operations, given in Table 1.

The first and last correspond to majority and minority respectively. The second, third and fifth correspond to semiprojections, and the other three correspond to Pixley operations.

Finally, suppose ω is a minimal weighted operation of arity 4 or greater. Every f with $\omega(f) > 0$ must become a projection when we identify any two variables. Thus, by the Świerczkowski Lemma (Lemma 1) each such f must be a semiprojection. $\square$

Table 1. Sharp ternary operations

Input	1	2	3	4	5	6	7	8
(x,x,y)	x	x	x	x	y	y	y	y
(x,y,x)	x	x	y	y	x	x	y	y
(y,x,x)	x	y	x	y	x	y	x	y

4   Simple Weighted Clones

In classical clone theory, every minimal clone is generated by a single operation. Rosenberg's classification of minimal operations [26] gives unary operations (retractions and cyclic permutations of prime orders), binary idempotent operations, majority operations, minority operations, and semiprojections.

Definition 9. *For any k-ary operation f we define the **canonical weighted operation** of f, ω_f, to be $\{(k, f)\}$.*

In other words, ω_f assigns weight k to f, and weight -1 to each projection.

In the rest of this section we prove that for some minimal operations f, the canonical weighted operation ω_f is a minimal weighted operation. In particular, we prove this for retractions, certain binary operations, majority operations, and minority operations.

Theorem 3. *If f is a retraction, then ω_f is a minimal weighted operation.*

Proof. Let f be a minimal unary operation which is a retraction; i.e. $f(f(x)) = f(x)$ for all $x \in D$. Let ω_f be the canonical weighted operation of f. Since f is a retraction, it is the only non-trivial operation in $\mathrm{Clone}(f)$. Hence, given any $\mu \in \mathrm{wClone}^{(k)}(\omega_f)$, translating by $\left\langle e_1^{(k)}, \ldots, e_k^{(k)} \right\rangle$ and applying a suitable scaling yields ω_f.   □

Theorem 4. *If f is a binary operation, then ω_f is minimal whenever f is a semilattice operation or a conservative commutative operation.*

Proof. Whenever f is a conservative commutative operation or a semilattice operation, we have that f is the only non-trivial binary operation in $\mathrm{Clone}(f)$. Thus, given any $\mu \in \mathrm{Clone}^{(k)}(\omega_f)$ we can find some tuple of binary projections $\mathbf{t}$ satisfying $g[\mathbf{t}] = f(x_1, x_2)$, for some g with $\mu(g) > 0$. That is, $\mu' = \mu[\mathbf{t}]$ is a binary weighted operation with $\mu'(f) > 0$. Finally, since f is commutative, the weighted operation obtained from μ' by Lemma 2 must be equal to ω_f.   □

Theorem 5. *If f is a majority operation, then ω_f is a minimal weighted operation.*

Proof. It is well known that any ternary operation generated by f is a majority operation since f is a majority operation. (This can be proved by induction on the number of occurrences of f.) We want to show that ω_f is minimal; that is, given $\mu \in \mathrm{wClone}(\omega_f)$, we need to show that $\omega_f \in \mathrm{wClone}(\mu)$.

Let μ be a k-ary weighted operation from $\mathrm{wClone}(\omega_f)$ such that $\mu(g) > 0$ for some non-projection g, where $g \in \mathrm{Clone}^{(k)}(f)$. From the argument above, there exists some k-tuple of ternary projections, $\mathbf{t}$, such that $g[\mathbf{t}]$ is a majority operation. Let $\mu' = \mu[\mathbf{t}]$. If $\mu' = c\omega_f$ for some $c > 0$ then we are done. Otherwise, by Lemma 2, there is ternary $\mu' \in \mathrm{wClone}(\mu)$ such that μ' assigns weight -1 to projections and positive weight to some (possibly different) majority operations $g_1, \ldots, g_k \in \mathrm{Clone}^{(3)}(f)$.

Translating μ' by $\langle x_j, x_j, f \rangle$, for $j \in [3]$, gives the weighted operation $2\omega_{j,f}$, where

$$\omega_{j,f}(g) = \begin{cases} -1 & g = e_j \\ +1 & g = f \\ 0 & \text{otherwise} \end{cases} . \tag{2}$$

Since $\omega_f = \omega_{1,f} + \omega_{2,f} + \omega_{3,f}$, we have proved that $\omega_f \in \text{wClone}(\mu)$.   □

Theorem 6. *If f is a minimal minority operation, then ω_f is a minimal weighted operation.*

Proof. Recall that a minority operation $f : D^3 \to D$ is minimal if and only if $f(x, y, z) = x - y + z$, where addition is taken over an elementary 2-group $\langle D, + \rangle$. An elementary 2-group $\langle D, + \rangle$ satisfies $2x = 0$ for all $x \in D$. Thus, we can conclude that f is the only ternary operation in $\text{Clone}(f)$. Now, given any $\mu \in \text{wClone}^{(k)}(\omega_f)$, we can find some k-tuple of ternary projections $\mathbf{t}$ such that $\mu[\mathbf{t}](f) > 0$. Then, using Lemma 2, we can obtain a ternary weighted operation $\mu' \in \text{wClone}(\mu)$ which satisfies $\mu'(e_i) = 1$ for $i = 1, 2, 3$. Since f is the only ternary operation in $\text{Clone}(f)$ then, necessarily, $\mu' = \omega_f$.   □

Due to space constraints, we only state the following result:

Proposition 2. *Let f be the ternary semiprojection on $D = \{0, 1, 2\}$ which returns 0 on every input with all values distinct, and the value of the first input otherwise. The weighted clone $\text{wClone}(\omega_f)$ is not minimal.*

Proposition 2 tells us that not all minimal operations have canonical minimal weighted operations. It is known that the constraint languages preserved by semiprojections are not tractable, so the weighted clones supported by semiprojection clones are of less interest to us.

An operation f is **tractable** if the set of cost functions invariant under f, denote by $\text{Inv}(f)$, is a tractable valued constraint language; see [14] for more details. Having proved minimality of weighted clones corresponding to well-known tractable operations, we finish this section with a conjecture.

Conjecture 1. If f is a minimal tractable operation, then ω_f is a minimal weighted operation.

5   Boolean Classification

In this section, we consider minimal weighted clones on Boolean domain $D = \{0, 1\}$. Since there are no semiprojections on a Boolean domain, we only need to consider the first three cases of Theorem 2. Moreover, for the third case, we need only consider weighted operations assigning negative weight to Mnrty and Mjrty. Post [25] has classified the minimal clones on a Boolean domain.

Theorem 7. *Every minimal clone on a Boolean domain is generated by one of the following operations:*

1. $f_0(x) = 0$
2. $f_1(x) = 1$
3. $f(x) = 1 - x$
4. $\min(x_1, x_2)$ *returns the minimum of the two arguments*
5. $\max(x_1, x_2)$ *returns the maximum of the two arguments*
6. $\mathrm{Mnrty}(x_1, x_2, x_3)$ *returns the minority of the three arguments*
7. $\mathrm{Mjrty}(x_1, x_2, x_3)$ *returns the majority of the three arguments*

First, we show that the canonical weighted operations corresponding to the minimal operations given in Theorem 7 are minimal.

Theorem 8. *For each minimal Boolean operation f, the weighted operation ω_f is minimal.*

Proof. Let $f(x) = 1 - x$. Notice that $f^2(x) = x$; that is, f is a cyclic permutation of order 2. Therefore, the only non-trivial unary operation in $\mathrm{Clone}(f)$ is f. Moreover, for any $k > 1$, the only non-trivial operations in $\mathrm{Clone}^{(k)}(f)$ are of the form $g(x) = 1 - x_i$ for some $i \in [k]$. Translating an operation of this form by the k-tuple of unary projections will yield f. Thus, given any non-zero $\mu \in \mathrm{wClone}^{(k)}(\omega_f)$, we can translate by the k-tuple of unary projections and apply a suitable scaling to obtain ω_f. Hence, ω_f is minimal. All other cases follow from Theorems 3, 4, 5, and 6.   □

Next, we show that there are precisely two other minimal weighted operations on a Boolean domain.

Theorem 9. *On a Boolean domain, there are precisely two minimal weighted operations other than the 7 canonical weighted operations arising from the minimal operations. These are the binary weighted operations $\{(1, \min), (1, \max)\}$ and $\{(1, \mathrm{Mnrty}), (2, \mathrm{Mjrty})\}$.*

Proof We first consider the binary case. Every binary minimal operation other than $\omega_{\min}$ and $\omega_{\max}$ must be of the form $\omega_a = \{(a, \min), (2 - a, \max)\}$ $(0 < a < 2)$. We will show that ω_a is minimal if and only if $a = 1$.

First, suppose $a = 1$. Let $\omega = \omega_1$. It is easy to check that the only non-zero translation is $\omega[e_1, e_2]$. Thus, by Proposition 1, every non-zero weighted operation in $\mathrm{wClone}^{(2)}(\omega)$ is equal to $c\omega$, for some $c > 0$.

There is precisely one sharp operation of arity ≥ 3 in $\mathrm{Clone}(\min, \max)$: the majority operation Mjrty. Since $\{(3, \mathrm{Mjrty})\} \notin \mathrm{wClone}(\omega)$ (we can check this using Proposition 1), it follows that any non-zero $\mu \in \mathrm{wClone}^{(k)}(\omega)$ must assign weight to an operation of the form $\min(x_i, x_j)$ or $\max(x_i, x_j)$, or a non-sharp operation of arity k, for any $k > 2$. We can translate any such μ by a k-tuple of binary projections to obtain some non-zero $\mu' \in \mathrm{wClone}^{(2)}(\mu)$. Since μ' must necessarily be contained in $\mathrm{wClone}(\omega)$, and since every binary weighted operation in $\mathrm{wClone}(\omega)$ is equal to $c\omega$, for some constant $c > 0$, it follows that $\omega \in \mathrm{wClone}(\mu)$. Hence, ω is minimal.

Now, suppose $a < 1$ (the other case is symmetric). Consider the weighted operations $\mu_i = \omega_a + \frac{a}{1-a}\omega_a[e_i, \min]$ $(i = 1, 2)$, which by Proposition 1 are contained in wClone(ω_a). Since $\min(x, \min(x, y)) = \min(x, y)$, we have that min is assigned weight $a - 1$ in $\omega_a[e_i, \min]$, and hence 0 in μ_i. To be precise, μ_i is the weighted operation which assigns weight $a-1$ to e_i, -1 to $e_{\bar{i}}$ ($\bar{i} \in \{1, 2\} \backslash \{i\}$), and $2 - a$ to max. Thus, by adding μ_1 and μ_2 and applying a suitable scaling, we can obtain the weighted operation $\{(2, \max)\}$. Since $\{(2, \max)\}$ generates a minimal clone which does not contain ω_a, we can conclude that ω_a is not minimal.

We now move on to the ternary case. Suppose ω is a ternary weighted operation and $\omega \notin$ wClone(ω_f) for $f \in \{\text{Mnrty}, \text{Mjrty}\}$. From Theorem 2 and the fact that there are no Boolean semiprojections, ω can only assign positive weight to Mjrty, Mnrty and the three Boolean Pixley operations f_1, f_2 and f_3 (corresponding to the fourth, sixth and seventh columns of Table 1). We first show that we can restrict our attention to weighted operations assigning weight 0 to all Pixley operations.

Let ω be a ternary weighted operation which assigns positive weight to some Pixley operations. Composing $\langle f_1, f_2, f_3 \rangle$ with the tuples of projections $\langle e_2, e_3, e_1 \rangle$ and $\langle e_3, e_1, e_2 \rangle$ yields $\langle f_2, f_3, f_1 \rangle$ and $\langle f_3, f_1, f_2 \rangle$ respectively. Thus, the weighted operation $\frac{1}{3}\omega + \frac{1}{3}\omega[e_2, e_3, e_1] + \frac{1}{3}\omega[e_3, e_1, e_2]$ assigns equal weight to each Pixley operation. Hence, from here on we assume we are working with a weighted operation ω which assigns equal weight to each Pixley operation, as well as assigning weight -1 to each projection (see Lemma 2).

Suppose each Pixley operation is assigned weight $a < 1$ by ω, so at least one of Mjrty and Mnrty is assigned positive weight. We observe that $f_i(f_1, f_2, f_3) = e_i$ for each $i = 1, 2, 3$. Moreover, Mjrty(f_1, f_2, f_3) = Mnrty and Mnrty(f_1, f_2, f_3) = Mjrty. Thus, the weighted operation $\omega + a\omega[f_1, f_2, f_3]$ is non-zero and assigns weight 0 to each Pixley operation.

Next, suppose each Pixley operation is assigned weight 1 by ω. Let $\mu_1 = \omega[e_1, e_2, f_1]$. Since $f_1(e_1, e_2, f_1) = \text{Mjrty}$, $f_2(e_1, e_2, f_1) = e_1$ and $f_3(e_1, e_2, f_1) = e_2$, we have that μ_1 assigns weight -1 to f_1, $+1$ to Mjrty, and is 0 everywhere else. For $i = 2, 3$, we can obtain μ_i, which assigns weight -1 to f_i and $+1$ to Mjrty, by a similar translation. Then the weighted operation obtained as $\omega + \mu_1 + \mu_2 + \mu_3$ will be equal to $\{(3, \text{Mjrty})\}$.

Thus, the weighted clone generated by any minimal ternary weighted operation will contain a non-zero ternary weighted operation assigning weight 0 to all Pixley operations. Hence, when searching for minimal ternary weighted operations other than ω_{Mnrty} and ω_{Mjrty}, we can restrict our attention to weighted operations of the form $\omega_a = \{(a, \text{Mnrty}), (3 - a, \text{Mjrty})\}$ ($0 < a < 3$). We will now show that ω_a is minimal if and only if $a = 1$.

Let $\omega = \omega_1$. Using Proposition 1, we can check that every ternary weighted operation in wClone(ω) which assigns positive weight to Mnrty and Mjrty only is of the form $c\omega$ for some $c > 0$. Since there are no semi-projections, we can translate any non-zero $\mu \in$ wClone$^{(k)}(\omega)$ by a k-tuple of ternary projections to obtain ternary non-zero $\mu' \in$ wClone(ω). We have shown that we can obtain some non-zero $\mu'' \in$ wClone(μ') which assigns positive weight to Mnrty and Mjrty only. Since μ'' must be in wClone(ω), it follows that $\mu'' = c\omega$, for some $c > 0$, so we can obtain ω by scaling. Hence, ω is a minimal weighted operation.

Suppose $a < 1$. Let $\mu_i = \omega_a + \frac{a}{1-a}\omega_a[e_i, e_i, \mathrm{Mnrty}]$ $(i \in \{1, 2, 3\})$. It is easy to check that $\mu_i(e_i) = -1+a$, $\mu_i(e_j) = -1$ $(j \neq i)$, $\mu_i(\mathrm{Mjrty}) = 3-a$, and $\mu_i(f) = 0$ everywhere else. Then, as in the binary case, we can obtain $\{(3, \mathrm{Mjrty})\}$ by adding μ_1, μ_2, and μ_3 and applying a suitable scaling. Similarly, if $a > 1$ we can show $\{(3, \mathrm{Mnrty})\} \in \mathrm{wClone}(\omega_a)$. In both cases, we have found non-zero $\mu \in \mathrm{wClone}(\omega_a)$ such that $\omega_a \notin \mathrm{wClone}(\mu)$, so ω_a cannot be minimal. $\qquad\square$

We remark that the proof of maximality of $\omega_{\langle\min,\max\rangle}$ in Theorem 9 actually proves a stronger result: minimality of $\omega_{\langle\min,\max\rangle}$ over arbitrary distributive lattices with min and max being the lattice meet and join operations.

6 Conclusions

We have studied minimal weighted clones using the algebraic theory for valued constraint languages developed by Cohen et al. [14]. Thus we have shown that the general theory from [14] can be used to answer interesting questions on the complexity of valued constraint languages.

We have shown an analogue of Rosenberg's classification of minimal clones for weighted clones. Furthermore, we have shown minimality of several weighted clones whose support clone is generated by a single minimal operation. On the other hand, we have demonstrated that this is not true in general: there are minimal operations which give rise to non-minimal weighted clones. We have conjectured that minimal *tractable* operations give rise to minimal weighted clones. Finally, we have classified all Boolean weighted clones. Consequently, we have been able to determine all maximal Boolean valued constraint languages, using proofs based on the algebraic characterisation of [11,14]. This has been originally proved in [13] using gadgets.

We believe that the techniques presented in this paper will be useful in identifying new tractable valued constraint languages and proving maximality of valued constraint languages.

References

1. Barto, L., Kozik, M., Maróti, M., Niven, T.: CSP dichotomy for special triads. Proceedings of the American Mathematical Society 137(9), 2921–2934 (2009)
2. Barto, L., Kozik, M., Niven, T.: The CSP dichotomy holds for digraphs with no sources and no sinks. SIAM Journal on Computing 38(5), 1782–1802 (2009)
3. Barto, L.: The dichotomy for conservative constraint satisfaction problems revisited. In: Proc. of LICS 2011 (2011)
4. Barto, L., Kozik, M.: Constraint Satisfaction Problems of Bounded Width. In: Proc. of FOCS 2009, pp. 461–471 (2009)
5. Berman, J., Idziak, P., Marković, P., McKenzie, R., Valeriote, M., Willard, R.: Varieties with few subalgebras of powers. Trans. of AMS 362(3), 1445–1473 (2010)
6. Bulatov, A., Krokhin, A., Jeavons, P.: The complexity of maximal constraint languages. In: Proc. of STOC 2001, pp. 667–674 (2001)
7. Bulatov, A.: A Graph of a Relational Structure and Constraint Satisfaction Problems. In: Proc. of LICS 2004, pp. 448–457 (2004)

8. Bulatov, A.: A dichotomy theorem for constraint satisfaction problems on a 3-element set. Journal of the ACM 53(1), 66–120 (2006)
9. Bulatov, A., Krokhin, A., Jeavons, P.: Classifying the Complexity of Constraints using Finite Algebras. SIAM Journal on Computing 34(3), 720–742 (2005)
10. Bulatov, A.A.: Tractable Conservative Constraint Satisfaction Problems. In: Proc. of LICS 2003, pp. 321–330 (2003)
11. Cohen, D.A., Cooper, M.C., Jeavons, P.G.: An Algebraic Characterisation of Complexity for Valued Constraints. In: Benhamou, F. (ed.) CP 2006. LNCS, vol. 4204, pp. 107–121. Springer, Heidelberg (2006)
12. Cohen, D.A., Cooper, M.C., Jeavons, P.G.: Generalising submodularity and Horn clauses: Tractable optimization problems defined by tournament pair multimorphisms. Theoretical Computer Science 401(1-3), 36–51 (2008)
13. Cohen, D.A., Cooper, M.C., Jeavons, P.G., Krokhin, A.A.: The Complexity of Soft Constraint Satisfaction. Artificial Intelligence 170(11), 983–1016 (2006)
14. Cohen, D., Creed, P., Jeavons, P., Živný, S.: An algebraic theory of complexity for valued constraints: Establishing a Galois connection. In: Murlak, F., Sankowski, P. (eds.) Mathematical Foundations of Computer Science 2011. LNCS, vol. 6907, pp. 231–242. Springer, Heidelberg (2011)
15. Creignou, N.: A dichotomy theorem for maximum generalized satisfiability problems. Journal of Computer and System Sciences 51(3), 511–522 (1995)
16. Creignou, N., Khanna, S., Sudan, M.: Complexity Classification of Boolean Constraint Satisfaction Problems. SIAM Monographs on Discrete Mathematics and Applications, vol. 7. SIAM, Philadelphia (2001)
17. Csákány, B.: Minimal clones – a minicourse. Algebra Universalis 54(1), 73–89 (2005)
18. Denecke, K., Wismath, S.: Universal Algebra and Applications in Theoretical Computer Science. Chapman and Hall/CRC Press (2002)
19. Feder, T., Vardi, M.: The Computational Structure of Monotone Monadic SNP and Constraint Satisfaction: A Study through Datalog and Group Theory. SIAM Journal on Computing 28(1), 57–104 (1998)
20. Jeavons, P.: On the Algebraic Structure of Combinatorial Problems. Theoretical Computer Science 200(1-2), 185–204 (1998)
21. Jeavons, P., Cohen, D., Gyssens, M.: Closure Properties of Constraints. Journal of the ACM 44(4), 527–548 (1997)
22. Kolmogorov, V., Živný, S.: The complexity of conservative finite-valued CSPs. Technical repport arXiv:1008.1555 (August 2010)
23. Kolmogorov, V., Živný, S.: The complexity of conservative valued CSPs (submitted for publication, 2011)
24. Nemhauser, G., Wolsey, L.: Integer and Combinatorial Optimization (1988)
25. Post, E.: The two-valued iterative systems of mathematical logic. Annals of Mathematical Studies, vol. 5. Princeton University Press, Princeton (1941)
26. Rosenberg, I.: Minimal Clones I: the five types. In: Lectures in Universal Algebra (Proc. Conf. Szeged 1983). Colloq. Math. Soc. Janos Bolyai, vol. 43, pp. 405–427. North-Holland, Amsterdam (1986)
27. Schaefer, T.: The Complexity of Satisfiability Problems. In: Proc. of STOC 1978, pp. 216–226 (1978)
28. Schrijver, A.: Theory of linear and integer programming (1986)
29. Schrijver, A.: Combinatorial Optimization: Polyhedra and Efficiency (2003)
30. Świerczkowski, S.: Algebras which are independently generated by every n elements. Fundamenta Mathematicae 49, 93–104 (1960)

Solving MAXSAT by Solving a Sequence of Simpler SAT Instances

Jessica Davies and Fahiem Bacchus

Department of Computer Science, University of Toronto,
Toronto, Ontario, Canada, M5S 3H5
{jdavies,fbacchus}@cs.toronto.edu

Abstract. MAXSAT is an optimization version of Satisfiability aimed at finding a truth assignment that maximizes the satisfaction of the theory. The technique of solving a sequence of SAT decision problems has been quite successful for solving larger, more industrially focused MAXSAT instances, particularly when only a small number of clauses need to be falsified. The SAT decision problems, however, become more and more complicated as the minimal number of clauses that must be falsified increases. This can significantly degrade the performance of the approach. This technique also has more difficulty with the important generalization where each clause is given a weight: the weights generate SAT decision problems that are harder for SAT solvers to solve. In this paper we introduce a new MAXSAT algorithm that avoids these problems. Our algorithm also solves a sequence of SAT instances. However, these SAT instances are always simplifications of the initial MAXSAT formula, and thus are relatively easy for modern SAT solvers. This is accomplished by moving all of the arithmetic reasoning into a separate hitting set problem which can then be solved with techniques better suited to numeric reasoning, e.g., techniques from mathematical programming. As a result the performance of our algorithm is unaffected by the addition of clause weights. Our algorithm can, however, require solving more SAT instances than previous approaches. Nevertheless, the approach is simpler than previous methods and displays superior performance on some benchmarks.

1   Introduction

MAXSAT is an optimization version of Satisfiability (SAT) that is defined for formulas expressed in Conjunctive Normal Form (CNF). Whereas SAT tries to determine whether or not a satisfying truth assignment exists, MAXSAT tries to find a truth assignment that maximizes the satisfaction of the formula. In particular, if each clause of the CNF formula is given a weight, MAXSAT tries to find a truth assignment that maximizes the sum of the weights of the clauses it satisfies (or equivalently minimizes the weight of the clauses it falsifies).

Various special cases can be defined. With only unit weights, MAXSAT becomes the problem of maximizing the number of satisfied clauses. If some of the clauses must be satisfied (**hard clauses**) they can be given infinite weight, while the other clauses are given unit weight indicating that they can be falsified if

J. Lee (Ed.): CP 2011, LNCS 6876, pp. 225–239, 2011.

necessary (**soft clauses**). In this case we have a Partial MAXSAT problem. If we allow non-unit weights, but no hard clauses, we have a Weighted MAXSAT problem. Finally, with non-unit weights and hard clauses we have a Weighted Partial MAXSAT problem.

In this paper we provide a new approach for solving MAXSAT problems that can be applied to any of these special cases. Our algorithm uses the approach of solving MAXSAT by solving a sequence of SAT tests. Recent international MAXSAT Evaluations have provided empirical evidence that the sequence of SAT tests approach tends to be more effective on the larger more industrially focused problems used in the evaluation. In contrast, the competitive approach of using branch and bound search seems to traverse its search space too slowly to tackle these larger problems effectively.

Previous works employing a sequence of SAT tests have used various techniques to convert the optimization problem into a sequence of decision problems, each of which is then encoded as a SAT problem and solved with a modern SAT solver. Letting W be the sum of the weights of the soft clauses, the typical decision problem used is "are $W - wt$ soft clauses along with all of the hard clauses satisfiable." Typically wt starts off at zero and is increased to the next feasible value every time the answer to the decision problem is no. The solution to the MAXSAT problem is the smallest value of wt for which the decision problem becomes satisfiable. This approach is very successful when only a few decision problems must be posed before a solution is found. However, each SAT decision problem is harder to solve than the previous, and performance can be significantly degraded as more and more decision problems must be solved.

In our approach, on the other hand, we utilize a sequence of SAT problems that become progressively easier. In particular, the SAT solver is only ever asked to solve problems that are composed of a subset of the clauses of the original MAXSAT problem. Our approach moves the arithmetic optimization component of the MAXSAT problem off into a different solver that is more suitable for such reasoning. Modern SAT solvers are based on resolution, and hence can have difficulties with inferences that require counting and other arithmetic reasoning. By separating the two components of satisfiability and optimization present in MAXSAT problems our approach can more effectively utilize the strengths of a SAT solver as well as exploiting the strengths of other solvers, like integer programming solvers, that are known to provide powerful arithmetic reasoning.

In the rest of the paper we first present some necessary background. After this we prove a simple theorem from which we obtain our new algorithm, prove its correctness, and then provide some further insights which allow us to improve our algorithm. The algorithm we present is very simple, but there are some issues that arise when implementing it. We discuss some of these next, followed by a discussion of the most closely related work. We then present various empirical results demonstrating that our approach is viable, and finally we close with some conclusions.

2 Background

A propositional formula in CNF is a conjunction of clauses, each of which is a disjunction of literals, each of which is a propositional variable or the negation of a propositional variable. Given a CNF formula a truth assignment is an assignment of *true* or *false* to all of the propositional variables in the formula.

A MAXSAT problem is specified by a CNF formula $\mathcal{F}$ along with a real valued weight for every clause in the formula (previous works have often required the weights to be integer but we do not require such restrictions in our approach). Let $wt(c)$ denote the weight of clause c. We require that $wt(c) > 0$ for every clause. (Clauses with weight zero can be removed from $\mathcal{F}$ without impact).

Some clauses might be hard clauses, indicated by them having infinite weight. Clauses with finite weight are called soft clauses. We use $hard(\mathcal{F})$ to indicate the hard clauses of $\mathcal{F}$ and $soft(\mathcal{F})$ the soft clauses. Note that $\mathcal{F} = hard(\mathcal{F}) \cup soft(\mathcal{F})$.

We define the function *cost* as follows: (a) if H is a set of clauses then $cost(H)$ is the sum of the clause weights in H ($cost(H) = \sum_{c \in H} wt(c)$); and (b) if π is a truth assignment to the variables in $\mathcal{F}$ then $cost(\pi)$ is the sum of the weights of the clauses falsified by π ($\sum_{\{c \mid \pi \not\models c\}} wt(c)$).

A solution to $\mathcal{F}$ is a truth assignment π to the variables of $\mathcal{F}$ with minimum cost. (Equivalently π maximizes the sum of the weights of the satisfied clauses). We let $mincost(\mathcal{F})$ denote the cost of a solution to $\mathcal{F}$.

For simplicity, in our formal results we will assume that $hard(\mathcal{F})$ is satisfiable and that $\mathcal{F}$ is unsatisfiable. It is straightforward to extend our formal results to deal with these corner cases, but doing so is a distraction from the core ideas. Furthermore, from a practical point of view both conditions can be easily tested with a SAT solver and if either is violated we immediately know $mincost(\mathcal{F})$: if $hard(\mathcal{F})$ is unsatisfiable then $mincost(\mathcal{F}) = \infty$ and any truth assignment is a "solution"; and if $\mathcal{F}$ is satisfiable then $mincost(\mathcal{F}) = 0$ and the SAT solution is also an MAXSAT solution.

A **core** κ for a MAXSAT formula $\mathcal{F}$ is a subset of $soft(\mathcal{F})$ such that $\kappa \cup hard(\mathcal{F})$ is unsatisfiable. That is, all truth assignments falsify at least one clause of $\kappa \cup hard(\mathcal{F})$. Cores can be fairly easily extracted from modern SAT solvers.

Given a set of cores $\mathcal{K}$ a **hitting set**, hs, of $\mathcal{K}$ is a set of soft clauses such that for all $\kappa \in \mathcal{K}$ we have that $hs \cap \kappa \neq \emptyset$. Since every core κ is a set of soft clauses it is not restrictive to also force hs to be a set of soft clauses. We say that hs is a **minimum cost hitting set** of $\mathcal{K}$ if it is (a) a hitting set and (b) $cost(hs) \leq cost(H)$ for every other hitting set H of $\mathcal{K}$.

There have been two main approaches to building MAXSAT solvers. The first approach is to utilize the logical structure of the CNF input to enable the computation of lower-bounds during a branch and bound search, e.g., [7,11]. The second approach is to reduce the problem to solving a sequence of SAT problems. In previous work (see Section 4) these SAT problems typically encode the decision problem: "is $mincost(\mathcal{F}) = k$." Starting with $k = 0$, when the answer from the SAT solver is no (i.e., the formula is unsatisfiable), the next lowest possible value k^+ for k is computed from the core returned by the SAT solver. The next SAT problem then encodes the decision problem "is $mincost(\mathcal{F}) = k^+$".

Recent MAXSAT Evaluations [3] have indicated that these two approaches have different coverage. That is, on some problems the branch and bound approach is significantly better, while on other problems the sequence of SAT problems approach is significantly better. In previous work we had investigated using clause learning to improve the lower bounds computed by a branch and bound solver [5]. In working to improve the performance of this lower bounding technique, related ideas were uncovered that lead to a new approach to solving MAXSAT using a sequence of SAT problems. Since this approach was likely to solve a different set of problems than our branch and bound solver we implemented these ideas in a new solver. This paper reports on our new approach.

3   Solving Maxsat with Simpler SAT Instances

The approach we present in this paper involves solving MAXSAT by solving a sequence of SAT problems. In contrast to prior approaches, however, the SAT problems we need to solve become simpler rather than more complex. In particular, the various encodings of the decision problem $mincost(\mathcal{F}) = k$ that have been used in previous work involve an increasing amount of arithmetic reasoning or involve increasing the size of the theory. For example, in the recent approach of [2] the decision problems contain an increasing number of pseudo-boolean constraints (linear constraints over boolean variables). Counting and arithmetic reasoning is often difficult for a SAT solver since such solvers are based on resolution. There are a number of known examples, e.g., the Pigeon Hole Principle, where resolution requires an exponential number of steps to reach a conclusion that can be quickly deduced by, e.g., reasoning directly with linear equations.

In our approach we split the problem into two parts. In one part we compute minimum cost hitting sets, while in the other part we test the satisfiability of *subsets* of the original problem. In this way we move the arithmetic reasoning into the hitting set solver, allowing the SAT solver to deal with only the logical/satisfiability structure of the original problem. Furthermore, the sequence of satisfiability problems that have to be solved can only become easier. However, the hitting set computations can and do become harder. Our thesis is that by splitting the problem in this manner we can more effectively exploit both the strengths of modern SAT solvers as well the strengths of solvers that are effective at performing the arithmetic reasoning required, e.g., integer programming solvers like CPLEX. Our empirical results provide some evidence in support of our thesis, but also indicate that there is a rich design space in exactly how best to perform this split between satisfiability testing and hitting set computations that remains to be more fully explored.

Our approach is based on a simple theorem.

Theorem 1. *If $\mathcal{K}$ is a set of cores for the MAXSAT problem $\mathcal{F}$, hs is a minimum cost hitting set of $\mathcal{K}$, and π is a truth assignment satisfying $\mathcal{F} - hs$ then $mincost(\mathcal{F}) = cost(\pi) = cost(hs)$.*

Proof: $mincost(\mathcal{F}) \leq cost(\pi)$ as $mincost(\mathcal{F})$ is the minimum over all possible truth assignments. $cost(\pi) \leq cost(hs)$ as the clauses π falsifies are a subset of hs

---

Algorithm 1. Algorithm 1 for Solving MAXSAT

---

1 MAXSAT-**solver-1** $(\mathcal{F})$
2 $\mathcal{K} = \emptyset$
3 **while** *true* **do**
4      $\quad$ $hs = \text{FindMinCostHittingSet}(\mathcal{K})$
5      $\quad$ $(\text{sat?},\kappa) = \text{SatSolver}(\mathcal{F} - hs)$
     $\quad$; // If SAT, κ contains the satisfying truth assignment.
     $\quad$; // If UNSAT, κ contains an UNSAT core.
6      $\quad$ **if** *sat?* **then**
7          $\quad\quad \lfloor$ **break** ; // Exit While Loop
     $\quad$ // Add new core to set of cores
8      $\quad$ $\mathcal{K} = \mathcal{K} \cup \{\kappa\}$
9 **return** $(\kappa, \; cost(\kappa))$

(π satisfies all clauses in $\mathcal{F} - hs$). On the other hand $mincost(\mathcal{F}) \geq cost(hs)$. Any truth assignment must falsify at least one clause from every core $\kappa \in \mathcal{K}$. Thus for any truth assignment τ, $cost(\tau)$ must include at least the cost of a hitting set of $\mathcal{K}$. This cannot be any less than $cost(hs)$ which has minimum cost. ∎

Theorem 1 immediately yields the simple algorithm for solving MAXSAT shown as Algorithm 1. The algorithm starts off with an empty set of cores $\mathcal{K}$. At each stage it computes a minimum cost hitting set hs via the function "FindMin-CostHittingSet" and calls a SAT solver to determine if $\mathcal{F} - hs$ is satisfiable. If it is the SAT solver returns (*true*, κ) with κ set to a satisfying assignment for $\mathcal{F} - hs$, otherwise the SAT solver returns (*false*, κ) with κ set to a core of $\mathcal{F} - hs$. New cores are added to $\mathcal{K}$, while satisfying assignments cause the algorithm to terminate.

Observation 1. *Algorithm 1 correctly returns a solution to the inputted* MAXSAT *problem $\mathcal{F}$. That is, it returns a truth assignment κ for $\mathcal{F}$ that achieves* $mincost(\mathcal{F})$.

Proof: First we observe that Algorithm 1 only returns when it breaks out of the while loop, and this occurs only when the current $\mathcal{F} - hs$ is satisfiable. Since in this case hs is a minimum cost hitting set of a set of cores and κ is a truth assignment satisfying $\mathcal{F} - hs$, we have by Theorem 1 that $cost(\kappa) = mincost(\mathcal{F})$. This shows that the algorithm is sound.

Second, to show that the algorithm is complete we simply need to observe that it must terminate. Notice, that since $\mathcal{F}$ is a finite set of clauses, the set of cores of $\mathcal{F}$ must also be finite. Each iteration of the while loop computes a new core of $\mathcal{F}$ and adds it to $\mathcal{K}$. This core cannot be the same as any previous core, hence the while loop must eventually terminate. Consider the hitting set hs computed at line 4 prior to the computation of κ at line 5. $\kappa \cap hs = \emptyset$ since $\kappa \subseteq (\mathcal{F} - hs)$. However, for any previously computed core κ^- we have that $\kappa^- \cap hs \neq \emptyset$ since hs is a hitting set of all previous cores. Hence for all previous cores κ^- we have that $\kappa \neq \kappa^-$. ∎

3.1   Realizable Hitting Sets

In this section we show that the hitting sets considered by Algorithm 1 can be further constrained. This can benefit both the time spent calculating the hitting sets, and the overall number of iterations or SAT solving episodes.

Definition 1. *A hitting set H (i.e., a set of clauses) is* **realizable** *in a* MAXSAT *problem $\mathcal{F}$ if there exists a truth assignment τ such that (a) for each clause $c \in H$, $\tau \not\models c$, and (b) $\tau \models hard(\mathcal{F})$. Otherwise H is said to be* **unrealizable**.

An example of an unrealizable hitting set is one that contains clauses c_1, c_2 with a variable $x \in c_1$ and $\neg x \in c_2$, since all truth assignments satisfy either c_1 or c_2. Next, we show that Algorithm 1 does not gain anything by encountering such unrealizable minimum hitting sets.

Corollary 1 (Of Theorem 1). *Let $\mathcal{K}$ be a set of cores of $\mathcal{F}$ and hs be a minimum cost hitting set of $\mathcal{K}$. If hs is unrealizable, then $\mathcal{F} - hs$ is unsatisfiable.*

Proof: For contradiction, suppose $\pi \models \mathcal{F} - hs$. Then $\pi \models hard(\mathcal{F})$ and since hs is unrealizable, π satisfies some clause in hs. So F_π the set of clauses falsified by π (a) is a strict subset of hs and (b) is a hitting set of $\mathcal{K}$. But then $cost(\mathcal{F}_\pi) < cost(hs)$ which contradicts the fact that hs is a minimum cost hitting set of $\mathcal{K}$.   ∎

Corollary 1 means that any time line 5 of Algorithm 1 returns an unrealizable hs, at least one more iteration of the while loop will be required. Yet in fact, there might be enough information already in the set of cores $\mathcal{K}$ to terminate right away. To see this, remember the aim in solving MAXSAT is to find a truth assignment of minimum cost. Let π be any truth assignment and let $F_\pi = \{c | \pi \not\models c\}$ be the set of clauses falsified by π. Given a set of cores $\mathcal{K}$ we know that π must falsify at least one clause from each core in $\mathcal{K}$. This means that we can partition F_π into two sets, hs_π a hitting set of $\mathcal{K}$, and $F_\pi - hs_\pi$ the remaining falsified clauses. This also partitions the cost of π into two components, $cost(\pi) = cost(hs_\pi) + cost(F_\pi - hs_\pi)$.

Theorem 1 says that if $cost(hs_\pi)$ is minimum (less than or equal to the cost of any hitting set of $\mathcal{K}$), and $cost(F_\pi - hs_\pi)$ is zero (i.e., $F_\pi - hs_\pi = \emptyset$), then π must be a minimum cost truth assignment as no other truth assignment can achieve a lower cost. Looking more closely, however, we can see that the first condition is more stringent than necessary. We do not need hs_π to be a minimum cost hitting set of $\mathcal{K}$, we only need that $cost(hs_\pi) \leq cost(hs_\tau)$ for all other truth assignments τ. We will then have that $cost(\pi) = cost(hs_\pi) + 0 \leq cost(hs_\tau) + cost(F_\tau - hs_\tau) = cost(\tau)$ for all other truth assignments τ. That is, π will be a solution. Going even further we see that we do not need to consider all truth assignments τ. If τ falsifies a hard clause of $\mathcal{F}$ it will immediately have cost ∞, and thus will necessarily be at least as expensive as π.

Realizable hitting sets are relevant because the minimum cost hitting set of $\mathcal{K}$ might not be realizable. In particular, given the current set of cores $\mathcal{K}$ in Algorithm 1, there might be some truth assignment π which satisfies $\mathcal{F} - hs_\pi$

Algorithm 2. Algorithm 2 for Solving MAXSAT

---

1 MAXSAT-**solver-2** $(\mathcal{F}, COND)$
   ; // $COND$ must be satisfied by all hitting sets realizable in $\mathcal{F}$.
   Identical to Algorithm 1 except we replace
   $hs = \text{FindMinCostHittingSet}(\mathcal{K})$
   by
   $hs = \text{FindMinCostHittingSetSatisfyingCondition}(\mathcal{K}, COND)$

(i.e., $F_\pi - hs_\pi = \emptyset$) and for which $cost(hs_\pi) \leq cost(hs_\tau)$ for any other truth assignment τ where $\tau \models hard(\mathcal{F})$. This means that (a) hs_π is a minimum cost realizable hitting set of $\mathcal{K}$, (b) if we pass $\mathcal{F} - hs_\pi$ to the SAT solver it will return π (or some equally good truth assignment) as a satisfying assignment, and (c) we have solved $\mathcal{F}$.

However, hs_π might not be a minimum cost hitting set of $\mathcal{K}$. There might be another hitting set hs that has minimum cost that is lower than the cost of hs_π, but is unrealizable. In Algorithm 1, hs would be selected and the SAT solver invoked with $\mathcal{F} - hs$. This will necessarily cause another core to be returned, and Algorithm 1 will then have to go through another iteration.

Corollary 1 indicates that we can improve on Theorem 1 and Algorithm 1 by computing minimum cost *realizable* hitting sets rather than unconstrained minimum cost hitting sets. Realizability requires a SAT test so it can be expensive. Hence, we improve Theorem 1 and Algorithm 1 in a more general way. In particular, we can search for a minimum cost hitting set that satisfies any condition that is satisfied by all realizable hitting sets. For example, realizability is one such condition. A simpler condition that is easy to test is to ensure that no clauses in the hitting set contain conflicting literals: this condition is also satisfied by all realizable hitting sets.

Theorem 2. *If $\mathcal{K}$ is a set of cores for the MAXSAT problem $\mathcal{F}$, $COND$ is a condition satisfied by all hitting sets that are realizable in $\mathcal{F}$, hs is a hitting set of $\mathcal{K}$ that satisfies $COND$ and has minimum cost among all hitting sets of $\mathcal{K}$ satisfying $COND$, and π is a truth assignment satisfying $\mathcal{F} - hs$ then $mincost(\mathcal{F}) = cost(\pi) = cost(hs)$.*

Proof: $mincost(\mathcal{F}) \leq cost(\pi) \leq cost(hs)$ by exactly the same argument as for Theorem 1. Furthermore $mincost(\mathcal{F}) \geq cost(hs)$. Any truth assignment that satisfies $hard(\mathcal{F})$ must falsify a hitting set of $\mathcal{K}$ that satisfies $COND$. Thus for any truth assignment τ, $cost(\tau)$ must include at least the cost of a hitting set of $\mathcal{K}$ that is at least as great as $cost(hs)$: $cost(hs)$ is minimum among all hitting sets of $\mathcal{K}$ satisfying $COND$. ∎

The improved version of Algorithm 1 is shown as Algorithm 2. Algorithm 2 takes as input a condition satisfied by all hitting sets that are realizable in $\mathcal{F}$. It now searches for a minimum cost hitting set that satisfies this condition. This can potentially cut down the number of iterations of the **while** loop, reducing the number of cores that have to be generated.

Observation 2. *Algorithm 2 correctly returns a solution to the inputted* MAXSAT *problem $\mathcal{F}$.*

Proof: The proof that Algorithm 1 is correct applies using Theorem 2 in place of Theorem 1.   ∎

Finally, we close this section with a brief comment about complexity. The worst case complexity of solving MAXSAT with a branch and bound solver is $2^{O(n)}$ where n is the number of variables. However, the worst case complexity of our algorithm is worse. There are $2^{O(m)}$ possible cores where m is the number of clauses. This provides a worst case bound on the number of iterations executed in the algorithm. Each iteration requires solving a SAT problem of $2^{O(n)}$ and a hitting set problem of $2^{O(m)}$ (one has to examine sets of clauses to find a hitting set). This leaves us with $2^{O(m)} \times 2^{O(m)} = 2^{O(m)}$ as the worst case complexity. Typically the number of clauses m is much larger than the number of variables n.

However, from a practical point of view we only expect our algorithm to work well when the number of cores it has to compute is fairly small. The empirical question is whether or not this tends to occur on problems that arise in various applications.

3.2   Implementation Techniques

There are two issues to be addressed in implementing our algorithm. First is the use of a SAT solver to compute new cores, and second is the computation of minimum cost hitting sets.

Extracting Cores. We use MiniSat-2.0 to compute cores and satisfying assignments. There is a simple trick that can be employed in MiniSat to make extracting cores easy. Following previous work we add a unique "relaxation variable" to each clause of $soft(\mathcal{F})$. So soft clause c_i becomes $c_i \cup \{b_i\}$ where b_i appears nowhere else in the new theory. The hard clauses of $\mathcal{F}$ are unchanged. If b_i is set to *true*, c_i becomes true and imposes no further constraints on the theory. If b_i is set to *false*, c_i is returned to its original state. To solve $\mathcal{F} - hs$ we set the b variables associated with the clauses in hs to *true*, and all other b variables to *false*. These b variable assignments are added as "assumptions" in MiniSat. MiniSat then solves the remaining problem $\mathcal{F} - hs$ and if this is UNSAT it computes a conflict clause over the assumptions—the set of assumptions that lead to failure. The *true* b variables do not impose any constraints so they cannot appear in the conflict clause. Instead, the conflict claused contains the set of *false* b variables that caused UNSAT. The core is simply the set of clauses associated with the b variables of the computed conflict.

An important factor in the performance of our algorithm is the diversity of the cores returned by the SAT solver. In the first phase, we compute as many disjoint cores as possible. The hitting set problems for disjoint cores are easy, and the cost of the minimum cost hitting set increases at each iteration. Typically, however, it is necessary to continue beyond this disjoint phase. Nevertheless we want the

SAT solver to return a core that is as different as possible from the previous cores. To encourage this to happen we employ the following two techniques in the SAT solver. (1) Although it can be shown to be sound to retain learnt clauses and reuse them in subsequent SAT solving calls, we found that doing so reduces the diversity of the returned core. Hence we removed all previously learnt clauses at the start of each SAT call. (2) We inverted the VSIDS scores that were computed during the previous SAT call. The VSIDS score makes the SAT solver branch on variables appearing most frequently in the learnt clauses of the previous SAT call. By inverting these scores the SAT solver tends to explore a different part of the space and tends to find a more diverse new core. Finally, it is also useful to obtain cores that are as small as possible (such cores are more constraining so they make the hitting set problem easier to solve). So after computing a core κ we feed it back into the SAT solver to see if a subset of κ can be detected to be UNSAT. We continue to do this until κ cannot be minimized any further.

Computing a minimal cost hitting set. We employed two different techniques for computing minimal cost hitting sets. The first technique is to encode the problem as an integer linear program (ILP) and invoke an ILP solver to solve it. In our case we utilized the CPLEX solver. The minimal cost hitting set problem is the same as the minimum cost set cover problem and standard ILP encodings exist, e.g., [13]. We used the encoding previously given in [5]. Briefly, for each clause c_i appearing in a core there is a 0/1 variable x_i; for each core there is the constraint that the sum over the x_i variables of the clauses it contains is greater or equal to 1; and the objective is to minimize the sum of $wt(c_i) \times x_i$. Using CPLEX worked well, but it is not clear how to solve for minimal cost realizable hitting sets—to do so would seem to require adding the satisfiability constraints of the hard clauses to the ILP model, and it is well known that ILP solvers are not very effective at dealing with these highly disjunctive constraints.

The second approach we used was our own branch and bound hitting set solver. We utilized a dancing links representation of the hitting set problem [9], and at each node branched on whether or not a clause was to be included or excluded from the hitting set. The main advantage of the dancing links representation is that it allowed us to simplify the representation after each decision. We performed two types of simplification. First, we simplified the representation to account for the decision made (e.g., if we decide to include a clause c_i we could remove all cores that c_i hit from the remaining hitting set problem). These simplifications are well described by Knuth in [9]. Second, we use the simplifications provided in [14] to further reduce the remaining problem. These latter simplifications involve two rules (a) if a core κ_1 has now become a subset of another core κ_2 we know that in hitting κ_1 we must also hit κ_2 so κ_2 can be removed; and (b) if a clause c_1 now appears in a subset of the cores that another clause c_2 appears in and $wt(c_1) \geq wt(c_2)$ we know that we can replace c_1 with c_2 in any hitting set so c_1 can be removed. These simplifications take time but overall in our implementation we found that they yielded a net improvement in solving times.

We additionally experimented with various lower bounds in the hitting set solver. In particular, we tried both of the simple to compute lower bounds given in [5]. Eventually, however, we found that a linear programming relaxation, although more expensive, yielded sufficiently superior bounds so as to improve the overall solving times. This LP relaxation was simply the current reduced hitting set problem encoded using the ILP encoding specified above with the integrality constraints removed. We used CPLEX to solve the LP.

We found that our branch and bound solver did not solve the hitting set problem as efficiently as CPLEX with the ILP encoding. However, with it we were able to implement the realizability condition forcing the solver to find a minimum cost realizable hitting set. This was accomplished by making additional calls to a SAT solver. At each node of the search tree, we performed the following test. If H was the set of clauses currently selected by the branch and bound solver to be in the hitting set, then we applied unit propagation to the theory containing all of the hard clauses of $\mathcal{F}$ along with the negation of every literal in every clause in H. If unit propagation revealed an inconsistency, we backtracked from the node since it could not lead to a realizable hitting set. Whenever branch and bound found a better-cost hitting set, we used the complete SAT test to check if it was realizable. Enforcing realizability also forced us to turn off the second simplification rule given above: removing a clause c_i because it is subsumed by another clause c_j is no longer valid as c_i rather than c_j might be needed for the hitting set to be realizable.

With the addition of realizability we found that our branch and bound hitting set solver was much more competitive with CPLEX on some problems. There are still a number of other improvements to our branch and bound that remain to be tested, including OR-Decomposition [8], caching, and alternate lower bounding techniques like Lagrangian relaxation [15].

4   Related Work

The main prior works utilizing a sequence of SAT tests to solve MAXSAT began with the work of Fu and Malik [6], and include SAT4J [4], WPM1, PM2, and WPM2 [1,2], and Msuncore [12]. As mentioned above there has also been work on branch and bound based solvers but such solvers are not directly comparable with the sequence of SAT solvers: each type of solver is best suited for different types of problems.

All of the sequence of SAT solvers utilize relaxation variables added to the soft clauses of $\mathcal{F}$ as described in Section 3.2, along with arithmetic constraints on which of these relaxation variables can true. Let $soft(\mathcal{F}) = \{c_1, \ldots, c_k\}$ and the corresponding relaxation variables be $\{b_1, \ldots, b_k\}$. SAT4J adds to $\mathcal{F}$ the constraint $\sum_{i=1}^{i=k} wt(c_i)b_i < UB$ encoded in CNF where UB is the current upper bound on $mincost(\mathcal{F})$. If this theory (with the numeric constraint encoded into SAT) is satisfiable UB is decreased and satisfiability retested until the theory transitions from SAT to UNSAT.

The other algorithms, like our approach, work upwards from UNSAT to SAT. And like SAT4J they add arithmetic constraints on the b variables as more cores are discovered. PM2 works only with unweighted clauses. At each iteration that produces a core, PM2 increments the upper bound on the total number of b variables that can be true. PM2 also uses the cores to derive *lower bounds* on different subsets of b variables. In the case of WPM2, each SAT test that returns UNSAT yields a core. This core is widened to include all previous cores it intersected with, and then an arithmetic constraint is added saying that the sum of the b variables in the widened core must have an increased weight of true b variables. Simultaneously another arithmetic constraint is added placing an upper bound on the weight of true b variables in the widened core. These constraints are formulated in such a manner that when the theory transitions from UNSAT to SAT, $mincost(\mathcal{F})$ has been computed.

The arithmetic constraints used in WPM1 and Msuncore are simpler. However, the theory is becoming more complex as the approach involves duplicating clauses. In particular, all of the clauses of the discovered core are duplicated. One copy gets a new b variable and a clause weight equal to the minimum weight clause of the core, while the other copy has the same weight subtracted from it. Finally, a new constraint is added to make the new b variables sum to one.

In contrast to these approaches the approach we present here involves a sequence of simpler SAT problems. There are no arithmetic constraints added to the SAT problem and no clauses are duplicated. Instead, the arithmetic constraints specifying that at least one clause from every core needs to be falsified are dealt with directly by the minimum hitting set solver. In addition, none of the previous approaches have looked at the issue of making sure that the relaxed clauses (i.e., the clauses with turned on b variables) are realizable.

Another closely related work is [5]. Although this work was focused on a branch and bound method, it also utilized the deep connection between hitting sets and MAXSAT solutions that we were able to further exploit here.

5   Empirical Results

We investigated the performance of our proposed algorithms on a variety of industrial and crafted instances, covering all weight categories: unweighted (MS), partial (PMS), weighted (WMS) and weighted partial (WPMS) MAXSAT. Our results suggest that our approach can solve 17 problems that have not been solved before, and can reasonably handle a variety of MAXSAT problems. We also present results on problems with diverse weights, to further illustrate the advantages of our approach.

We ran experiments with all available MAXSAT solvers that use a sequence of SAT problem approach: Msuncore, WBO [12], PM2, WPM1, WPM2 [1,2], SAT4J [4], and Qmaxsat [10].

In order to evaluate the effectiveness of our approach on industrial instances, we ran tests on all 1034 unsatisfiable Industrial instances from the 2009 MAXSAT Evaluation [3], as well as the 116 unsatisfiable WMS instances from the Crafted category. All experiments were conducted with a 1200 second timeout and 2.5GB memory limit, on 2.6GHz AMD Opteron 2535 processors.

In Table 1, we report the number of instances solved and the total runtime on solved instances, by benchmark family. Results are shown for SAT4J, WPM1 and WPM2, since these three solvers represent all existing algorithms that use a sequence of SAT approach and can handle weighted clauses (WPM1 solved more instances overall than Msuncore and WBO). The last two columns show our results for a version of our solver that implements Algorithm 1 and uses CPLEX to solve the ILP formulation of the hitting set problem. Although we don't solve the most problems overall, the families where we do perform best are highlighted in bold. In general, Algorithm 2 solved fewer problems than Algorithm 1 so its results are omitted from this table.

However, there were four benchmark families in which enforcing the realizability condition paid off. In particular, Algorithm 2 solved 44 instances that Algorithm 1 could not solve. These instances are shown in Table 2, which lists the number of instances solved, their average optimum, the average number of iterations Algorithm 1 performed before the timeout, and the number of iterations and runtime for Algorithm 2. We observe that the number of iterations that Algorithm 2 requires to solve the problem is usually significantly fewer than Algorithm 1 performs. This demonstrates that constraining the hitting sets to be realizable can reduce the number of iterations, on some problems.

Table 1. The number of instances solved, and total runtime on solved instances for the 2009 MAXSAT Evaluation industrial and WMS crafted instances

Family	#	SAT4J #	SAT4J Time	WPM1 #	WPM1 Time	WPM2 #	WPM2 Time	Alg1:CPLEX #	Alg1:CPLEX Time
ms/CirDeb	9	7	600	9	178	8	1051	9	395
ms/Sean	108	27	2890	86	6952	73	7202	73	6775
pms/bcp-fir	59	10	38	55	1470	48	2379	21	1873
pms/bcp-simp	138	132	415	131	796	137	1272	131	1326
pms/bcp-SU	38	9	591	13	1596	21	5299	19	3287
pms/bcp-msp	148	96	698	24	731	69	3282	5	2085
pms/bcp-mtg	215	199	1280	181	2651	215	172	102	2384
pms/bcp-syn	**74**	**24**	**2851**	**33**	**731**	**34**	**511**	**60**	**2761**
pms/CirTrace	4	4	2013	0	0	4	1193	0	0
pms/HapAsbly	**6**	**0**	**0**	**2**	**771**	**5**	**143**	**5**	**85**
pms/pbo-logenc	128	128	4229	72	5535	72	8799	78	856
pms/pbo-rtg	15	15	3236	15	16	15	131	14	453
pms/PROT	12	3	876	1	22	3	486	1	9
wpms/up-10	**20**	**20**	**71**	**20**	**109**	**20**	**525**	**20**	**62**
wpms/up-20	20	20	74	20	119	20	601	20	78
wpms/up-30	20	20	77	20	124	20	658	20	146
wpms/up-40	20	20	76	20	134	20	731	20	94
wms/KeXu	34	8	3774	1	395	16	1978	10	1342
wms/RAM	15	4	186	2	326	2	208	1	2
wms/CUT-DIM	62	2	0	4	0	3	0	4	847
wms/CUT-SPIN	5	1	7	0	0	0	0	1	132
Total	1150	749	23990	709	22665	805	36631	614	25002

Table 2. Results on instances Algorithm 2 can solve within 1200 s but Algorithm 1 cannot

		Avg	Alg1:CPLEX	Alg2:B&B	
Family	#	OPT	Iter	Iter	Time
ms/Sean	4	1	13	67	434
pms/bcp-msp	26	99	460	121	204
pms/bcp-mtg	13	8	2198	757	258
pms/bcp-syn	1	6	80	53	295

Table 3. Detailed results on newly solved instances, from the industrial PMS bcp-syn family. '-' in the Time columns indicates timeout.

			Alg1:CPLEX					Alg1:B&B				Alg2:B&B		
Instance	OPT	Iter	|Core|	MxN	HS	Time	Iter	Nodes	HS	Time	Iter	Nodes	HS	Time
saucier.r	6	80	2885	40x2167	15	-	3	1195		-	53	5	5	295
1_1_10_15	10	89	12	44x77	0	26	86	10	0	40	85	11	0	39
1_1_10_10	12	95	10	47x75	0	44	93	10	0	78	93	12	1	117
300_10_20	17	96	14	48x147	1	148	94	14	1	142	97	17	1	152
300_10_14	19	93	11	46x130	0	35	89	12	0	46	88	16	0	37
300_10_15	19	99	12	49x144	0	62	95	13	1	106	96	17	1	134
300_10_10	21	95	9	47x119	0	13	95	14	0	47	95	18	0	42
ex5.r	37	285	28	132x294	0	116	281	24	4	1187	260	46	5	-
ex5.pi	65	304	25	137x267	0	72	301	23	3	924	271	50	2	511
pdc.r	94	413	10	176x212	0	14	408	19	0	99	389	86	1	537
test1.r	110	278	6	119x176	0	3	277	9	0	17	271	85	0	67
rot.b	115	626	23	288x453	0	304	363	40	4	-	345	91	4	-
bench1.pi	121	330	8	149x290	0	25	331	28	1	298	328	113	1	264
max1024.r	245	747	5	323x377	0	153	734	28	1	1016	635	179	2	-
max1024.pi	259	724	5	310x358	0	200	720	25	2	-	663	187	2	-
prom2.r	278	935	6	385x498	0	61	968	21	0	717	733	225	2	-
prom2.pi	287	914	6	372x484	0	40	966	26	1	846	747	249	2	-
Average	100	364	180	159x368	1	82	347	18	71	397	308	83	2	200

In Table 3 we present more detailed results on 17 instances amoung those in Table 1. These were selected based on the fact that none of the competing solvers were able to solve them, and furthermore, they weren't solved by any other solver in the 2009 and 2010 MAXSAT Evaluations. We report results of using Algorithms 1 and 2 with our B&B solver for the hitting set problem, as well as Algorithm 1 with CPLEX for the hitting set. For each version of our solver, and each instance, we list the number of iterations (i.e. SAT episodes), the average time to solve the hitting set problems (columns 'HS'), and the total runtime. We also report some information about the size of the hitting set problems encountered. Column '|Core|' reports the average number of clauses in the cores. Column 'MxN' reports the average dimensions of the hitting set problem given to CPLEX after the simplification rules have been applied. The 'Nodes' columns give the average number of nodes searched by B&B while solving the hitting set problems. The time the SAT solver takes to generate each core is always

Table 4. The number of iterations and runtimes (s) for an industrial WPMS instance as the number k of distinct weights is increased. '-' indicates failure to solve within 1200 s.

k	Opt	SAT4J Iter	Time	WPM1 Iter	Time	WPM2 Iter	Time	WBO Iter	Time	Alg1:CPLEX Iter	Time
1	101	1	3	101	2	102	13	80	4	199	4
2	149	1	-	112	3	133	16	80	4	191	3
4	250	1	-	122	3	140	17	79	4	227	3
8	441	1	-	128	4	163	20	80	2	190	2
10	554	2	-	129	4	175	24	80	4	193	3
16	750	1	-	125	5	3751	-	80	3	161	2
32	1621	3	-	127	7	3066	-	79	2	218	4
64	2857	1	-	126	8	3104	-	80	4	172	3
100	4667	1	-	122	16	95	-	80	4	247	5
128	5994	1	-	126	17	3900	-	79	3	192	2
1000	47187	1	-	128	125	1644	-	80	2	193	3
10000	480011	4	763	127	1069	3074	-	80	3	182	2
100000	5057882	1	-	47	-	3108	-	80	4	184	3

less than 0.02s, so this is not included in the table. Our algorithms seem to be particularly suited to these problems. All three versions of our solver do well, whereas all previous MAXSAT methods fail. This is somewhat surprising since all of the instances are of the PMS type, with no clause weights. However, most of these instances have quite large optimums and therefore require many clauses to be relaxed. This is challenging for prior sequence of SAT approaches, even though the cores of the original MAXSAT theory are quite small. Our approach is able to succeed on these instances because it better exploits the SAT solver's ability to very quickly generate many cores of the original theory.

Sequence of SAT solvers are well suited to industrial problems, which are very large but easily refuted by existing SAT solvers. However, their performance can be adversely affected by the distribution of weights on the soft clauses. At the moment, most of the industrial WPMS benchmark problems have a very small number of distinct weight values. Many real-world applications will require a greater diversity of weights.

In order to investigate our solver's performance on problems with diverse weights, we created a new set of WPMS instances by increasing the diversity of weights on an existing benchmark instance. We selected an industrial problem that is easy for sequence of SAT solvers, the Linux Upgradeability family in the WPMS Industrial category of the 2009 Max-SAT Evaluation. Note that all instances in this family already have the same underlying CNF, just different weights. We generated 13 new instances for an increasing number $k \in \{2^0, 2^1, ..., 2^6\} \cup \{10^1, 10^2, ..., 10^6\}$ of distinct weights. Given k, the weight for each soft clause was randomly chosen (with replacement) from the set $\{1, 2, ..., k\}$. The number of iterations and the runtime on each instance is shown in Table 4. We see that WBO and our solver are immune to this type of weight diversification. Their number of SAT solving episodes and their runtimes remain steady as the number of distinct weights is increased. Although the number of iterations required by WPM1 also doesn't increase with k, the runtimes do increase. We observe that both the number of iterations required, and the runtimes increase significantly for WPM2. SAT4J also has difficulty with these problems.

6   Conclusion

We have presented a new approach to solving MAXSAT via a sequence of SAT problems. We proposed to separate the arithmetic reasoning from the satisfiability testing, allowing the sequence of SAT problems to be simpler rather than more difficult as in previous approaches. The new technique is competitive with previous solvers, and is able to solve some problems previous approaches could not solve. It is also a very simple approach that opens the door for many future improvements.

References

1. Ansótegui, C., Bonet, M.L., Levy, J.: Solving (weighted) partial maxsat through satisfiability testing. In: Proceedings of Theory and Applications of Satisfiability Testing (SAT), pp. 427–440 (2009)
2. Ansótegui, C., Bonet, M.L., Levy, J.: A new algorithm for weighted partial maxsat. In: Proceedings of the AAAI National Conference (AAAI), pp. 3–8 (2010)
3. Argelich, J., Li, C.M., Manyà, F., Planes, J.: The First and Second Max-SAT Evaluations. JSAT 4(2-4), 251–278 (2008)
4. Berre, D.L., Parrain, A.: The sat4j library, release 2.2. JSAT 7(2-3), 56–59 (2010)
5. Davies, J., Cho, J., Bacchus, F.: Using learnt clauses in maxsat. In: Cohen, D. (ed.) CP 2010. LNCS, vol. 6308, pp. 176–190. Springer, Heidelberg (2010)
6. Fu, Z., Malik, S.: On solving the partial MAX-SAT problem. In: Theory and Applications of Satisfiability Testing (SAT), pp. 252–265 (2006)
7. Heras, F., Larrosa, J., Oliveras, A.: Minimaxsat: An efficient weighted max-sat solver. Journal of Artificial Intelligence Research (JAIR) 31, 1–32 (2008)
8. Kitching, M., Bacchus, F.: Exploiting decomposition in constraint optimization problems. In: Stuckey, P.J. (ed.) CP 2008. LNCS, vol. 5202, pp. 478–492. Springer, Heidelberg (2008)
9. Knuth, D.E.: Dancing links. In: Proceedings of the 1999 Oxford-Microsoft Symposium in Honour of Sir Tony Hoare, pp. 187–214. Palgrave, Oxford (2000)
10. Koshimura, M., Zhang, T.: Qmaxsat, http://sites.google.com/site/qmaxsat
11. Li, C.M., Manyà, F., Mohamedou, N.O., Planes, J.: Resolution-based lower bounds in maxsat. Constraints 15(4), 456–484 (2010)
12. Manquinho, V., Marques-Silva, J., Planes, J.: Algorithms for weighted boolean optimization. In: Proceedings of Theory and Applications of Satisfiability Testing (SAT), pp. 495–508 (2009)
13. Vazirani, V.: Approximation Algorithms. Springer, Heidelberg (2001)
14. Weihe, K.: Covering trains by stations or the power of data reduction. In: Proceedings of Algorithms and Experiments (ALEX 1998), pp. 1–8 (1998)
15. Wolsey, L.A.: Integer Programming. Wiley, Chichester (1998)

Filtering Algorithms for Discrete Cumulative Problems with Overloads of Resource

Alexis De Clercq, Thierry Petit, Nicolas Beldiceanu, and Narendra Jussien

École des Mines de Nantes, LINA UMR CNRS 6241, 4, rue Alfred Kastler,
FR-44307 Nantes, France
{ADeClercq,TPetit,NBeldice,NJussien}@mines-nantes.fr

Abstract. Many cumulative problems are such that the horizon is fixed and cannot be delayed. In this situation, it often occurs that all the activities cannot be scheduled without exceeding the capacity at some points in time. Moreover, this capacity is not necessarily always the same during the scheduling period. This article introduces a new constraint for solving this class of problems. We adapt two filtering algorithms to our context: Sweep and P. Vilím's Edge-Finding algorithm. We emphasize that in some problems violations are imposed. We design a new filtering procedure specific to this kind of events. We introduce a search heuristic specific to our constraint. We successfully experiment our constraint.

1 Introduction

Scheduling problems consist of ordering activities. In *cumulative scheduling*, each activity has a duration and requires for its execution the availability of a certain amount of a renewable resource, its *consumption* (or *capacity demand*). Usually the objective is to minimize the *horizon* (maximum due date of an activity in the schedule), while at any point in time the cumulated consumption of activities should not exceed a limit on the available resource, the *capacity*.

However, many industrial problems require of their activities to be scheduled within a given time window, that is, the horizon is fixed and cannot be delayed. In this situation, it may occur that all the activities cannot be scheduled without exceeding the capacity at some points in time. To obtain a solution, exceeds can be tolerated under a certain limit provided operational rules that guarantee the practical feasibility are satisfied. Furthermore, in some problems the time window is partitioned: the capacity is not the same for each interval of the partition. Figure 1 depicts such a situation with overloads.

We introduce a new constraint, SOFTCUMULATIVE, which extends the work presented in [9] to consider overloaded cumulative problems where different local capacities are defined for disjoint intervals of time. Several violation measures can be used for quantifying exceeds of local capacities as well as for computing the global objective value: one may wish to minimize the highest overload, or to minimize the sum of overloaded areas.

J. Lee (Ed.): CP 2011, LNCS 6876, pp. 240–255, 2011.

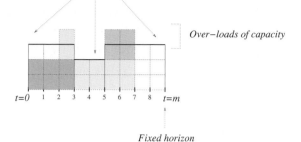

Three intervals with capacities 3, 2 and 3

Over−loads of capacity

$t=0$ 1   2   3   4   5   6   7   8 $t=m$

Fixed horizon

Fig. 1. A cumulative problem with a fixed horizon ($m = 9$) and 3 intervals with capacities respectively equal to 3, 2 and 3. Each activity requires 2 units of resource. The first one starts at $t = 0$ and ends at $t = 3$, the second one starts at $t = 2$ and ends at $t = 7$, the third one starts at $t = 5$ and ends at $t = 7$. There are two overloads of capacity: one in the first interval at time 2, one in the third interval at times 5 and 6.

We discuss concrete problems that can be encoded using SOFTCUMULATIVE together with additional constraints. Some of these constraints may lead to situations where overloads are imposed at some intervals in time. The need of this propagation for imposed violations emphasizes that, for solving over-constrained applications, it is not always sufficient to consider only maximum violation values.

Our main contribution is a new filtering algorithm associated with SOFTCUMU-LATIVE, which also considers imposed overloads, decomposed into three phases. The first phase is an adaptation of the $O(n \cdot log(n))$ sweep algorithm for CUMULA-TIVE [4], where n is the number of activities. In our case, the time complexity also depends on the number p of user-defined local capacities: $O((n + p) \cdot log(n + p))$. The advantages of sweep are preserved: the profile is computed and the starting time variables of activities are pruned in one sweep, and the complexity does not depend on the number of points in time. To perform an energetic reasoning[1] complementary to the profile-based reasoning of sweep, in a second phase we adapt the $O(k \cdot n \cdot log(n))$ Edge-Finding algorithm of P. Vilím [13], where k is the number of distinct capacity demands. In our case, time complexity is $O(p \cdot k \cdot n \cdot log(n))$. In the two phases lower bounds of the objective are included into pruning conditions without increasing the complexity. The third phase is a new specific propagation for events on minimum values of variables which express violations of local capacities, without increasing the time complexity.

Section 2 presents the background for understanding our contributions and defines SOFTCUMULATIVE. Section 3 presents some motivating examples. Section 4 describes the filtering algorithm of SOFTCUMULATIVE. Section 5 presents a new dedicated search strategy and the experiments we performed using CHOCO [1].

---

[1] Deductions based on the comparison between the consumed and available resource.

2   Definitions and Notations

We consider a set A of non-preemptive activities, that is, activities which cannot be interrupted. An activity is defined by some variables. Given a variable x, $\underline{x}$ (resp. $\overline{x}$) denotes the minimum (resp. maximum) value in its domain $D(x)$.

Definition 1 (Activity). *An activity $a_i \in A$ is defined by four variables: sa_i represents its starting point in time; da_i, its duration; ca_i, its completion date such that $ca_i = sa_i + da_i$; and $ra_i \geq 0$, the discrete amount of resource consumed by a_i at any point in time between its start and its completion.*

We denote by $\underline{e}(a_i)$ the *minimum energy* of an activity $a_i \in A$, equal to $\underline{da_i} *$ $\underline{ra_i}$. Given $\Omega \subseteq A$, $\underline{e}(\Omega)$ is the minimum energy of Ω, equal to $\sum_{a_i \in \Omega} \underline{e}(a_i)$. We denote $\underline{mins}(\Omega) = \min_{a_i \in \Omega}(\underline{sa_i})$, $\underline{maxs}(\Omega) = \min_{a_i \in \Omega}(\overline{sa_i})$, $\overline{minc}(\Omega) = \max_{a_i \in \Omega}(\underline{ca_i})$, $\overline{maxc}(\Omega) = \max_{a_i \in \Omega}(\overline{ca_i})$. The *time horizon* m is the maximum possible ending time of activities. We impose $\forall a_i \in A, ca_i \leq m$. At last, *an instantiation of A is an assignment of all variables defining activities in A.*

In CP, cumulative problems can be encoded using the CUMULATIVE constraint [2]. We first recall its definition before introducing SOFTCUMULATIVE.

Definition 2 (Height). *Given one resource and an instantiation of a set A of n activities, at each point in time t the cumulated height h_t of the activities overlapping t is $h_t = \sum_{a_i \in A, sa_i \leq t < ca_i} ra_i$.*

Definition 3 (CUMULATIVE). *Given one resource with a capacity limited by capa and an instantiation of a set A of n activities, the CUMULATIVE$(A, capa)$ constraint is satisfied iff the two following constraints are both satisfied:*

- *C1: For each activity $a_i \in A$, $sa_i + da_i = ca_i$, and*
- *C2: At each point in time t, $h_t \leq capa$.*

We now define the new SOFTCUMULATIVE, a constraint representing cumulative problems with a fixed horizon, cost variables expressing overloads of capacity at some intervals in time, and an objective variable aggregating the costs.

Definition 4 (SOFTCUMULATIVE). *Consider one resource with a capacity limited by capa and a set A of n activities such that $\overline{maxc}(A) \leq m$. We define:*

- *A partition $P = [p_0, \ldots, p_{k-1}]$ of $[0, m)$ in p consecutive intervals such that each p_j is defined by its start and its end : $p_j = [sp_j, ep_j)$.*
- *A sequence of local capacities $Loc = [lc_0, \ldots, lc_{k-1}]$ one-to-one mapped with P, such that a local capacity $lc_j \leq capa$ is associated with each interval p_j.*
- *A sequence of integer cost variables $Cost = [cost_0, \ldots, cost_{k-1}]$ one-to-one mapped with P, such that a variable $cost_j$ is associated with the interval p_j.*
- *An objective variable obj.*
- *A flag $costC \in \{max, sum\}$ indicating how variables in $Cost$ are computed (i.e. considering the maximum exceed or the surface on top).*
- *A flag $objC \in \{max, sum\}$ indicating how the variable obj is computed (i.e. considering the maximum or the sum of the variables in $Cost$).*

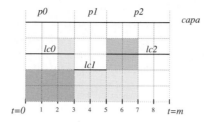

Fig. 2. An instance of SOFTCUMULATIVE representing the problem of Figure 1. If $costC= max$, $cost_0 = 1$, $cost_1 = 0$, $cost_2 = 1$ and if $objC= max$, $obj = 1$, if $objC=$ sum, $obj = 2$. If $costC= sum$, $cost_0 = 1$, $cost_1 = 0$, $cost_2 = 2$. If $objC= max$, and if $objC= max$, $obj = 2$, if $objC= sum$, $obj = 3$.

Given an instantiation of A, the SOFTCUMULATIVE*(A, capa, P, Loc, Cost, obj,costC ,objC) constraint is satisfied iff the four following conditions are all satisfied:*

- *C1 and C2 (see* Definition 3*).*
- *C3:* $\forall j \in [0, k-1]$*:* $cost_j = costC_{t \in p_j}(\max(0, h_t - lc_j))$
- *C4: An objective constraint:* $obj = objC_{j \in [0,k-1]}(cost_j)$.

Compared to SOFTCUMULATIVESUM [9], our constraint splits the time horizon in different intervals with its own length and capacity. overloads are quantified by a cost variable on each interval, depending on $costC$, and an objective variable aggregating the costs and depending on $objC$ (see Figure 2).

Notation 1. *For a given point in time t,* $p_j(t) = [sp_j(t), ep_j(t))$*,* $cost_j(t)$ *and* $lc_j(t)$ *are respectively the interval* $p_j \in P$*, the variable* $cost_j \in Cost$ *and the local capacity* $lc_j \in Loc$ *such that* $t \in p_j$.

3 Practical Problems

Cumulative problems with a fixed horizon may involve additional constraints on variables in $Cost$, to distinguish solutions having a practical interest from solutions that will be rejected by the end-user [9]. We discuss two usual cases.

Fair distribution of overloads. In many applications, e.g., time tabling problems where employees have to perform extra-hours of work to achieve their activities in overloaded periods, exceeds of local capacities have to be fairly distributed. This need was highlighted in [11]. Later, several global constraints were designed for balancing solutions [8,10,12]. For simple cases, classical cardinality constraints can be used. Using SOFTCUMULATIVE, one may define a partition on the set $Cost$ and impose in each class of the partition that the minimum number of cost variables equal to 0 is strictly positive (see Figure 3).

Smooth cost variations. A frequent requirement consists in limiting the number of big variations w.r.t. overloads. This can be done by adding on $Cost$ variables an instance of SMOOTH$(N, tol, Cost)$ [3], where N is a variable and tol an

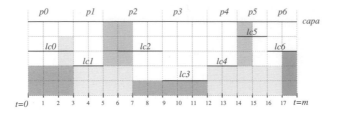

Fig. 3. A solution satisfying additional cardinality constraints on the partition $\{(cost_0, cost_1), (cost_2, cost_3), (cost_4, cost_5, cost_6)\}$ with $costC = max$: at least one cost equal to 0.

integer. It imposes that the number of times that $|cost_{i+1} - cost_i| > tol$ is equal to the value of N (i.e. N represents the limit). For example, when a company hires extra-employees their number should not vary too much from one day to another. Figure 3 is a solution satisfying both SOFTCUMULATIVE and SMOOTH($N, tol, Cost$) with $N = 1$ and $tol = 1$. In some applications, imposing primitive constraints of type $|cost_{i+1} - cost_i| \leq tol$ is convenient.

Overloads lead to violations of capacities and cumulative problems with a fixed horizon can be viewed as over-constrained problems. In [9], experiments show that, in over-constrained problems with additional constraints on variables representing violations, propagating efficiently additional constraints is mandatory to solve instances. In the case of fairly distributed solutions, such a propagation corresponds to events occurring when the maximum value of a cost variable is reduced. More generally, when solving over-constrained problems, it is admitted that violations should be minimized and are never imposed [7]. The example of smooth cost variations contradicts this assumption. Consider the case where the primitive constraint $|cost_{i+1} - cost_i| \leq 1$ is imposed. If $cost_i = 2$ then it is mandatory to have $cost_{i+1} \geq 1$. Therefore, to be efficient in all possible contexts, the filtering of SOFTCUMULATIVE should deal with events on minimum values for variables in *Cost*. Section 4.5 presents a filtering algorithm dedicated to such events. Regarding the state of the art, in [5] this kind of propagation is studied for SOFTALLDIFFERENT and SOFTALLEQUAL.

4 Filtering Algorithms

4.1 Background

Sweep for CUMULATIVE The goal is to reduce the domains of *start* variables according to the cumulated profile, which is built from compulsory parts.

Definition 5 (Compulsory part [6]). *The* Compulsory Part $cp(a_i)$ *of an activity* $a_i \in A$ *is the intersection of all feasible schedules of* a_i. *It is defined by* $[\overline{sa_i}, \underline{ca_i})$ *(therefore, it is not empty iff* $\overline{sa_i} < \underline{ca_i}$*), and a height equal to* $\underline{ra_i}$ *on* $[\overline{sa_i}, \underline{ca_i})$, *and null elsewhere.*

Definition 6 (Cumulated profile). *The* Cumulated Profile *CumP is the minimum cumulated resource consumption, over time, of all the activities. For a given point in time t, the height of CumP at t is equal to $\sum_{a_i \in A, t \in [\overline{sa_i}, \underline{ca_i})} \underline{ra_i}$. That is, the sum of the contributions of all compulsory parts that overlap t.*

The sweep algorithm [4] moves a vertical line Δ on the time axis from one event to the next event. In one sweep, it builds the cumulated profile and prunes activities in order not to exceed *capa*. An *event* corresponds either to the start or the end of a compulsory part, or to the release date $\underline{sa_i}$ of an activity $a_i \in A$. All events are initially computed and sorted in increasing order according to their date. The position of Δ is δ. At each step of the algorithm, a list *ActToPrune* contains the activities to prune.

- Compulsory part events are used for building *CumP*: All such events at date δ are used to update the height sum_h of the current rectangle in *CumP*, by adding the height if it is the start of a compulsory part or removing the height otherwise. The first compulsory part event with a date strictly greater than δ gives the end δ' of the rectangle, finally denoted by $\langle [\delta, \delta'), sum_h \rangle$.
- Events corresponding to release dates $\underline{sa_i}$ such that $\delta < \underline{sa_i} < \delta'$ add some new candidate activities to prune, according to $\langle [\delta, \delta'), sum_h \rangle$ and *capa* (activities overlapping $\langle [\delta, \delta'), sum_h \rangle$). They are added to the list *ActToPrune*.

For each $a_i \in ActToPrune$ that has no compulsory part in the rectangle $\langle [\delta, \delta'), sum_h \rangle$, if its height is greater than $capa - sum_h$ then we prune its starting time so that a_i doesn't overlap the current rectangle of *CumP*. If $\overline{ca_i} \leq \delta'$ then a_i is removed from *ActToPrune*. After pruning activities, δ is updated to δ'.

Pruning Rule 1. *If $a_i \in ActToPrune$ has no compulsory part in $\langle [\delta, \delta'), sum_h \rangle$ and $sum_h + \underline{ra_i} > capa$ then $]\delta - \underline{da_i}, \delta')$ can be removed from $D(sa_i)$.*

Time complexity of Sweep is $O(n \cdot log(n))$ where n is the number of activities.

Edge-Finding for CUMULATIVE This section summarizes Vilím's edge-finding two steps algorithm [13]. First, it detects precedences among activities, and then it prunes starting dates of activities. In both steps, it uses an energetic reasoning: It compares the resource required by a set of activities in a given interval $I = [a, b)$ of points in time with the available resource within this interval. This available resource is given by the capacity *capa* and the size of the interval.

Definition 7. (Available area). *Given an interval in time $I = [a, b)$, we denote by $Area(a, b)$ the maximum available resource, equal to $(b - a) * capa$.*

(Energy envelope). *Let Ω be a set of activities s.t. $\Omega \subseteq A$. The* energy envelope *of Ω is: $Env(\Omega) = \max_{\Theta \subseteq \Omega}(Area(0, \underline{mins}(\Theta)) + \underline{e}(\Theta))$.*

(Precedence). *An activity $a_i \in A$ ends before the end of an activity $a_j \in A$ iff, in all solutions $ca_i \leq ca_j$. It is denoted by the relation $a_i \lessdot a_j$. It can be extended to a set of activities Ω: $\Omega \lessdot a_j$.*

To detect precedences w.r.t. an activity a_j, we consider all the activities a_i having a latest completion time $\overline{ca_i}$ less than or equal to $\overline{ca_j}$.

Definition 8 (Left Cut). *The* Left Cut *of A by an activity $a_j \in A$ is a set of activities such that: $LCut(A, a_j) = \{a_i \in A, \overline{ca_i} \leq \overline{ca_j}\}$.*

Given $\Omega \subseteq A$ (in the algorithm systematically a Left Cut of A by an activity), the energy envelope is used to compute a lower bound $lb(\overline{minc}(\Omega))$ for the earliest completion time $\overline{minc}(\Omega)$ of Ω. From [13], $lb(\overline{minc}(\Omega)) = \lceil Env(\Omega)/capa \rceil$. Once the energy envelopes are available, it is possible to detect precedences.

Precedence Rule 1. *If* $lb(\overline{minc}(LCut(A, a_j) \ \cup \ \{a_i\})) \ > \ \overline{ca_j}$, *then* $LCut(A, a_j) \lessdot a_i$, *which is equivalent to: If* $Env(LCut(A, a_j) \cup \{a_i\}) > Area(0, \overline{ca_j})$, *then* $LCut(A, a_j) \lessdot a_i$.

From precedences, Vilím's algorithm updates the starting time $\underline{sa_i}$ for each activity that ends necessarily after the end of a set of activities Ω. It is based on the notion of *competition*: Ω competes with a_i iff, $\underline{e}(\Omega) > Area(\underline{mins}(\Omega), \overline{maxc}(\Omega)) - \underline{ra_i} * (\overline{maxc}(\Omega) - \underline{mins}(\Omega))$.

Pruning Rule 2. *If $\Omega \lessdot a_i$ and Ω competes with a_i then* $[\underline{sa_i}, \ \underline{mins}(\Omega) + \left\lceil \frac{\underline{e}(\Omega) - Area(\underline{mins}(\Omega), \overline{maxc}(\Omega)) + \underline{ra_i} * (\overline{maxc}(\Omega) - \underline{mins}(\Omega))}{\underline{ra_i}} \right\rceil)$ *can be removed from $D(\underline{sa_i})$.*

Vilím's algorithm uses a tree data structure to compute the energy envelope $Env(\Omega)$ for a given set $\Omega \subseteq A$, the Θ-tree, leading to an overall time complexity of $O(k \cdot n \cdot log(n))$ where k is the number of distinct $\underline{ra_i}$ for activities a_i in A.

4.2   Filtering from Maximum Costs

Some deductions can be made from events on upper bounds of variables in *Cost*. Since interactions with variable *obj* correspond to classical sum or max constraints, we focus on the filtering of start variables.

Sweep for SOFTCUMULATIVE The pruning does not only depend on the capacity *capa*, but also on the maximum values of the variables in *Cost*, and thus on *costC*. The notion of cumulative profile is the same. We add a new class of events: the start and the end of each user-interval $p_j \in P$. As a result, the rectangle defined by $\langle [\delta, \delta'), sum_h \rangle$ has a unique local capacity lc_j and corresponds to a unique cost variable $cost_j$. We have two properties: (1) These new events do not modify the incremental computation of sum_h within the sweep. (2) Contrary to Pruning Rule 1, the maximum capacity $capa_j$ to consider for a given rectangle depends on lc_j, $\overline{cost_j}$ and *costC*. We first consider $costC = max$.

Pruning Rule 3 ($costC = max$). *Let $a_i \in ActToPrune$, which has no compulsory part recorded within the rectangle $\langle [\delta, \delta'), sum_h \rangle$. If $sum_h + \underline{ra_i} > lc_j + \overline{cost_j}$ then $]\delta - \underline{da_i}, \delta')$ can be removed from $D(\underline{sa_i})$.*

Proof. Any a_i in *ActToPrune* is such that there exists at least one point in time t in $[\underline{sa_i}, \overline{ca_i})$ such that $\delta \le t < \delta'$. By Definitions 2 and 6, the height h_t of any solution extending the current partial instantiation is such that $h_t \ge sum_h + \underline{ra_i}$. Therefore, if $sum_h + \underline{ra_i} - lc_j > \overline{cost_j}$, constraint $C3$ of Definition 4 is violated. The same reasoning applies on each point in time within $[\delta, \delta') \cap [\underline{sa_i}, \overline{ca_i})$.   □

If $costC = sum$, in each user-defined interval p_j, $cost_j$ corresponds to the area that exceeds the local capacity lc_j within this interval. Recall that in a given interval $[\delta, \delta')$ defined in the sweep algorithm, the local capacity lc_j and the height of the profile sum_h remain constant by definition. The consumption of the profile is $sum_h * (\delta' - \delta)$ and the total available area that does not lead to an overload is $lc_j * (\delta' - \delta)$. We try to add an activity a_i which has a release date $\underline{sa_i}$ within the interval $[\delta, \delta')$. If a_i has a minimum duration such that a_i can fit in $[\delta, \delta')$, then its minimum energy in this interval is $\underline{e}(a_i)$. Otherwise, its minimum completion date is outside $[\delta, \delta')$, and its energy within this interval is $(\delta' - \underline{sa_i}) * \underline{ra_i}$. We compare the total energy $(\delta' - \delta) * sum_h + \min((\delta' - \underline{sa_i}) * \underline{ra_i}, \underline{e}(a_i))$ to the maximum available resource $lc_j * (\delta' - \delta) + \overline{cost_j}$. We prune $\underline{sa_i}$ if $\overline{cost_j}$ is exceeded.

Pruning Rule 4 (*costC = sum*). *Let $a_i \in ActToPrune$, which has no compulsory part recorded within the rectangle $\langle [\delta, \delta'), sum_h \rangle$ and such that $\delta \le \underline{sa_i} < \delta'$. If $(\delta' - \delta) * sum_h + \min((\delta' - \underline{sa_i}) * \underline{ra_i}, \underline{e}(a_i)) > lc_j * (\delta' - \delta) + \overline{cost_j}$ then*

$$[\underline{sa_i}, \min(\delta', \delta' - \lfloor (\overline{cost_j} + (lc_j - sum_h) * (\delta' - \delta))/(\underline{ra_i}) \rfloor))$$

can be removed from $D(\underline{sa_i})$.

Proof. Given $a_i \in A$ such that $\delta \le \underline{sa_i} < \delta'$, assume a_i starts at $t = \underline{sa_i}$. If $\underline{ca_i} < \delta'$, its minimum energetic contribution is $\underline{e}(a_i)$ in $[\delta, \delta')$, else it is $\underline{ra_i} * (\delta' - t)$. By Definitions 2 and 6, $(\delta' - \delta) * h_t \ge (\delta' - \delta) * (sum_h + \underline{ra_i})$ and $(\delta' - \delta) * (sum_h + \underline{ra_i}) \ge (\delta' - \delta) * sum_h + \min((\delta' - t) * \underline{ra_i}, \underline{e}(a_i))$. Therefore, if $(\delta' - \delta) * sum_h + \min((\delta' - t) * \underline{ra_i}, \underline{e}(a_i)) - lc_j * (\delta' - \delta) > \overline{cost_j}$ (pruning condition), constraint $C3$ of Definition 4 is violated. $\overline{cost_j} + (lc_j - sum_h) * (\delta' - \delta)$ is the area remaining available and $\lfloor \frac{\overline{cost_j} + (lc_j - sum_h) * (\delta' - \delta)}{\underline{ra_i}} \rfloor$ is the number of points in time that can be taken by a_i in $[\delta, \delta')$ without violating the pruning condition. a_i cannot start before δ', which leads to $\min(\delta', \delta' - \lfloor (\overline{cost_j} + (lc_j - sum_h) * (\delta' - \delta))/(\underline{ra_i}) \rfloor)$.   □

The number of events in the sweep depends both on the number of user-intervals and the number of activities. Time complexity is $O((n + p) \cdot log(n + p))$.

Edge-Finding for SOFTCUMULATIVE To extend Vilím's algorithm to the SOFT-CUMULATIVE case, we consider intervals in P and local capacities in Loc instead of a single capacity *capa*. Definition 7 (available area) needs to be adapted. Within an interval $I = [a, b)$, the available resource depends on the local capacities and the maximum values of the variables in *Cost*. We need to study the case where a and b are in the same user interval and the case where $p_j(a) \ne p_j(b)$.

Definition 9 (Available area). *Given an interval in time $I = [a, b)$, we denote by $Area(a, b)$ the maximum available resource. We distinguish two cases:*

- *If $costC = max$*
  - *If $p_j(a) = p_j(b)$, $Area(a, b) = (b - a) * (lc_j(a) + \overline{cost_j}(a))$*
  - *Else, $Area(a, b) = (ep_j(a) - a) * (lc_j(a) + \overline{cost_j}(a)) + (b - sp_j(b)) * (lc_j(b) + \overline{cost_j}(b)) + \sum_{p_i \in (p_j(a), p_j(b))} (ep_i - sp_i) * (lc_i + \overline{cost_i})$*
- *If $costC = sum$*
  - *If $p_j(a) = p_j(b)$, $Area(a, b) = (b - a) * lc_j(a) + \overline{cost_j}(a)$*
  - *Else, $Area(a, b) = (ep_j(a) - a) * lc_j(a) + \overline{cost_j}(a) + (b - sp_j(b)) * lc_j(b) + \overline{cost_j}(b) + \sum_{p_i \in (p_j(a), p_j(b))} ((ep_i - sp_i) * lc_i + \overline{cost_i})$*

Definition 10 (Free area). *Given an interval in time $I = [a, b)$, we denote by $FreeArea(a, b)$ the maximum resource available without creating any new increase in overloads. The calculation is similar to Definition 9 except that maximum values of cost variables ("$\overline{cost_j}$" and "$\overline{cost_i}$") are replaced by 0.*

The principles for computing the energy envelope and the left cut (see Definitions 7 and 8) remain the same as in the CUMULATIVE case, except that the available area is now computed according to Definition 9. Furthermore, Precedence Rule 1 remains also the same. To prove this, we introduce the following notation (there is no need to explicitly compute this quantity in the algorithm).

Notation 2 (*inf*). *Given a set Ω of activities in A, and its energy envelope $Env(\Omega)$, $inf(\Omega)$ is the greatest index j such that $Area(sp_0, sp_j) \leq Env(\Omega)$.*

As in the CUMULATIVE case, given a set of activities $\Omega \subseteq A$ (which is, within the algorithm, systematically a Left Cut), we adapt the calculation of a lower bound $lb(\overline{minc}(\Omega))$ for the earliest completion time $\overline{minc}(\Omega)$ in the case where $costC = max$. [2] Recall $sp_{inf(\Omega)}$ is the start of the user-defined interval of $inf(\Omega)$.

Proposition 1. $lb(\overline{minc}(\Omega)) = sp_{inf(\Omega)} + \left\lceil \dfrac{Env(\Omega) - Area(sp_0, sp_{inf(\Omega)})}{lc_{inf(\Omega)} + \overline{cost_{inf(\Omega)}}} \right\rceil$

Proof. $lb(\overline{minc}(\Omega))$ is the first point in time before which $Env(\Omega)$ can fit, starting from sp_0 (see [13]). By Definition 2, $sp_{inf(\Omega)} \leq lb(\overline{minc}(\Omega)) < sp_{inf(\Omega)+1}$. $Env(\Omega) - Area(sp_0, sp_{inf(\Omega)})$ fits in $[sp_{inf(\Omega)}, sp_{inf(\Omega)+1})$ in a minimum number of points in time $\lceil (Env(\Omega) - Area(sp_0, sp_{inf(\Omega)})) / (lc_{inf(\Omega)} + \overline{cost_{inf(\Omega)}}) \rceil$. $\square$

From Proposition 1, the equivalence of precedence rule 1 remains true.

Property 1. The two following conditions are equivalent: (1) $lb(\overline{minc}(LCut(A, a_j) \cup \{a_i\})) > \overline{ca_j}$. (2) $Env(LCut(A, a_j) \cup \{a_i\}) > Area(sp_0, \overline{ca_j})$.

---

[2] We only give the proof in the case where $costC = max$. In the case where $costC = sum$ the demonstration is the same, except the computation of $lb(\overline{minc}(\Omega))$ which is equal to $lb(\overline{minc}(\Omega)) = sp_{inf(\Omega)} + \lceil \dfrac{Env(\Omega) - Area(sp_0, sp_{inf(\Omega)}) - \overline{cost_{inf(\Omega)}}}{lc_{inf(\Omega)}} \rceil$.

Proof. From Proposition 1 and Definition 7, with $\Omega = LCut(A, a_j) \cup \{a_i\}$.   □

With the new computation of the available area, the notion of competition and Pruning Rule 2 remains the same as for CUMULATIVE. At each leaf of Vilím's Θ-tree, the available area takes $O(p)$ instead of $O(1)$ (see Definition 9). The computation of internal nodes remains the same as in Vilím's algorithm. Therefore, updating of starting times of activities takes $O(n \cdot p)$, while detecting precedences and thus the overall complexity is $O(p \cdot k \cdot n \cdot log(n))$.

4.3   Lower Bounds of Costs and Objective

This section shows how we can update the minimum of cost variables and we can compute lower bounds of the objective, from the domains of activity variables. These lower bounds can be used to update $\underline{obj}$.

Within the sweep algorithm. Variables in *Cost* can be directly updated within the sweep algorithm, while the profile is computed.

Pruning Rule 5. *Consider the current rectangle $\langle [\delta, \delta'), sum_h \rangle$ in the sweep.*

- *If (costC = max) then if $sum_h - lc_j(\delta) > \underline{cost_j}(\delta)$ then $[\underline{cost_j}(\delta), sum_h - lc_j(\delta))$ can be removed from $D(cost_j(\delta))$.*
- *If (costC = sum) then if $(\delta' - \delta) * (sum_h - lc_j(\delta)) > \underline{cost_j}(\delta)$ then $[\underline{cost_j}(\delta), (sum_h - lc_j(\delta)) * (\delta' - \delta))$ can be removed from $D(cost_j(\delta))$.*

Proof. From Definitions 5 and 6.   □

Lower bounds for the objective variable are: if $objC = sum$ then $LB = \sum_{j \in [0,k-1]} \underline{cost_j}$ and if $objC = max$ then $LB = max_{j \in [0,k-1]}(\underline{cost_j})$. These lower bounds can be incrementally computed without any increase in time complexity.

Within the Edge-Finding algorithm. Deductions on the minimum values of variables in *Cost* using edge-finding are weak. Therefore, we only focus on the computation of a lower bound for the objective.

For each activity $a_i \in A$, the minimum energy of $\underline{e}(LCut(A, a_i))$ is computed by the Edge-finding algorithm. This energy should fit within the area defined by the interval $[sp_0, \overline{ca_i})$ by Definition 8. If not, it implies overloads and it is likely to modify the minimum value of the objective variable. Following this process, for each activity we compute a specific lower bound $LB(a_i)$ for the objective variable.

To keep a simple computation of each $LB(a_i)$, the following proposition considers that there is no maximum limit on the cost of each interval. We denote by $\mathcal{P}$ a set containing all the user intervals p_j such that $sp_j \leq \overline{ca_i}$.

Proposition 2. *Let a_i be an activity in A, and $LCut(A, a_i)$ the Left Cut of A by a_i. If $\underline{e}(LCut(A, a_i)) > FreeArea(sp_0, \overline{ca_i})$ then*

- If $(costC = max$ and $objC = sum)$ then $LB(a_i) = \lceil \frac{\underline{e}(LCut(A,a_i)) - FreeArea(sp_0, \overline{ca_i})}{\max_{p_j \in \mathcal{P}}(min(\overline{ca_i}, sp_{j+1}) - sp_j)} \rceil$.

- If $(costC = max$ and $objC = max)$ then $LB(a_i) = \lceil \frac{\underline{e}(LCut(A,a_i)) - FreeArea(sp_0, \overline{ca_i})}{\overline{ca_i} - sp_0} \rceil$.

- If $(costC = sum$ and $objC = sum)$ then $LB(a_i) = \underline{e}(LCut(A, a_i)) - FreeArea(sp_0, \overline{ca_i})$.

- If $(costC = sum$ and $objC = max)$ then $LB(a_i) = \lceil \frac{\underline{e}(LCut(A,a_i)) - FreeArea(sp_0, \overline{ca_i})}{|\mathcal{P}|} \rceil$.

Proof. By Definition 8, $\underline{e}(LCut(A, a_i))$ is the minimum energy that is necessarily placed before $\overline{ca_i}$. The maximum energy that fits within $[sp_0, \overline{ca_i})$ without leading to an overload is $FreeArea(sp_0, \overline{ca_i})$ by Definition 10. As a result, if $\underline{e}(LCut(A, a_i)) > FreeArea(sp_0, \overline{ca_i})$ then it induces a lower bound on $\underline{obj}$. Assume $costC = max$ and $objC = sum$. W.l.o.g. we consider that all the overloading area can be put in the maximum length interval I starting at sp_j, that is, we consider $\max_{p_j \in \mathcal{P}}(min(\overline{ca_i}, sp_{j+1}) - sp_j)$: considering one or more additional intervals having, by definition, a length less than or equal to the length of I, would necessarily lead to a greater or equal total sum of overloads (recall that we do not consider maximum limits on costs). $LB(a_i)$ is equal to $\lceil \frac{\underline{e}(LCut(A,a_i)) - FreeArea(sp_0, \overline{ca_i})}{\max_{p_j \in \mathcal{P}}(min(\overline{ca_i}, sp_{j+1}) - sp_j)} \rceil$. If $costC = max$ and $objC = max$ then we spread out the overload on the greatest possible interval that is $[sp_0, \overline{ca_i})$. If $costC = sum$ and $objC = sum$, the lower bound is the same whatever the distribution of overloads is among the user-defined intervals. If $costC = sum$ and $objC = max$, by spreading out the overload $\underline{e}(LCut(A, a_i)) - FreeArea(sp_0, \overline{ca_i})$ on the intervals in $\mathcal{P}$ we obtain the smallest maximum possible cost. $\square$

Note that considering maximum limits on cost can only increase the computed lower bounds. The computation of $LB(a_i)$ is integrated in the edge-finding algorithm and is performed in $O(p)$. Therefore, the overall complexity when integrating this algorithm within edge-finding is still $O(k \cdot p \cdot n \cdot log(n))$.

4.4   Integrating Objective Lower Bounds

In this section, we consider that filtering procedures 4.2 have been performed. Our aim is to filter activity variables using the lower bounds of the objective variable computed in section 4.3.

We perform this integration in two phases. The first one is a second sweep procedure, while the second one is an energetic reasoning. Without loss of generality, we consider that $\underline{obj} = LB$.

Sweep. In this section we use the lower bound LB of the objective computed in Section 4.3. We consider activities that have no compulsory part in the current rectangle $\langle [\delta, \delta'), sum_h \rangle$, and the corresponding local capacity lc_j.

Recall that LB and $\underline{cost_j}$ have been computed in the first sweep phase. There-fore, if $costC = max$ then $\underline{cost_j} \geq max(sum_h - lc_j, 0)$, and if $costC = sum$ then $\underline{cost_j} \geq (\delta' - \delta) * max(sum_h - lc_j, 0)$.

We try to add an activity a_i in the interval $[\delta, \delta')$, and then we compute the cost obtained by assuming that a_i is scheduled in $[\delta, \delta')$. If the computed cost is strictly superior to $\underline{cost_j}$, then we can consider an increased LB under the condition that a_i is scheduled in $[\delta, \delta')$.

Definition 11. *Let* $a_i \in ActToPrune$, *which has no compulsory part recorded within the rectangle* $\langle [\delta, \delta'), sum_h \rangle$, *and* p_j *the unique interval containing* $[\delta, \delta')$. *We define* $cost_j^{a_i}$ *as:*

- *If(costC = max) then* $cost_j^{a_i} = max(sum_h + \underline{ra_i} - lc_j, 0)$.
- *If(costC = sum) then we consider only activities* a_i *such that* $\delta \leq \underline{sa_i} < \delta'$ *and* $cost_j^{a_i} = max((\delta' - \delta) * (sum_h - lc_j) + min((\delta' - \underline{sa_i}) * \underline{ra_i}, \underline{e}(a_i)), 0)$.

Pruning Rule 6. *Let* $a_i \in ActToPrune$, *which has no compulsory part recorded within the rectangle* $\langle [\delta, \delta'), sum_h \rangle$, *and* p_j *the unique interval containing* $[\delta, \delta')$.

- *If(costC = max and objC = sum) then if* $LB + max(cost_j^{a_i} - \underline{cost_j}, 0) > \overline{obj}$ *then* $]\delta - \underline{da_i}, \delta')$ *can be removed from* $D(sa_i)$.
- *If(costC = max and objC = max) then if* $cost_j^{a_i} > \overline{obj}$ *then* $]\delta - \underline{da_i}, \delta')$ *can be removed from* $D(sa_i)$.
- *If(costC = sum and objC = sum) then if* $LB + max(cost_j^{a_i} - \underline{cost_j}, 0) > \overline{obj}$ *then*

$$[\underline{sa_i}, min(\delta', \delta' - \left\lfloor \frac{(\overline{obj} - LB + \underline{cost_j}) + (lc_j - sum_h) * (\delta' - \delta)}{\underline{ra_i}} \right\rfloor))$$

can be removed from $D(sa_i)$.
- *If(costC = sum and objC = max) then if* $cost_j^{a_i} > \overline{obj}$ *then*

$$[\underline{sa_i}, min(\delta', \delta' - \left\lfloor \frac{\overline{obj} + (lc_j - sum_h) * (\delta' - \delta)}{\underline{ra_i}} \right\rfloor))$$

can be removed from $D(sa_i)$.

Proof. $cost_j^{a_i}$ represents the minimum cost within an interval $[\delta, \delta') \subseteq p_j$ if we add the activity a_i to $[\delta, \delta')$. By Definition 4, the increase in LB is $max(cost_j^{a_i} - \underline{cost_j}, 0)$ if $objC = sum$. If this increase is superior to the margin allowed by $\overline{obj}$, then we can prune sa_i. If $costC = max$, any point in time taken by a_i in $[\delta, \delta')$ can be responsible for the increase then $]\delta - \underline{da_i}, \delta')$ can be removed from $D(sa_i)$. If $costC = sum$, the maximum $cost_j$ allowed by $\overline{obj}$ is $\overline{obj} - LB + \underline{cost_j}$. We then prune the interval the same way as in Pruning Rule 4. The reasoning is similar for $objC = max$ except that we do not measure an increase, but we directly compare the induced cost with $\overline{obj}$. $\qquad \square$

Energetic reasoning. The Edge-finding algorithm computes, for each activity $a_i \in A$, the minimum energy of $\underline{e}(LCut(A, a_i))$. We then consider the lower bound $LB(a_i)$ of the objective variable computed in Section 4.3. We try to add an activity a_j such that $sa_j < \overline{ca_i}$ and $a_j \notin LCut(A, a_i)$ in the interval $[sp_0, \overline{ca_i})$. Then we compute the total energy obtained by assuming that a_j is scheduled in $[sp_0, \overline{ca_i})$. If the computed energy minus the available area in this interval is strictly greater than $LB(a_i)$, then we can consider an increased $LB(a_i)$ under the condition that a_i is scheduled in $[sp_0, \overline{ca_i})$. Then if this lower bound is strictly greater than $\overline{obj}$, we can prune sa_i.

Definition 12. *Let a_i and a_j two activities such that $sp_0 \leq \underline{sa_j} < \overline{ca_i}$. We define $e(a_i, a_j)$ as the energy of a_j in this interval under the condition that a_j begins at $\underline{sa_j}$: $e(a_i, a_j) = min(\underline{e}(a_j), (\overline{ca_i} - \underline{sa_j}) * ra_j)$.*

We focus here on $costC = max$ and $objC = sum$. Other cases are similar.

Pruning Rule 7 (**$costC = max$ and $objC = sum$**). *Let a_i and a_j be two activities in A s.t. $\underline{sa_j} < \overline{ca_i}$ and $a_j \notin LCut(A, a_i)$, and $LB(a_i)$ the lower bound of obj computed in 4.3. If $LB(a_i) + \lceil \frac{e(a_i, a_j)}{\max_{p_k \in \mathcal{P}}(min(\overline{ca_i}, sp_{k+1}) - sp_k))} \rceil > \overline{obj}$,*

$$[\underline{sa_j}, min(\overline{ca_i}, \overline{ca_i} - \lfloor \frac{(\overline{obj} - LB(a_i)) * (\max_{p_j \in \mathcal{P}}(min(\overline{ca_i}, sp_{j+1}) - sp_j))}{ra_j} \rfloor)) \ can \ be \ removed$$

from $D(sa_j)$.

Proof. $LB(a_i)$ ignores $a_j \notin LCut(A, a_i)$. From Proposition 2, the rule holds. □

4.5   Filtering from Minimum Costs

In most cases, in CP, we prune activities from upper-bounds of the cost variables. Section 3 shows that performing deductions from increases on minimum of domains of variables in *Cost* can be of interest. We introduce a technique based on the notion of enveloping part which is dual to the notion of compulsory part.

Definition 13. (Enveloping part). *The Enveloping Part $ep(a_i)$ of an activity $a_i \in A$, is the union of all feasible schedules of a_i. It is defined by the interval $[\underline{sa_i}, \overline{ca_i})$ and a height equal to $\overline{ra_i}$ on $[\underline{sa_i}, \overline{ca_i})$, and null elsewhere.*

(Enveloping cumulated profile). *The Enveloping cumulated Profile $EnvP$ is the maximum cumulated resource consumption, over time, of all the activities. For a given point in time t, the height of $EnvP$ at t is equal to $\sum_{a_i \in A, t \in [\underline{sa_i}, \overline{ca_i})} \overline{ra_i}$ (sum of the contributions of all envelopes overlapping t).*

To prune activities from minimum values of cost variables, we apply a sweep procedure on the enveloping cumulated profile and on the profile of compulsory parts. To do so, we propose to add a new class of events: the start and the end of the envelope of each activity. These new events do not modify the incremental computation of sum_h within the sweep. Additionally, we consider a new height sum_e, which is the height of the cumulated envelope profile in the current rectangle. Intuitively, the principle of the pruning is the following: While building $EnvP$, at each event equal to the start of a user-interval sp_j we check if there is a unique rectangle $\langle [\delta, \delta'), sum_e \rangle$ in $EnvP$ between sp_j and ep_j such that $sum_e \geq lc_j + \underline{cost_j}$. If it is true we prune $a_i \in A$ with the following rule.

1. Remove from $EnvP$ the contribution of a_i.
2. Prune the bounds of $D(sa_i)$ in order to ensure that if a_i starts at $\underline{sa_i}$ or $\overline{sa_i}$ then at any point in time t between 0 and m, $EnvP$ can reach $\underline{cost_j}(t)$.

Pruning Rule 8 ($costC = max$). *Consider a rectangle $\langle [\delta, \delta'), sum_e \rangle$ and an interval p_j such that $\langle [\delta, \delta'), sum_e \rangle$ is the unique rectangle satisfying $sum_e \geq lc_j + \underline{cost_j}$. Let $a_i \in ActToPrune$, if $sum_e - \overline{ra_i} < lc_j + \underline{cost_j}$ then: $[\underline{sa_i}, \delta - \overline{da_i}]$ and $[\delta', \overline{sa_i}]$ can be removed from $D(sa_i)$.*

Proof. If $sum_e - \overline{ra_i} < lc_j + \underline{cost_j}$ then a_i should intersect $[\delta, \delta')$, otherwise in any solution extending the current partial instantiation no point in time t in $[\delta, \delta')$ will satisfy $h_t \geq lc_j + \underline{cost_j}$. Constraint C3 of Definition 4 will be violated.   □

We consider that, for each event corresponding to the start of a user-defined interval we try to apply Pruning Rule 8 according to the previous user-defined interval. This can be done in $O(1)$. We add $O(n)$ events to the sweep and the existence and position of the unique rectangle $\langle [\delta, \delta'), sum_e \rangle$ satisfying $sum_e \geq lc_j + \underline{cost_j}$ can be maintained in $O(1)$. The overall complexity does not change.

5   Search Strategies and Experiments

We designed SCSTRATEGY, a search strategy specific to the problem represented by our constraint. It is based on two priority rules. (1) Variable selection: Select the set of activities maximizing the height, and among them select the start variable of one activity maximizing the duration. (2) Value selection: Given the selected variable, compute the set of points in time minimizing the increase in the objective, thanks to a sweep. Order this set according to the energy remaining free when adding the activity at this point, in a non decreasing order.

We implemented SOFTCUMULATIVE using CHOCO [1], with $costC = max$ and $objC = sum$. Benchmarks were randomly generated w.r.t. durations (between 1 and 4), heights (between 1 and 3), local capacities (between 3 and 6) and user-intervals length. Maximum costs were fixed at 6. Activities can be scheduled between 0 and the horizon. Results in tables are average on 50 instances for each class of problem, using a 2.53 Ghz Intel Core 2 CPU with 4 GB.

In a first benchmark we checked the scalability of our constraint, with 16 or 32 user-intervals. With our implementation, using only the sweep algorithm to find a first solution is the most effective approach w.r.t. time. The top table gives the results obtained by unplugging the Edge-finding algorithm, and shows that SOFTCUMULATIVE can be used to find a solution for problems involving 1000 activities. SCSTRATEGY generally provides, more quickly, a solution with a better objective value ($\pm 20\%$), compared with an heuristic assigning statically

Table 1. Top: Average time and number of backtracks for finding a first solution. Comparison of a Random strategy with SCStrategy. # solved is the number of solved instances with, in parenthesis, the number of instances where the objective variable is the smallest among the instances that can be solved by both strategies. Bottom: Average time and number of backtracks for finding an optimum solution with side constraints. W.r.t to the number of proved unfeasible and solved instances, "EF" means we used the Edge Finding algorithm, while "No EF" means we unplugged it.

# activities / # user-intervals	user interval max length	# solved (with the best obj)		average time (# backtracks)	
		Random	SCStrategy	Random	SCStrategy
500 / 16	40	48 (1)	49 (47)	2.2s (51)	2.1s (46)
500 / 32	20	50 (0)	50 (50)	3.5s (59)	2.8s (11)
1000 / 16	80	49 (1)	39 (38)	31.7s (221)	22.4s (150)
1000 / 32	40	49 (1)	46 (45)	67.3s (382)	49.5s (136)

# activities / # user-intervals	user-interval max length	# proved unfeasible		# solved with $obj = 0$		# solved with $obj \neq 0$		average time (#backtracks) for $obj \neq 0$	
		No EF	EF	No EF	EF	No EF	EF	No EF	EF
50 / 4	20	0	10	11	11	0	27	> 2mn	1.0s (2183)
50 / 8	10	0	6	9	9	0	32	> 2mn	8.1s (7512)
100 / 4	41	0	12	8	8	0	27	> 2mn	4.9s (5534)
100 / 8	21	0	2	8	8	0	33	> 2mn	21.8s (11494)
125 / 4	51	0	6	8	8	0	34	> 2mn	9.6s (8540)
125 / 8	25	0	2	5	5	0	36	> 2mn	47.5s (19058)

start variables with a random value (the best default heuristic in CHOCO w.r.t. our instances). As time complexity of the sweep depends on the number of intervals, finding a solution takes more time when there are more intervals.

In a second benchmark we try to find optimum solutions. The bottom table shows clearly that, in this case, using Edge-Finding improves the solving process. Instances involve either 4 or 8 user-intervals, and side constraints. To define such constraints we partitioned the costs by classes of 4 variables, on which we impose: (1) At least one cost variable equal to 0 within each class of the partition, and (2) $\forall i$ such that $0 \leq i < |Cost| - 1$, $|cost_{i+1} - cost_i| \leq 2$. Instances in the second table were run using the default search heuristic in CHOCO, as SCStrategy is not relevant for proving optimum. This second table highlights that, using Edge-Finding, we are able to find optimum solutions for problems with 125 activities.

6   Conclusion

We presented a new constraint for solving overloaded cumulative problems. We adapted a sweep algorithm and Vilím's Edge-Finding algorithm to our context. We proposed a filtering procedure specific to overloads imposed from outside. We designed a dedicated search heuristic. Future work will attempt to consider also relaxation of precedence relations among activities.

References

1. Choco: An open source Java CP library (2011), http://choco.mines-nantes.fr
2. Aggoun, A., Beldiceanu, N.: Extending CHIP in order to solve complex scheduling and placement problems. Mathl. Comput. Modelling 17(7), 57–73 (1993)

3. Beldiceanu, N., Carlsson, M.: Revisiting the cardinality operator and introducing the cardinality-path constraint family. In: Codognet, P. (ed.) ICLP 2001. LNCS, vol. 2237, pp. 59–73. Springer, Heidelberg (2001)
4. Beldiceanu, N., Carlsson, M.: A new multi-resource *cumulatives* constraint with negative heights. In: Van Hentenryck, P. (ed.) CP 2002. LNCS, vol. 2470, pp. 63–79. Springer, Heidelberg (2002)
5. Hebrard, E., O'Sullivan, B., Razgon, I.: A soft constraint of equality: Complexity and approximability. In: Stuckey, P.J. (ed.) CP 2008. LNCS, vol. 5202, pp. 358–371. Springer, Heidelberg (2008)
6. Lahrichi, A.: The notions of Hump, Compulsory Part and their use in Cumulative Problems. C.R. Acad. sc., t. 294, 209–211 (1982)
7. Larrosa, J., Schiex, T.: Solving weighted csp by maintaining arc consistency. Artificial Intelligence 159(1-2), 1–26 (2004)
8. Pesant, G., Régin, J.-C.: Spread: A balancing constraint based on statistics. In: van Beek, P. (ed.) CP 2005. LNCS, vol. 3709, pp. 460–474. Springer, Heidelberg (2005)
9. Petit, T., Poder, E.: Global propagation of side constraints for solving over-constrained problems. Annals OR 184(1), 295–314 (2011)
10. Petit, T., Régin, J.-C.: The ordered distribute constraint. In: ICTAI, pp. 431–438 (2010)
11. Petit, T., Régin, J.-C., Bessière, C.: Meta constraints on violations for over constrained problems. In: Proc. IEEE-ICTAI, pp. 358–365 (2000)
12. Schaus, P., Deville, Y., Dupont, P.E., Régin, J.-C.: The deviation constraint. In: Van Hentenryck, P., Wolsey, L.A. (eds.) CPAIOR 2007. LNCS, vol. 4510, pp. 260–274. Springer, Heidelberg (2007)
13. Vilím, P.: Edge finding filtering algorithm for discrete cumulative resources in $O(kn\log(n))$. In: Gent, I.P. (ed.) CP 2009. LNCS, vol. 5732, pp. 802–816. Springer, Heidelberg (2009)

Synthesis of Search Algorithms from High-Level CP Models*

Samir A. Mohamed Elsayed** and Laurent Michel

Computer Science Department, University of Connecticut

Abstract. The ability to specify CP programs in terms of a declarative model and a search procedure is instrumental to the industrial CP successes. Yet, writing search procedures is often difficult for novices or people accustomed to model & run approaches. The viewpoint adopted in this paper argues for the synthesis of a search from the declarative model to exploit the problem instance structures. The intent is not to eliminate the search. Instead, it is to have a default that performs adequately in the majority of cases while retaining the ability to write full-fledged procedures. Empirical results demonstrate that the approach is viable, yielding procedures approaching and sometimes rivaling hand-crafted searches.

1 Introduction

Constraint programming (CP) techniques are successfully used in various industries and quite successful when confronted with hard constraint satisfaction problems. Parts of this success can be attributed to the considerable amount of flexibility that arises from the ability to write completely tailored search procedures. The main drive is based on the belief that

$$CP = Model + Search$$

where the model provides a declarative specification of the constraints, while the search specifies how to explore the search space. In some CP languages, the search can be quite sophisticated. It can concisely specify variable and value selection heuristics, search phases [14], restarting strategies [9], large neighborhood search [1], exploration strategies like depth-first-search, best-first search, or limited discrepancy search [12] to name just a few. This flexibility is mostly absent in mathematical programming where the so-called *black-box* search is controlled through a collection of parameters affecting pre-processing, cut generation, or the selection of predefined global heuristics. Users of mathematical programming solely rely on modeling techniques and reformulations to indirectly influence and hopefully strengthen the search process effectiveness.

Newcomers discovering CP often overlook the true potential of open (i.e., *white-box*) search specification and fail to exploit it. The observation prompted

---

* This work is partially supported through NSF award IIS-0642906.
** The author is partially supported by Helwan University, Cairo, Egypt.

a number of efforts to rethink constraint programming tools and mold them after LP and MIP solvers by *eliminating open search procedures* in favors of intelligent black-box procedures. Efforts of this type include [14] and [6] while others, e.g., [21] provide a number of predefined common heuristics. Our contention is that it is possible to get the best of both worlds: retaining the ability to write tailored search procedures, and *synthesizing* instance-specific search procedures that are competitive with procedures hand-crafted by experts.

The central contribution of this paper is CP-AS, a model-driven automatic search procedure generator written in COMET [24]. CP-AS analyzes a CP model instance at runtime, examines the variable declarations, the arithmetic and logical constraints, as well as the global constraints and synthesizes a procedure that is likely to perform reasonably well on this instance. Empirical results on a variety of representative problems (with non-trivial tailored search procedures) demonstrate the effectiveness of the approach. The rest of the paper is organized as follows: Section 2 presents related work. Section 3 provides details about the synthesis process, while Section 4 illustrates the process on a popular CP application. Experimental results are reported in Section 5 and Section 6 concludes.

2   Related Work

The oldest general purpose heuristics follow the fail-first principle [11] and order variables according to the current size of their domains. Impacts [18] were introduced as a generic heuristic driven by the effect of labeling decisions on the search space contraction. *wdeg* and *dom/wdeg* [3] are inspired by SAT solvers and use conflicts to drive a variable ordering heuristic. Activity-based search [15] is driven by the number of variables involved in the propagation after each decision and is the latest entry among black-box general purpose heuristics.

MINION [6] offers a black-box search and combines it with matrix based modeling, aiming for raw speed alone to produce 'model and run' solutions. CPHYDRA [17] is a portfolio approach exploiting a knowledge base of solved instances. It combines machine learning techniques with the partitioning of CPU-time among portfolio members to maximize the expected number of solved instances within a fixed time budget. Model-driven derivation of search first appeared in [26] for Constraint-Based Local Search (CBLS). Given a model, a CBLS synthesizer derives a local search algorithm for the chosen meta-heuristic. It analyzes the instance and synthesizes neighborhoods as well as any other necessary components. The AEON synthesizer [16] targets the scheduling domain where combinatorial structures are easier to recognize and classify. Note that AEON handles both complete and incomplete (CBLS) solvers. The first extension to generic CP models was proposed in [4] and is extended here with a larger rule set for global constraints that now uses many variable and value selection heuristics.

3   The Synthesis Process

CP-AS defines rules meant to recognize combinatorial structures for which good heuristics exist. Each rule, when fired, produces a set of *recommendations* characterized by a fitness score, a subset of variables, and two heuristics for variable and value selection as well as dynamic value symmetry breaking whenever appropriate. This set of recommendations is the blueprint for the search itself. The section describes the entire process.

3.1   Preliminaries

A CSP (Constraint Satisfaction Problem) is a triplet $\langle X, D, C \rangle$, where X is a set of variables, D is a set of domains, and C is a set of constraints. Each $x \in X$ is associated with a domain $D(x)$, i.e., with a totally ordered finite set (i.e., a well-ordered set) of discrete values over some universe $\mathcal{U}$. A constraint $c(x_1, \cdots, x_n)$, specifies a subset of the Cartesian product $D(x_1) \times \cdots \times D(x_n)$ of mutually-compatible variable assignments. $\mathbb{X}$ is the type of a variable, while $\mathbb{X}[]$ denotes the type of an "array of variables". $\mathbb{D} = 2^{\mathcal{U}}$ is the type of a domain and $\mathbb{C}$ is the type of a constraint. A COP (Constraint Optimization Problem) $\langle X, D, C, O \rangle$ is a CSP with an objective function O.

Common notations. $vars(c)$ denotes the variables appearing in constraint c while $cstr(x)$ is the subset of constraints referring to variable x. The static degree $deg(x)$ of variable x is $deg(x) = \sum_{c \in cstr(x)} (|vars(c)| - 1)$. Variables can be organized as arrays in the model and this is captured by a special tautological "constraint" `array(x)` that states that the subset of variables $x \subseteq X$ forms an array. $T(c)$ denotes the type of a constraint c (e.g., `knapsack, sequence, array`, etc.). Finally, $T(C) = \{T(c) : c \in C\}$ is the set of constraint types in C.

Definition 1. *A variable ordering heuristic $h_x : \mathbb{X}[] \to \mathbb{N} \to \mathbb{X}$ is a function which, given an array of n variables $[x_0, \cdots, x_{n-1}]$, defines a permutation π of $0..n-1$ that produces a partial function $[0 \mapsto x_{\pi(0)}, \cdots, n-1 \mapsto x_{\pi(n-1)}] : \mathbb{N} \to \mathbb{X}$.*

Example 1. The static variable ordering denoted h_{static} simply produces the variable ordering partial function $h_{static} = [0 \mapsto x_0, \cdots, n - 1 \mapsto x_{n-1}]$.

Example 2. The static degree ordering denoted h_{deg} uses a permutation $\pi : \mathbb{N} \to \mathbb{N}$ of $0..n - 1$ satisfying

$$\forall i, j \in 0..n - 1 : i \leq j \Rightarrow deg(x_{\pi(i)}) \geq deg(x_{\pi(j)})$$

to define the partial function $h_{deg} = [0 \mapsto x_{\pi(0)}, \cdots, n - 1 \mapsto x_{\pi(n-1)}]$.

Example 3. The classic *dom* variable ordering denoted h_{dom} will, when given an array of variables x, uses a permutation $\pi : \mathbb{N} \to \mathbb{N}$ of $0..n - 1$ satisfying

$$\forall i, j \in 0..n - 1 : i \leq j \Rightarrow |D(x_{\pi(i)})| \leq |D(x_{\pi(j)})|$$

to produce a partial function capturing a permutation of x. For instance, invoking $h_{dom}([x_1, x_2, x_3])$ with $D(x_1) = \{1, 2, 3\}, D(x_2) = \{1\}, D(x_3) = \{3, 4\}$ returns the partial function $[0 \mapsto x_2, 1 \mapsto x_3, 2 \mapsto x_1]$. The result produced by h_{dom} is dynamic, i.e., the embedded permutation π will use the domains of the variables in x when it is invoked.

Example 4. The *dom/wdeg* [3] variable ordering denoted h_{wdeg} will, when given an array of variables x, use a permutation $\pi : \mathbb{N} \to \mathbb{N}$ of $0..n-1$ satisfying

$$\forall i,j \in 0..n-1 : i \leq j \Rightarrow \frac{|D(x_{\pi(i)})|}{\alpha_{wdeg}(x_{\pi(i)})} \geq \frac{|D(x_{\pi(j)})|}{\alpha_{wdeg}(x_{\pi(j)})}$$

with $\alpha_{wdeg}(x_i) = \sum_{c \in C} weight[c] \, | \, vars(c) \ni x_i \wedge |futVars(c)| > 1$. Following [3], $weight[c]$ is a counter associated to constraint c that tracks the number of conflicts discovered by c during the search. The expression $futVars(c)$ denotes the set of uninstantiated variables in c.

Definition 2. *A value ordering heuristic $h_v : \mathbb{D} \to \mathbb{N} \to \mathcal{U}$ is a function which, given a domain $d = \{v_0, \cdots, v_{k-1}\}$ of cardinality k, uses a permutation π to produce a serialization function for d defined as $[0 \mapsto v_{\pi(0)}, \cdots k-1 \mapsto v_{\pi(k-1)}]$.*

Example 5. The min-value heuristic (denoted h_{mv}) applied to the domain $D(x) = \{v_0, \cdots, v_{k-1}\}$ of a variable x uses a permutation $\pi : \mathbb{N} \to \mathbb{N}$ satisfying

$$\forall a,b \in 0..k-1 : a \leq b \Rightarrow v_{\pi(a)} \leq v_{\pi(b)}$$

to produce a serialization partial function $[0 \mapsto v_{\pi(0)}, \cdots, k-1 \mapsto v_{\pi(k-1)}]$. For instance, invoking $h_{mv}(\{3,7,1,5\})$ returns $[0 \mapsto 1, 1 \mapsto 3, 2 \mapsto 5, 3 \mapsto 7]$.

Definition 3. *A value symmetry breaking heuristic $h_s : \mathbb{D} \to \mathbb{D}$ is a function that maps a set of k values from $\mathcal{U}$ to a subset of non-symmetric values.*

3.2 Rules and Recommendations

Definition 4. *Given a CSP $\langle X, D, C \rangle$, a rule r is a tuple $\langle \mathcal{G}, \mathcal{S}, \mathcal{V}, \mathcal{H} \rangle$ where*

$\mathcal{G} : 2^C \to 2^{2^C}$ *is a partitioning function that breaks C into $G_1 \cdots G_n$ such that $\cup_{i=1}^n G_i \subseteq C$ and $G_i \cap G_j = \emptyset \; \forall i \neq j$.*
$\mathcal{S} : \langle 2^X, 2^D, 2^C \rangle \to \mathbb{R}$ *is a scoring function,*
$\mathcal{V} : \langle 2^X, 2^D, 2^C \rangle \to 2^X$ *is a variable extraction function,*
$\mathcal{H} : \langle 2^X, 2^D, 2^C \rangle \to \langle h_x, h_v \rangle$ *is a heuristic selection function.*

All scores are normalized in $0..1$ with 1 representing the strongest fit.

Definition 5. *Given a rule $\langle \mathcal{G}, \mathcal{S}, \mathcal{V}, \mathcal{H} \rangle$, a CSP $\langle X, D, C \rangle$, and a partition $\mathcal{G}(C) = \{G_1 \cdots G_n\}$ the rule's recommendations are $\{\langle S_i, V_i, H_i \rangle : 0 < i \leq n\}$ with $S_i = \mathcal{S}(X, D, G_i), V_i = \mathcal{V}(X, D, G_i)$, and $H_i = \mathcal{H}(X, D, G_i)$.*

Generic Partitioning. Several rules use the same partitioning scheme $\tilde{\mathcal{G}}$. A rule r focusing on constraints of type t uses the function $\tilde{\mathcal{G}}$ to only retain constraints of type t and yields one group per constraint. Namely, let $n = |\{c \in C : T(c) = t\}|$ in $\tilde{\mathcal{G}}(C) = \{\{c_1\}, \cdots, \{c_n\}\}$ with all the c_i constraints in C of type t.

3.3   Rules Library

Rules are meant to exploit combinatorial structures expressed with arrays, global constraints, arithmetic constraints, and logical constraints. Structures can be explicit (e.g., global constraints), or implicit (e.g., the static degree of a variable). CP-AS offers one rule per combinatorial structure that can produce a set of recommended labeling decisions. Global constraints play a prominent role in the analysis and their rules are described first. A brief discussion of a generic scoring function used by most rules starts the section.

Generic Scoring. The generic scoring applies to a group (i.e., a subset) $G \subseteq C$ of constraints and attempts to capture two characteristics: the homogeneity of the entire set C and the coupling of the variables in each constraint of the group G. A homogeneous constraint set contains few distinct constraint types that might be easier to deal with. The homogeneity of C is measured by $\frac{1}{|T(C)|}$ which ranges in 0..1 and peaks at 1 when only one type of constraint is present in C. The variable coupling for a single constraint $c \in G$ is an indicator of the amount of filtering to be expected from c.

When $vars(c)$ is a super-set of a user-specified array from the model, the ratio of the maximal variable degree in $vars(c)$ to the maximal overall degree ($r_1(c)$ below) is used to estimate c's coupling. Otherwise, the simpler ratio $r_2(c)$ is used.

$$r_1(c) = \frac{\max_{x \in vars(c)} deg(x)}{\max_{x \in X} deg(x)} \qquad r_2(c) = \frac{|vars(c)|}{|\bigcup_{k \in C : T(k) = T(c)} vars(k)|}$$

The generic scoring function for $G \subseteq C$ is then

$$\tilde{S}(G) = \frac{1}{|T(C)|} \cdot \max_{c \in G} \left(\begin{cases} r_1(c) \ \exists \ a \in C : T(a) = \mathtt{array} \wedge vars(c) \supseteq vars(a) \\ r_2(c) \ \text{otherwise} \end{cases} \right)$$

Observe how $r_1(c)$ and $r_2(c)$ are both in the range 0..1 delivering a generic score in the 0..1 range. The rest of the section defines the rules. Each definition specifies the partitioning $\mathcal{G}$, scoring $\mathcal{S}$, variable extraction $\mathcal{V}$, and the heuristic selection $\mathcal{H}$ functions. Each of these function names is subscripted by a two letter mnemonic that refers to the rule name.

Alldifferent(ad) Rule. The `alldifferent(x)` constraint over the array x of n variables holds when all variables are pairwise distinct. The rule uses the generic partitioning $\tilde{\mathcal{G}}$ and the generic scoring $\tilde{S}$. The variable selection heuristic is simply h_{dom} (i.e., the smallest domain), while the value selection heuristic is h_{mv} (i.e., min-value). The variable extraction simply restricts the scope of the rule to the variables of the constraint, namely $\mathcal{V}_{ad}(X, D, \{c\}) = vars(c)$. The heuristic selection $\mathcal{H}_{ad}$ returns $\langle h_{dom}, h_{mv} \rangle$. Note that $\mathcal{V}_{ad}$ will always receive a singleton as the rule uses the generic partitioning that always produces partitions with singletons. The rule is thus $\langle \tilde{\mathcal{G}}, \tilde{S}, \mathcal{V}_{ad}, \mathcal{H}_{ad} \rangle$.

Knapsack(ks) Rule. The `knapsack(w,x,b)` constraint over the array x of n variables holds when $\sum_{i=0}^{n-1} w_i \cdot x_i \leq b$. The knapsack rule uses the generic partitioning $\tilde{\mathcal{G}}$ and the generic scoring $\tilde{S}$.

A customized variable ordering heuristic is desirable when a user-specified array of variables coincides with the array x. If true, the rule favors a variable ordering for x based on decreasing weights in w and breaks ties according to domain sizes. Let $\pi : \mathbb{N} \to \mathbb{N}$ be a permutation of the indices $0..n-1$ into x satisfying

$$\forall i, j \in 0..n - 1 : i \leq j \Rightarrow \langle w_{\pi(i)}, -|D(x_{\pi(i)})|\rangle \succeq \langle w_{\pi(j)}, -|D(x_{\pi(j)})|\rangle$$

where $\succeq$ denotes the lexicographic ordering over pairs. The variable ordering is then a partial function $h_{ks} = [0 \mapsto x_{\pi(0)}, \cdots, n-1 \mapsto x_{\pi(n-1)}]$. When x does not correspond to a model array, the heuristic is simply h_{dom}. The heuristic selection function $\mathcal{H}$ is

$$\mathcal{H}_{ks}(X, D, \{c\}) = \left\langle \begin{array}{ll} h_{ks} & \text{if } \exists\, a \in C : T(a) = \text{array} \wedge vars(a) = vars(c) \\ h_{dom} & \text{otherwise} \end{array} , h_{mv} \right\rangle$$

The variable extraction simply restricts the scope of the rule to the variables of the constraint, namely $\mathcal{V}_{ks}(X, D, \{c\}) = vars(c)$. The rule is thus $\langle \tilde{\mathcal{G}}, \tilde{S}, \mathcal{V}_{ks}, \mathcal{H}_{ks}\rangle$.

Spread(sp) Rule. The `spread(x,s,δ)` constraint over an array x of n variables and a spread variable δ holds whenever $s = \sum_{i=0}^{n-1} x_i \wedge N \cdot \sum_{i=0}^{n-1}(x_i - s/n)^2 \leq \delta$ holds. It constrains the mean to the constant s/n and states that δ is an upper bound to the standard deviation of x [19]. The rule uses the generic partitioning and generic scoring functions. To minimize δ, one must minimize each term in the sum and thus bias the search towards values in $D(x_i)$ closest to s/n. This suggests both a variable and a value selection heuristic. The value selection can simply permute the values of the domain to first consider those values closer to s/n. Namely, let $\pi : \mathbb{N} \to \mathbb{N}$ be a permutation of the range $0..k-1$ satisfying

$$\forall i, j \in 0..k - 1 : i \leq j \Rightarrow |v_{\pi(i)} - \frac{s}{n}| \leq |v_{\pi(j)} - \frac{s}{n}|$$

in the definition of the value ordering $h_{vsp} = [0 \mapsto v_{\pi(i)}, \cdots, k \mapsto v_{\pi(k-1)}]$ for the domain $D(x) = \{v_0, \cdots, v_{k-1}\}$. Given h_{vsp}, the ideal variable ordering is maximum regret. Namely, the variable with the largest difference between the first two values suggested by its h_{vsp} ought to be labeled first. Let $\tau : \mathbb{N} \to \mathbb{N}$ be a permutation for the range $0..n-1$ satisfying

$$\forall i, j \in 0..n - 1 : i \leq j \Rightarrow$$
$$h_{vsp}(D(x_{\tau(i)}))(1) - h_{vsp}(D(x_{\tau(i)}))(0) \geq h_{vsp}(D(x_{\tau(j)}))(1) - h_{vsp}(D(x_{\tau(j)}))(0)$$

in the variable ordering $h_{xsp} = [0 \mapsto x_{\tau(0)}, \cdots, n - 1 \mapsto x_{\tau(n-1)}]$. Note how the value ordering $h_{vsp} : \mathbb{D} \to \mathbb{N} \to \mathcal{U}$ is passed the domains of the two chosen variables $x_{\tau(i)}$ and $x_{\tau(j)}$ to form the regret between the best two values according to h_{vsp}. The heuristic selection $\mathcal{H}_{sp}$ returns $\langle h_{xsp}, h_{vsp}\rangle$ and the variable extraction $\mathcal{V}_{sp}$ returns x (the variables of the spread) in the rule $\langle \tilde{\mathcal{G}}, \tilde{S}, \mathcal{V}_{sp}, \mathcal{H}_{sp}\rangle$.

Sequence(sq) Rule. The classic `sequence(x,d,p,q,V)` global constraint [2] requires that for every window of length q in array x, at most p variables take their values in V and the demands in d for values in V are met by the sequence. The sequence rule overrides the partitioning function $\tilde{\mathcal{G}}$ to group sequence constraints that pertain to the same sequence x and same demand d, to exploit the tightness of the various sequencing requirement and to yield better variable and value orderings. Let $\mathcal{G}_{sq}(C) = \{G_1, \cdots, G_k\}$ where G_1 through G_k satisfy

$$\forall a, b \in G_i : vars(a) = vars(b) \wedge d(a) = d(b) \wedge T(a) = T(b) = \text{sq}$$

The refined scoring function

$$\mathcal{S}_{sq}(X, D, G) = \tilde{\mathcal{S}}(X, D, G) \cdot \frac{\left(\sum_{c \in G} U(c)\right)}{|G|} \quad \text{where } U(c) = \frac{c.q}{c.p} \cdot \frac{\sum_{j \in c.V} d_j}{n}$$

scales the generic score $\tilde{S}$ with the average constraint tightness of a group G and the tightness of a single sequence constraint. The tightness of sequence c is proportional to $c.q/c.p$ and to the overall demand for values in $c.V$.

Following [20], the ideal variable and value selection heuristics attempt to avoid gaps in the sequence while labeling and give preference to values that contribute the most to the constraint tightness. The permutation $\pi_x : \mathbb{N} \to \mathbb{N}$ of $0..n-1$ satisfies

$$\forall i, j \in 0..n-1 : i \leq j \to |x_{\pi_x(i)} - n/2| \leq |x_{\pi_x(j)} - n/2|$$

(π_x prefers variables that are closer to the middle of the sequence) and is used to define the variable ordering $h_{xsq} = [0 \mapsto x_{\pi_x(0)}, \cdots, n-1 \mapsto x_{\pi_x(n-1)}]$. The value selection heuristic is driven by the tightness of a value j in all the constraints of group G

$$\bar{U}(j) = \sum_{c \in G} U(c) \cdot (j \in c.V)$$

The permutation π_v of the values in $D(x) = 0..k-1$ makes sure that i precedes j in π_v if it has a higher utility, i.e., π_v satisfies

$$\forall i, j \in 0..k-1 : i \leq j \Rightarrow \bar{U}(\pi_v(i)) \geq \bar{U}(\pi_v(j))$$

and leads to the value ordering $h_{vsq} = [0 \mapsto v_{\pi_v(0)}, \cdots, k-1 \mapsto v_{\pi_v(k-1)}]$. The heuristic selection $\mathcal{H}_{sq}$ returns $\langle h_{xsq}, h_{vsq} \rangle$ while the variable extraction function $\mathcal{V}_{sq}$ returns $\cup_{c \in G} vars(c)$ for a group G of sequence constraints. The sequence rule is $\langle \mathcal{G}_{sq}, \mathcal{S}_{sq}, \mathcal{V}_{sq}, \mathcal{H}_{sq} \rangle$.

Weighted-Sum(ws) Rule. The rule applies to a COP $\langle X, D, C, O \rangle$ with $O \equiv \sum_{i=0}^{n-1} w_i \cdot x_i$ where all the w_i are positive coefficients. The objective (without loss of generality, a minimization) can be normalized as a linear constraint c defined as $o = \sum_{i=0}^{n-1} w_i \cdot x_i$ with a fresh variable o. The partitioning function $\mathcal{G}_{ws}$ returns the singleton $\{o = \sum_{i=0}^{n-1} w_i \cdot x_i\}$ while the scoring function $\mathcal{S}_{ws}$

always returns 1. To minimize the objective, it is natural to first branch on the term with the largest weight and choose a value that acts as the smallest multiplier. Yet, variables in o are subject to constraints linking them to other decision variables and it might be preferable to first branch on those if these variables are more tightly coupled. Let $Z(x) = \cup_{i \in 0..n-1} \cup_{c \in cstr(x_i)} vars(c) \setminus \{x\}$ denotes the set of variables one "hop" away from variables in array x. The decision to branch on x or on $Z(x)$ can then be based upon an estimation of the coupling among these variables. Like in the generic scoring, the expression $\max_{y \in S} deg(y)$ can be used to estimate the coupling within set S and drives the choice between x and $Z(x)$ delivering a simple variable extraction function $\mathcal{V}_{ws}$

$$\mathcal{V}_{ws}(X, D, \{c\}) = \begin{cases} x & \text{if } \max_{y \in x} deg(y) \geq \max_{y \in Z(x)} deg(y) \\ Z(x) & \text{otherwise} \end{cases}$$

The variable ordering over x can directly use the weights in the objective. But a variable ordering operating on $Z(x)$ must first determine the contributions of a variable $y \in Z(x)$ to the terms of the objective function. Note how $Z(y) \cap x$ identifies the terms of the objective function affected by a decision on y. It is therefore possible to define a weight function that aggregates the weights of the term affected by a decision on y. Let

$$w(y) = \sum_{z \in Z(y) \cap x} c.w(z) \quad : \forall y \in Z(x)$$

denote the aggregate weights for variable y where $c.w(z)$ is the actual weight of variable z in the objective. A permutation $\pi : \mathbb{N} \to \mathbb{N}$ of the variable indices ranging over the n variables in x (respectively, over the n variables in $Z(x)$) satisfies

$$\forall i, j \in 0..n-1 : i \leq j \Rightarrow w(x_{\pi(i)}) \geq w(x_{\pi(j)})$$

and is key to define the variable ordering $h_{ws} = [0 \mapsto x_{\pi(0)}, \cdots, n-1 \mapsto x_{\pi(n-1)}]$. The heuristic selection function $\mathcal{H}_{ws}$ returns $\langle h_{ws}, h_{mv} \rangle$ (the value selection is min-value) and the entire rule is $\langle \mathcal{G}_{ws}, \mathcal{S}_{ws}, \mathcal{V}_{ws}, \mathcal{H}_{ws} \rangle$.

Pick-Value-First(pv) Rule. If the number of values to consider far outnumbers the variables to label, it is desirable to first choose a value and then a variable to assign it to. This rule generates one recommendation for each variable array and the partitioning function is thus $\mathcal{G}_{pv}(C) = \{\{c\} \in C : T(c) = \texttt{array}\}$. The scoring function measures the ratio array size to number of values

$$\mathcal{S}_{pv}(X, D, \{\texttt{array}(x)\}) = \begin{cases} 1 - \frac{|x|}{|\cup_{a \in x} D(a)|} & \text{if } |\cup_{a \in x} D(a)| \geq |x| \\ 0 & \text{otherwise} \end{cases}$$

The variable extraction function $\mathcal{V}_{pv}$ simply returns the variables in the array x while $\mathcal{H}_{pv}(X, D, \{\texttt{array}(x)\}) = \langle h_{static}, h_{mv} \rangle$. The rule is $\langle \mathcal{G}_{pv}, \mathcal{S}_{pv}, \mathcal{V}_{pv}, \mathcal{H}_{pv} \rangle$.

Degree(deg) Rule. The rule partitions C with $\mathcal{G}_{deg}(C) = \{\{c\} \in C : T(c) = \texttt{array}\}$ and issues and uses a scoring that conveys the diversity of the static degrees of the variables in the arrays. The index of diversity is based on the relative frequencies of each member of the collection [8] and is the first factor in the definition of $\mathcal{S}_{deg}$. The index tends to 1 for diverse populations and to 0 for uniform populations. The second factor captures the relative coupling of the variables in the array and also belongs to the 0..1 range. The score function is

$$\mathcal{S}_{deg}(X, D, \{\texttt{array}(x)\}) = \left(1 - \sum_{d=1}^{z} p_d^2 \right) \cdot \frac{\max_{y \in x} deg(y)}{\max_{y \in X} deg(y)}$$

where z is the number of distinct degrees, $p_d = freq_d/|x|$ and $freq_d = |\{a \in x : deg(a) = d\}|$. Note that, when all the variables in x have the same static degree the diversity index is equal to 0, sending the overall score to 0. The variable extraction is $\mathcal{V}_{deg}(X, D, \{\texttt{array}(x)\}) = x$. The variable ordering follows h_{deg}, i.e., it selects variables with largest degree first. The value selection is h_{mv} leading to a definition for the heuristic selection $\mathcal{H}_{deg}$ that returns $\langle h_{deg}, h_{mv} \rangle$ and the rule is $\langle \mathcal{G}_{deg}, \mathcal{S}_{deg}, \mathcal{V}_{deg}, \mathcal{H}_{deg} \rangle$.

The Default Rule. The rule ensures that all variables are ultimately labeled and its score is the lowest (i.e., a small constant ϵ bounded away from 0). The rule could effectively use any black-box heuristic like Activity-based search, Impact-based search, *dom/wdeg*, *dom/ddeg*, or even the simple *dom* heuristic. In the following, it defaults to the *dom* heuristic. $\mathcal{G}_{def}(C) = C$, $\mathcal{S}_{def}(X, D, C) = \epsilon$. $\mathcal{V}_{def}(X, D, C) = X$ to make sure that all variables are labeled. The variable ordering is h_{dom} and the value ordering is h_{mv}. The overall heuristic selection function $\mathcal{H}_{def}$ returns $\langle h_{dom}, h_{mv} \rangle$ and the rule boils down to $\langle \mathcal{G}_{def}, \mathcal{S}_{def}, \mathcal{V}_{def}, \mathcal{H}_{def} \rangle$.

3.4 Symmetry Breaking

The symmetry-breaking analysis is global, i.e., it considers the model as a whole to determine whether symmetries can be broken dynamically via the search procedure. When conclusive, the analysis offers a partitioning of the values into equivalence classes that the search can leverage.

While breaking symmetries statically is appealing for its simplicity, it can interfere with the dynamic variable and value selection heuristics. Breaking symmetries dynamically through the search sidesteps the issue. A global symmetry analysis of the model identifies equivalence classes among values in domains and avoid the exploration of symmetric labeling decisions. The automatic derivation of *value* symmetry breaking in CP-AS follows [23,5], where the authors propose a compositional approach that detects symmetries by exploiting the properties of the combinatorial sub-structures expressed by global constraints.

```
1  forall(r in rec.getKeys()) by (−rec{r}.getScore()) {
2      rec{r}.label();
3      if (solver.isBound()) break;
4  }
```

Fig. 1. A Skeleton for a Synthesized Search Template

3.5 Obtaining and Composing Recommendations

Given a CSP $\langle X, D, C \rangle$ and a set of rules $\mathcal{R}$, the synthesis process computes a set of recommendations rec defined as follows

$$\text{let } \{G_1, \cdots, G_k\} = \mathcal{G}_r(C)$$
$$\text{in}$$
$$rec = \bigcup_{r \in \mathcal{R}} \left(\cup_{i \in 1..k} \{ \langle \mathcal{S}_r(\langle X, D, G_i \rangle), \mathcal{V}_r(\langle X, D, G_i \rangle), \mathcal{H}_r(\langle X, D, G_i \rangle) \rangle \} \right)$$

Namely, each rule decomposes the set of constraints according to its partitioning scheme and proceeds with the production of a set of recommendations, one per partition. When a rule does not apply, it simply produces an empty set of recommendations. Once the set rec is produced, the search ranks the recommendation based on their scores and proceeds with the skeleton shown in

```
1  interface Recommendation {
2      void label();
3      var<CP>{int}[] getVars();
4      set{int} getValues(var<CP>{int} x);
5      int hx(var<CP>{int}[] x,int rank);
6      int hv(set{int} vals,int rank);
7  }
8  class VariableRecommendation implements Recommendation { ...
9      void label() {
10         var<CP>{int}[] x = getVars();
11         forall(rank in x.getRange()) {
12             var<CP>{int} pxi = hx(x, rank);
13             if (|D(pxi)| == 1) continue;
14             set{int} d = getValues(pxi);
15             int vr = 0;
16             while (vr < |d|) {
17                 int pvr = hv(d,vr++);
18                 if (pvr ∈ pxi)
19                     try<cp> cp.label(pxi, pvr); | cp.diff(pxi, pvr);
20             }
21         }
22     }
23 }
24 class ValueRecommendation implements Recommendation ...
```

Fig. 2. The Variable/Value Recommendation Classes

Figure 1. Line 2 invokes the polymorphic labeling method of the recommendation. The search ends as soon as all the variables are bound (line 3). Note that since

$$\bigcup_{\langle S_r, V_r, H_r \rangle \in rec} (\cup_{x \in V_r}) = X$$

the search is guaranteed to label all the variables. Figure 2 depicts the *label* method for a *variable first recommendation*, i.e., a recommendation that first selects a variable and then chooses a value. Line 10 retrieves the variables the recommendation operates on, and line 12 selects a variable according to the variable ordering h_x embedded in the recommendation. Line 14 retrieves the values that are to be considered for the chosen variable *pxi*. The `getValues` method is responsible for only returning non-symmetrical values when value symmetries can be broken (it returns the full domain of *pxi* otherwise). The index *vr* spans over the ranks of these values in *d* and line 17 retrieves the vr^{th} value from *d*. If the value is still in the domain, line 19 uses it to label *pxi*. Line 24 alludes to the fact that value-first recommendation also have their own implementation of the `Recommendation` interface to support their control flow.

4   A Walk-Through Example

The synthesis process is illustrated in detail on one representative COP featuring arithmetic, reified as well as global constraints. In the scene allocation problem, shown in Figure 3, one must schedule a movie shoot and minimize the production costs. At most 5 scenes can be shot each day and actors are compensated per day of presence on the set. The decision variable `shoot[s]` (line 2) represents the day scene `s` is shot while variable `nbd[a]` represents the number of days an actor `a` appears in the scenes.

The objective function is a weighted sum leading to a score of 1 for the *ws* rule. On a given instance, all the `nbd` variables have the same static degree (16) while the remaining variables (`shoot`) all have a static degree of 18. Therefore, $\max_{y \in nbd} deg(y) < \max_{y \in shoot} deg(y)$ and the rule recommends to branch on the connected (1-hop away) variables $Z(\mathtt{nbd})$, i.e., on the `shoot` variables. The rule proceeds and creates synthetic weights for each entry in `shoot` that aggregates the weight of terms influenced by the scene being shot.

```
1 Solver<CP> m();
2 var<CP>{int} shoot[Scenes](m,Days);
3 var<CP>{int} nbd[Actor](m,Days);
4 int up[i in Days] = 5;
5 minimize<m> sum(a in Actor) fee[a] * nbd[a] subject to {
6     forall(a in Actor)
7        m.post(nbd[a]==sum(d in Days) (or(s in which[a]) shoot[s]==d));
8     m.post(atmost(up,shoot),onDomains);
9 }
```

Fig. 3. A Model for the Scene Allocation Problem

Table 1. Experimental Results

Benchmark	Tailored			CPAS			ABS			IBS			WDEG		
	$\mu(T)$	$\sigma(T)$	TO	$\mu(T)$	$\sigma(T)$	TO	$\mu(T)$	$\sigma(T)$	TO	$\mu(T)$	$\sigma(T)$	TO	$\mu(T)$	$\sigma(T)$	TO
car-1	0.1	0.0	0	0.1	0.0	0	80.7	63.1	1	300.0	0.0	25	88.3	111.1	5
car-2	0.1	0.0	0	0.1	0.0	0	38.8	42.2	0	221.2	95.7	14	53.7	78.9	1
car-3	0.7	0.1	0	0.6	0.0	0	266.4	66.1	19	300.0	0.0	25	276.8	80.2	23
debruijn	0.6	0.1	0	0.5	0.0	0	300.0	0.0	25	301.2	0.7	25	300.0	0.0	25
gap	13.8	1.3	0	10.5	0.3	0	44.7	2.3	0	15.4	0.6	0	91.1	5.9	0
golomb	3.4	0.3	0	2.6	0.2	0	32.3	14.8	0	137.2	60.0	1	15.3	0.2	0
color	24.9	2.5	0	193.6	0.7	0	300.0	0.0	25	300.0	0.0	25	300.0	0.0	25
gcolor(5-6)	2.7	0.2	0	2.3	0.1	0	22.1	14.3	0	5.3	0.8	0	83.8	1.0	0
knapCOP-1	0.8	0.0	0	0.0	0.0	0	0.5	0.0	0	0.4	0.1	0	1.3	0.0	0
knapCOP-2	10.4	0.1	0	3.2	0.1	0	2.7	0.5	0	5.0	2.0	0	13.4	0.3	0
knapCOP-3	300.0	0.0	25	34.6	0.5	0	64.7	13.8	0	213.7	64.4	3	300.0	0.0	25
knapCSP-1	0.6	0.0	0	0.1	0.0	0	0.1	0.1	0	0.1	0.1	0	0.3	0.2	0
knapCSP-2	3.2	0.0	0	0.8	0.0	0	1.0	0.4	0	2.0	1.0	0	4.2	2.5	0
knapCSP-3	300.0	0.0	25	9.3	0.1	0	13.8	11.4	0	63.0	37.9	0	282.4	40.8	20
magic Sq-10	4.6	4.2	0	300.0	0.0	25	2.3	2.8	0	1.3	1.6	0	89.2	126.5	6
magic Sq-11	7.9	9.2	0	300.0	0.0	25	9.2	17.2	0	3.8	2.5	0	249.6	87.6	16
magicseries	5.8	0.7	0	5.7	0.1	0	2.8	1.6	0	2.7	0.4	0	1.9	3.0	0
market	5.8	0.2	0	5.2	0.1	0	30.4	21.9	0	37.2	27.1	0	47.3	36.5	0
nurse(z3)	0.3	0.0	0	4.6	0.1	0	40.3	17.2	0	18.9	6.9	0	163.4	49.8	0
nurse(z5)	0.1	0.0	0	2.1	0.0	0	53.8	6.0	0	13.0	9.4	0	61.4	15.6	0
perfectSq	0.2	0.0	0	0.2	0.0	0	300.0	0.0	25	300.0	0.0	25	300.0	0.0	25
progressive1	0.1	0.0	0	0.1	0.0	0	67.3	96.4	2	41.1	34.7	0	3.7	2.3	0
progressive2	0.6	0.0	0	0.7	0.0	0	112.3	125.7	7	278.8	64.6	22	175.4	114.8	9
progressive3	0.1	0.0	0	0.1	0.0	0	19.2	58.8	1	46.2	84.4	2	153.4	142.7	11
radiation1	2.3	0.0	0	0.5	0.0	0	0.4	0.1	0	1.7	0.1	0	0.1	0.0	0
radiation2	7.3	0.8	0	300.0	0.0	25	2.2	0.4	0	8.7	1.3	0	0.6	0.2	0
radiation3	198.1	3.9	0	300.0	0.0	25	0.5	0.1	0	2.4	0.2	0	0.1	0.0	0
radiation4	2.0	0.0	0	0.2	0.0	0	1.0	0.2	0	5.5	0.2	0	0.6	0.3	0
radiation5	0.0	0.0	0	12.4	0.1	0	1.1	0.2	0	5.6	0.5	0	0.3	0.2	0
radiation6	1.1	0.0	0	300.0	0.0	25	1.1	0.2	0	6.5	0.9	0	0.2	0.0	0
radiation7	1.3	0.0	0	11.2	0.3	0	1.3	0.4	0	10.0	0.7	0	0.2	0.1	0
radiation8	6.8	0.0	0	300.0	0.0	25	2.1	0.6	0	9.5	2.8	0	0.5	0.1	0
radiation9	300.0	0.0	25	4.8	0.1	0	2.1	0.5	0	9.5	0.7	0	1.1	0.6	0
RRT	4.7	0.0	0	4.9	0.1	0	145.4	131.9	10	243.2	105.9	17	91.3	94.8	3
scene	0.4	0.0	0	0.7	0.0	0	156.7	45.8	0	47.1	16.1	0	300.0	0.0	25
slab1	5.3	0.0	0	2.6	0.4	0	300.0	0.0	25	300.0	0.0	25	290.6	47.2	24
slab2	2.9	0.0	0	3.6	0.2	0	300.0	0.0	25	300.0	0.0	25	266.3	93.5	22
slab3	300.0	0.0	25	7.7	0.5	0	300.0	0.0	25	300.0	0.0	25	288.1	59.5	24
sport	6.6	1.1	0	5.4	0.1	0	151.2	123.9	7	255.3	96.3	20	131.8	111.1	5
Total	1526		100	2131		150	3170		197	4113		279	4428		294

Beyond *ws*, two rules produce additional recommendations. The degree rule produces a single recommendation, while the default rule produces another. Yet, the score of the degree rule is 0 since all the variables have the same degree forcing the diversity index to 0. The default rule issues a recommendation with a score of ϵ to label any remaining variables not handled by the *ws* recommendation.

The value-symmetry analysis determines that the value (days) assigned to the scenes (i.e., `shoot`) are fully interchangeable as reported in [13]. The symmetries are broken dynamically with the `getValues` method of the recommendation. The method returns the subset of values (days) already in use (these are no longer symmetric and each one forms one equivalence class) along with *one* unused day. Comparatively, the tailored search in [22] iterates over the scenes and always chooses to first label the scene with the smallest domain and to break ties based on the costliest scene first.

5   Experimental Results

Experiments were carried out on a mix of feasible CSP and COP that benefit from non-trivial tailored search procedures. Each benchmark is executed 25 times with a timeout at 300 seconds. Results are reported for Activity Based Search (ABS), Impact-Based Search (IBS), Weighted Degree search (WDEG), a state-of-the-art hand-written tailored search, and the search synthesized by CP-AS. ABS, IBS and WDEG all use a slow restarting strategy based on an initial failure limit of $3 \cdot |X|$ and a growth rate of 2 (i.e., the failure limit in round i is $l_i = 2 \cdot l_{i-1}$. Table 1 reports the average CPU time $\mu(T)$ (in seconds), its standard deviation $\sigma(T)$ and the number of runs that timed out (TO). The analysis time for CP-AS is negligible. Timeouts are "charged" 300 seconds in the averages.

The tailored search procedures are taken from the literature and do exploit symmetry breaking when appropriate. The steel mill instances come from CSPLib [7,10] and the hand-crafted search is from [25]. The car sequencing instances come from CSPLib and the tailored search uses the best value and variable orderings from [20]. The nurse rostering search and instances are from [19]. The progressive party instances come from [7] and the tailored search labels a period fully (using first-fail) before moving to the next period. The multi-knapsack as well as the magic square instances are from [18]. The tailored search for the magic square uses restarts, a semi-greedy variant of h_{dom} for its variable ordering and a randomized (lower or upper first) bisection for domain splitting. Grid coloring and radiation models and instances were obtained from the MiniZinc Challenge[1]. All the COP searches are required to find a global optimum and prove optimality. All results are based on COMET 3.0 on 2.8 GHz Intel Core 2 Duo machine with 2GB RAM running Mac OS X 10.6.7.

Rule's adequacy. The intent of CP-AS was to produce code reasonably close to procedures produced by experts and competitive with generic black-box searches. The evaluation suite contains additional benchmarks (quite a few classic CSP) that terminate extremely quickly for all the search algorithms and are therefore providing no insights into CP-AS's behavior. Figure 4 graphically illustrates how often the various rules contribute to the search procedure of a model. Unsurprisingly, a rule like "pick-value-first" is used extremely rarely (only on the perfect square) as the overwhelming majority of benchmarks do not have this property. The other rules are used substantially more often. The fallback rule is used fairly rarely as well. Overall, the rules do not overfit the benchmarks, i.e., we are far from equating one-rule with one benchmark.

Tailored Search. Procedures written by experts are often sophisticated with symmetry breaking and rich variable/value ordering using multiple criteria. The performance of custom searches is therefore a target to approach and possibly match on a number of benchmarks. CP-AS is successful in that respect and only falls short

---

[1] Available at http://www.g12.csse.unimelb.edu.au/minizinc/

on models like radiation (it cannot generate a bisecting search), or graph coloring (it branches on the chromatic number too early). On the magic square CP-AS cannot exploit semantics not associated with any one global constraint.

Black-box searches. Compared to black-box searches, CP-AS is generally competitive, especially in terms of robustness. Sometimes, the black-box heuristics perform better (e.g., on radiation) and this needs to be further investigated with a much lengthier set of experiments with and without restarting. Finally, it is possible and maybe even desirable to switch to a fallback rule that uses an effective black-box search techniques that dominates a plain *dom* heuristic. This was intentionally left out to avoid confusions about the true causes

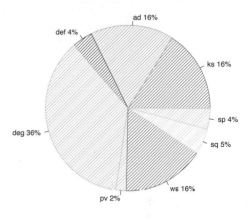

Fig. 4. Rule Usage

of CP-AS behavior. The grand total of running times and number of timeouts across the 5 searches is particularly revealing.

6 Conclusion

CP-AS automatically generates search algorithms from high-level CP models. Given a CP model, CP-AS recognizes and classifies its structures to synthesize an appropriate algorithm. Empirical results indicate that the technique can be competitive with state-of-the-art procedures on several classic benchmarks. CP-AS is able to generate searches that split variables into groups/phases and uses specialized variable and value ordering heuristics within each group. CP-AS also relies on a *global* value symmetry breaking analysis that follows [23,5] and whose results are exploited within each group of variables.

References

1. Ahuja, R.K., Ergun, Ö., Orlin, J.B., Punnen, A.P.: A survey of very large-scale neighborhood search techniques. Discrete Appl. Math. 123(1-3), 75–102 (2002)
2. Beldiceanu, N., Contejean, E.: Introducing global constraints in CHIP. Mathematical and Computer Modelling 20(12), 97–123 (1994)
3. Boussemart, F., Hemery, F., Lecoutre, C., Sais, L.: Boosting Systematic Search by Weighting Constraints. In: Proceedings of the Sixteenth Eureopean Conference on Artificial Intelligence, ECAI 2004, pp. 146–150. IOS Press, Amsterdam (2004)
4. Elsayed, S.A.M., Michel, L.: Synthesis of search algorithms from high-level CP models. In: Cohen, D. (ed.) CP 2010. LNCS, vol. 6308, pp. 186–200. Springer, Heidelberg (2010)

5. Eriksson, M.: Detecting symmetries in relational models of CSPs. Master's thesis, Department of Information Technology,Uppsala University, Sweden (2005)
6. Gent, I.P., Jefferson, C., Miguel, I.: Minion: A fast, scalable, constraint solver. In: ECAI 2006: 17th European Conference on Artificial Intelligence, August 29-September 1, Riva del Garda, Italy, p. 98 (2006)
7. Gent, I.P., Walsh, T.: CSPLib: a benchmark library for constraints. In: Jaffar, J. (ed.) CP 1999. LNCS, vol. 1713, pp. 480–481. Springer, Heidelberg (1999)
8. Gibbs, J.P., Martin, W.T.: Urbanization, technology, and the division of labor: International patterns. American Sociological Review 27(5), 667–677 (1962)
9. Gomes, C.P., Selman, B., Crato, N., Kautz, H.: Heavy-tailed phenomena in satisfiability and constraint satisfaction problems. Journal of automated reasoning 24(1), 67–100 (2000)
10. Belgian Constraints Group. Data and results for the steel mill slab problem, http://becool.info.ucl.ac.be/steelmillslab, Technical report, UCLouvain
11. Haralick, R.M., Elliott, G.L.: Increasing tree search efficiency for constraint satisfaction problems. Artificial Intelligence 14(3), 263–313 (1980)
12. Harvey, W.D., Ginsberg, M.L.: Limited discrepancy search. In: International Joint Conference on Artificial Intelligence, vol. 14, pp. 607–615 (1995)
13. Van Hentenryck, P., Flener, P., Pearson, J., Ågren, M.: Tractable Symmetry Breaking for CSPs with Interchangeable Values. In: IJCAI, pp. 277–284 (2003)
14. SA ILOG. ILOG Concert 2.0
15. Michel, L., Van Hentenryck, P.: Impact-based versus Activity-based Search for Black-Box Contraint-Programming Solvers (2011), http://arxiv.org/abs/1105.6314
16. Monette, J.N., Deville, Y., Van Hentenryck, P.: Aeon: Synthesizing scheduling algorithms from high-level models. Operations Research and Cyber-Infrastructure, 43–59 (2009)
17. OMahony, E., Hebrard, E., Holland, A., Nugent, C., OSullivan, B.: Using case-based reasoning in an algorithm portfolio for constraint solving. In: 19th Irish Conference on AI (2008)
18. Refalo, P.: Impact-based search strategies for constraint programming. In: Wallace, M. (ed.) CP 2004. LNCS, vol. 3258, pp. 557–571. Springer, Heidelberg (2004)
19. Schaus, P., Hentenryck, P., Régin, J.-C.: Scalable load balancing in nurse to patient assignment problems. In: van Hoeve, W.-J., Hooker, J.N. (eds.) CPAIOR 2009. LNCS, vol. 5547, pp. 248–262. Springer, Heidelberg (2009)
20. Smith, B.M.: Succeed-first or fail-first: A case study in variable and value ordering. In: Malyshkin, V.E. (ed.) PaCT 1997. LNCS, vol. 1277, pp. 321–330. Springer, Heidelberg (1997)
21. Gecode Team. Gecode: Generic constraint development environment (2006), http://www.gecode.org
22. Van Hentenryck, P.: Constraint and integer programming in OPL. INFORMS Journal on Computing 14(4), 345–372 (2002)
23. Van Hentenryck, P., Flener, P., Pearson, J., Ågren, M.: Compositional derivation of symmetries for constraint satisfaction. Abstraction, Reformulation and Approximation, 234–247 (2005)
24. Van Hentenryck, P., Michel, L.: Constraint-based local search. The MIT Press, Cambridge (2005)
25. Van Hentenryck, P., Michel, L.: The steel mill slab design problem revisited. In: Trick, M.A. (ed.) CPAIOR 2008. LNCS, vol. 5015, pp. 377–381. Springer, Heidelberg (2008)
26. Van Hentenryck, P., Michel, L.: Synthesis of constraint-based local search algorithms from high-level models. In: AAAI 2007, pp. 273–278. AAAI Press, Menlo Park (2007)

Revisiting the tree Constraint

Jean-Guillaume Fages and Xavier Lorca

École des Mines de Nantes, INRIA, LINA UMR CNRS 6241,
FR-44307 Nantes Cedex 3, France
{Jean-guillaume.Fages,Xavier.Lorca}@mines-nantes.fr

Abstract. This paper revisits the tree constraint introduced in [2]
which partitions the nodes of a n-nodes, m-arcs directed graph into a
set of node-disjoint anti-arborescences for which only certain nodes can
be tree roots. We introduce a new filtering algorithm that enforces generalized arc-consistency in $O(n + m)$ time while the original filtering
algorithm reaches $O(nm)$ time. This result allows to tackle larger scale
problems involving graph partitioning.

1 Introduction

In the recent history of constraint programming, global constraints constitute a
powerful tool for both modeling and resolution. Today still, the most commonly
used global constraints are based on an intensive use of concepts stemming from
graph theory. Of these, the most important are cardinality constraints [12,13]
and automaton based constraints [8,9,7]. More generally, the reader should refer
to the catalogue of constraints [1] to gain a more complete idea of the graph
properties used in global constraints. In the same way, difficult problems modeled
and solved thanks to graph theory have been successfully tackled in constraint
programming and, more particularly, thanks to global constraints. This mainly
consists of constraints around graph and subgraph isomorphism [17,19], search
paths in graphs [11,10,16], even minimum cost spanning trees [14] and graph
partitioning constraints like the tree constraint [2] Such a constraint is mainly
involved in practical applications like vehicle routing, mission planning, DNA
sequencing, or phylogeny.

The tree constraint enforces the partitioning of a directed graph $G = (V, E)$
into a set of L node-disjoint anti-arborescences, where $|V| = n$, $|E| = m$ and L is
an integer variable. In [2], it is shown that Generalized Arc-Consistency (GAC)
can be enforced in $O(nm)$ time, while feasibility can be checked in $O(n + m)$
time. The bottleneck of the filtering algorithm relies on the computation of
strong articulation points which, at this moment, could not be performed in
linear time. However, based on the works of [15,3], Italiano et. al. [5] solved
this open problem by giving an $O(n + m)$ time algorithm for computing strong
articulation points of a directed graph G. Their main contribution is the link
they made between the concept of strong articulation point in a directed graph
and the concept of dominator in a directed flow graph. This recent improvement

J. Lee (Ed.): CP 2011, LNCS 6876, pp. 271–285, 2011.

in graph theory made us revisit the `tree` constraint to see whether the complete filtering algorithm could now be computed in linear time or not.

In this paper, Section 2 first recalls some basic notions of graph theory as well as the integration of graph theory in a classical constraint programming framework. Next, Section 3 proposes a short survey about the `tree` constraint. First, a decomposition of the constraint is discussed in Section 3.1. Next, Section 3.2 shows that dominator nodes were already used in a different way to enforce reachability between nodes. Finally, Section 3.3 proposes a brief sum up of the original `tree` constraint filtering algorithm. This leads us to discuss the relevance of the approach showing that strong articulation points is a much too strong notion for this problem whereas the notion of dominators in a flow graph perfectly fits our needs. Thus, Section 4 presents a new complete filtering algorithm, closer to the definition of a tree, that runs in $O(n + m)$ worst-case time complexity. Finally, Section 5 concludes the paper with a short evaluation of the algorithm to illustrate how large scale problems can be tackled thanks to this new filtering algorithm.

2   Graph Theory Definitions

A *graph* $G = (V, E)$ is the association of a set of nodes V and a set of edges $E \subseteq V^2$. $(x, y) \in E$ means that x and y are connected. A *directed graph* (*digraph*) is a graph where edges are directed from one node to another, it is generally noted $G = (V, A)$. $(x, y) \in A$ means that an arc goes from x to y but does not provide information about whether an arc from y to x exists or not.

A *connected component* (*CC*) of a digraph $G = (V, A)$ is a maximal subgraph $G_{CC} = (V_{CC}, A_{CC})$ of G such that a chain exists between each pair of nodes. A *strongly connected component* of a digraph $G = (V, A)$ is a maximal subgraph $G_{SCC} = (V_{SCC}, A_{SCC})$ of G such that a directed path exists between each pair of nodes. A graph is said (strongly) *connected* if it consists in one single (strongly) connected component.

A *strong articulation point* (*SAP*) of a digraph $G = (V, A)$ is a node $s \in V$ such that the number of strongly connected components of $G\backslash\{s\}$ is greater than the one of G. In other words $s \in V$ is a SAP of G if there exists two nodes x and y in V, $x \neq s$, $y \neq s$, such that each path from x to y goes through s and a path from y to x exists.

A *flow graph* $G(r)$ of a directed graph $G = (V, E)$ is a graph rooted in the node $r \in V$ which maintains the following property: for each node $v \in V$ a directed path from r to v exists. A *dominator* of a flow graph $G(r)$ where $G = (V, A)$ is a node $d \in V$, $d \neq r$ such that there exists at least one node $v \in V$, $v \neq d$, for which all paths from the root r to v go through d. We extend this notion to arcs as following: an *arc-dominator* of a flow graph $G(r)$ where $G = (V, A)$ is an arc $(x, y) \in A$, $x \neq y$, such that there exists at least one node $v \in V$, for which all paths from the root r to v go through (x, y). This definition can easily be simplified into: an arc $(x, y) \in A$ is an *arc-dominator* of $G(r)$ if and only if $x \neq y$ and all paths from the root r to y go through (x, y).

A *tree* $T = (V, E)$ is an acyclic, connected and undirected graph. One of its directed variants is the *anti-arborescence*, a directed graph $T = (V, A)$ such that every node $v \in V$ has exactly one successor $w \in V$ and with one root $r \in V$, such that $(r, r) \in A$ and for each node $v \in V$, a directed path from v to r exists. It can be seen that an anti-arborescence can be transformed into a tree easily. In the paper we study the case of an anti-arborescence but use for simplicity the term tree rather than anti-arborescence. Thus the following definitions will be used as references:

Definition 1. *A tree $T = (X, Y)$ is a connected digraph where every node $v \in X$ has exactly one successor $w \in X$ and with one root $r \in X$ such that $(r, r) \in Y$ and for each node $v \in X$, a directed path from v to r exists.*

Definition 2. *Given a digraph $G = (V, A)$, a tree partition of G is a subgraph $P = (V, A_2)$, $A_2 \subseteq A$, such that each connected component is a tree.*

Then, the two previous definitions directly provide the proposition:

Proposition 1. *Given a digraph $P = (V, A_2)$, subgraph of a digraph $G = (V, A)$, and a set $R = \{r | r \in V, (r, r) \in A_2\}$, then P is a tree partition of G if and only if each node in V has exactly one successor in P and for each node $v \in V$ there exists a node $r \in R$ such that a directed path from v to r exists in P.*

In a constraint programming context a *solution* to the **tree** constraint is a tree partition of an input graph $G = (V, A)$. A *Graph Variable* is used to model the partitioning of G. It is composed of two graphs: the *envelope*, $G_E = (V, A_E)$, contains all arcs that potentially occur in at least one solution (Figure 1(a)) whereas the *kernel*, $G_K = (V, A_K)$, contains all arcs that occur in every solution (Figure 1(b)). It has to be noticed that $A_K \subseteq A_E \subseteq A$. During the resolution, filtering rules will remove arcs from A_E and decisions that add arcs to A_K will be applied until the Graph Variable is instantiated, i.e. when $A_E = A_K$ (Figure 1(c)). The problem has no solution when $|A_E| < |V|$.

Definition 3. *An instantiated Graph Variable is a tree partition of a digraph G, if and only if its kernel G_K is a tree partition of G. A partially instantiated Graph Variable can lead to a tree partition of a digraph G, if and only if there exists at least one tree partition of its envelope G_E.*

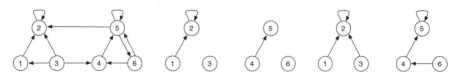

(a) Envelope $G_E = (V, A_E)$ (b) Kernel $G_K = (V, A_K)$ (c) A solution ($A_E = A_K$)

Fig. 1. A graph variable associated with a directed graph $G = (V, A)$

In the following, a node $r \in V$ is a *root* if and only if $(r, r) \in A_K$. It is called a *potential root* if $(r, r) \in A_E$.[1]

3   The `tree` Constraint: A Survey

This section introduces first a decomposed constraint programming model for the `tree` constraint. Such a model does not ensure any consistency level for the constraint. Next, we show how the `DomReachability` constraint can be used as a propagator for the `tree` constraint. Finally, we recall the initial GAC filtering algorithm of the constraint.

3.1   A Basic Decomposition

Our objective in this section is to convince the reader of the importance in proposing a global constraint for directed tree partitioning. In order to do so, we will introduce a broken down model for this problem. It is necessary to define an integer variable L characterizing the number of trees admitted in the partition. Next, taking $G = (V, E)$ a graph of order n, we link to each node i an integer variable v_i of enumerated domain $[1; n]$ defining the successor of i in G, an integer variable r_i of bounded domain $[0; n-1]$ defining the height of i in a solution and a boolean variable b_i characterizing the root property for node i. Note that the set of decision variables (to be used for branching) is v and that r is introduced to prevent from the creation of circuits. As such, the problem can be defined in the following way:

$$v_i = j \wedge i \neq j \Rightarrow r_i > r_j, \ \forall i \in [1; n] \tag{1}$$

$$b_i \Leftrightarrow v_i = i, \ \forall i \in [1; n] \tag{2}$$

$$L = \sum_{i=1}^{n} b_i \tag{3}$$

The correctness of the model is proved when we consider the following cases: (1) the model does not accept a solution containing more than L well-formed trees, (2) the model does not admit a solution containing fewer than L well-formed trees, (3) the model does not accept a solution containing a circuit and (4) the model does not accept a solution containing a single node without a loop. Given $G = (V, E)$, a directed graph of order n and F a partition of G into α well-formed trees:

- case (1), let us suppose that $\alpha > L$ so that if $\alpha > \sum_{i=1}^{n} b_i$ this means that there are more well-formed trees in F than nodes which are potential roots, which is impossible according to constraint (2);
- case (2), let us suppose that $\alpha < L$ so that if $\alpha < \sum_{i=1}^{n} b_i$ this means that F contains more loops than trees so that some contain more than one loop. However, since each node has exactly one successor, it is a contradiction;

---

[1] Notice that in this definition, a root is also a potential root.

- case (3), if there is $f \in F$ such that f contains a cycle, then, there are two nodes i and j in f such that we have an elementary path from i to j and an elementary path from j to i and, consequently, according to the constraint(1) we have $r_i < r_j$ and $r_j < r_i$: it is a contradiction;
- case (4) is obvious because each variable must be fixed to a value, which is equivalent to saying that each node must have exactly one successor.

3.2 The `DomReachability` Constraint

Luis Quesada et. al. introduced the `DomReachability` constraint [11,10,16] for solving path partitioning problems. It uses a similar graph variable description [4] .Their constraint maintains structural relationships between a flow graph, its dominator tree and its transitive closure. In particular, it can ensure that all nodes are reachable from a given source node, which is very close to the concept of a tree. Plus, and as it will be shown in the next subsection, dominance relationships are very useful information in that context. Thus one could think that it could be a good propagator for solving tree partitioning problems. We will show that the use of such a constraint is not appropriate.

`DomReachability` runs in $O(nm)$ worst case time complexity. This cost is due to the algorithm used for maintaining the transitive closure, which is not necessary for tree partitioning. The first algorithm [11] consisted in performing one DFS per node whereas the current algorithm [16] works on a reduced graph.

`DomReachability` does not enable to build a tree partition directly. As it needs a single source node it can only compute a single tree. To get a tree partition of cardinality k, then a trick would consist in adding a fictive source node s to the input graph and declare that each of its successors is a root node of a tree and add a propagator which would ensure that the outdegree of s is k. In the same way, even if one single tree is expected, when the root node is not known in advance then it is necessary to use the previous trick with $k = 1$.

`DomReachability` does not ensure GAC over tree partitioning. This is pretty obvious because the reachability property does not exclude cycles whereas tree properties do. Nevertheless they use `DomReachability` for path partitioning through the global constraint Simple Path with Mandatory Nodes (SPMN) [11,10,16]. As tree partitioning is a polynomial relaxation of path partitioning, a complete filtering over tree partitioning could be expected. However, to the best of our knowledge, SPMN does not reap the benefit of dominators by missing the following major pruning rule: if i dominates j then the arc (j, i) does not belong to any solution which, regarding their notation, can be expressed as:

$$\frac{\langle i, j \rangle \in Edges(Min(EDG))}{Edges(Max(FG)) := Edges(Max(FG)) \setminus \{\langle j, i \rangle\}} \tag{4}$$

For a better understanding of this rule, it has to be considered that they work on arborescences instead of anti-arborescences.

3.3   The Original `tree` Constraint

This part is a fast sum up of the tree constraint described in [2]. The constraint is composed of two main algorithms. The first one enables to check whether a partially instantiated *Graph Variable* can lead to at least one solution or not. This algorithm can be run in $O(n + m)$ worst case time complexity. The second algorithm enables to prune every arc that does not belong to any solution in $O(nm)$ worst case time complexity. It is the focus of this paper.

Feasibility Condition. The original paper defines an integer variable $L = [\underline{\ell}; \overline{\ell}]$ that represents the cardinality of the tree partition and two bounds: $\underline{\ell}^*$, the number of sink components[2], and $\overline{\ell}^*$, the number of potential roots. Those two bounds can easily be evaluated in linear time: all the strongly connected components of G_E can be computed in $O(n + m)$ using Tarjan's algorithm [18]. Thus, the sink components can be detected in $O(m)$ time, which provides $\underline{\ell}^*$. Moreover a simple breadth first search exploration of G_E enables to compute $\overline{\ell}^*$.

The feasibility condition can be decomposed into two parts. The first one is directly related to the number of trees allowed into the partition, while the second one is related to the definitions of directed tree: $dom(L) \cap [\underline{\ell}^*; \overline{\ell}^*] \neq \emptyset$, and all sink components of G_E must contain at least one potential root. The original paper provides the proof of sufficiency of those conditions which can obviously be checked in linear time.

Complete Filtering Algorithm. The complete filtering algorithm can be split into two propagators: bound filtering and structural filtering. The bound filtering focuses on the cardinality of the expected partition whereas the structural filtering ensures the generalized arc-consistency over tree partitioning properties. Both algorithms are complementary and form together a complete filtering algorithm for tree constraint.

The bound filtering is pretty simple. First of all, it consists in ensuring that $dom(L) \cap [\underline{\ell}^*; \overline{\ell}^*] \neq \emptyset$ by removing the values of L that are out of range. Secondly, it consists in pruning infeasible arcs when L is instantiated to one of its extrema: If $dom(L) = \{\underline{\ell}^*\}$ then any potential root in a non sink component is infeasible and thus removed from the envelope; If $dom(L) = \{\overline{\ell}^*\}$ then any potential root must be instantiated as a root thus all their outgoing arc that are not a loop are removed from the envelope.

The structural filtering detects all arcs that belong to no tree partition. For this purpose, several notations are required: A *door* is a vertex $v \in V$ such that there exists $(v, w) \in A_E$ where w does not belong to the same strongly connected component as v. A *winner* is a vertex $v \in V$ which is a potential root or a door. Let's consider S, a strongly connected component of G_E, and p a strong articulation point in S; Δ^p is the set of the new strongly connected components obtained by the removal of p from S: $\Delta^p = \{S_i | S_i \text{ strongly connected component of } S \setminus \{p\}\}$. Δ_{in}^p is the subset of Δ^p such that all paths from each of its strongly

---

[2] The number of strongly connected components with no outgoing arcs.

connected component to any winner of S go through p. Δ^p_{out} is the subset of Δ^p such that a path exists from each of its strongly connected component to a winner of S without going through p. Remark, $\Delta^p_{in} \oplus \Delta^p_{out} = \Delta^p$. Pruning is then performed according to three following rules:

1. If a sink component of G_E contains one single potential root r, then all the outgoing arc of r except the loop (r, r) are infeasible.
2. If a strongly connected component $C \subseteq G_E$ contains no potential root but one single door d, then all arcs $(d, v), v \in C$ are infeasible.
3. An outgoing arc (p, v) of a strong articulation point p of G_E that reaches a vertex v of a strongly connected component of Δ^p_{in} is infeasible.

Rules 1 and 2 are obvious. Rule 3 basically means that enforcing such an arc would lead to some strongly connected components with no winners, thus sinks with no potential roots which is a contradiction.

About time complexity, pruning among rules 1 and 2 can easily be performed in linear time but when the paper was published, computing efficiently the strong articulation points of a digraph remained an open problem and the worst case time of the pruning procedure was thus $O(nm)$. In response to that claim, Italiano et. al. [5] recently showed an $O(m+n)$ worst case time complexity algorithm for computing strong articulation points of a digraph. This work enabled to fasten the pruning in practice. However, the theoretic time complexity remains $O(nm)$: rule 3 needs to withdraw strong articulation points one by one and compute new strongly connected components each time. The strongly connected components can be computed in $O(n + m)$ time using Tarjan's algorithm but there can be up to n strong articulation points, thus the total processing has a $O(n^2 + nm) = O(nm)$ worst case time complexity.

We will now show that the concept of strong articulation point is not well appropriate and propose a new formulation of the pruning conditions based on dominance relationship.

4   Linear Time Algorithm for the **tree** Constraint

The contribution of this paper relies on a new formulation of the filtering rule related to the strong articulation points. The first point to notice is that, given a strong articulation point p of a strongly connected component $SCC_i \subseteq G_E$, Δ^p_{in} may be empty (Figure 2(a)), thus the initial algorithm may perform several expensive and useless computations. The second important point is that the initial filtering algorithm does not require the concepts of doors, winners, strong articulation points and strongly connected components. Actually, their use, which implies paths in two directions, is not natural in our context because only a one way path from each node to a root is required. For instance, given three nodes u, v and w in V such that w is the unique potential root reachable from u. If every path from u to w requires v, then any path from v to u has to be forbidden (Figure 2(b)).

The filtering rule proposed by the initial algorithm can be reformulated by: Any arc $(x, y) \in SCC_i \subseteq G_E, x \neq y$ is infeasible if and only if all paths from y to

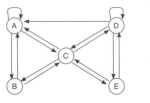 

(a) A strong articulation point C such that $\Delta_{in}^C = \emptyset$ (b) Main pruning rule

Fig. 2. Structural pruning observations

any winner of SCC_i go through x. However, as a winner in a strongly connected component is either a potential root, or a door that can thus lead to a potential root (each sink has at least one potential root), it can be rephrased: Any arc $(x, y) \in SCC_i \subseteq G_E, x \neq y$ is infeasible if and only if all paths from y to any potential root of G_E go through x. Moreover, assume (x, y) is an arc of the digraph G_E and there exists a path from y to x then x and y belong to the same strongly connected component, so the condition can be simplified in the following way: Any arc $(x, y) \in G_E, x \neq y$ is infeasible if and only if all paths from y to any potential root of G_E go through x. This condition is much closer to definition 1, it can be noted that it is also quite similar with the dominance definition: Let R be the set of potential roots, i.e. $R = \{v | v \in V, (v, v) \in A_E\}$. Let us consider the graph $G_{ES} = (V \cup s, A_E \cup S)$ where $s \notin V$ and $S = \bigcup_{r \in R}((r, s) \cup (s, r))$. Let the digraph G_{ES}^{-1} be the inverse graph of G_{ES} (obtained by reversing the orientation of arcs of G_{ES}). The previous definition can be transposed into: $(x, y) \in G_E, x \neq y$, is infeasible if and only if x is a dominator of y in the flow graph $G_{ES}^{-1}(s)$. The main interest is that algorithms do exist to find dominators of a flow graph in linear time [15,3].

4.1 Feasibility and Filtering Conditions

We now consider a partially instantiated graph variable $GV = (G_E, G_K)$ that represents a subgraph of an input directed graph $G = (V, A)$. We have $G_E = (V, A_E)$, $G_K = (V, A_K)$ and $A_K \subseteq A_E \subseteq A$ (Section 2).

Proposition 2. *Given a partially instantiated graph variable GV of a digraph G, there exists a tree partition of G if and only if for each node $v \in V$ the two following conditions hold:*

1. $|\{(v, w)|(v, w) \in A_E\}| \geq 1$ and $|\{(v, w)|(v, w) \in A_K\}| \leq 1$ and
2. there exists a potential root $r \in V$ such that a directed path from v to r exists in G_E.

Proof. If there exists a node $v \in V$ such that $|\{(v, w) \mid (v, w) \in A_K\}| > 1$ then v has more than one successor in all solutions, if $|\{(v, w) \mid (v, w) \in A_E\}| < 1$

then v has no successors in A_E and thus in all solutions because $A_K \subseteq A_E$. Both cases are in contradiction with Proposition 1 thus cannot lead to any tree partitioning. If there exists a node $v \in V$ such that v can reach no potential root with a directed path in G_E then, as $A_K \subseteq A_E$, v cannot reach any root in any solution which is in contradiction with Proposition 1 and thus cannot lead to any tree partitioning.

Let us now suppose that conditions 1 and 2 are respected. Let us instantiate all potential roots $r \in V$, i.e. add all arcs $(r,r) \in A_E$ to A_K and delete all other outgoing arcs of r from A_E. At this step condition 2 still holds so for each node $v \in V$ there exists a potential root $r \subset V$ such that a path from v to r exists in G_E. Let's add that path in G_K (by adding its arcs to A_K). The result of this procedure is an instantiated *Graph Variable* that is a tree partition of G.   □

Remark 1. Condition 1 did not appear in previous models because they used integer variables which immediately ensured that property.

Proposition 3. *Given a partially instantiated graph variable GV of a digraph G, if there exists a tree partition of G then, an arc $(x,y) \in A_E$, $x \neq y$, does not belong to any solution if and only if one of the following conditions holds:*

1. *there exists a node $w \in V, w \neq y$, such that $(x,w) \in A_K$,*
2. *all directed paths in G_E from y to any potential root $r \in V$ go through x.*

Proof. Let x and w be two nodes in V such that $(x,w) \in A_K$ then w is a successor of x in every solution. Definition 1 implies that w is the unique successor of x, thus any arc $(x,y) \in A_E$ such that $y \neq w$ belongs to no solution. Let x and y be two distinct nodes of V such that all directed paths in G_E from y to any potential root $r \in V$ go through x and that $(x,y) \subset A_E$. Then Proposition 1 implies that there will be a directed path from y to x in every solution. Using arc $(x,y) \in A_E$ would thus create a cycle which is in contradiction with definition 1 so (x,y) belong to no solution.

Let now suppose that there exists an arc $(x,y) \in A_E$ which belongs to no solution and such that conditions 1 and 2 are both false. Condition 1 is false if and only if $(x,y) \in A_K$ or no outgoing arc of x belongs to A_K. If $(x,y) \in A_K$ then all solutions contains arc (x,y) which is a contradiction so it can be supposed that no outgoing arc of x belongs to A_K. As condition 2 is false then at least one directed path exists in G_E from y to any potential root without going through x. If (x,y) is added to A_K then the two conditions of Proposition 2 hold, thus the graph variable GV still lead to at least one solution which is a contradiction.   □

Proposition 4. *Given a partially instantiated graph variable GV of a digraph G, if each infeasible arc has been removed from GV, then an arc $(x,y) \in A_E$, $x \neq y$, belongs to all solutions if and only if all paths in G_E from x to any potential root go through the arc (x,y).*

Proof. Given an arc $(x,y) \in A_E$, if all paths from x to any potential root go through (x,y), as a path should exist from x to a potential root in each solution, (x,y) belongs to all solutions. Given an arc $(x,y) \in A_K$, then x has only one single successor y in G_E, otherwise all infeasible arcs have not been pruned (because each node should have exactly one successor). Thus all outgoing paths of x go through (x, y) and as the problem is feasible at least one path from x to any potential root exists.   □

4.2   Filtering Algorithm

Keeping the previous notations about the graph variable GV, we assume that any graph is represented by two arrays of lists: successors and predecessors of nodes. The list of index i in the successors array represents the successors of the node $i \in V$. In order to make the complexity study easier, we introduce several basic notations: $n = |V|$, $m = |A|$, $m_E = |A_E|$ with $m_E \leq m$ (Section 2).

Proposition 5. *An $O(m + n)$ worst case time complexity algorithm exists to check whether GV can lead or not to a tree partition of G.*

Proof. Considering the list representation of the graph, condition 1 of Proposition 2 can be checked in $O(n)$ by computing the size of the list of successors of each node, once in G_E and once in G_K.

Let R be the set of potential roots, i.e. $R = \{v | v \in V, (v, v) \in A_E\}$. Let's consider the graph $G_{ES} = (V \cup s, A_E \cup S)$ where $s \notin V$, $A_E \cap S = \emptyset$ and $S = \bigcup_{r \in R}((r, s) \cup (s, r))$. Let the digraph G_{ES}^{-1} be the graph inverse of G_{ES} (obtained by reversing the orientation of arcs of G_{ES}). A simple Depth-First Search (DFS) exploration of G_{ES}^{-1} from node s will check whether each node $v \in V$ is reachable or not from s using directed paths in G_{ES}^{-1}. So it checks whether each node $v \in V$ can reach or not a potential root using a directed path in G_E. Thus it checks condition 2 of Proposition 2. The time complexity of a DFS of a graph of m_E arcs is $O(m_E)$. The total worst case time complexity of this algorithm is so $O(n + m_E)$. As $A_E \subseteq A$, $m_E \leq m$. Thus this algorithm runs in $O(n + m)$ worst case time complexity.   □

Proposition 6. *If the graph variable GV, associated with the digraph G to partition, can lead to a tree partition of G, an $O(m + n)$ worst case time complexity algorithm exists to detect and remove all the arcs $(x, y) \in A_E$ that do not belong to any tree partition of G.*

Proof. In this context pruning an arc (x, y) consists in removing it from A_E. We will now describe such an algorithm, which relies upon two main steps that respectively correspond to conditions 1 and 2 of Proposition 3.

Condition 1: for each node $v \in V$, either v has one successor in G_K or v has no successor in G_K. If v has one successor w in G_K then the list of successors of v in G_E is cleared and (v, w) is put back into G_E. This is done in constant time so the whole complexity of step 1 is $O(n)$.

Condition 2: let us consider the graph G_{ES}^{-1} previously described. Then condition 2 of Proposition 3 to ensure that the arc $(x, y) \in G_E$ belongs to no solution is equivalent to "x dominates y in the flow graph $G_{ES}^{-1}(s)$". Several algorithms enable to find immediate dominators in a flow graph [15,3] in $O(n + m_E)$ worst case time complexity. Let's compute I the dominance tree of the flow graph $G_{ES}^{-1}(s)$ with one of those algorithms.

Then a node $p \in V$ dominates $v \in V$ in G_{ES}^{-1} if and only if p is an ancestor of v in I. Such a query can be answered in constant time thanks to a $O(n)$ space and $O(n+m)$ time preprocessing. Let's create two n-size arrays $opening$ and $closure$, perform a depth first search of I from s and record pre-order and post-order numbers of each node in respectively $opening$ and $closure$. Then, p is an ancestor of v if and only if: $opening[p] < opening[v]$ and $closure[p] > closure[v]$. There are at most m_E requests (one for each arc) so the whole worst case time complexity of step two is $O(n+m)$. □

Proposition 7. *If the graph variable GV, associated with the digraph G to partition, can lead to a tree partition of G and if all its infeasible arcs have been pruned, an $O(m+n)$ worst case time complexity algorithm exists to add all the arcs $(x,y) \in A_E, x \neq y$, that belong to all tree partitions of G, into A_K.*

Proof. In this context enforcing an arc (x,y) consists in adding it to A_K. Let's consider the previously introduced flow graph $G_{ES}^{-1}(s)$. It should be noticed that the condition for enforcing an arc $(x,y) \in A_E$ of Proposition 4 is equivalent to: $(x,y) \in A_E$ belong to all solutions if and only if (y,x) is an arc-dominator in $G_{ES}^{-1}(s)$. Thus computing arc-dominators of $G_{ES}^{-1}(s)$ is all we have got left.

In [5] and [10], it is suggested to insert a fictive node inside each arc of the input graph and then compute dominators (in linear time). If a dominator is a fictive node, then the corresponding arc is an arc-dominator. Thus, the total processing time remains in $O(n+m)$ worst case time complexity. However, (y,x) is an arc-dominator of a flow graph $G(s)$ if and only if y is the immediate dominator of x in $G(s)$ and for each predecessor p of x such that $p \neq y$, x dominates p in $G(s)$. Thus we present an alternative method which we claim to be faster in practice and less space-consuming.

We assume that the pruning algorithm has been performed. Thus the dominance tree I, of G_{ES}^{-1}, is already computed and the preprocessing for ancestor relationships in I introduced in Proposition 6 has been done. A Depth First Search (DFS) exploration of G_{ES}^{-1} is then performed from the node s. For each encountered arc (y,x), such that $(x,y) \in I$ and $(x,y) \notin A_K$, for each predecessor p of x, a request to know whether x is an ancestor of p in I is computed. If one of those queries return false then (y,x) is not an arc-dominator of $G_{ES}^{-1}(s)$. Otherwise (x,y) can be enforced i.e. added into A_K. This algorithm computes $O(m)$ constant time queries. It is thus in $O(n+m)$ worst case time complexity. □

Remark 2. In our problem, each node has exactly one successor and all infeasible arcs are detected. Thus it is not useful to compute arcs that belong to all solutions explicitly: they will be deduced from the filtering algorithm. However in the general case, unlike integer variables, graph variables enable a node to have 0 or many outgoing arcs. Then the identification of arcs that belong to all solutions cannot be immediately deduced from pruning and thus provides important additional information.

Proposition 8. *Given the input graph G and an integer variable L, a partition of G into L trees, if one exists, can be found within $O(nm)$ worst case time complexity.*

Proof. Each of the n nodes must have exactly one successor. Then $n \leq m$. If the decision used in the propagation engine is "*enforce an arc $a \in A_E$, $a \notin A_K$*" then, as the pruning is complete the number of nodes in the tree search is $O(n)$. Plus it has just been shown that each propagation runs in $O(n+m)$ worst case time complexity. Thus the total solving time is $O(n(n+m)) = O(nm)$ worst case time complexity.   □

4.3   Implementation Details

The new `tree` constraint consists in the conjunction of 3 propagators: `OneSucc` enforces that each node must have exactly one successor; `Ntrees` controls the cardinality of the partition as described in [2]; `TreeProps` ensures a complete filtering over tree partitioning properties, which is the focus of the paper.

Algorithm 1. `TreeProps` propagator of the `tree` constraint

Require: two digraphs $G_E = (V_E, A_E)$, G_E^{-1} s.t. $s \notin V_E$ is its unique source
Ensure: each arc of G_E that does not belong to any solution has been removed
1: $T_E \leftarrow$ `dominatorTree`(G_E^{-1}, s); {dominance tree of G_E^{-1}}
2: int[] opening, closure $\leftarrow$ `ancestorPreProcess`(T_E, s); {pre/post-order of T_E}
3: **for all** node $v \in V_E$ **do**
4:      **for all** node $w \in A_E$.`getSucc`(v) s.t. $w \neq v$ **do**
5:          **if** opening$[v] <$ opening$[w] \wedge$ closure$[v] >$ closure$[w]$ **then**
6:              $A_E \leftarrow A_E \setminus \{(v, w)\}$;
7:          **end if**
8:      **end for**
9: **end for**

The structural filtering of `TreeProps` is based on the `dominatorTree`(G, s) algorithm which computes the immediate dominators of the flow graph $G(s)$ and return its dominance tree. It can be run in $O(n+m)$ worst case time [15,3]. However, for practical reasons, the current implementation uses the Lengauer-Tarjan algorithm [6] which runs in $O(m\alpha(n, m))$ worst case time complexity, where $\alpha(n, m)$ is the inverse of the Ackermann function and thus grows very slowly. The function `ancestorPreProcess`(T, s) returns the pre-order and the post-order (starting from node s) labels of the nodes involved in the tree T. This can be done in $O(n)$ time if T involves n nodes.

5   Experimental Study

This section enables to compare several previously exposed models: the decomposition model of Section 3.1, the original `tree` constraint of Section 3.3 and the new linear time algorithm introduced by Section 4. Each algorithm consists in providing a tree partition of a randomly generated input graph. For practical interest, two cases of the new tree constraint have been tested. Both uses exactly the same constraint implementation but one uses graph variables with a matrix representation whereas the second one uses adjacency lists. Technically, the matrix representation uses `bitset` arrays instead of `boolean` matrix. For homogeneity reasons, all those experiments use the same branching strategy which consists in enforcing a randomly selected arc. All algorithms are implemented within the Choco open source Java Library. The source code is not included in the current distribution but is available on demand. The experiment has been performed on a Mac mini 4.1, with a 2.4 Ghz Intel core 2 duo processor and 3 Go of memory allocated to the Java Virtual Machine.

As the study focuses on structural filtering, the cardinality of the expected partition has not been restricted and input graphs were generated connected. We note d the density of the input graph and $\overline{d^+}$ the average outdegree of its nodes. We have $d = \frac{m}{n^2} = \frac{\overline{d^+}}{n}$. For each parameters combination $(n, \overline{d^+})$ thirty graphs have been randomly generated and partitioned into trees. Then, for each method, the number of solved instances and their mean solving time have been recorded. The time limit has been set to one minute. This enables to get information about the stability of those algorithms and about the relevance of our measures.

Table 1 highlights that all approaches with a complete pruning are stable whereas the decomposition is unreliable. The computation time (column *time*) is provided in seconds, while the *solved* column denotes the percentage of solved instances. The decomposition is the worst choice for sparse graphs whereas it is better than the original **tree** constraint for dense graphs. This is due to the fact that the decomposition pruning is faster and that the denser the input graph, the higher the chance of any given arc to belong to at least one solution.

Figure 3 shows that the new **tree** constraint clearly outperforms the previous version by an important scaling factor. It can solve problems with up to 750 vertices when the graph is complete and up to 4500 vertices when the graph is sparse. Those results confirm the complexity of $O(nm)$ in theory (Proposition 8)

Table 1. Stability and performance study

Instances		Decomp.		Original		Matrix		List	
n	d+	time	solved	time	solved	time	solved	time	solved
	5	1.1	80	0.5	100	0	100	0	100
50	20	0.1	100	1.3	100	0	100	0	100
	50	0.1	100	1.2	100	0	100	0	100
	5	2.6	60	4.5	100	0	100	0	100
150	20	3.1	80	11.3	100	0	100	0	100
	50	0.6	87	25.3	100	0.1	100	0.2	100
	150	2.8	100	-	0	0.3	100	1.4	100
	5	0.1	20	51.6	100	0.1	100	0	100
300	20	0.4	47	-	0	0.2	100	0.3	100
	50	1.7	53	-	0	0.5	100	1	100
	300	17.7	77	-	0	2.4	100	30	100

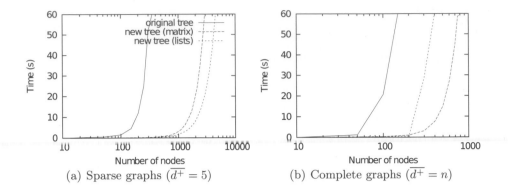

(a) Sparse graphs $(\overline{d^+} = 5)$ (b) Complete graphs $(\overline{d^+} = n)$

Fig. 3. Scalability and data structure

and $O(nm\alpha(n, m))$ in practice (Section 4.3). Moreover they highlight the impact of the chosen data structure according to the input graph density. We observed a critical density $d_c = \frac{35}{n}$: when $d < d_c$ a list representation should be preferred whereas a matrix representation should be more relevant for denser graphs.

The last experiments we provide concerns scalability. For this purpose, the time limit is increased from one minute to two minutes and we observe the size of the graphs which can be treated within this time. In the case of sparse digraphs, a list representation in our algorithm improves the size of the largest treated digraph by 31% (up to 5900 nodes), while the original approach only allows to handle digraphs about 17% bigger (about 350 nodes). In the case of complete digraphs, a matrix representation in our algorithm improves the results by 20% (up to 900 nodes), while the original approach reaches 28% (about 160 nodes).

6   Conclusion

In this paper we have presented a non incremental linear time filtering algorithm that ensures generalized arc consistency for the `tree` constraint. Its correctness and worst case time complexity have been demonstrated and enforced by an experimental study. Even with an implementation in $O(m\alpha(n, m))$ of the filtering phase (due to the Lengauer-Tarjan algorithm) the constraint gains a mean scale factor of approximately ten. Moreover, two different types of data structures have been tested: matrix and adjacency lists. We experimentally showed that the lists representation clearly outperforms the matrix representation for sparse graphs and that this trend reverses when the input graph density grows enough. All those results are encouraging for further works as path partitioning. Also, we might work on incremental algorithms, however the dominance property seems too global to let us hope in significant improvements.

References

1. Beldiceanu, N., Carlsson, M., Demassey, S., Petit, T.: Global Constraint Catalog: Past, Present and Future. Constraints 12(1), 21–62 (2007)
2. Beldiceanu, N., Flener, P., Lorca, X.: The tree constraint. In: Barták, R., Milano, M. (eds.) CPAIOR 2005. LNCS, vol. 3524, pp. 64–78. Springer, Heidelberg (2005)
3. Buchsbaum, A.L., Kaplan, H., Rogers, A., Westbrook, J.R.: A new, simpler linear-time dominators algorithm. ACM Transactions on Programming Languages and Systems 20, 1265–1296 (1998)
4. Dooms, G., Deville, Y., Dupont, P.: CP(graph): Introducing a graph computation domain in constraint programming. In: van Beek, P. (ed.) CP 2005. LNCS, vol. 3709, pp. 211–225. Springer, Heidelberg (2005)
5. Italiano, G.F., Laura, L., Santaroni, F.: Finding Strong Bridges and Strong Articulation Points in Linear Time. In: Wu, W., Daescu, O. (eds.) COCOA 2010, Part I. LNCS, vol. 6508, pp. 157–169. Springer, Heidelberg (2010)
6. Lengauer, T., Tarjan, R.E.: A fast algorithm for finding dominators in a flowgraph. TOPLAS 1(1) (1979)
7. Menana, J., Demassey, S.: Sequencing and counting with the `multicost-regular` constraint. In: van Hoeve, W.-J., Hooker, J.N. (eds.) CPAIOR 2009. LNCS, vol. 5547, pp. 178–192. Springer, Heidelberg (2009)
8. Pesant, G.: A regular language membership constraint for finite sequences of variables. In: Wallace, M. (ed.) CP 2004. LNCS, vol. 3258, pp. 482–495. Springer, Heidelberg (2004)
9. Pesant, G.: A regular language membership constraint for finite sequences of variables. In: Wallace, M. (ed.) CP 2004. LNCS, vol. 3258, pp. 482–495. Springer, Heidelberg (2004)
10. Quesada, L.: Solving constrained graph problems using reachability constraints based on transitive closure and dominators. PhD thesis, Université Catholique de Louvain (2006)
11. Quesada, L., van Roy, P., Deville, Y., Collet, R.: Using dominators for solving constrained path problems. In: Van Hentenryck, P. (ed.) PADL 2006. LNCS, vol. 3819, pp. 73–87. Springer, Heidelberg (2005)
12. Régin, J.-C.: A filtering algorithm for constraints of difference in CSP. In: AAAI 1994, pp. 362–367 (1994)
13. Régin, J.-C.: Generalized arc consistency for global cardinality constraint. In: AAAI 1996, pp. 209–215 (1996)
14. Régin, J.-C.: Simpler and incremental consistency checking and arc consistency filtering algorithm for the weighted tree constraint. In: Trick, M.A. (ed.) CPAIOR 2008. LNCS, vol. 5015, pp. 233–247. Springer, Heidelberg (2008)
15. Lauridsen, P.W., Alstrup, S., Harel, D., Thorup, M.: Dominators in linear time. SIAM J. Comput. 28(6), 2117–2132 (1999)
16. Sellmann, M.: Cost-based filtering for shortest path constraints. In: Rossi, F. (ed.) CP 2003. LNCS, vol. 2833, pp. 694–708. Springer, Heidelberg (2003)
17. Sorlin, S., Solnon, C.: A global constraint for graph isomorphism problems. In: Régin, J.-C., Rueher, M. (eds.) CPAIOR 2004. LNCS, vol. 3011, pp. 287–301. Springer, Heidelberg (2004)
18. Tarjan, R.E.: Depth-first search and linear graph algorithms. SIAM J. Comput. 1, 146–160 (1972)
19. Zampelli, S., Devilles, Y., Solnon, C., Sorlin, S., Dupont, P.: Filtering for subgraph isomorphism. In: Bessière, C. (ed.) CP 2007. LNCS, vol. 4741, pp. 728–742. Springer, Heidelberg (2007)

Half Reification and Flattening

Thibaut Feydy, Zoltan Somogyi, and Peter J. Stuckey

National ICT Australia and the University of Melbourne, Victoria, Australia
{tfeydy,zs,pjs}@csse.unimelb.edu.au

Abstract. Usually propagation-based constraint solvers construct a constraint network as a conjunction of constraints. They provide propagators for each form of constraint c. In order to increase expressiveness, systems also usually provide propagators for reified forms of constraints. A reified constraint $b \leftrightarrow c$ associates a truth value b with a constraint c. With reified propagators, systems can express complex combinations of constraints using disjunction, implication and negation by flattening. In this paper we argue that reified constraints should be replaced by half-reified constraints of the form $b \rightarrow c$. Half-reified constraints do not impose any extra burden on the implementers of propagators compared to unreified constraints, they can implement reified propagators without loss of propagation strength (assuming c is negatable), they extend automatically to global constraints, they simplify the handling of partial functions, and can allow flattening to give better propagation behavior.

1 Introduction

Constraint programming propagation solvers solve constraint satisfaction problems of the form $\exists V. \wedge_{c \in C} c$, that is an existentially quantified conjunction of primitive constraints c. But constraint programming modeling languages such as OPL [16], Zinc/MiniZinc [9,10] and Essence [6] allow much more expressive problems to be formulated. Modeling languages map the more expressive formulations to existentially quantified conjunction through a combination of loop unrolling, and flattening using reification.

Example 1. Consider the following "complex constraint" written in Zinc syntax

```
constraint i <= 4 -> a[i] * x >= 6;
```

which requires that if $i \leq 4$ then the value in the ith position of array a multiplied by x must be at least 6. This becomes the following existentially quantified conjunction through flattening and reification:

```
constraint b1 <-> i <= 4;    % b1 holds iff i <= 4
constraint element(i,a,t1);  % t1 is the ith element of a
constraint mult(t1,x,t2);    % t2 is t1 * x
constraint b2 <-> t2 >= 6;   % b2 holds iff t2 >= 6
constraint b1 -> b2          % b1 implies b2
```

J. Lee (Ed.): CP 2011, LNCS 6876, pp. 286–301, 2011.

The complex logic (implication) is encoded by "reifying" the arguments and in effect naming their truth value using new Boolean variables $b1$ and $b2$. The term structure is encoded by "flattening" the terms and converting the functions to relations, introducing the new integer variables $t1$ and $t2$. Note that the newly introduced variables are existentially quantified.   □

The translation given in the above example is well understood, but potentially flawed, for three reasons. The first is that the flattening may not give the intuitive meaning when functions are partial.

Example 2. Suppose the array a has index set 1..5, but i takes the value 7. The constraint `element`$(i, a, t1)$ will fail and no solution will be found. Intuitively if $i = 7$ the constraint should be trivially true.   □

The simple flattening used above treats partial functions in the following manner. Application of a partial function to a value for which it is not defined gives value $\perp$, and this $\perp$ function percolates up through every expression to the top level conjunction, making the model unsatisfiable. For the example $(t1 \equiv)$ $a[7] = \perp$, $(t2 \equiv)$ $\perp \times x = \perp$, $(b2 \equiv)$ $\perp \geq 6 = \perp$, $(b1 \equiv)$ $7 \leq 4 = false$, $false \rightarrow \perp = \perp$. This is known as the *strict* semantics [5] for modeling languages.

The usual choice for modeling partial functions in modeling languages is the *relational* semantics [5]. In the relational semantics the value $\perp$ percolates up through the term until it reaches a Boolean subterm where it becomes *false*. For the example $(t1 \equiv)$ $a[7] = \perp$, $(t2 \equiv)$ $\perp \times x = \perp$, $(b2 \equiv)$ $\perp \geq 6 = false$, $(b1 \equiv)$ $7 \leq 4 = false$, $false \rightarrow false = true$. But in order to implement the relational semantics, the translation of the original complex constraint needs to be far more complex.

Example 3. The tool `mzn2fzn` unrolls, flattens, and reifies MiniZinc models implementing the relational semantics. Assuming i takes values in the set 1..8, and a has an index set 1..5, its translation of the constraint in Example 1 is

```
constraint b1 <-> i <= 4;    % b1 holds iff i <= 4
constraint element(t3,a,t1);% t1 is the t3'th element of a
constraint mult(t1,x,t2);    % t2 is t1 * x
constraint b2 <-> t2 >= 6;   % b2 holds iff t2 >= 6
constraint t3 in 1..5        % t3 in index set of a
constraint b3 <-> i = t3;    % b3 holds iff i = t3
constraint b3 <-> i <= 5;    % b3 holds iff i in index set of a
constraint b4 <-> b2 /\ b3   % b4 holds iff b2 and b3 hold
constraint b1 -> b4          % b1 implies b4
```

The translation forces the partial function application `element` to be "safe" since $t3$ is constrained to only take values in the index set of a. The reified constraints defining $b3$ force $t3$ to equal i iff i takes a value in the index set of a.   □

A second weakness of reification, independent of the problems with partial functions, is that each reified version of a constraint requires further implementation to create, and indeed most solvers do not provide any reified versions of their global constraints.

Example 4. Consider the complex constraint

```
constraint i <= 4 -> alldifferent([i,x-i,x]);
```

The usual flattened form would be

```
constraint b1 <-> i <= 4;    % b1 holds iff i <= 4
constraint minus(x,i,t1);    % t1 = x - i
constraint b2 <-> alldifferent([i,t1,x]);
constraint b1 -> b2          % b1 implies b2
```

but no solver we are aware of implements the third primitive constraint.[1]   □

Reified global constraints are not implemented because a reified constraint $b \leftrightarrow c$ must also implement a propagator for $\neg c$ (in the case that $b = false$). While for some global constraints, e.g. `alldifferent`, this may be reasonable to implement, for most, such as `cumulative`, the task seems to be very difficult.

A third weakness of the full reification is that it may keep track of more information than is required. In a typical finite domain solver, the first reified constraint $b1 \leftrightarrow i \leq 4$ will wake up whenever the lower bound of i changes in order to check whether it should set $b1$ to *false*. But setting $b1$ to *false* will *never* cause any further propagation. There is no reason to check this.

Flattening with half-reification is an approach to mapping complex constraints to existentially quantified conjunctions that improves upon all these weaknesses of flattening with full reification.

- Flattening with half reification can naturally produce the relational semantics when flattening partial functions in positive contexts.
- Half reified constraints add no burden to the solver writer; if they have a propagator for constraint c then they can straightforwardly construct a half reified propagator for $b \rightarrow c$.
- Half reified constraints $b \rightarrow c$ can implement fully reified constraints without any loss of propagation strength (assuming reified constraints are negatable).
- Flattening with half reification can produce more efficient propagation when flattening complex constraints.

Our conclusion is that propagation solvers *only* need to provide half reified version of all constraints. This does not burden the solver writer at all, yet it provides more efficient translation of models, and more expressiveness in using global constraints.

2   Propagation Based Constraint Solving

We consider a typed set of variables $\mathcal{V} = \mathcal{V}_I \cup \mathcal{V}_B$ made up of *integer* variables, $\mathcal{V}_I$, and *Boolean* variables, $\mathcal{V}_b$. We use lower case letters such as x and y for integer variables and letters such as b for Booleans. A *domain* D is a complete mapping from $\mathcal{V}$ to finite sets of integers (for the variables in $\mathcal{V}_I$) and to subsets of $\{true, false\}$ (for the variables in $\mathcal{V}_b$). We can understand a domain D as a

---

[1] Although there are versions of soft `alldifferent`, they do not define this form.

formula $\wedge_{v \in \mathcal{V}}(v \in D(v))$ stating for each variable v that its value is in its domain. A *false domain* D is a domain where $\exists v \in \mathcal{V}.D(v) = \emptyset$, and corresponds to an unsatisfiable formula.

Let D_1 and D_2 be domains and $V \subseteq \mathcal{V}$. We say that D_1 is *stronger* than D_2, written $D_1 \sqsubseteq D_2$, if $D_1(v) \subseteq D_2(v)$ for all $v \in \mathcal{V}$ and that D_1 and D_2 are *equivalent modulo* V, written $D_1 =_V D_2$, if $D_1(v) = D_2(v)$ for all $v \in V$. The *intersection* of D_1 and D_2, denoted $D_1 \sqcap D_2$, is defined by the domain $D_1(v) \cap D_2(v)$ for all $v \in \mathcal{V}$. We assume an *initial domain* D_{init} such that all domains D that occur will be stronger i.e. $D \sqsubseteq D_{init}$.

A *valuation* θ is a mapping of integer and Boolean variables to correspondingly typed values, written $\{x_1 \mapsto d_1, \ldots, x_n \mapsto d_n, b_1 \mapsto tf_1, \ldots, b_m \mapsto tf_m\}$. We extend the valuation θ to map expressions or constraints involving the variables in the natural way. Let *vars* be the function that returns the set of variables appearing in an expression, constraint or valuation. In an abuse of notation, we define a valuation θ to be an element of a domain D, written $\theta \in D$, if $\theta(v) \in D(v)$ for all $v \in vars(\theta)$.

A constraint is a restriction placed on the allowable values for a set of variables. We define the *solutions* of a constraint c to be the set of valuations θ that make that constraint true, i.e. $solns(c) = \{\theta \mid (vars(\theta) = vars(c)) \wedge (\models \theta(c))\}$.

We associate with every constraint c a *propagator* f_c. A propagator f_c is a monotonically decreasing function on domains such that for all domains $D \sqsubseteq D_{init}$: $f_c(D) \sqsubseteq D$ and $\{\theta \in D \mid \theta \in solns(c)\} = \{\theta \in f_c(D) \mid \theta \in solns(c)\}$. This is a weak restriction since, for example, the identity mapping is a propagator for any constraint.

A domain D is *domain consistent* for constraint c if $D(v) = \{\theta(v) \mid \theta \in solns(c) \wedge \theta \in D\}$, for all $v \in vars(c)$. A domain D is *bounds(Z) consistent* for constraint c over variables $v_1, \ldots v_n$ if for each $i \in \{1, \ldots, n\}$ there exists $\theta \in solns(c) \cap D$ s.t. $\theta(v_i) = \min D(v_i)$ and $\min D(v_j) \leq \theta(v_j) \leq \max D(v_j), 1 \leq j \neq i \leq n$, and similarly exists $\theta \in solns(c) \cap D$ s.t. $\theta(v_i) = \max D(v_i)$ and $\min D(v_j) \leq \theta(v_j) \leq \max D(v_j), 1 \leq j \neq i \leq n$. For Boolean variables v we assume *false* < *true*. A domain D is *bounds(R) consistent* for constraint c if the same conditions as for bounds(Z) consistency hold except $\theta \in solns(c')$ where c' is the *real relaxation* of c. Note that we assume Booleans can only take Boolean values in the real relaxation.

Note that for the pure Boolean constraints domain, bounds(Z) and bounds(R) consistency coincide.

A propagator f_c is X-consistent if $f(D)$ is always X consistent for c, where X could be domain, bounds(Z) or bounds(R).

A *propagation solver* for a set of propagators F and current domain D, $solv(F, D)$, repeatedly applies all the propagators in F starting from domain D until there is no further change in the resulting domain. $solv(F, D)$ is the weakest domain $D' \sqsubseteq D$ which is a fixpoint (i.e. $f(D') = D'$) for all $f \in F$. In other words, $solv(F, D)$ returns a new domain defined by $solv(F, D) = \text{gfp}(\lambda d.iter(F, d))(D)$ where $iter(F, D) = \sqcap_{f \in F} f(D)$, where gfp denotes the greatest fixpoint w.r.t $\sqsubseteq$ lifted to functions.

2.1   A Language of Constraints

For simplicity of presentation we restrict ourselves in this paper to the following simple grammar of constraints (a subset of MiniZinc), in which the cons nonterminal defines constraints, and the term nonterminal defines integer terms:

cons $\longrightarrow$ true | false | bvar| term relop term
$\longrightarrow$ not cons | cons /\ cons | cons \/ cons | cons -> cons | cons <-> cons
$\longrightarrow$ pred(term$_1$, ..., term$_n$)
term $\longrightarrow$ int | ivar | term arithop term | array[term] | bool2int(cons)

The grammar uses the symbols bvar for Boolean variables, relop for relational operators { ==, <=, <, !=, >=, > }, pred for names of builtin predicate constraints, int for integer constants, ivar for integer variables, arithop for arithmetic operators { +, -, *, div } and array for array constants. The main missing things are looping constructs, long linear and Boolean constraints, and local variables.

We assume each integer variable x is separately declared with a finite initial set of possible values $D_{init}(x)$. We assume each array constant is separately declared as a mapping $\{i \mapsto d \mid i \in idx(a)\}$ where its index set $idx(a)$ is a finite integer range. Given these initial declarations, we can determine the set of possible values of any term t in the language as $\{\theta(t) \mid \theta \in D_{init}\}$. Note also while it may be prohibitive to determine the set of possible values for any term t, we can efficiently determine a superset of these values by building a superset for each subterm bottom up using approximation.

Given a cons term defining the constraints of the model we can split its cons subterms as occurring in kinds of places: positive contexts, negative contexts, and mixed contexts. A Boolean subterm t of constraint c, written $c[t]$, is in a *positive context* iff for any solution θ of c then θ is also a solution of $c[true]$, that is c with subterm t replaced by *true*. Similarly, a subterm t of constraint c is in a *negative context* iff for any solution θ of c then θ is also a solution of $c[false]$. The remaining Boolean subterms of c are in mixed contexts.

Example 5. Consider the constraint expression c

constraint i <= 4 -> x + bool2int(b) = 5;

then $i \leq 4$ is in a negative context, $x + \texttt{bool2int}(b) = 5$ is in a positive context, and b is in a mixed context. If the last equality were $x + \texttt{bool2int}(b) \geq 5$ then b would be in a positive context.   □

One can classify most contexts as positive or negative using a simple top-down analysis of the form of the expression. The remaining contexts can be considered mixed without compromising the correctness of the rest of the paper.

Our small language contains two partial functions: div returns ⊥ if the divisor is zero, while $a[i]$ returns ⊥ if the value of i is outside the domain of a. We can categorize the *safe* terms and constraints of the language, as those where no ⊥ can ever arise in any subterm. A term or constraint is *safe* if all its arguments are safe, and either the term is not a division or array access, or it is a division term t_1 div t_2 and the set of possible values of t_2 does not include 0, or it is an array access term $a[t]$ and the set of possible values of t are included in $idx(a)$.

3   Flattening with Full Reification

Since the constraint solver only deals with a flat conjunction of constraints, modeling languages that support more complex constraint forms need to *flatten* them into a form acceptable to the solver. The usual method for flattening complex formula of constraints is full reification. Given a constraint c the *full reified form* for c is $b \leftrightarrow c$, where $b \notin vars(c)$ is a Boolean variable naming the satisfied state of the constraint c.

The pseudo-code for flatc(b,c) flattens a constraint expression c to be equal to b, returning a set of constraints implementing $b \leftrightarrow c$. We flatten a whole model c using flatc($true, c$). In the pseudo-code the expressions **new** b and **new** v create a new Boolean and integer variable respectively.

The code assumes there are reified versions of the basic relational constraints r available, as well as reified versions of the Boolean connectives. Flattening of arbitrary constraint predicates aborts if not at the top level of conjunction. The code handles unsafe terms by capturing them when they first arrive at a Boolean context using safen.

flatc(b,c)
   switch c
   case true: **return** $\{b\}$
   case false: **return** $\{\neg b\}$
   case b' (bvar): **return** $\{b \leftrightarrow b'\}$
   case $t_1 \ r \ t_2$ (relop): **return** safen(b, flatt(**new** i_1, t_1) $\cup$ flatt(**new** i_2, t_2)) $\cup \{b \leftrightarrow i_1 \ r \ i_2\}$
   case not c_1: **return** flatc(**new** b_1, c_1) $\cup \{b \leftrightarrow \neg b_1\}$
   case $c_1 \ /\backslash \ c_2$: **if** $(b \equiv true)$ **return** flatc($true, c_1$) $\cup$ flatc($true, c_2$)
                          else return flatc(**new** b_1, c_1) $\cup$ flatc(**new** b_2, c_2) $\cup \{b \leftrightarrow (b_1 \wedge b_2)\}$
   case $c_1 \ \backslash/ \ c_2$: **return** flatc(**new** b_1, c_1) $\cup$ flatc(**new** b_2, c_2) $\cup \{b \leftrightarrow (b_1 \vee b_2)\}$
   case $c_1 \ \texttt{->} \ c_2$: **return** flatc(**new** b_1, c_1) $\cup$ flatc(**new** b_2, c_2) $\cup \{b \leftrightarrow (b_1 \rightarrow b_2)\}$
   case $c_1 \ \texttt{<->} \ c_2$: **return** flatc(**new** b_1, c_1) $\cup$ flatc(**new** b_2, c_2) $\cup \{b \leftrightarrow (b_1 \leftrightarrow b_2)\}$
   case $p \ (t_1, \ldots, t_n)$ (pred):
      if $(b \equiv true)$ **return** safen($b, \bigcup_{j=1}^{n}$flatt(**new** v_j, t_j)) $\cup \{p(v_1, \ldots, v_n)\}$
      else abort

The code flatt(v, t) flattens an integer term t, creating constraints that equate the term with variable v. It creates new variables to store the values of subterms, replaces integer operations by their relational versions, and array lookups by element.

flatt(v,t)
   switch t
   case i (int): **return** $\{v = i\}$
   case v' (ivar): **return** $\{v = v'\}$
   case $t_1 \ a \ t_2$ (arithop): **return** flatt(**new** v_1, t_1) $\cup$ flatt(**new** v_2, t_2) $\cup \{a(v_1, v_2, v)\}$
   case $a \ [\ t_1 \ ]$: **return** flatt(**new** v_1, t_1) $\cup \{$element$(v_1, a, v)\}$
   case bool2int(c_1): **return** flatc(**new** b_1, c_1) $\cup \{$bool2int$(b_1, v)\}$)

The procedure safen(b, C) enforces the relational semantics for unsafe expressions, by ensuring that the unsafe relational versions of partial functions are made safe. Note that to implement the *strict semantics* as opposed to the relational semantics we just need to define $\mathsf{safen}(b, C) = C$. If $b \equiv true$ then the relational semantics and the strict semantics coincide, so nothing needs to be done. The same is true if the set of constraints C is safe. For $div(x, y, z)$, the translation introduces a new variable y' which cannot be 0, and equates it to y if $y \neq 0$. The constraint $div(x, y', z)$ never reflects a partial function application. The new variable b' captures whether the partial function application returns a non $\bot$ value. For $\mathtt{element}(v, a, x)$, it introduces a new variable v' which only takes values in $idx(a)$ and forces it to equal v if $v \in idx(a)$. A partial function application forces $b = false$ since it is the conjunction of the new variables b'. The %HALF% comments will be explained later.

$\mathsf{safen}(b, C)$
   if $(b \equiv true)$ **return** C
   if $(C$ is a set of safe constraints) **return** C
   $B := \emptyset;\ S := \emptyset$
   foreach $c \in C$
      if $(c \equiv div(x, y, z)$ and y can take value 0)
         $B := B \cup \{\mathbf{new}\ b'\}$
         $S := S \cup \{\mathbf{new}\ y' \neq 0, b' \leftrightarrow y \neq 0, b' \leftrightarrow y = y', div(x, y', z)\}$
         %HALF% $S := S \cup \{b' \leftrightarrow y \neq 0, b' \rightarrow div(x, y, z)\}$
      else if $c \equiv \mathtt{element}(v, a, x)$ and v can take a value outside the domain of $a)$
         $B := B \cup \{\mathbf{new}\ b'\}$
         $S := S \cup \{\mathbf{new}\ v' \in idx(a), b' \leftrightarrow v \in idx(a), b' \leftrightarrow v = v', \mathtt{element}(v', a, x)\}$
         %HALF% $S := S \cup \{b' \leftrightarrow v \in idx(a), b' \rightarrow \mathtt{element}(v, a, x)\}$
      else $S := S \cup \{c\}$
   return $S \cup \{b \leftrightarrow \wedge_{b' \in B} b'\})$

The flattening algorithms above can produce suboptimal results in special cases, such as input with common subexpressions. Our implementation avoids generating renamed-apart copies of already-generated constraints, but for simplicity of presentation, we omit the algorithms we use to do this.

4   Half Reification

Given a constraint c, the *half-reified version* of c is a constraint of the form $b \rightarrow c$ where $b \notin vars(c)$ is a Boolean variable.

We can construct a propagator $f_{b \rightarrow c}$ for the half-reified version of c, $b \rightarrow c$, using the propagator f_c for c.

$$f_{b \rightarrow c}(D)(b) = \{false\} \cap D(b) \quad \text{if } f_c(D) \text{ is a false domain}$$
$$f_{b \rightarrow c}(D)(b) = D(b) \qquad\qquad\ \text{otherwise}$$
$$f_{b \rightarrow c}(D)(v) = D(v) \qquad\qquad\ \text{if } v \not\equiv b \text{ and } false \in D(b)$$
$$f_{b \rightarrow c}(D)(v) = f_c(D)(v) \qquad\ \text{if } v \not\equiv b \text{ and } false \notin D(b)$$

In practice most propagator implementations for c first check whether c is satisfiable, before continuing to propagate. For example, $\sum_i a_i x_i \leq a_0$ determines

$L = \sum_i min_D(a_i x_i) - a_0$ and fails if $L > 0$ before propagating; Regin's domain propagator for `alldifferent`$([x_1, \ldots, x_n])$ determines a maximum matching between variables and values first, if this is not of size n it fails before propagating; the timetable `cumulative` constraint determines a profile of necessary resource usage, and fails if this breaks the resource limit, before considering propagation. We can implement the propagator for $f_{b \to c}$ by only performing the checking part until $D(b) = \{true\}$.

Half reification naturally encodes the relational semantics for partial function applications in positive contexts. We associate a Boolean variable b with each Boolean term in an expression, and we ensure that all unsafe constraints are half-reified using the variable of the nearest enclosing Boolean term.

Example 6. Consider flattening of the constraint of Example 1. First we will convert it to an equivalent expression with only positive contexts

```
i > 4 \/ a[i] * x >= 6
```

There are three Boolean terms: the entire constraint, $i > 4$ and $a[i] \times x \geq 6$, which we name b_0, b_1 and b_2 respectively. The flattened form using half reification is

```
constraint b1 -> i > 4;
constraint b2 -> element(i,a,t1);
constraint mult(t1,x,t2);
constraint b2 -> t2 >= 6;
constraint b1 \/ b2;
```

The unsafe `element` constraint is half reified with the name of its nearest enclosing Boolean term. Note that if $i = 7$ then the second constraint makes $b2 = false$. Given this, the final constraint requires $b1 = true$, which in turn requires $i > 4$. Since this holds, the whole constraint is *true* with no restrictions on x.   ⊓⊔

Half reification can handle more constraint terms than full reification if we assume that each global constraint predicate p is available in half-reified form. Recall that this places no new burden on the solver implementer.

Example 7. Consider the constraint of Example 4. Half reification results in

```
constraint b1 -> i > 4;
constraint minus(i,x,t1);    % t1 = i - x
constraint b2 -> alldifferent([i,t1,x]);
constraint b1 \/ b2          % b1 or b2
```

We can easily modify any existing propagator for `alldifferent` to support the half-reified form, hence this model is executable by our constraint solver.   ⊔

Half reification can lead to more efficient constraint solving, since it does not propagate unnecessarily.

Example 8. Consider the task decomposition of a `cumulative` constraint (see e.g. [15]) which includes constraints of the form

```
constraint sum(i in Tasks where i != j)
  (bool2int(s[i] <= s[j] /\ s[i]+d[i] > s[j]) * r[i]) <= L - r[j];
```

which requires that at the start time $s[j]$ of task j, the sum of resources r used by it and by other tasks executing at the same time is less than the limit L. Flattening with full reification produces constraints like this:

```
constraint b1[i] <-> s[i] <= s[j];
constraint plus(s[i],d[i],e[i]);     % e[i] = s[i] + d[i]
constraint b2[i] <-> e[i] > s[j];
constraint b3[i] <-> b1[i] /\ b2[i];
constraint bool2int(b3[i], a[i]);    % a[i] = bool2int(b3[i])
constraint sum(i in Tasks where i != j)( a[i] * r[i] )\! <= L - r[j];
```

Whenever the start time of task i is constrained so that it does not overlap time $s[j]$, then $b3[i]$ is fixed to *false* and $a[i]$ to 0, and the long linear sum is awoken. But this is useless, since it cannot cause failure. The Boolean expression appears in a negative context, and half-reification produces

```
constraint b1[i] -> s[i] > s[j];
constraint plus(s[i],d[i],e[i]);     % e[i] = s[i] + d[i]
constraint b2[i] -> e[i] <= s[j];
constraint b3[i] -> b1[i] \/ b2[i];
constraint b4[i] <-> not b3[i];
constraint bool2int(b4[i], a[i]);    % a[i] = bool2int(b4[i])
constraint sum(i in Tasks where i != j)( a[i] * r[i] ) <= L - r[j];
```

which may seem to be more expensive since there are additional variables (the $b4[i]$), but since both $b4[i]$ and $a[i]$ are implemented by views [14], there is no additional runtime overhead. This decomposition will only wake the linear constraint when some task i is guaranteed to overlap time $s[j]$.   □

Half reification can cause propagators to wake up less frequently, since variables that are fixed to *true* by full reification will never be fixed by half reification. This is advantageous, but a corresponding disadvantage is that variables that are fixed can allow the simplification of the propagator, and hence make its propagation faster. We can reduce this disadvantage by fully reifying Boolean connectives (which have low overhead) where possible in the half reification.

Flattening with Half Reification. The procedure halfc(b, c) defined below returns a set of constraints implementing the half-reification $b \to c$. We flatten a whole model c using halfc($true, c$). The half-reification flattening transformation uses half reification whenever it is in a positive context. If it encounters a constraint c_1 in a negative context, it negates the constraint if it is safe, thus creating a new positive context. If this is not possible, it defaults to the usual flattening approach using full reification. Note how for conjunction it does not need to introduce a new Boolean variable. Negating a constraint expression is done one operator at a time, and is defined in the obvious way. For example, negating $t_1 < t_2$ yields $t_1 >= t_2$, and negating $c_1 /\ c_2$ yields not $c_1 \/$ not c_2. Any negations on subexpressions will be processed by recursive invocations of the algorithm.

halfc(b,c)
  switch c
  case true: **return** $\{\}$
  case false: **return** $\{\neg b\}$
  case b' (bvar): **return** $\{b \to b'\}$
  case $t_1\ r\ t_2$ (relop): **return** halft(b, **new** i_1, t_1) $\cup$ halft(b, **new** i_2, t_2) $\cup$ $\{b \to i_1\ r\ i_2\}$
  case not c_1:
    if (c_1 is safe) **return** halfc(b, negate(c_1))
    else return flatc(**new** b_1, not c_1) $\cup$ $\{b \to b_1\}$
  case $c_1\ /\backslash\ c_2$: **return** halfc(b, c_1) $\cup$ halfc(b, c_2)
  case $c_1\ \backslash/\ c_2$: **return** halfc(**new** b_1, c_1) $\cup$ halfc(**new** b_2, c_2) $\cup$ $\{b \to (b_1 \vee b_2)\}$
  case $c_1\ \text{->}\ c_2$: **return** halfc(b, not $c_1\ \backslash/\ c_2$)
  case $c_1\ \text{<->}\ c_2$: **return** flatc(**new** b_1, c_1) $\cup$ flatc(**new** b_2, c_2) $\cup$ $\{b \to (b_1 \leftrightarrow b_2)\}$
  case $p\ (t_1, \ldots, t_n)$ (pred): **return** $\cup_{j=1}^n$halft(b, **new** v_j, t_j) $\cup$ $\{b \to p(v_1, \ldots, v_n)\}$

Half reification of terms returns a set of constraints that enforce $v = t$ if the term t is safe, and $b \to v = t$ otherwise. The most complex case is bool2int(c_1), which half-reifies c_1 if it is in a positive context, negates c_1 and half-reifies the result if c_1 is safe and in a negative context, and uses full flattening otherwise.

halft(b,v,t)
  if (t is safe) **return** flatt(v, t)
  switch t
  case i (int): **return** $\{b \to v = i\}$ % unreachable
  case v' (ivar): **return** $\{b \to v = v'\}$ % unreachable
  case $t_1\ a\ t_2$ (arithop): halft(b, **new** v_1, t_1) $\cup$ halft(b, **new** v_2, t_2) $\cup$ $\{b \to a(v_1, v_2, v)\}$
  case $a\ [\ t_1\ ]$: halft(b, **new** v_1, t_1) $\cup$ $\{b \to$ element$(v_1, a, v)\}$
  case bool2int(c_1):
    if (c_1 is in a positive context) **return** halfc(**new** b_1, c_1) $\cup$ $\{b \to$ bool2int$(b_1, v)\}$)
    else if (c_1 is safe and in a negative context)
      halfc(**new** b_1, negate(c_1)) $\cup$ $\{b \to$ bool2int(**new** $b_2, v), b_2 \leftrightarrow \neg b_1\}$)
    else return flatc(**new** b_1, c_1) $\cup$ $\{b \to$ bool2int$(b_1, v)\}$

Half reified constraints can also simplify the process of enforcing the relational semantics for full reification, since we have a half-reified version of the div and element constraints. The safen operation can be improved by replacing the lines above those labeled %HALF% by the lines labeled %HALF%.

Full Reification using Half Reification. Usually splitting a propagator into two will reduce the propagation strength. We show that modeling $b \leftrightarrow c$ for primitive constraint c using half-reified propagators as $b \to c, b \leftrightarrow \neg b', b' \to \neg c$ does not do so.

To do so independent of propagation strength, we define the behaviour of the propagators of the half-reified forms in terms of the full reified propagator.

$$f_{b \to c}(D)(b) = D(b) \cap (\{false\} \cup f_{b \leftrightarrow c}(D)(b))$$
$$f_{b \to c}(D)(v) = D(v) \qquad \text{if } v \not\equiv b, false \in D(b)$$
$$f_{b \to c}(D)(v) = f_{b \leftrightarrow c}(D)(v) \qquad \text{if } v \not\equiv b, \text{otherwise}$$

and

$$f_{b' \to \neg c}(D)(b') = D(b') \qquad \text{if } \{false\} \in f_{b \leftrightarrow c}(D)(b)$$
$$f_{b' \to \neg c}(D)(b') = D(b') \cap \{false\} \text{ otherwise}$$
$$f_{b' \to \neg c}(D)(v) = D(v) \qquad \text{if } v \not\equiv b', false \in D(b')$$
$$f_{b' \to \neg c}(D)(v) = f_{b \leftrightarrow c}(D)(v) \quad \text{if } v \not\equiv b, \text{otherwise}$$

These definitions are not meant describe implementations, only to define how the half reified split versions of the propagator should act.

Theorem 1. $\forall D. \, solv(\{f_{b \leftrightarrow c}, f_{b' \leftrightarrow \neg b}\})(D) = solv(\{f_{b \to c}, f_{b' \to \neg c}, f_{b' \leftrightarrow \neg b}\}, D).$

Proof. Let $V = vars(c)$. We only consider domains D at a fixpoint of the propagators $f_{b' \leftrightarrow \neg b}$, i.e. $D(b') = \{\neg d \mid d \in D(b)\}$. The proof is by cases of D. **(a)** Suppose $D(b) = \{true, false\}$. **(a-i)** If $\exists \theta \in solns(c)$ where $\theta \in D$ (c can still be true) and $\exists \theta' \in D$ where $vars(\theta) = V$ and $\theta \notin solns(c)$ (c can still be false). then $f_{b \leftrightarrow c}$ does not propagate. Clearly neither do either of $f_{b \to c}$ or $f_{b' \to \neg c}$. **(a-ii)** Suppose c cannot still be false ($\forall \theta \in D$ where $vars(\theta) = V$ then $\theta \in solns(c)$) then $f_{b \leftrightarrow c}(D)(b) = \{true\}$ and similarly $f_{b' \to \neg c}(D)(b') = \{false\}$ using the second case of its definition. The propagator for $f_{b' \leftrightarrow \neg b}$ will then make the domain of b equal $\{true\}$. There is no other propagation in any case. **(a-iii)** Suppose c cannot still be true ($\neg(\exists \theta \in D \cap solns(c))$) then $f_{b \to c}(D)(b) = \{false\}$ and $f_{b \to c}(D)(b) = \{false\}$ using the first case of its definition. Again there is no other propagation in any case except making the domain of b' equal $\{true\}$. **(b)** If $D(b) = \{true\}$ then clearly $f_{b \leftrightarrow c}$ and $f_{b \to c}$ act identically on variables in $vars(c)$. **(c)** If $D(b) = \{false\}$ then $D(b') = \{true\}$ and clearly $f_{b \leftrightarrow c}$ and $f_{b' \to \neg c}$ act identically on variables in $vars(c)$. □

The reason for the generality of the above theorem which defines the half-reified propagation strength in terms of the full reified propagator is that we can now show that for the usual notions of consistency, replacing a fully reified propagator leads to the same propagation. Note that the additional variable b' can be implemented as a view [14] in the solver and hence adds no overhead.

Corollary 1. *A domain (resp. bounds(Z), bounds(R)) consistent propagator for $b \leftrightarrow c$ propagates identically to domain (resp. bounds(Z), bounds(R)) consistent propagators for $b \to c$, $b \leftrightarrow \neg b'$, $b' \to \neg c$.* □

5   Experiments

We ran our experiments on a PC with a 2.80GHz Intel i7 Q860 CPU and 4Gb of memory. www.cs.mu.oz.au/~pjs/half has our experimental MiniZinc models and instances. The first experiment considers "QCP-max" problems which are defined as quasi-group completion problems where the alldifferent constraints are soft, and the aim is to satisfy as many of them as possible.

```
int: n; % size
array[1..n,1..n] of 0..n: s; % 0 = unfixed 1..n = fixed
array[1..n,1..n] of var 1..n: q; % qcp array;
```

Table 1. QCP-max problems: Average time (in seconds), number of solved instances (300s timeout)

Instances	FD			FD + Explanations		
	full	half	half-g	full	half	half-g
qcp-10 (x15)	20.1 14	20.0 14	20.0 14	0 15	0 15	0 15
qcp-15 (x15)	204.6 6	179.9 7	174.1 7	2.5 15	1.5 15	1.0 15
qcp-20 (x15)	300.0 0	289.0 1	286.0 1	115.7 11	127.5 10	114.2 10

```
constraint forall(i,j in 1..n where s[i,j] > 0)(q[i,j] = s[i,j]);
solve maximize
    sum(i in 1..n)(bool2int(alldifferent([q[i,j] | j in 1..n]))) +
    sum(j in 1..n)(bool2int(alldifferent([q[i,j] | i in 1..n])));

predicate alldifferent(array[int] of var int: x) =
    forall(i,j in index_set(x) where i < j)(x[i] != x[j]);
```

Note that this is not the same as requiring the maximum number of disequality constraints to be satisfied. The `alldifferent` constraints, while apparently in a mixed context, are actually in a positive context, since the maximization in fact is implemented by inequalities forcing at least some number to be true.

In Table 1 we compare three different resulting programs on QCP-max problems: full reification of the model above, using the `alldifferent` decomposition defined by the predicate shown (full), half reification of the model using the `alldifferent` decomposition (half), and half reification using a half-reified global `alldifferent` (half-g) implementing arc consistency (thus having the same propagation strength as the decomposition). We use standard QCP examples from the literature, and group them by size. We compare both a standard finite domain solver (FD) and a learning lazy clause generation solver (FD + Explanations). We use the same fixed search strategy of labeling the matrix in order left-to-right from highest to lowest value for all approaches to minimize differences in search.

Half reification of the decomposition is more efficient, principally because it introduces fewer Boolean variables, and the direct implementation of the half reified constraint is more efficient still. Note that learning can be drastically changed by the differences in the model and full solves one more instance in qcp-20, thus winning in that case. Apart from this instance, the half reified versions give an almost uniform improvement.

The second experiment shows how half reification can reduce the overhead of handling partial functions correctly. Consider the following model for determining a prize collecting path, a simplified form of prize collecting traveling salesman problem [2], where the aim is define an acyclic path from node 1 along weighted edges to collect the most weight. Not every node needs to be visited ($pos[i] = 0$).

Table 2. Prize collecting paths: Average time (in seconds) and number of solved instances with a 300s timeout for various number of nodes

Nodes	FD			FD + Explanations		
	full	half	extended	full	half	extended
15-3-5 (x 10)	0.31 10	0.25 10	0.26 10	0.21 10	0.17 10	0.17 10
18-3-6 (x 10)	1.79 10	1.37 10	1.52 10	0.70 10	0.51 10	0.58 10
20-4-5 (x 10)	5.30 10	4.04 10	4.51 10	1.28 10	0.97 10	1.17 10
24-4-6 (x 10)	46.03 10	34.00 10	40.06 10	7.28 10	4.91 10	6.37 10
25-5-5 (x 10)	66.41 10	50.70 10	57.51 10	9.75 10	6.58 10	8.28 10
28-4-7 (x 10)	255.06 5	214.24 8	241.10 6	38.54 10	23.27 10	34.83 10
30-5-6 (x 10)	286.48 1	281.00 2	284.34 1	100.54 10	60.65 10	92.19 10
32-4-8 (x 10)	300.00 0	297.12 1	300.00 0	229.86 5	163.73 10	215.16 8

```
int: n; % size
array[1..n,0..n] of int: p; % prize for edge (i,j) Note p[i,0] = 0
array[1..n] of var 0..n: next; % next posn in tour
array[1..n] of var 0..n: pos;  % posn on node i in path, 0 = notin
array[1..n] of var int: prize = [p[i,next[i]] | i in 1..n];
                        % prize for outgoing edge
constraint forall(i in 1..n)(
    (pos[i] = 0 <-> next[i] = 0) /\
    (next[i] > 1 -> pos[next[i]] = pos[i] + 1));
constraint alldifferent_except_0(next) /\ pos[1] = 1;
solve minimize sum(i in 1..n)(prize[i]);
```

It uses the global constraint alldifferent_except_0 which constrains each element in the *next* array to be different or equal 0. The model has one unsafe array lookup $pos[next[i]]$. We compare using full reification (full) and half reification (half) to model this problem. Note that if we extend the *pos* array to have domain $0..n$ then the model becomes safe. We also compare against this model (extended). We use graphs with both positive and negative weights for the tests. The search strategy fixes the *next* variables in order of their maximum value. First we note that extended is slightly better than full because of the simpler translation, while half is substantially better than extended since most of the half reified element constraints become redundant. Learning increases the advantage because the half reified formulation focusses on propagation which leads to failure which creates more reusable nogoods.

In the final experiment we compare resource constrained project scheduling problems (RCPSP) where the cumulative constraint is defined by the task decomposition as in Example 8 above, using both full reification and half-reification. We use standard benchmark examples from PSPlib [12]. Table 3 compares RCPSP instances using full reification and half reification. We compare using J30 instances (J30) and instances due to Baptiste and Le Pape (BL). Each line in the table shows the average run time and number of solved instances. The search strategy tries to schedule the task with the earliest possible start time.

Table 3. RCPSP: Average time (in seconds) and number of solved instances with a 300s timeout

Instances	FD		FD + Explanations	
	full	half	full	half
BL (x 40)	277.2 5	269.3 5	17.1 39	15.4 39
J30 (x 480)	116.1 300	114.3 304	16.9 463	12.9 468

We find a small and uniform speedup for half over full across the suites, which improves with learning, again because learning is not confused by propagations that do not lead to failure.

6   Related Work and Conclusion

Half reification on purely Boolean constraints is well understood, this is the same as detecting the *polarity* of a gate, and removing half of the clausal representation of the circuit (see e.g. [11]). The flattening of functions (partial or total) and the calculation of polarity for Booleans terms inside bool2int do not arise in pure Boolean constraints.

Half reified constraints have been used in constraint modeling but are typically not visible as primitive constraints to users, or produced through flattening. Indexicals [17] can be used to implement reified constraints by specifying how to propagate a constraint c, propagate its negation, check disentailment, and check entailment, and this is implemented in SICstus Prolog [4]. A half reified propagator simply omits entailment and propagating the negation. Half reified constraints appear in some constraint systems, for example SCIP [1] supports half-reified real linear constraints of the form $b \rightarrow \sum_i a_i x_i \leq a_0$ exactly because the negation of the linear constraint $\sum_i a_i x_i > a_0$ is not representable in an LP solver so full reification is not possible.

While flattening is the standard approach to handle complex formula involving constraints, there are a number of other approaches which propagate more strongly. Schulte [13] proposes a generic implementation of $b \leftrightarrow c$ propagating (the flattened form of) c in a separate constraint space which does not affect the original variables; entailment and disentailment of c fix the b variable appropriately, although when b is made *false* the implementation does not propagate $\neg c$. This can also be implemented using propagator groups [8]. Brand and Yap [3] define an approach to propagating complex constraint formulae called controlled propagation which ensures that propagators that cannot affect the satisfiability are not propagated. They note that for a formula without negation, they could omit half their control rules, corresponding to the case for half reification of a positive context. Jefferson *et al* [7] similarly define an approach to propagating positive constraint formulae by using watch literal technology to only wake propagators for reified constraints within the formula when they can affect the final result. They use half reified propagators, which they call the "reifyimplied" form of a constraint, in some of their constraint models, though they do not

compare half reified models against full reified models. We can straightforwardly
fit these stronger propagation approaches to parts of a constraint formula into
the flattening approach by treating the whole formula as a predicate, and the
implementation of the stronger propagation as its propagator.

We suggest that all finite domain constraint solvers should move to supporting
half-reified versions of all constraints. This imposes no further burden on solver
implementors, it allows more models to be solved, it can be used to implement
full reification, and it can allow translation to more efficient models.

We are currently extending the translator from MiniZinc to FlatZinc, mzn2fzn,
to also support half-reification. This means also extending FlatZinc to include
half-reified versions of constraints.

Acknowledgments. NICTA is funded by the Australian Government as represented by the Department of Broadband, Communications and the Digital
Economy and the Australian Research Council.

References

1. Achterberg, T., Berthold, T., Koch, T., Wolter, K.: Constraint integer programming: A new approach to integrate CP and MIP. In: Trick, M.A. (ed.) CPAIOR
2008. LNCS, vol. 5015, pp. 6–20. Springer, Heidelberg (2008)
2. Balas, E.: The prize collecting traveling salesman problem. Networks 19, 621–636
(1989)
3. Brand, S., Yap, R.: Towards "Propagation = Logic + Control". In: Etalle, S.,
Truszczyński, M. (eds.) ICLP 2006. LNCS, vol. 4079, pp. 102–106. Springer, Heidelberg (2006)
4. Carlsson, M., Ottosson, G., Carlson, B.: An open-ended finite domain constraint
solver. In: Hartel, P.H., Kuchen, H. (eds.) PLILP 1997. LNCS, vol. 1292, pp. 191–
206. Springer, Heidelberg (1997)
5. Frisch, A., Stuckey, P.: The proper treatment of undefinedness in constraint languages. In: Gent, I.P. (ed.) CP 2009. LNCS, vol. 5732, pp. 367–382. Springer,
Heidelberg (2009)
6. Frisch, A.M., Grum, M., Jefferson, C., Hernandez, B.M., Miguel, I.: The design of
ESSENCE: A constraint language for specifying combinatorial problems. In: Procs.
of IJCAI 2007 (2007)
7. Jefferson, C., Moore, N.C.A., Nightingale, P., Petrie, K.E.: Implementing logical
connectives in constraint programming. Artif. Intell. 174(16-17), 1407–1429 (2010)
8. Lagerkvist, M.Z., Schulte, C.: Propagator groups. In: Gent, I.P. (ed.) CP 2009.
LNCS, vol. 5732, pp. 524–538. Springer, Heidelberg (2009)
9. Marriott, K., Nethercote, N., Rafeh, R., Stuckey, P., Garcia de la Banda, M.,
Wallace, M.: The design of the Zinc modelling language. Constraints 13(3), 229–
267 (2008)
10. Nethercote, N., Stuckey, P., Becket, R., Brand, S., Duck, G., Tack, G.: Minizinc:
Towards a standard CP modelling language. In: Bessière, C. (ed.) CP 2007. LNCS,
vol. 4741, pp. 529–543. Springer, Heidelberg (2007)
11. Plaisted, D., Greenbaum, S.: A structure-preserving clause form translation. Journal of Symbolic Computation 2, 293–304 (1986)
12. PSPlib (Project scheduling problem library), http://129.187.106.231/psplib/

13. Schulte, C.: Programming deep concurrent constraint combinators. In: Pontelli, E., Santos Costa, V. (eds.) PADL 2000. LNCS, vol. 1753, pp. 215–229. Springer, Heidelberg (2000)
14. Schulte, C., Tack, G.: Views and iterators for generic constraint implementations. In: van Beek, P. (ed.) CP 2005. LNCS, vol. 3709, pp. 817–821. Springer, Heidelberg (2005)
15. Schutt, A., Feydy, T., Stuckey, P., Wallace, M.: Why cumulative decomposition is not as bad as it sounds. In: Gent, I.P. (ed.) CP 2009. LNCS, vol. 5732, pp. 746–761. Springer, Heidelberg (2009)
16. Van Hentenryck, P.: The OPL Optimization Programming Language. MIT Press, Cambridge (1999)
17. Van Hentenryck, P., Saraswat, V., Deville, Y.: Constraint processins in cc(FD) (1991) (manuscript)

The Parameterized Complexity of Local Consistency*

Serge Gaspers and Stefan Szeider

Institute of Information Systems, Vienna University of Technology, Vienna, Austria
gaspers@kr.tuwien.ac.at, stefan@szeider.net

Abstract. We investigate the parameterized complexity of deciding whether a constraint network is k-consistent. We show that, parameterized by k, the problem is complete for the complexity class co-W[2]. As secondary parameters we consider the maximum domain size d and the maximum number ℓ of constraints in which a variable occurs. We show that parameterized by $k + d$, the problem drops down one complexity level and becomes co-W[1]-complete. Parameterized by $k + d + \ell$ the problem drops down one more level and becomes fixed-parameter tractable. We further show that the same complexity classification applies to strong k-consistency, directional k-consistency, and strong directional k-consistency.

Our results establish a super-polynomial separation between input size and time complexity. Thus we strengthen the known lower bounds on time complexity of k-consistency that are based on input size.

1 Introduction

Local consistency is one of the oldest and most fundamental concepts of constraint solving and can be traced back to Montanari's 1974 paper [26]. If a constraint network is locally consistent, then consistent instantiations to a small number of variables can be consistently extended to an additional variable. Hence local consistency avoids certain dead-ends in the search tree, in some cases it even guarantees backtrack-free search [1,20]. The simplest and most widely used form of local consistency is arc-consistency, introduced by Mackworth [25], and later generalized to k-consistency by Freuder [19]. A constraint network is k-consistent if each consistent assignment to $k - 1$ variables can be consistently extended to any additional k^{th} variable.

Consider a constraint network of *input size* s where the constraints are given as relations. It is easy to see that k-consistency can be checked by brute force in time $O(s^k)$ [10]. Hence, if k is a fixed constant, the check is polynomial. However, the algorithm runs in "nonuniform" polynomial time in the sense that the order of the polynomial depends on k, hence the running time scales poorly in k and becomes impractical already for $k \geq 3$. Also more sophisticated algorithms for k-consistency achieve only a nonuniform polynomial running time [8].

---

* This research was funded by the ERC (COMPLEX REASON, 239962).

J. Lee (Ed.): CP 2011, LNCS 6876, pp. 302–316, 2011.

In this paper we investigate the possibility of a uniform polynomial-time algorithm for k-consistency, i.e., an algorithm of running time $O(f(k)s^c)$ where f is an arbitrary function and c is a constant independent of k. We carry out our investigations in the theoretical framework of *parameterized complexity* [15,17,27] which allows to distinguish between uniform and nonuniform polynomial time. Problems that can be solved in uniform polynomial time are called *fixed-parameter tractable* (FPT), problems that can be solved in nonuniform polynomial time are further classified within a hierarchy of parameterized complexity classes forming the chain FPT $\subseteq$ W[1] $\subseteq$ W[2] $\subseteq$ W[3] $\subseteq \cdots$, where all inclusions are believed to be strict.

Results. We pinpoint the exact complexity of k-consistency decision in general and under restrictions on the given constraint network in terms of domain size d and the maximum number ℓ of constraints in which a variable occurs.

We show that deciding k-consistency is co-W[2]-complete for parameter k, co-W[1]-complete for parameter $k + d$, and fixed-parameter tractable for parameter $k + d + \ell$. Hence, subject to complexity theoretic assumptions, k-consistency cannot be decided in uniform polynomial-time in general, but admits a uniform polynomial-time solution if domain size and variable occurrence are bounded. The hardness results imply a super-polynomial separation between input size and running time for k-consistency algorithms.

We further show that all three complexity results also hold for deciding *strong* k-consistency, for deciding *directional* k-consistency, and for deciding *strong directional* k-consistency. A constraint network is strongly k-consistent if it is j-consistent for all $1 \le j \le k$. Directional local consistency takes a fixed ordering of the variables into account, the variable to which a local instantiation is extended is ordered higher than the previously instantiated variables [12].

Known Lower Bounds. In previous research, lower bounds on the running time of k-consistency algorithms have been obtained [8,10]. These lower bounds are based on instances of large input size, and the observation that any k-consistency algorithm needs to read the entire input. For instance, to decide whether a given constraint network on n variables is k-consistent one needs to check each constraint of arity $r \le k$ at least once (the arity of a constraint is the number of variables that occur in the constraint). Since there can be $\sum_{i=1}^{k} \binom{n}{i}$ such constraints, $\Omega(n^k)$ provides a lower bound on the running time of any k-consistency algorithm. Taking the domain size d into account, this lower bound can be improved to $\Omega((dn)^k)$ [10]. However, the constraint networks to which this lower bound applies are of size $s = \Omega((dn)^k)$. Therefore the known lower bounds do not provide a separation between input size and running time.

2   Preliminaries

2.1   Constraint Networks and Local Consistency Problems

A *constraint network* (or *CSP instance*) N is a triple (X, D, C), where X is a finite set of *variables*, D is a finite set of *values*, and C is a finite set of *constraints*.

Each constraint $c \in C$ is a pair (S, R), where $S = var(C)$, the *constraint scope*, is a finite sequence of distinct variables from X, and R, the *constraint relation*, is a relation over D whose arity matches the length of S, i.e., $R \subseteq D^r$ where r is the length of S. The size of N is $s = |N| = |X| + |D| + \sum_{(S,R) \in C} |S| \cdot (1 + |R|)$.

Let $N = (X, D, C)$ be a constraint network. A *partial instantiation* of N is a mapping $\alpha : X' \to D$ defined on some subset $var(\alpha) = X' \subseteq X$. We say that α *satisfies* a constraint $c = ((x_1, \ldots, x_r), R) \in C$ if $var(c) \subseteq var(\alpha)$ and $(\alpha(x_1), \ldots, \alpha(x_r)) \in R$. If α satisfies all constraints of N then it is a *solution* of N; in this case, N is satisfiable. We say that α is consistent with a constraint $c \in C$ if either $var(c)$ is not a subset of $var(\alpha)$ or α satisfies c. If α is consistent with all constraints of N we call it consistent. The restriction of a partial assignment α to a set of variables Y is denoted $\alpha|_Y$. It has scope $var(\alpha) \cap Y$ and $\alpha|_Y(x) = \alpha(x)$ for all $x \in var(\alpha|_Y)$.

Let $k > 0$ be an integer. A constraint network $N = (X, D, C)$ is *k-consistent* if for all consistent partial instantiations α of N with $|var(\alpha)| = k - 1$ and all variables $x \in X \setminus var(\alpha)$ there is a consistent partial instantiation α' such that $var(\alpha') = var(\alpha) \cup \{x\}$, and $\alpha'|_{var(\alpha)} = \alpha$. In such a case we say that α' *consistently extends* α to x. A constraint network is *strongly k-consistent* if it is j-consistent for all $j = 1, \ldots, k$.

For further background on local consistency we refer to other sources [2,11]. We consider the following decision problem.

k-CONSISTENCY
Input: A constraint network $N = (X, D, C)$ and an integer $k > 0$.
Question: Is N k-consistent?

The problem STRONG k-CONSISTENCY is defined analogously, asking whether N is strongly k-consistent.

It is easy to see that k-CONSISTENCY is co-NP-hard if k is unbounded. Take an arbitrary constraint network $N = (X, D, C)$ and form a new network N' from N by adding a new variable x, and $|X| + 1$ new constraints with empty relations, namely the constraint whose scope contains all variables, and all possible constraints of arity $|X|$ having x in their scope. Let $k = |X| + 1$. Now N' is k-consistent if and only if N is not satisfiable. Since k is large this reduction seems somehow unnatural and breaks down for bounded k. This suggests to "deconstruct" this hardness proof (in the sense of [24]) and to parameterize by k.

The constraint network N is *directionally k-consistent* with respect to a total order $\leq$ on its variables if every consistent partial instantiation α of $k-1$ variables of N can be consistently extended to every variable that is higher in the order $\leq$ than any variable of $var(\alpha)$. The corresponding decision problem is defined as follows.

DIRECTIONAL k-CONSISTENCY
Input: A constraint network $N = (X, D, C)$, a total order $\leq$ on X, and an integer $k > 0$.
Question: Is N directionally k-consistent with respect to $\leq$?

A constraint network is *strongly directionally k-consistent* if and only if it is directionally j-consistent for all $j = 1, \ldots, k$. The strong counterpart of the DI-RECTIONAL k-CONSISTENCY problem is called STRONG DIRECTIONAL k-CONSISTENCY.

We will consider parameterizations of these four problems by k, by $k + d$, and by $k + d + \ell$, where $d = |D|$ and ℓ denotes the maximum number of constraints in which a variable occurs.

2.2   Parameterized Complexity

We define the basic notions of Parameterized Complexity and refer to other sources [15,17] for an in-depth treatment. A parameterized problem can be considered as a set of pairs (I, k), the instances, where I is the main part and k is the parameter. The parameter is usually a non-negative integer. A parameterized problem is *fixed-parameter tractable* if there exists an algorithm that solves any instance (I, k) of size n in time $f(k)n^{O(1)}$, where f is a computable function. FPT denotes the class of all fixed-parameter tractable decision problems.

Parameterized complexity offers a completeness theory, similar to the theory of NP-completeness, that allows the accumulation of strong theoretical evidence that some parameterized problems are not fixed-parameter tractable. This theory is based on a hierarchy of complexity classes

$$\text{FPT} \subseteq \text{W}[1] \subseteq \text{W}[2] \subseteq \text{W}[3] \subseteq \cdots.$$

where all inclusions are believed to be strict. A $\text{W}[i+1]$-complete problem is considered harder than a $\text{W}[i]$-complete problem similar to a classical problem that is complete for the $i+1$-th level of the Polynomial Hierarchy is considered harder than one that is complete for the i-th level. Hence it is of significance to identify the exact location of a parameterized problem within the W-hierarchy. Each class $\text{W}[i]$ contains all parameterized decision problems that can be reduced to a canonical parameterized satisfiability problem P_i under *parameterized reductions*. These are many-to-one reductions where the parameter for one problem maps into the parameter for the other. More specifically, a parameterized problem L reduces to a parameterized problem L' if there is a mapping R from instances of L to instances of L' such that (i) (I, k) is a YES-instance of L if and only if $(I', k') = R(I, k)$ is a YES-instance of L', (ii) there is a computable function g such that $k' \leq g(k)$, and (iii) there is a computable function f and a constant c such that R can be computed in time $O(f(k) \cdot n^c)$, where n denotes the size of (I, k).

A parameterized problem is in co-$\text{W}[i]$, $i \in \mathbb{N}$, if its complement is in $\text{W}[i]$, where the *complement* of a parameterized problem is the parameterized problem resulting from reversing the YES and NO answers. If any co-$\text{W}[i]$-complete problem is fixed-parameter tractable, then co-$\text{W}[i] = \text{FPT} = \text{co-FPT} = \text{W}[i]$ follows, which causes the Exponential Time Hypothesis to fail [17]. Hence co-$\text{W}[i]$-completeness provides strong theoretical evidence that a problem is not fixed-parameter tractable.

2.3   Tries, Turing Machines, and Gaifman Graphs

Tries. A *trie* [9,18] is a tree for storing strings in which there is one node for every prefix of a string. Let T be a trie that stores a set S of strings on an alphabet Σ. At a given node v of T, corresponding to the prefix $p(v)$, there is an array with one entry for every character c of Σ. If $p(v).c$ is a prefix of a string of S, the entry corresponding to c has a pointer to the node corresponding to the prefix $p(v).c$ (the dot denotes a concatenation). If $p(v).c$ is not a prefix of a string of S, the entry corresponding to c has a null pointer. Thus, a trie uses space $O(|S| \cdot |\Sigma|)$, while inserting or searching a string s can be done in time $O(|s|)$ using the ordinal values for characters as array indices.

Turing Machines. A *nondeterministic Turing Machine (NTM)* [4,17] with t tapes is an 8-tuple $M = (Q, \Gamma, \beta, \$, \Sigma, \delta, q_0, F)$, where

- Q is a finite set of *states*,
- the *tape alphabet* Γ is a finite set of symbols,
- $\beta \in \Gamma$ is the *blank symbol*, the only symbol allowed to occur on the tape(s) infinitely often,
- $\$ \in \Gamma$ is a delimiter marking the (left) end of a tape,
- $\Sigma \subseteq \Gamma$ is the set of *input symbols*,
- $q_0 \in Q$ is the *initial state*,
- $F \subseteq Q$ is the set of *final* states,
- $\sigma \subseteq Q \setminus F \times \Gamma^t \times Q \times \Gamma^t \times \{L, N, R\}^t$ is the *transition relation*. A transition $(q, (a_1, \ldots, a_t), q', (a'_1, \ldots, a'_t), (d_1, \ldots, d_t)) \in \sigma$ allows the machine, when it is in state q and the head of each tape T_i is positioned on a cell containing the symbol a_i, to transition in one computation step into the state q', writing the symbol a'_i into the cell on which the head of each tape T_i is positioned, and shifting this head one position to the left if $d_i = L$, one position to the right if $d_i = R$, or not at all if $d_i = N$. On each tape, \$ cannot be overwritten and allows only right transitions, which is formally achieved by imposing that whenever $(q, (a_1, \ldots, a_t), q', (a'_1, \ldots, a'_t), (d_1, \ldots, d_t)) \in \sigma$, then for all $i \in \{1, \ldots, t\}$ we have $a_i = \$$ if and only if $a'_i = \$$, and $a_i = \$$ implies $d_i = R$.

Initially, the first tape contains $\$w\beta\beta\ldots$, where $w \in \Sigma^*$ is the input word, all other tapes contain $\$\beta\beta\ldots$, M is in state q_0, and all heads are positioned on the first cell to the right of the \$ symbol. We speak of a *single-tape* NTM if $t = 1$ and of a *multi-tape* NTM if $t > 1$. M accepts the input word w in k steps if there exists a transition path that takes M with input word w to a final state in k computation steps.

Graphs. The *Gaifman graph* $\mathcal{G}(N)$ of a constraint network $N = (X, D, C)$ has the vertex set $V(\mathcal{G}(N)) := X$ and its edge set $E(\mathcal{G}(N))$ contains an edge $\{u, v\}$ if u and v occur together in the scope of a constraint of C. In a graph $G = (V, E)$, the *(open) neighborhood* of a vertex v is the subset of vertices sharing an edge with v and is denoted $\Gamma(v)$, its *closed neighborhood* is $\Gamma[v] := \Gamma(v) \cup \{v\}$, and the *degree* of v is $d(v) := |\Gamma(v)|$. The maximum vertex degree of G is denoted $\Delta(G)$. For a vertex set S, $\Gamma[S] := \bigcup_{v \in S} \Gamma[v]$. S is *independent* in G if no two vertices of S are adjacent in G. S is *dominating* in G if $\Gamma[S] = V$.

3 k-Consistency Parameterized by k

In this section, we consider the most natural parameterization of k-CONSISTENCY. Theorem 1 shows that the problem is co-W[2]-hard, parameterized by k, and Theorem 2 shows that it is in co-W[2]. These results are also extended to the strong and directional versions of the problem, resulting in Corollary 1, which says that all four problems are co-W[2]-complete when parameterized by k.

Theorem 1. *Parameterized by k, the following problems are* co-W[2]*-hard:* k-CONSISTENCY, STRONG k-CONSISTENCY, DIRECTIONAL k-CONSISTENCY, *and* STRONG DIRECTIONAL k-CONSISTENCY.

Proof. We show a parameterized reduction from INDEPENDENT DOMINATING SET to the complement of k-CONSISTENCY. The INDEPENDENT DOMINATING SET problem was shown to be W[2]-hard by Downey and Fellows [13] (see also [7] where W[2]-completeness is established).

INDEPENDENT DOMINATING SET
Input: A graph $G = (V, E)$ and an integer $k \geq 0$.
Parameter: k.
Question: Is there a set $S \subseteq V$ of size k that is independent and dominating in G?

Let $G = (V, E)$ and $k \geq 0$ be an instance of INDEPENDENT DOMINATING SET. We construct a constraint network $N = (X, D, C)$ as follows. We take $k + 1$ variables and put $X = \{x_1, \ldots, x_{k+1}\}$. For $1 \leq i \leq k + 1$ we put $D(x_i) = V$. The set C contains $\binom{k+1}{2}$ constraints $c_{i,j} = ((x_i, x_j), R_E)$, $1 \leq i < j \leq k + 1$, where $R_E = \{ (v, u) \in V \times V \mid u \neq v, \{u, v\} \notin E \}$. This completes the definition of the constraint network N.

Claim 1. *G has an independent dominating set of size k if and only if N is not $(k+1)$-consistent.*

We refer to [23] for the proof of Claim 1, which has been omitted here due to space restrictions.

Evidently N can be obtained from G in polynomial time. Thus we have established a parameterized reduction from INDEPENDENT DOMINATING SET to the complement of k-CONSISTENCY. The co-W[2]-hardness of k-CONSISTENCY, parameterized by k, now follows from the W[2]-hardness of INDEPENDENT DOMINATING SET.

The co-W[2]-hardness of STRONG k-CONSISTENCY, parameterized by k, is proved analogously by reducing from the variant of INDEPENDENT DOMINATING SET which asks for an independent dominating set of size *at most* k. This variant is also W[2]-hard, as shown by Downey et al. [16].

To show that the directional versions of the problem are co-W[2]-hard, parameterized by k, we use the same reductions and additionally specify a total ordering of the vertices. We use the total order by increasing indices of the variables, and observe that the variable to which the partial order α cannot be extended is the last variable in this order in both directions of the proof of Claim 1. Thus, this modification of the reductions shows that DIRECTIONAL k-CONSISTENCY and STRONG DIRECTIONAL k-CONSISTENCY are also co-W[2]-hard parameterized by k.

The reductions of Theorem 1 actually show somewhat stronger results, namely that the four problems are co-W[2]-hard when parameterized by $k + \ell$. This follows from the observation that the number of variables in the target problems is $k + 1$. From Theorem 2, the co-W[2]-membership of this parameterization will follow. Thus, the problems are co-W[2]-complete when parameterized by $k + \ell$.

For the co-W[2]-membership proof, we build a multi-tape nondeterministic Turing machine that reaches a final state in $f(k)$ steps, for some function f, if and only if N is not k-consistent. As this reduction needs to be a parameterized reduction, we need avoid that the size of the Turing machine (and the time needed to compute it) depends on $O(|X|^k)$ or $O(d^k)$ terms, which would have been very handy to model constraint scopes and constraint relations. We counter this issue via organizing the states of the NTM in tries. There is a first level of tries to determine whether a certain subset of variables is the scope of some constraint. There is a second level of tries to find out whether a certain partial instantiation is allowed by a constraint relation. A second issue that needs particular attention is the size of the transition table. The number of tapes of the NTM is $d + 4$, and we cannot afford a transition for each combination of characters that the head of each tape might be positioned on. We use Cesati's information hiding trick [4] to avoid this issue, which means that the machine does the computations in such a way that in each state, it knows for most tapes (i.e., all, except a constant number of tapes) which characters are in the cell on which the corresponding head is positioned.

Theorem 2. *Parameterized by k, the following problems are in* co-W[2]*: k-*CONSISTENCY, STRONG k-CONSISTENCY, DIRECTIONAL k-CONSISTENCY, *and* STRONG DIRECTIONAL k-CONSISTENCY.

Proof. Cesati [4] showed that the following parameterized problem is in W[2].

SHORT MULTI-TAPE NTM COMPUTATION
Input: A multi-tape NTM M, a word w on the input alphabet of M, and an integer $k > 0$.
Parameter: k.
Question: Does M accept w in at most k steps?

We reduce the complement of k-CONSISTENCY to SHORT MULTI-TAPE NTM COMPUTATION. Let $(N = (X, D, C), k)$ be an instance for k-CONSISTENCY. We will construct an instance (M, w, k') which is a YES-instance for SHORT MULTI-TAPE NTM COMPUTATION if and only if (N, k) is a NO-instance for k-CONSISTENCY.

Let us describe how $M = (Q, \Gamma, \beta, \$, \Sigma, q_0, F, \sigma)$ operates. M has $d + 4$ tapes, named $Gx, Gd, Gx_k, S, d_1, \ldots, d_d$, and the input word w is empty. Thus, all the information about N is encoded in the states and transitions of M. The tape alphabet of M is $\Gamma = \{\beta, \$\} \cup X \cup D \cup \{T, F, 1, 0\}$.

In the initialization phase, M writes a 'T' symbol on the tapes $d_1, \ldots, d_d$ and it positions the head of each tape on the first blank symbol of this tape. This can be done in one computation step.

In the guess phase, M nondeterministically guesses $x(1), \ldots, x(k) \in X$ such that $x(i) < x(i+1)$ for all $i \in \{1, \ldots, k-2\}$, and it guesses $d(1), \ldots, d(k-1) \in D$. Here, $\leq$ is an arbitrary order on the variables, and $a < b$ means $a \leq b$ and $a \neq b$. It appends $x(1), \ldots, x(k-1)$ to the tape Gx, it appends $d(1), \ldots, d(k-1)$ to the tape Gd, and it appends $x(k)$ to the tape Gx_k. The goal is to make M halt in a final state after a number of steps only depending on k if and only if the partial instantiation α, with $\alpha(x(i)) = d(i), 1 \leq i \leq k-1$, is consistent, but α cannot be consistently extended to $x(k)$. See Figure 1 for a typical content of the tapes during the execution of M.

The remaining states of M are partitioned into $|X|$ parts, one part for each choice of $x(k)$. M reads $x(k)$ on the tape Gx_k and moves to the initial state in the part corresponding to $x(k)$.

Gx:	\$	$x(1)$	$x(2)$	$x(3)$	$\cdots$	$x(k-1)$
Gd:	\$	$d(1)$	$d(2)$	$d(3)$	$\cdots$	$d(k-1)$
Gx_k:	\$	$x(k)$				
S:	\$	0	0	1	$\cdots$	0
d_1:	\$	T	F	F		
d_2:	\$	T				
d_3:	\$	T	F			
$\cdots$						
d_d:	\$	T	F	F		

Fig. 1. A typical content of the tapes during an execution of M (blank symbols are omitted)

On the S tape, M now enumerates all binary 0/1 strings of length $k-1$. The strings in $\{0,1\}^{k-1}$ represent subsets of $\{x(1), \ldots, x(k-1)\}$, i.e., all possible scopes of the constraints that could be violated by the partial instantiation α. For each such binary string, representing a subset X' of $\{x(1), \ldots, x(k-1)\}$, M moves to a state representing X' if there is a constraint with scope X', otherwise it moves to a state calculating the next subset X'. This is achieved by a trie of states; each node of this trie represents a subset X'' of X which is the subset of the first few variables of the scope of some constraint (i.e., X'' represents the prefix of a constraint scope, if we imagine all constraint scopes to be strings of increasing variable names). Thus, the size of this trie does not exceed $O(|C| \cdot |X|)$, and the node corresponding to X' (or the evidence that there is no node corresponding to X') is found in $O(|X'|) = O(k)$ steps. Without loss of generality, we may assume that for each subset of X, there is at most one constraint with that scope; otherwise merge constraints with the same scope. If there is a node representing X', there is a constraint c with scope X'. A trie of states starting at this node represents all tuples that belong to the constraint relation R of c. This trie has size $O(|R| \cdot |X'|)$. Moreover, M can determine in time $O(|X'|)$ whether the tuple t, setting $x(i)$ to $d(i)$ for each i such that $x(i) \in X'$, is in R. If so, it moves to a state representing t, otherwise it moves to a non-accepting state where is loops forever (as the selected partial instantiation α is not consistent). At the state representing t, it appends 'F' to all tapes d_j such that there exists a constraint with scope $X' \cup \{x(k)\}$ and its constraint relation does not contain the tuple setting $x(i)$ to $d(i)$ for each $x(i) \in X'$ and setting $x(k)$ to d_j. Then, it moves to the state computing the next set X'. The machine can only move to a final state if the last symbol on each d_i-tape is 'F', meaning that the calculated partial instantiation $\alpha(x(i)) = d(i), 1 \le i \le k - 1$ is consistent (otherwise the machine loops forever in a non-accepting state), but cannot be consistently extended to $x(k)$ (otherwise some d_i-tape does not end in 'F'), which certifies that (N, k) is a No-instance for k-CONSISTENCY.

The number of states of M is clearly polynomial in $|N| + k$. The transition relation has also polynomial size as we use Cesati's information hiding trick [4], and place the head of the tapes $d_1, \dots, d_d$ always on the first blank symbol, except for the final check of whether M moves into a final state. If the machine can reach a final state, it can reach one in a number of steps which is a function of k only. This proves the co-W[2]-membership of k-CONSISTENCY, parameterized by k.

Checking whether a network is a No-instance for STRONG k-CONSISTENCY can be done by checking whether it is a No-instance for j-CONSISTENCY for some $j \in \{1, \dots, k\}$. Thus, it is sufficient to build k NTMs as we described, one for each value of $j \in \{1, \dots, k\}$, nondeterministically guess the integer j for which N is not j-consistent in case N is a No-instance, and move to the initial state of the jth NTM checking whether N is a No-instance for j-CONSISTENCY. Thus, STRONG k-CONSISTENCY parameterized by k is in co-W[2].

For the directional variants of the problem, the order $\le$ is the one given in the input. It is sufficient to additionally require $x(k)$ to represent a variable that is higher in the order $\le$ than all variables $x(1), \dots, x(k-1)$. Thus, our condition that $x(i) < x(i+1)$ for all $i \in \{1, \dots, k-2\}$ is extended to $i \in \{1, \dots, k-1\}$. We conclude that the parameterizations of DIRECTIONAL k-CONSISTENCY and STRONG DIRECTIONAL k-CONSISTENCY by k are in co-W[2] as well.

From Theorems 1 and 2, we obtain the following corollary.

Corollary 1. *Parameterized by k, the following problems are* co-W[2]*-complete: k-CONSISTENCY, STRONG k-CONSISTENCY, DIRECTIONAL k-CONSISTENCY, and STRONG DIRECTIONAL k-CONSISTENCY.*

As mentioned before, the corollary also holds for the parameterization by $k + \ell$.

4 k-Consistency Parameterized by $k + d$

In our quest to find parameterizations that make local consistency problems tractable, we augment the parameter by the domain size d. We find that, with this parameterization, the problems become co-W[1]-complete. The co-W[1]-hardness follows from a parameterized reduction from INDEPENDENT SET.

Theorem 3. *Parameterized by* $k + d$, *the following problems are hard for* co-W[1]: k-CONSISTENCY, STRONG k-CONSISTENCY, DIRECTIONAL k-CONSISTENCY, *and* STRONG DIRECTIONAL k-CONSISTENCY.

Proof. To show that the complement of k-CONSISTENCY is W[1]-hard, we reduce from INDEPENDENT SET, which is well-known to be W[1]-hard [14].

INDEPENDENT SET
Input: A graph $G = (V, E)$ and an integer $k \geq 0$.
Parameter: k.
Question: Is there an independent set of size k in G?

Let $G = (V, E)$ with $V = \{v_1, \ldots, v_n\}$ and $k \geq 0$ be an instance of INDEPENDENT SET. We construct a constraint network $N = (X, D, C)$ as follows.

The set of variables is $X = \{x_1, \ldots, x_n, c\}$. The set of values is $D = \{0, \ldots, k\}$. The constraint set C contains the constraints

(a) $((x_i, x_j), \{(a, b) : a, b \in \{0, \ldots, k\}$ and $(a = 0$ or $b = 0)\})$, for all $v_i v_j \in E$, constraining at least one of x_i and x_j to take the value 0 if $v_i v_j \in E$,

(b) $((x_i, c), \{(a, b) : a, b \in \{0, \ldots, k\}$ and $(a = 0$ or $a \neq b)\})$, for all $i \in \{1, \ldots, n\}$, constraining c to be set to a value different from j if any x_i is set to $j > 0$, and

(c) $((c), \{(1), \ldots, (k)\})$, restricting the domain of c to $\{1, \ldots, k\}$.

This completes the definition of the constraint network N. See Figure 2 for an illustration of N.

Claim 2. *G has an independent set of size k if and only if N is not $(k + 1)$-consistent.*

To show the ($\Rightarrow$)-direction, suppose $S = \{v_{s(1)}, \ldots, v_{s(k)}\}$ is an independent set in G. Consider the partial instantiation α such that $\alpha(x_{s(i)}) = i$, $i = 1, \ldots, k$. This partial instantiation is consistent, but cannot be consistently extended to c.

To show the ($\Leftarrow$)-direction, suppose α is a consistent partial instantiation of k variables and x is a variable such that α cannot be consistently extended to x. As the only constraint preventing a variable to be set to 0 is the constraint (c) restricting the domain of c to $\{1, \ldots, k\}$, we have that $x = c$. Now, that c cannot take any of the values in $\{1, \ldots, k\}$ is achieved by the constraints of type (b) by having α bijectively map k variables $x_{s(1)}, \ldots, x_{s(k)}$ to the set $\{1, \ldots, k\}$ without violating any constraint. As two distinct vertices can only be assigned values different from 0 each if they are not adjacent, by the constraints of type (a), we have that $\{x_{s(1)}, \ldots, x_{s(k)}\}$ is an independent set of size k. Hence Claim 2 is shown true.

Evidently N can be obtained from G in polynomial time. Thus we have established a parameterized reduction from INDEPENDENT SET to the complement of k-CONSISTENCY with $d = k + 1$. The co-W[1]-hardness of k-CONSISTENCY, parameterized by $k + d$, now follows from the W[1]-hardness of INDEPENDENT SET.

For the co-W[1]-hardness of STRONG k-CONSISTENCY, parameterized by $k + d$, just observe that any partial instantiation of fewer than k variables can be extended to any other variable. Thus, G has an independent set of size k if and only if N is not strongly k-consistent, and the co-W[1]-hardness of STRONG k-CONSISTENCY, parameterized by $k + d$, follows analogously.

For the directional versions of the problem, we use the same reduction and define the ordering in the target problem to be some ordering which has c as its last element. Observing that c is the variable to which the partial instantiation α cannot be extended in both directions of the proof of Claim 2, the co-W[1]-hardness of DIRECTIONAL k-CONSISTENCY and STRONG DIRECTIONAL k-CONSISTENCY, parameterized by $k + d$, follows.

It remains to show co-W[1]-membership, which easily follows from the parameterized reduction from Theorem 2 (we designed the proof of Theorem 2 in such a way that the same parameterized reduction shows co-W[1]-membership for the parameterization by $k + d$).

Theorem 4. *Parameterized by $k + d$, the following problems are in* co-W[1]: k-CONSISTENCY, STRONG k-CONSISTENCY, DIRECTIONAL k-CONSISTENCY, *and* STRONG DIRECTIONAL k-CONSISTENCY.

Proof. Cesati and Di Ianni [6] showed that the following parameterized problem is in W[1] (see also [3] where W[1]-completeness is established for the single-tape version of the problem).

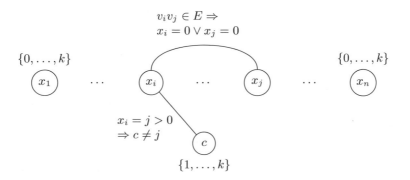

Fig. 2. The target constraint network in the parameterized reduction from INDEPENDENT SET

SHORT BOUNDED-TAPE NTM COMPUTATION
Input: A t-tape NTM M, a word w on the input alphabet of M, and an integer $k > 0$.
Parameter: $k + t$.
Question: Does M accept w in at most k steps?

Now, the proof follows from the proof of Theorem 2, which gives a parameterized reduction from the four problems to SHORT MULTI-TAPE NTM COMPUTATION where the number of tapes is bounded by $d + 4$.

From Theorems 3 and 4, we obtain the following corollary.

Corollary 2. *Parameterized by* $k + d$, *the following problems are* co-W[1] *-complete:* k-CONSISTENCY, STRONG k-CONSISTENCY, DIRECTIONAL k-CONSISTENCY, *and* STRONG DIRECTIONAL k-CONSISTENCY.

5 k-Consistency Parameterized by $k + d + \ell$

We further augment the parameter by ℓ, the maximum number of constraints in which a variable occurs. For this parameterization, we are able to show that the considered problems are fixed-parameter tractable. Bounding both d and ℓ is a reasonable restriction, as it still admits constraint networks whose satisfiability is NP-complete. For instance, determining whether a graph with maximum degree 4 is 3-colorable is an NP-complete problem [22] that can be naturally expressed as a constraint network with $d = 3$ and $\ell = 4$.

For checking whether there is a partial assignment that cannot be extended to a variable x, our FPT algorithm uses the fact that the number of constraints involving x is bounded by a function of the parameter. As constraints with a scope on more than k variables are irrelevant, it follows that the number of variables whose instantiation could prevent x from taking some value can also be bounded by a function of the parameter. For strong k-consistency, these observations are already sufficient to obtain an FPT algorithm as all instantiations of subsets of size at most $k - 1$ of the relevant variables can be enumerated. For (non-strong) k-consistency, the algorithm tries to select some independent variables to complete the consistent partial assignment, which must be of size exactly $k - 1$. If such a set of independent variables does not exist, the size of the considered constraint network is actually bounded by a function of the parameter and can be solved by a brute-force algorithm.

Theorem 5. *Parameterized by* $k + d + \ell$, *the following problems are fixed-parameter tractable:* k-CONSISTENCY, STRONG k-CONSISTENCY, DIRECTIONAL k-CONSISTENCY, *and* STRONG DIRECTIONAL k-CONSISTENCY.

Proof. Consider an input instance $N = (X, D, C)$ for k-CONSISTENCY. In a first step, discard all constraints c with $|var(c)| > k$, as they cannot influence whether N is k-consistent. The algorithm goes over all $|X|$ possibilities for choosing the vertex x to which a consistent partial instantiation α on $k - 1$ variables cannot be extended. If $|X| \leq k \cdot (1 + k \cdot \ell)$, then the number of constraints is at most $|X| \cdot \ell \leq k \cdot (1 + k \cdot \ell) \cdot \ell$ and each constraint has size at most $k \cdot (1 + d^k)$. It follows that

$$|N| \leq k \cdot (1 + k \cdot \ell) + d + (1 + k \cdot \ell) \cdot k^2 \cdot \ell \cdot (1 + d^k).$$

Thus, N is a kernel, i.e., its size is a function of the parameter, and any algorithm solving k-CONSISTENCY for N (brute-force search or Cooper's algorithm [8]) has a running time that can be bounded by a function of the parameter only.

Therefore, suppose $|X| > k \cdot (1 + k \cdot \ell)$. Let $G := \mathcal{G}(N)$ be the Gaifman graph of N. The algorithm chooses a set S of $k - 1$ variables for the scope of α. To do this, it goes over all $\delta = 0, \ldots, k - 1$, where δ represents the number of variables in $S \cap \Gamma(x)$. The number of possibilities for choosing these δ variables is at most $\binom{k \cdot \ell}{\delta}$ as $d(x) \leq k \cdot \ell$. The remaining $k - 1 - \delta$ variables of S need to be chosen from $V \setminus \Gamma[S \cup \{x\}]$. Note that these variables do not influence whether α can be extended to x as they do not occur in a constraint with x. So, it suffices to choose them such that α remains consistent if $\alpha|_{\Gamma(x)}$ was consistent. To do this, the algorithm chooses an independent set of size $k - 1 - \delta$ in $G \setminus \Gamma[S \cup \{x\}]$, which exists and can be obtained greedily due to the lower bound on $|X|$ and because every variable has degree at most $k \cdot \ell$. This terminates the selection of the $k - 1$ variables for the scope of α. The algorithm then goes over all d^{k-1} partial instantiations with scope S. For each such partial instantiation α, check in polynomial time whether it is consistent, and if so, whether it can be consistently extended to x. If any such check finds that α is consistent, but cannot be consistently extended to x, answer NO, otherwise answer YES. This part of the algorithm takes time $2^{k \cdot \ell} \cdot d^{k-1} \cdot |N|^{O(1)}$. We conclude that k-CONSISTENCY, parameterized by $k + d + \ell$, is fixed-parameter tractable.

The algorithm for the STRONG k-CONSISTENCY problem is simpler. After having chosen x, there is no need to consider variables that do not occur in a constraint with x. To choose S, it goes over all subsets of $\Gamma(x)$ of size at most $k - 1$, and proceeds as described above.

To solve the DIRECTIONAL k-CONSISTENCY and STRONG DIRECTIONAL k-CONSISTENCY problems, after having chosen x, the algorithm deletes all variables from N that occur after x in the ordering $\leq$, and it also removes the constraints whose scope contains at least one of the deleted variables. Then, the algorithm proceeds as above.

Using Frick and Grohe's meta-theorem [21], we can extend this result and show that k-CONSISTENCY parameterized by $k+d$ is fixed-parameter tractable for constraint networks whose Gaifman graph (obtained after discarding all constraints on more than k variables) belongs to a graph class of *locally bounded treewidth*. In contrast, if we bound the *average number* $\hat{\ell}$ of constraints in which a variable occurs, then k-CONSISTENCY parameterized by $k + d$ is co-W[1]-complete, as we can use Theorem 3 and bound $\hat{\ell}$ by a padding argument.

Once a local inconsistency in a constraint network is detected, one can add a new (redundant) constraint to the network that excludes this local inconsistency. More specifically, if we detect that a constraint network $N = (X, D, C)$ is not

k-consistent because some partial instantiation α to a set $S = \{x_1, \ldots, x_{k-1}\}$ of variables cannot be extended to some variable x, we add the redundant constraint $((x_1, \ldots, x_{k-1}), D^{k-1} \setminus \{(\alpha(x_1), \ldots, \alpha(x_{k-1}))\})$ to the network. We repeat this process until we end up with a network N^* that is k-consistent. One says that N^* is obtained from N by *enforcing k-consistency* [2]. Similar notions can be defined for strong/directional k-consistency.

It is obvious that the computational task of enforcing k-consistency is at least as hard as deciding k-consistency. Hence, by Theorems 1 and 3, enforcing (strong/directional) k-consistency is co-W[1]-hard when parameterized by $k + d$ and co-W[2]-hard when parameterized by k.

The fixed-parameter tractability result of Theorem 5 does not directly apply to enforcing, since one can construct instances with small d and ℓ that require the addition of a large number of redundant constraints that exceeds any fixed-parameter bound. However, we can obtain fixed-parameter tractability by restricting the enforced network N^*. Let ℓ^* denote the maximum number of constraints in which a variable occurs after k-consistency is enforced. The proof of Theorem 5 shows that enforcing k-consistency is fixed-parameter tractable when parameterized by $k + d + \ell^*$.

6   Conclusion

In recent years numerous computational problems from various areas of computer science have been identified as fixed-parameter tractable or complete for a parameterized complexity class W[i] or co-W[i]. The list includes fundamental problems from combinatorial optimization, logic, and reasoning (see, e.g., Cesati's compendium [5]). Our results place fundamental problems of constraint satisfaction within this complexity hierarchy.

It is perhaps not surprising that the general local consistency problems are fixed-parameter intractable. The drop in complexity from co-W[2] to co-W[1] when we include the domain size as a parameter shows that domain size is of significance for the complexity of local consistency. Somewhat surprising to us is Theorem 5 which shows that under reasonable assumptions there is still hope for fixed-parameter tractability. This result suggests to look for other less restricted cases for which local consistency checking or even enforcing is fixed-parameter tractable.

References

1. Atserias, A., Bulatov, A.A., Dalmau, V.: On the power of k-consistency. In: Arge, L., Cachin, C., Jurdziński, T., Tarlecki, A. (eds.) ICALP 2007. LNCS, vol. 4596, pp. 279–290. Springer, Heidelberg (2007)
2. Bessiere, C.: Constraint propagation. In: Rossi, F., van Beek, P., Walsh, T. (eds.) Handbook of Constraint Programming, ch. 3. Elsevier, Amsterdam (2006)
3. Cai, L., Chen, J., Downey, R.G., Fellows, M.R.: On the parameterized complexity of short computation and factorization. Archive for Mathematical Logic 36(4-5), 321–337 (1997)

4. Cesati, M.: The Turing way to parameterized complexity. Journal of Computer and System Sciences 67, 654–685 (2003)
5. Cesati, M.: Compendium of parameterized problems (September 2006), http://bravo.ce.uniroma2.it/home/cesati/research/compendium.pdf
6. Cesati, M., Ianni, M.D.: Computation models for parameterized complexity. Mathematical Logic Quarterly 43, 179–202 (1997)
7. Chen, Y., Flum, J.: The parameterized complexity of maximality and minimality problems. Annals of Pure and Applied Logic 151(1), 22–61 (2008)
8. Cooper, M.C.: An optimal k-consistency algorithm. Artificial Intelligence 41(1), 89–95 (1989)
9. De La Briandais, R.: File searching using variable length keys. In: IRE-AIEE-ACM 1959 (Western), pp. 295–298. ACM, New York (1959)
10. Dechter, R.: From local to global consistency. Artificial Intelligence 55(1), 87–107 (1992)
11. Dechter, R.: Constraint Processing. Morgan Kaufmann, San Francisco (2003)
12. Dechter, R., Pearl, J.: Network-based heuristics for constraint-satisfaction problems. Artificial Intelligence 34(1), 1–38 (1987)
13. Downey, R.G., Fellows, M.R.: Fixed-parameter tractability and completeness. In: Proceedings of the Twenty-first Manitoba Conference on Numerical Mathematics and Computing (Winnipeg, MB, 1991), vol. 87, pp. 161–178 (1992)
14. Downey, R.G., Fellows, M.R.: Fixed-parameter tractability and completeness. II. On completeness for $W[1]$. Theoretical Computer Science 141(1-2), 109–131 (1995)
15. Downey, R.G., Fellows, M.R.: Parameterized Complexity. Monographs in Computer Science. Springer, New York (1999)
16. Downey, R.G., Fellows, M.R., McCartin, C.: Parameterized approximation problems. In: Bodlaender, H.L., Langston, M.A. (eds.) IWPEC 2006. LNCS, vol. 4169, pp. 121–129. Springer, Heidelberg (2006)
17. Flum, J., Grohe, M.: Parameterized Complexity Theory. Texts in Theoretical Computer Science. An EATCS Series, vol. XIV. Springer, Berlin (2006)
18. Fredkin, E.: Trie memory. Communications of the ACM 3, 490–499 (1960)
19. Freuder, E.C.: Synthesizing constraint expressions. Communications of the ACM 21(11), 958–966 (1978)
20. Freuder, E.C.: A sufficient condition for backtrack-bounded search. Journal of the ACM 32(4), 755–761 (1985)
21. Frick, M., Grohe, M.: Deciding first-order properties of locally tree-decomposable structures. Journal of the ACM 48(6), 1184–1206 (2001)
22. Garey, M.R., Johnson, D.R.: Computers and Intractability. W. H. Freeman and Company, New York (1979)
23. Gaspers, S., Szeider, S.: The parameterized complexity of local consistency. Electronic Colloquium on Computational Complexity (ECCC), Technical Report TR11-071 (2011)
24. Komusiewicz, C., Niedermeier, R., Uhlmann, J.: Deconstructing intractability - a multivariate complexity analysis of interval constrained coloring. Journal of Discrete Algorithms 9(1), 137–151 (2011)
25. Mackworth, A.K.: Consistency in networks of relations. Artificial Intelligence 8, 99–118 (1977)
26. Montanari, U.: Networks of constraints: fundamental properties and applications to picture processing. Information Sciences 7, 95–132 (1974)
27. Niedermeier, R.: Invitation to Fixed-Parameter Algorithms. Oxford Lecture Series in Mathematics and its Applications. Oxford University Press, Oxford (2006)

Symmetry Breaking in Numeric Constraint Problems

Alexandre Goldsztejn[1], Christophe Jermann[1],
Vicente Ruiz de Angulo[2], and Carme Torras[2]

[1] Université de Nantes/CNRS LINA (UMR-6241),
2 rue de la Houssinière, Nantes, F-44300 France
name.surname@univ-nantes.fr
[2] Institut de Robòtica i Informàtica Industrial (CSIC-UPC),
Llorens i Artigas 4-6, 08028-Barcelona, Spain
surname@iri.upc.edu

Abstract. Symmetry-breaking constraints in the form of inequalities between variables have been proposed for a few kind of solution symmetries in numeric CSPs. We show that, for the variable symmetries among those, the proposed inequalities are but a specific case of a relaxation of the well-known LEX constraints extensively used for discrete CSPs. We discuss the merits of this relaxation and present experimental evidences of its practical interest.

Keywords: Symmetries, Numeric constraints, Variable symmetries.

1 Introduction

Numeric constraint solvers are nowadays beginning to be competitive and even to outperform, in some cases, classical methods for solving systems of equations and inequalities over the reals. As a consequence, their application has raised interest in fields as diverse as neurophysiology and economics [18], biochemistry, crystallography, robotics [13] and, more generally, in those related to global optimization [9]. Symmetries naturally occur in many of these applications, and it is advisable to exploit them in order to reduce the search space and, thus, to increase the efficiency of the solvers.

Considerable work on symmetry breaking has been performed for discrete Constraint Satisfaction Problems (CSPs) in the last decades [7,19]. Two main symmetry-breaking strategies have been pursued: 1) to devise specialized search algorithms that avoid symmetric portions of the search space [14,8]; and 2) to add *symmetry-breaking constraints* (SBCs) that filter out redundant subspaces [5,16]. Contrarily to this, there exists very little work on symmetry breaking for numerical problems. For cyclic variables permutations, an approach divides the initial space into boxes and eliminates symmetric ones before the solving starts [17]. The addition of SBCs has also been proposed, but only for specific problems or specific symmetry classes, as inequalities between variables [6,11,3].

In Section 2, we show that such inequalities are but a relaxation of the lexicographic-ordering based SBCs [4] widely used by the discrete CSP community. This relaxation allows us to generalize these previous works to any variable symmetry and can be derived automatically knowing the symmetries of a problem. In Section 3 we discuss its

J. Lee (Ed.): CP 2011, LNCS 6876, pp. 317–324, 2011.

merits with respect to lexicographic-ordering based SBCs. In Section 4 we assess its practical interest. We provide tracks for future developments in Section 5.

2   Symmetry-Breaking Constraints for NCSPs

We are interested in solving the following general *Numeric Constraint Satisfaction Problem* (NCSP) (X, D, C): Find all points $X = (x_1, \ldots, x_n) \in D \subseteq \mathbb{R}^n$ satisfying the constraint $C(X)$, a relation on $\mathbb{R}^n$, typically a conjunction of non-linear equations and inequalities.

A function $s : \mathbb{R}^n \to \mathbb{R}^n$ is a *symmetry* of a NCSP if it maps bijectively solutions to solutions[1], i.e., for all $X \in D$ such that $C(X)$ holds, $s(X) \in D$ and $C(s(X))$ also holds. In this case, we say X and $s(X)$ are *symmetric solutions*, and by extension for any point $Y \in D$, $s(Y)$ is a *symmetric point*. We consider only symmetries that are permutations of variables. Let $\mathcal{S}_n$ be the set of all permutations of $\{1, \ldots, n\}$. The image of i by a permutation σ is i^σ, and σ is described by $[1^\sigma, 2^\sigma, \ldots, n^\sigma]$. A symmetry s is a *variable symmetry* iff there is a $\sigma \in \mathcal{S}_n$ such that for any $X \in D$, $s(X) = (x_{1^\sigma}, \ldots, x_{n^\sigma})$. We identify such symmetries with their associated permutations and denote both by σ in the following. Consequently, the set of variable symmetries of a NCSP is isomorphic to a permutation subgroup of $\mathcal{S}_n$, which are both identified and denoted by Σ in the following.

Example 1. The 3-cyclic roots problem is: find all $(x_1, x_2, x_3) \in \mathbb{R}^3$ satisfying $(x_1 + x_2 + x_3 = 0) \wedge (x_1 x_2 + x_2 x_3 + x_3 x_1 = 0) \wedge (x_1 x_2 x_3 = 1)$. This problem has six variable symmetries including identity, $\Sigma = \{[1, 2, 3], [1, 3, 2], [2, 1, 3], [2, 3, 1], [3, 1, 2], [3, 2, 1]\}$. Hence, all its variables are interchangeable. ◇

We say that the symmetries of a CSP are completely broken when a single representative in each set of symmetric solutions is retained. To this end, it is possible to add *symmetry-breaking constraints* (SBCs) which will exclude all but a single representative of the symmetric solutions [7,19]. Crawford *et al.* [4] proposed *lexicographic ordering constraints* (LEX) that completely break any variable symmetry. Recall that given X and Y both in $\mathbb{R}^n$ the lexicographic order is defined inductively as follows:

for $n = 1$, $\quad X \preceq_{lex} Y \equiv (x_1 \leq y_1)$

for $n > 1$, $\quad X \preceq_{lex} Y \equiv (x_1 < y_1) \vee \left((x_1 = y_1) \wedge (X_{2:n} \preceq_{lex} Y_{2:n}) \right)$

where $X_{2:n} = (x_2, \ldots, x_n)$, and the same for Y. For a given symmetry σ, Crawford *et al.* define the corresponding SBC $\mathrm{LEX}_\sigma(X) \equiv X \preceq_{lex} \sigma(X)$. Intuitively, this constraint imposes a total order on the symmetric solutions, hence allowing to retain a single one w.r.t. a given symmetry σ. One such constraint is thus imposed for each of the symmetries of a problem in order to break them all. The strength of these constraints is that they reduce the search space by a factor equal to $\#\Sigma$, the order of the symmetry group Σ of the problem. One critical issue however is that the number of SBCs can be exponential with respect to the number of variables.

---

[1] Nothing is required for non-solution points, i.e., we consider *solution symmetries* [1].

Example 2. Excluding the identity permutation, a symmetry of any problem which is irrelevant to break, the LEX constraints for the symmetries of the 3-cyclic-roots problem are: $(x_1, x_2, x_3) \preceq_{lex} (x_1, x_3, x_2)$, $(x_1, x_2, x_3) \preceq_{lex} (x_2, x_1, x_3)$, $(x_1, x_2, x_3) \preceq_{lex} (x_2, x_3, x_1)$, $(x_1, x_2, x_3) \preceq_{lex} (x_3, x_1, x_2)$, and $(x_1, x_2, x_3) \preceq_{lex} (x_3, x_2, x_1)$.   ◇

Since they offer a good trade-off between the solving time reduction they allow, and the difficulty to handle them, *partial SBCs* (PSBCs), that retain *at least* one representative of the symmetric solutions, have often been considered. Especially for NC-SPs, several classes of variable symmetries have been broken using PSBCs having the form of inequalities between variables. For instance, Gasca *et al.* [6] proposed PSBCs $x_i \leq x_{i+1}$ ($i \in \{1, \ldots, n-1\}$) for full permutations ($\Sigma = \mathcal{S}_n$), and PSBCs $x_1 \leq x_i$ ($i \in \{2, \ldots, n\}$) for cyclic permutations ($\Sigma = \mathcal{C}_n)^2$. Similar PSBCs have been proposed for numeric optimization problems with more peculiar symmetry groups, e.g., $\Sigma = \mathcal{C}_2 \times \mathcal{S}_n$ in [3] and $\Sigma = \prod_i \mathcal{S}_{p_i}$ in [11].

Example 3. Considering again the 3-cyclic-roots problem, Gasca *et al.*'s PSBCs are: $x_1 \leq x_2$ and $x_2 \leq x_3$. Indeed, these inequalities filter out all but a single of the six symmetries of any solution to this problem.   ◇

The corner stone of our approach is to note that all the PSBCs mentioned above can be obtained by relaxing Crawford's SBCs as follows: For $\sigma \in \mathcal{S}_n$ different from the identity permutation, and $X = (x_1, \ldots, x_n)$, we define the constraint RLEX$_\sigma(X) \equiv x_{k_\sigma} \leq x_{k_\sigma{}^\sigma}$, where k_σ is the smallest integer in $\{1, \ldots, n\}$ such that $k_\sigma \neq k_\sigma{}^\sigma$. The following proposition establishes that this constraint is a relaxation of a LEX constraint, i.e., a PSBC: it cannot remove any solution preserved by LEX constraint.

Proposition 1. LEX$_\sigma(X) \Longrightarrow$ RLEX$_\sigma(X)$

Proof. Since $i < k_\sigma$ implies $i = i^\sigma$, we have $x_i = x_{i^\sigma}$ for all $i < k_\sigma$. Therefore LEX$_\sigma(X)$, which is $X \preceq_{lex} \sigma(X)$, is actually equivalent to $X_{k_\sigma:n} \preceq_{lex} \sigma(X)_{k_\sigma:n}$, i.e.,

$$\left(x_{k_\sigma} < x_{k_\sigma{}^\sigma}\right) \vee \left(\left(x_{k_\sigma} = x_{k_\sigma{}^\sigma}\right) \wedge \left(X_{k_\sigma+1:n} \preceq_{lex} \sigma(X)_{k_\sigma+1:n}\right)\right),$$

which logically implies $\left(x_{k_\sigma} < x_{k_\sigma{}^\sigma}\right) \vee \left(x_{k_\sigma} = x_{k_\sigma{}^\sigma}\right)$, that is RLEX$_\sigma(X)$.   □

The ad-hoc inequalities proposed so far to partially break specific classes of variable symmetries in NCSPs are just special cases of the RLEX constraints. For instance, when $\Sigma = \mathcal{S}_n$, Gasca *et al.*'s PSBCs are $x_i \leq x_{i+1}$ ($i \in \{1, \ldots, n-1\}$) [6]. In this case, k_σ takes all possible values in $\{1, \ldots, n-1\}$ and $k_\sigma{}^\sigma$ all possible values in $\{k_\sigma+1, \ldots, n\}$. Hence the corresponding RLEX constraints are $x_i \leq x_j$ ($i < j$). Since all the inequalities $x_i \leq x_j$ with $i+1 < j$ among them are redundant, they can be eliminated, yielding the inequalities proposed by Gasca *et al.*. A similar verification is easily carried out for the other specific variables symmetries tackled in [6,3,11]. Hence, RLEX constraints generalize these PSBCs to any variable symmetries.

Example 4. Continuing Example 2, the corresponding RLEX constraints are respectively: $x_2 \leq x_3$, $x_1 \leq x_2$, $x_1 \leq x_2$, $x_1 \leq x_3$ and $x_1 \leq x_3$. This set of inequalities can be simplified to $x_1 \leq x_2$ and $x_2 \leq x_3$, i.e., that presented in Example 3.   ◇

---

^{2} $\mathcal{C}_n = \{[k, \ldots, n, 1, \ldots, k-1] : k \in \{1, \ldots, n\}\}$.

3   RLEX VS LEX

Advantages. First, we draw the reader's attention to the simplicity of the relaxed constraints w.r.t. the original ones: RLEX constraints are just binary inequalities while LEX constraints involve all the variables of the symmetries in a large combination of logical operations. Hence, we expect it is much more efficient to prune RLEX constraints (no specific algorithm is required) and to propagate the obtained reductions (successful reductions trigger only constraints depending on two variables), than LEX constraints.

Second, and more prominently, the number of RLEX constraint is always smaller than the number of LEX constraints, and it is bounded upward by $\frac{n(n-1)}{2}$ (number of different pairs (x_i, x_j) with $i < j$), or only $n-1$ if one considers a non-redundant subset of inequalities as we explained previously. In contrast, there can be exponentially many LEX constraints, one for each permutation in $\mathcal{S}_n$. As remarked by Crawford *et al.*, this makes the use of LEX constraints impractical in general and has yielded research towards simplifying and relaxing them [4]. Oppositely, adding $O(n)$ RLEX constraints to a CSP model should never be a problem for its practical treatment by a solver.

Similar constraints $x_{k_\sigma} < x_{k_\sigma}{}^\sigma$ were proposed by Puget in [15] as SBCs for (discrete) problems where the variables are subject to an all different constraint. It is thus possible to obtain the RLEX constraints without having to compute all LEX constraints by applying the group theory results already used by Puget: From a generating set of the symmetries Σ of a problem, it is possible to derive a *stabilizer chain*, i.e., a sequence of permutation subgroups such that each is contained in the preceding and the permutations in the ith subgroup map all integers in $\{1, \ldots, i\}$ to themselves. The orbit of the integer $i + 1$ in the ith subgroup, i.e., all the integers it can be mapped to by any permutation in this subgroup, thus define exactly the pairs for which we must impose an inequality. These pairs can be obtained with the Shreier-Sims algorithm which runs in $O(n^2 \log^3(\#\Sigma) + tn\log(\#\Sigma))$, where t is the cardinality of the input generating set[3]. Since $\#\Sigma$ is at most $n!$ (when $\Sigma = \mathcal{S}_n$), this algorithm runs in polynomial time in n and t.

Hence, RLEX constraints constitute a generalization of the inequalities proposed so far for NCSPs that remains of tractable size and can be computed in polynomial time for any variable symmetries.

Drawbacks. The RLEX constraints break only partially the symmetries that LEX constraints break completely. Let us describe more precisely symmetric solutions which are discarded by LEX but not by RLEX.

Given a symmetry σ and a solution $X = (x_1, \ldots, x_n)$, if $\sigma(X)$ is discarded by the corresponding LEX constraint, it means that there exists i such that $x_i < x_{i^\sigma}$ and $\forall j \in \{1, \ldots, i-1\}$, $x_j = x_{j^\sigma}$. If $\sigma(X)$ is not discarded by the corresponding RLEX constraint $x_{k_\sigma} \leq x_{k_\sigma}{}^\sigma$, it means that $k_\sigma < i$. Thus, $x_{k_\sigma} = x_{k_\sigma}{}^\sigma$ while $k_\sigma \neq k_\sigma{}^\sigma$ by definition, i.e., X must lie on a given hyperplane $H_{uv} = \{X | x_u = x_v\}$.

Hence, all the symmetric solutions that are discarded by LEX constraints (w.r.t. all the symmetries of the problem) but not by RLEX constraints belong to such hyperplanes. Because the volume of these hyperplanes is null in $\mathbb{R}^n$, the set of points filtered out

---

[3] A minimal generating set is $O(n)$ for any subgroup of variable symmetries.

by LEX constraints and preserved by RLEX constraints represents a null volume of the search space. We conclude that RLEX constraints reduce the search space volume by a factor $\#\Sigma$ identical to that achieved with LEX constraints.

Moreover, numerical constraint solvers cannot eliminate these *singular* symmetric solutions even with LEX constraints since they do not distinguish strict and non-strict inequalities. Indeed, they perform computations using intervals and thus cannot approximate open sets differently from closed ones.

In conclusion, since the aim of PSBCs is essentially to enhance the solvers performances by allowing quick and easy reduction of the search space, it appears RLEX constraints are a very good trade-off between simplicity and efficiency: they are easy to derive, simple to handle, and still filter out most of the symmetric search space.

4 Experimental Results

We provide experimental evidences of the important performance gains RLEX constraints can bring when solving symmetric NCSPs. Indeed, the solving time of a given NCSP is in general proportional to its search space. We expect RLEX constraints allow to quickly eliminate large portions of the search space, isolating an asymmetric sub-search space whose volume is divided by $\#\Sigma$ w.r.t. the initial search space. As a result, we expect to observe computation time gains proportional to $\#\Sigma$.

All experiments are conducted on a dual-core equipped machine (2.5GHz, 4Gb RAM) using the Realpaver [10] constraint solver with default settings.

Preliminary analysis: We first consider homemade scalable problems whose solutions either lie outside any hyperplane H_{uv} (problems P_1, P_2), all lie on such hyperplanes (problems P_3, P_4), or lie at the intersection of all these hyperplanes (problems P_5, P_6). In all cases, we consider problems with only cyclic permutations (P_1, P_3, P_5) and others with full permutations (P_2, P_4, P_6), i.e., problems for which the volume of the asymmetric search space is $\frac{1}{n}$ and $\frac{1}{n!}$ of that of the initial search-space respectively :

P_1 : $X \in [-n,n]^n, \prod_{\sigma \in \mathcal{C}_n} ||\sigma(X) - X^*|| - 0$

P_2 : $X \in [-n,n]^n, \prod_{\sigma \subset S_n} ||\sigma(X) - X^*|| = 0$

P_3 : $X \in [-2,2]^n, \prod_{j=1}^n (\sum_{i=1}^n (x_{((i+j) \bmod n)} + (-1)^i)^2) = 0$

P_4 : $X =\in [0,1]^n, \forall i \in 1..n \ \sum_{j\neq i} x_j^2 + x_i \cos(\sum_{j=1}^n x_j) = 0$

P_5 : $X \in [-2,2]^n, \sum_{i=1}^n (x_i^2 - 1)^2 = 0$

P_6 : $X \in [0,1]^n, \forall i \in 1..n \ \sum_{j=1}^{n-1} (\prod_{l=1}^{n-1} x_{(i+j+l) \bmod n}) = 1$

where X^* is the point $(1,\dots,n) \in \mathbb{R}^n$. The solutions of P_1 are all cyclic permutations of X^* while that of P_2 are all permutations of X^*. The solutions of P_3 are the cyclic permutations[4] of $(-1,1,\dots,-1,1) \in \mathbb{R}^n$; that of P_4 are all points of the form $\{-1,1\}^n$. P_5 and P_6 both have a single (very symmetric) solution: 0^n.

---

[4] Note there are only 2 different solutions when n is even, n solutions when it is odd.

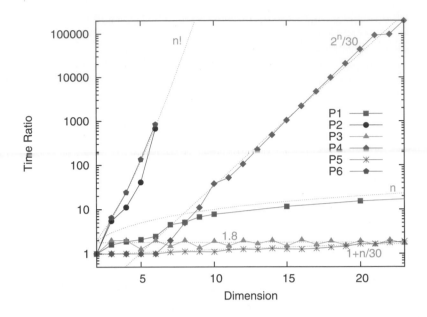

Fig. 1. Time ratios for homemade problems

Figure 1 presents the variation of the ratio between the computation time without RLEX and the computation time with it (called *gain* in the following) when the dimension n varies. In addition to the measured gains, the figure displays (in dotted gray) the functions of n that best approximate them.

The gains for P_1 and P_2 follow very closely the reduction factor of their search space volume, hence confirming our expectations. Note that although the gains are not as impressive for P_1 as for P_2, they are already significant: E.g., for $n = 50$ the computation time is 1124s (> 18min) without RLEX and 29s with RLEX. For P_2 they are really outstanding: E.g., for $n = 6$, the computations time is 12863s (> 3.5h) without RLEX but only 19s with RLEX.

For the other problems, the results are more varied: P_3 presents only an (almost) constant gain; P_4 shows a gain closer to the reduction factor of the size of its solution set than to its search space volume reduction factor; P_5 offers a (quite flat) linear gain, i.e., proportional to its search space volume reduction factor; the gain for P_6 follows closely its search space volume reduction factor[5]. The factors that could explain this diversity of behaviors are numerous (e.g., relative pruning power of the original constraints w.r.t. the added PSBCs, proportion of symmetric solutions with and without RLEX, ...). Further experiments will be necessary to distinguish the exact effects of all these factors.

The conclusion we draw from these results is that one cannot always expect as much gain as the search space volume reduction factor, especially when the problem has *singular* solutions; still, the gains can be outstanding, and adding RLEX constraints did not induce any uncompensated overhead in any of the settings we have considered.

---

[5] Computations for P_6 could not be performed further because the timings were becoming too large, e.g., 41751s (> 11.5h) for $n = 6$ without RLEX, as compared to 49.5s with it.

Table 1. Results for various problems from the literature

Problem	n	Sol	$\#\Sigma$	Time w/RLEX	Time w RLEX	gain
Brown	5	S	$n!$	0.95	0.24	3.9
	8			1218	5.32	229.0
Cyclic	4	GS*	$2n$	260	32.1	8.1
roots	5	S		46.6	4.7	9.7
	6	S		2017	183	10.9
Cyclohexane	3	S	$n!$	0.24	0.16	1.5
Extended	20	S	$\frac{n}{2}!$	0.41	0.26	1.6
Freudenstein	140			422	315	1.3
Extended	16	S	$n\frac{n}{2}!$	1.42	0.03	47.3
Powell	30			844	0.1	8442.0
Feigenbaum	11	GS	n	7.30	0.81	9.0
	23			10924	1027	10.6

Standard benchmark: We also consider a benchmark composed of standard problems picked from [2]. Their characteristics and the results obtained are reported in Table 1. For scalable problems we report timings for the smallest and largest dimension n we tested, allowing one to imagine the gain variation with the dimension. Column "Sol" indicates the type of solutions of the problem: G=Generic (i.e., out of any hyperplane H_{uv}) and S=Singular. Note that most of these standard problems are of type S. Problem *4-cyclic-roots* is marked GS^* because this problem has a continuous solution set which intersects some H_{uv} hyperplanes. For this problem, timings correspond to paving its solution manifold with 10^{-2}-wide boxes.

For problems *Brown*, *Cyclic-roots* and *Extended-Powell*, the gain closely follows the search space volume reduction factor (column $\#\Sigma$). Still, for problems *Extended-Freudenstein* and *Feigenbaum* the gains remain almost constant as the dimension grows. These experiments support the preliminary analysis we have performed: We can achieve important gains for highly symmetric problems and the introduction of RLEX constraints at least does not appear counterproductive.

5   Conclusion and Future Prospects

We have presented a generalization of the PSBCs proposed so far for variable symmetries in NCSPs. It corresponds to a relaxation of the famous LEX constraints used for breaking symmetries essentially for discrete CSPs so far. We have discussed the merits of this relaxation w.r.t. LEX constraints and illustrated its practical interest for NCSPs.

All the arguments we have used are also valid for continuous optimization and constrained optimization problems. Considering that many of them are not specific to numeric problems or solvers, it would also be interesting to consider this relaxation in discrete domains. Hence, we should also consider Mixed-Integer Linear/Nonlinear Programming and Integer Linear Programming where some of the PSBCs we have generalized have been proposed [3,12].

References

1. Cohen, D., Jeavons, P., Jefferson, C., Petrie, K., Smith, B.: Symmetry definitions for constraint satisfaction problems. Constraints 11(2-3), 115–137 (2006)
2. COPRIN: The inria project COPRIN examples webpage (2011),
   http://www-sop.inria.fr/coprin/logiciels/ALIAS/Benches/
3. Costa, A., Liberti, L., Hansen, P.: Formulation symmetries in circle packing. Electronic Notes in Discrete Mathematics 36, 1303–1310 (2010)
4. Crawford, J., Ginsberg, M., Luks, E., Roy, A.: Symmetry-breaking predicates for search problems. In: KR, pp. 148–159 (1996)
5. Flener, P., Frisch, A., Hnich, B., Kiziltan, Z., Miguel, I.: Breaking row and column symmetries in matrix models. In: Van Hentenryck, P. (ed.) CP 2002. LNCS, vol. 2470, pp. 462–476. Springer, Heidelberg (2002)
6. Gasca, R., Valle, C.D., Cejudo, V., Barba, I.: Improving the computational efficiency in symmetrical numeric constraint satisfaction problems. In: Marín, R., Onaindía, E., Bugarín, A., Santos, J. (eds.) CAEPIA 2005. LNCS (LNAI), vol. 4177, pp. 269–279. Springer, Heidelberg (2006)
7. Gent, I., Petrie, K., Puget, J.-F.: Symmetry in constraint programming. In: Handbook of Constraint Programming, pp. 329–376. Elsevier, Amsterdam (2006)
8. Gent, I.P.: Groups and constraints: Symmetry breaking during search. In: Van Hentenryck, P. (ed.) CP 2002. LNCS, vol. 2470, pp. 415–430. Springer, Heidelberg (2002)
9. Goldsztejn, A., Lebbah, Y., Michel, C., Rueher, M.: Capabilities of constraint programming in safe global optimization. In: International Symposium on Nonlinear Theory and its Applications, pp. 601–604 (2008)
10. Granvilliers, L., Benhamou, F.: Algorithm 852: Realpaver: an interval solver using constraint satisfaction techniques. ACM T. on Mathematical Software 32, 138–156 (2006)
11. Ji, X., Ma, F., Zhang, J.: Solving global unconstrained optimization problems by symmetry-breaking. In: 8th IEEE/ACIS International Conference on Computer and Information Science, pp. 107–111 (2009)
12. Margot, F.: Symmetry in integer linear programming. In: 50 Years of Integer Programming 1958-2008, pp. 647–686. Springer, Heidelberg (2010)
13. Merlet, J.-P.: Interval analysis for certified numerical solution of problems in robotics. Applied Mathematics and Computer Science 19(3), 399–412 (2009)
14. Meseguer, P., Torras, C.: Exploiting symmetries within constraint satisfaction search. Artif. Intell. 129(1-2), 133–163 (2001)
15. Puget, J.F.: Breaking symmetries in all different problems. In: Proc. 19th International Joint Conference on Artificial Intelligence (IJCAI), pp. 272–277 (2005)
16. Puget, J.-F.: Symmetry breaking revisited. Constraints 10(1), 23–46 (2005)
17. Ruiz de Angulo, V., Torras, C.: Exploiting single-cycle symmetries in continuous constraint problems. Journal of Artificial Intelligence Research 34, 499–520 (2009)
18. Vu, X.H., Schichl, H., Sam-Haroud, D.: Interval propagation and search on directed acyclic graphs for numerical constraint solving. J. Global Optimization 45(4), 499–531 (2009)
19. Walsh, T.: Parameterized complexity results in symmetry breaking. In: Raman, V., Saurabh, S. (eds.) IPEC 2010. LNCS, vol. 6478, pp. 4–14. Springer, Heidelberg (2010)

On Minimal Constraint Networks*

Georg Gottlob

Computer Science Department and Oxford Man Institute,
University of Oxford - Oxford OX1 3QD UK
gottlob@cs.ox.ac.uk

Abstract. In a minimal binary constraint network, every tuple of a constraint relation can be extended to a solution. It was conjectured that computing a solution
to such a network is NP hard. We prove this conjecture. We also prove a conjecture by Dechter and Pearl stating that for $k \geq 2$ it is NP-hard to decide whether
a constraint network can be decomposed into an equivalent k-ary constraint network, and study related questions.

1 Introduction

In his seminal 1974 paper [11], Montanari introduced the concept of *minimal constraint
network*. Roughly, a minimal network is a constraint network where each partial instantiation corresponding to a tuple of a constraint relation can be extended to a solution.
Each arbitrary binary network N having variables $\{X_1, \ldots, X_v\}$ can be transformed
into an equivalent binary minimal network $M(N)$ by computing the set $sol(N)$ of all
solutions to N and creating for $1 \leq i < j \leq v$ a constraint c_{ij} whose scope is (X_i, X_j)
and whose constraint relation consists of the projection of $sol(N)$ to (X_i, X_j). The
minimal network $M(N)$ is unique and its solutions are exactly those of the original
network, i.e., $sol(N) = sol(M(N))$.

Obviously, $M(N)$, which can be considered a heavily pruned compiled version of N,
is hard to compute. However, with $M(N)$ at hand, we can answer a number of queries
in polynomial time that would otherwise be NP hard. Typically, these are queries that
involve one or two variables only, for example, "Is there a solution for which $X_5 < 8$?"
or "what is the maximal value of X_3 such that X_7 is minimized?". In applications such
as computer-supported interactive product configuration, such queries arise frequently,
but it would be useful to be able to exhibit at the same time a full solution together with
the query answer, that is, an assignment of values to all variables witnessing this answer.
It was even unclear if it is tractable to compute an arbitrary single solution on the basis of $M(N)$. Gaur [7] formulated this as an open problem. He showed that a stronger
version of the problem, where solutions restricted by specific value assignments to a
pair of variables are sought, is NP hard, but speculated that finding arbitrary solutions
could be tractable. However, since the introduction of minimal networks in 1974, no
one came up with a polynomial-time algorithm for this task. This led Dechter to conjecture that this problem is hard [4]. Note that this problem deviates in two ways from

---

* Future improvements and extended versions of this paper will be published in CORR
  at http://arxiv.org/abs/1103.1604

J. Lee (Ed.): CP 2011, LNCS 6876, pp. 325–339, 2011.
© Springer-Verlag Berlin Heidelberg 2011

classical decision problems: First, it is a search problem rather than a decision problem, and second, it is a *promise problem*, where it is "promised" that the input networks, which constitute our problem instances, are indeed minimal — a promise whose verification is itself NP-hard (see Section 4.1). We therefore have to clarify what is meant by NP-hardness, when referring to such problems. The simplest and probably cleanest definition is the following: The problem is NP hard if any polynomial algorithms solving it would imply the existence of a polynomial-time algorithm for NP-hard decision problems, and would thus imply NP=P. In the light of this, we can formulate Dechter's conjecture as follows:

Conjecture 1 (Dechter[4]). *Unless P=NP, computing a single solution to a non-empty minimal constraint network cannot be done in polynomial time.*

While the problem has interested a number of researchers, it has not been solved until recently. Some progress was made by Bessiere in 2006. In his well-known handbook article "Constraint Propagation" [1], he used results of Cros [2] to show that no backtracking-free algorithm for computing a solution from a minimal network can exist unless the Polynomial Hierarchy collapses to its second level (more precisely, until $\Sigma_2^p = \Pi_2^p$). However, this does not mean that the problem is intractable. A backtrack-free algorithm according to Bessiere must be able to recognize *each* partial assignment that is extensible to a solution. In a sense, such an algorithm, even if it computes only one solution, must have the potential to compute all solutions just by changing the choices of the variable-instantiations made at the different steps. In more colloquial terms, backtrack-free algorithms according to Bessiere must be *fair to all solutions*. Bessiere's result does not preclude the existence of a less general algorithm that computes just one solution, while being unable to recognize all partial assignments, and thus unfair to some solutions.

In the first part of this paper, we prove Dechter's conjecture by showing that every polynomial-time search algorithm A that computes a single solution to a minimal network can be transformed into a polynomial-time decision algorithm A^* for the classical satisfiability problem 3SAT. The proof is carried-out in Section 3. We first show that each SAT instance can be transformed in polynomial time into an equivalent one that is highly symmetric (Section 3.1). Such symmetric instances, which we call *k-supersymmetric*, are then polynomially reduced to the problem of computing a solution to a minimal binary constraint network (Section 3.2). The minimal networks in the proof, however, have an unbounded number of domain values. We further consider the case of bounded domains, that is, when the input instances are such that the cardinality of the overall domain of all values that may appear in the constraint relation is bounded by some fixed constant c. We show that even in the bounded domain case, the problem of computing a single solution remains NP-hard (Section 3.3).

In Section 4, we deal with problems of network minimality checking and structure identification. In Section 4.1, we generalize and slightly strengthen a result by Gaur [7] by showing that it is NP hard to determine whether a k-ary network is minimal, even in case of bounded domains. Then, in Section 4.2, we study the complexity of checking whether a network N consisting of a single constraint relation (typically of arity $\geq k$) can be represented by an equivalent k-ary constraint network. Note that this is precisely the case iff there exists a k-ary minimal network for N. Dechter and Pearl [5] conjectured that this problem is NP-hard for $k \geq 2$. We prove this conjecture.

The paper is concluded in Section 5 by a brief discussion of the practical significance of our main result, a proposal for the enhancement of minimal networks, and a hint at possible future research.

2   Preliminaries and Basic Definitions

While most of the definitions in this section are adapted from the standard literature on constraint satisfaction, in particular [4,1], we sometimes use a slightly different notation which is more convenient for our purposes.

Constraints, networks, and solutions. A *k-ary constraint* c is a tuple $(scope(c), rel(c))$. The scope $scope(c)$ of c is a sequence of k variables $scope(c) = (X_{i_1}, \ldots, X_{i_k})$, where each variable X_{i_j} has an associated finite domain $dom(X_{i_j})$. The relation $rel(c)$ of c is a subset of the Cartesian product $dom(X_{i_1}) \times dom(X_{i_2}) \times \cdots \times dom(X_{i_k})$. The arity $arity(c)$ of a constraint c is the number of variables in $scope(c)$. The set $\{X_{i_1}, \ldots, X_{i_k}\}$ of all variables occurring in constraint c is denoted by $var(c)$.

A *Constraint Network* N consists of

- a finite set of variables $var(N) = \{X_1, \ldots, X_v\}$ with associated domains $dom(X_i)$ for $1 \leq i \leq v$, and
- a set of constraints $cons(N) = \{c_1, \ldots, c_m\}$, where for $1 \leq i \leq m$, $var(c_i) \subseteq var(N)$.

The *domain* $dom(N)$ of a constraint network N as defined above consists of the union of all variable domains: $dom(N) = \bigcup_{X \in var(N)} dom(X)$. The *schema* of N is the set $schema(N) = \{scope(c) | c \in cons(N)\}$ of all scopes of the constraints of N. We call N *binary* (*k-ary*) if $arity(c) = 2$ ($arity(c) = k$) for each constraint $c \in cons(N)$.

Let N be a constraint network. An *instantiation mapping* for a set of variables $W \subseteq var(N)$ is a mapping $W \longrightarrow dom(W)$, such that for each $X \in var(N)$, $\theta(X) \in dom(X)$. We call $\theta(W)$ an *instantiation* of W. An instantiation of a proper subset W of $var(N)$ is called a *partial instantiation* while an instantiation of $var(N)$ is called a *full instantiation* (also *total instantiation*). A constraint c of N is *satisfied* by an instantiation mapping $\theta : W \longrightarrow dom(W)$ if whenever $var(c) \subseteq W$, then $\theta(scope(c)) \in rel(c)$. An instantiation mapping $\theta : W \longrightarrow dom(W)$ is *consistent* if it is satisfied by all constraints. By abuse of terminology, in case θ is understood and is consistent, then we also say that $\theta(W)$ is consistent. A *solution* to a constraint network N is a consistent full instantiation for N. The set of all solutions of N is denoted by $sol(N)$. Whenever useful, we will identify the solution set $sol(N)$ with a single constraint whose scope is $var(N)$ and whose relation consists of all tuples in $sol(N)$. We assume without loss of generality, that for each set of variables $W \subseteq var(N)$ of a constraint network, there exists at most one constraint c such that the variables occurring in $scope(c)$ are precisely those of W. (In fact, if there are two or more constraints with exactly the same variables in the scope, an equivalent single constraint can always be obtained by intersecting the constraint relations.)

Complete networks. We call a k-ary constraint network N *complete*, if for each set U of k of variables, there is a constraint c such that $U = var(c)$. For each fixed constant k, each k-ary constraint network N can be transformed by a trivial polynomial reduction into an equivalent complete k-ary network N^+ with $sol(N) = sol(N^+)$. In fact, for each set $U = \{X_{i_1}, \ldots, X_{i_k}\}$ that is in no scope of N, we may just add the trivial constraint $\top_U$ with $scope(\top_U) = (X_{i_1}, \ldots, X_{i_k})$ and $rel(\top_U) = dom(X_{i_1}) \times dom(X_{i_2}) \times dom(X_{i_k})$. For this reason, we may, without loss of generality, restrict our attention to complete networks. Some authors, such as Montanari [11] who studies binary networks, make this assumption explicitly, others, such as Dechter [4] make it implicitly. We here assume unless otherwise stated, that k-ary networks are complete. In particular, we will assume without loss of generality, that when a binary constraint network N is defined over variables $X_1, \ldots, X_v$, that are given in this order, then the constraints are such that their scopes are precisely all pairs (X_i, X_j) such that $1 \leq i < j \leq v$. For a binary constraint network N over variables $\{X_1, \ldots, X_v\}$, we denote the constraint with scope (X_i, X_j) by c_{ij}^N.

Intersections of networks, containment, and projections. Let N_1 and N_2 be two constraint networks defined over the same schema S (that is, the same set S of constraint scopes). The *intersection* $M = N_1 \cap N_2$ of N_1 and N_2 consists of all constraints c^s, for each $s \in S$, such that $scope(c^s) = s$ and $rel(c^s) = rel(c_1^s) \cap rel(c_2^s)$, where c_1 and c_2 are the constraints having scope s of N_1 and N_2, respectively. The intersection of arbitrary families of constraint networks defined over the same schema is defined in a similar way. For two networks N_1 and N_2 over the same schema S, we say that c_1 is *contained in* c_2, and write $N \subseteq N'$, if for each $s \in S$, and for $c_1 \in cons(N_1)$ and $c_2 \in cons(N_2)$ with $scope(c_1) = scope(c_2) = s$, $rel(c_1) \subseteq rel(c_2)$. If c is a constraint over a set of variables $W = \{X_1, \ldots, X_v\}$ and $V \subseteq W$, then the projection $\Pi_V(c)$ is the constraint whose scope is V, and whose relation is the projection over V of $rel(c)$. Let c be a constraint and S a schema consisting of one or more scopes contained in $scope(c)$, then $\Pi_S(c) = \{\Pi_s(c) | s \in S\}$. If N is a constraint network and S a schema all of whose variables are contained in $var(N)$, then $\Pi_S(N) = \{\Pi_S(c) | c \in N\}$.

Minimal networks. If c is a constraint over variables $var(c) = \{X_1, \ldots, X_v\}$, we denote by $S_k(c)$ the k-ary schema over $var(c)$ having as scopes precisely all (ordered) lists of k variables from $var(c)$, i.e., all scopes $(X_{i_1}, X_{i_2}, \ldots, X_{i_k})$, where $1 \leq i_1 < i_2 < \cdots < i_{k-1} < i_k \leq v$. Thus $\Pi_{S_k}(c)$ is the constraint network obtained by projecting c over all ordered lists of k variables from $var(C)$. In particular, $\Pi_{S_2}(c)$ consists of all constraints $\Pi_{X_i,X_j}(c)$ such that X_i and X_j are variables from $var(c)$ with $i < j$.

It was first observed in [11] that for each binary constraint network N, there is a unique binary *minimal network* $M(N)$ that consists of the intersection of all binary networks N' for which $sol(N') = sol(N)$. Minimality here is with respect to the above defined "$\subseteq$"-relation among binary networks. More generally, for $k \geq 2$, each k-ary network there is a unique k-ary minimal network $M_k(N)$ that is the intersection of all k-ary networks N' for which $sol(N') = sol(N)$. (For the special case $k = 2$ we have $M_2(N) = M(N)$.) The following is well-known [11,12,4,1] and easy to see:

- $M_k(N) = \Pi_{S_k}(sol(N))$;
- $M_k(N) \subseteq N'$ for all k-ary networks N' with $sol(N') = sol(N)$;
- A k-ary network N is minimal iff $\Pi_{S_k}(sol(N)) = N$.
- A k-ary network N is minimal iff $M_k(N) = N$.
- A k-ary network N is satisfiable (i.e., has at least one solution) iff $M_k(N)$ is nonempty.

It is obvious that for $k \geq 2$, $M_k(N)$, is hard to compute. In fact, just *deciding* whether for a network N, $M_k(N)$ is the empty network (i.e., has only empty relations as constraint relations) is co-NP complete, because this decision problem is equivalent to deciding whether N has no solution. (Recall that deciding whether a network N has a solution is NP-complete [8].) In this paper, however, we are not primarily interested in computing $M_k(N)$, but in computing a single solution, in case $M_k(N)$ has already been computed and is known.

Graph theoretic characterization of minimal networks. An *n-partite graph* is a graph whose vertices can be partitioned into n disjoint sets so that no two vertices from the same set are adjacent. It is well-known (see, e.g., [13]) that each binary constraint network N on n variables can be represented as n-partite graph G_N. The vertices of G_N are possible instantiations of the variables by their corresponding domain values. Thus, for each variable X_i and possible domain value $a \in dom(X_i)$, there is a vertex X_i^a. Two vertices X_i^a and X_j^b are connected by an edge in G_N iff the relation of the constraint c_{ij}^N with scope (X_i, Y_j) contains the tuple (a, b). Gaur [7] gave the following nice characterization of minimal networks: A solvable complete binary constraint network N on n variables is minimal iff each edge of N is part of a clique of size n of G_N. Note that by definition of G_N as an n-partite graph, there cannot be any clique in G_N with more than n vertices, and thus the cliques of n vertices are precisely the maximum cliques of G_N.

Satisfiability problems. An instance C of the *Satisfiability (SAT)* problem is a conjunction of clauses (often just written as a *set* of clauses), each of which consists of a disjunction (*often written as set*) of literals, i.e., of positive or negated *propositional variables*. Propositional variables are also called *(propositional) atoms*. If α is a set of clauses or a single clause, then we denote by $propvar(\alpha)$ the set of all propositional variables occurring in α.

3 NP Hardness of Computing Minimal Network Solutions

To show that computing a single solution from a minimal network is NP hard, we will do exactly the contrary of what people — or automatic constraint solvers — usually do whilst solving a constraint network or a SAT instance. While everybody aims at breaking symmetries, we will actually *introduce additional symmetry* into a SAT instance and its corresponding constraint network representation. This will be achieved by the *Symmetry Lemma* to be proved in the next section.

3.1   The Symmetry Lemma

Definition 1. *A SAT instance C is k-supersymmetric if C is either unsatisfiable or if for each set of k propositional variables $\{p_1, \ldots, p_k\} \subseteq propvar(C)$, and for each arbitrary truth value assignment η to $\{p_1, \ldots, p_k\}$, there exists a satisfying truth value assignment τ for C that extends η.*

Lemma 1 (Symmetry Lemma). *For each fixed integer $k \geq 1$, there exists a polynomial-time transformation that transforms each 3SAT instance C into a k-supersymmetric instance C^* which is satisfiable if and only if C is satisfiable.*

Proof. We first prove the lemma for $k = 2$. Consider the given 3SAT instance C. Let us create for each propositional variable $p \in propvar(C)$ a set $New(p) = \{p_1, p_2, p_3, p_4, p_5\}$ of fresh propositional variables. Let $Disj^+(p)$ be the set of all disjunctions of three distinct positive atoms from $New(p)$ and let $Disj^-$ be the set of all disjunctions of three distinct negative literals corresponding to atoms in $New(p)$. Thus, for example $(p_2 \vee p_4 \vee p_5) \in Disj^+(p)$ and $(\bar{p}_1 \vee \bar{p}_4 \vee \bar{p}_5) \in Disj^-(p)$. Note that $Disj^+(p)$ and $Disj^-(p)$ each have exactly $\binom{5}{3} = 10$ elements (we do not distinguish between syntactic variants of equivalent clauses containing the same literals).

Consider the following transformation T, which eliminates all original literals from C, yielding C^*:

Function T:
BEGIN $C' := C$.
WHILE $propvar(C) \cap propvar(C') \neq \emptyset$ DO
    { pick any $p \in propvar(C) \cap propvar(C')$; $C' := elim(C', p)$};
Output(C')
END.

Here $elim(C', p)$ is obtained from C' and p as follows:

FOR each clause K of C' in which p occurs positively or negatively DO

BEGIN
let δ be the disjunction of all literals in K different from p and from $\neg p$;[1]
if p occurs positively in K, replace K in C' by the conjunction $\Gamma^+(K)$ of all clauses
    of the form $\alpha \vee \delta$, where $\alpha \in Disj^+(p)$;
if p occurs negatively in K, replace K in C' by the conjunction $\Gamma^-(K)$ of all clauses
    of the form $\alpha \vee \delta$, where $\alpha \in Disj^-(p)$;
END.

Let $C^* = T(C)$ be the final result of T. C^* contains no original variable from $propvar(C)$. Note that C^* can be computed in polynomial time from C. In fact, note that every clause of three literals of C gives rise to exactly $\binom{5}{3}^3 = 10^3 = 1000$ clauses of 9 literals each in C^*. We can actually replace each clause of C at once and independently by the corresponding 1000 clauses, which –assuming appropriate data

---

[1] An empty δ is equal to *false*, and it is understood that $\alpha \vee$ *false* is simply α.

structures– can be done in linear time. The entire transformation from C to C^* can thus be done in linear time.

We now need to prove (1) that C^* is satisfiable iff C is and (2) that C^* is 2-supersymmetric.

Fact 1: C^* is satisfiable iff C is. It is sufficient to show that, when at each step of algorithm T, C' is transformed into its next value $C'' = elim(C', p)$, then C' and C'' are satisfaction-equivalent. The statement then follows by induction. Assume C' is satisfied via a truth value assignment τ'. Then let τ'' be any truth value assignment to the propositional variables of C'' with the following properties:

- For each propositional variable q of C'' different from p, $\tau''(q) = \tau'(q)$;
- if $\tau'(p) = true$, then at least 3 of the variables in $New(p)$ are set true by τ'', and
- if $\tau'(p) = false$, then at most two of the variables in $New(p)$ is set true by τ'' (and at least three are thus set false).

By definition of C'', τ'' must satisfy C''. In fact, assume first $\tau'(p) = true$. Let K be a clause of C in which p occurs positively. Then, given that at least three variables in $New(p)$ are set true by τ'', each element of $Disj^+(p)$ must have at least one atom made true by τ'', and thus each of the clauses $\Gamma^+(K)$ of C'' evaluates to true via τ''. All other clauses of C'' stem from clauses of C' that were made true by literals corresponding to an atom q different from p. But, by definition of τ, these literals keep their truth values, and hence make the clauses true. In summary, all clauses of C'' are satisfied by τ''. In a very similar it is shown shown that τ'' satisfies C'' if, $\tau(p) = false$. Vice-versa, assume some truth value assignment τ'' satisfies C''. Then it is not hard to see that C' must be satisfied by the truth value assignment τ' to C' defined as follows: If a majority (i.e. 3 or more) of the five atoms in $New(p)$ are made true via τ'', then let $\tau'(p) = true$, otherwise let $\tau'(p) = false$; moreover, for all propositional variables $q \notin New(p)$, let $\tau'(q) = \tau''(q)$.

To see that τ' satisfies C', consider first the case that three or more of the propositional variables of $New(p)$ are assigned *true* by τ''. Note that all clauses of C' that neither contain p nor $\bar{p}$ are trivially satisfied by τ', as τ' and τ'' coincide on their atoms. Now let us consider any clause K of C' in which p occurs positively. Then the only clauses that contain positive occurrences of elements of $New(p)$ of C'' are the sets $\Gamma^+(K)$. If τ'' is such that it makes at least three of the five atoms in $New(p)$ true, then any clause in $\Gamma^+(K)$ is made true by atoms of $Newp$. Thus when replacing these atoms by p and assigning p true, the resulting clause K remains true. Now consider a clause $K = \bar{p} \vee \delta$ of C' in which p occurs negatively. The only clauses containing negative $New(p)$-literals in C'' are, by definition of C'', those in $\Gamma^-(K)$. Recall we assumed that that τ'' satisfies at least three distinct atoms from $New(p)$. Let three of these satisfied atoms be p_i, p_j, and p_k. By definition, $\Gamma^-(K)$ contains a clause of the form $\bar{p}_i \vee \bar{p}_j \vee \bar{p}_k \vee \delta$. Given that this clause is satisfied by τ'', but τ'' falsifies $\bar{p}_i \vee \bar{p}_j \vee \bar{p}_k$, δ is satisfied by τ'', and since δ contains no $New(p)$-literals, δ is also satisfied by τ'. Therefore, $K = \bar{p} \vee \delta$ is satisfied by τ'. This concludes the case where three or more of the propositional variables of $New(p)$ are assigned *true* by τ''. The case where three or more of the propositional variables of $New(p)$ are assigned *false* by τ'' is completely symmetric, and can thus be settled in a totally similar way.   ◇

Fact 2: Proof that C^* is 2-supersymmetric Assume C^* is satisfiable by some truth value assignment η. Then C is satisfiable by some truth value assignment τ, and thus C^* is satisfiable by some truth value assignment τ^* constructed inductively as described in the proof of Fact 1. Note that, for any initially fixed pair of propositional variables $p_i, q_j \in propvar(C^*)$, where $1 \leq i,j \leq 5$, the construction of τ^* gives us a large enough degree of freedom so to choose τ^* in order to let p_i, q_j take on any arbitrary truth value assignment among of the four possible joint truth value assignments. In fact, however we choose the truth value assignments for two among the variables in $\{p_1, \ldots, p_5, q_1, \ldots, q_5\}$, there is always enough flexibility for assigning the remaining variables in this set some truth values that ensure that the majority of variables has the truth value required by the proof of Statement 1 for representing the original truth value of p via τ'. (This holds even in case p and q are one and the same variable, and we thus want to force two elements from $\{p_1, \ldots, p_5\}$ to take on some truth values, see the second example below.) Let us give two examples that illustrate the two characteristic cases to consider. First, assume p and q are distinct and τ satisfies p and falsifies q. We would like to construct, for example, a truth value assignment τ^* that falsifies p_2 and simultaneously satisfies q_4. In constructing τ^*, the only requirements on $New(p)$ and $New(q)$ are that more than three variables from $New(p)$ need to be satisfied by τ^*, but no more than two from $New(q)$ need to be satisfied by τ^*. For instance, we may then set $\tau^*(p_1) = \tau^*(p_3) = \tau^*(p_4) = \tau^*(p_5) = true$ and $\tau^*(p_2) = false$ and $\tau^*(q_1) = \tau^*(q_2) = \tau^*(q_3) = \tau^*(q_5) = false$ and $\tau^*(q_4) = true$. This achieves the desired truth value assignment to p_2 and q_4. An extension to a full satisfying truth value assignment τ^* for C^* is guaranteed. Now, as a second example, assume that $\tau(p) = false$, but we would like $\tau(p_1)$ and $\tau(p_2)$ to be simultaneously true in a truth value assignment satisfying C^*. Note that in this case, the only requirement on $New(p)$ in the construction of τ^* is that at most two atoms from $New(p)$ must be assigned $true$. Here we have a single option only: set $\tau^*(p_1) = \tau^*(p_2) = true$ and $\tau^*(p_3) = \tau^*(p_4) = \tau^*(p_5) = false$. This option works perfectly, and assigns the desired truth values to p_1 and p_2. In summary, C^* is 2-supersymmetric. ◇

The proof of for $k > 2$ is totally analogous, except for the following modifications:

- Instead of creating for each propositional variable $p \in propvar(C)$ a set $New(p) = \{p_1, p_2, \ldots, p_5\}$ of five new variables, we now create a set $New(p) = \{p_1, p_2, \ldots, p_{2k+1}\}$ of $2k + 1$ new propositional variables.
- The set $Disj^+$ is now defined as the set of all disjunctions of $k + 1$ positive atoms from $New(p)$. Similarly, $Disj^-$ is now defined as the set of all disjunctions of $k + 1$ negative literals obtained by negating atoms from $New(p)$.
- Whe replace the numbers 2 and 3 by k and $k + 1$, respectively.
- We note that now each clause of C is replaced no longer by $\binom{5}{3}^3$ clauses but by $\binom{2k+1}{k+1}^3$ clauses.
- We note that the resulting clause set C^* is now a $3(k + 1)$-SAT instance.

It is easy to see that the proofs of Fact 1 and Fact 2 above go through with these modifications.

Finally, let us observe that any 2-supersymmetric SAT instance is trivially also 1-supersymmetric, which settles the theorem for the case $k = 1$ (that we consider for completeness reasons only). $\square$

3.2   Intractability of Computing Solutions

Let us use the Symmetry Lemma for proving our main result about the intractability of computing solutions from a minimal constraint network.

Theorem 2. *For each fixed constant $k \geq 2$, unless NP=P, computing a single solution from a minimal k-ary constraint network N cannot be done in polynomial time. The problem remains intractable even if the cardinality of each variable-domain is bounded by a fixed constant.*

Proof. We first prove the theorem for $k = 2$. Assume A is an algorithm that computes in time $p(n)$, where p is some polynomial, a solution $A(N)$ to each nonempty minimal binary constraint network N of size n. We will construct a polynomial-time 3SAT-solver Λ^* from A. The Theorem then follows.

Let us first define a simple transformation S from SAT instances to equivalent binary constraint networks. S transforms each clause set $C = \{K_1, \ldots, K_r\}$ into a binary constraint network $S(C) = N_C$ as follows. The set of variables $var(N_C)$ is defined by $var(N_C) = C = \{K_1, \ldots, K_r\}$. For each variable K_i of N_C, the domain $dom(K_i)$ consists exactly of all literals appearing in K_i. For each distinct pair of clauses (K_i, K_j), $i < j$, there is a constraint c_{ij} having $scope(c_{ij}) = (K_i, K_j)$ and $rel(c_{ij}) = (dom(K_i) \times dom(K_j)) - \{(p, \bar{p}), (\bar{p}, p) \mid p \in propvar(C)\}$. It is easy to see that C is satisfiable iff N_C is solvable. Basically, N_C is solvable, iff we can pick one literal per clause such that the set of all picked literal contains no atom together with its negation. But this is just equivalent to the satisfiability of C. Obviously, the transformation S is feasible in polynomial time.

Let us now look at constraint networks $N_{C^*} = S(C^*)$, where C^* is obtained via transformation T as in Lemma 1 from some 3SAT instance C, i.e., $C^* = T(C)$. In a precise sense, N_{C^*} inherits the high symmetry present in C^*. In fact, if C^* is satisfiable, then, by Lemma 1, for every pair ℓ_1, ℓ_2 of distinct non-contradictory literals, there is a satisfying assignment that makes both literals true. In case N_{C^*} is solvable, given our particular construction of N_{C^*}, this means that for every constraint c_{ij}, we may pick each pair (ℓ_1, ℓ_2) in $rel(c_{ij})$ as part of a solution. No such pair is useless. It follows that if N_{C^*} is solvable, then $M(N_{C^*}) = N_{C^*}$. On the other hand, if C^* (and thus C) is not satisfiable, then $M(N_{C^*})$ is the empty network. Thus C is satisfiable iff $M(N_{C^*}) = N_{C^*}$ i.e., iff N_{C^*} is minimal[2] Note that C^*, as constructed in the proof of Theorem 2, is a 9SAT instance, hence the cardinality of the domain of each variable of N_{C^*} is bounded by 9.

We are now ready for specifying our 3SAT-solver A^* that works in polynomial time, and hence witnesses NP=P. To a 3-SAT input instance C, A^* first applies T and computes $C^* = T(C)$ in polynomial time. Then A^* transforms C^* via S in polynomial time to N_{C^*}. If N_{C^*} is empty, then, C^* and C are not satisfiable, and A^* outputs "unsatisfiable" and stops. Otherwise, A^* submits N_{C^*} to A and proceeds as follows:

---

[2] From this, by the way, it follows that checking whether a given binary network is minimal is NP-hard, and thus NP-complete; see also Section 4.1.

1. If A on input N_{C^*} does not produce any output after $p(|N_{C^*}|)$ steps, then A^* outputs unsatisfiable and stops. (This is justified as follows: if C^* (and hence C) was satisfiable, then, by construction, N_{C^*} would be a satisfiable minimal network, and hence, by definition of A, $A(N_{C^*})$ would output a solution after at most $p(|N_{C^*}|)$ steps. Contradiction.)
2. If A produces an output w, then A^* checks if w is effectively a solution to N_{C^*}.
3. If w is not a solution to N_{C^*}, then N_{C^*} cannot be minimal. Thus A^* outputs "unsatisfiable" and stops.
4. If w is a solution to N_{C^*}, then N_{C^*} is solvable, and so is C^* and C. Thus A^* outputs "satisfiable" and stops.

In summary, A^* is a polynomial-time 3SAT checker. The theorem for $k = 2$ follows.

For $k > 2$, the proof is analogous to the one for $k = 2$. The only significant change is that now the transformation S now creates a k-ary constraint c_K for each ordered list of k clauses from C, rather than a binary one. The resulting constraint $N_{C^*} = S(C^*)$, where C^* is as constructed in Lemma 1 then does the job. □

3.3   The Case of Bounded Domains

Theorem 2 says that the problem of computing a solution from a non-empty minimal binary network is intractable even in case the cardinalities of the domains of all variables are bounded by a constant. However, if we take the total domain $dom(N)$, which is the set of *all* literals of C^*, its cardinality is unbounded. We show that even in case $|dom(N)|$ is bounded, computing a single solution from a minimal network N is hard.

Theorem 3. *For each fixed $k \geq 2$, unless NP=P, computing a single solution from a minimal k-ary constraint network N cannot be done in polynomial time, even in case $|dom(N)|$ is bounded by constant.*

Proof sketch. We prove the result for $k = 2$; for higher values of k, the proof is totally analogous. The key fact we exploit here is that each variable K_a of N_{C^*} in the proof of Theorem 2 has a domain of exactly nine elements, corresponding to the nine literals occurring in clause K_a of C^*. We "standardize" these domains by simply renaming the nine literals for each variable by the numbers 1 to 9. Thus for each K_a we have a bijection $f_a : dom(K_a) \longleftrightarrow \{1, 2, \ldots, 9\}$. Of course the same literal ℓ may be represented by different numbers for different variable-domains, i.e., it may well happen that $f_a(\ell) \neq f_b(\ell)$. Similarly, a value i in for X_a may correspond to a completely different literal than the same number i for X_b, i.e., $f_a^{-1}(i)$ may well differ from $f_b^{-1}(i)$. Let us thus simply translate N_{C^*} into a network $N_{C^*}^\#$, where each literal ℓ in each column of a variable X_a is replaced by $f_a(\ell)$. It is easy to see that N_{C^*} and $N_{C^*}^\#$ are equivalent and that the solutions of N_{C^*} and $N_{C^*}^\#$ are in a one-to-one relationship. Obviously, $N_{C^*}^\#$ inherits from N_{C^*} the property to be minimal in case it is solvable. Therefore, computing a solution to a network in which only nine values occur in total in the constraint relations is intractable unless NP=P. □

4   Minimal Network Recognition and Structure Identification

In this section we first study the complexity of recognizing whether a k-ary network M is the minimal network of a k-ary network N. We then analyze the problem of deciding whether a k-ary network M is the minimal network of a single constraint.

4.1   Minimal Network Recognition

An algorithmic problem of obvious relevance is recognizing whether a given network is minimal. Using the graph-theoretic characterization of minimal networks described in Section 2, Gaur [7] has shown the following for binary networks:

Proposition 1 (Gaur [7]). *Deciding whether a complete binary network N is minimal is NP-complete under Turing reductions.*

We generalize Gaur's result to the k-ary case and slightly strengthen it by showing NP completeness under the standard notion of polynomial-time many-one reductions:

Theorem 4. *For each $k \geq 2$, deciding whether a complete k-ary network N is minimal is NP-complete, even in case of bounded domain sizes.*

Proof. Membership in NP is easily seen: We just need to guess a candidate solution s_t from $sol(N)$ for each of the polynomially many tuples t of each constraint c of N, and check in polynomial time that s_t is effectively a solution and that the projection of s_t over $scope(c)$ yields t. For proving hardness, revisit the proof of Theorem 2 . For each $k \geq 2$, from a 3SAT instance C, we there construct in polynomial time a highly symmetric k-ary network with bounded domain sizes N_{C^*}, such that N_{C^*} is minimal (i.e., $M_k(N_{C^*}) = N_{C^*}$ iff C is satisfiable). This is clearly a standard many-one reduction from 3SAT to network minimality.   □

4.2   Structure Identification and k-Representability

This section is dedicated to the problem of representing single constraints (or single-constraint networks)through equivalent k-ary minimal networks with smaller relations. By a slight abuse of terminology, we will here identify a single-constraint network $\{\rho\}$ with its unique constraint ρ.

Definition 2. *A complete k-ary network M is a* minimal k-ary network *of ρ iff*

1. *$sol(M) = \rho$, and*
2. *every k-tuple occurring in some constraint r of M is the projection of some tuple t of ρ over $scope(r)$.*

We say that a constraint relation ρ is k-representable if there exists a (not necessarily complete) k-ary constraint network M such that $sol(M) = \rho$. The following proposition seems to be well-known and follows very easily from Definition 2 anyway.

Proposition 2. *Let ρ be a constraint. The following three statements are equivalent: (i) ρ has a minimal k-ary network; (ii) $sol(\Pi_{S_k}(\rho)) = \rho$; (iii) ρ is k-representable.*

Note that the equivalence of ρ being k-representable and of ρ admitting a minimal k-ary network emphasizes the importance and usefulness of minimal networks. In a sense this equivalence means that the minimal network of ρ, if it exists, already represents all k-ary networks that are equivalent to ρ.

The complexity of deciding whether a minimal network for a relation ρ exists has been stated as an open problem by Dechter and Pearl in [5]. More precisely, Dechter and Pearl consider the equivalent problem of deciding whether $sol(\Pi_{S_k}(\rho)) = \rho$ holds, and refer to this problem as a problem of *structure identification in relational data* [5]. The idea is to identify the class of relations ρ that have the structural property of being equivalent to the k-ary network $\Pi_{S_k}(\rho)$, and thus, of being k-representable. Dechter and Pearl formulated the following conjecture:

Conjecture 5 (Dechter and Pearl [5]). *For each positive integer $k \geq 2$, deciding whether $sol(\Pi_{S_k}(\rho)) = \rho$ is NP-hard[3].*

As already observed by Dechter and Pearl in [5], there is a close relationship between the k-representability of constraint relations and some relevant database problems. Let us briefly digress on this. It is common knowledge that a single constraint ρ can be identified with a *data relation* in the context of relational databases (cf. [4]). The decomposition of relations plays an important role in the database area, in particular in the context of normalization [9]. It consists of decomposing a relation ρ without loss of information into smaller relations whose natural join yields precisely ρ. If ρ is a concrete data relation (i.e., a relational instance), and S is a family of subsets (subschemas) of the schema of ρ, then the decomposition of ρ over S consists of the projection $\Pi_S = \{\Pi_s(\rho) \mid s \in S\}$ of ρ over all schemes in S. This decomposition is *lossless* iff the natural join of all $\Pi_s(\rho)$ yields precisely ρ, or, equivalently, iff ρ satisfies the *join dependency* $*[S]$. We can thus reformulate the concept of k-decomposability in terms of database theory as follows: A relation ρ is k-decomposable iff it satisfies the join dependency $*[S_k]$, i.e., iff the decomposition of ρ into schema S_k is lossless. The following complexity result was shown as early as 1981 in [10][4].

Proposition 3 (Maier, Sagiv, and Yannakakis [10]). *Given a relation ρ and a family S of subsets of the schema of ρ, it is coNP-complete to determine whether ρ satisfies the join dependency $*[S]$, or equivalently, whether the decomposition of ρ into schema S is lossless.*

Proposition 3 is weaker than Conjecture 5 and does not by itself imply it, nor so does its proof given in [10]. In fact, Conjecture 5 speaks about the very specific sets S_k for $k \geq 2$, which are neither mentioned in Proposition 3 nor used in its proof. To prove Conjecture 5 we thus developed an new and independent hardness argument.

---

[3] Actually, the conjecture stated in [5] is somewhat weaker: Given a relation ρ and an integer k, deciding whether $sol(\Pi_{S_k}(\rho)) = \rho$ is NP-hard. Thus k is not fixed and part of the input instance. However, from the context and use of this conjecture in [5] it is clear that Dechter and Pearl actually intend NP-hardness for each fixed $k \geq 2$.

[4] As mentioned by Dechter and Pearl [5], Jeff Ullman has proved this result, too. In fact, Ullman, on a request by Judea Pearl, while not aware of the specific result in [10], has produced a totally independent proof in 1991, and sent it as a private communication to Pearl. The result is also implicit in Moshe Vardi's 1981 PhD thesis.

Theorem 6. *Given a single constraint ρ and an integer $k \geq 2$, deciding whether $sol(\Pi_{S_k}(\rho)) = \rho$, and thus whether ρ is k-decomposable, is co-NP complete.*

Proof. We show that deciding whether $sol(\Pi_{S_k}(\rho)) \neq \rho$ is NP-complete.

Membership. Note that membership already follows from Proposition 3, but let us still give a short proof here for reasons of self-containment. Clearly, $\rho \subset sol(\Pi_{S_k}(\rho))$. Thus $sol(\Pi_{S_k}(\rho)) \neq \rho$ iff the containment is proper, which means that there exists a tuple t in $sol(\Pi_{S_k}(\rho))$ not contained in ρ. One can guess such a tuple t in polynomial time and check in polynomial time that for each k-tuple of variables $X_{i_1}, \ldots, X_{i_k}$ of $var(\rho)$, $i < j$, the projection of t to $(X_{i_1}, \ldots, X_{i_k})$ is indeed a tuple of the corresponding constraint of S_k. Thus determining whether $sol(\Pi_{S_k}(\rho)) \neq \rho$ is in NP.

Hardness. We first show hardness for the binary case, that is, the case where $k = 2$. We use the NP-hard problem 3COL of deciding whether a graph $G = (V, E)$ with set of vertices $V = \{v_1, \ldots, v_n\}$ and edge set E is three-colorable. Let r, g, b be three data values standing intuitively for the three colors red, green, and blue, respectively. Let $N_{3\mathrm{COL}}$ be the following constraint network: $var(N_{3\mathrm{COL}}) = \{X_1, \ldots, X_n\}$, $dom(X_i) = \{r, g, b\}$ for $1 \leq i \leq n$, and the schema of $N_{3\mathrm{COL}}$ be precisely S_2. Moreover for all $1 \leq i < j \leq n$, $N_{3\mathrm{COL}}$ has a constraint c_{ij} with schema (X_i, X_j) and constraint relation r_{ij} defined as follows: if $(i, j) \in E$, then r_{ij} the set of pairs representing all legal vertex colorings, i.e., $r_{ij} = \{(r, g), (g, r), (r, b), (b, r), (g, b), (b, g)\}$; otherwise $r_{ij} = \{r, g, b\}^2$. $N_{3\mathrm{COL}}$ is thus a straightforward encoding of 3COL over schema S_2, and obviously G is 3-colorable iff $sol(N_{3\mathrm{COL}}) \neq \emptyset$. Thus the deciding $sol(N_{3\mathrm{COL}}) \neq \emptyset$ is NP hard. Now let us construct from $N_{3\mathrm{COL}}$ a single constraint ρ with schema $\{X_1, \ldots, X_n\}$ and constraint relation s as follows. For each constraint c_{ij} of $N_{3\mathrm{COL}}$, ρ contains a tuple t whose X_i and X_j correspond to those of r_{ij}, and whose X_ℓ value, for all $1 \leq \ell \leq n$, $\ell \neq i$, $\ell \neq j$, is a fresh "dummy" constant d_{ij}^t, different from all other used values. We claim that $sol(\Pi_{S_2}(\rho)) \neq \rho$ iff $sol(N_{3\mathrm{COL}}) \neq \emptyset$ (and thus iff G is 3-colorable. This clearly implies the NP-hardness of deciding $sol(\Pi_{S_k}(\rho)) \neq \rho$.

We now show that the claim holds. Trivially, $\rho \subseteq sol(\Pi_{S_2}(\rho))$. It thus follows that $sol(\Pi_{S_2}(\rho)) \neq \rho$ iff there exists a tuple $t_0 \in sol(\Pi_{S_k}(\rho))$ such that $t_0 \notin \rho$. We will argue that t_0 can contain values from $\{r, g, b\}$ only and must be a solution of $N_{3\mathrm{COL}}$. First, assume that t_0 contains two distinct "dummy" constants, say, d, in column X_a and d' in column X_b with $a < b$. This would mean that $\Pi_{X_a X_b}(\rho)$ contains the tuple (d, d'), and thus, that ρ itself contains a tuple with the two *distinct* dummy values d, and d', which clearly contradicts the definition of ρ. It follows that at most one dummy value d may occur in t_0. However, each such dummy value $d = d_{ij}^t$ occurs precisely in one single tuple t of ρ, and thus each relation of $\Pi_{S_k}(\rho)$ has at most one tuple containing d. It follows that there is only one tuple containing d_{ij}^t in $sol(\Pi_{S_k}(\rho))$, which is t itself, but $t \in \rho$. Therefore, t_0 cannot contain any dummy value at all, and can be made of "color" elements from $\{r, g, b\}$ only. However, by definition of ρ, each tuple $t_{ij} \in \{r, g, b\}^2$ occurring in a relation with schema (X_i, X_j) of $\Pi_{S_2}(\rho)$ also occurs in the corresponding relation of $N_{3\mathrm{COL}}$, and vice-versa. Thus $sol(\Pi_{S_k}(\rho)) \neq \rho$ iff $sol(N_{3\mathrm{COL}}) \neq \emptyset$ iff G is 3-colorable, which proves our claim.

For each fixed $k > 2$ we can apply exactly the same line of reasoning. We define $N_{3\mathrm{COL}}^k$ as the complete network on variables $\{X_1, \ldots, X_n\}$ of all k-ary correct "coloring" constraints, where the relation with schema $X_{i_1}, \ldots, X_{i_k}$ expresses the correct colorings of vertices $v_{i_1}, \ldots, v_{i_k}$ of graph G. We then define ρ in a similar way as for $k = 2$: each k-tuple of a relation of $N_{3\text{COL}}^k$ is extended by use of a distinct dummy value to an n-tuple of ρ. Given that k is fixed, ρ can be constructed in polynomial time, and so $\Pi_{S_k}(\rho)$. It is readily seen that two distinct dummy values cannot jointly occur in a tuple of $sol(\Pi_{S_k}(\rho))$, and that each tuple of $sol(\Pi_{S_k}(\rho))$ that contains a dummy value is already present in ρ because for each dummy value d, each relation of $\Pi_{S_k}(\rho)$ contains at most one tuple involving d. Hence, any tuple in $sol(\Pi_{S_k}(\rho)) - \rho$ involves values from $\{r, g, b\}$ only, and is a solution to $N_{3\text{COL}}^k$ and thus a valid 3-coloring of G.   □

5 Discussion and Future Research

In this paper we have tackled and solved two long standing complexity problems related to minimal constraint networks:

- As solution of an open problem posed by Gaur [7] in 1995, and later by Dechter [4], we proved Dechter's conjecture and showed that computing a solution to a minimal constraint network is NP hard.
- We proved a conjecture made in 1992 by Dechter and Pearl [5] by showing that for $k \geq 2$, it is coNP complete to decide whether $sol(\Pi_{S_k}(\rho)) = \rho$, and thus whether ρ is k-decomposable.

We wish to make clear that our hardness results do not mean that we think minimal networks are useless. To the contrary, we are convinced that network minimality is a most desirable property when a solution space needs to be efficiently represented for applications such as computer-supported configuration [6]. For example, a user interactively configuring a PC constrains a relatively small number of variables, say, by specifying a maximum price, a minimum CPU clock rate, and the desired hard disk type and capacity. The user then wants to quickly know whether a solution exists, and if so, wants to see it. In presence of a k-ary minimal constraint network, the satisfiability of queries involving k variables only can be decided in polynomial time. However, our Theorem 2 states that, unless NP=P, in case the query is satisfiable, there is no way to witness the satisfiability by a complete solution (in our example, by exhibiting a completely configured PC satisfying the user requests).

Our Theorem 2 thus unveils a certain deficiency of minimal networks, namely, the failure of being able to exhibit full solutions. However, we have a strikingly simple proposal for redressing this deficiency. Rather than just storing k-tuples in a k-ary minimal network $M_k(N)$, we may store a full solution t^+ with each k-tuple, where t^+ coincides with t on the k variables of t. Call the so extended minimal network $M_k^+(N)$. Complexity-wise, $M_k^+(N)$ is not harder to obtain than $M_k(N)$. Moreover, in practical terms, given that the known algorithms for computing $M_k(N)$ from N require to check for each k-tuple t whether it occurs in some solution t^+, why not just memorizing t^+ on the fly for each "good" tuple t? Note also that the size of $M_k^+(N)$ is still polynomial, and at most by a factor $|var(N)|$ larger than the size of $M_k(N)$.

We currently work on the following problem: Show that deciding if ρ is k-decomposable remains coNP complete for bounded domains, even if $k = 3$ and $dom(\rho)$ is 2-valued, or if $k = 2$ and $dom(\rho)$ is 3-valued. This will hopefully allow us to confirm a further conjecture (Conjecture 3.27 in [5]) about the identification of CNF formulas. Note that for $k = 2$ and two-valued domains, the problem is tractable for reasons similar to those for which binary 2-valued constraint networks can be solved and minimized in polynomial time [3,7]. Another interesting research problem is the following. We may issue queries of the following form against $M_k^+(N)$: SELECT A SOLUTION WHERE ϕ. Here ϕ is Boolean combination on constraints on the variables of N. Queries, where ϕ is a simple combination of range restrictions on k variables can be answered in polynomial time. But there are much more complicated queries that can be answered efficiently, for example, queries that involve aggregate functions and/or re-use of quantified variables. It would thus be nice and useful to identify very large classes of queries to $M_k^+(N)$ for which a single solution – if it exists – can be found in polynomial time.

Acknowledgments. Work funded by EPSRC Grant EP/G055114/1 "Constraint Satisfaction for Configuration: Logical Fundamentals, Algorithms, and Complexity". We thank C. Bessiere, R. Dechter, D. Gaur, M. Vardi, M. Yannakakis, S. Živný, and the referees for useful comments and/or pointers to earlier work.

References

1. Bessiere, C.: Constraint propagation. In: Rossi, F., van Beek, P., Walsh, T. (eds.) Handbook of Constraint Programming, ch. 3, pp. 29–83 (2006)
2. Cros, H.: Compréhension et apprentissage dans les résaux de contraintes, Université de Montpellier, "PhD thesis, cited in [1], currently unavailable" (2003)
3. Dechter, R.: From local to global consistency. Artif. Intell. 55(1), 87–108 (1992)
4. Dechter, R.: Constraint processing. Morgan Kaufmann, San Francisco (2003)
5. Dechter, R., Pearl, J.: Structure identification in relational data. Artif. Intell. 58, 237–270 (1992)
6. Fleischanderl, G., Friedrich, G., Haselböck, A., Schreiner, H., Stumptner, M.: Configuring large systems using generative constraint satisfaction. IEEE Intell. Systems 13(4), 59–68 (1998)
7. Gaur, D.R.: Algorithmic complexity of some constraint satisfaction problems, Master of Science (MSc) Thesis, Simon Fraser University (April 1995), Currently available at: http://ir.lib.sfu.ca/bitstream/1892/7983/1/b17427204.pdf
8. Mackworth, A., Freuder, E.: The complexity of some polynomial network consistency algorithms for constraint satisfaction problems. Artif. Intelligence 25(1), 65–74 (1985)
9. Maier, D.: The theory of relational databases. Computer Science Press, Rockville (1983)
10. Maier, D., Sagiv, Y., Yannakakis, M.: On the complexity of testing implications of functional and join dependencies. J. ACM 28(4), 680–695 (1981)
11. Montanari, U.: Networks of constraints: Fundamental properties and applications to picture processing. Information Sciences 7, 95–132 (1974)
12. Montanari, U., Rossi, F.: Fundamental properties of networks of constraints: A new formulation. In: Kanal, L., Kumar, V. (eds.) Search in Artificial Intelligence, pp. 426–449 (1988)
13. Tsang, E.: Foundations of constraint satisfaction. Academic Press, London (1993)

Structural Tractability of Constraint Optimization

Gianluigi Greco[1] and Francesco Scarcello[2]

[1] Dept. of Mathematics
[2] DEIS, University of Calabria, 87036, Rende, Italy
ggreco@mat.unical.it, scarcello@deis.unical.it

Abstract. Several variants of the Constraint Satisfaction Problem have been proposed and investigated in the literature for modeling those scenarios where solutions are associated with costs. Within these frameworks, computing an optimal solution (short: MIN problem), enumerating the best K solutions (TOP-K), and computing the next solution following one that is given at hand (NEXT) are all NP-hard problems. In fact, only some restricted islands of tractability for them have been singled out in the literature. The paper fills the gap, by studying the complexity of MIN, TOP-K, and NEXT over classes of acyclic and nearly acyclic instances, as they can be identified via structural decomposition methods. The analysis is provided for both monotone cost-functions and non-monotone ones (which have been largely ignored so far). Also, multi-criteria optimization is considered, as instances may have a number of cost functions to be minimized together, according to a given precedence relationship. Large islands of tractability are identified and, for classes of bounded-arity instances, the tractability frontier of constraint optimization is precisely charted.

1 Introduction

By solving a Constraint Satisfaction Problem (CSP) instance we usually mean finding an assignment of values to variables satisfying all the constraints (see, e.g., [7]). However, whenever assignments are associated with some cost because of the semantics of the underlying application domain, computing an arbitrary solution might not be enough. In these cases, one is rather interested in the corresponding *optimization problem* of computing the solution of minimum cost (short: MIN problem), whose modeling is accounted for in several variants of the basic CSP framework, such as fuzzy, probabilistic, weighted, lexicographic, penalty, valued, and semiring-based CSPs (see [25,2], and the references therein). Moreover, one is also often interested in the TOP-K problem of enumerating the best K solutions in a ranked manner (see, e.g., [8,4]),[1] or even in the recently formalized and analyzed NEXT problem of computing the next solution following one that is given at hand [3].

---

[1] Relevant related works and results on graphical models, conjunctive query evaluation, and computing homomorphisms are transparently recalled hereinafter in the context of constraint satisfaction.

J. Lee (Ed.): CP 2011, LNCS 6876, pp. 340–355, 2011.

Since solving CSPs—and the above extensions—is an NP-hard problem, much research has been spent to identify classes of instances over which (the best) solutions can efficiently be computed. In this paper, *structural decomposition methods* are considered [12], which identify tractable classes by exploiting the structure of constraint scopes as it can be formalized either as a hypergraph (whose nodes correspond to the variables and where each group of variables occurring in some constraint induces a hyperedge) or as a suitable binary encoding of such a hypergraph. In fact, motivated by the tractability of *acyclic* instances [30], such methods are aimed at transforming any given cyclic instance into an equivalent acyclic one, by organizing its atoms or variables into a polynomial number of clusters, and by arranging these clusters as a tree, called *decomposition tree*. The original CSP instance is then evaluated via this tree, with a cost that is exponential in the cardinality of the largest cluster, also called *width* of the decomposition, and polynomial if the width is bounded by some constant.

Several deep and useful results have been achieved for structural decomposition methods applied to classical CSPs (see, e.g., [14,19,15,20,16,17,9,6,5]). In particular, the tractability frontier has precisely been charted in the bounded-arity case, i.e., over classes of instances whose constraints involve k variables at most, where $k > 0$ is some fixed natural number—for instance, $k - 2$ gives rise to classes of *binary* CSPs. Indeed, on bounded-arity instances, *tree decomposition* [27] emerged as the most powerful decomposition method [20,17]. On unbounded-arity instances, instead, things are not that clear, as various methods have been proposed, but none of them has been shown to precisely chart the tractability frontier. In fact, by relaxing the polynomial-time tractability requirement and by focusing instead on fixed-parameter tractability, certain tight characterizations have been shown for a notion called *submodular* width [24].

Structural methods for CSP extensions tailored to model optimization problems have received considerably less attention in the literature. Basically, we just knew that MIN is feasible in polynomial time and TOP-K with polynomial delay[2] over CSP instances equipped (essentially) with monotonic functions, and whose underlying hypergraphs are acyclic [21], have bounded treewidth [10,8], or have bounded *hypertree width* [11,26]. Instead, NEXT can be (weakly) NP-hard even in these settings, except for specific kinds of optimization frameworks [3]. Thus, the following questions did not find any answer in earlier literature:

(i) Can tractability results for MIN, TOP-K, and NEXT be extended to more general kinds of functions, possibly non-monotonic?
(ii) Can we precisely chart the tractability frontier for MIN, TOP-K and NEXT (at least in the bounded-arity case)?
(iii) Can we exhibit classes of queries over which TOP-K is feasible not only with polynomial delay, but also in polynomial space?

---

[2] As CSP instances may have exponentially many solutions, a class is said tractable if the solutions of its instances may be computed *with polynomial delay* (WPD): The first solution is computed in polynomial time, and any other solution is computed within polynomial time from the previous one.

Problem	No Restriction	Monotone	Smooth
MIN	NP-hard	in P	in P
NEXT	NP-hard	NP-hard	in P
TOP-K	NP-hard	WPD	WPD & PS

Fig. 1. Left: Summary of complexity results for acyclic instances. Right: Relationships among the different kinds of evaluation functions studied in the paper.

1.1 Contribution

In this paper, we depict a clear picture of the complexity issues arising with constraint optimization problems, by providing positive answers to the questions illustrated above. Our contributions are as follows—see Figure 1:

(1) We define a framework to study constraint optimization problems, where solutions are ranked according to *evaluation functions* defined on top of totally ordered domains, or of domains that are made total via some *linearization* [3]. In particular, we study both monotone functions and non-monotone ones, with the latter being largely ignored by earlier complexity studies. As an extension, the framework allows the user to equip each instance with an arbitrary number of evaluation functions, and a lexicographical mechanism is adopted to provide semantics to multi-criteria optimization.

(2) We analyze the complexity of MIN, TOP-K, and NEXT on *acyclic* CSP instances equipped with arbitrary evaluation functions. It emerges that non-monotonicity is a serious obstruction to tractability, as all the problems are NP-hard even in very simple settings.

(3) We re-consider the computational complexity of the above problems over monotone functions and again over acyclic CSP instances. In this setting (where NEXT is NP-hard [3]), MIN and TOP-K turned out to be feasible in polynomial time and with polynomial delay, respectively, even in the case of lexicographic multi-criteria optimization.

(4) As a trade-off between monotone and non-monotone functions, we define the notion of *smooth evaluation functions*, i.e., of functions that manipulate "small" (in fact, polynomially-bounded) values and that can be even non-monotone—see Figure 1, for an illustration. These functions are likely to occur in many practical applications, but they were not analyzed in earlier literature. As an example, finding a solution minimizing the number of variables that are mapped to a given domain value can be modeled as a smooth evaluation function, as its possible output values are bounded by the total number of variables. Note that this function is smooth *and* monotone, as it is often the case for functions based on counting. Instead, as an example of non-monotone smooth evaluation-function, consider the following function assigning the least value to those solutions with an odd number of variables mapped to some element, say 'a': for any solution, take the product of weights associated with variable assignments, where every variable mapped to 'a' is weighed -1, and all the others get 1. In general, such functions involving multiplications are non-monotone, but they are smooth if their output values are polynomially bounded (w.r.t. the input size).

(5) We show that MIN and NEXT can be efficiently solved on acyclic CSP instances equipped with smooth evaluation functions. To deal with non-monotone functions, we found useful and simple to exploit a technical machinery based on non-deterministic alternating Turing machines, which do not find any counterpart in earlier approaches for solving constraint optimization problems. As an immediate consequence of such positive results, it emerges that TOP-K can be solved, in this scenario, with polynomial delay *and* polynomial space (PS). Establishing such (stronger) tractability result for TOP-K was a major motivation for addressing the NEXT problem in [3].

(6) We point out that all the above tractability results can be extended to classes of *nearly acyclic* CSPs for which a decomposition tree can efficiently be constructed via decomposition methods. Moreover, on classes of bounded-arity instances, we show that having bounded treewidth is a necessary and sufficient condition for tractability, under typical complexity assumptions.

Organization. The rest of the paper is organized as follows. Section 2 reports basic notions. Section 3 illustrated the formal framework for CSP optimization exploited in the paper. Complexity results for arbitrary, monotone, and smooth evaluation functions are reported in Section 4, Section 5, and Section 6, respectively. The tractability frontier for the bounded-arity case is charted in Section 7.

2   Preliminaries

Constraint Satisfaction. Assume that a set *Var* of variables and a domain $\mathcal{U}$ of constants are given. Following [22], we shall exploit the logic-based characterization of a CSP instance as a pair (Φ, DB), where DB is the *constraint database*, i.e., a set of ground atoms of the form $r_i(a_1, ..., a_k)$, and where Φ is the *constraint formula*, i.e., a conjunction of atoms of the form $r_1(\mathbf{u_1}) \wedge \cdots \wedge r_m(\mathbf{u_m})$ such that $\mathbf{u_1}, ..., \mathbf{u_m}$ are lists of terms (i.e., variables in *Var* or constants in $\mathcal{U}$). The set of all atoms occurring in Φ is denoted by $atoms(\Phi)$. A *solution* to the instance (Φ, DB) is a substitution $\theta : \bar{X} \mapsto \mathcal{U}$ such that $\bar{X} = Var$ and $r_j(\theta(\mathbf{u_j})) \in \mathrm{DB}$, for each atom $r_j(\mathbf{u_j}) \in atoms(\Phi)$. The set of all solutions to (Φ, DB) is denoted by Φ^{DB}.

Substitutions are always intended from variables (in some $\bar{X} \subseteq Var$) to constants in $\mathcal{U}$, and will sometimes extensively denoted as the set of all pairs of the form X/u, where $u \in \mathcal{U}$ is the value to which variable X is mapped. A substitution θ is *partial* if it is undefined on some variable, i.e., $|\bar{X}| < |Var|$.

Structural Properties. The structure of a constraint formula Φ is best represented by its associated hypergraph $\mathcal{H}(\Phi) = (V, H)$, where $V = Var$ and where, for each atom in $atoms(\Phi)$, the set H of hyperedges contains a hyperedge including all its variables; and no other hyperedge is in H. A hypergraph $\mathcal{H}$ is *acyclic* iff it has a join tree [1]. A *join tree* $JT(\mathcal{H})$ for a hypergraph $\mathcal{H}$ is a tree whose vertices are the hyperedges of $\mathcal{H}$ such that, whenever the same node $X \in V$ occurs in two hyperedges h_1 and h_2 of $\mathcal{H}$, then X occurs in each vertex on the unique path linking h_1 and h_2 in $JT(\mathcal{H})$.

Orders. Let $\mathbb{D}$ be a domain of values, and $\succeq$ be a binary relation over $\mathbb{D} \times \mathbb{D}$. We say that $\succeq$ is a *preorder* if it is reflexive (i.e., $x \succeq x$) and transitive (i.e., $x \succeq y$ and $y \succeq z$ implies $x \succeq z$). For the preorder $\succeq$, we denote by $\succ$ the binary relation such that $x \succ y$ if, and only if, $x \succeq y$ and $y \not\succeq x$, i.e., $y \succeq x$ does not hold. A preorder $\succeq$ that is antisymmetric (i.e., $x \succeq y$ and $y \succeq x$ implies $x = y$) is a *partial order*. A partial order is a *total order* if $x \not\succeq y$ implies that $y \succeq x$. If $\succeq$ is a total order, then $\succ$ is a *strict total order*.

Computational Setting. In all complexity results, we assume that functions are explicitly listed in the input. Moreover, we adopt the usual simple approach of counting 1 each ("mathematical") operation. Observe that in this approach one may compute in polynomial-time (operations) values whose size is exponential w.r.t. the input size. We thus explicitly care about the size of values computed during the execution of algorithms, and look for output polynomial-space algorithms where the size of these values is bounded by the size of actual results.

3   Formal Framework

Throughout the following sections, assume that a set *Var* of variables and a domain $\mathcal{U}$ of constants are given.

Constraint Optimization Formulas. Let $\mathbb{D}$ be a domain of values and let $\succeq$ be a total order over it. Then, a *valuation function* $\mathcal{F}$ over $\mathbb{D}$ and $\succeq$ is a tuple $\langle w, \oplus \rangle$ with $w : Var \times \mathcal{U} \mapsto \mathbb{D}$ and where $\oplus$ is a commutative, associative, and closed binary operator with identity element over $\mathbb{D}$. For a substitution $\theta \neq \emptyset$, $\mathcal{F}(\theta)$ is the value $\bigoplus_{X/u \in \theta} w(X, u)$; and, conventionally, $\mathcal{F}(\emptyset)$ is the identity w.r.t. $\oplus$.

The evaluation function $\mathcal{F} = \langle w, \oplus \rangle$ is *monotone* if $\mathcal{F}(\theta) \succeq \mathcal{F}(\theta')$ implies that $\mathcal{F}(\theta) \oplus \mathcal{F}(\theta'') \succeq \mathcal{F}(\theta') \oplus \mathcal{F}(\theta'')$, for each substitution θ''.

Let $L = [\mathcal{F}_1, ..., \mathcal{F}_m]$ be a list of evaluation functions, where $\mathcal{F}_i$ is defined over a domain $\mathbb{D}_i$ and a total order $\succeq_i$, $\forall i \in \{1, ..., m\}$. Then, for any substitution θ, $L(\theta)$ denotes the vector of values $(\mathcal{F}_1(\theta), ..., \mathcal{F}_m(\theta)) \in \mathbb{D}_1 \times \cdots \times \mathbb{D}_m$.

To compare elements of $\mathbb{D}_1 \times \cdots \times \mathbb{D}_m$, we consider the total order $\succeq_{lex}$, inducing a hierarchy over the preference relations in each domain. Let $\mathbf{x} = (x_1, ..., x_m)$ and $\mathbf{y} = (y_1, ..., y_m)$ be two vectors with $x_i, y_i \in \mathbb{D}_i$, for each $i \in \{1, ..., m\}$. Then, $\mathbf{x} \succeq_{lex} \mathbf{y}$, if either $\mathbf{x} = \mathbf{y}$, or there is an index $i \in \{1, ..., m\}$ such that $x_i \succ_i y_i$ and $x_j = y_j$ holds, for each $j \in \{1, ..., i-1\}$.

Let $L = [\mathcal{F}_1, ..., \mathcal{F}_m]$ be a list of evaluation functions. Then, we define $\succeq_L$ as the binary relation such that, for each pair θ_1 and θ_2 of substitutions, $\theta_1 \succeq_L \theta_2$ if, and only if, $L(\theta_1) \succeq_{lex} L(\theta_2)$. Note that $\succeq_L$ is a preorder, which might be not antisymmetric, as $L(\theta_1) = L(\theta_2)$ does not imply that $\theta_1 = \theta_2$.

A constraint formula Φ equipped with a list L of evaluation functions is called a *constraint optimization formula*, and is denoted by Φ_L.

Example 1. Let $\mathcal{U}$ be the domain $\{a, b\}$ of constants, and let *Var* be the set $\{X_1, ..., X_4\}$ of variables. Consider the constraint optimization formula Φ_L where Φ is the constraint formula $r_1(X_1, X_2, X_3) \wedge r_2(X_1, X_4) \wedge r_3(X_4, X_3)$, and where

L is the list $[\mathcal{F}_1, \mathcal{F}_2]$ of the evaluation functions over the set of real values $\mathbb{R}$ (compared according to the standard ordering $\geq$) defined as follows. For each $i \in \{1, 2\}$, $\mathcal{F}_i$ is the pair $\langle w_i, + \rangle$ where:

- $w_1(X_1/a) = 1$, $w_1(X_1/b) = 0$, and $w_1(X_i/u) = 0$, $\forall i \in \{2, 3, 4\}$ and $\forall u \in \mathcal{U}$;
- $w_2(X_4/a) = 0$, $w_2(X_4/b) = 1$, and $w_2(X_i/u) = 0$, $\forall i \in \{1, 2, 3\}$ and $\forall u \in \mathcal{U}$.

Consider now the three substitutions $\theta_1 = \{X_1/b, X_2/b, X_3/b, X_4/b\}$, $\theta_2 = \{X_1/b, X_2/b, X_3/b, X_4/a\}$, and $\theta_3 = \{X_1/b, X_2/a, X_3/a, X_4/b\}$, and note that $L(\theta_1) = (0, 1)$, $L(\theta_2) = (0, 0)$, and $L(\theta_3) = (0, 1)$. Thus, $\theta_1 \succ_L \theta_2$ and $\theta_3 \succ_L \theta_2$. In fact, $\succeq_L$ is not antisymmetric as $\theta_1 \succeq_L \theta_3$ and $\theta_3 \succeq_L \theta_1$, but $\theta_1 \neq \theta_3$. $\triangleleft$

As the ordering induced over the solutions of a constraint formula might even not be a partial order at all, it is natural to exploit linearization techniques, as discussed in [3]. In this paper, we adopt a very simple and natural linearization method, based on variable and domain orderings (in fact, analyzed in [3]).

Let $\succeq_{\mathcal{U}}$ be an arbitrary total order defined over $\mathcal{U}$. Let $\ell = [X_1, ..., X_n]$ be a list including all the variables in Var, hereinafter called *linearization*. Then, we define $\succeq_L^\ell$ as the binary relation such that, for each pair θ_1 and θ_2 of substitutions, $\theta_1 \succeq_L^\ell \theta_2$ if, and only if, (i) $\theta_1 = \theta_2$, or (ii) $\theta_1 \succeq_L \theta_2$ and $\theta_2 \not\succeq_L \theta_1$, or (iii) $\theta_1 \succeq_L \theta_2$, $\theta_2 \succeq_L \theta_1$, and there is a variable X_i such that $\theta_1(X_i) \succ_{\mathcal{U}} \theta_2(X_i)$, and $\theta_1(X_j) = \theta_2(X_j)$, for each $j \in \{1, ..., i-1\}$.

Note that $\succeq_L^\ell$ is a total order, where ties in $\succeq_L$ are resolved according to ℓ and the total order $\succeq_{\mathcal{U}}$ over $\mathcal{U}$. In fact, $\succeq_L^\ell$ is a refinement of $\succeq_L$. For instance, consider again Example 1, assume that $a \succ_{\mathcal{U}} b$, and let ℓ be the linearization $[X_1, X_2, X_3, X_4]$. Then, $\succeq_L^\ell$ is the total order: $\theta_3 \succ_L^\ell \theta_1 \succ_L^\ell \theta_2$.

Computational Problems. Three problems that naturally arise with evaluation functions are stated below. All of them receive as input a set of variables Var, a domain $\mathcal{U}$ with an associated ordering $\succeq_{\mathcal{U}}$, a constraint optimization formula Φ_L, a constraint database DB, and a linearization ℓ:[3]

MIN$(\Phi_L, \text{DB}, \ell)$: Compute the solution $\theta \in \Phi^{\text{DB}}$ such that there is no solution $\theta' \in \Phi^{\text{DB}}$ with $\theta \succ_L^\ell \theta'$; Answer NONE, if $\Phi^{\text{DB}} = \emptyset$.

NEXT$(\Phi_L, \text{DB}, \ell, \theta)$: Given a solution $\theta \in \Phi^{\text{DB}}$, compute the solution $\theta' \in \Phi^{\text{DB}}$ such that $\theta' \succ_L^\ell \theta$ and there is no solution $\theta'' \in \Phi^{\text{DB}}$ such that $\theta' \succ_L^\ell \theta'' \succ_L^\ell \theta$. Answer NOMORE if there is no such a solution.

TOP-$K(\Phi_L, \text{DB}, \ell)$: Compute the list $[\theta_1, ..., \theta_{K'}]$, where $K' = \min\{K, |\Phi^{\text{DB}}|\}$ and for each $j \in \{1..., K'\}$, there is no $\theta' \in \Phi^{\text{DB}} \setminus \bigcup_{i=1}^{j-1} \theta_i$ with $\theta_j \succ_L^\ell \theta'$.

Note that, for $K = |\mathcal{U}|^{|Var|}$, TOP-$K$ coincides with the problem of enumerating all solutions in Φ^{DB} according to $\succeq_L^\ell$.

Example 2. Consider again the setting discussed in Example 1. Moreover, consider the constraint database $\overline{\text{DB}}$ over $\mathcal{U} = \{a, b\}$ such that $\overline{\text{DB}} = \{r_1(b, b, b), r_1(b, a, a), r_2(b, b), r_2(b, a), r_3(b, b), r_3(a, b), r_3(b, a)\}$. Then, it is easily seen that θ_1, θ_2, and θ_3 are all the solutions in Φ^{DB}. Thus, the answer to MIN$(\Phi_L, \text{DB}, \ell)$ is the solution θ_2, the answer to TOP-$K(\Phi_L, \text{DB}, \ell)$, with $K = 3$, is the list $[\theta_2, \theta_1, \theta_3]$, and (e.g.) the answer to NEXT$(\Phi_L, \text{DB}, \ell, \theta_2)$ is the solution θ_1. $\triangleleft$

---

[3] For the sake of simplicity, $Var, \mathcal{U}$, and $\succeq_{\mathcal{U}}$ are always assumed to be given as input, and thus are not listed explicitly.

4   Arbitrary Evaluation Functions

In this section, we analyze the complexity of MIN, NEXT, and TOP-K, in case of arbitrary (in particular, not necessarily monotone) valuation functions. Results are bad news about their tractability, even on classes of acyclic instances.

Theorem 1. MIN *is NP-hard for any linearization, even on classes of constraint optimization formulas* Φ_L *where* $\mathcal{H}(\Phi)$ *is acyclic (and where L is a list of formulas defined over a domain with two elements at most).*

Proof. Let $\psi = c_1 \wedge \ldots \wedge c_m$ be a Boolean formula in conjunctive normal form over a set $\{X_1, ..., X_n\}$ of variables, where $m \geq 2$ and each clause contains three variables. Recall that deciding the satisfiability of such formulas is NP-hard.

Let Var be the set $\{X_i^j \mid i \in \{1, ..., n\}, j \in \{1, ..., m\}\}$ of variables, and let $\mathcal{U}$ be the set $\{t, f\}$, where the constant t (resp., f) is meant to encode the fact that a variable evaluates true (resp., false).

Consider the CSP instance (Φ, DB) built as follows. For each clause c_j, with $j \in \{1, ..., m\}$, over the variables X_α, X_β, and X_γ, let a_j denote the atom $clause_j(X_\alpha^j, X_\beta^j, X_\gamma^j)$, and define $\Phi = a_1 \wedge \cdots \wedge a_m$. Moreover, for the clause c_j, DB contains all the ground atoms of the form $clause_j(u_\alpha, u_\beta, u_\gamma)$ such that c_j is satisfied by mapping X_α, X_β, and X_γ to the truth values encoded in u_α, u_β, and u_γ. No further atoms are in DB. Note that each variable occurs in one constraint at most and hence $\mathcal{H}(\Phi)$ is clearly acyclic.

Let us now equip Φ with a list of evaluation functions. To this end, for each $i \in \{1, ..., n\}$ and $j \in \{2, ..., m\}$, let $\mathcal{F}_i^j$ be the *monotone* evaluation function $\langle w_i^j, \times \rangle$ over $\{-1, 1\}$ (with $1 \succ -1$) such that:

- $w_i^j(X_i^1, t) = 1$; $w_i^j(X_i^1, f) = -1$; $w_i^j(X_i^j, t) = -1$; $w_i^j(X_i^j, f) = 1$;
  $w_i^j(X_i^{j'}, t) = w_i^j(X_i^{j'}, f) = 1$, for each $j' \in \{1, ..., m\} \setminus \{1, j\}$; and
- $w_i^j(X_{i'}^{j'}, t) = w_i^j(X_{i'}^{j'}, f) = 1$, for each $i' \in \{1, ..., n\} \setminus \{i\}$ and $j' \in \{1, ..., m\}$.

Let L be any arbitrary listing of all functions of the form $\mathcal{F}_i^j$, and $\theta : Var \mapsto \mathcal{U}$ be a substitution. Let $i \in \{1, ..., n\}$ and note that, for any $j \in \{2, ..., m\}$, $F_i^j(\theta) = -1$ if, and only if, $\theta(X_i^j) = \theta(X_i^1)$. It follows that $L(\theta) = -\mathbf{1}$ (i.e., the vector where each component is -1) if, and only if, for each $i \in \{1, ..., n\}$ and for each $j \in \{2, ..., m\}$, $\theta(X_i^j) = \theta(X_i^1)$. That is, $L(\theta) = -\mathbf{1}$ if, and only if, θ induces a truth assignment σ to the variables of ψ, such that $\sigma(X_i)$ evaluates to true (resp., false) if $\theta(X_i^1) = t$ (resp., $\theta(X_i^1) = f$). Moreover, given the construction of the constraint database DB, a solution $\theta \in \Phi^{\text{DB}}$ is such that $L(\theta) = -\mathbf{1}$ if, and only if, the assignment σ satisfies ψ.

In order to conclude the proof, note that $L(\theta') \succ_{lex} -\mathbf{1}$ holds, for each substitution θ' such that $L(\theta') \neq -\mathbf{1}$. It follows that the answer θ to $\text{MIN}(\Phi_L, \text{DB}, \ell)$ is such that $L(\theta) = -\mathbf{1}$ if, and only if, ψ is satisfiable—in particular, note that the linearization ℓ is immaterial. Computing this answer is therefore NP-hard. $\square$

As just computing the minimum element is NP-hard, the enumeration problem is NP-hard as well.

Corollary 1. TOP-K *is NP-hard for any linearization, even on classes of constraint optimization formulas* Φ_L *where* $\mathcal{H}(\Phi)$ *is acyclic (and where L is a list of formulas defined over a domain with two elements at most).*

We now complete the picture by addressing the complexity of NEXT. In fact, NEXT has already been shown to be NP-hard on acyclic structures and monotone functions [3], by exhibiting a reduction to the weakly NP-hard *subset sum* problem. Here, we observe that with arbitrary evaluation functions, a strong NP-hardness result can be obtained.

Theorem 2. NEXT *is NP-hard for any linearization, even on classes of constraint optimization formulas* Φ_L *where* $\mathcal{H}(\Phi)$ *is acyclic (and where L is a list of formulas defined over a domain with three elements at most).*

Proof (Idea). Modify the construction in the proof of Theorem 1 as follows: add a novel constant o getting value -2 in all evaluation functions, and add a number of constraints so that the overall structure is a chain (instead of a set of disconnected hyperedges). The role of these constraints is just to guarantee that, in any solution, either all variables are mapped to o, or no variable is mapped to o. Thus, the solution following the best one (where all variables are mapped to o) coincides with the best solution in the original reduction, whose computation allows us to decide the satisfiability of the given Boolean formula.   □

5   Monotone Evaluation Functions

The main source of complexity identified in the above section lies in the non-monotonicity of the evaluation functions. In this section, we study whether the setting where lists of monotone evaluation functions are considered is any easier.

We start by recalling the bad news proven in [3], suitably reformulated to fit our framework.

Proposition 1 (cf. [3]). NEXT *is NP-hard for any linearization, even on classes of constraint optimization formulas* $\Phi_{[\mathcal{F}]}$ *where* $\mathcal{H}(\Phi)$ *is acyclic, and $\mathcal{F}$ is a monotone evaluation function.*

Concerning the MIN problem, its tractability is already known in the literature for classes of acyclic instances and by considering one monotone function to be optimized (see, e.g., [21,10,8,11,26]). Here, we strengthen the result by showing that it remains tractable over acyclic instances even if the goal is to lexicographically optimize a list of (possibly many) monotone functions.

Theorem 3. *On classes of constraint optimization formulas* Φ_L *where* $\mathcal{H}(\Phi)$ *is acyclic and where L is a list of monotone evaluation functions, MIN is feasible in polynomial time and output-polynomial space.*

Proof (Idea). We propose a polynomial time and output-polynomial space algorithm, which is based on a dynamic-programming scheme implemented on top of a given join tree provided as input. The algorithm is based on two notions:

Total Order '$\succeq_{L_\ell}$': Let $\ell = [X_1, ..., X_n]$ be a linearization and let $\mathcal{U}$ be the underlying domain of constants equipped with the total order $\succeq_{\mathcal{U}}$. Let $r_{\mathcal{U}} : \mathcal{U} \mapsto \{0, ..., |\mathcal{U}| - 1\}$ be the bijective mapping such that $r_{\mathcal{U}}(u) > r_{\mathcal{U}}(v)$ if, and only if, $u \succ_{\mathcal{U}} v$, and consider the evaluation function $\mathcal{F}_\ell = \langle w_\ell, + \rangle$ over $\mathbb{R}$ such that $w_\ell(X_i, u) = |\mathcal{U}|^{n-i} \times r_{\mathcal{U}}(u)$. Let $L = [\mathcal{F}_1, ..., \mathcal{F}_m]$ be a list of monotone evaluation functions and define L_ℓ as the list $[\mathcal{F}_1, ..., \mathcal{F}_m, \mathcal{F}_\ell]$. It is immediate to check that $\theta_1 \succeq_L^\ell \theta_2$ if, and only if, $\theta_1 \succeq_{L_\ell} \theta_2$.

Conformance: For a pair of substitutions θ_1, θ_2, we say that θ_1 is *conform* with θ_2, denoted by $\theta_1 \approx \theta_2$, if for each variable X_i that the domains of θ_1 and θ_2 have in common, $X_i/u \in \theta_1 \Leftrightarrow X_i/u \in \theta_2$.

Armed with the notions above, the idea is then to solve $\mathrm{MIN}(\Phi_L, \mathrm{DB}, \ell)$ by traversing a given join tree $T = (N, E)$ of $\mathcal{H}(\Phi)$ from the leaves to the root r, by means of a bottom-up procedure. Recall first that each vertex $v \in N$ corresponds to a hyperedge of $\mathcal{H}(\Phi)$ and, hence, (w.l.o.g.) to one atom a_v in $atoms(\Phi)$, and define (initially) rel_v as the set of all solutions in a_v^{DB} (i.e., the CSP restricted to the one atom a_v). Then, in the bottom-up procedure, at each (non-leaf) vertex v, for each child c of v in T, we find the substitution $\bar{\theta}_c$ in rel_c with $\theta_v \approx \bar{\theta}_c$ and such that $\theta_c \cup \theta_v \succeq_{L_\ell} \bar{\theta}_c \cup \theta_v$, over all the possible substitutions $\theta_c \in rel_c$ with $\theta_v \approx \theta_c$. That is, we find the solution for the constraints associated with vertices in the subtree of T rooted at c, which is the best one (w.r.t. $\succeq_L^\ell$) over all solutions conforming with θ_v. Eventually, θ_v is enlarged to include $\bar{\theta}_c$. Thus, after that an internal node v is processed, rel_v contains solutions that are substitutions for all the variables that occur in the subtree of T rooted at v. Hence, after that the root r is reached, a solution is computed as one getting the best evaluation over those in rel_r. As it is based on a dynamic programming scheme, correctness of the approach can be shown by structural induction on the subtrees of T. □

An important consequence of the above result is the tractability of TOP-K.

Theorem 4. *On classes of constraint optimization formulas Φ_L where $\mathcal{H}(\Phi)$ is acyclic and where L is a list of monotone evaluation functions, TOP-K is feasible with polynomial delay.*

Proof (Sketch). The result can be established by exploiting a method proposed by Lawler [23] for ranking solutions to discrete optimization problems. In fact, the method has been already discussed in the context of inference in graphical models [8] and in conjunctive query evaluation [21]. Reformulated in the CSP context, for a CSP instance over n variables, the idea is to first compute the optimal solution (w.r.t. the functions specified by the user), and then recursively process n constraint databases, obtained as suitable variations of the database at hands where the current optimal solution is no longer a solution (and no relevant solution is missed). By computing the optimal solution over each one of

---

Input: A set *Var* of variables,
a CSP instance (Φ, DB), a smooth list $L = [\mathcal{F}_1, ..., \mathcal{F}_k]$ of evaluation functions,
where $\mathcal{F}_i = \langle w_i, \oplus_i \rangle$ is a function over $\mathbb{D}_i$, for each $i \in \{1, ..., k\}$,
a vector $(v_1, ..., v_k) \in \mathbb{D}_1 \times \cdots \times \mathbb{D}_k$, and
a join tree $T = (N, E)$ of the hypergraph $\mathcal{H}(\Phi)$;
Output: TRUE if, and only if, there is a solution $\theta \in \Phi^{\mathrm{DB}}$ such that $L(\theta) = (v_1, ..., v_k)$;

Procedure $findSolution(v \in N, \; \theta_p, \theta_v : Var \mapsto \mathcal{U}, \; (a_1, ..., a_k) \in \mathbb{D}_1 \times \cdots \times \mathbb{D}_k))$;
begin
    let $c_1, ..., c_r$ be the children of v in T;
    for each $i \in \{1, ..., r\}$ **do**
        guess a vector $(a_1^{c_i}, ..., a_k^{c_i}) \in \mathbb{D}_1 \times \cdots \times \mathbb{D}_k$;
        guess a substitution $\theta_{c_i} \in rel_{c_i}$;
    end for
    let $\theta_v' := \theta_v \setminus \theta_p$;
    check that all the following conditions hold
        C1: $(a_1, ..., a_k) = (\mathcal{F}_1(\theta_v') \oplus_1 a_1^{c_1} \oplus_1 \cdots \oplus_1 a_1^{c_r}, ..., \mathcal{F}_k(\theta_v') \oplus_k a_k^{c_1} \oplus_k \cdots \oplus_k a_k^{c_r})$;
        C2: $\theta_v \approx \theta_{c_1}, ..., \theta_v \approx \theta_{c_r}$;
    if this check fails **then return** FALSE;
    for each $i \in \{1, ..., r\}$ **do**
        if not $findSolution(c_i, \theta_v, \theta_{c_i}, (a_1^{c_i}, ..., a_k^{c_i}))$ **then return** FALSE;
    return TRUE;
end;

---

begin (* MAIN *)
    let r be the root of T;
    guess a substitution $\theta_r \in rel_r$;
    return $findSolution(r, \emptyset, \theta_r, (v_1, ..., v_k))$;
end.

Fig. 2. Algorithm SolutionExistence

these new constraint databases, we get n candidate solutions that are progressively accumulated in a priority queue over which operations (e.g., retrieving any minimal element) take logarithmic time w.r.t. its size. Therefore, even when this structure stores data up to *exponential space*, its operations are feasible in polynomial time. The procedure is repeated until K (or all) solutions are returned. Thus, whenever the MIN problem of computing the optimal solution is feasible in polynomial time (over the instances generated via this process), we can solve with WPD the TOP-K problem of returning the best K-ranked ones. $\qquad\square$

6 Smooth Evaluation Functions

In this section, we focus on a class of non-monotone evaluation functions.

An evaluation function $\mathcal{F}$ is *smooth* (w.r.t. Φ and DB) if, for each substitution θ, $\mathcal{F}(\theta)$ is polynomially-bounded by the size of Φ, DB, and $\mathcal{F}$. A list L of evaluation functions is *smooth* if it consists of k smooth evaluation functions, where k is some fixed natural number. Note that, by requiring that smooth lists comprise a constant number of functions, we focus in fact on polynomially-many combinations of polynomially-bounded values. This is to inhibit the source of intractability emerged in the hardness construction in Theorem 1, which is based on a *long* list of smooth evaluation functions.

Before facing problems MIN and NEXT, we find convenient to consider the problem CHECK$(\Phi_L, \mathrm{DB}, (v_1, ..., v_k))$ of deciding whether there is a solution $\theta \in \Phi^{\mathrm{DB}}$ such that $L(\theta)$ coincides with a given vector $(v_1, ..., v_k)$ of values. In fact, CHECK is NP-hard even on acyclic instances (as it can be easily seen by inspecting the proof of Theorem 1). Below, we show that it becomes tractable on smooth evaluation functions.

Consider the *non-deterministic* algorithm SOLUTIONEXISTENCE, shown in Figure 2—notation is the same as in the proof of Theorem 3. In a nutshell, SOLUTIONEXISTENCE is based on a recursive non-deterministic Boolean function *findSolution* that, at the generic step, receives as its inputs a node v of the join tree, a solution $\theta_v \in rel_v$, a solution for the parent p of v in T (which is the empty set if v is the root), and a vector $(a_1, ..., a_k)$ of values. For each child c_i of v, the function guesses a substitution θ_{c_i} and a vector $(a_1^{c_i}, ..., a_k^{c_i})$, thus revealing its non-deterministic nature. Then, it checks that θ_{c_i} conforms with θ_v, so that θ_{c_i} can be seen as an attempt of extending the current solution θ_v to the variables covered at the vertex c_i. Moreover, it checks that each entry a_j of the vector provided as input can be written as the aggregation (w.r.t. $\oplus_j$) of the corresponding values guessed over the children, plus the value given by the evaluation function $\mathcal{F}_j(\theta'_v)$, where θ'_v is the restriction of θ_v over the variables occurring for the first time in v, in a top-down visit of the join tree.

Lemma 1. *On classes of constraint optimization formulas Φ_L where $\mathcal{H}(\Phi)$ is acyclic and where L is smooth, CHECK is feasible in polynomial time.*

Proof (Idea). Because of its non-deterministic nature, it is not hard (though, rather technical) to check that SOLUTIONEXISTENCE is correct. Concerning its running time, by exploiting the arguments introduced in [13], we can note that SOLUTIONEXISTENCE can be implemented as a logspace alternating Turing machine M with a polynomially-bounded computation tree, from which feasibility in polynomial time (actually, membership in the class LOGCFL) follows by the results in [29]. Indeed, each guess of SOLUTIONEXISTENCE can be implemented with existential configurations of M, while checks can be implemented with universal configurations. Importantly, all the information that has to be kept in each configuration of the machine can be encoded in logspace. In fact, solutions associated with each vertex of the join tree can be indexed in logspace. Moreover, values associated with each of the k smooth evaluation functions are polynomially-bounded. Thus, they can be again represented in logspace, as k is a fixed constant. The only sensible issue is that *findSolution* is invoked recursively for each child c of v, and requires logspace for storing the information associated with each child c (and, hence, in principle polynomial space). Here, the problem can be faced by a pre-processing step, which modifies T into a binary tree such that v has two children at most (and by allowing duplicate nodes in join trees). Binarization is always possible, and is feasible in polynomial time.   □

Good news on CHECK imply good news on MIN and NEXT.

Theorem 5. *On classes of constraint optimization formulas* Φ_L *where* $\mathcal{H}(\Phi)$ *is acyclic and where* L *is smooth,* MIN *and* NEXT *are feasible in polynomial time and polynomial space.*

Proof (Sketch). Let us consider MIN on input Φ_L, DB, and ℓ. As L is smooth, the set of all vectors $L(\theta)$ for any substitution θ contains polynomially-many elements. Thus, we can iterate over them starting with the minimum possible one according to $\succeq_L$: Given the current vector, we decide in polynomial time whether there is an actual solution with such an associated vector (by Lemma 1), and we stop as soon as the test succeeds or if all vectors have been tested and no solution was found. In the latter case, we conclude that the answer to MIN is NONE. Otherwise, let $(a_1, ..., a_k)$ be the vector such that CHECK$(\Phi_L, \text{DB}, (v_1, ..., v_k))$ was noticed to be true. The goal of the remaining part of the computation is to find the solution $\bar{\theta}$ such that $\theta \succ_{L_\ell} \bar{\theta}$, for each solution $\theta \neq \bar{\theta}$ with $L(\theta) = L(\bar{\theta})$.

Let $\ell = [X_1, ..., X_n]$ and let $[u_1, ..., u_m]$ be the list of all the elements of the underlying domain $\mathcal{U}$ agreeing with the total order $\succeq_\mathcal{U}$. For a pair $i \in \{1, ..., n\}$ and $j \in \{1, ..., m\}$, and for a substitution θ over $X_1, ..., X_{i-1}$, let $\Phi_{i,j,\theta} = \Phi \wedge r_1(X_1) \wedge \cdots \wedge r_i(X_i)$, where $r_1, ..., r_i$ are fresh relational symbols, and let $\text{DB}_{i,j,\theta}$ be the database obtained by adding to DB the ground atoms $r_1(\theta(X_1)), ..., r_{i-1}(\theta(X_{i-1}))$, and $r_i(u_{m-j+1})$. Note that $\mathcal{H}(\Phi_{i,j,\theta})$ is acyclic as long as $\mathcal{H}(\Phi)$ is acyclic. Then, we proceed as follows: Starting with $\theta = \emptyset$ and $i = 1$, we repeatedly check whether CHECK$(\Phi_{i,j,\theta_L}, \text{DB}_{i,j,\theta}, (v_1, ..., v_k))$ evaluates to true for increasing values of j. Assume that $\bar{j}$ is the first index where CHECK is true. Then, we include in θ the substitution $X_i/u_{m-\bar{j}+1}$, and we repeat the process for the subsequent value of i. At the end of the process, i.e., when all possible values of i have been processed, θ is returned as the answer to MIN. In fact, as we know that there is at least one solution with associated value $(a_1, ..., a_k)$, the goal of the procedure is construct one solution starting from the most significant variable and assigning to it the least significant domain value, and iterating over all the remaining variables.

A similar line of reasoning can be applied to solve NEXT on input Φ_L, DB, ℓ, and θ. In fact, note that we can find the best solution $\bar{\theta}$ restricted over the set of solutions having an associated value following $L(\theta)$ exactly as discussed above. The difference is that we need now also to check whether there is another solution $\bar{\theta}$ following θ in the linearization and such that $L(\bar{\theta}) = L(\theta)$. To this end, we can adapt the method above, by checking whether there is a solution obtained modifying θ by changing the assignment starting from the least significative variable, and testing the values that follow the current one in θ. □

As a consequence of the above results, we get that TOP-K is feasible with polynomial delay and polynomial space. Indeed, in polynomial time (thus, space) we can find the best solution and any next solution following the one given at hand, till the desired K solutions are obtained or no further solution exists.

Corollary 2. *On classes of constraint optimization formulas* Φ_L *where* $\mathcal{H}(\Phi)$ *is acyclic and where* L *is smooth,* TOP-K *is feasible with polynomial delay and output-polynomial space.*

7   Beyond Acyclicity and the Tractability Frontier

Many attempts have been made in the literature for extending good results about acyclic instances to relevant classes of *nearly acyclic* structures, by exploiting decomposition methods that are based on "acyclicization".

In fact, those positive results for constraint optimization formulas that hold over acyclic instances can be straightforwardly extended to classes of nearly acyclic ones for which a decomposition tree can efficiently be computed. Indeed, given a decomposition tree for a CSP instance (Φ, DB), it is possible to build in polynomial time an acyclic CSP instance (Φ', DB') that is equivalent to the original one, i.e., solutions and their associated costs are preserved (cf. [11]). Hence, tractability results in Figure 1 hold for all classes of instances having hypertree width [14] or treewidth [27] bounded by some fixed constant $k > 0$.

A natural question is then to find the largest class of nearly-acyclic instances over which (optimal) solutions can be efficiently computed. On plain CSPs, it is known that, over classes of bounded-arity instances, the tree decomposition method is essentially the most powerful one: Let $\mathbf{C}$ be any recursively enumerable class of bounded-arity constraint formulas. Under standard complexity theoretic assumptions (FPT$\neq$ W[1]), deciding whether $\Phi^{\mathrm{DB}} \neq \emptyset$, for every formulas $\Phi \in \mathbf{C}$ and constraint database DB, is feasible in polynomial time *if, and only if,* $\mathbf{C}$ has bounded treewidth modulo homomorphic equivalence [20]. Moreover, assuming that $\mathbf{C}$ is closed under taking minors, computing all solutions over any given set of desired variables O, for every formula $\Phi \in \mathbf{C}$ and database DB, is feasible with polynomial delay *if, and only if,* $\mathcal{C}$ has bounded treewidth [17].

In this section, we provide dichotomy results for NEXT, MIN and TOP-K, which show that tree decomposition precisely charts the tractability frontier for constraint optimization problems. In particular, differently from known results for plain CSPs, note that homomorphic equivalence will not play any role, and that we will not need to focus the analysis on classes closed under taking minors.

For any problem P, let P$(\mathbf{C})$ be restriction of P over the set of all the possible instances receiving as input a constraint formula $\Phi \in \mathbf{C}$, and P[SM]$(\mathbf{C})$ the further restriction over smooth lists of evaluation functions.

Theorem 6. *Assume* FPT $\neq$ W[1]. *Let* $\mathbf{C}$ *be any recursively-enumerable bounded-arity class of constraint formulas. Then, the following are equivalent:*

(1) $\mathbf{C}$ *has bounded treewidth;*
(2) MIN[SM]$(\mathbf{C})$ *can be solved in polynomial time and polynomial space;*
(3) NEXT[SM]$(\mathbf{C})$ *can be solved in polynomial time and polynomial space;*
(4) MIN$(\mathbf{C})$ *can be solved in polynomial time and output-polynomial space;*
(5) TOP-K[SM]$(\mathbf{C})$ *can be solved with polynomial delay and output-polynomial space;*
(6) TOP-$K(\mathbf{C})$ *can be solved with polynomial delay.*

Proof (Sktech). From our results and given the definition of the problems, we have that $(1) \Rightarrow (2) \wedge (3) \wedge (4)$; $(2) \wedge (3) \Rightarrow (5)$; $(4) \Rightarrow (6)$; $(6) \Rightarrow (4)$; and $(5) \Rightarrow (2)$. The fact that $(2) \Rightarrow (1)$ and $(4) \Rightarrow (1)$ hold can be shown by applying results in [18], and details are omitted due to space limits. To complete the picture we show that $(3) \Rightarrow (1)$, by providing a self-contained proof idea.

Let G be a graph instance of the W[1]-hard p-CLIQUE problem of deciding whether G has a clique of cardinality h, where $h \geq 2$ is the fixed parameter of the problem. We enumerate the recursively enumerable class $\mathbf{C}$ until we eventually find a constraint formula Φ whose Gaifman graph contains as a minor the $(h \times H)$-grid, where $H = \binom{h}{2}$, which exists by the Excluded Grid Theorem [28]. Let k be the treewidth of $\mathcal{H}(\Phi)$. Note that searching for Φ and computing its treewidth k depend on the fixed parameter h only (in particular, it is independent of G).

We now claim that, for any graph G, we can build in fixed-parameter polynomial time a constraint database $\mathrm{DB}_{\Phi,G}$ and a set of constants $\mathcal{U}(X)$, for each variable X in Φ, such that: there is a solution $\theta \in \Phi^{\mathrm{DB}_{\Phi,G}}$ with $\theta(X) \in \mathcal{U}(X)$, $\forall X \Leftrightarrow G$ contains an h-clique. Indeed, the result follows by inspecting the proof of the grid-based construction in [20]. In that construction, based on Φ, the database $\mathrm{DB}_{\Phi,G}$ is build such that, if Q is a core, then G contains an h-clique if and only if $\Phi^{\mathrm{DB}_{\Phi,G}}$ is not empty. In fact, constants in $\mathrm{DB}_{\Phi,G}$ are "typed" w.r.t. the variables of Φ, and the role of the core is precisely to guarantee that each variable X is mapped into a constant taken from $\mathcal{U}(X)$.

W.l.o.g., assume that $\mathcal{H}(\Phi)$ is connected—otherwise, just modify Φ as to include a fresh variable connected with all the other ones, via binary relations taking in the constraint database all possible pairs of values in the domain. Let DB' be the database obtained by adding into $\mathrm{DB}_{\Phi,G}$ a new fact $r(o, ..., o)$, of the appropriate arity, for each relation r, and where o is fresh constant. Thus, for each solution $\theta \in \Phi^{\mathrm{DB}_{\Phi,G}}$, either θ maps each variable to o, or no variable is mapped to o. Consider now the smooth evaluation function $\mathcal{F} = \langle w, + \rangle$ such that $w(X, u) = 1$ if $u \in \mathcal{U}(X)$; $w(X, o) = 0$, and $w(X, u') = 2$ if $u' \notin \mathcal{U}(X) \cup \{o\}$, for each variable X. Let n be the number of variables, and note that for each substitution θ, $\mathcal{F}(\theta) = n$ if, and only if, $\theta(X) \in \mathcal{U}(X)$, for each variable X. Hence, there is a solution $\theta \in \Phi^{\mathrm{DB}_{\Phi,G}}$ such that $\mathcal{F}(\theta) = n$ if, and only if, G contains an h-clique. Moreover, there is no solution $\theta \in \Phi^{\mathrm{DB}_{\Phi,G}}$ such that $\mathcal{F}(\theta) < n$ and $\mathcal{F}(\theta) > 0$, while $\mathcal{F}(\bar{\theta}) = 0$, where $\bar{\theta}$ is the solution such that $\bar{\theta}(X) = o$, for each variable X. It follows that G contains an h-clique if, and only if, the answer to NEXT$(\Phi_{[\mathcal{F}]}, \mathrm{DB}_{\Phi,G}, \ell, \bar{\theta})$ is any solution θ with $\mathcal{F}(\theta) = n$—here the linearization is immaterial. Therefore, we have a fixed parameter algorithm that, given a solution to NEXT, can decide whether G has a clique of cardinality h. This is impossible, under the assumption that FPT $\neq$ W[1]. Hence, $(3) \Rightarrow (1)$ holds. $\square$

References

1. Bernstein, P.A., Goodman, N.: The power of natural semijoins. SIAM Journal on Computing 10(4), 751–771 (1981)
2. Bistarelli, S., Montanari, U., Rossi, F., Schiex, T., Verfaillie, G., Fargier, H.: Semiring-Based CSPs and Valued CSPs: Frameworks, Properties, and Comparison. Constraints 4(3), 199–240 (1999)

3. Brafman, R.I., Rossi, F., Salvagnin, D., Venable, K.B., Walsh, T.: Finding the Next Solution in Constraint- and Preference-Based Knowledge Representation Formalisms. In: Proc. of KR 2010, pp. 425–433 (2010)
4. Bulatov, A., Dalmau, V., Grohe, M., Marx, D.: Enumerating Homomorphism. In: Proc. of STACS 2009, pp. 231–242 (2009)
5. Chen, H., Dalmau, V.: Beyond Hypertree Width: Decomposition Methods Without Decompositions. In: van Beek, P. (ed.) CP 2005. LNCS, vol. 3709, pp. 167–181. Springer, Heidelberg (2005)
6. Cohen, D.A., Jeavons, P., Gyssens, M.: A unified theory of structural tractability for constraint satisfaction problems. J. of Computer and System Sciences 74(5), 721–743 (2008)
7. Dechter, R.: Constraint Processing. Morgan Kaufmann, San Francisco (2003)
8. Flerova, N., Dechter, R.: M best solutions over Graphical Models. In: Proc. of Constraint Reasoning and Graphical Structures, CP 2010 Workshop (2010)
9. Flum, J., Frick, M., Grohe, M.: Query evaluation via tree-decompositions. Journal of the ACM 49(6), 716–752 (2002)
10. de Givry, S., Schiex, T., Verfaillie, G.: Exploiting Tree Decomposition and Soft Local Consistency In Weighted CSP. In: Proc. of AAAI 2006 (2006)
11. Gottlob, G., Greco, G., Scarcello, F.: Tractable Optimization Problems through Hypergraph-Based Structural Restrictions. In: Albers, S., Marchetti-Spaccamela, A., Matias, Y., Nikoletseas, S., Thomas, W. (eds.) ICALP 2009. LNCS, vol. 5556, pp. 16–30. Springer, Heidelberg (2009)
12. Gottlob, G., Leone, N., Scarcello, F.: A comparison of structural CSP decomposition methods. Artificial Intelligence 124(2), 243–282 (2000)
13. Gottlob, G., Leone, N., Scarcello, F.: Computing LOGCFL Certificates. Theoretical Computer Science 270(1-2), 761–777 (2002)
14. Gottlob, G., Leone, N., Scarcello, F.: Hypertree decompositions and tractable queries. J. of Computer and System Sciences 64(3), 579–627 (2002)
15. Gottlob, G., Miklós, Z., Schwentick, T.: Generalized hypertree decompositions: NP-hardness and tractable variants. Journal of the ACM 56(6) (2009)
16. Greco, G., Scarcello, F.: The power of tree projections: local consistency, greedy algorithms, and larger islands of tractability. In: Proc. of PODS 2010, pp. 327–338 (2010)
17. Greco, G., Scarcello, F.: Structural Tractability of Enumerating CSP Solutions. In: Cohen, D. (ed.) CP 2010. LNCS, vol. 6308, pp. 236–251. Springer, Heidelberg (2010)
18. Greco, G., Scarcello, F.: The tractability frontier of computing K best solutions. Techinical Report, University of Calabria (2011)
19. Grohe, M., Marx, D.: Constraint solving via fractional edge covers. In: Proc. of SODA 2006, pp. 289–298 (2006)
20. Grohe, M.: The complexity of homomorphism and constraint satisfaction problems seen from the other side. Journal of the ACM 54(1) (2007)
21. Kimelfeld, B., Sagiv, Y.: Incrementally computing ordered answers of acyclic conjunctive queries. In: Etzion, O., Kuflik, T., Motro, A. (eds.) NGITS 2006. LNCS, vol. 4032, pp. 33–38. Springer, Heidelberg (2006)
22. Kolaitis, P.G., Vardi, M.Y.: Conjunctive-query containment and constraint satisfaction. Journal of Computer and System Sciences 61(2), 302–332 (1998)
23. Lawler, E.L.: A procedure for computing the k best solutions to discrete optimization problems and its application to the shortest path problem. Management Science 18, 401–405 (1972)

24. Marx, D.: Tractable Hypergraph Properties for Constraint Satisfaction and Conjunctive Queries. In: Proc. of STOC 2010, pp. 735–744 (2010)
25. Meseguer, P., Rossi, F., Schiex, T.: Soft Constraints. In: Handbook of Constraint Programming. Elsevier, Amsterdam (2006)
26. Ndiaye, S., Jégou, P., Terrioux, C.: Extending to Soft and Preference Constraints a Framework for Solving Efficiently Structured Problems. In: Proc. of ICTAI 2008, pp. 299–306 (2008)
27. Robertson, N., Seymour, P.D.: Graph minors III: Planar tree-width. Journal of Combinatorial Theory, Series B 36, 49–64 (1984)
28. Robertson, N., Seymour, P.D.: Graph minors V: Excluding a planar graph. Journal of Combinatorial Theory, Series B 41, 92–114 (1986)
29. Ruzzo, W.L.: Tree-size bounded alternation. Journal of Computer and System Sciences 21, 218–235 (1980)
30. Yannakakis, M.: Algorithms for acyclic database schemes. In: Proc. of VLDB 1981, pp. 82–94 (1981)

Models and Strategies for Variants of the Job Shop Scheduling Problem

Diarmuid Grimes[1] and Emmanuel Hebrard[2]

[1] Cork Constraint Computation Centre,
University College Cork, Ireland
d.grimes@4c.ucc.ie
[2] LAAS; CNRS,
Universit de Toulouse, France
hebrard@laas.fr

Abstract. Recently, a variety of constraint programming and Boolean satisfiability approaches to scheduling problems have been introduced. They have in common the use of relatively simple propagation mechanisms and an adaptive way to focus on the most constrained part of the problem. In some cases, these methods compare favorably to more classical constraint programming methods relying on propagation algorithms for global unary or cumulative resource constraints and dedicated search heuristics. In particular, we described an approach that combines restarting, with a generic adaptive heuristic and solution guided branching on a simple model based on a decomposition of disjunctive constraints.

In this paper, we introduce an adaptation of this technique for an important subclass of job shop scheduling problems (JSPs), where the objective function involves minimization of earliness/tardiness costs. We further show that our technique can be improved by adding domain specific information for one variant of the JSP (involving time lag constraints). In particular we introduce a dedicated greedy heuristic, and an improved model for the case where the maximal time lag is 0 (also referred to as no-wait JSPs).

1 Introduction

Scheduling problems come in a wide variety and it is natural to think that methods specifically engineered for each variant would have the best performance. However, it was recently shown this is not always true. Tamura et al. introduced an encoding of disjunctive and precedence constraints into conjunctive normal form formulae [22]. Thanks to this reformulation they were the first to report optimality proofs for all open shop scheduling instances from three widely studied benchmarks. Similarly the hybrid CP/SAT solver lazy-FD [10] was shown to be extremely effective on Resource-Constrained Project scheduling (RCPSP) [21].

Previously, we introduced an approach for open and job shop problems with a variety of extra constraints [12,13] using simple reified binary disjunctive constraints combined with a number of generic SAT and AI techniques: weighted degree variable ordering [5], solution guided value ordering [3], geometric restarting [25] and nogood recording from restarts [15]. It appears that the weighted degree heuristic efficiently detects the most constrained parts of the problem, focusing search on a fraction of the variables.

J. Lee (Ed.): CP 2011, LNCS 6876, pp. 356–372, 2011.

The simplicity of this approach makes it easy to adapt to various constraints and objective functions. One type of objective function that has proven troublesome for traditional CP scheduling techniques involves minimizing the sum of earliness/tardiness costs, primarily due to the weak propagation of the sum objective [8]. In this paper we show how our basic JSP model can be adapted to handle this objective. Experimental results reveal that our approach is competitive with the state of the art on the standard benchmarks from the literature.

Moreover, we introduce two refinements of our approach for problems with maximum time lags between consecutive tasks, where we incorporate domain specific information to boost performance. These time lag constraints, although conceptually very simple, change the nature of the problem dramatically. For instance, it is not trivial to find a feasible schedule even if we do not take into account any bound on the total makespan (unless scheduling jobs back to back). This has several negative consequences. Firstly, it is not possible to obtain a trivial upper bound of reasonable quality may be found by sequencing the tasks in some arbitrary order. The only obvious upper bound is to sequence the jobs consecutively. Secondly, since relaxing the makespan constraint is not sufficient to make the problem easy, our approach can have difficulty finding a feasible solution for large makespans, even though it is very effective when given a tighter upper bound. However because the initial upper bound is so poor, even an exploration by dichotomy of the objective variable's domain can take a long time.

We introduce a simple search strategy which, when given a large enough upper bound on the makespan, guarantees a limited amount of backtracking whilst still providing good quality solutions. This simple strategy, used as an initial step, greatly improves the performance of our algorithm on this problem type. We report several new best upper bounds and proofs of optimality on these benchmarks. Moreover, we introduce another improvement in the model of the particular case of *No wait* JSP where the tasks of each job must be directly consecutive. This variant has been widely studied, and efficient metaheuristics have been proposed recently. We report 5 new best upper bound, and close 9 new instances in standard data sets.

Finally, because there are few comparison methods in the literature for problems with strictly positive time lags, we adapted a job shop scheduling model written in Ilog Scheduler by Chris Beck [3], to handle time lag constraints. Our method outperforms this model when time lag constraints are tight (short lags), however when time lags are longer, the Ilog Scheduler model together with geometric restarts and solution guided search is better than our method.

2   Background and Previous Work

An $n \times m$ job shop problem (JSP) involves a set of nm *tasks* $\mathcal{T} = \{t_i \mid 1 \leq i \leq nm\}$, partitioned into n *jobs* $\mathcal{J} = \{J_x \mid 1 \leq x \leq n\}$, that need to be scheduled on m *machines* $\mathcal{M} = \{M_y \mid 1 \leq y \leq m\}$. Each job $J_x \in \mathcal{J}$ is a set of m tasks $J_x = \{t_{(x-1)*m+y} \mid 1 \leq y \leq m\}$. Conversely, each machine $M_y \in \mathcal{M}$ denotes a set of n tasks (to run on this machine) such that: $\mathcal{T} = (\bigcup_{1 \leq x \leq n} J_x) = (\bigcup_{1 \leq y \leq m} M_y)$.

Each task t_i has an associated duration, or processing time, p_i. A *schedule* is a mapping of tasks to time points consistent with sequencing and resource constraints. The former ensure that the tasks of each job run in a predefined order whilst the latter ensure that no two tasks run simultaneously on any given machine. In the rest of the paper, we shall identify each task t_i with the variable standing for its start time in the schedule. We define the sequencing (2.1) and resource (2.2) constraints in Model 1.

Moreover, we shall consider two objective functions: *total makespan*, and *weighted earliness/tardiness*. In the former, we want to minimize the the total duration to run all tasks, that is, $C_{max} = max_{t_i \in \mathcal{T}}(t_i + p_i)$ if we assume that we start at time 0. In the latter, each job $J_x \in \mathcal{J}$ has a due date, d_x. There is a linear cost associated with completing a job before its due date, or the tardy completion of a job, with coefficient w_x^e and w_x^t, respectively. (Note that these problems differ from Just in Time job shop scheduling problems[2], where each *task* has a due date.) If t_{xm} is the last task of job J_x, then $t_{xm} + p_{xm}$ is its completion time, hence the cost of a job is then given by: $ET_{sum} = \sum_{J_x \in \mathcal{J}}(max(w_x^e(d_x - t_{xm} - p_{xm}), w_x^t(t_{xm} + p_{xm} - d_x)))$

---

model 1 . JSP

$$t_i + p_i \leq t_{i+1} \qquad \forall J_x \in \mathcal{J}, \forall t_i, t_{i+1} \in J_x \qquad (2.1)$$

$$t_i + p_i \leq t_j \lor t_j + p_j \leq t_i \qquad \forall M_y \in \mathcal{M}, t_i \neq t_j \in M_y \qquad (2.2)$$

2.1 Boolean Model

In previous work [13] we described the following simple model for open shop and job shop scheduling. First, to each task, we associate a variable t_i taking its value in $[0, \infty]$ that stands for its starting time. Then, for each pair of tasks sharing a machine we introduce a Boolean variable that stands for the relative order of these two tasks. More formally, for each machine $M_y \in \mathcal{M}$, and for each pair of tasks $t_i, t_j \in M_y$, we have a Boolean variable b_{ij}, and constraint (2.2) can be reformulated as follows:

$$b_{ij} = \begin{cases} 0 \Leftrightarrow t_i + p_i \leq t_j \\ 1 \Leftrightarrow t_j + p_j \leq t_i \end{cases} \qquad \forall M_y \in \mathcal{M}, t_i \neq t_j \in M_y \qquad (2.3)$$

Finally, the tasks of each job J_x, are kept in sequence with a set of simple precedence constraints $t_i + p_i \leq t_{i+1}$ for all $t_i, t_{i+1} \in J_x$.

For n jobs and m machines, this model therefore involves $nm(n-1)/2$ Boolean variables, as many disjunctive constraints, and $n(m-1)$ precedence constraints. Bounds consistency (BC) is maintained on all constraints. Notice that state of the art CP models use instead m global constraints to reason about unary resources. The best known algorithms for filtering unary resources constraints implement the edge finding, not-first/not-last, and detectable precedence rules with a $O(n \log n)$ time complexity [24]. One might therefore expect our model to be less efficient as n grows. However, the quadratic number of constraints – and Boolean variables – required to model a resource in our approach has not proven problematic on the academic benchmarks tested on to date.

2.2   Search Strategy

We refer the reader to [12] for a more detailed description of the default search strategy used for job shop variants, and we give here only a brief overview.

This model does not involve any global constraint associated to a strong propagation algorithm. However, it appears that decomposing resource constraints into binary disjunctive elements is synergetic with adaptive heuristics, and in particular the *weighted-degree*-based heuristics [5]. (We note that the greater the minimum arity of constraints in a problem, the less discriminatory the weight-degree heuristic can be.) A constraint's weight is incremented by one each time the constraint causes a failure during search. This weight can then be projected on variables to inform the heuristic choices.

It is sufficient to decide the relative sequencing of the tasks, that is, the value of the Boolean variables standing for disjuncts. Because the domain size of these variables are all equal, we use a slightly modified version of the *domain over weighted-degree* heuristic, where weights and domain size are taken on the two tasks whose relative ordering is decided by the Boolean variable. Let $w(t_i)$ be the number of times search failed while propagating any constraint involving task t_i, and let $min(t_i)$ and $max(t_i)$ be, respectively, the minimum and maximum starting time of t_i at any point during search. The next disjunct b_{ij} to branch on is the one minimizing the value of:

$$(max(t_i) \mid max(t_j) - min(t_i) - min(t_j) + 2)/(w(t_i) + w(t_j))$$

A second important aspect is the use of restarts. It has been observed that weighted heuristics also have a good synergy with restarts [11]. Indeed, failures tend to happen at a given depth in the search tree, and therefore on constraints that often do not involve variables corresponding to the first few choices. As a result, early restarts will tend to favor diversification until enough weight has been given to a small set of variables, on which the search will then be focused. We use a geometric restarting strategy [25] with random tie-breaking. The geometric strategy is of the form $s, sr, sr^2, sr^3, \ldots$ where s is the base and r is the multiplicative factor. In our experiments the base was 256 failures and the multiplicative factor was 1.3. Moreover, after each restart, the dead ends of the previous explorations are stored as clausal nogoods [15].

A third very important feature is the idea of guiding search (branching choices) based on the best solution found so far. This idea is a simplified version of the solution guided approach (SGMPCS) proposed by Beck for JSPs [3]. Thus our search strategy can be viewed as variable ordering guided by past failures and value ordering guided by past successes.

Finally, before using a standard Branch & Bound procedure, we first use a dichotomic search to reduce the gap between lower and upper bound. At each step of the dichotomic search, a satisfaction problem is solved, with a limit on the number of nodes.

3   Job Shop with Earliness/Tardiness Objective

In industrial applications, the length of the makespan is not always the preferred objective. An important alternative criterion is the minimization of the cost of a job finishing early/late. An example of a cost for early completion of a job would be storage costs incurred, while for late completion of a job these costs may represent the impact on customer satisfaction.

Although the only change to the problem is the objective function, our model requires a number of additional elements. When we minimize the sum of earliness and tardiness, we introduce $4n$ additional variables. For each job J_x we have a Boolean variable e_x that takes the value 1 iff J_x is finished early and the value 0 otherwise. In other words, e_x is a reification of the precedence constraint $t_{xm} + p_{xm} < d_x$. Moreover, we also have a variable E_x standing for the duration between the completion time of the last task of J_x and the due date d_x when J_x is finished early: $E_x = e_x(d_x - t_{xm} - p_{xm})$. Symmetrically, for each job J_x we have Boolean variable l_x taking the value 1 iff J_x is finished late, and an integer variable L_x standing for the delay (Model 2).

---

model 2. ET-JSP

$$minimise\ ET_{sum}\ \text{subject to :}$$

$$ET_{sum} = \sum_{J_x \in \mathcal{J}} (w_x^e E_x + w_x^t L_x) \tag{3.1}$$

$$e_x \Leftrightarrow (t_{xm} + p_{xm} < d_x) \qquad \forall J_x \in \mathcal{J} \tag{3.2}$$

$$E_x = e_x(d_x - t_{xm} - p_{xm}) \qquad \forall J_x \in \mathcal{J} \tag{3.3}$$

$$l_x \Leftrightarrow (t_{xm} + p_{xm} > d_x) \qquad \forall J_x \in \mathcal{J} \tag{3.4}$$

$$L_x = l_x(t_{xm} + p_{xm} - d_x) \qquad \forall J_x \in \mathcal{J} \tag{3.5}$$

$$\text{(constraints 2.1) \& (constraints 2.3)}$$

Unlike the case where the objective involves minimizing the makespan, branching only on the disjuncts is not sufficient for these problems. Thus we also branch on the early and late Boolean variables, and on the variables standing for start times of the last tasks of each job. For these extra variables, we use the standard definition of domain over weighted degree.

4   Job Shop Scheduling Problem with Time Lags

Time lag constraints arise in many scheduling applications. For instance, in the steel industry, the time lag between the heating of a piece of steel and its moulding should be small [27]. Similarly when scheduling chemical reactions, the reactives often cannot be stored for a long period of time between two stages of a process to avoid interactions with external elements [19].

4.1   Model

The objective to minimise is represented by a variable C_{max} linked to the last task of each job by n precedence constraints: $\forall x \in [1, \ldots, n]\ t_{xm} + p_{xm} \leq C_{max}$. The maximum time lag between two consecutive tasks is simply modelled by a precedence constraint with negative offset. Letting $L(i)$ be the maximum time lag between the tasks t_i and t_{i+1}, we use the following model:

model 3. TL-JSP

$$minimise\ C_{max}\ \text{subject to :}$$

$$C_{max} \geq t_{xm} + p_{xm} \qquad\qquad \forall J_x \in \mathcal{J} \qquad\qquad (4.1)$$

$$t_{i+1} - (p_i + L(i)) \leq t_i \qquad \forall J_x \in \mathcal{J},\ \forall t_i, t_{i+1} \in J_x \qquad (4.2)$$

(constraints 2.1) & (constraints 2.3)

4.2 Greedy Initialization

In the classical job shop scheduling problem, one can consider tasks in any order compatible with the jobs and schedule them to their earliest possible start time. The resulting schedule may have a long makespan, however such a procedure usually produces reasonable upper bounds. With time lag constraints, however, scheduling early tasks of a job implicitly fixes the start times for later tasks, thus making the problem harder. Indeed, as soon as tasks have been fixed in several jobs, the problem becomes difficult even if there is no constraint on the length of the makepsan. Standard heuristics can thus have difficulty finding feasible solutions even when the makespan is not tightly bounded. In fact, we observed that this phenomenon is critical for our approach.

Once a relatively good upper bound is known our approach is efficient and is often able to find an optimal solution. However, when the upper bound is, for instance, the trivial sum of durations of all tasks, finding a feasible solution with such a relaxed makespan was in some cases difficult. For some large instances, no non-trivial solution was found, and on some instances of more moderate size, much computational effort was spent converging towards optimal values.

We therefore designed a search heuristic to find solutions of good quality, albeit very quickly. The main idea is to move to a new job only when all tasks of the same machine are completely sequenced between previous jobs. Another important factor is to make decisions based on the maximum completion time of a job, whilst leaving enough freedom within that job to potentially insert subsequent jobs instead of moving them to the back of the already scheduled jobs.

Algorithm 1. Greedy initialization branching heuristic

$fixed\_jobs \leftarrow \emptyset;\ jobs\_to\_schedule \leftarrow \mathcal{J};$
$fixed\_jobs \leftarrow \emptyset;\ jobs\_to\_schedule \leftarrow \mathcal{J};$
while $jobs\_to\_schedule \neq \emptyset$ **do**
    pick and remove a random job J_y in $jobs\_to\_schedule$; $fixed\_jobs \leftarrow fixed\_jobs \cup \{J_y\}$;
    $next\_decisions \leftarrow \{b_{ij} \mid J_{x(i)}, J_{x(j)} \in fixed\_jobs\}$;
    while $next\_decisions \neq \emptyset$ **do**
1   pick and remove a random disjunct b_{ij} from $next\_decisions$;
        if $J_{x(i)} = J_y$ **then** branch on $t_i + p_i \leq t_j$ **else** branch on $t_j + p_j \leq t_i$;
2   branch on $t_{xm} \leq min(t_{(x-1)m+1}) + \texttt{stretched}(J_y)$;

We give a pseudo-code for this strategy in Algorithm 1. The set $jobs\_to\_schedule$ stands for the jobs for which sequencing is still open, whilst $fixed\_jobs$ contains the currently processed job, as well as all the jobs that are completely sequenced. On the first iteration of the outer "while" loop, a job is chosen. There is no disjunct satisfying the condition in Line 1, so this job's completion time is fixed to a value given by the stretched procedure (Line 2), that is, the minimum possible starting time of its first task, plus its total duration, plus the sum of the possible time lags.

On the second iteration and beyond, a new job is selected. We then branch on the sequencing decisions between this new job and the rest of the set $fixed\_jobs$ before moving to a new job. We call $J_{x(i)}$ the job that contains task t_i, and observe that for any unassigned Boolean variable b_{ij}, either $J_{x(i)}$ or $J_{x(j)} \in fixed\_jobs$ must be the last chosen job J_y. The sequencing choice that sets a task of the new job *before* a task of previously explored jobs is preferred, i.e., considered in the left branch. Observe that a failure due to time lag constraints can be raised only in the inner "while" loop. Therefore, if the current upper bound on the makespan is large enough, this heuristic will ensure that we never backtrack on a decision on a task. We randomize this heuristic and use several iterations (1000 in the present set of experiments) to find a good initial solution.

4.3   Special Case: Job Shop with No-Wait problems

The job shop problem with no-wait refers to the case where the maximum time-lag is set to 0, i.e. each task of a job must start directly after its preceding task has finished. In this case one can view the tasks of the job as one block.

In [12] we introduced a simple improvement for the no-wait class based on the following observation: if no delay is allowed between any two consecutive tasks of a job, then the start time of every task is functionally dependent on the start time of any other task in the job. The tasks of each job can thus be viewed as one block. We therefore use a single variable J_x standing for the starting times of the job of same name.

We call $J_{x(i)}$ the job of task t_i, and we define h_i as the total duration of the tasks coming before task t_i in its job $J_{x(i)}$. That is, $h_i = \sum_{k \in \{k \mid k < i \,\wedge\, t_k \in J_{x(i)}\}} p_k$. For every pair of tasks $t_i \in J_x, t_j \in J_y$ sharing a machine, we use the same Boolean variables to represent disjuncts as in the original model, however linked by the following constraints:

$$b_{ij} = \begin{cases} 0 \Leftrightarrow J_x + h_i + p_i - h_j \leq J_y \\ 1 \Leftrightarrow J_y + h_j + p_j - h_i \leq J_x \end{cases}$$

Although the variables and constants are different, these are the same constraints as used in the basic model. The no-wait JSP can therefore be reformulated as shown in Model 4, where the variables $J_1, \ldots, J_n$ represent the start time of the jobs and $f(i,j) = h_i + p_i - h_j$.

However, we can go one step further. For a given pair of jobs J_x, J_y the set of disjunct between tasks of these jobs define as many *conflict intervals* for the start time of one job

model 4. NW-JSP

$$minimise \ C_{max} \ \text{subject to :}$$

$$C_{max} \geq J_x + \sum_{t_i \in J_x} p_i \qquad\qquad \forall J_x \in \mathcal{J} \qquad\qquad (4.3)$$

$$b_{ij} = \begin{cases} 0 \Leftrightarrow J_{x(i)} + f(i,j) \leq J_{x(j)} \\ 1 \Leftrightarrow J_{x(j)} + f(j,i) \leq J_{x(i)} \end{cases} \qquad \forall M_y \in \mathcal{M}, \ t_i \neq t_j \in M_y \qquad (4.4)$$

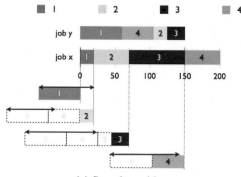

Machine	1	2	3	4
t_i, t_j	t_1, t_5	t_2, t_7	t_3, t_8	t_4, t_6
p_i	20	50	80	50
h_i	0	20	70	150
p_j	60	20	25	45
h_j	0	105	125	60
$-f(j,i)$	-60	-105	-80	45
$f(i,j)$	20	-35	25	140

(a) Sample problem

(b) Values of p, h and f

Fig. 1. Computation of conflict intervals

relative to the other. For two tasks t_i and t_j, we have $J_{x(j)} \notin \ ]J_{x(i)} - f(j,i), J_{x(i)} + f(i,j)[$. However, these intervals may overlap or subsume each other. It is therefore possible to tighten this encoding by computing larger intervals, that we shall refer to as *maximal forbidden intervals*, hence resulting in fewer disjuncts. We first give an example, and then briefly describe a procedure to find maximal forbidden intervals.

In Figure 1a we illustrate two jobs $J_x = \{t_1, t_2, t_3, t_4\}$ and $J_y = \{t_5, t_6, t_7, t_8\}$. The number and shades of grey stand for the machine required by each task. The length of the tasks are respectively $\{20, 50, 80, 50\}$ for J_x and $\{60, 45, 20, 25\}$ for J_y. In Figure 1b we give, for each machine, the pair of conflicting tasks, their durations and the corresponding forbidden intervals.

For each machine M_k, let t_i be the task of J_x and t_j the task of J_y that are both processed on machine M_k. Following the reasoning used in Model 4, we have a conflict interval (represented by black arrows in Figure 1a) for each pair of tasks sharing the same machine: $J_y \notin \ ]J_x - f(j,i), J_x + f(i,j)[$. In the example the forbidden intervals for J_y are therefore: $]J_x - 60, J_x + 20[\dots]J_x - 105, J_x - 35[\dots]J_x - 80, J_x + 25[\dots]J_x + 45, J_x + 140[$. However, these intervals can be merged, yielding larger (maximal) forbidden intervals, in which case we have: $J_y \notin]J_x - 105, J_x + 25[\wedge J_y \notin]J_x + 45, J_x + 140[$.

Given two jobs J_x and J_y, Algorithm 2 computes all maximal forbidden intervals efficiently (in $O(m \log m)$ steps). First, we build a list of pairs whose first element is an end point of a conflict interval, and second element is either $+1$ if it is the start, and -1 otherwise. Then these pairs are sorted by increasing first element. Now we can scan these pairs and count, thanks to the second element, how many intervals are

---

Algorithm 2. `get-F-intervals`.

Data: $J_x = \{t_{x_1}, \ldots, t_{x_m}\}$, $J_y = \{t_{y_1}, \ldots, t_{y_m}\}$, $\mathcal{M}$

$I_{in} \leftarrow []$;

foreach $t_{x_i} \in J_x, t_{y_j} \in J_y$ *such that* $\mathcal{M}(t_{x_i}) = \mathcal{M}(t_{y_j})$ **do**

  $I_{in} \leftarrow I_{in}$ extended with $[(-f(j,i), +1), (f(i,j), -1)]$;

sort I_{in} by increasing first element;

$I_{out} \leftarrow []$; $open \leftarrow 0$;

while $not\text{-}empty(I)$ **do**

  $(a, z) \leftarrow$ remove first element from I_{in};

  if $open = 0$ **then** append a to I_{out};

  $open \leftarrow open + z$;

  if $open = 0$ **then** append a to I_{out};

return I_{out};

---

simultaneously open. When we go from 0 to 1 open intervals, this marks the start of a maximal forbidden interval, and conversely the end when we go from 1 to 0 open intervals. The list I_{out} has $2k$ elements, and the $2i + 1^{th}$ and $2i + 2^{th}$ elements are read as the start and end of a forbidden interval.

Given this set of forbidden intervals, we can represent the conflicts between J_x and J_y with the following set of Boolean variables and disjunctive constraints:

$$b_{xy}^{105,25} = \begin{cases} 0 \Leftrightarrow J_y + 105 \leq J_x \\ 1 \Leftrightarrow J_x + 25 \leq J_y \end{cases} b_{xy}^{45,140} = \begin{cases} 0 \Leftrightarrow J_y - 45 \leq J_x \\ 1 \Leftrightarrow J_x + 140 \leq J_y \end{cases}$$

In the previous encoding we would have needed 4 Boolean variables and as many disjunctive constraints (one for each pair of tasks sharing a machine). We believe, however, that the main benefit is not the reduction in size of the encoding. Rather, it is the tighter correlation between the model and the real structure of the problem which helps the heuristic to make good choices.

---

model 5. NW-JSP

---

minimise C_{max} subject to :

$$C_{max} \geq J_x + \sum_{t_i \in J_x} p_i \qquad \forall J_x \in \mathcal{J} \qquad (4.5)$$

$$b_{ij}^{a,b} = \begin{cases} 0 \Leftrightarrow J_y - a \leq J_x \\ 1 \Leftrightarrow J_x + b \leq J_y \end{cases} \qquad \forall J_x \neq J_y \in \mathcal{J}, [a,b] \in \text{get-F-intervals}(J_x, J_y, \mathcal{M}) (4.6)$$

---

5   Experimental Evaluation

The full experimental results, with statistics for each instance, as well as benchmarks and source code are online: http://homepages.laas.fr/ehebrard/jsp-experiment.html.

5.1 Job Shop with Earliness/Tardiness Objective

The best complete methods for handling these types of problem are the CP/LP hybrid of Beck and Refalo [4] and the MIP approaches of Danna et al. [9], and Danna and Perron [8], while more recently Kebel and Hanzalek proposed a pure CP approach [14]. Danna and Perron also proposed an incomplete approach based on large neighborhood search [8].

Our experiments were run on an Intel Xeon 2.66GHz machine with 12GB of ram on Fedora 9. Each algorithm run on a problem had an overall time limit of 3600s, and there were 10 runs per instance. We report our results in terms of the best and worst run. We tested our method on two benchmarks which have been widely studied in the literature. The comparison experimental results are taken from [9] and [8], where all experiments were performed on a 1.5 GHz Pentium IV system running Linux. For the first benchmark, these algorithms had a time limit of 20 minutes per instance, while for the second benchmark the algorithms had a time limit of 2 hours.

The comparison methods are as follows:

- *MIP*: Default CPLEX in [9], run using a modified version of ILOG CPLEX 8.1
- *CP*: A pure constraint programming approach introduced by Beck and Refalo in [4], run using ILOG Scheduler 5.3 and ILOG Solver 5.3
- *CRS-ALL*: A CP/LP hybrid approach proposed by Beck and Refalo in [4], run using ILOG CPLEX 8.1, ILOG Hybrid 1.3.1, ILOG Scheduler 5.3 and ILOG Solver 5.3
- *uLNS*: An unstructured large neighborhood search MIP method proposed by Danna and Peron in [8], run using a modified version of ILOG CPLEX 8.1
- *sLNS*: A structured large neighborhood search CP/LP method proposed by Danna and Peron in [8], run using ILOG Scheduler 5.3, ILOG Solver 5.3 and ILOG CPLEX 8.1

The first benchmark consists of 9 sets of problems generated by Beck and Refalo [4] using the random JSP generator of Watson et al. [26]. For instance size $\mathcal{J}x\mathcal{M}$, there were three sets of ten JSPs of size 10x10, 15x10 and 20x10 generated. The second benchmark is taken from the genetic algorithms (GA) literature and was proposed by Morton and Pentico [18]. There are 12 instances, with problem size ranging from 10x3 to 50x8. Jobs in these problems do have release dates. Furthermore earliness and tardiness costs of a job are equal.

We present results on the randomly generated ETJSPs in Table 1 in terms of number of problems solved to optimality and sum of the upper bounds, for each algorithm.[1] Here, the column "Best" for our method means the number of problems solved to optimality on at least one of the ten runs on the instance, while the column "Worst" refers to the number of problems solved to optimality on all ten runs. We also report the mean cpu time in seconds for our method.

We first consider the number of problems solved to optimality (columns "Opt."). While there is little difference in the performance of our method and that of uLNS and CRS-ALL on the looser instances (looseness factor of 1.3 and 1.5), we see that our method is able to close three of the 23 open problems in the set with looseness factor

---

[1] Note that sLNS is not complete, hence it never proved optimality.

Table 1. ET-JSP - Random Problems, Number Proven Optimal and Upper Bound Sum

lf	MIP		CP		uLNS		sLNS	CRS-All		Model 2				
										Best		Worst		Avg.
	opt.	$\sum$ub	opt.	$\sum$ub	opt.	$\sum$ub	$\sum$ub	opt.	$\sum$ub	opt.	$\sum$ub	opt.	$\sum$ub	Time (s)
1.0	0	654,290	0	1,060,634	0	156,001	52,307	7	885,546	**10**	**30,735**	8	38,416	2534.86
1.3	14	26,930	6	1,248,618	**30**	8,397	**8,397**	**30**	**8,397**	**30**	**8,397**	**30**	**8,397**	0.36
1.5	27	7,891	6	1,672,511	**30**	6,964	**6,964**	**30**	**6,964**	**30**	**6,964**	**30**	**6,964**	0.18

Notes: Comparison results taken from [9], except uLNS, taken from [8].
Figures in bold are the best result over all methods.

1.0. An obvious reason for this improvement with our method would be the difference in time limits and quality of machines. However, analysis of the results reveals that of the 68 problems solved to optimality on every run of our method, only 8 took longer than one second on average, and only one took longer than one minute (averaging 156s). Furthermore, uLNS only solved two problems to optimality when the time limit was increased to two hours [8]. Clearly our method is extremely efficient at proving optimality on these problems.

The previous results suggest that CRS-ALL is much better than uLNS on these problems. However, as was shown by Danna et al. [9], this may not be the case when the algorithms are compared based on the sum of the upper bounds found over the 30 "hard" instances (i.e. with looseness factor 1.0). In order to assess whether there was a similar deterioration in the performance of our method as for CRS-ALL on the problems where optimality was not proven, we report this data in the columns "$\sum$ub" of Table 1.

We find, on the contrary, that the performance of our approach is even more impressive when algorithms are compared using this metric. The two large neighborhood search methods found the best upper bounds of the comparison algorithms with sLNS the most efficient by a factor of 2 over uLNS. However, there are a couple of points that should be noted here. Firstly sLNS is an incomplete method so cannot prove optimality, and secondly the sum of the worst upper bounds found by our method was still significantly better than that found by sLNS. Indeed, there was very little variation in performance for our method across runs, with an average difference of 256 between the best and worst upper bounds found.

Danna and Perron also provided the sum of the best upper bounds found on the hard instances over all methods they studied [8], which was 36,459. This further underlines the quality of the performance of our method on these problems. Finally, we investigated the hypothesis that the different time limit and machines used for experiments could explain these results. We compared the upper bounds found by our method after the dichotomic search phase, where the maximum runtime of this phase over all runs per instance was 339s. The upper bound sums over the hard instances were 32,299 and 49,808 for best and worst respectively, which refutes this hypothesis.

Table 2 provides results on the second of the benchmarks (taken from the GA literature). Following the convention of previous work on these problems [23][4][9], we report the cost normalized by the weighted sum of the job processing times. We include the best results found by the GA algorithms as presented by Vázquez and Whitley [23]. We also provide an aggregated view of the results of each algorithm using the geometric

Table 2. ET-JSP - GA Problems, Normalized upper bounds

Instance	Size	MIP	CP	uLNS	sLNS	CRS-All	GA Best	Model 2 Best	Model 2 Worst
jb1	10x3	**0.191***	0.474	**0.191***	**0.191**	**0.191***	0.474	**0.191***	**0.191***
jb2	10x3	**0.137***	0.746	**0.137***	**0.137**	0.531	0.499	**0.137***	**0.137***
jb4	10x5	**0.568***	0.570	**0.568***	**0.568**	**0.568***	0.619	**0.568***	**0.568***
jb9	15x3	**0.333***	0.355	**0.333***	**0.333**	1.216	0.369	**0.333***	**0.333***
jb11	15x5	0.233	0.365	**0.213***	**0.213**	**0.213***	0.262	0.221	0.235
jb12	15x5	**0.190***	0.239	**0.190***	**0.190**	**0.190***	0.246	**0.190***	**0.190***
	GMR	1.015	1.774	**1**	**1**	1.555	1.610	1.006	1.017
ljb1	30x3	**0.215***	0.847	**0.215***	**0.215**	0.295	0.279	0.215	0.221
ljb2	30x3	0.622	1.268	**0.508**	**0.508**	1.364	0.598	0.590	0.728
ljb7	50x5	0.317	0.614	0.123	**0.110**	0.951	0.246	0.166	0.256
ljb9	50x5	1.373	1.737	1.270	1.015	2.571	**0.739**	1.157	1.513
ljb10	50x8	0.820	1.569	0.558	0.525	1.779	0.512	**0.499**	0.637
ljb12	50x8	1.025	1.368	0.488	0.605	1.601	**0.399**	0.537	0.623
	GMR	1.943	3.233	1.213	**1.170**	4.098	1.220	1.299	1.686
Overall GMR		1.329	2.434	1.084	**1.068**	2.305	1.408	1.118	1.256

Comparison results taken from [9]. Figures in bold indicate best upper bound
found over the different algorithms. "*" indicates optimality was proven by the algorithm.

mean ratio (GMR), which is the geometric mean of the ratio between the normalized upper bound found by the algorithm and the best known normalized upper bound, across a set of instances.

The performance of our method was less impressive for these problems, solving two fewer problems to optimality than uLNS, and achieving a worse GMR than either of the large neighborhood search methods. However, we remind the reader that all comparison methods had a 2 hour time limit on these instances, except the GA approaches for which the time limit was not reported. We further note that we find an improved solution for one instance (ljb10) and outperform all methods other than uLNS and sLNS.

5.2 Job Shop Scheduling Problem with positive Time Lags

These experiments were run using the same settings as in Section 5.1. However, because of the large number of instances and algorithms, we used only 5 random runs per instance.

There are relatively few results reported for benchmarks with positive maximum time lag constraints, as most publications focus on the "no wait" case. Caumond et al. introduced a genetic algorithm [7]. Then, Artigues et al. introduced a Branch & Bound procedure that allowed them to find lower bounds of good quality [1]. Therefore, in order to get a better idea of the efficiency of our approach, we adapted a model written by Chris Beck for Ilog Scheduler (version 6.3) to problems featuring time lag constraints. This model was used to showcase the SGMPCS algorithm [3]. We used the following two strategies: In the first, the next pair of tasks to schedule is chosen following the Texture heuristic/goal predefined in Ilog Scheduler and restarts following the Luby sequence [16] are performed, this was one of the default strategies used as a reference point in [3]. In the second, branching decisions are selected with the same "goal", however the previous best solution is used to decide wich branch should be explored first, and geometric restarts [25] are performed, instead of the Luby sequence. In other words, this is SGMPCS with a singleton elite solution. We denote the first method Texture-Luby and the second method Texture-Geom+Guided. These two methods were run on the same hardware with the same time limit and number of random runs as our method. Finally, we report results for our approach without the greedy initialization heuristic (Algorithm 1) in order to evaluate its importance.

We used the benchmarks generated by Caumond et al. in [7] by adding maximal time lag constraints to the Lawrence JSP instances of the OR-library[2]. Given a job shop instance N, and two parameters x and y, a new instance N_x_y is produced. For each job all maximal time lags are given the value ym, where m is the average processing time over tasks of this job. The first parameter x corresponds to minimal time lags and will always be 0 in this paper.

Table 3. TL-JSP - Comparison with related work (Time & Upper bound)

Instance	[AHL]		[CLT]		Model 3	
	time (s)	C_{max}	time (s)	C_{max}	time (s)	C_{max}
la06_0_10	707.00	927	0.00	**926**	0.03	**926**
la06_0_1	524.00	1391	1839.00	1086	70.60	**926**
la07_0_10	518.00	1123	25.00	**890**	3600.00	**890**
la07_0_1	754.00	1065	1914.00	1032	3600.00	**896**
la08_0_10	260.00	**863**	2.00	**863**	0.07	**863**
la08_0_1	587.00	1052	1833.00	1048	615.80	**892**
average	558.33	1070	935.50	974	1314.41	898
PRD		18.88		8.32		0.00

Due to space limitations, we present most of our results in terms of each solver's average percentage relative deviation (PRD) given by the following formula: $PRD = ((C_{Alg} - C_{Ref})/C_{Ref}) * 100$, where C_{Alg} is the best makespan found by the algorithm and C_{Ref} is the best upper bound among all considered algorithms[3]. In Table 3, we first report a comparison with the genetic algorithm described in [7], denoted [CLT] and the adhoc Branch & Bound algorithm introduced in [1], denoted [AHL]. We used only instances for which results were reported in both papers, and where the time lags were strictly positive, hence the relatively small data set. Despite that, and despite the difference in hardware and time limit, it is quite clear that our approach outperforms both the complete and heuristic methods on these benchmarks.

Next, in Table 4, we report results on all modified Lawrence instances for both Ilog Scheduler models, and the two version of Model 3, with and without the greedy initialization heuristic. Since there are 280 instances in total, the results are aggregated by the

---

[2] http://people.brunel.ac.uk/~mastjjb/jeb/info.html
[3] To the best of our knowledge, these are the best known upper bounds.

Table 4. TL-JSP - Comparison with Ilog Scheduler (Proofs of optimality & Upper bound PRD)

Instance Sets	Texture				Model 3			
	Luby		Geom+Guided		no init.		init. heuristic	
	Opt.	PRD	Opt.	PRD	Opt.	PRD	Opt.	PRD
la[1,40]_0_0	0.12	25.37	0.12	16.15	**0.37**	10.42	0.35	**0.06**
la[1,40]_0_0.25	0.20	22.98	0.25	12.01	0.37	3.46	**0.40**	**0.00**
la[1,40]_0_0.5	0.22	19.47	0.25	5.17	0.37	2.62	**0.42**	**0.00**
la[1,40]_0_1	0.35	15.76	0.42	1.18	0.40	17.43	**0.45**	0.47
la[1,40]_0_2	0.67	7.35	**0.75**	**0.13**	0.67	74.16	0.70	0.37
la[1,40]_0_3	0.75	3.47	**0.92**	**0.00**	0.75	95.91	0.77	0.29
la[1,40]_0_10	0.95	0.10	**0.97**	**0.00**	0.92	0.04	0.92	0.05

level of tightness of the time lag constraints. For each set, we give the ratio of instances that were solved to optimality in at least one of the five runs in the first column, as well as the mean PRD in the second column.

First, we notice the great impact of the new initialization heuristic on our method. Without it, the Ilog Scheduler model was more efficient for instances with $y = 1$, and the overall results are extremely poor for larger values of y. However, the mean results are deceptive. Without initialization, Model 3 can be very efficient, although in a few cases no solution at all can be found. Indeed, relaxing the makespan does not necessarily makes the problem easy for this model. The weight of these bad cases in the mean value can be important, hence the poor PRD. On the other hand, we can see that the Ilog Scheduler model is more robust to this phenomenon: a non-trivial upper bound is found in every case. It is therefore likely that the impact of the initialization heuristic will not be as important on the Ilog model as on Model 3.

We also notice that solution guidance and geometric restarts greatly improve Ilog Scheduler's performance. Interestingly, we observe that our approach is best when the time lag constraints are tight. On the other hand, Scheduler is slightly more efficient on instances with loose time lag constraints and in particular proves optimality more often on these instances. However, whereas our method always finds near-optimal solutions (the worst mean PRD is 0.47 for instances with $y = 1$), both scheduler models find relatively poor upper bounds for small values of y.

5.3 Job Shop Scheduling Problem with no wait constraints

For the no-wait job shop problem, the best methods are a tabu search method by Schuster (TS [20]) and a hybrid constructive/tabu search algorithm introduced by Bożejko and Makuchowski in 2009 (HTS [6]). We also report the results of a Branch & Bound procedure introduced by Mascis and Pacciarelli [17]. This algorithm was run on a Pentium II 350 MHz.

For the no-wait class we used the same data sets as Schuster [20] and Bożejko et al. [6] where null time lags are added to instances of the OR-library. We report the best results of each paper in terms of average PRD. It should be noted that for HTS, the authors reported two sets of results. The former were run with a time limit based on

Table 5. NW-JSP - Comparison with related work (Upper bound PRD)

Instance	Mascis et al. B&B	Schuster TS	Bożejko et al. HTS	HTS+	Model 4 $tdom+bw$	$tdom/tw$	Model 5 $tdom+bw$	$tdom/tw$
la[1-10]	**0.00**	4.43	1.77	*1.77*	**0.00**	**0.00**	**0.00**	**0.00**
la[11-20]	31.66	7.93	3.49	*0.95*	0.14	0.10	**0.00**	0.31
la[21-30]	61.09	10.43	7.25	*0.08*	1.16	0.57	**0.25**	0.84
la[31-40]	73.73	10.95	8.33	*0.15*	4.42	1.77	2.68	**1.36**
ab2[5-9]	17.04	9.01	5.95	*0.78*	2.47	1.14	**1.13**	1.20
orb[1-10]	**0.00**	2.42	0.77	*0.77*	**0.00**	**0.00**	**0.00**	**0.00**
swv[1-5]	60.85	3.94	3.67	*0.00*	2.54	0.77	**0.00**	0.43
swv[6-10]	57.82	4.99	4.19	*0.00*	4.78	1.71	**0.44**	1.00
swv[11-15]	70.98	**0.68**	2.48	*0.60*	19.50	6.53	17.54	5.18
swv[16-20]	76.81	5.71	3.98	*0.00*	10.92	68.94	4.47	**3.17**
yn[1-4]	72.74	12.40	8.85	*0.32*	5.60	5.75	**2.37**	2.88
overall	44.72	6.51	4.36	*0.52*	3.53	5.50	1.97	**1.13**

Table 6. NW-JSP - New best upper bounds and optimality proofs

Instance	BKS	Schuster TS	Bożejko HTS	HTS+	Model 4 $tdom+bw$	$tdom/tw$	Model 5 $tdom+bw$	$tdom/tw$
la11_0_0	2821	1737	1704	1621	1622	**1619**	**1619***	1621
la13_0_0	2650	1701	1696	**1580**	1582	1590	**1580***	**1580**
la14_0_0	2662	1771	1722	1610	**1578**	**1578**	**1578***	1612
la15_0_0	2765	1808	1747	1686	1692	1679	**1671***	1691
la26_0_0	4268	2664	2738	2506	2624	2511	**2488**	2540
la28_0_0	4478	2886	2741	2552	2640	2605	**2546**	2569
la30_0_0	4097	2939	2791	**2452**	**2452**	**2452**	**2452***	2508
la34_0_0	6380	3957	3936	3659	3914	3693	3817	**3657**
la39_0_0	4295	2804	2725	2687	**2660**	**2660**	**2660***	**2660**
swv01	3824	2396	2424	**2318**	2344	2343	**2318***	2333
swv02	3800	2492	2484	**2417**	2440	2418	**2417***	**2417**
swv05	3836	2482	2489	**2333**	2433	**2333**	**2333***	**2333**
yn2	4025	2705	2647	2370	2486	2603	2427	**2353**
yn4	4109	2705	2630	2513	2532	2573	**2499**	2582

the runtimes reported in [20] and varying from 0.25 seconds for the easiest instances to 2360 seconds for the hardest. The latter (in italic font, and referred to as HTS+ in Table 5) were run "without limit of computation time". We use bold face to mark the best result amongst methods that had time limits, i.e. excluding HTS+. We ran two variable ordering heuristics for our method. First, the heuristics used for ET-JSP and TL-JSP, where the Boolean variable minimizing the value of $(max(t_i) + max(t_j) - min(t_i) - min(t_j) + 2)/(w(t_i) + w(t_j))$ is chosen first, denoted $tdom/tw$. Second, we used another heuristic, denoted $tdom+bw$ that selects the next Boolean variable to branch on solely according to the tasks' domain sizes $(max(t_i) + max(t_j) - min(t_i) - min(t_j) + 2)$, and break ties with the Boolean variable's own weight $w(b_{ij})$.

In Table 6 we report the results on no-wait instances for which we obtained new upper bounds (5 instances) or new proofs of optimality (9 instances), thanks to the model introduced here.

6   Conclusions

We have shown that the simple constraint programming approach introduced in [13] can be successfully adapted to handle the objective of minimizing the sum of earliness/tardiness costs. These problems have traditionally proven troublesome for CP approaches because of the weak propagation of the sum objective [8].

Then we introduced a new heuristic to find good initial solutions for job shop problems with maximal time lag constraints. The resulting method greatly improves over state of the art algorithms for this problem. However, as opposed to the other aspects of the method (adaptive variable heuristic, solution guided branching, restarts with nogood storage) this new initialization heuristic is dedicated to job shop problems with time lag constraints.

Finally, we showed that domain-specific information can also be used to improve our model for no-wait job shop scheduling problems, allowing us to provide several improved upper bounds and prove optimality in many cases.

References

1. Artigues, C., Huguet, M.-J., Lopez, P.: Generalized Disjunctive Constraint Propagation for Solving the Job Shop Problem with Time Lags. EAAI 24(2), 220–231 (2011)
2. Baptiste, P., Flamini, M., Sourd, F.: Lagrangian Bounds for Just-in-Time Job-shop Scheduling. Computers & OR 35(3), 906–915 (2008)
3. Beck, J.C.: Solution-Guided Multi-Point Constructive Search for Job Shop Scheduling. JAIR 29, 49–77 (2007)
4. Beck, J.C., Refalo, P.: A Hybrid Approach to Scheduling with Earliness and Tardiness Costs. Annals OR 118(1-4), 49–71 (2003)
5. Boussemart, F., Hemery, F., Lecoutre, C., Sais, L.: Boosting Systematic Search by Weighting Constraints. In: ECAI, pp. 482–486 (2004)
6. Bozejko, W., Makuchowski, M.: A Fast Hybrid Tabu Search Algorithm for the No-wait Job Shop Problem. Computers & Industrial Engineering 56(4), 1502–1509 (2009)
7. Caumond, A., Lacomme, P., Tchernev, N.: A Memetic Algorithm for the Job-shop with Time-lags. Computers & OR 35(7), 2331–2356 (2008)
8. Danna, E., Perron, L.: Structured vs. unstructured large neighborhood search: A case study on job-shop scheduling problems with earliness and tardiness costs. Technical report, ILOG (2003)
9. Danna, E., Rothberg, E., Le Pape, C.: Integrating Mixed Integer Programming and Local Search: A Case Study on Job-Shop Scheduling Problems. In: CPAIOR (2003)
10. Feydy, T., Stuckey, P.J.: Lazy Clause Generation Reengineered. In: Gent, I.P. (ed.) CP 2009. LNCS, vol. 5732, pp. 352–366. Springer, Heidelberg (2009)
11. Grimes, D.: A Study of Adaptive Restarting Strategies for Solving Constraint Satisfaction Problems. In: AICS (2008)

12. Grimes, D., Hebrard, E.: Job Shop Scheduling with Setup Times and Maximal Time-Lags: A Simple Constraint Programming Approach. In: Lodi, A., Milano, M., Toth, P. (eds.) CPAIOR 2010. LNCS, vol. 6140, pp. 147–161. Springer, Heidelberg (2010)
13. Grimes, D., Hebrard, E., Malapert, A.: Closing the Open Shop: Contradicting Conventional Wisdom. In: Gent, I.P. (ed.) CP 2009. LNCS, vol. 5732, pp. 400–408. Springer, Heidelberg (2009)
14. Kelbel, J., Hanzálek, Z.: Solving production scheduling with earliness/tardiness penalties by constraint programming. J. Intell. Manuf. (2010)
15. Lecoutre, C., Sais, L., Tabary, S., Vidal, V.: Nogood Recording from Restarts. In: IJCAI, pp. 131–136 (2007)
16. Luby, M., Sinclair, A., Zuckerman, D.: Optimal Speedup of Las Vegas Algorithms. In: ISTCS, pp. 128–133 (1993)
17. Mascis, A., Pacciarelli, D.: Job-shop Scheduling with Blocking and No-wait Constraints. EJOR 143(3), 498–517 (2002)
18. Morton, T.E., Pentico, D.W.: Heuristic Scheduling Systems. John Wiley and Sons, Chichester (1993)
19. Rajendran, C.: A No-Wait Flowshop Scheduling Heuristic to Minimize Makespan. The Journal of the Operational Research Society 45(4), 472–478 (1994)
20. Schuster, C.J.: No-wait Job Shop Scheduling: Tabu Search and Complexity of Problems. Math. Meth. Oper. Res. 63, 473–491 (2006)
21. Schutt, A., Feydy, T., Stuckey, P.J., Wallace, M.: Why Cumulative Decomposition Is Not as Bad as It Sounds. In: Gent, I.P. (ed.) CP 2009. LNCS, vol. 5732, pp. 746–761. Springer, Heidelberg (2009)
22. Tamura, N., Taga, A., Kitagawa, S., Banbara, M.: Compiling Finite Linear CSP into SAT. In: Benhamou, F. (ed.) CP 2006. LNCS, vol. 4204, pp. 590–603. Springer, Heidelberg (2006)
23. Vázquez, M., Whitley, L.D.: A comparison of genetic algorithms for the dynamic job shop scheduling problem. In: GECCO, p. 1011 (2000)
24. Vilím, P.: Filtering Algorithms for the Unary Resource Constraint. Archives of Control Sciences 18(2) (2008)
25. Walsh, T.: Search in a Small World. In: IJCAI, pp. 1172–1177 (1999)
26. Watson, J.-P., Barbulescu, L., Howe, A.E., Whitley, L.D.: Algorithm performance and problem structure for flow-shop scheduling. In: AAAI, pp. 688–695 (1999)
27. Wismer, D.A.: Solution of the Flowshop-Scheduling Problem with No Intermediate Queues. Operations Research 20(3), 689–697 (1972)

MaxRPC Algorithms Based on Bitwise Operations

Jinsong Guo[1,2], Zhanshan Li[1,2], Liang Zhang[1,2], and Xuena Geng[1,2]

[1] Key Laboratory of Symbolic Computation and Knowledge Engineering for
Ministry of Education, Jilin University, Changchun, 130012, China
[2] College of Computer Science and Technology, Jilin University,
Changchun, 130012, China
zslizsli@163.com

Abstract. Max Restricted Path Consistency (maxRPC) is a promising domain filtering consistency for binary constraints. In existing algorithms, the process of searching for PC-witnesses requires most constraint checks. And the computing speed of this process significantly affects the efficiency of the whole algorithm. In this paper, we propose a new method based on bitwise operations to speed up the computations of this process. Two algorithms maxRPC^{bit} and maxRPC^{bit+rm} utilizing this new method are proposed. Both algorithms and their light versions outperform the best ones among existing algorithms by a large margin. Significantly, our experiments, which compare the search algorithms applying light maxRPC with the one maintaining arc consistency, demonstrate that maxRPC is a much more promising filtering technique than what we thought.

1 Introduction

Filtering techniques are used to remove some local inconsistencies in the search algorithms solving the instances of the Constraint Satisfaction Problem (CSP). They can be used in a preprocessing step or during the search. In [1], a promising local consistency property has been proposed: the *max-restricted path consistency* (maxRPC). Computational experiments give evidence that maxRPC offers a particularly good compromise between computational cost and pruning efficiency [2]. Stronger than AC, maxRPC removes not only the values that have no AC-supports, but also those that have no PC-supports. A value (x_j, b) is an AC-support of value (x_i, a) if $((x_i, a), (x_j, b))$ is allowed by c_{ij}. An AC-support (x_j, b) of (x_i, a) is a PC-support of (x_i, a) iff at least one PC-witness exists in the domain of each third variable x_k which is constrained with both x_i and x_j. A PC-witness of the value pair $((x_i, a), (x_j, b))$ is a value which is consistent with both (x_i, a) and (x_j, b).

Several algorithms have been proposed to enforce maxRPC. The first one maxRPC1 [1] is a fine-grained algorithm and requires a relatively high space cost. To reduce the space cost, a coarse-grained algorithm maxRPC2 [3] was proposed. Both maxRPC1 and maxRPC2 are not suited for use during search, thus in [4], maxRPC^{rm} was proposed, it makes use of the residues[5, 6] and can be better suited for use during search. Recently in [7], it was pointed out that the two coarse-grained algorithms

J. Lee (Ed.): CP 2011, LNCS 6876, pp. 373–384, 2011.

maxRPC2 and maxRPC^{rm} both suffer from the overhead caused by the redundant constraint checks in the process of searching for PC-witnesses, and although maxRPC1 doesn't perform these redundant checks, it requires higher space cost. Recently, maxRPC3 [7] and maxRPC3^{rm} [7] were proposed, they can largely eliminate the redundant constraint checks with lower space complexity than maxRPC1. The experiments in [7] showed that maxRPC3, lmaxRPC3 and lmaxRPC3^{rm} are the most efficient algorithms among existing algorithms when used stand-alone, and lmaxRPC3^{rm} displays the best performance during search.

The key of improving the performance of maxRPC algorithms is to speed up the process of searching for PC-witnesses since this process can be performed many times and the most constraint checks are performed in this process. The outstanding performances of (l)maxRPC3 and (l)maxRPC^{rm} are mainly due to the improvement of searching for PC-witnesses. In this paper, we propose a new method of searching for PC-witnesses. Our method exploits the bitwise operations to speed up the computations. If the computer is equipped with a x-bit processor, when searching for a PC-witness in $D(x_k)$, the new method tests x values of x_k simultaneously instead of testing them one by one as the existing algorithms do. Based on this new method, we give a precise description of two coarse-grained algorithms maxRPC^{bit} and maxRPC^{bit+rm} which can be regarded as the variants of maxRPC2 and maxRPC3^{rm} respectively. Our experiments compare the new algorithms with the most efficient ones among the existing maxRPC algorithms. The results demonstrate that all the new algorithms outperform existing algorithms by a large margin when used stand-alone, and lmaxRPC^{bit+rm} displays a much better performance than lmaxRPC3^{rm} during search. Most importantly, the improvement of searching for PC-witnesses enables maintaining lmaxRPC outperforms MAC on much more problems.

2 Background

A Constraint Satisfaction Problem (CSP) is defined as a triple (X, D, C), where X is a finite set of variables, D is the set of domains, and C is a finite set of constraints. Each domain in $D(x_i) \in D$ denotes the current domain of x_i, i.e. it denotes the possible values for x_i. Each constraint $c \in C$ involves a subset of variables of X, called the scope of c and denoted by $vars(c)$, and has an associated relation, denoted $rel(c)$, which specifies the allowed combinations of values for the variables in $vars(c)$. In this paper, we assume that all the constraints are binary, i.e., each constraint $c_{ij} \in C$ is defined over two variables x_i and x_j. If $((x_i, a), (x_j, b)) \in rel(c_{ij})$, we then say that (x_j, b) is an AC-support of (x_i, a) on c_{ij}. An instantiation I of a set of n variables S is an indexed set of n values s.t. the ith value I_i belongs to the domain of the ith variable x_i in S. An instantiation I satisfies a constraint c_{ij} if $\{x_i, x_j\} \not\subseteq S$ or $((x_i, I_i), (x_j, I_j)) \in rel(c_{ij})$. An instantiation is consistent if it satisfies all the constraints.

Definition 1 (PC-support [1]). A pair of values $((x_i, a), (x_j, b))$ is path consistent if $\forall x_k \in X$ s.t. $x_j \neq x_k \neq x_i \neq x_j$, this pair of values can be extended to a consistent instantiation of $\{x_i, x_j, x_k\}$. (x_j, b) is a PC-support of (x_i, a) if $((x_i, a), (x_j, b))$ is path consistent.

Definition 2 (maxRPC [1]). A binary CN is max-restricted path consistent iff $\forall x_i \in X$, $D(x_i)$ is a non empty arc consistent domain and, $\forall a \in D(x_i)$, for all $x_j \in X$ linked to x_i, $\exists b \in D(x_j)$ s.t. $((x_i, a), (x_j, b)) \in rel(c_{ij})$ and for all $x_k \in X$ linked to both x_i and x_j, $\exists c \in D(x_k)$ s.t. $((x_i, a), (x_k, c)) \in rel(c_{ik}) \wedge ((x_k, c), (x_j, b)) \in rel(c_{jk})$.

Light maxRPC [4] is an approximation of maxRPC that only propagates the loss of AC-supports and not the loss of PC-witnesses. Several algorithms have been proposed to establish maxRPC and light maxRPC. maxRPC1 is a fine-grained algorithm. It has optimal $O(end^3)$ time complexity but it requires $O(end)$ space complexity. maxRPC2 has a smaller space complexity $O(ed)$ and an optimal time complexity $O(end^3)$. (l)maxRPC^{rm} makes use of the residues and can be better suited for use during search. However, both maxRPC2 and maxRPC^{rm} suffer from the overhead as following. When searching for a PC-witness for a pair of values $((x_i, a), (x_j, b))$ in a third variable x_k, they always start the search from scratch, i.e. from the first available value in $D(x_k)$. As these searches can be repeated many times during search, there can be many redundant constraint checks [7]. In contrast, maxRPC3 and maxRPC3^{rm} eliminate the redundant constraint checks with lower space complexity than maxRPC1. maxRPC3 has a good performance when used during the preprocessing step. And the light version of maxRPC3^{rm} which takes advantage of residues is very efficient when used during search. Both maxRPC3 and maxRPC3^{rm} utilize data structures called *LastPC* and *LastAC*. For each value (x_i, a), maxRPC3 uses $LastPC_{x_i, a, x_j}$ and $LastAC_{x_i, a, x_j}$ to record the smallest PC and AC-supports of (x_i, a) in $D(x_j)$, while maxRPC3^{rm} uses them to record the most recently discovered PC and AC-supports.

When searching for a PC-witness for a pair of values $((x_i, a), (x_j, b))$ in a third variable x_k, all existing algorithms need to perform constraint checks to confirm whether a value (x_k, c) satisfies $((x_i, a), (x_k, c)) \in rel(c_{ik})$ and $((x_j, b), (x_k, c)) \in rel(c_{jk})$. The differences at this process in these algorithms are from which value in $D(x_k)$ the search starts. maxRPC2 and maxRPC^{rm} start the search from scratch thus there are redundant constraint checks, maxRPC1 and maxRPC3 avoid these redundant constraint checks, and maxRPC3 requires only two constraint checks when $LastAC_{x_i, a, x_k}$ or $LastAC_{x_j, b, x_k}$ happens to be the PC-witness, but this is not always the case.

In the new method proposed below, bitwise operations are performed instead of constraint checks when searching for PC-witnesses. Assuming that the size of $D(x_k)$ is d and the computer is equipped with a 32-bit processor, in the worst case, only $2*\lceil d/32 \rceil$ bitwise operations need to be performed. The idea of exploiting bitwise operations to improve the efficiency of local arc consistency algorithms is not new. In particular, AC3^{bit} [8] which exploits bitwise operations can save a large amount of constraint checks in the process of determining whether or not a value has an AC-support. In [8], the arrays of words were used to represent domains and constraints. An array of words can be regarded as a bit sequence since each word is a sequence of 32 bits. Two 2-dimensional arrays *bitdom* and *bitSup* were introduced to respectively present domains and constraints. Each bit in *bitdom[X]* can be associated with the index of any value in the domain of X. When a bit is set to 1 (resp. 0), it means that the corresponding value is present in the domain (resp. absent from it). *bitSup[c$_{ij}$, x$_i$, a]* represents the binary representation of the supports of (x_i, a) in c_{ij}. For each value in the domain of x_j, there is a corresponding bit in $bitSup[c_{ij}, x_i, a]$ to mark whether this value is a support of (x_i, a).

The algorithms introduced in this paper are based on the same binary representations as [8]. In the paper, *length* is used to denote the size of an array and we consider that the computer is equipped with a 32-bit processor, thus if the domain of x_j has a size of d, the size of $bitdom[x_j]$ and $bitSup[c_{ij}, x_i, a]$ is $\lceil d/32 \rceil$, i.e. both $bitdom[x_j]$ and $bitSup[c_{ij}, x_i, a]$ consist of $\lceil d/32 \rceil$ words.

3   Exploiting Bitwise Operations to Enforce maxRPC

3.1   A New Method of Searching for PC-Witnesses

In existing algorithms, when testing whether a value (x_k, c) is a PC-witness of the value pair $((x_i, a), (x_j, b))$, constraint checks need to be performed to judge whether $((x_i, a), (x_k, c)) \in rel(c_{ik})$ and $((x_j, b), (x_k, c)) \in rel(c_{jk})$. The values of x_k need to be tested one by one until a PC-witness is found. This manner is not very efficient.

The new method tests 32 values simultaneously each time and aims at finding out whether there is at least one PC-witness instead of finding out which value is the PC-witness. Based on the binary representations in [8], the following instructions can be used when determining if a value pair $((x_i, a), (x_j, b))$ has at least one PC-witness in a third variable x_k:

```
1.    foreach w∈{0, … , bitSup[c , x , a].length-1} do
                                  ik   i

2.          if (bitSup[c  , x , a][w] AND bitSup[c  , x , b][w]
                       ik   i                     jk   j

            AND bitdom[x ][w])  ≠ ZERO
                       k

3.              then return true;

4.    return false;
```

ZERO denotes a sequence of 32 bits all set to 0. AND is the bitwise operator that simultaneously performs a logical AND operation on 32 pairs of corresponding bits. If the result of "$bisup[C_{ik}, x_i, a][w]$ **AND** $bisup[C_{jk}, x_j, b][w]$" is not *ZERO*, there must be common supports for (x_i, a) and (x_j, b) in the initial domain of x_k. Thus, if the result of the logical operations in line 2 is not equal to ZERO, there must be at least one PC-witness in the current domain of x_k. This method is very efficient, consider that x_k has a domain with the size of 100, only 8 bitwise operations need to be performed in the worst case, and these 8 bitwise operations can test all the values in x_k, in contrast, 8 constraint checks can only test 4 to 8 values in existing algorithms.

3.2   (l)maxRPC[bit], (l)maxRPC[bit+rm]

In this section, we propose two coarse-grained algorithms called maxRPC[bit] and maxRPC[bit+rm]. In the new algorithms, the process of searching for PC-witnesses uses

---

Algorithm 1. $\text{maxRPC}^{\text{bit}}/\text{maxRPC}^{\text{bit+rm}}$

```
/*  Initialization  */
1:   for each xᵢ ∈ X do
2:      for each a ∈ D(xᵢ) do
3:         for each xⱼ∈ X s.t. cᵢⱼ ∈ C do
4:            if HavenoPCsup(xᵢ, a, xⱼ) then
5:               SetbitFalse(bitdom[xᵢ], a);
6:               if D(xᵢ) ≠ ∅ then
7:                  Dellist = Dellist∪{xᵢ};
8:               else return false;
   /*  Propagation  */
9:  while Dellist ≠ ∅ do
10:     Dellist = Dellist - {xⱼ};
11:     for each xᵢ ∈ X s.t. cᵢⱼ ∈ C do
12:        for each a ∈ D(xᵢ) do
13:           if LastPC_{xᵢ, a, xⱼ} ∉ D(xⱼ) and HavenoPCsup
                  (xᵢ, a, xⱼ) then
14:              SetbitFalse(bitdom[xᵢ], a);
15:              if D(xᵢ) ≠ ∅ then
16:                 Dellist = Dellist∪{xᵢ};
17:              else return false;
18:           else
19:              if PCwitLose(xᵢ, a, xⱼ) then
20:                 SetbitFalse(bitdom[xᵢ], a);
21:                 if D(xᵢ) ≠ ∅ then
22:                    Dellist = Dellist∪{xᵢ};
23:                 else return false;
24:  return true;
```

the new method based on bitwise operations. Meanwhile the advantages of existing algorithms are kept. maxRPC^{bit} can be regarded as a variant of maxRPC2, and maxRPC^{bit+rm} can be regarded as the variant of maxRPC3^{rm}. The pseudo code for the unified description of maxRPC^{bit} and maxRPC^{bit+rm} is given in Algorithms 1 to 6. A Boolean variable rm is used to determine whether the algorithm presented is instantiated to maxRPC^{bit} or to maxRPC^{bit+rm}. If rm is true, the algorithm used is maxRPC^{bit+rm}. Otherwise, the algorithm is maxRPC^{bit}.

As described in Algorithm 1, both algorithms consist of two main steps: the initialization step and the propagation step. During the initialization phase, for each value a of each variable x_i, we check if it is maxRPC. For each value (x_i, a) which is not maxRPC, the corresponding bit in $bitdom$ is set to false. And each variable which has its domain filtered is added to the propagation list called $Dellist$. In the propagation step, until $Dellist$ is not empty, we extract a variable x_j from $Dellist$. And for each variable x_i constrained with x_j, we establish whether it is still maxRPC. If $LastPC_{x_i, a, x_j}$ is not valid and (x_i, a) has no other PC-supports in $D(x_j)$, the corresponding bit of a in $bitdom$ is set to false. Otherwise, $PCwitLose(x_i, a, x_j)$ is called to check the PC-witness loss in $D(x_j)$.

Algorithm 2. $HavenoPCsup(x_i, a, x_j)$:**boolean**

```
1:    if ¬ rm and LastPC_{x_i, a, x_j} ≠ NIL then

2:           v = LastPC_{x_i, a, x_j}+1;

3:    else

4:           v = first value in D(x_j);

5:    for each b ∈ D(x_j), b ≥ v do

6:           PCwitness=true;

7:           if IsbitTrue( bitSup[c_{ij}, x_i, a], b) then

8:                  for each x_k ∈ X s.t. c_{ik} ∈ C and c_{jk} ∈ C do

9:                         if ¬ HavePCwit( x_i, a, x_j, b, x_k) then

10:                               PCwitness=false; break;

11:           if PCwitness ≠ false then

12:                  LastPC_{x_i, a, x_j} = b;

13:                  if rm then

14:                         LastPC_{x_j, b, x_i} = a; LastAC_{x_i, a, x_j} = b div 32;

15:                  return false;

16:    return true;
```

maxRPC^{bit} uses $LastPC_{x_i, a, x_j}$ to record the smallest PC-support of (x_i, a) in $D(x_j)$ as maxRPC2 does. maxRPC^{bit+rm} uses $LastPC$ and $LastAC$ as residues. Differently from maxRPC3^{rm}, in maxRPC^{bit+rm}, whenever a PC-witness is detected, $LastAC$ records its position in $bitSup$, i.e. in which word of $bitSup$ the corresponding bit of the PC-witness is. In both maxRPC^{bit} and maxRPC^{bit+rm}, $LastPC$ and $LastAC$ are set to a special value NIL initially.

HavenoPCsup(x_i, a, x_j) (Algorithm 2) determines if (x_i, a) has a PC-support in $D(x_j)$. maxRPC^{bit} starts the search from the value after $LastPC_{x_i, a, x_j}$ since $LastPC_{x_i, a, x_j}$ was the smallest PC-support of (x_i, a). While maxRPC^{bit+rm} searches from the first value in $D(x_j)$, it is because in maxRPC^{bit+rm}, $LastPC$ is used as a residue and it does not always record the smallest PC-support. To find a value (x_j, b) such that $((x_i, a), (x_j, b)) \in rel(c_{ij})$, function *IsbitTrue* is called, it returns true if the corresponding bit of b in $bitSup[c_{ij}, x_i, a]$ is 1. If such a value is found, for each third variable x_k, *HavePCwit*(x_i, a, x_j, b, x_k) is called to establish whether at least one PC-witness of $((x_i, a), (x_j, b))$ exists in $D(x_k)$, if not, *PCwitness* is set to false and the value after b in $D(x_j)$ is to be checked. When a PC-support b is found, then maxRPC^{bit} sets $LastPC_{x_i, a, x_j}$ to b. Like maxRPC3^{rm},

```
Algorithm 3.   HavePCwit( x_i, a, x_j, b, x_k):boolean

1:  if rm then
2:      if LastAC_{x_i, a, x_k} ≠ NIL then
3:          i = LastAC_{x_i, a, x_k};
4:          if ( bitSup[c_{ik}, x_i, a][i] AND bitSup[c_{jk}, x_j, b][i]
               AND bitdom[x_k][i]) ≠ ZERO
5:          then return true;
6:      if LastAC_{x_j, b, x_k} ≠ NIL then
7:          j= LastAC_{x_j, b, x_k};
8:          if ( bitSup[c_{ik}, x_i, a][j] AND bitSup[c_{jk}, x_j, b][j]
               AND bitdom[x_k][j]) ≠ ZERO
9:          then return true;
10: for each i∈{0, … , bitSup [c_{ik}, x_i, a].length-1} do
11:     if ( bitSup[c_{ik}, x_i, a][i] AND bitSup[c_{jk}, x_j, b][i]
            AND bitdom[x_k][i]) ≠ ZERO then
12:         if rm then
13:             LastAC_{x_i, a, x_k} = i; LastAC_{x_j, b, x_k} = i;
14:         return true;
15: return false;
```

maxRPC^{bit+rm} exploits the multi-directionality of residues, it sets $LastPC_{x_i, a, x_j}$ to b and sets $LastPC_{x_j, b, x_i}$ to a. However, it does not set $LastAC_{x_i, a, x_j}$ to b as maxRPC3^{rm} does, as in line 13, $LastAC_{x_i, a, x_j}$ is set to the position of b in $bitSup$.

HavePCwit(x_i, a, x_j, b, x_k) (Algorithm 3) checks whether at least one PC-witness of $((x_i, a), (x_j, b))$ exists in $D(x_k)$. In this process, the method introduced in Section 3 is utilized. In maxRPC^{bit+rm}, the residual position is first checked, and when one PC-witness is detected, its position in $bitSup$ is recorded.

PCwitLose(x_i, a, x_j) (Algorithm 4) is called to check for the PC-witness loss. For each variable x_k constrained with both x_i and x_j, if $LastPC_{x_i, a, x_k}$ is valid, it checks whether there is still a PC-witness of the value pair $((x_i, a), (x_k, LastPC_{x_i, a, x_k}))$ in $D(x_j)$. If such a PC-witness exists, $LastPC_{x_i, a, x_k}$ is still the PC-support of (x_i, a). If $LastPC_{x_i, a, x_k}$ is not valid or it is no longer the PC-support of (x_i, a), as in line 6 to 8, we need to establish whether some other value in $D(x_k)$ can be found as the PC-support of (x_i, a).

Algorithm 4.   *PCwitLose*(x_i, a, x_j) :**boolean**

1:    **for each** $x_k \in X$ s.t. $c_{ik} \in C$ and $c_{jk} \in C$ **do**

2:        *witloss* = true;

3:        **if** $LastPC_{x_i, a, x_k} \in D(x_k)$ **then**

4:            **if** *HavePCwit*(x_i, a, x_k, $LastPC_{x_i, a, x_k}$, x_j) **then**

5:                *witloss* = false;

6:        **if** *witloss* and exists $c > LastPC_{x_i, a, x_k} \in D(x_k)$ **then**

7:            **if** $\neg$ *HavenoPCsup*(x_i, a, x_k) **then**

8:                *witloss* = false;

9:        **if** *witloss* **then return** true;

10:   **return** false;

Algorithm 5 and Algorithm 6 give the details of two basic functions. t is an array of words. *SetbitFalse*(t, a) is used to set the corresponding bit of value a in t to 1, and *IsbitTrue*(t, a) is used to verify whether the corresponding bit of value a in t is 1. For both functions, i denotes in which word of t the value a is, and j denotes which bit of $t[i]$ is the corresponding bit of value a. *div* denotes the integer division, *mod* the remainder operator. Like in [8], the structure *masks1*(resp. *masks0*) is a predefined array of 32 words that contains in its ith square a value that represents a sequence of 32 bits which are all set to 0 (resp. 1) except for the ith one.

Two algorithms lmaxRPC^{bit} and lmaxRPC^{bit+rm} which are respectively the light versions of maxRPC^{bit} and maxRPC^{bit+rm} can be used to enforce light maxRPC. They can be obtained by omitting the call to the *PCwitLose* function in Algorithm 1 since light maxRPC only propagates the loss of AC-supports. lmaxRPC^{bit+rm} can be used during search. And when it is used during search, the step of initialization is omitted and *Dellist* is initialized with the currently assigned variable.

Algorithm 5.   *SetbitFalse* (*t*, *a*)

```
1:    i = a div 32;

2:    j = a mod 32;

3:    t[i] = t[i] AND masks0[j];
```

Algorithm 6.   *IsbitTrue* (*t*, *a*): **boolean**

```
1:    i = a div 32;

2:    j = a mod 32;

3:    return ( t[i] AND masks1[j] ) • ZERO;
```

Actually, (l)maxRPC^{bit} can be regarded as the variant of (l)maxRPC2, which transforms the step of searching PC-witnesses through constraint checks into the new method exploiting bitwise operations. In the new method of searching for PC-witnesses, a relatively large number of constraint checks are saved and only several bitwise operations need to be performed, but the time complexity of the new method is the same as the old one. Although in the worst case, only $2*\lceil d/32 \rceil$ bitwise operations need to be performed, the time complexity of searching for a PC-witness is still $O(d)$. Since the time costs of (l)maxRPC^{bit} and (l)maxRPC2 are both bound by the cost of searching for PC-witnesses, (l)maxRPC^{bit} has the same time complexity as (l)maxRPC2 which is $O(end^3)$. In a similar way, the time complexities of lmaxRPC^{bit+rm} and maxRPC^{bit+rm} are the same as maxRPC3^{rm} and lmaxRPC3^{rm} respectively since (l)maxRPC^{bit+rm} can be regarded as the variant of (l)maxRPC3^{rm}. When used stand alone, the time comlexities of lmaxRPC^{bit+rm} and maxRPC^{bit+rm} are $O(end^4)$ and $O(en^2d^4)$ respectively. And when lmaxRPC^{bit+rm} is used during search, it also has a time complexity of $O(end^4)$.

The extra space required by the binary representations cause an overhead of $O(ed^2)$. It is not suitable for the problems with huge domains. However, the space costs of the new algorithms are acceptable in most problems because in both arrays *bitdom* and *bitSup*, representing each domain requires only $\lceil d/32 \rceil$ words.

4   Experiments

In order to show the practical interest of the algorithms presented in this paper, we have performed experiments on series of structured CSP problems which are available from *http://www.cril.univ-artois.fr/~lecoutre/benchmarks.html*. We compare the new algorithms with the most efficient ones among existing algorithms. Performances have been measured in terms of cpu time in seconds (*cpu*) and the number of constraint checks (*#ccks*). Note that for the new algorithms, *#ccks* corresponds to the number of bitwise operations. Average results for all the instances are grouped into specific problem classes. Both satisfiable and unsatisfiable instances are contained.

382   J. Guo et al.

Table 1 compares the performance of algorithms used stand-alone. We can observe that the numbers of bitwise operations performed by the new algorithms are much smaller than that of constraint checks performed by the old ones. Benefiting from these substantial reductions of operations, our algorithms are 4 to 7 times faster than the old ones. And the results also show that our algorithms have the similar performances. We have also compared the performances of search algorithms that apply $lmaxRPC^{bit+rm}$ and $lmaxRPC3^{rm}$. Both search algorithms use the *dom/wdeg* [9] heuristic. Table 2 demonstrates that $lmaxRPC^{bit+rm}$ always outperforms $lmaxRPC3^{rm}$ when used during search. In most problems, a speed-up of more than 3 times can be obtained.

Table 1. Average stand-alone performance on series of structured instances; cpu time (*cpu*) given in seconds

		maxRPC3	lmaxRPC3	lmaxRPC3^{rm}	
Graphs (14 instances)	cpu	7.471	7.342	7.677	
	#ccks	32.67M	32.19M	32.5M	
		maxRPC^{bit}	maxRPC^{bit+rm}	lmaxRPC^{bit}	lmaxRPC^{bit+rm}
	cpu	1.500	1.545	1.455	1.446
	#ccks	5.01M	5.29M	4.65M	5.00M
ehi-85 (20 instances)		maxRPC3	lmaxRPC3	lmaxRPC3^{rm}	
	cpu	1.626	1.624	1.391	
	#ccks	1.75M	1.75M	1.88M	
		maxRPC^{bit}	maxRPC^{bit+rm}	lmaxRPC^{bit}	lmaxRPC^{bit+rm}
	cpu	0.404	0.418	0.399	0.343
	#ccks	0.98M	1.06M	0.98M	1.06M
rlfapScens (11 instances)		maxRPC3	lmaxRPC3	lmaxRPC3^{rm}	
	cpu	5.726	5.950	6.333	
	#ccks	20.98M	20.93M	20.93M	
		maxRPC^{bit}	maxRPC^{bit+rm}	lmaxRPC^{bit}	lmaxRPC^{bit+rm}
	cpu	2.257	3.671	1.827	1.353
	#ccks	4.19M	4.68M	4.08M	4.01M
jobshop enddr1 (9 instances)		maxRPC3	lmaxRPC3	lmaxRPC3^{rm}	
	cpu	2.031	2.026	2.159	
	#ccks	5.39M	5.39M	5.48M	
		maxRPC^{bit}	maxRPC^{bit+rm}	lmaxRPC^{bit}	lmaxRPC^{bit+rm}
	cpu	0.348	0.465	0.348	0.349
	#ccks	1.57M	1.93M	1.57M	1.93M
jobshop ewddr2 (10 instances)		maxRPC3	lmaxRPC3	lmaxRPC3^{rm}	
	cpu	2.772	2.728	2.842	
	#ccks	8.76M	8.76M	8.91M	
		maxRPC^{bit}	maxRPC^{bit+rm}	lmaxRPC^{bit}	lmaxRPC^{bit+rm}
	cpu	0.418	0.431	0.410	0.418
	#ccks	2.01M	1.99M	2.01M	1.99M

Table 2. Average search performance on series of structured instances; cpu time (*cpu*) given in seconds

		lmaxRPC3^{rm}	lmaxRPC$^{\text{bit+rm}}$
Graphs (14 instances)	*cpu*	9.713	2.975
	#ccks	35.93M	7.23M
jobshop ewddr2 (10 instances)	*cpu*	3.560	0.994
	#ccks	11.66M	5.04M
jobshop enddr1 (9 instances)	*cpu*	2.722	0.796
	#ccks	7.34M	4.08M
jobshop enddr2 (6 instance)	*cpu*	3.463	1.012
	#ccks	11.35M	4.89M
rlfapScens (11 instances)	*cpu*	10.285	1.910
	#ccks	23.49M	5.04M
ModeScens (12 instances)	*cpu*	18.532	1.304
	#ccks	39.72M	3.58M

Table 3. Some instances on which the search algorithms applying lmaxRPC outperforms MAC; cpu time (*cpu*) given in seconds

		lmaxRPC3^{rm}	lmaxRPC$^{\text{bit+rm}}$	AC^{rm}
queenAttacking5	*cpu*	2.016	0.953	19.766
	#ccks	4.84M	5.32M	3.98M
queensKnights-15-15-5 -mul	*cpu*	64.093	21.438	54.985
	#ccks	262.06M	89.65M	22.91M
scen3-f11	*cpu*	13.75	3.781	7.047
	#ccks	27.58M	12.88M	1.71M
scen11-f8	*cpu*	32.797	9.562	145.562
	#ccks	55.08M	22.51M	36.48M
scen6-w1-f2	*cpu*	1.359	0.672	11.438
	#ccks	2.31M	1.01M	3.54M
scen6-w1-f3	*cpu*	1.172	0.609	5.312
	#ccks	1.94M	0.71M	1.99M
scen9-w1-f3	*cpu*	1.922	0.516	1.266
	#ccks	4.23M	1.03M	0.69M
qcp-order15-holes120-balanced-21-QWH-15	*cpu*	39.938	4.843	6.344
	#ccks	7.17M	5.96M	0.43M

The experiments in [7] showed that a search algorithm applying lmaxRPC can be competitive with MAC on many instances. In our experiments, we found that because of the speed-up of the process of searching for PC-witnesses, maintaining lmaxRPC during search can outperform MAC much more than we thought. We found that there are many instances on which MAC is not outperformed by lmaxRPC3^{rm} but by lmaxRPC^{bit+rm} (e.g. queensKnights-15-15-5-mul and scen3-f11). And for the instances on which lmaxRPC3^{rm} outperforms MAC, lmaxRPC^{bit+rm} outperforms MAC by a much larger margin (e.g. queenAttacking5 and scen11-f8). Some such instances are shown in Table 3, the version of MAC used is MAC^{rm}[5, 6].

5 Conclusions

In this paper, we have introduced a method based on bitwise operations to speed up the processes of searching for PC-witnesses. Based on the new method, we presented two algorithms maxRPC^{bit} and maxRPC^{bit+rm}. Both algorithms and their light versions outperform the best ones among existing algorithms by a large margin. Significantly, our experiments show that maxRPC is a much more promising filtering technique than what we thought because lmaxRPC^{bit+rm} outperforms MAC on a much larger number of instances and by a larger margin than lmaxRPC^{rm} does. In the future, we will do further research to find out in which situations can maxRPC be more preferable than AC.

Acknowledgement. This paper is supported in part by NSFC under Grant Nos.60773097, 60873148 and 60973089; Jilin Province Science and Technology Development Plan under Grant Nos.20071106, 20080107, 20101501 and 20100185.

References

1. Debruyne, R., Bessière, C.: From restricted path consistency to max-restricted path consistency. In: Smolka, G. (ed.) CP 1997. LNCS, vol. 1330, pp. 312–326. Springer, Heidelberg (1997)
2. Debruyne, R., Bessière, C.: Domain Filtering Consistencies. JAIR 14, 205–230 (2001)
3. Grandoni, F., Italiano, G.: Improved Algorithms for Max-Restricted Path Consistency. In: Rossi, F. (ed.) CP 2003. LNCS, vol. 2833, pp. 858–862. Springer, Heidelberg (2003)
4. Vion, J., Debruyne, R.: Light Algorithms for Maintaining Max-RPC During Search. In: Proceedings of SARA 2009 (2009)
5. Likitvivatanavong, C., Zhang, Y., Shannon, S., Bowen, J., Freuder, E.: Arc Consistency during Search. In: Proceedings of IJCAI 2007, pp. 137–142 (2007)
6. Lecoutre, C., And Hemery, F.: A Study of Residual Supports in Arc Consistency. In: Proceedings of IJCAI 2007, pp. 125–130 (2007)
7. Balafoutis, T., Paparrizou, A., Stergiou, K., Walsh, T.: Improving the performance of maxRPC. In: Cohen, D. (ed.) CP 2010. LNCS, vol. 6308, pp. 69–83. Springer, Heidelberg (2010)
8. Lecoutre, C., Vion, J.: Enforcing Arc Consistency using Bitwise Operations. Constraint Programming Letters 2, 21–35 (2008)
9. Boussemart, F., Hemery, F., Lecoutre, C., Sais, L.: Boosting Systematic Search by weighting Constraints. In: Proceedings of ECAI 2004, pp. 146–150 (2004)

Grid-Based SAT Solving with Iterative Partitioning and Clause Learning

Antti E.J. Hyvärinen, Tommi Junttila, and Ilkka Niemelä

Aalto University,
Department of Information and Computer Science,
PO Box 15400, FI-00076 AALTO, Finland
{Antti.Hyvarinen,Tommi.Junttila,Ilkka.Niemela}@aalto.fi

Abstract. This work studies the solving of challenging SAT problem instances in distributed computing environments that have massive amounts of parallel resources but place limits on individual computations. We present an abstract framework which extends a previously presented iterative partitioning approach with clause learning, a key technique applied in modern SAT solvers. In addition we present two techniques that alter the clause learning of modern SAT solvers to fit the framework. An implementation of the proposed framework is then analyzed experimentally using a well-known set of benchmark instances. The results are very encouraging. For example, the implementation is able to solve challenging SAT instances not solvable in reasonable time by state-of-the-art sequential and parallel SAT solvers.

1 Introduction

This work studies the solving of hard instances of the propositional satisfiability problem (SAT) using a massively parallel master-worker environment such as a grid or a cloud where several clusters are scattered around a large geographical area. Grids and clouds typically provide large amounts of computing power at a relatively low cost making them increasingly appealing for users.

This work considers a grid computing model where each worker executes a job for a limited amount of time and can communicate the results only to the master. The run time limits are typically quite low, in this work approximately one hour. Jobs with modest computing requirements are in many ways beneficial in practice. For example, a job requiring a single CPU core for a relatively short time can often be scheduled to a time slot unsuitable for jobs requiring several CPUs for an extended time period. Furthermore, should a job fail, e.g., due to a service break in a cluster, the cost of recovering from the failure is at most the duration of the job.

Most approaches to parallel SAT solving fall into the following two categories:

- In the *portfolio* approach the speed-up results from running slightly varied solvers with the same input simultaneously and obtaining the result from the first finishing solver (see, e.g., [10]). The idea generalizes to many related algorithms [18,12].
- In the *guiding path* approach the instance is constrained to several solution disjoint subproblems solved in parallel, usually aided with load balancing for dealing with unequally sized subproblems [25,27,22].

J. Lee (Ed.): CP 2011, LNCS 6876, pp. 385–399, 2011.

It is not straightforward to implement approaches from either of the two categories in an environment which limits job run times, as they naturally assume unlimited run times.

This work discusses an iterative partitioning approach which scales to thousands of jobs. Even current grid middlewares with relatively high latencies allow us to run tens of jobs simultaneously. The approach was introduced in [13] and further developed in [15]. A job for solving an instance is first submitted to the parallel environment, and at the same time constrained to several solution disjoint formulas. These *derived formulas* are then also submitted and the constraining applied iteratively to each derived formula resulting in a recursively constructed *partition tree*. During the solving process the solvers learn clauses that are used to prune the search space of the instance they are solving [20]. This work extends [15] by taking the clauses produced by a timed out job and integrating them to the partition tree to constrain the search spaces of the subsequent jobs. The challenge in this is that the learned clauses may depend on the partitioning constraints. As a solution to this problem we present two ways of determining how the learned clauses depend on the constraints.

The resulting implementation is able to solve several challenging SAT instances, some of which were not solved in the SAT Competition 2009 (see http://www.satcompetition.org/).

The learning partition tree approach compares favorably to several state-of-the-art parallel shared memory SAT solvers as well as to grid-based approaches.

1.1 Related Work

The iterative partitioning approach differs from the portfolio approach in that the derived formulas become increasingly constrained and hopefully easier to solve deeper in the partition tree. The approach is closely related to divide-and-conquer approaches such as the guiding path. However, in the iterative partitioning approach the search is organized redundantly (see Sect. 3). While this might seem counter-intuitive, it has proved to be a surprisingly good strategy; for example, it can be shown that the redundancy in solving can help prevent some anomalies related to increasing expected run times in unsatisfiable formulas [16]. The constraints used for producing derived formulas in this work are not limited to unit clauses, but can instead be arbitrarily long formulas. We are not aware of guiding path implementations that would use such constraints. Most literature, to our knowledge, assumes unbounded run times for jobs, while in [13,14,15] the current authors have studied SAT solving in environments where maximum run time of a job is much lower than typical time required to solve an instance.

The guiding path type constraining dates at least back to [25,4]. Much work has been invested in finding "good" guiding paths (see, e.g. [6], as an improper construction results in the worst case in increased expected run times [16]. The partition tree approach followed in this work attempts to solve both a formula and all its derived formulas in parallel being therefore immune to the increase. The partitioning approaches used in this work are described in [13] and [15]. Similar ideas based on running the VSIDS heuristic [23] to produce good constraints are discussed in [21].

Guiding path based parallel SAT solvers for distributed computing environments have been implemented both without clause learning [17,27] and with different strategies for sharing the learned clauses [3,24,5]. The approach discussed in this work differs from these by limiting the run time of jobs, by using the iterative partitioning approach for the basis of parallelism and by using a more general approach to constructing the derived formulas. In particular the latter strengthens the clauses as they need not be logical consequences of the original instance. Although this makes clause sharing tedious to implement efficiently, the approach performs well in experiments.

Algorithm portfolio based parallel solvers with clause sharing (see, e.g, [9,2]) work surprisingly well in shared memory environments. They have been adapted also to grid environments by the current authors as the CL-SDSAT framework [14] while the learning partition tree approach discussed in this work can be seen as an extension of CL-SDSAT.

2   Preliminaries

We assume the standard notations of satisfiability and basic knowledge conflict-driven clause learning (CDCL) SAT solvers (see e.g. [19]). Let V be a set of Boolean variables. The set $\{x, \neg x \mid x \in V\}$ is the set of *literals*, a *clause* is a set (disjunction) of literals and formula a conjunction of clauses. A formula is satisfiable if there is a set of literals τ such that for no $x \in V$ both $x, \neg x \in \tau$ and each clause contains a literal from τ. Such a τ is called a satisfying truth assignment, and in case one does not exist, the formula is unsatisfiable. Let ϕ and ψ be formulas. If all satisfying truth assignments of ψ satisfy ϕ, then ϕ is a *logical consequence* of ψ, denoted $\psi \vDash \phi$. If ψ and ϕ are satisfied by exactly the same truth assignments, they are logically equivalent and we write $\psi \equiv \phi$.

Many of the ideas in this work are based on the fact that a CDCL SAT solver, while solving a formula ϕ, produces during the search huge amounts of clauses C such that $\phi \vDash C$. The clauses are used in guiding the further search so that in general the size of the search space decreases. Typically one clause is learned each time the solver finds that a truth assignment does not satisfy the formula. Of particular interest are learned clauses containing a single literal l. Since l is true in any satisfying truth assignment of ϕ, its negation $\neg l$ can be removed from all clauses, resulting not only in smaller remaining search space but also in shorter clauses, decreased memory foot print and better cache performance.

3   Iterative Partitioning with Clause Learning

In this section, we first review and formalize the partition tree approach used, e.g., in [13]. We then extend the approach to allow the use of learned clauses, i.e., clauses that are logical consequences of the original formula or of the iteratively partitioned *derived formulas* in the partition tree, and discuss how they can be found and maintained in practice. Two implementation approaches that can make a modern CDCL SAT solver to produce such learned clauses are then described in the next section.

3.1   Partition Trees

The idea in the iterative partitioning approach is to construct a partition tree of formulas rooted at ϕ such that the satisfiability of ϕ can be deduced once a sufficient amount of the formulas in the tree have been solved.

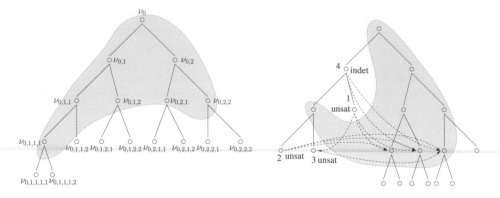

Fig. 1. The Iterative Partitioning approach. Nodes represent derived formulas, and the nodes in the shaded area are being solved simultaneously. Terminated jobs are marked either indet or unsat depending on whether they run out of resources or prove unsatisfiability, and annotated with the termination order (1 terminates first and 4 last). Some learned clauses from earlier terminated jobs can be transferred to the newly submitted jobs, illustrated by the dashed arrows. The tree is constructed in breadth-first order.

Given a formula ψ, the partitioning function computes the set of partitioning constraints $\mathcal{P}(\psi) = \{\Pi_1, \dots, \Pi_n\}$ that, when conjoined with ψ, result in the formulas $\psi_i = \psi \wedge \Pi_i$ such that (i) $\psi \equiv \psi_1 \vee \dots \vee \psi_n$, and (ii) $\psi_i \wedge \psi_j$ is unsatisfiable whenever $i \neq j$. A trivial way to get a partitioning function would be to select two variables a and b occurring in the formula ψ, and letting $\mathcal{P}(\psi) = \{a \wedge b, a \wedge \neg b, \neg a \wedge b, \neg a \wedge \neg b\}$.

In the following discussion we make a distinction between the nodes of the tree and the formulas representing the nodes. Formally, the partition tree $\mathcal{T}_\psi$ of a formula ψ is a rooted finite n-ary tree with the set of nodes $\mathcal{N}$. Each node $\nu \in \mathcal{N}$ is labeled with the partitioning constraint $constr(\nu)$ as follows:

1. The root node ν_0 is constrained with $constr(\nu_0) = \mathbf{true}$ (i.e. the empty conjunction).
2. Let ν_k be a node in the tree, $\nu_0\nu_1 \dots \nu_k$ the path from the root node ν_0 to ν_k, and $\nu_{k,1}, \dots, \nu_{k,n}$ the child nodes of ν_k. The constraints $constr(\nu_{k,i}) = \Pi_i$ are then obtained by computing the set $\mathcal{P}(\psi \wedge constr(\nu_0) \wedge \dots \wedge constr(\nu_k)) = \{\Pi_1, \dots, \Pi_n\}$.

Given a node ν_k, the formula $form(\nu_k) = \psi \wedge constr(\nu_0) \wedge \dots \wedge constr(\nu_k)$ is the *derived formula* at ν_k. Based on the properties of partitioning functions it is evident that (i) if a derived formula is satisfiable, then so is the original formula ψ, and (ii) if the leaves of a sub-tree rooted at ψ are all unsatisfiable, then so is the formula ψ.

Example 1. Figure 1 illustrates how the partition tree is constructed on-the-fly in breadth-first order starting from the root using eight CPU cores in a grid and when the partition factor $n = 2$. In the left tree the derived formulas at nodes are sent to the environment to be solved (in parallel) with a SAT solver, and the nodes are further partitioned into child nodes at the same time. The derived formula at the root node ν_0 (i.e., the original formula ψ) is first sent to be solved in the environment; while it is being solved, the root

ν_0 is partitioned into nodes $\nu_{0,1}, \nu_{0,2}$ and these are sent to be solved in the environment; then partitioning is applied to $\nu_{0,1}, \nu_{0,2}$ and so on in the similar breadth-first manner, until finally the derived formulas in the shaded nodes are running simultaneously. If the derived formula at a node were found satisfiable, then the original formula would be declared satisfiable and the process would end. In the right tree, the nodes $\nu_{0,1,2}$ and $\nu_{0,1,1,1}$ are first solved, and shown unsatisfiable. We therefore know that all derived instances below these are unsatisfiable, and are therefore not submitted. Instead the nodes $\nu_{0,1,1,2}$ and $\nu_{0,2,1,1}$ are submitted to the newly freed cores. Later the node $\nu_{0,1,1,2}$ is shown unsatisfiable. We could now finish the solving of $\nu_{0,1,1}$ since we know it unsatisfiable. The solving is not terminated in the example as the clauses learned there might still prove useful in other parts of the partition tree, and instead the next node $\nu_{0,2,1,2}$ is submitted. Finally the node $\nu_{0,1}$ times out and the derived formula in node $\nu_{0,2,2,1}$ is submitted for solving.

3.2   Adding Clause Learning

Since its introduction and popularization in *Grasp* [20] and *zChaff* [23] solvers, *conflict driven clause learning* has been a major search space pruning technique applied in sequential SAT solvers. Basically, at each conflict reached during the search the SAT solver adds a new *learned clause* C that (i) is a logical consequence of the formula ϕ under consideration, and (ii) prevents similar conflicts from happening in future search. In this paper, our main goal is to exploit such learned clauses produced during *solving one derived formula* when *solving other derived formulas* in a partition tree. As a learned clause produced when solving a derived formula may depend on the partitioning constraints, it is not necessarily a logical consequence of some other derived formulas and cannot thus be used when solving those. We first give a very abstract framework of partitioning trees where arbitrary logical consequences can be incorporated and then discuss the current realization of the framework based on using learned clauses derived during the search tree construction.

Assume a node ν_k in the tree with the associated derived formula $form(\nu_k) = \psi \wedge constr(\nu_0) \wedge \ldots \wedge constr(\nu_k)$. A formula $form(\nu_k)'$ is a *simulating derived formula*, denoted by $form(\nu_k)' \sim form(\nu_k)$, if it is of form $\psi' \wedge constr(\nu_0) \wedge \Sigma(\nu_0) \wedge constr(\nu_1) \wedge \Sigma(\nu_1) \wedge \ldots \wedge constr(\nu_k) \wedge \Sigma(\nu_k)$ such that (i) $\psi' \equiv \psi$, and (ii) for each $0 \leq i \leq k$, $\psi \wedge constr(\nu_0) \wedge \ldots \wedge constr(\nu_i) \models \Sigma(\nu_i)$. That is, (i) the original formula ψ may be substituted with an equivalent one (in practice: simplified with additional information obtained during the tree construction) and (ii) "learned clauses" $\Sigma(\nu_i)$ can be added as long as they are logical consequences of the corresponding partitioning constraints. Now the second rule in the definition of the partition tree $\mathcal{T}_\psi$ can be replaced with

2'. Let ν_k be a node in the tree, $\nu_0\nu_1\ldots\nu_k$ the path from the root node ν_0 to ν_k, and $\nu_{k,1}, \ldots, \nu_{k,n}$ the child nodes of ν_k. The constraints $constr(\nu_{k,i}) = \Pi_i$ are then obtained by computing the set $\mathcal{P}(\psi' \wedge \Sigma(\nu_0) \wedge constr(\nu_1) \wedge \Sigma(\nu_1) \wedge \ldots \wedge constr(\nu_k) \wedge \Sigma(\nu_k)) = \{\Pi_1, \ldots, \Pi_n\}$

Similarly, any simulating formula $form(\nu)' \sim form(\nu)$ at a node ν can be sent to be solved in the distributed computing environment instead of $form(\nu)$. Due to the definition of simulating derived instances, the same construction algorithms and termination criteria can be applied as in the base case of partition trees without learning.

Let S be a CDCL solver. If a simulating derived formula $\phi = form(\nu_k)'$ is found satisfiable by S, then the original formula ψ is also satisfiable and the construction of the partition tree can be terminated. However, if S found ϕ unsatisfiable or S could not solve ϕ within the imposed resource limits, we would like to obtain new learned clauses to help in solving other nodes in the partitioning tree. That is, we would like S to produce new sets Σ_i' of clauses such that for each $0 \le i \le k$, $\psi \wedge constr(\nu_1) \wedge \ldots \wedge constr(\nu_i) \vDash \Sigma_i'$. Each new clause set Σ_i' can be used when solving any node having ν_i as its ancestor, since the constraints of ν_i are a subset of the constraints of its descendant by the rule 2'. Naturally, of particular interest are the *partitioning constraint independent learned clauses* Σ_0' that can be used when solving any node in the tree; the transfer of these clauses is illustrated by the dashed arrows in the right tree of Fig. 1. Two techniques for obtaining such clauses are discussed in the next section.

In the experiments discussed in this work, we currently use two schemes for maintaining the sets of learned clauses. Firstly, we maintain a database of partitioning constraint independent learned clauses; when such new learned clauses are obtained from a job, they are inserted into the database. To limit the size of the database, only a fixed amount of clauses are kept in it; currently we prefer to keep the shortest learned clauses found. The found unit learned clauses are used to simplify the database. Secondly, we maintain for each node ν_k a limited set $\Sigma(\nu_k)$ of learned clauses specific to that node (i.e. $form(\nu_k) \vDash \Sigma(\nu_k)$). For the sake of space efficiency, these sets currently contain only unary learned clauses.

3.3 Partitioning Functions

This work considers two partitioning functions studied earlier in [15]. Both approaches take as input the formula $form(\nu_k)'$ and produce n partitioning constraints. The first, called *vsids* in this work, is based on running a SAT solver with the VSIDS branching heuristic [23] for a fixed amount of time (5 minutes in the experiments) and using the obtained heuristic values to pick literals l_j^i to construct the partitioning constraints

$$
\Pi_i = \begin{cases}
(l_1^1) \wedge \ldots \wedge (l_{d_1}^1) & \text{if } i = 1, \\
(\neg l_1^1 \vee \ldots \vee \neg l_{d_1}^1) \wedge \ldots \wedge (\neg l_1^{i-1} \vee \ldots \vee \neg l_{d_{i-1}}^{i-1}) \wedge \\
\quad (l_1^i) \wedge \ldots \wedge (l_{d_i}^i) & \text{if } 1 < i < n, \\
(\neg l_1^1 \vee \ldots \vee \neg l_{d_1}^1) \wedge \ldots \wedge (\neg l_1^{n-1} \vee \ldots \vee \neg l_{d_{n-1}}^{n-1}) & \text{if } i = n.
\end{cases}
$$

The resulting constraints are not necessarily sets of unit clauses, but instead might contain clauses of length d_i. The value of d_i is selected so that the partitions have equal search spaces (see [15] for details).

The second partitioning function is based on the *unit propagation lookahead* [11], where the idea is to always branch on the most propagating literal. The *lookahead* partitioning function is analyzed further in [15], while in this work we chose not to produce the disjunctions as above, but instead to use constraints of unit clauses.

4   Learned Clause Tagging CDCL Solvers

We now study the problem of determining the "constraint dependency" of new learned clauses as discussed above. Assume a partition tree node ν_k with a simulating derived formula $form(\nu_k)' = \psi \wedge \Sigma(\nu_0) \wedge constr(\nu_1) \wedge \Sigma(\nu_1) \wedge \ldots \wedge constr(\nu_k) \wedge \Sigma(\nu_k)$, sent to the grid to be solved with a CDCL solver S, and that the solving terminates either due to exhausting the resource limits or to conclusion that $form(\nu_k)'$ is unsatisfiable. To further exploit the work done by the solver S, we would like the solver to give new learned clauses to help in solving other nodes in the partition tree. That is, we would like S to produce new sets $\Sigma(\nu_i)'$ of clauses such that $\psi \vDash \Sigma(\nu_0)'$ and, for each $1 \leq i \leq k$, $\psi \wedge constr(\nu_1) \wedge \ldots \wedge constr(\nu_i) \vDash \Sigma(\nu_i)'$. A clause set $\Sigma(\nu_i)'$ can always be used when solving any descendant node of ν_i; we are therefore particularly interested in the partitioning constraint independent learned clauses $\Sigma(\nu_0)'$ that can be used when solving any node in the tree.

In this section we describe two techniques that can be used to "tag" the learned clauses produced by a CDCL solver so that they can be classified as either partitioning constraint independent (i.e. belong to $\Sigma(\nu_0)'$) or belonging to a set $\Sigma(\nu_i)'$ for some $1 \leq i \leq k$.

4.1   Assumption-Based Learned Clause Tagging

Our first, more fine grained clause tagging technique uses the concept of *assumption variables* for tagging partition constraints. Each constraint Π is annotated with a newly introduced variable a with the conjunction $\Pi \vee \neg a$. The constraint Π is then enabled by setting a true. When learned clauses are deduced by the CDCL solver during its search, these special literals are "inherited" in learned clauses, thus also tagging which partition constraints the newly derived learned clause depended on. The assumption variable technique was introduced in [7] for dynamically adding and removing clauses in a formula between subsequent satisfiability tests in the context of bounded model checking; it has also been used in a folklore method for unsatisfiability core extraction [1].

Given a simulating derived formula $form(\nu_k)' = \psi' \wedge \Sigma(\nu_0) \wedge constr(\nu_1) \wedge \Sigma(\nu_1) \wedge \ldots \wedge constr(\nu_k) \wedge \Sigma(\nu_k)$, the idea in the assumption based tagging is that the CDCL solver considers the straightforward CNF translation of the formula $form(\nu_k)^\star = \psi' \wedge \Sigma(\nu_0) \wedge (\neg a_1 \vee (constr(\nu_1) \wedge \Sigma(\nu_1))) \wedge \ldots \wedge (\neg a_k \vee (constr(\nu_k) \wedge \Sigma(\nu_k)))$ instead, where $a_1, \ldots, a_k$ are k disjoint *assumption variables* not occurring in $form(\nu_k)'$. Thus, for each clause $C = (l_1 \vee \ldots \vee l_m)$ in a "constraint subformula" $constr(\nu_i) \wedge \Sigma(\nu_i)$ in $form(\nu_k)'$, there is a corresponding "a_i-triggered clause" $(\neg a_i \vee l_1 \vee \ldots \vee l_m)$ in $form(\nu_k)^\star$. Obviously, both $form(\nu_k)'$ and $form(\nu_k)$ are satisfiable if and only if $form(\nu_k)^\star \wedge (a_1) \wedge \ldots \wedge (a_k)$ is.

To deduce whether $form(\nu_k)^\star \wedge (a_1) \wedge \ldots \wedge (a_k)$ is satisfiable (and thus whether $form(\nu_k)$ is), the CDCL solver is now invoked on $form(\nu_k)^\star$ with a list of "assumptions" $[a_1, \ldots, a_k]$. That is, its branching heuristic is forced to always branch on these variables first and to make the assumption that their values are true; these assumptions activate the "a_i-triggered clauses". After the assumptions the search continues as usual in a CDCL solver; the beauty of this technique is that when a learned clause is deduced

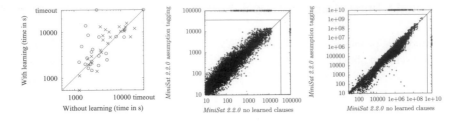

Fig. 2. The effect of learning in partition trees with assumption based tagging

during the search because a conflict was encountered, then the learned clause will in-clude the literal $\neg a_i$ iff the deduction of the clause depended on any clause in the derived formula $constr(\nu_i) \wedge \Sigma(\nu_i)$ (this follows from [7]). Therefore, recalling that $\psi' \equiv \psi$ and $\psi' \wedge constr(\nu_1) \wedge \ldots \wedge constr(\nu_i) \vDash \Sigma(\nu_i)$ for each $1 \leq i \leq k$, we get for each learned clause $C = (\neg a_1 \vee \ldots \vee \neg a_j \vee l_1 \vee \ldots \vee l_m)$ where a_j is the assumption variable with the largest index occurring in C, that $\psi' \wedge \bigwedge_{0 \leq i \leq j} constr(\nu_i) \vDash (l_1 \vee \ldots \vee l_m)$. Thus the learned clause $(l_1 \vee \ldots \vee l_m)$ can be used in the learned clause set $\Sigma(\nu_j)$ in the simulating derived formula $form(\nu_n)$ of any child node of ν_j. The important special case is when $j = 0$ and thus $(l_1 \vee \ldots \vee l_m)$ can be used in the partitioning constraint independent learned clause set $\Sigma(\nu_0)$ in the simulating derived formula $form(\nu)$ of *any* node ν in the partition tree.

In addition to learned clause tagging, the assumption variables can also be used to deduce an *unsatisfiability level* $0 \leq U \leq k$ such that, if $form(\nu_k)^* \wedge (a_1) \wedge \ldots \wedge (a_k)$ is unsatisfiable, then so is $\psi' \wedge \bigwedge_{1 \leq i \leq U} constr(\nu_i)$. This is because at the end of the search, when the solver deduces that not all the assumptions can be true at the same time (and thus $form(\nu_k)^* \wedge (a_1) \wedge \ldots \wedge (a_k)$ is unsatisfiable), it can invoke a special form of conflict analysis that deduces on which assumptions this "final conflict" depended on; this is implemented, e.g., in the current version 2.2.0 of MiniSat solver. Thus if $U < k$, we know that already the derived formula $form(\nu_U)$ of the ancestor node ν_U of ν_k is unsatisfiable and can *backjump* to ν_{U-1} (or report that the original formula ψ is unsat-isfiable if $U = 0$) and skip all the other children of ν_U. Unfortunately, our preliminary experiments show that such backjumping rarely occurs in real life benchmarks when a non-naive partitioning function is applied; it seems that the partitioning constraints imposed by the function are almost never totally irrelevant for the unsatisfiability proof found by the solver for $form(\nu_k)^* \wedge (a_1) \wedge \ldots \wedge (a_k)$ (and thus for $form(\nu_k)'$). Thus, and due to space limits, we do not analyze this tree backjumping technique further in this paper.

In Fig. 2 we analyze the assumption-based tagging approach using 36 application category instances from SATCOMP-2009. The instances are selected so that most of them are challenging for modern SAT solvers; 19 of them were not solved by any solver in the competition. We attempted solving of all the instances with the parti-tion tree approach both with and without learning, constructing the subproblems with *lookahead* and *vsids* partitioning functions. The leftmost figure is a scatter plot compar-ing the learning and non-learning partition tree approaches, where each point represents an instance solved either with *lookahead* or *vsids* (marked ○ and ×, respectively). Based on the results the learning, in fact, slows down the solving process compared to the approach without learning. The two rightmost figures illustrate the reason for this slow-down. Each point in the figures represents one job that was constructed while running the learning partition tree approach in the leftmost figure. Note that a single point in the leftmost figure might correspond to thousands of such points. The middle figure shows the run time of the jobs both with and without the learned clauses. The vertical axis is the run time with learned clauses solved with an assumption-based learned clause tagging solver, whereas the horizontal axis is the run time without learned clauses solved with an unaltered solver. Hence if a point is above the diagonal in the figure, the over-head caused by learning is not compensated by the reduction of the search space by the learned clauses. In particular it is interesting to note that the number of failures, shown as dots on the edges of the graph, is much higher when learning is used. Most of these result from memory exhaustion. The rightmost figure shows that the number of decisions made in the jobs decreases with learning. We may draw the conclusion that the solver with assumption based tagging consumes significantly more memory than the unaltered solver. This perhaps surprising result can be explained as follows. The conflict clauses deduced during the search can, for some real life formulas, contain large amounts of literals that (i) are implied by unit propagation after the assumption variables have been set to true, but (ii) are not (or have not been found to be by the solver) logical consequences of $form(\nu_k)^\star = \psi' \wedge \Sigma(\nu_0) \wedge (\neg a_1 \vee (constr(\nu_1) \wedge \Sigma(\nu_1))) \wedge \ldots \wedge (\neg a_k \vee (constr(\nu_k) \wedge \Sigma(\nu_k)))$. If the CDCL solver would consider $form(\nu_k)' = \psi' \wedge \Sigma(\nu_0) \wedge constr(\nu_1) \wedge \Sigma(\nu_1) \wedge \ldots \wedge constr(\nu_k) \wedge \Sigma(\nu_k)$ as a "flat formula" without assumption variables instead, such implied literals would not be in-cluded in conflict clauses as they are logical consequences of $form(\nu_k)'$. Such long clauses can consume excessive amounts of memory and also slow down the solver. We will shortly return to this perhaps surprising result in Example 2. The phenomenon has not, to our knowledge, been reported previously in parallel SAT solving, and we believe it plays a role also in the approaches based purely on guiding paths.

4.2 Flag-Based Learned Clause Tagging

To overcome the previously described challenge in assumption-based learned clause tagging, we describe here a light-weight version for clause learning similar to the one used in [26]. The intuition is to over-approximate the dependency of a learned clause from the constraints by flagging clauses which potentially depend on the assumptions.

Given a node ν_k with a simulating derived formula $form(\nu_k)' = \psi' \wedge \Sigma(\nu_0) \wedge constr(\nu_1) \wedge \Sigma(\nu_1) \wedge \ldots \wedge constr(\nu_k) \wedge \Sigma(\nu_k)$, our second clause tagging technique executes a CDCL solver "as is" on the formula except that in the beginning it marks the clauses in $\phi \wedge \Sigma(\nu_0)$ as "safe". Whenever a new learned clause (including learned unit clauses which are expressed as new "decision level 0" implied literals inside the solver) is derived, it is also marked "safe" if its derivation depended only on "safe" clauses. As a consequence, and recalling $\phi \vDash \Sigma(\nu_0)$, learned clauses marked "safe" are logical consequences of ϕ and can thus be included in the constraint-independent learned clause set $\Sigma(\nu_0)$ in any other node μ_m of the partition tree. The learned clauses not marked "safe" may depend on $constr(\nu_1) \wedge \Sigma(\nu_1) \wedge \ldots \wedge constr(\nu_k) \wedge \Sigma(\nu_k)$ and are thus

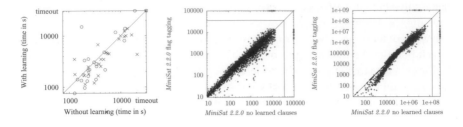

Fig. 3. The effect of learning in partition trees with flag based tagging

only guaranteed to be logical consequences of $\phi \wedge constr(\nu_0) \wedge \ldots \wedge constr(\nu_k)$; they can only be included in the constraint-dependent clause set $\Sigma(\nu_k)$ when considering any descendant node ν_l of ν_k.

This technique has the advantage of solving the above discussed "long clause problem" and adding only a very minimal overhead on the CDCL solver but, as shown below, the disadvantage that it can produce fewer constraint-independent learned clauses than the assumption based technique.

Figure 3 illustrates the effect of using flag-based learned clause tagging to the run time of the partition tree approach and to each job. We first note that based on the results in the leftmost graph using learned clauses seems to provide speed-up to the solving in most of the instances from the benchmark set. The per-job results in the two rightmost figures show that the previously observed failures are roughly equally common both with the flag-based solver with learned clauses and the unaltered solver without learned clauses. In particular the more difficult instances seem to be solved faster with the learned clauses (middle figure). The effect is also seen in the number of decisions (rightmost figure).

To shortly illustrate the two tagging techniques and to see that the assumption based one can produce more constraint-independent, although longer, learned clauses, consider the following simple example.

Example 2. Let the original formula ϕ include the clauses $(x_1 \vee x_2 \vee x_3) \wedge (x_2 \vee \neg x_3)$ and let $constr(\nu_1) = (\neg x_1)$ while $\Sigma(\nu_0) = \Sigma(\nu_1) = \emptyset$.

In the assumption based tagging, the solver will start with the formula ϕ extended with the assumption-encoded clause $(a_1 \vee \neg x_1)$. Making first the assumption branch on $\neg a_1$ and then the non-assumption branch on $\neg x_2$, the solver will learn the constraint-independent learned clause $(x_1 \vee x_2)$; note that $\neg x_1$ is not (necessarily) a logical consequence of ϕ and thus $(x_1 \vee x_2)$ is not simplified to x_2 by resolving on $\neg x_1$.

When using flag based tagging, the solver starts with an instance having the clauses $(x_1 \vee x_2 \vee x_3)^{\mathsf{S}} \wedge (x_2 \vee \neg x_3)^{\mathsf{S}} \wedge (\neg x_1)$ where the superscript s denotes a "safe" clause. Similarly branching on $\neg x_2$ results in a non-safe (and thus, correctly, constraint-dependent) learned clause (x_2); here $\neg x_1$ is trivially a logical consequence of the input formula $\phi \wedge constr(\nu_1)$ and thus $(x_1 \vee x_2)$ is simplified to x_2 by resolving on the non-safe unit clause $\neg x_1$.

5   The Main Experimental Results

This section compares our implementation of the iterative partitioning approach with clause learning to some other SAT solver implementations using all the 292 SATCOMP-2009 application benchmarks. These main experiments use the flag based learned clause tagging with the vsids heuristic, as it seems to perform slightly better than the lookahead heuristic (see the leftmost graph in Fig. 3). The remaining parameters, discussed in this section, are not particularly tuned for the benchmark set. They can be seen as reasonable guesses, but a closer study would likely reveal better values for these instances. The comparison uses the implementations below.

- *MiniSat 2.2.0*, a sequential SAT solver we have used as a basis for the grid-based approaches.
- *Part-Tree*, a grid-based iterative partitioning implementation without clause sharing [15].
- *Part-Tree-Learn*, a grid-based implementation of the learning iterative partitioning approach described in this work.
- *Cl-Sdsat*, a grid-based portfolio approach [14]. Learned clauses are collected from the timed-out jobs and used in subsequent jobs. Underlying solver is *MiniSat 2.2.0*.
- *ManySat 1.1* and *ManySat 1.5*, multi-core portfolio solvers using 4 cores [9].
- *Plingeling* 276, a multi-core portfolio solver which won the SAT-Race 2010. The results reported in this work are obtained with 12 cores [2].

The *Cl-Sdsat*, *Part-Tree*, and *Part-Tree-Learn* approaches use the M-grid environment currently consisting of nine clusters with CPUs purchased between 2006 and 2009. For more detailed information, see http://wiki.hip.fi/gm-fi/. The learned clauses transferred with the jobs are limited so that they contain in total 100 000 literals in these approaches. The other implementations were run using twelve-core AMD Opteron 2435 nodes from the year 2009.

As discussed before, each grid-based approach consists of a work flow of several relatively short lived jobs. The jobs enter the clusters through a batch queue system after a varying queuing time $d_{queuing}$ which is affected, for example, by the background load of the grid. Figure 4 shows the cumulative distribution of the queuing time measured over 200 000 jobs between 2010 and 2011; time t is shown on the horizontal axis, and the vertical axis gives the probability that the queuing time $d_{queuing}$ is at most t; median queuing time is approximately two minutes.

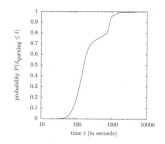

Fig. 4. Cumulative queuing time distribution in M-grid

The queuing time is included in the reported run times of the grid based approaches. Actual parallelism in the grid experiments depends on the queuing time and on the time required to construct the jobs, which in these experiments is at most 43 seconds per derived formula. As a result, the amount of parallelism varies typically between 8 and 60 simultaneously running jobs.

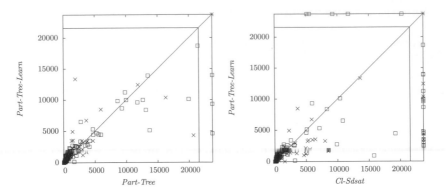

Fig. 5. Comparing *Part-Tree-Learn* to *Part-Tree* (left), and *Cl-Sdsat* (right). Satisfiable instances are marked with crosses (×) and unsatisfiable with boxes (□).

5.1   Comparing the Grid-Based Approaches

We first compare the grid-based *Part-Tree* and *Part-Tree-Learn* implementations in left of Fig. 5. The crosses (×) denote satisfiable and boxes (□) unsatisfiable instances from the SATCOMP-2009 benchmarks, and a mark below the diagonal means that *Part-Tree-Learn* performed better on that instance. An instance not solved in 6 hours is considered timed out. The 6 hour limit is marked on the graphs with the two inner lines on top and on the right of the graphs, and timed out instances are placed on the edges of the graph. The results suggest that learning may slow down the solving of easy instances but, as the run time of *Part-Tree* increases, the learned clauses decrease the run time of *Part-Tree-Learn*. The initial learned clauses are usually long and cause overhead in the search. The "quality" of the learned clauses improves as the search proceeds, which probably explains the speed-up for the more difficult instances.

The second experiment compares *Cl-Sdsat* against *Part-Tree-Learn*. The high number of time-outs for *Cl-Sdsat* compared to *Part-Tree-Learn* suggests that usually *Part-Tree-Learn* performs better than *Cl-Sdsat*. This is an interesting result, since most state-of-the-art parallel SAT solvers are based on a *Cl-Sdsat*-style portfolio approach, where several SAT solvers are running in parallel and sharing learned clauses. However, *Cl-Sdsat* is able to solve some instances not solved by *Part-Tree-Learn*, an indication that search space partitioning might not be the best solving approach for all instances.

5.2   Comparison to Parallel SAT Solvers

We now compare *Part-Tree-Learn* to three multi-core SAT solvers and the sequential *MiniSat 2.2.0* underlying *Part-Tree-Learn*. The jobs of *Part-Tree-Learn* ran in the grid with 2GB memory and approximately 1 hour time limit. All other solvers ran with 24GB memory and 6 hour time limit in relatively modern 12-core nodes so that no other process could cause, e.g., memory bus intereference with the solver. As the nodes are to our knowledge faster than the nodes in the grid and each job of *Part-Tree-Learn* experienced in addition the queue delay, we feel that the comparison should be relatively fair to our "competitors". The number of cores used by the other solvers is lower

Table 1. Instances that were not solved in SATCOMP-2009

Name	Type	Plingeling	ManySat 1.1	ManySat 1.5	Part-Tree-Learn	Part-Tree
9dlx_vliw_at_b_iq8	Unsat	3256.41	2950.52	**2750.39**	—	—
9dlx_vliw_at_b_iq9	Unsat	5164.00	4240.00	**3731.00**	—	—
AProVE07-25	Unsat	—	—	—	**9967.24**	9986.58
dated-5-19-u	Unsat	4465.00	11136.00	18080.00	**2522.40**	4104.30
eq.atree.braun.12.unsat	Unsat	—	—	—	**4691.99**	5247.13
eq.atree.braun.13.unsat	Unsat	—	—	—	**9972.47**	12644.24
gss-24-s100	Sat	2929.92	—	6575.00	3492.01	**1265.33**
gss-26-s100	Sat	18173.00	**1232.17**	—	10347.41	16308.65
gus-md5-14	Unsat	—	—	—	13890.05	**13466.18**
ndhf_xits_09_UNSAT	Unsat	—	—	—	**9583.10**	11769.23
rbcl_xits_09_UNKNOWN	Unsat	—	—	—	9818.59	**8643.21**
rpoc_xits_09_UNSAT	Unsat	—	—	—	**8635.29**	9319.52
sortnet-8-ipc5-h19-sat	Sat	**2699.62**	10785.00	7901.00	4303.93	20699.58
total-10-17-u	Unsat	**3672.00**	6392.00	10755.00	4447.26	5952.43
total-5-15-u	Unsat	—	—	—	**18670.33**	21467.79

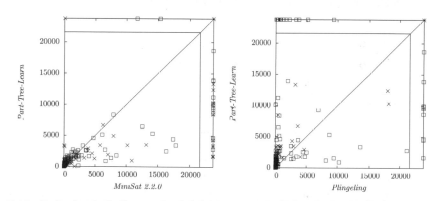

Fig. 6. Learning Partition Tree against *MiniSat 2.2.0* (left) and *Plingeling* (right)

than that used by *Part-Tree-Learn*, but we see this as an architectural limitation. For *Plingeling* we experimented with several numbers of cores. The 12-core configuration seemed to give the best result, whereas the default 4-core configuration was used for *ManySat 1.1* and *ManySat 1.5*. Of course, *MiniSat 2.2.0* was run with a single core.

Table 1 reports those of the 63 instances not solved in SATCOMP-2009 that were solved by at least one of the implementations in our experiments. The solvers *MiniSat 2.2.0* and *Cl-Sdsat* are omitted as they solved none of the unsolved instances. Based on the results, both *Part-Tree* and *Part-Tree-Learn* perform well on these hard instances, solving more instances than the other implementations. However, we do note that there are two instances from this benchmark set that *Part-Tree* and *Part-Tree-Learn* could not solve and three more where the solving time was lower in some other approach.

The *Part-Tree-Learn* approach is compared against *MiniSat 2.2.0* and *Plingeling* on the left and right hand side of Fig. 6, respectively, using the full set of application instances from SATCOMP-2009. We first note that *Part-Tree-Learn* performs in almost all more difficult instances significantly better than *MiniSat 2.2.0*. There are still some instances that cannot be solved with *Part-Tree-Learn*, an indication that the bounded job run times might limit the capabilities of *Part-Tree-Learn*. The comparison to the winner of SAT-Race 2010 *Plingeling* reveals that from the 292 instances, *Part-Tree-Learn* could solve 227 and *Plingeling* 234. Based on the scatter plot there are several instances that are much faster solved with *Plingeling* although the number of cores available to *Plingeling* was lower. It is interesting to note that there are still many instances that solved quickly with *Part-Tree-Learn* which, based on the results in Table 1, are such that they are difficult for many other solvers competing in SATCOMP-2009. One could read the right-hand side plot of Fig. 6 so that if an instance can be solved, it is either solved quickly with *Plingeling* or *Part-Tree-Learn*. It is interesting, although beyond the scope of this work, to contemplate whether an implementation of *Part-Tree-Learn* based on *Plingeling* would indeed result in an even higher performance.

Finally we report that we could use *Part-Tree-Learn* to show unsatisfiable a challenge instance called aes-top-22-symmetryBreaking posed in a footnote of [8] in approximately 45 hours. Neither *Plingeling*, *ManySat 1.1*, *ManySat 1.5*, nor *MiniSat 2.2.0* could produce the result in three days, and this is indeed the fastest wall-clock time known computation of unsatisfiability for this instance.

6   Conclusions

This work introduces a new approach to solving hard SAT instances in a grid or cloud computing environment where a master sends jobs to workers having tight limits on their resources. The approach is based on partitioning iteratively a given formula to increasingly constrained derived formulas while maintaining a learned clause collection of heuristically increasing quality. Promising sets of learned clauses are selected from the collection for each job based on the constraints of the corresponding derived formula. Two techniques for clause learning in the workers are studied: the more fine-grained assumption-based tagging and the light-weight flag-based tagging. Two partition functions are used to produce the partitioning constraints.

The results indicate that the clause-learning partition tree approach compares favorably to state-of-the-art SAT solvers particularly in the most challenging SAT instances.

Acknowledgments. The authors are grateful for the financial support of the Academy of Finland (project 122399) and the valuable comments of the anonymous reviewers.

References

1. Asín, R., Nieuwenhuis, R., Oliveras, A., Rodríguez-Carbonell, E.: Practical algorithms for unsatisfiability proof and core generation in SAT solvers. AI Communications 23(2-3), 145–157 (2010)
2. Biere, A.: Lingeling, Plingeling, PicoSAT and PrecoSAT at SAT race 2010. Technical Report 10/1, Institute for Formal Models and Verification, Johannes Kepler University (2010)
3. Blochinger, W., Sinz, C., Küchlin, W.: Parallel propositional satisfiability checking with distributed dynamic learning. Parallel Computing 29(7), 969–994 (2003)
4. Böhm, M., Speckenmeyer, E.: A fast parallel SAT-solver: Efficient workload balancing. Annals of Mathematics and Artificial Intelligence 17(4-3), 381–400 (1996)
5. Chrabakh, W., Wolski, R.: GridSAT: a system for solving satisfiability problems using a computational grid. Parallel Computing 32(9), 660–687 (2006)
6. Chu, G., Schulte, C., Stuckey, P.J.: Confidence-based work stealing in parallel constraint programming. In: Gent, I.P. (ed.) CP 2009. LNCS, vol. 5732, pp. 226–241. Springer, Heidelberg (2009)

7. Eén, N., Sörensson, N.: Temporal induction by incremental SAT solving. Electronic Notes in Theoretical Computer Science 89(4) (2003)
8. Fuhs, C., Schneider-Kamp, P.: Synthesizing shortest linear straight-line programs over GF(2) using SAT. In: Strichman, O., Szeider, S. (eds.) SAT 2010. LNCS, vol. 6175, pp. 71–84. Springer, Heidelberg (2010)
9. Hamadi, Y., Jabbour, S., Sais, L.: ManySAT: a parallel SAT solver. Journal on Satisfiability, Boolean Modeling and Computation 6, 245–262 (2009)
10. Hamadi, Y., Jabbour, S., Sais, L.: Constrol-based clause sharing in parallel SAT solving. In: Proc. IJCAI 2009, pp. 499–504 (2009)
11. Heule, M., van Maaren, H.: Look-ahead based SAT solvers. In: Handbook of Satisfiability. Frontiers in Artificial Intelligence and Applications, vol. 185, pp. 155–184. IOS Press, Amsterdam (2009)
12. Huberman, B.A., Lukose, R.M., Hogg, T.: An economics approach to hard computational problems. Science 275(5296), 51–54 (1997)
13. Hyvärinen, A.E.J., Junttila, T., Niemelä, I.: A distribution method for solving SAT in grids. In: Biere, A., Gomes, C.P. (eds.) SAT 2006. LNCS, vol. 4121, pp. 430–435. Springer, Heidelberg (2006)
14. Hyvärinen, A.E.J., Junttila, T., Niemelä, I.: Incorporating clause learning in grid-based randomized SAT solving. Journal on Satisfiability, Boolean Modeling and Computation 6, 223–244 (2009)
15. Hyvärinen, A.E.J., Junttila, T., Niemelä, I.: Partitioning SAT instances for distributed solving. In: Fermüller, C.G., Voronkov, A. (eds.) LPAR-17. LNCS, vol. 6397, pp. 372–386. Springer, Heidelberg (2010)
16. Hyvärinen, A.E.J., Junttila, T., Niemelä, I.: Partitioning search spaces of a randomized search. Fundamenta Informaticae 107(2-3), 289–311 (2011)
17. Jurkowiak, B., Li, C., Utard, G.: A parallelization scheme based on work stealing for a class of SAT solvers. Journal of Automated Reasoning 34(1), 73–101 (2005)
18. Luby, M., Sinclair, A., Zuckerman, D.: Optimal speedup of Las Vegas algorithms. Information Processing Letters 47(4), 173–180 (1993)
19. Marques-Silva, J., Lynce, I., Malik, S.: Conflict-driven clause learning SAT solvers. In: Handbook of Satisfiability. IOS Press, Amsterdam (2009)
20. Marques-Silva, J., Sakallah, K.: GRASP: A search algorithm for propositional satisfiability. IEEE Transactions on Computers 48(5), 506–521 (1999)
21. Martins, R., Manquinho, V., Lynce, I.: Improving search space splitting for parallel SAT solving. In: Proc. ICTAI 2010, pp. 336–343. IEEE Press, Los Alamitos (2010)
22. Michel, L., See, A., van Hentenryck, P.: Parallelizing constraint programs transparently. In: Bessière, C. (ed.) CP 2007. LNCS, vol. 4741, pp. 514–528. Springer, Heidelberg (2007)
23. Moskewicz, M., Madigan, C., Zhao, Y., Zhang, L., Malik, S.: Chaff: Engineering an efficient SAT solver. In: Proc. DAC 2001, pp. 530–535. ACM, New York (2001)
24. Schubert, T., Lewis, M., Becker, B.: PaMiraXT: Parallel SAT solving with threads and message passing. Journal on Satisfiability, Boolean Modeling and Computation 6, 203–222 (2009)
25. Speckenmeyer, E., Monien, B., Vornberger, O.: Superlinear speedup for parallel backtracking. In: Houstis, E.N., Polychronopoulos, C.D., Papatheodorou, T.S. (eds.) ICS 1987. LNCS, vol. 297, pp. 985–993. Springer, Heidelberg (1988)
26. Wieringa, S., Niemenmaa, M., Heljanko, K.: Tarmo: A framework for parallelized bounded model checking. In: Proc. PDMC 2009. EPTCS, vol. 14, pp. 62–76 (2009)
27. Zhang, H., Bonacina, M., Hsiang, J.: PSATO: A distributed propositional prover and its application to quasigroup problems. Journal of Symbolic Computation 21(4), 543–560 (1996)

Large Neighborhood Search
for Dial-a-Ride Problems

Siddhartha Jain and Pascal Van Hentenryck

Brown University, Department of Computer Science,
Box 1910, Providence, RI 02912, U.S.A.
{sj10,pvh}@cs.brown.edu

Abstract. Dial-a-Ride problems (DARPs) arise in many urban transportation applications. The core of a DARP is a pick and delivery routing with multiple vehicles in which customers have ride-time constraints and routes have a maximum duration. This paper considers DARPs for which the objective is to minimize the routing cost, a complex optimization problem which has been studied extensively in the past. State-of-the-art approaches include sophisticated tabu search and variable neighborhood search. This paper presented a simple constraint-based large neighborhood search, which uses constraint programming repeatedly to find good reinsertions for randomly selected sets of customers. Experimental evidence shows that the approach is competitive in finding best-known solutions and reaches high-quality solutions significantly faster than the state of the art.

1 Introduction

The Dial-a-Ride Problem (DARP) is a variant of the Pickup and Delivery Problem (PDP), frequently arising in door-to-door transportation services for elderly and disabled people or in services for patients. In recent years, dial-a-ride services have been steadily increasing in response to popular demand. [8]. A DARP consists of n customers who want to be transported from an origin to a destination. Requests can be classified as *outbound* (say from home to the hospital) or *inbound* (from hospital back to the home). DARPs can be rather diverse and there is no standard formulation in literature. Various formulations try to balance the cost of the route and user inconvenience via soft and hard constraints. One formulation minimizes the weighted sum of total routing cost, time-window violations, and the number of vehicles used [1]. Another has multiple depots, a heterogeneous fleet, service times, time windows, and maximum customer ride times [13]. Yet another minimizes the weighted sum of the customer transportation times, the excess customer ride time with respect to direct and maximum ride time, time-window violations, customer waiting time and excess work time [10]. A survey of various DARP models and the algorithms used to solve them is given in [8].

This paper studies the formulation of Cordeau et al. [7] defined in terms of a fixed number m of vehicles, which makes sense in practice. There is only one depot. There are time-window constraints on the pickup or delivery vertex depending on whether the request is inbound or outbound. We also have service times, maximum ride time, and maximum route duration constraints. The objective is to minimize the total routing cost,

J. Lee (Ed.): CP 2011, LNCS 6876, pp. 400–413, 2011.

i.e., the travel distance. A tabu-search procedure to solve the *static* version of the problem where the requests are known in advance was presented by Cordeau et al [7] while a Variable Neighborhood Search procedure was proposed recently by Parragh et al. [11]. A procedure for testing the *satisfiability* of an instance was given by Berbeglia et al. [5]. A procedure for testing the satisfiability for the *dynamic* version of the problem, where only a subset of requests is known in advance, was presented in [4]. In general, one is interested in finding high-quality solutions to DARPs since, as the name indicates, customers call for a service.

This paper presents a large neighborhood search for DARPs and makes the following contributions:

1. It proposes a large neighborhood search LNS-FFPA (FFPA will be defined in Section 6) which significantly outperforms the traditional LNS algorithm used in vehicle routing (e.g., [12,3,2]).
2. It shows that LNS-FFPA significantly improves the quality of the routings found under tight time constraints compared to the state-of-the-art variable neighborhood search and tabu-search algorithms.
3. It shows that LNS-FFPA compares very well with the state-of-the-art constraint-programming approach to find feasible solutions to DARPs.

From a technical standpoint, LNS-FFPA features two novelties. First, it does not impose that the neighborhood search must find an improving solution. Second, LNS-FFPA terminates the neighborhood search after finding a feasible solution. This solution is accepted using a Probabilistic criterion, which allows worse solutions to be accepted for subsequent iterations. As mentioned earlier, the diversification resulting from these two design decisions is key in finding high-quality solutions under time constraints. It is also important to emphasize that LNS-FFPA, which is a very generic search technique, improves solution quality under very tight constraints over highly dedicated local search implementations. This makes it ideal for the highly dynamic environments in which DARPs arise.

The rest of the paper is organized as follows. We first present the problem formulation and give an overview of the state-of-the-art. This review should give readers a sense of the sophistication of the existing approaches. We then present our large neighborhood algorithm LNS-FFPA, report the experimental results, and conclude the paper.

2   Formulation

The input to DARP consists of the number m of vehicles, n requests, the maximum ride time L for customers, the maximum route duration D, and the planning time horizon T, i.e., the hours between which the vehicles can operate. A DARP is defined on a complete graph $G = (V, E)$ where $V = \{v_0, v_1, \ldots, v_{2n}\}$ is the set of vertices and $E = \{(v_i, v_j) : v_i, v_j \in V, i \neq j\}$ is the set of edges. Vertex v_0 denotes the depot. Each request i ($1 \leq i \leq n$) consists of a pair of vertices (v_i, v_{i+n}). With each vertex v_j is associated a service duration $d_j \geq 0$, a load q_j and a time window $[e_j, l_j]$. We also have $d_0 = 0$, $q_0 = 0$, and $e_0 = 0, l_0 = T$. Service duration is the time needed to service a vertex. Requests are either *inbound* or *outbound*. If i is an outbound request, then the pickup vertex v_i has the time window $[0, T]$ and is called *non-critical*, whereas the delivery vertex is called *critical*. If i is an inbound request, then the delivery vertex v_{i+n} has time window $[0, T]$ and is non-critical whereas the pickup vertex is critical. The matrix $t_{i,j}$ also denotes the distance between vertices i and j. Given these definitions, a DARP consists in finding a route for each of the m vehicles such that (1) the route begins and ends at the depot; (2) The load of a vehicle k never exceeds its capacity Q_k; (3) The total duration (i.e., the difference between the end time and the start time) never exceeds a preset bound T_k; (4) For each request i, v_i and v_{i+n} are serviced by the same vehicle and v_{i+n} is visited after v_i; (5) The ride time of any customer (i.e., the difference between the serving time at the delivery vertex and the departure time at the pickup vertex) does not exceed L; (6) For each vertex v_i, the starting time of its service lies between $[e_i, l_i]$; and (7) The total routing cost of all vehicles is minimized. In our formulation as in [7], the total routing cost is equal to the total distance traveled by the vehicles.

3   A Constraint Programming Approach

Berbeglia et al [5] use a Constraint Programming (CP) approach for the DARP formulation in [7], except they do not model the route duration constraint and do not attempt to minimize the routing cost. Their focus is to check the satisfiability of DARP instances.

The Model. Each vertex v_i has a successor variable $s[i]$ and there is an *AllDifferent* constraint on all successor variables. The precedence, time window, ride time, and maximum vehicle capacity constraints are modeled via auxiliary variables representing the load, serving vehicle, and serving time for each vertex. The routes are constructed by branching on the successor variables.

Variable Selection. Let S be the set of all successor variables with the smallest domains. For every value v in the domain of some variable in S, the CP algorithm computes $v^{\#}$, the number of times that value appears in the domain of some variable in S. Denote by S' the set of all variables in S for which the sum $\sum_{v \in domain(S_i)} v^{\#}$ is maximized. The CP algorithm randomly select a variable from S'.

Value Selection. Let s be the chosen variable. The partial route of s is defined as the sequence of vertices $v_i, v_{i+1}, \ldots, v_j$ such that the successor $s[v_k]$ of v_k is v_{k+1} and $v_j = s$. The value-selection heuristic considers the following vertices in sequence:

1. a delivery vertex whose corresponding pickup vertex is in the partial route of s;
2. a pickup vertex randomly selected from the domain of s;
3. a delivery or a depot vertex.

Filtering Algorithms. Berbeglia et al. [5] developed two dedicated filtering algorithms for DARPs. The first filtering algorithm is based on solving exactly the Pickup and Delivery Problem with Fixed Partial Routes (PDP-FPR), a relaxed version of the DARP. The PDP-FPR takes into account the precedence and the capacity constraints and is strongly NP-complete [6]. The authors proposed a dynamic-programming algorithm to solve it exactly and use that to develop a filtering algorithm for PDP-FPR.

The second filtering algorithm is a partial filtering algorithm for the basic DARP with Ride Time Constraint problem, also a relaxation of the original problem with only the ride time constraint which is NP-complete [6]. For every unassigned successor variable s, the algorithm examines every pickup vertex p in the partial route of s and calculates a lower bound on the minimum time needed to get from p to the corresponding delivery vertex d. If this bound exceeds the maximum ride time, then some values from the domain of s can be removed. A similar procedure is executed for the delivery vertices in the partial routes of the vertices in the domain of s. The filtering algorithms are too complex to be described given space constraints but readers can consult [5] for the full details.

4   A Tabu Search Approach

A Tabu-Search approach was developed by Cordeau et al. [7]. The algorithm starts with a random initial solution s_0 and, at every iteration t, moves from solution s_t to a solution in its neighborhood. To prevent cycling, certain attributes of previous solutions are declared tabu unless those attributes form part of a new best solution. A diversification mechanism is in place to reduce the likelihood of being trapped in a local minimum. In addition, every κ iterations, every request is sequentially removed from its current route and inserted in the best possible location. Some important aspects of the algorithm are briefly described 1below.

Relaxation Mechanism.   One of the key features of the tabu-search algorithm is that it allows the exploration of infeasible solutions. The time window, ride time, capacity, and route duration constraints are relaxed and their violation is penalized in the objective. The objective is defined as $f(s) = c(s) + \alpha q(s) + \beta d(s) + \gamma w(s) + \tau t(s)$ where $\alpha, \beta, \gamma, \tau$ are self-adjusting positive parameters, $c(s)$ is the routing cost, $q(s)$ the load violation, $d(s)$ the route duration violation, $w(s)$ the time window violation, and $t(s)$ the ride-time violation. The search tries to minimize the routing cost and the violations simultaneously to get good solutions that satisfy all the constraints.

Neighborhood.   The neighborhood of a solution consists of moving a request i from a route r to a route r'. In such a case, the attribute (i, r) is put in the tabu list. If an attribute (i, r') is in the tabu list, then the request i cannot be moved to route r'. As a form of aspiration, if moving request i to route r' would result in a smaller cost than the best known solution *which has request i in route r'*, then the tabu status of the attribute (i, r') is revoked.

Penalty Adjustment.   The penalties for the violations are adjusted dynamically through the course of the search. At every iteration, if a constraint is being violated in the current solution, the penalty for that constraint is multiplied by a factor $(1 + \delta)$ $(\delta > 0)$. If on the other hand, the constraint is not violated, the penalty is divided by the same factor. If a penalty reaches a fixed upper bound, then it is reset to 1.[1]

---

[1] This particular aspect is not mentioned in [7] but was learned through personal communication.

Neighborhood Evaluation. Cordeau et al. [7] uses three different schemes for choosing where to insert a request on a route. The simplest one only minimizes the time-window violations. The second does the same and also minimizes the route duration violations without increasing the ride-time violations. Both are linear time algorithms. The third evaluation procedure minimizes first the time-window violations, then the route duration violations and then the ride-time violations without increasing the time window or route duration violations. It is a quadratic time procedure. To reduce the size of the neighborhood, the algorithm first looks for the best insertion place for the critical vertex (ride-time violations are ignored in this step) and then the best insertion place for the non-critical vertex, while keeping the critical vertex in its best insertion place. In particular, different insertion places for the critical vertex are not considered.

5   A Variable Neighborhood Approach

A Variable Neighborhood Search (VNS) procedure for the DARP was proposed by [11]. The search starts with an initial solution s_0 generated by taking into account the spatial and temporal closeness of vertices. Then, at every iteration t with solution s_t, a random solution s' is generated in the neighborhood $N_k(s_t)$ in a step called *shaking*. Here k indicates which neighborhood is being used. The heuristic uses three different types of neighborhoods with multiple neighborhood sizes for a total of 13 different neighborhoods. Following that, a local search step is applied to s' to get solution s''. A simulated annealing type criterion is used to decide whether s'' replaces s_t and become the new incumbent solution. If s_t is not replaced, the next (larger) neighborhood is tried. Otherwise, s'' replaces s_t and the search begins with the first neighborhood, i.e., k is reset to 1. If k reaches 13, the maximum number of neighborhoods, it is also reset to 1. Infeasible solutions are also permitted in this framework and they are incorporated into the objective as in [7]. The neighborhood evaluation is also the same. Their results are competitive with the results obtained by [7]. A few other important aspects of the solver are highlighted below.

Neighborhood Structure. Three different types of neighborhoods are employed. In the *swap* neighborhood, two sequences of requests are chosen from two randomly selected routes. Those requests are then ejected from their current route and inserted in the other selected route in the best possible position. The *chain* neighborhood applies the ejection chain idea [9]. First two routes are randomly chosen and a sequence of requests is ejected from the first route and inserted in the best possible way in the second route. Then a sequence of requests which would decrease the evaluation function value *of that route* the most is ejected from the second route and moved to a third route (which may even be the first route). This last step is repeated a fixed number of times. The size of the sequences is also fixed. The third type of neighborhood is the *zero-split* neighborhood which is parameterless. Define a natural sequence to be one where the load at the beginning and end of the sequence is zero. Then the neighborhood is based on the idea that quite often multiple such natural sequences exist in routes. Thus a random number of such natural sequences are ejected from a route. Each of them is then inserted independently in a random route at their best insertion point. By varying the parameters of the first two neighborhoods, along with the zero-split neighborhood, a sequence of 13 different neighborhoods is obtained.

Local Search. After the shaking step, a local search step is applied. Requests are sequentially removed from their current position and inserted in the first position that would improve the route's evaluation function value. If no such position exists for a request, then the request is kept at its original place. Since this procedure is time-consuming, it is only called if the solution after the shaking step is considered a promising solution, i.e., a solution that has a good possibility of becoming the new incumbent solution. Further details are in [11].

6   The LNS-FFPA Algorithm

The large neighborhood search algorithm (LNS-FFPA) is the main contribution of the paper. LNS-FFPA, where FFPA stands for First Feasible Probabilistic Acceptance, is inspired by the LNS algorithm described in [12,2,3] to minimize the travel distance for vehicle routing problems in [12] and pickup and delivery problems in [2]. However, LNS-FFPA contains some novel design decisions which are key to obtaining high-quality solutions on DARPs.

The Model. Each vertex v_i has a successor variable s_i. The routes are constructed by inserting a non-scheduled request r_i with pickup vertex v_i and delivery vertex v_j in the route. The pickup vertex is inserted in between two other vertices v_p and v_s which are parts of a route and similarly for the delivery vertex. In other words, each branching decision in LNS-FFPA corresponds to the insertion of a request in a route. Every time LNS-FFPA branches, it adds the following constraints for both the pickup and the delivery vertex of the request

$$b_i \geq b_p + d_p + t_{p,i}$$
$$b_s \geq b_i + d_i + t_{i,s}$$

where b_i is the serving time of the pickup or delivery vertex in question, d_i is the serving duration of a vertex and $t_{i,j}$ is the distance between two vertices as specified in Section 2. These constraints are removed upon backtracking.

The Feasibility Search. At a high level, LNS-FFPA is a constraint-programming search to find a feasible solution to DARPs, coupled with a large neighborhood algorithm to minimize travel distance. Algorithm 1 describes the algorithm for finding feasible solutions. The algorithm receives a partial solution, i.e., a set of partial routes for the vehicles. As long as there are unassigned customers, the algorithm selects such a request r (line 3). It then considers all its possible insertion points (line 4) and calls the algorithm recursively for each such insertion point p (line 6–8). If the recursive call finds a feasible solution, the algorithm returns. Otherwise, it removes the request and tries the remaining insertion points. Note that the insertion points are explored in increasing order of $e(r, p)$ which is defined as (α and β are positive constants)

$$\alpha \cdot costIncrease(r, p) - \beta \cdot slackAfterInsertion(r, p)$$

Algorithm 1. Tree-Search($PartialSolution$)

1: **if** no unassigned requests left **then**
2:      **return** PartialSolution
3: $r \leftarrow$ GetUnassignedRequest()
4: **for** all feasible insertion points p for r in increasing order of $e(r,p)$ **do**
5:      Insert r at point p in the PartialSolution
6:      ret = Tree-Search(PartialSolution)
7:      **if** ret is a solution **then**
8:          Return ret {Feasible solution found in sub-branch}
9:      Remove r from PartialSolution
10: **return** False {No feasible solution found for this sub-branch}

The Algorithm for Finding a Feasible Solution Given a Partial Solution.

Algorithm 2. GetUnassignedRequest()

1: $S_1 \leftarrow \{r : r$ is an unassigned request and the number of routes in which r can be inserted is minimized$\}$.
2: $S_2 \leftarrow \{r : r \in S_1$ and the number of insertion points for r is minimized$\}$.
3: $S_3 \leftarrow \{r : r \in S_2$ and the best insertion point for r increases $e(r,p)$ by the least amount$\}$.
4: **return** a randomly chosen element from S_3.

Request Selection Heuristic

---

where $costIncrease(r,p)$ denotes the increase in routing cost produced by inserting request r at insertion point p and $slackAfterInsertion(r,p)$ denotes the gap between the serving times of the pickup and delivery vertices and their successors and predecessors after the insertion. The gap for a vertex v_i is given by

$$servingTime[succ(v_i)] - servingTime[v_i] + servingTime[v_i] - servingTime[pred(v_i)]$$

and the gap for the pickup and delivery vertices is the sum of the gaps of the individual vertices. In other words, the insertion points are chosen to minimize the increase in the routing cost and maximize the available slack.

Algorithm 2 specifies which requests are inserted first, i.e., how line 3 in Algorithm 1 is implemented. It selects a request which can be inserted in the fewest vehicles (set S_1), which has the fewest insertion points (set S_2), and whose best insertion point produces the smallest amount in objective value.

Algorithm 1 is used both for finding an initial solution and for reinserting vertices during the large neighborhood search. In [12,2,3], the corresponding algorithm uses Limited Discrepancy Search (LDS) and limits the number of feasible insertion points explored at every search node. Moreover, such a neighborhood search is constrained to produce only improving solutions. In contrast, no such restrictions are imposed on Algorithm 1: It is a pure depth-first search algorithm, exploring all potential insertion points and returning the first feasible solution extending the input partial configuration.

For some instances with high (number of requests/number of vehicle) ratios, restarts improve performance: Algorithm 1 restarts after $max(\gamma \cdot m, \tau)$ failures where γ and τ are positive constants. This is only used for finding an initial feasible solution.

Algorithm 3. MinimizeRoutingCost($s, maxSize, range, numIter, timeLimit, d$)

1:
2: best ← s
3: current ← s
4: **for** $i \leftarrow 2; i \leq$ maxSize-range; $i \leftarrow i + 1$ **do**
5:   **for** $j \leftarrow 0; j \leq$ range; $j \leftarrow j + 1$ **do**
6:     **for** $k \leftarrow 0; k \leq$ numIter; $k \leftarrow k + 1$ **do**
7:       RelaxedSolution ← Randomly select $i + j$ requests and
8:       remove them from current
9:       $new \leftarrow$ Tree-Search(RelaxedSolution)
10:       $pr \leftarrow$ random number between 0 and 1
11:       **if** f(new) < f(current) OR $pr < d$ **then**
12:         current = new
13:         **if** f(current) < f(best) **then**
14:           best = current
15:       **if** timeLimit reached **then**
16:         **return** best
17: **return** best

The LNS-FFPA Algorithm for DARPs.

The Large Neighborhood Search **Algorithm 3** describes the LNS-FFPA algorithm to minimize the routing cost. It takes as input an initial feasible solution s and an upper bound on the number of requests that can be relaxed *maxSize*. To explore smaller neighborhoods first, LNS-FFPA uses a parameter *range* to increase the neighborhood size progressively. Finally, the procedure receives as inputs the number of iterations per neighborhood (t), the time limit for running the algorithm (*timeLimit*) and the probability d of accepting a worse solution. In addition, the function f used in the procedure returns the routing cost of a solution. The current solution is first initialized to the initial solution passed in to the procedure (line 3). Then the neighborhood is explored as given in lines 4-6. The number of requests that can be relaxed is steadily increased (line 4). Once it reaches the upper bound, it is effectively reset to 1. For a particular neighborhood size, a small range of neighborhoods starting from that size are explored (line 5). Every neighborhood size in that range is explored for *numIter* iterations (line 6). The number of requests equal to the neighborhood size are relaxed (line 7). The requests to relax are chosen at random. More sophisticated methods to select the requests to relax including the one used in [12,2,3] were tried but the random heuristic was significantly better for DARPs. Our conjecture is that the side constraints in DARPs, in particular the ride time, make it much harder to select a set of spatially related requests that could lead to a better solution than for more traditional VRPs without the ride constraint [12,2,3]. The search then attempts to complete the relaxed solution by calling Algorithm 1 to find a satisfying solution (line 9). The current solution is replaced by the new solution (which might be the same as the old solution) if either (1) the routing cost of the new solution is lower than the current solution; or (2) with some probability d (line 10). If the current solution is better than the best solution, then the best solution is updated (line 13). At the end or if the time limit is reached, the best solution found is returned (line 14-15 and line 16).

LNS-FFPA has some unique features compared to the standard LNS algorithms. First, during the neighborhood exploration, LNS-FFPA does not search for a solution with a routing cost better than the current solution, just a feasible solution. This diversifies the search and, equally importantly, enables LNS-FFPA to explore many reinsertions effectively. Indeed, since the selection of the requests to relax is randomized, it is not very likely that the search can discover better solutions for a given reinsertion set. Hence, it is not cost-effective to explore the sub-neighborhood exhaustively in the hope of finding a better solution. We could limit the number of insertion points per requests as is done in [12,2,3] but the algorithm would still take significant time on unsuccessful searches, while reducing the probability of finding high-quality solutions. Instead, we simply let Algorithm 1 find the first feasible, but not necessarily improving, solution, its variable and value heuristics guiding the search towards good solutions. Since finding a feasible solution is fast, LNS-FFPA explores many reinsertions, while providing a good diversification. This aspect is critical and led to significant improvements in quality, as will be demonstrated shortly.

7   Numerical Results

This section presents the experimental results, justifies the design decisions underlying our LNS-FFPA algorithm, and compares the algorithm with prior algorithms.

The Algorithms. We compared our LNS-FFPA algorithm against the CP approach of Berbeglia et al. [5], the tabu search by Cordeau et al. [7], and the variable neighborhood search by Parragh et al. [11]. For the parameters for Algorithm 1, we set $\alpha = 80$ and $\beta = 1$. For the parameters for the restart strategy, we set $\gamma = 200$ and $\tau = 1000$. For the LNS Search, we set $maxSize = n/2$, where n is the number of requests, $range = 4$, $numIter = 300$, and $d = 0.07$.

The LNS-FFPA and Variable Neighborhood Search algorithms[2] were tested on a Intel Core 2 Quad Q6600 machine with 3 GB of RAM. The Comet language was used to implement the LNS-FFPA algorithm and is in general 3–5x slower than comparable C++ code. As the code for VNS and Tabu Search is implemented in C++, we conservatively divide the amount of time LNS-FFPA takes by a factor of 3 for this evaluation.

The code for the the tabu search was unavailable and hence, we can only compare with the tables given in [7] which report results for only one or two runs of the algorithm.[3] This comparison is much less reliable than the comparison with the most recent Variable Neighborhood Search [11] but is given for completeness.

The Instances. The Dial-a-Ride instances are taken from Parragh et al. [11] and Cordeau et al. [7]. They are based on realistic assumptions and data provided by the Montreal Transit Commission (MTC). Half of the requests are outbound and half inbound. They are divided into classes a and b, the difference being that class a instances have tighter time windows. In the instances, m denotes the number of vehicles and n is the number of requests.

---

[2] Many thanks to Parragh et al. for providing us with the code for the VNS search.

[3] As the tabu search was run on a 2 GHZ machine, when it is compared with the LNS-FFPA algorithm, the time for LNS-FFPA is divided by 2.5 instead of 3.

Table 1. The Benefits of LNS-FFPA

Class *a*		LNS		LNS-FFPA		Class *b*		LNS		LNS-FFPA	
5 minute run						**5 minute run**					
m	*n*	Mean	Best	Mean	Best	*m*	*n*	Mean	Best	Mean	Best
3	24	191.14	190.02	190.77	190.02	3	24	170.29	167.78	164.46	164.46
4	36	302.77	296.36	292.86	291.71	4	36	263.27	252.99	248.31	248.21
5	48	318.50	312.12	304.45	303.03	5	48	318.51	308.51	301.67	299.27
6	72	537.10	526.54	505.15	494.91	6	72	509.89	494.97	477.75	469.73
7	72	577.13	547.69	547.39	542.83	7	72	548.22	530.45	504.69	494.01
8	108	768.08	736.14	711.60	696.51	8	108	682.50	647.85	633.51	620.54
9	96	660.67	636.50	595.05	588.80	9	96	611.66	595.32	566.48	557.61
10	144	987.70	950.01	911.18	891.98	10	144	952.60	918.76	857.95	838.65
11	120	722.87	696.95	662.56	653.57	11	120	671.87	650.27	610.33	602.19
13	144	915.34	905.03	832.74	816.79	13	144	870.30	846.16	785.13	771.69
Avg.		598.13	579.74	555.38	547.02	*Avg.*		559.91	541.31	515.03	506.64

The Benefits of LNS-FFPA. Before comparing LNS-FFPA with prior art, it is useful to evaluate our main design decision and compare LNS and LNS-FFPA. Standard LNS algorithms (e.g., [12,3,2]) always search for an improving solution and limit the number of insertion points to explore the "good" parts of the subproblems. In contrast, LNS-FFPA does not require the subproblem to find an improving solution: It simply searches for the first feasible solution to the subproblem using the heuristic to drive the search toward a high-quality solution. Moreover, LNS-FFPA may accept the solution to the subproblem even if it degrades the best-known solution, using a Probabilistic acceptance criterion.

Table 1 compares LNS and LNS-FFPA and reports the mean and best solutions found over 10 different 5-minute runs for each instance. In the table, m denotes the number of vehicles and n the number of requests. The experimental results indicate that LNS-FFPA leads to solutions of significantly higher quality and to a more robust algorithm. The average improvement for the Class a instances is about 8% and is higher for the larger instances. For Class b, the average improvement is also around 8% and, for larger instances, improvement of almost 10% are observed. It is also important to stress how robust LNS-FFPA is, since the difference in quality between the best and the average solutions is rather small.

Table 2 evaluates the impact of the two novel aspects of LNS-FFPA: It reports the results of LNS-FF which never accepts any worse solution. The results show that the two additional components of LNS-FFPA are complementary but with the First Feasible criterion having a slighly larger effect. Indeed, without Probabilistic acceptance criterion, the average improvement drops from 8% to 4.2% on Class a instances and from 8% to 4.5% on Class b.

It is also important to mention that simply adding the Probabilistic criterion to the standard LNS was not effective. In other words, accepting the best solution found in the neighborhood with a Probabilistic criterion actually deteriorated performance, indicating that it is the combination of stopping at the first feasible solution and using the Probabilistic criterion which is key to obtain enough search diversity. A potential

Table 2. The Impact of the Acceptance Criterion

5 minute run					5 minute run				
Class a		LNS		LNS-FF	Class b		LNS		LNS-FF	
m	n	Mean	Best	Mean	Best	m	n	Mean	Best	Mean	Best
3	24	191.14	190.02	190.224	190.019	3	24	170.29	167.78	166.57	164.46
4	36	302.77	296.36	297.419	293.038	4	36	263.27	252.99	257.02	255.96
5	48	318.50	312.12	307.449	304.051	5	48	318.51	308.51	309.43	299.02
6	72	537.10	526.54	518.945	507.672	6	72	509.89	494.97	488.90	478.19
7	72	577.13	547.69	556.872	546.893	7	72	548.22	530.45	526.87	511.35
8	108	768.08	736.14	736.739	714.860	8	108	682.50	647.85	645.20	624.61
9	96	660.67	636.50	626.956	598.675	9	96	611.66	595.32	593.90	574.23
10	144	987.70	950.01	937.208	912.302	10	144	952.60	918.76	903.58	883.29
11	120	722.87	696.95	685.016	670.116	11	120	671.87	650.27	640.77	615.96
13	144	915.34	905.03	875.007	849.761	13	144	870.30	846.16	811.58	795.23
Avg.		598.13	579.74	573.18	558.74	Avg.		559.91	541.31	534.38	520.28

explanation is that LNS-FFPA can exploit the diversification of accepting a worse solution a lot better since it explores a lot more neighborhoods whereas the standard LNS algorithm spends too much time trying to find a better solution in fewer neighborhoods.

Overall, these results show that LNS-FFPA is a critical aspect of this research. For Dial-a-Ride problems, more diversification is key to improving quality. This diversification can be obtained either by accepting worse solutions or by exploring more neighborhoods since the search terminates as soon as a feasible solution is found.

Comparison with the Variable Neighborhood Search. We now compare LNS-FFPA with the state-of-the-art Variable Neighborhood Search (VNS) of Parragh et al. [11]. Table 3 depicts the results for class a instances.[4] Except for small instances with three vehicles, LNS-FFPA produces results that are consistently better on average and frequently better in terms of the best solutions. As the n/m ratio rises, the difficulty and the instance size increase and the LNS-FFPA produces increasing benefits. For the 1.6 min runs, LNS-FFPA improves the quality of the solution by 6.1% in average and by 24.2% in the best case. For the 5 min runs, LNS-FFPA produces improvement of about 3% in average and 14% in the best case.

These results indicates that LNS-FFPA is a very effective approach to find high-quality solutions under severe time constraints to complex Dial-a-Ride problems.

Comparison with the Tabu Search. Table 4 compares LNS-FFPA and the tabu search of [7] on short runs for the classes a and b. As mentioned earlier, Cordeau did not release his algorithm whose results seem very hard to reproduce. The table reports the tabu-search results as given in [7] where the quality of a single solution, and the time to obtain it, are given. The results for LNS-FFPA are obtained by snapshots of the execution, selecting the best-found solution within the time reported by the tabu search. The tabu

---

[4] A comparison against the class b instances was not possible as the solver seemed to require some user interaction during the search on those instances.

Table 3. Comparing VNS and LNS-FFPA

1.6 minute run						5 minute run					
Class a		VNS		LNS-FFPA		Class a		VNS		LNS-FFPA	
m	n	Mean	Best	Mean	Best	m	n	Mean	Best	Mean	Best
3	24	190.02	190.02	191.02	190.79	3	24	190.02	190.02	190.77	190.02
4	36	294.42	291.71	294.00	291.71	4	36	293.77	291.71	292.86	291.71
5	48	306.10	302.45	305.30	303.39	5	48	305.84	302.45	304.45	303.03
6	72	507.54	501.31	506.65	494.91	6	72	507.21	501.31	505.15	494.91
7	72	553.85	536.23	548.76	542.94	7	72	552.54	536.23	547.39	542.83
8	108	843.64	783.24	723.64	699.95	8	108	730.48	701.71	711.60	696.51
9	96	611.86	592.91	607.06	597.98	9	96	610.30	602.40	595.05	588.80
10	144	1223.18	1189.36	926.98	909.51	10	144	1059.52	1021.72	911.18	891.98
11	120	724.52	681.1	667.45	655.16	11	120	686.11	672.23	662.56	653.57
13	144	991.18	976.85	856.84	846.56	13	144	885.67	869.56	832.74	816.79
Avg.		624.63	604.48	562.77	553.29	Avg.		582.15	568.93	555.38	547.02

Table 4. Comparing Tabu Search and LNS-FFPA

Class a		Tabu		LNS-FFPA		Class b		Tabu		LNS-FFPA	
m	n	1 Run	Time	Mean	Mean Time	m	n	1 Run	Time	Mean	Mean Time
3	24	191.05	0.19	191.13	0.40	3	24	165.31	0.19	167.67	0.40
4	36	292.80	0.44	296.99	0.40	4	36	253.04	0.42	255.45	0.40
5	48	304.04	0.81	306.73	0.80	5	48	304.73	0.83	305.99	0.80
6	72	506.62	2.4	506.65	2.40	6	72	495.31	2.29	480.27	2.00
7	72	550.48	1.72	549.84	1.60	7	72	510.86	1.85	509.38	1.60
8	108	732.12	5.51	711.60	5.20	8	108	657.96	5.13	632.89	4.80
9	96	597.32	2.88	602.15	2.80	9	96	563.24	3.12	570.02	2.80
10	144	933.22	8.75	909.17	8.40	10	144	909.58	9.24	857.49	9.20
11	120	691.55	4.62	664.58	4.40	11	120	615.36	5.43	616.31	5.20
13	144	870.66	5.39	834.40	5.20	13	144	810.65	7.37	788.33	7.20
Avg.		566.99	3.27	557.32	3.16	Avg.		528.60	3.59	518.38	3.44

search is slightly better on the small instances. However, as the instances get larger and harder with the n/m ratio increasing, LNS-FFPA gives much better results. In the best case, LNS-FFPA produces a 5.7% improvement while producing a 1.1% improvement on average. However, when restricting attention to larger instances ($m > 5$), LNS-FFPA algorithm produces an improvement of about 2% which becomes 3% if the largest three instances are considered. Given the high-quality and sophistication of both the VNS and the tabu-search algorithm, these improvements are significant.

These results are particularly appealing given the severe time constraints. For many problems, a dedicated local search produces solutions of higher quality than LNS early on, since LNS is a general-purpose technique on top of an existing optimization algorithm and does not have dedicated neighborhood operators. On Dial-a-Ride problems however, LNS-FFPA produces better solutions than highly-tuned tabu search or variable neighborhood search within short time limits, especially on the large instances.

This gives LNS-FFPA a significant advantage in dynamic settings since high-quality solutions would need to be found quickly in that scenario. A potential explanation is that the complexity of the side-constraints increases the cost of local moves in tabu and variable neighborhood searches, making LNS-FFPA very competitive.

Comparison with the Constraint-Programming Approach. We conclude this section with a comparison to the constraint-programming approach of Berbeglia et al. [5] who report the time taken to find a satisfying solution for their CP solver and for the tabu-search solver. These feasibility problems are tested on different instances: They have vertices located in a $[-20, 20]^2$ square, over a time horizon of 12 hours, with time windows of 15 minutes, and vehicle capacity of 3 for instances from set a and 6 for instances from set b. The ride time is 30 minutes. The time taken by Algorithm 1 to find a satisfying solution is 0.5-2 seconds which is comparable to the time taken by tabu search and, on average, 12 times faster than the CP approach of Berbeglia et al [5]. The exception is instance b5-40 where it cannot find a solution for a time limit of 60s. Algorithm 1 can also detect infeasibility in less than a second for all the infeasible instances described in [5] which were obtained by reducing the maximum ride time.

8   Conclusions and Future Work

This paper considered Dial-a-Ride applications, which are complex multiple-vehicle routing problems with pickups and deliveries, time windows, and constraints on the ride time. Moreover, these applications are typically dynamic, as customers dial for rides. As a result, optimization algorithms must return high-quality solutions quickly.

The paper presented a novel large neighborhood search LNS-FFPA, which contains two key technical contributions. First, LNS-FFPA does not search the neighborhoods for improving solutions and rather returns the first feasible solution. Second, such a feasible solution is accepted if it improves the existing incumbent solution or using a Probabilistic criterion.

Experimental results for benchmarks based on realistic assumptions and data provided by the Montreal Transit Commission (MTC) show the effectiveness of LNS-FFPA. On short runs (of 1.6 and 5.0 minutes), LNS-FFPA significantly outperforms the state-of-the-art VNS and tabu search algorithms which are both rather sophisticated. LNS-FFPA also compares very favourably with the constraint-programming approach for finding feasible solutions, often producing significant improvements in efficiency. The experimental results also demonstrate the benefits of LNS-FFPA over a traditional LNS approach, as it improves solution quality by about 8%. Finally, LNS-FFPA was particularly effective on the largest instance, where its benefits are larger.

Future work will study if the spatial and temporal structure of Dial-A-Ride applications can be exploited in the choice of the neighborhood instead of relying on pure random selections. Moreover, it would be interesting to study the dynamic problem in the framework of online stochastic optimization to evaluate if stochastic information would be valuable in this setting.

References

1. Baugh, J., John, W.K., Reddy, G.K., Stone, J.R.: Intractability of the dial-a-ride problem and a multiobjective solution using simulated annealing. Engineering Optimization 30, 91–123 (1998)
2. Bent, R., Hentenryck, P.V.: A two-stage hybrid algorithm for pickup and delivery vehicle routing problems with time windows. Comput. Oper. Res. 33, 875–893 (2006)
3. Bent, R., Van Hentenryck, P.: A two-stage hybrid local search for the vehicle routing problem with time windows. Transportation Science 38, 515–530 (2004)
4. Berbeglia, G., Cordeau, J.-F., Laporte, G.: A hybrid tabu search and constraint programming algorithm for the dynamic dial-a-ride problem. Submitted to INFORMS Journal on Computing (2010)
5. Berbeglia, G., Pesant, G., Rousseau, L.-M.: Checking the feasibility of dial-a-ride instances using constraint programming. Transportation Science (2010)
6. Berbeglia, G., Pesant, G., Rousseau, L.-M.: Feasibility of the pickup and delivery problem with fixed partial routes: A complexity analysis. Submitted to Transportation Science (2010)
7. Cordeau, J.-F., Laporte, G.: A tabu search heuristic for the static multi-vehicle dial-a-ride problem. Transportation Research Part B: Methodological 37(6), 579–594 (2003)
8. Cordeau, J.-F., Laporte, G.: The dial-a-ride problem: models and algorithms. Annals of Operations Research 153, 29–46 (2007), 10.1007/s10479-007-0170-8
9. Glover, F.: Ejection chains, reference structures and alternating path methods for traveling salesman problems. Discrete Applied Mathematics 65(1-3), 223–253 (1996); First International Colloquium on Graphs and Optimization
10. Jorgensen, R.M., Larsen, J., Bergvinsdottir, K.B.: Solving the dial-a-ride problem using genetic algorithms. Journal of the Operational Research Society 58(11), 1321–1331 (2007)
11. Parragh, S.N., Doerner, K.F., Hartl, R.F.: Variable neighborhood search for the dial-a-ride problem. Computers & Operations Research 37(6), 1129–1138 (2010)
12. Shaw, P.: Using constraint programming and local search methods to solve vehicle routing problems. In: Maher, M.J., Puget, J.-F. (eds.) CP 1998. LNCS, vol. 1520, pp. 417–431. Springer, Heidelberg (1998)
13. Toth, P., Vigo, D.: Heuristic algorithms for the handicapped persons transportation problem. Transportation Science, 60–71 (1997)

On Deciding MUS Membership with QBF

Mikoláš Janota[1] and Joao Marques-Silva[1,2]

[1] INESC-ID, Lisbon, Portugal
[2] University College Dublin, Ireland

Abstract. This paper tackles the problem of deciding whether a given clause belongs to some minimally unsatisfiable subset (MUS) of a formula, where the formula is in conjunctive normal form (CNF) and unsatisfiable. Deciding MUS-membership helps the understanding of *why* a formula is unsatisfiable. If a clause does not belong to any MUS, then removing it will certainly not contribute to restoring the formula's consistency. Unsatisfiable formulas and consistency restoration in particular have a number of practical applications in areas such as software verification or product configuration. The MUS-membership problem is known to be in the second level of polynomial hierarchy, more precisely it is Σ_2^P-complete. Hence, quantified Boolean formulas (QBFs) represent a possible avenue for tackling the problem. This paper develops a number of novel QBF formulations of the MUS-membership problem and evaluates their practicality using modern off-the-shelf solvers.

1 Introduction

Unsatisfiable formulas, representing refutation proofs or inconsistencies, appear in various areas of automated reasoning. This article focuses on helping us to understand *why* a certain formula is unsatisfiable. If a formula is represented in conjunctive normal form (CNF), it is sufficient to consider only certain subsets of clauses to see why it is unsatisfiable. In particular, a set of clauses is called a minimally unsatisfiable subset (MUS) if it is unsatisfiable and any of its proper subsets is satisfiable. The question addressed in this article is to determine whether a given clause belongs to some MUS of a formula. This is referred to as the MUS-MEMBERSHIP problem.

Deciding whether a clause belongs to some MUS is important when one wants to *restore consistency* of a formula: removing a clause that is *not* part of any MUS, will certainly not restore consistency. Restoring consistency is an active area of research in the area of *product configuration* [20,22]. For example, when configuring a product, some sets of its features result in an inconsistent configuration. Approaches for resolving conflicting features often involves user intervention, e.g. to decide which features to deselect. Clearly, it is useful for the user to know if a feature is relevant for the inconsistency.

Earlier work on the MUS-MEMBERSHIP problem consisted on complexity characterizations [13,12] and an algorithm based on heuristically-guided MUS enumeration [7]. In contrast, this article proposes four alternative solutions for solving MUS-MEMBERSHIP problem with Quantified Boolean Formulas (QBF).

J. Lee (Ed.): CP 2011, LNCS 6876, pp. 414–428, 2011.
© Springer-Verlag Berlin Heidelberg 2011

Two of these solutions follow directly from the problem's definition, and either involve a $\mathrm{QBF}_{3,\exists}$ formula or a $\mathrm{QBF}_{2,\exists}$ formula that grows quadratically with the size of the original formula. The paper also exploits the relationship between MUSes and Maximally Satisfiable Subsets (MSSes), and derives a $\mathrm{QBF}_{2,\exists}$ model for the MUS-MEMBERSHIP problem that grows linearly with the size of the original formula. Furthermore, this relationship is also used for relating the MUS-MEMBERSHIP with the problem of *inference in propositional circumscription*, which can be represented as a $\mathrm{QBF}_{2,\exists}$ with a specific structure. In turn, this enables the use of specialized algorithms for propositional circumscription [8]. Experimental results obtained on representative classes of problem instances demonstrate that the recent abstraction refinement algorithm [8] consistently outperforms all other approaches.

The paper is organized as follows. Section 2 introduces the notation and definitions used throughout the paper. Section 3 develops different models for solving the MUS-MEMBERSHIP problem. Section 4 analyzes results obtained on representative classes of problem instances. Finally, Section 5 concludes the paper.

2   Preliminaries

Throughout this paper, ϕ and ψ denote Boolean formulas, defined on a set of variables $X = \{x_1, \ldots, x_n\}$. Where necessary, additional sets of variables are considered, e.g. R, X'. A Boolean formula ϕ in Conjunctive Normal Form (CNF) is a conjunction of disjunctions of literals and a literal is a variable or its negation. A disjunction of literals is called a *clause* and it is preferably represented by ω. Unless specified otherwise, ϕ is assumed to be of the form $\{\omega_1, \ldots, \omega_n\}$. Where appropriate, a CNF formula is interpreted as a set of sets of literals.

A *truth assignment* μ_X is a mapping from a set of variables X to $\{0, 1\}$, $\mu_X : X \to \{0, 1\}$. A truth assignment is represented by the set M_X of true variables in μ_X, $M_X = \{x_i \in X \mid \mu_X(x_i) = 1\}$. In what follows, truth assignments will be represented by the set of true variables, since the definition of μ_X is implicit, given X and M_X. Moreover, $M_X \models \phi$ is used to denote that truth assignment μ_X is a *model* of ϕ, i.e. that μ_X satisfies all clauses in ϕ. Truth assignments will also be defined for other sets of variables, as needed, e.g. M_S, M_{S_a}, M_{S_b}. When a formula is defined over distinct sets of variables, e.g. X and S, $M_S, M_X \models \phi$ denotes that the truth assignment to the variables in S and the variables in X satisfies ϕ. Finally, a truth assignment represented by M_X implicitly denotes that $M_X \subseteq X$. Similarly, M_R implicitly denotes that $M_R \subseteq R$. To simplify the notation, the set containment relation will be omitted in all formulas.

A *QBF* is a Boolean formula where each variable is either universally or existentially quantified. We write $\mathrm{QBF}_{k,\exists}$ to denote the class of formulas of the form $\mathcal{Q}_1 X_1 \ldots \mathcal{Q}_k X_k. \; \phi$ where $\mathcal{Q}_i = \exists$ if i is odd and $\mathcal{Q}_i = \forall$ if i is even. In the context of QBF we write $\phi(X)$ to denote a formula that is built on the variables from X. An important result from the complexity theory is that the validity of a formula in $\mathrm{QBF}_{k,\exists}$ is Σ_k^P-complete [18].

2.1 Minimal Unsatisfiability and Maximal Satisfiability

This section introduces the concepts of minimally unsatisfiable and maximally satisfiable sets of clauses as well as related decision problems.

Definition 1 (MUS). *A set of clauses $\psi \subseteq \phi$ is a* Minimally Unsatisfiable Subset *(MUS) iff ψ is unsatisfiable and any set $\psi' \subsetneq \psi$ is satisfiable.*

Definition 2 (MSS). *A set of clauses $\psi \subseteq \phi$ is a* Maximally Satisfiable Subset *(MSS) iff ψ is satisfiable and any set $\psi' \subseteq \phi$ such that $\psi \subsetneq \psi'$ is unsatisfiable.*

Definition 3 (MCS). *A set of clauses $\psi \subseteq \phi$ is a* Minimally Correction Subset *(MCS) if $\phi \setminus \psi$ is satisfiable and for any subset $\psi' \subsetneq \psi$, $\phi \setminus \psi'$ is unsatisfiable.*

Deciding whether a CNF formula is an MUS is D^P-complete [21]. Algorithms for computing MUSes have been the subject of comprehensive research over the years [6,2,16]. Moreover, this article considers the following decision problems.

Name: MUS-MEMBERSHIP
Given: A CNF formula ϕ and a clause $\omega \in \phi$.
Question: Is there an MUS ψ of ϕ such that $\omega \in \psi$?

Name: MUS-OVERLAP
Given: CNF formulas ϕ and $\gamma \subseteq \phi$.
Question: Is there an MUS ψ of ϕ such that $\gamma \cap \psi \neq \emptyset$?

Name: MSS-MEMBERSHIP
Given: A CNF formula ϕ and a clause $\omega \in \phi$.
Question: Is there an MSS ψ of ϕ such that $\omega \notin \psi$?

We make several observations regarding the definitions. MUS-OVERLAP can be expressed as a disjunction of k instances of MUS-MEMBERSHIP, where k is the number of clauses in the formula γ. Hence, we mainly focus on MUS-MEMBERSHIP. We require $\omega \in \phi$, which is done convenience, and the decision problems for $\omega \notin \phi$ are trivial. In MUS-MEMBERSHIP we are looking for an MUS containing ω whereas in MSS-MEMBERSHIP, we are looking for an MSS that does *not* contain ω. Later on we show that the problems are convertible to one another.

To obtain the complexity classification of MUS-MEMBERSHIP, we realize that an MUS is a special case of irredundancy: an MUS is a subset-minimal representation that is equivalent to the original formula. The question whether a clause belongs to some minimal irredundant representation is known to be Σ_2^P-complete [13]. Hence, MUS-MEMBERSHIP is in Σ_2^P. In fact, it has been shown that MUS-MEMBERSHIP itself is Σ_2^P-hard (and therefore complete) [12].

2.2   Propositional Circumscription

Circumscription was introduced by McCarthy as a form of nonmonotonic reasoning [17]. While the original definition of circumscription is for first-order logic, for the purpose of this article we consider its propositional version.

Definition 4 (Circumscription). *Let P, Z be sets of variables and ϕ a formula on the variables $P \cup Z$. Circumscription of ϕ is defined as follows:*

$$CIRC(\phi; P; Z) = \phi(P, Z) \wedge (\forall P', Z')((\phi(P', Z') \wedge (P' \to P)) \to (P \to P')) \quad (1)$$

where $P' \to P$ stands for $\bigwedge_{x \in P}(x' \to x)$.

We should note that circumscription often considers another set of variables Q, which comprises variables that remain fixed. However, this set is not needed for the purpose of this article. Circumscription is closely related to model minimization introduced by the following two definitions.

Definition 5 (Model Orderings). *Let M and N be models of ϕ and let P be a set of variables. We write $M \preceq_P N$ iff $M \cap P \subseteq N \cap P$ and we write $M \prec_P N$ iff $M \preceq_P N$ and $M \neq N$.*

Definition 6 (Minimal Models). *A model M of ϕ is P-minimal iff there is no model N of ϕ such that $N \prec_P M$. We write $MM(\phi, P)$ to denote the set of all P-minimal models of ϕ. For formulas ϕ and ψ we write $\phi \models_P^{circ} \psi$ iff ψ holds in all P-minimal models of ϕ.*

In short, the ordering $\preceq$ is a bit-wise ordering on the variables from P and minimal models are the minimal elements of this ordering. The relation between circumscription and minimal models is well-known [19,15,1,3]. The following well-known result is used throughout the paper [1].

Proposition 1. *Let ϕ and ψ be formulas using only variables from $P \cup Z$. It holds that $CIRC(\phi; P; Z) \models \psi$ iff $\phi \models_P^{circ} \psi$.*

Proposition 1 tells us that inference from the set of minimal models is equivalent to inference from circumscription. Another observation we make is that the entailment in propositional circumscription is immediately expressible as a 2-level QBF.

Observation 1. *For formulas ϕ and ψ, $CIRC(\phi; P; Z) \nvDash \psi$ iff*

$$\exists P, Z. \neg\psi(P, Z) \wedge \phi(P, Z) \wedge (\forall P', Z')((\phi(P', Z') \wedge (P' \to P)) \to (P \to P')) \quad (2)$$

Note that the QBF above expresses that P, Z should satisfy (1) and violate ψ, and thus serve as a counterexample to the entailment. Naturally, the entailment can be expressed positively by negating the QBF.

Hence, propositional circumscription can be seen as reasoning over minimal models or as a special case of a QBF; in the remainder of the paper we treat these properties of propositional circumscription interchangeably.

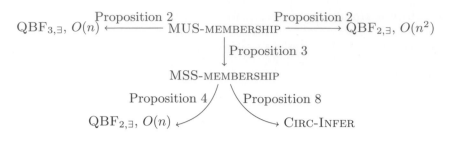

Fig. 1. Translating between problems

Name: CIRC-INFER

Given: CNF formulas ϕ and ψ and sets of variables P and Q.

Question: Does ψ hold in all $\langle P, Q\rangle$-minimal models of ϕ, i.e. $\phi \models^{circ}_{\langle P,Q\rangle} \psi$?

2.3 Related Work

The MUS-MEMBERSHIP problem has been studied mostly from a theoretical perspective [13,12]. Motivated by practical applications, recent work addressed the development of algorithms for this problem [7]. These algorithms are based on explicit and implicit enumeration of MUSes. A simple algorithm for solving the MUS-MEMBERSHIP problem is to run an MUS enumerator (e.g. [14]) and check whether any MUS contains the target clause $\omega \in \phi$. This algorithm was improved in [7] where heuristics are proposed for reducing the sets of clauses to consider. The tool cmMUS [10] represents recent work on the MUS membership problem. cmMUS builds upon the work described in the present paper, namely the connection between MUS membership and propositional circumscription, which is detailed in Section 3.3.

3 Deciding MUS-MEMBERSHIP

Figure 1 depicts the relations between the problems investigated in the remainder of this section. The motivation for these translations is to derive QBF formulas for the MUS-MEMBERSHIP problem. We show that a direct translation of MUS-MEMBERSHIP leads to $QBF_{3,\exists}$ despite the problem being in Σ_2^P. Alternatively, we propose a $QBF_{2,\exists}$ model, that is quadratic in the size of the original problem. Alternative QBF formulations are developed by exploiting the relationship between MUSes and MSSes. As a result, we derive a $QBF_{2,\exists}$ that is linear in the size of the original problem, and also relate MSS-MEMBERSHIP with CIRC-INFER. The QBF models can be solved with standard QBF algorithms, whereas for the CIRC-INFER, a dedicated algorithm can be used [8].

3.1 MUS-MEMBERSHIP with QBF

This section investigates the translation of MUS-MEMBERSHIP to QBF. Since MUS-MEMBERSHIP has been shown to be Σ_2^P-complete [13], the problem must be expressible as a $QBF_{2,\exists}$ formula. We begin by a straightforward translation from the problem statement following the following schema:

exists $\psi \subseteq \phi$ s.t. $\omega \in \psi$ **and** ψ is unsatisfiable **and forall** $\psi' \subsetneq \psi$ is satisfiable

To be able to quantify over subsets of ϕ, we introduce its relaxed form.

Definition 7 (relaxation ϕ^*). *Let ϕ be a set of clauses then its relaxation ϕ^* is defined as follows:*

$$\phi^* = \{\omega \vee r_\omega \mid \omega \in \phi\} \tag{3}$$

where r_ω are variables not appearing in ϕ. We refer to r_ω as the relaxation variable of the clause ω and if r_ω has the value 1, we say that the clause ω is relaxed.

In the following text we use R to denote the set of relaxation variables (and X for the set of original variables as before). The intuition behind relaxation variables is that once a clause is relaxed, it is equivalent to not having the clause in the formula. For succinctness, we introduce a dual term of *selected clauses*, which are clauses that are *not* relaxed.

Definition 8. *Let ϕ^* be a relaxation of ϕ and M_R be a subset of the pertaining relaxation variables. The set of* selected clauses $\mathcal{S}(\phi^*, M_R)$ *is defined as follows:*

$$\mathcal{S}(\phi^*, M_R) = \{\omega \mid r_\omega \notin M_R\} \tag{4}$$

Example 1. Let $\phi = \{x, \neg x, y\}$, then $\phi^* = \{x \vee r_1, \neg x \vee r_2, y \vee r_3\}$. Let $M_R = \{r_1, r_2\}$ then $\mathcal{S}(\phi^*, M_R) = \{y\}$. Observe that for any M_X s.t. $y \in M_X$ the interpretation $M_R \cup M_X$ is a model of ϕ^*: when the clauses x and $\neg x$ are relaxed, they do not need to be satisfied. However, if a clause is not relaxed (the corresponding relaxation variable is 0), the clause must be satisfied. Hence for a given M_R, satisfying ϕ^* is equivalent to satisfying $\mathcal{S}(\phi^*, M_R)$.

The following observation establishes a relation between the set of selected clauses and the relaxed formula.

Observation 2. *An assignment $M_R \cup M_X$ is a model of ϕ^* iff M_X is a model of $\mathcal{S}(\phi^*, M_R)$.*

In the following QBF the relaxed formula appears in two versions: a non-primed version $(\phi^*(R, X))$, and, a primed version—where all the variables are replaced with their primed copy $(\phi^*(R', X'))$.

Observe that relaxing a clause results into removing it from the set of selected clauses, and therefore for any relaxations M_R and M'_R, the requirement $\mathcal{S}(\phi^*, M_R) \subseteq \mathcal{S}(\phi^*, M'_R)$ is equivalent to $M'_R \subseteq M_R$. In the following QBFs, the requirement $M'_R \subseteq M_R$ is captured by the formula $R < R'$ defined as follows:

$$R < R' \equiv \bigwedge_{z \in R} z \rightarrow z' \wedge \bigvee_{z \in R} \neg z \wedge z' \tag{5}$$

Now let us express the MUS-MEMBERSHIP as a QBF formula:

$$\exists R. \, \neg r_\omega \wedge (\forall X. \neg \phi^*(R, X)) \wedge (\forall R'.(R < R') \rightarrow \exists X'.\phi^*(R', X')) \tag{6}$$

The formula expresses that we are searching for a relaxation R for which the clause ω is not relaxed ($\neg r_\omega$). The set of selected clauses induced by the relaxation R is unsatisfiable ($\forall X.\neg\phi^*(R, X)$). If R is relaxed anymore, then the induced set of selected clauses is satisfiable ($\forall R'.(R < R') \rightarrow \exists X'.\phi^*(R', X')$).

Formula (6) can be reformulated if we realize that a set of clauses is an MUS iff removing any clause yields a satisfiable set of clauses:

$$\exists R. \ \neg r_\omega \wedge (\forall X.\neg\phi^*(R, X)) \wedge \bigwedge_{r_{\omega_i} \in R} (\neg r_{\omega_i} \rightarrow \exists X^{\omega_i}.\phi^*[r_{\omega_i}/1](R, X^{\omega_i})) \qquad (7)$$

Where $\phi^*[r_{\omega_i}/1]$ is the substitution of 1 for r_{ω_i} in ϕ^* and X^{ω_i} is a fresh copy of the variables X for each $r_{\omega_i} \in R$.

Since the variables X appear only in the first half of the formula, it can be rewritten into 2QBF as follows:

$$\exists R \exists X^{\omega_1} \ldots \exists X^{\omega_n} \forall X. \ \neg r_\omega \wedge \neg\phi^*(R, X) \wedge \bigwedge_{r_{\omega_i} \in R} (\neg r_{\omega_i} \rightarrow \phi^*[r_{\omega_i}/1](R, X^{\omega_i})) \quad (8)$$

Altogether, a solution M_R to either of the formulas (6), (7), or (8) represents an MUS containing the clause ω, which enables us to state the following proposition.

Proposition 2. *The clause ω belongs to some MUS of the formula ϕ iff* (6), (7), *or* (8) *is valid.*

3.2   QBF for MUS-MEMBERSHIP Using MSS-MEMBERSHIP

We observe that the equations developed above are problematic from a practical perspective. Equation (6) uses 3 levels of quantifiers despite the problem being in Σ_2^P [12]. Equation (8) has only 2 levels of quantifiers but uses a quadratic number of variables.

The following describes how to construct a QBF with 2 quantifiers using a linear number of variables by first translating the problem to MSS-MEMBERSHIP. In order to get to show the relation between MUS-MEMBERSHIP and MSS-MEMBERSHIP, we invoke the following lemma [11]:

Lemma 1 (Lemma 4.3 in [11]). *Let* $\mathrm{MU}(\phi)$ *denote the set of all MUSes of ϕ and let* $\mathrm{MS}(\phi)$ *denote the set of all MSSes of ϕ. Then the following equality holds:*

$$\bigcup \mathrm{MU}(\phi) = \phi \setminus \bigcap \mathrm{MS}(\phi) \qquad (9)$$

An immediate consequence of Lemma 1 is that a clause ω is included in some MUS of ϕ if and only if ω is *not* included in some MSS of ϕ. This consequence is stated in the following proposition.

Proposition 3. *A clause ω belongs to some MUS of ϕ iff there exists an MSS ψ of ϕ such that $\omega \notin \psi$.*

Example 2. Let $\phi = \{\neg x, x, z\}$. The formula ϕ has only one MUS $\{\neg x, x\}$ while it has two MSSes $\{x, z\}$ and $\{\neg x, z\}$. Observe that the clause z is in both MSSes and not in the MUS; for both of the clauses x, $\neg x$ there is an MSS without the clause and both are in the MUS.

The relation between MUSes and MSSes established by Proposition 3 motivates the following quantified Boolean formula for MUS-MEMBERSHIP (again we use the notation $R' < R$ introduced earlier).

$$\exists R \exists X \forall R' \forall X'. \, (r_\omega \wedge \phi^*(R, X) \wedge (R' < R \to \neg \phi^*(R', X'))) \qquad (10)$$

The formula expresses that we are looking for a relaxation in which ω is relaxed (r_ω). The relaxation is satisfiable ($\phi^*(R, X)$) and any relaxation relaxing less clauses yields an unsatisfiable set of clauses ($R' < R \to \neg \phi^*(R', X')$). Altogether, a solution M_R to the equation (10) corresponds to an MSS that does *not* contain the clause ω.

Proposition 4. *The answer to* MUS-MEMBERSHIP *is "yes" iff* (10) *is valid.*

Observe that the quantified formula has two levels of quantifiers and linear number of variables.

Equation (10) provides a solution for testing whether a clause ω is included in an MUS of ϕ. However, it does not provide a *witness*, i.e. an MUS containing ω. Nevertheless, a witness can be computed by exploiting the properties of MSSes and MUSes.

Lemma 2. *Let ψ be an MSS of ϕ such that $\omega \notin \psi$, than any MUS of $\psi \cup \{\omega\}$ contains ω.*

Proof (sketch). Since ψ is an MSS, adding *any* clause from ϕ to ψ will make the result unsatisfiable. Therefore, adding ω to ψ, $\psi' = \psi \cup \{\omega\}$, results in an unsatisfiable formula. Let $\psi'' \subseteq \psi'$ be an MUS of ψ', then $\omega \in \psi''$ as otherwise $\psi'' \subseteq \psi$ would lead to a contradiction because ψ is satisfiable.

Lemma 2 enables the use of standard MUS extraction algorithms to extract an MUS witness given an MSS not containing ω.

Proposition 5. *Let ϕ be a CNF formula and $\omega \in \phi$. For a clause ω, if the answer to the* MUS-MEMBERSHIP *problem is "yes", then a witness for the* MUS-MEMBERSHIP *problem is any MUS of an MSS not containing ω.*

Proof. Immediate consequence of Proposition 4 and Lemma 2.

3.3   MUS-MEMBERSHIP **with** CIRC-INFER

Proposition 3 lets us translate MUS-MEMBERSHIP to MSS-MEMBERSHIP. In this section we show how to translate MSS-MEMBERSHIP to CIRC-INFER.

Recall that CIRC-INFER is the problem of deciding whether a formula ψ holds in all P-minimal models of a formula ϕ, for some set of variables P (Proposition 1). We begin by showing a relation between minimal models and MSSes.

As in the previous section, we operate on the relaxed formula ϕ^* where setting the relaxation variable r_ω to 1 effectively eliminates the clause (relaxes the clause). Dually, setting the variable r_ω to 0 results into adding the clause ω into the set of selected clauses (Definition 8). Consequently, MSSes correspond to minimal models of the relaxed formula, which is captured by the following proposition.

Proposition 6. *For an interpretation M_R, the set of selected clauses $\mathcal{S}(\phi^*, M_R)$ is an MSS of ϕ iff there exists M_X such that $M_R \cup M_X$ is an R-minimal model of ϕ^*.*

Proof (sketch). If the set $\mathcal{S}(\phi^*, M_R)$ is an MSS, then it must be satisfiable and therefore it must have some model M_X. Due to Observation 2, $M_R \cup M_X$ is a model of ϕ^*. The model $M_R \cup M_X$ must be R-minimal because otherwise we would obtain a relaxation corresponding to a strict superset of $\mathcal{S}(\phi^*, M_R)$ rendering it not maximal. If $M_R \cup M_X$ is an R-minimal model of ϕ^* then $\mathcal{S}(\phi^*, M_R)$ is satisfied by M_X due to Observation 2. The set $\mathcal{S}(\phi^*, M_R)$ must be an MSS otherwise $M_R \cup M_X$ would not be R-minimal.

Example 3. Let $\phi = \{x, \neg x, y \vee z, \neg y \vee \neg z\}$, then $\phi^* = \{x \vee r_1, \neg x \vee r_2, y \vee z \vee r_3, \neg y \vee \neg z \vee r_4\}$ for the relaxation variables $R = \{r_1, r_2, r_3\}$. In order to achieve consistency, one of the clauses x and $\neg x$ must be relaxed. Hence, the formula ϕ^* has the following four R-minimal models: two models have the clause $\neg x$ relaxed $\{r_2, x, y\}, \{r_2, x, z\}$ and two models have the clause x relaxed $\{r_1, y\}, \{r_1, z\}$. These models correspond to the MSSes $\{x, y \vee z, \neg y \vee \neg z\}$ and $\{\neg x, y \vee z, \neg y \vee \neg z\}$. Observe that the clauses $y \vee z$ and $\neg y \vee \neg z$ are in both MSSes, which means that the corresponding variables r_2 and r_3 have the value 0 in all R-minimal models (they never need to be relaxed).

Proposition 6 establishes a relation between the MSSes of a formula and minimal models of the corresponding relaxed formula. Consequently, in order to solve MUS-MEMBERSHIP for a clause ω, we need to look for a minimal model with the clause relaxed.

Proposition 7. *A clause ω belongs to some MUS of ϕ iff there exists a model $M \in MM(\phi, R)$ such that $M \models r_\omega$, equivalently:*

$$\phi^* \not\models_R^{circ} \neg r_\omega \tag{11}$$

Proof (sketch). A clause ω belongs to some MUS of ϕ iff there exists an MSS $\psi \subseteq \phi$ s.t. $\omega \notin \psi$ (Proposition 3). There exists an MSS ψ of ϕ s.t. $\omega \notin \psi$ iff there exists an R-minimal model M of ϕ^* s.t. $M \models r_\omega$ (Proposition 6). To relate to the circumscription inference notation we observe that there exists an R-minimal model M s.t. $M \models r_\omega$ iff $\phi^* \models_R^{circ} \neg r_\omega$ does *not* hold.

Proposition 7 is easily generalized for MUS-OVERLAP by observing that we only need to find a minimal model where at least one of the clauses in question is relaxed.

Proposition 8. *A set of clauses* $\omega_1, \ldots, \omega_n$ *overlaps with some MUS of* ϕ *iff there exists* $M \in MM(\phi, R)$ *such that* $M \models r_{\omega_1} \vee \cdots \vee r_{\omega_n}$, *equivalently:*

$$\phi^* \not\models_R^{circ} (\neg r_{\omega_1} \wedge \cdots \wedge \neg r_{\omega_n}) \tag{12}$$

Observe that in Propositions 6 and 8 CIRC-INFER appears in a negative sense. This again agrees with the known complexity classification, as MUS-MEMBERSHIP is Σ_2^P-complete [12] and circumscription is Π_2^P-complete [3]. Moreover, although the relationship with QBF is simple (see Section 2.2), we opt to solve CIRC-INFER with a dedicated algorithm [8].

3.4   Algorithms for MUS-MEMBERSHIP

The previous two sections develop a number of properties of the MUS-MEMBERSHIP problem. This section summarizes the concrete algorithms that these properties enable us to consider. The algorithms are classified into three classes: enumeration, QBF, and circumscription inference. These classes are discussed in turn.

The simplest approach for deciding MUS-MEMBERSHIP is to enumerate MUSes (e.g. [14]). Practical algorithms for MUS-MEMBERSHIP follow this approach [7], but are coupled with heuristics for reducing the number of MUSes to enumerate. An alternative solution, also based on enumeration, consists of enumerating MSSes, using Proposition 3. Given that MUS enumeration algorithms start by enumerating MSSes [14], an algorithm based on enumerating MSSes is guaranteed to outperform naïve solutions based on MUS enumeration. It should be noted that existing algorithms (e.g. [14]) are based on MCS enumeration. However, since an MCS is the complement of an MSS, a clause is in an MUS iff it is included in some MCS.

A second class of algorithms consists of using the mapping to QBF and solving the resulting problem instances with a QBF solver. This paper develops 3 alternative approaches for encoding MUS-MEMBERSHIP into QBF (see Figure 1). The first approach uses 3 levels of quantifiers and produces a formula linear in the size; second approach uses 2 levels of quantifiers but produces a formula of quadratic size; the third approach uses the relation between MUSes and MSSes and provides a 2-level formulation of linear size.

Finally, a third class of algorithms exploits the relationship between MSSes and CIRC-INFER. As noted in preliminaries, CIRC-INFER is a special case of a 2-level QBF formula. Hence, a general QBF solver could be used. However, this formulation also enables the use of specialized algorithms for CIRC-INFER [8].

4   Experimental Results

Following the discussion in Section 3.4, the following concrete tools were used for the evaluation.

MUSer is a tool for extracting MUSes [16]. The tool was used to obtain a witness MUS in approaches based on MSSes (see Proposition 5).

AReQS is a recently developed solver, implemented by the authors, for 2QBF formulas based on counterexample guided refinement (CEGAR). The solver was used for all QBF formulas with 2 levels of quantifiers since previous research showed that it consistently outperforms the available solvers on these types of formulas [9].

cmMUS is a tool that solves MSS-MEMBERSHIP using propositional circumscription (implemented by the authors) [10]. Just as AReQS, it uses counterexample guided abstraction refinement approach but tailored for propositional circumscription [8].

look4MUS is a tool dedicated to MUS-MEMBERSHIP based on MUS enumeration, guided by heuristics based on a measure of inconsistency [7].

QuBE 7.1 is a QBF solver[1] which solved the most instances in the 2CNF track of QBF Evaluation 2010[2] and overall ranks high in all categories. QuBE has a powerful built-in preprocessor, which significantly improves its performance [5] (all of the preprocessing techniques were switched on for the purpose of the evaluation). The solver was used to evaluate 3-level formulas (see (6)). The downside of QuBE 7.1 is that it does not provide a model. Hence, even though a solution to (6) is immediately an MUS containing the desired clause, it cannot be retrieved from the answer of QuBE 7.1.

sSolve is a QBF solver which returns a solution for valid formulas, unlike QuBE 7.1 [4]. The solver was used to evaluate 3-level formulas (see (6)).

MSS enum. The tool CAMUS [14] was used to enumerate MSSes of the given formula. If the enumeration is looking for an MSS that overlaps with a set of clauses γ, then it immediately stops once it finds an MSS ψ that does not contain at least one of the clauses from γ, i.e. $\gamma \smallsetminus \psi \neq \emptyset$.

4.1 Benchmarks

A variety of unsatisfiable formulas was selected from SAT competitions benchmarks[3] and from well-known applications of SAT (namely ATPG and product configuration). The selected formulas are relatively easy for modern SAT solvers because MUS-MEMBERSHIP is significantly harder than satisfiability. Even so, instances with tens of thousands of clauses were used (e.g. dining philosophers).

For each of these formulas, the MUS-OVERLAP was computed using the various approaches. The 1st, 3rd, 5th, and 7th clauses in the formula's DIMACS representation were chosen as the set γ for which the overlap was to be determined—this evaluation methodology was also used in [7].

4.2 Results

All experimental results were obtained on an Intel Xeon 5160 3GHz with 4GB of memory. The experiments were obtained with a memory limit of 2GB and time limit of 1,000 seconds. The results of the measurements are presented by Table 1 and Figure 2. Table 1 presents the number of solved instances by each of the approaches for each set of benchmarks. Figure 2 presents the computation

---

[1] Available at www.star.dist.unige.it/~qube/
[2] http://www.qbflib.org/
[3] http://www.satcompetition.org/

Table 1. Number of solved instances by the different approaches

	cmMUS	look4MUS	MSS enum.	2lev. lin.
Nemesis (bf) (223)	**223**	**223**	31	29
Daimler-Chrysler (84)	46	13	**49**	36
dining phil. (22)	**17**	**17**	4	8
dimacs (87)	**87**	82	51	51
ezfact (41)	**20**	11	11	10
total (457)	**393**	346	146	134

	2lev. qv.	3lev. lin. (QuBE)	3lev. lin. (sSolve)
Nemesis (bf) (223)	9	13	0
Daimler-Chrysler (84)	0	4	0
dining phil. (22)	2	1	0
dimacs (87)	18	25	4
ezfact (41)	0	0	0
total (457)	29	43	4

times with *cactus plots*—the horizontal axis represents the number of instances that were solved within the time represented by the vertical axis.

The QBFs derived in Section 3.1 and Section 3.2 are denoted as: 2-level linear—2-level linear formula using MSS; 2-level quadratic—2-level quadratic formula directly yielding a witnessing MUS; 3-level linear—3-level linear formula directly yielding a witnessing MUS. The results for the approaches that first find an MSS include the runtime of MUSer, which was used to obtain the witnessing MUS (see Section 3.2).

Out of the presented approaches, the circumscription-based approach (cmMUS) turned out to be the most robust one: it has solved the most instances (393) and except for one class of benchmarks it exhibits the shortest overall running times. The set of benchmarks where cmMUS came second are the Daimler-Chrysler, for which the simple MSS enumeration solved 3 more instances.

The dedicated algorithm look4MUS came second in terms of the number of solved instances (346). However, it turned out not to be robust, e.g. a small number of instances were solved for Daimler-Chrysler and ezfact.

The use of general QBF solvers yielded significantly poorer results. As expected, out of these, the 2-level linear formulation (solved by AReQS +MUSer) had the best performance with 134 solved instances. Even though both AReQS and cmMUS use CEGAR to solve the problem, cmMUS uses a refinement specific to circumscription (cf. [8,9]) and that turned out to be important for the performance. The 3-level linear approach using QuBE 7.1 solved significantly more than both sSolve with 3-level approach and AReQS with quadratic 2-level formulation. However, we recall that QuBE 7.1 does not provide a model. In most cases when the quadratic formulation approach did not succeed it was because of exceeding the memory limit.

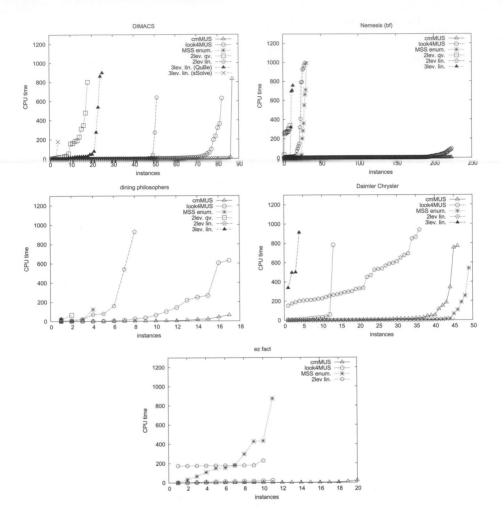

Fig. 2. Cactus plots for the measurements (number of instances x solved in less than y seconds)

We should note that the runtime of `MUSer` affected very little the overall runtimes of the approaches based on MSSes. Mostly, the runtime of `MUSer` was below 1 second. Only two instances where the desired MUS was not found in time appeared (in dining philosophers and ezfact).

5   Conclusions

This article addresses the problem of deciding whether a given clause belongs to some minimal unsatisfiable subset (MUS) of some CNF formula. This is a well-known Σ_2^P-complete problem [13,12], for which recent work proposed heuristic-guided algorithms based on enumeration of MUSes [7]. In contrast, this paper develops new solutions for the MUS-MEMBERSHIP problem based on QBF. Some of the QBFs follow from the problem's definition, whereas the others exploit the relationship between MUSes and MSSes [11]. The proposed solutions include one $QBF_{3,\exists}$ and two $QBF_{2,\exists}$ formulations. One additional solution consists of mapping MUS-MEMBERSHIP to CIRC-INFER, the propositional circumscription inference problem, itself expressible as a $QBF_{2,\exists}$. Given well-known mappings of propositional circumscription to other formalisms, this yields additional algorithms to solve the MUS-MEMBERSHIP problem. Experimental results obtained on a wide range of well-known benchmarks, demonstrate that the most effective approach consists of using a recent counterexample guided abstraction refinement algorithm for the propositional circumscription inference problem [8].

The promising experimental results suggest considering the use of dedicated algorithms for propositional circumscription inference in other settings, namely other Σ_2^P-complete and Π_2^P-complete decision problems.

Acknowledgement. This work is partially supported by SFI PI grant BEACON (09/IN.1/I2618), EC FP7 project MANCOOSI (214898), FCT grants ATTEST (CMU-PT/ELE/0009/2009), and INESC-ID multiannual funding from the PIDDAC program funds.

References

1. Cadoli, M., Lenzerini, M.: The complexity of closed world reasoning and circumscription. In: AAAI Conference on Artificial Intelligence, pp. 550–555 (1990)
2. Desrosiers, C., Galinier, P., Hertz, A., Paroz, S.: Using heuristics to find minimal unsatisfiable subformulas in satisfiability problems. J. Comb. Optim. 18(2), 124–150 (2009)
3. Eiter, T., Gottlob, G.: Propositional circumscription and extended closed-world reasoning are Π_2^P-complete. Theor. Comput. Sci. 114(2), 231–245 (1993)
4. Feldmann, R., Monien, B., Schamberger, S.: A distributed algorithm to evaluate quantified Boolean formulae. In: AAAI/IAAI, pp. 285–290 (2000)
5. Giunchiglia, E., Marin, P., Narizzano, M.: An effective preprocessor for QBF prereasoning. In: 2nd International Workshop on Quantification in Constraint Programming, QiCP (2008)
6. Grégoire, É., Mazure, B., Piette, C.: On approaches to explaining infeasibility of sets of Boolean clauses. In: International Conference on Tools with Artificial Intelligence, pp. 74–83 (November 2008)
7. Grégoire, E., Mazure, B., Piette, C.: Does this set of clauses overlap with at least one MUS? In: Schmidt, R.A. (ed.) CADE-22. LNCS, vol. 5663, pp. 100–115. Springer, Heidelberg (2009)
8. Janota, M., Grigore, R., Marques-Silva, J.: Counterexample guided abstraction refinement algorithm for propositional circumscription. In: Proceeding of the 12th European Conference on Logics in Artificial Intelligence, JELIA (2010)
9. Janota, M., Marques-Silva, J.: Abstraction-based algorithm for 2QBF. In: Sakallah, Simon (eds.) [23]
10. Janota, M., Marques-Silva, J.: cmMUS: a circumscription-based tool for MUS membership testing. In: Delgrande, J.P., Faber, W. (eds.) LPNMR 2011. LNCS, vol. 6645, pp. 266–271. Springer, Heidelberg (2011)

11. Kullmann, O.: An application of matroid theory to the SAT problem. In: IEEE Conference on Computational Complexity, pp. 116–124 (2000)
12. Kullmann, O.: Constraint satisfaction problems in clausal form: Autarkies and minimal unsatisfiability. ECCC 14(055) (2007)
13. Liberatore, P.: Redundancy in logic I: CNF propositional formulae. Artif. Intell. 163(2), 203–232 (2005)
14. Liffiton, M.H., Sakallah, K.A.: Algorithms for computing minimal unsatisfiable subsets of constraints. J. Autom. Reasoning 40(1), 1–33 (2008)
15. Lifschitz, V.: Some results on circumscription. In: NMR, pp. 151–164 (1984)
16. Marques-Silva, J., Lynce, I.: On improving MUS extraction algorithms. In: Sakallah, Simon (eds.) [23]
17. McCarthy, J.: Circumscription - a form of non-monotonic reasoning. Artif. Intell. 13(1-2), 27–39 (1980)
18. Meyer, A.R., Stockmeyer, L.J.: The equivalence problem for regular expressions with squaring requires exponential space. In: Switching and Automata Theory (1972)
19. Minker, J.: On indefinite databases and the closed world assumption. In: Conference on Automated Deduction, pp. 292–308 (1982)
20. O'Callaghan, B., O'Sullivan, B., Freuder, E.C.: Generating corrective explanations for interactive constraint satisfaction. In: van Beek, P. (ed.) CP 2005. LNCS, vol. 3709, pp. 445–459. Springer, Heidelberg (2005)
21. Papadimitriou, C.H., Wolfe, D.: The complexity of facets resolved. J. Comput. Syst. Sci. 37(1), 2–13 (1988)
22. Papadopoulos, A., O'Sullivan, B.: Relaxations for compiled over-constrained problems. In: Stuckey, P.J. (ed.) CP 2008. LNCS, vol. 5202, pp. 433–447. Springer, Heidelberg (2008)
23. Sakallah, K.A., Simon, L. (eds.): The 14th International Conference on Theory and Applications of Satisfiability Testing (SAT). Springer, Heidelberg (2011)

On the Relative Efficiency of
DPLL and OBDDs with Axiom and Join*

Matti Järvisalo

Department of Computer Science, University of Helsinki, Finland

Abstract. This paper studies the relative efficiency of ordered binary decision diagrams (OBDDs) and the Davis-Putnam-Logemann-Loveland procedure (DPLL), two of the main approaches to solving Boolean satisfiability instances. Especially, we show that OBDDs, even when constructed using only the rather weak axiom and join rules, can be exponentially more efficient than DPLL or, equivalently, tree-like resolution. Additionally, by strengthening via simple arguments a recent result—stating that such OBDDs do not polynomially simulate unrestricted resolution—we also show that the opposite holds: there are cases in which DPLL is exponentially more efficient out of the two considered systems. Hence DPLL and OBDDs constructed using only the axiom and join rules are polynomially incomparable. This further highlights differences between search-based and compilation-based approaches to Boolean satisfiability.

1 Introduction

Many algorithms for Boolean satisfiability (SAT) are based on either resolution (including most state of the art search-based solvers today) or (reduced) ordered binary decision diagrams (OBDDs). Recently, there has been a lot of interest in the relative efficiency of satisfiability checking methods based on resolution and OBDDs [1,2,3,4,5,6]. While OBBDs in general are known to be in cases exponentially more efficient that unrestricted resolution [7], it has been recently shown [6] that the restricted OBDD$_{aj}$ proof system, consisting only of the rather weak *Axiom* and *Join* rules which correspond to the *Apply* OBDD operator (i.e., disallowing symbolic quantifier elimination and reordering), does not polynomially simulate unrestricted resolution. In other words, there is an infinite family $\{F_n\}_n$ of unsatisfiable CNF formulas such that (i) there is a polynomial-size resolution proof of F_n w.r.t. n for every n, whereas (ii) minimum-size OBDD$_{aj}$ proofs of F_n for every n are of exponential size w.r.t. n (and of super-polynomial size w.r.t. the number of clauses in F_n). A practical implication of this result is that OBDD$_{aj}$ (under any variable ordering) does not polynomially simulate typical restarting conflict-driven clause learning SAT solvers—often the most efficient ones for practical applications of SAT, and which have been recently shown to polynomially simulate unrestricted resolution [8]. However, the results in [6] leave open the question of pinpointing the (in)efficiency of OBDD$_{aj}$ more exactly: Does it even polynomially simulate the Davis-Putnam-Logemann-Loveland procedure (DPLL) [9,10] that is known to be exponentially weaker than clause learning? Does DPLL polynomially simulate OBDD$_{aj}$?

* This work is financially supported by Academy of Finland (grant 132812).

J. Lee (Ed.): CP 2011, LNCS 6876, pp. 429–437, 2011.
© Springer-Verlag Berlin Heidelberg 2011

In this paper we show that the answer to both of these questions is negative: 1. We show that DPLL (with an optimal branching heuristic) does not polynomially simulate $OBDD_{aj}$ (using a suitable variable ordering). 2. Strengthening the result of [6] via simple arguments, we show that the $OBDD_{aj}$ proof system (under any variable ordering) does not polynomially simulate DPLL (known to be equivalent to the tree-like resolution refinement). Hence $OBDD_{aj}$ and DPLL are *polynomially incomparable*.

Theorem 1. *OBDDs constructed using the Axiom and Join rules and* DPLL *(equivalently, tree-like resolution) are polynomially incomparable.*

This provides further understanding on the general question of the relative efficiency of DPLL and variants of OBDDs, highlighting further the differences between search-based and compilation-based approaches to Boolean satisfiability.

2   Preliminaries

CNF Satisfiability. A literal is a Boolean variable x or its negation $\neg x$. A *clause* is a disjunction ($\vee$) of literals and a CNF formula is a conjunction ($\wedge$) of clauses. When convenient, we view a clause as a finite set of literals and/or a CNF formula as a finite set of clauses. The set of variables occurring in a CNF formula F is denoted by $\mathsf{vars}(F)$, and the set of literals occurring in a clause C by $\mathsf{lits}(C)$. An *assignment* τ is a function that maps literals to elements in $\{0, 1\}$, where 1 and 0, resp., stand for *true* and *false*, resp. If $\tau(x) = v$, then $\tau(\neg x) = 1 - v$, and vice versa. A clause is *satisfied* by τ if it contains at least one literal l such that $\tau(l) = 1$. An assignment τ *satisfies* a CNF formula if it satisfies every clause in the formula.

DPLL. The DPLL procedure [9,10] is a classical complete search algorithm for deciding satisfiability of CNF formulas. It can be summarized as the following non-deterministic algorithm.

> DPLL(F)
> > **If** F is empty **report** *satisfiable* and **halt**
> > **If** F contains the empty clause **return**
> > **Else** *choose a variable* $x \in \mathsf{vars}(F)$
> > > DPLL(F_x)
> > > DPLL($F_{\neg x}$)

Here F_x denotes the formula resulting from applying *unit propagation* until fixpoint on F, i.e., removing all clauses containing x and all occurrences of $\neg x$ from F, and repeating until fixpoint for all single-literal clauses in F. Practical implementations make DPLL deterministic by implementing a branching heuristic for choosing a variable. However, here we do not restrict this non-deterministic choice. A DPLL proof of an unsatisfiable CNF formula F is a search tree of DPLL(F). The size of a DPLL proof is the number of nodes in the tree.

Resolution. The well-known Resolution proof system (RES) is based on the *resolution rule* that allows one to *directly derive* the clause $(C \cup D) \setminus \{x, \neg x\}$ from the clauses $\{x\} \cup C$ and $\{\neg x\} \cup D$ by *resolving on* the variable x. Given an unsatisfiable CNF formula F, a RES *proof* of F is a sequence of clauses $\pi = (C_1, C_2, \ldots, C_m = \emptyset)$, where each C_i, $1 \leq i \leq m$, is either (i) a clause in F (an *initial clause*) or (ii) directly derived with the resolution rule from two clauses C_j, C_k where $1 \leq j, k < i$. The *size* of π, denoted by $|\pi|$, is m. Any RES proof $\pi = (C_1, C_2, \ldots, C_m = \emptyset)$ can be presented as a directed acyclic graph. The clauses occurring in π label the nodes. The edge relation is defined so that there are edges from C_i and C_j to C_k, if and only if C_k has been directly derived from C_i and C_j. *Tree-like Resolution* (T-RES) proofs are representable as trees. It is well-known that T-RES proofs are polynomially equivalent to search trees traversed by the DPLL procedure.

In *Extended Resolution* (E-RES) [11] one can first apply the *extension rule* to add a conjunction of clauses (an *extension*) to a CNF formula F in a restricted manner, before using the resolution rule to construct a RES proof of the resulting formula. In more detail, for a given CNF formula F, the extension rule allows for iteratively adding definitions of the form $x \equiv l_1 \wedge l_2$ (i.e. the clauses $(x \vee \neg l_1 \vee \neg l_2)$, $(\neg x \vee l_1)$, and $(\neg x \vee l_2)$) to F, where x is a new variable and l_1, l_2 are literals in the current formula. The resulting formula $F \wedge E$ then consists of the original formula F and the extension E, the conjunction of the clauses iteratively added to F using the extension rule.

OBDDs with Axiom and Join. A *binary decision diagram* (BDD) over a set of Boolean variables V is a rooted directed acyclic graph that consists of (i) *decision nodes* labelled with distinct variables from V and (ii) two terminal nodes (of out-degree zero) labelled with 0 and 1. Each decision node v has two children, low(v) and high(v). The edge from v to low(v) (to high(v), resp.) represents assigning v to 0 (to 1, resp.). A BDD is *ordered* according to a total variable order $\prec$ if its variables appear in the order given by $\prec$ on all paths from the root to the terminal nodes. An ordered BDD is *reduced* (simply, an OBDD from here on) if its (i) isomorphic subgraphs have been merged, and (ii) the nodes that have isomorphic children have been eliminated. Given any propositional formula ϕ and a total variable order $\prec$ over vars(ϕ), there is a unique OBDD $\mathsf{B}(\phi, \prec)$ that represents ϕ. The *size* of $\mathsf{B}(\phi, \prec)$, denoted by size$(\mathsf{B}_i(\phi_i, \prec))$, is the number of its nodes.

Given an unsatisfiable CNF formula F and a total variable order $\prec$ over vars(F), an OBDD$_\mathsf{aj}$ *proof* of F (i.e., an OBDD$_\mathsf{aj}$ *derivation* of the OBDD for 0) is a sequence $\rho = (\mathsf{B}_1(\phi_1, \prec), \ldots, \mathsf{B}_m(\phi_m, \prec))$ of OBDDs, where (i) $\mathsf{B}_m(\phi_m, \prec)$ is the single-node OBDD representing 0, and (ii) for each $i \in \{1, \ldots, m\}$, either

- ϕ_i is a clause in F, or
- $\phi_i = \phi_j \wedge \phi_k$ for some $\mathsf{B}_j(\phi_j, \prec)$ and $\mathsf{B}_k(\phi_k, \prec)$, $1 \leq j < k < i$, in ρ.

In the former case $\mathsf{B}_i(\phi_i, \prec)$ is an *axiom*, and in the latter $\mathsf{B}_i(\phi_i, \prec)$ is the *join* of $\mathsf{B}_j(\phi_j, \prec)$ and $\mathsf{B}_k(\phi_k, \prec)$. The size of an OBDD$_\mathsf{aj}$ proof ρ is $\Sigma_{i=1}^{m}$size$(\mathsf{B}_i(\phi_i, \prec))$.

3 DPLL Does Not Polynomially Simulate OBDD$_\mathsf{aj}$

In this section we show that DPLL does not polynomially simulate OBDD$_\mathsf{aj}$. For the separation, we consider so-called *pebbling contradictions* $\mathrm{Peb}(G)$, first introduced in [12], based on the structure of a directed acyclic graph (DAG) G. Taking two variables $x_{i,0}$ and $x_{i,1}$ for each node in G, $\mathrm{Peb}(G)$ is the conjunction of the following clauses.

- $(x_{i,0} \lor x_{i,1})$ for each source node (in-degree 0) i of G;
- $(\neg x_{i,0})$ and $(\neg x_{i,1})$ for each sink node (out-degree 0) i of G;
- $(\neg x_{i_1,a_1} \lor \cdots \lor \neg x_{i_k,a_k} \lor x_{j,0} \lor x_{j,1})$ for each non-source node j, where $i_1, \ldots, i_k$ are the predecessors of j, and for each $(a_1, \ldots, a_k) \in \{0,1\}^k$.

The following theorem helps us in achieving polynomial-size OBDD$_{aj}$ proofs.

Theorem 2 ([13]). *For any Boolean function f over n variables, and any variable order $\prec$, $\mathrm{size}(\mathrm{B}(f, \prec)) = \mathcal{O}(2^n/n)$.*

Corollary 1. *For any unsatisfiable CNF formula F over n variables, and any variable order $\prec$, there is an OBDD$_{aj}$ proof of F of size $2^{\mathcal{O}(n)}$.*

The following two lemmas play a key role in this work. For proving the lemmas we rely on a similar proof strategy as the one applied in [14] used in a different context (for showing that tree-like resolution does not polynomially simulate *ordered resolution*).

Lemma 1. *Let G be a DAG on n nodes, and j a node in G with parents $i_1, \ldots, i_k$ where $k = \mathcal{O}(\log n)$. Consider the clauses $(x_{i_1,0} \lor x_{i_1,1}), \ldots, (x_{i_k,0} \lor x_{i_k,1})$ and $(\neg x_{i_1,a_1} \lor \cdots \lor \neg x_{i_k,a_k} \lor x_{j,0} \lor x_{j,1})$ for all $(a_1, \ldots, a_k) \in \{0,1\}^k$. For any variable order $\prec$, there is a polynomial-size OBDD$_{aj}$ derivation of $\mathrm{B}((x_{j,0} \lor x_{j,1}), \prec)$ from these clauses.*

Proof. Consider the unsatisfiable CNF formula consisting of the clauses $(x_{i_1,0} \lor x_{i_1,1})$, $\ldots, (x_{i_k,0} \lor x_{i_k,1})$ and $(\neg x_{i_1,a_1} \lor \cdots \lor \neg x_{i_k,a_k})$ for all $(a_1, \ldots, a_k) \in \{0,1\}^k$. The number of variables in this formula is $\mathcal{O}(\log n)$, and hence by Corollary 1 there is a polynomial-size OBDD$_{aj}$ proof of this formula for any variable order $\prec$. Such an OBDD$_{aj}$ proof can be transformed into a OBDD$_{aj}$ derivation of $\mathrm{B}((x_{j,0} \lor x_{j,1}), \prec')$ by defining $\prec'$ as $\prec$ to which $x_{j,0}$ and $x_{j,1}$ have been added as the last two elements, and by replacing $\mathrm{B}(\phi, \prec)$ with $\mathrm{B}(\phi \lor x_{j,0} \lor x_{j,1}, \prec)$ for each $\mathrm{B}(\phi, \prec)$ in the proof such that either ϕ is $(\neg x_{i_1,a_1} \lor \cdots \lor \neg x_{i_k,a_k})$ or $\mathrm{B}(\phi, \prec)$ has been derived starting from the axiom $\mathrm{B}((\neg x_{i_1,a_1} \lor \cdots \lor \neg x_{i_k,a_k}), \prec)$. For each such $\mathrm{B}(\phi, \prec)$, $\mathrm{B}(\phi \lor x_{j,0} \lor x_{j,1}, \prec)$ is $\mathrm{B}(\phi, \prec)$ with the terminal node 0 replaced by $\mathrm{B}((x_{j,0} \lor x_{j,1}), \prec)$. $\qquad\square$

Lemma 2. *There are polynomial-size OBDD$_{aj}$ proofs of $\mathrm{Peb}(G)$ for any DAG G with node in-degree bounded by $\mathcal{O}(\log n)$.*

Proof. Fix any ordering $\prec$ of the variables in $\mathrm{Peb}(G)$ that respects a topological ordering of G. Label each source j of G with $\mathrm{B}((x_{j,0} \lor x_{j,1}), \prec)$. For each non-source node j of G with parents $i_1, \ldots, i_k$, $k = \mathcal{O}(\log n)$, replace j with the polynomial-size OBDD$_{aj}$ derivation of $\mathrm{B}((x_{j,0} \lor x_{j,1}), \prec)$ (Lemma 1) under $\prec$. The result is a polynomial-size OBDD$_{aj}$ derivation of $\mathrm{B}((x_{t,0} \lor x_{t,1}), \prec)$ for the single sink t of G (analogously for multiple sinks). To complete the proof, join $\mathrm{B}((x_{t,0} \lor x_{t,1}), \prec)$ with the axioms $\mathrm{B}((\neg x_{t,0}), \prec)$ and $\mathrm{B}((\neg x_{t,1}), \prec)$. $\qquad\square$

Combined with the following lemma, we have that DPLL (equivalently, T-RES) does not polynomially simulate OBDD$_{aj}$ (using a suitable variable order for OBDD$_{aj}$).

Lemma 3 ([12]). *There is an infinite family $\{G_n\}$ of DAGs with constant node in-degree (from [15]) such that minimum-size T-RES proofs of $\mathrm{Peb}(G_n)$ are of size $2^{\Omega(n/\log n)}$.*

4 OBDD$_{aj}$ Does Not Polynomially Simulate DPLL

In [6] it was shown that OBDD$_{aj}$ does not polynomially simulate unrestricted resolution RES. In this section we show the stronger result that OBDD$_{aj}$ is not only weaker than RES, but also exponentially weaker than DPLL (equivalently, T-RES).

4.1 OBDD$_{aj}$ Does Not Benefit from the Extension Rule

As an auxiliary result, we prove the following lemma as an extension of [6, Lemma 8]. The original lemma was restricted to a particular CNF formula PHP_n^{n+1} and a particular extension of PHP_n^{n+1}. This more general version states that OBDD$_{aj}$ proofs cannot be made smaller by first adding an extension to the input unsatisfiable CNF formula.

Lemma 4. *Assume an arbitrary unsatisfiable CNF formula F and extension E to F, and any satisfiable $F' \subset F$ and $E' \subseteq E$. Then, for every variable order $\prec$ over $\mathsf{vars}(F') \cup \mathsf{vars}(E')$, $\mathsf{size}(\mathsf{B}(F' \wedge E', \prec)) \geq \mathsf{size}(\mathsf{B}(F', \prec))$.*

Following the proof strategy for [6, Lemma 8], we first state a simple extension of [6, Lemma 7], simply stating that no extension E of a CNF formula F can affect the set of satisfying assignments of F (restricted to F).

Lemma 5. *Assume an arbitrary CNF formula F and extension E to F, any satisfiable $F' \subset F$ and $E' \subseteq E$, and an assignment τ that satisfies F'. Then there is an assignment τ' such that (i) $\tau'(x) = \tau(x)$ for each $x \in \mathsf{vars}(F')$, and (ii) τ' satisfies $F' \wedge E'$.*

Proof. Assume that the clauses in $E = C_1 \wedge \cdots \wedge C_k$ were introduced using the extension rule in the order of the sequence $(C_1, \ldots, C_k)$. Fix an arbitrary satisfiable $F' \subseteq F$ and assignment τ that satisfies F'. Let $\tau'(x) = \tau(x)$ for each $x \in \mathsf{vars}(F')$. By induction, assume that, for an arbitrary i, τ' satisfies all C_j for $j < i$. Let C_i be part of a definition $x_i \equiv l \wedge l'$. To satisfy C_i, we extend τ' as follows. If both l and l' are assigned under τ', then assign x_i so that the semantics of $x_i \equiv l \wedge l'$ is respected. If l (or l', resp.) is not assigned under τ' (this is possible in case l or l' do not appear in F'), first assign it an arbitrary value.   □

For the following, a function f *depends essentially* on a variable x if $f|_{x=0} \neq f|_{x=1}$, where $f|_{x=c}$ denotes the function f with x assigned to a constant $c \in \{0,1\}$. Again following [6], we make use of a structural theorem from [16].

Theorem 3 ([16]). *For any Boolean function $f(x_1, \ldots, x_n)$ and $i < n$, let S_i be the set $\{f|_{x_1=c_1,\ldots,x_{i-1}=c_{i-1}} : c_1, \ldots, c_{i-1} \in \{0,1\}\}$ of sub-functions which depend essentially on x_i. Then the OBDD for f under the variable order $x_1 \prec \cdots \prec x_n$ contains exactly $|S_i|$ nodes labelled with x_i in correspondence with the sub-functions in S_i.*

In the following, for an assignment τ over a set X of variables and a variable order $\prec$ over V, let $\tau_{\prec x}$ be the restriction of τ to the variables preceding $x \in X$ under $\prec$.

Proof of Lemma 4. We show that, for any $F', E', \prec, i < |\mathsf{vars}(F')|$, and $x_i \in \mathsf{vars}(F')$, where x_i is the ith variable in $\mathsf{vars}(F')$ under $\prec$, it holds that if $\mathsf{B}(F', \prec)$ has k nodes labelled with x_i, then $\mathsf{B}(F' \wedge E', \prec)$ has at least k nodes labelled with x_i.

Take any satisfying assignment τ over vars(F') such that $F'|_{\tau_{\prec x_i}}$ depends essentially on x_i. By Theorem 3, corresponding to any such $F'|_{\tau_{\prec x_i}}$ there is a node $n_{\tau_{\prec x_i}}$ in $\mathrm{B}(F', \prec)$ labelled with x_i. Based on τ, consider an assignment τ' for $F' \wedge E'$ as in Lemma 5. By the construction of τ', $(F' \wedge E')|_{\tau'_{\prec x_i}}$ depends essentially on x_i. By Theorem 3, for any such $n_{\tau_{\prec x_i}}$, there is a distinct node $n_{\tau'_{\prec x_i}}$ (corresponding to $(F' \wedge E')|_{\tau'_{\prec x_i}}$) in $\mathrm{B}(F' \wedge E', \prec)$.   □

The following is an immediately corollary of Lemma 4.

Corollary 2. *Let F be an unsatisfiable CNF formula and E an extension to F. For any variable order $\prec$ over vars$(F) \cup$ vars(E), if $F \wedge E$ has a $\mathrm{OBDD}_{\mathsf{aj}}$ proof of size s, then F has a $\mathrm{OBDD}_{\mathsf{aj}}$ proof of size s.*

4.2   DPLL and the Extension Rule

Let F be an arbitrary unsatisfiable CNF formula and let $\pi_F = (C_1, \ldots, C_m = \emptyset)$ be a RES proof of F. We define the extension $\mathrm{E}(\pi_F)$ of F based on π_F, defining new variables $e_i \equiv C_i$ for $i = 1, \ldots, m-1$ using the extension rule, as the CNF formula

$$\mathrm{E}(\pi_F) := \bigwedge_{i=1}^{m-1} \left((\neg e_i \vee C_i) \wedge \bigwedge_{l \in \mathrm{lits}(C_i)} (e_i \vee \neg l) \right).$$

This formulation originates from a construction that was used to polynomially simulate Frege systems by tree-like Frege systems [17], and was also applied in [18].

Lemma 6. *Let F be an unsatisfiable CNF formula and let π_F be a RES proof of F. There is a DPLL proof of $F \wedge \mathrm{E}(\pi_F)$ of size $\mathcal{O}(|\pi_F|)$.*

Proof. Choose variables in the order $e_1 \prec \cdots \prec e_{m-1}$. For each $i = 1, \ldots, m-1$, the call DPLL$(F \wedge \mathrm{E}(\pi_F)_{e_1, \ldots, e_{i-1}, \neg e_i})$ returns immediately since $F \wedge \mathrm{E}(\pi_F)_{e_1, \ldots, e_{i-1}, \neg e_i}$ contains the empty clause due to emptying either a clause in F, or one of the two clauses in π_F used to directly derive the resolvent C_i. The call DPLL$(F \wedge \mathrm{E}(\pi_F)_{e_1, \ldots, e_{m-1}})$ returns immediately since there are the two unit clauses (x) and $(\neg x)$ in π_F for some variable x.   □

In fact, as similarly observed in [18], full one-step lookahead with unit propagation is enough for constructing the DPLL proof presented in the proof of Lemma 6.

4.3   Separating DPLL from $\mathrm{OBDD}_{\mathsf{aj}}$

The well-known *pigeon-hole principle* states that there is no injective mapping from an m-element set into an n-element set if $m > n$ (that is, m pigeons cannot sit in fewer than m holes so that every pigeon has its own hole). We will consider the case $m = n + 1$ encoded as the CNF formula

$$\mathrm{PHP}_n^{n+1} := \bigwedge_{i=1}^{n+1} \left(\bigvee_{j=1}^{n} p_{i,j} \right) \wedge \bigwedge_{j=1}^{n} \bigwedge_{i=1}^{n} \bigwedge_{i'=i+1}^{n+1} (\neg p_{i,j} \vee \neg p_{i',j}),$$

where each $p_{i,j}$ is a Boolean variable with the interpretation "$p_{i,j}$ is 1 if and only if the ith pigeon sits in the jth hole". Notice that PHP_n^{n+1} contains $O(n^2)$ clauses.

Theorem 4 ([19]). *There is no polynomial-size* RES *proof of* PHP_n^{n+1}.

In contrast, Cook [20] showed that there is a polynomial-size E-RES proof of PHP_n^{n+1}. Cook basically applies the E-RES extension rule to add a conjunction EXT_n of $O(n^3)$ clauses to PHP_n^{n+1}, based on defining new variables $p_{i,i}^k \equiv p_{i,j}^{k-1} \vee (p_{i,n}^{k-1} \wedge p_{n+1,j}^{k-1})$, where $1 \leq i \leq n$, $1 \leq j \leq n-1$, $1 \leq k \leq n-1$, and each $p_{i,j}^0$ is the variable $p_{i,j} \in \mathrm{vars}(\mathrm{PHP}_n^{n+1})$. These equivalences[1] are presented as the CNF formula $\mathrm{EXT}_n := \bigwedge_{k=1}^{n-1} \bigwedge_{i=1}^{n} \bigwedge_{j=1}^{n-1}$
$$\left(\left(p_{i,j}^k \vee \neg p_{i,j}^{k-1}\right) \wedge \left(p_{i,j}^k \vee \neg p_{i,n}^{k-1} \vee \neg p_{n+1,j}^{k-1}\right) \wedge \left(\neg p_{i,j}^k \vee p_{i,j}^{k-1} \vee p_{i,n}^{k-1}\right) \wedge \left(\neg p_{i,j}^k \vee p_{i,j}^{k-1} \vee p_{n+1,j}^{k-1}\right) \right).$$

Theorem 5 ([20]). *There is a* RES *proof of* $\mathrm{PHP}_n^{n+1} \wedge \mathrm{EXT}_n$ *of size* $O(n^4)$.

Explicit constructions of a RES proof of size $O(n^4)$ of $\mathrm{PHP}_n^{n+1} \wedge \mathrm{EXT}_n$ are presented in [18,6]. On the other hand, these proofs are not tree-like, and it is not apparent whether there is a polynomial-size DPLL proof of $\mathrm{PHP}_n^{n+1} \wedge \mathrm{EXT}_n$. However, we can use the extension trick from Sect. 4.2 for achieving a short DPLL proof.

Corollary 3. *There is an extension E to* PHP_n^{n+1} *such that there is a polynomial-size* DPLL *proof of* $\mathrm{PHP}_n^{n+1} \wedge E$.

Proof. Take an arbitrary RES proof π of $\mathrm{PHP}_n^{n+1} \wedge \mathrm{EXT}_n$ such that $|\pi| \in O(n^4)$ (there is such a π by Theorem 5). Define E as $\mathrm{EXT}_n \wedge \mathrm{E}(\pi)$. By Lemma 6 there is a polynomial-size DPLL proof of $\mathrm{PHP}_n^{n+1} \wedge \mathrm{EXT}_n \wedge \mathrm{E}(\pi)$.   □

To separate DPLL from OBDD_{aj}, we observe the following.

Theorem 6 ([6]). *For any variable order $\prec$, minimum size* OBDD_{aj} *proofs of* PHP_n^{n+1} *are of size* $2^{\Omega(n)}$.

Corollary 4. *Let E be an arbitrary extension of* PHP_n^{n+1}. *For any variable order $\prec$, minimum-size* OBDD_{aj} *proofs of* $\mathrm{PHP}_n^{n+1} \wedge E$ *are of size* $2^{\Omega(n)}$.

Proof. Follows directly from Corollary 2 and Theorem 6.   □

The fact that OBDD_{aj} does not polynomially simulate DPLL (equivalently, T-RES) now follows directly from Corollaries 3 and 4.

5 Conclusions

We showed that the standard DPLL procedure and OBDDs constructed using the *axiom* and *join* rules (OBDD_{aj}) are polynomially incomparable. This further highlights the differences between search-based and compilation-based approaches to Boolean

---

[1] Although Cook introduces directly clauses representing $p_{i,i}^k \equiv p_{i,j}^{k-1} \vee (p_{i,n}^{k-1} \wedge p_{n+1,j}^{k-1})$ which does not follow the original definition of the extension rule, it is easy to see that this can be simulated with the original rule by first introducing an auxiliary variable for $(p_{i,n}^{k-1} \wedge p_{n+1,j}^{k-1})$. This more general way of defining the extension does not affect the results of this paper.

satisfiability. Especially, although $OBDD_{aj}$ is intuitively rather weak, it can still be exponentially more efficient than DPLL. However, in contrast to DPLL, $OBDD_{aj}$ cannot exploit particular types of redundancy in CNF (introduced by the extension rule). As a result, DPLL can be in cases exponentially more efficient than $OBDD_{aj}$.

Whether there is a resolution refinement that polynomially simulate $OBDD_{aj}$ is an interesting open question. Another interesting question is the relative efficiency of tree-like and DAG-like $OBDD_{aj}$ proofs. Especially, the $OBDD_{aj}$ proofs constructed in Lemma 2 are not tree-like.

References

1. Groote, J.F., Zantema, H.: Resolution and binary decision diagrams cannot simulate each other polynomially. Discrete Applied Mathematics 130(2), 157–171 (2003)
2. Atserias, A., Kolaitis, P.G., Vardi, M.Y.: Constraint propagation as a proof system. In: Wallace, M. (ed.) CP 2004. LNCS, vol. 3258, pp. 77–91. Springer, Heidelberg (2004)
3. Sinz, C., Biere, A.: Extended resolution proofs for conjoining BDDs. In: Grigoriev, D., Harrison, J., Hirsch, E.A. (eds.) CSR 2006. LNCS, vol. 3967, pp. 600–611. Springer, Heidelberg (2006)
4. Segerlind, N.: On the relative efficiency of resolution-like proofs and ordered binary decision diagram proofs. In: Proc. CCC, pp. 100–111. IEEE Computer Society, Los Alamitos (2008)
5. Peltier, N.: Extended resolution simulates binary decision diagrams. Discrete Applied Mathematics 156(6), 825–837 (2008)
6. Tveretina, O., Sinz, C., Zantema, H.: Ordered binary decision diagrams, pigeonhole formulas and beyond. Journal on Satisfiability, Boolean Modeling and Computation 7, 35–58 (2010)
7. Chen, W., Zhang, W.: A direct construction of polynomial-size OBDD proof of pigeon hole problem. Information Processing Letters 109(10), 472–477 (2009)
8. Pipatsrisawat, K., Darwiche, A.: On the power of clause-learning SAT solvers as resolution engines. Artificial Intelligence 175(2), 512–525 (2011)
9. Davis, M., Putnam, H.: A computing procedure for quantification theory. Journal of the ACM 7(3), 201–215 (1960)
10. Davis, M., Logemann, G., Loveland, D.: A machine program for theorem proving. Communications of the ACM 5(7), 394–397 (1962)
11. Tseitin, G.S.: On the complexity of derivation in propositional calculus. In: Slisenko, A.O. (ed.) Studies in Constructive Mathematics and Mathematical Logic, Part II. Seminars in Mathematics, V.A.Steklov Mathematical Institute, Leningrad, vol. 8, pp. 115–125. Consultants Bureau (1969) (originally in Russian)
12. Ben-Sasson, E., Wigderson, A.: Short proofs are narrow - resolution made simple. Journal of the ACM 48(2), 149–169 (2001)
13. Liaw, H.T., Lin, C.S.: On the OBDD-representation of general boolean functions. IEEE Transactions on Computers 41(6), 661–664 (1992)
14. Buresh-Oppenheim, J., Pitassi, T.: The complexity of resolution refinements. Journal of Symbolic Logic 72(4), 1336–1352 (2007)
15. Paul, W.J., Tarjan, R.E., Celoni, J.R.: Space bounds for a game on graphs. Mathematical Systems Theory 10, 239–251 (1977)
16. Sieling, D., Wegener, I.: NC-algorithms for operations on binary decision diagrams. Parallel Processing Letters 3, 3–12 (1993)

17. Krajicek, J.: Speed-up for propositional frege systems via generalizations of proofs. Commentationes Mathematicae Universitas Carolinae 30(1), 137–140 (1989)
18. Järvisalo, M., Junttila, T.: Limitations of restricted branching in clause learning. Constraints 14(3), 325–356 (2009)
19. Haken, A.: The intractability of resolution. Theoretical Computer Science 39(2-3), 297–308 (1985)
20. Cook, S.A.: A short proof of the pigeon hole principle using extended resolution. SIGACT News 8(4), 28–32 (1976)

Min CSP on Four Elements: Moving beyond Submodularity

Peter Jonsson[1,*], Fredrik Kuivinen[2], and Johan Thapper[3,**]

[1] Department of Computer and Information Science, Linköpings universitet
SE-581 83 Linköping, Sweden
petej@ida.liu.se, frekui@gmail.com
[2] École polytechnique, Laboratoire d'informatique (LIX),
91128 Palaiseau Cedex, France
thapper@lix.polytechnique.fr

Abstract. We report new results on the complexity of the valued constraint satisfaction problem (VCSP). Under the unique games conjecture, the approximability of finite-valued VCSP is fairly well-understood. However, there is yet no characterisation of VCSPs that can be solved exactly in polynomial time. This is unsatisfactory, since such results are interesting from a combinatorial optimisation perspective; there are deep connections with, for instance, submodular and bisubmodular minimisation. We consider the MIN and MAX CSP problems (i.e. where the cost functions only attain values in $\{0, 1\}$) over four-element domains and identify all tractable fragments. Similar classifications were previously known for two- and three-element domains. In the process, we introduce a new class of tractable VCSPs based on a generalisation of submodularity. We also extend and modify a graph-based technique by Kolmogorov and Živný (originally introduced by Takhanov) for efficiently obtaining hardness results in our setting. This allow us to prove the result without relying on computer-assisted case analyses (which is fairly common when studying VCSPs). The hardness results are further simplified by the introduction of powerful reduction techniques.

Keywords: Constraint satisfaction problems, combinatorial optimisation, computational complexity, submodularity, bisubmodularity.

1 Introduction

This paper concerns the computational complexity of an optimisation problem with strong connections to the *constraint satisfaction problem* (CSP). An instance of the constraint satisfaction problem consists of a finite set of variables, a set of values (the domain), and a finite set of constraints. The goal is to determine whether there is an assignment of values to the variables such that all

---

* Partially supported by the *Swedish Research Council* (VR) under grant 621-2009-4431.
** Supported by the *LIX-Qualcomm Postdoctoral Fellowship*.

J. Lee (Ed.): CP 2011, LNCS 6876, pp. 438–453, 2011.

the constraints are satisfied. CSPs provide a general framework for modelling a wide variety of combinatorial decision problems [4].

Various optimisation variations of the constraint satisfaction framework have been proposed and many of them can be seen as special cases of the *valued constraint satisfaction problem* (VCSP). This is an optimisation problem which is general enough to express such diverse problems as MAX CSP, where the goal is to maximise the number of satisfied constraints, and the minimum cost homomorphism problem (MIN HOM), where all constraints must be satisfied, but each variable-value tuple in the assignment is given an independent cost. We have the following formal definition.

Definition 1. *Let D be a finite domain, and let Γ be a set of functions $f_i : D^{k_i} \to \mathbb{Q}_{\geq 0} \cup \{\infty\}$. By VCSP($\Gamma$) we denote the following minimisation problem:*

Instance: *A set of variables V, and a sum $\sum_{i=1}^{m} \varrho_i f_i(\mathbf{x_i})$, where $\varrho_i \in \mathbb{Q}_{\geq 0}$, $f_i \in \Gamma$, and $\mathbf{x_i}$ is a list of k_i variables from V.*
Solution: *A function $\sigma : V \to D$.*
Measure: *$m(\sigma) = \sum_{i=1}^{m} \varrho_i f_i(\sigma(\mathbf{x_i}))$, where $\sigma(\mathbf{x_i})$ is the list of elements from D obtained by applying σ component-wise to $\mathbf{x_i}$.*

The set Γ is referred to as the *constraint language*. We say that a class of VCSPs X is polynomial-time solvable if VCSP(Γ) is polynomial-time solvable for every $\Gamma \in X$. Finite-valued functions, i.e. functions with a range in $\mathbb{Q}_{\geq 0}$, are sometimes called *soft constraints*. A prominent example is given by functions with a range in $\{0, 1\}$; they can be used to express instances of the well-known MIN CSP and MAX CSP problems (which, for instance, include MAX k-CUT, MAX k-SAT, and NEAREST CODEWORD as subproblems). On the other side we have *crisp constraints* which represent the standard type of CSP constraints. These can be expressed by cost functions taking values in $\{0, \infty\}$.

A systematic study of the computational complexity of the VCSP was initiated by Cohen et al. [2]. This led to a large number of complexity results for VCSP: examples include complete classifications of conservative constraint languages (i.e. languages containing all unary cost functions) [5,9], $\{0, 1\}$ languages on three elements [8], and the MIN IIOM problem [16]. We note that some of these results have been proved by computer-assisted search—something that drastically reduces the readability, and insight gained from the proofs. We also note that there is no generally accepted conjecture stating which VCSPs are polynomial-time solvable.

The picture is clearer concerning the approximability of finite-valued VCSP. Raghavendra [14] has presented algorithms for approximating any finite-valued VCSP. These algorithms achieve an optimal approximation ratio for the constraint languages that cannot be solved to optimality in polynomial time, given that the unique games conjecture (UGC) is true. For the constraint languages that can be solved to optimality, one gets a PTAS. No characterisation of the set of constraint languages that can be solved to optimality follows from Raghavendra's result. Thus, Raghavendra's result does not imply the complexity results discussed above (not even conditionally under the UGC).

The goal of this paper is to study VCSPs with $\{0,1\}$ cost functions over four-element domains: we show that every such problem is either solvable in polynomial time or NP-hard. Such a dichotomy result is not known for CSPs on four-element domains (and, consequently, not for unrestricted VCSPs on four-element domains). Our result proves that, in contrast to the two-element, three-element, and conservative case, submodularity is not the only source of tractability. In order to outline the proof, let Γ denote a constraint language with $\{0,1\}$ cost functions over a four-element domain D. We will need one new tractability result for our classification; this result can be found in Section 3 and our algorithm is based on a combination of submodular and bisubmodular minimisation [6,12,15]. The hardness proof consists of three parts. Section 4 concerns the problem of adding (crisp) constant unary relations to Γ without changing the computational complexity of the resulting problem, and Section 5 introduces a graph construction for studying Γ. This graph provides information about the complexity of VCSP(Γ) based on the two-element sublanguages of Γ. Similar graphs have been used repeatedly in the study of VCSP, cf. [9,16]. Equipped with these tools, we prove our main classification result, Theorem 18, in Section 6. Due to space constraints, some proofs have been left out.

2   Preliminaries

Throughout this paper, we will assume that Γ is a finite set of $\{0,1\}$-valued functions. By MIN CSP(Γ) we denote the problem VCSP(Γ). Note that MIN CSP(Γ) is polynomial-time equivalent to MAX CSP($\{1 - f \mid f \in \Gamma\}$). This implies, for instance, that the dichotomy theorem for MAX CSP over domains of size three also can be viewed as a dichotomy result for MIN CSP. It turns out to be convenient to work with a slightly more general problem, in which we allow additional crisp constraints on the solutions.

Definition 2. *Let Γ be a set of $\{0,1\}$-valued functions on a domain D, and let Δ be a set of finitary relations on D. By MIN CSP(Γ, Δ) we denote the following minimisation problem:*

Instance: *A MIN CSP(Γ)-instance $\mathcal{I}$, and a finite set of constraint applications $\{(\mathbf{y_j}; R_j)\}$, where $R_j \in \Delta$ and $\mathbf{y_j}$ is a matching list of variables from V.*
Solution: *A solution σ to $\mathcal{I}$ such that $\sigma(\mathbf{y_j}) \in R_j$ for all j.*
Measure: *The measure of σ as a solution to $\mathcal{I}$.*

2.1   Weighted pp-Definitions and Expressive Power

We continue by defining two closure operators that are useful in studying the complexity of MIN CSP. Let $\mathcal{I}$ be an instance of MIN CSP(Γ, Δ), and let $\mathbf{x} = (x_1, \ldots, x_s)$ be a sequence of distinct variables from $V(\mathcal{I})$. Let $\pi_{\mathbf{x}} \text{Optsol}(\mathcal{I})$ denote the set $\{(\sigma(x_1), \ldots, \sigma(x_s)) \mid \sigma \text{ is an optimal solution to } \mathcal{I}\}$, i.e. the projection of the set of optimal solutions onto $\mathbf{x}$. We say that such a relation has a *weighted pp-definition in* (Γ, Δ) (cf. *primitive positive* (pp-) definitions in predicate logic.) Let $\langle \Gamma, \Delta \rangle_w$ denote the set of relations which have a weighted pp-definition in (Γ, Δ). For an instance $\mathcal{J}$ of MIN CSP, we define $\mathsf{Opt}(\mathcal{J})$ to be the optimal value of a solution to $\mathcal{J}$, and to be undefined if no solution exists. The following definition is a variation of the concept of the *expressive power* of a valued constraint language, see for example Cohen et al. [2]. Define the function $\mathcal{I}_{\mathbf{x}} : D^k \to \mathbb{Q}_{\geq 0}$ by letting $\mathcal{I}_{\mathbf{x}}(a_1, \ldots, a_k) = \mathsf{Opt}(\mathcal{I} \cup \{(x_i; \{a_i\}) \mid 1 \leq i \leq k\})$. We say that $\mathcal{I}_{\mathbf{x}}$ is *expressible over* (Γ, Δ). Let $\langle \Gamma, \Delta \rangle_{fn}$ denote the set of *total functions* expressible over (Γ, Δ).

Proposition 3. *Let* $\Gamma' \subseteq \langle \Gamma, \Delta \rangle_{fn}$ *and* $\Delta' \subseteq \langle \Gamma, \Delta \rangle_w$ *be finite sets. Then,* MIN CSP(Γ', Δ') *is polynomial-time reducible to* MIN CSP(Γ, Δ).

Proof (sketch): The reduction from MIN CSP(Γ', Δ') to MIN CSP(Γ, Δ') is a special case of Theorem 3.4 in [2]. We allow weights as a part of our instances, but this makes no essential difference. To prove that there is a polynomial-time transformation from MIN CSP(Γ, Δ') to MIN CSP(Γ, Δ), we need a way to 'force' constraints in $\Delta' \setminus \Delta$ to hold in every optimal solution. This can quite easily be guaranteed by using large weights, and one sees that the representation size of these weights needs to grow only linearly in the size of the instance.   ⊔

2.2   Multimorphisms and Submodularity

We now turn our attention to *multimorphisms* and tractable minimisation problems. Let D be a finite set. Let $f : D^k \to D$ be a function, and let $\mathbf{x}_1, \ldots, \mathbf{x}_k \in D^n$, with components $\mathbf{x}_i = (x_{i1}, \ldots, x_{in})$. Then, we let $f(\mathbf{x}_1, \ldots, \mathbf{x}_k)$ denote the n-tuple $(f(x_{11}, \ldots, x_{k1}), \ldots, f(x_{1n}, \ldots, x_{kn}))$. A (binary) *multimorphism* [2] of Γ is a pair of functions $f, g : D^2 \to D$ such that for any n-ary $h \in \Gamma$, and tuples $\mathbf{x}, \mathbf{y} \in D^n$, $h(f(\mathbf{x}, \mathbf{y})) + h(g(\mathbf{x}, \mathbf{y})) \leq h(\mathbf{x}) + h(\mathbf{y})$.

Definition 4 (Multimorphism Function Minimisation). *Let X be a finite set of triples* $(D_i; f_i, g_i)$*, where D_i is a finite set and f_i, g_i are functions mapping D_i^2 to D_i. MFM(X) is a minimisation problem with*

Instance: *A positive integer n, a function* $j : \{1, \ldots, n\} \to \{1, \ldots, |X|\}$*, and a function* $h : D \to \mathbb{Z}$ *where* $D = \prod_{i=1}^{n} D_{j(i)}$*. Furthermore,*

$$h(\mathbf{x}) + h(\mathbf{y}) \geq h(f_{j(1)}(x_1, y_1), f_{j(2)}(x_2, y_2), \ldots, f_{j(n)}(x_n, y_n)) +$$
$$h(g_{j(1)}(x_1, y_1), g_{j(2)}(x_2, y_2), \ldots, g_{j(n)}(x_n, y_n))$$

for all $\mathbf{x}, \mathbf{y} \in D$*. The function h is given to the algorithm as an oracle, i.e., for any* $\mathbf{x} \in D$ *we can query the oracle to obtain $h(\mathbf{x})$ in unit time.*
Solution: *A tuple* $\mathbf{x} \in D$*.*
Measure: *The value of $h(\mathbf{x})$.*

For a finite set X we say that MFM(X) is *oracle-tractable* if it can be solved in time $O(n^c)$ for some constant c. It is easy to see that when (f, g) is a multimorphism of Γ, and MFM$(D; f, g)$ is oracle-tractable, then MIN CSP(Γ) is tractable. However, MFM is more general than the problem of minimising a function with a specific multimorphism; each coordinate may have its own domain and its own pair of functions.

We now give two examples of oracle-tractable problems. A partial order on D is called a *lattice* if every pair of elements $a, b \in D$ has a greatest lower bound $a \wedge b$ (meet) and a least upper bound $a \vee b$ (join). A *chain* on D is a lattice which is also a total order. For $i = 1, \ldots, n$, let L_i be a lattice on D_i. The *product lattice* $L_1 \times \cdots \times L_n$ is defined on the set $D_1 \times \cdots \times D_n$ by extending the meet and join component-wise. A function $f : D^k \to \mathbb{Z}$ is called *submodular* on the lattice $L = (D; \wedge, \vee)$ if $f(\mathbf{a} \wedge \mathbf{b}) + f(\mathbf{a} \vee \mathbf{b}) \leq f(\mathbf{a}) + f(\mathbf{b})$ for all $\mathbf{a}, \mathbf{b} \in D^k$. A set of functions Γ is submodular on L if every function in Γ is submodular on L. This is equivalent to $(\wedge, \vee)$ being a multimorphism of Γ. It follows from known algorithms for submodular function minimisation that MFM(X) is oracle-tractable for any finite set X of finite *distributive lattices* (e.g. chains) [6,15].

The second example is strongly related to submodularity, but here we use a partial order that is not a lattice to define the multimorphism. Let $D = \{0, 1, 2\}$, and define the functions $u, v : D^2 \to D$ by letting $u(x, y) = \min\{x, y\}$, $v(x, y) = \max\{x, y\}$ if $\{x, y\} \neq \{1, 2\}$, and $u(x, y) = v(x, y) = 0$ otherwise. A function $h : D^k \to \mathbb{Z}$ is *bisubmodular* if h has the multimorphism (u, v). The main result of [12] implies that MFM($\{D; u, v\}$) is oracle-tractable.

3   A New Tractable Class

In this section, we introduce a new class of multimorphisms which ensures tractability for MIN CSP (and more generally for VCSP).

Definition 5. *Let b and c be two distinct elements in D. Let $(D; <)$ be a partial order which relates all pairs of elements except for b and c. Assume that $f, g : D^2 \to D$ are two commutative functions satisfying the following conditions:*

- *If $\{x, y\} \neq \{b, c\}$, then $f(x, y) = x \wedge y$ and $g(x, y) = x \vee y$.*
- *If $\{x, y\} = \{b, c\}$, then $\{f(x, y), g(x, y)\} \cap \{x, y\} = \varnothing$, and $f(x, y) < g(x, y)$.*

We call $(D; f, g)$ a 1-defect chain (over $(D; <)$), and say that $\{b, c\}$ is the defect of $(D; f, g)$. If a function has the multimorphism (f, g), then we also say that (f, g) is a 1-defect chain multimorphism.

Three types of 1-defect chains are shown in Fig. 1(a–c). Note this is not an exhaustive list, e.g. for $|D| > 4$, there are 1-defect chains similar to Fig. 1(b), but with $f(b, c) < g(b, c) < b, c$. When $|D| = 4$, type (b) is precisely the product lattice shown in Fig. 1(d). We denote this lattice by L_{ad}.

Example 6. Let $D = \{a, b, c, d\}$, and assume that $(D; f, g)$ is a 1-defect chain, with defect $\{b, c\}$, and that $a = f(b, c), d = g(b, c)$. If $a < b, c < d$, then f and g are the meet and join of L_{ad}, cf. Fig. 1(d). When $a < d < b, c$ we have the situation in Fig. 1(a), and when $b, c < a < d$ we have the situation in Fig. 1(c).

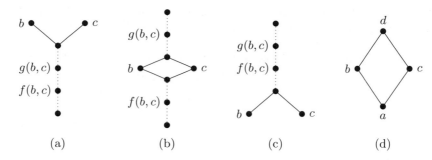

Fig. 1. Three types of 1-defect multimorphisms with defect $\{b, c\}$. (a) $f(b, c) < g(b, c) < b, c$. (b) $f(b, c) < b, c < g(b, c)$. (c) $b, c < f(b, c) < g(b, c)$. (d) The Hasse diagram of the lattice L_{ad}, a special case of (b).

In the two latter cases, f and g are given by the two following multimorphisms (rows and columns are listed in the order a, b, c, d, e.g. $g_1(c, d) = c$):

$$f_1 : \begin{array}{cccc} a & a & a & a \\ a & b & a & d \\ a & a & c & d \\ a & d & d & d \end{array} \qquad g_1 : \begin{array}{cccc} a & b & c & d \\ b & b & d & b \\ c & d & c & c \\ d & b & c & d \end{array} \qquad f_2 : \begin{array}{cccc} a & b & c & a \\ b & b & a & b \\ c & a & c & c \\ a & b & c & d \end{array} \qquad g_2 : \begin{array}{cccc} a & a & a & d \\ a & b & d & d \\ a & d & c & d \\ d & d & d & d \end{array}$$

The proof of tractability for languages with 1-defect chain multimorphisms is inspired by Krokhin and Larose's [10] result on maximising supermodular functions on Mal'tsev products of lattices. First we will need some notation and a general lemma on oracle-tractability of MFM problems.

For an equivalence relation θ on D we use $x[\theta]$ to denote the equivalence class containing $x \in D$. The relation θ is a *congruence* on $(D; f, g)$, if $f(x_1, y_1)[\theta] = f(x_2, y_2)[\theta]$ and $g(x_1, y_1)[\theta] = g(x_2, y_2)[\theta]$ whenever $x_1[\theta] = x_2[\theta]$ and $y_1[\theta] = y_2[\theta]$. We use D/θ to denote the set $\{x[\theta] \mid x \in D\}$ and $f/\theta : (D/\theta)^2 \to D/\theta$ to denote the function $(x[\theta], y[\theta]) \mapsto f(x, y)[\theta]$.

Lemma 7. *Let f, g be two functions that map D^2 to D. If there is a congruence relation θ on $(D; f, g)$ such that 1) $MFM(D/\theta; f/\theta, g/\theta)$ is oracle-tractable; and 2) $MFM(\{(X; f|_X, g|_X) \mid X \in D/\theta\})$ is oracle-tractable, then $MFM(D; f, g)$ is oracle-tractable.*

Proof. Let $h : D^n \to \mathbb{Z}$ be the function we want to minimise. We define a new function $h' : (D/\theta)^n \to \mathbb{Z}$ by

$$h'(z_1, z_2, \ldots, z_n) = \min_{x_i \in z_i} h(x_1, x_2, \ldots, x_n).$$

It is clear that $\min_{\mathbf{z} \in (D/\theta)^n} h'(\mathbf{z}) = \min_{\mathbf{x} \in D^n} h(\mathbf{x})$. By assumption 2 in the statement of the lemma we can compute h' in polynomial time given $z_1, z_2, \ldots, z_n$. To simplify the notation we let $u = f/\theta$ and $v = g/\theta$. We will now prove that h' is an instance of $MFM(D/\theta; u, v)$.

Let $\mathbf{x}, \mathbf{y} \in D^k$ and choose $x_i' \in x_i[\theta]$ and $y_i' \in y_i[\theta]$ so that $h'(\mathbf{x}[\theta]) = h(\mathbf{x}')$ and $h'(\mathbf{y}[\theta]) = h(\mathbf{y}')$. We then have

$$h'(\mathbf{x}[\theta]) + h'(\mathbf{y}[\theta]) = h(\mathbf{x}') + h(\mathbf{y}') \tag{1}$$
$$\geq h(f(\mathbf{x}', \mathbf{y}')) + h(g(\mathbf{x}', \mathbf{y}')) \tag{2}$$
$$\geq h'(f(\mathbf{x}', \mathbf{y}')[\theta]) + h'(g(\mathbf{x}', \mathbf{y}')[\theta]) \tag{3}$$
$$= h'(f(\mathbf{x}, \mathbf{y})[\theta]) + h'(g(\mathbf{x}, \mathbf{y})[\theta])) \tag{4}$$
$$= h'(u(\mathbf{x}[\theta], \mathbf{y}[\theta])) + h'(v(\mathbf{x}[\theta], \mathbf{y}[\theta])). \tag{5}$$

Here (1) follows from our choice of $\mathbf{x}'$ and $\mathbf{y}'$, (2) follows from the fact that h is an instance of $\mathrm{MFM}(D; f, g)$, (3) follows from the definition of h', and finally (4) and (5) follows as θ is a congruence relation of f and g. Hence, h' is an instance of $\mathrm{MFM}(D/\theta; u, v)$ and can be minimised in polynomial time by the first assumption in the lemma. $\qquad\square$

Armed with this lemma and the oracle-tractability of submodular and bisubmodular functions described in the previous section, we can now present a new tractable class of MIN CSP-problems.

Proposition 8. *If Γ has a 1-defect chain multimorphism, then* MIN CSP(Γ) *is tractable.*

Proof. Assume that Γ has a 1-defect chain multimorphism (f, g) over $(D; <)$ with defect $\{b, c\}$. We prove that $\mathrm{MFM}(D; f, g)$ is oracle-tractable.

Assume that b and c are maximal elements, i.e. $x < b, c$ for all $x \in D \setminus \{b, c\}$. In this case the equivalence relation θ with classes $A = D \setminus \{b, c\}$, $B = \{b\}$, $C = \{c\}$ is a congruence relation of $(D; f, g)$. Furthermore, $\mathrm{MFM}(\{A, B, C\}; f/\theta, g/\theta)$ and $\mathrm{MFM}(A; f|_A, g|_A)$ are oracle-tractable [12,15]. It now follows from Lemma 7 that $\mathrm{MFM}(D; f, g)$ is oracle-tractable. The same argument works for the case when b and c are minimal elements.

If $f(b, c) < g(b, c) < b, c$, but b and c are not maximal, then we can use the congruence relation θ' with classes $A = \{x \mid x \leq b \text{ or } x \leq c\}$ and $B = D \setminus A$. Here, $(\{A, B\}; f/\theta', g/\theta')$ and $(B; f|_B, g|_B)$ are chains, and $(A; f|_A, g|_A)$ is a 1-defect chain of the previous type. One can show that when $\mathrm{MFM}(X)$ and $\mathrm{MFM}(Y)$ are both oracle-tractable, then so is $\mathrm{MFM}(X \cup Y)$. Combining this with the technique used above, we can now solve the minimisation problem. An analoguous construction works in the case when $b, c < f(b, c), g(b, c)$, using the congruence consisting of the class $\{x \mid x \geq b \text{ or } x \geq c\}$ and its complement. Finally, when $f(b, c) < b, c < g(b, c)$, we can use the congruence relation θ'' with classes $B = \{x \mid x \leq b\}$ and $C = \{x \mid x \geq c\}$. Here, $(\{B, C\}, f/\theta'', g/\theta'')$, $(B, f|_B, g|_B)$, and $(C, f|_C, g|_C)$ are all chains and thus the MFM problem for these triples is oracle-tractable [15]. $\qquad\square$

We now turn to prove a different property of functions with 1-defect chain multimorphisms. It is based on the following result for submodular functions on chains, which was derived by Queyranne et al. [13].

Lemma 9. *A function $f : D^k \to \mathbb{Z}$ is submodular on a chain $(D; \wedge, \vee)$ if and only if the following holds: every binary function obtained from f by replacing any given $k - 2$ variables by any constants is submodular on this chain.*

It is straightforward to extend this lemma to products of chains, such as L_{ad}. Here, we outline the proof of the corresponding property for arbitrary 1-defect chains, which will be needed in Section 6.

Lemma 10. *A function $h : D^k \to \mathbb{Z}$, $k \geq 2$, has the 1-defect chain multimorphism (f, g) if and only if every binary function obtained from h by replacing any given $k - 2$ variables by any constants has the multimorphism (f, g).*

Proof (sketch): Every function obtained from h by fixing a number of variables is clearly invariant under every 1-defect chain multimorphism of h. For the opposite direction, assume that h does not have the multimorphism (f, g). We want to prove that there exist vectors $\mathbf{x}, \mathbf{y} \in D^k$ such that

$$h(\mathbf{x}) + h(\mathbf{y}) < h(f(\mathbf{x}, \mathbf{y})) + h(g(\mathbf{x}, \mathbf{y})), \tag{6}$$

with $d_H(\mathbf{x}, \mathbf{y}) = 2$, where d_H denotes the *Hamming distance* on D^k, i.e. the number of coordinates in which $\mathbf{x}$ and $\mathbf{y}$ differ.

Assume to the contrary that the result does not hold. We can then choose a function h of minimal arity such that $\min\{ d_H(\mathbf{x}, \mathbf{y}) \mid \mathbf{x}$ and $\mathbf{y}$ satisfy (6) $\} > 2$. The arity of h must in fact be equal to the least $d_H(\mathbf{x}, \mathbf{y})$. Otherwise, we could obtain a function h' of strictly smaller arity by fixing the variables in h on which $\mathbf{x}$ and $\mathbf{y}$ agree. This would contradict the minimality in the choice of h.

This means that for any vectors which share an element in some coordinate, the reverse (non-strict) inequality holds in (6). It is possible to combine such inequalities to prove that there are $\mathbf{x}$ and $\mathbf{y}$, with $d_H(\mathbf{x}, \mathbf{y}) = k$, and satisfying (6), such that $\{x_i, y_i\} \neq \{b, c\}$ for all i, where $\{b, c\}$ is the defect of (f, g).

Let $D' = D \setminus \{b, c\} \cup \{B\}$. For each i, let $\varphi_i : D' \to D$ be an injection which fixes $D \setminus \{b, c\}$, and sends B to b or c in such a way that $\{x_i, y_i\} \subseteq \varphi_i(D)$. Let $(D'; f', g')$ be the chain defined by $x <' y$ if $x, y \neq B$ and $x < y$, $x <' B$ if $x < b, c$, and $B <' y$ if $b, c < y$. Then, $\varphi_i(f'(x, y)) = f(\varphi_i(x), \varphi_i(y))$, and $\varphi_i(g'(x, y)) = g(\varphi_i(x), \varphi_i(y))$, for all i. Let $\varphi(\mathbf{z}) = (\varphi_1(z_1), \ldots, \varphi_k(z_k))$, and let $\mathbf{x}', \mathbf{y}' \in (D')^k$ be such that $\varphi(\mathbf{x}') = \mathbf{x}$ and $\varphi(\mathbf{y}') = \mathbf{y}$. Define $h'(\mathbf{z}') = h(\varphi(\mathbf{z}'))$. Then, $h'(\mathbf{x}') + h'(\mathbf{y}') = h(\mathbf{x}) + h(\mathbf{y}) < h(f(\mathbf{x}, \mathbf{y})) + h(g(\mathbf{x}, \mathbf{y})) = h'(f'(\mathbf{x}', \mathbf{y}')) + h'(g'(\mathbf{x}', \mathbf{y}'))$. It follows that h' is not submodular on (D', f', g'). By Lemma 9, there are elements $\mathbf{z}', \mathbf{w}' \in (D')^k$ with $d_H(\mathbf{z}', \mathbf{w}') = 2$ such that $h'(\mathbf{z}') + h'(\mathbf{w}') < h'(f'(\mathbf{z}', \mathbf{w}')) + h'(g'(\mathbf{z}', \mathbf{w}'))$. Hence, $h(\varphi(\mathbf{z}')) + h(\varphi(\mathbf{w}')) = h'(\mathbf{z}') + h'(\mathbf{w}') < h'(f'(\mathbf{z}', \mathbf{w}')) + h'(g'(\mathbf{z}', \mathbf{w}')) = h(f(\varphi(\mathbf{z}'), \varphi(\mathbf{w}'))) + h(g(\varphi(\mathbf{z}'), \varphi(\mathbf{w}')))$, and we have $d_H(\varphi(\mathbf{z}'), \varphi(\mathbf{w}')) = 2$. This contradicts the original choice of h.   □

4   Endomorphisms, Cores and Constants

In this section, we show that under a natural condition, it is possible to add constant unary relations to Γ without changing the computational complexity of the corresponding MIN CSP-problem. Let $h : D^k \rightarrow \{0,1\}$. A function $g : D \rightarrow D$ is called an *endomorphism* of h if for every k-tuple $(x_1, \ldots, x_k) \in D^k$, it holds that $h(x_1, \ldots, x_k) = 0 \implies h(g(x_1), \ldots, g(x_k)) = 0$. The function g is an endomorphism of Γ if it is an endomorphism of each function in Γ. A set of functions, Γ, is said to be a *core* if all of its endomorphisms are injective. The idea is that if Γ is not a core, then we can apply a non-injective endomorphism to every function in Γ, and obtain a polynomial-time equivalent problem on a strictly smaller domain. We can then use results previously obtained for smaller domains [2,8]. Thus, we can restrict our attention to the case when Γ is a core.

The set of all endomorphisms of Γ is denoted by $\text{End}(\Gamma)$. Recall that a bijective endomorphism is called an *automorphism* and that the automorphisms of Γ form a group under composition.

Jeavons et al. [7] defined the notion of an *indicator problem of order k* for CSPs. We will exploit indicator problems of order 1 here, adapted to the setting of MIN CSP. Let Γ be a finite set of $\{0,1\}$-valued functions over D. Let X_D denote the set containing a variable x_d for each $d \in D$, and for $\mathbf{a} = (a_1, \ldots, a_k) \in D^k$, let $\mathbf{x_a} = (x_{a_1}, \ldots x_{a_k}) \in X_D^k$. The indicator problem $\mathcal{IP}(\Gamma)$ is defined as the instance of MIN CSP(Γ) with variables X_D, and sum $\sum_{f_i \in \Gamma} \sum_{\mathbf{a} \in f_i^{-1}(0)} f_i(\mathbf{x_a})$, where k_i is the arity of the function f_i.

Let $\mathcal{C}_D = \{\{d\} \mid d \in D\}$ be the set of constant unary relations over D. The proof of the following result follows the lines of similar results for related problems, such as the CSP decision problem.

Proposition 11. *Let Γ be a core over D. Then, MIN CSP$(\Gamma, \mathcal{C}_D)$ is polynomial-time reducible to MIN CSP(Γ).*

Proof. Let $\iota : D \rightarrow X_D$ be the function defined by $\iota(d) = x_d$. Theorem 3.5 in [7] implies the following property of $\mathcal{IP}(\Gamma)$: the set of optimal solutions to $\mathcal{IP}(\Gamma)$ is equal to $\{\sigma : X_D \rightarrow D \mid \sigma \circ \iota \in \text{End}(\Gamma)\}$.

Let $\mathcal{J}$ be an instance of MIN CSP$(\Gamma, \mathcal{C}_D)$. The only way for $\mathcal{J}$ to be unsatisfiable is if it contains two contradicting constraint applications $(y; \{a\})$ and $(y; \{b\})$, with $a \neq b$. This is easily checked in polynomial time.

Otherwise, let $\mathbf{x}$ be a list of the variables X_D, and let $R = \pi_{\mathbf{x}}\text{Optsol}(\mathcal{IP}(\Gamma))$. Now modify $\mathcal{J}$ to an instance $\mathcal{J}'$ of MIN CSP(Γ, R) as follows. Add the variables in X_D to $V(\mathcal{J}')$, and add the constraint application $(\mathbf{x}; R)$. Furthermore, remove each constraint $(y; \{a\})$, and replace y by x_a throughout the instance. Let σ' be an optimal solution to $\mathcal{J}'$. Since Γ is a core, $g = \sigma'|_{X_D} \circ \iota$ is an automorphism of Γ, and so is its inverse, g^{-1}. Hence, $\sigma = g^{-1} \circ \sigma'$ is also an optimal solution to $\mathcal{J}'$. From σ we easily recover a solution to $\mathcal{J}$ of equal measure, and conversely, any solution to $\mathcal{J}$ can be interpreted as a solution to $\mathcal{J}'$. It follows that we have a reduction from MIN CSP$(\Gamma, \mathcal{C}_D)$ to MIN CSP(Γ, R). By Proposition 3, we finally have a reduction from MIN CSP(Γ, R) to MIN CSP(Γ). $\square$

For $a, b \in D$, let $e_{ab} : D \rightarrow D$ denote the function $e_{ab}(a) = b$ and $e_{ab}(x) = x$ for $x \neq a$. The proof of the following lemma is straightforward.

Lemma 12. *If $e_{ab} \notin \mathrm{End}\,(\Gamma)$, then $\langle \Gamma, \mathcal{C}_D \rangle_{fn}$ contains a unary $\{0,1\}$-valued function u such that $u(a) = 0$ and $u(b) = 1$.*

5   A Graph of Partial Multimorphisms

Let Γ be a core over D. In this section, we define a graph $G = (V, E)$ which encodes either the **NP**-hardness of MIN CSP$(\Gamma, \mathcal{C}_D)$ or provides a multimorphism for the binary functions in $\langle \Gamma, \mathcal{C}_D \rangle_{fn}$. The graph is a variation of a graph defined by Kolmogorov and Živný [9].

Let V be the set of partial functions $(f, g) : D^2 \to D^2$ such that (1) f and g are defined on a subset $\{a, b\} \subseteq D$; (2) f and g are idempotent and commutative; and (3) $\{f(a,b), g(a,b)\} = \{a, b\}$ or $\{f(a,b), g(a,b)\} \cap \{a, b\} = \varnothing$. We allow $a = b$ in the definition of V so there is precisely one vertex for each singleton in D. For $a, b \in D$, we let $G[a, b]$ denote the graph induced by the set of vertices defined on $\{a, b\}$. Let $(f_1, g_1) \in G[a_1, b_1]$ and $(f_2, g_2) \in G[a_2, b_2]$. There is an edge in E between (f_1, g_1) and (f_2, g_2) if there is a binary function $h \in \langle \Gamma, \mathcal{C}_D \rangle_{fn}$ such that

$$\min\{h(a_1, a_2) + h(b_1, b_2), h(a_1, b_2) + h(b_1, a_2)\} <$$
$$h(f_1(a_1, b_1), f_2(a_2, b_2)) + h(g_1(a_1, b_1), g_2(a_2, b_2)). \quad (7)$$

We can now see how G describes multimorphisms of binary functions in $\langle \Gamma, \mathcal{C}_D \rangle_{fn}$.

Lemma 13. *Let $I \subseteq V$ be an independent set in G with precisely one vertex $(f_{\{x,y\}}, g_{\{x,y\}})$ from each subgraph $G[x, y]$. Then, every binary function $h \in \langle \Gamma, \mathcal{C}_D \rangle_{fn}$ has the multimorphism (f, g) defined by $f(x, y) = f_{\{x,y\}}(x, y)$ and $g(x, y) = g_{\{x,y\}}(x, y)$.*

Proof. Assume to the contrary that (f, g) is not a multimorphism of h. Then, there are tuples $(a_1, a_2), (b_1, b_2) \in D^2$ such that

$$h(a_1, a_2) + h(b_1, b_2) < h(f(a_1, b_1), f(a_2, b_2)) + h(g(a_1, b_1), g(a_2, b_2)).$$

But this would imply that $\{(f_{\{a_1,b_1\}}, g_{\{a_1,b_1\}}), (f_{\{a_2,b_2\}}, g_{\{a_2,b_2\}})\} \in E$, which is a contradiction since I is an independent set.   □

For distinct $a, b \in D$, let $\overrightarrow{ab}$ denote the vertex $(f, g) \in G[a, b]$ such that $f(a, b) = a$ and $g(a, b) = b$. We say that such a vertex is *conservative*. Let V' denote the set of all conservative vertices, and let $G' = G[V']$ be the subgraph of G induced by V'. Let $V'_\Gamma \subseteq V'$ be the set of vertices $\overrightarrow{xy}$ such that $\{x, y\} \in \langle \Gamma, \mathcal{C}_D \rangle_w$. For conservative vertices $\overrightarrow{a_1 b_1}$ and $\overrightarrow{a_2 b_2}$, condition (7) reduces to:

$$h(a_1, b_2) + h(b_1, a_2) < h(a_1, a_2) + h(b_1, b_2). \quad (8)$$

For a vertex $x = (f, g)$, we let $\overline{x}$ denote the vertex (g, f). It follows immediately from (7) that $\{x, y\} \in E$ iff $\{\overline{x}, \overline{y}\} \in E$. We also need to establish a number of additional properties of the graph G.

Lemma 14. *If $\{\overrightarrow{a_1b_1}, \overrightarrow{a_2b_2}\} \in E$, then there exists a function $h \in \langle \Gamma, \mathcal{C}_D \rangle_{fn}$ such that $h(a_1, b_2) = h(b_1, a_2) < h(a_1, a_2) = h(b_1, b_2)$.*

The proof of Lemma 14, and of properties (1–3) of the following lemma are very similar to the proof of Lemma 11 in Kolmogorov and Živný [9]. The main difference is that we do not have access to all unary functions, so we must be a bit more careful. Property (4) provides a way to deduce the existence of a set of neighbours for non-isolated conservative vertices; (5) and (6) follow from (4).

Lemma 15. *Let $x_1, \ldots, x_n$ be conservative vertices.*

1. *If $\{x_1, x_2\}, \{x_2, x_3\} \in E$ and $x_2 \in V'_\Gamma$, then $\{x_1, \overline{x_3}\} \in E$.*
2. *Let $(x_1, \ldots, x_n), n \geq 2$, be a path in G, with $x_2, \ldots, x_{n-1} \in V'_\Gamma$. If n is even, then $\{x_1, x_n\} \in E$, otherwise $\{x_1, \overline{x_n}\} \in E$.*
3. *If $(x_1, \ldots, x_n, x_1)$, $n \geq 3$ is an odd cycle in G and $x_2, \ldots, x_n \in V'_\Gamma$, then there is a loop on x_1.*
4. *If $\{\overrightarrow{a_1b_1}, \overrightarrow{a_2b_2}\} \in E$, then for each element $x \neq a_2, b_2$, either $\{\overrightarrow{a_1b_1}, \overrightarrow{a_2x}\} \in E$ or $\{\overrightarrow{a_1b_1}, \overrightarrow{xb_2}\} \in E$.*
5. *If $\{\overrightarrow{xy}, \overrightarrow{yx}\}, \{\overrightarrow{yz}, \overrightarrow{zy}\} \in E$ and $\{\overrightarrow{xy}, \overrightarrow{yz}\} \notin E$, then $\{\overrightarrow{xy}, \overrightarrow{zx}\}, \{\overrightarrow{yz}, \overrightarrow{zx}\} \in E$.*
6. *If there is a loop on $\overrightarrow{xz}$, but $\overrightarrow{xy}$ and $\overrightarrow{yz}$ are loop-free, then $\{\overrightarrow{xy}, \overrightarrow{yz}\} \in E$.*

6   Classification for $|D| = 4$

We will now completely classify the complexity of MIN CSP over a four-element domain. From here on, we assume that D is the domain $\{a, b, c, d\}$. First, we prove a result which describes the structure of the unary functions in $\langle \Gamma, \mathcal{C} \rangle_{fn}$, when Γ is a core. Let $\Sigma = \{\{x, y\} \subseteq D \mid x \neq y\}$, $\Sigma_0 = \Sigma \setminus \{\{b, c\}, \{a, d\}\}$, and let $\Sigma_\Gamma = \langle \Gamma, \mathcal{C}_D \rangle_w \cap \Sigma$. For distinct $x, y \in D$, let $u_{xy}(z) = 0$ if $z \in \{x, y\}$, and $u_{xy}(z) = 1$ otherwise.

Proposition 16. *Let Γ be a core over $\{a, b, c, d\}$ and assume that $\{b, c\} \notin \Sigma_\Gamma$. Then, $\Sigma_0 \subseteq \Sigma_\Gamma$ and for all unary functions $u \in \langle \Gamma, \mathcal{C}_D \rangle_{fn}$, we have $u(a) + u(d) \leq u(b) + u(c)$. If $\Sigma_0 = \Sigma_\Gamma$, then $u(a) + u(d) = u(b) + u(c)$.*

Proof (sketch): Let $\mathcal{U}$ be the set of unary functions in $\langle \Gamma, \mathcal{C}_D \rangle_{fn}$. If $\{b, c\} \notin \Sigma_\Gamma$, then $u_{bc} \notin \mathcal{U}$. Since Γ is a core, $e_{ba}, e_{ca}, e_{bd}, e_{cd} \notin \text{End}(\Gamma)$, so by Lemma 12, there must be a number of unary $\{0, 1\}$-valued functions in $\mathcal{U}$ to witness this. The set $\{u_{bd}, u_{cd}, u_{ab}, u_{ac}\}$ fulfils this condition, and due to the absence of u_{bc}, one can argue that this set must indeed lie entirely in $\mathcal{U}$. The last part of the proposition can be shown using the observation that this set can express every unary function u such that $u(a) + u(d) = u(b) + u(c)$, and considering what happens when one adds a function v with $v(a) + v(d) < v(b) + v(c)$.   □

We can link properties of G' to the existence of certain multimorphisms. Note that if $\{x, y\} \in \Sigma_\Gamma$, then $\overrightarrow{xy}, \overrightarrow{yx} \in V'_\Gamma$. Proposition 16 therefore gives us good control over the size of V'_Γ. In general $G[V'_\Gamma]$ needs to be bipartite unless MIN CSP(Γ) is **NP**-hard (cf. the proof of Theorem 18), so a lower bound on Σ implies that a large induced subgraph of G' needs to be bipartite. This connection is made formal by the following proposition, the proof of which is deferred to Appendix A. We are then ready to state and prove the main theorem.

Proposition 17. *Assume $\Sigma_0 \subseteq \Sigma_\Gamma$. If G' is bipartite, then the set of binary functions in $\langle \Gamma, \mathcal{C}_D \rangle_{fn}$ is submodular on a chain. Otherwise, if $G[V'_\Gamma]$ is bipartite, then the set of binary functions in $\langle \Gamma, \mathcal{C}_D \rangle_{fn}$ has a 1-defect chain multimorphism.*

Theorem 18. *Let Γ be a core over $D = \{a, b, c, d\}$. If Γ is submodular on a chain, or if Γ has a 1-defect chain multimorphism, then $\mathrm{MIN}\ \mathrm{CSP}(\Gamma)$ is tractable. Otherwise, it is NP-hard.*

Proof. Assume that $G[V'_\Gamma]$ has a loop on a vertex $\overrightarrow{xy}$. It then follows from Lemma 14 that there is a function $h \in \langle \Gamma, \mathcal{C}_D \rangle_{fn}$ such that $h(x, y) = h(y, x) < h(x, x) = h(y, y)$, and $\{x, y\} \in \langle \Gamma, \mathcal{C}_D \rangle_w$. By Proposition 5.1 in [2], the problem $\mathrm{MIN}\ \mathrm{CSP}(\Gamma, \mathcal{C}_D)$ is NP-hard. By Proposition 11, $\mathrm{MIN}\ \mathrm{CSP}(\Gamma, \mathcal{C}_D)$ reduces to $\mathrm{MIN}\ \mathrm{CSP}(\Gamma)$. Hence, the latter problem is NP-hard as well.

If instead $G[V'_\Gamma]$ is loop-free, then it is bipartite, by Lemma 15(3). We may assume that $\Sigma_0 \subseteq \Sigma_\Gamma$: this is trivial if $\Sigma_\Gamma = \Sigma$. If Σ_Γ is strictly contained in Σ, then up to an automorphism we may assume that $\{b, c\} \notin \Sigma_\Gamma$, and the inclusion follows by Proposition 16. For a k-ary function $h \in \Gamma$, let $\Phi(h)$ be the set of binary functions which can be obtained from h by fixing $k - 2$ variables, and let Γ' be the union of $\Phi(h)$ over all $h \in \Gamma$.

Now, if G' is bipartite, then by Proposition 17, the set of binary functions in $\langle \Gamma, \mathcal{C}_D \rangle_{fn}$ is submodular on a chain. Since this set contains Γ', we may conclude, by Lemma 9, that Γ is submodular on this chain as well. It follows that $\mathrm{MIN}\ \mathrm{CSP}(\Gamma)$ is tractable [15].

Otherwise, G' is not bipartite, and by Proposition 17, the set of binary functions in $\langle \Gamma, \mathcal{C}_D \rangle_{fn}$ have a 1-defect chain multimorphism. Since this set contains Γ', we may conclude, by Lemma 10 this time, that Γ has a 1-defect chain multimorphism. It now follows from Proposition 8 that $\mathrm{MIN}\ \mathrm{CSP}(\Gamma)$ is tractable. □

7 Discussion

We have presented a complete complexity classification for $\mathrm{MIN}\ \mathrm{CSP}$ over a four-element domain. More importantly, we have compiled a powerful set of tools which will allow further systematic study of this problem. In particular, we have shown that it is possible to add (crisp) constants to an arbitrary core, without changing the complexity of the problem. This result holds in the more general case of finite-valued VCSP as well, thus answering Question 4 in Živný [17]. We have also demonstrated that the techniques used by Krokhin and Larose [10] for lattices can be used effectively in the context of arbitrary algebras, and in doing so, we have given the first example of an instance of $\mathrm{MIN}\ \mathrm{CSP}$ where submodularity does not suffice to explain tractability. Finally, we have shown that graph representations such as the one defined by Kolmogorov and Živný [9] can be used to great effect, even in a non-conservative setting.

The curious readers may ask themselves several questions at this point, and the following one is particularly important: do 1-defect chain multimorphisms define genuinely new tractable classes? There is still a possibility that the tractability can be explained in terms of submodularity. We answer this question negatively with the following example.

Example 19. Consider the language $\Gamma = \{u_{bd}, u_{cd}, u_{ab}, u_{ac}, h\}$ where $h : D^2 \rightarrow \{0,1\}$ is defined such that $h(x,y) = 1$ if and only if $x = c$ or $y = b$. Γ is a core on $\{a,b,c,d\}$ but it is not submodular on any lattice. However, Γ has the 1-defect chain multimorphisms (f_1, g_1) and (f_2, g_2) from Example 6.

A related question is why bisubmodularity does not appear in the classification of MIN CSP over domains of size three [8]. The reason is that for any cost function $h : \{0,1,2\}^k \rightarrow \{0,1\}$ which is bisubmodular, the tuple $(0,0,\ldots,0)$ minimises h. It follows that any $\{0,1\}$ constraint language over three elements which is bisubmodular is not a core.

There are several ways of extending this work, and one obvious way is to study VCSP instead of MIN CSP. It is known that the *fractional polymorphisms* of the constraint language, introduced by Cohen et al. [1], characterise the complexity of this problem (see also [3]). Multimorphisms are a special case of fractional polymorphisms. As for MIN CSP, it is currently not known whether submodularity over every finite lattice implies tractability for VCSP. This is known to be true for distributive lattices, and for certain constructions on lattices, e.g. homomorphic images and Mal'tsev products [10]. The five element modular non-distributive lattice (also known as the diamond) implies tractability for *unweighted* VCSP [11]. Finally, it is known that submodularity over finite modular lattices implies containment in **NP ∩ coNP** [11]. It is thus clear that in order to approach further classification of either MIN CSP or VCSP, it will be necessary to study the complexity of minimising submodular cost functions over new finite lattices.

References

1. Cohen, D., Cooper, M., Jeavons, P.: An algebraic characterisation of complexity for valued constraint. In: Benhamou, F. (ed.) CP 2006. LNCS, vol. 4204, pp. 107–121. Springer, Heidelberg (2006)
2. Cohen, D., Cooper, M., Jeavons, P., Krokhin, A.: The complexity of soft constraint satisfaction. Artif. Intell. 170(11), 983–1016 (2006)
3. Cohen, D., Creed, P., Jeavons, P., Živný, S.: An algebraic theory of complexity for valued constraints: Establishing a Galois connection. In: Murlak, F., Sankowski, P. (eds.) MFCS 2011. LNCS, vol. 6907, pp. 231–242. Springer, Heidelberg (to appear, 2011)
4. Creignou, N., Kolaitis, P.G., Vollmer, H. (eds.): Complexity of Constraints. LNCS, vol. 5250. Springer, Heidelberg (2008)
5. Deineko, V., Jonsson, P., Klasson, M., Krokhin, A.: The approximability of MAX CSP with fixed-value constraints. J. ACM 55(4), 1–37 (2008)
6. Iwata, S., Fleischer, L., Fujishige, S.: A combinatorial strongly polynomial algorithm for minimizing submodular functions. J. ACM 48(4), 761–777 (2001)

7. Jeavons, P., Cohen, D., Gyssens, M.: How to determine the expressive power of constraints. Constraints 4(2), 113–131 (1999)
8. Jonsson, P., Klasson, M., Krokhin, A.: The approximability of three-valued MAX CSP. SIAM J. Comput. 35(6), 1329–1349 (2006)
9. Kolmogorov, V., Živný, S.: The complexity of conservative finite-valued CSPs. CoRR, abs/1008.1555 (2010)
10. Krokhin, A., Larose, B.: Maximizing supermodular functions on product lattices, with application to maximum constraint satisfaction. SIAM J. Discrete Math. 22(1), 312–328 (2008)
11. Kuivinen, F.: Algorithms and Hardness Results for Some Valued CSPs. PhD thesis, Linköping University (2009)
12. McCormick, S.T., Fujishige, S.: Strongly polynomial and fully combinatorial algorithms for bisubmodular function minimization. Math. Program. 122(1), 87–120 (2010)
13. Queyranne, M., Spieksma, F., Tardella, F.: A general class of greedily solvable linear programs. Math. Oper. Res. 23(4), 892–908 (1998)
14. Raghavendra, P.: Optimal algorithms and inapproximability results for every CSP? In: Proceedings of the 40th Annual ACM Symposium on Theory of Computing (STOC 2008), pp. 245–254 (2008)
15. Schrijver, A.: A combinatorial algorithm minimizing submodular functions in strongly polynomial time. J. Comb. Theory, Ser. B 80(2), 346–355 (2000)
16. Takhanov, R.: A dichotomy theorem for the general minimum cost homomorphism problem. In: Proceedings of the 27th International Symposium on Theoretical Aspects of Computer Science (STACS 2010), pp. 657–668 (2010)
17. Živný, S.: The Complexity and Expressive Power of Valued Constraints. PhD thesis, Oxford University Computing Laboratory (2009)

A   Proof of Proposition 17

We will need three supporting lemmas, which are stated here without proofs. They follow without too much difficulty from the definition of the graph G, Lemma 15, and Proposition 16. Let $\Sigma_{ad} = \Sigma \setminus \{\{b, c\}\}$.

Lemma 20. *If $\Sigma_0 \subseteq \Sigma_\Gamma$, and $x \in V'$ is not isolated in G', then $\{x, \overline{x}\} \in E$.*

Lemma 21. *Assume that $\Sigma_\Gamma \subseteq \Sigma_{ad}$ and that there is an edge $\{(f, g), z\} \in E$, $z \in V'$. Then, $\{\overrightarrow{ab}, z\} \in E$ or $\{\overrightarrow{ac}, z\} \in E$, and $\{\overrightarrow{bd}, z\} \in E$ or $\{\overrightarrow{cd}, z\} \in E$.*

Lemma 22. *Assume that $\Sigma_\Gamma \subseteq \Sigma_0$. If there is a loop on $\overrightarrow{bc}$ or $\overrightarrow{ad}$, then there is a loop on at least one of the vertices $\overrightarrow{ab}$, $\overrightarrow{ac}$, $\overrightarrow{bd}$, $\overrightarrow{cd}$.*

Proposition 17. *Assume $\Sigma_0 \subseteq \Sigma_\Gamma$. If G' is bipartite, then the set of binary functions in $\langle \Gamma, \mathcal{C}_D \rangle_{fn}$ is submodular on a chain. Otherwise, if $G[V'_\Gamma]$ is bipartite, then the set of binary functions in $\langle \Gamma, \mathcal{C}_D \rangle_{fn}$ has a 1-defect chain multimorphism.*

Proof. We start by proving the case when G' is bipartite. For an independent set I in G', let R_I denote the binary relation on D defined by $(x, y) \in R_I$ iff $\overrightarrow{xy} \in I$. Let $\{I, J\}$ be a 2-colouring of the subgraph of G' induced by the non-isolated vertices. We first show that R_I is a partial order on D. Let $(x,y),(y,z) \in R_I$. Then, $\overrightarrow{xy}$ and $\overrightarrow{yz}$ have the same colour in I, and it follows that $\{\overrightarrow{xy}, \overrightarrow{yz}\} \notin E$. Hence, by Lemma 15(5), we have $\{\overrightarrow{xy}, \overrightarrow{zx}\}, \{\overrightarrow{yz}, \overrightarrow{zx}\} \in E$. By Lemma 20, $\{\overrightarrow{zx}, \overrightarrow{xz}\} \in E$, so $\overrightarrow{xz} \in I$ and $(x,z) \in R_I$. Now, let $(D;<)$ be a linear extension of R_I (i.e. a total order on D containing R_I), and let $I' \supseteq I$ be the corresponding subset of V'. The set I' is independent since I is independent and $I' \setminus I$ is a set of isolated vertices in G'. Since there are no edges from V' to the singleton vertices in G, we can add all of these to I' as well. Thus, by Lemma 13, every binary function in $\langle \Gamma, \mathcal{C}_D \rangle_{fn}$ is submodular on the chain $(D; \wedge, \vee)$, where $\wedge$ and $\vee$ are defined with respect to $(D;<)$.

Let (f,g) denote the vertex in G given by $f(b,c) = f(c,b) = a$ and $g(b,c) = g(c,b) = d$. We follow a similar strategy for the case when G' is not bipartite. However, instead of using G' we now consider the graph $G[V'_{ad} \cup \{(f,g),(g,f)\}]$, where $V'_{ad} = V' \setminus \{\overrightarrow{bc}, \overrightarrow{cb}\}$. First, we show that $G[V'_{ad}]$ is bipartite. If $\Sigma_\Gamma = \Sigma_{ad}$, then $G[V'_{ad}] = G[V'_\Gamma]$ is bipartite by assumption. Otherwise, $\Sigma_\Gamma = \Sigma_0$. Since $G[V'_\Gamma] = G[V'_0]$ is loop-free, we know from Lemma 22 that there is no loop on $\overrightarrow{bc}$, nor on $\overrightarrow{ad}$. Thus, by Lemma 15(3), $G[V'_{ad}]$ is bipartite.

Assume for the moment that the following holds:

$$\text{For } y \in D \setminus \{b,c\}, \text{ there is an odd path in } G[V'_{ad}] \text{ from } \overrightarrow{by} \text{ to } \overrightarrow{yc}. \tag{9}$$

Let $\{I,J\}$ be a 2-colouring of the subgraph of $G[V'_{ad}]$ induced by the non-isolated vertices. We claim that R_I is a partial order on D. Let $(x,y),(y,z) \in R_I$ and observe that (9) implies $\{x,z\} \neq \{b,c\}$. As in the case for bipartite G', we can argue that $\overrightarrow{xz}$ is connected by even paths to both $\overrightarrow{xy}$ and $\overrightarrow{yz}$. Since $\{x,z\} \neq \{b,c\}$, it follows that $(x,z) \in I$. Now take a transitive extension of R_I which orders all pairs of elements except for b and c, and let $I' \supseteq I$ be the corresponding subset of V'_{ad}. We can assume (possibly by swapping I and J) that $\overrightarrow{ad} \in I'$.

Next we show that $I' \cup \{(f,g)\}$ is independent. This will ensure that $f(b,c) = a < d = g(b,c)$ holds in the constructed multimorphism. If (f,g) is not connected to any vertex in V'_{ad}, then $I' \cup \{(f,g)\}$ is trivially independent. Otherwise, by Lemma 21, (9), and Lemma 20, we can show that from any $z \in V'_{ad}$ such that $\{(f,g),z\} \in E$, there are odd paths in $G[V'_{ad}]$ to each vertex in the set $S = \{\overrightarrow{ab}, \overrightarrow{ac}, \overrightarrow{bd}, \overrightarrow{cd}\}$. Since $G[V'_{ad}]$ is bipartite, it follows that $\{\overrightarrow{ab}, \overrightarrow{bd}\} \notin E$, so $\{\overrightarrow{ab}, \overrightarrow{da}\} \in E$ by Lemma 15(5). Hence, $I' = I = S \cup \{\overrightarrow{ad}\}$, and $z \notin I'$.

It remains to verify that $I' \cup \{(f,g)\}$ together with the singleton vertices in G also form an independent set. By condition (7) this is equivalent to saying that each unary function obtained from a binary function in $\langle \Gamma, \mathcal{C}_D \rangle_{fn}$ by fixing one argument to a constant is submodular on L_{ad}. This follows from Proposition 16. By Lemma 13, every binary function in $\langle \Gamma, \mathcal{C}_D \rangle_{fn}$ has the 1-defect chain multimorphism corresponding to $I' \cup \{(f,g)\}$.

Finally, we prove property (9). If $\Sigma_\Gamma = \Sigma_{ad}$, then by Lemma 15(3), and the fact that G' contains an odd cycle, we have a loop on $\overrightarrow{bc}$. Since $\overrightarrow{by}$ and $\overrightarrow{yc}$ are loop-free for $y \in D \setminus \{b,c\}$, we have $\{\overrightarrow{by}, \overrightarrow{yc}\} \in E$ by Lemma 15(6). Otherwise, $\Sigma_\Gamma = \Sigma_0$. We argued above that G' does not contain any loop in this case.

Thus, by Lemma 15(3), every odd cycle C in G' must intersect both $\{\overrightarrow{bc}, \overrightarrow{cb}\}$ and $\{\overrightarrow{ad}, \overrightarrow{da}\}$. Now, by repeatedly applying Lemma 15(2) to C, we obtain a triangle on a subset of $\{\overrightarrow{bc}, \overrightarrow{cb}, \overrightarrow{ad}, \overrightarrow{da}\}$. By Lemma 20, we can conclude that G' in fact contains the complete graph on these four vertices. In particular, we have both $\{\overrightarrow{ad}, \overrightarrow{bc}\} \in E$ and $\{\overrightarrow{da}, \overrightarrow{bc}\} \in E$. By Lemma 15(4), we therefore have either $\{\overrightarrow{ad}, \overrightarrow{ba}\} \in E$ or $\{\overrightarrow{ad}, \overrightarrow{ac}\} \in E$, and furthermore, either $\{\overrightarrow{da}, \overrightarrow{ba}\} \in E$ or $\{\overrightarrow{da}, \overrightarrow{ac}\} \in E$. Since there is no loop on $\overrightarrow{ad}$, we conclude that either the path $(\overrightarrow{ba}, \overrightarrow{ad}, \overrightarrow{da}, \overrightarrow{ac})$ or the path $(\overrightarrow{ba}, \overrightarrow{da}, \overrightarrow{ad}, \overrightarrow{ac})$ is in $G[V'_{ad}]$. In the same way, we find an odd path from $\overrightarrow{bd}$ to $\overrightarrow{dc}$. $\square$

Algorithm Selection and Scheduling

Serdar Kadioglu[1], Yuri Malitsky[1], Ashish Sabharwal[2],
Horst Samulowitz[2], and Meinolf Sellmann[2]

[1] Brown University, Dept. of Computer Science, Providence, RI 02912, USA
{serdark,ynm}@cs.brown.edu
[2] IBM Watson Research Center, Yorktown Heights, NY 10598, USA
{ashish.sabharwal,samulowitz,meinolf}@us.ibm.com

Abstract. Algorithm portfolios aim to increase the robustness of our ability to solve problems efficiently. While recently proposed algorithm selection methods come ever closer to identifying the most appropriate solver given an input instance, they are bound to make wrong and, at times, costly decisions. Solver scheduling has been proposed to boost the performance of algorithm selection. Scheduling tries to allocate time slots to the given solvers in a portfolio so as to maximize, say, the number of solved instances within a given time limit. We show how to solve the corresponding optimization problem at a low computational cost using column generation, resulting in fast and high quality solutions. We integrate this approach with a recently introduced algorithm selector, which we also extend using other techniques. We propose various static as well as dynamic scheduling strategies, and demonstrate that in comparison to pure algorithm selection, our novel combination of scheduling and solver selection can significantly boost performance.

1 Introduction

The constraint reasoning community has a long tradition of introducing and refining ideas whose practical impact often goes far beyond the field's scope. One such contribution is that of robust solvers based on the idea of *algorithm portfolios* (cf. [28,11,20,21,41,25]). Motivated by the observation that solvers have complementary strengths and therefore exhibit incomparable behavior on different problem instances, algorithm portfolios run multiple solvers in parallel or select one solver, based on the features of a given instance. Portfolio research has led to a wealth of different approaches and an amazing boost in solver performance in the past decade. One of the biggest success stories is that of SATzilla [40], which combines existing Boolean Satisfiability (SAT) solvers and has now dominated various categories of the SAT Competition for about half a decade [29]. Another example is CP-Hydra [25], a portfolio of Constraint Programming (CP) solvers which won the CSP 2008 Competition. Instead of choosing a single solver for an instance, Silverthorn and Miikkulainen [30] proposed a Dirichlet Compound Multinomial distribution to create a schedule of solvers to be run in sequence. Other approaches (e.g., [17]) dynamically switch between a portfolio of solvers

J. Lee (Ed.): CP 2011, LNCS 6876, pp. 454–469, 2011.

based on the predicted completion time. Alternatively, ArgoSmart [24] and Hydra [38] focus on not only choosing the best solver for an instance, but also the best parametrization of that solver. For a further overview of the state-of-the-art in portfolio generation, see the thorough survey by Smith-Miles [31].

A recently proposed algorithm selector for SAT based on nearest-neighbor classification [23] serves as the foundation for our work here. First, we present two extensions to it involving distance-based weighting and cluster-guided adaptive neighborhood sizes, demonstrating moderate but consistent performance improvements. Then we develop a new hybrid portfolio that combines algorithm selection and algorithm scheduling, in static and dynamic ways. To this end we present a heuristic method for computing solver schedules efficiently, which O'Mahony et al. [25] identified as an open problem. This also enables us to quantify the impact of various scheduling strategies and to report those findings accordingly. Finally, we are able to show that a completely new way of solver scheduling consisting of a combination of static schedules and solver selection is able to achieve significantly better results than plain algorithm selection.

Using SAT as the testbed, we demonstrate through extensive numerical experiments that our approach is able to handle even highly diverse benchmarks, in particular a mix of random, crafted, and industrial instance categories, with a *single* portfolio. This is in contrast to, for example, SATzilla, which has historically excelled only in different versions that were specifically tuned for each category. Our approach also works well even when the training set is not fully representative of the test set that needs to be solved.

2   Nearest-Neighbor-Based Algorithm Selection

Malitsky et al. [23] recently proposed a simple yet highly effective algorithm selector for SAT based on nearest-neighbor classification. We review this approach here, before proposing two improvements to it in Section 3 and algorithm schedules in Section 4.

Nearest-neighbor classification (k-NN) is a classic machine learning approach. In essence, we base our decision for a new instance on prior experience with the k training instances most similar to it. As the similarity measure between instances, we simply use the Euclidean or L^2 distance on 48 core features of SAT instances that SATzilla is based on [40]. Each feature is (linearly) normalized to fit the interval $[0, 1]$ across all training instances. As the solver performance measure, we use the PAR10 score of the solver on these k instances. PAR10 score for a given timelimit T is a hybrid measure, defined as the average of the runtimes for solved instances and of $10 \times T$ for unsolved instances. It is thus a combined measure of number of instances solved and average solution time.

It is well-known in machine learning that 1-NN (i.e., $k = 1$) often does not generalize well to formerly unseen examples, as it tends to over-fit the training data. A very large value of k, on the other hand, defeats the purpose of considering local neighborhoods. To find the "right" value of k, we employ another classic strategy in machine learning, namely *random sub-sampling validation*. The idea

---

Algorithm 1. Algorithm Selection using Nearest-Neighbor Classification

---

1 k-NN-Algorithm-Selection Phase

    Input   : a problem instance F

    Params: nearest neighborhood size k, candidate solvers $\mathcal{S}$, training instances
            $\mathcal{F}_{\text{train}}$ along with feature vectors and solver runtimes

    Output: a solver from the set $\mathcal{S}$

2 begin

3   compute normalized features of F

4 $\mathcal{F} \leftarrow$ set of k instances from $\mathcal{F}_{\text{train}}$ that are closest to F

5   **return** solver in $\mathcal{S}$ that has the best PAR10 score on $\mathcal{F}$

6 end

7 Training Phase

    Input   : candidate solvers $\mathcal{S}$, training instances $\mathcal{F}_{\text{train}}$, time limit $T_{\max}$

    Params: neighborhood range $[k_{\min}, k_{\max}]$, number of sub-samples m, split ratio
            m_b/m_v

    Output: best performing k, reduced $\mathcal{F}_{\text{train}}$ along with feature and runtimes

8 begin

9   run each solver $S \in \mathcal{S}$ for time $T_{\max}$ on each $F \in \mathcal{F}_{\text{train}}$; record runtimes

10   remove from $\mathcal{F}_{\text{train}}$ instances solved by no solver, or by all within 1 second

11   compute feature vectors for each $F \in \mathcal{F}_{\text{train}}$

12   **for** $k \in [k_{min}, k_{max}]$ **do**

13   score$[k] \leftarrow 0$

14   **for** $i \in [1..m]$ **do**

15 $(\mathcal{F}_{\text{base}}, \mathcal{F}_{\text{validation}}) \leftarrow$ a random m_b/m_v split of $\mathcal{F}_{\text{train}}$

16   add to score$[k]$ performance of k-NN portfolio on $\mathcal{F}_{\text{validation}}$ using
                training instances $\mathcal{F}_{\text{base}}$ and solver selection based on PAR10

17   score$[k] \leftarrow$ score$[k]/m$; $k_{\text{best}} \leftarrow \text{argmin}_k$ score$[k]$

18   **return** $(k_{\text{best}}, \mathcal{F}_{\text{train}}$, feature vectors, runtimes)

19 end

---

is to repeat the following process several times: Randomly split the training data into a base set and a validation set, train on the base set, and assess how well the learned approach performs on the validation set. We use a 67/33 base-validation split and perform random sub-sampling 100 times. We then finally choose the k that yields the best PAR10 performance averaged across the 100 validation sets.

Algorithm 1 gives a more formal description of the entire algorithm, in terms of its usage as a portfolio solver (i.e., algorithm selection given a new instance, as described above) and the random sub-sampling based training phase performed to compute the best value for k to use. The training phase starts out by computing the runtimes of all solvers on all training instances. It then removes all instances that cannot be solved by any solver in the portfolio within the time limit, or are solved by every solver in the portfolio within marginal time (e.g., 1 second for reasonably challenging benchmarks); learning to distinguish between solvers based on data from such instances is pointless. Along with the estimated best k, the training phase passes along this reduced set of training instances, their runtimes for each solver, and their features to the main solver

Table 1. Comparison of Baseline Solvers, Portfolios, and VBS Performances: PAR10, average runtime in seconds, and number of instances solved (timeout 1,200 seconds)

| | Pure Solvers | | | | | | | Portfolios | | VBS |
	agw-sat0	agw-sat+	**gnov-elty+**	SAT-enstein	march	pico-sat	kcnfs	SAT-zilla	**k-NN**	VBS
PAR10	5940	6017	5874	5892	8072	10305	6846	3578	**3151**	2482
Avg Time	634	636	626	625	872	1078	783	452	**442**	341
# Solved	290	286	293	292	190	83	250	405	**427**	457
% Solved	50.9	50.2	51.4	51.2	33.3	14.6	43.9	71.1	**74.9**	80.2

selection phase. We emphasize that the training phase does not learn any sophisticated model (e.g., a runtime prediction model); rather, it simply memorizes the training performances of all solvers and "learns" only the value of k.

Despite the simplicity of this approach – compared, for example, to the description of SATzilla [40] – it is highly efficient and outperforms SATzilla2009_R, the Gold Medal winning solver in the random category of SAT Competition 2009. In Table 1 we compare simple k-NN algorithm selection with SATzilla_R, using the 2,247 random category instances from SAT Competitions 2002-2007 as the training set and the 570 such instances from SAT Competition 2009 as the test set. Both portfolios are based on the following local search solvers: Ag2wsat0 [36], Ag2wsat+ [37], gnovelty+ [26], Kcnfs04 [8], March_dl04 [16], Picosat 8.46 [3], and SATenstein [19], all in the versions that are *identical* to the ones that were used when SATzilla09_R [39] entered the 2009 competition. To make the comparison as fair as possible, k-NN uses only the 48 core instance features that SATzilla is based on and is trained for Par10-score. For both training and testing, we use a time limit of 1,200 seconds. Table 1 shows that SATzilla boosts performance of individual solvers dramatically.[1] The pure k-NN approach pushes the performance level substantially further. It solves 22 more instances and closes about one third of the gap between SATzilla_R and the virtual best solver (VBS),[2] which solves 457 instances.

3   Improving Nearest-Neighbor-Based Solver Selection

We now discuss two mutually orthogonal techniques to further improve the performance of the algorithm selector outlined in Section 2.

Distance-Based Weighting. A natural extension of k-NN is to scale the scores of the k neighbors of an instance based on the Euclidean distance to it. Intuitively speaking, inspired by O'Mahony et al. [25], we assign larger weights to instances that are closer to the test instance assuming that closer instances more accurately

---

[1] The exact runtimes in Table 1 are lower than the ones reported in [23] due to faster machines: dual Intel Xeon 5540 (2.53 GHz) quad-core Nehalem processors with 24 GB of DDR-3 memory. The relative drop in the performance of *kcnfs*, we believe, is also due to this hardware difference.

[2] VBS refers to the "oracle" that always selects the solver that is fastest on the given instance. Its performance is the best one can hope to achieve with algorithm selection.

reflect the properties of the instance at hand. Hence, in Lines 5 and 16 of Algorithm 1, when computing the PAR10 score for solver selection for an instance F, we scale a solver S's penalized runtime (i.e., actual runtime or $10 \times T_{\max}$) on a neighbor F' by $\left(1 - \frac{dist(F, F')}{totalDist}\right)$, where $totalDist$ corresponds to the sum of all distances from F to instances in the neighborhood under consideration.

Clustering-Based Adaptive Neighborhood Size. Rather than learning a single value for k, we adapt the size of the neighborhood based on the properties of the given test instance. To this end, we partition the instance feature space by clustering the training instances using g-means clustering [13]. An instance is considered to belong to the cluster it is nearest to (breaking ties arbitrarily). Algorithm 1 can be easily adapted to learn one k for each cluster. Given a test instance, we first determine the cluster to which it belongs and then use the value of k learned for this cluster during training. We note that our clustering is used to select only the *size* of the neighborhood based on instance features, not to limit the neighborhood itself; neighboring instances from other clusters can still be used when determining the best solver based on PAR10 score.

3.1   Experimental Setup and Evaluation

We now describe the benchmark used for portfolio evaluation in the rest of this paper. Note that such a benchmark involves not only training and testing instances but also the base solvers used for building portfolios. The challenging benchmark setting we consider mixes incomplete and complete SAT solvers, as well as industrial, crafted, and random instances. After describing these, we will assess the impact of weighting, clustering, and their combination, on pure k-NN. Note that the reported runtimes include all overhead incurred by our portfolios.

Benchmark Solvers. We consider the following 21 state-of-the-art complete and incomplete SAT solvers: 1. Clasp[9], 2. CryptoMiniSat [32], 3. Glucose [1], 4. Lineling [5], 5. LySat i [12], 6. LySat c [12], 7. March-hi [14], 8. March-nn [15], 9. MiniSAT 2.2.0 [33], 10. MXC [6], 11. PrecoSAT [4], 12. Adaptg2wsat2009 [22], 13. Adaptg2wsat2009++ [22], 14. Gnovelty+2 [27], 15. Gnovelty+2-H [27], 16. HybridGM3 [2], 17. Kcnfs04SAT07 [8], 18. Picosat [3], 19. Saps [18], 20. TNM [35], and 21. SATenstein [19]. We in fact use six different parametrizations of SATenstein, resulting in a total of 26 base solvers. In addition, we preprocess all industrial and crafted instances with SatElite (version 1.0, with default option '+pre') and let the following solvers run on both original and preprocessed version of each instance:[3] 1. Clasp, 2. CryptoMiniSat, 3. Glucose, 4. Lineling, 5. LySat c, 6. LySat i, 7. March-hi, 8. March-nn, 9. MiniSat, 10. MXC, and 11. Precosat. Our portfolio is thus composed of 37 solvers.

Benchmark Instances. We selected 5,464 instances from all SAT Competitions and Races during 2002 and 2010 [29], whereby we discarded all instances that

---

[3] Preprocessing usually does not improve performance on random instances.

Table 2. Average Performance Comparison of Basic *k*-NN, Weighting, Clustering, and the combination of both using the *k*-NN Portfolio. Numbers in braces show in how many of the 10 training-test splits does incorporating weighting and clustering outperform basic *k*-NN (column 2).

	Basic *k*-NN	Weighting	Clustering	**Weight.+Clust.**
# Solved	1609	1611	1615	**1617** (9/10)
# Unsolved	114	112	108	**106** (9/10)
% Solved	93.5	93.6	93.8	**93.9** (9/10)
Avg Runtime	588	584	584	**577** (7/10)
PAR10 Score	3518	3459	3369	**3314** (8/10)

cannot be solved by any of the aforementioned solvers within the competition time limit of 5,000 seconds (i.e., the VBS can solve 100% of all instances).

Now, we need to partition these instances into disjoint sets of training and testing instances. In research papers, we often find that only one training-test split of the instances is considered. Moreover, commonly this split is computed at random, thereby increasing the likelihood that the training set is quite representative of the test set. We propose to adopt some best practices from machine learning and to consider *multiple splits* as well as *a more challenging partitioning* into training and test sets. Our objective for the latter is to generate splits where entire benchmark families are completely missing in the training set, while for other families some instances are present in both the training and in the test partition. To asses which instances are related, we use the the first three characters in the prefix of an instance name and assume that instances starting with the same three characters belong to the same benchmark family. We select, at random, about 5% of benchmark *families* and include them fully in the test partition; this typically resulted in roughly 15% of all instances being in the test partition. Next, we randomly add more instances to the test partition until it has about 30% of all instances, resulting in a 70-30 split. The 10 such partitions used in our experimentation are available online for future reference.[4]

Results. Table 2 summarizes the performance gain from using weighting, clustering, and the combination of the two. We show the average performance (across the 10 training-test splits mentioned above) in terms of number of instances solved/not solved, average runtime, and PAR10 score. Depending on the performance measure, the combination of weighting and clustering is able to improve performance of basic *k*-NN on anywhere from 7 to 9 out of the 10 splits (shown in braces in the rightmost column). The gain is modest but serves as a good incremental step for the rest of this paper.

For completeness, we remark that these modest gains also translate to the benchmark discussed in Table 1, where the combination of weighting and clustering solves 7 more instances than basic *k*-NN and 29 more than SATzilla_R. We will return to this benchmark towards the end of this paper.

---

[4] http://www.cs.toronto.edu/~horst/CP2011-Training-Test-Splits.zip

4   Building Solver Schedules

To further increase the robustness of our approach we consider computing schedules that define a sequence of solvers to try, along with individual time limits, given an instance. The general idea was previously introduced by Streeter [34] and in CP-Hydra [25]. In fact, Streeter [34] uses the idea of scheduling to *generate* algorithm portfolios. While he suggested using schedules that can suspend solvers and let them continue later on in exactly the same state they were suspended in, we will focus on solver schedules without preemption, i.e., each solver will appear in the schedule at most once. This setting was also used in CP-Hydra, which computes a schedule of CP solvers based on k nearest neighbors.

We note that a solver schedule can never outperform the VBS. In fact, a schedule is no better than the VBS *with a reduced captime of the longest running solver in the schedule*. Therefore, trivial schedules that split the available time evenly between all solvers have inherently limited performance. The reason why we may be interested in solver schedules nevertheless is to hedge our bets: We often observe that instances that cannot be solved by one solver even in a very long time can in fact be solved by another very quickly. Consequently, by allocating a reasonably small amount of time to other solvers we can provide a safety net in case our solver selection happens to be unfortunate.

4.1   Static Schedules

The simplest approach is to compute a static schedule of solvers. For example, we could compute a schedule that solves the most training instances within the allowed time (cf. [25]). We propose to do slightly more, namely to compute a schedule that, first, solves most training instances and that, second, requires the lowest amount of time among all schedules that are able to solve the same amount of training instances. We can formulate this problem as an integer program (IP), more precisely as a resource constrained set covering problem (RCSCP), where the goal is to select a number of solver-runtime pairs that together "cover" (i.e., solve) as many training instances as possible:

Solver Scheduling IP:

$$\min \quad (C+1)\sum_i y_i + \sum_{S,t} t x_{S,t} \tag{1}$$

$$s.t. \quad y_i + \sum_{(S,t)\,|\,i\in V_{S,t}} x_{S,t} \geq 1 \qquad \forall i \tag{2}$$

$$\sum_{S,t} t x_{S,t} \leq C \tag{3}$$

$$y_i, x_{S,t} \in \{0,1\} \qquad \forall i, S, t \tag{4}$$

Binary variables $x_{S,t}$ correspond to sets of instances that can be solved by solver S within a time t. These sets have cost t and a resource consumption coefficient t. To make it possible that all training instances can be covered even when they remain unsolved, we introduce additional binary variables y_i. These correspond to the set that contains only item i, they have cost $C + 1$ and time resource consumption coefficient 0. The constraints (2) in this model enforce that we cover all training instances, the additional resource constraint (3) that we do not exceed the overall captime C. The objective is to minimize the total cost. Due to the high costs for variables y_i (which will be 1 if and only if instance i cannot be solved by the schedule), schedules that solve most instances are favored, and among those the fastest schedule is chosen (as the cost of $x_{S,t}$ is t).

4.2   A Column Generation Approach

The main problem with the above formulation is the sheer number of variables. For our most up-to-date benchmark with 37 solvers and more than 5,000 training instances, solving the above problem is impractical, even when we choose the timeouts t smartly such that from timeout $t1$ to the next timeout $t2$ at least one more instance can be solved by the respective solver ($V_{S,t1} \subsetneq V_{S,t2}$). In our experiments we found that the actual time to solve these IPs may at times still be tolerable, but the memory consumption was often prohibitively high.

We therefore propose to solve the above problem approximately, using column generation (aka Dantzig-Wolfe decomposition) – a well-known technique for handling linear programs (LPs) with a lot of variables [7,10]. We discuss it briefly in the general setting. Consider the LP:

$$\min c^T x \quad \text{s.t. } A x \geq b, x \geq 0 \tag{5}$$

In the presence of too many variables, it is often not practical to solve the large system (5) directly. The core observation underlying column generation is that only a few variables (i.e., "columns") will be non-zero in any optimal LP solution (at most as many as there are constraints). Therefore, if we knew which variables are important, we could consider a much smaller system $A' x' = b$ where A' contains only a few columns of A. When we choose only some columns in the beginning, LP duality theory tells us which columns that we have left out so far are of interest for the optimization of the global LP. Namely, only columns with *negative reduced costs* (which are defined based on the optimal duals of the system $A' x' = b$) can help the objective to decrease further.

Column generation proceeds by considering, in turn, a *master problem* (the reduced system $A' x' = b$) and a *subproblem* where we select a new column to be added to the master based on its current optimal dual solution. This process is iterated until there is no more column with a negative reduced cost. At this point, we know that an optimal solution to (5) has been found – even though most columns have never been added to the master problem!

When using standard LP solvers to solve the master problem and obtain its optimal duals, all that is left is solving the subproblem. To develop a subproblem generator, we need to understand how exactly the reduced costs are computed. Assume we have a dual value $\lambda_i \geq 0$ for each constraint in A'. Then, the reduced

Algorithm 2. Subproblem: Column Generation

---

begin
    minRedCosts ← ∞
    forall *Solvers S* **do**
        $T \leftarrow 0$
        forall *i* **do**
            $j \leftarrow \pi(i);$ $T \leftarrow T + \lambda_j;$ $\hat{t} \leftarrow \text{Time}(S, j)$
            redCosts ← $\hat{t}(1 - \mu) - T$
            if *redCosts < minRedCosts* **then**
                Solver ← S
                timeout ← $\hat{t}$
                minRedCosts ← redCost

    if *minRedCosts < 0* **then return** $x_{\text{Solver},\text{timeout}}$
    else return None
end

---

cost of a column $\alpha := (\alpha_1, \ldots, \alpha_z)^{\mathrm{T}}$ is defined as $\bar{c}_\alpha = c_\alpha - \sum_i \lambda_i \alpha_i$, where c_α is the cost of column α.

Equipped with this knowledge, we can apply column generation to solve the continuous relaxation of the Solver Scheduling IP. To this end, we begin the process by adding, at the start, all columns corresponding to variables y to our reduced system A'. Next, we repeatedly generate and solve a subproblem whose goal is to suggest a solver-runtime pair that is likely to increase the objective value of the (continuous) master problem the most. Hence, each column we add regards an $x_{S,t}$ variable, specifically the one with minimal reduced cost.

To find such an $x_{S,t}$, first, for all solvers S, we compute a permutation π of the instances such that the time that S needs to solve instance $\pi_S(i)$ is less than or equal that the solver needs to solve instance $\pi_S(i+1)$ (for appropriate i). See Algorithm 2. Obviously, we only need to do this once for each solver and not each time we want to generate a new column. Now, let us denote with $\lambda_i \geq 0$ the optimal dual value for the restriction to cover instance i (2). Moreover, denote with $\mu \leq 0$ the dual value of the resource constraint (3) (since that constraint enforces a lower-or-equal restriction μ is guaranteed to be non-positive). Finally, for each solver S we iterate over i and compute the term $T \leftarrow \sum_{k \leq i} \lambda_{\pi_S(k)}$ (which in each iteration we can obviously derive from the previous value for T). Let $\hat{t}$ denote the time that solver S needs to solve instance $\pi(i)$. Then, the reduced costs of the column that corresponds to variable $x_{S,t}$ are $\hat{t} - \hat{t}\mu - T$. We choose the column with the most negative reduced costs and add it to the master problem. If there is no more column with negative reduced costs, we stop.

We would like to point out two things. First, note that what we have actually done is to pretend that all columns were present in the matrix and computed the reduced costs for all of them. This is not usually the case in column generation approaches where most columns are usually found to have larger reduced costs *implicitly* rather than explicitly. Second, note that the solution returned from this process will in general not be integer but contain fractional values. Therefore, the solution obtained cannot be interpreted as a solver schedule directly.

This situation can be overcome in two ways. The first is to start branching and to generate more columns – which may still be needed by the optimal integer solution even though they were superfluous for the optimal fractional solution. This process is known in the literature as branch-and-price.

What we propose, and that is in fact the reason why we solved the original problem by means of column generation in the first place, is to stick to the columns that were added during the column generation process and to solve the remaining system as an IP. Obviously, this is just a heuristic that may return sub-optimal schedules for the training set. However, we found that this process is very fast and nevertheless provides high quality solutions (see empirical results in Section 4.4). Even when the performance on the training set is at times slightly worse than optimal, the performance on the test set often turned out as good or sometimes even better than that of the optimal training schedule – a case where the optimal schedule overfits the training data.

The last aspect that we need to address is the case where the final schedule does not utilize the entire available time. Recall that we even deliberately minimize the time needed to solve as many instances as possible. Obviously, at runtime it would be a waste of resources not to utilize the entire time that is at our disposal. In this case, we scale each solver's time in the schedule equally so that the total time of the resulting schedule will be exactly the captime C.

4.3   Dynamic Schedules

O'Mahony et al. [25] found that static schedules work only moderately well. Therefore, they introduced the idea of computing *dynamic* schedules: At runtime, for a given instance, CP-Hydra considers the ten nearest neighbors (in case of ties, up to fifty) and computes a schedule that solves as many of these instances as possible in the given time limit. Accordingly, the constraints in the Solver Scheduling IP are limited to the few instances in the neighborhood, which allows CP-Hydra to use a brute-force approach to compute dynamic schedules at runtime. This is reported to work well thanks to the small neighborhood size and the fact that CP-Hydra only has three constituent solvers.

Our column generation approach, yielding potentially sub-optimal but usually high quality solutions, works fast enough to handle even 37 solvers and over 5,000 instances within seconds. This allows us to embed the idea of dynamic schedules in the previously developed nearest-neighbor approach which selects optimal neighborhood sizes by random subsampling validation – which requires us to solve hundreds of thousands of these IPs.

Both cluster-guided adaptive neighborhood size and weighting discussed earlier can be incorporated into solver schedules as well. For the latter, we suggest a slightly different approach than CP-Hydra. Specifically, when given an instance F, we adapt the objective function in the Solver Scheduling IP by multiplying the costs for the variables y_i, which were originally $C + 1$, with $2 - \frac{\text{dist}(F, F_i)}{\text{totalDist}}$. This favors schedules that solve more training instances that are closer to F.

We thus obtain four variations of dynamic schedules. We also used a setting inspired by the CP-Hydra approach: size 10 neighborhood size and weighting

Table 3. Average performance of semi-static schedules compared with no schedules and with static schedules based only on the available solvers. Numbers in braces show in how many of the 10 training-test splits does semi-static scheduling with weighting and clustering outperform the same approach without scheduling (column 2).

	No Sched. Wtg+Clu	Static Sched. Wtg+Clu	Semi-Static Schedules			
			Basic k-NN	Weighting	Clustering	**Wtg+Clu**
# Solved	1617	1572	1628	1635	1633	**1636** (7/10)
# Unsolved	106	151	95	88	90	**87** (7/10)
% solved	93.9	91.2	94.6	94.9	94.8	**95.0** (7/10)
Avg Runtime	577	562	448	451	**446**	449 (10/10)
PAR10 score	3314	4522	2896	2728	2789	**2716** (8/10)

scheme as in [25]. We refer to this approach as SAT-Hydra. In our experiments with dynamic schedules as well as SAT-Hydra, we found the gain over and above k-NN solver selection with weights and clustering (the rightmost column in Table 2) was marginal. SAT-Hydra and dynamic schedule without weights and clustering, for example, each solved only 4 more instances. Due to limited space, we omit detailed experimental numbers and instead move on to scheduling strategies that turned out to be more effective.

4.4   Semi-static Solver Schedules

Observe that the four algorithm selection portfolios that we developed in Section 2 can themselves be considered solvers. We can add the portfolio itself to our set of constituent solvers and compute a "static" schedule for this augmented collection of solvers. We quote "static" here because the resulting schedule is of course still instance-specific. After all, the algorithm selector portfolio chooses one of the constituent solvers based on the test instance's features. We refer to the result of this process as *semi-static solver schedules*.

Depending on which of our four portfolios from Section 2 we use, we obtain four semi-static schedules. We report their performance Table 3. We observe that semi-static scheduling improves the overall performance in anywhere from 7 to 10 of the 10 training-test splits considered, depending on the performance measure used (compare with column 2 in the table for the best results without scheduling). All semi-static schedules here solve at least 20 more instances within the time limit. Again, the combination of weighting and clustering achieves the best performance and it narrows the gap to VBS in percentage of instances solved to nearly 5%. For further comparison, in the column 3 we show the performance of a static schedule that was trained on the entire training set and is the same for all test instances. We can confirm the earlier finding [25] that static solver schedules are indeed inferior to dynamic schedules, and find that they are considerably outperformed by semi-static solver schedules.

Quality of results generated by Column Generation. Table 4 illustrates the performance of our Column Generation approach. We show a comparison of the resulting performance achieved by the *optimal* schedule. In order to compute the optimal solution to the IP we used Cplex on a machine with sufficient memory

Table 4. Comparison of Column Generation and the Solution to the Optimal IP

Schedule by	# Solved	# Unsolved	% Solved	Avg Runtime (s)	PAR10 score
Optimal IP	1635.8	87.1	95.0	442.5	2708.4
Column Generation	1635.7	87.2	95.0	448.9	2716.2

and a 15 second resolution to fit the problem into the available memory. As we can observe the column generation is able to determine a high quality schedule that results in a performance that nearly matches the one of the (coarse-grained) optimal schedule according to displayed measures.

4.5   Fixed-Split Selection Schedules

Based on this success, we consider a parametrized way of computing solver schedules. As discussed earlier, the motivation for using solver schedules is to increase robustness and hedge against an unfortunate selection of a long-running solver. At the same time, the best achievable performance of a portfolio is that of the VBS *with a captime of the longest individual run.* In both dynamic and semi-static schedules, the runtime of the longest running solver(s) was determined by the column generation approach working solely on training instances. This procedure inherently runs the risk of overfitting the training set.

Consequently, we consider splitting the time between an algorithm selection portfolio and the constituent solvers based on a parameter. For example, we could allocate 90% of the available time for the solver selected by the portfolio. For the remaining 10% of the time, we run a static solver schedule. We refer to these schedules as *90/10-selection schedules.* Note that choosing a fixed amount of time for the schedule of constituent solvers is likely to be suboptimal for the training set but offers the possibility of improving test performance.

Table 5 captures the corresponding results. We observe that using this restricted application of scheduling is able to outperform our best approach so far (semi-static scheduling, shown again in the first column, which is outperformed consistently in 9 out of 10 training-test splits). We are able to solve nearly 1642 instances on average which is 6 more than we were able to solve before and the gap to the virtual best solver is narrowed down to 4.69%. Recall that we

Table 5. Average performance comparison of basic k-NN, weighting, clustering, and the combination of both using the k-NN Portfolio with a 90/10 fixed-split static schedule. Numbers in braces show in how many of the 10 training-test splits does fixed-split scheduling with weighting and clustering outperform the same approach with semi-static scheduling (column 2).

	Semi-Static Wtg+Clu	Fixed-Split Schedules		
		Basic k-NN	Weighting	Clustering	**Wtg+Clu**
# Solved	1636	1637	1641	1638	**1642** (9/10)
# Unsolved	87	86	82	85	**81** (9/10)
% solved	95.0	95.0	95.3	95.1	**95.3** (9/10)
Avg Runtime	449	455	446	452	**445** (9/10)
PAR10 score	2716	2683	2567	2652	**2551** (9/10)

consider a highly diverse set of benchmark instances from the Random, Crafted, and Industrial categories. Moreover, we do not work with plain random splits, but splits where complete families of instances in the test set are not represented in the training set at all.

Compared to the plain k-NN approach of Malitsky et al. [23] that we started with (column 2 of Table 2), the fixed-split selection schedules close roughly one third of the gap to the VBS. The performance gain, as measured by Welch's T-test, is significant in most of the training-test splits. For example, the p-value for the T-test of an instance being solved or not by the two approaches has a median value of 0.05. Similarly, the median p-value across the 10 splits for the penalized runtime is 0.04, indicating the improvements are statistically significant.

5   Summary and Discussion

We considered the problem of algorithm selection and scheduling so as to maximize performance when given a hard time limit within which we need to provide a solution. We considered two improvements for simple nearest-neighbor solver selection, weighting and adaptive neighborhood sizes based on clustering. Then, we developed a light-weight optimization algorithm to compute near-optimal schedules for a given set of training instances. This allowed us to provide an extensive comparison of pure algorithm selection, static solver schedules, dynamic solver schedules, and semi-static solver schedules which are essentially static schedules combined with an algorithm selector.

While quantifying the performance of the various scheduling strategies we found out that dynamic schedules are only able to achieve rather minor improvements and that semi-static schedules work the best among these options. Finally, we compared two alternatives: use the optimization component or use a fixed percentage of the allotted time when deciding how much time to allocate to the solver suggested by the algorithm selector. In either case, we used a static schedule for the remaining time. This latter parametrization allowed us to avoid overfitting the training data and overall resulted in the best performance.

We tested this approach on a highly diverse benchmark set with random, crafted, and industrial SAT instances where we even deliberately removed entire families of instances from the training set. 90/10 fixed-split selection schedules demonstrated a convincing performance and solved, on average, over 95% of the instances that the virtual best solver is able to solve.

As an insight into the selection strategy of our fixed-split selection schedule, Figure 1 shows the fraction of test instances across all training-test splits on which any given solver was chosen and resulted in a successful run. The special bar labeled 'unsolved' shows how often the portfolio made a choice that resulted in failing to solve an instance (which here equals the gap to the VBS). Note that out of the 37 possible choices, our portfolio chose only 18 solvers in successful runs. Further, the black portion of the bars indicates how often was the selected solver nearly the best possible choice, defined as the solver taking within 10% of VBS time or solving the instance within 5 seconds. The predominant black

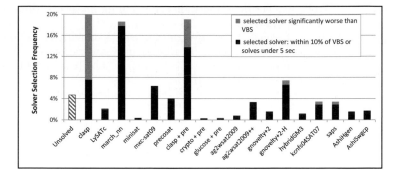

Fig. 1. Frequency of solver selection by 90-10 fixed-split schedule

Table 6. Comparison of Major Portfolios for the SAT-Rand Benchmark (570 test instances, timeout 1,200 seconds). Values in braces denote p-value of Welch's T-test for the considered solver improving upon SATzilla_R as the baseline.

	SATzilla_R	SAT-Hydra	k-NN	90-10	VBS
# Solved	405	419	427 (0.071)	**135** (0.022)	457
# Unsolved	165	151	143 —	**135** —	113
% solved	71.5	73.5	74.9 —	**76.3** —	80.2
Avg Runtime	452	489	442 (0.367)	**400** (0.042)	341
PAR10 score	3578	3349	3151 (0.085)	**2958** (0.022)	2482

regions, with the exception of Clasp, indicate that our portfolio often selected solvers with performance close to that of the VBS.

As a final remark, in Table 6, we close the loop and consider again the first benchmark set from Section 2 which compared portfolios for SAT Competition's random category instances, based on the same solvers as the gold-medal winning SATzilla_R. Overall, we go up from 405 (88.6% of VBS) for SATzilla_R to 435 (95.1% of VBS) instances solved for our fixed-split solver schedules. In other words, fixed-split selection schedule closes over 50% of the performance gap between SATzilla_R and the VBS. The p-values of Welch's T-test being below 0.05 (shown within braces) indicate that the performance achieved by our fixed-split selection schedule is statistically significantly better than SATzilla_R.

References

1. Audemard, G., Simon, L.: GLUCOSE: a solver that predicts learnt clauses quality. SAT Competition, 7–8 (2009)
2. Balint, A., Henn, M., Gableske, O.: hybridGM. Solver description. SAT Competition (2009)
3. Biere, A.: Picosat version 846. Solver description. SAT Competition (2007)
4. Biere, A.: Pre,icoSATSC 2009. SAT Competition, 41–43 (2009)
5. Biere, A.: Lingeling. SAT Race (2010)
6. Bregman, D.R.: The SAT Solver MXC, Version 0.99. SAT Competition, 37–38 (2009)

7. Dantzig, G.B., Wolfe, P.: The decomposition algorithm for linear programs. Econometrica 29(4), 767–778 (1961)
8. Dequen, G., Dubois, O.: kcnfs. Solver description. SAT Competition (2007)
9. Gebser, M., Kaufmann, B., Schaub, T.: Solution Enumeration for Projected Boolean Search Problems. In: van Hoeve, W.-J., Hooker, J.N. (eds.) CPAIOR 2009. LNCS, vol. 5547, pp. 71–86. Springer, Heidelberg (2009)
10. Gilmore, P.C., Gomory, R.E.: A linear programming approach to the cutting stock problem. Operations Research 9, 849–859 (1961)
11. Gomes, C.P., Selman, B.: Algorithm Portfolios. Artificial Intelligence 126(1-2), 43–62 (2001)
12. Hamadi, Y., Jabbour, S., Sais, L.: LySAT: solver description. SAT Competition, 23-24 (2009)
13. Hamerly, G., Elkan, C.: Learning the K in K-Means. NIPS (2003)
14. Heule, M., van Marren, H.: march hi: solver description. SAT Competition, 27–28 (2009)
15. Heule, M., van Marren, H.: march nn, http://www.st.ewi.tudelft.nl/sat/download.php
16. Heule, M., Zwieten, J., Dufour, M., Maaren, H.: March_eq: implementing additional reasoning into an efficient lookahead SAT solver. In: Hoos, H.H., Mitchell, D.G. (eds.) SAT 2004. LNCS, vol. 3542, pp. 345–359. Springer, Heidelberg (2005)
17. Huberman, B., Lukose, R., Hogg, T.: An Economics Approach to Hard Computational Problems. Science 265, 51–54 (2003)
18. Hutter, F., Tompkins, D.A.D., Hoos, H.H.: Scaling and probabilistic smoothing: Efficient dynamic local search for SAT. In: Van Hentenryck, P. (ed.) CP 2002. LNCS, vol. 2470, pp. 233–248. Springer, Heidelberg (2002)
19. KhudaBukhsh, A.R., Xu, L., Hoos, H.H., Leyton-Brown, K.: SATenstein: Automatically Building Local Search SAT Solvers From Components. In: IJCAI (2009)
20. Lagoudakis, M.G., Littman, M.L.: Learning to select branching rules in the DPLL procedure for satisfiability. In: SAT (2001)
21. Leyton-Brown, K., Nudelman, E., Andrew, G., McFadden, J., Shoham, Y.: A Portfolio Approach to Algorithm Selection. In: IJCAI, pp. 1542–1543 (2003)
22. Li, C.M., Wei, W.: Combining Adaptive Noise and Promising Decreasing Variables in Local Search for SAT. Solver description. SAT Competition (2009)
23. Malitsky, Y., Sabharwal, A., Samulowitz, H., Sellmann, M.: Non-Model-Based Algorithm Portfolios for SAT. SAT (to be published, 2011)
24. Nikolic, M., Maric, F., Janici, P.: Instance Based Selection of Policies for SAT Solvers. In: Kullmann, O. (ed.) SAT 2009. LNCS, vol. 5584, pp. 326–340. Springer, Heidelberg (2009)
25. O'Mahony, E., Hebrard, E., Holland, A., Nugent, C., O'Sullivan, B.: Using Case-based Reasoning in an Algorithm Portfolio for Constraint Solving. In: Irish Conference on Artificial Intelligence and Cognitive Science (2008)
26. Pham, D.N., Gretton, C.: gnovelty+. Solver description. SAT Competition (2007)
27. Pham, D.N., Gretton, C.: gnovelty+ (v.2). Solver description. SAT Competition (2009)
28. Rice, J.R.: The algorithm selection problem. Advances in Computers, 65–118 (1976)
29. SAT Competition, http://www.satcomptition.org
30. Silverthorn, B., Miikkulainen, R.: Latent Class Models for Algorithm Portfolio Methods. In: AAAI (2010)
31. Smith-Miles, K.A.: Cross-disciplinary perspectives on meta-learning for algorithm selection. ACM Comput. Surv. 41(1), 6:1–6:25 (2009)

32. Soos, M.: CryptoMiniSat 2.5.0. Solver description. SAT Race (2010)
33. Sorensson, N., Een, N.: MiniSAT 2.2.0 (2010), http://minisat.se
34. Streeter, M., Golovin, D., Smith, S.F.: Combining Multiple Heuristics Online. In: AAAI, pp. 1197–1203 (2007)
35. Wei, W., Li, C.M.: Switching Between Two Adaptive Noise Mechanisms in Local Search for SAT. Solver description. SAT Competition (2009)
36. Wei, W., Li, C.M., Zhang, H.: Combining adaptive noise and promising decreasing variables in local search for SAT. Solver description. SAT Competition (2007)
37. Wei, W., Li, C.M., Zhang, H.: Deterministic and random selection of variables in local search for SAT. Solver description. SAT Competition (2007)
38. Xu, L., Hoos, H.H., Leyton-Brown, K.: Hydra: Automatically Configuring Algorithms for Portfolio-Based Selection. In: AAAI (2010)
39. Xu, L., Hutter, F., Hoos, H.H., Leyton-Brown, K.: SATzilla2009: an Automatic Algorithm Portfolio for SAT. Solver description. SAT Competition (2009)
40. Xu, L., Hutter, F., Hoos, H.H., Leyton-Brown, K.: SATzilla: Portfolio-based Algorithm Selection for SAT. JAIR 32(1), 565–606 (2008)
41. Xu, L., Hutter, F., Hoos, H.H., Leyton-Brown, K.: SATzilla-07: The Design and Analysis of an Algorithm Portfolio for SAT. In: Bessière, C. (ed.) CP 2007. LNCS, vol. 4741, pp. 712–727. Springer, Heidelberg (2007)

Incorporating Variance in Impact-Based Search

Serdar Kadioglu[1], Eoin O'Mahony[2], Philippe Refalo[3], and Meinolf Sellmann[4]

[1] Brown University, Dept. of Computer Science, Providence, RI 02912, USA
serdark@cs.brown.edu
[2] Cornell University, Dept. of Computer Science, Ithaca, NY 14850, USA
eoin@cs.cornell.edu
[3] IBM, 1681 route des Dolines, 06560 Sophia-Antipolis, France
philippe.refalo@fr.ibm.com
[4] IBM Watson Research Center, Yorktown Heights, NY 10598, USA
meinolf@us.ibm.com

Abstract. We present a simple modification to the idea of impact-based search which has proven highly effective for several applications. Impacts measure the average reduction in search space due to propagation after a variable assignment has been committed. Rather than considering the mean reduction only, we consider the idea of incorporating the variance in reduction. Experimental results show that using variance can result in improved search performance.

Keywords: Search Strategies, Impact-based Search, Robust Search.

1 Introduction

Impact-based search strategies give efficient variable and value ordering heuristics to solve decision problems in constraint programming [12]. This method learns information about the importance of variables and values choices by averaging the observed search space reduction due to constraint propagation after an assignment. It's a simple way to exploit parts of the search tree that are apparently not useful because they do not lead to a solution.

Other impact measures have been designed and subjected to experimental validation. They refine or take into account more information in order to obtain better strategies. In [14] the solution density of constraints and occurrences of values in constraints' feasible assignments are used to guide search. In [1] the measure of the impact of an assignment is based on explanations provided by the constraint programming solver. These approaches can be more effective than regular impacts on some problems.

We propose in this paper a new way to refine the classical averaging of impact observations by taking into account the *variance* of the observations. In practice, when one needs to choose between two variables that have the same average impact, one can break this tie by taking into account the distribution of the observed impacts. Assuming that the two distributions have different variances, a risk-free choice will choose the variable with the smallest variance, while an optimistic choice will choose the variable with the largest variance.

Incorporating variance in impact based search is rather natural since impacts are based on taking the mean of observed domain reductions. Moreover, in practice, impact

J. Lee (Ed.): CP 2011, LNCS 6876, pp. 470–477, 2011.
© Springer-Verlag Berlin Heidelberg 2011

values are normally distributed [13]. Experimental validation was performed to determine the best way to use variance in practice. We present our results on quasi-group completion problems, magic squares and on the Costas array problem. Our results show that including variance can be rewarding in several cases and that it is an enhancement to be considered for impact-based search implementations.

2   Impact-Based Search

In constraint programming (CP) we strive to find feasible solutions, and our main inference mechanism is constraint propagation. Namely, by considering the problem constraints, one at a time, we eliminate potential values for the variables involved in the constraint. We iterate this process until no one constraint alone can eliminate values from the domain of variables anymore.

If we want to avoid an explicit enumeration of all potential solutions, we must obviously rely on constraint propagation to discard most of these solution candidates *implicitly*. Therefore, the way how we partition the space needs to enable constraint propagation to function well.

There are several ways how search methods try to provide the underlying inference mechanism with the necessary "grip." One traditional method is based on the fail-first principle which states: "To succed, try first where you are most likely to fail." [7]. To list only a few others, solution-density guided search [14] finds a constraint where one variable clearly favors one value in the sense that in most assignments that obey this constraint the variable is overwhelmingly assigned to the respective value. The method branches over that variable in the hope that the constraint will fail quickly when one of the other values is assigned to it. [1]

In mathematical programming a well-known and successful technique is pseudo-cost branching. While solution-density guided search looks ahead, pseudo-cost branching keeps a running average of the change in relaxation objective value due to the branching on a variable. That is, pseudo-cost branching extrapolates the past search experience to make predictions which search partition is likely to affect the inference mechanism the most.

Impact-based search in constraint programming is following the same motivation. Lacking an objective function, [12] proposes to keep a running average of the reduction in search space that is observed after committing a variable assignment $X = v$. Assume the Cartesian product of the variables' domains *before* committing the assignment has size $B \in \mathbb{N}$ and the product of all domain sizes *after* committing and propagating the assignment is $A \in \mathbb{N}$. Then, the impact of the assignment is defined as

$$I(X = v) = 1 - \frac{A}{B}.$$

The running average of these values is denoted with $\bar{I}(X = v)$.

From these values we can derive the expected search space reduction factor (ERF) for a variable. Namely, the sum of the Cartesian products of all domain sizes after

---

[1] Note that this is our summary which does not quite align with the motivation given in [14].

committing in turn $X = v$ for all values v in the domain $D(X)$ is expected to be multiplied by

$$\text{ERF}(X) = 1 - \sum_{v \in D(X)} \bar{I}(X = v).$$

In [12] it was proposed to branch over the variable with the lowest corresponding ERF: As we assume that we are searching an infeasible part of the search space, we expect that all alternative values for X must be explored. The lower the ERF, the smaller we expect the union of the remaining search spaces to be after committing assignments $X = v$ for all $v \in D(X)$. This method has since proven to work very well in various domains such as latin square completion, magic square, and multi-knapsack problem.

3   Impact Variance

Obviously, when estimating the ERF by computing a running average of reductions in search space that we observe, our estimate will come with some uncertainty.

3.1   Variance

To assess the confidence that we have in our estimate, variance is the statistical quantity that comes to mind first. Between two variables that have the same low ERF, being risk averse clearly we would favor the one that has exhibited less variance in search space reduction. On the other hand, if we are optimistic we might want to choose a variable that offers the potential of significantly reducing the search space.

If we incorporate variance, we now have two quantities that we want to optimize. The natural question is what should be the right trade-off between both objectives. If we assumed that the ERFs of a variable are normally distributed, then

- with about **68%** probability the real reduction factor will be lower than the mean **plus the standard deviation** (i.e., the square root of the variance),
- with about **95%** probability the real reduction factor will be lower than the mean plus **two times** the standard deviation, and
- with about **99.7%** probability the real reduction factor will be lower than the mean plus **three times** the standard deviation.

Alternatively, if we take the optimistic viewpoint and value variables with larger potential more, for a normal distribution we can argue that

- with about **32%** probability the real reduction factor will be lower than the mean **minus the standard deviation**, and
- with about **5%** probability the real reduction factor will be even lower than the mean minus **two times** the standard deviation.

Even though we cannot assume that the real reduction factors will be exactly normally distributed, the trend will be the same for all distributions. We therefore propose to choose an $\alpha \in \mathbb{Q}$ (where $\alpha > 0$ means we are risk averse, and $\alpha < 0$ means "we are feeling lucky") and to compute the *adjusted reduction factor*

$$\mathrm{ARF}_\alpha(X) = \mathrm{ERF}(X) + \alpha\sqrt{\mathrm{VAR}(X)}.$$

Then, we choose as branching variable

$$X = \mathrm{argmin}_Y \mathrm{ARF}_\alpha(Y).$$

If we choose a large α, then we compare variables by their ability to shrink the search space which we can expect with some higher probability. On the other hand, if we choose a low value for α, we compare variables based on their potential to shrink the search space a lot.

Note that the idea to use a factor $\alpha < 0$ somewhat resembles the idea of *upper confidence trees (UCTs)* [10]. As a very high-level description, in the UCT method we probe a tree and achieve estimates of the quality of a subtree by the samples drawn from the probes over the different child nodes. The question arises which probes should be launched next. Based on a very nice theory it was proven that it pays off to optimistically consider subtrees first which combine a good current estimate and larger uncertainty [10].

Our situation is of course different, as each "probe" can incur a significant cost. Essentially, without nogood-learning, with each unfortunate choice of the branching variable we could multiply the minimally required search effort. Therefore, in this paper we compare risk-averse and optimistic impact-based search in an empirical study.

3.2 Computing a Variance-Estimate

To implement the approach outlined above we obviously need to assess the quantity $\mathrm{VAR}(X)$. We can achieve this based on the variance that we observe for the variable assignment impacts $I(X = v)$. Since the random variable ERF is based on the sum of these random variables, if we assume that the $I(X = v)$ (for various v) are independent, then the variance of the ERF will be simply the sum of the variances of the $I(X - v)$. In other words, the variance can be estimated as

$$\mathrm{VAR}(X) = \sum_{v \in D(X)} \mathrm{VAR}(X = v).$$

All that is left to develop now is a way for estimating the variance of the $I(X = v)$. We could of course keep a history of these values and compute the variance from scratch. However, there is a much more elegant way, namely, after a new value for $I(X = v)$ or $\mathrm{ERF}(X)$ is observed, we can update the variance *online*.

This is trivial for the mean of a sequence. Given numbers $a_1, \ldots, a_{n-1}$ and their mean $\mu_{n-1} = \frac{\sum_i a_i}{n-1}$, and a new number a_n, for the new mean it obviously holds

$$\mu_n = \frac{(n-1)\mu_{n-1} + a_n}{n}.$$

A similar update rule holds for the sum of square differences $SD_{n-1} = \sum_i (a_i - \mu_{n-1})^2$ [9]:

$$SD_n = SD_{n-1} + (a_n - \mu_n)(a_n - \mu_{n-1}).$$

Therefore, we maintain three numbers for each $I(X = v)$: The number of times n we have observed a value, the current mean μ_n, and the current sum of square differences SD_n. Then, to choose a branching variable we use the unbiased [9] variance estimate $\frac{SD_n}{n-1}$.

4   Numerical Results

We now present empirical results demonstrating the benefits obtained by incorporating variance information as well as impacts when branching. We implemented the new heuristic in IBM Ilog Solver, and studied a number of problems. The goal of our experiments is to compare the relative performance of these three different variable selection heuristics:

- Impact-based search (IBS).
- Impact-based search with addition of variable variance. That is, α is set to 1 or to 2, which means we favor variables with low variance.
- Impact-based search with subtraction of variable variance. That is, α is set to -1 or to -2, which means we favor variables with high variance.

To conduct a fair test of the different variable selection heuristics we use a randomized value selection strategy and perform multiple runs of the same instance with different random seeds. The initial mean and variance value are obtained by probing each value of the domain of the variable. This gives a first impact for each value. Then a second impact is computed by performing a few steps of a dichotomic search to approximate impacts as described in [12]. Thus we have enough values at the beginning to compute the impact mean and the unbiased variance. In the instances we consider here, the overhead of probing the whole variable domain is negligible compared to the solution time. All approaches ran on identical models with the DFS search implementation of IBM ILOG Solver. The experiments were run on dual processor dual core Intel Xeon 2.8 GHz computers with 8GB of RAM.

4.1   Quasigroup Completion

Problem Definition. *A quasigroup completion problem [5] is tasked with completing an $n \times n$ partially filled matrix such that the numbers from 1 to n exactly once in each row and column*

Quasigroup completion problems are a well-known combinatorial problem. These problems, unlike latin square or quasigroup with holes problems, are not strictly satisfiable. We consider two sets of 100 instances. One set with order 40 and 640 unassigned cells ("holes"), and another one with order 50 and 1250 unassigned cells. They are generated randomly using a standard tool provided by the authors of [5]. We used depth-first search to solve the problems and four standard deviation factors $\alpha = \{-2, -1, 1, 2\}$.

Table 1. Results for the Quasigroup Completion Problem (order = 40, holes = 640)

α value	-2	-1	0 (IBS)	1	2
Time	**302**	320	336	374	408
# Success	**596**	555	523	439	355

Table 2. Results for the Quasigroup Completion Problem (order = 50, holes = 1250)

α value	-2	-1	0 (IBS)	1	2
Time	**166**	187	184	247	333
# Success	**864**	825	805	739	567

When setting α to 0, the strategy is simply the standard impact-based strategy. We perform 10 runs for each instance with as many different random seeds. The time limit is 2000 seconds. We report the average running time in seconds and the number of instance solved (the maximum is 1000 for each set).

The results of our evaluation is presented in Table 1 and Table 2. We can see that a risk-optimistic approach outperforms both the classical and risk-averse impact-based search on the instances. The optimistic strategy solves considerably more instances in substantially less time. On the other hand, risk-averse strategy marks the worse performance. It is slower and solves the least number of instances.

4.2   Magic Square

Problem Definition: *A magic square [11] of order n is an $n \times n$ square that contains all numbers from 1 to n^2 such that each row, column and both main diagonals add up to the "magic sum" $n(n^2 \quad 1)/2$.*

Magic squares are a much studied problem in the domain of combinatorial solvers. Although polynomial-time construction methods exist for creating magic squares, the problem poses a challenge for constraint programming based approaches. The current best systematic approach was presented in [4] and can only construct magic squares of orders up to 18 efficiently.

We again evaluate the performance of impact based search (when α is 0) and impact based search incorporated with standard deviation using factors $\alpha = \{-2, -1, 1, 2\}$. We consider magic squares of orders between 5 and 16. We use 50 different seeds for each order. The time limit is set to 2000 seconds. We compare the average runtime and the average number of successful trials.

Table 3 summarizes our results for the magic square problem. We observe that risk-optimistic approaches and impact-based search perform similarly, while the best performance is achieved when $alpha$ is set to -2, i.e., when the most risk-optimistic strategy is used. On the contrary, risk-averse approaches depict an inferior performance in terms of both running time and number of successful trials.

Table 3. Results for the Magic Square Problem

α value	-2	-1	0 (IBS)	1	2
Time	**680**	691	686	705	735
# Success	**34.3**	34.2	34.2	33.8	33

Table 4. Results for the Costas array problem

α value	-2	-1	0 (IBS)	1	2
Time	224	**218**	220	234	234
# Success	46.8	**46.9**	46.8	46.4	46.8

4.3 Costas Array

Problem Definition: *A Costas array [6] is a pattern of n marks on a $n \times n$ grid, such that each column or row contains only one mark, and all of the $n(n-1)/2$ vectors between the marks are all different.*

Costas arrays are a mathematical structure that is studied in a number of domains. It is a combinatorial structure with links to number theory, and is used to provide a template for generating radar and sonar signals with ideal ambiguity functions [2,3].

We consider Costas arrays of orders between 10 and 19, and evaluate impact-based search, and impact-based search with standard deviation incorporated using factors $alpha = \{-2, -1, 1, 2\}$. We use 50 different seeds for each order. The time limit is set to 2000 seconds. We compare the average running time, and the average number of successful trials.

Our results are presented in Table 4. While the best performance is achieved with a risk-optimistic approach, it is better than impact-based search with only a small margin. The risk-averse approaches again perform worse than other strategies.

Overall, we tried to determine the best way to use variance information in practice on three different constraint satisfaction problems. We have shown that including variance in a risk-optimistic setting can improve the search performance in several cases. We attribute the improved performance of the optimistic strategy to its ability to select variables that have high potential to reduce the search space.

5 Conclusion

In this paper we presented a new search heuristic which is based on a simple modification to impact-based search. The modification is to take variance information into account as well as impact values when selecting a branching variable. We consider a risk-averse and a risk-optimistic version of impact-based search with different coefficients, and provide experimental results that compare their relative performance on three different problems. Our findings suggest that a risk-optimistic approach can improve the search performance, hence it has potential to be a useful search heuristic, and, in general, variance information is an enhancement to be considered for impact-based search implementations.

References

1. Cambazard, H., Jussien, N.: Identifying and Exploiting Problem Structures using Explanation-Based Constraint Programming. Constraints 11(4), 295–313 (2006)
2. Costas, J.P.: A Study of a Class of Detection Waveforms Having Nearly Ideal Range-Doppler Ambiguity Properties. Proceedings of IEEE 72(8), 996–1009 (1984)
3. Freedman, A., Levanon, N.: Staggered Costas signals. IEEE Trans. Aerosp. Electron Syst. AES-22(6), 695–701 (1986)
4. Gomes, C.P., Sellmann, M.: Streamlined constraint reasoning. In: Wallace, M. (ed.) CP 2004. LNCS, vol. 3258, pp. 274–287. Springer, Heidelberg (2004)
5. Gomes, C.P., Shmoys, D.: Completing Quasigroups or Latin Squares: A Structured Graph Coloring Problem. In: Proceedings of Computational Symposium on Graph Coloring and Generalizations (2002)
6. Golomb, S.W., Taylor, H.: Two Dimensional Synchronization Patterns for Minimum Ambiguity. IEEE Trans. Informat. Theory IT-28(4), 600–604 (1982)
7. Haralick, R.M., Elliott, G.L.: Increasing Tree Search Efficiency for Constraint Satisfaction. Artificial Intelligence 14, 263–314 (1980)
8. IBM. IBM ILOG Reference manual and user manual. V6.4. IBM (2009)
9. Knuth, D.-E.: The Art of Computer Programming. seminumerical algorithms, vol. 2(3), p. 232. Addison-Wesley Longman Publishing Co., Inc., Amsterdam (1997)
10. Levente, K., Csaba, S.: Bandit Based Monte-Carlo Planning. Machine Learning ECML (2006)
11. Moran, J.: The Wonders of Magic Squares. Vintage, New York (1982)
12. Refalo, P.: Impact-Based Search Strategies for Constraint Programming. In: Wallace, M. (ed.) CP 2004. LNCS, vol. 3258, pp. 557–571. Springer, Heidelberg (2004)
13. Refalo, P.: Learning in Search. In: Hybrid Optimization. Springer, Heidelberg (2011)
14. Zanarini, A., Pesant, G.: Solution Counting Algorithms for Constraint-Centered Search Heuristics. Constraints 14(3), 392–413 (2009)

A Quadratic Edge-Finding Filtering Algorithm for Cumulative Resource Constraints

Roger Kameugne[1,2], Laure Pauline Fotso[3],
Joseph Scott[4], and Youcheu Ngo-Kateu[3]

[1] University of Maroua, Higher Teachers' Training College, Dept. of Mathematics,
P.O. Box 55 Maroua-Cameroon
[2] University of Yaoundé I, Faculty of Sciences, Dept. of Mathematics, P.O. Box 812,
Yaoundé, Cameroon
rkameugne@yahoo.fr, rkameugne@gmail.com
[3] University of Yaoundé I, Faculty of Sciences, Dept. of Computer Sciences, P.O. Box
812, Yaoundé, Cameroon
lpfotso@ballstate.bsu.edu, mireille_youcheu@yahoo.fr
[4] Uppsala University, Dept. of Information Technology, Computing Science Division,
Box 337, SE-751 05 Uppsala Sweden
joseph.scott@it.uu.se

Abstract. The cumulative scheduling constraint, which enforces the sharing of a finite resource by several tasks, is widely used in constraint-based scheduling applications. Propagation of the cumulative constraint can be performed by several different filtering algorithms, often used in combination. One of the most important and successful of these filtering algorithms is edge-finding. Recent work by Vilím has resulted in a $\mathcal{O}(kn \log n)$ algorithm for cumulative edge-finding, where n is the number of tasks and k is the number of distinct capacity requirements. In this paper, we present a sound $\mathcal{O}(n^2)$ cumulative edge-finder. This algorithm reaches the same fixpoint as previous edge-finding algorithms, although it may take additional iterations to do so. While the complexity of this new algorithm does not strictly dominate Vilím's for small k, experimental results on benchmarks from the Project Scheduling Problem Library suggest that it typically has a substantially reduced runtime. Furthermore, the results demonstrate that in practice the new algorithm rarely requires more propagations than previous edge-finders.

1 Introduction

Edge-finding is a filtering technique commonly used in solving resource-constrained project scheduling problems (RCPSP). An RCPSP consists of a set of resources of finite capacities, a set of tasks of given processing times, an acyclic network of precedence constraints between tasks, and a horizon (a deadline for all tasks). Each task requires a fixed amount of each resource over its execution time. The problem is to find a start time assignment for every task satisfying the precedence and resource capacity constraints, with a makespan (i.e., the time at which all tasks are completed) equal at most to the horizon. Edge-finding reduces

J. Lee (Ed.): CP 2011, LNCS 6876, pp. 478–492, 2011.

the range of possible start times by deducing new ordering relations between the tasks: for a task i, an edge-finder searches for a set of tasks Ω that *must* end before the end (or alternately, start before the start) of i. Based on this newly detected precedence, the earliest start time (or latest completion time) of i is updated. Note that we consider here only non-preemptive scheduling problems; that is, once started a task executes without interruption until it is completed. For disjunctive scheduling (i.e., scheduling on a resource of capacity $C = 1$) on a set of n tasks, there are well-known $\mathcal{O}(n \log n)$ edge-finding algorithms [3], [11]. In cumulative scheduling, where tasks may have different capacity requirements, edge-finding is more challenging. Early work by Nuijten [9] and Baptiste [2] resulted in cumulative edge-finding algorithms of complexity $\mathcal{O}(n^2 k)$ (where k is the number of distinct capacity requirements among the tasks) and $\mathcal{O}(n^2)$, respectively. Mercier and Van Hentenryck [8] demonstrated that both of these algorithms were incomplete, and provided a correct $\mathcal{O}(n^2 k)$ algorithm. More recently, Vilím [13] gave a $\mathcal{O}(kn \log n)$ algorithm, using an extension of the Θ-tree data structure which had previously been used [11] to improve the complexity of disjunctive edge-finding.

In this paper, we present a new cumulative edge-finding algorithm with a complexity of $\mathcal{O}(n^2)$. This algorithm uses the maximum density and minimum slack of sets of tasks to quickly locate the set Θ that provides the strongest update to the bounds of i.

The paper is organized as follows. Section 2 defines the cumulative scheduling problem, and the notations used in the paper. Section 3 gives a formal definition of the edge finding rules; Section 4 provides dominance properties of these rules. Section 5 presents the new edge-finding algorithm and a proof of its soundness. Section 6 discusses the overall complexity of the algorithm. Section 7 reports experimental results.

2   Cumulative Scheduling Problem

The cumulative scheduling problem (CuSP) is a sub-problem of the RCPSP, where precedence constraints are relaxed and a single resource is considered at a time; both problems are NP-complete [1]. In a CuSP, there is a finite set of tasks or activities with fixed processing times and resource requirements. Each task has a defined earliest start and latest completion time. The problem consists of deciding when to execute each task so that time and resource constraints are satisfied. Tasks are assumed to be processed without interruption. Formally, this problem is defined as follows:

Definition 1 (Cumulative Scheduling Problem). *A Cumulative Scheduling Problem (CuSP) is defined by a set T of tasks to be performed on a resource of capacity C. Each task $i \in T$ must be executed without interruption over p_i units of time between an earliest start time r_i (release date) and a latest end time d_i (deadline). Moreover, each task requires a constant amount of resource c_i. It is assumed that all data are integer. A solution of a CuSP is a schedule that assigns*

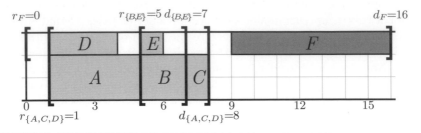

Fig. 1. A scheduling problem of 6 tasks sharing a resource of capacity $C = 3$

a starting date s_i to each task i such that:

$$\forall i \in T : r_i \leq s_i \leq s_i + p_i \leq d_i \tag{1}$$

$$\forall \tau : \sum_{i \in T, \ s_i \leq \tau < s_i + p_i} c_i \leq C \tag{2}$$

The inequalities in (1) ensure that each task is assigned a feasible start and end time, while (2) enforces the resource constraint. An example of a CuSP is given in Fig. 1.

We define the energy of a task i as $e_i = c_i \cdot p_i$. This notation, along with that of earliest start and latest completion time, may be extended to non-empty sets of tasks as follows:

$$r_\Omega = \min_{j \in \Omega} r_j, \quad d_\Omega = \max_{j \in \Omega} d_j, \quad e_\Omega = \sum_{j \in \Omega} e_j \tag{3}$$

By convention, if Ω is the empty set, $r_\Omega = +\infty$, $d_\Omega = -\infty$, and $e_\Omega = 0$. Throughout the paper, we assume that for any task $i \in T$, $r_i + p_i \leq d_i$ and $c_i \leq C$, otherwise the problem has no solution. We let $n = |T|$ denote the number of tasks, and $k = |\{c_i, i \in T\}|$ denote the number of distinct capacity requirements.

Clearly, if there exists a set of tasks $\Omega \subseteq T$ which cannot be scheduled in the window from r_Ω to d_Ω without exceeding the capacity, then the CuSP has no feasible solution. *Overload checking* algorithms typically enforce the following relaxation of this feasibility condition, which may be computed in $\mathcal{O}(n \log n)$ time [12], [14]:

Definition 2 (E-Feasibility). *[8] A problem is E-feasible if* $\forall \Omega \subseteq T$, $\Omega \neq \emptyset$

$$C \left(d_\Omega - r_\Omega \right) \geq e_\Omega . \tag{4}$$

It is obvious that a CuSP that fails the E-feasibility condition cannot have a feasible solution. In the rest of the paper, we only consider E-feasible CuSPs.

3   The Edge-Finding Rule

The main idea of edge-finding is to discover a set of tasks $\Omega \subset T$ and a task $i \notin \Omega$ such that, in any solution, all the tasks in Ω end before the end of i;

following [13], we denote this relationship $\Omega \lessdot i$. Once an appropriate Ω and i have been located, the earliest start time of i can be adjusted using the following rule:

$$\Omega \lessdot i \implies r_i \geq r_\Theta + \left\lceil \frac{1}{c_i} \operatorname{rest}(\Theta, c_i) \right\rceil \tag{5}$$

for all $\Theta \subseteq \Omega$ such that $\operatorname{rest}(\Theta, c_i) > 0$, where

$$\operatorname{rest}(\Theta, c_i) = \begin{cases} e_\Theta - (C - c_i)(d_\Theta - r_\Theta) & \text{if } \Theta \neq \emptyset \\ 0 & \text{otherwise} \end{cases} . \tag{6}$$

The condition $\operatorname{rest}(\Theta, c_i) > 0$ states that the total energy e_Ω that must be scheduled in the window $[r_\Omega, d_\Omega)$ is strictly larger than the energy that could be scheduled without making any start time of i in that window infeasible. The proof of these results can be found in [2], [9].

It remains to define what tasks and sets of tasks satisfy the condition $\Omega \lessdot i$. Proposition 1 provides conditions under which all tasks of a set Ω of an E-feasible CuSP end before the end of a task i.

Proposition 1. *Let Ω be a set of tasks and let $i \notin \Omega$ be a task of an E-feasible CuSP.*

$$e_{\Omega \cup \{i\}} > C\left(d_\Omega - r_{\Omega \cup \{i\}}\right) \Rightarrow \Omega \lessdot i \ , \tag{EF}$$
$$r_i + p_i \geq d_\Omega \quad \Rightarrow \quad \Omega \lessdot i \ . \tag{EF1}$$

Proof. (EF) is the traditional edge-finding rule; proof can be found in [9,2]. The addition of (EF1), proposed in [13], strengthens the edge-finding rule; the proof follows trivially from the fact that $r_i + p_i \geq d_\Omega$ implies that task i ends before all tasks in the set Ω. $\qquad\square$

In the example shown in Fig. 1, the rule (EF) correctly detects $\Omega \lessdot F$ for $\Omega = \{A, B, C, D, E\}$. Using the set $\Theta = \Omega$ in formula (5), shows that the release date of F may be updated to 5; however, allowing $\Theta = \{B, E\}$ instead yields an updated bound of 6. A value of $\Omega = \{B, E\}$ would not meet the edge-finding condition in (EF); the set $\{A, B, C, D, E\}$ is needed to detect the precedence condition.

Combining (EF) and (EF1) with (5) gives us a formal definition of an edge-finding algorithm:

Definition 3 (Specification of a complete edge-finding algorithm). *An edge-finding algorithm receives as input an E-feasible CuSP, and produces as output a vector of updated lower bounds for the release times of the tasks $\langle LB_1, \ldots, LB_n \rangle$, where:*

$$LB_i = \max\left(r_i, \max_{\substack{\Omega \subseteq T \\ i \notin \Omega \\ \alpha(\Omega, i)}} \max_{\substack{\Theta \subseteq \Omega \\ \operatorname{rest}(\Theta, c_i) > 0}} r_\Theta + \left\lceil \frac{1}{c_i} \operatorname{rest}(\Theta, c_i) \right\rceil \right) \tag{7}$$

with

$$\alpha\left(\Omega, i\right) \stackrel{def}{=} \left(C\left(d_\Omega - r_{\Omega \cup \{i\}}\right) < e_{\Omega \cup \{i\}}\right) \vee \left(r_i + p_i \geq d_\Omega\right) \tag{8}$$

and

$$\text{rest}(\Theta, c_i) = \begin{cases} e_\Theta - (C - c_i)(d_\Theta - r_\Theta) & \text{if } \Theta \neq \emptyset \\ 0 & \text{otherwise} \end{cases} \tag{9}$$

4   Dominance Properties of the Rules

Clearly an edge-finder cannot efficiently consider all sets $\Theta \subseteq \Omega \subset T$ to update a task i. In order to reduce the number of sets which must be considered, we first consider the following definition:

Definition 4 (Task Intervals). *(After [4]) Let $L, U \in T$. The task intervals $\Omega_{L,U}$ is the set of tasks*

$$\Omega_{L,U} = \{j \in T \mid r_L \leq r_j \wedge d_j \leq d_U\} \ . \tag{10}$$

It is demonstrated in [8] that an edge-finder that only considers sets $\Omega \subseteq T$ and $\Theta \subseteq \Omega$ which are also task intervals can be complete. Furthermore, we can reduce the number of intervals that must be checked according to the following propositions:

Proposition 2. *[8] Let i be a task and Ω, Θ be two task sets of an E-feasible CuSP with $\Theta \subseteq \Omega$. If the edge-finding rule (EF) applied to task i with pair (Ω, Θ) allows to update the earliest start time of i then*

(i) there exists four tasks L, U, l, u such that $r_L \leq r_l < d_u \leq d_U < d_i \wedge r_L \leq r_i$
(ii) the edge-finding rule (EF) applied to task i with the pair $(\Omega_{L,U}, \Omega_{l,u})$ allows at least the same update of the earliest start time of task i.

Proposition 3. *Let i be a task and Ω, Θ be two task sets of an E-feasible CuSP with $\Theta \subseteq \Omega$. If the edge-finding rule (EF1) applied to task i with pair (Ω, Θ) allows to update the earliest start time of i then*

(i) there exists four tasks L, U, l, u such that $r_L \leq r_l < d_u \leq d_U < d_i$
(ii) the edge-finding rule (EF1) applied to task i with the pair $(\Omega_{L,U}, \Theta_{l,u})$ allows at least the same update of the earliest start time of task i.

Proof. The proof of Proposition 3 is similar to that of Proposition 2, given in [8].

5   A New Edge-Finding Algorithm

In this section, we present a quadratic edge-finding algorithm that reaches the same fix point as the well known edge-finding algorithm proposed by Vilím [13].

We start by considering the $\mathcal{O}(n^2)$ edge-finding algorithm proposed in [2] and [9], which finds the set Θ for the inner maximization of Definition 3 by locating the task intervals with the minimum *slack*, as given by the following definitions.

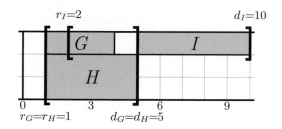

Fig. 2. Three tasks to be scheduled on a resource of capacity $C = 3$

Definition 5. *Let Ω be a task set of an E-feasible CuSP. The* slack *of the task set Ω, denoted SL_Ω, is given by:* $SL_\Omega = C(d_\Omega - r_\Omega) - e_\Omega$.

Definition 6. *Let i and U be two tasks of an E-feasible CuSP. $\tau(U, i)$, where $r_{\tau(U,i)} \leq r_i$, defines the task intervals with the* minimum slack: *for all $L \in T$ such that $r_L \leq r_i$,*

$$C(d_U - r_{\tau(U,i)}) - e_{\Omega_{\tau(U,i),U}} \leq C(d_U - r_L) - e_{\Omega_{L,U}} \ .$$

For a given task i, the algorithm detects $\Omega \lessdot i$ by computing $SL_\Omega < e_i$ for all $\Omega = \Omega_{\tau(U,i),U}$ such that $d_U < d_i$ and $r_{\tau(U,i)} \leq r_i$. Furthermore, if the interval $\Theta_{l,u}$ that yields the strongest update to r_i is such that $r_l \leq r_i$, then $\Theta_{l,u}$ will be the interval of minimum slack. This is the situation shown in Fig. 2. Rather than determine r_l, the new algorithm computes a potential update to r_i using rest(Ω, c_i). However, if the strongest updating interval $\Theta_{l,u}$ has $r_i < r_l$, then $\Theta_{l,u}$ need not be the interval of minimum slack. For this case, we introduce the notion of interval *density*.

Definition 7. *Let Θ be a task set of an E-feasible CuSP. The* density *of the task set Θ, denoted $Dens_\Theta$, is given by:* $Dens_\Theta = \frac{e_\Theta}{d_\Theta - r_\Theta} \ .$

Definition 8. *Let i, u be two tasks of an E-feasible CuSP. $\rho(u, i)$, where $r_i < r_{\rho(u,i)}$, defines the task intervals with the* maximum density: *for all task $l \in T$ such that $r_i < r_l$,*

$$\frac{e_{\Theta_{l,u}}}{d_u - r_l} \leq \frac{e_{\Theta_{\rho(u,i),u}}}{d_u - r_{\rho(u,i)}} \ .$$

If the strongest updating interval $\Theta_{l,u}$ has $r_i < r_l$, then $\Theta_{l,u}$ will be the interval of maximum density. Consequently, the new algorithm computes a second potential update for each r_i: for each task u such that $d_u \leq d_U$, the task intervals of maximum density $\Theta_{\rho(u,i),u}$ with $r_{\rho(u,i)} > r_i$ is computed according to Definition 8, and the strongest update of any of these intervals becomes the second potential update. The algorithm does not determine in advance whether $r_l \leq r_i$ or not; that is, whether minimum slack or maximum density is the correct method to locate the strongest update. For each i, both potential updates are computed, and the stronger update is applied.

Consider the scheduling problem shown in Fig. 1. With $\Omega = \{A, B, C, D, E\}$ and $i = F$, the rule (EF) detects the condition $\Omega \lessdot i$. However, the algorithm from [9] fails to adjust r_F, because for all $\Theta \subseteq \Omega$ we have $r_\Theta > r_F$. We can update r_F using a task intervals of maximum density, $\Theta_{\rho(u,i),u}$ where $d_u \leq d_\Omega$. For $u \in \{A, C, D\}$, the interval of maximum density is $\Theta_{A,D} = \{A, B, C, D, E\}$, which has a density of $18/7 \approx 2.6$. Using (5) with $\Theta_{A,D}$ shows that we can strengthen the release date of F to $r_F \geq 5$. For $u \in \{B, E\}$, however, the interval of maximum density is $\Theta_{B,E} = \{B, E\}$, which has a density of $5/2 = 2.5$. Using (5) with $\Theta_{B,E}$ yields a new release date for F of $r_F \geq 6$, which is in fact the strongest update we can make.

Algorithm 1 performs these computations for all $i \in T$ in $\mathcal{O}(n^2)$ time. The outer loop (line 3) iterates through the tasks $U \in T$ forming the possible upper bounds of the task intervals, selected in the order of non-decreasing deadlines. The first inner loop (line 5) selects the tasks $i \in T$ that comprise the possible lower bounds for the task intervals, in non-increasing order by release date. If $d_i \leq d_U$, then the energy and density of $\Omega_{i,U}$ are calculated; if the new density is higher than $\Omega_{\rho(U,i),U}$, $\rho(U,i)$ becomes i. If $d_i > d_U$, then instead the potential update $Dupd_i$ to the release date of i is calculated, based on the current $\rho(U,i)$. This potential update is stored only if it is greater than the previous potential update value calculated for this task using the maximum density. The second inner loop (line 16) selects i in non-decreasing order by release date. The energies stored in the previous loop are used to compute the slack of the current interval $\Omega_{i,U}$. If the slack is lower than that of $\Omega_{\tau(U,i),U}$, $\tau(U,i)$ becomes i. Any task with a deadline greater than d_U is checked to see if it meets either edge-finding criteria (EF) or (EF1); if it does, a new potential update $SLupd_i$ for the task's release date is calculated using $\tau(U,i)$. This potential update is stored only if it is greater than the previous potential update value calculated for this task using the minimum slack. At the next iteration of the outer loop, $\rho(U,i)$ and $\tau(U,i)$ are re-initialized.

Before showing that Algorithm 1 is correct, let us prove some properties of its inner loops.

Proposition 4. *For each task i, Algorithm 1 calculates a potential update $Dupd_i$ to r_i based on the task intervals of maximum density such that*

$$Dupd_i = \max_{U:\, d_U < d_i \wedge \mathrm{rest}(\Theta_{\rho(U,i),U}, c_i) > 0} \left(r_{\rho(U,i)} + \left\lceil \mathrm{rest}(\Theta_{\rho(U,i),U}, c_i) \cdot \frac{1}{c_i} \right\rceil \right) . \quad (11)$$

Proof. Let $i \in T$ be any task. Each choice of $U \in T$ in the outer loop (line 3) starts with the values $r_\rho = -\infty$ and $maxEnergy = 0$. The inner loop at line 5 iterates through all tasks $i' \in T$ (T sorted in non-increasing order of release date). For any task $i' \in T$ such that $r_{i'} > r_i$, if $d_{i'} \leq d_U$, then $i' \in \Theta_{i',U}$, so $e_{i'}$ is added to $Energy$ (line 7). Hence $Energy = e_{\Theta_{i',U}}$ at each iteration. The test on line 8 ensures that r_ρ and $maxEnergy = e_{\Theta_{\rho,U}}$ are updated to reflect $\rho(U,i)$ for the current task intervals $\Theta_{i',U}$. Therefore, at the ith iteration of the inner loop, if $d_i > d_U$ then line 11 computes $\mathrm{rest}(i, U) = \mathrm{rest}(\Theta_{\rho(U,i),U}, c_i)$, and the potential update value: $r_\rho + \lceil \mathrm{rest}(i, U) \cdot \frac{1}{c_i} \rceil$ if $\mathrm{rest}(i, U) > 0$, and $-\infty$ otherwise. On

---

Algorithm 1. Edge-finding algorithm in $\mathcal{O}(n^2)$ time and $\mathcal{O}(n)$ space

Require: T is an array of tasks
Ensure: A lower bound LB_i' is computed for the release date of each task i

1   **for** $i \in T$ **do**
2      $LB_i' := r_i, \quad Dupd_i := -\infty, \quad SLupd_i := -\infty;$
3   **for** $U \in T$ *by non-decreasing deadline* **do**
4      $Energy := 0, \quad maxEnergy := 0, \quad r_\rho := -\infty;$
5   **for** $i \in T$ *by non-increasing release dates* **do**
6   **if** $d_i \le d_U$ **then**
7             $Energy := Energy + e_i;$
8   **if** $\left(\frac{Energy}{d_U - r_i} > \frac{maxEnergy}{d_U - r_\rho} \right)$ **then**
9                 $maxEnergy := Energy, \quad r_\rho := r_i \;;$
10   **else**
11             $rest := maxEnergy - (C - c_i)(d_U - r_\rho);$
12   **if** $(rest > 0)$ **then**
13                 $Dupd_i := \max(Dupd_i, \quad r_\rho + \lceil \frac{rest}{c_i} \rceil);$
14         $E_i := Energy \;;$
15      $minSL := +\infty, r_\tau := d_U \;;$
16   **for** $i \in T$ *by non-decreasing release date* **do**
17   **if** $(C(d_U - r_i) - E_i < minSL)$ **then**
18             $r_\tau := r_i, \quad minSL := C(d_U - r_\tau) - E_i \;;$
19   **if** $(d_i > d_U)$ **then**
20             $rest' := c_i(d_U - r_\tau) - minSL \;;$
21   **if** $(r_\tau \le d_U \wedge rest' > 0)$ **then**
22                 $SLupd_i := \max(SLupd_i, r_\tau + \lceil \frac{rest'}{c_i} \rceil);$
23   **if** $(r_i + p_i \ge d_U \vee minSL - e_i < 0)$ **then**
24             $LB_i' := \max(LB_i', Dupd_i, SLupd_i);$
25   **for** $i \in T$ **do**
26      $r_i := LB_i';$

---

line 13, $Dupd_i$ is updated only if $r_\rho + \lceil \text{rest}(i,U) \cdot \frac{1}{c_i} \rceil$ is larger than the current value of $Dupd_i$; since the outer loop selects the task U in non-decreasing order by d_U, we have:

$$Dupd_i = \max_{U\,:\,d_U < d_i \wedge \text{rest}(i,U) > 0} r_\rho + \lceil \text{rest}(i, U) \cdot \frac{1}{c_i} \rceil \,. \tag{12}$$

Hence formula (11) holds and the proposition is correct. □

Proposition 5. *For each task i, Algorithm 1 calculates a potential update $SLupd_i$ to r_i based on the task intervals of minimum slack such that*

$$SLupd_i = \max_{U\,:\,d_U < d_i \wedge \text{rest}(\Omega_{\tau(U,i)}, U, c_i) > 0} \left(r_{\tau(U,i)} + \left\lceil \text{rest}(\Omega_{\tau(U,i)}, U, c_i) \cdot \frac{1}{c_i} \right\rceil \right) \,. \tag{13}$$

Proof. Let $i \in T$ be any task. Each choice of U in the outer loop (line 3) starts with the values $r_\tau = d_U$ and $minSL = +\infty$ (line 15). The inner loop at line 16 iterates through all tasks $i' \in T$ (T sorted in non-decreasing order of release dates). For every task $i' \in T$, $e_{\Omega_{i',U}}$ has already been computed in the first loop and stored as Ei' (line 14); this is used to compute the slack of $\Omega_{i',U}$. If $SL_{\Omega_{i',U}} < minSL$, the values $r_\tau = r_{i'}$ and $minSL = C(d_U - r_{i'}) - e_{\Omega_{i',U}}$ are updated to reflect $\tau(U, i)$ for the current task intervals $\Omega_{i',U}$. At the ith iteration, if $d_i > d_U$, then line 20 computes $rest'(i, U) = \text{rest}(\Omega_{\tau(U,i),U}, c_i)$, and the potential update value: $r_\tau + \lceil rest'(i, U) \cdot \frac{1}{c_i} \rceil$ if $r_\tau \leq d_U \wedge rest'(i, U) > 0$, and $-\infty$ otherwise. On line 22, $SLupd_i$ is updated only if $r_\tau + \lceil rest'(i, U) \cdot \frac{1}{c_i} \rceil$ is larger than the current value of $SLupd_i$. Since the outer loop selects the task U in non-decreasing order by d_U we have:

$$SLupd_i = \max_{U \,:\, d_U \leq d_i \wedge r_\tau \leq d_U \wedge rest'(i,U) > 0} r_\tau + \lceil rest'(i, U) \cdot \frac{1}{c_i} \rceil \,. \tag{14}$$

Hence formula (13) holds and the proposition is correct.   □

We now provide a proof that the edge-finding condition (EF) can be checked using minimum slack.

Theorem 1. *For any task $i \in T$ and set of tasks $\Omega \subseteq T \setminus \{i\}$,*

$$e_{\Omega \cup \{i\}} > C(d_\Omega - r_{\Omega \cup \{i\}}) \vee r_i + p_i \geq d_\Omega \tag{15}$$

if and only if

$$e_i > C\left(d_U - r_{\tau(U,i)}\right) - e_{\Omega_{\tau(U,i),U}} \vee r_i + p_i \geq d_U \tag{16}$$

for some task $U \in T$ such that $d_U < d_i$, and $\tau(U, i)$ as specified in Definition 6.

Proof. Let $i \in T$ be any task.

It is obvious that (EF1) can be checked by $r_i + p_i \geq d_U$ for all tasks $U \in T$ with $d_i > d_\Omega$. In the rest of the proof, we focus on the rule (EF). We start by demonstrating that (15) implies (16). Assume there exists a subset $\Omega \subseteq T \setminus \{i\}$ such that $C(d_\Omega - r_{\Omega \cup \{i\}}) < e_\Omega + e_i$. By (EF), $\Omega \lessdot i$. By Proposition 2, there exists a task intervals $\Omega_{L,U} \lessdot i$, such that $d_i > d_U$ and $r_L \leq r_i$. By Definition 6 we have

$$C(d_U - r_{\tau(U,i)}) - e_{\Omega_{\tau(U,i),U}} \leq C(d_U - r_L) - e_{\Omega_{L,U}} \,. \tag{17}$$

Adding $-e_i$ to both sides of (17) and using the fact that

$$C(d_U - r_L) < e_{\Omega_{L,U}} + e_i \,, \tag{18}$$

it follows that

$$C\left(d_U - r_{\tau(U,i)}\right) < e_{\Omega_{\tau(U,i),U}} + e_i \,. \tag{19}$$

Now we show that (16) implies (15). Let $U \in T$ such that $d_U < d_i$, and $\tau(U, i) \in T$, be tasks that satisfy (16). By the definition of task intervals, $d_i > d_U$ implies $i \notin \Omega_{\tau(U,i),U}$. Since $r_{\tau(U,i)} \leq r_i$, we have

$$e_{\Omega_{\tau(U,i),U}} + e_i > C(d_U - r_{\tau(U,i)}) \geq C(d_{\Omega_{\tau(U,i),U}} - r_{\Omega_{\tau(U,i),U} \cup \{i\}}) \,. \tag{20}$$

Hence, (15) is satisfied for $\Omega = \Omega_{\tau(U,i),U}$.   □

Proposition 5 has shown that $\tau(U, i)$ and the minimum slack are correctly computed by the loop at line 16. Combined with Theorem 1 this justifies the use of $minSL - e_i < 0$ on line 23 to check (EF), where the condition (EF1) is also checked. Thus, for every task i Algorithm 1 correctly detects the sets $\Omega \subseteq T \setminus \{i\}$ for which rules (EF) and (EF1) demonstrate $\Omega \lessdot i$.

A complete edge-finder would always choose the set Θ for each task i that yielded the strongest update to the bound of i. In the following theorem, we demonstrate that our algorithm has the slightly weaker property of soundness; that is, the algorithm updates the bounds correctly, but might not always make the strongest adjustment to a bound on the first iteration.

Theorem 2. *For every task $i \in T$, and given the strongest lower bound LB_i as specified in Definition 3, Algorithm 1 computes some lower bound LB'_i, such that $r_i < LB'_i \le LB_i$ if $r_i < LB_i$, and $LB'_i = r_i$ if $r_i = LB_i$.*

Proof. Let $i \in T$ be any task. LB'_i is initialized to r_i. Because the value LB'_i is only updated by $\max(Dupd_i, SLupd_i, LB'_i)$ (line 24) after each detection, it follows that $LB'_i \ge r_i$. If the equality $LB_i = r_i$ holds, then no detection is found by Algorithm 1, and thus $LB'_i - r_i$ holds from the loop at line 25. In the rest of the proof, we assume that $r_i < LB_i$. By Propositions 2 and 3, there exist two task sets $\Theta_{l,u} \subseteq \Omega_{L,U} \subseteq T \setminus \{i\}$ such that $r_L \le r_l < d_u \le d_U < d_i$ and $r_L \le r_i$, for which the following holds:

$$\alpha\left(\Omega_{L,U}, i\right) \quad \wedge \quad LB_i = r_{\Theta_{l,u}} + \left\lceil \frac{1}{c_i} \operatorname{rest}(\Theta_{l,u}, c_i) \right\rceil . \tag{21}$$

As demonstrated by Proposition 5 and Theorem 1, Algorithm 1 correctly detects the edge-finding condition; it remains only to demonstrate the computation of update values. Since (EF) and (EF1) use the same inner maximization, the following two cases hold for both rules:

1. $r_i < r_l$: Here we prove that the update can be made using the task intervals of maximum density. According to Definition 8, we have

$$\frac{e_{\Theta_{l,u}}}{d_u - r_l} \le \frac{e_{\Theta_{\rho(u,i),u}}}{d_u - r_{\rho(u,i)}} . \tag{22}$$

Since $(\Omega_{L,U}, \Theta_{l,u})$ allows the update of the release date of task i, we have $\operatorname{rest}(\Theta_{l,u}, c_i) > 0$. Therefore,

$$\frac{e_{\Theta_{l,u}}}{d_{\Theta_{l,u}} - r_{\Theta_{l,u}}} > C - c_i . \tag{23}$$

By relations (22) and (23), it follows that $\operatorname{rest}(\Theta_{\rho(u,i),u}, c_i) > 0$. $r_i < r_{\rho(u,i)}$ implies $r_{\rho(u,i)} + \left\lceil \frac{1}{c_i} \operatorname{rest}(\Theta_{\rho(u,i),u}, c_i) \right\rceil > r_i$. According to Proposition 4, the value $Dupd_i = r_{\rho(u,i)} + \left\lceil \frac{1}{c_i} \operatorname{rest}(\Theta_{\rho(u,i),u}, c_i) \right\rceil > r_i$ is computed by Algorithm 1 at line 13. Therefore, after the detection condition is fulfilled at line 23, the release date of task i is updated to $LB'_i = \max(Dupd_i, SLupd_i) \ge Dupd_i > r_i$.

2. $r_l \leq r_i$: Here we prove that the update can be made using the task intervals of minimal slack. By Definition 6, we have:

$$C(d_u - r_{\tau(u,i)}) - e_{\Theta_{\tau(u,i),u}} \leq C(d_u - r_l) - e_{l,u} \ . \tag{24}$$

Adding $-c_i(d_u - r_{\tau(u,i)}) - c_i \cdot r_{\tau(u,i)}$ to the left hand side and $-c_i(d_u - r_l) - c_i \cdot r_l$ to the right hand side of (24) we get

$$-c_i \cdot r_{\tau(u,i)} - \text{rest}(\Theta_{\tau(u,i),u}, c_i) \leq -c_i \cdot r_l - \text{rest}(\Theta_{l,u}, c_i) \ . \tag{25}$$

Therefore,

$$r_{\tau(u,i)} + \frac{1}{c_i} \text{rest}(\Theta_{\tau(u,i),u}, c_i) \geq r_l + \frac{1}{c_i} \text{rest}(\Theta_{l,u}, c_i) \tag{26}$$

and

$$r_{\tau(u,i)} + \frac{1}{c_i} \text{rest}(\Theta_{\tau(u,i),u}, c_i) > r_i \tag{27}$$

since $r_l + \frac{1}{c_i} \text{rest}(\Theta_{l,u}, c_i) > r_i$. From inequality (27), it follows that

$$\text{rest}(\Theta_{\tau(u,i),u}, c_i) > 0 \tag{28}$$

since $r_{\tau(u,i)} \leq r_i$. According to Proposition 5, the value

$$SLupd_i = r_{\tau(u,i)} + \frac{1}{c_i} \text{rest}(\Theta_{\tau(u,i),u}, c_i) > r_i \tag{29}$$

is computed by Algorithm 1 at line 20. Therefore, after the detection condition is fulfilled at line 23, the updated release date of task i satisfies $LB'_i > r_i$.

Hence, Algorithm 1 is sound.   □

6   Overall Complexity

According to Theorem 2, Algorithm 1 will always make some update to r_i if an update is justified by the edge-finding rules, although possibly not always the strongest update. As there are a finite number of updating sets, Algorithm 1 must reach the same fixpoint as other correct edge-finding algorithms. This "lazy" approach has recently been used to reduce the complexity of not-first/not-last filtering for cumulative resources [6], [10]; the situation differs from the previous quadratic edge-finder [9], which missed some updates altogether. Now we demonstrate that in most cases Algorithm 1 finds the strongest update immediately; when it does not, it requires at most $n - 1$ propagations.

Theorem 3. *Let $i \in T$ be any task of an E-feasible CuSP. Let $\Theta \subseteq T \setminus \{i\}$ be a set used to perform the maximum adjustment of r_i by the edge-finding rule. Let $\rho(u, i)$ be a task as given in Definition 8, applied to $i, u \in T$ with $d_u = d_\Theta$. Then Algorithm 1 performs the strongest update of r_i in the following number of iterations:*

1. *If $r_\Theta \leq r_i$, then on the first iteration,*
2. *If $r_i < r_\Theta$ then:*
   (a) If $r_i < r_\Theta \leq r_{\rho(u,i)}$, then also on the first iteration,
   (b) If $r_i < r_{\rho(u,i)} \leq r_\Theta$, then after at most $n - 1$ iterations.

Proof. Given $i \in T$, let $\Theta \subseteq T \setminus \{i\}$ be a task set used to perform the maximum adjustment of r_i by the edge-finding rule. Let $\rho(u, i)$ be the task of Definition 8 applied to i and $u \in T$ with $d_u = d_\Theta$.

1. Assume $r_\Theta \leq r_i$. By Propositions 1 and 2, and the proof of the second item of Theorem 2, formula (26) holds. By Proposition 5, when Algorithm 1 considers u in the outer loop and i in the second inner loop, it sets

$$Dupd_i = r_{\tau(u,i)} + \left\lceil \frac{1}{c_i} \text{rest}(\Theta_{\tau(u,i),u}, c_i) \right\rceil \geq r_\Theta + \left\lceil \frac{1}{c_i} \text{rest}(\Theta, c_i) \right\rceil . \quad (30)$$

   As the adjustment value of Θ is maximal, r_i is updated to $r_\Theta + \lceil \frac{1}{c_i} \text{rest}(\Theta, c_i) \rceil$.
2. Assume $r_i < r_\Theta$. We analyze two subcases:
   (a) $r_i < r_\Theta \leq r_{\rho(u,i)}$: According to definition of task $\rho(u, i)$, we have

$$\frac{e_\Theta}{d_\Theta - r_\Theta} \leq \frac{e_{\Theta_{\rho(u,i),u}}}{d_u - r_{\rho(u,i)}} . \quad (31)$$

   Removing $\frac{e_{\Theta_{\rho(u,i),u}}}{d_\Theta - r_\Theta}$ from each side of (31), we get

$$e_\Theta - e_{\Theta_{\rho(u,i),u}} \leq \frac{e_{\Theta_{\rho(u,i),u}}}{d_u - r_{\rho(u,i)}} (r_{\rho(u,i)} - r_\Theta) . \quad (32)$$

   As the problem is E-feasible, we have

$$\frac{e_{\Theta_{\rho(u,i),u}}}{d_u - r_{\rho(u,i)}} \leq C . \quad (33)$$

   Combining inequalities (32) and (33) gives

$$C r_\Theta + e_\Theta \leq C r_{\rho(u,i)} + e_{\Theta_{\rho(u,i),u}} . \quad (34)$$

   Obviously, inequality (34) is equivalent to

$$r_\Theta + \left\lceil \frac{1}{c_i} \text{rest}(\Theta, c_i) \right\rceil \leq r_{\rho(u,i)} + \left\lceil \frac{1}{c_i} \text{rest}(\Theta_{\rho(u,i),u}, c_i) \right\rceil . \quad (35)$$

   Proposition 4 shows that when Algorithm 1 considers u in the outer loop and i in the first inner loop, it sets

$$Dupd_i = r_{\rho(u,i)} + \left\lceil \frac{1}{c_i} \text{rest}(\Theta_{\rho(u,i),u}, c_i) \right\rceil \geq r_\Theta + \left\lceil \frac{1}{c_i} \text{rest}(\Theta, c_i) \right\rceil . \quad (36)$$

   As the adjustment value of Θ is maximal, r_i is updated to $r_\Theta + \lceil \frac{1}{c_i} \text{rest} (\Theta, c_i) \rceil$.
   (b) $r_i < r_{\rho(u,i)} \leq r_\Theta$: Let $\Theta^k_{\leq i} := \{j, j \in T \wedge r_j \leq r_i \wedge d_j \leq d_\Theta\}$ and $\Theta^k_{>i} := \{j, j \in T \wedge r_j > r_i \wedge d_j \leq d_\Theta\}$ be sets of tasks defined at the kth iteration of Algorithm 1. If the maximum adjustment is not found after this iteration, then at least one task is moved from $\Theta^k_{>i}$ to $\Theta^k_{\leq i}$. Indeed, if at the kth and $k{+}1^{\text{th}}$ iteration, $\Theta^k_{\leq i} = \Theta^{k+1}_{\leq i}$, $\Theta^k_{>i} = \Theta^{k+1}_{>i}$ and the maximum adjustment is not found, then the tasks $\tau(u, i) \in \Theta^k_{\leq i} = \Theta^{k+1}_{\leq i}$ (Definition 6) and $\rho(u, i) \in \Theta^k_{>i} = \Theta^{k+1}_{>i}$ (Definition 8) are the same for both iterations. Therefore, at the $k{+}1^{\text{th}}$ iteration, no new adjustment

is found, yet the maximum adjustment of the release date of task i is
not reached, thus contradicting the soundness of Algorithm 1. Hence,
the maximum adjustment of the release date of task i is reached after at
most $|\Theta^1_{>i}| \leq n - 1$ iterations.   □

We argue that, in practice, the possibility of our algorithm using multiple propagations to find the strongest bound is not significant. In the first place, edge-
finders are not idempotent; adjustment to the release dates and deadlines of the
tasks is not taken into account during one iteration, so additional propagations
are always required to reach a recognizable fixpoint. Furthermore, in actual cumulative problems, there are typically a relatively small number of task sets
that could be used to update the start time of a given task, so the number of
propagations should not normally approach the worst case. This claim is borne
out by the experimental observations reported in the next section.

7   Experimental Results

The new edge-finding algorithm presented in section 5 was implemented in C++
using the Gecode 3.4.2 [5] constraint solver. The Gecode cumulative propagator
for tasks of fixed duration is a sequence of three filters: the $\mathcal{O}(kn \log n)$ edge-
finding algorithm from [13], overload checking, and time tabling. We tested this
propagator against a modified version that substituted the new quadratic edge-
finding filter for the Θ-tree filter.

Tests were performed on the single-mode J30, J60, and J90 test sets of the
well-established benchmark library PSPLib [7]. Each data set consists of 480
instances, of 30, 60, and 90 tasks respectively; these tasks require multiple shared
resources, each of which was modeled with a cumulative constraint. Precedence
relations were enforced as a series of linear relations between task start and end
times. Branch and bound search was used to find the minimum end time for
the project; variables were selected by minimum domain size, with ties broken
by selecting the variable occuring in the most propagators, while values were
selected starting with the minimum. Tests were performed on a 3.07 GHz Intel
Core i7 processor with a time limit of 300 seconds; only tests for which both
propagators were able to find the best solution within 300 seconds are included
in Fig. 3 (8 instances in which only the quadratic propagator was able to find
a solution in the time available were discarded)[1]. Each instance was run three
times, with the best result for each filtering algorithm reported.

Our tests showed that the quadratic edge-finder was faster in almost all test
instances, with a proportional speedup increasing with the size of the instance.
Of the 1034 instances solved by both filters, only four instances from the j3036
group and the j601_1 instance were solved more quickly by the Θ-tree filter.
Figure 3a compares the runtimes of the hardest instances (with runtime greater
than 1 second on the Θ-tree filter).

---

[1] Detailed experimental results: http://user.it.uu.se/~jossc163/quadef2011.

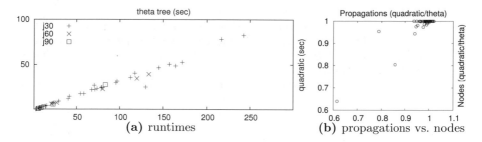

Fig. 3. Two comparisons of Θ-tree vs. quadratic edge-finding: (a) runtimes for instances where both methods found the best solution, and (b) the proportion of quadratic to Θ-tree propagation counts, and node counts.

In order to determine the difference in propagation strength between the two filters, we instrumented the two propagators to count the number of executions of the cumulative propagator in each of the 1034 solved instances. As expected, the number of propagations was different in 122 of these instances; however, only in 35 of those instances was the number of propagations required by the quadratic filter greater. While this could suggest that the quadratic filter reaches fixpoint more quickly than the Θ-tree filter in some cases, a more likely explanation is that the domain reductions made by the two filters before reaching fixpoint were different enough to affect the filtering strength of the other propagators used in the problem. Figure 3b compares the number of propagations (shown as the proportion of quadratic propagations to Θ-tree propagations) to the number of nodes in the search tree for each algorithm. We observe that, even in those instances where the quadratic filter required a larger number of propagations, the number of nodes in the search tree of the quadratic algorithm was always less than equal to those in the Θ-tree filter search tree, implying that the quadratic algorithm reaches at least as strong a fixpoint as the Θ-tree filter.

8   Conclusion

In this paper, we have presented a quadratic edge-finding filtering rule for cumulative scheduling that reaches the same fixpoint as previous algorithms, possibly after more propagations. While its complexity does not strictly dominate that of Vilím's $\mathcal{O}(kn \log n)$ algorithm, experimental results demonstrate that on a standard benchmark suite our algorithm is substantially faster. Future work will focus on finding a complete quadratic edge-finder, a similar algorithm for extended edge-finding, and investigating the use of Θ-trees to increase the efficiency of finding maximum density.

Acknowledgements. The third author is supported by grant 2009-4384 of the Swedish Research Council (VR). The authors would also like to thank Christian Schulte for his assistance with the Gecode cumulative propagator.

References

1. Baptiste, P., Le Pape, C.: Constraint propagation and decomposition techniques for highly disjunctive and highly cumulative project scheduling problems. In: Smolka, G. (ed.) CP 1997. LNCS, vol. 1330, pp. 375–389. Springer, Heidelberg (1997)
2. Baptiste, P., Le Pape, C., Nuijten, W.: Constraint-based scheduling: applying constraint programming to scheduling problems. Kluwer, Boston (2001)
3. Carlier, J., Pinson, E.: Adjustment of heads and tails for the job-shop problem. European Journal of Operational Research 78, 146–161 (1994)
4. Caseau, Y., Laburthe, F.: Improved CLP scheduling with task intervals. In: Van Hentenryck, P. (ed.) ICLP94, pp. 369–383. MIT Press, Boston (1994)
5. Gecode Team: Gecode, a generic constraint development environment (2006), http://www.gecode.org
6. Kameugne, R., Fotso, L.P.: A not-first/not-last algorithm for cumulative resource in $\mathcal{O}(n^2 \log n)$ (2010) (accepted to CP 2010 Doctoral Program)
7. Kolisch, R., Sprecher, A.: PSPLIB – A project scheduling problem library. European Journal of Operational Research 96(1), 205–216 (1997)
8. Mercier, L., Van Hentenryck, P.: Edge finding for cumulative scheduling. INFORMS Journal on Computing 20(1), 143–153 (2008)
9. Nuijten, W.: Time and resource constrained scheduling: a constraint satisfaction approach. PhD thesis, Eindhoven University of Technology (1994)
10. Schutt, A., Wolf, A.: A New $\mathcal{O}(n^2 \log n)$ Not-First/Not-Last Pruning Algorithm for Cumulative Resource Constraints. In: Cohen, D. (ed.) CP 2010. LNCS, vol. 6308, pp. 445–459. Springer, Heidelberg (2010)
11. Vilím, P.: Global constraints in scheduling. PhD thesis, Charles University, Prague (2007)
12. Vilím, P.: Max energy filtering algorithm for discrete cumulative resources. In: van Hoeve, W.-J., Hooker, J.N. (eds.) CPAIOR 2009. LNCS, vol. 5547, pp. 66–80. Springer, Heidelberg (2009)
13. Vilím, P.: Edge Finding Filtering Algorithm for Discrete Cumulative Resources in $\mathcal{O}(kn \log n)$. In: Gent, I.P. (ed.) CP 2009. LNCS, vol. 5732, pp. 802–816. Springer, Heidelberg (2009)
14. Wolf, A., Schrader, G.: $\mathcal{O}(n \log n)$ overload checking for the cumulative constraint and its application. In: Umeda, M., Wolf, A., Bartenstein, O., Geske, U., Seipel, D., Takata, O., et al. (eds.) INAP 2005. LNCS (LNAI), vol. 4369, pp. 88–101. Springer, Heidelberg (2006)

A CSP Solver Focusing on FAC Variables *

Éric Grégoire, Jean-Marie Lagniez, and Bertrand Mazure

Université Lille-Nord de France,
CRIL - CNRS UMR 8188,
Artois, F-62307 Lens
{gregoire,lagniez,mazure}@cril.fr

Abstract. The contribution of this paper is twofold. On the one hand, it introduces a concept of FAC variables in discrete Constraint Satisfaction Problems (CSPs). FAC variables can be discovered by local search techniques and powerfully exploited by MAC-based methods. On the other hand, a novel synergetic combination schema between local search paradigms, generalized arc-consistency and MAC-based algorithms is presented. By orchestrating a multiple-way flow of information between these various fully integrated search components, it often proves more competitive than the usual techniques on most classes of instances.

1   Introduction

These last decades, many research efforts have been devoted in the Artificial Intelligence community to the design of general algorithms and solvers for discrete Constraint Satisfaction Problems (in short, CSPs). Tracing back to the seminal work on simulated annealing by Kirkpatrick *et al.* [17], stochastic local-search approaches (SLS) were investigated successfully in early pioneering works, mainly based on the so-called *min-conflicts* heuristic developed by Minton *et al.* [24]. They were considered powerful paradigms for CSPs -and their specific SAT case- in light of the results by e.g. Gu [13], Selman *et al.* [27] and Cheeseman *et al.* [4].

However, apart from the specific SAT domain and with only a few exceptions (e.g. [10], [16], [7], [8]), the current mainstream approaches to general CSPs solving rely on complete methods that do not include SLS components as main tools (*e.g.*, Abscon [23,19], Choco [29], Mistral [14], Sugar [28], etc.). One reason lies in the fact that SLS is not an exhaustive search paradigm and does not allow by itself to prove the absence of any solution for a CSP. Moreover, SLS often entails significant computations and search-space explorations that advanced complete techniques are expected to attempt to avoid, at least partially. Finally, it is sometimes (but wrongly) believed that SLS should merely be devoted to situations where solutions are densely distributed throughout the state space, justifying some possible random aspects in the search.

---

* Part of this work was supported by the French Ministry of Higher Education and Research, Nord/Pas-de-Calais Regional Council and E.C. FEDER program through the 'Contrat de Projets État/Région (CPER) 2007-2013' and by the French National Research Agency (ANR) through the UNLOC and TUPLES projects.

J. Lee (Ed.): CP 2011, LNCS 6876, pp. 493–507, 2011.

On the contrary, this paper shows that complete and SLS techniques for solving CSPs can benefit one another. More precisely, it presents a synergetic combination of local search and elements of complete techniques that often outperforms the usual complete, SLS, or basic hybrid approaches involving (generalized) arc-consistency and SLS, in the following sense. This method is not only complete, it is also robust in the sense that it solves both satisfiable or unsatisfiable (structured or random) CSPs instances quite indifferently. Actually, our comprehensive experimental studies show that it solves more instances than the currently existing techniques.

One key issue is that the SLS computation that is guided as much as possible towards the most difficult subparts of the CSP can provide powerful oracles and information when some further steps of a complete search are required. Although this latter idea was already exploited in some previous works in the SAT domain [21], it is refined here thanks to an original concept of FAC variables. FAC variables of a CSP, as **F**alsified in **A**ll **C**onstraints, are variables occurring in all falsified constraints under some intrepretation, and thus in at least one constraint per minimal core (also called MUC, for Minimal Unsatisfiable Core) of the CSP when such cores exist. Interestingly, SLS often allows FAC variables to be detected efficiently and complete MAC-based techniques focusing first on FAC variables can have their efficiency boosted on many instances. Likewise, e.g. powerful heuristics (especially the $dom/wdeg$ [3]) developed within complete CSP techniques can play an essential role in the SLS computation. Actually, the proposed method, called FAC-SOLVER, is an elaborate imbrication of SLS and steps of complete techniques that orchestrates a multiple-way flow of information between various fully integrated search components.

The paper is organized as follows. In the next Section, some basic technical background about CSPs is provided. Then, the FAC variable concept is presented. In Section 4, the architecture of the FAC-SOLVER method is presented globally, before each component is detailed. Comprehensive experimental studies are discussed in Section 5. In the conclusion, the focus is on perspectives and promising paths for future research.

2   CSPs Technical Background

A CSP or *Constraint Network* $\mathcal{CN}$ is a pair $\langle \mathcal{X}, \mathcal{C} \rangle$ where $\mathcal{X}$ is a finite set of n variables s.t. each variable X of $\mathcal{X}$ is associated with a finite set $dom(X)$ of candidate values for X. $\mathcal{C}$ is a finite set of m constraints on variables from $\mathcal{X}$ s.t. each constraint C in $\mathcal{C}$ is associated with one relation $rel(C)$ indicating the set of tuples of authorized values for the variables occurring in C. An assignment $\mathcal{I}$ of $\mathcal{CN}$ associates a value $\mathcal{I}(X) \in dom(X)$ to every variable $X \in \mathcal{X}$. We note $false(\mathcal{X}, \mathcal{C}, \mathcal{I})$ the set of variables that appear in at least one falsified constraint under the assignment $\mathcal{I}$. $\langle \mathcal{X}, \mathcal{C} \rangle|_{X=v}$ is the resulting CSP obtained from the CSP $\langle \mathcal{X}, \mathcal{C} \rangle$ by reducing $dom(X)$ to the singleton $\{v\}$ while $\langle \mathcal{X}, \mathcal{C} \rangle|_{X \neq v}$ is obtained by deleting the v value in $dom(X)$. We say that the assignment $\mathcal{I}$ is a local minimum for $\mathcal{CN}$ when no single change of value of any variable leads to a decrease of the total number of falsified constraints of $\mathcal{CN}$.

Solving a constraint network $\mathcal{CN}$ consists in checking whether $\mathcal{CN}$ admits at least one assignment that satisfies all constraints of $\mathcal{CN}$ and in delivering such an assignment in the positive case.

In the following, we consider both binary and non-binary constraints. Most current complete approaches to solve constraints networks are based on algorithms implementing *maintaining arc consistency* techniques (in short, MAC) [25]. Roughly, these techniques perform a depth-first search procedure with backtracking, while maintaining some forms of local (Generalized Arc) Consistency (in short GAC and AC), which are filtering techniques expelling detected forbidden values (see e.g. [20,2,18]).

3   FAC Variables

One key factor of the efficiency of the FAC-SOLVER approach relies on the following FAC *(Falsified in All Constraints) variable* concept.

Definition 1. *Let CN be a constraint network under an assignment $\mathcal{I}$. A FAC variable is a variable occurring in every falsified constraint of CN under $\mathcal{I}$.*

This concept can be related to the notion of *boundary* point introduced by Goldberg in the SAT domain [12]. For a CNF formula, a variable is boundary under an assignment of all propositional variables if this variable belongs to all clauses that are falsified by the assignment. This definition is similar to the FAC one, but we have adopted an alternative name for a simple reason: in the CSP context, this kind of variables is not at the so-called "boundary", *i.e.*, a situation where it is sufficient to inverse the truth value of a boundary variable to satisfy all falsified clauses. A FAC variable in the SAT domain thus draws a boundary line between satisfiabiliy and unsatisfiability of a part of the formula. In CSP, changing the value of a FAC variable does not ensure that constraints become satisfied. Accordingly, the notion of boundary as underlied by Goldberg cannot be applied in theCSP domain. For this reason we have decided to not use the same name. Nevertheless some interesting properties of boundary are preserved which can help understand the possible role of FAC variables for solving unsatisfiable CSPs.

Property 1. Any FAC variable X of CN occurs in at least one constraint per MUC of CN when CN is unsatisfiable.

Indeed, under any assignment $\mathcal{I}$, any MUC contains at least one falsified constraint. Thus, if a variable occurs within all constraints that are falsified under $\mathcal{I}$, it occurs within at least one constraint per MUC.

Property 2. Unsatisfiable CSPs that exhibit at least two MUCs sharing no variable do not possess any FAC variable.

FAC variables can play a key role in the inconsistency of a CSP since they are involved in all of its unresolvable minimal sets of conflicting constraints. Accordingly, focusing a MAC-based search component first on FAC variables (when they exist) might thus help.

In the worst case, checking whether a constraint belongs to at least one MUC, belongs to the Σ_2^p complexity class [9]. Moreover, a CSP can possess an exponential number of MUCs. Thus, detecting FAC variables by first computing all MUCs is untractable in the worst case. On the contrary, SLS provides a heuristic way to detect FAC variables at low cost. One direct but inefficient way to detect some of them would consist in looking for FAC variables for each assignment crossed by SLS. For efficiency reasons, we will look for FAC variables only for assignments that are local minima w.r.t. the number of currently falsified constraints of the CSP.

Satisfiable CSPs can also exhibit FAC variables. Interestingly, it appears that FAC variables can also be expected to play a positive role for solving those CSPs. Indeed, to some extent, these variables can also be expected to take part in the difficult part of those CSPs since they are involved in all falsified constraints under at least one assignment. Accordingly, it could be also useful to focus on them during a complete search.

Finally, it must be noted that when some variables are instantiated, a new CSP is actually created. FAC variables w.r.t. this new CSP can exist; they are not necessarily FAC variables w.r.t. the initial CSP.

In the FAC-SOLVER method, all FAC variables that can be detected when local minima are reached during a SLS will be collected. When a MAC-based component must be run thereafter, it will focus first on the FAC variables in hope for an improved efficiency.

Using FAC variables in a further systematic search component appears to be a refinement of some heuristics e.g. used in the SAT framework and involving hybrid SLS-DPLL algorithms. For example, [21] advocates to select the next variables to be assigned in a DPLL-based search for satisfiability among the variables belonging to the most often falsified clauses during a preliminary failed SLS, as those variables probably belong to minimal cores of the instance. Also [11] recommends the use of critical clauses, *i.e.*, falsified clauses during a failed SLS that are such that any flip of a variable causes at least another clause to be falsified. Critical clauses were also shown to often belong to minimal cores. Branching on variables occurring in them appeared to boost the further complete search process [1]. FAC variables do not only occur in one minimal core but in all of them. Branching on them might thus increase the efficiency of the search process even more significantly. The FAC-SOLVER method described in the next Section was intended to implement and check these ideas on a large panel of instances.

4   FAC-SOLVER Approach

The FAC-SOLVER approach deeply integrates three search components in a novel synergetic way: a SLS, a MAC and an hybrid solver, which is itself mixing SLS and GAC. These components interact in several ways and share all information about the current global search process. The global architecture of FAC-SOLVER is described in Figure 1. Roughly, the process starts with a call to one SLS solver, then in the case of failure a hybrid solver is run followed by a limited MAC. Calls between different components depend on dynamical threshold values for two variables that play a strategic role, namely $SLSprogress$ and $\#conflicts$.

Algorithm 1 describes the FAC solver. First, a call to GAC ensures arc-consistency (or delivers a final inconsistency proof) and leads to some possible filterings (lines 4-5). Next, while a solution is not found or the problem is not proved inconsistent, the solver sequentially performs the three components described in the next sections. The number of conflicts $maxConf$ controls the restart associated to the Hybrid and MAC parts. It is initialized to 10 (line 2) and is geometrically increased at each iteration step of the

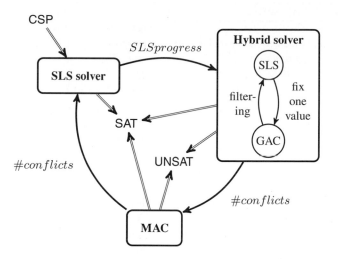

Fig. 1. Interactions between FAC-SOLVER basic search components

main loop (line 16). The complete assignment used by the local search is initialized randomly. The CSP $\langle \mathcal{X}, \mathcal{C} \rangle$ is shared by all components. It is simplified by successive assignments and refutations. At each new iteration, this CSP is reinitialized (only the filtering computed at level 0 are kept (line 9)). The $SLSprogress$ variable controls the duration of the SLS component run. It is initialized to $maxConf \times 8$. This variable will be increased and decreased by the SLS component. All components are detailed in the next sections.

4.1   The SLS Component

Let us detail the SLS procedure first which is described in a simplified way in the algorithm named Procedure SLS. It is a random-walk local search procedure *à la walksat* [26] with a *novelty* escape strategy [22]. In parallel, this SLS also tries to detect FAC variables each time a local minimum is reached. The variable controlling the progress of the SLS is $SLSprogress$, which is increased in two situations: when the number of falsified constraints reaches a new minimum value (line 13) and when FAC variables are discovered (line 5). It is decreased when no FAC variable is discovered in a local minimum (line 6). This variable is initialized to 10.000 if the CSP is binary and to 1.000 otherwise. This way to estimate the progress of the SLS is inspired from the adaptive noise introduced by Hoos *et al.* in [15]. When the SLS fails to prove the consistency of the CSP but seems rather stuck in its exploration, the $SLSprogress < 0$ test (line 7) allows the so-called Hybrid component to be activated, which will exploit in its turn all the information collected so-far. Intuitively, in addition to looking for an assignment satisfying the CSP, the SLS solver collects information about FAC variables. Due to the larger increment of the $SLSprogress$ control variable when FAC variables are discovered, it focuses its exploration on assignments that are close to local minima involving FAC variables.

Algorithm 1. FAC-solver

Data: A CSP $\langle \mathcal{X}, \mathcal{C} \rangle$
Result: *true* if the CSP is satisfiable, *false* otherwise

1   $result \longleftarrow unknown$;
2   $maxConf \longleftarrow 10$;
3   $S_e \longleftarrow \emptyset$;   //Set of FAC var. found with their FAC values
4   GAC() ;
5   **if** $\exists X \in \mathcal{X}$ *s.t.* $dom(X) = \emptyset$ **then return** *false* ;
6   $\mathcal{A} \longleftarrow$ a random assignment of $\mathcal{X}$;
7   **while** *(result = unknown)* **do**
8   initialize $SLSprogress$ variable ;
9   Backjump(*0*) ;   // backjump to level 0
10   SLS() ;
11   **if** *(result ≠ unknown)* **then return** *true* ;
12   Hybrid() ;
13   **if** *(result ≠ unknown)* **then return** *result* ;
14   MAC() ;
15   **if** *(result ≠ unknown)* **then return** *result* ;
16      $maxConf \longleftarrow maxConf \times 1.5$;

The SLS procedure is also used by the hybrid component. When this procedure is called by the hybrid component, the SLS works on a sub-CSP that is downsized by the various calls to the FIX procedure which is described in the next section. At the opposite, during the initial local search, SLS is handling the full CSP.

4.2 Hybrid SLS-GAC Component

The hybrid component allows to focus on expected difficult subparts of the instance. This allows to get FAC variables that are linked to the (expected) most difficult subparts to satisfy. This component is described in Procedure Hybrid. Roughly, starting with the current assignment $\mathcal{A}$ provided by the SLS component, a variable in a violated constraint is selected and is assigned according to $\mathcal{A}$ (lines 4-5). The $dom/wdeg$ heuristic [3] is used as a tiebreaker amongst the set of variables of a violated constraint. A call is made to the FIX procedure (line 6), which operates and propagates GAC (Generalized Arc-Consistency) filtering steps. This procedure detects also conflicts (*i.e.*, empty domains for variables in $\mathcal{X}$) which trigger a backtrack on the last fixed variables (line 4-11). The GAC version used in the solver is based on AC3 [20]. The FIX procedure reduces the domain variables of $\mathcal{X}$ which is shared by all components. In fact, during the Hybrid procedure, SLS is still running but waits for decisions and does neither revise them nor the propagations done by the FIX procedure. The assignment $\mathcal{A}$, used by SLS, is thus in part fixed by this hybridization. In some sense, those fixed variables are tabu for SLS.

The variable $\#conf$ measures the number of encountered conflicts. After the FIX procedure and when this number has become strictly larger than the dynamical $maxConf$ threshold, it is estimated that the hybrid component is stuck and a call to MAC is made. When this threshold is not reached the search goes back to the SLS component, the collected filtering information being preserved.

Procedure.   SLS

---

1 **while** $\exists C \in \mathcal{C}$ *s.t.* C *is violated by* $\mathcal{A}$ **do**
2   **if** *a local minimum is reached* **then**
3   **if** $\exists$ FAC *variables* **then**
4   add new FAC variables to $\mathcal{S}_e$;
5              $SLSprogress \longleftarrow SLSprogress + 1000$;
6   **else** $SLSprogress \longleftarrow SLSprogress - 1$;
7   **if** $SLSprogress < 0$ **then return**;
8   **else**
9   Change the value in $\mathcal{A}$ of one var. of $\mathcal{X}$ according to the novelty escape strategy ;
10   **else**
11   Change the value in $\mathcal{A}$ of one var. of $\mathcal{X}$ s.t. the number of violated constraints decreases ;
12   **if** *A new best configuration is obtained* **then**
13         $SLSprogress \longleftarrow SLSprogress + 1000$;
14 $result \longleftarrow true$;

Procedure.   Hybrid

---

1 $level \longleftarrow 0$;
2 $\#conf \longleftarrow 0$;
3 **while** $(\#conf < maxConf)$ **do**
4      $X \longleftarrow$ pick a variable according to $dom/wdeg$ s.t. X appears in violated constraint by $\mathcal{A}$;
5      $v \longleftarrow$ the value of X in $\mathcal{A}$;
6   FIX(X, v) ;
7   **if** $(result = false)$ **then return** ;
8   SLS() ;

4.3   MAC-Based Component

The MAC-based component starts with the initial CSP with the exception of filterings computed at level 0 during the SLS and the calls to FIX (line 1). This procedure is a standard MAC algorithm except that the focus is on collected FAC variables. The heuristic used to selected variable is $dom/wdeg$. For the first choices (lines 8-9), the variable is selected amongst the FAC variables collected during the SLS procedure. The next choices (line 11) are made within all variables. The use of FAC variables only for the first choices can be explained by the fact that the $dom/wdeg$ heuristics allows to focus on the same inconsistent part (*i.e.,* on the same core) whereas fixing another FAC variable can lead the search to be dispersed and slowing down the discovery of a small proof of inconsistency.

The weights used by the $dom/wdeg$ heuristic are preserved from one iteration to the next one in Algorithm 1, and are shared by all search components.

Moreover, this MAC procedure does not necessarily perform a complete search since if the number of conflicts $\#conf$ becomes larger than the $maxConf$ before a final

Procedure. FIX (X, v)

1 $dom(X) \longleftarrow \{v\}$;
2 $level \longleftarrow level + 1$;
3 GAC() ;
4 **while** $\exists X' \in \mathcal{X}$ s.t. $dom(X') = \emptyset$ **do**
5   **if** $level = 0$ **then**
6        $result \longleftarrow false$;
7   **return**;
8   Backtrack() ;
9     $level \longleftarrow level - 1$;
10    $\#conf \longleftarrow \#conf + 1$;
11    $dom(X) \longleftarrow dom(X) \setminus \{v\}$;
12   GAC() ;

decision is obtained, then the process goes back to the SLS component. In this latter case, the $maxConf$ control variable is increased in a geometric manner.

As $maxConf$ is increased whenever the MAC component fails, this component will eventually give a final result when this boundary becomes larger than the number of conflicts needed by MAC to solve the CSP. Accordingly, FAC-SOLVER is complete.

Procedure. MAC

1 Backjump(*0*) ;   // backjump to level 0
2 $level \longleftarrow 0$;
3 $\#conf \longleftarrow 0$;
4 **while** *($\#conf < maxConf$)* **do**
5   **if** $\mathcal{X} = \emptyset$ **then**
6        $result \longleftarrow true$;
7   **return** ;
8   **if** *($\#conf = 0$)* **and** *($\exists X \in \mathcal{S}_e \cap \mathcal{X}$)* **then**
9        $X \longleftarrow$ pick a variable in $\mathcal{S}_e$;
10   **else**
11       $X \longleftarrow$ pick a variable according to $dom/wdeg$;
12    $v \longleftarrow$ pick randomly a value in $dom(X)$;
13   FIX(X, v) ;
14   **if** *($result = false$)* **then return** ;

5   Experimental Results

In order to assess the efficiency of FAC-SOLVER, we have considered benchmarks from the last CSP competitions [5,6], which include binary vs. non-binary, random vs. real-life, satisfiable vs. unsatisfiable CSP instances. They were classified according to four types: 635 CSPs made of binary constraints in extension (BIN-EXT), 696 CSPs made of binary constraints in intension (BIN-INT), 704 CSPs involving n-ary constraints in extension (N-EXT) and 716 instances of CSPs of n-ary constraints in intention (N-INT). We have run four methods on all those instances: namely, our own implementation of SLS Walksat+Novelty, of an hybrid method combining SLS and GAC, of MAC and FAC-SOLVER. All tests have been conducted on a Xeon 3.2 GHz (2 G RAM) under Linux 2.6. Time-out has been set to 1200 seconds while a space limit has been set to 900 Mbytes. Note that the MAC version used in the experimentations makes use of a geometric restart policy that is similar way to our solver. Similarly, the SLS solver (Walksat+Novelty) used in our experimental comparison uses the same novelty heuristic than our solver. Note that, the solved unsatisfiable instances by novelty have been solved by GAC on the initial instance.

Table 1 summarizes the results in terms of the numbers of satisfiable and unsatisfiable instances that were solved. In each horizontal "total"-line, the solver that solves the most instances has been emphasized in gray. The main result is that FAC-SOLVER managed to solve more instances than any of the other methods globally for either satisfiable (SAT) or unsatisfiable (UNSAT) instances, and considering the subclasses of instances separately, for three types of CSPs. For the last type (binary CSP in extension), let us stress that the best solver is different in each of the three columns (SAT, UNS(AT) and TOT(AL)) and in each case, the number of solved instances by FAC-SOLVER is very close to the best one.

In Figure 2, five scatter points diagrams are given for a more detailed analysis. In each of them, two of the methods are pairwise compared w.r.t. instances that were solved by at least one of them. The X-axis represents the computing times in seconds by FAC-SOLVER whereas the Y-axis provides the performance of the second method. Results are expressed in seconds and represented according to a logarithmic scale. Instances were divided within the four classes detailed above. We provide separate diagrams for SAT and UNSAT instances. FAC-SOLVER is not compared with Walksat+Novelty on UNSAT instances since these instances are out of scope for the latter technique. The main information that can be drawn from these diagrams is as follows.

- More instances are located on the Y=1200 line than on the X=1200 one. This shows, as Table 1 summarizes it, that FAC-SOLVER solves more instances than any of the other considered methods.
- With the exceptions of UNSAT instances for MAC, there are more points located above the diagonals showing that FAC-SOLVER is generally more efficient than the other methods. Also, for UNSAT instances, the difference of time performance between pairs of methods is globally smaller than for SAT instances (points are less dispersed and are closer to the diagonal). FAC-SOLVER is generally more efficient than a mere combination of SLS and GAC. It is also more efficient than MAC on SAT instances (mainly due to the power of SLS). But there is no free lunch, the time spent on SLS by FAC-SOLVER on UNSAT instances leads to some small and very acceptable time overheads, compared with MAC. This is perhaps the price to pay to solve more unsatisfiable instances than MAC within the same price constraints, thanks to the collected information by SLS.

An important issue is the way according to which the efficiency of FAC-SOLVER might depend on the specific initial assignment selected by its SLS component. Actually, it appears that, on average, this dependency is weak and is not a serious troubling factor affecting the results. To show this robustness, we have selected 96 instances within the above benchmarks in a random fashion but according to their relative importance in each of the four classes of instances. For each of these instances, 50 successive runs of FAC-SOLVER have been conducted with a different initial (randomly generated) assignment. When an instance was solved by at least one run, it was also solved by the 49 other runs in 97 % of the situations, with a very low 2.52 seconds average deviation.

To show the importance of FAC variables, we have run our solver with and without computing and using the FAC variables. Table 2 provides typical results. The use of FAC variables allows more instances to be solved. Most of the time, the use of FAC variables can solve benchmarks more quickly. In rare cases, the use of FAC variables wastes time. This is because the solver wastes time to compute FAC variables that are not used when the instance is solved directly by the SLS solver or when the benchmarks is globally inconsistent. In this case, all variables are potentially FAC variables and their computation also wastes time.

Table 1. Experimental results

		NOVELTY			SLS+GAC			MAC			FAC-SOLVER		
		SAT	UNS	TOT	SAT	UNS	TOT	SAT	UNS	TOT	SAT	UNS	TOT
2-EXT	ACAD	7	0	7	7	2	9	7	2	9	7	2	9
	PATT	106	0	106	100	38	138	83	38	121	99	39	138
	QRND	24	0	24	24	51	75	24	51	75	24	51	75
	RAND	206	0	206	197	105	302	194	110	304	193	106	299
	REAL	6	0	6	7	0	7	7	0	7	7	0	7
	TOTAL	349	0	349	335	196	531	315	201	516	330	198	528
2-INT	ACAD	38	7	45	37	40	77	37	40	77	38	40	78
	BOOL	0	1	1	0	1	1	0	1	1	0	1	1
	PATT	112	0	112	150	60	210	146	62	208	152	62	214
	REAL	47	74	121	74	102	176	75	103	178	75	103	178
	TOTAL	197	82	279	261	203	464	258	206	464	265	206	471
N-EXT	BOOL	70	1	71	74	75	149	74	70	144	74	74	148
	PATT	6	0	6	30	0	30	29	0	29	30	0	30
	QRND	43	0	43	40	40	80	33	40	73	45	40	85
	RAND	70	0	70	68	32	100	72	34	106	70	34	104
	REAL	41	29	70	45	114	159	47	115	162	47	115	162
	TOTAL	230	30	260	257	261	518	255	259	514	266	263	529
N-INT	ACAD	40	0	40	39	23	62	36	23	59	40	23	63
	BOOL	145	1	146	156	12	168	146	12	158	162	13	175
	PATT	88	5	93	103	19	122	95	20	115	102	18	120
	REAL	85	2	87	152	3	155	150	3	153	152	3	155
	TOTAL	358	8	366	450	57	507	427	58	485	456	57	513
	TOTAL	**1134**	**113**	**1247**	**1293**	**717**	**2010**	**1255**	**724**	**1979**	**1317**	**724**	**2041**

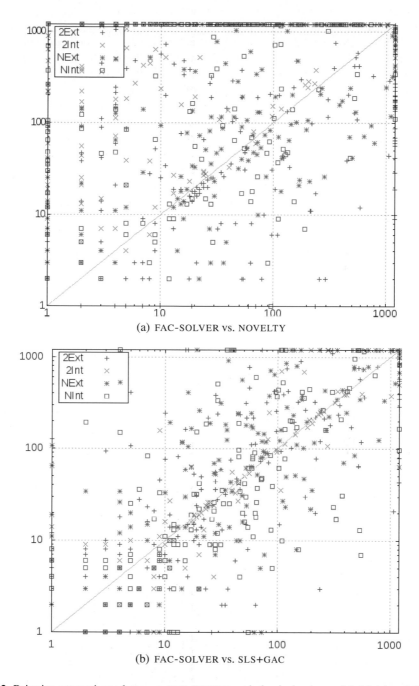

(a) FAC-SOLVER VS. NOVELTY

(b) FAC-SOLVER VS. SLS+GAC

Fig. 2. Pairwise comparisons between FAC-SOLVER and classical solvers: (a) (b) (c) satisfiable instances/(d) (e) unsatisfiable instances

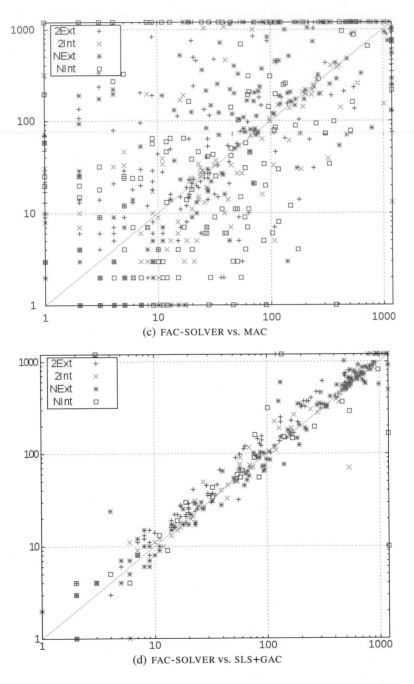

(c) FAC-SOLVER vs. MAC

(d) FAC-SOLVER vs. SLS+GAC

Fig. 2. (*continued*)

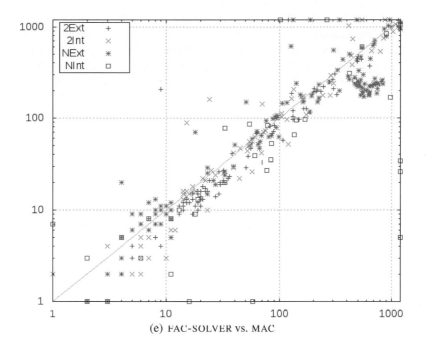

(e) FAC-SOLVER vs. MAC

Fig. 2. (*continued*)

Table 2. Using or not FAC variables in FAC-SOLVER: typical results

Instance	SAT/UNSAT?	time (FAC-SOLVER)	time (FAC-SOLVER without FAC variables)
uclid-elf-rf8	UNSAT	**305.15**	time out
uclid-37s-smv	UNSAT	**387.50**	659.58
par-16-5	SAT	**168.87**	329.06
primes-10-40-2-7	SAT	**891.01**	time out
primes-20-20-2-7	SAT	976.68	**313.31**
queensKnights-100-5-add	UNSAT	**1,120.18**	time out
queensKnights-100-5-mul	UNSAT	**1,165.81**	time out
queensKnights-80-5-mul	UNSAT	**343.68**	time out
rand-2-40-18	UNSAT	41.47	**1.61**

6   Perspectives and Conclusions

In this paper a FAC variables concept has been introduced and investigated w.r.t. CSP solving. One goal of this study was to develop a CSP solving method that would at least match the efficiency of each best current approach on each class of traditional CSPs instances. In this respect, our experimental results show the extent to which this goal has been met.

One question that naturally arises is the extent to which the various findings and components implemented in FAC-SOLVER do actually take part in the increased efficiency. Actually, it appears that *each* finding and search component (FAC variables, use of *dom/wdeg* heuristic in SLS, hybrid method involving SLS and filtering techniques) were necessary to ensure the supremacy of the method. Especially, we have e.g. measured that FAC variables were detected in 56 % of the instances and that they play a crucial role even in consistent instances.

FAC-SOLVER remains a basic algorithm and could be fine-tuned in several ways. Especially, comprehensive experimental studies could allow to optimize its various control variables and factors, which we fixed quite arbitrarily. Moreover, our implementation does not include usual CSP simplification techniques like the exploitation of symmetries or global constraints. We believe that the integration of these techniques could also dramatically improve FAC-SOLVER. Also, it would be interesting to explore the relaxation of the FAC variable concept to encompass also variables that occur in *most* or *some preferred* falsified contraints (instead of all of them). This could prove useful for e.g. CSP instances containing non-overlapping MUCs.

Finally, we believe that the FAC variable concept is a good trade-off between the effective computational cost spent by SLS to find some of them, and what would be the theoretically best branching variable for MAC-based algorithm giving rise to the shortest proofs. FAC variables are variables taking part in all unsatisfiable minimal subsets of constraints, which often appear to be the difficult parts of unsatisfiable CSPs. However, it is easy to find out unsatisfiable CSPs where FAC variables do not conceptually take part in the real causes of unsatisfiability but rather simply appear as variables occurring in all MUCs while, at the same time, they are not related to the actual conflicting information. Refining the FAC variable concept to better capture the essence of unsatisfiability while keeping efficient heuristics that can help finding them remains an exciting challenge.

References

1. Audemard, G., Lagniez, J.M., Mazure, B., Saïs, L.: Boosting local search thanks to CDCL. In: Fermüller, C.G., Voronkov, A. (eds.) LPAR-17. LNCS, vol. 6397, pp. 474–488. Springer, Heidelberg (2010)
2. Bessière, C., Régin, J.C., Yap, R., Zhang, Y.: An optimal coarse-grained arc consistency algorithm. Artificial Intelligence 165(2), 165–185 (2005)
3. Boussemart, F., Hemery, F., Lecoutre, C., Saïs, L.: Boosting systematic search by weighting constraints. In: ECAI 2004, pp. 146–150 (2004)
4. Cheeseman, P., Kanefsky, B., Taylor, W.: Where the really hard problems are. In: IJCAI 1991, pp. 331–340 (1991)
5. Third international CSP solver competition (2008), http://cpai.ucc.ie/08/
6. Fourth international CSP solver competition (2009), http://cpai.ucc.ie/09/
7. Eisenberg, C., Faltings, B.: Making the breakout algorithm complete using systematic search. In: IJCAI 2003, pp. 1374–1375 (2003)
8. Eisenberg, C., Faltings, B.: Using the breakout algorithm to identify hard and unsolvable subproblems. In: Rossi, F. (ed.) CP 2003. LNCS, vol. 2833, pp. 822–826. Springer, Heidelberg (2003)

9. Eiter, T., Gottlob, G.: On the complexity of propositional knowledge base revision, updates and counterfactuals. Artificial Intelligence 57, 227–270 (1992)
10. Galinier, P., Hao, J.K.: Tabu search for maximal constraint satisfaction problems. In: Smolka, G. (ed.) CP 1997. LNCS, vol. 1330, pp. 196–208. Springer, Heidelberg (1997)
11. Gégoire, É., Mazure, B., Piette, C.: Local-search extraction of muses. Constraints 12(3), 325–344 (2007)
12. Goldberg, E.: Boundary points and resolution. In: Kullmann, O. (ed.) SAT 2009. LNCS, vol. 5584, pp. 147–160. Springer, Heidelberg (2009)
13. Gu, J.: Design efficient local search algorithms. In: Belli, F., Radermacher, F.J. (eds.) IEA/AIE 1992. LNCS, vol. 604, pp. 651–654. Springer, Heidelberg (1992)
14. Hébrard, E.: Mistral 1.529 (2006), `http://4c.ucc.ie/~ehebrard/mistral/doxygen/html/main.html`
15. Hoos, H.: An adaptive noise mechanism for walksat. In: AAAI 2002, pp. 655–660 (2002)
16. Jussien, N., Lhomme, O.: Combining constraint programming and local search to design new powerful heuristics. In: MIC 2003 (2003)
17. Kirkpatrick, S., Gelatt Jr., D., Vecchi, M.: Optimization by simulated annealing. Science 220(4598), 671–680 (1983)
18. Lecoutre, C., Hemery, F.: A study of residual supports in arc consistency. In: IJCAI 2007, pp. 125–130 (2007)
19. Lecoutre, C., Tabary, S.: Abscon 112: towards more robustness. In: CSC 2008, pp. 41–48 (2008)
20. Mackworth, A.: Consistency in networks of relations. Artificial Intelligence 8(1), 99–118 (1977)
21. Mazure, B., Saïs, L., Grégoire, É.: Boosting complete techniques thanks to local search methods. Annals of Mathematics and Artificial Intelligence 22(3-4), 319–331 (1998)
22. McAllester, D., Selman, B., Kautz, H.: Evidence for invariants in local search. In: AAAI 1997, pp. 321–326 (1997)
23. Merchez, S., Lecoutre, C., Boussemart, F.: Abscon: A prototype to solve CSPs with abstraction. In: Walsh, T. (ed.) CP 2001. LNCS, vol. 2239, pp. 730–744. Springer, Heidelberg (2001)
24. Minton, S., Johnston, M., Philips, A., Laird, P.: Minimizing conflicts: A heuristic repair method for constraint satisfaction and scheduling problems. Artificial Intelligence 58(1-3), 161–205 (1992)
25. Sabin, D., Freuder, E.: Contradicting conventional wisdom in constraint satisfaction. In: ECAI 1994, pp. 125–129 (1994)
26. Selman, B., Kautz, H., Cohen, B.: Noise strategies for improving local search. In: AAAI 1994, pp. 337–343 (1994)
27. Selman, B., Levesque, H., Mitchell, D.: A new method for solving hard satisfiability problems. In: AAAI 1992, pp. 440–446 (1992)
28. Tamura, N., Taga, A., Kitagawa, S., Banbara, M.: Compiling finite linear CSP into SAT. Constraints 14(2), 254–272 (2009)
29. Choco Team. Choco: an open source Java constraint programming library. Research report 10-02-INFO, Ecole des Mines de Nantes (2010)

Constraint Reasoning and Kernel Clustering for Pattern Decomposition with Scaling

Ronan LeBras[1], Theodoros Damoulas[1], John M. Gregoire[2],
Ashish Sabharwal[3], Carla P. Gomes[1], and R. Bruce van Dover[4]

[1] Dept. of Computer Science, Cornell University, Ithaca, NY 14853, USA
[2] School of Engr. and Applied Sciences, Harvard University, Cambridge, MA 02138
[3] IBM Watson Research Center, Yorktown Heights, NY 10598, USA
[4] Dept. of Materials Science and Engr., Cornell University, Ithaca, NY 14853, USA

Abstract. Motivated by an important and challenging task encountered in material discovery, we consider the problem of finding K basis patterns of numbers that jointly compose N observed patterns while enforcing additional spatial and scaling constraints. We propose a Constraint Programming (CP) model which captures the exact problem structure yet fails to scale in the presence of noisy data about the patterns. We alleviate this issue by employing Machine Learning (ML) techniques, namely kernel methods and clustering, to decompose the problem into smaller ones based on a global data-driven view, and then stitch the partial solutions together using a global CP model. Combining the complementary strengths of CP and ML techniques yields a more accurate and scalable method than the few found in the literature for this complex problem.

1 Introduction

Consider a setting where our goal is to infer properties of a system by observing patterns of numbers (e.g., discretized waveforms, locations of peak intensities in a signal, etc.) at N sample points. Suppose these N patterns are a combination of K unobserved basis patterns. The *pattern decomposition problem* seeks to identify, given patterns at the N sample points as input, K basis patterns that generate the observed patterns and which of these basis patterns appear at any given sample point. The sample points are often embedded in the Euclidean space, enforcing a constraint that points near each other should generally be explained by a similar subset of patterns (except for a few transition boundaries).

Variants of this problem arise in a number of scenarios. For example, in the well-known *cocktail party problem*, the observed patterns are mixtures of voices of people as recorded by various microphones and the task is to decompose the signal at each microphone into the voices of individuals – the basis patterns – contributing to that signal. The microphones observe a spatial correlation, in the sense that if person's voice is heard at a microphone, it is likely that it is also heard at a neighboring microphone but not at a far away one.

Problems such as these fall under the category of *source separation problems*. Typically, purely data-driven methods are used for these, relying heavily on pattern recognition from a global analysis of the available data. A limitation of this

J. Lee (Ed.): CP 2011, LNCS 6876, pp. 508–522, 2011.

approach, however, is that it makes it very difficult to enforce *hard constraints*. While one may argue that the spatial and other requirements in problems such as the cocktail party problem are somewhat "soft", the setting we consider in this paper is motivated by a materials science problem that imposes hard constraints dictated by physics. When solving this problem, even slight deviation from the requirements of the underlying physics makes "solutions" meaningless. Moreover, in this setting, observed patterns are allowed to be superpositions of basis patterns *stretched* by a small multiplicative scaling factor, leading to what we call the *Decomposition Problem With Scaling*. This problem generalizes a known NP-complete problem, namely, the Set Basis Problem [19].

Faced with the challenge of handling hard constraints and scaling factors, we propose a Constraint Programming (CP) approach to solve our variant of the pattern decomposition problem. Our CP formulation captures the desired constraints in a detailed and exact fashion. However, as expected, it does not scale well with problem size once we introduce errors and noise in the input data. To alleviate this issue, we turn to Machine Learning (ML) and use kernel-based clustering as a way to guide the CP solver by creating multiple smaller sub-problems within its reach. After solving these smaller sub-problems with CP, we take a step back and combine the multiple partial solutions into a consistent global solution, using the original, global CP model.

Our contributions include bringing this intriguing and challenging problem to the CP community, providing a CP model for it, and enhancing the global scalability of the model while preserving local accuracy by exploiting ML methods for designing a divide-and-conquer approach. Using data from our material discovery application as a testbed, we demonstrate that the proposed hybrid ML-CP approach yields more accurate and meaningful solutions than existing, mostly data-driven approaches.

1.1   Pattern Decomposition for Material Discovery

The particular variant of the pattern decomposition problem considered in this paper is motivated by an important application in the area of material discovery. Specifically, a detailed analysis of libraries of inorganic materials has become an increasingly useful technique in this line of work, as evident from the number and variety of recently published methods for combinatorial materials research [e.g., 2, 16]. These libraries can be screened for a desired property, providing an understanding of the underlying material system. This is an important direction in *computational sustainability* [8], and aims to achieve the best possible use of our available material resources.

A fundamental property of inorganic materials is their crystallographic phase, and thus creating a "phase map" of an inorganic library across various compositions is a key aspect of combinatorial materials science. Often, correlations between the phase map and other material properties provide important insights into the behavior of the material system. For example, a recent study of a Platinum-Tantalum library revealed an important correlation between crystallographic phase and improved catalytic activity for fuel cell applications [10].

The most common technique for creating such a phase map is to first use Xray diffraction to generate diffraction patterns (continuous waveforms) for sample points with different compositions. Inferring the phase map from these diffraction patterns is then done using a laborious manual inspection. Doing this automatically, without human interaction, is a long standing problem in combinatorial crystallography. Several recent algorithms have been proposed which correctly solve the phase map for limited cases [3, 4, 14, 15]. In 2007, Long et al. [15] suggested a *hierarchical agglomerative clustering* (HAC) approach which aims to cluster the observed patterns that involve the same subset of basis patterns, but relies on a manual inspection in order to discover the actual basis patterns. In a follow-up paper, Long et al. [14] applied *non-negative matrix factorization* (NMF), which approximates (through gradient descent) the observed diffraction patterns with a linear combination of positive basis patterns. A main limitation of both approaches lies in the assumption that peaks of a phase will always appear at the same position and with the same relative intensities in any pattern. However, the position and intensity of diffraction peaks typically *scale* as a function of composition due to chemical alloying. Also, these approaches are unable to enforce hard constraints such as connectivity requirements.

Our goal is to take the actual physics behind the crystallographic process (e.g., the nature of scalings in the patterns and connectivity) into account in order to design a robust and scalable method for solving this problem in the presence of experimental noise.

2   Problem Description

From a computational perspective, we are interested in solving the following constraint reasoning (and optimization) problem. We will define this problem over rational numbers, $\mathbb{Q}$, rather than reals as this ensures that the problem is within NP; if there is a solution, using rational numbers will allow us to compactly represent and verify its correctness. We will refer to a set $P \subseteq \mathbb{Q}^+$ of positive rationals as a *pattern* over positive rational. For a scaling factor $s \in \mathbb{Q}$, let us define the *scaled pattern* sP as the pointwise scaled version of the pattern P, namely, $sP = \{sp \mid p \in P\}$.

Informally speaking, the problem is the following. Suppose we are given a graph over N vertices and, associated with each vertex v_i, a pattern P_i consisting of a finite set of numbers. Given $K \leq N$, the goal is to decompose these N patterns into K patterns that form a "basis" in the following sense: each P_i must be the union of at most M scaled basis patterns (i.e., scaled versions of at most M basis patterns must *appear* at each vertex), and the subgraph formed by the vertices where the k-th basis pattern appears must be connected.

The problem, illustrated in Figure 1, is formally defined as follows:

Definition 1 (Problem: Pattern Decomposition With Scaling). *Let*

- $G = (V, E)$ *be an undirected graph with* $V = \{v_1, \ldots, v_N\}$,
- $\mathcal{P} = \{P_1, \ldots, P_N\}$ *be a collection of* N *patterns over a finite set* $S \subseteq \mathbb{Q}^+$,

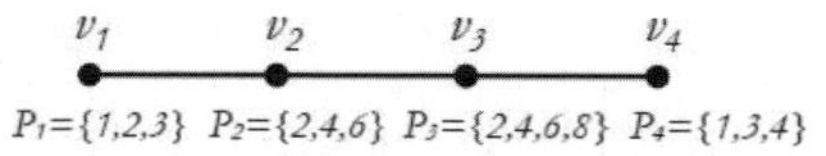

Fig. 1. Left: Toy example illustrating Def. 1. Right: Solution for $M = K = 2$ and $\delta = 2$

- $M \leq K \leq N$ be positive integers, and $\delta \geq 1$ be a rational.

Determine whether there exists a collection $\mathcal{B}$ of K basis patterns over S and scaling factors $s_{ik} \in \{0\} \cup [1/\delta, \delta]$ for $1 \leq i \leq N, 1 \leq k \leq K$, such that:

(a) $\forall i$: P_i is the union of scaled basis patterns, i.e., $P_i = \bigcup_{k=1}^{K} s_{ik} B_k$;
(b) $\forall i$: the number of basis patterns with a non-zero coefficient at vertex v_i is at most M, i.e., $|\{k \mid s_{ik} > 0\}| \leq M$; and
(c) $\forall k$: the subgraph of G induced by $V_k = \{v_i \in V \mid s_{ik} > 0\}$ is connected.

Noisy Data. In practice, one may not have accurate information about the pattern P_i at each vertex v_i. Indeed, in our material discovery application to be discussed shortly, it is very common for several types of *noise* to be present in the patterns provided as input to this problem. For the purposes of this paper, we will assume that *there may be false negatives in the N observed patterns, but no false positives*. In other words, our models will be designed to tolerate *missing elements* in patterns, by relaxing the first condition in the problem definition to $P_i \subseteq \bigcup_k s_{ik} B_k$ rather than requiring a strict equality. Note that this relaxation severely limits the propagation that a constraint enforcing this condition might be able to perform, as we can no longer remove an element from a candidate basis pattern B_k even if that element (appropriately scaled) does not appear in the observed pattern P_i. We will discuss this issue in more detail in Section 3.

Further, we will make the assumption that for every basic pattern, there is *at least one recurrent element* that is not missing in every observed pattern involving this basic pattern. This assumption is often quite realistic in many applications where elements of a pattern are, for example, locations of peaks in a waveform. Indeed, even though the highest peak of a given basic pattern might not be observed as the highest one in each pattern where it appears, it is quite unlikely to completely disappear due to noise.

Other Dimensions to the Elements of a Pattern. Depending on the particular application under consideration, the elements of a pattern may have associated with them other dimensions as well that an algorithm may be able to exploit. E.g., when elements correspond to "locations" of peaks in a waveform, they naturally have *height* and *width* of the corresponding peaks associated with them as well. We will use these additional dimensions, specifically height, in the material discovery application experiments in order to control the amount of tolerable error. The machine learning part of our hybrid method will also exploit height and width indirectly when computing the similarity between patterns.

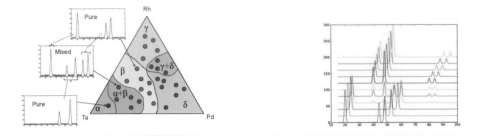

Fig. 2. Left: Pictorial depiction of the problem, showing 29 sample locations each corresponding to a composition and associated with an observed x-ray diffraction pattern. The green, blue, yellow, and red colored regions denote pure phase regions. Also shown are two mixed regions, formed by the overlap of $\alpha + \beta$ and $\gamma + \delta$. Right: Multiplicative *shift* in waveforms as one moves from one point to an adjacent one; waveforms are shown stacked up vertically to highlight the shift.

2.1   Motivating Application: Phase Identification in Materials

A combinatorial method for discovering new materials involves sputtering three metals (or oxides) onto a silicon wafer, resulting in a so-called thin film. The goal is to identify structural regions in thin films. Any location on a thin film corresponds to a crystal with a particular composition of the three sputtered metals (or oxides); a number of such locations are sampled during experimentation, as shown with black dots in Figure 2. The structural information of this crystal lattice is usually characterized by its x-ray diffraction pattern – a continuous waveform obtained by electromagnetic radiation. The resulting diffraction pattern associated with each location represents the intensity of the electromagnetic waves as a function of the scattering angle of radiation (see Figure 2).

The pattern observed at any location is often a superposition of a number of basis patterns, known as *phases*, possibly *stretched* by a small multiplicative scaling factor; the shifts are depicted in the right panel of Figure 2 where adjacent lines correspond to waveforms observed at adjacent locations. In other words, a thin film involves a small number of basic crystallographic phases, and the crystal corresponding to each sampled location lies either in a *pure region* comprising of just one phase, or a *mixed region* made from a superposition of multiple, possibly stretched phases (e.g., the waveform shown in the middle of the left panel of Figure 2 is the superposition of the ones shown above and below it).

Given the diffraction patterns at N sampled locations, the problem is to compute the most likely *phase map*, i.e., the set of phases that are involved at any location of the thin film and in which proportion. A sub-problem, often considered in the literature [e.g., 15], is to cluster the sampled locations such that locations in each cluster are superpositions of the same subset of phases.

When three metals are used for this experiment, the result is referred to as a *ternary diagram*. A physical constraint in a ternary diagram is that independent of the total number of phases present, the number of phases that may appear at any given location is at most 3. Furthermore, if 3 phases do appear at a location, then it does not leave any degree of freedom for the aforementioned shifts to happen, i.e., only pure regions or mixed regions comprising 2 phases exhibit shifting.

We can cast this problem as the Pattern Decomposition With Scaling problem discussed earlier, with an additional constraint enforcing scaling factors to be precisely 1 when 3 phases appear at a location. The idea is to pre-process these x-ray diffraction patterns by performing *peak detection*, for which reliable techniques are available in the context of materials science. This results in a finite set of scattering angles – a pattern in our earlier notation – at which peaks are observed at a given sampled location. Specifically, N is the number of sampled locations, G is obtained by Delaunay triangulation over the sampled points based on their given x-y coordinates on the thin film, $\mathcal{P}$ is the set of such patterns associated with each location, $M = 3$, δ is typically 1.15 (i.e., allowing shifts by a maximum scaling factor of 15%), K is the number of underlying phases or basis patterns we are interested in discovering. Without loss of generality, we fix S to be the set of all scattering angles (i.e., pattern elements) at which a peak is observed in the sampled locations.

In general, the goal from a material discovery perspective is two-fold: explain the diffraction patterns observed at the N locations with the fewest number K of phases, while also minimizing the error resulting from missing peaks and other noise in the data. We will assume for the purposes of this paper that although we might miss some peaks (i.e., false negatives), the scattering angle where we do observe a peak is accurate (i.e., no false positives). Given the small range of K in reality (typically 5-8), we will take K to be a parameter of the problem and attempt to minimize error introduced due to missing peaks. As a practically relevant *objective function*, we use the *sum of the estimated heights of missing peaks*. Note that "heights" and "peaks" are not part of the formal definition of the satisfaction problem, Pattern Decomposition With Scaling. Nonetheless, this data is readily available for this material discovery application and we use it to enhance the problem with a realistic objective function. In fact, when discussing the machine learning part to boost scalability, we will use for computing "similarity" between locations not only the scattering angles where peaks appear but also a discretized version of the complete waveforms.

2.2   NP-Completeness

In order to prove that the Pattern Decomposition With Scaling problem as defined above is NP-hard, we simplify it in three steps to what is called the Set Basis Problem, which is known to be NP-complete. First, let $M = K$, i.e., allow the K basis patterns to appear at any vertex. Second, let the underlying graph G be a clique, thereby trivially satisfying the third condition in the problem definition (subgraph connectivity). Finally, let $\delta = 1$, thereby forcing all scaling factors s_{ij} to be either 0 or 1. With these three modification steps, our problem simplifies to what is known in the literature as the Set Basis Problem, defined as follows and known to be NP-complete [19]:

Definition 2 (Set Basis Problem [19]). *Given a collection $\mathcal{P} = \{P_1, \ldots, P_N\}$ of N subsets of S and an integer K satisfying $2 \leq K \leq N$, is there a collection $\mathcal{B}$ of K subsets of S such that for all $1 \leq i \leq N$ there exist $\mathcal{B}_i \subseteq \mathcal{B}$ such that $P_i = \cup_{B \in \mathcal{B}_i} B$?*

To see that the Pattern Decomposition With Scaling problem is within NP, we observe that given a candidate solution to the problem, namely a collection $\mathcal{B}$ of K subsets of S and scaling factors $s_{ik} \in \mathbb{Q}$ for $1 \leq i \leq N, 1 \leq k \leq K$, one can easily verify in polynomial time that all requirements of the problem are satisfied. Note that defining the problem over $\mathbb{Q}$ rather than the reals ensures that if an instance has a solution, then there is also one with all $s_{ik} \in \mathbb{Q}$, allowing succinct representation and efficient verification of a candidate solution.

Together, these imply that this problem is NP-complete.

3   A Constraint Programming Formulation

We first describe a CP formulation of this problem assuming no errors, i.e., no missing elements in patterns nor experimental noise in the element value. A natural way to encode this problem is to have one variable for each element of each of the N patterns indicating which of the K basic patterns "explains" this element. This formulation, however, results in too many variables and also fails to account for overlaps, i.e., that an element of an observed pattern may in fact be explained by *multiple* basic patterns (since we take the union of basic patterns in the problem definition). An alternative formulation can try to analyze the N given patterns to identify which elements are shared between neighboring vertices of G, and use this as a basis for creating basis patterns. This formulation too results in too many variables and constraints. We present below a formulation that proved to be the most successful. This formulation explicitly uses the underlying basis patterns as the central variables, and merges sets of large numbers of constraints into global ones in order to reduce memory consumption.

In a preprocessing step, we compute the set r_{ij} as P_i normalized by its jth element. For example, if P_5 corresponds to $\{1, 2, 4\}$, then $r_{5,2}$ becomes $\{1/2, 1, 2\}$.

Variables. We model whether a basis pattern k is present in a pattern P_i using a *decision variable* p_{ki}. According to the assumption mentioned in Section 2, there is at least one element of any basis pattern that appears in all sample points in which this basis pattern is present. As a result, if we use this element as a normalizing one, the set of elements of this basis pattern becomes the same in all of these sample points. We represent the normalizing element of basis pattern k in sample point P_i as p_{ki}, whose domain is $\{0, 1, ..., |P_i|\}$ and where value 0 denotes that basis pattern k is not present in pattern P_i. Furthermore, *auxiliary Boolean variable* a_{ki} indicates whether basis pattern k appears in P_i while *auxiliary set variable* q_k represents the normalized elements of pattern k and initially ranges over all possible scaled elements. The domain representation used for the q_{ik} variables is the classical subset-bound, yet more advanced representations ([see eg. 7, 11]) might further enhance the model.

Constraints. We first express the relationship between the auxiliary variables a_{ki} and the decision variables p_{ki} as follows:

$$(a_{ki} = 0) \iff (p_{ki} = 0) \qquad\qquad \forall\, 1 \le k \le K, 1 \le i \le n \qquad (1)$$

At this point, we can directly enforce that a pattern has to be composed of at least one basis pattern, and at most M:

$$1 \le \sum_{s=1}^{K} a_{si} \le M \qquad\qquad \forall\, 1 \le i \le n \qquad (2)$$

Next, anytime a pattern P_i involves a particular basis pattern k, every element of k has to match one of the normalized elements of P_i. Formally:

$$(p_{ki} = j) \Rightarrow (q_k \subseteq r_{ij}) \qquad\qquad \forall\, 1 \le k \le K, 1 \le i \le n, 1 \le j \le |P_i| \qquad (3)$$

Nonetheless, in order to fully determine q_k from the p_{ki}'s, we require that all elements of a pattern appear in one of the basis patterns that compose this point. First, if a pattern is made of only one basis pattern, their elements should be identical, up to a scaling factor. It means that if p_{ki} is set to be equal to j, then r_{ij} also has to be a subset of q_k. Second, if a pattern P_i is made of two basic patterns k and k', then every element of P_i has to appear in q_k or in q'_k, when normalized by their respective scaling factor. The first case translates into:

$$(p_{ki} - j \wedge \sum_{s=1}^{K} a_{si} = 1) \Rightarrow (r_{ij} \subseteq q_k) \qquad \forall\, 1 \le k \le K, 1 \le i \le n, 1 \le j \le |P_i| \qquad (4)$$

while the second one entails the following equation:

$$(p_{ki} = j \wedge p_{k'i} = j' \wedge \sum_{s=1}^{K} a_{si} = 2) \Rightarrow \big(member(r_{ij}[j''], q_k) \vee member(r_{ij'}[j''], q_{k'})\big)$$

$$\forall\, 1 \le k, k' \le K, 1 \le i \le n, 1 \le j, j', j'' \le |P_i| \qquad (5)$$

Similarly, we derive constraints for points that are made of g basis patterns, where $3 \le g \le M$. Then, we guarantee that the scaling factors of a basis pattern belong to a valid range. For two patterns to be composed of the same basis pattern, these constraints require that the two respective normalizing elements are not too far apart in the pattern. This step relies as well on a preprocessing step of the data, in order to compute the relative distances and to post the required constraints. For a given $\delta \ge 1$, we consider that this preprocessing step yields a set $\Phi = \{(i, j, i', j') \mid \frac{P_i[j]}{P'_i[j']} < 1/\delta \vee \frac{P_i[j]}{P'_i[j']} > \delta, i < i'\}$ of pairs of elements that do not satisfy this property (typically $\delta \le 1.15$). It yields:

$$(p_{ki} = j) \Rightarrow (p_{ki'} \ne j') \qquad\qquad \forall\, 1 \le k \le K, (i, j, i', j') \in \Phi \qquad (6)$$

Finally, we implement a special-purpose global constraint, called *basisPattern-Connectivity* which maintains the set of basis patterns in every connected component. Formally, if $a_{ki_1} = 1$ and $a_{ki_t} = 1$, then there exists an undirected path $i_1 \to i_2 \cdots \to i_t$ such that $a_{ki_u} = 1$ for all $1 \le u \le t$. We could perform propagation based on component and bridge information [see 13, 17], however in practice this extra filtering does not seem to justify the added overhead for our particular problem setting. Instead we simply make sure that the aforementioned statement is not violated. We define this constraint as:

$$basisPatternConnectivity(\{a_{ki}|1 \leq i \leq n\}) \qquad \forall\, 1 \leq k \leq K \qquad (7)$$

During search, the branching variables are the p_{ki}s. The variable ordering using an arbitrary BFS on G to statically order the vertices v_i, and dynamically select k such that a neighbor of v_i has set its phase k, proved to be the most successful.

Symmetry Breaking. In order to break symmetries, we systematically assign either an already existing basis pattern or the lowest one available. This means that for example, given the three basis patterns q_1, q_2 and q_3, and considering a new pattern P_i, the variables $p_{5,i}, ..., p_{K,i}$ must be assigned value 0. This is reminiscent, for example, of work on the *Steel Mill Slab Design* [12].

3.1   Handling Errors and Noisy Data

In order to handle missing elements, we adapt constraints (3) to allow for elements of q_k not to appear in P_i, even if the sample point P_i involves basis pattern k. Therefore, the propagation of constraints (3) gets weaker, as we can no longer filter out an element of q_k that is anomalously missing from a sample point (see following section). Also, to avoid a trivial solution in which all possible elements belong to q_k, we introduce an optimization objective that aims to minimize either the overall number of missing elements or the overall relative importance of the missing elements. The importance of an element is application specific, and in the case of our motivating application, a natural way to penalize for a missing peak is to consider its inferred height: the higher the missing peak, the worse the solution. Finally, note that handling missing elements does not affect constraints (4) nor (5), as we do not allow for false positives.

Also, in order to account for noise, we introduce a precision value that represents how far off an observed value can be from its true one. Thus, in constraints (3) to (5), when checking whether an element belongs to a set, we use this precision to assess whether the element appears as a slightly different value.

3.2   Limitations of the Pure CP Approach: Scaling

Although this CP model captures the details of the problem very well, it scales very poorly – especially when errors are introduced in the data in terms of missing peaks. In Table 1, we show the running time of the CP model on (small) instances of various sizes from our material discovery application. Experiments were conducted using IBM ILOG CP Solver version 6.5 deployed on 3.8 GHz Intel Xeon machines with 2GB memory running Linux 2.6.9-22.ELsmp. The time limit used was 1,200 seconds. The observed patterns in each of these instances can, in reality, be explained by $K = 6$ basic patterns. We create simpler versions of the problem by *fixing* some of these basic patterns as a partial solution, leaving $K' \in \{0, 1, ..., 6\}$ unknown basic patterns, for each of which we have a row in

Table 1. Scaling of the pure CP model, without errors (pure) and with errors. Rows: num. of unknown basic patterns. Cols: num. of observed patterns. Timeout 1,200 sec.

	$N = 10$		$N = 15$		$N = 18$		$N = 28$		$N = 219$	
	pure	errors	pure	errors	pure	errors	pure	errors	pure	errors
$K' = 0$	0.0	0.0	0.0	0.0	0.0	0.1	0.0	0.1	1.1	3.5
$K' = 1$	0.0	0.1	0.0	0.1	0.0	0.3	0.1	0.4	115.3	343.2
$K' = 2$	0.0	0.2	0.0	0.3	1.0	—	1.4	—	—	—
$K' = 3$	0.5	717.3	0.5	—	384.8	—	276.0	—	—	—
$K' = 4$	668.5	—	824.2	—	—	—	—	—	—	—
$K' = 5$	—	—	—	—	—	—	—	—	—	—

the table ($K' = 6$ is omitted as all instances timed out in this case). As we see, for all N, the instances go from being solvable in a fraction of a second to not solvable in 20 minutes extremely fast. Moreover, when errors are introduced in the form of missing peaks, the scaling behavior becomes worse. Finally, even with a very small problem size such a $N = 10$ and the ideal case of no errors, we cannot solve for all 6 (or even 5) basic patterns. It becomes evident that we need a methodology that can allow us to scale to instances of realistic sizes (e.g., over 100 patterns and with $K' = 6$). This will be the subject of the rest of this paper.

4   Boosting Scalability: Exploiting Kernel-Based Clustering to Guide the CP Formulation

The CP approach discussed thus far attempts to accurately solve the full problem under certain assumptions and, as we saw, fails to scale up to instance sizes of interest as soon as errors are introduced. We discuss in this section how we can leverage ideas from machine learning (ML), specifically kernel-based similarity measures and clustering, in order to make the problem solving task easier for the CP formulation. This integration of the two approaches is inspired by their complementary strengths: While CP techniques are excellent at enforcing detailed constraints at a local level, data-driven ML methods are more robust to noise and good at recognizing global patterns of similarity.

The integration uses the following 4-step "divide-and-conquer" process:

i. use kernel methods to analyze the patterns P_i at a global scale in order to compute a robust similarity measure between pairs of patterns;
ii. use clustering with this similarity measure to "over-segment" the N vertices into J clusters and choose a set $V^{(j)}$ of vertices associated with each cluster based on their distance to the cluster centroid; the vertices in these $V^{(j)}$ are expected to be explained by the same subset of basis patterns;
iii. solve the CP formulation, without the connectivity constraint, on the subgraph induced by the vertices in each $V^{(j)}$ to obtain a partial solution defined by a collection of basis patterns $\mathcal{B}^{(j)}$ each of size at most M; and
iv. glue the basis patterns $\mathcal{B}^{(j)}$ found for the J sub-problems together using a global CP formulation in order to obtain the full set $\mathcal{B}$ of K basis patterns.

4.1   Kernels as Robust Similarity Measures

Assuming D is an upper bound on the number of elements in each input pattern, we will think of the N input patterns as the input dataset $\mathbf{X} \in \mathbb{Q}^{N \times D}$ where each of the N patterns is represented by its D "features" in the D-dimensional space. One can model rich, non-linear relationships between the D base features by instead representing the N patterns in a much larger feature space, one of dimension $L \gg D$. Thus, instead of modeling non-linear relationships directly in D dimensions, one achieves the same effect more easily by still modeling linear relationships but in a much higher dimensional space, using an expanded feature representation $\phi(\mathbf{X}) \in \mathbb{Q}^{N \times L}$.

The problem, of course, is that explicitly constructing this L-dimensional space and working in it can be computationally prohibitive. Kernel methods solve this issue by allowing us to directly model the desired inner product, i.e., the "similarity" measure, $\langle \phi(\mathbf{X}), \phi(\mathbf{X}) \rangle$, and reduce the dimensionality we must deal with while leaving open, in principle, the possibility of even an infinite-dimensional underlying feature expansion ($L = \infty$). Note that this inner product computation results in the construction of a symmetric positive semi-definite $N \times N$ matrix, independent of the dimension L of the much expanded feature space. This matrix is known as the *kernel*.

Typically used generic kernel functions include the *linear* or *cosine* kernel $\mathbf{x}_i^\mathsf{T} \mathbf{x}_j$, the *polynomial* kernel $(\mathbf{x}_i^\mathsf{T} \mathbf{x}_j + 1)^k$ of degree k, and the *Gaussian* or *radial basis function (RBF)* kernel $\exp(-\frac{||\mathbf{x}_i - \mathbf{x}_j||^2}{2\sigma^2})$. Two specific material-discovery characteristics, however, pose a big challenge when computing similarity between x-ray diffraction waveforms – the inherent peak *shifts* (with multiplicative scaling) and varying peak *intensity* or height levels. This is especially true in cases where the presence of small peaks indicates a novel phase and the existence of a new crystal structure. In order to address this we propose to use the *dynamic time warping* technique [18] to construct a global alignment kernel. Such a kernel was recently used successfully in the context of Bayesian classification [6]. The idea is to construct a kernel from *minimum-cost alignment* of two sequences $\mathbf{x}_i, \mathbf{x}_j$ based on DTW: $\mathbf{k}_{\mathrm{DTW}}(\mathbf{x}_i, \mathbf{x}_j) = \exp\left(-\frac{||\mathbf{c}_i - \mathbf{c}_j||^2}{2\sigma^2}\right)$ where $\mathbf{c}_i$ is the ith row of the minimum-cost alignment matrix. We refer the reader to Damoulas et al. [6] for further details.

4.2   Clustering and Sample Selection

Having constructed the kernel matrix capturing similarity between the patterns at the N vertices of our underlying graph G, we now seek to create small subsets $V^{(j)}, 1 \leq j \leq J$, of the vertices such that all vertices within each $V^{(j)}$ are the unions of the *same* subset of basis patterns, scaled appropriately. The subproblems induced by these small subsets will be passed on to the CP model to be solved exactly to discover the basic patterns appearing in each of these subsets. Therefore, we would ideally like these subsets to be small enough to be solvable by the CP model, and at the same time large enough so that if there is shifting involved, the corresponding scaling factor can be recovered by the CP model.

To this end, we use *k-means* algorithm [5] with multiple initializations (centroids of clusters) and the Euclidean distance $d(\mathbf{k}_i, \mathbf{k}_j) = \left(\sum_{n=1}^{N} (k_{in} - k_{jn})^2 \right)^{1/2}$ as metric. We over-segment the kernel by choosing a large number of clusters when performing k-means. The final proposed vertices, $V^{(j)}$, are chosen from within each cluster based on their proximity to the cluster centroid.

4.3   Scaling CP: Solving Sub-problems and Fusing Solutions

Assuming the vertices of $V^{(j)}$ are the unions of the same subset of basis patterns, we know by definition of the problem that at most M basis patterns compose all the patterns of these vertices. Therefore, this is in fact a pattern decomposition problem with scaling by itself, where $N = |V^{(j)}|$ and $K = M$. If this subproblem is within the reach of the CP model (cf. Section 3.2), then we will have uncovered M of the initial K basis patterns. Otherwise, or if our previous assumption about the vertices of $V^{(j)}$ turns out to be wrong, the CP model will simply not be able to solve the instance, and will then consider the next cluster of points. Hence, every cluster may provide up to M basis patterns and contribute to a pool of basis patterns. After taking care of redundancy within this pool (which, is in the worst case, exponential in M), the pool is made of at most K basis patterns, and is used to initialize the basis patterns of the global CP model, thus typically becoming a much simpler problem (again, cf. Section 3.2).

5   Empirical Validation

In order to evaluate the performance of the hybrid method described above, we use our material discovery application as the testbed. As discussed in Section 3.2, the pure CP approach suffers from very poor scaling. On the other end, data-driven approaches such as non-negative matrix factorization (NMF) used in the literature [14] for such problems suffer, as we will show, from low accuracy – to the point that "solutions" found by them for material discovery instances can be meaningless. Our hybrid method avoids both of these extreme kinds of failures, in scaling and in accuracy.

Instance Generation. We use the same underlying known phase map for the Al-Li-Fe system [1] that was used for the instances discussed in Section 3.2. Specifically, this is a ternary system composed of 6 phases or basis patterns, $\alpha, \beta, \gamma, \delta, \epsilon$, and ζ; see Figure 3 for a pictorial depiction. These 6 phases appear together at various locations in the "triangle" in different combinations to generate 7 mixed regions, such as $\{\alpha, \delta\}$, $\{\alpha, \gamma, \delta\}$, etc. Recall that each location in the ternary diagram corresponds to a certain composition of the three constituent elements, in this case Al, Li, and Fe and these compositions can be sampled at various granularities. For the rest of this paper, we will focus on a realistic instance size, 219, and a smaller instance size, 91.

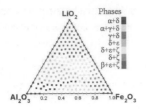

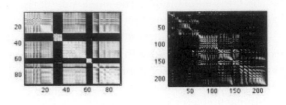

Fig. 3. Ternary system com-posed of Al, Li, and Fe

Fig. 4. DTW-Gaussian kernel as a similarity mea-sure. Left: $N = 91$. Right: $N = 219$

For these instances, we generated synthetic x-ray diffraction data by start-ing with known diffraction patterns of constituent phases from the JCPDS database [1] with parameters reflecting those of a recently developed combi-natorial crystallography technique [9]. This diffraction data was then converted into a set of peaks to generate discrete patterns with typically 20-30 peaks. The effect of experimental noise on the inability to detect low-intensity peaks was simulated by the random removal of Gaussian peaks from the synthetic data with probability proportional to the square of the inverse peak height. The total heights of the peaks removed was provided as a parameter for instance genera-tion. This noise model intends to legitimately reflect not only the true underlying physics (e.g., overlapping peaks), but also experimental imperfections of the thin film on which the metals/oxides are sputtered during experimentation.

Results. All experiments were conducted on the same machine and using the same CP solver as in Section 3.2. We first used the DTW-Gaussian kernel as a measure of similarity between sampled locations. Figure 4 depicts the resulting similarity matrix for $N = 91$ and 219; the latter is admittedly hard to understand visually because of too fine a granularity. A point (x, y) in this symmetric matrix is depicted as white if x and y are deemed to be similar, and 0 otherwise; e.g., the main diagonal, representing (x, x) similarity, is white. A similarity matrix such as this is generally considered to be good if areas within it have clear rectangular boundaries, thus identifying small groups of points that are similar to each other but different from the rest of the points. Compared to other standard kernels, we found this DTW-Gaussian kernel to perform the best.

Starting with this kernel as the similarity measure, we used k-means cluster-ing to obtain 50 clusters and asked for 4 points closest to the resulting cluster centroids to generate 50 very small sub-problems for the CP model. Note that these 50 sub-problems are not necessarily disjoint. We then solved each sub-problem with a corresponding CP model (without the connectivity constraint, as mentioned earlier), each of which was either easily solved (average 0.4 sec) when feasible or discarded after 30 seconds if no solution was found in that time. Note that we need to solve a sub-problem this way first for $M = 1$ and then for $M = 2$, which takes 60 seconds in the worst case. When solved, each of them identified 1 or 2 basic patterns or phases; recall that the sub-problem

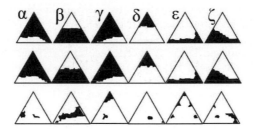

Fig. 5. Results: appearance (white) or not (black) of the 6 phases underlying the Al-Li-Fe system. Top: the true values. Middle: phases found by our hybrid method. Bottom: phases found by the competing NMF approach.

data is insufficient to distinguish between 1 and 3 basic patterns. In the final 'global' phase, we used these partial solutions to initialize a full CP model of the complete instance as discussed in Section 4.3.

The resulting 6 basic patterns found by the hybrid model are depicted in Figure 5, where the spread of each basis pattern over the composition space appears in white. The top line shows the true answer, which we know from the construction of the instance. The middle row shows the result as produced by our hybrid method. We observe that this solution is extremely close to the true answer in each one of the 6 basic patterns, except for some noise at the boundaries, and it translates into a precision/recall performance across all sampled points, averaged over individual phases of 77.4% / 84.2%.

The bottom row shows the results obtained by the NMF approach recently proposed for this problem. Comparatively, it results in a precision/recall performance of 39.5% / 77.9%. We see that this "solution" is in fact nowhere close to the true answer. Moreover, it violates the hard constraints imposed by physics, such as connectivity (violated for patterns β and ζ) and no more than 3 basis patterns appearing at any location (violated essentially everywhere). This highlights the inability of purely data-driven approaches to effectively deal with hard constraints — a clear strength of CP based approaches.

On the instance with fewer locations (91), we also obtained similar results (and faster) but we omit them here due to lack of space.

6   Conclusion

We explored the use of CP techniques to solve a challenging and interesting problem studied for the most part by researchers in data-driven sub-fields of computer science, or by application domain experts such as physicists in the case of our motivating application — a deeper understanding and discovery of new materials. Our CP model captures the details of the Pattern Decomposition With Scaling problem much better than, say, a matrix factorization or clustering approach, but at the high expense of poor scaling. We therefore introduce a hybrid model that avoids the pitfalls of CP and ML individually, and results in meaningful solutions respecting hard constraints while preserving scalability.

Acknowledgments. Supported by NSF (Expeditions in Computing award for Computational Sustainability, grant 0832782; NSF IIS award 0514429) and IISI, Cornell Univ. (AFOSR grant FA9550-04-1-0151). LeBras was partially funded by a NSERC fellowship. Gregoire and van Dover acknowledge support from the Energy Materials Center at Cornell (USDE award DE-SC0001086). Work done while Gregoire and Sabharwal were at Cornell University.

References

[1] Powder Diffract. File, JCPDS Internat. Centre Diffract. Data, PA (2004)
[2] Barber, Z.H., Blamire, M.G.: High throughput thin film materials science. Mat. Sci. Tech. 24(7), 757–770 (2008)
[3] Barr, G., Dong, W., Gilmore, C.J.: Polysnap3: a computer program for analysing and visualizing high-throughput data from diffraction and spectroscopic sources. J. Appl. Cryst. 42, 965 (2009)
[4] Baumes, L.A., Moliner, M., Corma, A.: Design of a full-profile-matching solution for high-throughput analysis of multiphase samples through powder x-ray diffraction. Chem. Eur. J. 15, 4258 (2009)
[5] Bishop, C.M.: Pattern Recognition and Machine Learning. Springer, NY (2006)
[6] Damoulas, T., Henry, S., Farnsworth, A., Lanzone, M., Gomes, C.: Bayesian Classification of Flight Calls with a novel Dynamic Time Warping Kernel. In: ICMLA 2010, pp. 424–429. IEEE, Los Alamitos (2010)
[7] Gervet, C., Hentenryck, P.V.: Length-lex ordering for set csps. In: AAAI (2006)
[8] Gomes, C.P.: Computational Sustainability: Computational methods for a sustainable environment, economy, and society. The Bridge, NAE 39(4) (2009)
[9] Gregoire, J.M., Dale, D., Kazimirov, A., DiSalvo, F.J., van Dover, R.B.: High energy x-ray diffraction/x-ray fluorescence spectroscopy for high-throughput analysis of composition spread thin films. Rev. Sci. Instrum. 80(12), 123905 (2009)
[10] Gregoire, J.M., Tague, M.E., Cahen, S., Khan, S., Abruna, H.D., DiSalvo, F.J., van Dover, R.B.: Improved fuel cell oxidation catalysis in pt1-xtax. Chem. Mater. 22(3), 1080 (2010)
[11] Hawkins, P., Stuckey, P.J.: Solving set constraint satisfaction problems using robdds. Journal of Artificial Intelligence Research 24, 109–156 (2005)
[12] Van Hentenryck, P., Michel, L.: The steel mill slab design problem revisited. In: Trick, M.A. (ed.) CPAIOR 2008. LNCS, vol. 5015, pp. 377–381. Springer, Heidelberg (2008)
[13] Holm, J., de Lichtenberg, K., Thorup, M.: Poly-logarithmic deterministic fully-dynamic algorithms for connectivity, minimum spanning tree, 2-edge, and biconnectivity. In: STOC 1998, New York, NY, USA, pp. 79–89 (1998)
[14] Long, C.J., Bunker, D., Karen, V.L., Li, X., Takeuchi, I.: Rapid identification of structural phases in combinatorial thin-film libraries using x-ray diffraction and non-negative matrix factorization. Rev. Sci. Instruments 80(103902) (2009)
[15] Long, C.J., Hattrick-Simpers, J., Murakami, M., Srivastava, R.C., Takeuchi, I., Karen, V.L., Li, X.: Rapid structural mapping of ternary metallic alloy systems using the combinatorial approach and cluster analysis. Rev. Sci. Inst. 78 (2007)
[16] Potyrailo, R.A., Maier, W.F.: Combinatorial and High-Throughput Discovery and Optimization of Catalysts and Materials. CRC Press, Boca Raton (2007)
[17] Prosser, P., Unsworth, C.: A connectivity constraint using bridges. In: ECAI 2006, The Netherlands, pp. 707–708 (2006)
[18] Sakoe, H., Chiba, S.: Dynamic programming algorithm optimization for spoken word recognition. Readings in Speech Recognition, 159 (1990)
[19] Stockmeyer, L.J.: The set basis problem is np-complete. Technical Report Report No. RC-5431, IBM Watson Research Center, East Lansing, Michigan (1975)

Solving Qualitative Constraints Involving Landmarks*

Weiming Liu[1], Shengsheng Wang[2], Sanjiang Li[1], and Dayou Liu[2]

[1] Centre for Quantum Computation and Intelligent Systems,
Faculty of Engineering and Information Technology,
University of Technology Sydney, Australia
[2] College of Computer Science and Technology, Jilin University, Changchun, China

Abstract. Consistency checking plays a central role in qualitative spatial and temporal reasoning. Given a set of variables V, and a set of constraints Γ taken from a qualitative calculus (e.g. the Interval Algebra (IA) or RCC-8), the aim is to decide if Γ is consistent. The consistency problem has been investigated extensively in the literature. Practical applications e.g. urban planning often impose, in addition to those between undetermined entities (variables), constraints between determined entities (constants or landmarks) and variables. This paper introduces this as a new class of qualitative constraint satisfaction problems, and investigates the new consistency problem in several well-known qualitative calculi, e.g. IA, RCC-5, and RCC-8. We show that the usual local consistency checking algorithm works for IA but fails in RCC-5 and RCC-8. We further show that, if the landmarks are represented by polygons, then the new consistency problem of RCC-5 is tractable but that of RCC-8 is NP-complete.

1 Introduction

Qualitative constraints are widely used in temporal and spatial reasoning (cf. [1,10,7]). This is partially because they are close to the way humans represent and reason about commonsense knowledge, easy to specify, and provide a flexible way to deal with incomplete knowledge.

Usually, these constraints are taken from a qualitative calculus, which is a set $\mathcal{M}$ of relations defined on an infinite universe U of entities [8]. Well-known qualitative calculi include the Interval Algebra [1], RCC-5 and RCC-8 [10], and the cardinal direction calculus (for point-like objects) [7]. A central problem of reasoning with such a qualitative calculus is the *consistency problem*. For a qualitative calculus $\mathcal{M}$ on U, an instance of the consistency problem over $\mathcal{M}$ is a network Γ of constraints like $x\alpha y$, where x, y are variables taken from a finite set V, and α is a relation in $\mathcal{M}$. Unlike classical constraint solving, the domain of the variables appeared in a qualitative constraint is usually infinite.

Consistency checking has applications in many areas, e.g. temporal or spatial query preprocessing, planning, natural language understanding; and the consistency problem has been extensively studied for many different qualitative calculi (cf. [3]). These works

* This work was partially supported by an ARC Future Fellowship (FT0990811), an open project program of the MOE Key Lab of Symbolic Computation and Knowledge Engineering (93K-17-2009-K03), and by Jilin University Research Project (200903178).

J. Lee (Ed.): CP 2011, LNCS 6876, pp. 523–537, 2011.

almost unanimously assume that qualitative constraints involve only *unknown* entities. In other words, the precise (geometric) information of *every* object is totally unknown. In practical applications, however, we often meet constraints that involve both known and unknown entities, i.e. constants and variables.

For example, consider a class scheduling problem in a primary school. In addition to constraints between unknown intervals (e.g. a Math class is *followed by* a Music class), we may also impose constraints involving determined intervals (e.g. a P.E. class should be *during* afternoon).

Constraints involving known entities are especially common in spatial reasoning tasks such as urban planning. For example, to find a best location for a landfill, we need to formulate constraints between the unknown landfill and significant landmarks, e.g. lake, university, hospital etc.

In this paper, we explicitly introduce *landmarks* (defined as known entities) into the definition of the consistency problem, and call the consistency problem involving landmarks the *hybrid* consistency problem. In comparison, we call the usual consistency problem (involving no landmarks) the *pure* consistency problem.

In general, solving constraint networks involving landmarks is different from solving constraint networks involving no landmarks. For example, consider the simple RCC-5 algebra. Suppose x, v_1, v_2, v_3 are spatial variables which are interpreted as regions in the plane. Consider the following RCC-5 constraint network:

$$\Gamma = \{v_1\mathbf{PO}v_2, v_1\mathbf{PO}v_3, v_2\mathbf{PO}v_3\} \cup \{x\mathbf{PP}v_1, x\mathbf{PP}v_2, x\mathbf{PP}v_3\}.$$

where **PP** is the proper part relation, **PO** is the partially overlap relation. It is clear that Γ is consistent, and a solution of Γ is shown in the following figure (left), where v_1, v_2, v_3, x are interpreted by regions l_1, l_2, l_3, a respectively.

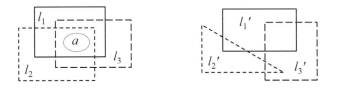

Therefore, the network

$$\Gamma_1 = \{x\mathbf{PP}l_1, x\mathbf{PP}l_2, x\mathbf{PP}l_3\},$$

which involves three landmarks l_1, l_2, l_3, is consistent. Note that the RCC-5 constraint between any two landmarks is the actual RCC-5 relation between them,

Suppose l_1', l_2', l_3' are regions shown in the above figure (right). The network

$$\Gamma_2 = \{x\mathbf{PP}l_1', x\mathbf{PP}l_2', x\mathbf{PP}l_3'\}$$

is not consistent, because $l_1' \cap l_2' \cap l_3' = \varnothing$. The RCC-5 relation between any two of l_1', l_2', l_3' is **PO**, which is the same relation as that between any two landmarks l_1, l_2, l_3 in Γ_1. Therefore, the consistency problem for RCC-5 networks involving landmarks can not be decided by the RCC-5 relations between the landmarks alone. Note that (l_1, l_2, l_3) and (l'_1, l'_2, l'_3) are partial solutions of Γ, so the problem is equivalent to decide whether a particular partial solution can be extended to a global one.

The aim of this paper is to investigate how landmarks affect the consistency of constraint networks in several very important qualitative calculi. The rest of this paper proceeds as follows. Section 2 introduces basic notions in qualitative constraint solving and examples of qualitative calculi. The new consistency problem, as well as several basic results, is also presented here. Assuming that all landmarks are represented as polygons, Section 3 then provides a polynomial decision procedure for the consistency of hybrid basic RCC-5 networks. Besides, if the network is consistent, a solution is constructed in polynomial time; Section 4 shows that consistency problem for hybrid basic RCC-8 networks is NP-hard. The last section then concludes the paper.

2   Qualitative Calculi and the Consistency Problem

Most qualitative approaches to spatial and temporal knowledge representation and reasoning are based on qualitative calculi. Suppose U is a universe of spatial or temporal entities. Write $\mathbf{Rel}(U)$ for the algebra of binary relations on U. A qualitative calculus on U is a sub-Boolean algebra of $\mathbf{Rel}(U)$ generated by a set $\mathcal{B}$ of jointly exhaustive and pairwise disjoint (JEPD) relations on U. Relations in $\mathcal{B}$ are called basic relations of the qualitative calculus. We next recall the well-known Interval Algebra (IA) [1] and the two RCC algebras.

Example 1 (Interval Algebra). Let U be the set of closed intervals on the real line. Thirteen binary relations between two intervals $x = [x^-, x^+]$ and $y = [y^-, y^+]$ are defined by comparing the order relations between the endpoints of x and y. These are the basic relations of IA.

Example 2 (RCC-5 and RCC-8 Algebras[1]). Let U be the set of bounded regions in the real plane, where a region is a nonempty regular set. The RCC-8 algebra is generated by the eight topological relations

$$\mathbf{DC}, \mathbf{EC}, \mathbf{PO}, \mathbf{EQ}, \mathbf{TPP}, \mathbf{NTPP}, \mathbf{TPP}^\sim, \mathbf{NTPP}^\sim, \tag{1}$$

where $\mathbf{DC}, \mathbf{EC}, \mathbf{PO}, \mathbf{TPP}$ and $\mathbf{NTPP}$ are defined in Table 1, $\mathbf{EQ}$ is the identity relation, and $\mathbf{TPP}^\sim$ and $\mathbf{NTPP}^\sim$ are the converses of $\mathbf{TPP}$ and $\mathbf{NTPP}$, respectively, see the following figure for illustration. The RCC-5 algebra is the sub-algebra of RCC-8 generated by the five part-whole relations

$$\mathbf{DR}, \mathbf{PO}, \mathbf{EQ}, \mathbf{PP}, \mathbf{PP}^\sim, \tag{2}$$

where $\mathbf{DR} = \mathbf{DC} \cup \mathbf{EC}, \mathbf{PP} = \mathbf{TPP} \cup \mathbf{NTPP}$, and $\mathbf{PP}^\sim = \mathbf{TPP}^\sim \cup \mathbf{NTPP}^\sim$.

A qualitative calculus provides a useful constraint language. Suppose $\mathcal{M}$ is a qualitative calculus defined on an infinite domain U. Relations in $\mathcal{M}$ can be used to express

---

[1] We note that the RCC algebras have interpretations in arbitrary topological spaces. In this paper, we only consider the most important interpretation in the real plane.

Table 1. A topological interpretation of basic RCC-8 relations in the plane, where a, b are two bounded plane regions, and $a°, b°$ are the interiors of a, b, respectively

Relation	Meaning	Relation	Meaning
DC	$a \cap b = \varnothing$	**TPP**	$a \subset b, a \not\subset b°$
EC	$a \cap b \neq \varnothing, a° \cap b° = \varnothing$	**NTPP**	$a \subset b°$
PO	$a \not\subseteq b, b \not\subseteq a, a° \cap b° \neq \varnothing$	**EQ**	$a = b$

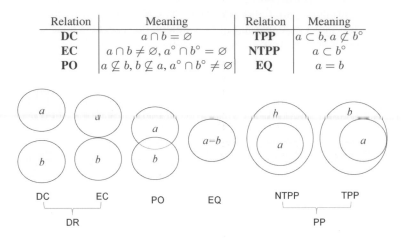

constraints about variables which takes values in U. A constraint has the form $x_1 \alpha x_2$, where α is a relation in $\mathcal{M}$, x_i is either a constant in U (called *landmark* in this paper), or a variable. Such a constraint is *basic* if α is a basic relation in $\mathcal{M}$.

Given a finite set Γ of constraints, we write $V(\Gamma)$ ($L(\Gamma)$, resp.) for the set of variables (constants, resp.) appearing in Γ, and assume that the constraint between two landmarks a, b is the actual basic relation in $\mathcal{M}$ that relates a to b. A solution of Γ is an assignment of values in U to variables in $V(\Gamma)$ such that all constraints in Γ are satisfied. If Γ has a solution, we say Γ is *consistent* or *satisfiable*. Two sets of constraint Γ and Γ' are *equivalent* if they have the same set of solutions.

A set Γ of constraints is said to be a *complete constraint network* if there is a unique constraint between each pair of variables/constants appearing in Γ. It is straightforward to show that a non-complete constraint network Γ can be transformed into an equivalent complete constraint network Γ' in polynomial time.

Definition 1. *Let $\mathcal{M}$ be a qualitative calculus on U. The hybrid consistency problem of $\mathcal{M}$ is, given a constraint network Γ in $\mathcal{M}$, decide the consistency of Γ in $\mathcal{M}$, i.e. decide if there is an assignment of elements in U to variables in Γ that satisfies all the constraints in Γ. The pure consistency problem of $\mathcal{M}$ is the sub-consistency problem that considers constraint networks that involve no landmarks.*

The hybrid consistency problem of $\mathcal{M}$ can be approximated by a variant of the path-consistency algorithm. We say a complete constraint network Γ is *path-consistent* if for any three objects l_i, l_j, l_k in $V(\Gamma) \cup L(\Gamma)$, we have

$$\alpha_{ij} = \alpha_{ji}^{\smile} \ \& \ \alpha_{ij} \subseteq \alpha_{ik} \circ_w \alpha_{kj}, \qquad (3)$$

where $\circ_w$ is the weak composition [6,8] in $\mathcal{M}$ and $\alpha \circ_w \beta$ is defined to be the smallest relation in $\mathcal{M}$ which contains the usual composition of α and β, i.e.

$$\alpha \circ_w \beta = \bigcup \{\gamma \text{ is a basic relation in } \mathcal{M} : \gamma \cap \alpha \circ \beta \neq \varnothing\}. \qquad (4)$$

We note that the above notion of path-consistency for qualitative constraint network is very different from the classical notion (cf. [5,3]).

It is clear that each complete network can be transformed in polynomial time into an equivalent complete network that is path-consistent. Because the consistency problem is in general NP-hard, we do not expect that a local consistency algorithm can solve the general consistency problem. However, it has been proved that the path-consistency algorithm suffices to decide the pure consistency problem for large fragments of some well-known qualitative calculi, e.g. IA, RCC-5, and RCC-8 (cf. [3]). This shows that, at least for these calculi, the pure consistency problem can be solved by path-consistency algorithm and by applying the backtracking method to constraints [3].

The remainder of this paper will investigate the hybrid consistency problem for the above calculi. In the following discussion, we assume Γ is a complete basic network that involves at least one landmark.

For IA, we have

Proposition 1. *Suppose Γ is a basic network of IA constraints that involves landmarks and variables. Then Γ is consistent iff it is path-consistent.*

Proof. If we replace each landmark in Γ by a new interval variable, and constrain any two new variables with the actual relation between the corresponding landmarks, then we obtain a basic network Γ^* of IA constraints that involves no landmarks. Note that each path-consistent IA basic network is globally consistent. The landmarks (as a partial solution of Γ^*) can also be extended to a solution.   □

This result shows that, for IA, the hybrid consistency problem can be solved in the same way as the pure consistency problem. Similar conclusion also holds for some other calculi, e.g. the Point Algebra, the Rectangle Algebra, and the Cardinal Direction Calculus (for point-like objects) [7].

This property, however, does not hold in general. Take the RCC-5 as example. If a basic network Γ involves no landmark, then we know Γ is consistent if it is path-consistent. If Γ involves landmarks, we have seen in the introduction a path-consistent but inconsistent basic RCC-5 network.

In the next two sections, we investigate how landmarks affect the consistency of RCC-5 and RCC-8 topological constraints. We stress that, in this paper, we *only consider* the standard (and the most important) interpretation of the RCC language in the real plane, as given in Example 2. When restricting landmarks to polygons, we first show that the consistency of a hybrid basic RCC-5 network can still be decided in polynomial time (Section 4), but that of RCC-8 networks is NP-hard.

3   The Hybrid Consistency Problem of RCC-5

We begin with a short review of the realization algorithm for pure consistency problem of RCC-5 [4,5]. Suppose Γ involves only spatial variables $v_1, v_2, \cdots, v_n$. We define a finite set X_i of *control points* for each v_i as follows:

- Add a point P_i to X_i;
- For any $j > i$, add a new point P_{ij} to both X_i and X_j if $(v_i\mathbf{PO}v_j) \in \Gamma$;
- For any j, put all points in X_i into X_j if $(v_i\mathbf{PP}v_j) \in \Gamma$.

Take $\varepsilon > 0$ such that the distance between any two different points in $\bigcup_{i=1}^n X_i$ is greater than 2ε. Let $B(P, \varepsilon)$ be the closed disk with radius ε centred at P. By the choice of ε, different disks are disjoint. Let $a_i = \bigcup\{B(P, \varepsilon) : P \in X_i\}$. It is easy to check that the assignment is a solution of Γ, if Γ is consistent.

Assume Γ is a basic RCC-5 network involving landmarks $L = \{l_1, \cdots, l_m\}$ in the real plane and variables $V = \{v_1, \cdots, v_n\}$. Write ∂L for the union of the boundaries of the landmarks. A *block* is defined to be a maximal connected component of $\mathbb{R}^2 \setminus \partial L$, which is an open set. It is clear that the complement of the union of all landmarks (which are bounded) is the unique unbounded block. We write $\mathbb{B}$ for the set of all blocks.

For each landmark l_i, we write $I(l_i)$ for the set of blocks that l_i contains, and write $E(l_i)$ for the set of rest blocks, i.e. the blocks that are disjoint from l_i. That is,

$$I(l_i) = \{b \in \mathbb{B} : b \subseteq l_i\}, \qquad E(l_i) = \{b \in \mathbb{B} : b \cap l_i = \varnothing\}. \tag{5}$$

It is clear that each block is in either $I(l_i)$ or $E(l_i)$, but not both, i.e., $I(l_i) \cup E(l_i) = \mathbb{B}$ and $I(l_i) \cap E(l_i) = \varnothing$.

These constructions can be extended from landmarks to variables as

$$I(v_i) = \bigcup\{I(l_j) : l_j\mathbf{PP}v_i\}, \tag{6}$$

$$E(v_i) = \bigcup\{I(l_j) : l_j\mathbf{DR}v_i\} \cup \bigcup\{E(l_j) : v_i\mathbf{PP}l_j\}. \tag{7}$$

Intuitively, $I(v_i)$ is the set of blocks that v_i must contain, and $E(v_i)$ is the set of blocks that should be excluded from v_i. We now give an example.

Example 3. Consider the network Γ_1 that involves landmarks l_1, l_2, l_3 and variable v, where $l_2\mathbf{DR}l_3$ and $l_1 = l_2 \cup l_3$ (see the following figure). The constraints in Γ_1 are specified as $v\mathbf{PP}l_1, v\mathbf{DR}l_2$ and $v\mathbf{DR}l_3$. We have $\mathbb{B} = \{b_1, b_2, b_3\}$, and

$$
\begin{aligned}
I(l_1) &= \{b_1, b_2\}, & I(l_2) &= \{b_1\}, & I(l_3) &= \{b_2\}, \\
E(l_1) &= \{b_3\}, & E(l_2) &= \{b_2, b_3\}, & E(l_3) &= \{b_1, b_3\}, \\
I(v) &= \varnothing & E(v) &= E(l_1) \cup I(l_2) \cup I(l_3) = \mathbb{B}.
\end{aligned}
$$

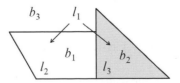

The following proposition claims that no block can appear in both $I(v_i)$ and $E(v_i)$.

Proposition 2. *Suppose Γ is a basic RCC-5 constraint network that involves at least one landmark. If Γ is path-consistent, then $I(v_i) \cap E(v_i) = \varnothing$.*

Proof. Assume $b \in I(v_i) \cap E(v_i)$. There exists some l_j such that $l_j \mathbf{PP} v_i$ and $b \in I(l_j)$. Furthermore, there exists some l_k such that either (i) $l_k \mathbf{DR} v_i$ and $b \in I(l_k)$, or (ii) $v_i \mathbf{PP} l_k$ and $b \in E(l_k)$.

Both cases lead to contradiction. For the first case, we know that $b \subseteq l_j \cap l_k$, while the path-consistency of Γ implies that $l_j \mathbf{DR} l_k$. For the second case, the path-consistency of Γ implies $l_j \mathbf{PP} l_k$, but $b \subseteq l_j$ and $b \cap l_k = \varnothing$. $\square$

We have the following theorem.

Theorem 1. *Suppose Γ is a basic RCC-5 constraint network that involves at least one landmark. If Γ is consistent, then we have*

- *For any $v_i \in V$,*
$$E(v_i) \subsetneq \mathbb{B}. \tag{8}$$
- *For any $v_i \in V$ and $w \in L \cup V$ such that $(v_i \mathbf{PO} w) \in \Gamma$,*
$$E(v_i) \cup E(w) \subsetneq \mathbb{B}, \tag{9}$$
$$E(v_i) \cup I(w) \subsetneq \mathbb{B}, \tag{10}$$
$$I(v_i) \cup E(w) \subsetneq \mathbb{B}. \tag{11}$$
- *For any $v_i \in V$ and $l_j \in L$ such that $(v_i \mathbf{PP} l_j) \in \Gamma$,*
$$I(v_i) \subsetneq I(l_j). \tag{12}$$
- *For any $v_i \in V$ and $l_j \in L$ such that $(l_j \mathbf{PP} v_i) \in \Gamma$,*
$$E(v_i) \subsetneq E(l_j). \tag{13}$$
- *For any $v_i, v_j \in V$ such that $(v_i \mathbf{PP} v_j) \in \Gamma$,*
$$I(v_i) \cup E(v_j) \subsetneq \mathbb{B}. \tag{14}$$

Proof. Note the inclusion part of these equations are clear. We only focus on the inequality. Suppose $\{\bar{v}_1, \cdots, \bar{v}_n\}$ is a solution of Γ. Because each $\bar{v}_i$ has nonempty interior, there exists at least one block b such that $b \cap \bar{v}_i$ is nonempty. Clearly, $b \notin E(v_i)$ since blocks in $E(v_i)$ are all disjoint from $\bar{v}_i$. Therefore, $E(v_i) \neq \mathbb{B}$.

If $(v_i \mathbf{PO} w) \in \Gamma$, then by assumption we have $\bar{v}_i \mathbf{PO} \bar{w}$, where $\bar{w}$ is l_j if $w = l_j$. By definition of **PO** (see Table 1), we know $\bar{v}_i$ and $\bar{w}$ have a common interior point. This implies that there exists a block b that contains an interior point of $\bar{v}_i \cap \bar{w}$. This block is neither in $E(v_i)$ nor in $E(w)$. That is, $E(v_i) \cup E(w) \neq \mathbb{B}$. Similarly, we know neither $E(v_i) \cup I(w)$ nor $I(v_i) \cup E(w)$ is $\mathbb{B}$. If $(v_i \mathbf{PP} l_j) \in \Gamma$, then $\bar{v}_i \mathbf{PP} l_j$. Because l_j is the regularized union of all the blocks it contains, we know there exists at least one block in $I(l_j)$ that is not in $I(v_i)$. This shows $I(v_i) \neq I(l_j)$. The rest situations are similar. $\square$

These conditions are also sufficient to determine the consistency of a path-consistent basic RCC-5 network. We show this by devising a realization algorithm. The construction is similar to that for the pure consistency problem. For each v_i, we define a finite set X_i of control points as follows, where for clarity, we write
$$P(v_i) = \mathbb{B} - I(v_i) - E(v_i). \tag{15}$$

- For each block b in $P(v_i)$, select a fresh point in b and add the point into X_i.
- For any $j > i$ with $(v_i \mathbf{PO} v_j) \in \Gamma$, select a fresh point in some block b in $P(v_i) \cap P(v_j)$ (if it is not empty), and add the point into X_i and X_j.
- For any j, put all points in X_j into X_i if $(v_j \mathbf{PP} v_i) \in \Gamma$.

We note that the points selected from a block b for different v_i, or in different steps, should be pairwise different. Recall that each point in $\bigcup_{i=1}^n X_i$ is not at the boundary of any block. We choose $\varepsilon > 0$ such that $B(P, \varepsilon)$ does not intersect either the boundary of a block or another disk $B(Q, \varepsilon)$. Furthermore, we can assume that ε is small enough such that the union of all the disks $B(P, \varepsilon)$ does not cover any block in $\mathbb{B}$.

Let

$$\hat{a}_i = \bigcup \{B(P, \varepsilon) : P \in X_i\} \cup \bigcup \{l_j : l_j \mathbf{PP} v_i\}. \tag{16}$$

We claim that $\{\hat{a}_1, \cdots, \hat{a}_t\}$ is a solution of Γ. We first prove the following lemma.

Lemma 1. *Let Γ be a path-consistent basic RCC-5 constraint network that involves at least one landmark. Suppose $\mathbb{B}$ is the block set of Γ. Then, for each $b \in \mathbb{B}$, we have*

- *$b \in I(v_i)$ iff $b \subseteq \hat{a}_i$.*
- *$b \in E(v_i)$ iff $b \cap \hat{a}_i = \varnothing$.*
- *$b \in P(v_i)$ iff $b \not\subseteq \hat{a}_i$ and $b \cap \hat{a}_i \neq \varnothing$.*

Proof. We first prove the necessity part.

Suppose $b \in I(v_i)$. There exists a landmark l such that $l\mathbf{PP}v_i$ and $b \subseteq l$. The first statement follows directly from $b \subseteq l$ and $l \subseteq \hat{a}_i$.

Assume $b \in E(v_i)$. By definition, there is a landmark l such that either (i) $b \subseteq l$ and $l\mathbf{DR}v_i$ or (ii) $b \cap l = \varnothing$ and $v_i \mathbf{PP} l$. In both cases, we have $b \cap l' = \varnothing$ for any landmark l' with $l'\mathbf{PP}v_i$. We next show $b \cap B(P, \varepsilon) = \varnothing$ for any P in X_i, which is equivalent to that there is no control point in X_i in b. Now suppose P is a control point in X_i and $P \in b$. Since $b \in E(v_i)$, we know P is not generated by the first two rules. That is, P must be a control point of some v_j and $v_j \mathbf{PP} v_i$. In this case, it can be proved that $b \in E(v)$ by path-consistency. Therefore we find a different variable v_j such that $b \in E(v_j)$ and $b \cap \hat{a}_j \neq \varnothing$. Because the variables are finite, we will get a contradiction by repeating this procedure. As a conclusion, we have $b \cap \hat{a}_i = \varnothing$ whenever $b \in E(v_i)$.

Now assume $b \in P(v_j)$. The first step of the construction algorithm shows that a control point of v_j is taken from b. Therefore, $b \cap \hat{a}_j \neq \varnothing$. Since $b \notin I(v_j)$, we know b is not contained in any landmark l with $l\mathbf{PP}v_i$. Moreover, b is not contained in the union of all $B(P, \varepsilon)$ due to the choice of ε. This implies $b \not\subseteq \hat{a}_i$.

Since $\{I(v_i), E(v_i), P(v_i)\}$ is a partition of the blocks in B, it is easy to see the conditions are also sufficient.   □

We next prove that $\{\hat{a}_1, \cdots, \hat{a}_t\}$ is a solution of Γ.

Theorem 2. *Suppose Γ is a complete basic RCC-5 network involving landmarks L and variables V. Assume Γ is path-consistent and satisfies the conditions in Theorem 1. Then Γ is consistent and $\{\hat{a}_1, \cdots, \hat{a}_t\}$, as constructed in (16), is a solution of Γ.*

Proof. By (8) we know there is at least one block b in either $I(v_i) \cup P(v_i)$. By Lemma 1 we know $\hat{a}_i$ is nonempty. We next prove all constraints in Γ are satisfied.

We first consider the constraint $v_i \alpha l_j$ between variable v_i and landmark l_j. The cases that $\alpha = \mathbf{PP}, \mathbf{PP}^\sim, \mathbf{DR}$ can be directly checked by Lemma 1. Now suppose $v_i \mathbf{PO} l_j$. By (9), we know that $E(v_i) \cup E(l_j) \subsetneq \mathbb{B}$. That is, there is some block b in $I(l_j)$ but outside $E(v_i)$. By Lemma 1, we know $b \cap \hat{a}_i \neq \varnothing$. By $b \subseteq l_j$, $\hat{a}_i$ and l_j have a common interior point. Furthermore, by $E(v_i) \cup I(l_j) \subsetneq \mathbb{B}$ (10), we know there is a block b' in $E(l_j)$ that is outside $E(v_i)$. By $b' \in E(l_j)$, we have $b' \cap l_j = \varnothing$; by $b' \notin E(v_i)$ and Lemma 1, we have $b' \cap \hat{a}_i \neq \varnothing$. So $\hat{a}_i \not\subseteq l_j$. Similarly, we can show $l_j \not\subseteq \hat{a}_i$. Therefore, $\hat{a}_i \mathbf{PO} l_j$.

Now we consider constraints between two variables v_i and v_j.

(1) If $(v_i \mathbf{PP} v_j) \in \Gamma$, we have $X_i \subset X_j$ and $I(v_i) \subseteq I(v_j)$. By definition, $\hat{a}_i \subseteq \hat{a}_j$. Moreover, by $I(v_i) \cup E(v_j) \subsetneq \mathbb{B}$ (14), we know there is a block b that is outside both $I(v_i)$ and $E(v_j)$. By Lemma 1, this implies that $b \not\subseteq \hat{a}_i$ and $b \cap \hat{a}_j \neq \varnothing$. If $b \cap \hat{a}_i = \varnothing$ or $b \subseteq \hat{a}_j$, then $\hat{a}_i \neq \hat{a}_j$. If otherwise, then $b \in P(v_j)$. Hence, there is a fresh control point P of v_j in b. By the choice of P, we know P is not in X_i, hence not in $\hat{a}_i$. So in this case we also have $\hat{a}_i \neq \hat{a}_j$. Therefore, we have $\hat{a}_i \mathbf{PP} \hat{a}_j$.

(2) If $(v_i \mathbf{PP}^\sim v_j) \in \Gamma$, we know that Γ also contains constraint $(v_j \mathbf{PP} v_i)$. Because we have proved that $\hat{a}_j \mathbf{PP} \hat{a}_i$, constraint $v_i \mathbf{PP}^\sim v_j$ is also satisfied by $\hat{a}_i$ and $\hat{a}_j$.

(3) If $(v_i \mathbf{DR} v_j) \in \Gamma$, we show that $X_i \cap X_j = \varnothing$. Otherwise, there exists some v_k such that $v_k \mathbf{PP} v_i$ and $v_k \mathbf{PP} v_j$, which contradicts $v_i \mathbf{DR} v_j$ by path-consistency. It remains to prove $X_i \cap l = \varnothing$ if $(l \mathbf{PP} v_j) \in \Gamma$, and $X_j \cap l' = \varnothing$ if $(l' \mathbf{PP} v_i) \in \Gamma$.

Let P be a control point of v_i, and l is a landmark such that $l \mathbf{PP} v_j$. We next show $P \notin l$. By $v_i \mathbf{DR} v_j$ and $l \mathbf{PP} v_j$, we know $l \mathbf{DR} v_i$. Hence $E(l) \subseteq E(v_i)$. For any block $b \in E(l)$, by $b \in E(v_i)$ and Lemma 1, we know $b \cap \hat{a}_i = \varnothing$. Because $P \in \hat{a}_i$, we know $P \notin b$ for any $b \in E(l)$. This implies that $P \notin l$. Therefore, $X_i \cap l = \varnothing$ if $l \mathbf{PP} v_j$. That $X_j \cap l' = \varnothing$ if $l' \mathbf{PP} v_j$ is similar. In conclusion, we have $\hat{a}_i \mathbf{DR} \hat{a}_j$.

(4) If $(v_i \mathbf{PO} v_j) \in \Gamma$, we show $\hat{a}_i$ and $\hat{a}_j$ have a common interior point. We prove this by contradiction. Suppose $v_i \mathbf{PO} v_j$ but $\hat{a}_i$ and $\hat{a}_j$ have no common interior point. For any $b \in I(v_i)$, we have $b \subseteq \hat{a}_i$. Since b is an open set, $b \cap \hat{a}_j$ cannot be nonempty (otherwise $\hat{a}_i$ and $\hat{a}_j$ shall have a common interior point). Therefore $b \in E(v_j)$, according to Lemma 1. In other words, $I(v_i) \subseteq E(v_j)$. Symmetrically, we have $I(v_j) \subseteq E(v_i)$. Hence $I(v_i) \cup I(v_j) \cup E(v_i) \cup E(v_j) = E(v_i) \cup E(v_j)$. Note the right hand side of the above equation is a proper subset of $\mathbb{B}$ (cf. (9)). This implies that $P(v_i) \cap P(v_j) \neq \varnothing$. By the construction of control points, we know there exists $P \in X_i \cap X_j$, where P is a control point selected from a block in $P(v_i) \cap P(v_j)$. Because P is a common interior point of both $\hat{a}_i$ and $\hat{a}_j$, this clearly contradicts our assumption. Therefore, $\hat{a}_i$ and $\hat{a}_j$ have a common interior point. That $\hat{a}_i$ and $\hat{a}_j$ are incomparable is similar to the case of $(v_i \mathbf{PO} l_j)$. As a result, we know $\hat{a}_i \mathbf{PO} \hat{a}_j$.

In summary, all constraints are satisfied and $\{\hat{a}_1, \cdots, \hat{a}_t\}$ is a solution of Γ. $\square$

It is worth noting that the complexity of deciding the consistency of a hybrid basic RCC-5 network includes two parts, viz. the complexity of computing the blocks, and that of checking the conditions in Theorem 1. The latter part alone can be completed in $O(|\mathbb{B}|n(n+m))$ time, where $|\mathbb{B}|$ is the number of the blocks. In the worst situation, the number of blocks may be up to 2^m. This suggests that the decision method described above is in general inefficient. The following theorem, however, asserts that this method is still polynomial in the size of the input instance, provided that the landmarks are all represented as polygons.

Before proving Theorem 3, we review some notions and results in computational geometry. The reader is referred to [2] and references therein for more details. A *(planar) subdivision* is the map induced by a planar embedding of a graph. The embedding of nodes (arcs, resp.) of the graph is called *vertices* (*edges*, resp.) in the subdivision, where each edge is required to be a straight line segment. A *face* of the subdivision is a maximal connected subset of the remaining part of the plane excluded by all the edges and vertices. The *complexity of a subdivision* is defined to be the sum of the number of vertices, the number of edges, and the number of faces in the subdivision. The *overlay* of two subdivisions S_1 and S_2 is the subdivision of the plane induced by all the edges from S_1 and S_2. Let S_1 and S_2 be two subdivisions with complexities n_1 and n_2. The overlay of S_1 and S_2 can be computed in $O(n \log n + k \log n)$ time, where $n = n_1 + n_2$ and k is the complexity of the overlay [2, Section 2.3]. Note that this complexity is sensitive to the output. Polygons can be viewed as special cases of subdivisions.

Theorem 3. *Suppose Γ is a basic RCC-5 constraint network, and $V(\Gamma) = \{v_1, \cdots, v_n\}$ and $L(\Gamma) = \{l_1, \cdots, l_m\}$ are the set of variables and, respectively, the set of landmarks appearing in Γ. Assume each landmark l_i is represented by a planar subdivision with complexity k_i. Let K be the sum of all k_i. Then the consistency of Γ can be decided in $O((n + m)^3 + n(n + m)K^2 + m^2 K^2 \log K)$ time.*

Proof. We first compute the overlay of all landmarks. Then we calculate $I(l_i)$ and $E(l_i)$ for each landmark (l_i), and $I(v_i)$ and $E(v_i)$ for each variable v_i. Finally we check the conditions listed in Theorem 1.

Let $\mathcal{O}_k$ be the overlay of the first k landmarks, and write $\mathcal{O} = \mathcal{O}_m$. Recall each overlay is a subdivision. We show that the complexity of $\mathcal{O}$ is $O(K^2)$. Each vertex in the subdivision $\mathcal{O}$ is either a vertex of some landmark, or the intersection of two edges of the landmarks. Because the total number of vertices (edges, resp.) is less than K, we have that the number of vertices in $\mathcal{O}$ is $O(K^2)$. Each edge in $\mathcal{O}$ is clearly a part of an edge of some landmark. Moreover, each edge in a landmark is divided into at most K edges in $\mathcal{O}$, so the number of edges in $\mathcal{O}$ is $O(K^2)$. Let l_i' be the subdivision obtained by replacing the line segments in l_i with lines. [2] It is obvious that the overlay $\mathcal{O}'$ of all l_i' is finer than $\mathcal{O}$. Because K lines partition the plane into at most $1 + 1 + 2 + \cdots + K = O(K^2)$ faces, we know that the number of faces in $\mathcal{O}'$ is $O(K^2)$, which further implies that the number of faces in $\mathcal{O}$ is also $O(K^2)$. In summary, the complexity of subdivision $\mathcal{O}$ is $O(K^2)$. It is clear that the faces in $\mathcal{O}$ are actually the blocks we defined.

Now consider how to compute subdivision $\mathcal{O}_{i+1}$, the overlay of subdivision $\mathcal{O}_i$ and landmark l_{i+1}. Regarded as a subdivision, the complexity of l_{i+1} is $O(K)$. The complexities of $\mathcal{O}_k$ and $\mathcal{O}_{i+1}$ are no more than that of $\mathcal{O}$, which is $O(K^2)$. By the computational geometry result stated before the theorem, the subdivision $\mathcal{O}_{i+1}$ can be computed in $O(K^2 \log K)$ time. Therefore, the overlay $\mathcal{O}$ of all the landmarks can be computed in $O(mK^2 \log K)$ time.

---

[2] Note here we allow the edges in a subdivision to be rays.

To record whether a face is contained in a landmark or not, we attach to each face f (in some overlay $\mathcal{O}_i$) a label which is the set of landmarks that contain face f. When computing the overlay $\mathcal{O}_{i+1}$ of $\mathcal{O}_i$ and l_{i+1}, the labels of faces in $\mathcal{O}_{i+1}$ can be computed as well. This is because, each face in $\mathcal{O}_{i+1}$ is the intersection of some face f_1 from $\mathcal{O}_i$ and some face f_2 from l_{i+1}, and its label is the union of the labels of f_1 and f_2, which can be computed in $O(m)$ time. Computing the labels of faces increases the complexity of calculating the subdivision $\mathcal{O}$ to $O(m^2 K^2 \log K)$ time.

For each landmark l_i, $I(l_i)$ is the set of faces in $\mathcal{O}$ such that the labels of which contain l_i. So $I(l_i)$ can be obtained by scanning the labels of all the faces in $\mathcal{O}$. This takes $O(K^2)$ time, since the number of faces in $\mathcal{O}$ is $O(K^2)$. Therefore, all $I(l_i)$ and $E(l_i)$ can be computed in $O(mK^2)$ time. By definition, all $I(v_i)$ and $E(v_i)$ can be computed in $O(nmK^2)$ time. Each of the $O(n(n+m))$ conditions in Theorem 1 can be checked in $O(K^2)$ time, so these conditions can be checked in $O(n(n+m)K^2)$ time if the overlay is computed. In conclusion, the consistency can be checked in $O((n + m)^3 + n(n+m)K^2 + m^2 K^2 \log K)$ time, where the term $(n+m)^3$ is the time needed to decide the path-consistency of the network. □

4   The Hybrid Consistency Problem of RCC-8

Suppose Γ is a complete basic RCC-8 network that involves no landmarks. Then Γ is consistent if it is path-consistent [9,11]. Moreover, a solution can be constructed for each path-consistent basic network in cubic time [4,5]. This section shows that, however, when considering polygons, it is NP-hard to determine if a complete basic RCC-8 network involving landmarks has a solution. We achieve this by devising a polynomial reduction from 3-SAT.

In this section, for clarity, we use upper case letters A, B, C (with indices) to denote landmarks, and use lower case letters u, v, w (with indices) to denote spatial variables.

The NP-hardness stems from the fact that two externally connected polygons, say A, B, may have more than one tangential points. Assume v is a spatial variable that is required to be a tangentially proper part of A but externally connected to B. Then it is undetermined at which tangential point(s) v and B should meet.

Precisely, consider the configuration shown in Fig. 1 (a), where A and B are two externally connected landmarks, meeting at two tangential points, say Q^+ and Q^-. Assume $\{u, v, w\}$ are variables that are subject to the following constraints

$$u\mathbf{TPP}A, u\mathbf{EC}B,$$
$$v\mathbf{TPP}B, v\mathbf{EC}A, w\mathbf{TPP}B, w\mathbf{EC}A,$$
$$u\mathbf{EC}v, u\mathbf{DC}w, v\mathbf{DC}w.$$

It is clear that u is required to meet B at either Q^+ or Q^-, but not both (cf Fig. 1(b,c)). The correspondence between these two configurations and the two truth values (true or false) of a propositional variable is exploited in the following reduction.

Let $\phi = \bigwedge_{k=1}^{m} \varphi_k$ be a 3-SAT instance over propositional variables set $\{p_1, \cdots, p_n\}$. Each clause φ_k has the form $p_r^* \vee p_s^* \vee p_t^*$, where literal p_i^* is either p_i or $\neg p_i$ for $i = r, s, t$. We next construct a set of polygons L and a complete basic RCC-8 network Γ_ϕ, such that ϕ is satisfiable iff Γ_ϕ is satisfiable.

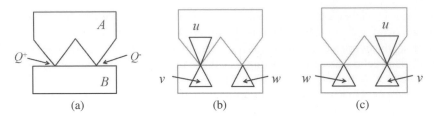

Fig. 1. Two landmarks A, B that are externally connected at two tangential points Q^+ and Q^-

First, we define $A, B_1, B_2, \cdots, B_n$ such that for each $1 \leq i \leq n$, A is externally connected to B_i at two tangential points Q_i^+ and Q_i^-, as shown in Fig. 2.

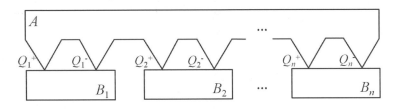

Fig. 2. Illustration of landmarks $A, B_1, \cdots, B_n$

The variable set of Γ is $V = \{u, v_1, \cdots, v_n, w_1, \cdots, w_n\}$. We impose the following constraints to the variables in V.

$$u\mathbf{TPP}A, \qquad u\mathbf{EC}B_i, \qquad\qquad\qquad\qquad\qquad (17)$$
$$v_i\mathbf{EC}A, \qquad v_i\mathbf{TPP}B_i, \qquad v_i\mathbf{DC}B_j \ (j \neq i), \qquad (18)$$
$$w_i\mathbf{EC}A, \qquad w_i\mathbf{TPP}B_i, \qquad w_i\mathbf{DC}B_j \ (j \neq i), \qquad (19)$$
$$u\mathbf{EC}v_i, \qquad u\mathbf{DC}w_i, \qquad\qquad\qquad\qquad\qquad (20)$$
$$v_i\mathbf{DC}w_j, \qquad v_i\mathbf{DC}v_j \ (j \neq i), \qquad w_i\mathbf{DC}w_j \ (j \neq i). \qquad (21)$$

Therefore, u is required to meet each B_i, at either Q_i^- or Q_i^+ but not both.

For each clause φ_k, we introduce an additional landmark C_k, which externally connects A at three tangential points, and partially overlaps B_i. The three tangential points of C_k and A are determined by the literals in φ_k. Precisely, suppose $\varphi_k = p_r^* \vee p_s^* \vee p_t^*$, then the first tangential point of A and C_k is constructed to be Q_r^+ if $p_r^* = p_r$, or Q_r^- if $p_r^* = \neg p_r$. The second and the third tangential points are selected from $\{Q_s^+, Q_s^-\}$ and $\{Q_t^+, Q_t^-\}$ similarly. Take clause $p_r \vee \neg p_s \vee p_t$ for example, the tangential points between landmarks C_k and A should be Q_r^+, Q_s^-, and Q_t^+, as shown in Fig. 3.

The constraints between C_k and variables in V are specified as

$$u\mathbf{ECC}_k, \qquad v_i\mathbf{POC}_k, \qquad w_i\mathbf{POC}_k. \qquad (22)$$

Since C_k and A have three tangential points, the constraints $u\mathbf{TPP}A$ and $u\mathbf{ECC}_k$ imply that u should occupy at least one of the three tangential points. This corresponds

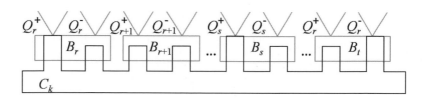

Fig. 3. Illustration of landmark C_k

to the fact that if φ_k is true under some assignment, then at least one of its three literals is assigned true.

Lemma 2. *Suppose* $\phi = \bigwedge_{k=1}^{m} \varphi_k$ *is a 3-SAT instance over propositional variables set* $\{p_1, p_2, \cdots, p_n\}$. *Let* Γ_ϕ *be the basic RCC-8 network composed with constraints in (17)-(22), involving landmarks* $\{A, B_1, \cdots, B_n, C_1, \cdots, C_m\}$ *and spatial variables* $\{u, v_1, \cdots, v_n, w_1, \cdots, w_n\}$. *Then* ϕ *is satisfiable iff* Γ_ϕ *is satisfiable.*

Proof. Suppose ϕ is satisfiable and $\pi : P \rightarrow \{$true, false$\}$ is a truth value assignment that satisfies ϕ. We construct regions $u, v_1, \cdots, v_n, w_1, \cdots, w_m$ that satisfy all constraints in Γ_ϕ.

Region $\bar{u}$ is composed of n pairwise disjoint triangles in A. The lower vertex of the i-th triangle is Q_i^+ if $\pi(p_i) =$ true, and Q_i^- otherwise. Fig. 4 shows the case that $\pi(p_1) =$ true, $\pi(p_2) =$ false, $\pi(p_n) =$ true.

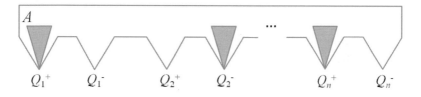

Fig. 4. Construction of variable u

Regions $\bar{v}_i$ and $\bar{w}_i$ are constructed as, respectively, a triangle inside B_i. If $\pi(p_i) =$ true, then Q_i^+ is a vertex of $\bar{v}_i$ and Q_i^- is a vertex of $\bar{w}_i$ (see Fig. 5(a)). Oppositely, if $\pi(p_i) =$ false, then Q_i^- is a vertex of $\bar{v}_i$ and Q_i^+ is a vertex of $\bar{w}_i$ (see Fig. 5(b)). Moreover, $\bar{v}_i$ and $\bar{w}_i$ are properly chosen to make them partially overlap with each C_k.

By the construction, it is easy to see that all constraints in (17)-(22), except $u\mathbf{ECC}_k$, are satisfied. We next show $u\mathbf{ECC}_k$ is also satisfied. That is, $\bar{u}\mathbf{ECC}_k$. Because π satisfies ϕ, it also satisfies φ_k. That is, at least one of the three literals in φ_k, say p_r^*, is true under the assignment π. If $p_r^* = p_r$, then Q_r^+ is at the boundary of C_k by construction. In this case, we have $\pi(p_r) =$ true. By the construction of $\bar{u}$, we know Q_r^+ is also at the boundary of $\bar{u}$. Similarly, if $p_r^* = \neg p_r$, then we can prove Q_r^- is a tangential point of C_k and $\bar{u}$. Therefore, in both cases, the RCC-8 relation between C_k and u is **EC**. This shows that the constructed regions $\bar{u}, \bar{v}_1, \cdots, \bar{v}_n, \bar{w}_1, \cdots, \bar{w}_m$ satisfy all constraints in Γ_ϕ. Hence, Γ_ϕ is satisfiable.

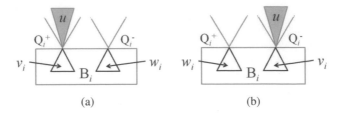

Fig. 5. Construction of variable v_i and w_i. $\pi(p_i) =$ true (a), $\pi(p_i) =$ false (b)

On the other hand, suppose $\{\bar{u}, \bar{v}_1, \cdots, \bar{v}_n, \bar{w}_1, \cdots, \bar{w}_n\}$ is a solution of the network Γ_ϕ. It is straightforward to verify that $\bar{v}_i$ has exactly one tangential point with A, namely either Q_i^- or Q_i^+. We define a truth value assignment $\pi : P \to \{\text{true}, \text{false}\}$ as

$$\pi(p_i) = \begin{cases} \text{true,} & \text{if } \bar{v}_i \cap A = Q_i^+, \\ \text{false,} & \text{otherwise.} \end{cases} \tag{23}$$

We assert that $\pi(\varphi_k) = $ true for each φ_k in ϕ. Otherwise, suppose $\pi(\varphi_k) = $ false for some $\varphi_k = p_r^* \vee p_s^* \vee p_t^*$ in ϕ. This only happens when $\pi(p_i^*) = $ false for $i = r, s, t$. Therefore, for $i = r, s, t$, if p_i^* is positive, then by (23), we know that $\bar{v}_i \cap A = Q_i^-$. Since $\bar{u} \subset A$ and $\bar{v}_i \mathbf{EC} \bar{u}$, we have $Q_i^- \in \bar{u}$, which implies Q_i^+ is not in $\bar{u}$. Similarly if p_i^* is negative, then Q_i^- is not in $\bar{u}$. This is to say, all the three tangential points of A and C_k are not in $\bar{u}$, which contradicts with $\bar{u}\mathbf{EC}C_k$. Therefore, ϕ is satisfiable. $\square$

Corollary 1. *Deciding the consistency of a complete basic RCC-8 network involving landmarks is NP-hard.*

Is this problem still in NP? As long as the landmarks are polygons, the answer is yes! Recall that we write $\mathcal{O}$ for the overlay of all landmarks (cf. Theorem 3). As a subdivision, $\mathcal{O}$ consists of faces, edges and vertices. For RCC-5, only faces in $\mathcal{O}$ (i.e., the blocks) affect the consistency. For RCC-8, the vertices and the edges in $\mathcal{O}$ also need to be considered. We denote $I(l_i)$ ($E(l_i)$, $B(l_i)$ resp.) for the set of faces, edges, and vertices contained in the interior (exterior, boundary resp.) of landmark l_i, and define $I(v_i)$ ($E(v_i)$ resp.) to be the set of faces, edges and vertices that are required to be in the interior (exterior resp.) of variable v_i. Each RCC-8 constraint between a variable v and a landmark l is equivalent to several requirements about $I(v)$, $E(v)$ and the boundary of v, with respect to $I(l)$, $E(l)$ and $B(l)$. For example, $v\mathbf{TPP}l$ is equivalent to (i) $E(v) \supseteq E(l)$, (ii) $I(v) \subset I(l)$, and (iii) the boundary of v has nonempty intersection with some edge or vertex in $B(l)$. The NP-hardness of the hybrid consistency problem of RCC-8 is mainly related to the last kind of requirement which involves the boundary of v, i.e., to decide whether a vertex is on the boundary of variable v. This can be resolved by a non-deterministic algorithm that guesses whether each vertex in $\mathcal{O}$ is on the boundary of v. Once the guessing is made, we can prove that, for example, either (iii) automatically holds, or it is satisfiable iff $I(v) \cup E(v) \nsupseteq B(l)$, moreover, the RCC-8 constraint network can be expressed by a set of necessary conditions about $I(v_i)$ and $E(v_i)$, without involving the boundary of v_i. These conditions are also sufficient and can be checked in polynomial time.

Theorem 4. *Suppose all landmarks in a hybrid basic RCC-8 network are represented by (complex) polygons. Then deciding the consistency of a complete basic RCC-8 network involving at least one landmark is an NP-complete problem.*

5   Conclusion and Further Discussions

In this paper, we introduced a new paradigm of consistency checking problem for qualitative calculi, which supports definitions of constraints between a constant (landmark) and a variable. Constraints like these are very popular in practical applications such as urban planning and schedule planning. Therefore, this hybrid consistency problem is more practical. Our examinations showed that for some well-behaved qualitative calculi such as PA and IA, the new hybrid consistency problem can be solved in the same way; while for some calculi e.g. RCC-5 and RCC-8, the usual composition-based reasoning approach fails to solve the hybrid consistency problem. We provided necessary and sufficient conditions for deciding if a hybrid basic RCC-5 network is consistent. Under the assumption that each landmark is represented as a polygon, these conditions can be checked in polynomial time. As for the RCC-8, we show that it is NP-complete to determine the consistency of a basic network that involves polygonal landmarks.

The hybrid consistency problem is equivalent to determining if a partial solution can be extended to a complete solution. This is usually harder than the pure consistency problem. More close connections between the pure and hybrid consistency problems are still unknown. For example, suppose the consistency problem is in NP (decidable, resp.), is the hybrid consistency problem always in NP (decidable, resp.)?

References

1. Allen, J.F.: Maintaining knowledge about temporal intervals. Commun. ACM 26(11), 832–843 (1983)
2. de Berg, M., Ceong, O., van Kreveld, M., Overmars, M.: Computational Geometry: Algerithms and Applications, 3rd edn. Springer, Heidelberg (2008)
3. Cohn, A.G., Renz, J.: Qualitative spatial reasoning. In: van Harmelen, F., Lifschitz, V., Porter, B. (eds.) Handbook of Knowledge Representation. Elsevier, Amsterdam (2007)
4. Li, S.: On topological consistency and realization. Constraints 11(1), 31–51 (2006)
5. Li, S., Wang, H.: RCC8 binary constraint network can be consistently extended. Artif. Intell. 170(1), 1–18 (2006)
6. Li, S., Ying, M.: Region connection calculus: Its models and composition table. Artif. Intell. 145(1-2), 121–146 (2003)
7. Ligozat, G.: Reasoning about cardinal directions. J. Vis. Lang. Comput. 9(1), 23–44 (1998)
8. Ligozat, G., Renz, J.: What is a qualitative calculus? A general framework. In: Zhang, C., Guesgen, H.W., Yeap, W.K. (eds.) PRICAI, pp. 53–64. Springer, Heidelberg (2004)
9. Nebel, B.: Computational properties of qualitative spatial reasoning: First results. In: Wachsmuth, I., Rollinger, C.R., Brauer, W. (eds.) KI, pp. 233–244. Springer, Heidelberg (1995)
10. Randell, D.A., Cui, Z., Cohn, A.G.: A spatial logic based on regions and connection. In: KR, pp. 165–176 (1992)
11. Renz, J., Nebel, B.: On the complexity of qualitative spatial reasoning: A maximal tractable fragment of the region connection calculus. Artif. Intell. 108(1-2), 69–123 (1999)

Searching for Doubly Self-orthogonal Latin Squares*

Runming Lu[1,2], Sheng Liu[1,2], and Jian Zhang[1]

[1] State Key Laboratory of Computer Science,
Institute of Software, Chinese Academy of Sciences
{lurm,lius,zj}@ios.ac.cn
[2] Graduate University, Chinese Academy of Sciences

Abstract. A Doubly Self Orthogonal Latin Square (DSOLS) is a Latin square which is orthogonal to its transpose to the diagonal and its transpose to the back diagonal. It is challenging to find a non-trivial DSOLS. For the orders $n = 2$ (mod 4), the existence of DSOLS(n) is unknown except for $n = 2, 6$. We propose an efficient approach and data structure based on a set system and exact cover, with which we obtained a new result, i.e., the non-existence of DSOLS(10).

1 Introduction

Latin squares (quasigroups) are very interesting combinatorial objects. Some of them have special properties. It can be quite challenging to know, for which positive integer n, a latin square of size n (with certain properties) exists. Mathematicians have proposed several construction methods to generate bigger Latin squares from smaller ones. For the small Latin squares, some can be found or constructed by hand easily, but the others are very hard to generate. Computer search methods can be helpful here. In fact, many open cases in combinatorics have been solved by various programs [2,8].

In this paper, we study a special kind of Latin square named *doubly self-orthogonal Latin square* (DSOLS) which is related to the so-called perfect Latin squares [4]. In [1], Du and Zhu proved the existence of DSOLS(n) for $n = 0, 1, 3$ (mod 4), except for $n = 3$. For the orders $n = 2$ (mod 4), the existence of DSOLS(n) is unknown except for $n = 2, 6$. So the existence of DSOLS(10) is the smallest open case.

2 Preliminaries and Notations

A Latin square L of order n is an $n \times n$ table where each integer $0, 1, \ldots, n-1$ appears exactly once in each row and each column. We call each of the n^2 positions of the table a cell. For instance, the position at row x column y is called cell (x, y) and the value of cell (x, y) is denoted as $L(x, y)$, where $x, y, L(x, y)$ all take values from $[0, n-1]$. If $\forall i \in [0, n-1], L(i, i) = i$, L is called an idempotent Latin square.

Two Latin squares L_1 and L_2 are orthogonal if each pair of elements from the two squares occurs exactly once, or alternatively,

$$L_1(x_1, y_1) = L_1(x_2, y_2) \wedge L_2(x_1, y_1) = L_2(x_2, y_2) \rightarrow x_1 = x_2 \wedge y_1 = y_2$$

* This work is partially supported by the National Natural Science Foundation of China (NSFC) under grant No. 60673044. Corresponding author: Jian Zhang. We are grateful to the anonymous reviewers for their comments, to Lie Zhu and Feifei Ma for their help in this research.

J. Lee (Ed.): CP 2011, LNCS 6876, pp. 538–545, 2011.

Definition 1. *A DSOLS of order* n, *denoted as DSOLS(n), is a Latin square* A *which is orthogonal to both its transpose to the diagonal* A^T *and its transpose to the back diagonal* A^*.

A DSOLS A of order n can also be characterized using first order logic formulas:

$$A(x, y) = A(x, z) \rightarrow y = z \tag{1}$$

$$A(x, y) = A(z, y) \rightarrow x = z \tag{2}$$

$$A(x_1, y_1) = A(x_2, y_2) \wedge A(y_1, x_1) = A(y_2, x_2) \rightarrow x_1 = x_2 \wedge y_1 = y_2 \tag{3}$$

$$A(x_1, y_1) = A(x_2, y_2) \wedge A(n - 1 - y_1, n - 1 - x_1) = A(n - 1 - y_2, n - 1 - x_2)$$

$$\rightarrow x_1 = x_2 \wedge y_1 = y_2 \tag{4}$$

Table 1 gives an example of DSOLS(4).

Table 1. A DSOLS(4) and Its two Transposes

0	2	3	1		0	3	1	2		3	0	2	1
3	1	0	2		2	1	3	0		1	2	0	3
1	3	2	0		3	0	2	1		0	3	1	2
2	0	1	3		1	2	0	3		2	1	3	0

$$A \qquad\qquad\qquad A^T \qquad\qquad\qquad A^*$$

A closely related concept is *doubly diagonal orthogonal latin squares* (DDOLS) [3], which refers to a pair of orthogonal latin squares with the property that each square has distinct elements on the main diagonal as well as on the back diagonal. A DSOLS can be viewed as a special kind of a DDOLS. The existence problem for DDOLS has been solved completely later on.

3 Finding a DSOLS Using SAT and CSP

3.1 SAT Encoding of the Problem

We first encode the problem of finding DSOLS(n) into a SAT instance. Since each cell of Latin square can take one and only one value from the domain $[0, n-1]$, we introduce one boolean variable for each possible value of each cell. For each row $i \in [0, n - 1]$, each column $j \in [0, n-1]$ and each candidate value $k \in [0, n-1]$, a boolean variable V_{ijk} is introduced. The variables V_{ijk} should satisfy some inherent constraints. For instance, each cell should take a value from $[0, n - 1]$, so we have:

$$\forall i, j \in [0, n - 1], V_{ij0} \vee V_{ij1} \vee \cdots \vee V_{ij(n-1)}$$

But each cell should not take more than one values from $[0, n - 1]$ at the same time, so $\forall i, j \in [0, n - 1]$, we have formulas like the following:

$$\neg V_{ij0} \vee \neg V_{ij1} \qquad \neg V_{ij0} \vee \neg V_{ij2} \qquad \cdots \qquad \neg V_{ij(n-2)} \vee \neg V_{ij(n-1)}$$

Besides these constraints, we also have to encode the problem-specific constraints in formulas 1, 2, 3, 4 into SAT clauses. There can also be other constraints. For instance, we may add unit clauses $V_{iii}(i \in [0, n-1])$ to force the cell (i, i) to take the value i.

Then we send the SAT instance to the state-of-the-art SAT solver MiniSAT. The tool is very efficient. But we still can not solve DSOLS(10) in one week.

3.2   Classical Constraint Satisfaction Problem (CSP)

In [2], Dubois and Dequen employ the CSP model and develop a specific quasigroup generator qgs for QG2, another well known combinatorial problem which is quite difficult. With qgs, they first proved the non-existence of QG2(10) in 140 days of sequential computation. Due to the similarity of QG2 and DSOLS, we tried to use the technique of qgs to find DSOLS(10).

From the CSP's viewpoint, DSOLS can be formulated as a series of overlapping Alldifferent constraints in which no two variables involved are allowed to take the same value. For each cell of DSOLS(n), $\forall i, j \in [0, n-1]$, we associate a variable $A(i, j)$ with a domain $D_n = [0, n-1]$. The constraints of DSOLS can be formulated as follows:

$$\text{Alldifferent}\{A(i, j) | i \in [0, n-1]\}, \forall j \in [0, n-1] \tag{5}$$

$$\text{Alldifferent}\{A(i, j) | j \in [0, n-1]\}, \forall i \in [0, n-1] \tag{6}$$

$$\text{Alldifferent}\{A(j, i) | A(i, j) = v\}, \forall v \in [0, n-1] \tag{7}$$

$$\text{Alldifferent}\{A(n-1-j, n-1-i) | A(i, j) = v\}, \forall v \in [0, n-1] \tag{8}$$

When a variable $A(a, b)$ is assigned a value v_0 in the domain D_n, the constraint propagation procedure would be enabled. For example, in every Alldifferent constraint in which $A(a, b)$ appears, the value v_0 will be deleted from the domains of the other variables of the constraint. Some Alldifferent constraints will be changed dynamically as well based on constraint 7 and 8. For example, the assignment of v_0 to $A(a, b)$ will affect the variables $A(b, a)$ and $A(n-1-b, n-1-a)$ involved in the following constraints

$$\text{Alldifferent}\{A(j, i) | A(i, j) = v_0\}$$

$$\text{Alldifferent}\{A(n-1-j, n-1-i) | A(i, j) = v_0\}$$

Once enabled, the constraint propagation procedure will be carried out recursively until no propagation can be done.

We developed a solver based on the classical CSP model. The basic idea of the solver was similar to the method by Dubois and Dequen [2]. In the implementation, arc-consistency was enforced for the Alldifferent constraints, but the propagation method was light-weight and we did not use any novel techniques for constraint propagation. But for the Alldifferent constraints 7 and 8, since the variables in the constraints dynamically depend on the values of other cells, we designed a specific propagator to maintain the constraints instead of using a general-purpose CSP solver. We also used some simple techniques like fixing all the cells on the diagonal to break symmetry and tried several common heuristics for selecting variables and for assigning values. With the tool, we still failed to solve the DSOLS(10) problem in one week.

4   An Approach Based on Set System and Exact Cover

Combinatorial objects can also be viewed as set systems [6]. A set system is defined as a collection of subsets of a given set X, $S = \{S_1, S_2, ..., S_m\}$ $(S_i \subseteq X)$, which has some additional properties. From the set system's point of view, some combinatorial object searching problems can be formulated as the clique problem [6]. Thus the solution to a set system can be constructed via cliques in certain problem-specific graphs. In the set system representation, lots of inherent symmetries like value symmetry automatically do not exist any more, as compared with other representations. So in some cases, the set system representation may induce surprisingly efficient performance on some combinatorial object searching problem. Based on this observation, Vasquez [7] developed an efficient algorithm for the queen graph coloring problem and obtained some new results. Motivated by this idea, we treat the constraints of DSOLS as a set system.

The set X consists of all cells of the Latin square and $S = \{S_1, S_2, ..., S_{2^{|X|}-1}\}$ is the powerset of X where $S_i \subseteq X (i \in [1, 2^{|X|} - 1])$ (the empty set is not included). For all i, define $S_i^T = \{(y, x)|(x, y) \in S_i\}$ and $S_i^* = \{(n-1-y, n-1-x)|(x, y) \in S_i\}$.

Definition 2 (admissible). S_i is admissible iff S_i satisfies the following constraints:

(1) $|S_i| = n$
(2) $\forall (x_1, y_1), (x_2, y_2) \in S_i$, if $(x_1, y_1) \neq (x_2, y_2)$, then $x_1 \neq x_2$ and $y_1 \neq y_2$
(3) if $(x, y) \in S_i$ and $x \neq y$ then $(y, x) \notin S_i$
(4) if $(x, y) \in S_i$ and $(x, y) \neq (n-1-y, n-1-x)$ then $(n-1-y, n-1-x) \notin S_i$

Definition 3 (compatible). Two elements of S (S_i and S_j, $i \neq j$) are compatible iff

(1) $S_i \cap S_j = \varnothing$
(2) $|S_i \cap S_j^T| = 1$
(3) $|S_i \cap S_j^*| = 1$

Theorem 1. There exists a solution to DSOLS(n) if and only if there is a collection of n admissible subsets of X each pair of which are compatible.

It is easy to prove that the theorem holds. On the one hand, if there exists a DSOLS(n), we can partition the n^2 cells into n sets such that cells are in the same set if and only if they have the same value. According to the definition of DSOLS, it is obvious that these n sets are admissible subsets of X and they are mutually compatible. On the other hand, suppose there are a collection of n admissible subsets of X and they are compatible. The cells in the same set can be assigned with the same value while the cells in different sets can be assigned with different values. The Latin square constructed by these n^2 cells is a DSOLS(n).

A set system of DSOLS(n) can be represented as a graph whose vertices correspond to the admissible sets and edges correspond to the compatible set pairs. Any clique of this graph is also a set system and a clique with n vertices corresponds to a solution of DSOLS(n). If the number of vertices in each maximum clique of the graph is less than n, we can conclude the non-existence of DSOLS(n); otherwise we can conclude the existence of a DSOLS(n).

Algorithm Framework and Data Structure

It is straightforward to use clique algorithms to construct a (partial) solution of a given combinatorial problem which is represented as a set system. If the solution of the combinatorial problem corresponds to the exact cover of the set system, a substantially more efficient algorithm can be utilized because of this property.

Definition 4 (**exact cover**). *Given a set X and a collection S of subsets of X, an exact cover is a subcollection T of S such that each element in X falls into exactly one element of T.*

T is actually a partition of X. If the element $e \in X$ is contained in the set $t \in T$, then the element e is said to be covered by the set t.

Knuth uses an efficient data structure DLX to index the subsets in the exact cover problem, and develops Algorithm X to solve the classical exact cover problem [5]. In DSOLS(n), all elements in X should also be covered because each cell should be assigned a value. However, a set system of DSOLS(n) is not the general exact cover problem since the compatibility of a pair of subsets requires additional constraints like $|S_i \cap S_j^T| = 1$ and $|S_i \cap S_j^*| = 1$ besides $S_i \cap S_j = \varnothing$. So the constraints of the set system of DSOLS(n) are tighter than those of the general exact cover problem.

Our algorithm for DSOLS(n) includes two steps. First, we enumerate all admissible sets of DSOLS(n), then from these admissible sets, we try to find n sets such that each pair of them are compatible. The framework of our algorithm is given below.

```
1:  if all cells have been labeled then
2:      A solution is found;
3:      return ;
4:  end if
5:  Select an unlabeled cell c from the set X and mark c as labeled;
6:  for each subset S_i containing c do
7:      S_* = S;
8:      S_* = S_* - {S_j|S_i ∩ S_j ≠ ∅};
9:      S_* = S_* - {S_j||S_j ∩ S_i^T| ≠ 1 OR |S_j ∩ S_i^*| ≠ 1};
10:     Search(S_*);
11: end for
12: restore c as unlabeled;
13: return ;
```

Algorithm 1. The Algorithm Search(S)

It is an exhaustive search algorithm with a filtering scheme to reduce the search space. When the algorithm chooses a subset S_i to constitute the solution, it applies a propagation procedure which removes the remaining subsets not compatible with S_i.

For computational reason, $\{S_j|S_i \cap S_j \neq \varnothing\}$ is removed first since these subsets can be indexed conveniently while removing $\{S_j||S_j \cap S_i^T| \neq 1 \text{ OR } |S_j \cap S_i^*| \neq 1\}$ needs to scan the whole remaining subsets to select the right ones to be removed. Suppose that a subset S_i is chosen to constitute the solution, m subsets remain and r subsets violate the constraint $S_i \cap S_j = \varnothing$, it takes $r \times n$ operations to remove the r subsets which are not compatible with S_i, $(m - r) \times n$ operations to compute the remaining subsets not compatible with S_i and at most $(m - r) \times n$ operations to remove them.

It seems that the computational complexity is very high since the number of admissible sets is huge. However, after selecting a subset S_i, the number of the remaining subsets which are compatible with S_i decreases dramatically. Table 2 shows the average number of admissible subsets at different levels of the backtracking search tree.

Table 2. Average Number of Admissible Subsets in Different Search Levels

	Level									
n	0	1	2	3	4	5	6	7	8	9
7	208.0	12.0	7.0	7.0	7.0	7.0	7.0	-	-	-
8	2784.0	124.8	11.5	8.4	8.2	8.0	8.0	8.0	-	-
9	20556.0	870.8	52.0	9.8	9.1	9.1	9.0	9.0	9.0	-
10	200960.0	8750.3	423.4	40.0	16.0	0	0	0	0	0

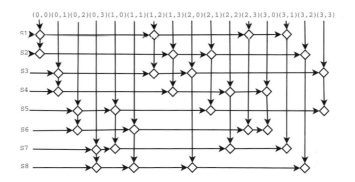

Fig. 1. Data Structure for DSOLS(4)

It does not take much time to enumerate all admissible sets of DSOLS(n) when n is not bigger than 10. Even using a naive method such as enumerating all permutation of n, the computation is only 10!=3628800 steps when $n = 10$. The first column of Table 2 shows the number of admissible sets of DSOLS(n) ($n \leqslant 10$). It is even impossible to store all pairs of these compatible sets in a desktop computer, not to speak of using general clique algorithms including stochastic algorithms to handle such a big graph.

For enumerating all compatible collections of size n in the set system of DSOLS(n), we modify the algorithm for exact cover to take into account the two extra compatibility constraints, $|S_i \cap S_j^T| = 1$ and $|S_i \cap S_j^*| = 1$. A big sparse table is used to index the subsets so that given a cell c it is convenient to access all subsets containing c and given a subset S_i it is convenient to access all cells in S_i. Each cell has a CELL list that contains all subsets covering this cell. Each subset T keeps a list recording the positions of T in the CELL lists besides the cells it covers. For example, DSOLS(4) has 8 admissible subsets $(S_1, S_2, \ldots, S_8)$ which are represented in the way shown in Fig. 1.

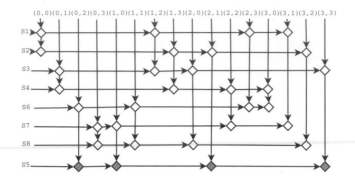

Fig. 2. Data Structure for DSOLS(4) after removing S_5

When removing a subset S_i, S_i in the subsets list and the nodes in the CELL lists representing S_i need to be removed. Instead of deleting these nodes from the lists directly, these nodes are moved to the end of the lists and the length of each list is decreased by 1. For example, after removing S_5 from Figure 1, the updated structure is shown in Figure 2. One benefit of this method is that, when the search needs to restore the subsets during the backtracking, the only operation needed is to recover the length of CELL lists no matter how many subsets had been removed.

5   Experimental Results

Using the algorithm and data structures described in the previous section, we developed a DSOLS generator named DSOLver. To compare the performance of different approaches, we carried out some experiments on a desktop computer (Fedora 10 with 1.5G memory, 2.13GHz CPU, Intel Core2 6400). Table 3 lists the time[1] and branch nodes of MiniSAT, light-weight CSP program (LCSP) and DSOLver on proving the existence of DSOLS(n) where n ranges from 6 to 9. Table 4 lists the time and branch nodes of LCSP and DSOLver on finding all idempotent solutions of DSOLS. Because classical MiniSAT only specializes in finding one solution but not in enumerating all solutions, we do not list its results in Table 4.

These two tables show that DSOLver is better on both CPU time and number of branches. Note that selecting one subset in DSOLver corresponds to assigning n different cells' values in CSP model. So one branch in DSOLver is equivalent to n branches in SAT and CSP. But even if the branch number of DSOLver is multiplied by n, the result is still much smaller than that of SAT and CSP. The reason probably is that each admissible subset has already summed up all the constraints of the n cells involved into one scheme. This kind of scheme can be reused as a package without considering the internal constraint structure again and again as compared with the classical CSP model.

---

[1] With a different SAT encoding, Hantao Zhang implemented a method which found the first solution of DSOLS(9) in 4 seconds (Private communication with Jian Zhang, July 2010).

Table 3. Comparison of MiniSAT, LCSP and DSOLver on finding one solution

DSOLS(n)		MiniSAT		LCSP		DSOLver	
n	exist?	time(second)	#branches	time(second)	#branches	time(second)	#branches
6	no	0.036	119	0.002	104	0	0
7	yes	0.125	47	0.005	1537	0	7
8	yes	0.716	6140	0.003	856	0.008	33
9	yes	48.201	137083	7.123	3140786	0.071	49

Table 4. Comparison of LCSP and DSOLver on finding all solutions of DSOLS

		LCSP		DSOLver	
n	#solutions	time(second)	#branches	time(second)	#branches
7	64	0.025	8966	0	116
8	1152	8.403	3421189	0.109	4710
9	28608	14515.26	1945836918	28.917	570365
10	0	-	-	83733	606458896

6   Conclusion

Finding a DSOLS is a hard combinatorial search problem. It can be a challenging benchmark for constraint solving and constraint programming. In this paper we discuss how to solve the problem using various techniques with different formulations. We propose an efficient exhaustive search algorithm based on the set system representation and exact cover, with which we obtained a new result, i.e., the non-existence of DSOLS(10). There remain some open cases on the existence of DSOLS(n). In the future, we plan to improve the current algorithm and design new data structures to handle even bigger open instances, e.g., DSOLS(14).

References

1. Du, B., Zhu, L.: Existence of doubly self-orthogonal Latin squares. Bulletin of the Institute of Combinatorics and its Applications (Bulletin of the ICA) 20, 13–18 (1997)
2. Dubois, O., Dequen, G.: The non-existence of (3, 1, 2)-conjugate orthogonal idempotent Latin square of order 10. In: Walsh, T. (ed.) CP 2001. LNCS, vol. 2239, pp. 108–120. Springer, Heidelberg (2001)
3. Heinrich, K., Hilton, A.J.W.: Doubly diagonal orthogonal latin squares. Discrete Mathematics 46(2), 173–182 (1983)
4. Kim, K., Prasanna-Kumar, V.K.: Perfect Latin squares and parallel array access. SIGARCH Comput. Archit. News 17(3), 372–379 (1989)
5. Knuth, D.E.: Dancing links. Arxiv preprint cs/0011047 (2000)
6. Östergård, P.R.J.: Constructing combinatorial objects via cliques. In: Webb, B.S. (ed.) Surveys in Combinatorics. London Mathematical Society Lecture Note Series, vol. 327, pp. 57–82. Cambridge University Press, Cambridge (2005)
7. Vasquez, M.: New results on the queens_n^2 graph coloring problem. J. of Heuristics 10(4), 407–413 (2004)
8. Zhang, H.: Combinatorial designs by SAT solvers. In: Biere, A., Heule, M., van Maaren, H., Walsh, T. (eds.) Handbook of Satisfiability, vol. 2. IOS Press, Amsterdam (2009)

QCSP on Partially Reflexive Forests

Barnaby Martin*

School of Engineering and Computing Sciences, Durham University,
Science Labs, South Road, Durham, DH1 3LE, UK
barnabymartin@gmail.com

Abstract. We study the (non-uniform) quantified constraint satisfaction problem QCSP($\mathcal{H}$) as $\mathcal{H}$ ranges over partially reflexive forests. We obtain a complexity-theoretic dichotomy: QCSP($\mathcal{H}$) is either in NL or is NP-hard. The separating condition is related firstly to connectivity, and thereafter to accessibility from all vertices of $\mathcal{H}$ to connected reflexive subgraphs. In the case of partially reflexive paths, we give a refinement of our dichotomy: QCSP($\mathcal{H}$) is either in NL or is Pspace-complete.

1 Introduction

The *quantified constraint satisfaction problem* QCSP($\mathcal{B}$), for a fixed *template* (structure) $\mathcal{B}$, is a popular generalisation of the *constraint satisfaction problem* CSP($\mathcal{B}$). In the latter, one asks if a primitive positive sentence (the existential quantification of a conjunction of atoms) φ is true on $\mathcal{B}$, while in the former this sentence may be positive Horn (where universal quantification is also permitted). Much of the theoretical research into CSPs is in respect of a large complexity classification project – it is conjectured that CSP($\mathcal{B}$) is always either in P or NP-complete [11]. This *dichotomy* conjecture remains unsettled, although dichotomy is now known on substantial classes (e.g. structures of size ≤ 3 [16,6] and smooth digraphs [13,3]). Various methods, combinatorial (graph-theoretic), logical and universal-algebraic have been brought to bear on this classification project, with many remarkable consequences. A conjectured delineation for the dichotomy was given in the algebraic language in [7].

Complexity classifications for QCSPs appear to be harder than for CSPs. Just as CSP($\mathcal{B}$) is always in NP, so QCSP($\mathcal{B}$) is always in Pspace. However, no overarching polychotomy has been conjectured for the complexities of QCSP($\mathcal{B}$), as $\mathcal{B}$ ranges over finite structures, but the only known complexities are P, NP-complete and Pspace-complete (see [4,14] for some trichotomies). It seems plausible that these complexities are the only ones that can be so obtained.

In this paper we study the complexity of QCSP($\mathcal{H}$), where $\mathcal{H}$ is a partially reflexive (undirected) forest, i.e. a forest with potentially some loops. CSP($\mathcal{H}$), in these instances, will either be equivalent to 2-*colourability* and be in L (if $\mathcal{H}$ is irreflexive and contains an edge) or will be trivial (if $\mathcal{H}$ contains no edges or some self-loop). Thus, CSP($\mathcal{H}$) is here always (very) easy. We will discover, however that QCSP($\mathcal{H}$) may be either in NL or be NP-hard (and is often Pspace-complete).

* The author is supported by EPSRC grant EP/G020604/1.

It is well-known that CSP($\mathcal{B}$) is equivalent to the *homomorphism problem* HOM($\mathcal{B}$) – is there a homomorphism from an input structure $\mathcal{A}$ to $\mathcal{B}$? A similar problem, SUR-HOM($\mathcal{B}$), requires that this homomorphism be surjective. On Boolean $\mathcal{B}$, each of CSP($\mathcal{B}$), SUR-HOM($\mathcal{B}$) and QCSP($\mathcal{B}$) display complexity-theoretic dichotomy (the first two between P and NP-complete, the last between P and Pspace-complete). However, the position of the dichotomy is the same for QCSP and SUR-HOM, while it is different for CSP. Indeed, the QCSP and SUR-HOM are cousins: a surjective homomorphism from $\mathcal{A}$ to $\mathcal{B}$ is equivalent to a sentence Θ of the form $\exists v_1, \ldots, v_k \theta(v_1, \ldots, v_k) \wedge \forall y(y = v_1 \vee \ldots \vee y = v_k)$, for θ a conjunction of atoms, being true on $\mathcal{B}$. This sentence is certainly not positive Horn (it involves some disjunction), but some similarity is there. Recently, a complexity classification for SUR-HOM($\mathcal{H}$), where $\mathcal{H}$ is a partially reflexive forest, was given in [12].[1] The separation between those cases that are in P and those cases that are NP-complete is relatively simple, those that are hard are precisely those in which, in some connected component (tree), the loops induce a disconnected subgraph. Their work is our principle motivation, but our dichotomy appears more complicated than theirs. Even in the basic case of partially reflexive paths, we find examples $\mathcal{P}$ whose loops induce a disconnected subgraph and yet QCSP($\mathcal{P}$) is in NL. In the world of QCSP, for templates that are partially reflexive forests $\mathcal{H}$, the condition for tractability may be read as follows. If $\mathcal{H}$ is disconnected (not a tree) then QCSP($\mathcal{H}$) is in NL. Otherwise, let λ_H be the longest distance from a vertex in H to a loop in $\mathcal{H}$. If either 1.) there exists no looped vertex or 2.) there exists a single reflexive connected subgraph $\mathcal{T}_0 \subseteq \mathcal{H}$, such that there is a λ_H-walk from any vertex of H to $\mathcal{T}_0$, then QCSP($\mathcal{H}$) is in NL (we term such an $\mathcal{H}$ *quasi-loop-connected*). In all other cases, QCSP($\mathcal{H}$) is NP-hard. In the case of partially reflexive paths, we may go further and state that all other cases are Pspace-complete.

In the world of partially reflexive trees, we derive our NL membership results through the algebraic device of polymorphisms, together with a logico-combinatorial characterisation of template equivalence given in [9]. In the first instance, we consider trees in which the loops induce a connected subgraph: so-called *loop-connected* trees – including irreflexive trees. Such trees $\mathcal{T}$ are shown to possess certain (surjective) polymorphisms, that are known to collapse the complexity of QCSP($\mathcal{T}$) to a polynomially-sized ensemble of instances of CSP($\mathcal{T}^c$) (the superscript suggesting an expansions by some constants) [8]. Although CSP($\mathcal{T}^c$) may no longer trivial, $\mathcal{T}^c$ still admits a majority polymorphism, so it follows that CSP($\mathcal{T}^c$) is in NL [10].

We prove that every loop-connected tree $\mathcal{T}$ admits a certain *majority* polymorphism, and deduce therefore that QCSP($\mathcal{T}$) is in NL. However, we also prove that loop-connected trees are the only trees that admit majority polymorphisms, and so we can take this method no further. In order to derive the remaining tractability results, we use the characterisation from [9] for equivalent templates – the first time this method has been used in complexity classification. If there

---

[1] Their paper is in fact about partially reflexive trees, but they state in the conclusion how their result extends to partially reflexive forests.

exist natural numbers t and s such that there are surjective homomorphisms from $\mathcal{T}^t$ to $\mathcal{S}$ and from $\mathcal{S}^s$ to $\mathcal{T}$ (the superscript here indicates direct power), then it follows that $\mathrm{QCSP}(\mathcal{T}) = \mathrm{QCSP}(\mathcal{S})$, i.e. $\mathcal{T}$ and $\mathcal{S}$ agree on all positive Horn sentences. Of course it follows immediately that $\mathrm{QCSP}(\mathcal{T})$ and $\mathrm{QCSP}(\mathcal{S})$ are of the same complexity. It turns out that for every quasi-loop-connected tree $\mathcal{T}$, there is a loop-connected tree $\mathcal{S}$ such that $\mathrm{QCSP}(\mathcal{T}) = \mathrm{QCSP}(\mathcal{S})$, and our tractability classification follows (indeed, one may even insist that the loops of $\mathcal{S}$ are always contiguous with some leaves).

For our NP-hardness proofs we use a direct reduction from *not-all-equal* 3-*satisfiability* (NAE3SAT), borrowing heavily from [15]. (In the paper [12] the NP-hardness results follow by reduction from the problem *matching cut*, which is proven NP-complete in [15] by reduction from NAE3SAT.) Our Pspace-hardness proofs, for partially reflexive paths only, use a direct reduction from *quantified not-all-equal 3-satisfiability* (QNAE3SAT). We require several different flavours of the same reduction in order to cover each of the outstanding cases. We conjecture that all NP-hardness cases for partially reflexive trees (forests) are in fact Pspace-complete.

The paper is organised as follows. After the preliminaries and definitions, we give the cases that are in NL in Section 3, and the cases that are NP-hard and Pspace-complete in Section 4. For the cases that are in NL, we first give our result for loop-connected trees. We then expand to the case of quasi-loop-connected paths (for pedagogy and as an important special subclass) before going on to all quasi-loop-connected trees. For the cases that are hard, we begin with the Pspace-completeness results for paths and then give the NP-hardness for the outstanding trees. A full version of this paper is available at `http://arxiv.org/abs/1103.6212`. The author is grateful for assistance with majority operations from Tomás Feder and Andrei Krokhin. We give here our main results.

Theorem 1 (Pspace Dichotomy). *Suppose $\mathcal{P}$ is a partially reflexive path. Then, either $\mathcal{P}$ is quasi-loop-connected, and $\mathrm{QCSP}(\mathcal{P})$ is in NL, or $\mathrm{QCSP}(\mathcal{P})$ is Pspace-complete.*

Proof. This follows immediately from Theorems 3 (tractability) and 4 (Pspace-completeness).

Theorem 2 (NP Dichotomy). *Suppose $\mathcal{H}$ is a partially reflexive forest. Then, either $\mathcal{H}$ is disconnected or quasi-loop-connected, and $\mathrm{QCSP}(\mathcal{H})$ is in NL, or $\mathrm{QCSP}(\mathcal{H})$ is NP-hard.*

Proof. For tractability, if $\mathcal{H}$ is a tree then we appeal to Corollary 1. If $\mathcal{H}$ is a forest that is not a tree, then it follows that $\mathcal{H}$ is disconnected, and that that $\mathrm{QCSP}(\mathcal{H})$ is equivalent to $\mathrm{QCSP}(\mathcal{H})$ with inputs restricted to the conjunction of sentences of the form "$\forall x \exists \overline{y} \varphi(x, \overline{y})$", where φ is a conjunction of positive atoms (see [14]). The evaluation of such sentences on any partially reflexive forest is readily seen to be in NL.

For NP-hardness, we appeal to Theorem 5.

2   Preliminaries and Definitions

Let $[n] := \{1, \ldots, n\}$. A graph $\mathcal{G}$ has vertex set G, of cardinality $|G|$, and edge set $E(\mathcal{G})$. Henceforth we consider partially reflexive trees, i.e. trees potentially with some loops (we will now drop the preface partially reflexive). For a sequence $\alpha \in \{0,1\}^*$, of length $|\alpha|$, let $\mathcal{P}_\alpha$ be the undirected path on $|\alpha|$ vertices such that the ith vertex has a loop iff the ith entry of α is 1 (we may say that the path $\mathcal{P}$ is *of the form* α). We will usually envisage the domain of a path with n vertices to be $[n]$, where the vertices appear in the natural order. The *centre* of a path is either the middle vertex, if there is an odd number of vertices, or between the two middle vertices, otherwise. Therefore the position of the centre of a path on m vertices is at $\frac{m+1}{2}$. In a path on an even number of vertices, we may refer to the pair of vertices in the middle as *centre vertices*. Call a path $\mathcal{P}$ *loop-connected* if the loops induce a connected subgraph of $\mathcal{P}$. Call a path *0-eccentric* if it is of the form $\alpha 1^b 0^a$ for $b \geq 0$ and $|\alpha| \leq a$. Call a path *weakly balanced* if, proceeding from the centre to each end, one encounters at some point a non-loop followed by a loop (if the centre is loopless then this may count as a non-loop for both directions). Call a weakly-balanced path $\mathcal{P}$ *0-centred* if the centre vertex is a non-loop (and $|P|$ is odd) or one of the centre vertices is a non-loop (and $|P|$ is even). Otherwise, a weakly-balanced path $\mathcal{P}$ is *1-centred*.

In a rooted tree, the *height* of the tree is the maximal distance from any vertex to the root. For a tree $\mathcal{T}$ and vertex $v \in T$, let $\lambda_T(v)$ be the shortest distance in $\mathcal{T}$ from v to a looped vertex (if $\mathcal{T}$ is irreflexive, then $\lambda_T(v)$ is infinite). Let λ_T be the maximum of $\{\lambda_T(v) : v \in T\}$. A tree is *loop-connected* if the self-loops induce a connected subtree. A tree $\mathcal{T}$ is *quasi-loop-connected* if either 1.) it is irreflexive, or 2.) there exists a connected reflexive subtree $\mathcal{T}_0$ (chosen to be **maximal** under inclusion) such that there is a walk of length λ_T from every vertex of $\mathcal{T}$ to $\mathcal{T}_0$. The quasi-loop-connected paths are precisely those that are 0-eccentric.

The problems $\mathrm{CSP}(\mathcal{T})$ and $\mathrm{QCSP}(\mathcal{T})$ each take as input a sentence ψ, and ask whether this sentence is true on $\mathcal{T}$. For the former, the sentence involves the existential quantification of a conjunction of atoms – *primitive positive* logic. For the latter, the sentence involves the arbitrary quantification of a conjunction of atoms – *positive Horn* logic.

The *direct product* $\mathcal{G} \times \mathcal{H}$ of two graphs $\mathcal{G}$ and $\mathcal{H}$ has vertex set $\{(x,y) : x \in G, y \in H\}$ and edge set $\{((x,u),(y,v)) : x,y \in G, u,v \in H, (x,y) \in E(\mathcal{G}), (u,v) \in E(\mathcal{H})\}$. Direct products are (up to isomorphism) associative and commutative. The kth power $\mathcal{G}^k$ of a graph $\mathcal{G}$ is $\mathcal{G} \times \ldots \times \mathcal{G}$ (k times). A homomorphism from a graph $\mathcal{G}$ to a graph $\mathcal{H}$ is a function $h : G \to H$ such that, if $(x,y) \in E(\mathcal{G})$, then $(h(x),h(y)) \in E(\mathcal{G})$ (we sometimes use $\longrightarrow$ to indicate existence of surjective homomorphism). A k-ary polymorphism of a graph is a homomorphism from $\mathcal{G}^k$ to $\mathcal{G}$. A ternary function $f : G^3 \to G$ is designated a *majority* operation if $f(x,x,y) = f(x,y,x) = f(y,x,x) = x$, for all $x, y \in G$.

In a matrix, we refer to the *leading* diagonal, running from the top left to bottom right corner, and the *rising* diagonal running from the bottom left to top right corner.

The computational reductions we use will always be comprised by local substitutions that can easily be seen to be possible in logspace – we will not mention this again. Likewise, we recall that QCSP($\mathcal{T}$) is always in Pspace, thus Pspace-completeness proofs will only deal with Pspace-hardness.

3   Tractable Trees

We now explore the tree templates $\mathcal{T}$ such that QCSP($\mathcal{T}$) is in NL. We derive our tractability results through majority polymorphisms and equivalence of template.

3.1   Loop-Connected Trees and Majority Polymorphisms

Majority operations on (irreflexive) trees It is known that all (irreflexive) trees admit a majority polymorphism [1]; however, not just any operation will suffice for our purposes, therefore we define a majority polymorphism of a certain kind on a rooted tree $\mathcal{T}$ **whose root could also be a leaf** (i.e. is of degree one). In a rooted tree let the root be labelled 0 and let the numbering propagate upwards from the root along the branches (probably non-uniquely). For $x, y \in T$ define the meet(x, y) to be the highest (first) point at which the paths from the root to x and the root to y meet. If x and y are on the same branch, and the closer to the root is x, then meet(x, y) is x. In the following definition, we sometimes write, e.g., $d\ [-1]$, to indicate that the function takes either value d or $d-1$: this is dependent on the dominant parity of the arguments which should be matched by the function. Define the following ternary function f on T.

$$f_0(x, y, z) := \begin{cases} d\ [-1] & x, y, z \text{ all the same parity; } d \text{ is highest of} \\ & \text{meet}(x, y), \text{meet}(y, z) \text{ and meet}(x, z) \qquad A \\ \text{meet}(u, v)\ [-1] & \text{two of } x, y, z \ (u \text{ and } v) \text{ same parity;} \\ & \text{other different} \qquad\qquad\qquad\qquad\qquad B \end{cases}$$

Lemma 1. *Let $\mathcal{T}$ be a rooted (irreflexive) tree whose root has degree one. Then f_0 is a majority polymorphism of $\mathcal{T}$.*

Majority operations on reflexive trees. It is known that reflexive trees admit a majority polymorphism [2], but it will be a simple matter for us to provide our own. If x, y, z are vertices of a (not necessarily reflexive) tree $\mathcal{T}$ then we define their *median* to be the unique point where the paths from x to y, y to z and x to z meet. It follows that median is a majority operation. If x, y and z are all on a single branch (path), then we have given the standard definition of median. On a tree, the median function need not be conservative (i.e. we do not in general have median$(x, y, z) \in \{x, y, z\}$). The following is easy to verify.

Lemma 2. *Let $\mathcal{T}$ be a reflexive tree. Then the median function is a majority polymorphism of $\mathcal{T}$.*

Amalgamating these operations. Let T be constructed by attaching rooted (irreflexive) trees – called *tree-components* – whose roots have degree one, to the branches of some reflexive tree – the *centre* – such that the resulting object is a partially reflexive tree (loop-connected, of course). The roots maintain their labels 0 despite now having a loop there. These special looped vertices are considered both part of their tree-component(s) and part of the centre. For the sake of well-definition, we preferentially see a vertex 0 as being in some tree-component. Thus a looped vertex 0 and the vertex 1 above it, in its tree-component, constitute two vertices in the same tree-component. It is possible that a looped vertex 0 is simultaneously the 0 in multiple tree-components. This will mean we have to verify well-definition. Define the following ternary operation on T.

$$
f_1(x,y,z) := \begin{cases}
f_0(x,y,z) & x,y,z \text{ in same tree-component} & A \\
\text{meet}(u,v) \ [-1] & \text{two of } x,y,z \ (u \text{ and } v) \text{ in the same} \\
& \text{tree-component; other elsewhere;} \\
& \text{and } u,v \text{ same parity} & B \\
0 \text{ from } \{u,v\}\text{'s comp.} & \text{two of } x,y,z \ (u \text{ and } v) \text{ in the same} \\
& \text{tree-component; other elsewhere;} \\
& \text{and } u,v \text{ different parity} & C \\
\text{median}(x,y,z) & \text{otherwise} & D
\end{cases}
$$

Lemma 3. *Let T be a loop-connected tree. Then f_1 is well-defined and a majority polymorphism of T.*

Proposition 1. *If T is a loop-connected tree, then $QCSP(T)$ is in NL.*

Proof. Since T admits a majority polymorphism, from Lemma 3, it follows from [8] that $QCSP(T)$ reduces to the verification of a polynomial number of instances of $CSP(T^c)$, each of which is in NL by [10]. The result follows.

In fact, for our later results, we only require the majority polymorphism on trees all of whose loops are in a connected component involving leaves. However, we give the fuller result because it is not much more difficult and because we can show these are the only trees admitting a majority polymorphism.

Proposition 2. *Let T be a tree that is not loop-connected, then T does not admit a majority polymorphism.*

3.2   Paths of the Form $\alpha 0^a$ Where $|\alpha| \leq a + 1$

We will now explore the tractability of paths of the form $\alpha 0^a$, where $|\alpha| \leq a+1$. In the proof of the following lemma we deviate from the normalised domain of $[n]$ for a path on n vertices, for pedagogical reasons that will become clear.

Lemma 4. *There is a surjective homomorphism from $\mathcal{P}_{10^m}{}^2$ to $\mathcal{P}_{0^m 10^m}$.*

Proof. Let $[a, b] := \{a, \dots, b\}$. Let $E(\mathcal{P}_{10^m}) := \{(i, j) : i, j \in [0, m], j = i + 1\} \cup \{(0, 0)\}$. Let $\mathcal{P}_{0^m 10^m}$ be the undirected $2m$-path (on $2m + 1$ vertices) such that the middle vertex has a self-loop but none of the others do. Formally, $E(\mathcal{P}_{0^m 10^m}) = \{(i, j) : i, j \in [-m, m], j = i + 1\} \cup \{(0, 0)\}$. The numbering of the vertices is important in the following proof. We will envisage $\mathcal{P}_{10^m}{}^2$ as a square $(m + 1) \times (m + 1)$ matrix whose top left corner is the vertex $(0, 0)$ which has the self-loop. The entry in the matrix tells one where in $\mathcal{P}_{0^m 10^m}$ the corresponding vertex of $\mathcal{P}_{10^m}{}^2$ is to map. It will then be a straightforward matter to verify that this is a surjective homomorphism. By way of example, we give the matrix for $m + 1 := 7$ in Figure 2 (for all smaller m one may simply restrict this matrix by removing rows and columns from the bottom right). 0 is sometimes written as -0 for (obvious) aesthetic reasons – we will later refer to the two parts *plus* and *minus* of the matrix.

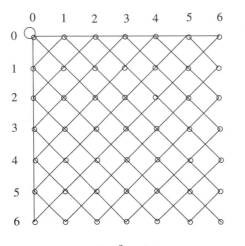

$$
\begin{array}{ccccccc}
-0 & 0 & -0 & 0 & -0 & 0 & -0 \\
1 & -1 & 1 & -1 & 1 & -1 & 1 \\
-0 & 2 & -2 & 2 & -2 & 2 & -2 \\
1 & -1 & 3 & -3 & 3 & -3 & 3 \\
-0 & 2 & -2 & 4 & -4 & 4 & -4 \\
1 & -1 & 3 & -3 & 5 & -5 & 5 \\
-0 & 2 & -2 & 4 & -4 & 6 & -6 \\
\end{array}
$$

Fig. 1. $\mathcal{P}_{10^6}{}^2$ and its ...   **Fig. 2.** ... homomorphism to $\mathcal{P}_{0^6 10^6}$

We refer to the far left-hand column as 0. Note that the leading diagonal enumerates $-0, \dots, -m$. Beneath the leading diagonal, the matrix is periodic in each column (with period two). In general, the jth column of this matrix will read, from top to bottom:

$$(-1)^{j-1}.0, \ (-1)^j.1, \ (-1)^{j+1}.2, \ \dots, \ (-1)^{j+j-2}.(j-1), \ -j, \ j+1, \ -j, \ j+1, \text{ etc.}$$

Further verification that this is a surjective homomorphism appears in the full version of this paper.

Proposition 3. *If $\mathcal{P}$ is of the form $\alpha 0^a$ where $|\alpha| \leq a+1$, then $QCSP(\mathcal{P})$ is in NL.*

Proof. Let $\mathcal{P}$ be of the form $\alpha 0^a$ where $|\alpha| \leq a + 1$. If $\mathcal{P}$ is irreflexive then the result follows from [14]. Otherwise, $\mathcal{P}$ contains a loop, the right-most of which is m vertices in from the right-hand end (on or left of centre). We claim that $\mathcal{P} \longrightarrow \mathcal{P}_{10^m}$ and $\mathcal{P}_{10^m}{}^2 \longrightarrow \mathcal{P}$. It then follows from [9] that $QCSP(\mathcal{P}) = QCSP(\mathcal{P}_{10^m})$, whereupon membership in NL follows from Proposition 1.

The surjective homomorphism from $\mathcal{P}$ to $\mathcal{P}_{10^m}$ is trivial: map all vertices to the left of the right-most loop of $\mathcal{P}$ to the loop of $\mathcal{P}_{10^m}$, and let the remainder of the map follows the natural isomorphism. The surjective homomorphism from $\mathcal{P}_{10^m}{}^2 \longrightarrow \mathcal{P}$ follows from the obvious surjective homomorphism from $\mathcal{P}_{0^m10^m}$ to $\mathcal{P}$, via Lemma 4.

3.3   Paths of the Form $\alpha 1^b 0^a$ Where $b \geq 1$ and $|\alpha| = a$

Proof of the following proceeds similarly to that of Lemma 4.

Lemma 5. *For $b \geq 1$, there is a surjective homomorphism from $\mathcal{P}_{1^a1^b0^a}{}^2$ to $\mathcal{P}_{0^a1^b0^a}$.*

Proposition 4. *If $\mathcal{P}$ is of the form $\alpha 1^b 0^a$ for $b \geq 1$ and $|\alpha| = a$, then $QCSP(\mathcal{P})$ is in NL.*

Proof. Let $\mathcal{P}$ be of the form $\alpha 1^b 0^a$ where $|\alpha| = a$ and $b \geq 1$. We claim that $\mathcal{P} \longrightarrow \mathcal{P}_{1^a1^b0^a}$ and $\mathcal{P}_{1^a1^b0^a}{}^2 \rightarrowtail \mathcal{P}$. It then follows from [9] that $QCSP(\mathcal{P}) = QCSP(\mathcal{P}_{1^a1^b0^a})$, whereupon membership in NL follows from Proposition 1.

The surjective homomorphism from $\mathcal{P}$ to $\mathcal{P}_{1^a1^b0^a}$ is the identity. The surjective homomorphism from $\mathcal{P}_{1^a1^b0^a}{}^2$ to $\mathcal{P}$ follows from the surjective homomorphism from $\mathcal{P}_{0^a1^b0^a}$ to $\mathcal{P}$ (the identity), via Lemma 5.

Theorem 3. *If $\mathcal{P}$ is quasi-loop-connected (0-eccentric), then $QCSP(\mathcal{P})$ is in NL.*

Proof. If $\mathcal{P}$ is quasi-loop-connected (0-eccentric), then either $\mathcal{P}$ is of the form $\alpha 0^a$, for $|\alpha| \leq a+1$, or $\alpha 1^b 0^a$, for $|\alpha| = a$ and $b \geq 1$ (or both!). The result follows from Propositions 3 and 4.

3.4   The Quasi-Loop-Connected Case

Suppose that $\mathcal{T}$ is a quasi-loop-connected tree, that is neither reflexive nor irreflexive, with associated $\mathcal{T}_0$ and λ_T, as defined in the preliminaries. Let $v_\lambda \in \mathcal{T}$ be such that there is no $(\lambda_T - 1)$-walk to a looped vertex but there is a λ_T-walk to the looped vertex l of the maximal (under inclusion) connected reflexive subtree $\mathcal{T}_0$ (such a v_λ exists). Let $\mathcal{T}_1$ be the maximal subtree of $\mathcal{T}$ rooted at l that contains v_λ.

Lemma 6. *If $\mathcal{T}$ and v_λ are as in the previous paragraph, then v_λ is a leaf.*

Proof. If not, then v_λ has a neighbour w on the path in the direction from l towards and beyond v. But the distance from this vertex to the connected component $\mathcal{T}_0$ containing l is $\lambda_T + 1$, which contradicts maximality of λ_T.

Note that if $\mathcal{T}$ were an arbitrary tree, i.e. not quasi-loop-connected, then there is no need for v_λ, at maximal distance from a loop, to be a leaf. E.g., let $\mathcal{P}_{101}$ be the path on three vertices, the two ends of which are looped. $\lambda_{\mathcal{P}_{101}} = 1$ and v_λ would be the centre vertex.

So, as before, let $\mathcal{T}$ be a quasi-loop-connected tree that is neither reflexive nor irreflexive, and let some $v_\lambda \in \mathcal{T}$ be given (v_λ, of course, need not be unique). There is an irreflexive path $\mathcal{P} \subseteq \mathcal{T}_1$ of length λ_T from the leaf v_λ to $l \in \mathcal{T}_0$. There may be other paths joining this path, of course. Let $\mathcal{T}'$ be $\mathcal{T}$ with these other paths pruned off (see Figure 3). We need to take a short diversion in which we consider graphs with a similar structure to $\mathcal{T}'$. Proof of the following is again similar to that of Lemma 4.

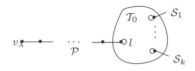

Fig. 3. Anatomy of $\mathcal{T}'$

Lemma 7. *Suppose $\mathcal{H}$ consists of a graph $\mathcal{G}$, with a looped vertex l, onto which an irreflexive path $\mathcal{P}$ of length λ is attached. Let $\mathcal{H}'$ be constructed as $\mathcal{H}$ but with the addition of two (disjoint) paths $\mathcal{P}$ onto the looped vertex l. Then there is a surjective homomorphism from $\mathcal{H}^2$ to $\mathcal{H}'$.*

Lemma 8. *There is a surjective homomorphism from $\mathcal{T}$ to $\mathcal{T}'$. There exists $p \in \mathbb{N}$ such that there is a surjective homomorphism from $(\mathcal{T}')^p$ to $\mathcal{T}$.*

Proof. The surjective homomorphism from $\mathcal{T}$ to $\mathcal{T}'$ takes the paths constituted by $\mathcal{T}_1 \setminus \mathcal{P}$ and folds them back towards l. These paths may have loops on them, but never at distance $< \lambda_T$ from v_λ, which explains why this will be a homomorphism.

The surjective homomorphism from $(\mathcal{T}')^p$ to $\mathcal{T}$ comes from the multiplication of the paths $\mathcal{P}$ – by iteration of Lemma 7 – in powers of $\mathcal{T}'$ (note that nothing may be further than λ_T from l in $\mathcal{T}_1$, without violating maximality of λ_T or uniqueness of $\mathcal{T}_0$). To cover $\mathcal{T}_1$ in $\mathcal{T}$ we require no more than $|\mathcal{T}_1|$ copies of the path $\mathcal{P}$. According to the previous lemma, we may take $p := |\mathcal{T}_1| - 1$ (in fact it is easy to see that $\lceil \log |\mathcal{T}_1| \rceil$ suffices).

Now, it may be possible that in $\mathcal{T}'$ there are subtrees $\mathcal{S}_1, \ldots, \mathcal{S}_k$ rooted in $\mathcal{T}_0$ whose first vertex, other than their root, is a non-loop (because we chose $\mathcal{T}_0$ to be maximal under inclusion). The height of these trees is $\leq \lambda_T$. Let $\mathcal{T}''$ be $\mathcal{T}'$ with these subtrees $\mathcal{S}_1, \ldots, \mathcal{S}_k$ being reflexively closed.

Lemma 9. *There is a surjective homomorphism from $\mathcal{T}'$ to $\mathcal{T}''$. There is a p such that there is a surjective homomorphism from $(\mathcal{T}'')^p$ to $\mathcal{T}'$.*

Corollary 1. *Let T be quasi-loop-connected, then $QCSP(T)$ is in NL.*

Proof. If T is actually loop-connected, then the result is Proposition 1. Otherwise, $QCSP(T) = QCSP(T') = QCSP(T'')$, and tractability of the last follows from Proposition 1.

4   Hard Cases

4.1   Pspace-Completeness Results for Paths That Are Not 0-Eccentric

$\mathcal{P}_{101}$ and weakly balanced 0-centred paths. In the following proof we introduce the notions of *pattern* and $\forall$-*selector* that will recur in future proofs.

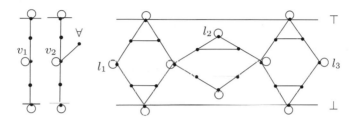

Fig. 4. Variable and clause gadgets in reduction to $QCSP(\mathcal{P}_{101})$

Proposition 5. *$QCSP(\mathcal{P}_{101})$ is Pspace-complete.*

Proof. For hardness, we reduce from QNAE3SAT, where we will ask for the extra condition that no clause has three universal variables (of course, any such instance would be trivially false). From an instance Φ of QNAE3SAT we will build an instance Ψ of $QCSP(\mathcal{P}_{101})$ such that Φ is in QNAE3SAT iff Ψ in $QCSP(\mathcal{P}_{101})$. We will consider the quantifier-free part of Ψ, itself a conjunction of atoms, as a graph, and use the language of homomorphisms. The constraint satisfaction problem, $CSP(\mathcal{P}_{101})$, seen in this guise, is nothing other than the question of homomorphism of this graph to $\mathcal{P}_{101}$. The idea of considering $QCSP(\mathcal{P}_{101})$ as a special type of homomorphism problem is used implicitly in [5][2] and explicitly in [14].

    We begin by describing a graph $\mathcal{G}_\Phi$, whose vertices will give rise to the variables of Ψ, and whose edges will give rise to the facts listed in the quantifier-free part of Ψ. Most of these variables will be existentially quantified, but a small handful will be universally quantified. $\mathcal{G}_\Phi$ consists of two reflexive paths, labelled $\top$ and $\bot$ which contain inbetween them gadgets for the clauses and variables of Φ. We begin by assuming that the paths $\top$ and $\bot$ are evaluated, under any

---

[2] The journal version of this paper was published much later as [4].

homomorphism we care to consider, to vertices 1 and 3 in P_{101}, respectively (the two ends of P_{101}); later on we will show how we can effectively enforce this. Of course, once one vertex of one of the paths is evaluated to, say, 1, then that whole path must also be so evaluated – as the only looped neighbour of 1 in $\mathcal{P}_{101}$ is 1. The gadgets are drawn in Figure 4. The pattern is the path $\mathcal{P}_{101}$, that forms the edges of the diamonds in the clause gadgets as well as the tops and bottoms of the variable gadgets. The diamonds are *braced* by two horizontal edges, one joining the centres of the top patterns and the other joining the centres of the bottom patterns. The ∀-selector is the path $\mathcal{P}_{10}$, which travels between the universal variable node v_2 and the labelled vertex ∀.

For each existential variable v_1 in Φ we add the gadget on the far left, and for each universal variable v_2 we add the gadget immediately to its right. There is a single vertex in that gadget that will eventually give rise to a variable in Ψ that is universally quantified, and it is labelled ∀. For each clause of Φ we introduce a copy of the clause gadget drawn on the right. We then introduce an edge between a variable v and literal l_i ($i \in \{1,2,3\}$) if $v = l_i$ (note that all literals in QNAE3SAT are positive). We reorder the literals in each clause, if necessary, to ensure that literal l_2 of any clause is never a variable in Φ that is universally quantified. It is not hard to verify that homomorphisms from $\mathcal{G}_\Phi$ to $\mathcal{P}_{101}$ (such that the paths ⊤ and ⊥ are evaluated to 1 and 3, respectively) correspond exactly to satisfying not-all-equal assignments of Φ. The looped vertices must map to either 1 or 3 – ⊤ or ⊥ – and the clause gadgets forbid exactly the all-equal assignments. Now we will consider the graph $\mathcal{G}_\Phi$ realised as a formula Ψ'', in which we will existentially quantify all of the variables of Ψ'' except: one variable each, $v_\top$ and $v_\bot$, corresponding respectively to some vertex from the paths ⊤ and ⊥; all variables corresponding to the centre vertex of an existential variable gadget; all variables corresponding to the centre vertex of a universal variable gadget, and all variables corresponding to the extra vertex labelled ∀ of a universal variable gadget. We now build Ψ' by quantifying, adding outermost and in the order of the quantifiers of Φ:

- existentially, the variable corresponding to the centre vertex of an existential variable gadget,
- universally, the variable corresponding to the extra vertex labelled ∀ of a universal variable gadget, and then existentially, the variable corresponding to the centre vertex of a universal variable gadget.

The reason we do not directly universally quantify the vertex associated with a universal variable is because we want it to be forced to range over only the looped vertices 1 and 3 (which it does as its unlooped neighbour ∀ is forced to range over all $\{1,2,3\}$). $\Psi'(v_\top, v_\bot)$ is therefore a positive Horn formula with two free variables, $v_\top$ and $v_\bot$, such that, Φ is QNAE3SAT iff $\mathcal{P}_{101} \models \Psi'(1,3)$. Finally, we construct Ψ from Ψ' with the help of two ∀-selectors, adding new variables $v'_\top$ and $v'_\bot$, and setting

$$\Psi := \forall v'_\top, v'_\bot \exists v_\top, v_\bot \; E(v'_\top, v_\top) \wedge E(v_\top, v'_\top) \wedge E(v'_\bot, v_\bot) \wedge E(v_\bot, v'_\bot) \wedge \Psi'(v_\top, v_\bot).$$

The purpose of universally quantifying the new variables $v'_\top$ and $v'_\bot$, instead of directly quantifying $v_\top$ and $v_\bot$, is to force $v'_\top$ and $v'_\bot$ to range over $\{1,3\}$ (recall that $E(v_\top, v_\top)$ and $E(v_\bot, v_\bot)$ are both atoms of Ψ). This is the same reason we add the vertex $\forall$ to the universal variable gadget.

We claim that $\mathcal{P}_{101} \models \Psi'(1,3)$ iff $\mathcal{P}_{101} \models \Psi$. It suffices to prove that $\mathcal{P}_{101} \models \Psi'(1,3)$ implies $\mathcal{P}_{101} \models \Psi'(3,1), \Psi'(1,1), \Psi'(3,3)$. The first of these follows by symmetry. The second two are easy to verify, and follow because the second literal in any clause is forbidden to be universally quantified in Φ. If both paths $\top$ and $\bot$ are w.l.o.g. evaluated to 1, then, even if some l_1- or l_3-literals are forced to evaluate to 3, we can still extend this to a homomorphism from $\mathcal{G}_\Phi$ to $\mathcal{P}_{101}$.

Proposition 6. *Let $\mathcal{P}_{0^a 10^b 10^c}$ be such that its centre is between its loops ($a + b \geq c$ and $b + c \geq a$). Then $QCSP(0^a 10^b 10^c)$ is Pspace-complete.*

Proposition 7. *Let $\mathcal{P}$ be a weakly balanced 0-centred path, then $QCSP(\mathcal{P})$ is Pspace-complete.*

$\mathcal{P}_{10101}$ and weakly balanced 1-centred paths. We begin with the simplest weakly balanced 1-centred path, $\mathcal{P}_{10101}$, which in some sense is also the trickiest.

Proposition 8. *$QCSP(\mathcal{P}_{10101})$ is Pspace-complete.*

Proof. We work as in Proposition 5, but with pattern $\mathcal{P}_{10101}$ and $\forall$-selector $\mathcal{P}_{10}$. We will need more sophisticated variable gadgets, along with some vertical bracing in the diamonds. The requisite gadgets are depicted in Figures 5 and 6. Finally,

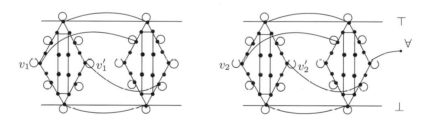

Fig. 5. Variable gadgets in reduction to $QCSP(\mathcal{P}_{10101})$

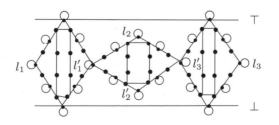

Fig. 6. Clause gadget in reduction to $QCSP(\mathcal{P}_{10101})$

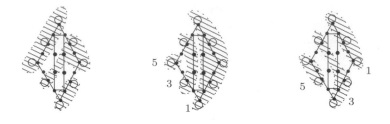

Fig. 7. Degenerate mappings in QCSP($\mathcal{P}_{10101}$)

not only is v_1 (likewise, v_2) connected by an edge to a literal l_i (if $v_1 = l_i$), but on the other side v_1' is also connected by an edge to l_i'. We assume for now that the paths $\top$ and $\bot$ are evaluated to 1 and 5. We need the extra edge from l_i' to v_1' as an evaluation of l_1 on a clause diamond to, e.g., 1, no longer, in itself, enforces that l_i' be evaluated to 5. In the existential variable gadgets, v_1 must be evaluated to either 1 or 5, and v_1' must be evaluated to the other. In a universal gadget, the loop adjacent to the vertex $\forall$ will be evaluated to any of 1, 3 or 5 – but v_2 and v_2' must still be evaluated to opposites in 1 and 5. We depict an example of the situation where the loop adjacent to $\forall$ is evaluated to 3, but the other vertices are mapped so as to set v_2 to 1 and v_2' to 5 (this is the left-hand diamond of Figure 7).

Finally, we must explain what happens in the degenerate cases in which $v_\top$ and $v_\bot$ are not evaluated to 1 and 5, respectively (or vice-versa). It is not hard to see that this is no problem, even when universal variables are evaluated anywhere. Two examples of these degenerate cases, when $v_\top$ and $v_\bot$ are evaluated firstly to 1 and 1, and, secondly, to 1 and 3 are drawn in the centre and right of Figure 7. In both cases, we consider what happens when the evaluation of a universal variable forces the left-hand node of the gadget to be evaluated to 5.

It may be asked why we did not consider using a pattern of $\mathcal{P}_{101}$ and $\forall$-selector $\mathcal{P}_{10}$ in the previous proof, while, instead of beginning with $\forall v_\top', v_\bot'$, using $\exists v_\top' \forall v_\bot'$. This would then select the centre loop for $v_\top$ along with at least once an outer loop for $v_\bot$. This proof would work for a simulation of the NP-hard NAE3SAT, but breaks down for the quantified variables of QNAE3SAT.

Proposition 9. *For all d, QCSP($\mathcal{P}_{101^d01}$) is Pspace-complete.*

Proposition 10. *If $\mathcal{P}$ is a weakly balanced 1-centred path, then QCSP($\mathcal{P}$) is Pspace-complete.*

Remaining path cases. We are close to having exhausted the possible forms that a partially reflexive path may take.

Proposition 11. *Let $\mathcal{P}$ be of the form $\alpha 1^b 0^a$ such that $\mathcal{P}$ is not 0-eccentric and $|\alpha| + 1 \leq \frac{|\alpha| + b + a + 1}{2} \leq |\alpha| + b$ (the centre is in the 1^b segment), then QCSP($\mathcal{P}$) is Pspace-complete.*

Theorem 4. *If $\mathcal{P}$ is not a 0-eccentric path, then $QCSP(\mathcal{P})$ is Pspace-complete.*

Proof. Suppose $\mathcal{P}$ is not a 0-eccentric path. Then, if $\mathcal{P}$ is weakly balanced, the result follows from Propositions 7 and 10. Otherwise, $\mathcal{P}$ is of the form of Proposition 11, and the result follows from that proposition.

4.2 NP-hardness for Remaining Trees

Theorem 5. *Let $\mathcal{T}$ be a tree that is not quasi-loop-connected. Then $QCSP(\mathcal{T})$ is NP-hard.*

Proof. Let $\mathcal{T}$ and its associated $\lambda := \lambda_T$ be given. Define $\mu(x, y)$ to be the minimum distance between some reflexive subtree $\mathcal{T}_x$ (at distance λ from x) and some reflexive subtree $\mathcal{T}_y$ (at distance λ from y). Note that we are considering all possible reflexive subtrees $\mathcal{T}_x$ and $\mathcal{T}_y$. In particular, since $\mu(x, y)$ is a minimum, it is sufficient to consider only such reflexive subtrees that are maximal under inclusion. Let $\mu := \max\{\mu(x, y) : x, y \in T\}$. Since $\mathcal{T}$ is not quasi-loop connected, $\mu > 1$. A subpath $\mathcal{P} \subseteq \mathcal{T}$ is said to have the *μ-property* if it connects two (maximal under inclusion) reflexive subtrees $\mathcal{T}_x$ and $\mathcal{T}_y$ that witness the maximality of μ, as just defined. Let ν be the size of the largest induced reflexive subtree of $\mathcal{T}$.

Let $\mathbb{P}$ be the set of induced subpaths $\mathcal{P}$ of $\mathcal{T}$ that have the μ-property, re-labelled with vertices $\{1, \ldots, n := |P|\}$ in the direction from $\mathcal{T}_x$ to $\mathcal{T}_y$. Note that the paths in $\mathcal{P}$ have loops on neither vertex 2 nor vertex $n - 1$. Note also that $\mathbb{P}$ is closed under reflection of paths (i.e., the respective mapping of $1, \ldots, n$ to $n, \ldots, 1$). We would like to reduce from NAE3SAT exactly as in the proof of Proposition 5, with pattern $\mathcal{P}_{10^{\mu-1}1}$ and $\forall$-selector $\mathcal{P}_{1^\nu 0^\lambda}$. The sentence we would create for input for $QCSP(\mathcal{T})$ has precisely two universal quantifiers, at the beginning (i.e. this is the only use of the $\forall$-selector). The point is that somewhere we would forcibly stretch $v_\top$ and $v_\perp$ to be at distance μ (when this distance is less, it will only make it easier to extend to homomorphism). However, this method will only succeed if there is the path $\mathcal{P}_{10^{\mu-1}1} \in \mathbb{P}$.

For $\mathcal{P} \in \mathbb{P}$, let $\Delta(\mathcal{P})$ be the distance from the end of the path $\mathcal{P}$ (vertex n) to the nearest loop. Let $\Delta := \max\{\Delta(\mathcal{P}) : \mathcal{P} \in \mathbb{P}\}$. We build an input Ψ for $QCSP(\mathcal{T})$ as in the proof of Proposition 5, with pattern $\mathcal{P}_{10^{\Delta-1}1}$, except for the point at which we have only the variables $v_\top$ and $v_\perp$ remaining free (i.e., the one place we would come to use a $\forall$-selector). Here, we use the $\forall$-selector $\mathcal{P}_{0^{\mu-1}1^\nu 0^\lambda}$ for $v_\top$ and $\mathcal{P}_{1^\nu 0^\lambda}$ for $v_\top$. For the correctness of this, note that a walk of $\mu - 1$ will always get you to the penultimate loop along a path $\mathcal{P} \in \mathbb{P}$, which is sometimes at distance Δ from the end (and is always at distance $\leq \Delta$ from the end).

References

1. Bandelt, H.J., Dhlmann, A., Schtte, H.: Absolute retracts of bipartite graphs. Discrete Applied Mathematics 16(3), 191–215 (1987)
2. Bandelt, H.-J., Pesch, E.: Dismantling absolute retracts of reflexive graphs. Eur. J. Comb. 10, 211–220 (1989)

3. Barto, L., Kozik, M., Niven, T.: The CSP dichotomy holds for digraphs with no sources and no sinks (a positive answer to a conjecture of Bang-Jensen and Hell). SIAM Journal on Computing 38(5), 1782–1802 (2009)
4. Börner, F., Bulatov, A.A., Chen, H., Jeavons, P., Krokhin, A.A.: The complexity of constraint satisfaction games and qcsp. Inf. Comput. 207(9), 923–944 (2009)
5. Börner, F., Krokhin, A., Bulatov, A., and Jeavons, P. Quantified constraints and surjective polymorphisms. Tech. Rep. PRG-RR-02-11, Oxford University (2002)
6. Bulatov, A.: A dichotomy theorem for constraint satisfaction problems on a 3-element set. J. ACM 53(1), 66–120 (2006)
7. Bulatov, A., Krokhin, A., Jeavons, P.G.: Classifying the complexity of constraints using finite algebras. SIAM Journal on Computing 34, 720–742 (2005)
8. Chen, H.: The complexity of quantified constraint satisfaction: Collapsibility, sink algebras, and the three-element case. SIAM J. Comput. 37(5), 1674–1701 (2008)
9. Chen, H., Madelaine, F., Martin, B.: Quantified constraints and containment problems. In: 23rd Annual IEEE Symposium on Logic in Computer Science, pp. 317–328 (2008)
10. Dalmau, V., Krokhin, A.A.: Majority constraints have bounded pathwidth duality. Eur. J. Comb. 29(4), 821–837 (2008)
11. Feder, T., Vardi, M.: The computational structure of monotone monadic SNP and constraint satisfaction: A study through Datalog and group theory. SIAM Journal on Computing 28, 57–104 (1999)
12. Golovach, P., Paulusma, D., Song, J.: Computing vertex-surjective homomorphisms to partially reflexive trees. In: Kulikov, A., Vereshchagin, N. (eds.) CSR 2011. LNCS, vol. 6651. Springer, Heidelberg (to appear, 2011)
13. Hell, P., Nešetřil, J.: On the complexity of H-coloring. Journal of Combinatorial Theory, Series B 48, 92–110 (1990)
14. Martin, B., Madelaine, F.: Towards a trichotomy for quantified H-coloring. In: Beckmann, A., Berger, U., Löwe, B., Tucker, J.V. (eds.) CiE 2006. LNCS, vol. 3988, pp. 342–352. Springer, Heidelberg (2006)
15. Patrignani, M., Pizzonia, M.: The complexity of the matching-cut problem. In: Brandstädt, A., Le, V.B. (eds.) WG 2001. LNCS, vol. 2204, pp. 284–295. Springer, Heidelberg (2001)
16. Schaefer, T.J.: The complexity of satisfiability problems. In: Proceedings of STOC 1978, pp. 216–226 (1978)

The Computational Complexity of Disconnected Cut and $2K_2$-Partition*

Barnaby Martin and Daniël Paulusma

School of Engineering and Computing Sciences, Durham University,
Science Laboratories, South Road, Durham DH1 3LE, United Kingdom
{barnaby.martin,daniel.paulusma}@durham.ac.uk

Abstract. For a connected graph $G = (V, E)$, a subset $U \subseteq V$ is called a disconnected cut if U disconnects the graph and the subgraph induced by U is disconnected as well. We show that the problem to test whether a graph has a disconnected cut is NP-complete. This problem is polynomially equivalent to the following problems: testing if a graph has a $2K_2$-partition, testing if a graph allows a vertex-surjective homomorphism to the reflexive 4-cycle and testing if a graph has a spanning subgraph that consists of at most two bicliques. Hence, as an immediate consequence, these three decision problems are NP-complete as well. This settles an open problem frequently posed in each of the four settings.

1 Introduction

We solve an open problem that showed up as a missing case (often *the* missing case) in a number of different research areas arising from connectivity theory, graph covers and graph homomorphisms. Before we explain how these areas are related, we briefly describe them first. Throughout the paper, we consider undirected finite graphs that have no multiple edges. Unless explicitly stated otherwise they do not have self loops either. We denote the vertex set and edge set of a graph G by V_G and E_G, respectively. If no confusion is possible, we may omit the subscripts. The *complement* of a graph $G = (V, E)$ is the graph $\overline{G} = (V, \{uv \notin E \mid u \neq v\})$. For a subset $U \subset V_G$, we let $G[U]$ denote the subgraph of G *induced by* U, which is the graph $(U, \{uv \mid u, v \in U$ and $uv \in E_G\})$.

1.1 Vertex Cut Sets

A maximal connected subgraph of G is called a *component* of G. A *vertex cut (set)* or *separator* of a graph $G = (V, E)$ is a subset $U \subset V$ such that $G[V \backslash U]$ contains at least two components.

Vertex cuts play an important role in graph connectivity, and in the literature various kinds of vertex cuts have been studied. For instance, a cut U of a graph $G = (V, E)$ is called a *k-clique cut* if $G[U]$ has a spanning subgraph consisting of k complete graphs; a *strict k-clique cut* if $G[U]$ consists of k components that are complete graphs; a *stable cut* if U is an independent set; and a *matching cut* if $E_{G[U]}$ is a matching. The problem

---

* This work is supported by EPSRC (EP/G020604/1 and EP/G043434/1).

J. Lee (Ed.): CP 2011, LNCS 6876, pp. 561–575, 2011.

that asks whether a graph has a k-clique cut is solvable in polynomial time for $k = 1$, as shown by Whitesides [22], and for $k = 2$ as shown by Cameron et al. [4]. The latter authors also showed that deciding if a graph has a strict 2-clique cut can be solved in polynomial time. On the other hand, the problems that ask whether a graph has a stable cut or a matching cut, respectively, are NP-complete, as shown by Chvátal [6] and Brandstädt et al. [1], respectively.

For a fixed constant $k \geq 1$, a cut U of a connected graph G is called a k-*cut* of G if $G[U]$ contains exactly k components. Testing if a graph has a k-cut is solvable in polynomial time for $k = 1$, whereas it is NP-complete for every fixed $k \geq 2$ [15]. For $k \geq 1$ and $\ell \geq 2$, a k-cut U is called a (k, ℓ)-*cut* of a graph G if $G[V \setminus U]$ consists of exactly ℓ components. Testing if a graph has a (k, ℓ)-cut is polynomial-time solvable when $k = 1$, $\ell \geq 2$, and NP-complete otherwise [15].

A cut U of a graph G is called *disconnected* if $G[U]$ contains at least two components. We observe that U is a disconnected cut if and only if $V \setminus U$ is a disconnected cut if and only if U is a (k, ℓ)-cut for some $k \geq 2$ and $\ell \geq 2$. The following question was posed in several papers [12,15,16] as an open problem.

Q1. How hard is it to test if a graph has a disconnected cut?

The problem of testing if a graph has a disconnected cut is called the DISCONNECTED CUT problem. A disconnected cut U of a connected graph $G = (V, E)$ is *minimal* if $G[(V \setminus U) \cup \{u\}]$ is connected for every $u \in U$. Recently, the corresponding decision problem called MINIMAL DISCONNECTED CUT was shown to be NP-complete [16].

1.2 H-Partitions

A *model graph* H with $V_H = \{h_0, \ldots, h_{k-1}\}$ has two types of edges: solid and dotted edges, and an H-*partition* of a graph G is a partition of V_G into k (nonempty) sets $V_0, \ldots, V_{k-1}$ such that for all vertices $u \in V_i$, $v \in V_j$ and for all $0 \leq i < j \leq k - 1$ the following two conditions hold. Firstly, if $h_i h_j$ is a solid edge of H, then $uv \in E_G$. Secondly, if $h_i h_j$ is a dotted edge of H, then $uv \notin E_G$. There are no such restrictions when h_i and h_j are not adjacent. Let $2K_2$ be the model graph with vertices $h_0, \ldots, h_3$ and two solid edges $h_0 h_2, h_1 h_3$, and $2S_2$ be the model graph with vertices $h_0, \ldots, h_3$ and two dotted edges $h_0 h_2, h_1 h_3$. We observe that a graph G has a $2K_2$-partition if and only if its complement $\overline{G}$ has a $2S_2$-partition.

The following question was mentioned in several papers [5,7,8,11,18] as an open problem.

Q2. How hard is it to test if a graph has a $2K_2$-partition?

One of the reasons for posing this question is that the (equivalent) cases $H = 2K_2$ and $H = 2S_2$ are the only two cases of model graphs on at most four vertices for which the computational complexity of the corresponding decision problem, called H-PARTITION, is still open; all other of such cases have been settled by Dantas et al. [7]. Especially, $2K_2$-partitions have been well studied, see e.g. three very recent papers of Cook et al. [5], Dantas, Maffray and Silva [8] and Teixeira, Dantas and de Figueiredo [18]. The first two papers [5,8] study the $2K_2$-PARTITION problem for several graph classes, and the second paper [18] defines a new complexity class of problems called $2K_2$-hard.

By a result on retractions of Hell and Feder [9], which we explain later, the list versions of $2S_2$-PARTITION and $2K_2$-PARTITION are NP-complete. A variant on H-partitions that allows empty blocks V_i in an H-partition is studied by Feder et al. [10], whereas Cameron et al. [4] consider the list version of this variant.

1.3 Graph Covers

Let G be a graph and $\mathcal{S}$ be a set of (not necessarily vertex-induced) subgraphs of G that has size $|\mathcal{S}|$. The set $\mathcal{S}$ is a *cover* of G if every edge of G is contained in at least one of the subgraphs in $\mathcal{S}$. The set $\mathcal{S}$ is a *vertex-cover* of G if every vertex of G is contained in at least one of the subgraphs in $\mathcal{S}$. If all subgraphs in $\mathcal{S}$ are *bicliques*, that is, complete connected bipartite graphs, then we speak of a *biclique cover* or a *biclique vertex-cover*, respectively. Testing whether a graph has a biclique cover of size at most k is polynomial-time solvable for any fixed k; it is even fixed-parameter tractable in k as shown by Fleischner et al. [12]. The same authors [12] show that testing whether a graph has a biclique vertex-cover of size at most k is polynomial-time solvable for $k = 1$ and NP-complete for $k \geq 3$. For $k = 2$, they show that this problem can be solved in polynomial time for bipartite input graphs, and they pose the following open problem.

Q3. How hard is it to test if a graph has a biclique vertex-cover of size 2?

The problem of testing if a graph has a biclique vertex-cover of size 2 is called the 2-BICLIQUE VERTEX-COVER problem. In order to answer question Q3 we may without loss of generality restrict to biclique vertex-covers in which every vertex is in exactly one of the subgraphs in $\mathcal{S}$ (cf. [12]).

1.4 Graph Homomorphisms

A *homomorphism* from a graph G to a graph H is a mapping $f : V_G \rightarrow V_H$ that maps adjacent vertices of G to adjacent vertices of H, i.e., $f(u)f(v) \in E_H$ whenever $uv \in E_G$. The problem H-HOMOMORPHISM tests whether a given graph G allows a homomorphism to a graph H called the *target* which is fixed, i.e., not part of the input. This problem is also known as H-COLORING. Hell and Nešetřil [14] showed that H-HOMOMORPHISM is solvable in polynomial time if H is bipartite, and NP-complete otherwise. Here, H does not have a self-loop xx, as otherwise we can map every vertex of G to x.

A homomorphism f from a graph G to a graph H is *surjective* if for each $x \in V_H$ there exists at least one vertex $u \in V_G$ with $f(u) = x$. This leads to the problem of deciding if a given graph allows a surjective homomorphism to a fixed target graph H, which is called the SURJECTIVE H-HOMOMORPHISM or SURJECTIVE H-COLORING problem. For this variant, the presence of a vertex with a self-loop in the target graph H does not make the problem trivial. Such vertices are called *reflexive*, whereas vertices with no self-loop are said to be *irreflexive*. A graph that contains zero or more reflexive vertices is called *partially reflexive*. In particular, a graph is *reflexive* if all its vertices are reflexive, and a graph is *irreflexive* if all its vertices are irreflexive. Golovach, Paulusma and Song [13] showed that for any fixed partially reflexive tree H, the SURJECTIVE H-HOMOMORPHISM problem is polynomial-time solvable if the (possibly empty) set of reflexive vertices in H induces a connected subgraph of H, and NP-complete otherwise [13]. They mention that the smallest open case is the case in which H is the reflexive 4-cycle denoted $\mathcal{C}_4$.

Q4. How hard is it to test if a graph has a surjective homomorphism to $\mathcal{C}_4$?

The following two notions are closely related to surjective homomorphisms. A homomorphism f from a graph G to an induced subgraph H of G is a *retraction* from G to H if $f(h) = h$ for all $h \in V_H$. In that case we say that G *retracts to* H. For a fixed graph H, the H-RETRACTION problem has as input a graph G that contains H as an induced subgraph and is to test if G retracts to H. Hell and Feder [9] showed that $\mathcal{C}_4$-RETRACTION is NP-complete.

We emphasize that a surjective homomorphism is vertex-surjective. A stronger notion is to require a homomorphism from a graph G to a graph H to be *edge-surjective*, which means that for any edge $xy \in E_H$ with $x \neq y$ there exists an edge $uv \in E_G$ with $f(u) = x$ and $f(v) = y$. Note that the edge-surjectivity condition only holds for edges $xy \in E_H$; there is no such condition on the self-loops $xx \in E_H$. An edge-surjective homomorphism is also called a *compaction*. If f is a compaction from G to H, we say that G *compacts to* H. The H-COMPACTION problem asks if a graph G compacts to a fixed graph H. Vikas [19,20,21] determined the computational complexity of this problem for several classes of fixed target graphs. In particular, he showed that $\mathcal{C}_4$-COMPACTION is NP-complete [19].

1.5   The Relationships between Questions Q1–Q4

Before we explain how questions Q1–Q4 are related, we first introduce some new terminology. The *distance* $d_G(u, v)$ between two vertices u and v in a graph G is the number of edges in a shortest path between them. The *diameter* $\mathrm{diam}(G)$ is defined as $\max\{d_G(u, v) \mid u, v \in V\}$. The *edge contraction* of an edge $e = uv$ in a graph G replaces the two end-vertices u and v with a new vertex adjacent to precisely those vertices to which u or v were adjacent. If a graph H can be obtained from G by a sequence of edge contractions, then G is said to be *contractible to* H. The biclique with partition classes of size k and ℓ is denoted $K_{k,\ell}$; it is called *nontrivial* if $k \geq 1$ and $\ell \geq 1$.

Proposition 1 ([15]). *Let G be a connected graph. Then statements (1)–(5) are equivalent:*

(1) G *has a disconnected cut.*
(2) G *has a $2S_2$-partition.*
(3) G *allows a vertex-surjective homomorphism to $\mathcal{C}_4$.*
(4) $\overline{G}$ *has a spanning subgraph that consists of exactly two nontrivial bicliques.*
(5) $\overline{G}$ *has a $2K_2$-partition.*

If $\mathrm{diam}(G) = 2$, then (1)–(5) are also equivalent to the following statements:

(6) G allows a compaction to C_4.

(7) G is contractible to some biclique $K_{k,\ell}$ for some $k, \ell \geq 2$.

Due to Proposition 1, questions Q1–Q4 are equivalent. Hence, by solving one of them we solve them all. Moreover, every graph of diameter 1 has no disconnected cut, and every graph of diameter at least 3 has a disconnected cut [12]. Hence, we may restrict ourselves to graphs of diameter 2. Then, by solving one of Q1–Q4 we also determine the computational complexity of C_4-COMPACTION on graphs of diameter 2 and BICLIQUE CONTRACTION on graphs of diameter 2; the latter problem is to test if a graph can be contracted to a biclique $K_{k,\ell}$ for some $k, \ell \geq 2$. Recall that Vikas [19] showed that C_4-COMPACTION is NP-complete. However, the gadget in his NP-completeness reduction has diameter 3 as observed by Ito et al. [16].

Our Result. We solve question Q4 by showing that the problem SURJECTIVE C_4-HOMOMORPHISM is NP-complete, even for graphs of diameter 2 that have a dominating non-edge. A pair of vertices in a graph is a *dominating (non-)edge* if the two vertices of the pair are (non-)adjacent, and any other vertex in the graph is adjacent to at least one of them. In contrast, Fleischner et al. [12] showed that this problem is polynomial-time solvable on input graphs with a dominating edge. As a consequence of our result, we find that the problems DISCONNECTED CUT, $2K_2$-PARTITION, $2S_2$-PARTITION, and 2-BICLIQUE VERTEX-COVER are all NP-complete. Moreover, we also find that the problems C_4-COMPACTION and BICLIQUE CONTRACTION are NP-complete even for graphs of diameter 2.

Our approach to prove NP-completeness is as follows. As mentioned before, we can restrict ourselves to graphs of diameter 2. We therefore try to reduce the diameter in the gadget of the NP-completeness proof of Vikas [19] for C_4-COMPACTION from 3 to 2. This leads to NP-completeness of SURJECTIVE C_4-HOMOMORPHISM, because these two problems coincide for graphs of diameter 2 due to Proposition 1. The proof that C_4-COMPACTION is NP-complete [19] has its roots in the proof that C_4-RETRACTION is NP-complete [9]. So far, it was only known that C_4-RETRACTION stays NP-complete for graphs of diameter 3 [16]. We start our proof by showing that C_4-RETRACTION is NP-compete even for graphs of diameter 2. The key idea is to base the reduction from an NP-complete homomorphism (constraint satisfaction) problem that we obtain only after a fine analysis under the algebraic conditions of Bulatov, Krokhin and Jeavons [3]. We perform this analysis in Section 2 and present our NP-completeness proof for C_4-RETRACTION on graphs of diameter 2 in Section 3. This leads a special input graph of the C_4-RETRACTION problem, which enables us to modify the gadget of the proof of Vikas [19] for C_4-COMPACTION in order to get its diameter down to 2, as desired. We explain this part in Section 4.

For reasons of space some simple proofs are omitted, these can be found in the full version of this paper [17].

2 Constraint Satisfaction

The notion of a graph homomorphism can be generalized as follows. A *structure* is a tuple $\mathcal{A} = (A; R_1, \ldots, R_k)$, where A is a set called the *domain* of $\mathcal{A}$ and R_i is an

n_i-ary *relation* on A for $i = 1, \ldots, k$, i.e., a set of n_i-tuples of elements from A. Note that a graph $G = (V, E)$ can be seen as a structure $G = (V; \{(u, v), (v, u) \mid uv \in E\})$. Throughout the paper we only consider *finite* structures, i.e., with a finite domain.

Let $\mathcal{A} = (A; R_1, \ldots, R_k)$ and $\mathcal{B} = (B; S_1, \ldots, S_k)$ be two structures, where each R_i and S_i are relations of the same arity n_i. Then a *homomorphism* from $\mathcal{A}$ to $\mathcal{B}$ is a mapping $f : A \to B$ such that $(a_1, \ldots, a_{n_i}) \in R_i$ implies $(f(a_1), \ldots, f(a_{n_i})) \in S_i$ for every i and every n_i-tuple $(a_1, \ldots, a_{n_i}) \in A^{n_i}$. The decision problem that is to test if a given structure $\mathcal{A}$ allows a homomorphism to a fixed structure $\mathcal{B}$ is called the $\mathcal{B}$-HOMOMORPHISM problem, also known as the $\mathcal{B}$-CONSTRAINT SATISFACTION problem.

Let $\mathcal{A} = (A; R_1, \ldots, R_k)$ be a structure. The *power structure* $\mathcal{A}^\ell$ has domain A^ℓ and for $1 \leq i \leq k$, has relations

$$R_i^\ell := \{((a_1^1, \ldots, a_\ell^1), \ldots, (a_1^{n_i}, \ldots, a_\ell^{n_i})) \mid (a_1^1, \ldots, a_1^{n_i}), \ldots, (a_\ell^1, \ldots, a_\ell^{n_i}) \in R_i\}.$$

An (l-ary) *polymorphism* of $\mathcal{A}$ is a homomorphism from $\mathcal{A}^\ell$ to $\mathcal{A}$ for some integer ℓ. A 1-ary polymorphism is an *endomorphism*. The set of polymorphisms of $\mathcal{A}$ is denoted $\mathrm{Pol}(\mathcal{A})$.

A binary function f on a domain A is a *semilattice* function if $f(h, (f(i, j)) = f(f(h, i), j)$, $f(i, j) = f(j, i)$, and $f(i, i) = i$ for all $i, j \in A$. A ternary function f is a *Mal'tsev* function if $f(i, j, j) = f(j, j, i) = i$ for all $i, j \in A$. A ternary function f is a *majority* function if $f(h, h, i) = f(h, i, h) = f(i, h, h) = h$ for all $h, i \in A$. On the Boolean domain $\{0, 1\}$, we may consider propositional functions. The only two semilattice functions on the Boolean domain are the binary function $\wedge$, which maps (h, i) to $(h \wedge i)$, which is 1 if $h = i = 1$ and 0 otherwise, and the binary function $\vee$ which maps (h, i) to $(h \vee i)$, which is 0 if $h = i = 0$ and 1 otherwise. We may consider each of these functions on any two-element domain (where we view one element as 0 and the other as 1). For a function f on B, and a subset $A \subseteq B$, let $f_{|A}$ be the restriction of f to A.

A structure is a *core* if all of its endomorphisms are *automorphisms*, i.e., are invertible. We will make use of the following theorem from Bulatov, Krokhin and Jeavons [3] (it appears in this form in Bulatov [2]).

Theorem 1 ([2,3]). *Let $\mathcal{B} = (B; S_1, \ldots, S_k)$ be a core and $A \subseteq B$ be a subset of size $|A| = 2$ that as a unary relation is in $\mathcal{B}$. If for each $f \in \mathrm{Pol}(\mathcal{B})$, $f_{|A}$ is not majority, semilattice or Mal'tsev, then $\mathcal{B}$-HOMOMORPHISM is NP-complete.*

Let $\mathcal{D}$ be the structure on domain $D = \{0, 1, 3\}$ with four binary relations

$$S_1 := \{(0, 3), (1, 1), (3, 1), (3, 3)\} \quad S_3 := \{(1, 3), (3, 1), (3, 3)\}$$
$$S_2 := \{(1, 0), (1, 1), (3, 1), (3, 3)\} \quad S_4 := \{(1, 1), (1, 3), (3, 1)\}.$$

Proposition 2. *The $\mathcal{D}$-HOMOMORPHISM problem is NP-complete.*

Proof. We use Theorem 1. We first show that $\mathcal{D}$ is a core. Let g be an endomorphism of $\mathcal{D}$. If $g(0) = 3$ then $g(1) = 3$ by preservation of S_2, i.e., as otherwise $(1, 0) \in S_2$ does not imply $(g(1), g(0)) \in S_2$. However, $(1, 1) \in S_4$ but $(g(1), g(1)) = (3, 3) \notin S_4$. Hence $g(0) \neq 3$. If $g(0) = 1$ then $g(3) = 1$ by preservation of S_1. However,

$(3,3) \in S_3$ but $(g(3), g(3)) = (1,1) \notin S_3$. Hence $g(0) \neq 1$. This means that $g(0) = 0$. Consequently, $g(1) = 1$ by preservation of S_2, and $g(3) = 3$ by preservation of S_1. Hence, g is the identity mapping, which is an automorphism, as desired.

Let $A = \{1,3\}$, which is in $\mathcal{D}$ in the form of $S_1(p,p)$ (or $S_2(p,p)$). Suppose that $f \in \text{Pol}(\mathcal{D})$. In order to prove Proposition 2, we must show that $f_{|A}$ is neither majority nor semilattice nor Mal'tsev.

Suppose that $f_{|A}$ is semilattice. Then $f_{|A} = \wedge$ or $f_{|A} = \vee$. If $f = \wedge$, then either $f(1,1) = 1$, $f(1,3) = 3$, $f(3,1) = 3$, $f(3,3) = 3$, or $f(1,1) = 1$, $f(1,3) = 1$, $f(3,1) = 1$, $f(3,3) = 3$ depending on how the elements $1,3$ correspond to the two elements of the Boolean domain. The same holds for $f = \vee$. Suppose that $f(1,1) = 1$, $f(1,3) = 3$, $f(3,1) = 3$, $f(3,3) = 3$. By preservation of S_4 we find that $f(1,3) = 1$ due to $f(3,1) = 3$. This is not possible. Suppose that $f(1,1) = 1$, $f(1,3) = 1$, $f(3,1) = 1$, $f(3,3) = 3$. By preservation of S_3 we find that $f(1,3) = 3$ due to $f(3,1) = 1$. This is not possible.

Suppose that $f_{|A}$ is Mal'tsev. By preservation of S_4, we find that $f(1,1,3) = 1$ due to $f(3,1,1) = 3$. However, because $f(1,1,3) = 3$, this is not possible.

Suppose that $f_{|A}$ is majority. By preservation of S_1, we deduce that $f(0,3,1) \in \{0,3\}$ due to $f(3,3,1) = 3$, and that $f(0,3,1) \in \{1,3\}$ due to $f(3,1,1) = 1$. Thus, $f(0,3,1) = 3$. By preservation of S_2, however, we deduce that $f(0,3,1) \in \{0,1\}$ due to $f(1,3,1) = 1$. This is a contradiction. Hence, we have completed the proof of Proposition 2.   □

3   Retractions

In the remainder of this paper, let H denote the reflexive 4-vertex cycle $\mathcal{C}_4$, on vertices $h_0, \ldots, h_3$, with edges $h_0 h_1$, $h_1 h_2$, $h_2 h_3$, $h_3 h_0$, $h_0 h_0$, $h_1 h_1$, $h_2 h_2$ and $h_3 h_3$. We prove that H-RETRACTION is NP-complete for graphs of diameter 2 by a reduction from $\mathcal{D}$-HOMOMORPHISM.

Let $\mathcal{A} = (A; R_1, \ldots, R_4)$ be an instance of $\mathcal{D}$-HOMOMORPHISM, where we may assume that each R_i is a binary relation. From $\mathcal{A}$ we construct a graph G as follows. We let the elements in $\mathcal{A}$ correspond to vertices of G. If $(p,q) \in R_i$ for some $1 \leq i \leq 4$, then we say that vertex p in G is of *type ℓ* and vertex q in G is of *type r*. Note that a vertex can be of type ℓ and r simultaneously, because it can be the first element in a pair in $R_1 \cup \cdots \cup R_4$ and the second element of another such pair. For each $(p,q) \in R_i$ and $1 \leq i \leq 4$ we introduce four new vertices a_p, b_p, c_q, d_q with edges $a_p p$, $a_p b_p$, $b_p p$, $c_q q$, $c_q d_q$ and $d_q q$. We say that a vertex a_p, b_p, c_q, d_q is of *type a, b, c, d*, respectively; note that these vertices all have a unique type.

We now let the graph H be an induced subgraph of G (with distinct vertices $h_0, \ldots, h_3$). Then formally G must have self-loops $h_0 h_0, \ldots, h_3 h_3$. However, this is irrelevant for our problem, and we may assume that G is irreflexive (since H is reflexive, it does not matter – from the perspective of retraction – if G is reflexive, irreflexive or anything inbetween). In G we join every a-type vertex to h_0 and h_3, every b-type vertex to h_1 and h_2, every c-type vertex to h_2 and h_3, and every d-type vertex to h_0 and h_1. We also add an edge between h_0 and every vertex of $\mathcal{A}$.

We continue the construction of G by describing how we distinguish between two pairs belonging to different relations. If $(p, q) \in R_1$, then we add the edges $c_q p$ and $q h_2$; see Figure 1. If $(p, q) \in R_2$, then we add the edges $h_2 p$ and $b_p q$; see Figure 2. If $(p, q) \in R_3$, then we add the edges $h_2 p$, $h_2 q$ and $a_p c_q$; see Figure 3. If $(p, q) \in R_4$, then we add the edges $h_2 p$, $h_2 q$ and $b_p d_q$; see Figure 4. We also add an edge between any two vertices of type a, between any two vertices of type b, between any two vertices of type c, and between any two vertices of type d. Note that this leads to four mutually vertex-disjoint cliques in G. We call G a $\mathcal{D}$-*graph*. The proof of Lemma 1 proceeds by a simple analysis (a diameter table appears in the full version of this paper [17]).

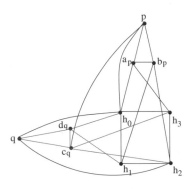

Fig. 1. The part of a $\mathcal{D}$-graph G for a pair $(p, q) \in R_1$

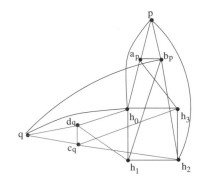

Fig. 2. The part of a $\mathcal{D}$-graph G for a pair $(p, q) \in R_2$

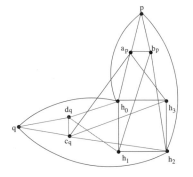

Fig. 3. The part of a $\mathcal{D}$-graph G for a pair $(p, q) \in R_3$

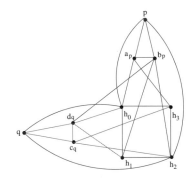

Fig. 4. The part of a $\mathcal{D}$-graph G for a pair $(p, q) \in R_4$

Lemma 1. *Every $\mathcal{D}$-graph has diameter 2 and a dominating non-edge.*

Recall that Feder and Hell [9] showed that H-RETRACTION is NP-complete. Ito et al. [16] observed that H-RETRACTION stays NP-complete on graphs of diameter 3. We need the following. Lemma 1 and Theorem 2 together imply that H-RETRACTION is NP-complete for graphs of diameter 2 that have a dominating non-edge.

Theorem 2. *The H-*RETRACTION *problem is* NP-*complete even for* $\mathcal{D}$-*graphs.*

Proof. We recall that H-RETRACTION is in NP, because we can guess a partition of the vertex set of the input graph G into four (non-empty) sets and verify in polynomial time if this partition corresponds to a retraction from G to H. From an instance $\mathcal{A}$ of $\mathcal{D}$-HOMOMORPHISM we construct a $\mathcal{D}$-graph G. We claim that $\mathcal{A}$ allows a homomorphism to $\mathcal{D}$ if and only if G retracts to H.

First suppose that $\mathcal{A}$ allows a homomorphism f to $\mathcal{D}$. We construct a mapping g from V_G to V_H as follows. We let $g(a) = h_i$ if $f(a) = i$ for all $a \in A$ and $g(h_i) = h_i$ for $i = 0, \dots, 3$. Because f is a homomorphism from $\mathcal{A}$ to $\mathcal{D}$, this leads to Tables 1–4, which explain where a_p, b_p, c_q and d_q map under g, according to where p and q map. From these, we conclude that g is a retraction from G to H. In particular, we note that the edges $c_q p$, $b_p q$, $a_p c_q$, and $b_p d_q$ each map to an edge or self-loop in H when (p, q) belongs to $R_1, \dots, R_4$, respectively.

Table 1. g-values when $(p, q) \in R_1$

p	q	a_p	b_p	c_q	d_q
h_0	h_3	h_0	h_1	h_3	h_0
h_1	h_1	h_0	h_1	h_2	h_1
h_3	h_1	h_3	h_2	h_2	h_1
h_3	h_3	h_3	h_2	h_3	h_0

Table 2. g-values when $(p, q) \in R_2$

p	q	a_p	b_p	c_q	d_q
h_1	h_0	h_0	h_1	h_3	h_0
h_1	h_1	h_0	h_1	h_2	h_1
h_3	h_1	h_3	h_2	h_2	h_1
h_3	h_3	h_3	h_2	h_3	h_0

Table 3. g-values when $(p, q) \in R_3$

p	q	a_p	b_p	c_q	d_q
h_1	h_3	h_0	h_1	h_3	h_0
h_3	h_1	h_3	h_2	h_2	h_1
h_3	h_3	h_3	h_2	h_3	h_0

Table 4. g-values when $(p, q) \in R_4$

p	q	a_p	b_p	c_q	d_q
h_1	h_1	h_0	h_1	h_2	h_1
h_1	h_3	h_0	h_1	h_3	h_0
h_3	h_1	h_3	h_2	h_2	h_1

To prove the reverse implication, suppose that G allows a retraction g to H. We construct a mapping $f : A \to \{0, 1, 2, 3\}$ by defining $f(a) = i$ if $g(a) = h_i$ for $a \in A$. We claim that f is a homomorphism from $\mathcal{A}$ to $\mathcal{D}$. In order to see this, we first note that g maps all a-type vertices to $\{h_0, h_3\}$, all b-type vertices to $\{h_1, h_2\}$, all c-type vertices to $\{h_2, h_3\}$ and all d-type vertices to $\{h_0, h_1\}$. We now show that $(p, q) \in R_i$ implies that $(f(p), f(q)) \in S_i$ for $i = 1, \dots, 4$.

Suppose that $(p, q) \in R_1$. Because p is adjacent to h_0, we obtain $g(p) \in \{h_0, h_1, h_3\}$. Because q is adjacent to h_0 and h_2, we find that $g(q) \in \{h_1, h_3\}$. If $g(p) = h_0$, then g maps c_q to h_3, and consequently, $g(q) = h_3$. If $g(p) = h_1$, then g maps c_q to h_2, and consequently d_q to h_1, implying that $g(q) = h_1$. If $g(p) = h_3$, then we do not investigate further; we allow g to map q to h_1 or h_3. Hence, we find that $(f(p), f(q)) \in \{(0, 3), (1, 1), (3, 1), (3, 3)\} = S_1$, as desired.

Suppose that $(p, q) \in R_2$. Because p is adjacent to h_0 and h_2, we find that $g(p) \in \{h_1, h_3\}$. Because q is adjacent to h_0, we find that $g(q) \in \{h_0, h_1, h_3\}$. If $g(q) = h_0$, then g maps b_p to h_1, and consequently, $g(p) = h_1$. If $g(q) = h_1$, then we do not investigate further; we allow g to map p to h_1 or h_3. If $g(q) = h_3$, then g maps b_p to h_2, and consequently, a_p to h_3, implying that $g(p) = h_3$. Hence, we find that $(f(p), f(q)) \in \{(1,0),(1,1),(3,1),(3,3)\} = S_2$, as desired.

Suppose that $(p,q) \in R_3$. Because both p and q are adjacent to both h_0 and h_2, we find that $g(p) \in \{h_1, h_3\}$ and $g(q) \in \{h_1, h_3\}$. If $g(p) = h_1$, then g maps a_p to h_0, and consequently, c_q to h_3, implying that $g(q) = h_3$. Hence, we find that $(f(p), f(q)) \in \{(1,3),(3,1),(3,3)\} = S_3$, as desired.

Suppose that $(p,q) \in R_4$. Because both p and q are adjacent to both h_0 and h_2, we find that $g(p) \in \{h_1, h_3\}$ and $g(q) \in \{h_1, h_3\}$. If $g(q) = h_3$, then g maps d_q to h_0, and consequently, b_p to h_1, implying that $g(p) = h_1$. Hence, we find that $(f(p), f(q)) \in \{(1,1),(1,3),(3,1)\} = S_4$, as desired. This completes the proof of Lemma 2. □

4 Surjective Homomorphisms

Vikas [19] constructed the following graph from a graph $G = (V, E)$ that contains H as an induced subgraph. For each vertex $v \in V_G \backslash V_H$ we add three new vertices u_v, w_v, y_v with edges $h_0 u_v, h_0 y_v, h_1 u_v, h_2 w_v, h_2 y_v, h_3 w_v, u_v v, u_v w_v, u_v y_v, v w_v, w_v y_v$. We say that a vertex u_v, w_v and y_v has *type* u, w, or y, respectively. We also add all edges between any two vertices $u_v, u_{v'}$ and between any two vertices $w_v, w_{v'}$ with $v \neq v'$. For each edge vv' in $E_G \backslash E_H$ we choose an arbitrary orientation, say from v to v', and then add a new vertex $x_{vv'}$ with edges $v x_{vv'}, v' x_{vv'}, u_v x_{vv'}, w_v x_{vv'}$. We say that this new vertex has *type* x. The new graph G' obtained from G is called an H-*compactor* of G. See Figure 5 for an example. This figure does not depict any self-loops, although formally G must have at least four self-loops, because G contains H as an induced subgraph. Just as for retractions, this is irrelevant, and we assume that G is irreflexive.

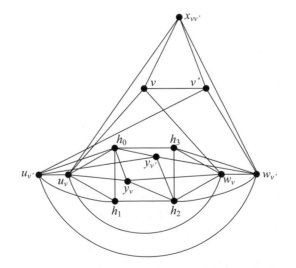

Fig. 5. The part of G' that corresponds to edge $vv' \in E_G \setminus E_H$ as displayed in [19]

Vikas [19] showed that a graph G retracts to H if and only if an (arbitrary) H-compactor G' of G retracts to H if and only if G' compacts to H. Recall that an H-compactor is of diameter 3 as observed by Ito et al. [16]. Our aim is to reduce the diameter in such a graph to 2. This forces us to make a number of modifications. Firstly, we must remove a number of vertices of type x. Secondly, we can no longer choose the orientations regarding the remaining vertices of type x arbitrarily. Thirdly, we must connect the remaining x-type vertices to H via edges. In more detail, let G be a $\mathcal{D}$-graph. For all vertices in G we create vertices of type u, v, w, y with incident edges as in the definition of a compactor. We then perform the following three steps.

1. Not creating all the vertices of type x
We do not create x-type vertices for the following edges in G: edges between two a-type vertices, edges between two b-type vertices, edges between two c-type vertices, and edges between two d-type vertices.

2. Choosing the "right" orientation of the other edges of G \ H
For $(p, q) \in R_i$ and $1 \leq i \leq 4$, we choose x-type vertices $x_{a_p p}$, $x_{p b_p}$, $x_{a_p b_p}$, $x_{q c_q}$, $x_{q d_q}$, and $x_{d_q c_q}$. In addition we create the following x-type vertices. For $(p, q) \in R_1$ we choose $x_{p c_q}$. For $(p, q) \in R_2$ we choose $x_{q b_p}$. For $(p, q) \in R_3$ we choose $x_{a_p c_q}$. For $(p, q) \in R_4$ we choose $x_{d_q b_p}$.

3. Connecting the created x-type vertices to H
We add an edge between h_0 and every vertex of type x that we created in Step 2. We also add an edge between h_2 and every such vertex.

We call the resulting graph a *semi-compactor* of G and give two essential lemmas (proof of the first proceeds by simple analysis – a diameter table appears in the full version of this paper [17]).

Lemma 2. *Let G be a $\mathcal{D}$-graph. Every semi-compactor of G has diameter 2 and a dominating non-edge.*

Lemma 3. *Let G'' be a semi-compactor of a $\mathcal{D}$-graph G. Then the following statements are equivalent:*

 (i) G retracts to H;
 (ii) G'' retracts to H;
 (iii) G'' compacts to H;
 (iv) G'' has a vertex-surjective homomorphism to H.

Proof. We show the following implications: $(i) \Rightarrow (ii)$, $(ii) \Rightarrow (i)$, $(ii) \Rightarrow (iii)$, $(iii) \Rightarrow (ii)$, $(iii) \Rightarrow (iv)$, and $(iv) \Rightarrow (iii)$.

"$(i) \Rightarrow (ii)$" Let f be a retraction from G to H. We show how to extend f to a retraction from G'' to H. We observe that every vertex of type u can only be mapped to h_0 or h_1, because such a vertex is adjacent to h_0 and h_1. We also observe that every vertex of type w can only be mapped to h_2 or h_3, because such a vertex is adjacent to h_2 and h_3. This implies the following. Let $v \in V_G \setminus V_H$. If $f(v) = h_0$ or $f(v) = h_1$, then w_v must be mapped to h_3 or h_2, respectively. Consequently, u_v must be mapped to h_0 or h_1, respectively, due to the edge $u_v w_v$. If $f(v) = h_2$ or $f(v) = h_3$, then u_v must be mapped to h_1 or h_0, respectively. Consequently, w_v must be mapped to h_2 or h_3, respectively, due to the edge $u_v w_v$. Hence, $f(v)$ fixes the mapping of the vertices u_v or w_v, and either u_v is mapped to h_1 or w_v is mapped to h_3. Note that both vertices are adjacent to y_v. Then, because y_v can only be mapped to h_1 or h_3 due to the edges $h_0 y_v$ and $h_2 y_v$, the mapping of y_v is fixed as well; if u_v is mapped to h_1 then y_v is mapped to h_1, and if w_v is mapped to h_3 then y_v is mapped to h_3.

What is left to do is to verify whether we can map the vertices of type x. For this purpose we refer to Table 5, where v, v' denote two adjacent vertices of $V_G \setminus V_H$. Every possible combination of $f(v)$ and $f(v')$ corresponds to a row in this table. As we have just shown, this fixes the image of the vertices u_v, $u_{v'}$, w_v, $w_{v'}$, $y_{v'}$ and y_v. For $x_{vv'}$ we use its adjacencies to v, v', u_v and $w_{v'}$ to determine potential images. For some cases, this number of potential images is not one but two. This is shown in the last column of Table 5; here we did not take into account that every $x_{vv'}$ is adjacent to h_0 and h_2 in our construction. Because of these adjacencies, every $x_{vv'}$ can only be mapped to h_1 or h_3. In the majority of the 12 rows in Table 5 we have this choice; the exceptions are row 4 and row 9. In row 4 and 9, we find that $x_{vv'}$ can only be mapped to one image, which is h_0 or h_2, respectively. By construction, we have that (v, v') belongs to

$$\{(a_p, p), (p, b_p), (a_p, b_p), (q, c_q), (q, d_q), (d_q, c_q), (p, c_q), (q, b_p), (a_p, c_q), (d_q, b_p)\}.$$

We first show that row 4 cannot occur. In order to obtain a contradiction, suppose that row 4 does occur, i.e., that $f(v) = h_1$ and $f(v') = h_0$ for some $v, v' \in V_G \setminus V_H$. Due to their adjacencies with vertices of H, every vertex of type a is mapped to h_0 or h_3, every vertex of type b to h_1 or h_2, every vertex of type c to h_2 or h_3 and every vertex of type d to h_0 or h_1. This means that v can only be p, q, b_p, or d_q, whereas v' can only be p, q, a_p or d_q. If $v = p$ then $v' \in \{b_p, c_q\}$. If $v = q$ then $v' \in \{c_q, d_q, b_p\}$. If $v = b_p$ then v' cannot be chosen. If $v = d_q$ then $v' \in \{c_q, b_p\}$. Hence, we find that $v = q$ and $v' = d_q$. However, then f is not a retraction from G to H, because c_q is adjacent to d_q, q, h_2, h_3, and f maps these vertices to h_0, h_1, h_2, h_3, respectively. Hence, row 4 does not occur.

We now show that row 9 cannot occur. In order to obtain a contradiction, suppose that row 9 does occur, i.e., that $f(v) = h_2$ and $f(v') = h_3$. As in the previous case, we deduce that every vertex of type a is mapped to h_0 or h_3, every vertex of type b to h_1 or h_2, every vertex of type c to h_2 or h_3 and every vertex of type d to h_0 or h_1. Moreover, every vertex of type ℓ or r cannot be mapped to h_2, because it is adjacent to h_0. Then v can only be b_p or c_q, and v' can only be p, q, a_p or c_q. However, if $v = b_p$ or $v = c_q$ then v' cannot be chosen. Hence, row 9 cannot occur, and we conclude that f can be extended to a retraction from G'' to H, as desired.

"$(ii) \Rightarrow (i)$" Let f be a retraction from G'' to H. Then the restriction of f to V_G is a retraction from G to H. Hence, this implication is valid.

"$(ii) \Rightarrow (iii)$" Every retraction from G'' to H is an edge-surjective homomorphism, so *a fortiori* a compaction from G'' to H.

"$(iii) \Rightarrow (ii)$" Let f be a compaction from G'' to H. We will show that f is without loss of generality a retraction from G'' to H. Our proof goes along the same lines as the proof of Lemma 2.1.2 in Vikas [19], i.e., we use the same arguments but in addition we must examine a few more cases due to our modifications in steps 1–3; we therefore include all the proof details below.

Table 5. Determining a retraction from G'' to H

v	v'	u_v	$u_{v'}$	w_v	$w_{v'}$	y_v	$y_{v'}$	$x_{vv'}$
h_0	h_0	h_0	h_0	h_3	h_3	h_3	h_3	h_0/h_3
h_0	h_1	h_0	h_1	h_3	h_2	h_3	h_1	h_1
h_0	h_3	h_0	h_0	h_3	h_3	h_3	h_3	h_0/h_3
h_1	h_0	h_1	h_0	h_2	h_3	h_1	h_3	h_0
h_1	h_1	h_1	h_1	h_2	h_2	h_1	h_1	h_1/h_2
h_1	h_2	h_1	h_1	h_2	h_2	h_1	h_1	h_1/h_2
h_2	h_1	h_1	h_1	h_2	h_2	h_1	h_1	h_1/h_2
h_2	h_2	h_1	h_1	h_2	h_2	h_1	h_1	h_1/h_2
h_2	h_3	h_1	h_0	h_2	h_3	h_1	h_3	h_2
h_3	h_0	h_0	h_0	h_3	h_3	h_3	h_3	h_0/h_3
h_3	h_2	h_0	h_1	h_3	h_2	h_3	h_1	h_3
h_3	h_3	h_0	h_0	h_3	h_3	h_3	h_3	h_0/h_3

We let U consist of h_0, h_1 and all vertices of type u. Similarly, we let W consist of h_2, h_3 and all vertices of type w. Because U forms a clique in G, we find that $f(U)$ is a clique in H. This means that $1 \leq |f(U)| \leq 2$. By the same arguments, we find that $1 \leq f(W) \leq 2$.

We first prove that $|f(U)| = |f(W)| = 2$. In order to derive a contradiction, suppose that $|f(U)| \neq 2$. Then $f(U)$ has only one vertex. By symmetry, we may assume that f maps every vertex of U to h_0; otherwise we can redefine f. Because every vertex of G'' is adjacent to a vertex in U, we find that G'' contains no vertex that is mapped to h_2 by f. This is not possible, because f is a compaction from G'' to H. Hence $|f(U)| = 2$, and by the same arguments, $|f(W)| = 2$. Because U is a clique, we find that $f(U) \neq \{h_0, h_2\}$ and $f(U) \neq \{h_1, h_3\}$. Hence, by symmetry, we assume that $f(U) = \{h_0, h_1\}$.

We now prove that $f(W) = \{h_2, h_3\}$. In order to obtain a contradiction, suppose that $f(W) \neq \{h_2, h_3\}$. Because f is a compaction from G'' to H, there exists an edge st in G'' with $f(s) = h_2$ and $f(t) = h_3$. Because $f(U)$ only contains vertices mapped to h_0 or h_1, we find that $s \notin U$ and $t \notin U$. Because we assume that $f(W) \neq \{h_2, h_3\}$, we find that st is not one of $w_v h_2, w_v h_3, h_2 h_3$. Hence, st is one of the following edges

$$vw_v, w_v y_v, vx_{vv'}, y_v h_2, vh_2, vh_3, vv', v'x_{vv'}, w_{v'} x_{vv'}, x_{vv'} h_2,$$

where $v, v' \in V_G \setminus V_H$. We must consider each of these possibilities.

If $st \in \{vw_v, w_v y_v, vx_{vv'}\}$ then $f(u_v) \in \{h_2, h_3\}$, because u_v is adjacent to $v, w_v, y_v, x_{vv'}$. However, this is not possible because $u_v \in \{h_0, h_1\}$. If $st = y_v h_2$, then $f(w_v) = h_2$ or $f(w_v) = h_3$, because w_v is adjacent to y_v and h_2. If $f(w_v) = f(y_v)$, then $f(w_v) \neq f(h_2)$, and consequently, $\{f(w_v), f(h_2)\} = \{h_2, h_3\}$. This means that $f(W) = \{h_2, h_3\}$, which we assumed is not the case. Hence, $f(w_v) \neq f(y_v)$. Then f maps the edge $w_v y_v$ to $h_2 h_3$, and we return to the previous case. We can repeat the same arguments if $st = vh_2$ or $st = vh_3$. Hence, we find that st cannot be equal to those edges either.

If $st = vv'$, then by symmetry we may assume without loss of generality that $f(v) = h_2$ and $f(v') = h_3$. Consequently, $f(u_v) = h_1$, because $u_v \in U$ is adjacent to v, and can only be mapped to h_0 or h_1 By the same reasoning, $f(u_{v'}) = h_0$. Because w_v is adjacent to v with $f(v) = h_2$ and to u_v with $f(u_v) = h_1$, we find that $f(w_v) \in \{h_1, h_2\}$. Because $w_{v'}$ is adjacent to v' with $f(v') = h_3$ and to $u_{v'}$ with $f(w_{v'}) = h_0$, we find that $f(w_{v'}) \in \{h_0, h_3\}$. Recall that $f(W) \neq \{h_2, h_3\}$. Then, because w_v and $w_{v'}$ are adjacent, we find that $f(w_v) = h_1$ and $f(w_{v'}) = h_0$. Suppose that $x_{vv'}$ exists. Then $x_{vv'}$ is adjacent to vertices v with $f(v) = h_2$, to v' with $f(v') = h_3$, to u_v with $f(u_v) = h_1$ and to w_v with $f(w_{v'}) = h_0$. This is not possible. Hence $x_{vv'}$ cannot exist. This means that v, v' are both of type a, both of type b, both of type c or both of type d. If v, v' are both of type a or both of type d, then $f(h_0) \in \{h_2, h_3\}$, which is not possible because $h_0 \in U$ and $f(U) \in \{h_0, h_1\}$. If v, v' are both of type b, we apply the same reasoning with respect to h_1. Suppose that v, v' are both of type c. Then both v and v' are adjacent to h_2. This means that $f(h_2) \in \{h_2, h_3\}$. Then either $\{f(v), f(h_2)\} = \{h_2, h_3\}$ or $\{f(v'), f(h_2)\} = \{h_2, h_3\}$. Hence, by considering either the edge vh_2 or $v'h_2$ we return to a previous case. We conclude that $st \neq vv'$.

If $st = v'x_{vv'}$ then $f(v) \in \{h_2, h_3\}$, because v is adjacent to v' and $x_{vv'}$. Then one of vv' or $vx_{vv'}$ maps to h_2h_3, and we return to a previous case. Hence, we obtain $st \neq v'x_{vv'}$. If $st = w_{v'}x_{vv'}$ then $f(v') \in \{h_2, h_3\}$, because v' is adjacent to w' and $x_{vv'}$. Then one of vv' or $v'x_{vv'}$ maps to h_2h_3, and we return to a previous case. Hence, we obtain $st \neq w_{v'}x_{vv'}$. If $st = x_{vv'}h_2$ then $f(w_{v'}) \in \{h_2, h_3\}$, because $w_{v'}$ is adjacent to $x_{vv'}$ and h_2. Because $f(W) \neq \{h_2, h_3\}$, we find that $f(w_{v'}) = f(h_2)$. Then $w_{v'}x_{vv'}$ is mapped to h_2h_3, and we return to a previous case. Hence, $st \neq x_{vv'}h_2$. We conclude that $f(W) = \{h_2, h_3\}$.

We now show that $f(h_0) \neq f(h_1)$. Suppose that $f(h_0) = f(h_1)$. By symmetry we may assume that $f(h_0) = f(h_1) = h_0$. Because $f(U) = \{h_0, h_1\}$, there exists a vertex u_v of type u with $f(u_v) = h_1$. Because w_v with $f(w_v) \in \{h_2, h_3\}$ is adjacent to u_v, we obtain $f(w_v) = h_2$. Because h_2 with $f(h_2) \in \{h_2, h_3\}$ is adjacent to h_1 with $f(h_1) = h_0$, we obtain $f(h_2) = h_3$. However, then y_v is adjacent to h_0 with $f(h_0) = h_0$, to u_v with $f(u_v) = h_1$, to w_v with $f(w_v) = h_2$, and to h_2 with $f(h_2) = h_3$. This is not possible. Hence, $f(h_0) \neq f(h_1)$. By symmetry, we may assume that $f(h_0) = h_0$ and $f(h_1) = h_1$. Because h_2 is adjacent to h_1 with $f(h_1) = h_1$, and $f(h_2) \in \{h_2, h_3\}$ we obtain $f(h_2) = h_2$. Because h_3 is adjacent to h_0 with $f(h_0) = h_0$, and $f(h_3) \in \{h_2, h_3\}$ we obtain $f(h_3) = h_3$. Hence, f is a retraction from G'' to H, as desired. "$(iii) \Rightarrow (iv)$" and "$(iv) \Rightarrow (iii)$" follow from the equivalence between statements 3 and 6 in Proposition 1, after recalling that G'' has diameter 2 due to Lemma 2.   □

Our main result follows from Lemmas 2 and 3, in light of Theorem 2 (note that all constructions may be carried out in polynomial time).

Theorem 3. *The* Surjective *H-*Homomorphism *problem is* **NP**-*complete even for graphs of diameter 2 with a dominating non-edge.*

References

1. Brandstädt, A., Dragan, F.F., Le, V.B., Szymczak, T.: On stable cutsets in graphs. Discrete Appl. Math. 105, 39–50 (2000)
2. Bulatov, A.: Tractable conservative constraint satisfaction problems. In: Proceedings of LICS 2003, pp. 321–330 (2003)
3. Bulatov, A., Krokhin, A., Jeavons, P.G.: Classifying the complexity of constraints using finite algebras. SIAM Journal on Computing 34, 720–742 (2005)
4. Cameron, K., Eschen, E.M., Hoáng, C.T., Sritharan, R.: The complexity of the list partition problem for graphs. SIAM J. Discrete Math. 21, 900–929 (2007)
5. Cook, K., Dantas, S., Eschen, E.M., Faria, L., de Figueiredo, C.M.H., Klein, S.: $2K_2$ vertex-set partition into nonempty parts. Discrete Math. 310, 1259–1264 (2010)
6. Chvátal, V.: Recognizing decomposable graphs. J. Graph Theory 8, 51–53 (1984)
7. Dantas, S., de Figueiredo, C.M.H., Gravier, S., Klein, S.: Finding H-partitions efficiently. RAIRO-Theoret. Inf. Appl. 39, 133–144 (2005)
8. Dantas, S., Maffray, F., Silva, A.: $2K_2$-partition of some classes of graphs. Discrete Applied Mathematics (to appear)
9. Feder, T., Hell, P.: List homomorphisms to reflexive graphs. J. Combin. Theory Ser. B 72, 236–250 (1998)
10. Feder, T., Hell, P., Klein, S., Motwani, R.: List partitions. SIAM J. Discrete Math. 16, 449–478 (2003)
11. de Figueiredo, C.M.H.: The P versus NP-complete dichotomy of some challenging problems in graph theory. Discrete Applied Mathematics (to appear)
12. Fleischner, H., Mujuni, E., Paulusma, D., Szeider, S.: Covering graphs with few complete bipartite subgraphs. Theoret. Comput. Sci. 410, 2045–2053 (2009)
13. Golovach, P.A., Paulusma, D., Song, J.: Computing vertex-surjective homomorphisms to partially reflexive trees. In: Kulikov, A., Vereshchagin, N. (eds.) CSR 2011. LNCS, vol. 6651, pp. 261–274. Springer, Heidelberg (2011)
14. Hell, P., Nešetřil, J.: On the complexity of H-colouring. Journal of Combinatorial Theory, Series B 48, 92–110 (1990)
15. Ito, T., Kamiński, M., Paulusma, D., Thilikos, D.M.: Parameterizing Cut Sets in a Graph by the Number of Their Components. In: Dong, Y., Du, D.-Z., Ibarra, O. (eds.) ISAAC 2009. LNCS, vol. 5878, pp. 605–615. Springer, Heidelberg (2009)
16. Ito, T., Kaminski, M., Paulusma, D., Thilikos, D.M.: On disconnected cuts and separators. Discrete Applied Mathematics (to appear)
17. Martin, B., Paulusma, D.: The Computational Complexity of Disconnected Cut and 2K2-Partition, http://arxiv.org/abs/1104.4779
18. Teixeira, R.B., Dantas, S., de Figueiredo, C.M.H.: The external constraint 4 nonempty part sandwich problem. Discrete Applied Mathematics 159, 661–673 (2011)
19. Vikas, N.: Computational complexity of compaction to reflexive cycles. SIAM Journal on Computing 32, 253–280 (2002)
20. Vikas, N.: Compaction, Retraction, and Constraint Satisfaction. SIAM Journal on Computing 33, 761–782 (2004)
21. Vikas, N.: A complete and equal computational complexity classification of compaction and retraction to all graphs with at most four vertices and some general results. J. Comput. Syst. Sci. 71, 406–439 (2005)
22. Whitesides, S.H.: An algorithm for finding clique cut-sets. Inform. Process. Lett. 12, 31–32 (1981)

Reducing the Search Space of Resource Constrained DCOPs

Toshihiro Matsui[1], Marius Silaghi[2], Katsutoshi Hirayama[3],
Makoto Yokoo[4], Boi Faltings[5], and Hiroshi Matsuo[1]

[1] Nagoya Institute of Technology, Gokiso-cho Showa-ku Nagoya 466-8555, Japan
{matsui.t,matsuo}@nitech.ac.jp
[2] Florida Institute of Technology, Melbourne FL 32901, United States of America
msilaghi@fit.edu
[3] Kobe University, 5-1-1 Fukaeminami-machi Higashinada-ku Kobe 658-0022, Japan
hirayama@maritime.kobe-u.ac.jp
[4] Kyushu University, 744 Motooka Nishi-ku Fukuoka 819-0395, Japan
yokoo@is.kyushu-u.ac.jp
[5] Swiss Federal Institute of Technology, Lausanne (EPFL),
CH-1015 Lausanne, Switzerland
boi.faltings@epfl.ch

Abstract. Distributed constraint optimization problems (DCOPs) have
been studied as a basic framework of multi-agent cooperation. The Resource Constrained DCOP (RCDCOP) is a special DCOP framework
that contains n-ary hard constraints for shared resources. In RCDCOPs,
for a value of a variable, a certain amount of the resource is consumed.
Upper limits on the total use of resources are defined by n-ary resource
constraints. To solve RCDCOPs, exact algorithms based on pseudo-trees
employ virtual variables whose values represent use of the resources. Although, virtual variables allow for solving the problems without increasing the depth of the pseudo-tree, they exponentially increase the size
of search spaces. Here, we reduce the search space of RCDCOPs solved
by a dynamic programming method. Several boundaries of resource use
are exploitable to reduce the size of the tables. To employ the boundaries, additional pre-processing and further filtering are applied. As a
result, infeasible solutions are removed from the tables. Moreover, multiple elements of the tables are aggregated into fewer elements. By these
modifications, redundancy of the search space is removed. One of our
techniques reduces the size of the messages by an order of magnitude.

1 Introduction

Distributed constraint optimization problems (DCOPs) [3,5,7,8,11,13] have been
studied as a basic framework of multi-agent cooperation. With DCOPs, the status of agents and the relationship between agents are represented as discrete
optimization problems that consist of variables, constraints and functions. Elements of the problem are placed at various agents. Therefore, the problem is
solved using a distributed search algorithm. The Resource Constrained DCOP

J. Lee (Ed.): CP 2011, LNCS 6876, pp. 576–590, 2011.
© Springer-Verlag Berlin Heidelberg 2011

(RCDCOP) [9] is a special DCOP framework that contains n-ary hard constraints for shared resources. In RCDCOPs, for a value of a variable, a certain amount of the resource is consumed. Upper limits on the total use of resources are defined by n-ary resource constraints. The resource constraint can be considered as a kind of global constraint. Several problems in multi-agent systems that consume shared energy or budget can be formalized as RCDCOPs. On the other hand, basic solvers for DCOPs that handle binary constraints/functions have to be extended to support the n-ary constraints of RCDCOPs. To solve RCDCOPs, exact algorithms based on pseudo-trees employ virtual variables whose values represent use of the resources. The virtual variables allow for solving the problems without increasing the depth of the pseudo-tree. However, the virtual variables exponentially increase the size of search spaces. Therefore, reducing the search space is an important problem. In a previous study [6], a dynamic programming method for a specialized class of RCDCOP has been proposed. The problem is motivated by a kind of power network and its characteristics are exploited to reduce the tables of the dynamic programming. Since their study mainly aims to handle this specific problem, several dedicated structures and constraints that represent feeder trees on the power supply network are employed in their formalism and solver. Therefore, their problem definition and representation is different from the RCDCOP in [9]. On the other hand, our contribution is to show several methods to reduce the search space of the RCDCOPs. Several issues about that point will be discussed in Section 2.4.

Here, we reduce the search space of RCDCOPs solved by a dynamic programming method. Several boundaries of resource use are exploitable to reduce the size of the tables. To employ the boundaries, additional pre-processing and further filtering is applied. As a result, infeasible solutions are removed from the tables. Moreover, multiple elements of the tables are aggregated into fewer elements. By these modifications, redundancy of the search space is removed. The rest of the paper is organized as follows. In Section 2, we give the background for the study, and related works are addressed. Our proposed methods are described in Sections 3. The methods are experimentally evaluated in Section 4, and we conclude our study in Section 5.

2   Background

2.1   Resource Constrained DCOP

A DCOP is defined by a set A of agents, a set X of variables and a set F of binary functions. Agent i has its own variable x_i. x_i takes a value from a discrete finite domain D_i. The value of x_i is controlled by agent i. The cost of an assignment $\{(x_i, d_i), (x_j, d_j)\}$ is defined by a binary function $f_{i,j}(d_i, d_j) : D_i \times D_j \to \mathbb{N}_0$. The goal is to find a global optimal solution $\mathcal{A}$ that minimizes the global cost function:

$$\sum_{f_{i,j} \in F,\ \{(x_i,d_i),(x_j,d_j)\} \subseteq \mathcal{A}} f_{i,j}(d_i, d_j). \tag{1}$$

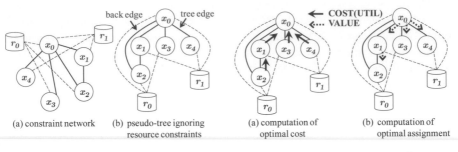

Fig. 1. Resource constrained DCOP   Fig. 2. Computation on pseudo-trees

In a RCDCOP, resource constraints are added to a DCOP. Resource constraints are defined by a set R of resources and a set U of resource requirements. A resource $r \in R$ has its capacity defined by $C(r) : R \to \mathbb{N}_0$. Each agent requires resources according to its assignment. For an assignment (x_i, d_i) and a resource r, a resource requirement is defined by $u_i(r, d_i) : R \times D_i \to \mathbb{N}_0$. For each resource, the total amount of requirements must not exceed its capacity. The global resource constraint is defined as follows: $\forall r \in R, \sum_{u_i \in U, \{(x_i, d_i)\} \subseteq \mathcal{A}} u_i(r, d_i) \leq C(r)$. The resource constraint takes arbitrary arity. In the following, we may use the notation $u_i(r, d)$ even if x_i does not relate to resource r. In that case, the values of $u_i(r, d)$ are always zero. An example of RCDCOP that consists of 5 variables and 2 resources is shown in Figure 1(a). In this example, x_0, x_2 and x_3 are constrained by resource r_0. x_0, x_1 and x_4 are constrained by resource r_1.

2.2   Pseudo Tree Ignoring Resource Constraints

Several exact solvers for DCOPs depend on a variable ordering defined by a pseudo-tree [4,13,14]. The edges of the original constraint network are categorized into tree edges and back edges of the pseudo-tree. The tree edges are the edges of the spanning tree. The other edges are back edges. The tree edges represent the partial order relation between the two variables. In the following, vertices, variables, and agents may not be strictly distinguished. The following notations are used:

- $prnt_i$: the parent variable of x_i.
- $Chld_i$: the set of child variables of x_i.
- $NbrU_i$ [1]: the partial set of neighboring ancestor variables of x_i. The variables in $NbrU_i$ are related to x_i by constraints.
- $AncSt_i$: the partial set of descendent-neighboring ancestor variables of x_i. Let x_k denote a variable in $AncSt_i$. For at least one variable x_j that is contained in the pseudo-tree rooted at x_i, x_k has the relationship $x_k \in NbrU_j$.

There is no edge between different subtrees. By employing this property, search processing can be performed in parallel.

---

[1]   In related works, $NbrU_i$ is called "pseudo parent".

When a DCOP contains an n-ary constraint, variables related to the constraint have to be placed in a single path of a pseudo-tree. That increases the depth of the pseudo-tree. Moreover, each variable depends on other ancestor variables related with the n-ary constraint. In such pseudo-trees, it is difficult to apply dynamic programming [13] because the size of its table exponentially increases with the arity of the n-ary constraint.

By employing certain properties of the resource constraints, search can be performed based on pseudo-trees that ignore resource constraints. An example of such pseudo-trees is shown in Figure 1(b). Because resource constraints relate to different subtrees of the pseudo tree, an additional scheme is necessary to share the resources between the subtrees. A known solution is based on virtual variables whose values represent use of the resources. Solvers process original variables and virtual variables based on the pseudo-trees. However, the virtual variables exponentially increase the size of search spaces. Therefore, reducing the search space arises as a new problem. In a previous study [6], a dynamic programming based solver called DPOP that employs a similar scheme has been applied to a specialized class of RCDCOPs. Its search space is reduced using several methods and characteristics of the problem.

2.3   DPOP with Virtual Variables

In this study, we focus on DPOP for general RCDCOPs. As the first step, we outline the cost computation using pseudo-trees without resource constraint [11,13]. In the following expressions, it is assumed that agents have already received both variables' values and cost values from other agents. Agent i's computation is based on the partial solution s_i of $AncSt_i$. s_i is called *context*. S_i denotes the set of all s_i. The local cost $\delta_i(s_i \cup \{(x_i, d)\})$ for context s_i and value d of variable x_i is defined as $\delta_i(s_i \cup \{(x_i, d)\}) = \sum_{(x_j, d_j) \in s_i, \, j \in NbrU_i} f_{i,j}(d, d_j)$. Optimal cost $g^*(s_i)$ for context s_i and the subtree routed at x_i are recursively defined as follows.

$$g_i^*(s_i) = \min_{d \in D_i} g_i(s_i \cup \{(x_i, d)\}) \qquad (2)$$

$$g_i(s_i \cup \{(x_i, d)\}) = \delta_i(s_i \cup \{(x_i, d)\}) + \sum_{j \in Chld_i} g_j^*(s_j) \text{ s.t. } s_j \subseteq (s_i \cup \{(x_i, d)\})$$

In dynamic programming, the computation of the optimal cost value of subtrees is performed from leaf agents to a root agent. Then the optimal assignments are decided from a root agent to leaf agents. There is no iterative processing. However, the size of the memory and of the messages is exponential in the induced width of the pseudo-trees because each agent i simultaneously computes $g^*(s_i)$ for all assignments of the variables contained in $AncSt_i$. When the globally optimal cost $g_r^*(\phi)$ is computed for the root variable x_r, r determines the optimal assignment of its variable. Similarly, an optimal solution for the rest of the problem can be computed in a top-down manner.

Message paths of the dynamic programming are shown in Figure 2. The processing consists of two phases of message propagation as follows.

1 $W_i \leftarrow \phi$.
2 **foreach** $s_i \cup \{(x_i, d)\}$ s.t. $s_i \in S_i, d \in D_i$ {
3    $g \leftarrow \delta_i(s_i \cup \{(x_i, d)\})$. $sv \leftarrow \phi$.
4   **foreach** r in R_i {
5   **if**(r relates to x_i){ $sv \leftarrow sv \cup \{(v_r, u_i(r, d))\}$. }**else**{ $sv \leftarrow sv \cup \{(v_r, 0)\}$. } }
6   computeTable($s_i \cup \{(x_i, d)\}$, g, sv, $Chld_i$).
7 }
8 **end**.
9 computeTable($s_i \cup \{(x_i, d)\}$, g, sv, $Chld$){
10   **if**($Chld$ is empty){
11   **if**(all assignments of sv are feasible){
12   **if**(x_i is root){ $sv \leftarrow \phi$. }
13   **if**(W_i contains element w s.t. $(t(w)_{\downarrow S} = s_i \wedge t(w)_{\downarrow V} = sv)$){
14         $g(w) \leftarrow \min(g(w), g)$. }**else**{ $W_i \leftarrow W_i \cup \{(s_i \cup sv, g)\}$. } }
15   }**else**{
16     $x_j \leftarrow$ the most prior element of $Chld$.
17   **foreach** w s.t. $w \in W_j, t(w)_{\downarrow S} \in s_i \cup \{(x_i, d)\}$ {
18       $sv' \leftarrow \phi$.
19   **foreach** (v_r, u) in sv {
20   **if**($t(w)_{\downarrow V}$ contains element $(v_r, u'))$){ $sv' \leftarrow sv' \cup \{(v_r, u + u')\}$.
21   }**else**{ $sv' \leftarrow sv' \cup \{(v_r, u)\}$. } }
22   computeTable($s_i \cup \{(x_i, d)\}$, $g + g(w)$, sv', $Chld \backslash \{x_j\}$).
23   } }
24 }

Fig. 3. Computation of table W_i

1. Computation of the globally optimal cost: as shown above, the globally optimal cost is computed in a bottom up manner. Using a COST message[2], each agent sends a table of optimal costs and assignments for the subtree rooted at the agent's variable. In the case of RCDCOP, the table also contains information on resource use.
2. Computation of globally optimal assignments: the globally optimal assignments are determined from the root agent to leaf agents. Using VALUE messages, each agent sends the optimal assignments. Additionally, the upper limit of resource use for each subtree is also sent.

In the case of RCDCOP, use of resources is represented using virtual variables. Let us denote by v_r the virtual variable for resource r. v_r takes a value between 0 and $C(r)$. Agent i knows a set R_i of resources that relates to the subtree routed at x_i. R_i can be computed by a bottom-up preprocessing as follows.

$$R_i = \{r | r \text{ relates to } x_i\} \cup \bigcup_{x_j \in Chld_i} R_j \qquad (3)$$

We also assume that agent i knows the capacity of the resources contained in R_i. That can be simultaneously propagated with R_i. Each agent i maintains values of virtual variables for R_i. When x_i takes a value d_i, one can think that the use of the resource r is aggregated as $v_{r,i} = u_i(r, d_i) + \sum_{x_j \in Chld_i} v_{r,j}$. However, this

---

[2] To represent the minimizing problem, we prefer to use COST instead of UTIL.

```
1  s_i^* ← φ. CSV_i^* ← φ. g_i^* ← ∞.
2  foreach (v_r, u) in sv*_{prnt_i,i}{ C(r) ← u. }
3  foreach d in D_i {
4    g ← δ_i(s*_{prnt_i} ∪ {(x_i, d)}). sv ← φ.
5    foreach r in R_i {
6      if(r relates to x_i){ sv ← sv ∪ {(v_r, u_i(r, d))}. }else{ sv ← sv ∪ {(v_r, 0)}. } }
7    computeAssign(s*_{prnt_i} ∪ {(x_i, d)}, g, sv, φ, Chld_i).
8  }
9  end.
10 computeAssign(s_i ∪ {(x_i, d)}, g, sv, CSV, Chld){
11   if(Chld is empty){
12     if(all assignments of sv are feasible){
13       if(g < g_i^*){ s_i^* ← s_i. CSV_i^* ← CSV. g_i^* ← g. } }
14   }else{
15     x_j ← the most prior element of Chld.
16     foreach w s.t. w ∈ W_j, t(w)_{↓S} ∈ s_i ∪ {(x_i, d)} {
17       sv' ← φ.
18       foreach (v_r, u) in sv {
19         if(t(w)_{↓V} contains element (v_r, u')){ sv' ← sv' ∪ {(v_r, u + u')}.
20         }else{ sv' ← sv' ∪ {(v_r, u)}. } }
21       computeAssign(s_i ∪ {(x_i, d)}, g + g(w), sv', CSV ∪ {(j, t(w)_{↓V})}, Chld\{x_j}).
22     } }
23 }
```

Fig. 4. Computation of optimal assignment s_i^* and cost allocation CSV_i^* for children

equation is insufficient because it ignores the assignments of pseudo parents' original variables in the subtree. Note that the use of resources depends on the assignments of the original variables. Moreover, the problem can contain multiple resources. Therefore, assignments of original and virtual variables have to be handled together.

For agent i, the combination T_i that represents the assignments S_i of original variables and the assignments SV_i of virtual variables is defined as $T_i = \{s \cup sv | s \in S_i, sv \in SV_i\}$. For an element t of T_i, the notations $t_{↓S}$ and $t_{↓V}$ define parts of t. $t_{↓S}$ is an element of S_i. $t_{↓V}$ is an element of SV_i. For the description of the computation, we use a set W_i of pairs (t, g). W_i represents the table of dynamic programming in agent i. t is an element of T_i. g is a cost value that is aggregated for t. We decompose an element $w = (t, g)$, into its components using notations $t(w)$ and $g(w)$.

When agent i has received all W_j from each child j such that $x_j \in Chld_i$, element (t, g) of W_i is computed as shown in Figure 3. Intuitively, this procedure computes the minimum value of g for each t. Each assignment t and its cost value g are recursively expanded and merged to W_i. Note that all combinations of assignments from children are explored. That is necessary, because the combinations implicitly represent different contexts of original variables. For an element (t, g) of W_i, if at least one assignment of a virtual variable v_r for resource r exceeds capacity $C(r)$, the element is infeasible. Therefore such an element is eliminated before the element is merged to W_i. This efficiently reduces the size of the search spaces when resource constraints are relatively tight. The assignment of x_i is removed from t when (t, g) is merged to W_i. To compute a minimum global cost value, assignments of resource variables are removed at the root agent. If the problem is globally infeasible, the W_i of the root agent i is empty. Otherwise, only one element is contained in the W_i of the root agent. Therefore, the element represents the optimal cost.

Once the computation of the optimal cost value propagates to the root agent, the root agent determines its optimal assignment, namely one whose cost corresponds to the optimal cost. Then, the optimal assignment is sent to child agents, and similar computations are propagated to leaf agents. When the agent i determines its optimal assignment, the computation of costs is also performed to evaluate assignments. The computation of the optimal assignments s_i^* is shown in Figure 4. While the computation resembles the computation of costs in Figure 3, there are three major differences. The first is that the assignment of $AncSt_i$ is fixed to the optimal assignment $s_{prnt_i}^*$ that is received from its parent node. The second difference is that, for the optimal assignment, the set CSV_i^* of assignments of virtual variables for all child agents is computed. The assignments $(j, sv_{i,j}^*)$ in CSV_i^* are sent to the child agent j with optimal assignment $s_{prnt_j}^*$. The last difference is that, by using assignments $sv_{prnt_i,i}^*$ of the virtual variables received from the parent, the maximum use of each resource for the optimal assignment is limited. Such computation of the virtual variables is similar to the "child allocation invariant" in ADOPT [11], which is an exact solver based on pseudo-trees.

2.4   Related Works

An extended DPOP algorithm for a specialized class of RCDCOPs has been proposed in [6]. Basically, their problem domain is the allocation of feeder trees on a power supply network. In their DCOP representation, each variable has a structure that represents a (partial) feeder tree. The variable also represents use of a resource. There are several hard constraints for the feeder trees. For each assignments of variables (i.e. partial feeder tree), a cost value is computed. Please see [6] for more detailed explanations. In our study, several similar approaches are applied to general RCDCOPs. The similar points of both methods are as follows. In [6], an operator called Composite Project generates a tuple of assignments. That resembles tuples of assignments of original/virtual variables in RCDCOPs, as shown in Section 2.3. Also, in [6], a pruning called Dominated Pruning is employed to integrate partial solutions. Moreover, an assignment that represents a feeder tree that has all leaves is replaced by its root node. That resembles removing assignments in COST(UTIL) propagation in DPOP for RCDCOPs, as shown in Section 2.3. On the other hand, several points are different between the two studies. Basically, the representation in [6] highly depends on the problem domain of feeder trees although several parts may be translated to generic RCDCOP. For example, the aggregation for assignments of variables that represents a (partial) feeder tree is different from the one in generic RCDCOPs. A single resource (i.e. electrical power) is considered in [6] while multiple resources are considered in RCDCOP. In [6], hard constraints and dedicated structures

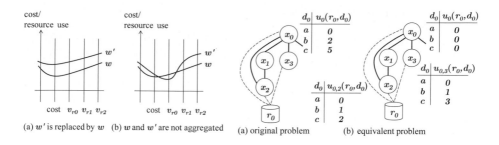

Fig. 5. Aggregation of assignments   Fig. 6. Moving evaluation of resource use

represent specific properties of the problem, including Kirchhoff's law and the capacity of the power line, while in RCDCOPs the hard constraints model the total amount of available resources.

In this study, we investigate several methods to reduce the size of the search space of DPOP. Our main contribution consists in a way of applying a set of techniques to reduce the size of tables in a variant of DPOP for RCDCOPs. While several ideas are based on related works, they are re-formalized for the RCDCOPs and the solver. Also, they can be consistently integrated. These techniques can be applied to the ADOPT-based solver shown in [9]. In [9], authors propose an efficient method that employs upper bounds on the use of resources. It can be considered as a simple version of the method shown in Section 3.5, that employ feasible solutions. However, its effect has been relatively small. We clarified the effect of the feasible solution and integrated it with other methods that employ infeasible solutions. In [1,12], extended classes of DCOPs that contains slightly different types of resource constraints are shown. Although modifications to handle the different types of the resource constraints are necessary, the methods shown in our study will be effective for those classes of problems.

3   Reducing Search Spaces

The basic algorithm shown in Section 2.3 already reduces search spaces by eliminating infeasible solutions. Here, we show additional methods to reduce the search spaces. These methods consist of preprocessing and/or add-on processing. In the following, to clarify the essence of these computations, we prefer to use recursive expressions. Actually, the preprocessing can be represented as a top-down or bottom-up distributed computations. All methods shown in this section can be consistently combined. While the method shown in Sections 3.3 and 3.4 modify evaluation functions of resource use, they do not contradict each other. The method in Section 3.5 extends the method in Sections 3.2. Several possible combinations of the methods are evaluated in Section 4.

3.1   Root Nodes of Resources

In the basic algorithm, assignments of virtual variables are removed at the root node of the pseudo-tree. If a resource only relates to variables in a subtree, the virtual variable for the resource can be removed at the root agent of that subtree. This approach resembles the method shown in [9]. For this modification, additional processing is applied to the computation of R_i shown in Expression 3. When agents compute R_i in a bottom-up manner, the number $n_{r,i}^R$ of variables that relate to resource r in the subtree routed at i is simultaneously computed as follows.

$$n_{r,i}^R = \sum_{x_j \in Chld_i, r \in R_j} n_{r,j}^R + \begin{cases} 1 \ x_i \text{ relates to } r \\ 0 \text{ otherwise} \end{cases} \tag{4}$$

To evaluate whether $n_{r,i}^R$ reaches the arity of the resource constraint for r, at least one agent that directly relates to the resource r leaks the arity. Then, the arity of r is also propagated in a bottom-up manner. If $n_{r,i}^R$ equals the arity of r, then the agent i is the root of resource r. Therefore, r, $n_{r,i}^R$ and the arity of r are eliminated when R_i is sent to i's parent. The limitation of R_i is effective when multiple resources relate to a small number of variables in a part of the pseudo-tree.

3.2   Aggregation of Assignments

In the computation shown in Figure 3, elements of W_i are aggregated when their assignments are completely equal. However, by employing a monotonicity of the assignments, more effective aggregation can be applied. Let w and w' denote elements of W_i. For two assignments $t(w)_{\downarrow V}$ and $t(w')_{\downarrow V}$, a relation $\succeq$ is defined as follows.

$$t(w)_{\downarrow V} \succeq t(w')_{\downarrow V} \text{ iff } \forall (v_r, u) \in t(w)_{\downarrow V} \forall (v_r, u') \in t(w')_{\downarrow V}, u \geq u' \tag{5}$$

$t(w)_{\downarrow V} \succeq t(w')_{\downarrow V}$ means that the resource use of $t(w')$ does not exceed the use of $t(w)$. By using this relation, the following aggregation is applied when $t(w)_{\downarrow S} = t(w')_{\downarrow S}$:

1. $t(w)_{\downarrow V} = t(w')_{\downarrow V} \wedge g(w) = g(w')$: w and w' are completely equal. They are integrated as shown in Figure 3.
2. $t(w)_{\downarrow V} \preceq t(w')_{\downarrow V} \wedge g(w) \leq g(w')$: w' is replaced by w.
3. $t(w)_{\downarrow V} \succeq t(w')_{\downarrow V} \wedge g(w) \geq g(w')$: w is replaced by w'.
4. otherwise: both w and w' are stored.

The first condition has the highest priority. This aggregation is based on the fact that if there is an assignment whose cost and resource uses are smaller than for other assignments, then the other assignments are redundant for minimizing costs. Figure 5 shows the concept of the aggregation. In this figure, (a) and (b) represent the second and last conditions. The effects of the aggregation depend on characteristics of assignments. If many assignments have the relationship of monotonicity, many assignments can be aggregated to a smaller number of assignments.

3.3   Global Lower Bounds of Resource Use

When the minimum value of resource use is greater than zero, a common amount of the use can be extracted as the global lower bound of the resource use. This modification is a simple case of soft arc consistency [2,10]. Because RCDCOPs in this work contain only unary functions of resource use, each agent only needs to consider the assignment of its variable. The lower bound $u_{i,r}^L$ for agent i's use of resource r is computed as follows: $u_{i,r}^L = \min_{d \in D_i} u_i(r, d)$. Then, function u_i is modified to subtract $u_{i,r}^L$. For all d in D_i, $u_i(r, d) \leftarrow u_i(r, d) - u_{i,r}^L$.

Values of $u_{i,r}^L$ are summed in a bottom-up manner. Agent i computes a total amount $u_{i,r}^{L*}$ of a lower bound of resource use as $u_{i,r}^{L*} = u_{i,r}^L + \sum_{x_j \in Chld_i} u_{j,r}^{L*}$. The computation propagates to the root agent of resource r. In the root agent i of r, the capacity of r is modified to subtract $u_{i,r}^{L*}$: $C(r) \leftarrow C(r) - u_{i,r}^{L*}$. Then, to update the capacity in descendant agents, $C(r)$ is propagated in a top-down manner. This computation implicitly propagates resource use among different subtrees. Because the capacities of resources are reduced, the number of infeasible solutions can be increased. Therefore, the number of elements in W_i can be reduced. Obviously, if $u_{i,r}^L$ is zero in all agents, the processing has no effect.

3.4   Moving Evaluation of Resource Use

To improve the efficiency of the pruning based on feasible solutions, the pruning should be applied in lower levels of the pseudo-trees. If the lowest agent that is related to a resource evaluates all assignments for the resource, that increases the number of infeasible assignments detected in the agent. This approach is similar to the serialization technique of the variables for n-ary constraints [1,12]. However, the extra assignments increase the size of the search space.

Instead of that, similar techniques can be applied for two variables that are directly related with an original cost function. Because assignments of the higher variable are already contained in assignments for $AncSt_i$ of the lower variable x_i, the modification does not increase the size of the search space. The evaluation of resource use is moved as follows. In the first phase, a bottom-up computation is performed to compute the set $X_{r,i,j}^L$ of lower peer variables of variable x_i. Each variable in $X_{r,i,j}^L$ directly relates to x_i with both a cost function and a resource r. For the bottom-up computation, descendant agent j of i maintains $X_{r,i,j}^L$ and propagates $X_{r,i,j}^L$ to its parent using the following steps.

1. $X_{r,i,j}^L \leftarrow \cup_{x_k \in Chld_j, k \text{ has } X_{r,i,k}^L} X_{r,i,k}^L$
2. if $(X_{r,i,j}^L$ is empty$) \wedge (x_j$ relates to x_i by a cost function$) \wedge (x_j$ and x_i relate to resource $r)$, then $X_{r,i,j}^L \leftarrow \{x_j\}$

As a result of the computation, agent i knows $X_{r,i,i}^L$, which represents lower peer variables of variable x_i. If there are lower peer variables in multiple subtrees, $X_{r,i,i}^L$ contains multiple variables. Then, for all d in D_i, agent i decides a share of resource use $u_{i,j}(r, d)$ for each variable x_j in $X_{r,i,i}^L$. In this study, the values of

$u_{i,j}(r,d)$ are shared by peer variables as evenly as possible. The value of $u_{i,j}(r,d)$ is subtracted from the function u_i of resource use. Then $u_{i,j}(r,d)$ is sent to x_j. Agent j aggregates $u_{i,j}(r,d)$ when the assignment of the virtual variable for r is computed. An example is shown in Figure 6. In this example, the resource use of x_0 is completely subtracted. Then, the resource use is shared with agents 2 and 3. These agents evaluate the use of the resource instead of agent 0.

3.5 Feasible Solutions

In the above, infeasible or redundant solutions are considered to reduce the number of elements in W_i. If capacities of resources are sufficient, it is unnecessary to consider any resource constraints. However, the effectiveness of the pruning methods based on infeasible solutions decreases when the capacity of resources increases. In completely feasible problems, they have no effects. Therefore, in easy problems, considering feasible solutions is necessary to reduce the number of elements of W_i. To detect the feasibility in a subtree, resource use in other parts of the pseudo-tree is necessary. Because we do not use iterative search processing for each context, upper bounds of the resource use are computed in a pre-processing. In the first step, a bottom-up processing is performed to compute the upper bounds in subtrees. Similarly to the computation shown in Section 3.3, the upper bounds $u_{i,r}^U$ for agent i and resource r are computed as $u_{i,r}^{U*} = \max_{d \in D_i} u_i(r,d) + \sum_{x_j \in Chld_i} u_{j,r}^{U*}$. Then, upper bounds $u_{i,r}^{U+}$ of resource use in other parts of the subtree are computed as follows.

$$u_{i,r}^{U+} = \max_{d \in D_{prnt_i}} u_{prnt_i}(r,d) + u_{prnt_i,r}^{U+} + \sum_{x_j \in Chld_{prnt_i} \setminus \{i\}} u_{j,r}^{U*} \qquad (6)$$

For element w of W_i, the feasibility of assignment $t(w)_{\downarrow V}$ is evaluated using $u_{i,r}^{U+}$. For all (v_r, u) in $t(w)_{\downarrow V}$, if $u + u_{i,r}^{U+} \leq C(r)$, then w is feasible.

Now the aggregation of the elements w and w' of W_i is generalized. When $t(w)_{\downarrow S} = t(w')_{\downarrow S}$, the feasibility of w and w' is evaluated. If both of w and w' are feasible, they are aggregated as follows.

1. $g(w) = g(w')$: one of w and w' is replaced by the other one.
2. $g(w) < g(w')$: w' is replaced by w.
3. $g(w) > g(w')$: w is replaced by w'.

Otherwise, the aggregation shown in Section 3.2 is applied.

In contrast to the pruning based on infeasible solutions, the aggregation of feasible solutions has almost no effect if resource constraints are relatively tight. Both effects are complementary. When the upper bound $u_{i,r}^{U+}$ of resource use is applied with the method shown in Section 3.4, $u_{i,r}^{U+}$ has to be revised to exclude the moved use of resource r.

3.6 Correctness and Complexity

The computation of the proposed methods basically resembles conventional methods based on pseudo-trees. Only redundant solutions are eliminated from

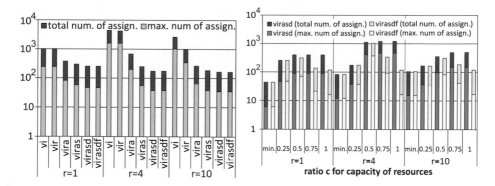

Fig. 7. Effects of methods ($n=20$, $u=5$, $c=0.25$)

Fig. 8. Effects of feasibility ($n=20$, $u=5$)

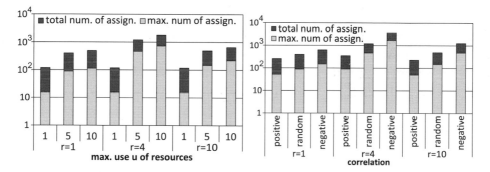

Fig. 9. Influence of combination of resource use ($n=20$, $c=1$, virasd)

Fig. 10. Influence of correlation between cost and resource use ($n=20$, $c=1$, virasd)

the tables of the dynamic programming. Therefore, the correctness of the solver is the same as for the conventional methods. In the worst case, the size of the table of agent i is $\prod_{j \in AncSt_i} |D_j| \cdot \prod_{r \in R_i} (C(r) + 1)$. Although the increments of computation depend on implementations, the total number of comparisons of two solutions in generating a table is up to the product of the number of solutions in the generated table and the number of solutions that are enumerated in the computation of dynamic programming. The encoding of the dynamic programming table of the new algorithm consists of the full list of assignments. It is true that the size of compact tables which are encoded as an array of all cost values that are sorted by an order of solutions can be smaller than the size of tables using the list of assignments, when the pruning is insufficient. On the other hand, if the pruning leaves less than 1 / (size of an assignment) of the assignments, the size of our tables is smaller than the size of compact tables.

4 Evaluation

The proposed methods are experimentally evaluated using random RCDCOPs. The RCDCOPs consist of n ternary variables, $1.1n$ binary cost functions and

Table 1. Influence of size of problems (total num. of assign., u=5, virasdf, incomplete results are not shown)

r	n	c				
		min.	0.25	0.5	0.75	1
1	20	44	254	314	137	118
	40	98	1219	1364	338	289
	60	181	5658	5695	801	733
	80	270	21859	23045	1979	1774
4	20	82	175	1041	235	119
	40	181	1302	26606	1522	289
	60	327	31607	-	16907	733
	80	490	-	-	-	1774
10	20	105	165	313	186	120
	40	237	701	-	8334	297
	60	434	-	-	-	736
	80	847	-	-	-	1780

r n-ary resource constraints. We prefer a very low density of cost functions, because we focus on the influence of the resource constraint. In the case that there are multiple resources, a resource relates to n/r agents. Although each agent consumes only one resource, agents have to maintain use of resources that relate to a part of pseudo-tree including the agent. Cost values of each cost function $f_{i,j}$ were randomly set from the interval $[1,5]$ based on a uniform distribution. For each value of the variables and each related resources, an amount in interval $[1,u]$ is consumed. To ensure the minimum resource use n for feasible solutions, resource use for one value of each variable is forced to the minimum of 1. Using parameter c, capacity $c \cdot u \cdot (n/r)$ of each resource is determined. Parameters u and c are common for all resources in a problem instance. The constraint networks are randomly generated. Results for fifty problem instances are averaged. We limited the maximum number of assignments in a table to 10^5. If the size of a table exceeded the limit value, the computation was aborted. The following methods are evaluated:

 - vi(a basic algorithm in Section 2.3. It removes infeasible assignments),
 - vir(vi with removing resource assignments in Section 3.1),
 - vira(vir with aggregation of assignments in Section 3.2),
 - viras(vira with extracting global lower bounds of resource use in Section 3.3),
 - virasd(viras with moving the evaluation of resource use in Section 3.4),
 - virasdf(vrasd with detection of feasibility in Section 3.5).

Figure 7 shows the size of tables. The total number of assignments, and the maximum number of assignments in an agent are evaluated. The resource constraints of these problems are relatively tight. Therefore, the methods viras and virasd that employ infeasibility are effective. virasd is better than other partial combinations. On the other hand, virasdf has almost no effect. vir efficiently eliminates virtual variable in the case of $r = 10$, because several resources are locally shared by few agents. Figure 8 shows effects of the feasibility. virasdf reduces the size of the table in loosely constrained problems.

The influence of combinations of resource use is shown in Figure 9. Although these problems are completely feasible, virasd does not exploit this feasibility.

Table 2. Approximate method (total num. of assign. and (error ratio), $u=10$, $c=0.5$, incomplete results are not shown)

r	n	e					
		0	1	2	3	10	20
1	20	313 (1)	263 (1.03)	229 (1.09)	203 (1.13)	160 (1.31)	159 (1.32)
	40	1265 (1)	945 (1.04)	775 (1.09)	652 (1.16)	452 (1.38)	446 (1.40)
	60	5349 (1)	3811 (1.03)	2890 (1.09)	2324 (1.16)	1252 (1.40)	1229 (1.43)
	80	17380 (1)	11806 (1.03)	8456 (1.09)	6585 (1.15)	3081 (1.39)	2881 (1.43)
4	20	1390 (1)	879 (1.03)	650 (1.07)	464 (1.11)	298 (1.30)	295 (1.31)
	40	-	17831	7346	4556	1079	1035
	60	-	-	-	47176	6801	5251
	80	-	-	-	-	-	24724
10	20	406 (1)	316 (1.02)	268 (1.04)	238 (1.07)	195 (1.18)	194 (1.19)
	40	-	-	13414	7647	1910	1633
	60	-	-	-	-	17451	15707

Therefore, the effect of the aggregation of assignments is emphasized. The effect decreases when summation of resource use takes various values.

The aggregation of the assignments depends on a monotonicity between the assignments. We attempted to emphasize this characteristics by sorting resource use $u_i(r,d)$. For each value d_i of variable x_i, a heuristic value $h_i^*(d_i) = \sum_j \max_{d_j \in D_j} f_{i,j}(d_i, d_j)$ is computed. Then, the resource uses are sorted to have positive or negative correlation with $h_i^*(d_i)$. The result shown in Figure 10 can be considered as an influence of the correlation. It can be considered that there are relatively small opportunities of the aggregation in the case of the negative correlation.

Table 1 shows results when the size of problems is changed. The scalability depends on the effects of the pruning methods. In complex problems, relaxation or approximation in the integration of solutions will be necessary. As a simple method, we can allow for a bounded error in the aggregation. If errors are allowed in the aggregation of the assignments of virtual variables, incorrect feasible or infeasible assignments may be inferred. Therefore, we tolerate the bounded errors for cost values. With the parameter e of the error, the second condition in Section 3.2 is modified as follows.

2. $t(w)_{\downarrow V} \preceq t(w')_{\downarrow V} \wedge g(w) \leq g(w') + e$: w' is replaced by w.

Similarly, the third condition can be modified. The modification abandons opportunities to reduce cost values by e. To avoid diffusion of the errors in W_i, only new assignments can be aggregated with other assignments existing in the table. Table 2 shows the effects of the approximating approaches when parameter e is changed. In this experiment, we used parameter $u = 10$ that increases the difficulty of the problems especially in the cases of multiple-resources. The size of tables is reduced in exchange for the errors.

5   Conclusions

In this study, we investigated several methods to reduce the search space of RCDCOPs solved by dynamic programming methods. The proposed methods are based on several boundaries of resource use. Infeasible or suboptimal solutions are removed from the tables. Multiple elements of the tables are aggregated into fewer elements. The feasibility of the assignments is also exploited and the solvers are generalized to process completely feasible problems. By these modifications, redundancy of the search space is removed.

Future work will include applying these efficient methods to other classes of resource constrained DCOPs, developing sophisticated criteria for the approximation methods, and conducting evaluation in practical problems.

Acknowledgments. This work was supported in part by KAKENHI, a Grant-in-Aid for Scientific Research (B), 23300060.

References

1. Bowring, E., Tambe, M., Yokoo, M.: Multiply constrained distributed constraint optimization. In: AAMAS 2006, pp. 1413–1420 (2006)
2. Cooper, M., Schiex, T.: Arc consistency for soft constraints. Artificial Intelligence 154(1-2), 199–227 (2004)
3. Farinelli, A., Rogers, A., Petcu, A., Jennings, N.R.: Decentralised coordination of low-power embedded devices using the max-sum algorithm. In: AAMAS 2008, pp. 639–646 (2008)
4. Freuder, E.C.: A sufficient condition for backtrack-bounded search. Journal of the ACM 32(14), 755–761 (1985)
5. Junges, R., Bazzan, A.L.C.: Evaluating the performance of DCOP algorithms in a real world, dynamic problem. In: AAMAS 2008, pp. 599–606 (2008)
6. Kumar, A., Faltings, B., Petcu, A.: Distributed constraint optimization with structured resource constraints. In: AAMAS 2009, pp. 923–930 (2009)
7. Maheswaran, R.T., Tambe, M., Bowring, E., Pearce, J.P., Varakantham, P.: Taking DCOP to the real world: Efficient complete solutions for distributed multi-event scheduling. In: Kudenko, D., Kazakov, D., Alonso, E. (eds.) AAMAS 2004. LNCS (LNAI), vol. 3394, pp. 310–317. Springer, Heidelberg (2005)
8. Mailler, R., Lesser, V.: Solving distributed constraint optimization problems using cooperative mediation. In: Kudenko, D., Kazakov, D., Alonso, E. (eds.) AAMAS 2004. LNCS (LNAI), vol. 3394, pp. 438–445. Springer, Heidelberg (2005)
9. Matsui, T., Silaghi, M., Hirayama, K., Yokoo, M., Matsuo, H.: Resource constrained distributed constraint optimization with virtual variables. In: AAAI 2008, pp. 120–125 (2008)
10. Matsui, T., Silaghi, M., Hirayama, K., Yokoo, M., Matsuo, H.: Directed soft arc consistency in pseudo trees. In: AAMAS 2009, pp. 1065–1072 (2009)
11. Modi, P.J., Shen, W., Tambe, M., Yokoo, M.: Adopt: Asynchronous distributed constraint optimization with quality guarantees. Artificial Intelligence 161(1-2), 149–180 (2005)
12. Pecora, F., Modi, P., Scerri, P.: Reasoning about and dynamically posting n-ary constraints in ADOPT. In: DCR at AAMAS 2006 (2006)
13. Petcu, A., Faltings, B.: A scalable method for multiagent constraint optimization. In: IJCAI 2005, pp. 266–271 (2005)
14. Schiex, T.: A note on CSP graph parameters. Technical report 1999/03, INRA (1999)

Proving Symmetries by Model Transformation[*]

Christopher Mears[1], Todd Niven[1], Marcel Jackson[2], and Mark Wallace[1]

[1] Faculty of IT, Monash University, Australia
[2] Department of Mathematics, La Trobe University, Australia
{Chris.Mears,Todd.Niven,Mark.Wallace}@monash.edu,
M.G.Jackson@latrobe.edu.au

Abstract. The presence of symmetries in a constraint satisfaction problem gives an opportunity for more efficient search. Within the class of matrix models, we show that the problem of deciding whether some well known permutations are model symmetries (solution symmetries on every instance) is undecidable. We then provide a new approach to proving the model symmetries by way of model transformations. Given a model M and a candidate symmetry σ, the approach first syntactically applies σ to M and then shows that the resulting model $\sigma(M)$ is semantically equivalent to M. We demonstrate this approach with an implementation that reduces equivalence to a sentence in Presburger arithmetic, using the modelling language MiniZinc and the term re-writing language Cadmium, and show that it is capable of proving common symmetries in models.

1 Introduction

Solving a constraint satisfaction problem (CSP) can be made more efficient by exploiting the symmetries of the problem. In short the efficiency is gained by omitting symmetric regions of the search space. The automated detection of symmetries in CSPs has recently become a topic of great interest. However, the majority of research into this area has been directed at individual instances of CSPs where the exact set of variables, constraints and domains are known before the detection takes place. The most accurate and complete methods for detecting solution symmetries are computationally expensive and so limited in the size of problem they can tackle (e.g. [10,8,1]).

A CSP *model* represents a class of CSPs and is defined in terms of some parameters. An *instance* is generated from the model by assigning values to the parameters. There are automatic symmetry detection methods for CSP models, as described in [13,14]. However they are problem-specific or can only detect a very small collection of simple symmetries, namely piecewise value and piecewise variable interchangeability.

[*] All four authors were supported under Australian Research Council's Discovery Projects funding scheme (project number DP110102258 for the first, second and fourth authors and project number DP1094578 for the third author).

J. Lee (Ed.): CP 2011, LNCS 6876, pp. 591–605, 2011.

Mears et al. [9] proposed a broader framework to detect model symmetries which only requires explicitly detecting solution symmetries on small instances. The framework can be described as performing the following steps:

1. Detect symmetries on some collection of small instances of the model,
2. Lift the detected symmetries to model permutations,
3. Filter the model permutations to keep only those that are likely to be symmetries for all instances of the model (candidate model symmetries),
4. Prove that the selected model permutations are indeed symmetries for every instance of the model (model symmetries).

Mears et al. [9] developed an automated implementation of this framework on matrix models (i.e. the variables of each instance have an underlying matrix structure) that tackles steps 1, 2 and 3 whilst preliminary attempts at 4, using graph techniques, can be found in [7]. These graph theoretic approaches were, however, ad hoc and not automated. Automating step 4 can be approached by way of automated theorem proving as in [6], where the authors represent their models in existential second order logic and use a theorem proving application to verify that a candidate model symmetry is a model symmetry. Whilst potentially quite powerful, this approach requires a large amount of work to translate a practical model into the required form.

The distinction between constraint symmetry and solution symmetry proves to be critical. This paper studies the problem of proving whether a given candidate symmetry is a model symmetry. One result that we provide is that, in general, deciding whether or not some well known candidate symmetries are model "solution" symmetries is undecidable and indeed undecidable under quite weak assumptions on the models. These results consider models that can be viewed as tiling problems and then utilises the standard method of encoding Turing machines into tiling problems introduced by Robinson [12].

From the other direction, when restricting to constraint symmetries, we provide a new method that can prove when a given candidate symmetry is a model symmetry by way of model transformations. Specifically, if we apply our candidate symmetry to our model and obtain an "equivalent" model in return, then we can deduce that our candidate symmetry is indeed a model symmetry (and indeed a constraint symmetry on every instance of the model). We implement this idea by attempting to reduce the problem of model equivalence to a first order sentence in some decidable theory.

Our implementation uses MiniZinc as the modelling language and Cadmium to perform model transformations and our method focuses on proving simple matrix symmetries (swapping dimensions, inverting dimensions and permutations of a dimension) on arbitrary matrix models. Two benefits of our method are:

1. we act directly on the MiniZinc model, being the same model that could be used in solving a given instance, and
2. the theoretical steps to transform the model are closely matched to the Cadmium rules that transform the MiniZinc model.

We present an application of our method to a set of well known bench marks.

2   Background

A CSP is a tuple (X, D, C) where X represents a set of variables, D a set of values and C a set of constraints. For a given CSP, a *literal* is defined to be an ordered pair $(x, d) \in X \times D$ and represents the expression $x = d$. We denote the set of all literals of a CSP P by $lit(P)$ and define $var(x, d) = x$, for all $(x, d) \in lit(P)$. An *assignment* A is a set of literals. An *assignment over a set of variables* $V \subseteq X$ has precisely one literal (x, d) for each variable $x \in V$. An assignment over X is called a *complete* assignment.

A constraint c is defined over a set of variables, denoted by $vars(c)$, and specifies a set of *allowed* assignments over $vars(c)$. An assignment A over $V \subseteq X$ *satisfies* constraint c if $vars(c) \subseteq V$ and the set $\{(x, d) \in A \mid x \in vars(c)\}$ is allowed by c. A *solution* is a complete assignment that satisfies every constraint in C.

A *solution symmetry* σ of a CSP P is a permutation on $lit(P)$ that preserves the set of solutions [1], i.e. σ is a bijection from $lit(P)$ to $lit(P)$ that maps solutions to solutions. A permutation f on the set of variables X induces a permutation σ_f on the set of literals $lit(P)$ in the obvious way, i.e. $\sigma_f(x, d) = (f(x), d)$. A *variable symmetry* is a permutation of the variables whose induced literal permutation is a solution symmetry. Similarly, a *value symmetry* is a solution symmetry $\sigma_f(x, d) = (x, f(d))$, for some permutation f on D. If d is a set, then f is a permutation on all possible elements of d. A *variable-value* symmetry is a solution symmetry that is neither a variable nor a value symmetry.

The *microstructure complement* of a CSP P is a graph with vertices $X \times D$, and a hyperedge between a set of vertices if that set represents an assignment disallowed by some constraint, or disallowed because it assigns distinct values to one variable. A *constraint symmetry* of a CSP P is an automorphism of the microstructure of P [1]. Note that every constraint symmetry of a problem is also a solution symmetry.

A CSP *model* is a parametrised form of CSP, where the overall structure of the problem is specified, but particular details such as size are omitted. A *model permutation* σ of a CSP model M is a function that takes an instance P of the model M and produces a permutation on $lit(P)$, i.e. $\sigma(P)$ is a permutation on $lit(P)$, for all instances P of M. A *model (constraint) symmetry* σ of a CSP model M is a model permutation such that $\sigma(P)$ is a solution (constraint) symmetry, for all instances P of M. For the purposes of this paper, a *matrix model* is a model M such that the variables of M form a single n-dimensional matrix of the following form:

$$\{x[i_1, i_2, \ldots, i_n] \mid 1 \le i_j \le d_j \text{ for all } 1 \le j \le n\},$$

where the d_j's indicate the size of each dimension and may be determined by the parameters of the model. See [3] and [4] for more on matrix models.

The models that we will be interested in are those that have parameters consisting of integers $p_1, p_2, \ldots, p_n$ and a fixed number of quantified constraints of the form

$$(\forall k_1, k_2, \ldots k_l)\Phi(k_1, k_2, \ldots, k_l, p_1, p_2, \ldots, p_n)$$
$$G(\{x[I_1], x[I_2], \ldots, x[I_m] \mid \Psi(I_1, I_2, \ldots, I_m, k_1, k_2, \ldots, k_l, p_1, p_2, \ldots, p_n)\}) \qquad (\star)$$

where

- G is a constraint (possibly global),
- each I_i represents a list of r (not necessarily distinct) variables for some fixed r (note that we do not allow nested indexing), and
- Φ and Ψ are arithmetic formulæ, with free variables among those within the corresponding parenthesis.

Example 1. The *N-Queens* problem of size N is to construct an $N \times N$ board where we are required to place N mutually non-attacking queens.

Below is a model of the Boolean N-queens problem of size N, where N is the parameter of the model. The model uses N^2 zero-one variables – one for each combination of row and column – where the variable $x[i, j]$ is one if and only if row i and column j has a queen placed.

$$X[N] = \{x[i, j] \mid i, j \in R = \{1, 2, \ldots, N\}\}$$
$$D[N] = \{0, 1\}$$
$$C[N] = \{(\forall j \in R) \sum_{1 \le i \le N} x[i, j] = 1,$$

$$(\forall i \in R) \sum_{1 \le j \le N} x[i, j] = 1,$$

$$(\forall k \in \{3, \ldots, 2N - 1\}) \sum \{x[i, j] \mid i, j \in R, i + j = k\} \le 1,$$

$$(\forall k \in \{2 - N, \ldots, N - 2\}) \sum \{x[i, j] \mid i, j \in R, i - j = k\} \le 1\}.$$

This problem has many model symmetries; one of them is that the i and j dimensions can be interchanged (diagonal reflection of the square).

The quantified constraints in the above example are equivalent to those of $(\star)$. Indeed,

$$(\forall j \in R) \sum_{1 \le i \le N} x[i, j] = 1$$

from above is equivalent to

$$(\forall k)1 \le k \wedge k \le N \sum \{x[i, j] \mid 1 \le i \wedge i \le N \wedge j = k\} = 1,$$

where the constraint G in this case is the global constraint of the sum equaling 1.

3   Undecidability of Model Symmetries

In this section we show that two common permutations cannot be algorithmically recognised as solution symmetries of CSP models. More precisely we show that the class of CSP models (with a single 2-dimensional matrix variable x) admitting the given solution symmetry is not recursively enumerable. As the consequences of a proof system form a recursively enumerable set, a sort of incompleteness theorem follows: any proof system for proving the existence of solution symmetries from CSP models is incomplete. We prove this for the domain inversion symmetry and the dimension swap symmetry, though other cases (those in Section 4.1) can be treated using similar ideas.

Mancini and Cadoli [6] have provided similar undecidability results with respect to *problem specifications* which formulates classes of CSPs via scond order logic. The results given here differ in that we only require a single matrix of variables, the constraints have extremely simple structure and the models relate to natural geometric constraint satisfaction problems of independent interest (symmetric tilings of the plane for example).

We consider CSP models related to tiling grids by square tiles with matching conditions dictating which tile can be placed in horizontal adjacency and which can be placed in vertical adjacency. This situation may be viewed as a kind of directed graph except with two binary relations $\sim_h$ and $\sim_v$ (representing allowed horizontal and vertical adjacencies resp.) instead of one.

The basic problem of tiling an $N \times N$ grid with tiles from $\{0, \ldots, n-1\}$ is as follows (here $\mathtt{x[i,j]} = k$ represents tile k being placed at position (i,j)).

$$X[N] = \{x[i,j] \mid 0 < i, j \leq N - 1\}$$
$$D[N] = \{0, 1, \ldots, n - 1\}$$
$$C[N] = \{(\forall i, j \in \{0, \ldots, N - 1\}, i > 0)x[i - 1, j] \sim_h x[i,j]$$
$$(\forall i, j \in \{0, \ldots, N - 1\}, j > 0)x[i, j - 1] \sim_v x[i,j]\}$$

It is well known that the problem of deciding if the full positive quadrant of the plane may be tiled starting from an arbitrary finite $\mathcal{T}$ is undecidable. This is usually proved by a simple encoding of a Turing machine program into the tiles so that successfully tiled rows of the plane correspond to successful steps of computation by the Turing machine. If the Turing machine eventually halts then the tiling cannot be completed. We exploit this idea by instead allowing completion of the tiling, but only in a way that violates some symmetry always present in nonhalting situations.

The results are proved using variations of this CSP model. Note that failure to exhibit a given solution symmetry is a Σ_1^0 property. Thus it remains to show Σ_1^0-hardness. We reduce the Halting Problem to the failure of a solution symmetry.

3.1   Basic Strategy

The arguments are extensions of the following idea. We use an easy variation of the Halting problem for deterministic Turing machine programs: given a Turing machine program T with no halting states, but with some distinguished state q, is the state q ever reached when T is started on the blank tape? This problem is Σ_1^0-complete.

Step 1. The program T can be encoded into a set of tiles $\mathcal{T}_T$ in a standard way (see Robinson [12] or Harel [5] for example). Successive tiled rows correspond to successive configurations of the machine running T. Let us assume that tile 0 encodes the Turing machine in initial state reading the blank symbol and that tile 1 encodes a transition into state q. Then the following problem is Σ_1^0-complete: given T, is there a number N and a tiling of the $N \times N$ grid using $\mathcal{T}_T$ with tile 0 at position $(0,0)$ and involving placement of tile 1?

Step 2. Duplicate some part (or all of) $\mathcal{T}_T$, creating the solution symmetry of interest. Then adjust the adjacency conditions applying to tile 1 and compared to its duplicate so that the solution symmetry is violated in sufficiently large models if and only if state q is reached by T.

3.2 Swapping of Dimension: $x[i,j] \mapsto x[j,i]$

Aside from the domain structure and the input parameter N, the constraints used in this construction involve only order and successor on indices. First, the tiling created at step 1 of the basic strategy is adjusted so that it exhibits the constraint symmetry $x[i,j] \mapsto x[j,i]$: moreover in every solution, the value of $x[i,j]$ is equal to the value of $x[j,i]$, and in no solution can tile 1 be placed on the diagonal. Step 2 of the basic strategy involves duplication of the distinguished tile 1: say that tile 2 is the exact duplicate of tile 1, with every adjacency condition for 1 applying identically to tile 2. Add one further constraint c dictating that tile 1 cannot be placed above the diagonal and that tile 2 cannot be placed below the diagonal.

If the Turing machine program T does not reach state q, then tile 1 cannot be placed, and the final constraint c is redundant. In this case the dimension swapping solution symmetry holds. However if T does eventually reach state q, then for sufficiently large N, a tiling of the $N \times N$ grid will involve, for some $i > j$, placement of 1 at some position $x[i,j]$ and 2 at position $x[j,i]$. This violates the solution symmetry.

3.3 Inversion of Domain: $x[i,j] \mapsto n - 1 - x[i,j]$

Aside from the domain structure and the input parameter N, the constraints used in this construction involve only successor on indices. Let us assume that the tiling created at step 1 of the basic strategy has tiles $0, \ldots, n-1$. For step 2 we duplicate these tiles to produce tiles $0, \ldots, n-1, n, \ldots, 2n-1$, with tile $i \leq n-1$ corresponding to tile $2n-1-i$: there are no adjacencies allowed between tiles from $0, \ldots, n-1$ and those from $n, \ldots, 2n-1$, but within these two blocks, the adjacency patterns are identical (except in reverse order).

Weaken the constraint $x[0,0] = 0$ to $x[0,0] \in \{0, 2n-1\}$: this CSP model exhibits inversion of domain as a constraint symmetry, and every solution corresponds to a tiling of an $N \times N$ grid with either the tiles $0, \ldots, n-1$ or the tiles $n, \ldots, 2n-1$. Now remove all adjacency capabilities for tile $2n-2$ (the duplicate of the special tile 1): so $2n-2$ cannot be placed. The inversion of domain solution symmetry can hold if and only if no solution involves placement of tile 1, which is equivalent to program T reaching state q.

4   Proving Symmetries by Model Transformation

Motivated by the matrix model permutations investigated in [9] (i.e. dimension swap, dimension inversion and dimension permutations), we describe an automated method that is capable of proving when such permutations are indeed model constraint symmetries. Specifically, given a common matrix permutation σ on the variables of a model M, we prove that σ is a symmetry of M by showing that $\sigma(M)$ is semantically equivalent to M. We say that a quantified constraint c in a model M is equivalent to a quantified constraint c' in the model $\sigma(M)$ if, for every instance of M, the quantified constraint c is equal to c' in the corresponding instance of $\sigma(M)$. Note that we are concerned here with "constraint symmetries" in contrast to the previous section where we found that it is undecidable to determine if such permutations are model solution symmetries.

Given a model with a set of quantified constraints C, and a symmetry σ, the method has the following steps:

1. Partition the quantified constraints into equivalence classes Θ_G where a quantified constraint $c \in \Theta_G$ if the constraint (refer to $(\star)$ in Section 2) in c is G.
2. Compute $\sigma(c)$ for each quantified constraint $c \in C$, giving the set $C' = \{\sigma(c) \mid c \in C\}$ with equivalence classes $\Theta'_G = \sigma(\Theta_G)$ (we assume that σ satisfies: if G is the constraint in c then G is also the constraint in $\sigma(c)$).
3. Normalise every quantified constraint $c' \in C'$ by reducing the expressions used as array indices to single variables by substitution.
4. For each bijection $\varphi : C \to C'$, that preserves the equivalence classes Θ_G, produce a sentence $\Phi_\varphi(c)$ (in some decidable theory) that expresses (if true) the equivalence of $c \in C$ with its matched constraint $\varphi(c) \in C'$.
5. Prove that the sentence $\bigvee_\varphi \bigwedge_{c \in C} \Phi_\varphi(c)$ is true.

Since item 4 requires two quantified constraints have the same constraint G before we attempt to match them, this method will not be complete for model constraint symmetries.

We now describe steps 2–4 in detail. We restrict ourselves to models in which the variables have integer, or set of integer, domains and the quantified constraints are of the form $(\star)$ where Φ and Ψ are first order formulæ in Presburger arithmetic (considered here to be the first order theory of $+, -, \leq, 0, 1$ over the integers; a well known decidable theory, see e.g. [2]).

4.1   Computing $\sigma(c)$

We consider the following five types of permutations acting on a matrix of variables (these include permutations from Section 3.)

- Swapping of dimensions j and k:
  $$x[i_1, i_2, \ldots, i_j, \ldots, i_k, \ldots, i_n] \mapsto x[i_1, i_2, \ldots, i_k, \ldots, i_j, \ldots, i_n],$$
  where $j < k$ and $d_j = d_k$,
- Inverting of dimension j:
  $$x[i_1, i_2, \ldots, i_j, \ldots, i_n] \mapsto x[i_1, i_2, \ldots, d_j - i_j + 1, \ldots, i_n],$$

- All permutations of dimension j:
  $x[i_1, i_2, \ldots, i_j, \ldots, i_n] \mapsto x[i_1, i_2, \ldots, \varphi(i_j), \ldots, i_n]$, where φ represents an arbitrary permutation on $\{1, 2, \ldots, d_j\}$,
- All permutations of values:
  $x[i_1, i_2, \ldots, i_n] \mapsto \varphi(x[i_1, i_2, \ldots, i_n])$, where φ represents an arbitrary permutation on the domain of values.
- Inverting of values:
  $x[i_1, i_2, \ldots, i_n] \mapsto u - (x[i_1, i_2, \ldots, i_n]) + l$, where l and u are the lower and upper bounds of the value domain.

These permutations appear commonly in matrix models. We define the quantified constraint $\sigma(c)$ by replacing each occurrence of $x[i_1, i_2, \ldots, i_n]$ in c with its image $\sigma(x[i_1, i_2, \ldots, i_n])$ as given above.

Example 2. One of the constraints of the N-Queens problem (Example 1) is:

$$(\forall k \in \{2 - N, \ldots, N - 2\}) \sum \{x[i, j] \mid i, j \in R, i - j = k\} \leq 1$$

where $R = \{1, 2, \ldots, N\}$. Let σ be the symmetry that swaps dimensions 1 and 2: $x[i, j] \mapsto x[j, i]$ By substituting $x[j, i]$ for $x[i, j]$, we see that $\sigma(c)$ is:

$$(\forall k \in \{2 - N, \ldots, N - 2\}) \sum \{x[j, i] \mid i, j \in R, i - j = k\} \leq 1$$

4.2   Substituting Complex Expressions

The goal of this step is to reduce all array accesses $x[e_1, e_2, \ldots, e_n]$, where each e_j is an expression, to the form $x[i_1, i_2, \ldots, i_n]$ where each i_j is a single variable (or constant) and the name of the variables i_j are in lexicographical order. In particular, the name of a variable i_j is lexicographically less than the name of i_k if $j < k$.

We introduce variables i_j that will ultimately take the place of the expressions e_j. We assume an expression e_j is a permutation f of a quantified variable q_j. For example, e_j could be the expression $\varphi(q_j)$ where $1 \leq q_j \leq N$ and φ is a permutation on the set $\{1, 2, \ldots, N\}$.

We introduce a new variable i_j and let $i_j = e_j$; therefore $q_j = f^{-1}(i_j)$. Using this identity, we replace all occurrences of q_j throughout the constraint with $f^{-1}(i_j)$ and as a result, e_j becomes i_j.

With the names of the introduced variables are generated in lexicographical order, we perform the substitution of the expressions e_j in order that they appear in the array access; this ensures that after simplification, the names of the i_j variables in $x[i_1, i_2, \ldots, i_n]$ are in lexicographical order.

Example 3. Consider again one of the constraints of the N-Queens problem (Example 1):

$$(\forall k \in \{2 - N, \ldots, N - 2\}) \sum \{x[i, j] \mid i, j \in R, i - j = k\} \leq 1$$

where $R = \{1, 2, \ldots, N\}$. Let σ be the symmetry that inverts dimension 1:

$$x[i, j] \mapsto x[N - i + 1, j]$$

By substituting $x[N - i + 1, j]$ for $x[i, j]$, we see that $\sigma(c)$ is:

$$(\forall k \in \{2 - N, \ldots, N - 2\}) \sum \{x[N - i + 1, j] \mid i, j \in R, i - j = k\} \leq 1$$

Let us now substitute the first expression in the array access. We introduce a new variables $\alpha = N - i + 1$ and $\beta = j$. We see that α is a function of the quantified variable i, and that $i = N - \alpha + 1$. Next, we replace each occurrence of the quantified variable i with $N - \alpha + 1$ and each occurrence of j with β, giving:

$$(\forall k \in S) \sum \{x[\alpha, \beta] \mid N - \alpha + 1, \beta \in R, N - \alpha + 1 - \beta = k\} \leq 1$$

where $S = \{2 - N, \ldots, N - 2\}$.

4.3   Equivalence via Presburger Forumlæ

In the previous subsections we described how we apply a candidate symmetry to the quantified constraints and to rewrite them into a reduced form that matches the form of one or more of the original constraints. We now want to determine if two model constraints are equivalent; if checking this can be formulated into a first order statement in some decidable theory, then a theorem prover can prove or disprove equivalence.

Example 4. In Example 3 we obtained the quantified constraint

$$(\forall k \in S) \sum \{x[\alpha, \beta] \mid N - \alpha + 1, \beta \in R \text{ and } N - \alpha + 1 - \beta = k\} \leq 1$$

where $R = \{1, \ldots, N\}$ and $S = \{2 - N, \ldots, N - 2\}$. Renaming α to i and β to j we obtain

$$(\forall k \in S) \sum \{x[i, j] \mid N - i + 1, j \in R \text{ and } N - i + 1 - j = k\} \leq 1.$$

It so happens that this quantified constraint is equivalent to one from the original model, namely

$$(\forall l \in \{3, \ldots, 2N - 1\}) \sum \{x[i, j] \mid i, j \in R \text{ and } i + j = l\} \leq 1.$$

Since the relations corresponding to the sum global constraint are identical in the two constraints whenever they have the same arity, the equivalence of the quantified constraints is equivalent to their scopes being the same; which corresponds to the following sentences holding in the integers:

$$(\forall i, j, N)(\forall k \in S)(N - i + 1 \in R) \wedge (j \in R) \wedge (N - i + 1 - j = k)$$
$$\Rightarrow (\exists l \in \{3, \ldots, 2N - 1\})(i \in R) \wedge (j \in R) \wedge (i + j = l)$$

and

$$(\forall i, j, N)(\forall l \in \{3, \ldots, 2N - 1\})(i \in R) \wedge (j \in R) \wedge (i + j = l)$$
$$\Rightarrow (\exists k \in S)(N - i + 1 \in R) \wedge (j \in R) \wedge (N - i + 1 - j = k)$$

These sentences are both true and can easily be seen to be equivalent to sentences in Presburger arithmetic.

4.4   An Exploration of N-Queens

In this section we further explore the model symmetry $\sigma(i,j) = (j,i)$ for the N-queens model described in Section 2.

This model involves two global constraints, both involving $\sum$. This gives us the two equivalence classes

$$\Theta_{(=1)} = \{(\forall j \in R) \sum_{1 \leq i \leq N} x[i,j] = 1, (\forall i \in R) \sum_{1 \leq j \leq N} x[i,j] = 1\} \text{ and}$$

$$\Theta_{(\leq 1)} = \{(\forall k \in \{3, \ldots, 2N-1\}) \sum \{x[i,j] \mid i,j \in R, i+j = k\} \leq 1,$$

$$(\forall k \in \{2-N, \ldots, N-2\}) \sum \{x[i,j] \mid i,j \in R, i-j = k\} \leq 1\}.$$

Applying σ to C we obtain $C' = \sigma(\Theta_{(=1)}) \cup \sigma(\Theta_{(\leq 1)})$, where

$$\sigma(\Theta_{(=1)}) = \{(\forall j \in R) \sum_{1 \leq i \leq N} x[j,i] = 1, (\forall i \in R) \sum_{1 \leq j \leq N} x[j,i] = 1\}$$

and

$$\sigma(\Theta_{(\leq 1)}) = \{(\forall k \in \{3, \ldots, 2N-1\}) \sum \{x[j,i] \mid i,j \in R, i+j = k\} \leq 1,$$

$$(\forall k \in \{2-N, \ldots, N-2\}) \sum \{x[j,i] \mid i,j \in R, i-j = k\} \leq 1\}.$$

Notice that, the constraints in C' are already essentially normalized (the indices are not lexicographically ordered, however this will not concern us), so we just need to find a bijection φ from C to C' that maps $\Theta_{(=1)}$ to $\sigma(\Theta_{(=1)})$ and $\Theta_{(\leq 1)}$ to $\sigma(\Theta_{(\leq 1)})$ such that for all $c \in C$, the quantified constraint $\varphi(c)$ is equivalent to c.

Let φ be a bijection from C to C' such that $\varphi(\Theta_{(=1)}) = \sigma(\Theta_{(=1)})$ and $\varphi(\Theta_{(\leq 1)}) = \sigma(\Theta_{(\leq 1)})$ (there are only 4 such maps). Since our quantified constraints are equivalent to those of the form $(\star)$, to determine if $c \in C$ is equivalent to $\varphi(c) \in C'$ amounts to proving sentences in Presburger like those we found in Section 4. In this case, the map φ that matches $c \in \Theta_{(\leq 1)}$ with its corresponding $\sigma(c)$ and matches $c \in \Theta_{(=1)}$ with $c' \in \Theta_{(\leq 1)}$ where $c' \neq \sigma(c)$, will produce true sentences, whilst all other φ will produce a sentence that is false.

5   Implementation

The transformations described in the previous section are implemented as Cadmium rules that act on a MiniZinc model. Before showing the details of our implementation, we describe briefly MiniZinc and Cadmium.

A MiniZinc model is a set of items. The items we are interested in are *constraint* items: it is these that we will be manipulating. Consider this example constraint item:

```
constraint forall (i,j in 1..N) ((sum (k in 1..N) (x[i,j,k]) = 1));
```

The token `constraint` introduces a constraint item. The `forall` indicates a quantification of some variable(s) over some range(s) of values. The first parenthesised part (`i,j in 1..n`) is called a generator and introduces the two variables that are to be quantified, and that both range over the set of integers from 1 to N inclusive. The body of the quantification is the second parenthesised part. The left hand side of the `=` constraint is a `sum` expression that introduces an index variable `k` which also ranges over the set 1 to N, and the expression as a whole evaluates to the sum of `x[i,j,k]` for a given `i` and `j` over those values of `k`. The right hand side is simply the constant 1. This constraint item therefore represents the constraint:

$$(\forall i,j \in R) \sum_{k \in R} x[i,j,k] = 1 \text{ where } R = \{1, 2, \ldots, N\}.$$

Since we only consider quantified constraints of the form (⋆) from Section 2, we only operate on a subset of Minizinc.

MiniZinc models are translated into terms to be manipulated by Cadmium rules. A Cadmium rule has the following form:

```
| Context \ Head <=> Guard | Body.
```

The meaning of a rule is that wherever `Head` occurs in the model it should be replaced by `Body`, but only if `Guard` is satisfied and if `Context` appears in the conjunctive context of `Head`. Roughly, the conjunctive context of a term is the set of all terms that are joined to it by conjunction. The `Context` and `Guard` parts are optional. Consider the following example Cadmium rules:

```
| -(-(X)) <=> X.
| constraint(C) <=> ID := unique_id("con") |
|                   (constraint_orig(ID,C) /\ constraint_to_sym(ID,C)).
```

The first rule implements a basic arithmetic identity. Identifiers such as `X` that begin with an uppercase letter are variables and can match any term. The head `-(-(X))` matches any term `X` that is immediately preceded by two negations, and such a term is replaced by the body `X`. The second rule is more complex. It matches any constraint item `constraint(C)` and replaces it with the conjunction `constraint_orig(ID,C) /\ constraint_to_sym(ID,C)`. The body of the constraint item `C` is duplicated into two items `constraint_orig(ID,C)` and `constraint_to_sym(ID,C)`, where the new names `constraint_orig` and `constraint_to_sym` are arbitrary and do not have any interpretation in MiniZinc. The guard `ID := unique_id("con")` calls the standard Cadmium function `unique_id` to supply a unique identifier to be attached to the constraints. This guard always succeeds; its purpose is to assign a value to `ID`.

Each step of the method corresponds to a set of Cadmium rules. In this section we show excerpts of the relevant parts of the Cadmium rules that implement these steps. Particular details of Cadmium will be explained as necessary.

5.1   Computing $\sigma(c)$

First, the constraints are duplicated and the symmetry is applied.

```
% Every constraint C is given a unique ID and is duplicated.
constraint(C) <=> ID := unique_id("con") |
                  (constraint_orig(ID,C) /\ constraint_to_sym(ID,C)).
% Every constraint in the duplicated set has the symmetry applied.
constraint_to_sym(ID,C) <=> constraint_sym(ID,sigma(C)).
```

The rule for **sigma** depends on the particular symmetry to be tested. Here are three possible definitions, corresponding to the first three kinds of permutation in Section 4.1. The "all-permutations" symmetries are represented by a syntactic construct that represents an arbitrary permutation.

```
% Dimensions 1 and 2 swap.  x[I,J,k] -> x[J,i,k]
sigma(aa(id("x"), t([I,J,K]))) <=> aa(id("x"), t([J,I,K])).
% Inverting of dimension 1:  x[i,j,k] -> x[n-i+1,j,k]
sigma(aa(id("x"), t([I,J,K]))) <=>
                        aa(id("x"), t([id("n")+(-I)+i(1),J,K])).
% All permutations of dimension 1:  x[i,j,k] -> x[phi(i),j,k]
sigma(aa(id("x"), t([I,J,K]))) <=>
                        aa(id("x"), t([permutation(phi,I),J,K])).

% Traverse the entire constraint term to apply the symmetry.
sigma(E) <=> '$arity'(E) '$==' 0 | E.
sigma(E) <=> [F|A] := '$deconstruct'(E) |
             '$construct'([F | list_map(sigma, A)]).
```

The term `aa(id("x"), t([I,J,K]))` represents a MiniZinc array access of the form `x[I,J,K]`, where I, J and K are arbitrary terms. The `id(S)` term represents an identifier with name S (a string), and the `t([...])` term represents a tuple (in this case the indices of the array).

The final two rules implement a top-down traversal of a term. Zero-arity terms, such as strings, are handled in the first rule: they are left unchanged. Compound terms, such as `constraint_to_sym(ID,C)`, are broken into their functor (`constraint_to_sym`) and their arguments (ID and C), and the symmetry is applied recursively to the arguments. The special `$deconstruct` and `$construct` functions respectively break a term into its parts or reconstruct a term from its parts.

5.2   Substituting Complex Expressions

In this step we find the expressions used in array accesses and replace them with single variables. Firstly, we find those expressions used in the array accesses.

```
% Extract array indices in the order that they are used.
% I,J,K may be complex expressions.
extract_indices(aa(_Array, t([I,J,K]))) <=> [I,J,K].
% (Traversal omitted.)
```

The result is a list of expressions that should be replaced with single variables. This list is passed as the first argument to the **rename_list** rule. Note that the order that the expressions were found in the array access is also the order in which they are renamed.

```
rename_list([], T) <=> T.
% Replace in term T the complex expression X with a fresh variable Y.
rename_list([X|Xs], T) <=>
        Y := unique_id("index") /\
        renaming(From, To) := compute_renaming(X, id(Y)) |
             substitute_ids([From 'maps_to' To], T).
```

The term X is the expression e_j to be replaced. The first part of the guard
Y := unique_id("index") generates the fresh variable i_j. As described in Section 4.2, we assume that $e_j = f(q_j)$ and replace all occurrences of q_j with
$f^{-1}(i_j)$. The rule compute_renaming computes this replacement $f^{-1}(i_j)$; the
standard Cadmium rule substitute_ids performs the replacement throughout
the term T.

The compute_renaming begins with the complex expression e_j as the first
argument, and the replacement variable i_j as the second argument. Parts of the
expression are moved to the second argument until the first argument is a single
variable (a bare identifier).

```
% The inverse of phi(X) is invphi(X).
compute_renaming(permutation(Phi, X), Y) <=>
  compute_renaming(X, inverse_permutation(Theta, Y)).

% If X is a global variable (e.g. a parameter), then move it to
% the right hand side.
% X + Y = Z  -->  Y = Z - X.
decl(int,id(X),_,global_var,_) \
  compute_renaming(id(X)+Y, Z) <=> compute_renaming(Y, Z + (-id(X))).
% -X = Y  ->  X = -Y.
compute_renaming(-(id(X)), Y) <=> compute_renaming(id(X), -(Y)).
% X + Y = Z  -->  X = Z - Y.
compute_renaming(id(X)+Y, Z) <=> compute_renaming(id(X), Z + -(Y)).
% -X + Y = Z  -->  X - Y = -Z.
compute_renaming(-(id(X))+Y, Z) <=> compute_renaming(id(X) + -(Y), -(Z)).

% When the left hand side is a mere identifier, the right hand side
% is the expression to replace it with.
compute_renaming(id(X), Y) <=> renaming(id(X), Y).
```

Note the use of the contextual guard decl(int,id(X),_,global_var,_) in the
second rule. This means that the identifier X is moved to the second argument
only if it is declared as a global variable somewhere in the conjunctive context
of the term being matched to the head. This contextual matching feature of
Cadmium allows parts of the model that occur in distant parts of the model to
be used when determining if a rule should apply. Also note that a pattern such
as id(X)+Y exploits the commutativity and associativity of addition; Cadmium
rearranges the expression as needed to make the pattern match.

5.3 Producing and Proving Presburger Formulæ

Finally, we attempt to match each quantified constraint in C with a quantified
constraint in C' that is in the same equivalence class Θ_G. Ensuring that the two
quantified constraints are in the same class is done by inspecting the structure of
the terms. The test for equivalence of the quantified constraints is then reduced
to a Presburger sentence. We extract from each quantified constraint the expressions for Φ and Ψ (see $(\star)$) and construct a Presburger sentence as described in
Section 4.3. The sentence is then passed to the Presburger solver *Omega*, which
uses the omega test [11] to prove or disprove the sentence.

For a given symmetry σ, if all constraints in $\sigma(C)$ can be shown to match a
constraint in C, then we state that σ is a model symmetry.

Table 1. Summary of Symmetries Proved

Problem	Variable Symmetries	
Latin Squares (Boolean)	`x[i,j,k]` $\mapsto$ `x[j,i,k]`	`x[i,j,k]` $\mapsto$ `x[i,k,j]`
	`x[i,j,k]` $\mapsto$ `x[N-i+1,j,k]`	`x[i,j,k]` $\mapsto$ `x[`φ`(i),j,k]`
	`x[i,j,k]` $\mapsto$ `x[i,`φ`(j),k]`	`x[i,j,k]` $\mapsto$ `x[i,j,`φ`(k)]`
Latin Squares (integer)	`x[i,j]` $\mapsto$ `x[j,i]`	`x[i,j]` $\mapsto$ `x[`φ`(i),j]`
	`x[i,j]` $\mapsto$ `x[i,`φ`(j)]`	`x[i,j]` $\mapsto$ φ`(x[i,j])`
Steiner Triples	`x[i,j]` $\mapsto$ `x[`φ`(i),j]`	`x[i,j]` $\mapsto$ `x[i,`φ`(j)]`
BIBD	`x[i,j]` $\mapsto$ `x[`φ`(i),j]`	`x[i,j]` $\mapsto$ `x[i,`φ`(j)]`
Social Golfers	`x[i,j]` $\mapsto$ `x[`φ`(i),j]`	`x[i,j]` $\mapsto$ `x[i,`φ`(j)]`
	`x[i,j]` $\mapsto$ φ`(x[i,j])`	
N-Queens (Boolean)	`x[i,j]` $\mapsto$ `x[j,i]`	`x[i,j]` $\mapsto$ `x[N-i+1,j]`
N-Queens (integer)	`x[i]` $\mapsto$ `x[N-i+1]`	`x[i]` $\mapsto$ `N-x[i]+1`

6   Results

We have tested our model transformation approach for symmetries found by
Mears et al. [9] in a suite of benchmark problems modelled in MiniZinc. Table 1
lists, for each problem, the symmetries that our implementation was able to
prove hold.

The results in Table 1 show that we can verify the existence of some common
variable and value symmetries in selected well-known matrix models. In addition,
we have tested symmetries that are known not to hold on the models and verified
that the implementation fails to prove them. Note that for the set variables in the
Social Golfers problem, the value symmetry acts on the elements of the set rather
than the sets themselves. The running time is negligible; for each benchmark,
the execution takes around one second.

Our implementation does not deal with variable-value symmetries that cannot
be expressed as a composition of a variable symmetry with a value symmetry
e.g. the solution symmetry σ taking the literal $x[i] = j$ to $x[j] = i$. One way
to step around this problem is to translate one's model into a Boolean model
(in an appropriate way), where now the value symmetries and variable-value
symmetries are simply variable symmetries.

7   Conclusion

The automatic detection of CSP symmetries is currently either restricted to problem instances, is limited to the class of symmetries that can be inferred from the
global constraints present in the model, or requires the use of (incomplete) automated theorem provers. This paper, whilst showing that the fundamental problem
is undecidable, provides a new way of proving the existence of model symmetries
by way of model transformations. We show that simple matrix permutations, such
as swapping and inverting dimensions, can be shown to be model symmetries using
this method. Pleasingly, our method has also been successful in showing that an
arbitrary permutation (which represents a large group of symmetries) applied to
a dimension of the matrix of variables is a model symmetry.

Acknowledgements. The authors would like to thank Leslie De Koninck and Sebastian Brand for assisting with the Cadmium development, and the G12 Project for supplying some of the MiniZinc models. We also thank Maria Garcia de la Banda for her invaluable suggestions.

References

1. Cohen, D., Jeavons, P., Jefferson, C., Petrie, K., Smith, B.: Symmetry definitions for constraint satisfaction problems. In: van Beek, P. (ed.) CP 2005. LNCS, vol. 3709, pp. 17–31. Springer, Heidelberg (2005)
2. Enderton, H.: A Mathematical Introduction to Logic, 2nd edn. Academic Press, Inc., London (2001)
3. Flener, P., Frisch, A.M., Hnich, B., Kiziltan, Z., Miguel, I., Walsh, T.: Matrix modelling. In: Proc. Formul 2001, CP 2001 Workshop on Modelling and Problem Formulation (2001)
4. Flener, P., Frisch, A., Hnich, B., Kiziltan, Z., Miguel, I., Pearson, J., Walsh, T.: Breaking row and column symmetries in matrix models. In: Van Hentenryck, P. (ed.) CP 2002. LNCS, vol. 2470, pp. 187–192. Springer, Heidelberg (2002)
5. Harel, D.: Effective transformations on infinite trees with applications to high undecidability, dominoes and fairness. J. ACM, 224–248 (1986)
6. Mancini, T., Cadoli, M.: Detecting and breaking symmetries by reasoning on problem specifications. In: Zucker, J.-D., Saitta, L. (eds.) SARA 2005. LNCS (LNAI), vol. 3607, pp. 165–181. Springer, Heidelberg (2005)
7. Mears, C.: Automatic Symmetry Detection and Dynamic Symmetry Breaking for Constraint Programming. Ph.D. thesis, Monash University (2009)
8. Mears, C., Garcia de la Banda, M., Wallace, M.: On implementing symmetry detection. Constraints 14 (2009)
9. Mears, C., Garcia de la Banda, M., Wallace, M., Demoen, B.: A novel approach for detecting symmetries in CSP models. In: Fifth International Conference on Integration of AI and OR Techniques in Constraint Programming for Combinatorial Optimization Problems (2008)
10. Puget, J.-F.: Automatic detection of variable and value symmetries. In: van Beek, P. (ed.) CP 2005. LNCS, vol. 3709, pp. 475–489. Springer, Heidelberg (2005)
11. Pugh, W.: The omega test: a fast and practical integer programming algorithm for dependence analysis. Communications of the ACM, 102–114 (1992)
12. Robinson, R.: Undecidability and nonperiodicity for tilings of the plane. Inventiones Math. 12, 177–209 (1971)
13. Roy, P., Pachet, F.: Using symmetry of global constraints to speed up the resolution of constraint satisfaction problems. In: ECAI 1998 Workshop on Non-binary Constraints (1998)
14. Van Hentenryck, P., Flener, P., Pearson, J., Agren, M.: Compositional derivation of symmetries for constraint satisfaction. In: Zucker, J.-D., Saitta, L. (eds.) SARA 2005. LNCS (LNAI), vol. 3607, pp. 234–247. Springer, Heidelberg (2005)

Value Ordering for Finding All Solutions: Interactions with Adaptive Variable Ordering

Deepak Mehta, Barry O'Sullivan, and Luis Quesada

Cork Constraint Computation Centre, University College Cork, Ireland
{d.mehta,b.osullivan,l.quesada}@4c.ucc.ie

Abstract. We consider the impact of value ordering heuristics on the search effort required to find all solutions, or proving none exist, to a constraint satisfaction problem in k-way branching search. We show that when the variable ordering heuristic is adaptive, the order in which the values are assigned to variables can make a significant difference in all measures of search effort. We study in depth an open issue regarding the relative merit of traditional value heuristics, and their complements, when searching for all solutions. We also introduce a lazy version of k-way branching and study the effect of value orderings on finding all solutions when it is used. This paper motivates a new and fruitful line of research in the study of *value ordering* heuristics for proving unsatisfiability.

1 Introduction

The entire search space of a constraint satisfaction problem (CSP) is explored when one is interested in finding all solutions, counting the number of solutions, or proving that the problem is unsatisfiable. The latter case may also appear as a sub-problem while solving a satisfiable problem when a globally inconsistent assignment to a subset of the variables is being explored. While most research in the area of search heuristics has focused on variable ordering, the question of determining which value should be assigned to the current variable has not received much attention. One reason is that it has been generally accepted that when the entire search space of a CSP is explored by a search algorithm that backtracks chronologically, the order in which the values are selected does not affect its search effort, e.g. the number of visited nodes, or the number of failures [4]. A well-known theorem states that this is true for both static and dynamic variable ordering heuristics [4]. In the case of search algorithms that perform *binary branching* recent work has shown that search effort is affected by the choice of value ordering [11]. However, that work was supportive of the conventional wisdom in the case of k-way branching.

In the case of search algorithms that perform *k-way branching* we advance the conventional wisdom related to the role of value ordering heuristics in the context of CSPs. We show that the conventional wisdom only applies when non-adaptive static/dynamic variable ordering heuristics are used. However, when adaptive dynamic variable ordering heuristics are used, value ordering heuristics can make a *significant* difference in the search-effort of a chronological backtrack

J. Lee (Ed.): CP 2011, LNCS 6876, pp. 606–620, 2011.

search algorithm, including the MAC [9] algorithm, even when the entire search space is explored using k-way branching. Furthermore, we show that static value ordering heuristics can make a difference in terms of the number of support checks for algorithms that maintain arc consistency during search even for k-way branching, even when there is no difference in the search effort. A preliminary investigation of how value ordering can affect the search to find all solutions is reported in [8]. Here, we present a more extensive investigation and explain how value ordering can affect search effort when using k-way branching.

We also introduce a *lazy version of k-way branching* whereby instead of selecting and assigning a value to a variable, a value is selected and *removed* from the domain of the selected variable. We show that postponing the assignment decision can help in reducing the number of failures. We further perform a detailed analysis and also demonstrate the effect of value ordering heuristics on the search effort when using lazy k-way branching. Finally, we perform a detailed study of value ordering heuristics and their corresponding anti-heuristics with respect to their relative efficiency. We demonstrate that one can dramatically out-perform the other depending on the context. A major contribution of this paper is that it motivates a new and fruitful line of research in the study of *value ordering* heuristics for proving unsatisfiability.

Although binary branching is theoretically more efficient than k-way branching [6], in practice the latter can be more efficient than the former on many classes of problem [1]. Our goal is not to compare the relative merits of different branching schemes but to show that value orderings can have a significant impact under all branching schemes. We show the various ways in which value ordering heuristics affect the various elements of search which contribute to an overall effect. The results presented in this paper complement and complete the analysis of the effects of value ordering on branching strategies introduced by Smith and Sturdy in [11] on binary branching.

2   Background

A CSP, $\mathcal{P}$, is a triple $(\mathcal{X}, \mathcal{C}, D)$ where $\mathcal{X}$ is a set of variables and $\mathcal{C}$ is a set of constraints. Each variable $X \in \mathcal{X}$ is associated with a finite domain, which is denoted by $D(X)$. We use n, d and e to denote the number of variables, the maximum domain size, and the number of constraints respectively. Each constraint is associated with a set of variables on which the constraint is defined. We restrict our attention to binary CSPs, where the constraints involve two variables. A binary constraint C_{XY} between variables X and Y is a subset of the Cartesian product of $D(X)$ and $D(Y)$ that specifies the allowed pairs of values for X and Y. We assume that there is only one constraint between a pair of variables. A value $b \in D(Y)$ is called a support for $a \in D(X)$ if $(a, b) \in C_{XY}$. Similarly $a \in D(X)$ is called a support for $b \in D(Y)$ if $(a, b) \in C_{XY}$.

A value $a \in D(X)$ is called arc-consistent (AC) if for every variable Y constraining X the value a is supported by some value in $D(Y)$. A CSP is AC if for every variable $X \in \mathcal{X}$, each value $a \in D(X)$ is AC. We use AC($\mathcal{P}$) to denote the CSP obtained after applying arc consistency. If there exists a variable with an empty domain in $\mathcal{P}$ then $\mathcal{P}$ is unsatisfiable and it is denoted by $\mathcal{P} = \bot$. Maintaining Arc Consistency (MAC) after each decision during search is one of the most efficient and generic approaches to solving CSPs. A *solution* of a CSP is an assignment of values to all the variables that satisfies all the constraints. A CSP is *satisfiable* if and only if it admits at least one solution; otherwise it is *unsatisfiable*. In general, determining the satisfiability of a CSP is NP-complete.

Branching Strategies. A branching strategy defines a search tree. The well-known branching schemes are k-way branching, binary branching [10] and split branching. In k-way, when a variable X with k values is selected for instantiation, k branches are formed. Here each branch corresponds to an assignment of a value to the selected variable. In binary branching, when a variable X is selected, its values are assigned via a sequence of binary choices. If the values are assigned in the order $v_1, v_2, \ldots, v_k$, then two branches are formed for the value v_1, associated with $X = v_1$ and $X \neq v_1$ respectively. The left branch corresponds to a positive decision and the right branch corresponds to a negative decision. The first choice creates the left branch; if that branch fails, or if all solutions are required, the search backtracks to the choice point, and the right branch is followed instead. Crucially, the constraint $X \neq v_1$ is propagated, before selecting another variable-value pair. In split branching, when a variable X is selected, its domain is divided in to two sets: $\{v_1, \ldots, v_j\}$ and $\{v_{j+1}, \ldots, v_k\}$, where $j = \lceil k/2 \rceil$. Two branches are formed by removing each set of values from $D(X)$ respectively.

Variable Ordering Heuristics. When a dynamic variable ordering is used the selection of the next variable to be considered at any point during search depends on the current node of the search tree. Examples of dynamic variable ordering heuristics are: dom/deg [2] and dom/wdeg [3]. The dom/deg heuristic selects a variable which has the smallest ratio of the current domain size to the original degree of the variable, while the *dom/wdeg* heuristic selects a variable which has the smallest ratio of the current domain size to the weighted degree of the variable. The dom/wdeg heuristic is adaptive while the dom/deg is non-adaptive. By adaptive we mean that the heuristic measure of a variable at a given node of the search tree is dependent on previous experience with the search process. For a non-adaptive variable ordering, the heuristic measure at a particular node in the search tree is same before and after backtracking to the node. However, this is not necessarily true for an adpative variable ordering heuristic.

Value Ordering Heuristics. A value ordering heuristic is used to select a value from the domain of a variable to instantiate that variable during search. Three value ordering heuristics are *total-cost*, *cruciality*, and *promise*, which are primarily based on selecting the least constrained value for a variable and are proposed in [5]. The heuristic *total-cost* associates each value from the domain of a variable with the sum of incompatible values in the domains of the other variables. The values are then considered in the increasing order of this count. The heuristic *cruciality* differs slightly from *total-cost*. It aggregates the percentage of the incompatible values in future domains. The heuristic *promise* associates each value with the product of the number of compatible values in the domain of each variable. The value with the highest product is chosen subsequently. For all these heuristics, the compatibility of each value a in the domain of a variable x is tested with each value b in the domain of each variable y constrained with x. This process requires $\mathcal{O}(n\,d^2)$ support checks in the worst-case after each variable selection during search. Several value ordering heuristics including *min-conflict* are presented in [4], which is, in fact, the same as the total-cost of [5].

3   Impact of Value Orderings on MAC

In this section we show that value ordering heuristics can affect the search effort (i.e. the number of visited nodes, failures etc.) of a backtrack search algorithm that forms k-way branching when the entire search space of a CSP is explored.

3.1   State-of-the-Art on Heuristic Interactions

Frost and Dechter [4] claim that value orderings have no impact on the search effort of a backtrack search algorithm, when all solutions of a CSP are searched, which includes when no solution exists. This claim has been made both for static and dynamic variable ordering heuristics [4]. Their argument is that when a variable X with k values is selected, k subtrees are explored *independently*, and the search spaces of these k subtrees are commutative. To find all solutions or to prove that there are none, every subtree must be explored and therefore the order in which values are assigned cannot make a difference in cumulative search effort.

Smith and Sturdy [11] claim that value orderings can make a difference in the algorithm's search effort when *binary-branching* is used, and agree that value ordering does not make a difference when k-way branching is used. Their argument is that in binary-branching, if a variable X and a value $x_1 \in D(X)$ is selected then two subtrees are created, $X = x_1$ and $X \neq x_1$. If $X = x_1$ fails, then the constraint $X \neq x_1$ is propagated, which can lead to further domain reduction. This propagation can remove one or more values from the current variable's domain which are not yet considered for instantiation. Hence, the order in which the values are assigned can affect the search effort even if the entire search space is explored.

In the following section we show that k subtrees are not always explored independently in k-way branching. It depends on whether a dynamic variable ordering heuristic is adaptive or non-adaptive. Notice that the heuristic measures of variables for a non-adaptive heuristic like *dom/deg* and an adaptive heuristic like *dom/wdeg* are changing during search. When the algorithm backtracks to a node the heuristic measures of all variables of a non-adaptive heuristic like dom/deg is restored to the same measures as they were before exploring that node. However, this does not hold for a dynamic variable ordering heuristic like dom/wdeg, which is adaptive. Consequently, the search spaces of k subtrees may

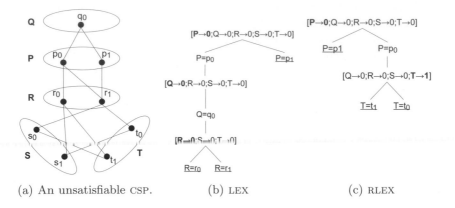

(a) An unsatisfiable CSP.   (b) LEX   (c) RLEX

Fig. 1. An unsatisfiable CSP with five variables (Figure 1(a)), and search trees with different value orderings (Figure 1(b) and Figure 1(c))

not necessarily be commutative. Therefore, when an adaptive dynamic variable ordering is used for searching all solutions, k-way branching is sensitive to the choice of value ordering heuristic.

3.2   The Role of Value Ordering: New Insights

Let us consider a trivial CSP whose micro-structure is depicted in Figure 1(a). There are five variables P, Q, R, S and T. Their domains are $D(P) = \{p_0, p_1\}$, $D(Q) = \{q_0\}$, $D(R) = \{r_0, r_1\}$, $D(S) = \{s_0, s_1\}$ and $D(T) = \{t_0, t_1\}$. There are five binary constraints. Here an edge corresponds to a pair of values that satisfy the constraint. For any two values a_i and a_j, we write $a_i <_l a_j$ if a_i is lexicographically smaller than a_j. Notice that the CSP is inconsistent. The reason for the inconsistency is the sub-problem restricted to the variables R, S and T.

The search trees shown in Figures 1(b) and 1(c) are the results of applying the MAC algorithm. The variable ordering heuristic employed by the search algorithm *selects a variable having the maximum number of wipeouts with a lexicographical tie breaker*. Initially, the number of wipeouts associated with each variable is set to 0. The number of wipeouts, v_x, associated with a variable x is written as $x \rightarrow v_x$. In the search trees, uninstantiated variables are enclosed in the square brackets in the lexicographical order, e.g. $[x \rightarrow v_x, \ldots, z \rightarrow v_z]$. The selected variable is indicated by making it bold. Each assignment of a value to the selected variable represents a node visited in the search tree. When a node is underlined, it indicates a failure.

The search tree in Figure 1(b) is the result of using the lexicographical value ordering heuristic (LEX). Initially, the number of wipeouts associated with each variable is 0, so the lexicographically smallest variable P is selected and it is instantiated to the lexicographically smallest value p_0. Enforcing AC at this point does not remove any value from any domain. The next lexicographically smallest variable is Q, which is then initialized to q_0. Again, enforcing AC makes no change in the domains. When the variable R is selected, each of its instantiations leads to a domain wipeout. When R is instantiated to r_0, first the domain of S is revised against the domain of R and s_0 is removed. Next, the domain of T is revised against the domains of R and S. This results in removing t_0 and t_1 and hence the domain wipeout occurs. When R is initialized to r_1, there is again a domain wipeout associated with T. The search process backtracks to P and initializes it to p_1. This again results in the domain wipeout associated with T, since r_0 is removed from R while revising its domain against the domain of P, which eventually results in the domain wipeout associated with T.

The search tree shown in Figure 1(c) is the result of using the reverse lexicographical value ordering heuristic (RLEX). First P is initialized to p_1 which results in a domain wipeout. This happens while revising the domain of T. At this point the number of wipeouts associated with T is incremented by 1. This influences the selection of the variable T after initializing P to p_0 in Figure 1(c). However, in Figure 1(b), due to a different value ordering, when P is initialized to p_0, Q is selected instead of T, which results in a different number of nodes.

When LEX is used the number of search nodes is 5 and when RLEX is used the number of nodes is 4. This difference is due to the interaction between the variable ordering and the value ordering heuristics. When an assignment fails the number of wipeouts associated with a variable changes. Different value ordering heuristics may change the number of wipeouts associated with different variables. Consequently, the ordering of the values in the previously explored subtrees may influence the decision of selecting the next variable in the subtrees that are yet to be explored. This shows that claims made in [4] and [11] that a search algorithm that forms k-way branching explores k subtrees independently is not always true. Hence, value orderings can affect the search tree of a backtrack algorithm when adaptive dynamic variable ordering heuristics are used with k-way branching for exploring the entire search space.

4   Impact of Value Orderings on AC

We show that static value ordering heuristics can have an impact on the efficiency of arc consistency algorithms. We focus on the static versions of the heuristics *total-cost*, *cruciality* and *promise*. The ordering based on these heuristics can be viewed as arranging the values in increasing order of their constrainedness. This can be advantageous while revising the domains of the variables, when trying to make the problem AC. More specifically, putting the least constrained value at the beginning of the domain list might help values of other domains to find their support more quickly during revision (on average). This may save failed support checks since the further the first support is from the start of the domain list, the more are the failed checks required to find that support for a given value.

To illustrate this, let us consider a constraint $X \leq Y$ and study the revision of $D(X)$ against $D(Y)$ as shown in Figures 2(a) and 2(b). If the values in $D(Y)$ are arranged in $\langle 1, 2, 3, 4 \rangle$ order, as shown in Figure 2(a), and the search for a support starts from 1, then the revision of $D(X)$ against $D(Y)$ will require 10

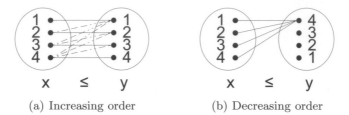

(a) Increasing order   (b) Decreasing order

Fig. 2. Visualization of the checks of the constraint $X \leq Y$ where dashed lines refer to failed checks and solid lines refer to successful checks

support checks in total, using the revise function of AC-3. If the values in $D(Y)$ are arranged in $\langle 4, 3, 2, 1 \rangle$ order, as shown in Figure 2(b), then the revision of $D(X)$ against $D(Y)$ will require only 4 support checks in total, using the revise function of AC-3. Obviously, different constraints may require different orderings of values. However, these orderings can be aggregated. For example, one can use total-cost or promise as measures to sort the values of the domain accordingly.

The fact that ordering the values can reduce support checks during revisions and thereby improves the average revision time does not seem to have been observed before. This is the reason that when a static value ordering heuristic is used in a search algorithm such as MAC, it can make a difference at least in terms of support checks even when the entire search space is explored.

5   Lazy K-Way Branching

In k-way branching a decision corresponds to an assignment of a value to a given variable and its dual can be seen as removing all but one value from the domain of the variable. An example of k-way branching is illustrated in Figure 3, where a box denotes a variable selection and an ellipse denotes selecting and assigning a value to the selected variable. Here X is the selected variable whose domain is $\{a_1, a_2, a_3, a_4, a_5\}$ and $k = 5$. A (positive) decision $X = a_1$, is equivalent to removing a_2, a_3, a_4 and a_5 from the domain of X, or in other words enforcing a conjunction of inequalities, i.e., $X \neq a_2 \land X \neq a_3 \land X \neq a_4 \land X \neq a_5$.

We propose a *lazy version* of the *k-way branching* scheme whereby instead of enforcing all $(k-1)$ inequalities at once each inequality is enforced separately, e.g., each assignment of a value in Figure 3 corresponds to a sequence of inequalities in Figure 4(a). The k-way branching scheme can be seen as being optimistic

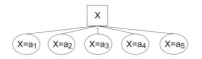

Fig. 3. k-way branching

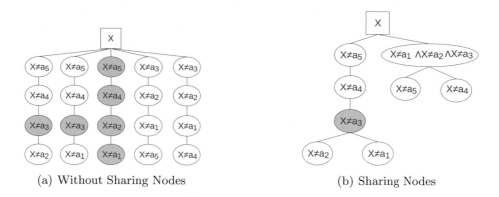

(a) Without Sharing Nodes   (b) Sharing Nodes

Fig. 4. Lazy k-way branching

whereby, based on some heuristic measure, a most optimistic value is selected and assigned to the selected variable. Lazy k-way branching can be seen as being pessimistic whereby a most pessimistic value is selected and removed from the selected variable. Postponing the instantiation of a variable may help in making better decisions, thus reducing the number of mistakes.

An additional advantage of enforcing each inequality separately is that one can infer dependencies between *explicitly* removed values of the selected variable as a result of making (negative) decisions, and the *implicitly* removed values of the selected variable as a result of enforcing local consistency, such as arc consistency in the case of MAC. These dependencies can be exploited to reduce the number of decisions. For example, let us assume that a_3 is removed from $D(X)$ when arc consistency is enforced after taking the negative decisions $X \neq a_5$ and $X \neq a_4$ in the first branch of Figure 4(a), which is shown by shading the decision node $X \neq a_3$. One can infer the following implication: $X \neq a_5 \wedge X \neq a_4 \rightarrow X \neq a_3$. This effectively means that there does not exist any solution in the resulting subproblem after selecting variable X where $X = a_3$. Therefore, if the decision of instantiating X to a_3 has not yet been tried, then there is no need to try it. Hence, the third branch of Figure 4(a) is not explored, which is equivalent to $X = a_3$. This is shown by shading all the corresponding negative decisions: $X \neq a_5$, $X \neq a_4$, $X \neq a_2$, and $X \neq a_1$. This is an original and novel way of reducing the number of useless branches and failures.

In k-way branching, if k branches are explored after selecting a variable, then each value is removed at most $(k - 1)$ times, and in algorithms like MAC, the work required for propagating the impact of removing a value will be repeated. This repetition can be reduced in lazy k-way branching. Remember that in lazy k-way branching each assignment of a value to a variable can be seen as a path consisting of at most $k - 1$ negative decisions starting after the selection of the variable and ending at a node when the variable's domain is singleton. Instead of having disjoint paths for each assignment of a value, as shown in Figure 4(a), the idea is to maximize the sharing of negative decisions among different paths in order to minimize the work required for propagation.

Algorithm 1. $\text{MAC}_{LK}(\mathcal{P}, Y)$

Require: $\mathcal{P}$: input CSP $(\mathcal{X}, \mathcal{C}, D)$; Y: current variable
1: **if** $\mathcal{X} = \emptyset$ **then**
2:        solution found
3: **else**
4:        **if** $Y = \texttt{null}$ **then** select and remove any variable X from $\mathcal{X}$
5:        **else** $X \leftarrow Y$
6:        $V \leftarrow \emptyset; D' \leftarrow D$
7:        **while** $\mathcal{P} \neq \perp \wedge |V| < |D(X)|$ **do**
8:              select and remove any value v from $D(X)$
9:              $V \leftarrow V \cup \{v\}; \mathcal{P} \leftarrow \text{AC}(\mathcal{P})$
10:       **if** $\mathcal{P} \neq \perp$ **then**
11:             **if** $|D(X)| = 1$ **then** $\text{MAC}_{LK}(\mathcal{P}, \texttt{null})$ **else** $\text{MAC}_{LK}(\mathcal{P}, X)$
12:       $D \leftarrow D'; D(X) \leftarrow V; \mathcal{P} \leftarrow \text{AC}(\mathcal{P})$
13:       **if** $\mathcal{P} \neq \perp$ **then**
14:             **if** $|D(X)| = 1$ **then** $\text{MAC}_{LK}(\mathcal{P}, \texttt{null})$ **else** $\text{MAC}_{LK}(\mathcal{P}, X)$

One way of implementing lazy k-way branching in order to share nodes (propagation) is shown in Algorithm 1. Notice that MAC_{LK} requires CSP $\mathcal{P}$ and the current variable Y. If Y is null then a new current variable is selected (Line 4–5). After the current variable, X, is determined, a set V for storing negative decisions is initialized to $\emptyset$, and the domains of the variables are saved in D' (Line 8). While $|V| < |D(X)|$ and there is no domain wipe-out, a value v is selected and removed from $D(X)$, it is added to the set V, and AC is enforced (Line 7–9). When the loop is terminated and if $\mathcal{P}$ is not empty then the left branch is created (Line 10–11). The right branch is created by restoring the domains to D' and setting $D(X)$ to the set of values that were removed in the loop (Line 12–14). If X is instantiated then MAC_{LK} is invoked by setting the current variable to $\texttt{null}$, otherwise it is invoked with the current variable X.

An example of sharing nodes is presented in Figure 4(b). In this example the loop is exited after visiting the node corresponding to $X \neq a_4$ (in the left branch). Notice that the decision associated with the last node and all those decisions preceding it are shared by all branches originating from this node, thus reducing the work required for propagation. When the algorithm backtracks it first removes all those values that are already tried as assignments to the current variable, e.g., $X \neq a_1 \wedge X \neq a_2$, as well as those values of X that were implicitly removed while enforcing arc consistency, e.g., $X \neq a_3$. This is done in Line 12 of MAC_{LK} when $D(X)$ is set to V, since V contains only a_4 and a_5. Notice that $X = a_3$ is never tried since it was inferred as inconsistent in the subproblem resulting from the selection of variable X.

Similar to the lazy version of k-way branching, lazy versions of binary branching and split branching are also possible. One can infer and exploit the dependencies between inequality constraints involving values of the same domain to reduce the number of failures in a lazy version of any branching scheme. However, this is beyond the scope of the current paper.

6   Experimental Results

The experiments were conducted using MAC as a backtrack search algorithm. AC-3 was used as its arc consistency component which was equipped with the residual support mechanism and revision condition [7]. We conducted experiments with the static versions of *min-conflict, max-conflict, cruciality, anti-cruciality, promise* and *anti-promise* value ordering heuristics. The information required for these value ordering heuristics was computed prior to search as a pre-processing step after making the problem initially arc-consistent. We also present the results obtained by using the default ordering of the values as specified by the problem instance which is denoted by *default*. Of course, these heuristics might not be the best or might be very expensive/inapplicable for one or more classes of problems. Nevertheless, the purpose of these experiments is not to prove the efficiency of these value ordering heuristics, but to show that different value ordering heuristics can have a significant impact on the search effort when the entire search space of a CSP is explored using MAC with k-way branching. We also wish to demonstrate the effectiveness of lazy k-way branching when compared with k-way branching.

Search effort was measured in terms of support checks ($\#c$), visited nodes ($\#n$), failures ($\#f$) and the solution time (time) in seconds. All algorithms are written in C. The experiments were carried out as a single thread on Dual Quad Core Xeon CPU, running Linux 2.6.25 x64, with 11.76 GB of RAM, and 2.66 GHz processor speed. We perform experiments on many instances of the problems that were used as benchmarks in the CP solver competition of the CPAI'05 workshop.[1]

Table 1 presents results for different value ordering heuristics when the dom/deg variable ordering is used to explore the complete search space. The search nodes for all value orderings is the same as depicted in the first column,

Table 1. Results for exploring the entire search space with dom/deg and k-way branching. Instances are: (a) bqwh $- 15 - 106 - 32$ ($\#n = 33168$), (b) frb50 $- 23 - 3 - bis$ ($\#n = 230746522$), (c) graph12_w1 ($\#n=177059$), (d) dual_ehi $- 85 - 297 - 10$ ($\#n$ 377649), (e) qk_12_12_5_mul ($\#n$ 1996472)

inst		default	min-conflict	max-conflict	promise	anti-promise
(a)	$\#c$	1,174,152	1,181,071	1,176,787	1,178,857	1,179,353
	time	0.535	0.534	0.528	0.537	0.533
(b)	$\#c$	98,657,596,677	93,687,374,052	103,998,537,736	93,537,311,214	104,177,841,288
	time	19,924.439	19,761.988	20,168.810	19,747.415	19,865.577
(c)	$\#c$	27,573,288	28,114,893	28,012,342	28,114,952	28,012,414
	time	2.565	2.695	2.610	2.624	2.619
(d)	$\#c$	374,657,413	363,435,461	382,601,651	362,105,766	382,003,776
	time	400.085	400.772	400.746	396.993	399.856
(e)	$\#c$	6,283,619,236	6,148,687,117	6,330,315,375	6,148,556,738	6,317,352,246
	time	127.459	124.576	127.909	125.882	126.916

---

[1] http://cpai.ucc.ie/05/Benchmarks.html

which is consistent with the conventional wisdom. However, there is a difference in terms of support checks. On average fewer checks are required when values are ordered based on a heuristic than with the corresponding anti-heuristic. The difference in terms of checks is not significant. The reason is that a huge number of support checks are replaced and reduced by auxiliary checks performed by the residual support mechanism and revision condition. For example, for the queens-knights instance qk_12_12_5_mul , 2% of the checks are saved when values are ordered by min-conflict when compared with that of max-conflict. However, if a standard AC-3 is used then 14% of the checks are saved by min-conflict when compared with max-conflict.

Table 2 presents results for different problem classes when the *dom/wdeg* variable ordering is used with different value ordering heuristics and the complete search space is explored using k-way branching. We have computed the ratio with respect to the default for each heuristic different to the default. For each instance, the highest/lowest result is written in bold/italic. The results clearly show that value ordering heuristics can make a significant difference in terms of the number of search nodes and time. It is worth emphasizing that for some problems a heuristic like min-conflict, cruciality, or promise performs better while on some others, its corresponding anti-heuristic performs better. We did some further investigation by solving the same instance with 2500 random value orderings. The results for some of them are presented in Figure 5; in these plots each point represents the probability of the search effort to solve an instance exceeding the corresponding number of search nodes on the x-axis. It again shows that value ordering heuristics can make a difference up to several orders-of-magnitude in terms of search nodes when the entire search space is explored; the first two graphs, in fact, exhibit a heavy-tail distribution in search effort.

Table 3 presents results for lazy k-way branching and k-way branching when the entire search space was explored with different value ordering heuristics. In the first three rows *dom/deg* was used while for the remaining *dom/wdeg* was used. The first observation is that when different value orderings are used in conjunction with lazy k-way branching they can result in different search effort when the entire search space is explored. More importantly, unlike k-way branching, the difference in the search effort is also observed for dom/deg as shown in 2nd and 3rd rows. This is because in the lazy k-way branching scheme a decision corresponds to selecting and removing a value, with AC being enforced after each value removal. Therefore, depending on the order in which the values are removed dependencies involving inequalities amongst the values of the same domain are inferred, which are exploited to reduce the number of decisions. Moreover, when dom/wdeg is used, the difference in the search effort is also due to the interaction between variable and value ordering heuristics as explained in Section 3. Table 3 also confirms that lazy k-way branching can reduce the number of failures by up to one order-of-magnitude for some instances when compared with k-way branching. The minimum number of failures between lazy

Table 2. Results for finding all solutions with dom/wdeg and k-way branching

instance		default	min-conflict	max-conflict	cruciality	anti-cruciality	promise	anti-promise
bqwh − 15 − 106 − 32	#c	*411,235.000*	**2.996**	1.665	1.452	2.451	1.460	2.452
(sat)	#n	*7,383.000*	**3.292**	1.664	1.483	2.520	1.486	2.520
	time	*0.197*	**2.995**	1.670	1.452	2.508	1.472	2.518
bqwh − 18 − 141 − 40	#c	602,681,284.000	**2.086**	1.087	1.788	*0.932*	1.470	0.988
(sat)	#n	10,779,400.000	**2.190**	1.075	1.846	*0.929*	1.502	0.981
	time	*321.383*	**2.083**	1.085	1.773	*0.926*	1.450	0.984
bqwh − 18 − 141 − 68	#c	21,995,315.000	0.942	0.786	1.595	*0.740*	**2.129**	0.929
(sat)	#n	371,375.000	0.951	0.748	1.596	*0.716*	**2.086**	0.898
	time	12.504	0.937	0.783	1.561	*0.734*	**2.099**	0.921
frb50 − 23 − 3 − *bis*	#c	*81,752,058,491.000*	*0.960*	1.082	0.960	1.082	1.012	**1.106**
(sat)	#n	*187,967,335.000*	1.007	1.023	1.007	1.023	**1.064**	1.042
	time	*16,512.675*	1.006	1.032	1.020	1.019	**1.053**	1.034
qa − 6	#c	*21,950,814,589.000*	**1.121**	1.019	1.117	1.084	1.097	1.015
(sat)	#n	134,884,052.000	1.089	1.002	**1.095**	1.063	1.071	*0.999*
	time	3,083.689	1.106	1.011	**1.108**	1.072	1.096	*0.998*
graph14_f28	#c	5,142,167.000	0.528	1.387	0.528	**1.387**	*0.528*	1.387
(unsat)	#n	28,177.000	*0.348*	1.310	0.348	1.310	0.348	**1.310**
	time	0.751	*0.397*	1.611	0.399	1.610	0.406	**1.617**
graph2_f25	#c	65,664,798.000	0.950	0.994	*0.029*	1.016	0.030	**1.016**
(unsat)	#n	275,917.000	1.000	1.004	*0.015*	1.029	0.015	**1.029**
	time	8.021	0.982	1.014	*0.019*	**1.037**	0.020	1.035
scen6_w1_f2	#c	19,978,058.000	1.114	*0.690*	1.115	0.741	**1.125**	0.697
(unsat)	#n	52,325.000	1.084	*0.627*	1.084	0.674	**1.107**	0.654
	time	0.662	**1.166**	*0.690*	1.156	0.740	1.162	0.705
dual_ehi − 90 − 315 − 97	#c	**11,283,716.000**	0.280	0.961	0.283	0.228	*0.219*	0.977
(unsat)	#n	6,288.000	0.308	1.022	0.314	*0.228*	0.253	**1.100**
	time	10.166	0.235	1.024	0.234	0.206	*0.160*	**1.069**
qk_20_20_5_add	#c	3,001,318,053.000	95.518	0.794	**95.518**	0.794	84.080	*0.304*
(unsat)	#n	237,139.000	**102.069**	0.785	28.996	*0.207*	91.023	0.291
	time	51.371	**96.175**	0.800	27.350	*0.222*	85.000	0.308
qk_20_20_5_mul(unsat)	#c	4,257,470,286.000	59.509	0.602	16.949	*0.149*	**69.584**	0.171
	#n	360,924.000	64.125	0.587	18.229	*0.131*	**75.216**	0.154
	time	78.117	58.306	0.586	16.619	*0.144*	**68.420**	0.167
composed − 75 − 1 − 40 − 7	#c	205,748.000	**1.170**	0.756	1.170	0.751	1.167	*0.707*
(unsat)	#n	1,089.000	1.448	0.684	1.448	*0.613*	**1.460**	0.613
	time	0.020	1.150	0.650	1.150	*0.600*	**1.200**	0.650
cril_unsat_b_1	#c	**297,178,340.000**	*0.810*	0.930	0.816	0.930	0.818	0.930
(unsat)	#n	**1,672,114.000**	0.886	*0.851*	0.886	0.851	0.888	0.851
	time	**32.854**	0.904	*0.879*	0.904	0.884	0.909	0.885

k-way and k-way branching schemes for each value ordering is made bold in each row of Table 3.

In some cases, despite failing more, the ratio of checks per node ($\#c/\#n$) is less for lazy k-way branching than with that of k-way branching, e.g., see the row corresponding to the qk_20_20_5_add instance. The reason is that when the problem is relatively hard, more nodes are explored. Consequently more nodes are shared among different branches. Hence, work required for constraint propagation is also shared, which improves the trade-off between the number of decision nodes and the work done on each of them.

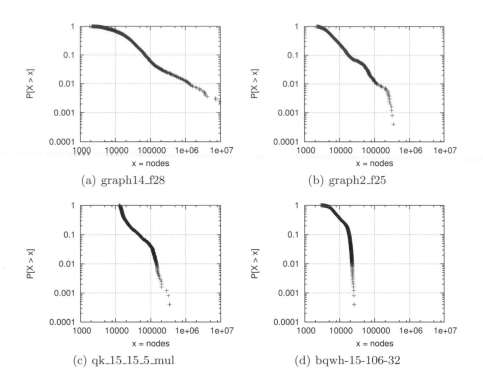

(a) graph14_f28

(b) graph2_f25

(c) qk_15_15_5_mul

(d) bqwh-15-106-32

Fig. 5. Search effort for exploring the entire search space of different instances with 2500 random value ordering heuristics and dom/wdeg as a variable ordering heuristic

Value ordering heuristics like min-conflict, cruciality, and promise are proposed in the literature to find one solution quickly, and not for exploring the entire search space. Thus, when it comes to exploring the entire search-space, it is not surprising to see that, for some problem instances, value ordering heuristics like min-conflict perform significantly better than anti-heuristics like max-conflict, while for others it is the other way around, and for some there is only a marginal difference in their performance. We are not aware of any work on value ordering heuristics for finding all solutions with k-way branching in the CSP context. In fact for a long time it has been believed that value orderings do not make any difference in the search effort of backtrack algorithm with k-way branching. Contrary to that, we have shown results where the difference in the search effort is up to several orders-of-magnitude because of using different value orderings. These results raise an interesting question: *what kind of value ordering heuristics should be used with (lazy) k-way branching and adaptive variable ordering heuristics like dom/wdeg when it comes to exploring the entire search space.*

Table 3. Results for lazy k-way branching and k-way branching with different value orderings

instance		lex		min-conflict		max-conflict		promise		anti-promise	
		lazy	k-way	lazy	k-way	lazy	k-way	lazy	k-way	lazy	k-way
bqwh − 15 − 106 − 32	#c/#n	35	35	35	35	35	35	35	35	35	35
(sat)	#f	16,568	16,568	16,568	16,568	16,568	16,568	16,568	16,568	16,568	16,568
(dom/deg)	time	0.547	0.535	0.545	0.534	0.549	0.528	0.548	0.537	0.548	0.533
graph12_w1	#c/#n	227	155	204	158	565	158	204	158	564	158
(unsat)	#f	62,029	146,056	62,041	146,056	42,058	146,056	62,041	146,056	42,058	146,056
(dom/deg)	time	2.295	2.565	2.406	2.695	2.667	2.610	2.398	2.624	2.662	2.619
qk_12.12_5_mul	#c/#n	578	3,147	676	3,079	825	3,170	676	3,079	839	3,164
(unsat)	#f	1,800,233	1,933,202	1,585,215	1,933,202	1,602,612	1,933,202	1,585,225	1,933,202	1,607,642	1,933,202
(dom/deg)	time	100.182	127.459	107.223	124.576	122.685	127.909	107.625	125.882	124.593	126.916
bqwh − 18 − 141 − 40	#c/#n	53	55	52	53	52	56	51	54	52	56
(sat)	#f	6,060,698	5,355,527	8,525,678	11,829,875	6,340,885	5,757,040	11,304,683	8,091,911	5,688,069	5,258,850
(dom/wdeg)	time	370.067	321.383	499.935	669.521	331.778	348.624	652.630	466.117	346.182	316.384
bqwh − 18 − 141 − 68	#c/#n	54	59	54	58	57	62	55	60	55	61
(sat)	#f	262,036	190,020	158,538	179,877	155,934	141,998	342,944	393,687	163,859	169,572
(dom/wdeg)	time	16.906	12.504	10.276	11.720	11.277	9.796	22.456	26.247	10.928	11.510
qa − 6	#c/#n	111	162	110	167	112	155	110	166	113	165
(sat)	#f	83,018,862	83,567,571	76,845,848	93,016,524	74,749,673	83,676,659	77,295,678	90,932,653	84,307,042	83,458,694
(dom/wdeg)	time	3,288.929	3,083.689	3,110.823	3,410.738	2,951.007	3,117.558	3,121.990	3,381.146	3,304.104	3,077.301
graph14_f28	#c/#n	117	182	107	276	164	193	107	276	164	193
(unsat)	#f	11,524	21,831	38,497	7,840	9,736	28,355	38,497	7,840	9,736	28,355
(dom/wdeg)	time	0.578	0.751	1.876	0.298	0.547	1.210	1.879	0.305	0.555	1.214
graph2_f25	#c/#n	170	237	151	226	158	235	246	481	158	234
(unsat)	#f	44,278	210,765	175,584	211,438	28,556	210,651	2,877	3,292	169,689	217,072
(dom/wdeg)	time	2.689	8.021	8.839	7.876	1.471	8.131	0.175	0.158	8.696	8.304
scen6_w1_f2	#c/#n	178	381	254	392	315	420	258	387	307	406
(unsat)	#f	15,128	46,091	22,016	49,963	12,512	28,894	19,300	51,022	16,125	30,158
(dom/wdeg)	time	0.485	0.662	0.783	0.772	0.512	0.457	0.710	0.769	0.698	0.467
dual_ehi − 90 − 315 − 97	#c/#n	1,289	1,794	1,314	1,631	1,488	1,686	1,513	1,552	1,492	1,594
(unsat)	#f	2,436	3,522	1,409	1,123	3,430	3,566	797	907	3,078	3,889
(dom/wdeg)	time	5.936	10.166	3.039	2.392	10.174	10.411	1.730	1.628	9.340	10.867
qk_20.20_5_add	#c/#n	1,215	12,656	1,374	11,844	1,587	12,805	1,374	11,630	1,606	13,232
(unsat)	#f	197,976	229,562	19,271,246	22,899,364	182,798	181,067	25,928,724	20,321,780	45,971	67,920
(dom/wdeg)	time	23.677	51.371	2,648.326	4,940.583	29.024	41.113	3,580.520	4,366.546	7.480	15.800
qk_20.20_5_mul	#c/#n	1,184	11,796	1,315	10,946	1,533	12,099	1,342	10,912	1,606	13,106
(unsat)	#f	327,484	748,717	25,290,613	21,841,327	210,111	205,860	24,401,630	25,633,431	43,872	54,894
(dom/wdeg)	time	40.181	48.718	3,446.613	4,554.656	33.562	45.809	5,344.759	5,633.491	7.675	13.037
cril_unsat_b_1	#c/#n	138	177	111	162	147	194	111	153	147	194
(unsat)	#f	677,349	1,505,510	723,522	1,158,780	700,502	1,110,120	730,559	1,162,132	700,502	1,110,120
(dom/wdeg)	time	32.862	33.145	30.141	29.815	32.113	28.920	30.429	29.831	32.103	29.042
composed − 75 − 1 − 40 − 7	#c/#n	128	188	109	152	188	208	111	150	176	217
(unsat)	#f	475	901	756	1,334	296	602	682	1,353	305	532
(dom/wdeg)	time	0.018	0.020	0.028	0.023	0.013	0.013	0.027	0.024	0.014	0.013

7   Conclusions

Given recent developments in the area of variable ordering heuristics, the conventional wisdom with respect to k-way branching and value ordering needed to be reconsidered. We have presented an analysis in this paper demonstrating that value ordering can make a considerable difference in search effort. We demonstrated this phenomenon across multiple problem classes, and for two forms of k-way branching. One of our k-way branching schemes, lazy k-way, is very novel and merits a deeper investigation in the context of CSP solving.

A major contribution of this paper is that it motivates a new and fruitful line of research in the study of *value ordering* heuristics for proving unsatisfiability.

Acknowledgments. We thank Marc van Dongen for providing the example of Figure 1(a) and Diarmuid Grimes for helpful discussions. This work was supported by Science Foundation Ireland Grant 08/CE/I1423. Barry O'Sullivan is also supported by Science Foundation Ireland Grant 10/IN.1/I3032.

References

1. Balafoutis, T., Stergiou, K.: Adaptive branching for constraint satisfaction problems. In: ECAI, pp. 855–860 (2010)
2. Bessière, C., Régin, J.-C.: MAC and combined heuristics: Two reasons to forsake FC (and CBJ?) on hard problems. In: Freuder, E.C. (ed.) CP 1996. LNCS, vol. 1118, pp. 61–75. Springer, Heidelberg (1996)
3. Boussemart, F., Hemery, F., Lecoutre, C., Saïs, L.: Boosting systematic search by weighting constraints. In: Procs of ECAI 2004 (2004)
4. Frost, D., Dechter, R.: Look-ahead value ordering for constraint satisfaction problems. In: Proceedings of the IJCAI 1995, pp. 572–578 (1995)
5. Geelen, P.A.: Dual viewpoint heuristics for binary constraint satisfaction problems. In: Proceedings of ECAI 1992, New York, NY, USA, pp. 31–35 (1992)
6. Hwang, J., Mitchell, D.G.: 2-way vs. d-way branching for csp. In: van Beek, P. (ed.) CP 2005. LNCS, vol. 3709, pp. 343–357. Springer, Heidelberg (2005)
7. Lecoutre, C.: Constraint Networks Techniques and Algorithms. Wiley, Chichester (2009)
8. Mehta, D., van Dongen, M.R.C.: Static value ordering heuristics for constraint satisfaction problems. In: Proceedings of CPAI 2005 Workshop held with CP 2005, pp. 49–62 (2005)
9. Sabin, D., Freuder, E.C.: Contradicting conventional wisdom in constraint satisfaction. In: Cohn, A.G. (ed.) ECAI 1994, pp. 125–129. John Wiley and Sons, Chichester (1994)
10. Sabin, D., Freuder, E.C.: Understanding and improving the MAC algorithm. In: Smolka, G. (ed.) Principles and Practice of Constraint Programming, pp. 167–181. Springer, Heidelberg (1997)
11. Smith, B.M., Sturdy, P.: Value ordering for finding all solutions. In: Proceedings of the IJCAI 2005, pp. 311–316 (2005)

Boolean Equi-propagation
for Optimized SAT Encoding

Amit Metodi[1], Michael Codish[1], Vitaly Lagoon[2], and Peter J. Stuckey[3]

[1] Department of Computer Science, Ben Gurion University of the Negev, Israel
[2] Cadence Design Systems, USA
[3] Department of Computer Science and Software Engineering, and
NICTA Victoria Laboratory, The University of Melbourne, Australia

Abstract. We present an approach to propagation based SAT encoding, Boolean equi-propagation, where constraints are modelled as Boolean functions which propagate information about equalities between Boolean literals. This information is then applied as a form of partial evaluation to simplify constraints prior to their encoding as CNF formulae. We demonstrate for a variety of benchmarks that our approach leads to a considerable reduction in the size of CNF encodings and subsequent speed-ups in SAT solving times.

1 Introduction

In recent years, Boolean SAT solving techniques have improved dramatically. Today's SAT solvers are considerably faster and able to manage far larger instances than yesterday's. Moreover, encoding and modeling techniques are better understood and increasingly innovative. SAT is currently applied to solve a wide variety of hard and practical combinatorial problems, often outperforming dedicated algorithms. The general idea is to encode a (typically, NP) hard problem instance, P, to a Boolean formula, φ_P, such that the solutions of P correspond to the satisfying assignments of φ_P. Given an encoding from problem instances to Boolean formula, a SAT solver is then applied to solve the problem instances.

Tailgating the success of SAT technology are a variety of tools which can be applied to specify and then compile problem instances to corresponding SAT instances. Typically, a constraint based modelling language is introduced and used to model instances. Then encoding techniques are applied to compile constraints to the language of an underlying solver such as SAT, SMT, or others. Some examples follow: In [5], Cadoli and Schaerf introduce NP-SPEC, a logic-based specification language which allows to specify combinatorial problems in a declarative way. At the core of this system is a compiler which translates specifications to CNF formula. Sugar [20], is a SAT-based constraint solver. To solve a finite domain linear constraint satisfaction problem it is first encoded to a CNF formula by Sugar, and then solved using the MiniSat solver [8]. MiniZinc [15], is a constraint modeling language which is compiled by a variety of solvers to the low-level target language FlatZinc. FlatZinc instances are solved by fzntini [13] by encoding them to CNF and in fzn2smt by encoding to SMT-LIB [2].

J. Lee (Ed.): CP 2011, LNCS 6876, pp. 621–636, 2011.
© Springer-Verlag Berlin Heidelberg 2011

The objective of all of these tools is to facilitate the process of providing a high-level description of how the (constraint) problem at hand is to be solved. Taking the analogy to programming languages, given such a description, a compiler can then provide a low-level executable for the underlying machine. Namely, in our context, a formula for the underlying SAT or SMT solver.

This paper takes a new approach, introducing the notion of equi-propagation. Similar to how unit propagation is about inferring unit clauses which can then be applied to simplify CNF formulae, equi-propagation is about inferring equational consequences. In contrast to unit propagation, equi-propagation derives information from the higher-level constraints, prior to their encoding to CNF. Each individual constraint is modelled as a Boolean function which propagates equalities between Boolean literals that it implies. Given this information, all of the constraints are simplified by partial evaluation, possibly leading to further equi-propagation. When equi-propagation provides no further information, the residual constraints are encoded to CNF.

Drawing on the programming languages analogy, we view our contribution as an optimizing compiler for SAT encoding where equi-propagation and partial evaluation facilitate optimization of the constraint model. This, fast (polynomial-time) optimization phase is followed by the more costly (exponential-time) SAT solving phase. A novel and efficient implementation of equi-propagation using binary decision diagrams (BDD's) [4] is described. Experiments demonstrate for a variety of constraint problems that equi-propagation significantly reduces the size of their encoding to CNF formulae as well as the solving time required for a SAT solver to find a solution.

2   Overview

In this section we illustrate the main ideas we apply to simplify a constraint model prior to its encoding as a CNF formula. To support the presentation we first introduce a core portion of the underlying modelling language. Here, constraints are about finite domain integer variables and viewed as Boolean functions about the low-level bit representation of these variables. Our compiler supports both unary and binary integer representations, however in the paper we focus on a unary representation, the *order encoding*. Consider the following three constructs in the modelling language.

$\boxed{1}$ $\text{unary}_n(X, [a, b])$ $\boxed{2}$ $\text{diff}(X_1, X_2)$ $\boxed{3}$ $\text{allDiff}([X_1, \ldots, X_n])$

A constraint $\text{unary}_n(X, [a, b])$ where $0 \leq a \leq b \leq n$ specifies a finite domain integer variable $X = \langle x_1, \ldots, x_n \rangle$, represented in n bits, which takes values in the interval $[a, b]$. We denote by $dom(X)$ the finite set of values that variable X can take. Initially, $dom(X) = \{a, \ldots, b\}$. When clear from the context, we drop n from the notation. A constraint, $\text{diff}(X_1, X_2)$, specifies that integer variables (bit vectors) X_1 and X_2 take different values from their respective domains. The third construct, $\text{allDiff}(Xs)$, specifies that integer variables $Xs = [X_1, \ldots, X_m]$

all take different values from their respective domains. The argument of this constraint is a list of bit vectors. We denote $dom(Xs) = \cup\{ dom(X_i) \mid 1 \le i \le m \}$.

In the *order encoding* (see e.g. [6,1]), the bit vector representation of integer variable $X = \langle x_1, \ldots, x_n \rangle$ constitutes a monotonic decreasing sequence. For example, the value 3 in 5 bits is represented as $\langle 1,1,1,0,0 \rangle$. The bit x_i (for $1 \le i \le n$) is interpreted as the statement $X \ge i$. Throughout the paper, for a bit vector $X = \langle x_1, \ldots, x_n \rangle$ representing an integer in the order-encoding, we assume implicit bits $x_0 = 1$ and $x_{n+1} = 0$, and denote $X(i) = x_i$ for $0 \le i \le n+1$.

An important property of a Boolean representation for finite domain integers is the ability to represent changes in the set of values a variable can take. It is well-known that the order-encoding facilitates the propagation of bounds. Consider an integer variable $X = \langle x_1, \ldots, x_n \rangle$ with values in the interval $[0, n]$. To restrict X to take values in the range $[a, b]$ (for $1 \le a \le b \le n$), it is sufficient to assign $x_a = 1$ and $x_{b+1} = 0$ (if $b < n$). The variables $x_{a'}$ for $0 \ge a' > a$ and $b < b' \le n$ are then determined true and false, respectively, by *unit propagation*. For example, given $X = \langle x_1, \ldots, x_9 \rangle$, assigning $x_3 = 1$ and $x_6 = 0$ propagates to give $X = \langle 1, 1, 1, x_4, x_5, 0, 0, 0, 0 \rangle$, signifying that $dom(X) \subseteq \{3, \ldots, 5\}$. This property is exploited in Sugar [20] which also applies the order encoding.

We observe an additional property of the order-encoding: its ability to specify that a variable cannot take a specific value $0 \le v \le n$ in its domain by equating two variables: $x_v = x_{v+1}$. This indicates that the order-encoding is well-suited not only to propagate lower and upper bounds, but also to represent integer variables with an arbitrary, finite set, domain. For example, for $X = \langle x_1, \ldots, x_9 \rangle$, equating $x_2 = x_3$ imposes that $X \ne 2$. Likewise $x_5 = x_6$ and $x_7 = x_8$ impose that $X \ne 5$ and $X \ne 7$. Applying these equalities to X gives, $X = \langle x_1, x_2, x_2, x_4, x_5, x_5, x_7, x_7, x_9 \rangle$, signifying that $dom(X) = \{0, 1, 3, 4, 6, 8, 9\}$.

The Boolean functions corresponding to constraints $\boxed{1}$ — $\boxed{3}$ are as follows (where $1 \le a \le b \le n$):

$$
\mathtt{unary}(\langle x_1, \ldots, x_n \rangle, [a, b]) - \bigwedge_{i=1}^{n} (x_{i-1} \leftarrow x_i) \wedge x_a \wedge \neg x_{b \mid 1}
$$

$$
\mathtt{diff}(\langle x_1, \ldots, x_n \rangle, \langle y_1, \ldots, y_n \rangle) = \bigvee_{i=1}^{n} (x_i \mathbin{\mathtt{xor}} y_i) \tag{1}
$$

$$
\mathtt{allDiff}([X_1, \ldots, X_m]) = \bigwedge_{1 \le i < j \le m} \mathtt{diff}(X_i, X_j)
$$

For constraint c with integer variable arguments, we denote by c_u the conjunction of c with the statement that its arguments are represented in the order-encoding. For example, $\mathtt{diff}_u(X, Y) = \mathtt{diff}(X, Y) \wedge \mathtt{unary}_n(X, [0, n]) \wedge \mathtt{unary}_n(Y, [0, n])$.

The idea in this paper is to simplify constraints, prior to their encoding to CNF, using a technique we call equi-propagation. We distinguish between *low-level constraints*, such as $\mathtt{unary}(X, [a, b])$ and $\mathtt{diff}(X_1, X_2)$, which are about a fixed number (one and two) of integer variables, and *high-level constraints*, such as $\mathtt{allDiff}([X_1, \ldots, X_m])$. Low-level constraints are simplified and then encoded directly to CNF, while high-level constraints are simplified and then decomposed to low-level constraints. We now demonstrate three types of simplification rules on the constraint $\mathtt{diff}(X, Y)$ where $X = \langle x_1, x_2, x_3, x_4 \rangle$ and $Y = \langle y_1, y_2, y_3, y_4 \rangle$ are integer variables in the unary, order-encoding.

(1) *equi-propagation*, where we propagate information about equalities between Boolean literals and constants. For example, assuming that $Y = \langle 1, 1, 0, 0 \rangle$ we propagate that $(x_2 = x_3)$ because $\mathtt{diff}_u(\langle x_1, x_2, x_3, x_4 \rangle, \langle 1, 1, 0, 0 \rangle) \models (x_2 = x_3)$. To see why, consider that X is in the order-encoding, so $x_2 \geq x_3$. Furthermore, also $x_2 \leq x_3$ as otherwise $x_2 = 1$ and $x_3 = 0$ which implies that $X = \langle 1, 1, 0, 0 \rangle$ (because also $x_1 \geq x_2$ and $x_3 \geq x_4$), contradicting $\mathtt{diff}(X, Y)$. When we detect such equalities, we apply them to simplify the constraints in a model.

(2) *redundant constraint elimination*, where we discover that, given information about equalities between Boolean literals and constants, a constraint is redundant. For example, when $Y = \langle 1, 1, 0, 0 \rangle$ and $x_2 = x_3$, then $\mathtt{diff}(X, Y)$ is redundant because $\mathtt{unary}(X, [0, 4]) \wedge (Y = \langle 1, 1, 0, 0 \rangle) \wedge (x_2 = x_3) \models \mathtt{diff}(X, Y)$.

(3) *constraint restriction*, where we discover that some bits in a constraint c are "dont-cares" and project c to the remaining variables. For example, when $x_1{=}1$ and $x_2{=}1$ then y_1 is a don't care and $\mathtt{diff}(X, Y)$ is equivalent to $\mathtt{diff}(X', Y')$ where $X' = \langle x_2, x_3, x_4 \rangle$ and $Y' = \langle y_2, y_3, y_4 \rangle$. To see why $\mathtt{unary}(X, [0, 4]) \wedge \mathtt{unary}(Y, [0, 4]) \wedge x_1 = 1 \wedge x_2 = 1 \models \mathtt{diff}(X, Y) \leftrightarrow \mathtt{diff}(X', Y')$, consider that if $y_1 = 0$ then also $y_2 = 0$ and both $\mathtt{diff}$ constraints are true, and if $y_1 = 1$ then $x_1 \mathtt{\ xor\ } y_1 = \mathit{false}$ and $\mathtt{diff}(X, Y) \leftrightarrow \mathtt{diff}(X', Y')$ follows.

In addition to simplification rules, we apply *decomposition rules* to high-level constraints. For example, an $\mathtt{allDiff}$ constraint decomposes naturally to a set of constituent $\mathtt{diff}$ constraints. The rule we apply to decompose $\mathtt{allDiff}$ constraints is as follows:

$$\mathtt{allDiff}([U_1, \ldots, U_m]) \mapsto \big\{ \, \mathtt{diff}(U_i, U_j) \, \big| \, 1 \leq i < j \leq m \, \big\}, \qquad (2)$$
$$\mathtt{permutation}_{\#}([U_1, \ldots, U_m])$$

where $\mathtt{permutation}_{\#}$ is a redundant constraint.[1] Its role is to introduce redundant clauses to accelerate SAT solving for the special case when the $\mathtt{allDiff}$ constraint specifies a permutation (m variables taking m different values). By delaying the special treatment of $\mathtt{allDiff}$ constraints which specify permutations we can often detect more permutations than prior to constraint simplification. The precise specification of the $\mathtt{permutation}_{\#}$ constraint is given in Section 4.

3   Boolean Equi-propagation

Let $\mathcal{B}$ be a set of Boolean variables. A *literal* is a Boolean variable $b \in \mathcal{B}$ or its negation $\neg b$. The negation of a literal ℓ, denoted $\neg \ell$, is defined as $\neg b$ if $\ell = b$ and as b if $\ell = \neg b$. The Boolean constants 1 and 0 represent *true* and *false*, respectively. The set of literals is denoted $\mathcal{L}$ and $\mathcal{L}_{0,1} = \mathcal{L} \cup \{0, 1\}$.

An *assignment*, A, is a partial mapping from Boolean variables to constants, often viewed as the set of literals: $\{ \, b \, | \, A(b) = 1 \, \} \cup \{ \, \neg b \, | \, A(b) = 0 \, \}$. For a formula φ and $b \in \mathcal{B}$, we denote by $\varphi[b]$ (likewise $\varphi[\neg b]$) the formula obtained by substituting all occurrences of $b \in \mathcal{B}$ in φ by *true* (*false*). This notation extends in the natural way for sets of literals. We say that A satisfies φ if $\varphi[A]$ evaluates

---

[1] The symbol $\#$ in the name of a constraint indicates that it is redundant.

to *true*. A *Boolean Satisfiability (SAT) problem* consists of a Boolean formula φ and determines if there exists an assignment which satisfies φ. The set of (free) Boolean variables that appear in a Boolean formula φ is denoted $vars(\varphi)$.

A *Boolean equality* is a constraint $\ell = \ell'$ where $\ell, \ell' \in \mathcal{L}_{0,1}$. An *equi-formula* E is a set of Boolean equalities understood as a conjunction. The set of equi-formulae is denoted $\mathcal{E}$, and (bi-)implication of equi-formulae is denoted $(\leftrightarrow) \supset$.

Equi-propagation is the process of inferring new equational consequences from the constraints of a model and existing equational information. An *equi-propagator* for Boolean formula φ is an extensive function $\mu_\varphi : \mathcal{E} \to \mathcal{E}$ defined s.t. for all equi-formula E, $\wedge\{\, e \in \mathcal{E} \,|\, \varphi \wedge E \models e \,\} \supset \mu_\varphi(E) \supset E$. That is, a conjunction of Boolean equalities, at least as strong as E, made true by $\varphi \wedge E$. We say that equi-propagator μ_φ is complete if $\mu_\varphi(E) \leftrightarrow \{\, e \in \mathcal{E} \,|\, \varphi \wedge E \models e \,\}$. We denote a complete equi-propagator for φ as $\hat{\mu}_\varphi$.

Example 1. Let $X = \langle x_1, x_2, x_3, x_4 \rangle$ and $Y = \langle y_1, y_2, y_3, y_4 \rangle$ and consider $E_1 = \{\, y_1 = 1, \ y_2 = 1, \ y_3 = 0, \ y_4 = 0 \,\}$ and $E_2 = \{\, x_2 = \neg y_3, \ x_3 = y_2 \,\}$. Then, $\hat{\mu}_{\mathtt{diff}_u(X,Y)}(E_1) = E_1 \sqcup \{x_2 = x_3\}$ and also $\hat{\mu}_{\mathtt{diff}_u(X,Y)}(E_2) = E_2 \cup E_1$.

The following theorem states that complete equi-propagation for a Boolean formula φ will determine at least as many fixed literals as unit propagation for *any* clausal representation of φ.

Theorem 1. *Complete equi-propagation is uniformly stronger than unit propagation.*

Proof. Let φ be a Boolean formula, $E \in \mathcal{E}$, and let ℓ be a literal that follows from unit propagation from some clasual representation of φ and E. Then $\varphi \wedge E \models \ell$ and hence $(\ell = 1) \in \hat{\mu}_\varphi(E)$.

Boolean Unifiers. It is convenient to view equi-formula in a generic "solved-form" as a substitution, θ_E, which is a (most general) unifier for the equations in E. Boolean substitutions generalize assignments in that variables can be bound also to literals. A Boolean *substitution* is an idempotent mapping $\theta : \mathcal{B} \to \mathcal{L}_{0,1}$ such that $dom(\theta) = \{\, b \in B \,|\, \theta(b) \neq b \,\}$ is finite and $\forall. b \in \mathcal{B}. \ \theta(b) \neq \neg b$. It is viewed as the set $\theta = \{\, b \mapsto \theta(b) \,|\, b \in dom(\theta) \,\}$. We can apply θ to another substitution θ', to obtain substitution $(\theta \cdot \theta') = \{\, b \mapsto \theta(\theta'(b)) \,|\, b \in dom(\theta) \cup dom(\theta') \,\}$. A *unifier* for equi-formula E is a substitution θ such that $\models \theta(e)$, for each $e \in E$. A *most-general unifier* for E is a substitution θ such that for any unifier θ' of E, there exists substitution γ where $\theta' = \gamma \cdot \theta$.

Example 2. Consider the equi-formula $E \equiv \{b_1 = \neg b_2, \neg b_3 = \neg b_4, b_5 = b_6, b_6 = b_4, b_7 = 1, b_8 = \neg b_7\}$ then a unifier θ for E is $\{b_2 \mapsto \neg b_1, b_4 \mapsto b_3, b_5 \mapsto b_3, b_6 \mapsto b_3, b_7 \mapsto 1, b_8 \mapsto 0\}$. Note that $\theta(E)$ is the trivially true equi-formula $\{b_1 = \neg\neg b_1, \neg b_3 = \neg b_3, b_3 = b_3, b_3 = b_3, 1 = 1, 0 = \neg 1\}$.

Let $\prec$ be a total (strict) order on $\mathcal{B}$, extended to an order on $\mathcal{L}_{0,1}$ such that $0 \prec 1$ and $\forall. b \in B, \ 1 \prec b$ and $b \approx \neg b$. We define a canonical most-general unifier for any satisfiable equi-formula E: $\mathtt{unify}_E = \lambda b. \min\{\, \ell \in \mathcal{L}_{0,1} \,|\, E \models b = \ell \,\}$. We can compute $\mathtt{unify}_E$ in almost linear (amortized) time using a variation of the union-find algorithm [21].

Example 3. For the equi-formula E and substitution θ from Example 2 we have that $\text{unify}_E = \theta$ where the ordering is $0 \prec 1 \prec b_1 \prec b_2 \prec \cdots \prec b_8$.

The following allows us to replace formula φ by $\text{unify}_E(\varphi)$, and provides an alternative, more efficient to implement, definition for complete equi-propagation.

Proposition 1.   **Proposition 2.**

$\varphi \wedge E \;\leftrightarrow\; \text{unify}_E(\varphi) \wedge E$ $\hat{\mu}_\varphi(E) \;\leftrightarrow\; E \wedge \{e \in \mathcal{E} \mid \text{unify}_E(\varphi) \models e\}$

Implementing complete equi-propagators. A complete equi-propagator is straightforward to implement using binary decision diagrams (BDDs). Consider Boolean formula φ and equi-formula E. Then, for equation $(\ell_1 = \ell_2)$, based on Proposition 2, we can test the condition, $\text{unify}_E(\varphi) \models (\ell_1 \leftrightarrow \ell_2)$ using a standard BDD containment test e.g., "bddLeq" in [19]. This test can be performed for all relevant equations involving variables from $\text{unify}_E(\varphi)$ (and constants 0,1).

Example 4. Consider the BDD shown in Figure 3(a) which represents the formula: $\varphi \equiv \text{unary}_3(A, [0,3]) \wedge \text{unary}_3(B, [0,3]) \wedge \text{diff}(A,B)$. Suppose that E is $\{\, B_1 = 1,\; B_2 = 1,\; B_3 = 0 \,\}$. The BDD for $\text{unify}_E(\varphi)$ is shown in Figure 3(b). It is easy to see from the BDD that equi-propagation determines that $\text{unify}_E(\varphi) \models A_2 = A_3$. Indeed $\hat{\mu}_\varphi(E) = E' = E \cup \{A_2 = A_3\}$.

We apply complete equi-propagation in cases when BDDs are guaranteed to be polynomial in the size of the constraints they propagate for. The following result holds for an arbitrary constraint φ, so it also holds for $\text{unify}_E(\varphi)$.

Proposition 3. *Let $c(Xs)$ be an arbitrary constraint about integer variables $Xs = [X_1, \ldots, X_k]$ each represented with n bits in the order encoding. Then, the number of nodes in the BDD representing $c(Xs)$ is bound by $O(n^k)$.*

Proof. (Sketch) There are only $n + 1$ legitimate states for each n bit unary variable, and the BDD cannot have more nodes than possible states.   □

Implementing ad-hoc equi-propagators. Most simple constraints have a fixed small arity and hence complete equi-propagators using BDD are polynomially bounded. However, this is not the case for global constraints where the arity is not fixed. In this case we define an ad-hoc, possibly incomplete, equi-propagator. We demonstrate this for the $\text{allDiff}([U_1, \ldots, U_m])$ constraint.

Example 5. Consider $Us = [U_1, \ldots, U_5]$ where the $U_i = \langle x_{i1}, \ldots, x_{i9} \rangle$ are integer variables in the range $[0, 9]$. Given E, we denote $\text{unify}_E(Us) = [U'_1, \ldots, U'_5]$ and illustrate equi-propagator $\mu_\varphi(E) = E \cup E'$ for $\varphi = \text{allDiff}_u(Us)$: **(1)** Consider $E = \{\, x_{12} = 1, x_{13} = 0 \,\}$. Denoting $E_a = \{\, x_{1j} = j \leq 2 \mid 1 \leq j \leq 9 \,\}$ (e.g. $U'_1 = 2$), and $E_b = \{\, x_{i2} = x_{i3} \mid 2 \leq i \leq 5 \,\}$ (e.g. $U'_i \neq 2$ for $i > 1$), the propagator adds $E' = E_a \cup E_b$. **(2)** Consider $E = E_b \cup E_c$ where $E_c = \{\, x_{i5} = 0 \mid 1 \leq i \leq 5 \,\}$ (e.g. $U_i \leq 4$) and E_b is from the previous case. In this case, only U_1 can take the value 2. So a propagator adds equations imposing that $U'_1 = \langle 1, 1, 0, \ldots, 0 \rangle$. **(3)** Consider $E = E_c \cup E_d$ where $E_d = \bigcup \{\, x_{i1} = x_{i2}, x_{i3} = x_{i4} \mid 3 \leq i \leq 5 \,\}$ (e.g. only U_1 and U_2 can take the values 1 and 3) and E_c is from the previous case. A propagator adds $E' = \cup \{\, x_{i1} = 1, x_{i2} = x_{i3}, x_{i4} = 0 \mid i \in \{1, 2\} \,\}$.

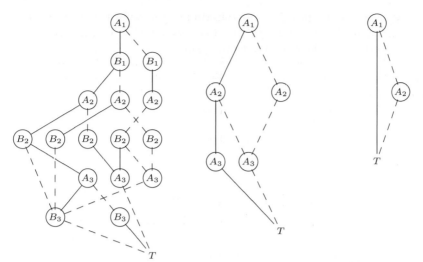

(a) BDD for $\mathtt{diff}_u(A, B)$ **(b)** Simpl'd wrt $B{=}[1,1,0]$ **(c)** Simpl'd wrt $A_2{=}A_3$

Fig. 1. BDDs for (a) $\varphi \equiv \mathtt{unary}_3(A, [0,3]) \wedge \mathtt{unary}_3(B, [0,3]) \wedge \mathtt{diff}(A, B)$ (b) $\mathtt{unify}_E(\varphi)$ where $E = \{B_1{=}1, B_2{=}1, B_3{=}0\}$ and (c) $\mathtt{unify}_{E'}(\varphi)$ where $E' = E \cup \{A_2{=}A_3\}$. Full (dashed) lines correspond to true (false) edges. Target "F" node is omitted for brevity.

The following is essentially the usual domain consistent propagator for the `allDiff` constraint [18] applied to the unary encoding.

Definition 1 (ad-hoc equi-propagator for `allDiff`). An equi-propagator for $\varphi = \mathtt{allDiff}_u(Us)$ where $Us = [U_1, \ldots, U_m]$ is defined as $\mu_\varphi(E) = E \cup E'$ where $E' = \{\, U_i'(v) = U_i'(v+1) \,|\, i \in \{1, \ldots, m\} - H, v \in V \,\}$ if there exists a Hall set $H \subseteq \{1, \ldots, m\}$ where $V = \cup_{i \in H} dom(U_i')$, $|V| = |H|$ and denoting $\mathtt{unify}_E(Us) - [U_1', \ldots, U_m']$. Otherwise, $E' = \emptyset$.

After a Hall set H is detected (and equi-propagation has triggered), we also apply an additional decomposition rule:

$$\mathtt{allDiff}(Us) \mapsto \mathtt{allDiff}([U_i \mid i \in H]) \wedge \mathtt{allDiff}([U_i \mid i \in \{1, \ldots, m\} - H])$$

The benefit arises because the first `allDiff` constraint is guaranteed to represent a permutation so the $\mathtt{permutation}_\#$ constraint gives an advantage.

For the three cases in Example 5 we have: **(1)** $H{=}\{1\}$ and $V{=}\{2\}$, **(2)** $H{=}\{2,3,4,5\}$, and $V{=}\{0,1,3,4\}$, and **(3)** $H{=}\{3,4,5\}$ and $V{=}\{0,2,4\}$. Indeed we can convert any finite domain propagator to an equi-propagator. The following holds simply because the unary encoding can represent arbitrary domains.

Proposition 4. *Let $E \in \mathcal{E}$ and $c(Xs)$ be a constraint over integer variables $Xs = [X_1, \ldots, X_m]$. Let $\mathtt{unify}_E(Xs) = [X_1', \ldots, X_m']$. Suppose D is the mapping from variables to sets of value $D(X_i) = dom(X_i')$ and suppose propagator f for $c(Xs)$ maps D to D'. Then a correct equi-propagator for $c(Xs)$ discovers new equality literals $E' = \{X_i'(v) = X_i'(v+1) \mid i \in \{1, \ldots, m\}, v \in D(X_i) - D'(X_i)\}$.*

Note that complete equi-propagators can determine more information than finite domain propagation as illustrated by the example for E_2 in Example 1. To complete this section, consider the following example.

x_{11}	x_{12}	x_{13}	x_{14}
x_{21}	x_{22}	x_{23}	x_{24}
x_{31}	x_{32}	x_{33}	x_{34}
x_{41}	x_{42}	x_{43}	x_{44}
x_{51}	x_{52}	x_{53}	x_{54}

$\xRightarrow{E_1}$

1	A	A	A
1	B	B	B
C	D	D	0
E	E	E	F
x_{51}	x_{52}	x_{53}	x_{54}

$\xRightarrow{E_2}$

1	A	A	A
1	$-A$	$-A$	$-A$
D	D	D	0
E	E	E	0
G	G	H	0

$\xRightarrow{E_3}$

1	A	A	A
1	$-A$	$-A$	$-A$
D	D	D	0
$-D$	$-D$	$-D$	0
1	1	1	0

(a)   (b)   (c)   (d)

Fig. 2. An example of equi-propagation (See Example 6)

Example 6. Consider constraint $\varphi = \mathtt{allDiff}(Xs)$ where $Xs = [X_1, \ldots, X_5]$ with each X_i in the interval $[0, 4]$, depicted as Fig. 2(a). Consider also the equi-formula E_1 which specifies that $X_1, X_2 \in \{1, 4\}$, $X_3 \in \{0, 1, 3\}$, $X_4 \in \{0, 3, 4\}$. Fig. 2(b) depicts $\mathtt{unify}_{E_1}(Xs)$. Constraint simplification proceeds in two steps. First, equi-propagation adds equi-formula E_2, the affect of which is depicted as Fig. 2(c) where φ is also decomposed: The upper part, $\mathtt{allDiff}(X_1, X_2)$, and the lower part $\mathtt{allDiff}(X_3, X_4, X_5)$. In the second step equi-propagation adds equi-formula E_3, the impact of which is depicted as Fig. 2(d). Constraint φ is now fully solved, Xs is represented using only 2 propositional variables and the CNF encoding will contain no clauses.

4   Optimized SAT Encodings Using Equi-propagation

Boolean equi-propagation is at the foundation of our optimizing CNF compiler. The compiler repeatedly applies: equi-propagation, constraint decomposition, restriction and elimination, and finally outputs CNF encodings. We assume that each constraint comes with an associated equi-propagator.

Given a conjunction Φ of constraints, we first apply equi-propagators. Each such application effectively removes at least one bit from the Boolean representation of Φ. During this process, when no further equi-propagators can be applied, we may apply a decomposition rule to a high-level constraint, introducing additional low-level constraints, but without introducing additional bits in the system. The actual implementation is of course less naive. It takes care to wakeup equi-propagators only when they may generate new information, and it makes use of the most efficient implementation of the equi-propagator possible, so avoiding BDD based propagators if we have an equivalent propagator implemented directly.

The complexity of the compiler is measured in the size of the constraint system Φ it is optimizing. Denote by $|\Phi|_c$, the total number of low-level constraints in Φ after decomposing all high-level constraints, and by $|\Phi|_b$ the total number of Boolean variables in the bit representation of Φ. Assuming that equi-propagators are of polynomial cost, then so is the cost of running the compiler itself.

Proposition 5. *Let Φ be a conjunction of high- and low-level (finite domain) constraints. Then the number of equi-propagation steps performed when compiling Φ is bound by $O(|\Phi|_c \times |\Phi|_b)$.*

Proof. (sketch) Each pass of the algorithm covers at most $|\Phi|_c$ constraints and removes at least one of the $|\Phi|_b$ Boolean variables from Φ. □

After equi-propagation and constraint decomposition triggers no more, we apply constraint restriction and elimination rules. We say that a constraint φ is redundant with respect to an equi-formula E if either (a) $\texttt{unify}_E(\varphi)$ is a tautology or (b) there exists another constraint φ' in the constraint store such that $\texttt{unify}_E(\varphi') \models \texttt{unify}_E(\varphi)$. Our implementation is tuned to identify a collection of ad-hoc cases. However in general, where BDDs have been applied to implement complete propagators, such tests are particularly easy. Testing for (a) is trivial. Testing for (b) is also straightforward for BDDs e.g., using "$\texttt{bddLeq}$" in [19]. However we only apply this rule in a restricted form due to the quadratic time-complexity of examining all pairs of constraints. Namely, to determine cases of the form $true_u(X_1, \ldots, X_n) \models c(X_1, \ldots, X_n)$ where the constraint is redundant with respect to the unary encoding of its variables.

Example 7. Take $\varphi = \texttt{diff}_u(A, B)$ and E' from Example 4. The BDD for $\varphi'' = \texttt{unify}_{E'}(\varphi)$ is shown in Figure 3(c). One can check that $\texttt{unary}(A, [0, 4]) \models \varphi''$ using "$\texttt{bddLeq}$" indicating that the original constraint $\texttt{diff}(A, B)$ is redundant.

In the final stage, when no further simplification applies, constraints are encoded to CNF formula. This can be performed either using their Boolean specification, or if BDD based propagators were applied, then we can read off the encoding from the BDD using standard techniques.

Redundant constraints (with subscript $\#$ in the name) that were introduced in the model only to improve equi-propagation need not be encoded to CNF clauses. However, when we expect such redundant clauses to facilitate unit propagation during SAT solving, then we do add them. For instance, we add clauses to encode redundant $\texttt{permutation}_\#$ constraints. Each such constraint $\varphi' = \texttt{permutation}_\#([U_1, \ldots, U_m])$ is affiliated with a corresponding $\texttt{allDiff}$ constraint. If $S = \cup_{i=1}^m dom(U_i)$, $|S| \neq m$ then the $\texttt{allDiff}$ constraint does not represent a permutation and nothing is added. Otherwise we create additional Boolean variables b_{iv} to represent the expressions $U_i = v, v \in S$. Let the unary encoding of U_i be $\langle u_1, \ldots, u_k \rangle$. We add clauses encoding $b_{iv} \leftrightarrow (u_v \wedge \neg u_{v+1})$ to connect these to the unary encoding, and the clauses $\vee_{i=1}^m b_{iv}, \forall v \in S$ to get better propagation from permutations.

5   Implementation, Experiments, and Extensions

All experiments were performed on an Intel Core 2 Duo E8400 3.00GHz CPU with 4GB memory under Linux (Ubuntu lucid, kernel 2.6.32-24-generic).[2] Our

---

[2] The benchmark instances and encodings can be viewed at
   http://www.cs.bgu.ac.il/~mcodish/Benchmarks/CP2011/

Table 1. QCP results for 25×25 instances with 264 holes

instance		compiler			Sugar		3D		CSP'08	OSC'09	FS'09
num	un/sat	compl (sec.)	cnf size (clauses)	SAT (sec.)	cnf size (clauses)	SAT (sec.)	cnf size (clauses)	SAT (sec.)	(sec.)	(sec.)	(sec.)
1	sat	0.41	6509	2.46	140315	37.36	6507	0.09	31.55	34.81	6.44
2	sat	0.33	7475	0.02	140920	234.70	7438	0.74	137.60	99.84	44.80
4	sat	0.38	6818	0.61	141581	90.64	6811	0.08	47.24	273.36	157.58
5	sat	0.35	7082	0.32	140431	206.03	7099	0.14	27.33	24.87	22.30
6	sat	0.33	7055	0.45	140625	67.84	7044	1.11	35.78	108.60	12.58
7	sat	0.33	7711	2.36	142200	60.97	7684	0.08	57.23	67.32	341.62
11	unsat	0.45	6491	0.05	140603	39.02	6534	0.03	19.47	30.02	5.20
12	unsat	0.23	1	0.00	139037	0.58	7393	0.00	0.36	0.05	0.81
14	unsat	0.28	1	0.00	140706	2.25	7173	0.00	1.40	0.29	0.80
15	unsat	0.38	6063	0.05	140224	35.93	6104	0.06	32.39	58.41	4.77

prototype constraint compiler is written in Prolog and run using SWI Prolog v5.10.2 64-bits. Complete propagators are implemented using the BDD package, CUDD v2.4.2. Comparisons with Sugar (v1.14.7) are based on the use of identical constraint models, apply the same SAT solver (CryptoMiniSat v2.5.1), and run on the same machine. Comparisons with Minion (v0.10) are based on the use of identical constraint models, and run on the same machine (with minor differences due to syntax). For each of the example problems we extend (our description of) the constraint modelling language as required for the benchmarks.

Quasigroup Completion Problems. (QCP) are given as an $n \times n$ board of integer variables (in the range $[1, n]$) in which some are assigned integer values. The task is to assign values to all variables, so that no column or row contains the same value twice. A model is a conjunction of `allDiff` constraints.

Table 1 illustrates results for 10 (of the largest) instances from the 2008 CSP competition[3] with data for our compiler (compilation time, number of clauses, SAT solving time), Sugar (number of clauses, subsequent SAT solving time), the so-called 3D SAT encoding of [12] (number of clauses after unit propagation, SAT solving time), and from: CSP'08 (the winning result from the 2008 competition), OSC'09 and FS'09 (results for lazy clause generation solvers reported in [16] and [9]). It is, by now, accepted that the 3D encoding is strong for QCP problems, a fact echoed by the results of Table 1. Observe that for 2 instances, unsatisfiable is detected directly by the compiler (where the CNF contains 1 empty clause).

Table 2 shows results for larger (40×40, satisfiable) instances[4] with 800-1000 holes. We compare the order-encoding (compiled) and the 3D-encoding (with unit propagation). The CNF sizes before compilation/unit propagation are

Table 2. QCP 40×40. CNF size in **million's** clauses

inst.	order enc.		3D enc.		inst.	order enc.		3D enc.	
800	CNF	SAT	CNF	SAT	1000	CNF	SAT	CNF	SAT
holes	mCl	(sec)	mCl	(sec)	holes	mCl	(sec)	mCl	(sec)
1	0.11	18.24	0.13	6.87	1	0.31	0.40	0.38	27.78
2	0.11	2.88	0.13	3.70	2	0.31	0.39	0.38	0.33
3	0.11	6.54	0.13	2.50	3	0.31	0.39	0.39	19.76
4	0.11	0.34	0.13	1.47	4	0.31	0.39	0.38	8.73
5	0.11	21.50	0.13	7.09	5	0.31	0.39	0.38	0.35
total		50.05		22.28	total		1.96		56.95

---

[3] http://www.cril.univ-artois.fr/CPAI08/

[4] Generated using lsencode from http://www.cs.cornell.edu/gomes/SOFT

circa 2.74 million clauses for the order-encoding and 3.74 for the 3D-encoding. The advantage of the 3D encoding is no longer clear.

This experiment indicates that our compiler competes with the 3D encoding for QCP. Other high level models are clearly inferior. The comparison with Sugar (stunning reduction in CNF size and faster SAT solving) is representative of all other experiments and hence not highlighted in the following result tables.

Nonogram Problems. are boards of cells to color black or white, given clues per row and column of a board. A clue is a number sequence indicating blocks of cells to be colored black. For example, the clue $\langle 4, 8, 3\rangle$ on a row indicates that it should contain contiguous blocks of $4, 8$ and 3 black cells (in that order) separated by non-empty sequences of white cells. A Nonogram puzzle is modeled as a Boolean matrix with constraints per row and column, each about a clue (number sequence) $\langle b_1, \ldots, b_k\rangle$, and about a Boolean vector, Vec (a row or column of the matrix). Each b_i is associated with an integer variable indicating the index in Vec where block b_i starts. For notation, if $U=\langle u_1, \ldots, u_n\rangle$ is an integer variable (order-encoding) then U^{+c} is U prefixed by c ones representing $U+c$. Similarly, if U is greater than c then $U^{-c} = \langle u_{c+1}, \ldots, u_n\rangle$ represents $U-c$. We introduce two additional constraints

Table 3. Human Nonograms Results

instance		compiler				
id	size	comp	cnf	sat	BGU	Walt.
9717	(30x30)	0.13	14496	124.43	∞	∞
10000	(50x40)	0.28	44336	40.66	∞	∞
9892	(40x50)	0.57	30980	0.44	∞	∞
2556	(45x65)	0.13	2870	0.00	15.85	0.4
10088	(63x52)	0.64	78482	1.26	0.27	0.08
2712	(47x47)	0.31	43350	0.92	5.98	4.95
6727	(80x80)	1.11	156138	2.86	0.5	0.17
8098	(19x19)	0.02	3296	0.06	209.54	8.63
6574	(25x25)	0.10	7426	0.03	37.56	2.94

$\boxed{4}$ $\texttt{block}(U_1, U_2, Vec)$ $\qquad\qquad$ $\boxed{5}$ $\texttt{leq}(U_1, U_2)$

The first specifies that for a bit vector Vec the variables in the indices greater than value U_1 and less equal value U_2 (with $U_1 \leq U_2$) are true. The second specifies that for integer variables U_1 and U_2 in the order-encoding, $U_1 \leq U_2$. The Boolean functions corresponding to constraints of these forms are as follows:

$$\texttt{block}(U_1, U_2, \langle x_1, \ldots, x_n\rangle) = \bigwedge_{i=1}^{n}(\neg U_1(i) \wedge U_2(i) \rightarrow x_i$$
$$\texttt{leq}(\langle x_1, \ldots, x_n\rangle, \langle y_1, \ldots, y_n\rangle) = \bigwedge_{i=1}^{n} x_i \rightarrow y_i \qquad (3)$$

Example 8. The constraints below model the position of block sequence $s = \langle 3, 1, 2\rangle$ in $X = \langle x_1, \ldots, x_9\rangle$. In the first column, integer variables, U_1, U_2, U_3 model the start positions of the three blocks. In the second column, the start position of a block is required to be at least one after the end position of its predecessor. In the third column, $\texttt{block}$ constraints specify the black cells in the vector X, and in the fourth column the white cells in the block $\bar{X} = \langle \neg x_1, \ldots, \neg x_9\rangle$.

$\texttt{unary}(U_1, [1,9])$ $\qquad\qquad\qquad\qquad$ $\texttt{block}(U_1^{-1}, U_1^{+3}, X)$ $\quad$ $\texttt{block}(0, U_1, \bar{X})$
$\texttt{unary}(U_2, [1,9])$ $\quad$ $\texttt{leq}(U_1^{+4}, U_2)$ $\quad$ $\texttt{block}(U_2^{-1}, U_2^{+1}, X)$ $\quad$ $\texttt{block}(U_1^{+4}, U_2, \bar{X})$
$\texttt{unary}(U_3, [1,9])$ $\quad$ $\texttt{leq}(U_2^{+2}, U_3)$ $\quad$ $\texttt{block}(U_3^{-1}, U_3^{+2}, X)$ $\quad$ $\texttt{block}(U_2^{+2}, U_3, \bar{X})$

Tables 3 & 4 compare ours to the two fastest documented Nonogram solvers: BGU (v1.0.2) [17] and Wolter (v1.09) [24]. Table 3 is about "human-designed" instances from [22]. These are the 10 hardest problems for the BGU solver. The first 8 puzzles have at least 2 solutions. The last 2 have a single solution. Solving time is for determining the number of solutions (0, 1, or more). For our compiler, the columns indicate: compilation time, cnf size (number of clauses) and sat solving time. The final two columns are about the solution times for the BGU and Wolter solvers (running on the same machine). The timeout for these solvers (indicated by ∞) is 300 sec. Table 4 reports on a collection of 5,000 random puzzles from [23]. For each of the three solvers we indicate how many puzzles it solves within the given allocated time. This experiment indicates that our compiler is superior to other known methods for Nonograms. We apply generic SAT solving compared to the other systems which are nonogram-specific.

Table 4. 5,000 Random Nonograms Results

	time (sec)	0.20	0.50	1.00	10.00	30.00	60.00
solver	BGU	279	3161	4871	4978	4989	4995
	Wolter	4635	4782	4840	4952	4974	4976
	Compiler	13	4878	4994	5000	5000	5000

BIBD Problems. (CSPlib problem 28) are defined by a 5-tuple of positive integers $\langle v, b, r, k, \lambda \rangle$ and require to partition v distinct objects into b blocks such that each block contains k different objects, exactly r objects occur in each block, and every two distinct objects occur in exactly λ blocks. To model BIBD problems we introduce three additional constraints

6 sumBits($[B_1, \ldots, B_n], U$)   7 uadder(U_1, U_2, U_3)

8 pairwise_and($[A_1, \ldots, A_n], [B_1, \ldots, B_n], [C_1, \ldots, C_n]$)

The first (high-level) constraint states that the sum of bits, $[B_1, \ldots, B_n]$ is the unary value U. It is defined by decomposition: split the bits into two parts, sum the parts, then add the resulting (unary) numbers. The sum of two unary numbers, $U_1 + U_2 = U_3$, is specified by the (low-level) constraint uadder(U_1, U_2, U_3). To compute the scalar product of vectors $[A_1, \ldots, A_n]$ and $[B_1, \ldots, B_n]$ we use the pairwise_and constraint in combination with sumBits.

The model for BIBD instance $\langle v, b, r, k, \lambda \rangle$ is a Boolean incidence matrix with constraints: sumBits(C, k) (sumBits(R, r)) for each column C (row R); and for each pair of rows R_i, R_j ($i < j$), pairwise_and(R_i, R_j, Vs) and sumBits(Vs, λ). To break symmetry, we reorder rows and columns of the matrix to assign fixed values in the first two rows and leftmost column: the first row contains r ones, followed by zeros. The second row contains λ ones, $r - \lambda$ zeros, $r - \lambda$ ones, and then zeros. The left column contains k ones followed by zeros. This information enables the compiler to simplify constraints.

Table 5 shows results comparing our compiler (compilation time, cnf size, and sat solving time) using the model we call SymB (for symmetry breaking) with the Minion constraint solver [11]. Ignore for now the last 3 columns about SATELITE. We will come back to explain these in Section 6. All experiments were run on the same computer. We consider three different models for Minion: [M'06] indicates

Table 5. BIBD results (180 sec. timeout)

instance	compiler (SymB)			Minion			SATELITE (SymB)		
$\langle v, b, r, k, \lambda \rangle$	comp (sec.)	cnf size (clauses)	SAT (sec.)	[M'06] (sec.)	SymB (sec.)	SymB$^+$ (sec.)	prepro (sec.)	cnf size (clauses)	SAT (sec.)
$\langle 7, 420, 180, 3, 60 \rangle$	1.65	698579	1.73	0.54	1.36	0.42	1.67	802576	2.18
$\langle 7, 560, 240, 3, 80 \rangle$	3.73	1211941	13.60	0.66	1.77	0.52	2.73	1397188	5.18
$\langle 12, 132, 33, 3, 6 \rangle$	0.95	180238	0.73	5.51	∞	1.76	1.18	184764	0.57
$\langle 15, 45, 24, 8, 12 \rangle$	0.51	116016	8.46	∞	∞	75.87	0.64	134146	∞
$\langle 15, 70, 14, 3, 2 \rangle$	0.56	81563	0.39	12.22	1.42	0.31	1.02	79542	0.20
$\langle 16, 80, 15, 3, 2 \rangle$	0.81	109442	0.56	107.43	13.40	0.35	1.14	105242	0.35
$\langle 19, 19, 9, 9, 4 \rangle$	0.23	39931	0.09	53.23	38.30	0.31	0.4	44714	0.09
$\langle 19, 57, 9, 3, 1 \rangle$	0.34	113053	0.17	∞	1.71	0.35	10.45	111869	0.14
$\langle 21, 21, 5, 5, 1 \rangle$	0.02	0	0.00	1.26	0.67	0.15	0.01	0	0.00
$\langle 25, 25, 9, 9, 3 \rangle$	0.64	92059	1.33	∞	∞	0.92	1.01	97623	8.93
$\langle 25, 30, 6, 5, 1 \rangle$	0.10	24594	0.06	∞	1.37	0.31	1.2	23828	0.05
Total		36.66				81.24		> 219.14	

results using the BIBD model described in [11], SymB uses the same model we use for the SAT approach, SymB$^+$, is an enhanced symmetry breaking model with all of the tricks applied also in the [M'06] model. For the columns with no timeouts we show total times (for the compiler this includes compile time and sat solving). Note that by using a clever modeling of the problem we have improved also the previous runtimes for Minion.

This experiment indicates that our compiler is significantly faster than Minion on its BIBD models ([M'06]). Only when tailoring our SymB model, Minion becomes competitive with ours (and still total Minion time is double).

Word Design for DNA. (Problem 033 of CSPLib) seeks the largest parameter n, s.t. there exist a set S of n eight-letter words over the alphabet $\Sigma = \{A, C, G, T\}$ with the following properties: (1) Each word in S has 4 symbols from $\{C, G\}$; (2) Each pair of distinct words in S differ in at least 4 positions; and (3) For every $x, y \in S$: x^R (the reverse of x) and y^C (the word obtained by replacing each A by T, each C by G, and vice versa) differ in at least 4 positions.

In [10], the authors present the "*template-map*" strategy for this problem. Letters are modelled by bit-pairs $\langle t_i, m_i \rangle$. For each eight-letter word, $\langle t_1, \ldots, t_8 \rangle$ is the *template* and $\langle m_1, \ldots, m_8 \rangle$ is the *map*. The authors pose conditions on a set of templates T and a set of maps M so that the Cartesian product $S = T \times M$ will satisfy the requirements of the original problem. It is this template-map strategy that we model in our encoding. The authors report a solution composed from two template-maps $\langle T_1, M_1 \rangle$ and $\langle T_2, M_2 \rangle$ where $|T_1| = 6$, $|M_1| = 16$, $|T_2| = 2$, $|M_2| = 6$. This forms a set S with $(6 \times 16) + (2 \times 6) = 108$ DNA words. Marc van Dongen reports a larger solution with 112 words.[5] To model this problem we introduce the two constraints (where V_i are vectors of bits).

$\boxed{9}$ lexleq($[V_1, \ldots, V_n]$) $\boxed{10}$ lexleq(V_1, V_2)

The first specifies that a list of vectors is ordered in the lexicographic order. It decomposes to low-level constraints (of the second form) that specify that pairs of vectors are ordered in the lexicographic order.

---

[5] See http://www.cs.st-andrews.ac.uk/~ianm/CSPLib/

Using our compiler, we find a template and map of size 14 and 8, the Cartesian product of which gives a solution with $14 \times 8 = 112$ words. The SAT solving time is less than 0.2 seconds. Håkan Kjellerstrand reports finding a 112 word solution in 36.5s using Comet.[6] To show that there is no template of size 15 and no map of size 9 takes 0.14 and 3.32 seconds respectively. This is a new result not obtainable using previous solving techniques. We obtain this result when symmetries are broken by ordering the vectors in T and in M lexicographically. Proving that there is no solution to the original DNA word problem with more than 112 words (not via the template-map strategy) is still an open problem.

6   Related Work and Conclusion

There is a considerable body of work on CNF simplification techniques with a clear trade-off between amount of reduction achieved and invested time. Most of these approaches determine binary clauses implied by the CNF, which is certainly enough to determine Boolean equalities. The problem is that determining all binary clauses implied by the CNF is prohibitive when the SAT model may involve many thousands of variables. Typically only some of the implied binary clauses are determined, such as those visible by unit propagation. The trade-off is regulated by the choice of the techniques applied to infer binary clauses, considering the power and cost. See for example [7] and the references therein. There are also approaches [14] that detect and use Boolean equalities during runtime, which are complementary to our approach.

In our approach, the beast is tamed by introducing a notion of locality. We do not consider the full CNF. Instead, by maintaining the original representation, a conjunction of constraints, each viewed as a Boolean formula, we can apply powerful reasoning techniques to separate parts of the model and maintain efficient preprocessing. Our specific choice, using BDD's for bounded sized formula, guarantees that reasoning is always polynomial in cost.

To illustrate one difference consider again Example 6 where equi-propagation simplifies the constraint so that it is expressed in 2 propositional variables and requires 0 clauses. In contrast, the CNF representing the `allDiff` constraint with the initial equations E_1 consists of 76 clauses with 23 variables and after applying SatELite [7] this is reduced to 57 clauses with 16 variables. Examining this reduced CNF reveals that it contains binary clauses corresponding to the equations in E_2 but not those from E_3.

Finally, we come back to (the last 3 columns in) Table 5 where a comparison with SatELite is presented. It is interesting to note that in some cases preprocessing results in smaller CNF and faster SAT solving, however in total (even if not counting the timeout for BIBD instance $\langle 15, 45, 24, 8, 12 \rangle$) equi-propagation is stronger.

Using equi-propagation on a high level view of the problem allows us to simplify the problem more aggressively than is possible with a CNF representation. The resulting CNF models can be significantly smaller than those

---

[6]   See http://www.hakank.org/comet/word_design_dna1.co

resulting from straight translation, and significantly faster to solve. Hence we believe that Boolean equi-propagation, combined with CNF simplification tools (such as SATELITE), makes an important contribution to the encoding of CSPs to SAT.

References

1. Bailleux, O., Boufkhad, Y.: Efficient CNF encoding of boolean cardinality constraints. In: Rossi, F. (ed.) CP 2003. LNCS, vol. 2833, pp. 108–122. Springer, Heidelberg (2003)
2. Barrett, C., Stump, A., Tinelli, C.: The Satisfiability Modulo Theories Library, SMT-LIB (2010), www.SMT-LIB.org
3. Bofill, M., Suy, J., Villaret, M.: A System for solving constraint satisfaction problems with SMT. In: Strichman, O., Szeider, S. (eds.) SAT 2010. LNCS, vol. 6175, pp. 300–305. Springer, Heidelberg (2010)
4. Bryant, R.: Graph-based algorithms for Boolean function manipulation. IEEE Transactions on Computers C-35(8), 677–691 (1986)
5. Cadoli, M., Schaerf, A.: Compiling problem specifications into SAT. Artificial Intelligence 162(1-2), 89–120 (2005)
6. Crawford, J., Baker, A.: Experimental results on the application of satisfiability algorithms to scheduling problems. In: Procs. AAAI 1994, pp. 1092–1097 (1994)
7. Eén, N., Biere, A.: Effective preprocessing in SAT through variable and clause elimination. In: Bacchus, F., Walsh, T. (eds.) SAT 2005. LNCS, vol. 3569, pp. 61–75. Springer, Heidelberg (2005)
8. Eén, N., Sörensson, N.: An extensible sat-solver. In: Giunchiglia, E., Tacchella, A. (eds.) SAT 2003. LNCS, vol. 2919, pp. 502–518. Springer, Heidelberg (2004)
9. Feydy, T., Stuckey, P.: Lazy clause generation reengineered. In: Gent, I.P. (ed.) CP 2009. LNCS, vol. 5732, pp. 352–366. Springer, Heidelberg (2009)
10. Frutos, A.G., Qinghua Liu, A.J.T., Sanner, A.M.W., Condon, A.E., Smith, L.M., Corn, R.M.: Demonstration of a word design strategy for DNA computing on surfaces. Journal of Nucleic Acids Research 25(23), 4748–4757 (1997)
11. Gent, I.P., Jefferson, C., Miguel, I.: Minion: A fast scalable constraint solver. In: Brewka, G., Coradeschi, S., Perini, A., Traverso, P. (eds.) ECAI. Frontiers in Artificial Intelligence and Applications, vol. 141, pp. 98–102. IOS Press, Amsterdam (2006)
12. Gomes, C., Shmoys, D.: Completing Quasigroups or Latin Squares: A structured graph coloring problem. In: Proceedings of the Computational Symposium on Graph Coloring and Extensions (2002)
13. Huang, J.: Universal Booleanization of constraint models. In: Stuckey, P.J. (ed.) CP 2008. LNCS, vol. 5202, pp. 144–158. Springer, Heidelberg (2008)
14. Li, C.M.: Equivalent Literal Propagation in the DLL Procedure. Discrete Applied Mathematics 130(2), 251–276 (2003)
15. Nethercote, N., Stuckey, P.J., Becket, R., Brand, S., Duck, G.J., Tack, G.: Minizinc: Towards a standard CP modelling language. In: Bessière, C. (ed.) CP 2007. LNCS, vol. 4741, pp. 529–543. Springer, Heidelberg (2007)
16. Ohrimenko, O., Stuckey, P., Codish, M.: Propagation via lazy clause generation. Constraints 14(3), 357–391 (2009)
17. Pomeranz, D., Raziel, B., Rabani, R., Berend, D., Goldberg, M.: BGU Nonogram solver (student project), http://www.cs.bgu.ac.il/~benr/nonograms (viewed March 2011)

18. Regin, J.-C.: A filtering algorithm for constraints of difference in CSP. In: Procs. AAAI 1994, pp. 362–367 (1994)
19. Somenzi, F.: CUDD: Colorado University Decision Diagram package (February 2009), http://vlsi.colorado.edu/~fabio/CUDD/ (Online, accessed April 13, 2011)
20. Tamura, N., Taga, A., Kitagawa, S., Banbara, M.: Compiling finite linear CSP into SAT. Constraints 14(2), 254–272 (2009)
21. Tarjan, R.: Efficiency of a good but not linear set union algorithm. JACM 22(2), 215–225 (1975)
22. Wolter, J.: Nonogram puzzle collection, http://webpbn.com/export.cgi (viewed March 2011)
23. Wolter, J.: Nonogram random puzzle collection, http://webpbn.com/survey/rand30.tgz (viewed March 2011)
24. Wolter, J.: Wolter Nonogram solver, http://webpbn.com/pbnsolve.html (viewed March 2011)

CP Models for Maximum Common Subgraph Problems

Samba Ndojh Ndiaye and Christine Solnon

Université de Lyon, CNRS
Université Lyon 1, LIRIS, UMR5205, F-69622, France

Abstract. The distance between two graphs is usually defined by means of the size of a largest common subgraph. This common subgraph may be an induced subgraph, obtained by removing nodes, or a partial subgraph, obtained by removing arcs and nodes. In this paper, we introduce two soft CSPs which model these two maximum common subgraph problems in a unified framework. We also introduce and compare different CP models, corresponding to different levels of constraint propagation.

1 Introduction

Graphs are used in many applications to represent structured objects such as, for example, molecules, images, or biological networks. In many of these applications, it is necessary to measure the distance between two graphs, and this problem often turns into finding a largest subgraph which is common to both graphs [1]. More precisely, we may either look for a maximum common induced subgraph (which has as many nodes as possible), or a maximum common partial subgraph (which has as many arcs as possible). Both problems are NP-hard in the general case [2], and have been widely studied, in particular in bioinformatic and chemoinformatic applications [3,4].

In this paper, we study how to solve these problems with CP. In Section 2, we recall definitions and we describe existing approaches. In Section 3, we introduce two soft CSPs which model these problems in a unified framework. In Section 4, we introduce different CP models, corresponding to different levels of constraint propagation. In Section 5, we experimentally compare these different models.

2 Background

2.1 Definitions

A graph G is composed of a finite set N_G of nodes and a set $A_G \subseteq N_G \times N_G$ of arcs. We implicitly consider directed graphs, such that each arc is a directed couple of nodes. Results introduced in this paper may be generalized to non directed graphs in a straightforward way, by associating two directed arcs (u, v) and (v, u) with every non directed edge linking u and v.

Let G and G' be two graphs. G is *isomorphic* to G' if there exists a bijective function $f : N_G \rightarrow N_{G'}$ which preserves arcs, *i.e.*, $\forall (u, v) \in N_G \times N_G, (u, v) \in$

J. Lee (Ed.): CP 2011, LNCS 6876, pp. 637 644, 2011.
© Springer-Verlag Berlin Heidelberg 2011

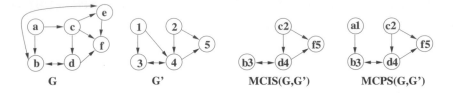

Fig. 1. Example of two graphs G and G' and their MCIS and MCPS

$A_G \Leftrightarrow (f(u), f(v)) \in A_{G'}$. An *induced subgraph* is obtained by removing nodes, *i.e.*, G' is an induced subgraph of G if $N_{G'} \subseteq N_G$ and $A_{G'} = A_G \cap N_{G'} \times N_{G'}$. A *partial subgraph* is obtained by removing nodes and arcs, *i.e.*, G' is a partial subgraph of G if $N_{G'} \subseteq N_G$ and $A_{G'} \subseteq A_G \cap N_{G'} \times N_{G'}$.

We denote $G_{\downarrow S}$ the subgraph obtained by keeping a subset S of components of G: If S is a subset of nodes, then $G_{\downarrow S}$ is the induced subgraph obtained by keeping these nodes (*i.e.*, $N_{G_{\downarrow S}} = S$ and $N_{G_{\downarrow S}} = A_G \cap S \times S$); if S is a subset of arcs, then $G_{\downarrow S}$ is the partial subgraph obtained by keeping these arcs (*i.e.*, $N_{G_{\downarrow S}} = \{u \in N_G \mid \exists v \in N_G, (u, v) \in S \vee (v, u) \in S\}$ and $A_{G_{\downarrow S}} = S$).

A *common subgraph* is a graph which is isomorphic to subgraphs of G and G'. The similarity of two graphs is usually defined by means of the size of a common subgraph [1]: the larger the subgraph, the more similar the graphs. The size of a subgraph is defined differently whether we consider induced or partial subgraphs: A *Maximum Common Partial Subgraph (MCPS)* is a common partial subgraph which has a maximum number of arcs, whereas a *Maximum Common Induced Subgraph (MCIS)* is a common induced subgraph which has a maximum number of nodes. Fig. 1 displays two graphs and an example of MCPS and MCIS.

2.2   Existing Complete Approaches for Solving MCIS and MCPS

Most complete approaches are based on a reformulation of the problem into a maximum clique problem in a compatibility graph (whose nodes correspond to couples of nodes that may be matched and edges correspond to pairs of compatible nodes) [5,6,7]. McGregor [8] proposes a different approach based on Branch & Bound: Each node of the search tree corresponds to the matching of two components, and a bounding function evaluates the number of components that can still be matched so that the current branch is pruned as soon as this bound becomes lower than the size of the largest known common subgraph.

Conte *et al* [9] compare these 2 approaches within a same programming framework on a large database of graphs. They show that no approach is outperforming the other: The best performing approach varies when changing graph features.

Vismara and Valery [10] show how to model and solve MCIS and MCPS with constraint programming. They consider particular cases of these two problems, where the subgraph must be connected, and they introduce a global connectivity constraint for this purpose. However, they ensure that node matchings are injective by using a set of binary difference constraints. They compare CP with a clique-based approach, and show that CP obtains better results.

3   Modeling MCIS and MCPS Problems as Soft CSPs

In this section, we introduce two soft CSPs which respectively model MCIS and MCPS problems for two graphs G and G'. These two models mainly differ with respect to their variables: For MCIS, variables are associated with nodes of G, whereas for MCPS, variables are associated with arcs. In both cases, the value assigned to the variable associated with a component (node or arc) of G corresponds to its matched component in G'. As some components may not be matched, we introduce a joker value $\bot$ which denotes the fact that a component is not matched. Hence, for MCIS, the domain of every variable x_u associated with a node $u \in N_G$ is $D(x_u) = N_{G'} \cup \{\bot\}$ whereas, for MCPS, the domain of every variable x_{uv} associated with an arc $(u, v) \in A_G$ is $D(x_{uv}) = A_{G'} \cup \{\bot\}$.

In both cases, there are two different kinds of constraints. A first set of binary constraints ensures that neighborhood relations defined by arcs are preserved. For MCIS, these binary constraints ensure that adjacency relations between matched nodes are preserved: Given two variables x_u and x_v respectively associated with nodes u and v of G, we define

$$C_{arc}(x_u, x_v) \equiv (x_u = \bot) \vee (x_v = \bot) \vee ((u, v) \in A_G \Leftrightarrow (x_u, x_v) \in A_{G'})$$

For MCPS, these binary constraints ensure that incidence relationships between matched arcs are preserved: Given two variables x_{uv} and x_{wy} respectively associated with arcs (u, v) and (w, y) of G, we define

$$C_{arc}(x_{uv}, x_{wy}) \equiv (x_{uv} = \bot) \vee (x_{wy} = \bot) \vee (R((u, v), (w, y), x_{uv}, x_{wy}))$$

where R is a predicate which checks that (u, v) and (w, y) have the same incidence relationships as the arcs of G' assigned to x_{uv} and x_{wy}, i.e.,
$R((u, v), (w, y), (u', v'), (w', y')) \equiv (u = v \Leftrightarrow u' = v') \wedge (u = w \Leftrightarrow u' = w') \wedge (u = y \Leftrightarrow u' = y') \wedge (v = w \Leftrightarrow v' = w') \wedge (v = y \Leftrightarrow v' = y') \wedge (w = y \Leftrightarrow w' = y')$.

Finally, we have to express that the matching must be injective (as two different components of G must be matched to two different components of G'). This kind of constraint could be modeled with a global $allDiffExcept\bot(X)$ constraint which enforces all variables in X to take distinct values, except those variables that are assigned to a joker $\bot$ value [11]. To find a maximum common subgraph, we search for a partial injective matching which matches as many components as possible, i.e., we have to minimize the number of variables assigned to $\bot$. This could be achieved by adding an $atmost(b - 1, X, \bot)$ constraint each time a feasible solution σ is found, where b is the number of variables assigned to $\bot$ in σ. However, this model achieves a weak filtering because it separates the evaluation of the cost function from the $allDiff$ constraint.

Stronger filterings may be achieved by using optimization constraints, which relate constraints with cost variables to be optimized, as proposed in [12]. In particular, the soft $allDiff$ constraint [13] relates a set X of variables to an additional $cost$ variable which is constrained to be equal to the number of variables of X that should change their value in order to satisfy the $allDiff(X)$ constraint, and which must be minimized (we consider variable-based violation costs).

To find an injective partial matching which minimizes the number of non matched components, we introduce an additional variable $x_\perp$ whose domain is $D(x_\perp) = \{\perp\}$ and we post a soft $allDiff(X \cup \{x_\perp\}, cost)$ constraint. Note that $x_\perp$ is always assigned to $\perp$: It ensures that all other variables are assigned to values different from $\perp$ whenever this is possible (*e.g.*, when G and G' are isomorphic).

Let us now formally define the two soft CSPs modeling MCIS and MCPS. For the MCIS, we define the soft CSP:

- Variables: $X = \{x_u \mid u \in N_G\} \cup \{x_\perp\}$
- Domains: $D(x_\perp) = \{\perp\}$ and $\forall u \in N_G, D(x_u) = N_{G'} \cup \{\perp\}$
- Hard constraints: $\forall \{u, v\} \subseteq N_G, C_{arc}(x_u, x_v)$
- Soft constraint: $allDiff(X, cost)$

For the MCPS, we define the soft CSP :

- Variables: $X = \{x_{uv} \mid (u, v) \in A_G\} \cup \{x_\perp\}$
- Domains: $D(x_\perp) = \{\perp\}$ and $\forall (u, v) \in A_G, D(x_{uv}) = A_{G'} \cup \{\perp\}$
- Hard constraints: $\forall \{(u, v), (w, y)\} \subseteq A_G, C_{arc}(x_{uv}, x_{wy})$
- Soft constraint: $allDiff(X, cost)$

Computing Maximum Common Subgraphs from soft CSP solutions. A solution is an assignment σ of the variables of X which satisfies all hard constraints, and which minimizes the violation cost of the soft constraint so that $\sigma(cost)$ is equal to this violation cost. Let $\sigma(X) \setminus \perp$ be the set of values different from $\perp$ which are assigned to variables of X. One can easily check that, for MCIS (resp. MCPS), $G'_{\downarrow\sigma(X)\setminus\perp}$ is isomorphic to an induced (resp. partial) subgraph of G.

Note that we cannot define the common induced subgraph by simply keeping every node of G whose associated variable is assigned to a value different from $\perp$. Indeed, when several nodes of G have the same neighborhood, it may happen that the variables associated with these nodes are assigned to a same value (different from $\perp$). Let us consider for example the graphs of Fig. 1. For MCIS, the assignment $\sigma = \{x_\perp = \perp, x_a = \perp, x_b = 3, x_d = 4, x_c = 2, x_f = 5, x_e = 4\}$ is an optimal solution. In this case, $\sigma(X) \setminus \perp = \{2, 3, 4, 5\}$ and $G'_{\downarrow\sigma(X)\setminus\perp}$ is the subgraph obtained by removing node 1 from G'. In this solution, both x_d and x_e are assigned to 4 because d and e have the same neighborhood.

The size of the common subgraph $G'_{\downarrow\sigma(X)\setminus\perp}$ is equal to $c - \sigma(cost)$ where c is the number of components of G ($c = |N_G|$ for MCIS and $c = |A_G|$ for MCPS), and $\sigma(cost)$ is the value of the cost variable of the soft $allDiff$ constraint. As the value of $cost$ is minimal, the size of $G'_{\downarrow\sigma(X)\setminus\perp}$ is maximal. On our previous example, we have $\sigma(cost) = 2$ and $|N| = 6$ so that $G'_{\downarrow\sigma(X)\setminus\perp}$ has 4 nodes.

Extension to Labeled Graphs. In labeled graphs, nodes and edges are associated with labels. In this case, the common subgraph must match components the labels of which are equal. This kind of constraints is handled in a straightforward way. For MCIS, we restrict the domain of every variable x_u to nodes which have the same label as u, and we ensure that arc labels are preserved in C_{arc} constraints. For MCPS, we restrict the domain of every variable x_{uv} to arcs which have the same label as (u, v) and whose endpoints have the same labels.

4   Constraint Propagation

The two soft CSP models introduced in the previous section are very similar: they both combine a set of binary hard constraints with a soft *allDiff* constraint. We consider different levels of propagation of these constraints.

Propagation of the soft allDiff *constraint.* We consider 3 levels of propagation. The strongest propagation, denoted *GAC(allDiff)*, ensures the generalized arc consistency as proposed in [13]. More precisely, we search for a maximum matching in the bipartite graph $G_b = (X, V, E_b)$ where X is the set of variables, V is the set of values in variable domains, and E_b is the set of edges $(x, v) \in X \times V$ such that $v \in D(x)$. A matching of G_b is a subset of edges of E_b such that no two edges share an endpoint. The cardinality of a largest matching of G_b gives the maximum number of variables that may be assigned to different values. Therefore the number of nodes which are not matched provides an upper bound for *cost*. When this number is larger than the lower bound of *cost*, we cannot filter variable domains. However, as soon as it is as large as the lower bound of *cost*, we can filter domains by searching for every edge (x, v) which does not belong to any maximum matching in G_b. As proposed in [13,14,15], we use the algorithm of [16] to compute a maximum matching, and we exploit the fact that this algorithm is incremental: at each node, we update the last computed maximum matching by removing edges corresponding to removed values, and we complete this matching until it becomes maximum.

We have considered a weaker filtering, denoted *bound(cost)+FC(diff)*. This filtering does not ensure the generalized arc consistency, but simply checks if there exists a matching of G_b such that the number of non matched nodes is greater than or equal to the lower bound of *cost*. This is done in an incremental and lazy way: at each node, once we have updated the last computed matching, we try to extend it only if its number of non matched nodes is strictly lower than the lower bound of *cost*. We combine this with a simple forward-checking of the binary decomposition of the *allDiff* constraint which simply removes a value v such that $v \neq \perp$ whenever v has been assigned to a variable.

The weakest propagation of the soft *allDiff* constraint, denoted *FC(diff)*, is a forward-checking of its binary decomposition which simply removes a value v such that $v \neq \perp$ whenever v has been assigned to a variable. The upper bound of the *cost* variable is updated each time a variable is assigned to $\perp$.

Propagation of the binary hard constraints C_{arc}. When the domain of the *cost* variable has not been reduced to a singleton by the propagation of the soft *allDiff* constraint, the joker value $\perp$ belongs to the domain of every non assigned variable. In this case, a forward-checking of C_{arc} constraints actually ensures arc consistency. Indeed, for every pair (x_i, x_j) of non assigned variables, and for every value $v \in D(x_i)$, the value $\perp$ belongs to $D(x_j)$ and is a support for v as $C_{arc}(x_i, x_j)$ is satisfied as soon as x_i or x_j is assigned to $\perp$.

When the domain of *cost* is reduced to a singleton, $\perp$ is removed from the domain of all non assigned variable. In this case, maintaining arc consistency

(MAC) may remove more values than a simple forward-checking (FC). Hence, we have considered two different levels of propagation: $FC(C_{arc})$ performs forward checking, whereas $MAC(C_{arc})$ maintains arc consistency (however, as FC ensures AC while $\perp$ has not been removed from domains, we still perform FC until $\perp$ is removed, and maintain AC only when $\perp$ has been removed).

5   Experimental Results

Compared models. We compare the five following models:

- FC = $FC(C_{arc})$+FC(diff);
- FC+bound = $FC(C_{arc})$+bound(cost)+FC(diff);
- FC+GAC = $FC(C_{arc})$+GAC(allDiff);
- MAC+bound = $MAC(C_{arc})$+bound(cost)+FC(diff);
- MAC+GAC = $MAC(C_{arc})$+GAC(allDiff).

The FC model basically corresponds to the Branch & Bound approach proposed by McGregor in [8], and to the CP model proposed in [10] (except that, in [10], a connectivity constraint is added in order to search for connected subgraphs). All models have been implemented in C. We have considered the *minDom* variable ordering heuristic, and values are assigned by increasing order of value.

Test Suites. We consider a synthetically generated database described in [9]. For each graph, there are 3 different labelings such that the number of different labels is equal to 33%, 50% or 75% of the number of nodes.

We report results obtained on 3 test suites of increasing hardness. Test suite 1 considers MCIS on directed and labeled graphs such that the number of labels is equal to 33% of the number of nodes (when increasing this ratio, the problem becomes easier). Test suite 2 considers MCIS on non directed and non labeled graphs. Test suite 3 considers MCPS on directed and non labeled graphs. We have adapted the size of the graphs with respect to the difficulty of these test suites so that they may be solved within a reasonable CPU time limit: in test suite 1 (resp. 2 and 3), we consider graphs with 40 (resp. 30 and 20) nodes. For each test suite, we report results obtained on different classes of graphs: randomly connected graphs with connectivity $\eta \in \{0.05, 0.2\}$ (r005 and r02); 2D, 3D, and 4D regular meshes (m2D, m3D, m4D); 2D, 3D, and 4D irregular meshes with $\rho = 0.6$ (m2Dr, m3Dr, and m4Dr); regular bounded valence graphs with $V \in \{3, 9\}$ (b03 and b09) and irregular bounded valence graphs with $V \in \{3, 9\}$ (b03m and b09m). Each class contains 150 pairs of graphs corresponding to the first 30 instances for each of the 5 possible sizes of the MCIS (*i.e.*, 10%, 30%, 50%, 70% and 90% of the number of nodes of the original graphs).

Discussion. Table 1 compares the 5 CP models on the 3 test suites. It shows us that the FC model (which basically corresponds to approaches proposed in [8] and [10]) is clearly outperformed by all other models, which perform stronger filterings. Indeed, FC achieves a kind of passive bounding on the *cost* variable, by simply counting the number of variables that must be assigned to $\perp$. All other models

Table 1. Comparison of the 5 CP models on the 3 test suites. Each line successively displays the name of the class and, for each model, the percentage of solved instances within a CPU time limit of 30mn (%S), the CPU time (time) in seconds on a 2.26 GHz Intel Xeon E5520 and the number of thousands of nodes (#Kn) in the search tree. CPU time and number of nodes are average results (if an instance is not solved within 30mn, we consider in the average results the CPU time and the number of nodes reached when the search was stopped).

		FC			FC+bound			FC+GAC			MAC+bound			MAC+GAC		
		%S	time	#Kn	%S	time	#Kn	%S	time	#Kn	%S	time	#Kn	%S	time	#Kn
Test Suite 1	b03	100	105.79	56074	100	20.81	6066	100	24.83	4831	100	**13.43**	3166	100	13.86	1502
	b03m	100	143.74	80297	100	26.17	7754	100	28.86	5651	100	16.91	4021	100	**15.06**	1742
	b09	100	0.11	50	100	0.07	19	100	0.08	17	100	**0.06**	15	100	0.08	10
	b09m	100	0.12	54	100	0.08	22	100	0.09	20	100	**0.07**	17	100	0.10	11
	m2D	100	98.62	53960	100	18.05	5200	100	20.19	3664	100	12.25	2876	100	**10.94**	1220
	m2Dr	100	8.06	3990	100	3.14	864	100	3.65	724	100	**2.21**	523	100	2.38	291
	m3D	100	15.05	7532	100	5.55	1536	100	5.82	1157	100	**3.69**	865	100	4.86	439
	m3Dr	100	3.90	1913	100	1.62	419	100	1.82	359	100	1.14	273	100	**1.13**	154
	m4D	100	97.33	50940	100	12.09	3147	100	12.94	2496	100	**8.17**	1832	100	9.28	835
	m4Dr	100	5.85	2745	100	1.87	471	100	2.04	387	100	**1.38**	325	100	1.50	169
	r005	100	19.47	10540	100	4.72	1295	100	5.68	1040	100	**3.17**	741	100	3.57	393
	r02	100	0.02	10	100	0.02	6	100	0.02	5	100	**0.01**	4	100	0.02	3
Test Suite 2	b03	72	756.25	312080	100	**68.87**	10256	100	77.93	7728	97	212.41	3679	98	231.77	2301
	b03m	57	1081.52	441952	100	**101.77**	14749	100	121.99	12043	97	343.77	6017	97	397.14	4010
	b09	100	147.80	62050	100	**35.09**	7709	100	40.27	6699	100	41.49	6068	100	44.69	3531
	b09m	99	342.89	149613	100	**86.07**	20054	100	94.98	16364	100	101.07	15347	100	103.71	8439
	m2D	61	985.35	394241	100	**103.17**	16003	100	131.48	13532	96	365.66	7582	95	411.89	4491
	m2Dr	62	998.30	383680	100	**171.70**	29757	100	201.49	24344	99	428.35	17228	98	482.21	9128
	m3D	76	737.81	277429	100	**81.78**	13206	100	101.71	11570	100	240.58	7538	100	284.13	4331
	m3Dr	83	681.18	266386	100	**115.49**	21872	100	156.56	20579	100	254.37	13715	100	316.93	8262
	m4D	46	1276.08	498405	100	**120.71**	17386	100	129.53	13257	100	360.14	8699	96	423.83	5704
	m4Dr	50	1448.08	549375	100	**165.51**	27849	100	195.86	23127	100	421.02	16238	100	467.62	8966
	r005	50	1236.75	515935	99	**142.04**	22122	98	175.62	17625	93	443.26	8601	92	494.76	5099
	r02	100	474.12	222831	100	246.16	67044	100	283.70	58036	100	**238.91**	53792	100	242.84	32445
Test Suite 3	b03	100	34.44	9364	100	8.67	1178	100	10.93	1163	100	**7.13**	582	100	8.37	392
	b03m	100	47.41	13809	100	9.62	1350	100	10.41	1172	100	7.33	700	100	**7.04**	386
	b09	0	-	-	0	-	-	0	-	-	0	-	-	0	-	-
	b09m	0	-	-	0	-	-	0	-	-	0	-	-	0	-	-
	m2D	100	214.00	59029	100	32.17	3933	100	33.69	3324	100	26.16	2159	100	**25.83**	1165
	m2Dr	0	-	-	0	-	-	0	-	-	0	-	-	0	-	-
	m3D	90	1122.39	263519	100	206.22	23399	100	282.27	24543	100	**187.90**	14170	100	226.57	9000
	m3Dr	0	-	-	0	-	-	0	-	-	0	-	-	0	-	-
	r005	100	11.28	4333	100	2.12	354	100	2.56	358	100	**1.39**	144	100	1.56	98
	r02	0	-	-	0	-	-	0	-	-	0	-	-	0	-	-

achieve an active bounding by checking that the number of variables that can be assigned to different values is large enough. The lazy bounding introduced in Section 4 drastically reduces the search space and CPU times of FC+bound are always significantly lower than those of FC. GAC(allDiff) reduces even more the search space but the difference is not so obvious so that CPU times of FC+GAC are always greater than those of FC+bound. This tendency is observed on the 3 test suites.

Replacing FC(C_{arc}) with MAC(C_{arc}) also significantly reduces the number of explored nodes but this stronger filtering has a higher time complexity so that it does not always reduce CPU times: it improves performances on Test suites 1 and 3 but deteriorates them on Test Suite 2. Hence, the best performing approaches are MAC+bound and MAC+GAC on Test suites 1 and 3 whereas the best performing approach is FC+bound on Test suite 2. These results may be explained by the fact that constraints of instances of Test suites 1 and 3 (such that graphs are directed or labeled) are tighter than those of Test suite 2.

Further works. Further work will concern the integration of symmetry breaking techniques and more advanced propagation techniques such as those proposed in [17,18,19] for graph and subgraph isomorphism. We shall also study the integration of ordering heuristics. Indeed, when solving an optimization problem, ordering heuristics aim at guiding the search towards the best assignments, thus allowing the bounding functions to prune more branches.

Acknowledgement. This work was done in the context of project Sattic (Anr grant Blanc07-1 184534).

References

1. Bunke, H., Sharer, K.: A graph distance metric based on the maximal common subgraph. Pattern Recognition Letters 19(3), 255–259 (1998)
2. Garey, M.R., Johnson, D.S.: Computer and intractability. Freeman, New York (1979)
3. Régin, J.-C.: Développement d'Outils Algorithmiques pour l'Intelligence Artificielle. Application à la Chimie Organique. PhD thesis, Université Montpellier II (1995)
4. Raymond, J.W., Willett, P.: Maximum common subgraph isomorphism algorithms for the matching of chemical structures. Journal of Computeraided Molecular Design 16(7), 521–533 (2002)
5. Balas, E., Yu, C.S.: Finding a maximum clique in an arbitrary graph. SIAM Journal on Computing 15(4), 1054–1068 (1986)
6. Durand, P.J., Pasari, R., Baker, J.W., Tsai, C.: An efficient algorithm for similarity analysis of molecules. Internet Journal of Chemistry 2 (1999)
7. Raymond, J.W., Gardiner, E.J., Willett, P.: Calculation of graph similarity using maximum common edge subgraphs. The Computer Journal 45(6) (2002)
8. McGregor, J.J.: Backtrack search algorithms and the maximal common subgraph problem. Software Practice and Experience 12(1), 23–34 (1982)
9. Conte, D., Foggia, P., Vento, M.: Challenging complexity of maximum common subgraph detection algorithms: A performance analysis of three algorithms on a wide database of graphs. Graph Algorithms and Applications 11(1), 99–143 (2007)
10. Vismara, P., Valery, B.: Finding maximum common connected subgraphs using clique detection or constraint satisfaction algorithms. Communications in Computer and Information Science 14(1), 358–368 (2008)
11. Beldiceanu, N., Carlsson, M., Demassey, S., Petit, T.: Global constraint catalog: Past, present and future. Constraints 12(1), 21–62 (2007)
12. Focacci, F., Lodi, A., Milano, M.: Cost-based domain filtering. In: Jaffar, J. (ed.) CP 1999. LNCS, vol. 1713, pp. 189–203. Springer, Heidelberg (1999)
13. Petit, T., Régin, J.-C., Bessière, C.: Specific filtering algorithms for over-constrained problems. In: Walsh, T. (ed.) CP 2001. LNCS, vol. 2239, pp. 451–464. Springer, Heidelberg (2001)
14. Régin, J.-C.: A filtering algorithm for constraints of difference in csps. In: AAAI 1994, pp. 362–367 (1994)
15. Gent, I., Miguel, I., Nightingale, P.: Generalised arc consistency for the alldiff constraint: An empirical survey. Artificial Intelligence 172(18), 1973–2000 (2008)
16. Hopcroft, J.E., Karp, R.M.: An n5/2 algorithm for maximum matchings in bipartite graphs. SIAM Journal on Computing 2(4), 225–231 (1973)
17. Sorlin, S., Solnon, C.: A parametric filtering algorithm for the graph isomorphism problem. Constraints 13(4), 518–537 (2008)
18. Zampelli, S., Deville, Y., Solnon, C.: Solving subgraph isomorphism problems with constraint programming. Constraints 15(3), 327–353 (2010)
19. Solnon, C.: Alldifferent-based filtering for subgraph isomorphism. Artificial Intelligence 174(12-13), 850–864 (2010)

Kangaroo: An Efficient Constraint-Based Local Search System Using Lazy Propagation

M.A. Hakim Newton[1,2], Duc Nghia Pham[1,2],
Abdul Sattar[1,2], and Michael Maher[1,3,4]

[1] National ICT Australia (NICTA) Ltd.
[2] Institute for Integrated and Intelligent Systems, Griffith University
[3] School of Computer Science and Engineering, University of New South Wales
[4] Reasoning Research Institute, Sydney

Abstract. In this paper, we introduce Kangaroo, a constraint-based local search system. While existing systems such as Comet maintain invariants after every move, Kangaroo adopts a lazy strategy, updating invariants only when they are needed. Our empirical evaluation shows that Kangaroo consistently has a smaller memory footprint than Comet, and is usually significantly faster.

1 Introduction

Constraint-based local search (CBLS) has been quite successful in solving problems that prove difficult for constraint solvers based on constructive search. Unfortunately, there is little published work on existing implementations that led to this success – most work has addressed language features [12,7,8] and applications [5,2]. In this paper we present Kangaroo, a new constraint-based local search system and expose key details of its implementation. We compare it with Comet, which has been the state-of-the-art in CBLS for several years.

Kangaroo differs from Comet in several aspects: it currently provides a C++ library, not a separate language; it employs a lazy strategy for updating invariants; it uses well-supported simulation to explore neighbourhoods, rather than directly using invariants as Comet seems to; and data structures are encapsulated at the system level instead of at the object level as Comet does. Nevertheless, Kangaroo provides many of the capabilities of Comet and is also very efficient. On a benchmark of well-known problems Kangaroo more frequently solves problems than Comet, and usually solves them faster. It also consistently uses about half the memory footprint of Comet.

The rest of the paper is organised as follows: Section 2 outlines constraint-based local search; Section 3 introduces Kangaroo terminology; Section 4 describes the Kangaroo system in detail; Section 5 discusses the experimental results and analyses; and finally, Section 6 presents conclusions and future work.

2 Constraint-Based Local Search

Constraint-based local search is based on a view of constraint satisfaction as an optimization problem. With every constraint c, there is a violation metric

J. Lee (Ed.): CP 2011, LNCS 6876, pp. 645–659, 2011.
© Springer-Verlag Berlin Heidelberg 2011

function μ_c that maps variable assignments[1] θ to non-negative numbers. We require of a violation metric only that $\mu_c(\theta) = 0$ iff c is satisfied by θ. For a set of constraints $\mathcal{C}$, constraint satisfaction is reformulated as the minimisation problem: $\mathsf{minimize}_\theta \mu_{\mathcal{C}}(\theta)$ where $\mu_{\mathcal{C}}(\theta) = \sum_{c \in \mathcal{C}} w_c \mu_c(\theta)$ and the weights w_c (often $w_c = 1$) are to guide the search. If the minimum value of $\mu_{\mathcal{C}}$ is 0 then $\mathcal{C}$ is satisfiable by the assignment that produces this value. If the minimum is non-zero then $\mathcal{C}$ is unsatisfiable, but the assignment that produces the minimum achieves a "best" partial solution of $\mathcal{C}$.

CBLS uses local search to try to solve this minimization problem. There are many variants of local search, but common to them all is a behaviour of moving from one variable assignment θ to another, in search of a better assignment, and the exploration of a neighbourhood $\mathcal{N}_\theta$ before selecting the next assignment. Since this behaviour is repeated continually, key to the performance of local search is the ability to sufficiently explore the neighbourhood and perform the move to the next variable assignment quickly.

Comet [6] provides two progressively higher level linguistic concepts to support the specification of these operations. *Invariants* are essentially equations $y = f(x_1, \ldots, x_n)$ which are guaranteed to hold after each move; as the value of the expression $f(x_1, \ldots, x_n)$ is changed by a move, the value of y is revised. Note that such an invariant induces a *dependency* of y on $x_1, \ldots, x_n$ and, transitively, y depends on the terms that any x_i depends on. *Differentiable constraints* associate, with each constraint c, several methods that are often implemented with many invariants; they provide a way to inspect the effect of neighbouring assignments on c and they support an abbreviated exploration of the neighbourhood, by providing an estimate of *gradients*: the amount that the violation measure might change by changing the value of a given variable. Objective functions, and expressions in general, can be differentiable.

The invariants and differentiable objects as discussed above provide certain guarantees, but the job of actually keeping the guarantees is performed by a CBLS system. Invariants are implemented in the Comet system by a two-phase algorithm based on a relatively standard approach for one-way constraints [1]: in a planning phase the invariants are topologically ordered according to the dependencies between them, and then the execution phase propagates the one-way constraints, respecting this order. Planning ensures that each invariant is propagated at most once in each move. In terms of Fig. 1, this is a bottom-up execution, where a change in a problem variable such as $Queens[k]$ is propagated through all invariants possibly affected by the change. This approach clearly keeps the guarantees.

An alternative approach is to perform a propagation only when it is needed. When a top-level term's value is needed (for example, the value of the objective function), those invariants that it depends on and are out-of-date are visited by a (top-down) depth-first search and recursively, when all children of a node have been visited, and are up-to-date, the propagation for the invariant at that node is executed. If an invariant's value is unchanged by its execution, we can

---

[1] A variable assignment maps each variable to a value in its domain.

avoid useless propagations. This approach requires that when a move is made all invariants that might be affected are marked as out-of-date before beginning evaluation. This approach, which is called mark-sweep, is also well-established [9]. It also keeps the guarantees. Kangaroo employs a variant of this approach.

There are several languages, toolkits and libraries supporting local search, including constraint-based local search. Local search frameworks or libraries such as HOTFRAME [3] and EasyLocal++ [4] focus on flexibility, rather than efficiency. They do not seem to support the light-weight inspection/exploration of neighbourhoods. Nareyek's system DragonBreath [11] is not described directly; it appears to require explicit treatment of incrementality (no invariants) and a devolved search strategy where, at each step, a constraint is delegated to choose a move. Localizer [10] is a precursor to Comet that incorporated invariants but not differentiability. The invariant library of the iOpt toolkit [14] is similar to Localizer in many ways, except it is a Java toolkit, rather than a language, and it employs a mark-sweep approach to invariants, rather than topological ordering. Among SAT solvers employing local search only [13] employs a dependency structure similar to CBLS systems, and it needs only a simple update strategy because each move is a single flip. Unfortunately, most of the published literature focuses on language features, APIs, etc. and their use in applications, rather than describe details of their implementation. We believe this is the first paper on CBLS with an implementation focus.

3 Kangaroo Terminology

We introduce some terminology and notation for discussing Kangaroo. Given a CBLS problem, there is a set $\mathcal{K}$ of constants and a set $\mathcal{V}$ of problem variables. Every variable v is assumed to have a finite domain of values it can take. The basic element of computation in Kangaroo is a *term*, denoted by τ. If a term τ has the form $f(p_1, \ldots, p_n)$, we refer to each p_i as a *parameter* and define $P(\tau) = \{p_1, \ldots, p_n\}$. Terms other than variables and constants are referred to as *dependent* terms. Some dependent terms may be known to have values that are independent of the values of any variables and hence will not need to be repeatedly evaluated; the remaining dependent terms are *computable*. A term is *updatable* if it is a variable or is computable. A *root* term is a term on which no term depends. Γ is the set of root terms. For each term τ, $D(\tau)$ denotes the set of terms that are *directly dependent* on τ.

After a move, the values of some terms may be explicitly required; these are called *requisite* terms. The set of requisite terms is denoted by $\mathcal{R}$. A computable term τ is called an *enforced* term if τ is a requisite term, or some requisite term depends on τ. All other computable terms are called *deferred* terms; their recomputations are deferred until they become enforced terms, or an explicit *one-shot* request is made (e.g. by the search algorithm).

An assignment θ maps each variable v to a value in its domain. A *partial assignment* maps only some variables to values. We write $v \in \theta$ if θ maps v to a value. In the running of Kangaroo, a committed assignment is an assignment θ that describes the current node of the local search. Any neighbouring assignment

θ' of the committed assignment θ can be described by θ and a partial assignment ϑ specifying the new values that some variables take. That is, a partial assignment specifies a possible move from the committed assignment θ to θ' where $\theta'(v) =$ if $v \in \vartheta$ then $\vartheta(v)$ else $\theta(v)$. Thus, a local search process that runs for N moves can be viewed as a sequence $\langle \theta_0, \vartheta_1, \cdots, \vartheta_N \rangle$ of an assignment followed by a number of partial assignments.

Given a partial assignment ϑ, an updatable term τ is called a *candidate* term if τ is a variable in ϑ or depends on such a variable. These are the terms that *might* be recomputed if the move described by ϑ is made. Given ϑ and a computable term τ, the *candidate* parameters are the parameters of τ that are candidate terms for ϑ; we denote the set of candidate parameters by $P_c(\tau, \vartheta)$.

Assume that a deferred term σ is last recomputed at iteration i and the latest iteration completed is j where $0 \le i < j \le N$. The *postponed* parameters $P_p(\sigma)$ are those parameters of σ that cause σ to recompute. We define them recursively as follows. A postponed parameter for σ wrt iterations $i \dots j$ is a parameter of σ that either (i) has actually changed value in an iteration between i and j (inclusive), or (ii) is a deferred term that has one or more postponed parameters wrt iterations $i \dots j$. A deferred term σ is said to be *out-of-date* at iteration j, if $P_p(\sigma)$ is non-empty; otherwise, the term is *up-to-date*[2].

4   Kangaroo System

The Kangaroo architecture as depicted in Fig. 1 has two components: Representation Component (RC) and Exploration Component (EC). The RC allows description of a given CBLS problem in a declarative way while the EC allows specification of the search algorithms and the heuristics/meta-heuristics. The RC consists of two units: Assignment Unit (AU) and Propagation Unit (PU). The AU holds all variables and constants, supports definition of the constants, and allows run-time assignments of new values to the variables by the EC. The PU holds all the dependent terms and provides the EC with the up-to-date values of the updatable terms under assignment of any new values to the variables. Overall, the RC is responsible for running an assignment-propagation cycle for each iteration of the search algorithm in the EC. On the other hand, the EC is responsible for any run-time decision during search, including selections of best or least-bad assignments and restarting the search at plateaus.

The Kangaroo architecture has a number of notable features: **i)** on-demand recomputation of the updatable terms using lazy propagation of the given assignments, **ii)** specialised incremental execution to compute aggregate formula, **iii)** specialised incremental simulation boosted by caching when ranges of values are tried but the variables remain the same or different sets of variables are tried but the sets differ by just one variable, **iv)** type-independent linearly ordered scalar view of domain values to allow unified selection over variables or values, **v)** low-level memory management to obtain fast and compact data

---

[2] Note that 'out-of-date' refers to terms that are *potentially* out-of-date; it may be that a term has the correct value but it is still regarded as out-of-date.

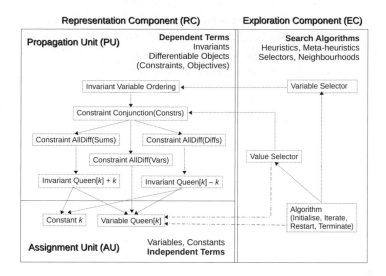

Fig. 1. The Kangaroo architecture and the view of queens problem

structures, **vi**) data encapsulation at the system level and unencapsulation at the object level to allow array-based data storage and faster access through non-virtual function calls, and **vii**) implementation as a C++ library to allow easier integration with large systems and also to get the complete support of a very well-known programming language and its powerful compiler.

Execution vs. Simulation

In Kangaroo, *computations* are performed in two different modes: execution and simulation. In the *execution mode*, variables can be assigned new values by accessing the AU. The PU then propagates the effect by recomputing the requisite terms in a top-down fashion. In the *simulation mode*, the AU and PU work in the same way, but the updates are temporary and the effects are not committed. The simulation mode thus allows a neighbourhood-exploration algorithm to investigate the effect of potential assignments and then to elect an assignment for the next execution. Kangaroo has two separate sets of data structures through out the entire system to run these two modes in an interleaving fashion. The interleaving facility allows execution of some deferred terms (with the last committed assignment), if required by the EC, in between performing two simulation runs.

Note that the simulation in Kangaroo and that in Comet have significantly different purposes. Comet uses simulation (i.e. the lookahead method) only in rare cases where moves are very complex and cannot be evaluated incrementally or are not supported by the differentiable API. The implementation of simulation in Comet performs execution for a given assignment, obtains the result, and then reverses the effect of the execution; the simulation is thus typically significantly slow [6]. In Kangaroo, simulation is at the centre of neighbourhood investigation.

Our simulation efficiently performs light-weight incremental computation for a
given assignment and does not require reverting to a previous state.

Incremental Computation

For some invariants, it is possible to perform a computation without accessing all the parameters. This is particularly attractive when there are many parameters and only a few are modified. Consider the invariant $S = \sum_{x \in X} x$.
When all parameters in X are assigned values for the first time, S is computed
anew, that is, from scratch. In later computation, when only a subset $X' \subset X$
of all parameters are changed, then the new value of S can be obtained as
S.oldval $+ \sum_{x \in X'}(x$.newval $- x$.oldval$)$. This type of computation is referred to
as *incremental computation* and involves only the parameters that are changed.
We formulate this as an undo operation with the old value of x and a redo operation with the new value of x, for each modified parameter x. Incremental
computations are useful in both execution and simulation modes.

Top-Down Computation

Kangaroo performs computation of a given term in a top-down fashion. In the
execution mode, when the effect of a partial assignment ϑ is to be propagated,
the PU performs a depth-first recursive exploration, starting from each requisite
term. During this exploration, each visited computable term τ first determines
the set of candidate parameters $P_c(\tau, \vartheta)$. If any candidate parameter p requires
recomputation, the depth-first exploration moves to that p. Recomputation of
a variable $v \in P_c(\tau, \vartheta)$ involves assigning it the value $\vartheta(v)$. When all candidate parameters are explored and recomputed, τ is recalculated from only those
candidate parameters that are actually modified.

This process is complicated when the given term τ is a deferred term. This
is tackled by maintaining a list of postponed parameters for each deferred term.
Whenever a term τ' has *actual* modification, it notifies each of its deferred
dependents σ to add τ' to $P_p(\sigma)$. This denotes σ might have a change because
of the modification of τ'. Consequently, each deferred dependent σ recursively
notifies its deferred dependents of its *potential* change, resulting in it being added
in their list of postponed parameters. During recomputation of any deferred
term, its postponed parameters are explored and recomputed.

The recomputation of τ is further complicated when an incremental computation is to deal with the actual modification of a parameter $p \in P_p(\tau)$ during
the iterations when τ was not recomputed. This is because an incremental computation, to ensure correctness, requires undoing the effect of p's value that was
used in τ's last recomputation. During next recomputation of τ, of course we
would need to redo for the latest value of p. Nevertheless, the undo operation is
performed when p is modified for the first time between these two recomputations. An undo operation also adds p to τ's list of *undone* parameters. This list
is used in recomputation of τ to determine which parameters need only redo.

In the simulation mode, recomputations are done in the same top-down recursive way as is done in the execution mode. In local search, each execution

normally follows a range of simulations that are closely related. For example, during exploration of values for a given variable, the variable remains the same for all simulation runs; or during exploration of pair-wise swapping between variables, many potential pairs have one shared variable. Kangaroo exploits this close relationship by caching once and reusing in all the simulations: the candidate parameters, computations performed for postponed parameters, and even undo operations for the candidate parameters.

It is worth emphasizing here that our lazy top-down approach is different from the mark-sweep approach taken in [9] for incremental attribute evaluation. For a given assignment, the mark-sweep approach marks all candidate terms. In our case, we need not mark the enforced terms; these terms will be explored by the top-down traversal algorithm starting from the requisite terms. We therefore mark only the deferred terms. An actually modified term marks only its deferred dependents, and consequently these marked deferred dependents recursively mark their deferred dependents.

Data Structures

While implementing Kangaroo, we found that the choice of certain representations and data structures are key to performance. Although the differential benefits are not accounted for each individual choices made, their combination appears to have significant impact on both speed and memory.

1. **System Clocks:** At the system level, there are two separate assignments ϑ_e and ϑ_s respectively for execution and simulation; to denote the time of change in the assignments, there are two clocks T_e' and T_s'. Also, there are two more clocks T_e and T_s to denote the current propagation cycle in the execution and simulation modes. Each term tracks when it was last computed, using timestamps T_e and T_s. Clocks T_e and T_s help avoid recomputations within the same cycle while clocks T_e' and T_s' help detect need for recomputation of the intra-term caches.

2. **Data Buffers:** Each term has three sets of data buffers – B_c, B_p, and B_n to hold respectively the result of currently completed execution, that of immediately previous execution, and that of the currently completed simulation (i.e. potentially the next execution). Simulations are always subject to the currently completed execution; if there is no such simulation, then $B_n = B_c$. The $\langle B_p, B_c \rangle$ pair is used in incremental execution while the $\langle B_c, B_n \rangle$ pair in incremental simulation. Note that each term also has two more boolean buffers to hold the values of $(B_c \neq B_p)$ and $(B_c \neq B_n)$, which saves repeated checking for actual change.

3. **Data Tables:** The data buffers described above are stored in array-based tables within the system and accessed using term indexes. This enables efficient access to the data without making costlier virtual function calls. However, this is a violation of data encapsulation at the term level; in the object-oriented paradigm, data is normally stored within the object. We deal with this by assigning such responsibilities to the system level.

4. **Term Lists:** Kangaroo keeps a list of root terms Γ and another list of requisite terms $\mathcal{R}$. The root terms are executed during initialisation or restarting of the system while the requisite terms are executed in incremental execution phase. The simulation mode does not require these lists as recomputations in this mode are performed only based on instant demand.

5. **Term Representations:** Each updatable term τ stores the dependents $D(\tau)$ and the deferred dependents $D_d(\tau)$. The key records for each dependent term δ are parameters $P(\delta)$, involved variables[3] $\mathcal{V}(\delta)$, postponed parameters $P_\mu(\delta)$, undone parameters $P_u(\delta)$, candidate parameters $P_c(\delta, \vartheta_e)$ for ϑ_e, candidate parameters $P_c(\delta, \vartheta_s)$ for ϑ_s, and, for each $v \in \mathcal{V}(\delta)$, the set $P_d(\delta, v)$ of updatable parameters of δ that depend on v. $P_d(\delta, v)$ is recomputed statically and is used to compute candidate parameters of δ using a simple set-union.

6. **Value Representations:** To facilitate implementation of type-independent selectors and search algorithms, Kangaroo takes the unified approach of using linear indexes to denote domain values. This eliminates costlier navigation on the value space through virtual function calls. For discrete variables, such indexes are a natural choice. For continuous variables, the assumption is to have a step size that allows discretisation of the value space.

7. **Customised Data Structures:** To obtain efficiency and better memory usage, we implemented customised data structures for arrays, heaps, hash-sets, and hash-maps. We also have timestamp-based arrays of flags to efficiently perform set-unions, marking and unmarking operations.

Recomputations

Both in execution and simulation modes, recomputation of a computable term could be done anew or incrementally. During anew recomputation, each computable term first invokes anew recomputation of all its updatable parameters, and then recalculates itself from scratch without requiring results of the previous iterations. Anew recomputations are needed when all the variables are initialised, and also when a complete restart is required. In this paper, we mainly describe the procedures required in incremental and deferred recomputations. Refer to Fig. 2 for pseudocode of the procedures.

1. **Potential Recomputations:** Initially all computable terms are deferred. When such a term is marked as a requisite term, its descendant computable terms recursively become enforced. For conditional terms such as if-then-else, only the conditional term becomes enforced; depending on the condition, the then or else term, if not enforced w.r.t. other terms, is executed only on one-shot request mode. Nevertheless, when a term is no longer a requisite term, its descendant enforced terms are notified. In this process, a computable

---

[3] For each dependent term δ, the set $\mathcal{V}(\delta)$ of *involved* variables of δ is the set of variables that δ depends on.

```
proc τ.execIncr
  // τ is computable.
  if τ.Te = Te then return;
  if |Pu(τ)| = 0 then τ.Bp = τ.Bc;
  if τ.T'e ≠ T'e then compute Pc(τ, ϑe);
  foreach p ∈ Pp(τ) ∪ Pc(τ, ϑe) do
    if p ∉ V then p.execIncr();
    if p ∉ Pu(τ) ∧ p.Bp ≠ p.Bc then
      undo(p.Bp), redo(p.Bc);
      // sum.Bc += p.Bc − p.Bp
  foreach p ∈ Pu(τ) do
    redo(p.Bc) // sum.Bc += p.Bc;
  if τ.Deferred then
    foreach p ∈ Pp(τ) ∪ Pu(τ) do
      p.notifyRecomp (τ);
  clear Pp(τ) and Pu(τ);
  if τ.Bc ≠ τ.Bp then
    foreach σ ∈ Dd(τ) do
      σ.notifyChange (τ,true);
    clear Dd(τ),
  τ.Te = Te;

proc σ.notifyChange(p, isActualChange)
  // σ is deferred.
  if isActualChange then
    if p ∈ Pu(σ) then return;
    Pu(σ) = Pu(σ) ∪ {p}
    if |Pu(σ)| = 1 then
      σ.Bp = σ.Bc;
      undo(p.Bp) // sum.Bc −= p.Dp,
  else
    if p ∈ Pp(σ) then return;
    Pp(σ) = Pp(σ) ∪ {p};
  foreach σ' ∈ Dd(σ) do
    σ'.notifyChange (σ, false);

proc τ.notifyRecomp(σ)
  //τ is updatable.
  Dd(τ) = Dd(τ) ∪ {σ}
```

```
proc τ.simulIncr
  // τ is computable.
  if τ.Ts = Ts then return;
  if τ.T's ≠ T's then
    compute Pc(τ, ϑs);
    // Cache = τ.Bc
  foreach p ∈ Pp(τ) \ Pc(τ, ϑs) do
    if p ∉ V then p.simulIncr();
    if p ∉ Pu(τ) ∧ p.Bn ≠ p.Bc
    then
      undo(p.Bc), redo(p.Bn);
      // Cache += p.Bn − p.Bc
  foreach p ∈ Pc(τ, ϑs) \ Pu(τ) do
    undo(p.Bc)
    // Cache −= p.Bc
  foreach p ∈ Pu(τ) \ Pc(τ, ϑs) do
    redo(p.Bc); // Cache += p.Bc
  // τ.Bn = Cache
  foreach p ∈ Pc(τ, ϑs) do
    if p ∉ V then p.simulIncr();
    redo(p.Bn)// τ.Bn += p.Bn
  τ.Ts = Ts;

proc v.execIncr
  // v is a variable.
  if v.Te = Te then return;
  v.Bp = v.Bc, v.Rc = ϑe(v);
  if v.Bc ≠ v.Bp then
    foreach σ ∈ Dd(v) do
      σ.notifyChange (v, true);
    clear Dd(v);
  v.Te = Te;

proc v.simulIncr
  // v is a variable.
  if v.Ts = Ts then return;
  v.Bn = ϑs(v), v.Ts = Ts;
```

Fig. 2. The Kangaroo algorithms using summation as an example

term, that is neither a requisite term itself nor an enforced term w.r.t. another requisite term, becomes deferred again. Computation of deferred terms is allowed only after the first iteration. At the end of first iteration, each deferred term executes notifyRecomp to notify each of its parameters that it has been computed. Each parameter p adds the deferred term to its $D_d(p)$ so that it can later notify its actual or potential changes to the deferred term.

2. **Incremental Execution:** During incremental execution, Procedure execIncr first checks the execution clock to determine whether execution has already been performed in the current cycle. During incremental execution of a variable v, B_c is saved in B_p and the new value $\vartheta_e(v)$ is assigned to B_c. For computable terms, B_c is saved in B_p, if there is no undone parameter; if there is any, notifyChange has already done this. Next, the candidate parameters are recomputed, if T'_e has changed. All postponed and candidate parameters are then executed incrementally, but calculation is performed for the given term only using those parameters that are not modified; the calculations involve un-

doing with B_{p} and redoing with B_{c}. Next, for undone parameters, only redo operations are performed; undo operations have already been performed in notifyChange. If the computable term τ is a deferred term, it then executes notifyRecomp to notify each parameter in $P_{\mathrm{p}}(\tau) \cup P_{\mathrm{u}}(\tau)$ that τ has been recomputed. The computable term then clears the lists of undone and postponed parameters. For both computable terms and variables, if the term being executed has a new value, it notifies this to its deferred dependents by executing their notifyChange and then clears the list. During execution of notifyChange, the deferred dependents need to perform undo operations and then recursively notify each of their deferred dependents about their potential modification. The execution of a term ends by updating its execution timestamp T_{e}.

3. **Incremental Simulation:** Procedure simulIncr performs incremental simulation. For variables, incremental simulation involves only assigning new values. For computable terms, candidate parameters are to be determined first, if T_{s}' has changed. For a new T_{s}', the cache inside the term also needs recomputation. Cache recomputation involves incremental simulation of all non-candidate postponed parameters and both undoing and redoing for the unmodified parameters. It also requires undoing for the candidate parameters (excluding undone parameters) and redoing for the undone parameters (excluding candidate parameters). Given the same assignment variables, each simulation run reuses the cached result and then incrementally simulates the candidate terms and performs redo for them. Notice that the cache mentioned above could be split into two parts: one for the postponed parameters, and the other for the candidate parameters. The cache for candidate parameters cannot be reused in the simulations with different assignment variables, but the cache for postponed parameters could still be reused. The use of cache could further be extended over assignments that have overlapping variables (e.g. a range of variable-value swappings with one variable in common).

Search Controls

Kangaroo currently implements a number of variable selectors, value selectors, and swap selectors. To support these selectors, especially the variable selectors, Kangaroo implements a specific type of invariant, called *variable ordering*. Such invariant utilises priority queues to maintain candidate variables for selection. In addition, the taboo heuristic is integrated into the *variable ordering* invariant, enabling Kangaroo to ignore calculation of tabooed variables. This is different from the way taboo variables are handled in Comet.

5   Experiments

We compared Kangaroo and Comet on a set of benchmarks from CSPLib: a problem library for constraints (www.csplib.org). We selected benchmarks that use representative elements of key features such as selectors, invariants, constraints, and taboo and restart heuristics. The benchmarks are: all interval series, golomb ruler, graph coloring, magic square, social golfer, and vessel loading. We also included the well-known n-queens problem. It is worth mentioning here that we only used satisfaction versions of the benchmarks, although some of them in CSPLib are optimisation problems. There was insufficient time to run optimisation benchmarks; we expect similar performance for those benchmarks.

We briefly describe the benchmarks, and also the constraint model and search algorithm to solve each benchmark. For detailed description of these benchmarks, please refer to CSPLib.

1. **all interval series:** The problem is to find a permutation $s = (s_1, ..., s_n)$ of $Z_n = \{0, 1, ..., n-1\}$ such that $V = (|s_2-s_1|, |s_3-s_2|, ...|s_n-s_{n-1}|)$ is a permutation of $Z_n - \{0\} = \{1, 2, ..., n-1\}$. Problem instances are generated for $n = 10, 15, 20$, and 25. The problem model includes an AllDifferent constraint on V. The search algorithm is based on swapping a pair of variables that leads to the minimum violation. The length of taboo on variables is 5.

2. **golomb ruler:** Given M and m, a Golomb ruler is defined as a set of m integers $0 = a_1 < a_2 < ... < a_m \leq M$ such that the $m(m-1)/2$ differences $a_j - a_i (1 \leq i < j \leq m)$ are distinct. In the problem model, the domain of a variable is dynamically restricted using the values of its neighbours. Problem instances are generated for $4 \leq m \leq 11$ and M to be equal or close to the minimum M known for m. The problem model includes an AllDifferent constraint on the differences. The search algorithm is based on assigning a variable causing maximum violation with a value that results in the minimum violation (max/min search). Taboo length is 5.

3. **graph coloring:** Given a k colorable graph generated with n vertices and the probability of having any edge being p, the problem is to assign k colors to the vertices such that no two adjacent vertices get the same color. Problems instances were generated using the graph generator programs written by Joseph Culberson[4] with parameter values $p = 0.5$, $k \in [3, 10]$, $n \in \{25, 50, 75, 100\}$ and 5 instances per setting.[5] The problem model uses a not-equal constraint for each pair of adjacent vertexes. It uses max/min search. Taboo length is 5.

4. **magic square:** Given a square S of dimension $n \times n$, the problem is to assign values $\{1, \cdots, n^2\}$ to the n^2 cells such that the sum of each row, column, and diagonal is equal to $C = n(n^2 + 1)/2$. The problem instances are generated for $n \in [10, 50]$ in step of 5. The search algorithm is based on swapping between a pair of variables that leads to the minimum violation. Taboo length is 5.

5. **n-queens:** Given a chess-board of dimension $n \times n$, put n queens on the board such that no two queens attack each other. Problems instances were generated for $n \in [1000, 50000]$. The problem model uses three AllDifferent constraints and an invariant on most violated queens (this is automatically maintained by the variable ordering invariant in Kangaroo – see Fig. 1). It uses max/min search.

6. **social golfer:** Given w weeks, g groups, and p persons per group, the problem is to find a golf playing schedule such that each person plays every week in a group with other persons, but no two persons fall in the same group more than once.

---

[4] The generator can be downloaded at
`http://webdocs.cs.ualberta.ca/~joe/Coloring/`

[5] For the graph coloring problem, generating good benchmark instances was difficult: the generated instances were either too difficult or too easy for both systems. We included instances that are roughly at the capability horizon of Comet.

Problems instances were generated for $w \in [3,9]$, $g \in [3,5]$, and $p \in [2,5]$. The problem model uses atmost and exactly constraints. It uses max/min search that also incorporates random restarts in every given $r \in \{1000, 5000, 15000\}$ iterations. Taboo length is 5.

7. **vessel loading:** Given a vessel of size $L \times W$, a number of containers are to be placed on the vessel such that there is no overlapping among the containers. The size of each container k is $l_k \times w_k$ where $l_k, w_k \in [D_{min}, D_{max}]$. Problems are generated with $10 \leq W \leq L \leq 20$, $D_{min} = 2, D_{max} = 5$ and the total area covered by the containers is varied between 25%, 50%, and 75% of the vessel area. The problem model uses If-then-else to determine the length and width of the containers based on their orientations, and the constraints required to ensure non-overlappings of the containers use invariants that maintain disjunctions. It uses max/min search. Taboo length is 5.

We ran experiments on the NICTA (www.nicta.com.au) cluster machine with a maximum limit on the iteration-count. The cluster has a number of machines each equipped with 2 quad-core CPUs (Intel Xeon @2.0GHz, 6MB L2 Cache) and 16GB RAM (2GB per core), running Rocks OS (a Linux variant for cluster). For each benchmark, a number of solvable instances were created, varying the complexity by specifying the parameters. Both Comet and Kangaroo were run 100 times for each problem instance and the instance distribution was considered to be non-parametric. When specifying problems, we tried our best to keep the specifications for Comet and Kangaroo as close as possible both in the problem models and in the search algorithms (for example, see Fig. 3). The experimental results of Kangaroo and Comet are summarised in Table 1 and presented in details in Fig. 4.

Comet.AllIntervalSeries

```
range Size = 0..(n − 1);
range Diff = 1..(n − 1);
// Create n vars with a domain Size
var{int} s[Size](m, Size);
// Post an alldiff constraint on intervals
S.post (alldifferent (all (i in Diff)
    abs(s[i] − s[i − 1])));
// Assign random permutation to s
RandomPermutation distr (Size);
forall( i in Size ) s[i] := distr.get ();
int tabu[Size] = 0;
while( S.violations() > 0 ){
    if it ≥ MaxIt then return;
    // Select two vars that, if swapped,
    // lead to the min violation delta
    selectMin( i in Size: tabu[i] ≤ it,
        j in Size: i < j∧ tabu[j] ≤ it )
        (S.getSwapDelta(s[i], s[j])) {
        s[i] :=: s[j]; // Swap the values
        tabu[i] = it + TabuLength;
        tabu[j] = it + TabuLength;
    }
    it = it + 1;
}
```

Kangaroo.AllIntervalSeries

```
defineSolver (Solver);
// Set the tabu tenure: effectively tell Kangaroo
// to automatically maintain the tabu heuristic
setTabuLength (Solver, TabuLength);
// Create n vars with domain [0, n − 1]
forall( i in 0..n − 1 )
    defineVar (Solver, s[i], 0, n − 1);
// Create n − 1 intervals abs(s[i] − s[i − 1])
forall( i in 1..n − 1 )
    defAbsDiff (Solver, v[i], s[i], s[i − 1]);
// Post an alldiff(v[i], i in 1..n-1) constraint
defAllDifferent (Solver, alldiffConstr, v);
// Create a Selector: selects two non-tabu variables
// leading to the min violation metric, if swapped
defTabuMinSwapSel (Solver, Selector, alldiffConstr);
assign a random permutation of [0..n-1] to s;
while( alldiffConstr.violations() > 0 ){
    if it ≥ MaxIt then return;
    run Selector to select a pair of vars (s[i], s[j]);
    swap the value of s[i] and s[j];
    it = it + 1;
}
```

Fig. 3. Problem specifications for Comet(left) and Kangaroo(right)

Table 1. Kangaroo and Comet comparison summary

Instances	Kangaroo				Comet			
	success rate (%)	#iteration	CPU time (in secs)	memory (in MBs)	success rate (%)	#iteration	CPU time (in secs)	memory (in MBs)
all interval series (4)	75%	21,734	1.6	20	50%	504,465	65.1	42
golomb ruler (11)	91%	681,452	8.0	21	45%	not computed		42
graph coloring (20)	100%	774	0.0	22	50%	590	0.3	44
magic square (9)	100%	212	172.6	22	100%	213	103.3	43
n-queens (18)	100%	8,532	104.7	111	100%	8,597	140.9	293
social golfer (16)	88%	987,822	21.7	22	19%	not computed		47
vessel loading (45)	100%	212	0.0	24	62%	3,741,397	96.4	43

For each benchmark, Table 1 reports the number of instances, the percentage success rate, the mean-of-median iteration-counts, the mean-of-median solution-time in seconds, and the mean-of-median memory usage in megabytes. The percentage success rate of a benchmark is calculated as the percentage of solved instances in that benchmark set. Here an instance is considered solved if its success rate is at least 50%. Medians are taken over all runs of each instance while the means are taken over the medians of the instances. Memory statistics are based on both successful and unsuccessful runs. However, statistics on iteration-count and solution-time are only on successful runs and when success rate is at least 50%. For each benchmark, Fig. 4 graphically presents the % success rate and the median solution-times over the successful runs. Note, when the success rate for an instance is below 50%, the solution time plotted is not completely meaningful.

Overall, we found that in all of the above benchmarks, Kangaroo consistently uses less than 50% of the memory required by Comet. The success rate of Kangaroo is significantly higher in all of the benchmarks except magic square and n-queens, where both systems could solve all problem instances. In terms of solution times, Kangaroo significantly outperforms Comet, except in magic square where Comet performs better than Kangaroo.

The models and the search algorithms for Comet and Kangaroo are best matched in magic square and n-queens. This is reflected by the similar number of iterations required by the two systems to solve instances in these two benchmarks. The performance of Kangaroo is better in n-queens than that of Comet. This clearly shows the performance advantage of the Kangaroo architecture.

In magic square Comet performs better than Kangaroo because it uses a specialised getSwapDelta method to compute the effect of a swap. This specialisation helps in magic square where constraints are based on summation of variables. When two variables belonging to the same summation are swapped, the summation result remains unchanged. Thus, there is no need to compute the effect of such a swap. In general, this specialisation can be exploited for all invariants where the changes in swapping variables would nullify each other. By contrast, Kangaroo currently implements a generic getSwapDelta method that emulates swaps as assignments of two variables simultaneously. In other words, Kangaroo

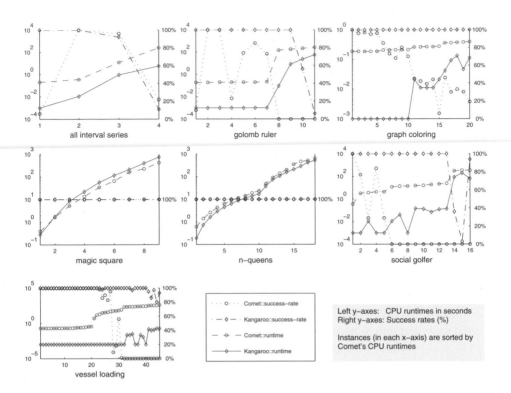

Fig. 4. Kangaroo vs Comet: a detailed comparison on success rate and runtime

has to simulate the changes in both variables and then adds them to obtain the new summation result. In future, we plan to eliminate such redundant calculation from Kangaroo.

However, there are many cases where parameters of an invariant consists of complex functions and a swap between two variables is not necessarily a no-op for that invariant although it may involve both variables. In such cases, it is a must to use the generic getSwapDelta method to compute the effect of a swap. There are also cases where the benefit of a specialised swap is not much different compared to a generic swap. A strong evidence for such situations is demonstrated in the all interval series benchmark. Here, a fresh computation of $|s_k - s_{k-1}|$ is cheaper than its incremental computation. Nevertheless, the success rates of Comet and Kangaroo are significantly different in this benchmark. From the chart, it appears that Comet search does not progress on the problem instances with ($n = 10$). For the time being, we cannot speculate on reasons for that.

In graph coloring, golomb ruler, vessel loading, and social golfer, we found Comet to be performing very poorly while Kangaroo showed notable performance. We reiterate that the models and search algorithms for those benchmarks are semantically matched. This variation must be due to differences in implementation but, unfortunately, the implementation details of Comet are not available to us.

6   Conclusion and Future Work

We have presented Kangaroo and key details of its implementation. Empirical results show it to improve on Comet in both time and memory usage. In the future, we hope to release Kangaroo under an open source license. We plan to provide a technical report with more details than could be presented in this paper, and hope to provide a FlatZinc interface, so that Zinc can be used as a frontend to the system.

Acknowledgements. NICTA is funded by the Australian Government as represented by the Department of Broadband, Communications and the Digital Economy and the Australian Research Council through the ICT Centre of Excellence program.

References

1. Alpern, B., Hoover, R., Rosen, B.K., Sweeney, P.F., Zadeck, F.K.: Incremental evaluation of computational circuits. In: SODA, pp. 32–42 (1990)
2. Pham, Q.D., Deville, Y., Van Hentenryck, P.: Constraint-based local search for constrained optimum paths problems. In: Lodi, A., Milano, M., Toth, P. (eds.) CPAIOR 2010. LNCS, vol. 6140, pp. 267–281. Springer, Heidelberg (2010)
3. Fink, A., Voss, S.: Hotframe: A heuristic optimization framework. In: Woodruff, D.L., Voss, S. (eds.) Optimization Software Class Libraries, pp. 81–154. Kluwer, Dordrecht (2002)
4. Di Gaspero, L., Schaerf, A.: EASYLOCAL++: An object-oriented framework for flexible design of local search algorithms. Software — Practice & Experience 33(8), 733–765 (2003)
5. Van Hentenryck, P., Coffrin, C., Gutkovich, B.: Constraint-based local search for the automatic generation of architectural tests. In: Gent, I.P. (ed.) CP 2009. LNCS, vol. 5732, pp. 787–801. Springer, Heidelberg (2009)
6. Van Hentenryck, P., Michel, L.: Constraint-Based Local Search. The MIT Press, Cambridge (2005)
7. Van Hentenryck, P., Michel, L.: Control abstractions for local search. Constraints 10(2), 137–157 (2005)
8. Van Hentenryck, P., Michel, L.: Differentiable invariants. In: Benhamou, F. (ed.) CP 2006. LNCS, vol. 4204, pp. 604–619. Springer, Heidelberg (2006)
9. Hudson, S.E.: Incremental attribute evaluation: A flexible algorithm for lazy update. ACM Trans. Program. Lang. Syst. 13(3), 315–341 (1991)
10. Michel, L., Van Hentenryck, P.: Localizer. Constraints 5(1/2), 43–84 (2000)
11. Nareyek, A.: Constraint-Based Agents. LNCS, vol. 2062. Springer, Heidelberg (2001)
12. Nareyek, A.: Using global constraints for local search. In: Freuder, E.C., Wallace, R.J. (eds.) Constraint Programming and Large Scale Discrete Optimization, pp. 9–28. American Mathematical Society Publications, Providence (2001)
13. Pham, D.N., Thornton, J., Sattar, A.: Building structure into local search for SAT. In: IJCAI, pp. 2359–2364 (2007)
14. Voudouris, C., Dorne, R., Lesaint, D., Liret, A.: iOpt: A software toolkit for heuristic search methods. In: Walsh, T. (ed.) CP 2001. LNCS, vol. 2239, pp. 716–719. Springer, Heidelberg (2001)

Pseudo-Tree-Based Incomplete Algorithm for Distributed Constraint Optimization with Quality Bounds

Tenda Okimoto[1], Yongjoon Joe[1], Atsushi Iwasaki[1],
Makoto Yokoo[1], and Boi Faltings[2]

[1] Kyushu University, Fukuoka 8190395, Japan
[2] Artificial Intelligence Laboratory, Swiss Federal Institute of Technology in Lausanne (EPFL),
CH-1015, Lausanne, Switzerland
{tenda@agent.,yongjoon@agent.,iwasaki@,yokoo@}inf.kyushu-u.ac.jp,
boi.faltings@epfl.ch

Abstract. A Distributed Constraint Optimization Problem (DCOP) is a fundamental problem that can formalize various applications related to multi-agent cooperation. Since it is NP-hard, considering faster incomplete algorithms is necessary for large-scale applications. Most incomplete algorithms generally do not provide any guarantees on the quality of solutions. Some notable exceptions are DALO, the bounded max-sum algorithm, and ADPOP.

In this paper, we develop a new solution criterion called p-optimality and an incomplete algorithm for obtaining a p-optimal solution. The characteristics of this algorithm are as follows: (i) it can provide the upper bounds of the absolute/relative errors of the solution, which can be obtained a priori/a posteriori, respectively, (ii) it is based on a pseudo-tree, which is a widely used graph structure in complete DCOP algorithms, (iii) it is a one-shot type algorithm, which runs in polynomial-time in the number of agents n assuming p is fixed, and (iv) it has adjustable parameter p, so that agents can trade-off better solution quality against computational overhead. The evaluation results illustrate that this algorithm can obtain better quality solutions and bounds compared to existing bounded incomplete algorithms, while the run time of this algorithm is shorter.

1 Introduction

A Distributed Constraint Optimization Problem (DCOP) is a fundamental problem that can formalize various applications related to multi-agent cooperation. A DCOP consists of a set of agents, each of which needs to decide the value assignment of its variables so that the sum of the resulting rewards is maximized. Many application problems in multi-agent systems can be formalized as DCOPs, in particular, distributed resource allocation problems including distributed sensor networks [8] and meeting scheduling [12]. Various complete algorithms have been developed for finding globally optimal solution to DCOPs, e.g., DPOP [12], ADOPT [8], and OptAPO [7]. However, finding optimal DCOP solutions is NP-hard, so considering faster incomplete algorithms is necessary for large-scale applications. Various incomplete algorithms have been developed, e.g., DSA [3], MGM/DBA [10,17], and ALS-DisCOP [18].

J. Lee (Ed.): CP 2011, LNCS 6876, pp. 660–674, 2011.

Most incomplete algorithms generally do not provide any guarantees on the quality of the solutions they compute. Notable exceptions are DALO [4], the bounded max-sum algorithm [13], and ADPOP [11]. Among these algorithms, DALO is unique since it can provide the bound of a solution a priori, i.e., the error bound is obtained before actually running the algorithm. Also, the obtained bound is independent of problem instances. On the other hand, the bounded max-sum algorithm and ADPOP can only provide the bound of a solution a posteriori, i.e., the error bound is obtained only after we actually run the algorithm and obtain an approximate solution. Having a priori bound is desirable, but a posteriori bound is usually more accurate.

In this paper, we develop an incomplete algorithm based on a new solution criterion called p-optimality. This algorithm can provide the upper bounds of the absolute/relative errors of the solution, which can be obtained a priori/a posteriori, respectively. Our priori bound is determined by the induced width of a constraint graph and the maximal value of reward functions. Thus, the bounds can be given independently from problem instances, i.e., all problem instances have the same bound as long as the induced width and the maximal reward value are the same. Induced width is a parameter that determines the complexity of many constraint optimization algorithms. This algorithm utilizes a graph structure called a pseudo-tree, which is widely used in complete DCOP algorithms such as ADOPT and DPOP. This algorithm can obtain an approximate solution with reasonable quality, while it is a one-shot type algorithm and runs in polynomial-time in the number of agents n assuming p is fixed. Thus, it is suitable for applications that need to obtain reasonable quality solutions (with quality guarantees) very quickly. Furthermore, in this algorithm, agents can adjust parameter p so that they can trade-off better solution quality against computational overhead.

DALO is an anytime algorithm based on the criteria of local optimality called k-size/t-distance optimality [4,9] and has adjustable parameters k/t. Compared to this algorithm, our algorithm is a one-shot type algorithm, while DALO is an anytime algorithm, which repeatedly obtains new local optimal solutions until the deadline and returns the best solution obtained so far. Also, our algorithm can provide tighter bounds a priori. Furthermore, in our algorithm, the increase of computation/communication costs by increasing parameter p is more gradual compared to those for k-size/t-distance-optimality.

The bounded max-sum algorithm is a one-shot type algorithm. Compared to this algorithm, our algorithm has adjustable parameter p, while this algorithm has no adjustable parameter. Also, our algorithm can obtain a priori bound. Thus, agents can adjust parameter p before actually running the algorithm to obtain a solution with a desirable bound. Furthermore, the bounded max-sum algorithm works on a factor graph, while our algorithm works on a standard constraint graph.

Our proposed algorithm is quite similar to ADPOP which is also one-shot type algorithm and has an adjustable parameter. However, in ADPOP, the variable ordering is found through a depth-first search, and cannot be chosen freely. In contrast, our algorithm allows choosing a variable ordering, which can sometimes be better than a DFS ordering. Furthermore, our algorithm can obtain a bound on the solution quality before propagation. We can consider p-optimality gives a simple but theoretically well-founded method to determine which edges to eliminate in ADPOP.

The rest of this paper is organized as follows. Section 2 formalizes DCOP and provides basic terms related to the graphs. Section 3 introduces our incomplete algorithm and provides methods for estimating the error bound obtained by our algorithm. Section 4 evaluates the solution quality and the accuracy of the error bounds obtained by our algorithm. Section 5 concludes this paper.

2   Preliminaries

In this section, we briefly describe the formalization of Distributed Constraint Optimization Problems (DCOPs) and the basic terms for graphs.

Definition 1 (DCOP). *A distributed constraint optimization problem is defined by a set of agents S, a set of variables X, a set of binary constraint relations C, and a set of binary reward functions F. An agent i has its own variable x_i. A variable x_i takes its value from a finite, discrete domain D_i. A binary constraint relation (i, j) means there exists a constraint relation between x_i and x_j. For x_i and x_j, which have a constraint relation, the reward for an assignment $\{(x_i, d_i), (x_j, d_j)\}$ is defined by a binary reward function $r_{i,j}(d_i, d_j) : D_i \times D_j \to \mathbb{R}$. For a value assignment to all variables A, let us denote*

$$R(A) = \sum_{(i,j) \in C, \{(x_i, d_i), (x_j, d_j)\} \subseteq A} r_{i,j}(d_i, d_j).$$

Then, an optimal assignment A^* is given as $\arg\max_A R(A)$, i.e., A^* is an assignment that maximizes the sum of the value of all reward functions.

In this paper, we assume all reward values are non-negative and that the maximal value of each binary reward function is bounded, i.e., we assume $\forall i, \forall j$, where $(i, j) \in C$, $\forall d_i \in D_i, \forall d_j \in D_j, 0 \le r_{i,j}(d_i, d_j) \le r_{max}$ holds.

A DCOP problem can be represented using a constraint graph, in which a node represents an agent/variable and an edge represents a constraint. A subgraph is obtained by removing several edges from the original constraint graph.

Definition 2 (Total ordering among nodes). *A total ordering among nodes o is a permutation of a sequence of nodes $\langle 1, 2, \ldots, n \rangle$. We say node i precedes node j (denoted as $i \prec j$), if i occurs before j in o. We also denote $\mathrm{ord}(i)$ for the i-th node in a total ordering o.*

Definition 3 (Ancestors). *For a graph $G = (V, E)$, a total ordering o, and a node $i \in V$, we call $A(E, o, i) = \{j \mid (i, j) \in E \wedge j \prec i\}$ as i's ancestors.*

Definition 4 (Chordal graph based on total ordering). *For a graph $G = (V, E)$ and a total ordering o, we say G is a chordal graph based on total ordering o when the following condition holds:*

- *$\forall i, \forall j, \forall k \in V$, if $j, k \in A(E, o, i)$, then $(j, k) \in E$.*

Definition 5 (Induced chordal graph based on total ordering). *For a graph* $G = (V, E)$ *and a total ordering* o, *we say a chordal graph* $G' = (V, E')$ *based on total ordering* o, *which is obtained by the following procedure, as an induced chordal graph* [1] *of G based on total ordering* o.

1. *Set E' to E.*
2. *Choose each node $i \in V$ from the last to the first based on o and apply the following procedure.*
   - *if $\exists j, \exists k \in A(E', o, i)$ s.t. $(j, k) \notin E'$, then set E' to $E' \cup \{(j, k)\}$.*
3. *Return $G' = (V, E')$.*

Next, we introduce a parameter called *induced width*, which can be used as a measure for checking how close a given graph is to a tree. For example, if the induced width of a graph is one, it is a tree. Also, the induced width of a complete graph with n variables is $n - 1$.

Definition 6 (Width based on total ordering). *For a graph $G = (V, E)$, a total ordering o, and a node $i \in V$, we call $|A(E, o, i)|$ as the width of node i based on total ordering o. Furthermore, we call $\max_{i \in V} |A(E, o, i)|$ as the width of graph G based on total ordering o and is denoted as $w(G, o)$.*

Definition 7 (Induced width based on total ordering). *For a graph $G = (V, E)$ and a total ordering o, we call $w(G', o)$ as the induced width of G based on total ordering o, where $G' = (V, E')$ is the induced chordal graph of G based on total ordering o.*

Example 1 (Induced width of induced chordal graph). Figure 1-(a) shows a constraint graph with ten nodes. (b) presents the induced chordal graph based on total ordering $o = 1 \prec \ldots \prec 10$. The ancestors of node 10 are nodes 7, 8, and 9. Since no edge exists between ancestors 7 and 9, edge $(7, 9)$ is added. Similarly, several new edges are added (shown as broken lines). The induced width of (b) is three.

A pseudo-tree is a special graph structure, where a unique root node exists and each non-root node has a parent node.

Definition 8 (Pseudo-tree representation of chordal graph based on total ordering). *A chordal graph $G = (V, E)$ based on total ordering o can be assumed as a pseudo-tree as follows: (i) the node that appears first in o is the root node, and (ii) for each non-root node i, i's parent is node j, where $j \in A(E, o, i)$ and $\forall k \in A(E, o, i)$ and $k \neq j$, $k \prec j$ holds.*

Definition 9 (Back-edge). *When assuming a chordal graph $G = (V, E)$ based on total ordering o as a pseudo-tree, we say an edge (i, j) is a back-edge of i, if $j \in A(E, o, i)$ and j is not i's parent. Also, when $(i, j_1), (i, j_2), \ldots, (i, j_k)$ are all back-edges of i, and $j_1 \prec j_2 \prec \ldots \prec j_k$ holds, we call $(i, j_1), (i, j_2), \ldots, (i, j_k)$ as first back-edge, second back-edge, $\ldots$, k-th back-edge, respectively. Clearly, a node has at most $w(G, o) - 1$ back-edges.*

---

[1] In constraint reasoning literature [2], such a graph is simply called an *induced* graph. However, the term *induced* is used in a more general meaning in graph theory. Thus, we use a more specific term, i.e., *induced chordal graph* in this paper.

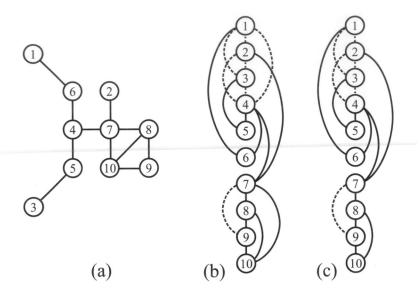

Fig. 1. (a) shows a constraint graph with ten nodes. (b) shows the induced chordal graph of (a) based on $o = 1 \prec \ldots \prec 10$. Induced width of (b) is three. (c) shows the subgraph of (b) obtained by removing edges $(1, 4)$ and $(7, 10)$. This graph is not chordal.

In the graph theory literature [2], a notion called *tree-width* is widely used. The tree-width of a graph G is defined as $\min_o w(G, o)$, where o is chosen from all possible total orderings. Finding a total ordering o that minimizes $w(G, o)$ is NP-hard in general. Thus, in this paper, we assume a particular total ordering o (which is obtained by some heuristic method and is not necessarily optimal) is given, and develop an approximate algorithm based on this total ordering.

3 Bounded Incomplete Algorithm Based on Induced Width

In this section, we describe our new incomplete algorithm based on the induced width of a constraint graph. The basic idea of this algorithm is that we remove several edges from a constraint graph [2], so that the induced width of the remaining graph is bounded. Then we compute the optimal solution of the remaining graph, which is used as the approximate solution of the original graph.

3.1 Incomplete Algorithm and p-Optimality

Our proposed incomplete algorithm has two phases:

Phase 1: Generate a subgraph from the induced chordal graph based on the total ordering by removing several edges, so that the induced width of the induced chordal graph obtained from the subgraph is bounded by parameter p.

---

[2] This idea is similar to edge removal approaches in belief propagation [5,14]. However, our method can bound the (maximum) number of removed edges a priori.

Phase 2: Find an optimal solution to the graph obtained in Phase 1 using any complete DCOP algorithms.

First, let us describe Phase 1. Our goal is to obtain a subgraph so that the induced width of the induced chordal graph obtained from the subgraph equals p. At the same time, we want to bound the number of removed edges. This is not easy. One might imagine that we can easily obtain such a subgraph by just removing the back-edges so that all nodes have at most $p - 1$ back-edges. However, by this simple method, we cannot guarantee that the remaining graph is a chordal graph and we might need to add some edges to make it a chordal graph. As a result, the induced width of the induced chordal graph can be more than p.

Example 2 (Simple method does not work). Figure 1-(c) presents the subgraph of (b) in Example 1. If we simply remove edges $(1, 4)$ and $(7, 10)$, each node has at most two edges with its ancestors (in (c)). However, the graph shown in (c) is not chordal, i.e., edge $(1, 4)$ is missing, while there exist edges $(1, 6)$ and $(4, 6)$.

We develop a method for Phase 1 as follows. We call the obtained subgraph a *p-reduced graph*.

Definition 10 (*p*-**reduced graph**). *For a induced chordal graph $G = (V, E)$ based on total ordering o, we say a graph $G' = (V, E')$ obtained by the following procedure as p-reduced graph of G (where $1 \leq p \leq w(G, o)$):*

1. *Set E' to E.*
2. *Repeat the following procedure $w(G, o) - p$ times*
   - *For each $i \in V$ where $p + 1 \leq ord(i) \leq w(G, o)$*
     remove the first back-edge in $G' = (V, E')$ from E' if there is one.
3. *Return $G' = (V, E')$.*

Assuming that the agents know the pseudo-tree among them, running this procedure by these agents is quite simple. For obtaining the p-reduced graph, each agent i ($p + 1 \leq ord(i) \leq w(G, o)$) simply removes its first back-edge, second back-edge, ..., $(w(G, o) - p)$-th back-edge.

Theorem 1. *For a induced chordal graph $G = (V, E)$ based on total ordering o, for any $1 \leq p \leq w(G, o)$, and G's p-reduced graph $G' = (V, E')$, the following conditions hold:*

1. *G' is a chordal graph based on total ordering o.*
2. *$w(G', o)$ is p.*

Proof. When obtaining p-reduced graph G', for each node i ($p + 1 \leq ord(i) \leq w(G, o)$), its first back-edge is repeatedly removed $w(G, o) - p$ times. Since the number of back-edges is at most $w(G, o) - 1$, the number of remaining back-edges is at most $p - 1$. Also, there exists at least one node who has exactly $w(G, o) - 1$ back-edges. Thus, since the remaining back-edges for the node are $p - 1$, $w(G', o)$, i.e., the width of G' based on o, is p.

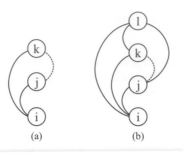

Fig. 2. (a) presents a part of p-reduced graph $G'' = (V, E'')$, where $j, k \in A(E'', o, i)$, and $(j, k) \notin E''$. (b) presents a situation where (j, k) is not j's first back-edge in G, i.e., there exists node l s.t. $l \prec k$, $(j, l) \in E$, and $(j, l) \notin E''$.

Next, we show that G' is a chordal graph based on total ordering o. Since p-reduced graph G' is obtained by repeatedly removing first back-edges for each node i ($p + 1 \leq ord(i) \leq w(G, o)$), it suffices to show that graph $G'' = (V, E'')$, which is obtained by removing first back-edges for each node i ($p+1 \leq ord(i) \leq w(G, o)$) in G, is a chordal graph based on total ordering o. We prove this fact by contradiction, i.e., we derive a contradiction by assuming that $\exists i \in V, \exists j, \exists k \in A(E'', o, i)$, s.t., $(j, k) \notin E''$. Without loss of generality, we can assume $k \prec j$ (Fig. 2-(a)).

Since $G = (V, E)$ is a induced chordal graph based on total ordering o, $(j, k) \in E$ holds. Furthermore, since $(j, k) \notin E''$, (j, k) must be the first back-edge of j in G. Also, since $k \in A(E'', o, i)$, $(i, k) \in E''$ holds. Thus, there exists node l s.t. $l \prec k$, $(i, l) \in E$, and $(i, l) \notin E''$ holds, i.e., (i, l) is i's first back-edge in G and is removed in G''. Furthermore, since $G = (V, E)$ is a induced chordal graph based on total ordering o, and $(i, l) \in E$ and $(i, j) \in E$ hold, $(j, l) \in E$ must hold (Fig. 2-(b)). However, since $l \prec k$, (j, k) cannot be j's first back-edge in G. This is a contradiction. Thus, $G'' = (V, E'')$ must be a chordal graph based on total ordering o. □

We introduce a new criterion for approximated solutions.

Definition 11 (p-optimality). *We say an assignment A is p-optimal for a distributed constraint optimization problem $\langle X, C, R \rangle$ and a total ordering o, when A maximizes the total rewards in $G'' = (X, C'')$, where $G' = (X, C')$ is an induced chordal graph of $G = (X, C)$ based on total ordering o, and $G'' = (X, C'')$ is the p-reduced graph of G'. More specifically, $\forall A', R_{C''}(A) \geq R_{C''}(A')$ holds.*

Next, let us describe Phase 2. To find a p-optimal solution, we can use any complete DCOP algorithms. We use the obtained p-optimal solution as an approximate solution of the original graph. In particular, since we already obtained a pseudo-tree whose induced width is bounded, using pseudo-tree-based DCOP algorithms would be convenient.

3.2   Quality Guarantees

We provide two methods for estimating the error of the solution obtained by our algorithm. One method estimates absolute error which can be obtained a priori. Thus, agents can choose parameter p based on the estimation before actually obtaining an approximate solution.

Theorem 2. *For a distributed constraint optimization problem $\langle X, C, R \rangle$, its constraint graph $G = (X, C)$, and a total ordering o, if A is p-optimal, then the following condition holds among $R(A^*)$ and $R(A)$, where A^* is an optimal assignment:*

$$R(A^*) - R(A) \leq r_{max} \times \sum_{k=1}^{w(G,o)-p} (|X| - (k+1))$$

Intuitively, the absolute error is given by the product of r_{max} and the maximal number of removed back-edges. To make a p-reduced graph, we first remove the first back-edges from all nodes, except the first and the second nodes in the total ordering, since they have no back-edge (note that we never remove a tree edge). Thus, the number of the removed first back-edge is at most $|X| - 2$. Next, we remove the second back-edges from all nodes, except the first, the second, and the third node. Thus, the number of the removed second back-edge is at most $|X| - 3$. As a result, the total number of removed back-edges is given as $\sum_{k=1}^{w(G,o)-p}(|X| - (k+1))$.

Furthermore, we can compute the upper bound of the relative error using a method similar to ADPOP [11]. Note that this error bound can be obtained only a posteriori, i.e., we first need to obtain an approximate solution, then, we know the upper-bound of the relative error. Intuitively, if we remove a back-edge connecting i and j, we add an edge that connects i and j', where j' is a copy of j but it is connected only to i and has no unary reward. If we add an equality constraint between j and j', this problem is equivalent to the original problem. By ignoring such a constraint, we obtain a relaxed problem. Note that the induced width of this relaxed problem is p. This method, which ignores some dependencies among variables, is similar to minibucket elimination scheme [2].

4 Experimental Evaluation

In this section, we evaluate the solution quality and the accuracy of the error bounds obtained by our algorithm and show comparisons with DALO-t [16] and the bounded max-sum algorithm [13]. In our evaluations, we use the following problem instances. The domain size of each variable is three, and we chose the reward value uniformly at random from the range [0,..., 99]. Each data point in a graph represents an average of 30 problem instances. We generate random graphs with a fixed induced width. For Phase 2 of our p-optimal algorithm, we use the DPOP algorithm with FRODO [6](version 2.7.1). For comparison, we use the DALO-t algorithm that obtains t-distance-optimal solutions, since [4] shows that the error bounds for t-distance-optimality are usually better than that for k-size optimality. In our comparison, we mostly use settings $p{=}1$ and $t{=}1$.

First, we show (a) the quality of an obtained solution, (b) the estimated quality of an optimal solution based on the relative error bound, and (c) the estimated quality of an optimal solution based on the absolute error bound for the p-optimal algorithm. The

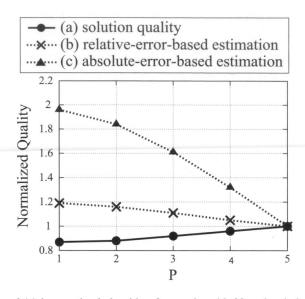

Fig. 3. (a), (b), and (c) in p-optimal algorithm for graphs with 20 nodes, induced width 5, and density 0.4. Value closer to 1 is desirable.

results of (a), (b), and (c) are normalized by the quality of an actual optimal solution, where (a) should be less than 1, and (b) and (c) should be more than 1. For all of them, a value closer to 1 is desirable. Figure 3 shows these values for graphs with 20 nodes, induced width 5, and the density of the binary constraints 0.4. We vary parameter p from 1 to 5. Note that when we set the number of nodes to 20 and the induced width to 5, we cannot create a graph whose density is greater than 0.6. We can see that the obtained solution quality and estimation are reasonable for most cases, except that (c) becomes rather inaccurate when $p = 1$. This is because the number of removed edges is large. In such a case, we need to increase p to obtain a better estimation.

Next, we compare our algorithm for p=1-optimality and DALO-t=1 for t=1-distance-optimality. Usually, DALO-t is used as an anytime algorithm, i.e., it continuously obtains t-optimal solutions. In this paper, we stop DALO-t when the first t-optimal solution is found. Figure 4-(i) shows (a), (b), and (c) in the p=1-optimal algorithm and in DALO-t=1 for graphs with 20 nodes and induced width 5, varying the density. A value closer to 1 is desirable. The broken lines indicate the results for DALO-t=1. We can see (a), (b), and (c) are better/more accurate in the p=1-optimal algorithm compared with DALO-t=1. Results (b) and (c) for the p=1-optimal algorithm become less accurate when the density increases. This is because the number of removed edges becomes large in the high density region. Figure 4-(ii) shows the results for graphs with 20 nodes and density 0.3, varying the induced width. We can see even the induced width is increased, (a), (b), and (c) for p=1-optimal algorithm are better/more accurate compared with DALO-t=1. Note that even if the induced width is 19, it does not mean we eliminate 18 edges from each node. 18 is the maximum value and for most of nodes, the number of eliminated edges is much smaller. Figure 4-(iii) shows the results for graphs with density 0.3 and induced width 3, varying the number of nodes. The obtained

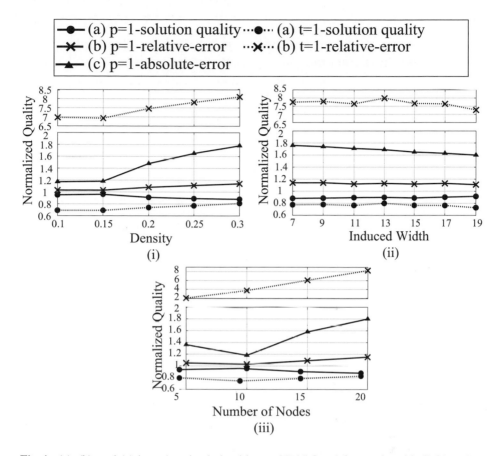

Fig. 4. (a), (b), and (c) in p=1-optimal algorithm and DALO-t=1 for graphs with (i) 20 nodes, induced width 5, (ii) 20 nodes, density 0.3, and (iii) density 0.3, induced width 3. Broken line indicates results for DALO-t=1. Value closer to 1 is desirable.

results are similar to Fig. 4-(i), i.e., (b) and (c) for the p=1-optimal algorithm become less accurate when the number of nodes increases.

Moreover, we show the results for large-scale problem instances. For them, obtaining an optimal solution is infeasible. Figure 5 shows the results for graphs with 1000 nodes and induced width 5, varying the density. Since we cannot obtain optimal solutions for these problem instances, we show the values of the obtained reward (which are not normalized). By setting the induced width to 5, we cannot create a graph whose density is greater than 0.01. We can see the rewards/run time for the p=1-optimal algorithm are greater/shorter compared to those for DALO-t=1.

Finally, we compare our algorithm for p=1-optimality and the bounded max-sum (bmaxsum) algorithm. We used graph coloring problems in the same settings presented in [13], except that the reward of each binary constraint is in the range [0,...,6]. Figure 6 shows the results for graphs with induced width 2, varying the number of nodes. A value closer to 1 is desirable. Broken lines indicate the results for the bounded

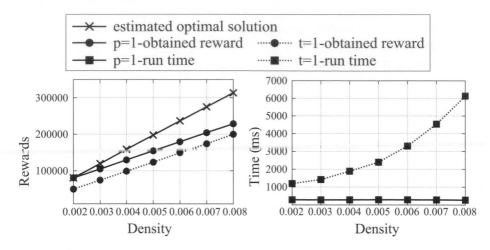

Fig. 5. Obtained rewards (not normalized) and run time (ms) for graphs with 1000 nodes and induced width 5. Broken line indicates results for DALO-t=1.

max-sum algorithm. We can see (a) and (b) (also (c)) are better in the $p=1$-optimal algorithm compared with the bounded max-sum algorithm.

We show the results for large-scale problem instances (graphs with 1000 nodes and induced width 2) in Fig. 7. Similar to the problem instances used in Fig. 5, obtaining an optimal solution is infeasible for these problem instances. By setting the induced width to 2, we cannot create a graph whose density is greater than 0.004. We show the values of the obtained reward (which are not normalized) as in Fig. 5. We can see the rewards/run time for the $p=1$-optimal algorithm are greater/shorter compared to those for the bounded max-sum algorithm.

In summary, these experimental results reveal that (i) the quality of the obtained solution of the $p=1$-optimal algorithm is much better compared with DALO-t=1 and bounded max-sum algorithms, (ii) the estimated quality of an optimal solution based on the absolute/relative error bounds for the $p=1$-optimal algorithm is more accurate than the other algorithms, and (iii) the run time of our algorithm is much shorter.

Although we did not show the results of ADPOP for space reasons, they are basically similar to our algorithms, since these two algorithms differ only in the methods to determine which edges to eliminate. The advantage of our algorithm is that it can provide the bound of a solution a priori.

Let us consider why our algorithm can obtain better results compared to DALO-t and the bounded max-sum algorithm. DALO-t obtains approximate solutions of the original problem, while our algorithm obtains an optimal solution for a relaxed problem. If the relaxed problem is not so different from the original problem, e.g., the induced width is small, our algorithm can find a better solution quickly.

It must be mentioned that we require knowledge of the induced width and r_{max} to obtain a priori bound based on p-optimality. On the other hand, the error bound obtained by k/t-optimality is independent from problem instances. If r_{max} can be extremely large, while the average of the binary rewards is rather small compared to r_{max}, the absolute error bound of p-optimality becomes less informative.

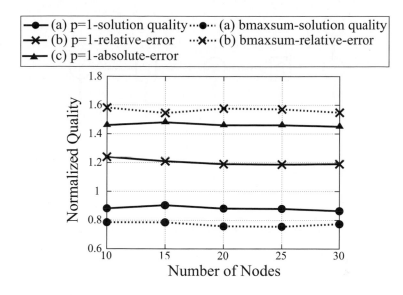

Fig. 6. (a), (b), and (c) in p–1-optimal algorithm and bounded max-sum algorithm for graphs with induced width 2. Broken line indicates results for bounded max-sum (bmaxsum) algorithm. Value closer to 1 is desirable.

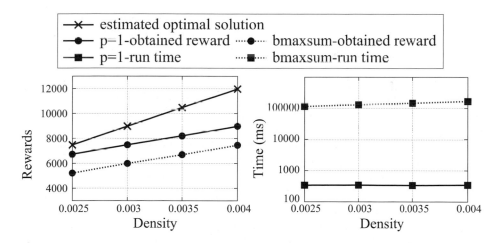

Fig. 7. Obtained rewards (not normalized) and run time (ms) for graphs with 1000 nodes and induced width 2. Broken line indicates results for bounded max-sum (bmaxsum) algorithm.

It might sound counter-intuitive that p=1-optimal algorithm performs much better compared to the bounded max-sum, since these two algorithms look quite similar, i.e., they remove edges from a constraint graph to make it cycle-free, and obtain optimal solutions for the remaining cycle-free graph. Furthermore, the bounded max-sum algorithm considers the importance of edges and removes less important edges, while p=1

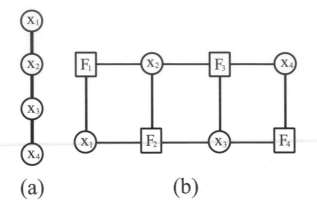

Fig. 8. (a) shows a chain constraint graph with four nodes. (b) shows the corresponding factor graph to (a). (b) contains a cycle, while (a) is a cycle free.

optimal algorithm does not consider such information and removes edges in a prede-fined way.

In reality, there exist some fundamental differences in these two algorithms. First, the graph structures used in these algorithms are completely different. The bounded max-sum algorithm works on a factor graph, while our algorithm works on a standard constraint graph. Even if a constraint graph is cycle-free, the corresponding factor graph inevitably contains a cycle, since a constraint is bi-directional in a DCOP [3]. Let us show an example. Figure 8-(a) shows a constraint graph with four nodes, which form a chain, and (b) shows the corresponding factor graph, where x_i and F_i represent variables and functions, respectively [4]. Clearly, (a) is cycle-free. On the other hand, to make (b) cycle-free, we need to remove at least three edges, e.g., edges between x_1 and F_1, x_2 and F_2, and x_3 and F_3, while our p=1-optimal algorithm does not need to remove any edges. In short, the bounded max-sum algorithm needs to remove more edges compared to our algorithm.

Second, the meaning of "optimal" solutions obtained by these two algorithms are different. Let us assume that we remove an edge between x_1 and F_1 from Figure 8-(b). This corresponds to make a copy of x_1 (which we call x_1'), and assume x_1' and x_1 are independent (so that the remaining factor graph is cycle-free). However, if we choose an arbitrary value for x_1', we cannot bound the solution quality. The bounded max-sum algorithm assumes that for each value of x_2, x_1''s value is chosen so that F_1 is minimized, i.e., the worst-case value for x_1' is chosen. In short, the bounded max-sum

---

[3] We can modify the original definition of a factor graph in [13] by assuming each function node corresponds to one constraint, so that a factor graph has less cycles. For example, in Fig. 8-(a), we introduce three function nodes F_1, F_2, F_3, where F_1 is related to x_1 and x_2, F_2 is related to x_2 and x_3, and F_3 is related to x_3 and x_4. Then, the obtained factor graph is cycle-free. We are not sure how this modification affects the performance of the bounded max-sum algorithm. Further evaluations are needed to clarify the effect of this modification for the bounded max-sum algorithm.

[4] Function F_i aggregates all reward functions related to x_i.

algorithm obtains a value assignment that optimizes the worst-case reward assuming we cannot control the value assignment of copied variables. Such a value assignment can be quite different from an optimal solution (where we can control all variables). On the other hand, our algorithm obtains an optimal solution for the remaining graph simply ignoring removed edges (assuming we obtain no reward from the removed edges).

5 Conclusion

We developed a new solution criterion called p-optimality and an incomplete algorithm for obtaining a p-optimal solution. This algorithm utilizes a graph structure called a pseudo-tree, which is widely used in complete DCOP algorithms. We provided the upper bounds of the absolute/relative errors of the solution, which can be obtained a priori/a posteriori, respectively. We showed that our algorithm for $p=1$-optimality can obtain better quality solutions and estimate more accurate error bounds compared with DALO-t for $t=1$-distance-optimality and the bounded max-sum algorithm. Furthermore, we showed that the run time for our algorithm for $p=1$-optimality is much shorter compared to these existing algorithms. Our future works include developing an anytime/complete algorithm that utilizes our algorithm as a preprocessing phase. A similar idea, i.e., using ADPOP as a preprocessing for ADOPT, is presented in [1]. Recently, a new criterion called c-optimality, which is a generalization of k-size/t-distance-optimality, has been proposed [15]. It provides quality guarantees for region optimal solutions and tighter bounds compared with k-size/t-distance-optimality. Our future work includes the comparison with this new criterion.

References

1. Atlas, J., Warner, M., Decker, K.: A memory bounded hybrid approach to distributed constraint optimization. In: Proceedings of the 11th International Workshop on Distributed Constraint Reasoning, pp. 37–51 (2008)
2. Dechter, R.: Constraint Processing. Morgan Kaufmann Publishers, San Francisco (2003)
3. Fitzpatrick, S., Meertens, L.: Distributed coordination through anarchic optimization. In: Lesser, V., Ortiz, C., Tambe, M. (eds.) Distributed Sensor Networks: A Multiagent Perspective, pp. 257–295. Kluwer Academic Publishers, Dordrecht (2003)
4. Kiekintveld, C., Yin, Z., Kumar, A., Tambe, M.: Asynchronous algorithms for approximate distributed constraint optimization with quality bounds. In: Proceedings of the 9th International Conference on Autonomous Agents and Multiagent Systems, pp. 133–140 (2010)
5. Kjaerulff, U.: Reduction of computational complexity in bayesian networks through removal of weak dependences. In: Proceedings of the 10th International Conference on Uncertainty in Artificial Intelligence, pp. 374–382 (1994)
6. Léauté, T., Ottens, B., Szymanek, R.: FRODO 2.0: An open-source framework for distributed constraint optimization. In: Proceedings of the 12th International Workshop on Distributed Constraint Reasoning, pp. 160–164 (2009)
7. Mailler, R., Lesser, V.: Using cooperative mediation to solve distributed constraint satisfaction problems. In: Proceedings of the 3rd International Conference on Autonomous Agents and Multiagent Systems, pp. 446–453 (2004)
8. Modi, P., Shen, W.-M., Tambe, M., Yokoo, M.: ADOPT: asynchronous distributed constraint optimization with quality guarantees. Artificial Intelligence 161(1-2), 149–180 (2005)

9. Pearce, J., Tambe, M.: Quality guarantees on k-optimal solutions for distributed constraint optimization problems. In: Proceedings of the 20th International Joint Conference on Artificial Intelligence, pp. 1446–1451 (2007)
10. Pearce, J., Tambe, M., Maheswaran, R.: Solving multiagent networks using distributed constraint optimization. AI Magazine 29(3), 47–66 (2008)
11. Petcu, A., Faltings, B.: Approximations in distributed optimization. In: van Beek, P. (ed.) CP 2005. LNCS, vol. 3709, pp. 802–806. Springer, Heidelberg (2005)
12. Petcu, A., Faltings, B.: A scalable method for multiagent constraint optimization. In: Proceedings of the 19th International Joint Conference on Artificial Intelligence, pp. 266–271 (2005)
13. Rogers, A., Farinelli, A., Stranders, R., Jennings, N.: Bounded approximate decentralised coordination via the max-sum algorithm. Artificial Intelligence 175(2), 730–759 (2011)
14. van Engelen, R.A.: Approximating bayesian belief networks by arc removal. IEEE Transactions on Pattern Analysis and Machine Intelligence 19, 916–920 (1997)
15. Vinyals, M., Shieh, E., Cerquides, J., Rodriguez-Aguilar, J.A., Yin, Z., Tambe, M., Bowring, E.: Quality guarantees for region optimal DCOP algorithms. In: Proceedings of the 10th International Conference on Autonomous Agents and Multiagent Systems, pp. 133–140 (2011)
16. Yin, Z.: USC dcop repository. University of Southern California, Department of Computer Science (2008)
17. Zhang, W., Wang, G., Xing, Z., Wittenburg, L.: Distributed stochastic search and distributed breakout: properties, comparison and applications to constraint optimization problems in sensor networks. Artificial Intelligence 161(1-2), 55–87 (2005)
18. Zivan, R.: Anytime local search for distributed constraint optimization. In: Proceedings of the 23rd National Conference on Artificial Intelligence, pp. 393–398 (2008)

A More Efficient BDD-Based QBF Solver

Oswaldo Olivo and E. Allen Emerson

Department of Computer Science,
The University of Texas, Austin TX-78712, USA
{olivo,emerson}@cs.utexas.edu

Abstract. In this paper we present a QBF solver that is based on BDD
technologies but includes optimizations from search-based algorithms.
We enhance the early quantification technique from model checking,
favoring aggressive quantification over conjunction of BDDs. BDD Constraint propagation is also described, a strategy inspired by the efficient simplifications applied to CNFs in DPLL-based algorithms . Some
dynamic variable elimination heuristics that enforce quantification and
bounded space usage are also presented, coping with the difficulties
faced by static heuristics included in previous BDD-based solvers. Experimental results show that our solver outperforms both symbolic and
search-based competitive solvers in formal verification benchmarks with
practical applications in equivalence checking and theorem proving, by
completing more problems or finishing in less time. Some preliminary
results also show that the solver is able to handle some other hard problems for symbolic solvers in the planning domain with similar efficiency.
The benchmarks we used contain QBFs of nearly up to 9000 variables
and are available at the QBFLIB website.

Keywords: Quantified boolean formulas, bounded model construction,
equivalence checking, theorem proving, conformant planning, symbolic
decision procedures.

1 Introduction

The satisfiability problem consists of determining whether a given formula is satisfiable or not. The main variations of the problem are satisfiability for boolean
propositional formulas (SAT) and satisfiability for quantified boolean propositional formulas (QBF)[18][15]. QBFs are the central topic in this paper. Some
problems traditionally expressed as QBFs are conformant planning[27], model
checking[5], equivalence checking[3] and theorem proving for modal logics[21].

Satisfiability solvers are commonly classified as search-based and symbolic.
Algorithms that belong to the search-based category are widely based on the
DPLL procedure[11][12]. In contrast, symbolic solvers proceed over a different
(but co-satisfiable) representation of the original formula, such as Binary Decision Diagrams, Zero-Suppressed Decision Diagrams, And-Inverted Graphs and
others, and then attempt to determine satisfiability of it. Symbolic satisfiability
solving has not been very successful so far according to experimental comparisons with search-based algorithms.

J. Lee (Ed.): CP 2011, LNCS 6876, pp. 675–690, 2011.
© Springer-Verlag Berlin Heidelberg 2011

In this paper we present a QBF solver that is based on BDD technologies but includes optimizations from search-based algorithms. We enhance the early quantification technique from model checking[7], favoring aggressive quantification over conjunction of BDDs. To our knowledge, our BDD Constraint propagation procedure is introduced for the first time, a strategy inspired by the efficient simplifications applied to CNFs in DPLL-based algorithms [11]. Some dynamic variable elimination heuristics that enforce quantification and bounded space usage are also presented, coping with the difficulties faced by static heuristics included in previous BDD-based solvers[1][15]. Conjunction of small sets of BDDs is sought and quantification is given precedence over conjunction as much as possible, typically resulting in the simplification of the clauses to a large extent before the conjunctions are performed.

We refer to our solver as eBDD-QBF (for Efficient BDD-based QBF solver) in the rest of the paper. We have compared eBDD-QBF with QuBE7.1[14] , Semprop[19] and DepQBF[20] on some equivalence checking[3], conformant planning[27] and theorem proving for modal logic[21] benchmarks publicly available in the QBFLIB website. These three solvers have been reported to perform best on the verification domain , and have dominated BDD-based state-of-the-art approaches; in fact, DepQBF won the main track of the QBFEVAL solver competition in 2010[21]. Instances of up to 9000 variables were solved by our tool, overcoming scalability issues of established BDD-based solving algorithms. eBDD-QBF performs best for equivalence checking, followed by Semprop and DepQBF, and then QuBe7.1. Our solver is mostly efficient on the adder circuit instances.

The eBDD-QBF solver performs comparably well on the conformant planning benchmarks, and is vastly superior on the theorem proving instances. Therefore, we conclude that our solver is better for the equivalence checking problem, significantly superior on theorem proving for modal logic, while being also robust enough to handle successfully problems in non-verification domains such as conformant planning.

Our goal was to improve previous algorithms for BDD-based solving, which were clearly dominated by search-based solvers according to experiments. The results shown in this paper suggest the importance of combining search-based simplifications in BDD solving in an effective manner to make this approach practical. The techniques presented in this paper can also be reused in larger frameworks that involve BDD processing at some point, such as AQME[25] and AIGSOLVE[23]. The paper is organized as follows : section 2 contains the background for this work, explaining QBFs, search-based and symbolic algorithms for the problem. In the third section we explain our algorithm for solving QBF, with emphasis on novel features. Section 4 contains the experimental results, and conclusions and future work are the subject of section 5.

2   Background

This section covers the necessary background for understanding the rest of the paper: QBFs, BDDs, search-based algorithms and symbolic decision procedures for QBF.

2.1   Quantified Boolean Formulas

Consider the formula $Q_1 X_1 Q_2 X_2 ... Q_n X_n \phi$, where $Q_i \in \{\forall, \exists\}$, X_i is a set of propositional variables and ϕ is a propositional formula over the variables defined in each X_i.

$Q_1 X_1 Q_2 X_2 ... Q_n X_n$ is called the quantifier prefix and ϕ the matrix. Each $Q_i X_i$ is called a quantifier, Q_i is the quantifier operator and X_i is the variable set of the quantifier.

The quantified boolean problem consists of determining if there is a satisfying assignment for the formula stated above. In this paper we deal with matrices in CNF , so the QBFs have the form:

$$(1) \qquad Q_1 X_1 Q_2 X_2 ... Q_n X_n (C_1 \wedge C_2 \wedge ... \wedge C_m)$$

where the quantifier prefix is as defined previously and each C_j is a disjunction of literals called clause.

2.2   Binary Decision Diagrams

A Binary Decision Diagram (BDD) is a directed acyclic graph (DAG) that represents all the satisfying assignments of a formula. Every inner node represents a variable x of the formula and has two children denoted as high child and low child; the subgraph starting from the high (low) child corresponds to assigning $x := true$ ($x := false$) in the formula represented by the parent node. The leaves of a BDD are the constants $true$ and $false$. Every path in the BDD that reaches the $true$ ($false$) node represents a(n) (un)satisfying a assignment of the formula. Imposing the condition that variables occur in the same order in all the paths, elimination of redundant nodes and merging of isomorphic subgraphs yields the concept of Reduced Ordered Binary Decision Diagrams (ROBDDs). This data structure was proposed by Bryant[6], with the accompanying $Apply(A, B, op)$ algorithm that generalizes binary operator applications for pairs of BDDs. Another important algorithm for ROBDDs is $RestrictBy(A, B)$, proposed by Coudert[9], which prunes the assignments of A that are inconsistent with B. The $RestrictBy$ function is important to the understanding of this paper, so the reader is encouraged to consult the algorithm in [9]. The intuition for the algorithm is provided below:

Restricting f by c corresponds to recursively applying shannon expansion over f according to the variable assignments provided for each variable in c.

2.3   Search-Based Algorithms

Search-based decision procedures for QBF are largely based on the DPLL algorithm[12], which consists of attempting to find a satisfying assignment in a top-down fashion. It is labeled as top-down because the main-algorithm consists of splitting the original formula by setting a variable to $true$ and to $false$ and solving recursively the two sub-formulas; hence, it is inspired by the divide-and-conquer framework.

The recursive procedure takes as input the QBF given by the quantifier prefix and matrix in CNF, selects a variable to assign at each step, checks that the sub-formula is satisfiable for at least one case if the variable is existential or for both cases if the variable is universal.

Also important are the unit propagation and pure-literal rules. The first corresponds to setting a clause with only one literal to the appropriate value and propagating the result throughout the formula. The second consists of setting the corresponding value to literals that occur either only positively or only negatively across the formula. The DPLL version that handles QBFs is traditionally referred to as Q-DPLL.

Resolution is another simplification rule that leads to a distinct range of search based approaches[11][28][24].

2.4   Symbolic Algorithms

The distinguishing feature of symbolic procedures for solving QBFs consists in operating over a co-satisfiable structure obtained from the formula, rather than the original representation. They typically employ BDDs[4][13][16], ZDDs[8][15], AIGs[23] and other diagrams. We will describe BDD-based solvers with more detail, as they form the basis for the work presented in this paper.

A naive procedure to solve a QBF is to create a BDD for each clause C_j in (1), conjoin all of them iteratively by Bryant's Apply algorithm into a monolithic BDD B, and then quantify out all variables, in the order given by the quantifier prefix, from inner to outermost fashion, i.e. quantify all variables over X_n, then all variables in X_{n-1} and so on. The limitation of this approach is that the monolithic BDD B generally becomes too big, making it impractical to solve formulas of over 200-300 variables.

All of this was noted initially in symbolic model checking, which eventually gave rise to the early quantification technique[7].

Consider a variable x_i in the innermost variable set X_n. Without loss of generality, suppose x_i occurs in the clauses $C_1, ..., C_k$ and doesn't appear in $C_{k+1}, ..., C_m$. Then we can rewrite (1) into:

$$(2) \qquad Q_1 X_1 Q_2 X_2 ... Q_{n-1} X_{n-1} Q_n (X_n - \{x_i\})$$
$$(Q_n x_i (C_1 \wedge C_2 \wedge ... \wedge C_k) \wedge C_{k+1} \wedge ... \wedge C_m)$$

The above formulation allows the procedure to focus on simplifying the inner quantified formula, which is frequently smaller than the original, and then solve the outer formula. This re-formulation can be done iteratively from inner to outermost fashion.

To the best of our knowledge, the principal BDD-based solvers[13][16][15] rely on a variant of directed bucket elimination with static heuristics for variable selection and conjunction scheduling. The variable ordering is generally calculated statically by using a wide range of graph heuristics, and the BDDs are then ordered according to this variable ordering before bucket elimination begins. The clauses are clustered according to the topmost variable of the BDDs, and then the clusters are selected according to the fixed ordering. Elimination of a variable consists of conjoining all the BDDs in the variable's bucket, performing the quantification and then putting the resulting BDD into the appropriate bucket. This is done until termination is detected (all buckets are empty or the Zero BDD was obtained) or when all variables have been eliminated.

There has been some work involving the combination of search and symbolic techniques in the past. For example, DPLL for ZDDs has been implemented[8]. Audemard proposed a BDD QBF solver that consists of using a SAT solver to find solutions and store them into a BDD, [2] but this method didn't produce a competitive solver. Similarly, sKizzo[4] uses a SAT solver as an oracle over a skolemnization of the original formula. CirCUs combines the power of AIGs, BDDs and SAT solvers into a tool[17]. eBDD-QBF is different in the sense that only BDD algorithms and operations are used, and no external SAT solvers or other search based procedure. That is, one of the main contributions of this work is the introduction of BDD constraint propagation procedures that allow a pure BDD-based solver to be competitive. Adapting the unit-clause and pure-literal rules for ZDDs was presented previously[8], but we are not aware of any approach of this kind involving BDDs.

3 New QBF Solver

We now describe the new BDD-based QBF solving algorithm implemented in this work. First, we explain our improvements over previous search and symbolic strategies that lead to a novel component of the solver : BDD constraint propagation. Then follows a presentation of the variable selection dynamic heuristics that cope to some extent with unsolved issues of static heuristics such as space explosion. Finally, the main solving algorithm is presented, which differs from the established bucket elimination framework in most BDD-based solvers in order to incorporate the new features developed in this work.

3.1 Enhanced Early Quantification

A variation of early quantification was implemented in the solver.

Recall (1) and (2) from the background section. Consider variable x_i in the innermost variable set X_n of (1). Without loss of generality, suppose x_i occurs in the clauses $C_1, ..., C_k$ and doesn't appear in $C_{k+1}, ..., C_m$.

If x_i is an existential variable then we rewrite (1) into (2) as discussed in the introduction.

If x_i is an universal variable then we make use of the distributivity property in predicate logic $\forall x.P(x) \wedge Q(x). \equiv \forall x.P(x). \wedge \forall x.Q(x).$, and (1) becomes :

$$(3) \qquad Q_1 X_1 Q_2 X_2 ... Q_{n-1} X_{n-1} \forall (X_n - \{x_i\})$$
$$((\forall x_i(C_1) \wedge \forall x_i(C_2) \wedge ... \wedge \forall x_i(C_k)) \wedge C_{k+1} \wedge ... \wedge C_m)$$

The simple reformulation in (3) enforces a more aggressive quantification mechanism than (2), eliminating the variable x_i for each of $C_1, ..., C_k$ before conjoining them, making use of the fact that quantification typically reduces the size of the diagram because a variable is eliminated from the support set - this argument is not immediately applicable to BDD conjunction.

After performing quantification individually, we conjoin all of the simplified BDDs, store the result and apply the early quantification procedure iteratively.[1]

3.2   BDD Constraint Propagation

The BDD constraint propagation strategies were inspired by the unit-propagation and pure literal rules that DPLL-based procedures employ for CNFs. We present the BDD unit propagation and BDD pure literal propagation algorithms in this section. Due to space limitations the detailed correctness proofs are to be consulted in [22].

Definition 1 (Unit Clause):[10] Let $f = C_1 \wedge C_2 \wedge .... \wedge C_{i-1} \wedge C_i \wedge C_{i+1} \wedge ... \wedge C_k$ be a CNF formula and $C_i = x_j$, where x_j is a literal. We call C_i a *unit clause* of f.   □

Definition 2 (Generalized Unit Clause): Let f be a boolean formula. If $\exists$ CNF $f' = C_1 \wedge C_2 \wedge .... \wedge C_{i-1} \wedge C_i \wedge C_{i+1} \wedge ... \wedge C_k$ such that $f' \equiv f$ and $C_i = x_j$, where x_j is a literal, then C_i is a *generalized unit clause* of f.   □

Definition 1 is the widely known version of unit clauses for CNF formulas. We propose definition 2 in order to apply a more general form of unit propagation in the context of BDDs. Since conjunction and quantification of BDDs results in intermediate BDDs that are not clauses, it is necessary to detect unit clauses that appear in equivalent CNF representations to make use of unit propagation during the solving procedure.

Theorem 1: Let C_i be a clause and $C_j = x_l$ be a unit clause (x_l is an existential literal). Then $RestrictBy(BDD(C_i), BDD(C_j)) = BDD(C_i[x_l := true])$.   □

Corollary 1: Let $f = C_1 \wedge C_2 \wedge ... \wedge C_k$ be a CNF and $C_j = x_l$ be a unit clause (where x_l is a unit literal). Then $RestrictBy(BDD(f), BDD(C_j)) = BDD(f[x_l := true])$.   □

Corollary 2: Let f be a non-trivial propositional formula and $C_j = x_l$ be a generalized unit clause of f (where x_l is an existential literal).
Then $RestrictBy(BDD(f), BDD(C_j)) = BDD(f[x_l := true])$.   □

The previous theorems and corollaries state that in order to apply unit propagation with regular and generalized unit clauses in the context of BDDs, it is sufficient to apply *RestrictBy* with the corresponding literal.

---

[1] It is also possible to avoid conjunction of the results, proceeding with the next variable elimination step, but we didn't detect any performance boost during our preliminary experiments.

Theorem 2: Let f be a non-trivial propositional formula, x_j a literal and f' an equivalent CNF representation of f obtained by applying distributivity of $\wedge$ and $\vee$ and removing trivial clauses. Then x_j is a generalized unit clause in f iff x_j is a unit clause in f'. $\qquad\square$

Theorem 3: Let f be a non-trivial propositional formula and x_j a literal. Then x_j is a generalized unit clause in f iff $f[x_j := false] = false$. $\qquad\square$

Corollary 3: Let f be a non-trivial propositional formula and x_l a literal. Then $C_j = x_l$ is a generalized unit clause in f iff $RestrictBy(BDD(f), BDD(\neg C_j)) = ZERO\_BDD$. $\qquad\square$

Corollary 3 gives us a procedure for extracting unit BDDs. It is important to note the CNF construction may be exponential in size, but we do not construct it explicitly in our algorithm; it is only employed for proving purposes. The reader should also note that extracting the unit BDDs is analogous to computing prime implicates of a formula, which is NP-Hard. However, our main algorithm only performs BDD extraction for one BDD at each iteration and not the complete formula, making the solving procedure computationally practical.

Lemma 1: Let f be a non-trivial propositional formula, and x_i, x_j two literals. Then $RestrictBy(BDD(f), BDD(x_i) \wedge BDD(x_j)) = RestrictBy(RestrictBy(BDD(f), BDD(x_i)), BDD(x_j))$. $\qquad\square$

Theorem 4: Let f be a non-trivial propositional formula and $C_{i_1}, ..., C_{i_m}$ be unit clauses of existential literals.
    Then $g(f, \{C_{i_1}, ..., C_{i_m}\}) = RestrictBy(f, C_{i_1} \wedge .... \wedge C_{i_m})$,
    where $g(f, l) = g(RestrictBy(f, C_{i_1}), \{C_{i_2}, ..., C_{i_m}\})$ if $l = \{C_{i_1}, .., C_{i_m}\}$ and f if $l = \emptyset$. $\qquad\square$

Theorem 4 justifies the fact that we can perform unit propagation in BDDs by first conjoining all of the unit BDDs and then applying the restriction operation.

The unit propagation rule is fairly intuitive when all of the BDDs represent clauses: we can extract BDDs with support set size equal to one and apply the unit propagation according to the above theorems. The previous procedure is somewhat limited because it fails to recognize BDDs containing inner unit BDDs, which occurs for non-clause formulas. This is why we need a unit BDD extraction algorithm to detect generalized unit clauses.

Considering that any propositional function can be written in CNF and that BDDs are canonical representations of these functions, then any formula (clause or non-clause) containing a generalized unit clause can be expressed as $l_i \wedge p$, where l_i is a literal and p is a propositional formula. Therefore, setting l_i to false makes the entire formula unsatisfiable. One can then conclude that for any variable x_i in the support set of a formula F, it holds that x_i is a positive (negative) generalized unit clause iff $F[x_i := false] \equiv false$ ($F[x_i := true] \equiv false$). Below is the algorithm for detecting inner unit BDDs for a given BDD b.

Now we will discuss the pure literal rule for BDDs.

---

algorithm. UnitBDDExtraction(BDD b, Quantifier Prefix qp):
Set of BDD $S := \{\}$
for each variable v in the support set of b do
    if RestrictBy(b,Not(bdd(v))) = $Zero\_BDD$ then
        if(isUniversal(v,qp)) then return $\{Zero\_BDD\}$
        else $S := S \cup \{bdd(b)\}$
    else if RestrictBy(b,bdd(v)) = $Zero\_BDD$ then
        if(isUniversal(v,qp)) then return $\{Zero\_BDD\}$
        else $S := S \cup \{Not(bdd(b))\}$
return S

Algorithm for unit BDD extraction

Definition 3 (Pure Literal):[10] Let $f = C_1 \wedge C_2 \wedge ... \wedge C_k$ be a CNF formula and x_j a literal, where x_j only appears positively (negatively) in f. We call x_j a *positive (negative) pure literal* of f. □

Definition 4 (Generalized Pure Literal): Let f be a boolean formula. If $\exists$ CNF $f' = C_1 \wedge C_2 \wedge .... \wedge C_k$ such that $f' \equiv f$ and x_j occurs only positively (negatively) in f', where x_j is a literal, then x_j is a *generalized positive (negative) pure literal* of f. □

Theorem 5: Let f be a non-trivial propositional formula, x_j a literal and f' an equivalent CNF representation of f obtained by applying distributivity of $\wedge$ and $\vee$ and removing trivial clauses. Then x_j is a generalized positive (negative) pure literal in f iff x_j is a positive (negative) pure literal in f'. □

Theorem 6: Let f be a non-trivial formula and x_j a literal. x_j is a generalized positive (negatively) pure literal in f iff $f[x_j := false] = \forall x_j(f)$ ($f[x_j := true] = \forall x_j(f)$). □

Theorem 6 entails an algorithm for calculating the polarity of a variable in a formula.

Corollary 4: Let f be a non-trivial formula and x_j a literal. x_j is positively (negatively) pure in $BDD(f)$ iff $RestrictBy(BDD(f), BDD(\neg(x_j))) = \forall x_j(BDD(f))$ ($RestrictBy(BDD(f), BDD(x_j)) = \forall x_j(BDD(f))$). □

The pure literal propagation algorithm first constructs the pure literal vector (which determines the polarity and purity of the variables) and then applies pure literal propagation accordingly. A universal pure literal is eliminated from the clauses and an existential pure literal entails the removal of clauses where it appears.

    Similarly to unit propagation, we first consider the case involving only clause BDDs. Setting a variable in the support set of the BDD to either *true* or *false* results in *true* iff the formula is a clause. By checking which assignment to the variable makes the formula satisfiable the polarity of the variable within the BDD can be detected. The polarity table is calculated as follows:

```
algorithm PolarityVectorClauseBDDs(Set of BDD bdds, int numVars):
Vector of Int v
for i = 1 to numVars do
    v[i] := −2
for each BDD b in bdds do
    for each variable v in the support set of b do
        if RestrictBy(b,bdd(v)) = One_BDD then updatePolarity(polarity,v,1)
        else if RestrictBy(b,not(bdd(v)))=One_BDD
            then updatePolarity(polarity,v,0)
    return polarity
```

Algorithm for calculating the polarity vector from a set of clause BDDs

Initially all variables hold the -2 value, stating that the polarity is undefined. *updatePolarity* sets the polarity to 1 or 0 if the polarity was undefined previously for the variable. Whenever the newly found polarity is different from the previously held, the polarity of the variable is changed into -1 permanently, and otherwise keeps the polarity unchanged. After constructing the polarity vector, the pure-literal propagation eliminates clauses with existential pure variables and eliminates universal pure variables.

```
algorithm PureLiteralClauseBDDs(Set of BDD bdds, int numVars, Quantifier Prefix
qp):
    boolean pure_var := true
    while pure_var do
        Vector of int polarity := PolarityVectorClauseBDDsPureLiteral(bdds, numVars)
        BDD polarityBDD := One_BDD
        pure_var := false
        for each variable v in polarity do
            if polarity[v] ≠  2 ∧ polarity[v] ≠  1 then
                pure_var := true
                if isUniversal(v,qp) then
                    polarityBDD := polarityBDD∧(polarity[v] = 1?not(bdd(v)) : bdd(v))
                else
                    polarityBDD := polarityBDD∧(polarity[v] = 1?bdd(v) : not(bdd(v)))
        for each BDD b in bdds do
            RestrictBy(b,polarityBDD)
    return bdds
```

Algorithm for applying the pure literal rule for clause BDDs

Whenever BDDs are not clauses, the polarity of the variables is not obviously determined. We use universal quantification in this case, according to corollary 4. Consider a formula F that contains a variable x_i. If F has x_i ($\neg x_i$) in all its clauses, then setting the variable to the appropriate truth value would be sufficient to determine the polarity. Distinction between containing both x_i and $\neg x_i$ in its clauses and containing only one of them is harder. In $\forall x_i.F$ the variable x_i is eliminated. If x_i is positively (negatively) pure in F then $F[x_i := false] \equiv \forall x_i.F$ ($F[x_i := true] \equiv \forall x_i.F$). Therefore we can quantify and compare with either $F[x_i := false]$ ($F[x_i := true]$) to determine if x_i is a generalized positive (negative) pure literal. In order to employ this pure-literal rule for non-clause BDDs we only need to change the polarity vector calculation procedure as follows:

---

algorithm   PolarityVectorNonClauseBDDsPureLiteral(Set   of   BDD   *bdds*,   int *numVars*):
    Vector of Int v
    for $i = 1$ to *numVars* do
        $v[i] := -2$
    for each BDD b in *bdds* do
        for each variable v in the support set of b do
            if RestrictBy(b,bdd(v)) = *One_BDD* then updatePolarity(*polarity*,v,1)
            else if RestrictBy(b,not(bdd(v))) = *One_BDD* then
                updatePolarity(*polarity*,v,0)
            else if $\forall v.b. \equiv$ RestrictBy(b,not(bdd(v))) then updatePolarity(*polarity*,v,1)
            else if $\forall v.b. \equiv$ RestrictBy(b,bdd(v)) then updatePolarity(*polarity*,v,0)
            else updatePolarity(*polarity*,v,$\neg polarity[v]$)
    return *polarity*

Algorithm for calculating the polarity vector from a set of non-clause BDDs

3.3   Variable Ordering Heuristics

Another feature of our implementation consists of dynamic heuristics for selecting variable elimination orders in BDD-based QBF solving. Although dynamic heuristics have been proposed in the context of model checking[26] and other areas, their effectiveness varies according to the problem domain, and to the best of our knowledge all BDD-Based SAT and QBF solvers employ static heuristics. The main reason is that bucket elimination with BDDs relies on eliminating only top variables at each iteration, so the ordering must be fixed before starting bucket processing. We have implemented the following: (1) Most occurring top variable, (2) Most occurring variable, (3) Least occurring top variable, (4) Least occurring variable, (5) Smallest BDD top variable, (6) Smallest BDD variable, (7) Bounded Most occurring variable with min.

3.4   Main Algorithm

The main procedure simply puts together all of the algorithms mentioned in the previous subsections.

```
algorithm BDD-QBF(CNF F, Quantifier Prefix qp, int numVars,int heuristic):
Set of BDD bdds := createBDDForEachClause(F)
bdds := ClauseBDDUnitPropagation(bdds,qp)
bdds := PureLiteralClauseBDDsPureLiteral(bdds,numVars,qp)
while qp ≠ {} do
    if bdds = {} then return QSAT
    if Zero_BDD ∈ bdds then return Q-UNSAT
    Quantifier q := innermostQuantifier(qp)
    qp := qp − {q}
    while variableSet(q) ≠ {} do
        if bdds = {} then return QSAT
        if Zero_BDD ∈ bdds then return Q-UNSAT
        int var := chooseVariable(bdds,variableSet(q),heuristic)
        variableSet(q) := variableSet(q) −{var}
        Set of BDD occ_bdds :=chooseBDDsWithVariable(bdds,var)
        bdds := bdds − occ_bdds
        if isUniversal(var,qp) then
            for each BDD b in occ_bdds do
                b := ∀var.(b).
        BDD bdd_conj := ∧_{b∈occ_bdds}b
        if isExistential(var,qp) then
            bdd_conj := ∃var.(bdd_conj).
        bdds := bdds ∪ {bdd_conj}
        Set of BDD unitBDD := UnitBDDExtraction(bdd_conj)
        if unitBDD ≠ {} then
            bdds := NonClauseBDDUnitPropagation(bdds,∧_{b∈unitBDDvector}b)
```

BDD-Based QBF Solver

4   Experiments

The solver was implemented in C++ and the underlying BDD package is CUDD[29] from the University of Colorado at Boulder. All experiments were run on the same machine, an Intel Dual Core 2.13GHz Unix desktop machine with 4 GB of RAM. We compared eBDD-QBF with other solvers that reportedly performed best on the verification domain, such as QuBE7.1[14], Semprop[19] and DepQBF[20]. They also dominated BDD-based solvers according to previous experiments. In fact, DepQBF is a solver that integrates dependency graphs with DPLL, and was the winner of the QBFEVAL '10 main competition[21]. Additionally, previous research had shown that the first two solvers clearly dominated BDD-based approaches, so we wanted to determine if our improved BDD-based algorithm was able to perform better in comparison[10].

We set a 30 minute timeout for each instance, meaning that if the solver took more than 30 minutes to complete an instance it stopped and went on to the next one.

We must mention the fact that we performed preliminary experiments in order to select a suitable dynamic variable elimination technique, and that the least occurring variable heuristic turned out as the overall best. This was the only parameter that needed to be decided before performing the experiments, so we ran all of the benchmarks using the least occurring variable heuristic. Due to space constraints, we only present a table summarizing the number of instances solved, total time taken, variable and clause range for each solver.

The full tables can be consulted in
http://www.cs.utexas.edu/~olivo/CP/App.pdf

First we present experiments for Ayari's benchmarks[3], which consists of QBF formulas that are satisfiable iff a given circuit has a satisfying word model of a bounded depth. The problem is called bounded model construction, and it is analogous to bounded model checking in the sense that a tool can iteratively generate QBF formulas for increasing bounds k until it has found a satisfying model or covered the complete state space.

The benchmarks formulate the problem for ripple-carry adder circuits, D-type flip-flops, Von Neumann machines, mutual exclusion and Szymanski protocols. These have practical applications in equivalence checking.

We noticed that the unit propagation and pure-literal rules were only effective at the start of the solving procedure, and decided to turn off these rules during variable elimination for this suite. That is, only outer unit propagation and pure-literal rules were applied in this case. We give detailed information for the entire suite, except for the Von Neumann instances; these were omitted because of the impossibility to handle variable indices over 80000 with CUDD. Therefore, any algorithm based on the current version of CUDD must do pre-processing before handling these instances, which was intentionally left out in our pure BDD-based solver.

Solver	Instances Solved	Total Time	Variable Range	Clause Range
eBDD-QBF	27	3257.83s	332-5833	127-6084
QuBE7.1	19	304.214s	332-252710	127-334058
Semprop	20	361.614 s	332-57143	127-74975
DepQBF	20	61.107s	332-4558	5-73065

Experimental results for Equivalence Checking instances

eBDD-QBF is the best solver in the overall suite, solving 27 instances, followed by Semprop and DepQBF with 20, and finally QuBE7.1 with 19. We should also point out the excellent performance of eBDD-QBF for the adder instances, which is mainly due, according to our inspections, to the dynamic heuristic and aggressive universal quantification rather than pure-literal and unit-propagation for BDDs. We later determined that eBDD-QBF solved Adder2-10-s with 8949 variables and 9664 clauses in 60m7.509s, driven by our curiosity to evaluate the limits of our tool for adder circuits; that was the largest instance it could handle, blowing up in space for the larger ones. On the other hand, eBDD-QBF performs badly on flip-flops, where the rest of the solvers have no trouble at all. We have determined that eBDD-QBF takes too much time executing the outer pure-literal and unit propagation rules, making it exceed the time limit. The total time of eBDD-QBF is also marred by a couple of instances in which it takes a little over 12 minutes to complete. All of this can be confirmed by reading the appendix on the website.

Presumably, similar preprocessing to that implemented in the other solvers would make eBDD-QBF more competitive for these instances.

We now present results for Rintanen's instances[27], which are encodings of conformant planning problems. The suite includes instances from the implication chains, sorting networks, blocksworld and bombs in the toilet problems. In our experiments, we exclude blocksworld problems, as their random generation is incompatible with the use of BDDs. For this benchmark we employed both inner and outer unit propagation, and outer pure-literal rule application for eBDD-QBF.

Solver	Instances Solved	Total Time	Variable Range	Clause Range
eBDD-QBF	30	246.75s	10-3290	18-19663
QuBE7.1	27	506.211s	10-2035	18-178750
Semprop	32	75.092s	10-3290	18-178750
DepQBF	23	1984.76s	10-2501	18-178750

Experimental results for Conformant Planning instances

Results are almost equal for the planning instances, Semprop being the overall winner with 32 benchmarks solved, eBDD-QBF is second with 30, and QuBE7.1 and DepQBF trail behind with 27 and 23 instances solved respectively. eBDD-QBF is only slower than Semprop for this suite.

We must stress the fact that symbolic methods have not been generally too successful in the past under this domain, given the structure of the instances. We attribute the competitive results obtained with eBDD-QBF to the BDD constraint propagation strategy.

As an additional note, eBDD-QBF was able to solve Castellini's bombs in the toilet benchmarks and Letz's tree instances[21] in just a matter of seconds. These are related to the conformant planning domain, but we don't report detailed results because of space constraints.

The third suite that we present results for consists of Pan's instances for Modal Logic K[21]. These are encodings of propositional formulas extended with the possibility and necessity operators. The problem of satisfiability in modal logics has applications in artificial intelligence, and program and hardware verification. Particularly, the instances used for the experiments in this paper have been proposed in the context of evaluating theorem provers.

Identically to the previous suite, eBDD-QBF was run with both inner and outer unit propagation, and outer pure-literal rule application.

Solver	Instances Solved	Total Time	Variable Range	Clause Range
eBDD-QBF	269	6283.38s	4-3004	5-131072
QuBE7.1	140	8148.41s	4-11130	5-355294
Semprop	242	10129.9s	4-5320	5-131072
DepQBF	140	12087.7s	4-4558	5-73065

Experimental results for Modal Logic instances

There is a markedly superior performance by eBDD-QBF in this case, both in the number of instances solved and total execution time. Again, the BDD adaptation of DPLL techniques was decisive in the excellent performance of our solver. A distinctive feature of these benchmarks is a larger alternation depth than in Ayari's and Rintanen's instances. This clearly favors the simplification of the BDDs by repeatedly applying our reformulation of universal variable elimination, under the assumption that eliminating variables reduces the size of the diagram.

5   Conclusions and Future Work

We have implemented a QBF solver based on BDDs that is competitive with other efficient decision procedures. The main features were the introduction of BDD constraint propagation, implementation of dynamic variable selection and enhanced early quantification. Our solver outperformed competitive search-based procedures in the verification domain (which in turn also outperformed previous BDD-based solvers according to previous experiments), dominating in the bounded model construction and modal logic benchmarks, and performing comparably for conformant planning - a domain where previous BDD-based approaches performed terribly.

We found that our solver had a rather complementary performance in comparison with the other solvers. For example, eBDD-QBF worked well on Adders and worse on Dflipflops for Ayari's benchmarks, whereas the other way around was the case for the rest of the tools; a similar pattern was present in Pan's instances. This suggests the idea of including our BDD algorithms into a more general framework involving search and symbolic techniques with more elaborate preprocessing. However, there is still work to do in identifying the structure of the formulas that are most efficiently handled by our solver, given that our work is substantially supported by empirical analysis instead of theoretical reasoning. We are incorporating the bottom-up approach with a top-down algorithm based on DPLL, that would potentially allow more flexible dynamic variable selection heuristics. The inclusion of preprocessing techniques and more robust BDD constraint propagation algorithms are also being implemented in order to obtain a comparable solver w.r.t. more elaborate tools such as AIGSOLVE[23] and AQME[25].

References

1. Aloul, F.A., Markov, I.L., Sakallah, K.A.: Faster SAT and Smaller BDDs via Common Function Structure. In: Technical Report #CSE-TR-445-01. University of Michigan (2001)
2. Audemard, G., Sas, L.: SAT Based BDD Solver for Quantified Boolean Formulas. In: 16th IEEE International Conference on Tools with Artificial Intelligence (ICTAI), pp. 82–89. IEEE Computer Society, Los Alamitos (2004)
3. Ayari, A., Basin, D.: Bounded Model Construction for Monadic Second-Order Logics. In: Emerson, E.A., Sistla, A.P. (eds.) CAV 2000. LNCS, vol. 1855, pp. 99–113. Springer, Heidelberg (2000)
4. Benedetti, M.: Evaluating QBFs via Symbolic Skolemization. In: Baader, F., Voronkov, A. (eds.) LPAR 2004. LNCS (LNAI), vol. 3452, Springer, Heidelberg (2005)
5. Biere, A., Cimatti, A., Clarke, E., Strichman, O., Zhu, Y.: Bounded model checking. J. Adv. Comp. Sci. 58 (2003)
6. Bryant, R.E.: Graph-Based Algorithms for Boolean Function Manipulation. IEEE Trans. on Comp. 35, 677–691 (1986)
7. Burch, J.R., Clarke, E.M., Mcmillan, K.L., Dill, D.L., Hwang, L.J.: Symbolic Model Checking: 10 20 States and Beyond. In: Fifth Annual IEEE Symposium on Logic in Computer Science, pp. 428–439. IEEE Comput. Soc. Press, Los Alamitos (1990)
8. Chatalic, P., Simon, L.: Zres:The old Davis-Putnam procedure meets ZBDDs. In: McAllester, D. (ed.) CADE 2000. LNCS (LNAI), vol. 1831, pp. 449–454. Springer, Heidelberg (2000)
9. Coudert, O., Madre, J.C.: A Unified Framework for the Formal Verification of Sequential Circuits. In: IEEE International Conference on Computer-Aided Design (ICCAD), pp. 126–129. IEEE, Los Alamitos (1990)
10. Darwiche, A., Pipatsrisawat, K.: Complete Algorithms. In: Biere, A., Heule, M., van Maaren, H., Walsh, T. (eds.) Handbook of Satisfiability. Frontiers in Artificial Intelligence and Applications, pp. 99–130. IOS Press, Amsterdam (2009)
11. Davis, M., Putnam, M.: A computing procedure for quantification theory. J. ACM 7, 201–215 (1960)
12. Davis, M., Logemann, G., Loveland, D.: A machine program for theorem-proving. Commun. ACM 5(7), 394–397 (1962)
13. Franco, J., Kouril, M., Schlipf, J.S., Ward, J., Weaver, S., Dransfield, M., Vanfleet, W.M.: SBSAT: A State-Based, BDD-Based Satisfiability Solver. In: Giunchiglia, E., Tacchella, A. (eds.) SAT 2003. LNCS, vol. 2919, pp. 398–410. Springer, Heidelberg (2004)
14. Giunchiglia, E., Narizzano, M., Tacchella, A., Tacchella, O.: QUBE: A system for deciding Quantified Boolean Formulas Satisfiability. In: IJCAR, pp. 364–369 (2001)
15. Giunchiglia, E., Marin, P., Narizzano, M.: QBF Reasoning. In: Biere, A., Heule, M., van Maaren, H., Walsh, T. (eds.) Handbook of Satisfiability. Frontiers in Artificial Intelligence and Applications, pp. 99–130. IOS Press, Amsterdam (2009)
16. Huang, J., Darwiche, A.: Toward good elimination orders for symbolic SAT solving. In: 16th IEEE International Conference on Tools with Artificial Intelligence (ICTAI), pp. 566–573 (2004)
17. Jin, H., Somenzi, F.: CirCUs: A hybrid satisfiability solver. In: International Conference on Theory and Applications of Satisfiability Testing (SAT), pp. 211–223 (2004)

18. Kleine, H., Bubeck, U.: QBF Theory. In: Biere, A., Heule, M., van Maaren, H., Walsh, T. (eds.) Handbook of Satisfiability. Frontiers in Artificial Intelligence and Applications, pp. 99–130. IOS Press, Amsterdam (2009)

19. Letz, R.: Lemma and Model Caching in Decision Procedures for Quantified Boolean Formulas. In: Egly, U., Fermüller, C. (eds.) TABLEAUX 2002. LNCS (LNAI), vol. 2381, pp. 160–175. Springer, Heidelberg (2002)

20. Lonsing, F., Biere, A.: DepQBF: A Dependency-Aware QBF Solver. J. Sat, Bool. Mod. and Comp. 7, 71–76 (2010)

21. Narizzano, M.: QBFLIB, The Quantified Boolean Formulas Satisfiability Library, http://www.qbflib.org/

22. Olivo, O., Emerson, E.A.: A More Efficient BDD-Based QBF Solver. In: Tech Report, http://www.cs.utexas.edu/~olivo/CP/More_Efficient_BDD_QBF_Tech_Report.pdf

23. Pigorsch, F., Schol, C.: Exploiting structure in an AIG based QBF solver. In: Proc. of DATE 2009 (2009) (to appear)

24. Plaisted, D.A., Biere, A., Zhu, Y.: A satisfiability procedure for quantified boolean formulae. J. Disc. App. Math. 130(2) (2003)

25. Pulina, L., Tacchella, A.: A multi-engine solver for quantified Boolean formulas. In: Bessière, C. (ed.) CP 2007. LNCS, vol. 4741, pp. 574–589. Springer, Heidelberg (2007)

26. Ranjan, R.K., Aziz, A., Brayton, R.K., Plessier, B., Pixley, C.: Efficient BDD Algorithms for FSM Synthesis and Verification. In: IEEE/ACM Proceedings International Workshop on Logic Synthesis. IEEE/ACM (1995)

27. Rintanen, J.: Constructing conditional plans by a theorem prover. J. A.I. 10, 323–352 (1999)

28. Sinz, C., Biere, A.: Extended resolution proofs for conjoining BDDs. In: Grigoriev, D., Harrison, J., Hirsch, E.A. (eds.) CSR 2006. LNCS, vol. 3967, pp. 600–611. Springer, Heidelberg (2006)

29. Somenzi, F.: CUDD: CU Decision Diagram Package, http://vlsi.colorado.edu/~fabio/CUDD/

Constraint Propagation for Efficient Inference in Markov Logic

Tivadar Papai[1], Parag Singla[2], and Henry Kautz[1]

[1] University of Rochester, Rochester NY 14627, USA
{papai,kautz}@cs.rochester.edu
[2] University of Texas, Austin TX 78701, USA
parag@cs.utexas.edu

Abstract. Many real world problems can be modeled using a combination of hard and soft constraints. Markov Logic is a highly expressive language which represents the underlying constraints by attaching real-valued weights to formulas in first order logic. The weight of a formula represents the strength of the corresponding constraint. Hard constraints are represented as formulas with infinite weight. The theory is compiled into a ground Markov network over which probabilistic inference can be done. For many problems, hard constraints pose a significant challenge to the probabilistic inference engine. However, solving the hard constraints (partially or fully) before hand outside of the probabilistic engine can hugely simplify the ground Markov network and speed probabilistic inference. In this work, we propose a generalized arc consistency algorithm that prunes the domains of predicates by propagating hard constraints. Our algorithm effectively performs unit propagation at a lifted level, avoiding the need to explicitly ground the hard constraints during the pre-processing phase, yielding a potentially exponential savings in space and time. Our approach results in much simplified domains, thereby, making the inference significantly more efficient both in terms of time and memory. Experimental evaluation over one artificial and two real world datasets show the benefit of our approach.

1 Introduction

Combining the power of logic and probability has been a long standing goal of AI research. The last decade has seen a significant progress towards this goal, with the emergence of the research area called statistical relational learning (SRL). Many different representation languages have been proposed which combine subsets of full-first order logic with various probabilistic graphical representations [4]. One such powerful language is Markov Logic [2], which represents a joint probability distribution over worlds defined by relationships over entities by attaching weights to formulas in first order logic.

A Markov logic theory can be seen as a combination of hard and soft constraints. Hard constraints are modeled by formulas with infinite weight, and must be satisfied in any world with non-zero probability. The typical approach to inference in Markov logic involves grounding out the theory and jointly dealing with

J. Lee (Ed.): CP 2011, LNCS 6876, pp. 691–705, 2011.
© Springer-Verlag Berlin Heidelberg 2011

both hard and soft constraints. For many problems, hard constraints can pose a significant challenge to the underlying probabilistic inference engine, making it difficult for a sampler to move between different modes. Much work has gone into the development of probabilistic inference algorithms that are robust in the face of hard constraints (for example, MC-SAT [11], SampleSearch [5]), but the general problem of efficiently handling hard constraints is far from solved.

The key idea in this paper is that, intuitively, each hard constraint in the knowledge base reduces the set of possible worlds that have a non-zero probability. In particular, a set of hard constraints together can restrict the number of groundings of a predicate about which we are uncertain (i.e., the probability of an instance of the predicate holding is strictly between 0 and 1). We refer to this phenomenon as *domain pruning*. Domain pruning can significantly simplify the ground network over which probabilistic inference needs to be done, as the pruned groundings can be treated as *evidence* (fully observed). Therefore, we propose an approach to probabilistic inference which has two components: 1) Solve the hard constraints (fully or partially) to identify the pruned domains 2) Use a standard probabilistic inference engine with pruned domains input as evidence. Building on ideas in the area of constraint satisfaction, we propose a novel generalized arc consistency algorithm for propagating the hard constraints. Since our algorithm deals only with hard constraints to prune the domains, it is guaranteed to produce the same solution as the standard techniques. Our algorithm can be seen as a form of lifted unit propagation. We show that our approach can use exponentially less space and time than performing unit propagation on the grounded theory. Experiments on three different datasets clearly show the advantage our approach.

The organization of this paper is as follows. We first present some background on Markov logic and constraint propagation. This is followed by the details of the generalized arc consistency algorithm. We present our results on two real and one artificial datasets. Next, we discuss some of the related work in this area. We conclude with the directions for future work.

2   Background

2.1   Markov Logic

First-order probabilistic languages combine graphical models with elements of first-order logic, by defining template features that apply to whole classes of objects at once. One such powerful language is *Markov logic* [2]. A *Markov logic network (MLN)* is a set of weighted first-order formulas. The weight of a formula represents the strength of the constraint. *Soft* constraints are formulas with finite weight, while *hard* constraints have infinite weight. A theory consists of a combination of hard and soft constraints. Together with a set of constants representing the objects of interest, it defines a Markov network with one node per ground atom and one feature per ground formula. The weight of a feature is the weight of the first-order formula that originated it. More formally,

Definition 1. *[2] A Markov logic network (MLN) L is a set of pairs (F_i, w_i), where F_i is a formula in first-order logic and w_i is a real number. Together with a finite set of constants $C = \{c_1, c_2, \ldots, c_{|C|}\}$, it defines a Markov network $M_{L,C}$ as follows:*

1. *$M_{L,C}$ contains one binary node for each possible grounding of each predicate (ground atom) appearing in L. The value of the node is 1 if the ground predicate is true, and 0 otherwise.*
2. *$M_{L,C}$ contains one feature for each possible grounding of each formula F_i (ground formula) in L. The value of this feature is 1 if the ground formula is true, and 0 otherwise. The weight of the feature is the w_i associated with F_i in L.*

For many problems, a set of ground atoms are known to be *true* or *false* before hand. These are known as *evidence atoms*. The ground atoms whose value is not known at the inference time are called *query atoms*. The ground Markov network $M_{L,C}$ defines the probability of an assignment y to the query atoms Y, given an assignment x to the evidence atoms X, as

$$P(Y = y | X = x) = \frac{1}{Z_x} \exp \left(\sum_k w_k f_k(y, x) \right) \tag{1}$$

where the summation is taken over all the ground formulas. w_k is the weight of the kth ground formula, $f_k = 1$ if the kth ground formula is true, and $f_k = 0$ otherwise, and Z_x is the normalization constant. For any state to have a non-zero probability, all the hard constraints have to be satisfied, in which case the corresponding weight term (infinite) can be factored out from the denominator as well as the numerator. The evidence atoms can be input to the inference procedure in the form of a set called *evidence database*. The value of evidence atoms is set by fixing the assignment of the corresponding nodes in the network to the respective truth value. A large evidence results in effectively pruning the network, as the corresponding nodes assignments can be fixed and removed from the network. Marginal inference corresponds to the problem of finding the probability of true assignment to each of the query nodes in the network. Inference can be done using standard inference techniques such as Gibbs sampling or belief propagation. More efficient techniques which exploit the nature of the formula (hard or soft) [11] or the structure of the network [16] have also been proposed. None of these techniques is able to exploit the fact that the set of hard constraints in the knowledge base can, in many instances, be solved very efficiently, thereby significantly pruning the domains of predicates and shrinking the number of ground formulas.

Any first-order knowledge base can be equivalently converted into a clausal form by a series of mechanical steps [12]. We deal with finite first order logic, and all the function evaluations are assumed to be known in advance [2]. Hence, any existential can be equivalently replaced by a disjunction of corresponding ground literals. Therefore, without loss of generality, we will deal explicitly with clauses in the following formulation.

2.2   Constraint Satisfaction and Local Consistency

A *Constraint Satisfaction Problem* (CSP) refers to a set of variables $X = \{X_1, \ldots, X_n\}$, their domains $R = \{R_1, \ldots, R_n\}$ and a set of constraints $C = \{C_1, \ldots, C_k\}$ over the variables in X. Every constraint $C_i \in C$ is a relation over some non-empty set of variables in X, and specifies the set of values the variables appearing in it can take. A solution to a CSP is a set of assignments S to the variables in X, such that every member $s \in S$ satisfies all the constraints in C. In many instances, finding such a set is computationally challenging. However, for many problems, for each variable X_i, we can efficiently eliminate a subset of the values which are not part of any solution to the CSP. Let $V_i \subseteq R_i$ be the set of allowed values of X_i after eliminating such a subset of values. A variable is *generalized arc consistent* (or hyper-arc consistent) with a constraint, if for every value in its allowed set of values, there is an assignment to the remaining variables which satisfies the constraint. Consistency with respect to a set of constraints is defined in a similar manner. Generalized arc consistency only ensures *local consistency* i.e. it does not directly enforce any constraints among the variables which do not share a constraint. One way to ensure generalized arc consistency is to initialize the set of allowed values, V_i, to the respective domain R_i, and then iteratively eliminate those values which are not generalized arc consistent with the set of constraints. The algorithm continues until none of the V_i sets changes. This simple iterative procedure can lead to significant reduction in domain size for many problems. There are other forms of local consistency which could be enforced. A partial assignment to a set S of variables is said to be consistent if it does not violate any constraints which involve variables only from S. i-consistency requires that every consistent assignment of $i - 1$ variables can be extended by a value of any other variable not violating any of the constraints, and strong i-consistency ensures k-consistency for every $1 \leq k \leq i$. For a thorough introduction to CSPs and local consistency, see [1].

3   Constraint Propagation in Markov Logic

A set of first order clauses impose a set of constraints on the truth assignment to the ground atoms which participate in the respective ground clauses. Generalized arc consistency ensures that allowed truth assignments (true/false) to any ground atom have a corresponding assignment for all the other atoms in the clause such that the clause is satisfied. An evidence database fixes the assignment of the ground atoms in the database to true or false. Given a set of first order clauses, and an evidence database, our goal then, is to devise an algorithm so that the ground atoms in the domain are generalized arc consistent with the constraints imposed by the set of ground clauses. Because each atom can take only two possible assignments, any pruning on the domain of an atom essentially means that we can fix its assignment (if the whole domain is pruned then the constraints are inconsistent). Hence, ensuring generalized arc consistency on a set of hard clauses in a theory is a way to infer the additional truth assignments for some of the originally unknown ground atoms. These can then be set to evidence with the inferred truth value for any following probabilistic inference procedure. This leads to huge simplification in the network over which probabilistic inference needs to be performed.

The key idea for enforcing generalized arc consistency is to look at each ground clause in turn, and identify a ground atom whose assignment needs to be fixed in order to satisfy the clause, given current assignment to other atoms in the clause. This can be done iteratively, until no more truth assignments can be fixed. The main caveat with this approach is that it explicitly involves grounding out the whole theory, which is often prohibitively expensive. Next, we describe an algorithm which alleviates this problem.

3.1   Generalized Arc Consistency Algorithm

For the notational convenience, we will explain our algorithm for the case of untyped predicates; extending it to the more general case is straightforward. Let KB be a knowledge base with a set of hard constraints. Let L denote a predicate (or its negation). Let each argument take the values from the set of constants T. Therefore, the domain of L, denoted as $R(L)$, is T^k. Further, let $D(L)$ be the subset of tuples $\mathbf{t} \in R(L)$, for which $L(t)$ can be true in some model, i.e. $\mathbf{t} \in D(L)$ if $L(\mathbf{t}) = true$ is possibly a part of some assignment satisfying the constraints in KB. Let $N(L)$ be the subset of tuples for which $L(t)$ is necessarily true in any given model, i.e. $\mathbf{t} \in N(L)$ if $L(\mathbf{t}) = true$ in every assignment satisfying the constraints in KB. Note that $N(L) = R(L) \setminus D(\neg L)$.

The goal of the generalized arc consistency algorithm is to find the maximal $N(L)$ for every predicate L, while propagating constraints through the hard clauses. The algorithm starts with an initial set $N(L)$ for every L, and iteratively increases the size of $N(L)$, using the hard constraints given in the knowledge base, until none of the $N(L)$ sets can be further extended. The starting points of the algorithm are the ground atoms supplied in the evidence database. The algorithm is most easily described in the case where each predicate in a clause contains the same set of variables. Consider, for example:

$$C = L_1(x) \vee \ldots \vee L_k(x) \tag{2}$$

where x is a vector of variables. For every $1 \le i \le k$: $N(L_i)$ can be updated as follows:

$$N(L_i) \leftarrow N(L_i) \bigcup \left[\bigcap_{i \ne j, 1 \le j \le k} N(\neg L_j) \right] \tag{3}$$

In words, for every tuple c in the domain of x, we can conclude that $L_i(c)$ is true in every possible world if every other $L_j(c)$ appearing in the clause is false in every possible world. To generalize the update rule for predicates with different sets of variables we employ the (database) *Join* and *Project* operations. We define *Join* for two sets of tuples each of which has a corresponding vector of variables associated with it. Let S_i be a set of tuples and X_i be the corresponding vector of variables $(i \in \{1, 2\})$. We overload the notation such that X_i also refers to the set of variables in the corresponding vector. For now, we assume that a variable cannot appear more than once in a vector of variables (we will relax this assumption later in the text). For a tuple $s \in S_i$ and a variable $x \in X_i$ let $s[x]$ denote the value of the variable x in the tuple s. Let $X = X_1 \bigcup X_2$ and $R(X)$ be the full domain formed by the Cartesian product of the individual domains of the variables in X in some ordering of the variables. The join of the sets of tuples S_i, given corresponding vector of variables X_i, is defined as follows:

$$Join\{\langle X_i, S_i \rangle\} = \langle X, \{c | c \in R(X) \land \forall i, \exists s \in S_i \ \forall x \in X_i : s[x] = c[x]\}\rangle \quad (4)$$

$Join$ is commutative and associative. The projection of a set S of tuples associated with a variable vector X to the variable vector Y is defined as follows:

$$Project(Y, \langle S, X \rangle) = \{c | c \in R(Y) \land \exists s \in S \ \forall y \in (Y \cap X) : s[y] = c[y]\} \quad (5)$$

For more details on natural join and project operations, see [3]. Using the above definitions we can extend the update rule to the general case (where each predicate in a clause can contain an arbitrary subset of variables):

$$N(L_i) \leftarrow N(L_i) \bigcup [Project(X_i, Join_{j \neq i}\{\langle X_j, N(\neg L_j)\rangle\})] \quad (6)$$

The space and time complexity of Equation (6) is sensitive to the order in which we perform the $Joins$ (they can be performed in any order since $Join$ is both commutative and associative). The worst case complexity (both space and time) is exponential in the number of variables involved in the operation. A number of different heuristic criteria could be used to decide the join order; we selected the literal L first with the smallest $N(L)$ set. Additionally, while performing a series of $Joins$, if the intermediate result contains a set of variables X' such that an $x \in X'$ variable does not occur in the remaining X_j sets, i.e., x is guaranteed not to appear on any other side of a $Join$ and x is also not a member of X_i, then, we can project this partial result to $X' \setminus \{x\}$. This re-ordering of join and project operations can substantially reduce the space and time complexity of the algorithm. Consider, e.g.,

$$H(x) \lor O_1(x, y_1) \lor O_2(x, y_2) \lor \ldots \lor O_k(x, y_k) \quad (7)$$

where H is a hidden predicate while $O_1, O_2, \ldots, O_k$ are all observed. Also, let $|R(H)| = N$ and for every $1 \leq i \leq n : |R(O_i)| = N^2$. For every $1 \leq i \leq k$ we can perform

$$Project(x, \langle (x, y_i), N(\neg O_i)\rangle) \quad (8)$$

and feed the results to the $Joins$ instead of using $N(\neg O_i)$ in the $Joins$, because every y_i occurs exactly in one predicate. This way, the space and time complexity of the algorithm reduces to $O(kN^2)$ from $O(N^{k+1})$.

Algorithm 1 shows the pseudo-code for our generalized arc consistency algorithm. Line 3 initializes the $N(L_i)$ sets based on the evidence database. In line 8 of the algorithm we start iterating through all the hard constraints. In line 10 we update the $N(L_i)$ sets for every positive or negative literal using Equation (6).

Algorithm 1. Update Algorithm for Generalized Arc Consistency on Clauses

```
1: for all C ∈ KB do
2:     for all Lᵢ literal ∈ C do
3:         N(Lᵢ) = {t|Lᵢ(t) = true; given the evidence database}
4:     end for
5: end for
6: repeat
7:     changed ← false
8:     for all C ∈ KB do
9:         for all Lᵢ literal ∈ C do
10:            Δ ← [Project(Xᵢ, Joinⱼ≠ᵢ{⟨Xⱼ, N(¬Lⱼ)⟩})]
11:            if Δ ≠ ∅ then
12:                changed ← changed ∨ N(Lᵢ) ≠ N(Lᵢ)⋃Δ
13:                N(Lᵢ) ← N(Lᵢ)⋃Δ
14:            end if
15:        end for
16:    end for
17: until ¬changed
```

The algorithm keeps iterating over all the hard constraints until none of the $N(L_i)$ sets change. It is easy to prove the convergence as well as the correctness of our generalized arc consistency algorithm. First, for convergence, clearly, the algorithm stops if in any iteration, none of the clauses results in a change in the $N(L_i)$ sets. Alternatively stated, each iteration results in at least one of the $N(L_i)$ sets increasing in size. Further, size of each $N(L_i)$ is upper bounded by the size of the corresponding domain $R(L_i)$. Therefore, the algorithm terminates in finite steps. By correctness we mean that, if $N(L_i)$ is the set obtained for predicate L_i at the end of the algorithm, then, for each tuple $t_i \in N(L_i)$, every model contains $L(t_i)$ in it, i.e. in any satisfying solution to the hard constraints $L_i(t_i) = true$. Let us prove it by induction. Initially, each $N(L_i)$ is set using the evidence database. Hence, the claim is true in the beginning. Next, let the claim holds at the kth update step (to any of the $N(L_i)$'s) during the execution of the algorithm. Considering $k + 1^{th}$ update, if an atom t_i is added to the set $N(L_i)$, then, there must have been a ground clause, $L_1(t_1) \vee L_2(t_2) \cdots \vee L_i(t_k) \cdots \vee L_k(t_k)$, such that each of $L_j(t_j) = false, \forall j \neq i$. This follows from the generalized arc consistency update rule (Equation (6)) and the fact that the claim holds true at the kth update step. Hence, $L(t_i)$ must be $true$ as setting it otherwise would lead to violation of this clause. Further, since we assumed the claim to be true at step k, and any new additions to the set $N(L_i)$ satisfy the claim by above argument, the claim is true at step $k + 1$. Hence, proved.

3.2 Extension to Other Cases

Existentials. We extend the update rule for clauses to allow existentially quantified conjunctions besides regular literals. E.g., consider the formula:

$$P(x) \vee \exists y \left[Q(x, y) \wedge R(z, y) \right] \tag{9}$$

For all the instantiations of x when $\exists y\,[Q(x,y) \wedge R(z,y)]$ is necessarily false $P(x)$ must be true. Thus, all we need to do is to extend the definition of $N(L_i)$ to allow L_i to be the negation of an existentially quantified conjunction.

Let $F = \neg\exists Y\,[L_1(X_1) \wedge \ldots \wedge L_k(X_k)]$ where $Y \subseteq \bigcup_i X_i$. Let $X = \bigcup_i X_i \setminus Y$ and $R(X)$ be the full domain formed by the Cartesian product of the individual domains of the non-quantified variables in X in some ordering of the variables. Then:

$$N(F) \leftarrow R(X) \setminus Project(X, Join_{1 \leq i \leq k}\{\langle X_i, R(L_i) \setminus N(\neg L_i)\rangle\}) \qquad (10)$$

$N(F)$ has to be updated if $N(\neg L_i)$ changes for any of the L_i's appearing in F.

Constant Arguments. If a predicate P in a clause has a constant argument c, we can do the following transformation of the clause to a new clause which provides an equivalent hard constraint without having constant arguments in the predicates:

$$P(x,c) \vee \ldots is\ replaced\ by P(x,y) \vee \neg E_c(y) \vee \ldots \qquad (11)$$

Where $E_c(y)$ is a fully observed predicate and is true if and only if $y = c$.

Repeated Arguments. If a predicate P in a clause has a variable argument which appears more than once, the following transformation could handle this case:

$$P(x,x) \vee \ldots is\ replaced\ by P(x,x') \vee \neg E(x,x') \vee \ldots \qquad (12)$$

Where x' is a variable not appearing in the original clause, and $E(x,x')$ is a fully observed predicate being true if and only if $x = x'$.

3.3   Relation to Unit Propagation

Running unit propagation on the ground hard clauses using the evidence would produce exactly the ground unit clauses which correspond to the N sets created by running the proposed generalized arc consistency algorithm.[1] Initially, the N sets are set according to the evidence, and to the unit clause hard constraints.[2] At this point the ground unit clauses available for unit propagation are exactly the ground unit clauses corresponding to the members of the N sets. Let the claim holds true after k updates to the N sets. Then, if unit propagation can derive a new ground unit clause so can the generalized arc consistency algorithm, because the new unit clause is the result of resolving a ground clause with ground unit clauses to each of which there is a corresponding member of N. This makes sure that the *Joins* and *Projects* in Equation (6) result in a

---

[1] This result holds in general when we do not perform any special pruning for existential quantifiers (Section 3.2). They are simply treated as disjunction of literals.

[2] Algorithm 1 initializes the N sets based only on evidence, but it is easy to see that both forms of initializations become equivalent after one step of running the original algorithm on unit clause hard constraints.

non-empty set containing a member corresponding to the newly derived ground unit clause. Also, when Equation (6) updates an $N(L_i)$ set based on the clause $C = L_1(X_1) \vee \ldots \vee L_n(X_n)$, it uses the values in $N(\neg L_1), \ldots, N(\neg L_j), \ldots N(\neg L_n)$ $(i \neq j)$. The ground unit clauses corresponding to these values are available to unit propagation, hence unit propagation can derive the ground unit clauses corresponding to the update of $N(L_i)$. Therefore, the claim holds true after $k+1$ updates to the N sets. Using the induction argument, the claim holds true for all values of k, and in particular, at the termination of the generalized arc consistency algorithm.

Although, the end result is the same, the generalized arc consistency algorithm can use significantly less space and time. Revisiting the example in Equation (7), there are $O(N^{k+1})$ ground clauses created, and hence, unit propagation would need $O(N^{k+1})$ space and time. However, as we pointed out earlier, generalized arc consistency algorithm requires only $O(kN^2)$ space and time.

3.4   Moving Beyond Generalized Arc Consistency

A natural question that may arise is why not use other forms of local consistency instead of generalized arc consistency (e.g. strong i-consistency). There is a trade-off between the strength of the consistency requirement and the time spent in processing the hard constraints. Stronger consistency requirements will typically result in better pruning but it comes at the cost of increased processing time. It is easy to see that if l is the maximum length of a clause in the Markov logic theory, then, strong i-consistency $(i \geq l)$ subsumes generalized arc consistency. Following example is illustrative in this regard. Consider the axioms:

1. $P(x) \wedge Q(x) \Rightarrow O(x)$
2. $S(x) \Rightarrow P(x)$
3. $S(x) \Rightarrow Q(x)$

where O is an observed predicate such that $R(O) = \{a, b, c, d\}$ and $D(O) = \{a, b, c\}$. Let $R = R(S) = R(P) = R(Q) = R(O)$. Together these imply that the domain of S is limited to $\{a, b, c\}$. But this cannot be inferred by generalized arc consistency on the CSP created from these axioms. Enforcing 3-consistency on the groundings of P, Q and O will ensure that both $P(d) = true$ and $Q(d) = true$ cannot hold at the same time. Moreover, enforcing 3-consistency on the groundings of P, Q and S ensures that for every $m \in R$ if at least one of $P(m)$ and $Q(m)$ is false then $S(m)$ must be false as well. Hence, we could try to enforce strong i-consistency on the CSP for some value of $i \geq 3$. But strong i-consistency requirements do not fall out naturally from the clausal structure imposed by the Markov logic theory. However, the same effect can be achieved by applying FOL resolution [12] to the axioms before creating the CSP. For instance, resolving 1 and 2 yields $\neg Q(x) \vee \neg S(x) \vee O(x)$. Resolving this with 3 yields $\neg S(x) \vee O(x)$. This new clause then does allow $D(S) = \{a, b, c\}$ to be inferred by generalized arc consistency.

Pre-processing a theory by resolving (hard) constraints can be done exhaustively or in a limited manner; for example, resolution could be performed in a breadth-first manner up to a fixed depth. Because a Markov logic theory contains no uninterpreted function symbols, even exhaustive resolution is guaranteed to terminate, although in the worst case an exponential number of resolvants would be created. We did some preliminary experiments with performing resolution to varying depths before applying generalized arc consistency, but little additional benefit was obtained on our test domains. Exploring this further is a direction for future work.

4   Experiments

We experimented on two real and one artificial datasets to compare the time and memory performances of CPI (Constraint Propagation based Inference) and the standard approach to inference (i.e. no prior pruning of the predicate domains is done). We used the freely available Alchemy [9] system for all our experiments. For the standard approach to inference, we used the Alchemy implementation as is. For the constraint propagation, we implemented a separate program to prune the domains by propagating the constraints amongst hard clauses. The output of this program was passed as additional evidence to Alchemy for the CPI. For the probabilistic inference in both the approaches, exactly the same knowledge base was used (including all the soft and hard rules). Since exact marginal inference was not tractable, we used the MCMC based MC-SAT [11] algorithm implemented in Alchemy. It was run to collect 1000 samples (default in Alchemy) for both the approaches. All the experiments were run on a cluster of nodes with processor speed of 2.4 GHz. We do not report accuracy since both the approaches are guaranteed to give the same results at the point of convergence of MC-SAT (Section 4.3 discusses some of the issues relating to the convergence of MC-SAT). We first describe the datasets in detail followed by our results.

4.1   Datasets

Cora. Entity resolution is the problem of determining which observations (e.g., records in a database) correspond to the same objects. We used the version of McCallum's Cora database available on the Alchemy website (Kok et al. 2007). The inference task was to de-duplicate citations, authors and venues (i.e., to determine which pairs of citations refer to the same underlying paper, and similarly for author fields and venue fields). We used the MLN (formulas and weights) used by Singla and Domingos [15] in their experiments. This contains first-order clauses stating regularities such as: if two fields have high TF-IDF similarity, they are (probably) the same; if two records are the same, their fields are the same, and vice-versa; etc. For each field, we added the hard rules for deciding that two fields are a non-match if their TF-IDF similarity was below a threshold. This effectively implements the canopies as described by McCallum [10], to eliminate obvious non-matches. We also added another set of rules deciding a pair of citations as non-match if any of the fields did not match. The final knowledge base contained 25 predicates and 52 formulas (6 hard and 46 soft). Maximum formula-arity was 4 and maximum predicate domain size was 71,000.

Capture the Flag (CTF). Our second dataset deals with the task of activity recognition. Sadilek and Kautz [13] collected this dataset by having subjects play the game of capture the flag on a University campus. The dataset contains the details of the GPS location of each player at each time step. The task is to determine all the captured events during the course of the game. The dataset contains information about 3 different games with 14 players (divided onto two teams), running for an average of 625 time steps. Each GPS location was uniquely snapped (model as hidden predicate) to one of the 6499 cells. We used the knowledge base hand-coded by Sadilek & Kautz (2010) stating hard facts such as "captured players stay at the same location" and soft rules such as "if two players from different teams are snapped to the same cell at a time step, then it is likely to result into a capture event". We added another hard rule stating if two agents are at same place, then they must be snapped to nearby cells. The original knowledge base involves some soft rules with real-valued features. Since current Alchemy implementation does not support them, we ignored these rules for our experiments. The final knowledge base contained 9 predicates and 17 formulas (15 hard and 2 soft). Maximum formula-arity was 4 and maximum predicate domain size was 29 million.

Library. We also experimented with an artificially generated online library dataset. The goal of the system is to recommend books to each user that they might like to read. Each user can read books in one or more of the four languages that they can speak. A user needs to read a book in order to like it. The system can recommend a book to a user if they have not already read it. These are modeled as hard constraints. The system recommends a book to a user if the user shares the liking of another book with a user who likes this book as well. This is modeled as a soft constraint. *Read*, *available* and *speaks* are modeled as fully observed. *Likes* is partially observed. The task is to predict *recommends*. The final knowledge base contained 5 predicates and 4 formulas (3 hard and 1 soft). Maximum formula-arity was 4 and maximum predicate domain size was 0.5 million.

We generated a dataset containing 100 users. The number of books was varied from 500 to 5000, at intervals of 500. For each user (book), the set of languages spoken (available) was chosen using a Bernoulli trial for each of the 4 languages. The parameters of the Bernoulli trials were set to model that certain languages are more popular than others. The number of books read by each user followed a Gaussian distribution with $\mu = 30$ and $\sigma = 5$. The subset of books read by a user was assigned uniformly at random from the set of books available in the languages that user could speak. A user left feedback for a book he read with 0.3 probability and the feedback was *likes* with 0.7 and *not likes* with 0.3 probability.

4.2   Results

Tables 1 presents the results on the three datasets. For Library, the reported results are for 2500 books. Standard (Stand.) and CPI refer to the standard approach to inference, and the constraint propagation based inference, respectively.

Table 1. Time and memory costs comparing the two inference approaches

Domain	Time (in mins)				Ground Tuples (in 1000's)			
	Const. Propagation		Prob. Inference		Const. Propagation		Prob. Inference	
	Stand.	CPI	Stand.	CPI	Stand.	CPI	Stand.	CPI
CTF	0	0.37	1536.6	528.0	0	585.5	2107.8	1308.7
Cora	0	0.07	181.1	26.2	0	153.6	488.2	81.4
Library	0	0.20	286.4	23.0	0	462.7	366.2	45.9

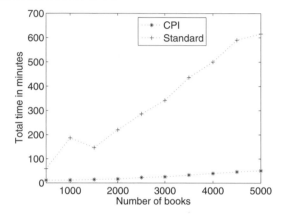

Fig. 1. Inference time for varying number of books

We report the running time of the two algorithms as well as the memory requirement, measured in terms of number of ground clauses created. For both time
and memory, results are split into two parts a) cost of constraint propagation b)
cost of probabilistic inference. First cost is zero for the standard inference. For
CPI, total time cost is the sum of two costs. As evident from the table, time
cost of constraint propagation is negligible compared to the cost for probabilistic
inference. On CTF, CPI is faster than standard inference by a factor of 3; on
Cora, by a factor of 7. On library, the gain is an order of magnitude.

Since we run the two inference pieces sequentially (constraint propagation
followed by probabilistic inference), memory cost for CPI is the maximum of the
cost for the two parts. For CTF, the cost of probabilistic inference dominates.
Memory cost for CPI for this dataset is about 60% of the standard inference.
For Cora and Library, constraint propagation dominates the memory cost. This
is due to the *join* operation in the generalized arc consistency algorithm, which
can turn out to be quite expensive. On Cora, CPI saves memory by more than
a factor of 4. On Library the gain is relatively less. Figure 1 shows the inference
time results for the Library dataset as the number of books is varied from 500 to
5000. The time cost for CPI stays almost constant, whereas, it goes linearly up
for standard inference. The number of ground clauses constructed (during actual
probabilistic inference) follows a similar trend. This is attributed to the fact that
as the number of books increases, the problem becomes sparser i.e. chances of two

people having liked the same book and hence, one causing the recommendation to the other decreases with increasing number of books. Most recommended groundings need not be considered for inference and CPI can take advantage of this. Standard inference, not being able to prune the domains, scales linearly with increasing number of books. It should be noted that the Library dataset had to be carefully hand-engineered for the standard inference approach to run on it, whereas CPI did not have any problems with the intuitive formulation of the knowledge base.[3] Exploring this further is a direction for future work.

Results above demonstrate that hard constraints in Markov logic can be used to significantly reduce both the time and memory cost of inference. The advantage can be huge for the problems where domains are already very sparse. Generalized arc consistency is extremely fast relative to the probabilistic inference. Its memory requirements can be relatively high sometimes, but still it saves significant memory in many cases, in comparison to the standard approach.

4.3   Note about MC-SAT Convergence

Alchemy does not give a way to detect if the MC-SAT algorithm has converged. But we compared the differences in the marginals obtained by two approaches at the end of 1000 steps of MC-SAT (all our results are obtained by running MC-SAT for 1000 steps.). On the Cora dataset, 99% of the differences were within 0.01 threshold. For Library, this number was 0.05. For Capture the Flag, we noticed a much larger variation. This is due the fact that it is a much bigger domain, and many more samples are needed to converge to the right marginals. Nevertheless, it should be noted that any increase in the number of samples during probabilistic inference would lead to even larger gain for our approach. This is because we have a much simpler network, and collecting each sample takes lesser time compared to the standard approach. For the same reason, we also expect a faster convergence (in terms of the number of samples needed) for our approach. Exploring these convergence issues in detail is a direction for future work.

5   Related Work

There has been some related work which exploits the structure of the network to make inference in Markov logic more efficient, but none has separately analyzed the hard constraints to reduce the size of the predicate domains over which network is constructed. LazySAT [15] exploits the fact that for many problems, most ground atoms are false and most ground clauses are satisfied, hence, a local solver (such as MaxWalkSAT [7]), does not need to explicitly instantiate them. Lifted Belief Propagation (LBP) [16] performs inference over a lifted network by clustering the nodes that would pass the same BP message in the ground network. None of these approaches are able to explicitly eliminate the nodes which are categorically false (or true) by virtue of the hard constraints. This

---

[3] Results reported above for the Library dataset are for the hand-engineered case.

may lead to sub-optimal inference, for instance, flipping a false (inferred) node in LazySAT, or, putting two false nodes in the different clusters for the case of LBP. Our approach is orthogonal to the benefits obtained by above algorithms, and thus can be used in conjunction with them. Jha et al. [6] recently proposed a lifted inference algorithm which uses techniques from logic and database literature. Their algorithm handles only the case for exact inference and that, too, for a small class of very simple MLNs.

Shavlik and Natarajan [14] present an approach to pre-process MLN theory to reduce the size of the ground Markov network. Their pre-processing effectively implements a fast index based algorithm to eliminate trivially satisfied (or unsatisfied) clauses. Each clause is processed independently. They do not allow information to be transferred from one clause to another, which is a key aspect of our approach. Alchemy already implements their pre-processing step, and hence, any benefits obtained by our approach are in addition to theirs.

Kisyński and Poole [8] analyze the use of different algorithms for constraint satisfaction in lifted inference. Their analysis is in the context of FOVE (first-order variable elimination) where factors are eliminated in some order. It's not directly applicable to approximate inference setting. Whether their lifted solver can be used in place of generalized arc consistency in our framework is a direction for future work.

Our work can be seen in the light of constraints specified using SQL queries in Relational Markov Networks (RMNs) [17]. Our approach is more general than theirs because constraints do not have to be repeated for each clause. Further, unlike their approach, we propagate information from one constraint to another, thereby potentially leading to even smaller predicate domains, over which to construct the network.

6   Conclusion and Future Work

We proposed a generalized arc consistency algorithm to effectively propagate the hard constraints in a Markov logic theory. We are able to do this at a lifted level, without ever explicitly grounding out the whole theory. Our algorithm significantly prunes the predicate domains, thereby, resulting in much simpler networks and allowing for significant efficiency gains during probabilistic inference. Directions for future work include experimenting with a wider variety of domains, trying out other forms of consistency requirements, symbolic manipulation of the theory to propagate the constraints more effectively, and combining our approach with lifted and lazy inference.

Acknowledgements. We are thankful to Ray Mooney for helpful discussions, and to Adam Sadilek for sharing the CTF dataset. This research was partly funded by ARO grant W911NF-08-1-0242 and NSF award 1012017. The views and conclusions contained in this document are those of the authors and should not be interpreted as necessarily representing the official policies, either expressed or implied, of ARO, NSF or the United States Government.

References

1. Dechter, R.: Constraint Processing. Morgan Kaufmann, San Francisco (2003)
2. Domingos, P., Lowd, D.: Markov Logic: An Interface Layer for Artificial Intelligence. Morgan & Claypool, San Rafael (2009)
3. Garcia-Molina, H., Ullman, J.D., Widom, J.D.: Database Systems: The Complete Book, 2nd edn. Prentice Hall, Englewood Cliffs (2008)
4. Getoor, L., Taskar, B. (eds.): Introduction to Statistical Relational Learning. MIT Press, Cambridge (2007)
5. Gogate, V., Dechter, R.: SampleSearch: Importance sampling in presence of determinism. Artificial Intelligence 175, 694–729 (2011)
6. Jha, A., Gogate, V., Meliou, A., Suciu, D.: Lifted inference seen from the other side: The tractable features. In: Advances in Neural Information Processing Systems 23 (NIPS 2010), pp. 973–981 (2010)
7. Kautz, H., Selman, B., Jiang, Y.: A general stochastic approach to solving problems with hard and soft constraints. In: Gu, D., Du, J., Pardalos, P. (eds.) The Satisfiability Problem: Theory and Applications. DIMACS Series in Discrete Mathematics and Theoretical Computer Science, vol. 35, pp. 573–586. American Mathematical Society, New York (1997)
8. Kisyński, J., Poole, D.: Constraint processing in lifted probabilistic inference. In: Proceedings of 25th Conference on Uncertainty in Artificial Intelligence (UAI 2009), pp. 292–302 (2009)
9. Kok, S., Sumner, M., Richardson, M., Singla, P., Poon, H., Lowd, D., Wang, J., Nath, A., Domingos, P.: The Alchemy system for statistical relational AI. Tech. rep., Department of Computer Science and Engineering, University of Washington (2010), http://alchemy.cs.washington.edu
10. McCallum, A.: Efficiently inducing features of conditional random fields. In: Proceedings of 19th Conference on Uncertainty in Artificial Intelligence (UAI 2003), Acapulco, Mexico, pp. 403–410 (August 2003)
11. Poon, H., Domingos, P.: Sound and efficient inference with probabilistic and deterministic dependencies. In: Proceedings of the Twenty-First National Conference on Artificial Intelligence (AAAI 2006), Boston, MA (2006)
12. Russell, S., Norvig, P.: Artificial Intelligence: A Modern Approach, 2nd edn. Prentice Hall, Upper Saddle River (2003)
13. Sadilek, A., Kautz, H.: Recognizing mutli-agent activities from GPS data. In: Proceedings of the 25th AAAI Conference on Artificial Intelligence, AAAI 2010 (2010)
14. Shavlik, J., Natarajan, S.: Speeding up inference in Markov logic networks by preprocessing to reduce the size of the resulting grounded network. In: Proceedings of the Twenty First International Joint Conference on Artificial Intelligence (IJCAI 2009), Hyederabad, India, pp. 1951–1956 (2009)
15. Singla, P., Domingos, P.: Discriminative training of Markov logic networks. In: Proceedings of the Twentieth National Conference on Artificial Intelligence (AAAI 2005), Pittsburgh, PA, pp. 868–873 (2005)
16. Singla, P., Domingos, P.: Lifted first-order belief propagation. In: Proceedings of the 23rd AAAI Conference on Artificial Intelligence (AAAI 2008), Chicago, IL, pp. 1094–1099 (2008)
17. Taskar, B., Abbeel, P., Koller, D.: Discriminative probabilistic models for relational data. In: Proceedings of 18th Conference on Uncertainty in Artificial Intelligence (UAI 2002), Edmonton, Canada, pp. 485–492 (2002)

Octagonal Domains for Continuous Constraints

Marie Pelleau, Charlotte Truchet, and Frédéric Benhamou

LINA, UMR CNRS 6241,
Université de Nantes, France
firstName.lastName@univ-nantes.fr

Abstract. Domains in Continuous Constraint Programming (CP) are generally represented with intervals whose n-ary Cartesian product (box) approximates the solution space. This paper proposes a new representation for continuous variable domains based on octagons. We generalize local consistency and split to this octagon representation, and we propose an octagonal-based branch and prune algorithm. Preliminary experimental results show promising performance improvements on several classical benchmarks.

1 Introduction

Continuous Constraint Programming (CP) relies on interval representation of the variables domains. Filtering and solution set approximations are based on Cartesian products of intervals, called boxes. In this paper, we propose to improve the Cartesian representation precision by introducing an n-ary octagonal representation of domains in order to improve filtering accuracy.

By introducing non-Cartesian representations for domains, we do not modify the basic principles of constraint solving. The main idea remains to reduce domains by applying constraint propagators that locally approximate constraint and domains intersections (filtering), by computing fixpoints of these operators (propagation) and by splitting the domains to search the solution space. Nevertheless, each of these steps has to be redesigned in depth to take the new domains into account, since we lose the convenient correspondence between approximate intersections and domain projections.

While shifting from a Cartesian to a relational approach, the resolution process is very similar. In the interval case, one starts with the Cartesian product of the initial domains and propagators reduce this global box until reaching a fixpoint. In the octagonal case, the Cartesian product of the initial domains is itself an octagon and each constraint propagator computes in turn the smallest octagon containing the intersection of the global octagon and the constraint itself, until reaching an octagonal fixpoint. In both cases, splitting operators drive the search space exploration, alternating with global domain reduction.

The octagon are chosen for different reasons: they represent a reasonable tradeoff between boxes and more complex approximation shapes (e.g. polyhedron, ellipsoids) and they have been studied in another context to approximate numerical computations in static analysis of programs. More importantly, we

J. Lee (Ed.): CP 2011, LNCS 6876, pp. 706–720, 2011.

show that octagons allows us to translate the corresponding constraint systems in order to incorporate classical continuous constraint tools in the resolution.

The contributions of this paper concern the different aspects of octagon-based solving. First, we show how to transform the initial constraint problem to take the octagonal domains into account. The main idea here is to combine classical constraint matrix representations and rotated boxes, which are boxes defined in different $\pi/4$ rotated bases. Second, we define a specific local consistency, oct-consistency, and propose an appropriate algorithm, built on top of any continuous filtering method. Third, we propose a split algorithm and a notion of precision adapted to the octagonal case.

After some preliminary notions on continuous CSPs and octagons (Section 2), we present in Section 3 the octagon representation and the notion of octagonal CSP. Section 4 addresses octagonal consistency and propagation. The general solver, including discussions on split and precision is presented in Section 5. Finally, experimental results are presented in Section 6, related work in Section 7, while conclusion and future work end the presentation of this work.

2   Preliminaries

This section recalls basic notions of CP and gives material on octagons from [9].

2.1   Notations and Definitions

We consider a Constraint Satisfaction Problem (CSP) on variables $\mathcal{V} = (v_1...v_n)$, taking their values in domains $\mathcal{D} = (D_1...D_n)$, with constraints $(C_1...C_p)$. The set of tuples representing the possible assignments for the variables is $D = D_1 \times ... \times D_n$. The solutions of the CSP are the elements of D satisfying the constraints. We denote by $\mathcal{S}$ the set of solutions, $\mathcal{S} = \{(s_1...s_n) \in \mathcal{D}, \forall i \in 1..n, C_i(s_1...s_n)\}$.

In the CP framework, variables can either be discrete or continuous. In this article, we focus on real variables. Domains are subintervals of $\mathbb{R}$ whose bounds are floating points, according to the norm IEEE 754. Let $\mathbb{F}$ be the set of floating points. For $a, b \in \mathbb{F}$, we can define $[a, b] = \{x \in \mathbb{R}, a \leq x \leq b\}$ the real interval delimited by a and b, and $\mathbb{I} = \{[a, b], a, b \in \mathbb{F}\}$ the set of all such intervals. Given an interval $I \in \mathbb{I}$, we write $\underline{I}$ (resp. $\overline{I}$) its lower (resp. upper) bound, and, for any real point x, $\underline{x}$ its floating-point lower approximation (resp. $\overline{x}$, upper). A cartesian product of intervals is called a box. For CSPs with domains in $\mathbb{I}$, constraint solver usually return a box containing the solutions, that is, an overapproximation for $\mathcal{S}$.

The notion of *local consistency* is central in CP. We recall here the definition of Hull-consistency, one of the most usual local consistency for continuous constraints.

Definition 1 (Hull-Consistency). *Let $v_1...v_n$ be variables over continuous domains represented by intervals $D_1...D_n \in \mathbb{I}$, and C a constraint. The domains $D_1...D_n$ are said Hull-consistent for C iff $D_1 \times ... \times D_n$ is the smallest floating-point box containing the solutions for C.*

Given a constraint C over domains $D_1...D_n$, an algorithm that computes the local consistent domains $D'_1...D'_n$, such that $\forall i \in 1...n, D'_i \subset D_i$ and $D'_1...D'_n$ are locally consistent for C, is called a *propagator* for C. The domains which are locally consistent for all constraints are the largest common fixpoints of all the constraints propagators [2,12]. Practically, propagators often compute overapproximations of the locally consistent domains. We will use the standard algorithm HC4 [3]. It efficiently propagates continuous constraints, relying on the syntax of the constraint and interval arithmetic [10]. It generally does not reach Hull consistency, in particular in case of multiple occurrences of the variables.

Local consistency computations can be seen as deductions, performed on domains by analyzing the constraints. If the propagators return the empty set, the domains are inconsistent and the problem has no solution. Otherwise, non-empty local consistent domains are computed. This is often not sufficient to accurately approximate the solution set. In that case choices are made on the variables values. For continuous constraints, a domain D is chosen and split into two (or more) parts, which are in turn narrowed by the propagators. The solver recursively alternates propagations and splits until a given precision is reached. In the end, the collection of returned boxes covers $\mathcal{S}$, under some hypotheses on the propagators and splits [2].

2.2   Octagons

In geometry, an octagon is a polygon having eight faces in $\mathbb{R}^2$[1]. In this paper, we use a more general definition given in [9].

Definition 2 (Octagonal constraints). *Let v_i, v_j be two real variables. An octagonal constraint is a constraint of the form $\pm v_1 \pm v_2 \leq c$ with $c \in \mathbb{R}$.*

For instance in $\mathbb{R}^2$, octagonal constraints define straight lines which are parallel to the axis if $i = j$, and diagonal if $i \neq j$. This remains true in $\mathbb{R}^n$, where the octagonal constraints define hyperplanes.

Definition 3 (Octagon). *Given a set of octagonal constraints $\mathcal{O}$, the subset of $\mathbb{R}^n$ points satisfying all the constraints in $\mathcal{O}$ is called an octagon.*

Remark 1. Here follows some general remarks on octagons :

- The geometric shape defined above includes the geometric octagons, but also other polygons (e.g. in $\mathbb{R}^2$, an octagon can have less than eight faces);
- an octagon can be defined with redundant constraints (for example $v_1 - v_2 \leq c$ and $v_1 - v_2 \leq c'$), but only one of them defines a face of the octagon (the one with the lowest constant in this example),
- in $\mathbb{R}^n$, an octagon has at most $2n^2$ faces, which is the maximum number of possible non-redundant octagonal constraints on n variables,
- an octagon is a set of *real* points, but, like the intervals, they can be restricted to have floating-points bounds ($c \in \mathbb{F}$).

In the following, octagons are restricted to floating-point octagons. Without loss of generality, we assume octagons to be defined with no redundancies.

---

[1] http://mathworld.wolfram.com/Octagon.html

2.3   Matrix Representation of Octagons

An octagon can be represented with a *difference bound matrix* (DBM) as described in [8,9]. This representation is based on a normalization of the octagonal constraints as follows.

Definition 4 (difference constraints). *Let* w, w' *be two variables. A difference constraint is a constraint of the form* $w - w' \leq c$ *for* c *a constant.*

By introducing new variables, it is possible to rewrite an octagonal constraint as an equivalent difference constraint: let $C = (\pm v_i \pm v_j \leq c)$ an octagonal constraint. Define the new variables $w_{2i-1} = v_i, w_{2i} = -v_i, w_{2j-1} = v_j, w_{2j} = -v_j$. Then

- for $i \neq j$
  - if $C \equiv (v_i - v_j \leq c)$, then C is equivalent to the difference constraints $(w_{2i-1} - w_{2j-1} \leq c)$ and $(w_{2j} - w_{2i} \leq c)$,
  - if $C \equiv (v_i + v_j \leq c)$, then C is equivalent to the difference constraints $(w_{2i-1} - w_{2j} \leq c)$ and $(w_{2j-1} - w_{2i} \leq c)$,
  - the two other cases are similar,
- for $i = j$
  - if $C \equiv (v_i - v_i \leq c)$, then C is pointless, and can be removed,
  - if $C \equiv (v_i + v_i) \leq c)$, then C is equivalent to the difference constraint $(w_{2i-1} - w_{2i} \leq c)$,
  - the two other cases are similar.

In what follows, regular variables are always written $(v_1...v_n)$, and the corresponding new variables are written $(w_1, w_2, ...w_{2n})$ with: $w_{2i-1} = v_i$, and $w_{2i} = -v_i$. As shown in [9], the rewritten difference constraints represent the same octagon as the original set of octagonal constraints, by replacing the positive and negative occurrences of the v_i variables by their w_i counterparts. Storing difference constraints is thus a suitable representation for octagons.

Definition 5 (DBM). *Let* $\mathcal{O}$ *be an octagon in* $\mathbb{R}^n$, *and its sequence of potential constraints as defined above. The octagon DBM is a* $2n \times 2n$ *square matrix, such that the element at row i, column j is the constant c of the potential constraint* $w_j - w_i \leq c$.

An example is shown on Figure 1(c): the element on row 1 and column 3 corresponds to the constraint $v_2 - v_1 \leq 2$ for instance.

At this stage, different DBMs can represent the same octagon. For example on Figure 1(c), the element row 2 and column 3 can be replaced with 100, for instance, without changing the corresponding octagon. In [9], an algorithm is defined so as to optimally compute the smallest values for the elements of the DBM. This algorithm is adapted from the Floyd-Warshall shortest path algorithm [6], modified in order to take advantage of the DBM structure. It exploits the fact that w_{2i-1} and w_{2i} correspond to the same variable. It is fully presented in [9].

3   Boxes Representation

In the following section we introduce a box representation for octagons. This representation, combined with the DBM will be used to define, from an initial set of continuous constraints, an equivalent system taking the octagonal domains into account.

3.1   Intersection of Boxes

In two dimensions, an octagon can be represented by the intersection of one box in the canonical basis for $\mathbb{R}^2$, and one box in the basis obtained from the canonical basis by a rotation of angle $\pi/4$ (see figure 1(b)). We generalize this remark to n dimensions.

Definition 6 (Rotated basis). *Let $B = (u_1, ..., u_n)$ be the canonical basis of $\mathbb{R}^n$. Let $\alpha = \pi/4$. The (i,j)-rotated basis $B_\alpha^{i,j}$ is the basis obtained after a rotation of α in the subplane defined by (u_i, u_j), the other vectors remaining unchanged:*
$B_\alpha^{i,j} = (u_1, ..., u_{i-1}, (cos(\alpha)u_i + sin(\alpha)u_j), ...u_{j-1}, (-sin(\alpha)u_i + cos(\alpha)u_j), ...u_n).$

By convention, for any $i \in \{1...n\}$, $B_\alpha^{i,i}$ represents the canonical basis. In what follows, α is always $\pi/4$ and will be omitted. Finally, every variable v living in the $B^{i,j}$ rotated basis and whose domain is D will be denoted by $v^{i,j}$ and its domain by $D^{i,j}$).

The DBM can also be interpreted as the representation of the intersection of one box in the canonical basis and $n(n-1)/2$ other boxes, each one living in a rotated basis. Let $\mathcal{O}$ be an octagon in $\mathbb{R}^n$ and its DBM M, with the same notations as above (M is a $2n \times 2n$ matrix). For $i, j \in \{1...n\}$, with $i \neq j$, let $\mathcal{B}_\mathcal{O}^{i,j}$ be the box $I_1 \times ... \times I_i^{i,j} \times ... \times I_j^{i,j} ... \times I_n$, in $B^{i,j}$, such that $\forall k \in \{1...n\}$

$$\underline{I_k} = -\tfrac{1}{2}M[2k-1, 2k] \qquad \overline{I_k} = \tfrac{1}{2}M[2k, 2k-1]$$
$$\underline{I_i^{i,j}} = -\tfrac{1}{\sqrt{2}}M[2j-1, 2i] \qquad \overline{I_i^{i,j}} = \tfrac{1}{\sqrt{2}}M[2j, 2i-1]$$
$$\underline{I_j^{i,j}} = -\tfrac{1}{\sqrt{2}}M[2j-1, 2i-1] \qquad \overline{I_j^{i,j}} = \tfrac{1}{\sqrt{2}}M[2j, 2i]$$

Proposition 1. *Let $\mathcal{O}$ be an octagon in $\mathbb{R}^n$, and $\mathcal{B}_\mathcal{O}^{i,j}$ the boxes as defined above. Then $\mathcal{O} = \bigcap_{1 \leq i,j \leq n} \mathcal{B}_\mathcal{O}^{i,j}$.*

Proof. Let $i, j \in \{1..n\}$. We have $v_i^{i,j} = 1/\sqrt{2}(v_i + v_j)$ and $v_j^{i,j} = 1/\sqrt{2}(v_i - v_j)$ by definition 6. Thus $(v_1...v_i^{i,j}...v_j^{i,j}...v_n) \in \mathcal{B}_\mathcal{O}^{i,j}$ iff it satisfies the octagonal constraints on v_i and v_j, and the unary constraints for the other coordinates, in the DBM. The box $\mathcal{B}_\mathcal{O}^{i,j}$ is thus the solution set for these particular octagonal constraints. The points in $\bigcap_{1 \leq i,j \leq n} \mathcal{B}_\mathcal{O}^{i,j}$ are exactly the points which satisfy all the octagonal constraints.

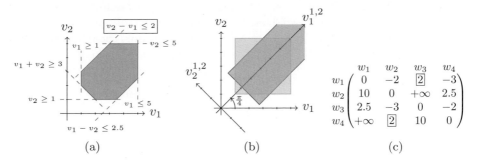

Fig. 1. Equivalent representations for the same octagon: the octagonal constraints 1(a), the intersection of boxes 1(b), and the DBM 1(c)

Example 1. Considering the DBM Figure 1(c), the boxes are $I_1 \times I_2 = [1, 5] \times [1, 5]$, and $I_1^{1,2} \times I_2^{1,2} = [3/\sqrt{2}, +\infty] \times [-2.5/\sqrt{2}, \sqrt{2}]$.

To summarize, an octagon with its DBM representation can also be interpreted as a set of octagonal constraints (definition in intension) or equivalently as an intersection of rotated boxes (definition in extension), at the cost of a multiplication / division with the appropriate rounding mode. We show below that the octagonal constraints (or the bounds in the case of boxes) can be inferred from the CSP.

3.2   Octagonal CSP

Consider a CSP on variables $(v_1...v_n)$ in $\mathbb{R}^n$. The goal is now to equip this CSP with an octagonal domain. We detail here how to build an octagonal CSP from a regular one, and show that the two systems are equivalent.

First, the CSP is associated to an octagon, by stating all the possible octagonal constraints $+v_i \pm v_j \leq c_k$ for $i, j \in \{1...n\}$. The constants c_k represent the bounds of the octagon boxes and are dynamically modified. They are initialized to $+\infty$.

The rotations defined in the previous section introduce new axes, that is, new variables $v_i^{i,j}$. Because these variables are redundant with the regular ones, they are also linked through the CSP constraints $(C_1...C_p)$, and these constraints have to be rotated as well.

Given a function f on variables $(v_1...v_n)$ in B, the expression of f in the (i, j)-rotated basis is obtained by symbolically replacing the i-th and j-th coordinates by their expressions in $B_\alpha^{i,j}$. Precisely, replace v_i by $\cos(\alpha)v_i^{i,j} - \sin(\alpha)v_j^{i,j}$ and v_j by $\sin(\alpha)v_i^{i,j} + \cos(\alpha)v_j^{i,j}$ where $v_i^{i,j}$ and $v_j^{i,j}$ are the coordinates for v_i and v_j in $B_\alpha^{i,j}$. The other variables are unchanged.

Definition 7 (Rotated constraint). *Given a constraint C_k holding on variables $(v_1...v_n)$, the (i, j)-rotated constraint $C_k^{i,j}$ is the constraint obtained by replacing each occurrence of v_i by $\cos(\alpha)v_i^{i,j} - \sin(\alpha)v_j^{i,j}$ and each occurrence of v_j by $\sin(\alpha)v_i^{i,j} + \cos(\alpha)v_j^{i,j}$.*

Given a continuous CSP $< v_1...v_n, D_1...D_n, C_1...C_p >$, we define an octagonal CSP by adding the rotated variables, the rotated constraints, and the rotated domains stored as a DBM. To sum up and fix the notations, the octagonal CSP thus contains:

- the regular variables $(v_1...v_n)$;
- the rotated variables $(v_1^{1,2}, v_2^{1,2}, v_1^{1,3}, v_3^{1,3}...v_n^{n-1,n})$, where $v_i^{i,j}$ is the i-th variable in the (i,j) rotated basis $B_\alpha^{i,j}$;
- the regular constraints $(C_1...C_p)$;
- the rotated constraints $(C_1^{1,2}, C_1^{1,3}...C_1^{n-1,n}...C_p^{n-1,n})$.
- the regular domains $(D_1...D_n)$;
- a DBM which represents the rotated domains. It it initialized with the bounds of the regular domains for the cells at position $2i, 2i-1$ and $2i-1, 2i$ for $i \in \{1...2n\}$, and $+\infty$ everywhere else.

In these conditions, the initial CSP is equivalent to this transformed CSP, restricted to the variables $v_1...v_n$, as shown in the following proposition.

Proposition 2. *Consider a CSP $< v_1...v_n, D_1...D_n, C_1...C_p >$, and the corresponding octagonal CSP as defined above. The solution set of the original CSP $\mathcal{S}$ is equal to the solution set of the $(v_1...v_n)$ variables of the octagonal CSP.*

Proof. Let $s \in \mathbb{R}^n$ a solution of the octogonal CSP for $(v_1...v_n)$. Then $s \in D_1 \times ... \times D_n$ and $C_1(s)...C_p(s)$ are all true. Hence s is a solution for the original CSP. Reciprocally, let $s' \in \mathbb{R}^n$ a solution of the original CSP. The regular constraints $(C_1...C_p)$ are true for s'. Let us show that there exist values for the rotated variables such that the rotated constraints are true for s'. Let $i, j \in \{1...n\}$, $i \neq j$, and $k \in \{1...p\}$ and $C_k^{i,j}$ the corresponding rotated constraint. By definition 7, $C_k^{i,j}(v_1...v_{i-1}, \cos(\alpha)v_i^{i,j} - \sin(\alpha)v_j^{i,j}, v_{i+1}... \sin(\alpha)v_i^{i,j} + \cos(\alpha)v_j^{i,j}...v_n) \equiv C_k(v_1...v_n)$. Let us define the two reals $s_i^{i,j} = cos(\alpha)s_i + sin(\alpha)s_j$ and $s_j^{i,j} = -sin(\alpha)s_i + cos(\alpha)s_j$, the image of s_i and s_j by the rotation of angle α. By reversing the rotation, $cos(\alpha)s_i^{i,j} - sin(\alpha)s_j^{i,j} = s_i$ and $sin(\alpha)s_i^{i,j} + cos(\alpha)s_j^{i,j} = s_j$, thus $C_k^{i,j}(s_1...s_i^{i,j}, ...s_j^{i,j}...s_n) = C_k(s_1...s_n)$ is true. It remains to check that $(s_1...s_i^{i,j}, ...s_j^{i,j}...s_n)$ is in the rotated domain, which is true because the DBM is initialized at $+\infty$. □

For a CSP on n variables, this representation has an order of magnitude n^2, with n^2 variables and domains, and $p\frac{n(n-1)}{2} + p$ constraints. Of course, many of these objects are redundant. We explain in the next sections how to use this redundancy to speed up the solving process.

4   Octagonal Consistency and Propagation

We first generalize the Hull-consistency definition to the octagonal domains, and define propagators for the rotated constraints. Then, we use the modified version of Floyd-Warshall (briefly described in section 2.3) to define an efficient propagation scheme for both octagonal and rotated constraints.

4.1   Octagonal Consistency for a Constraint

We generalize to octagons the definition of Hull-consistency on intervals for any continuous constraint. With the box representation, we show that any propagator for Hull-consistency on boxes can be extended to a propagator on the octagons. For a given n-ary relation on $\mathbb{R}^n$, there is a unique smallest octagon (wrt inclusion) which contains the solutions of this relation, as shown in the following proposition.

Remark 2. Consider a constraint C (resp. a constraint sequence $(C_1...C_p)$), and $\mathcal{S}_C$ its set of solutions (resp. $\mathcal{S}$). Then there exist a unique octagon $\mathcal{O}$ such that: $\mathcal{S}_C \subset \mathcal{O}$ (resp. $\mathcal{S} \subset \mathcal{O}$), and for all octagons $\mathcal{O}'$, $\mathcal{S}_C \subset \mathcal{O}'$ implies $\mathcal{O} \subset \mathcal{O}'$. $\mathcal{O}$ is the unique smallest octagon containing the solutions, wrt inclusion.

Definition 8 (Oct-Consistency). *Consider a constraint C (resp. a constraint sequence $(C_1...C_p)$), and $\mathcal{S}_C$ its set of solutions (resp. $\mathcal{S}$). An octagon is said Oct-consistent for this constraint iff it is the smallest octagon containing $\mathcal{S}_C$ (resp. $\mathcal{S}$), wrt inclusion.*

From remark 2, this definition is well founded. With the expression of an (i,j)-rotated constraint $C^{i,j}$, any propagator defined on the boxes can be used to compute the Hull-consistent boxes for $C^{i,j}$ (although such a propagator, as HC4, may not reach consistency). This gives a consistent box in basis $B^{i,j}$, and can be done for all the bases. The intersection of the Hull-consistent boxes is the Hull-consistent octagon.

Proposition 3. *Let C be a constraint, and $i,j \in \{1...n\}$. Let $\mathcal{B}^{i,j}$ be the Hull-consistent box for the rotated constraint $C^{i,j}$, and $\mathcal{B}$ the Hull consistent box for C. The Oct-consistent octagon for C is the intersection of all the $\mathcal{B}^{i,j}$ and $\mathcal{B}$.*

Proof. Let $\mathcal{O}$ be the Oct-consistent octagon. By definition 2, a box is an octagon. Since $\mathcal{O}$ is the smallest octagon containing the solutions, and all the $\mathcal{B}^{i,j}$ contain the solutions, for all $i,j \in \{1...n\}$, $i \neq j$ $\mathcal{O} \subset \mathcal{B}^{i,j}$ (the same holds for $\mathcal{B}$). Thus $\mathcal{O} \subset \bigcap_{1 \leq i,j \leq n} \mathcal{B}^{i,j}$. Reciprocally, we use the box representation for the Oct-consistent octagon: $\mathcal{O} = \bigcap_{1 \leq i,j \leq n} \mathcal{B}_o^{i,j}$, where $\mathcal{B}_o^{i,j}$ is the box defining the octagon in $B^{i,j}$. Because $\mathcal{O}$ contains all the solutions and $\mathcal{B}_o^{i,j}$ contains $\mathcal{O}$, $\mathcal{B}_o^{i,j}$ also contains all the solutions. Since $\mathcal{B}^{i,j}$ is the Hull-consistent box in $B_\alpha^{i,j}$, it is the smallest box in $B_\alpha^{i,j}$ which contains all the solutions. Thus $\mathcal{B}^{i,j} \subset \mathcal{B}_o^{i,j}$. From there, $\bigcap_{1 \leq i,j \leq n} \mathcal{B}^{i,j} \subset \bigcap_{1 \leq i,j \leq n} \mathcal{B}_o^{i,j} = \mathcal{O}$. Again, the same holds for $\mathcal{B}$. The two inclusions being proven, $\mathcal{O} = \bigcap_{1 \leq i,j \leq n} \mathcal{B}^{i,j}$.   □

4.2   Propagation Scheme

The propagation scheme presented in subsection 2.3 for the octagonal constraints is optimal. We thus rely on this propagation scheme, and integrate the non-octagonal constraints propagators in this loop. The point is to use the octagonal

float dbm[2n, 2n] /*the dbm containing the octagonal constraints*/
list propagList ← $(\rho_{C_1}, ...\rho_{C_p}, \rho_{C_1^{1,2}}...\rho_{C_p^{n-1,n}})$ /*list of the propagators to apply*/
while propagList $\neq \emptyset$ **do**
    apply all the propagators of propagList **to** dbm /*initial propagation*/
    propagList ← $\emptyset$
    for i,j from 1 to n **do**
        m ← minimum of (dbm$[2i-1, k]$+dbm$[k, 2j-1]$) for k from 1 to $2n$
        m ← minimum(m, dbm$[2i-1, 2i]$+dbm$[2j, 2j-1]$)
        if m < dbm$[2i-1, 2j-1]$ **then**
            dbm$[2i-1, 2j-1]$ ← m /*update of the DBM*/
            add $\rho_{C_1^{i,j}}...\rho_{C_p^{i,j}}$ **to** propagList /*get the propagators to apply*/
        end if
        repeat the 5 previous steps **for** dbm$[2i-1, 2j]$, dbm$[2i, 2j-1]$, **and** dbm$[2i, 2j]$
    end for
end while

Fig. 2. Pseudo code for the propagation loop mixing the Floyd Warshall algorithm (the *for* loop) and the regular and rotated propagators $\rho_{C_1}...\rho_{C_p}, \rho_{C_1^{1,2}}...\rho_{C_p^{n-1,n}}$, for an octagonal CSP as defined in section 3.2

constraints to benefit from the relational properties of the octagon. This can be done thanks to the following remark: all the propagators defined in the previous subsections are monotonic and complete (as is the HC4 algorithm). It results that they can be combined in any order in order to achieve consistency, as shown for instance in [2].

The key idea for the propagation scheme is to interleave the refined Floyd-Warshall algorithm and the constraint propagators. A pseudocode is given on figure 2. At the first level, the DBM is recursively visited so that the minimal bounds for the rotated domains are computed. Each time a DBM cell is modified, the corresponding propagators are added to the propagation list. The propagation list is applied before each new round in the DBM (so that a cell that would be modified twice is propagated only once). The propagation is thus guided by the additional information of the relational domain. This is illustrated on Figure 3: the propagators $\rho_{C_1}...\rho_{C_p}, \rho_{C_1^{1,2}}...\rho_{C_p^{n-1,n}}$ are first applied (3(a), 3(b)), then the boxes are made consistent wrt each other using the refined Floyd-Warshall algorithm.

We show here that the propagation as defined on figure 2 computes the consistent octagon for a sequence of constraints.

Proposition 4 (Correctness). *Let* $< v_1...v_n, D_1...D_n, C_1...C_p >$ *a CSP. Assume that, for all* $i, j \in \{1...n\}$, *there exists a propagator* ρ_C *for the constraint* C, *such that* ρ_C *reaches Hull consistency, that is,* $\rho_C(D_1 \times ... \times D_n)$ *is the Hull consistent box for* C. *Then the propagation scheme as defined on figure 2 computes the Oct-consistent octagon for* $C_1...C_p$.

Proof. This derives from proposition 3, and the propagation scheme of figure 2. The propagation scheme is defined so as to stop when propagList is empty. This

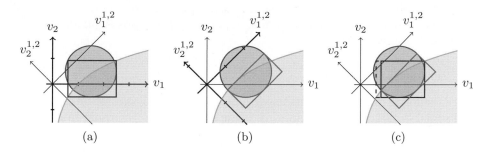

(a)   (b)   (c)

Fig. 3. Example of the Oct-consistency: an usual consistency algorithm is applied in each basis (Figures 3(a) and 3(b)) then the different boxes are made consistent using the modified Floyd-Warshall algorithm (Figure 3(c))

happens when $\forall i, j \in \{1...n\}, k \in \{1...2n\}, \text{dbm}[2i-1, k]+\text{dbm}[k, 2j-1], \text{dbm}[2i-1, 2i]+\text{dbm}[2j, 2j-1] \geq \text{dbm}[2i-1, 2j-1]$, the same holds for $\text{dbm}[2i-1, 2j]$, $\text{dbm}[2i, 2j-1]$, and $\text{dbm}[2i, 2j]$. The octagonal constraints are thus consistent. In addition, each time a rotated box is modified in the DBM, its propagators are added to propagList. Hence, the final octagon is stable by the application of all $\rho_{C_k^{i,j}}$, for all $k \in \{1...p\}$ and $i, j \in \{1...n\}$. By hypothesis, the propagators reach consistency, the boxes are thus Hull-consistent for all the (rotated and regular) constraints. By proposition 3, the returned octagon is Oct-consistent.   □

The refined Floyd-Warshall has a time complexity of $O(n^3)$. For each round in its loop, in the worst case we add p propagators in the propagation list. Thus the time complexity for the propagation scheme of figure 2 is $O(n^3 p^3)$. In the end, the octagonal propagation uses both representations of octagons. It takes advantage of the relational property of the octagonal constraints (Floyd-Warshall), and of the usual constraint propagation on boxes (propagators). This comes to the cost of computing the octagon, but is expected to give a better precision in the end.

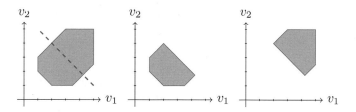

Fig. 4. Example of a split: the octagon on the left is cut in the $B^{1,2}$ basis

5   Solving

Besides the expected gain in precision obtained with octagon consistency, the box representation of octagons allows us to go a step further and define a fully

octagonal solver. We thus define an octagonal split, in order to be able to cut
the domains in any octagonal direction, and an octagonal precision, and end up
with a fully octagonal solver.

5.1   Octagonal Split

The octagonal split extends the usual split operator to octagons. Splits can be
performed in the canonical basis, thus being equivalent to the usual splits, or in
the rotated basis. It can be defined as follow:

Definition 9. *Given an octagonal domain defined with the box representation*
$D_1...D_n, D_1^{1,2}...D_1^{n-1,n}...D_n^{n-1,n}$, *such that* $D_k^{i,j} = [a,b]$, *a splitting operator for*
variable $v_k^{i,j}$, *computes the two octagonal subdomains* $D_1...[a, \overline{(a+b)/2}]...D_n^{n-1,n}$
and $D_1...[\underline{(a+b)/2}, b]...D_n^{n-1,n}$.

As for the usual split, the union of the two octagonal subdomains is the original
octagon, thus the split does not lose solutions. This definition does not take
into account the correlation between the variables of the different basis. We take
advantage again of the octagonal representation to communicate the domain
reduction to the other basis. A split is thus immediately followed by a Floyd-
Warshall propagation. Figure 4 shows an example of the split.

5.2   Precision

In most continuous solvers, the precision is defined as the size of the largest
domain. For octagons, this definition leads to a loss of information because it
does not take into account the correlation between the variables and domains.

Definition 10. *Let $\mathcal{O}$ be an octagon, and $I_1...I_n, I_1^{1,2}...I_n^{n-1,n}$ its box represen-*
tation. The octagonal precision is $\tau(\mathcal{O}) = min_{1 \leq i,j \leq n}(max_{1 \leq k \leq n}(\overline{I_k^{i,j}} - \underline{I_k^{i,j}}))$.

For a single regular box, τ would be the same precision as usual. On an octagon, we take the minimum precision of the boxes in all the bases because
it is more accurate, and it allows us to retrieve the operational semantics of
the precision, as shown by the following proposition: in an octagon of precision
r overapproximating a solution set $\mathcal{S}$, every point is at a distance at most r
from $\mathcal{S}$.

Proposition 5. *Let $< v_1...v_n, D_1...D_n, C_1...C_p >$ be a CSP, and $\mathcal{O}$ an octagon*
overapproximating $\mathcal{S}$. Let $r = \tau(\mathcal{O})$. Let $(v_1, ...v_n) \in \mathbb{R}^n$ be a point of $D_1 \times ... \times$
D_n. Then $\forall 1 \leq i \leq n, min_{s \in \mathcal{S}}|v_i - s_i| \leq r$, where $s = (s_1...s_n)$. Each coordinate
of all the points in $\mathcal{O}$ are at a distance at most r of a solution.

Proof. By definition 10, the precision r is the minimum of some quantities in all
the rotated basis. Let $B^{i,j}$ be the basis that realizes this minimum. Because the
box $\mathcal{B}^{i,j} = D_1 \times ... \times D_i^{i,j} \times ...D_j^{i,j}... \times D_n$ is Hull-consistent by proposition 3,
it contains $\mathcal{S}$. Let $s \in \mathcal{S}$. Because $r = max_k(\overline{D_k} - \underline{D_k})$, $\forall 1 \leq k \leq n, |s_k - v_k| \leq$
$\overline{D_k} - \underline{D_k} \leq r$. $\square$

```
Octogone oct
queue splittingList ← oct /*queue of the octagons*/
list acceptedOct ← ∅ /*list of the accepted octagons*/
while splittingList ≠ ∅ do
   Octogone octAux ← splittingList.top()
   splittingList.pop()
   octAux ← Oct-consistence(octAux)
   if τOct(octAux) < r or octAux contains only solutions then
      add octAux to acceptedOct
   else
      Octogone leftOct ← left(octAux) /*left and right are the split operators*/
      Octogone rightOct ← right(octAux)
      add leftOct to splittingList
      add rightOct to splittingList
   end if
end while
return acceptedOct
```

Fig. 5. Solving with octagons

5.3 Octagonal Solver

Figure 5 describes the octagonal solving process. By proposition 4, and the split property, it returns a sequence of octagons whose union overapproximate the solution space. Precisely, it returns either octagons for which all points are solutions, or octagons overapproximating solution sets with a precision r.

An important feature of a constraint solver is the variable heuristic. For continuous constraints, one usually choose to split the variable that has the largest domain. This would be very bad for the octagons, as the variable which has the largest domain is probably in a basis that is of little interest for the problem (it probably has a wide range because the constraints are poorly propagated in this basis). We thus define a default octagonal strategy which relies on the same remark as for definition 10: the variable to split is the variable $V_k^{i,j}$ which realizes the minimum of $min_{1 \leq i,j \leq n}(max_{1 \leq k \leq n}(\overline{D_k^{i,j}} - D_k^{i,j}))$. The strategy is the following: choose first a promising basis, that is, a basis in which the boxes are tight (choose i, j). Then take the worst variable in this basis as usual (choose k).

6 Experiments

This section compares the octagonal solver with a traditional interval solver on classical benchmarks.

6.1 Implementation

We have implemented a prototype of the octagonal solver, with Ibex, a C++ library for continuous constraints [4]. We use the Ibex implementation of *HC4-Revise* [3] to contract the constraints. The octagons are implemented with their

Table 1. Results on problems from the Coconut benchmark. The first column gives the name of the problem, the number of variable and the type of the constraints. In each cell, the number on the left is the CPU time in seconds. Upper right is the number of box in the computed solution, lower right the number of created boxes.

	First solution				All the solutions			
	$\mathbb{I}^n$		Oct		$\mathbb{I}^n$		Oct	
h75 5 $\leq$	41.40	*1* / 1 024 085	0.03	*1* / 149	> 3 hours		> 3 hours	
hs64 3 $\leq$	0.01	*1* / 217	0.05	*1* / 67	> 3 hours		> 3 hours	
h84 5 $\leq$	5.47	*1* / 87 061	2.54	*1* / 1 407	> 3 hours		7238.74	*10 214 322* / 22 066 421
KinematicPair 2 $\leq$	0.00	*1* / 45	0.00	*1* / 23	53.09	*424 548* / 893 083	16.56	*39 555* / 79 125
pramanik 3 $=$	28.84	*1* / 321 497	0.16	*1* / 457	193.14	*145 663* / 2 112 801	543.46	*210 371* / 1 551 157
trigo1 10 $=$	18.93	*1* / 10 667	1.38	*1* / 397	20.27	*12* / 11 137	28.84	*347* / 5 643
brent-10 10 $=$	6.96	*1* / 115 949	0.54	*1* / 157	17.72	*854* / 238 777	105.02	*142* / 100 049
h74 5 $= \leq$	305.98	*1* / 8 069 309	13.70	*1* / 138 683	1 304.23	*183 510* / 20 061 357	566.31	*700 669* / 1 926 455
fredtest 6 $= \leq$	3 146.44	*1* / 29 206 815	19.33	*1* / 3 281	> 3 hours		> 3 hours	

DBM representation. Additional rotated variables and constraints are posted and dealt with as explained above.

An important point is the rotation of the constraints. The HC4 algorithm is sensitive to multiple occurrences of the variables, and the symbolic rewriting defined in section 3.2 creates multiple occurrences. Thus, the HC4 propagation on the rotated constraints could be very poor if performed directly on the rotated constraints. It is necessary to simplify the rotated constraints wrt the number of multiple occurrences for the variables. We use the Simplify function of Mathematica to do this. The computation time indicated below does not include the time for this treatment, however, it is negligible compared to the solving times. The propagator is an input of our method: we used a standard one (HC4), but more recent propagator such as [1] will be considered in the future. It is sufficient for our needs that the consistency algorithms computes overapproximations of the Hull-consistent boxes, as it is often the case for continuous propagators.

6.2   Results

We have tested the prototype octagonal solver on problems from the Coconut benchmark[2]. These problems have been chosen depending on the type of the constraints (inequations, equations, or both).

---

[2] This benchmark can be found at
http://www.mat.univie.ac.at/~neum/glopt/coconut/

Experiments have been made, with Ibex 1.18, on a MacBook Pro Intel Core 2 Duo 2.53 GHz. Apart from the variable heuristic presented in subsection 5.3, the experiments have been done with the same configuration in Ibex, in particular, using the same propagators, so as to compare exactly the octagonal results with their interval counterparts. Table 1 compares the results obtained by the interval resolution to those obtained by the octagonal resolution. In the first four problems the constraints are inequalities, in the three following they are only equalities and in the last two they are mixed inequalities and equalities. The octagonal solver needs less time and created less boxes to find the first solution of a problem. We obtain better results on problems containing inequalities. Problems with equalities contain multiple occurrences of variables, which can explain the bad results obtained by the octagonal solver on those problems.

7   Related Works

Our work is related to [9], in static analysis of programs. Their goal is to compute overapproximations for the traces of a program. The octagons are shown to provide a good trade off between the precision of the approximation and the computation cost. We use their matrix representation and their version of the Floyd–Warshall algorithm.

Propagation algorithms for the difference constraints, also called *temporal*, have already presented in [5,11]. They have a better complexity than the one we use, but are not suited to the DBM case, because they do not take into account the doubled variables.

The idea of rotating variables and constraints has already been proposed in [7], in order to better approximate the solution set. Their method is dedicated to under-constrained systems of equations.

8   Conclusion

In this paper, we have proposed a solving algorithm for continuous constraints based on octagonal approximations. Starting from the remark that domains in Constraint Programming can be interpreted as components of a global multi-dimensional parallelepipedic domain, we have constructed octagonal approximations on the same model and provided algorithms for octagonal CSP transformations, filtering, propagation, precision and splitting. An implementation based on Ibex and preliminary experimental results on classical benchmarks are encouraging, particularly in the case of systems containing inequalities. Future work involves the experimental study of other interval-based propagators such as Mohc [1] and extensions to other geometric structures.

References

1. Araya, I., Trombettoni, G., Neveu, B.: Exploiting monotonicity in interval constraint propagation. In: Proceedings of the 24th AAAI Conference on Artificial Intelligence, AAAI 2010 (2010)

2. Benhamou, F.: Heterogeneous constraint solvings. In: Proceedings of the 5th International Conference on Algebraic and Logic Programming, pp. 62–76 (1996)
3. Benhamou, F., Goualard, F., Granvilliers, L., Puget, J.-F.: Revisiting hull and box consistency. In: Proceedings of the 16th International Conference on Logic Programming, pp. 230–244 (1999)
4. Chabert, G., Jaulin, L.: Contractor programming. Artificial Intelligence 173, 1079–1100 (2009)
5. Dechter, R., Meiri, I., Pearl, J.: Temporal constraint networks. In: Proceedings of the First International Conference on Principles of Knowledge Representation and Reasoning (1989)
6. Floyd, R.: Algorithm 97: Shortest path. Communications of the ACM 5(6) (1962)
7. Goldsztejn, A., Granvilliers, L.: A new framework for sharp and efficient resolution of ncsp with manifolds of solutions. In: Stuckey, P.J. (ed.) CP 2008. LNCS, vol. 5202, pp. 190–204. Springer, Heidelberg (2008)
8. Menasche, M., Berthomieu, B.: Time petri nets for analyzing and verifying time dependent communication protocols. In: Protocol Specification, Testing, and Verification (1983)
9. Miné, A.: The octagon abstract domain. Higher-Order and Symbolic Computation 19(1), 31–100 (2006)
10. Moore, R.: Interval Analysis. Prentice-Hall, Englewood Cliffs (1966)
11. Régin, J.-C., Rueher, M.: Inequality-sum: a global constraint capturing the objective function. RAIRO Operations Research (2005)
12. Schulte, C., Stuckey, P.J.: Efficient constraint propagation engines. Transactions on Programming Languages and Systems 31(1), 2:1–2:43 (2008)

A $\Theta(n)$ Bound-Consistency Algorithm for the Increasing Sum Constraint

Thierry Petit[1], Jean-Charles Régin[2], and Nicolas Beldiceanu[1]

[1]TASC team (INRIA/CNRS), Mines de Nantes, France
[2] Université de Nice-Sophia Antipolis, I3S UMR 6070, CNRS, France
{nicolas.beldiceanu,thierry.petit}@mines-nantes.fr, jcregin@gmail.com

Abstract. Given a sequence of variables $X = \langle x_0, x_1, \ldots, x_{n-1} \rangle$, we consider the INCREASINGSUM constraint, which imposes $\forall i \in [0, n-2]$ $x_i \leq x_{i+1}$, and $\sum_{x_i \in X} x_i = s$. We propose an $\Theta(n)$ bound-consistency algorithm for INCREASINGSUM.

1 Introduction

Many problems involve *sum constraints*, for instance optimization problems. In this paper we consider a specialization of the sum constraint enforcing that an objective variable should be equal to a sum of a set of variables. Given a sequence of variables $X = \langle x_0, x_1, \ldots, x_{n-1} \rangle$ and a variable s, we propose an $\Theta(n)$ BC algorithm for the INCREASINGSUM constraint, which imposes that $\forall i \in [0, n-2], x_i \leq x_{i+1} \wedge \sum_{x_i \in X} x_i = s$. INCREASINGSUM is a special case of the INEQUALITYSUM constraint [4], which represents a sum constraint with a graph of binary inequalities.[1]

INCREASINGSUM is useful for breaking symmetries in some problems. For instance, in bin packing problems some symmetries can be broken by ordering bins according to their use. For each bin i we introduce a variable x_i giving the sum of the heights of the items assigned to i. We can explicitly state that the sum of the x_i's is equal to the sum of the heights of all the items.

2 Sum Constraints in CP

This section discusses the time complexity for filtering sum constraints. Given $x_i \in X$, we denote by $D(x_i)$ the domain of x_i, $min(x_i)$ its minimum value and $max(x_i)$ its maximum value. We say that an assignment $A(X)$ of values to a set of integer variables in X is valid iff each value assigned to $x_i \in X$, denoted by $A(x_i)$, is such that $A(x_i) \in D(x_i)$ (the domain of x_i).

We first recall the usual definitions of GAC and BC.

---

[1] BC can be achieved on INEQUALITYSUM in $O(n \cdot (m + n \cdot log(n)))$ time complexity, where m is the number of binary inequalities (arcs of the graph) and n is the number of variables.

J. Lee (Ed.): CP 2011, LNCS 6876, pp. 721–728, 2011.

Definition 1 (GAC, BC). *Given a variable x_i and a constraint $C(X)$ such that $x_i \in X$, Value $v \in D(x_i)$*

- *has a* support *on $C(X)$ iff there exists a valid assignment $A(X)$ satisfying C with $A(x_i) = v$.*
- *has a* bounds-support *on $C(X)$ iff there exists an assignment $A(X)$ satisfying C with $A(x_i) = v$ and such that $\forall x_j \in X$, $x_j \neq x_i$, we have $A(x_j) \in [min(D(x_j)), max(D(x_j))]$.*

$C(X)$ *is* Generalized Arc-Consistent (GAC) *iff $\forall x_i \in X$, $\forall v \in D(x_i)$, v has a support on $C(X)$. $C(X)$ is* Bounds-Consistent (BC) *iff $\forall x_i \in X$, $min(D(x_i))$ and $max(D(x_i))$ have a bound-support on $C(X)$.*

Given a set X of integer variables and an integer k, we denote by $\sum_{=} k$ the problem consisting of determining whether there exists an assignment of values to variables in X such that $\sum_{x_i \in X} x_i = k$, or not. This problem is NP-Complete [4, p. 7]: The SUBSETSUM problem [2, p. 223], which is NP-Complete, is a particular instance of the feasibility check of a constraint $\sum_{x_i \in X} x_i = k$.

When we consider an objective variable s instead of an integer k, performing GAC on $\sum_{x_i \in X} x_i = s$ is NP-Hard since one has to check the consistency of all values in $D(s)$, which corresponds to the $\sum_{=} k$ problem.

Conversely, enforcing BC on $\sum_{x_i \in X} x_i = s$ is in P as well as achieving BC on $\sum_{x_i \in X, a_i \in \mathbb{N}} a_i \cdot x_i \leq s$ [3].

In practice the constraint $\sum_{x_i \in X} x_i = s$ is generally associated with some additional constraints on variables in X. Next section presents a BC algorithm for a sum with increasing variables. This constraint may occur in problems involving sum constraints on symmetrical variables.

3   BC Linear Algorithm for Increasing Sum

Given a sequence of variables $X = \langle x_0, x_1, \ldots, x_{n-1} \rangle$ and a variable s, this section presents an $\Theta(n)$ algorithm for enforcing BC on the constraint INCREASINGSUM$(X, s) = \forall i \in \{0, 1, \ldots n-2\}, x_i \leq x_{i+1} \wedge \sum_{x_i \in X} x_i = s$. Following Definition 1, and since we consider an algorithm achieving BC, **this section ignores holes in the domains of variables**.

Definition 2. *Let $x_i \in X$ be a variable. $D(x_i)$ is $\leq$-consistent iff there exists two assignments $A(X)$ and $A'(X)$ such that $A(x_i) = min(x_i)$ and $A'(x_i) = max(x_i)$ and $\forall j \in [0, n-2]$, $A(x_j) \leq A(x_{j+1})$ and $A'(x_j) \leq A'(x_{j+1})$. X is $\leq$-consistent iff $\forall x_i \in X$, $D(x_i)$ is $\leq$-consistent.*

W.l.o.g., **from now we consider that X is $\leq$-consistent**. In practice we can ensure $\leq$-consistency of X in $\Theta(n)$ by traversing X so as to make for each $i \in [0, n-2]$ the bounds of the variables x_i and x_{i+1} consistent with the constraint $x_i \leq x_{i+1}$. After making X $\leq$-consistent, it is easy to evaluate a lower bound and an upper bound of the sum s.

Lemma 1. *Given* INCREASINGSUM(X, s), *the intervals* $[min(s), \sum_{x_i \in X} min(x_i)[$ *and* $]\sum_{x_i \in X} max(x_i), max(s)]$ *can be removed from* $D(s)$.

Proof. $\sum_{x_i \in X} min(x_i) \leq \sum_{x_i \in X} x_i \leq \sum_{x_i \in X} max(x_i)$.   □

Lemma 1 docs not ensure that INCREASINGSUM is BC, since we can have $min(s) > \sum_{x_i \in X} min(x_i)$ and $max(s) < \sum_{x_i \in X} max(x_i)$. In this case, bounds of variables in X may not be consistent, and some additional pruning needs to be performed. Next example highlights this claim.

Example 1. We consider INCREASINGSUM(X, s), $D(s) = \{28, 29\}$ and the sequence $X = \langle x_0, x_1, \ldots, x_5 \rangle$. We denote by $\underline{sum}$ the minimum value of the sum of variables in X.

$D(x_0) = \{\ 2, 3, 4, 5, 6\ \}$, $\underline{sum}$ if $x_0 = 6 : 28 + 9 = 37$
$D(x_1) = \{\quad\ 4, 5, 6, 7\ \}$, $\underline{sum}$ if $x_1 = 7 : 28 + 9 = 37$
$D(x_2) = \{\quad\ 4, 5, 6, 7\ \}$, $\underline{sum}$ if $x_2 = 7 : 28 + 6 = 34$
$D(x_3) = \{\quad\quad 5, 6, 7\ \}$, $\underline{sum}$ if $x_3 = 7 : 28 + 3 = 31$
$D(x_4) = \{\quad\quad 6, 7, 8, 9\ \}$, $\underline{sum}$ if $x_4 = 9 : 28 + 5 = 33$
$D(x_5) = \{\quad\quad\quad 7, 8, 9\ \}$, $\underline{sum}$ if $x_5 = 9 : 28 + 2 = 30$.

For all $x_i \in X$, $min(x_i)$ is consistent since $\sum_{x_i \in X} min(x_i) = 28 = min(s)$, and $max(x_i)$ is not consistent. The increase in the sum corresponding to $max(x_i)$ (the bold values) is computed by considering that values assigned to variables having an index greater than i should be at least equal to $max(x_i)$. For instance, if $x_0 = 6$ then $\underline{sum} = 28 + 9 = 37$ with $9 = 4 + 2 + 2 + 1 + 0 + 0$, where 4 is the increase with respect to x_0, 2 the increase with respect to x_1, and so on.

Conversely, once s has been updated thanks to Lemma 1, all values between $min(s)$ and $max(s)$ are bound-consistent with INCREASINGSUM.

Property 1. Given INCREASINGSUM(X, s), if $min(s) \geq \sum_{x_i \in X} min(x_i)$, $max(s) \leq \sum_{x_i \subset X} max(x_i)$ and $min(s) \leq max(s)$ then $\forall v \in D(s)$ there exists an assignment $A(X)$ such that $\sum_{x_i \in X} A(x_i) = v$.

Proof. Let $\delta \geq 0$ such that $v \in D(s)$ and $v = \sum_{x_i \in X} min(x_i) + \delta$. If $\delta = 0$ then the property holds. Assume the property is true for $\delta = k$: there exists an assignment $A(X)$ with $\sum_{x_i \in X} A(x_i) = \sum_{x_i \in X} min(x_i) + k$. We prove that it remains true for $\delta = k + 1$, that is, $v = \sum_{x_i \in X} min(x_i) + k + 1$. First, if $v > \sum_{x_i \in X} max(x_i)$ the property holds (the condition is violated). Otherwise, consider $A(X)$. We have not $\forall i \in [0, n - 1], A(x_i) = max(x_i)$ since $v \leq \sum_{x_i \in X} max(x_i)$. Therefore, consider the greatest index $i \in [0, n - 1]$ such that $A(x_i) < max(x_i)$. All $x_j \in X$ such that $j > i$ (if $i = n - 1$ no such x_j exists) satisfy by definition $A(x_j) = max(x_j)$. Variables in X are range variables, thus $A(x_i) + 1 \in D(x_i)$. X is $\leq$-consistent: if $i < n - 1$ then $A(x_i) + 1 \leq A(x_{i+1})$. Moreover, if $i < n - 1$, $A(x_{i+1}) = max(x_{i+1})$ by definition of i. In all cases, $(i < n - 1$ or $i = n - 1)$, assignment $A'(X)$ such that $A'(x_i) = A(x_i) + 1$ is such that $\sum_{x_i \in X} A'(x_i) = \sum_{x_i \in X} min(x_i) + k + 1 = v$. The Property holds.   □

Once Property 1 is satisfied, we have to focus on bounds of variables in X. We restrict ourself to the maximum values in domains. The case of minimum values is symmetrical. We consider also that $D(s)$ is not empty after applying Lemma 1, which entails that no domain of a variable in X can become empty, *i.e.*, we have at least one feasible solution for INCREASINGSUM.

In Example 1, all maximum values of domains should be reduced. For all x_i in X, if we assign $max(x_i)$ to x_i the overload on $min(s)$ (bold values in Example 1) is too big, *i.e.*, $max(s)$ is exceeded. To reduce the upper bound of a variable x_i, we search for the greatest value v in $D(x_i)$ which leads to a value of s less than or equal to $max(s)$.

Notation 1. *Given a value $v \in D(x_j)$, we denote by $bp(X, j, v)$ (break point) the minimum value of the sum $\sum_{x_i \in X} x_i$ of an assignment $A(X)$ satisfying for each $i \in [0, n-2]$ the constraint $x_i \le x_{i+1}$ and such that $x_j = v$.*

To compute this quantity we introduce the notion of *last intersecting index*, which allows to split $\sum_{x_i \in X} x_i$ in three sub-sums that can be evaluated independently.

Definition 3. *Given INCREASINGSUM(X, s), let $i \in [0, n-1]$ be an integer. The last intersecting index $last_i$ of variable x_i is equal either to the greatest index in $[i+1, n-1]$ such that $max(x_i) > min(x_{last_i})$, or to i if no integer k in $[i+1, n-1]$ is such that $max(x_i) > min(x_k)$.*

Property 2. Given INCREASINGSUM(X, s), let $i \in [0, n-1]$ be an integer and $v \in D(x_i)$, $bp(X, i, v) =$

$$\left(\sum_{k \in [0, \dots, i-1]} min(x_k) \right) + bp(\langle x_i, \dots, x_{last_i} \rangle, i, v) + \left(\sum_{k \in [last_i+1, \dots, n-1]} min(x_k) \right)$$

Proof. By Definition 3, any variable x_k in $\{x_0, \dots, x_{i-1}\} \cup \{x_{last_i+1}, \dots, x_{n-1}\}$ can be assigned to its minimum $min(x_k)$ within an assignment of X where: (1) x_i is assigned to v, and (2) this assignment satisfies $\forall k \in [0, n-2], x_k \le x_{k+1}$. □

From Property 2, we know that to check the feasibility of the upper bound of x_i we have to compute $bp(\langle x_i, \dots, x_{last_i} \rangle, i, max(x_i))$.

Property 3. Given INCREASINGSUM(X, s), let $i \in [0, n-1]$ and $last_i$ be the last intersecting index of x_i, $bp(\langle x_i, \dots, x_{last_i} \rangle, i, max(x_i)) = \sum_{k \in [i, last_i]} max(x_i)$.

Proof. By Definition 3, $last_i$ is the *greatest* index, greater than i, such that $min(x_{last_i}) < max(x_i)$, or i if no such an index exists. All variables x_k in $\langle x_i, \dots, x_{last_i} \rangle$ are such that $min(x_k) \le max(x_i)$, thus assigning $max(x_i)$ to x_i implies assigning a value greater than or equal to $max(x_i)$ to any x_k such that $k \in [i+1, last_i]$, in order to satisfy $\forall l \in [i+1, last_i]$ the constraint $x_{l-1} \le x_l$. Since X is $\le$-consistent, for each $k \in [i, last_i]$ $max(x_i) \in D(x_k)$ and the minimum increase due to x_k compared with $\sum_{x_k \in [i, last_i]} min(x_k)$ if $x_i = max(x_i)$ is $max(x_i) - min(x_k)$. □

From Property 3 we obtain a consistency check for the maximum value of x_i. We use the following notations:

- $margin = max(s) - \sum_{k \in [0,n-1]} min(x_k)$; we consider $\sum_{k \in [0,n-1]} min(x_k)$ because our goal is here to reduce upper bounds of domains of variables in X according to $max(s)$.
- $\Delta_i = \sum_{k \in [i,last_i]}(max(x_i) - min(x_k))$; Δ_i is the minimum increase with respect to $\sum_{k \in [0,n-1]} min(x_k)$ under the hypothesis that x_i is fixed to $max(x_i)$.

Lemma 2. *Given* INCREASINGSUM(X, s) *and* $i \in [0, n-1]$, *if* $\Delta_i > margin$ *then* $max(x_i)$ *is not consistent.*

Proof. Obvious from Property 3. □

We now present our BC algorithm. Algorithm 1 prunes the maximum values in domains of variables in a $\leq$-consistent sequence X, using an incremental computation of Δ_i, starting from the last variable x_{n-1} and considering at each step the valid last intersection index. When the condition of Lemma 2 is satisfied, that is, $\Delta_i > margin$, Algorithm 1 calls the procedure FILTERMAXVAR$(x_i, last_i, \Delta_i, margin)$ to decrease $max(x_i)$. This procedure is described later.

Algorithm 1. FILTERMAXVARS(X, s)

1 $minsum := 0$;
2 **for** $i = 0$ *to* $n - 1$ **do** $minsum := minsum + min(x_i)$;
3 $margin := max(s) - minsum$; $i := n - 1$; $last_i := i$; $\Delta_i := max(x_i) - min(x_i)$;
4 **while** $i \geq 0$ **do**
5 $\quad$ **if** $\Delta_i \leq margin$ **then**
6 $\quad\quad$ $oldmax := max(x_i)$;
7 $\quad\quad$ $i := i - 1$;
8 $\quad\quad$ **if** $i > 0$ **then**
9 $\quad\quad\quad$ **while** $(min(x_{last_i}) \geq max(x_i)) \wedge (last_i > i)$ **do**
10 $\quad\quad\quad\quad$ $\Delta_i := \Delta_i - (oldmax - min(x_{last_i}))$;
11 $\quad\quad\quad\quad$ $last_i := last_i - 1$;
12 $\quad\quad\quad$ $\Delta_i := \Delta_i + max(x_i) - min(x_i) - (last_i - i) \cdot (oldmax - max(x_i))$;

13 $\quad$ **else** $(last_i, \Delta_i) :=$ FILTERMAXVAR$(x_i, last_i, \Delta_i, margin)$;
14 $\quad$ **if** $i > 0 \wedge max(x_{i-1}) > max(x_i)$ **then** $max(x_{i-1}) := max(x_i)$;

Figure 1 illustrates with an example of the incremental update of Δ_i (lines 9-12 of Algorithm 1) when $\Delta_i < margin$ and i is decremented by one.

We now describe how the procedure FILTERMAXVAR$(x_i, last_i, \Delta_i, margin)$ can be implemented to obtain a time complexity linear in the number of variables for Algorithm 1. We thus consider that the condition of Lemma 2 is satisfied, that is, $\Delta_i > margin$. It is required to reduce $max(x_i)$.

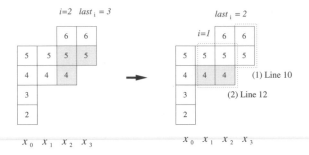

Fig. 1. Execution of Algorithm 1 with $margin = 4$ and 4 variables such that $D(x_0) = [2,5], D(x_1) = [4,5], D(x_2) = [4,6], D(x_3) = [5,6]$. On the left side, the current index is $i = 2$, $last_2 = 3$ and we have $\Delta_2 = 3$ (bolded values). Since $\Delta_2 < margin$ no pruning is performed and the algorithm moves to the next variable ($i = 1$). The right side shows that: (1) Δ_1 is first updated by removing the contributions computed with the previous maximum value of x_i ($oldmax = max(x_2)$) at the variable indexed by the previous last intersecting index $last_2 = 3$ (line 10 of Algorithm 1), and then $last_i$ is decreased (line 11). (2) According to the new $last_1 = 2$, Δ_1 is increased by the contribution of x_1, while the exceed over $max(x_2)$ of variables indexed between $i = 1$ and $last_1 = 2$ is removed from Δ_1 (line 12).

Our aim is then to update x_i and update both $last_i$ and Δ_i while preserving the property that the time complexity of Algorithm 1 is linear in the number of variables. The principle is the following.

Algorithm 2. FILTERMAXVAR(x_i, $last_i$, Δ_i, $margin$)

---
1 **while** $\Delta_i > margin$ **do**
2      $steps := min(\lceil \frac{\Delta_i - margin}{last_i - i + 1} \rceil, max(x_i) - min(x_{last_i}))$;
3      $D(x_i) := D(x_i) \setminus \,]max(x_i) - steps, max(x_i)]$;
4      $\Delta_i := \Delta_i - (last_i - i + 1) \cdot (steps)$;
5   **while** $(min(x_{last_i}) \geq max(x_i)) \wedge (last_i > i)$ **do** $last_i := last_i - 1$;

6 **return** $(last_i, \Delta_i)$;

If we assume that all variables $\langle x_i, x_{i+1}, \ldots, x_{last_i} \rangle$ will be assigned the same value then the minimum number of horizontal slices to remove (each slice corresponding to a same value, that can potentially be assigned to each variable in $\langle x_i, x_{i+1}, \ldots, x_{last_i} \rangle$) in order to absorb the exceed $\Delta_i - margin$ is equal to $\lceil \frac{\Delta_i - margin}{last_i - i + 1} \rceil$. Then, two cases are possible.

1. If $\lceil \frac{\Delta_i - margin}{last_i - i + 1} \rceil$ is strictly less (strictly since one extra slice is reserved for the common value assigned to $x_i, x_{i+1}, \ldots, x_{last_i}$, that is, the new maximum of x_i) than the number of available slices between $min(x_{last_i})$ and $max(x_i)$, namely $max(x_i) - min(x_{last_i}) + 1$, then removing $]max(x_i) - \lceil \frac{\Delta_i - margin}{last_i - i + 1} \rceil, max(x_i)]$ gives the feasible upper bound of x_i.

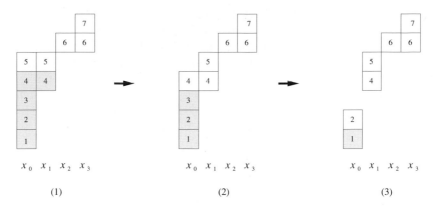

(1)   (2)   (3)

Fig. 2. Execution of Algorithm 2 with $i = 0$, $margin = 1$, $\Delta_i = 5$, and $last_0 = 1$. $D(x_0) = [1,5], D(x_1) = [4,5], D(x_2) = [6,6], D(x_3) = [6,7]$. (1) $\Delta_0 > margin$ so we compute $\lceil \frac{\Delta_0 - margin}{1 - 0 + 1} \rceil = 2$, which is not strictly less than $max(x_0) - min(x_1) + 1 = 2$, so $steps = max(x_0) - min(x_1) = 1$ and several phases may be required to prune x_0. (2) $D(x_0) := D(x_0)\backslash \,]5 - 1, max(x_0)] = [1,4]$. $\Delta_0 = \Delta_0 - (1 - 0 + 1) * 1 = 3$. $(min(x_1) \geq max(x_0)) \wedge (1 > 0)$ so $last_0 = 1 - 1 = 0$. (3) $\Delta_0 > margin$ so we compute $\lceil \frac{\Delta_0 - margin}{0 - 0 + 1} \rceil - \lceil \frac{3 - 1}{0 - 0 + 1} \rceil = 2$, which is strictly less than $max(x_0) - min(x_0) + 1 = 4$. $D(x_0) := D(x_0)\backslash \,]4 - 2, max(x_0)] = [1,2]$, and we have $\Delta_i = margin = 1$.

2. Otherwise, the quantity $q = max(x_i) - \lceil \frac{\Delta_i - margin}{last_i - i + 1} \rceil$ is not necessarily a feasible upper bound of x_i. In this case we decrease $max(x_i)$ down to $min(x_{last_i})$, that is, we consider the number of available slices consistent with the current $last_i$. Then we update $last_i$ and Δ_i and we repeat the process.

Algorithm 2 implements these principles. It takes as arguments the variable x_i, the last intersecting index $last_i$ of x_i, Δ_i and $margin$. It prunes the max of x_i and returns the updated pair $(last_i, \Delta_i)$. Figure 2 depicts an example where the pruning of x_i requires more than one step.

With respect to time complexity, recall $\leq$-consistency of X can be achieved in $\Theta(n)$ before runing Algorithm 1 by traversing the sequence and ensuring for each $i \in [0, n - 2]$ that bounds of variables are consistent with $x_i \leq x_{i+1}$. Therefore, the time complexity of for achieving BC is linear in the number of variables, since the following proposition holds with respect to Algorithm 1.

Proposition 1. *Time complexity of Algorithm 1 is $\Theta(n)$.*

Proof. An invariant of both Algorithm 2 and Algorithm 1 is that during the whole pruning of X, the index $last_i$ only decreases. Moreover, in Algorithm 2, if $steps = max(x_i) - min(x_{last_i}) + 1$ then $last_i$ decreases, otherwise $\Delta_i = margin$ and the algorithm ends. Thus, the cumulative time spent in the loop of line 5 in Algorithm 2 as well as the loop of lines 8-9 in Algorithm 1 is in n, the number of variables in X. Therefore, time complexity of Algorithm 1 is $O(n)$. Since to reduce domains of all the variables in X we have at least to update each of them, this time complexity is optimum. The proposition holds. $\square$

Furthermore, if minimum values of domains of variables in X are pruned after maximum values, there is no need to recompute those maximum values: increasing the lower bound $min(x_i)$ of a variable x_i leads to a diminution of *margin* and exactly the same diminution in Δ_i. Therefore, applying a second time Algorithm 1 cannot lead to more pruning. The reasoning is symmetrical if maximum values are filtered after minimum values. As a consequence, BC can be achieved in three phases: the first one to ensure $\leq$-consistency of X and adjust the bounds of s, the second one for maximum values in domains of variables in X, and the third one for minimum values in in domains of variables in X.

4   Conclusion and Future Work

We presented a $\Theta(n)$ BC algorithm for INCREASINGSUM(X, s), where $X = \langle x_0, x_1, \ldots, x_n \rangle$ is a sequence of variables and s is a variable. This constraint can be used in problems with variable symmetries involved in a sum. A Choco [1] implementation is available.

INCREASINGSUM can be used to enforce BC on the following generalization: $\forall i \in [0, n-2], x_i \leq x_{i+1} + cst \wedge \sum_{x_i \in X} x_i = s$, where cst is a constant. Indeed, we can add n additional variables X', one additional variable s' and $n+1$ mapping constraints: $\forall i \in [0, n-1], x_i' = x_i + cst \cdot i$ and $s' = s + \sum_{i \in [1, n-1]} i \cdot k$. Then enforcing BC on INCREASINGSUM(X', s') also enforces BC on variables in X and s since we use only mapping (equality) constraints. Time complexity remains $\Theta(n)$ because we add $O(n)$ variables.

With respect to GAC on INCREASINGSUM, Property 1 is not true when variables in X may have some holes in their domains. For instance, consider a sequence X of three variables with $D(x_0) = D(x_1) = D(x_2) = \{1, 3\}$ and a variable s with domain $D(s) = \{3, 6, 9\}$. Values 3 and 9 in $D(s)$ are consistent with INCREASINGSUM(X, s) while value 6 in $D(s)$ is not consistent with INCREASINGSUM(X, s). From this remark, enforcing GAC may require a check in $O(d^n)$ per value in s. A solution to INCREASINGSUM corresponds to a "sorted" solution of the SUBSETSUM problem, which does not make that problem easier.

References

1. Choco: An open source Java CP library, documentation manual (2011), http://www.emn.fr/z-info/choco-solver/
2. Garey, M.R., Johnson, D.S.: Computers and intractability: A guide to the theory of NP-completeness. W.H. Freeman and Company, New York (1979) ISBN 0-7167-1045-5
3. Harvey, W., Schimpf, J.: Bounds Consistency Techniques for Long Linear Constraints. In: Van Hentenryck, P. (ed.) CP 2002. LNCS, vol. 2470, pp. 39–46. Springer, Heidelberg (2002)
4. Régin, J.-C., Rueher, M.: Inequality-sum: a global constraint capturing the objective function. RAIRO - Operations Research 39, 123–139 (2005)

Automatic Generation of Constraints for Partial Symmetry Breaking

Christopher Jefferson[1] and Karen E. Petrie[2]

[1] Computer Science, University of St Andrews, UK
caj@cs.st-andrews.ac.uk
[2] School of Computing, University of Dundee, UK
karenpetrie@computing.dundee.ac.uk

Abstract. Constraint Satisfaction Problems (CSPs) are often highly symmetric. Symmetries can give rise to redundant search, since subtrees may be explored which are symmetric to subtrees already explored. To avoid this redundant search, constraint programmers have designed methods, which try to exclude all but one in each equivalence class of solutions. One problem with many of the symmetry breaking methods that eliminate all the symmetry is that they can have a large running overhead. To counter this flaw many CP practitioners have looked for methods that only eliminate a subset of the symmetries, so called partial symmetry breaking methods, but do so in an efficient manner. Partial symmetry breaking methods often work only when the problem is of a certain type. In this paper, we introduce a new method of finding a small set of constraints which provide very efficient partial symmetry breaking. This method works with all problem classes and modelling techniques.

1 Introduction

Constraint Satisfaction Problems (CSPs) are often highly symmetric. Symmetries may be inherent in the problem, as in placing queens on a chess board that may be rotated and reflected. Additionally, the modelling of a real problem as a CSP can introduce extra symmetry: problem entities which are indistinguishable may in the CSP be represented by separate variables, leading to n! symmetries between n variables. Symmetries may be found between variables or values or variable/value combinations.

Symmetries can give rise to redundant search, since subtrees may be explored which are symmetric to subtrees already explored. To avoid this redundant search, constraint programmers have designed methods which try to exclude symmetrically equivalent solutions.

In recent years CSP practitioners have created ways to automatically detect symmetry [1,2]. In this paper we consider how a constraint solving system such as Minion [3] should automatically exclude this detected symmetry. In particular, we wish to use a method that will increase the efficiency of search by effectively excluding part of the search space, without incurring an overhead. This will provide an efficient method for dealing with the occurrence of symmetry, without requiring user input.

J. Lee (Ed.): CP 2011, LNCS 6876, pp. 729–743, 2011.
© Springer-Verlag Berlin Heidelberg 2011

The symmetry breaking method considered here is the addition of constraints to the CSP, which exclude some or all symmetric equivalents. The focus of this paper is to find a small subset of symmetry breaking constraints, the placing of which has negligible effect on the solver; yet that efficiently excludes a large proportion of the symmetrically equivalent search space.

In the next section of the paper we discuss the previous work in the area of symmetry exclusion and in particular partial symmetry breaking. We then explain how our method choosing the set of symmetry breaking constraints to be placed. The final section of this paper provide detailed benchmarking for possible sets of symmetry breaking constraints, across multiple problems.

2   Background

Methods to eliminate symmetry in CSP fall into two broad categories: dynamic and static. Dynamic symmetry breaking methods eliminate symmetry during search. Static symmetry breaking methods eliminate symmetry before search commences. Both of these methods can add a large efficiency overhead to solving a CSP. To counter this CP practitioners have tried partial methods which eliminate only a subset of the symmetry. Partial methods have been experimented with in both the dynamic and static contexts. We will look at each of these in turn.

Symmetry Breaking During Search [4,5] is a dynamic symmetry elimination method which adds constraints on backtracking. McDonald and Smith [6] considered using a subset of the full symmetry functions which would be required for complete symmetry breaking, with SBDS to provide partial symmetry breaking. They proved that there is indeed a cross over point where by using an increased number of symmetry functions would not create the efficiency of solving the problem. The problem with dynamic symmetry breaking methods in general is that the framework to use them must be available in your solver, many modern solvers such as Gecode and Minion [3,7] do not have this framework.

Static symmetry breaking methods do not require solver support. The most common static symmetry breaking method is to add constraints to the CSP. Crawford et al. [8] give a systematic method for generating symmetry breaking constraints. Definition 1 explains Crawford ordering constraints.

Definition 1. *For a variable symmetry group of size s the Crawford ordering method produces a set of $s - 1$ lex constraints that provide complete symmetry breaking. We first decide on a canonical order for the variables in the CSP, then post constraints such that this ordering is less than or equal to the permutation of the ordering by each of the symmetries. Consider the following 2×3 matrix with the symmetries that the rows and columns can be swapped independently.*

$$x_{11} \; x_{12} \; x_{13}$$
$$x_{21} \; x_{22} \; x_{23}$$

If we choose a row-wise canonical variable ordering, in this case $x_{11} x_{12} x_{13} x_{21} x_{22} x_{23}$, then we can generate 11 lex constraints to break all the symmetries. For example the constraint generated for the permutation which swaps the rows of the matrix is:

$$x_{11} x_{12} x_{13} x_{21} x_{22} x_{23} \leq_{\text{lex}} x_{21} x_{22} x_{23} x_{11} x_{12} x_{13}$$

The flaw with this complete symmetry breaking method is that if a problem has many symmetries than a large number of symmetry breaking constraints will be needed to eliminate all the symmetry. To counter this problem CP practitioners have tried placing just a small subset of these constraints. The question then arises as to which subset should be placed? This is the question we tackle in this paper.

Puget and Smith [9,10] have previously looked at this question and shown that a small subset of constraints can provide complete symmetry breaking when there is an alldifferent constraint across all the problem variables.

The constraints presented by Puget and Smith can also be simply used to create a partial symmetry breaking method on problems without alldifferent constraints, as demonstrated in Example 1. We will consider these constraints later in this paper.

Example 1. The algorithm of Puget in [9] would generate for the example in Definition 1 the set of constraints:

$$x_{11} < x_{12}, \quad x_{11} < x_{21}, \quad x_{11} < x_{22}, \quad x_{11} < x_{23}, \quad x_{12} < x_{13}$$

These constraints are generating by truncating each Crawford ordering constraint at the first index where the variables are different. These can be transformed into a partial set of symmetry breaking constraints for any CSP by weakening them to:

$$x_{11} \leq x_{12}, \quad x_{11} \leq x_{21}, \quad x_{11} \leq x_{22}, \quad x_{11} \leq x_{23}, \quad x_{12} \leq x_{13}$$

It has also been proposed in SAT and CP that using just the group generators provided by Nauty [11], after automatic symmetry detection, provide an efficient set of symmetry breaking constraints [12,13,14]. Our method often improves on the performance given by the group generators produced by Nauty. While there has been work into automatically finding the symmetries of CP problems [1,2], so far the only general symmetry breaking method is to use the generators returned by the symmetry detection method into Crawford ordering constraints.

A discussion of partial symmetry breaking would not be complete without mention of Double Lex [15,16]. Double Lex is a method of placing lexicographic constraints to provide partial symmetry breaking on matrix models of CSPs. Double Lex is a very widely used symmetry breaking method. However, it has the limitation of only working when the problem is modelled as a matrix.

3   Overview of Group Theory Required for Our Method

In this section we explain the group theory required to understand how we choose a subset of constraints. Group theory is the mathematical study of symmetry.

Stabiliser chains provide an algorithmic method of constructing a small generating set [17,18] for any group and provide the inspiration for our algorithm. The stabiliser chain relies on the concept of the point wise stabiliser. We start by giving the definition of a stabiliser.

Definition 2. *Let G be a permutation group acting on the set of points Ω. Let $\beta \in \Omega$ be any point. The stabiliser of β is the subgroup of G defined by: $Stab_G(\beta) = \{g \in G \mid \beta^g = \beta\}$, which is the set of elements in G which fixes or stabilises the point β. The stabiliser of any point in a group G is a subgroup of G. The stabiliser of a set of points, denoted $Stab_G(i, j, \ldots)$, is the elements of G which move none of the points.*

The definition of the stabiliser chain follows.

Definition 3. *Stabiliser chains are built in an recursive fashion. Given a permutation group G and a point i, the first level of the stabiliser chain is built from an element of G which represents each of the places i can be mapped to. The next level of the stabiliser chain is built from applying this same algorithm to $Stab_G(i)$, again choosing representative elements for all the places some point $j \neq i$ can be mapped to. The stabiliser chain is finished when the stabiliser generated contains only the identity element.*

Stabiliser chains, in general, collapse quickly to the subgroup containing only the identity since the order of each new stabiliser must divide the order of the stabilisers above it. The following example shows the construction of a stabiliser chain.

Example 2. Consider the group consisting of all 24 permutations of $\{1, 2, 3, 4\}$. We compute a chain of stabilisers of each point, starting arbitrarily with 1 (denoted $Stab_{S_4}(1)$). 1 can be mapped to 2 by $[2, 1, 3, 4]$, 3 by $[3, 1, 2, 4]$ and 4 by $[4, 1, 2, 3]$. These group elements form the first level of the stabiliser chain.

   The second level is generated by looking at the orbit and stabiliser of 2 in $Stab_{S_4}(1)$. In the stabiliser of 1, 2 can be mapped to both 3 and 4 by the group elements $[1, 3, 2, 4]$ and $[1, 4, 2, 3]$. We now stabilise both 1 and 2, leaving only the group elements $[1, 2, 3, 4]$ and $[1, 2, 4, 3]$. Here 3 can be mapped to 4 by the second group element, and once 1, 2 and 3 are all stabilised the only element left is the identity and the algorithm finishes.

4   Methods of Creating Subset of Symmetry Breaking Constraints

In this section we will investigate methods of generating both partial and complete sets of symmetry breaking constraints. While in general complete symmetry breaking is NP-complete, for certain groups it is polynomial and by studying these groups we hope to derive general principles. We begin by proving a simple result about Crawford ordering constraints. This result will be used in the following sections.

Definition 4. *Given a permutation p on the ordered set $S = \{x_1, \ldots, x_n\}$ other than the identity permutation, the first moved point of p is the smallest i such that $p(x_i) \neq x_i$.*

Lemma 1. *Consider any permutation p on the ordered set $V = \{x_1, \ldots, x_n\}$ which is not the identity permutation, then the Crawford ordering constraint generated by p is logically equivalent to $x_i \leq p(x_i) \wedge (x_i = p(x_i) \rightarrow C)$, where x_i is the first moved point of p and C is some constraint on the elements of V.*

Proof. The Crawford ordering constraint generated from p is the constraint $[x_1, \ldots, x_n] \leq_{lex} [p(x_1), \ldots, p(x_n)]$. Up until the first moved point of p the variables in the two arrays are identical, so have no effect. At position i, the first moved point, the theorem follows from the definition of lexicographic ordering constraints, with C equal to the constraint $[x_{i+1}, \ldots, x_n] \leq_{lex} [p(x_{i+1}), \ldots, p(n)]$. $\qquad \square$

While Lemma 1 follows fairly directly from the definitions of the Crawford ordering and lexicographic ordering constraints, it is useful when analysing subsets of Crawford ordering constraints. In the next section we will show how important the first moved point is in generating good sets of partial symmetry breaking constraints.

4.1   Analysing the Complete Symmetry Group

The complete, or symmetric, group is the group which contains all permutations on some set. There are many problems which have the complete group of variable symmetries. There are already known methods of achieving complete symmetry breaking for the complete group. In this section we will produce a dichotomy which tells us all subsets of permutations which lead to sets of Crawford ordering constraints which break all symmetries.

Theorem 1. *Given a subset S of the complete symmetry group G on the set $\{x_1, \ldots, x_n\}$, the Crawford ordering constraints generated by S with the ordering $x_1, \ldots, x_n$ will be complete symmetry breaking constraints for G if and only if:*

$$\forall i \in \{1, \ldots, n-1\}. \, \exists p \in S. \, (p(x_i) = x_{i+1} \wedge \forall j \in \{1, \ldots, i-1\}. \, p(x_j) = x_j)$$

Proof. We will perform this proof in two parts. Firstly by Lemma 1 a permutation where $p(x_i) = x_{i+1} \wedge \forall j \in \{1, \ldots, i-1\}. \, p(x_j) = x_j$ implies $x_i \leq x_{i+1}$. Therefore these constraints together imply that any assignment to the x_i must be non-decreasing, which leads to complete symmetry breaking.

Now consider any permutation q where for some fixed c:

$$q(x_c) = x_{c+1} \wedge (\forall j \in \{1, \ldots, c-1\}. \, q(x_j) = x_j)$$

does not hold. Then by Lemma 1, the Crawford ordering constraint generated by this permutation is equivalent to $x_r \leq x_s \wedge (x_r = x_s \rightarrow C)$, where either $r \neq c$ or $s \neq c+1$.

Consider the assignment where $x_i = i$ for all i, and the assignment where $x_i = i$ for all i, except x_c is assigned $c + 1$ and x_{c+1} is assigned c. Both of these assignments are accepted by the Crawford ordering constraint generated from q, as both satisfy the constraint $x_r < x_s$ for all $r < s$, except in the case $r = c, s = c + 1$.

This implies that if there is any c where no permutation in S satisfies $q(x_c) = x_{c+1} \wedge \forall j \in \{1, \ldots, c-1\}. q(x_j) = x_j$, then the Crawford ordering constraints generated from S cannot break all symmetry.   □

Theorem 1 describes all sets of permutations which lead to a complete set of symmetry breaking constraints for the symmetric group. We can deduce some interesting properties from the requirements of Theorem 1.

Theorem 1 requires permutations which fix the first i variables of the ordering used for the Crawford ordering. Such permutations are generated by stabiliser-chain based algorithms, as these begin by looking for permutations which fix as many points as possible, in the order given to the algorithm. Such algorithms are unlikely to arise when chose at random. In particular, any set of permutations whose Crawford ordering constraints break all symmetry must include the permutation which fixes all but the last two variables.

While in general we cannot find a polynomial-sized set of permutations which break all symmetry, Theorem 1 suggests we should investigate sets which contain permutations which fix many initial points, even when these form a very small part of the full group.

4.2   Generating Stabiliser Chains

We introduced the concept of a stabiliser chain in Section 3. Nauty [11] and other graph-theoretic systems generate a stabiliser chain for a group. Permutations in a stabiliser chain for a group, form a set of generators for that group. Stabiliser chains also have many other useful properties. In this section we shall analyse the Crawford ordering constraints the permutations from stabiliser chains generate.

Algorithm 1 shows a very basic outline of an algorithm for finding stabiliser chains (in . Example 2 shows this algorithm in practice with no optimisations. Algorithms similar to this basic form are used by Nauty, GAP and other group-theoretic systems. Most of the complication of the algorithm occurs in line 5, where the majority of the work is done.

Algorithm 1. Generate Stabiliser Chain: $sc(G)$

Require: A group G defined over the points $[x_1, \ldots, x_n]$
1: Initialize $Gens$: Stabiliser chain for G
2: **for all** i in $[n, \ldots, 1]$ **do**
3:     **for all** j in $[n, \ldots, i+1]$ **do**
4:         **if** Optimisation Check Fails **then**
5:             **if** $\exists g \in G. (\forall k \in \{1, \ldots, i-1\}. g(x_k) = x_k) \wedge g(x_i) = x_j$ **then**
6:                 Record g as the permutation mapping x_i to x_j
7: **return** $Gens$

The interesting part for this paper is the optimisation function used to skip parts of search when some permutations have been found. These algorithms ensure that we find a complete set of generators for the group, while skipping parts of the search space.

In this paper we will consider two possible optimisation conditions, given in Definition 5. The **Nauty** optimisation condition is one of the techniques used by Nauty, Saucy and GAP. The **reduced** optimisation condition is the one we will be most interested in here. As the **reduced** optimisation condition is logically weaker than the **Nauty** condition, we do not have to prove that it is valid to use it to reduce search when searching for stabiliser chains. It should be noted that the set of constraints produced by the **Nauty** condition is always a subset of the subset of constraints obtained from the **Reduced** condition.

Definition 5.
*The **Nauty** optimisation condition for line 4 of Algorithm 1 is:*

$$\exists k.\ i \le k < j \text{ and a permutation mapping } x_k \text{ to } x_j \text{ was already found}$$

*The **Reduced** optimisation condition is:*

$$\exists k.\ i < k < j \text{ and a permutation mapping } x_k \text{ to } x_j \text{ was already found}$$

The reduced optimisation condition will produce a larger set of generators. These generators have the property that the Crawford ordering constraints generated from these permutations subsume the binary $\le$ constraints generated by Puget's algorithm, as given in Example 1.

Theorem 2. *Given a set of generators S for a group G on an ordered list $[x_1, \ldots, x_n]$ generated by Algorithm 1 with the **reduced** optimisation condition, the Crawford ordering constraints generated from S under the ordering $[x_1, \ldots, x_n]$ will imply $x_i \le x_j$ for every pair of variables if any of the full set of symmetry breaking constraints for G imply that constraint.*

Proof. If the Crawford ordering constraint for some $g \in G$ implies $x_i \le x_j$, then by Lemma 1, the permutation g must have smallest moved point x_i, which is moved to x_j. We shall prove that all such inequalities are implied by the Crawford ordering constraint generated from S by contradiction.

If some inequalities are not implied by the Crawford ordering constraints generated from S, consider some permutation g where the inequality $x_i \le x_j$ generated by g has the smallest possible value for $j - i$.

Now, as $g \in G$, then the algorithm would find g when looking for a permutation which mapped x_i to x_j while fixing all the x_z for $z < i$, unless this part of search was skipped over by the **reduced** optimisation condition. However in this case there must exist some k with $i < k < j$ such that a permutation mapping x_k to x_j was already found. In this situation there are two cases to consider:

1. S contains a permutation mapping x_i to x_k which fixes all $x_z, z < i$. In this case the Crawford ordering constraint generated by this permutation implies $x_i \leq x_k$ and the permutation mapping x_k to x_j which caused the **reduced** optimisation condition to trigger implies the constraint $x_k \leq x_j$. These constraints together imply $x_i \leq x_j$.
2. S does not contain a permutation mapping x_i to x_k which fixes all $x_z, z < i$. Such permutations certainly exist in G, by applying the permutation which maps x_i to x_j, and the inverse of the permutation which maps x_k to x_j. Therefore permutations of this kind must have been skipped by the **reduced** optimisation condition. Then either there exists some permutation in G which implies $x_i \leq x_k$ in which case we are done, or there does not, in which case as $k - i < j - i$ our assumption that x_i and x_j were the pair where the inequality $x_i \leq x_j$ was not generated and $j - i$ was minimised is false.   □

As we know that the binary inequalities break all symmetry in the presence of all different constraints, intuitively we might expect them to do well when breaking symmetries in general. Later in our experimental section we shall test this hypothesis.

5 Experimental Results

In this section we will compare a number of methods of generating both partial and complete sets of symmetry breaking constraints, to compare their effectiveness. In each case we automatically detect the symmetry of the problem using a variant of the algorithm given in [19] and Nauty. We consider 5 different methods:

> **Nauty:** Crawford ordering constraints created from the set of permutations generated by Nauty.
> **ArityOne:** $\leq$ constraints derived from Puget's algorithm, as in Example 1.
> **All:** Crawford ordering constraints created from all symmetries.
> **Reduced:** Crawford ordering constraints generated from our new algorithm, described as the reduced optimisation condition in Definition 5
> **Basic Stabiliser:** Crawford ordering constraints generated by running Algorithm 1 with no optimisation condition.

In order to fit our tables into a compressed space, we use a short-hand to label our results tables:

> C: The number of constraints added.
> T1: The time taken to find one solution.
> N1: The nodes taken to find one solution.
> TA: The time taken to find all solutions.
> NA: The nodes taken to find all solutions.
> S: The total number of solutions.

Due to space limitations, in some tables we use scientific notation to represent large numbers. For example, 1.3E8 is equal to 1.3×10^8.

5.1   Unconstrained Cycles

Firstly, we consider symmetry breaking in two closely related problems, the symmetric cycle and the non-symmetric cycle.

The symmetric cycle is given to Nauty as a graph on the n variables of the problem, with an edge between x_i and x_{i+1} for all i, as well as an edge between the first and last variables x_1 and x_n. This problem has $2n$ symmetries, as the variables can be rotated and also flipped, by mapping x_i to x_{n-i+1} for all i. We also consider the symmetric problem without the flip, by giving Nauty directed rather than undirected edges. There are no constraints in this problem other than the symmetry breaking constraints produced, meaning that it gives us a testbed for our method without having to worry about how the symmetry breaking constraints are interacting with the problem constraints.

The results are given in Table 1. In this problem we see the efficiency of **Nauty** in terms of the size of the generating sets it creates, with only 2 generators for the symmetric cycle and 1 generator for the non-symmetric cycle. However, these very small sets of constraints do not make good sets of symmetry breaking constraints. Our **reduced** algorithm produces 10 constraints which provide smaller times than both **Nauty** and **ArityOne** consistently.

In this problem, as in all the others, we found that the **Basic Stabiliser** method generated exactly the same sized search as the **Reduced** method, while taking longer and producing more constraints. Therefore we omit it.

Table 1. Solving the unconstrained cyclic problem. All node and solution counts given in millions. Problems specified as: "variable count . domain size". N = Not Symmetric cycle.

	ArityOne				Nauty				All				Reduced			
	C	TA	NA	S	C	TA	NA	S	C	TA	NA	S	C	TA	NA	S
10.4	9	0.6	2.6E6	1.3E6	2	1.1	6.9E6	3.4E6	19	0.3	1.1E6	0.4E6	10	0.4	1.4E6	0.6E6
11.4	10	2.7	13E6	6.5E6	2	5.4	34E6	17E6	21	1.3	4.9E6	2.2E6	10	1.8	8.0E6	3.7E6
12.4	11	13	64E6	32E6	2	25	164E6	82E6	23	6.2	22E6	10E6	11	7.4	31E6	14E6
13.4	12	62	31E7	15E7	2	127	82E7	41E7	25	31	10E7	4.6E7	12	38	17E7	8.1E7
11.5	10	16	83E6	41E6	2	39	252E6	125E6	21	9.0	36E6	16E6	10	11	54E6	25E6
11.5N	10	26	142E6	71E6	1	54	362E6	181E6	10	15	73E6	32E6	10	15	73E6	32E6

5.2   Graceful Graphs

Secondly we consider symmetry breaking in the Graceful Graphs problem [20]. A labelling f of the nodes of a graph with q edges is *graceful* if f assigns each node a unique label from $\{0, 1, ..., q\}$ and when each edge xy is labelled with $|f(x)-f(y)|$, the edge labels are all different (and form a permutation of $\{1, 2, ..., q\}$). This problem has both variable and value symmetry, in this paper we will consider only the variable symmetry.

The CP model we use has variables for each node of the graph and each edge. Assigning just the node variables is sufficient to break all symmetry, and these

Table 2. Solving instances of the Graceful Graphs problem. The last 4 methods all share a node and solution count.

Graph	Nauty				Complete Methods									
					ArityOne		All		Basic Stab		Reduced			
	C	TA	NA	S	C	TA	C	TA	C	TA	C	TA	NA	S
DW4	5	7.3	1.6E6	196	7	3.2	127	3.63	12	3.5	7	3.3	767,613	88
DW5	5	2700	6.9E8	9112	9	856	199	971	15	864	9	856	2.0E8	2432
K4xP2	3	2.7	739,461	572	7	0.2	47	0.2	10	0.2	7	0.2	62,473	30
K5xP2	20	194	4.7E7	20	9	18.2	239	22.16	15	18.1	15	18.1	5.0E6	2

variables must be all different. Therefore we know that the **ArityOne** constraints are sufficient to break all symmetry. In fact, we find that the **ArityOne**, **All**, **Basic Stabiliser** and **Reduced** problems all generate an identically sized search tree. Therefore in Table 2, we give the solution and node count for each of these problems only once.

We use double-wheel and KnxP2 instances of the Graceful Graphs problem as described in [20]. In Table 2 we see that **Reduced** and **ArityOne** are comparable. This is somewhat surprising as **ArityOne** provides complete symmetry breaking with less constraints then **Reduced**. The **Nauty** constraints perform quite poorly on this problem.

5.3   BIBD

The balanced incomplete block design problem is a commonly used problem to study symmetry breaking in constraint programming. A *balanced incomplete block design* (BIBD) [21] is a $v \times b$ Boolean matrix, with the columns summing to k, the rows summing to r, and exactly λ positions where two rows both have a 1, for any pair of rows.

Given a (non-) solution to a BIBD, it is possible to freely permute all of the rows of the matrix to get other (non-) solutions, and it is also possible to freely reorder the rows. Thus this problem has *row and column symmetry*. On this problem, it was not possible to generate the Crawford ordering constraints for the whole symmetry group, and the results for the ArityOne constraints timed out.

Our results for the BIBD are given in Table 3. In this particular problem, we note that all methods generate the same sized search space. Section 5.4 shows that this is not a characteristic of all problems involving row and column symmetry, even on domain size 2. As the **reduced** method generates more constraints, it is slightly slower on this problem.

It is interesting to note that the Crawford ordering constraints generated by Nauty for this, and other, problems with a two dimensional matrix with symmetries of the rows and columns is exactly the Double Lex set of constraints from [15].

Table 3. Solving BIBD models with various symmetry breaking methods

Problem	N1	NA	S	Nauty			Basic Stabiliser			Reduced		
				C	T1	TA	C	T1	TA	C	T1	TA
11,11,5,5,2	66	110	1	21	0.03	0.04	210	0.23	0.23	120	0.18	0.17
13,13,4,1,1	105	815	8	24	0.06	0.06	300	0.57	0.55	168	0.38	0.40
16,16,6,6,2	323	78,842	252	30	0.12	0.82	465	1.73	2.48	255	1.03	1.91
7,35,15,3,5	341	600,598	64,601	40	0.04	3.21	820	0.90	4.87	244	0.40	3.97
8,28,14,4,6	2955	1.8E7	2.0E6	34	0.05	123	595	0.73	137	223	0.42	132
7,49,21,3,7	778	3.2E7	2.2E6	54	0.06	194	1485	2.15	274	342	0.80	215
7,56,24,3,8	1107	1.7E8	1.0E7	61	0.08	1079	1891	3.02	1659	391	1.04	1231

5.4   Plain Row and Column Symmetry

To further investigate row and column symmetries, we tested finding all solutions to a problem with no constraints, placing only symmetry breaking constraints for row and column symmetries.

Table 4 summarises the results for this problem. Here we can see that the **Reduced** method produces both a smaller search and faster time than either the **Nauty** or **ArityOne** method. While generating **All** symmetry breaking constraints produces a smaller search, the time taken to solver the problem is much longer. As in the BIBD problem, the constraints generated by the **Nauty** method is the set of constraints commonly referred to as Double Lex. So on this problem the **Reduced** method outperforms Double Lex.

Table 4. Solving the unconstrained problem with row and column symmetries. Time limit one hour.

	ArityOne				All				Nauty				Reduced			
	C	TA	NA	S	C	TA	NA	S	C	TA	NA	S	C	TA	NA	S
2x5 D8	9	5.5	31E6	15E6	239	6.2	10E6	5E6	5	3.8	22E6	11E6	9	2.3	12E6	6.1E6
2x5 D10	9	40.6	23E7	11E7	239	51	9.3E7	4.5E7	5	30	18E7	9.4E7	9	19.7	10E7	5.2E7
3x3 D10	8	18	10E7	5.1E7	35	13	5.6E7	2.7E7	4	15	10E7	5.0E7	8	12	6.8E7	3.4E7
3x3 D4	14	9.0	47E6	23E6	719	6.3	3.5E6	1.7E6	6	1.4	8.4E6	4.2E6	14	1.3	6.1E6	3.0E6
4x4 D4	15	41	214E6	107E6	575	22	16E6	7.8E6	6	13	84E6	42E6	15	10	49E6	24E6
5x5 D2	24	0.8	3.2E7	1.6E7	14,399	1.2	11,269	5,624	8	0.05	162,567	81,284	24	0.03	38,459	19,230
5x5 D3	24	-	-	-	14,399	-	-	-	8	455	2.7E9	1.3E9	24	106	4.5E8	2.2E8

5.5   Randomly Generated Sets

So far we have compared various variants of stabiliser chains, and with the exception of the **Basic Stabiliser** method, we have found methods which generate more constraints produce smaller search trees while taking longer per node. In our experiments, the **Reduced** method does consistently well. In this section we will investigate two hypothesises by the use of randomly generated sets of permutations.

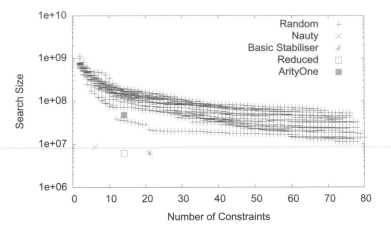

Fig. 1. Plot of solving a 3 by 5 matrix of variables with domain size 4

Firstly, we test the hypothesis that the sets of permutations we are using are better than a randomly generated set of the same size. In particular, we are not simply gaining by increasing the size of the set of permutations we use. Secondly, we test if in general a set of permutations being a generating set improves their effectiveness at symmetry breaking.

Arbitrary Random Sets. We consider one problem in depth, a 3 by 5 matrix of variables with domain size 4 and the Graceful graph problem of the "double wheel" of size 4. Figures 1 and 2 show how search size varies with the number of random constraints, compared to the specialised algorithms we have considered. These graphs clearly show how much our algorithms out-perform a random set of constraints. This shows that the **Reduced** method of generating constraints,is far better than just picking the same number of constraints at random.

Random sets of Generators. Set of generators are used to express groups compactly, and therefore it makes intuitive sense that they may make good sets of permutations to generate Crawford ordering constraints. We will investigate this intuition in this section.

There are two classes of generators we can consider, minimal and non-minimal. Non-minimal sets of generators are any set of permutations which generate the group in question. A minimal set of generators is the smallest number of generators needed to generate a group.

Random sets of constraints are very likely to be sets of generators for most groups. For example, in the 3 by 5 matrix problem given in Section 5.5, by experimentation we find over 91% of random sets of permutations of size 6 and 98% of random sets of permutations of size 8 are generating sets. This means that Figures 1 and 2 can be also be used as a comparison of random sets of generators, as well as random sets of permutations. Therefore the same results as Section 5.5 applies to generators – random sets of generators do not perform well as symmetry breaking constraints.

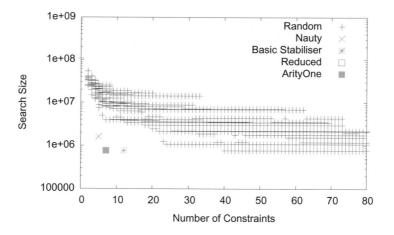

Fig. 2. Plot of solving the DW4 Graceful Graph instance

We shall consider in this section the issue of minimal sets of generators. In particular, we will study if a minimal set of generators produces better Crawford ordering constraints than an arbitrary set of permutations of the same size.

For each problem in Table 5, we created one thousand random sets of minimal generators. Then we created one thousand sets of random permutations of the same size as the minimal generating set. We then found all solutions for each of these pairs and compared how often an arbitrary random set won over a minimal generating set.

Table 5 shows the average and minimum performances, and also compares on each of the thousand runs which of the two methods was fastest. We can see there is no benefit to considering a set of random generators over an arbitrary random set of permutations. This table also shows the sizes these minimal generating sets took. We can see the range of sizes is very small, even when generating a thousand generating sets. Further, these algorithms performed extremely poorly when compared to the **Reduced** algorithm described in this paper. The experiments in Table 5 are a BIBD, a problem with no constraints & row and column symmetry and anna.col, a graph colouring problem from the Stanford Graphbase.

This section, and the previous one, show two important results. Firstly random sets of permutations form poor sets of symmetry breaking constraints, so the

Table 5. Solving problems with 1,000 randomly generated sets of minimal generators

Problem	Sizes	Average Nodes		Minimum		Wins		Nodes
		Gen	Any	Gen	Any	Gen	Any	Reduced
7,7,3,3,1 BIBD	2,3	112264	112056	39031	55837	500	500	23
3x5 D3	2,3,4	8,780,000	8,800,000	2,119,322	2,782,488	508	492	104,129
Anna.col	16	21,485,800	21,489,100	11,471,047	11,789,567	494	506	5,122,183

effort of defining particular subsets is worthwhile. Further, it is not important that the specialised sets of permutations we generate are generators, as in general generators perform no better than an arbitrary set of permutations.

6   Conclusion

The focus of this paper was to find a small reliable set of partial symmetry breaking constraints, which will work to efficiently eliminate symmetry for any problem modelled in any manner. To that end we have introduced the **Reduced** method of generating a set of partial symmetry breaking constraints. We have shown that in practice this method generates slightly more constraints than just using the generators produced by Nauty as the basis for constraints. Although, both methods are based on the stabiliser chain method. However, this slight increase in the number of constraints produced by the **Reduced** method, actually provides more efficient symmetry breaking than the Nauty based constraints. We have also shown that the **Reduced** method produces more constraints than Double Lex does, but again these constraints can provide more efficient symmetry breaking. In our BIBD experiment, where this was not the case, the two methods are comparable. Further, the **Reduced** method also outperforms a randomly chosen set of symmetry breaking constraints.

We have improved the understanding of small sets of symmetry breaking constraints. We show that **Nauty**, the method generally used in the past because of it's simplicity, is competitive, but not because it is a set of generators. We show strong evidence it is fixing many variables early in the variable ordering, rather than being generator sets, which make stabiliser chain based algorithms so effective at generating good sets of partial symmetry breaking constraints.

In general, we feel that the **Reduced** method is a very reliable way of providing a small set of partial symmetry breaking constraints, which perform well across a range of problems.

Acknowledgments. The authors wish to acknowledge that Dr Petrie is supported by a Royal Society Dorothy Hodgkins Research Fellow and Dr Jefferson by EPSRC grant number EP/H004092/1.

References

1. Puget, J.-F.: Automatic detection of variable and value symmetries. In: van Beek, P. (ed.) CP 2005. LNCS, vol. 3709, pp. 475–489. Springer, Heidelberg (2005)
2. Demoen, B., de la Banda, M.G., Mears, C., Wallace, M.: A novel approach for detecting symmetries in csp models. In: Proc. of The Seventh Intl. Workshop on Symmetry and Constraint Satisfaction Problems (2007)
3. Gent, I.P., Jefferson, C., Miguel, I.: Minion: A fast scalable constraint solver. In: Brewka, G., Coradeschi, S., Perini, A., Traverso, P. (eds.) Conf. ECAI 2006, pp. 98–102. IOS Press, Amsterdam (2006)
4. Gent, I.P., Smith, B.M.: Symmetry breaking in constraint programming. In: Proceedings of the 14th European Conference on Artificial Intelligence, ECAI 2000, Berlin, Germany, August 20-25, pp. 599–603. IOS Press, Amsterdam (2000)

5. Bjäreland, M., Jonsson, P.: Exploiting bipartiteness to identify yet another tractable subclass of CSP. In: Jaffar, J. (ed.) CP 1999. LNCS, vol. 1713, pp. 118–128. Springer, Heidelberg (1999)
6. McDonald, I., Smith, B.: Partial symmetry breaking. In: Van Hentenryck, P. (ed.) CP 2002. LNCS, vol. 2470, pp. 431–445. Springer, Heidelberg (2002)
7. Gecode Team: Gecode: Generic constraint development environment (2006), http://www.gecode.org
8. Crawford, J., Ginsberg, M., Luks, E., Roy, A.: Symmetry-breaking predicates for search problems. In: Proc. of the Intl. Conference Principles of Knowledge Representation and Reasoning, pp. 148–159 (1996)
9. Puget, J.F.: Breaking symmetries in all different problems. In: Proceedings of the 19th International Joint Conference on Artificial Intelligence, pp. 272–277. Morgan Kaufmann Publishers Inc., San Francisco (2005)
10. Smith, B.M.: Sets of symmetry breaking constraints. In: Proc. Symcon, Agaoka (2005)
11. McKay, B.: Practical graph isomorphism. In: Numerical Mathematics and Computing, Proc. 10th Manitoba Conf., Winnipeg/Manitoba 1980, Congr. Numerantium, vol. 30, pp. 45–87 (1981), http://cs.anu.edu.au/people/bdm/nauty
12. Aloul, F.A., Sakallah, K.A., Markov, I.L.: Efficient symmetry breaking for boolean satisfiability. IEEE Transactions on Computers, 271–276 (2003)
13. Aloul, F., Ramani, A., Markov, I., Sakallah, K.: Solving difficult sat instances in the presence of symmetries. In: Proceedings of the Design Automation Conference, pp. 731–736 (2002)
14. Katsirelos, G., Narodytska, N., Walsh, T.: Breaking generator symmetry. In: The Ninth International Workshop on Symmetry and Constraint Satisfaction Problems (2009)
15. Flener, P., Frisch, A.M., Hnich, B., Kiziltan, Z., Miguel, I., Pearson, J., Walsh, T.: Breaking row and column symmetries in matrix models (2002)
16. Katsirelos, G., Narodytska, N., Walsh, T.: On the complexity and completeness of static constraints for breaking row and column symmetry. In: Cohen, D. (ed.) CP 2010. LNCS, vol. 6308, pp. 305–320. Springer, Heidelberg (2010)
17. Jerrum, M.: A compact presentation for permutation groups. J. Algorithms 7, 71–90 (2002)
18. Seress, A.: Permutation group algorithms. Cambridge tracts in mathematics, vol. (152). Cambridge University Press, Cambridge (2002)
19. Mears, C., De La Banda, M.G., Wallace, M.: On implementing symmetry detection. Constraints 14, 443–477 (2009)
20. Petrie, K.E., Smith, B.M.: Symmetry breaking in graceful graphs. In: Rossi, F. (ed.) CP 2003. LNCS, vol. 2833, pp. 930–934. Springer, Heidelberg (2003)
21. Meseguer, P., Torras, C.: Solving strategies for highly symmetric csps. In: IJCAI (1999)

Beyond QCSP for Solving Control Problems

Cédric Pralet and Gérard Verfaillie

ONERA – The French Aerospace Lab, F-31055, Toulouse, France
{cedric.pralet,gerard.verfaillie}@onera.fr

Abstract. Quantified Constraint Satisfaction Problems (QCSP) are often claimed to be adapted to model and solve problems such as two-player games, planning under uncertainty, and more generally problems in which the goal is to control a dynamic system subject to uncontrolled events. This paper shows that for a quite large class of such problems, using standard QCSP or QCSP+ is not the best approach. The main reasons are that in QCSP/QCSP+, (1) the underlying notion of system state is not explicitly taken into account, (2) problems are modeled over a bounded number of steps, and (3) algorithms search for winning strategies defined as "memoryfull" policy trees instead of winning strategies defined as "memoryless" mappings from states to decisions. This paper proposes a new constraint-based framework which does not suffer from these drawbacks. Experiments show orders of magnitude improvements when compared with QCSP/QCSP+ solvers.

1 Introduction

Quantified Constraint Satisfaction Problems (QCSP [1]) were introduced to model and solve CSP involving uncertainty or uncontrollability on the value taken by some variables. From a formal point of view, a QCSP is defined by two elements: a set of constraints C, and a quantification sequence $Q = Q_1 x_1 \ldots Q_n x_n$ where each Q_i corresponds to an existential or universal quantifier ($\exists$ or $\forall$). A QCSP defined by $Q = \exists x_1 \forall x_2 \exists x_3 \forall x_4$ and $C = \{x_1 + x_3 < x_4, x_2 \neq x_1 - x_3\}$ is then to be interpreted as "Does there exist a value for x_1 such that for every value taken by x_2 there exists a value for x_3 such that for every value of x_4 constraints $x_1 + x_3 < x_4$ and $x_2 \neq x_1 - x_3$ are satisfied?". Solving a QCSP means answering yes or no to the previous question, and producing a winning strategy if the answer is yes. If $\mathbf{d}(x)$ denotes the domain of variable x and if A_x denotes the set of universally quantified variables that precede x in the quantification sequence, such a winning strategy is generally defined as a set of functions $f_x : \prod_{y \in A_x} \mathbf{d}(y) \to \mathbf{d}(x)$ (one function per existentially quantified variable x). This set of functions can be represented as a so-called *policy tree*. Various algorithms were defined in the last decade for solving QCSPs, from earlier techniques based on binary or ternary quantified arc-consistency (QAC [1,2]) or translation into quantified boolean formulas [3], to techniques based on pure value rules, n-ary quantified generalized arc consistency [4], conflict-based backjumping [5], solution repair [6], or right-left traversal of the quantification sequence [7]. Recently, an adaptation of QCSP called QCSP+ [8] was proposed to make QCSP

J. Lee (Ed.): CP 2011, LNCS 6876, pp. 744–758, 2011.

more practical from the modeling point of view. The idea in QCSP+ is to use restricted quantification sequences instead of standard quantification sequences. The former look like $\exists x_1[x_1 \geq 3] \, \forall x_2[x_2 \leq x_1] \, \exists x_3, x_4[(x_3 \neq x_4) \land (x_3 \neq x_1)] \, C$, and must be interpreted as "Does there exist a value for x_1 satisfying $x_1 \geq 3$ such that for every value of x_2 satisfying $x_2 \leq x_1$, there exists values for x_3 and x_4 satisfying $x_3 \neq x_4$ and $x_3 \neq x_1$ such that all constraints in C are satisfied?".

QCSP and QCSP+ can be used to model problems involving a few quantifier alternations such as adversary scheduling problems [8]. They can also be used to model problems involving a larger number of quantifier alternations, such as two-player games or planning under uncertainty. For two-player games, the goal is to determine a first play for player 1 such that for every play of player 2, there exists a play of player 1 such that for every play of player 2 ... player 1 wins the game. The size of the quantification sequence is fixed initially depending on the maximum number of turns considered. Planning under uncertainty can be seen as a game against nature and interpreted similarly. More generally, a large number of quantifier alternations are often useful when QCSP/QCSP+ is used to model problems of control of the state of a dynamic system subject to events.

The goal of this paper is to show that when that state is completely observable at each step and when the evolution of the current state is Markovian (i.e. the state of the system at a given step depends only on the last state and on the last event, and not on the whole history of events), then using pure QCSP/QCSP+ is (currently) not the best approach. The paper is organized as follows. We first illustrate why using pure QCSP/QCSP+ in this context is not always appropriate (Section 2). We then define a new framework called MGCSP for Markovian Game CSP (Section 3), and associated algorithms (Section 4). Experiments show orders of magnitude improvements on some standard QCSP benchmarks (Section 5). Proofs are omitted for space reasons.

2 Illustrating Example

Let us consider a QCSP benchmark called the *NimFibo* game. This game involves two players, referred to as A and B, who play alternatively. Initially, there are N matches on a table. At the first play, player A can take between 1 and N-1 matches. Then, at each turn, each player takes at least one match and at most twice the number of matches taken by the last player. The player taking the last match wins. The problem is to find a winning strategy for player A.

The QCSP/QCSP+ approach. Let us assume that N is odd. To model the Nim-Fibo game as a QCSP+, it is first possible to introduce N variables $r_1, \ldots, r_N$ of domain $[0..N]$ representing the number of matches remaining after each turn (N variables because there are at most N turns). It is also possible to introduce decision variables of domain $[1..N - 1]$ modeling the number of matches taken by each player at each turn: $a_1, a_3, \ldots, a_N$ for player A and $b_2, b_4, \ldots, b_{N-1}$ for player B. A QCSP+ modeling the NimFibo game is then:

$$\exists a_1, r_1 [r_1 = N - a_1] \, \forall b_2, r_2 [b_2 \leq 2a_1, r_2 = r_1 - b_2]$$
$$\exists a_3, r_3 [a_3 \leq 2b_2, r_3 = r_2 - a_3] \, \forall b_4, r_4 [b_4 \leq 2a_3, r_4 = r_3 - b_4] \ldots$$
$$\exists a_N, r_N [a_N \leq 2b_{N-1}, r_N = r_{N-1} - a_N] \ True$$

Figure 1(a) gives a winning strategy expressed as a policy tree for $N = 15$ matches. Nodes depicted by circles model all possible decisions of player B. Nodes depicted by squares represent decisions to be made by player A to win the game.

State-based approach. Basically, the state of the system at each step is defined by three state variables: one variable $p \in \{A, B\}$ specifying the next player, one variable $r \in [0..N]$ modeling the number of remaining matches, and one variable $l \in [1..N]$ specifying the number of matches taken by the last player. Two kinds of decisions modify the state (p, r, l): plays of player A and plays of player B, modeled respectively by decision variables a and b of domain $[1..N-1]$ representing the number of matches taken by each player at each turn. These decisions are sequentially made. Variable a is controllable by player A whereas variable b is not. The goal is to reach, whatever the plays of player B, a state such as $(B, 0, l)$ in which B cannot take any match, while ensuring that states of the form $(A, 0, l)$ in which A cannot take any match are never reached before. A solution to this control problem can be defined as a decision policy $\pi : \{(A, r, l) \mid r \in [1..N], l \in [1..N]\} \to \mathbf{d}(a)$ associating a value for a with states $s = (A, r, l)$ in which A must play and there is at least one remaining match. Policy π does not need to be specified for all states: it only needs to be specified for states which are reachable using π. A solution policy is given in Figure 1(b). Figure 1(c) gives the states which are reachable using this policy, as well as the possible transitions between states.

Comparison between the two approaches. With 15 matches, the policy tree contains 48 leaves and the decision policy contains only 19 (state,decision) pairs, although both policies induce the same sequences of states. The size ratio grows exponentially when the number of matches increases. The main reason is that the Markovian nature of the system considered together with the complete observability of the state at each step entail that the strategy encoded as a policy tree memorizes too many elements. For instance, on the reachability graph of Figure 1(c), the two sequences of plays $seq_1 : [a = 2, b = 1, a = 1, b = 1, a = 2]$ and $seq_2 : [a = 2, b = 3, a = 2]$ are equivalent because they end up in the same state, $(B, 8, 2)$. The only useful information to be taken into account to act from that state is the state itself, and not the entire trajectory used to reach it. Said differently, searching for strategies defined as "memoryfull" policy trees as in QCSP/QCSP+ is searching in a uselessly large search space, since searching for "memoryless" decision policies π is sufficient.

Second, explicitly reasoning over the notion of state enables to memorize whether a state s has already been successfully explored, which means that it has been already proved that the goal can always be reached from s. This is

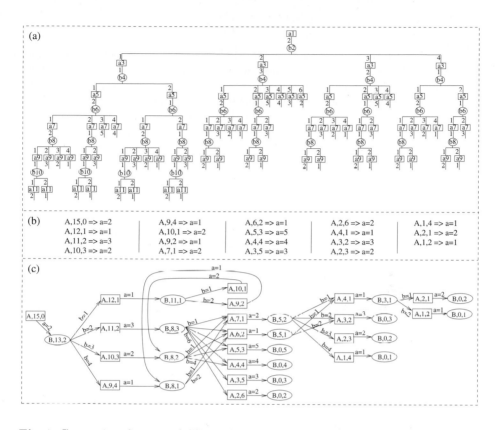

Fig. 1. Comparison between QCSP and state-based models on the NimFibo game: (a) QCSP policy tree; (b) state-based policy; (c) reachability graph using the policy

equivalent to memorizing *goods* over states. For example, when exploring reachable states of Figure 1(c), trajectories rooted in state $(B, 8, 2)$ do not need to be explored twice (once when $(B, 8, 2)$ is reached from $(A, 10, 1)$ and once when $(B, 8, 2)$ is reached from $(A, 10, 3)$). Similarly, if the exploration below state s leads to a dead-end, then s can be recorded as a nogood, potentially reused later during search to avoid exploring s again. These notions of goods and nogoods *over states* are not handled by QCSP solvers, which can only record goods and nogoods *over variables* of the unfolded model. Recording information about states already explored uses the principles of forward dynamic programming [9].

Third, the state-based approach is able to reason over unbounded horizons. It does not require the system evolutions to be unfolded over a fixed number of steps. This leads to models which are more compact than QCSP models.

For all these reasons, we believe that there is a need to introduce a new constraint-based framework based explicitly on the notion of state, in order to efficiently model and solve control problems for completely observable and Markovian dynamic systems.

3   Markovian Game-CSP (MGCSP)

In the following, S denotes the set of variables describing the system state. State variables used here differ from those used in Strategic CSP [10]. Every assignment $s \in \mathbf{d}(S)$ is called a state (given an ordered set of variables X, $\mathbf{d}(X)$ denotes the Cartesian product of the domains of the variables in X). We consider two additional sets of variables denoted C and U respectively, corresponding to the decision made by the $\exists$-player (resp. the $\forall$-player) at each decision step. Every assignment $c \in \mathbf{d}(C)$ (resp. $u \in \mathbf{d}(U)$) is called a controllable (resp. uncontrollable) decision.

3.1   Control Model

To represent the possible initial and final states, we use a relation $I \subseteq \mathbf{d}(S)$ ("init") and a relation $E \subseteq \mathbf{d}(S)$ ("end"). To represent that some decisions $c \in \mathbf{d}(C)$ (resp. $u \in \mathbf{d}(U)$) cannot be made in some states, due to game rules or to physical constraints, we use a relation $F_c \subseteq \mathbf{d}(S) \times \mathbf{d}(C)$ (resp. $F_u \subseteq \mathbf{d}(S) \times \mathbf{d}(U)$) called feasibility relation such that $F_c(s, c)$ (resp. $F_u(s, u)$) holds iff making decision c (resp. u) is possible in state s. The state evolution scheme is defined by a transition function $T_c : \mathbf{d}(S) \times \mathbf{d}(C) \to \mathbf{d}(S)$ (resp. $T_u : \mathbf{d}(S) \times \mathbf{d}(U) \to \mathbf{d}(S)$), such that $s' = T_c(s, c)$ (resp. $s' = T_u(s, u)$) means that s' is the state resulting from the application of decision c (resp. u) in state s.

Three assumptions are made to guarantee that system evolutions cannot be blocked: first, there exists at least one possible initial state s, that is one state such that $I(s) = true$; second, for every state s which is not terminal ($E(s) = false$), there exists at least one feasible decision c (resp. u), that is one decision such that $F_c(s, c) = true$ (resp. $F_u(s, u) = true$); third, for every state s which is not terminal and every decision c (resp. u) feasible in s, $T_c(s, c)$ (resp. $T_u(s, u)$) is defined; it may be undefined for infeasible decisions. These three assumptions are actually undemanding: if the first assumption is violated, then it is obvious that the goal cannot be reached; if the second assumption is violated, it suffices to add a dummy value for every variable in C (resp. U) to guarantee that at least doing nothing is always feasible; if the third assumption does not hold, then feasibility relation F_c (resp. F_u) can be strengthened by considering as infeasible decisions that induce no successor state. Relations I, E, F_c, F_u, T_c, and T_u are expressed by sets of constraints. All previous elements are gathered in the notion of Markovian Game CSP.

Definition 1. *A Markovian Game Constraint Satisfaction Problem (MGCSP) is a tuple $M = (S, I, E, C, U, F_c, T_c, F_u, T_u)$ with:*

- *S a finite set of finite domain variables called* state variables;
- *I a finite set of constraints over S called* initialization constraints;
- *E a finite set of constraints over S called* termination constraints;
- *C a finite set of finite domain variables called* controllable variables
- *U a finite set of finite domain variables called* uncontrollable variables;

– F_c and F_u finite sets of constraints over $S \cup C$ and $S \cup U$ respectively, called feasibility constraints;
– T_c and T_u finite sets of constraints over $S \cup C \cup S'$ and $S \cup U \cup S'$ respectively, called transition constraints;
– $\exists s \in \mathbf{d}(S),\ I(s)$;
– $\forall s \in \mathbf{d}(S),\ \neg E(s) \rightarrow ((\exists c \in \mathbf{d}(C),\ F_c(s, c)) \wedge (\exists u \in \mathbf{d}(U),\ F_u(s, u)))$;
– $\forall s \in \mathbf{d}(S),\ \neg E(s) \rightarrow ((\forall c \in \mathbf{d}(C),\ F_c(s, c) \rightarrow (\exists! s' \in \mathbf{d}(S),\ T_c(s, c, s'))) \wedge (\forall u \in \mathbf{d}(U),\ F_u(s, u) \rightarrow (\exists! s' \in \mathbf{d}(S),\ T_u(s, u, s'))))$ ("$\exists!$" stands for "there exists a unique").

To illustrate the framework, consider the NimFibo game again. In this example, the set of state variables S contains variables p, r, and l defined previously, representing respectively the next player (value in $\{A, B\}$), the number of remaining matches (value in $[0..N]$), and the number of matches taken at the last play (value in $[1..N]$). Set C (resp. U) contains a unique variable a (resp. b) of domain $[1..N-1]$ representing the number of matches taken by player A (resp. B). The different constraint sets are given below. I expresses that initially, there are N matches and variable l is assigned a default arbitrary value (since there is no last play). E expresses that the game ends when there is no match left. F_c and F_u express that at each step, a player can take at most twice the number of matches taken by the last player. T_c and T_u define the transition function of the system: e.g., the number of remaining matches r' is decreased by the number of matches taken (given a variable x, x' denotes the value of x at the next step).

$I : (p = A) \wedge (r = N) \wedge (l = N)$ $\qquad$ $E : (r = 0)$
$F_c : (a \leq r) \wedge (a \leq 2 \cdot l)$ $\qquad$ $F_u : (b \leq r) \wedge (b \leq 2 \cdot l)$
$T_c : (p' = B) \wedge (r' = r - a) \wedge (l' = a)$ $\quad$ $T_u : (p' = A) \wedge (r' = r - b) \wedge (l' = b)$

3.2   Reachability Control Problems

A MGCSP describes the dynamics of the system considered and induces a set of possible trajectories.

Definition 2. *Let $M = (S, I, E, C, U, F_c, T_c, F_u, T_u)$ be a MGCSP. The set of trajectories induced by M is the set of (possibly infinite) sequences of state transitions* $seq : s_1 \xrightarrow{c_1} s_2 \xrightarrow{u_2} s_3 \xrightarrow{c_3} s_4 \xrightarrow{u_4} s_5 \cdots$ *such that:*

– *$I(s_1)$ holds, and for every state s_i which is not the last state of the sequence, $E(s_i)$ does not hold (s_i is not terminal),*
– *for every transition $s_i \xrightarrow{c_i} s_{i+1}$ in seq, $F_c(s_i, c_i)$ and $T_c(s_i, c_i, s_{i+1})$ hold,*
– *for every transition $s_i \xrightarrow{u_i} s_{i+1}$ in seq, $F_u(s_i, u_i)$ and $T_u(s_i, u_i, s_{i+1})$ hold.*

In order to control the system and restrict its possible evolutions, we use so-called *decision policies* π, which are mappings from states $s \in \mathbf{d}(S)$ to decisions $c \in \mathbf{d}(C)$. $\pi(s) = c$ means that decision c is made when state s is encountered. Such a decision policy can be partial in the sense that $\pi(s)$ may be undefined for some states $s \in \mathbf{d}(S)$. Partial policies are useful to define the controller behavior only over the set of reachable states of the system. We are also interested in applicable policies, which have the particularity to specify only feasible decisions. These elements are formalized below.

Definition 3. *A policy for a MGCSP* $M = (S, I, E, C, U, F_c, T_c, F_u, T_u)$ *is a partial function* $\pi : \mathbf{d}(S) \to \mathbf{d}(C)$. *The domain of a policy* π *is defined as* $\mathbf{d}(\pi) = \{s \in \mathbf{d}(S) \mid \pi(s) \text{ defined}\}$.

The set of trajectories induced by π *is the set of trajectories for* M *of the form* $s_1 \xrightarrow{c_1} s_2 \xrightarrow{u_2} s_3 \xrightarrow{c_3} s_4 \xrightarrow{u_4} s_5 \cdots \xrightarrow{u_{i-1}} s_i$ *obtained by following* π, *i.e. such that* $c_j = \pi(s_j)$ *for every transition* $s_j \xrightarrow{c_j} s_{j+1}$ *in the sequence. The trajectory is said to be complete if it is infinite or if* $s_i \notin \mathbf{d}(\pi)$.

π *is said to be applicable iff for every trajectory* $s_1 \xrightarrow{c_1} s_2 \xrightarrow{u_2} s_3 \xrightarrow{c_3} s_4 \xrightarrow{u_4} s_5 \cdots \xrightarrow{u_{i-1}} s_i$ *induced by* π, *either* $s_i \notin \mathbf{d}(\pi)$, *or* $s_i \in \mathbf{d}(\pi)$ *and* $F_c(s_i, \pi(s_i))$ *(i.e. the policy specifies decisions which are feasible).*

Several requirements can be imposed on system-state trajectories. We focus here on *reachability* requirements, imposing to find an applicable policy π so that all trajectories induced by π satisfy a given condition at some step.

Definition 4. *A reachability control problem is a pair* (M, G) *with* M *a MGCSP over a set of state variables* S, *and* G *a finite set of constraints over* S *called goal constraints. A solution to this problem is an applicable policy* π *for* M *such that all complete trajectories* $s_1 \xrightarrow{c_1} s_2 \xrightarrow{u_2} s_3 \xrightarrow{c_3} s_4 \xrightarrow{u_4} s_5 \cdots$ *induced by* π *are finite and end in a state* s_n *such that* $G(s_n)$ *holds.*

The NimFibo problem corresponds to reachability control problem (M, G) with M the MGCSP defined in Section 3.1 and $G : (p = B) \wedge (r = 0)$ (requirement of reaching a state in which there is no match left and B must play). A possible solution policy π for $N = 15$ is given in Figure 1(b).

3.3   Relationship with QCSP/QCSP+

To relate QCSP and reachability control problems (M, G), let us consider the following QCSP+, which could be put in prenex normal form:

$$Q_N(M, G) : \forall S_1 [I(S_1)]$$
$$G(S_1) \vee (\neg E(S_1) \wedge \exists C_1, S_2 [F_c(S_1, C_1) \wedge T_c(S_1, C_1, S_2)]$$
$$G(S_2) \vee (\neg E(S_2) \wedge \forall U_2, S_3 [F_u(S_2, U_2) \wedge T_u(S_2, U_2, S_3)]$$
$$G(S_3) \vee (\neg E(S_3) \wedge \exists C_3, S_4 [F_c(S_3, C_3) \wedge T_c(S_3, C_3, S_4)]$$ \hfill (1)
$$G(S_4) \vee (\neg E(S_4) \wedge \forall U_4, S_5 [F_u(S_4, U_4) \wedge T_u(S_4, U_4, S_5)]$$
$$\dots$$
$$G(S_{N-1}) \vee (\neg E(S_{N-1}) \wedge \exists C_{N-1}, S_N [F_c(S_{N-1}, C_{N-1}) \wedge T_c(S_{N-1}, C_{N-1}, S_N)]$$
$$G(S_N))\dots))))$$

$Q_N(M, G)$ can be read as: "Does it hold that for every possible initial state s_1, either $G(s_1)$ is satisfied, or s_1 is not terminal and there exists a feasible decision

c_1 inducing successor state s_2 such that either the goal is reached in s_2, or s_2 is not a terminal state and for every feasible decision u_2, inducing successor state s_3, either the goal is reached in s_3 or s_3 is not terminal and there exists a feasible decision c_3 ... such that either $G(s_{N-1})$ holds or s_{N-1} is not terminal and there exists a feasible decision c_{N-1} inducing a state s_N satisfying the goal?".

Proposition 1. *There exists a winning strategy for QCSP $Q_N(M,G)$ given in Equation 1 if and only if there exists a solution policy $\pi : \mathbf{d}(S) \to \mathbf{d}(C)$ for reachability control problem (M,G) such that all complete trajectories induced by π have less than N steps.*

Proposition 1 implies that if a QCSP can be put in a form similar to $Q_N(M,G)$, in which the notion of state is made explicit, then searching for a solution policy for (M,G) suffices to solve the initial QCSP. However, there may exist a solution policy for (M,G) and no winning strategy for $Q_N(M,G)$ because $Q_N(M,G)$ models a control problem over a *bounded* horizon. It is possible to take N high enough, for instance equal to the number of possible states $(N = |\mathbf{d}(S)|)$. But as $|\mathbf{d}(S)|$ can be huge and as the number of variables and constraints in $Q_N(M,G)$ is linear in N, this approach may not be practically applicable. The problem does not arise with the MGCSP approach in which we just describe the transition function of the system instead of unfolding the model. In another direction, Proposition 1 can be seen as a counterpart of a property of Markov Decision Processes (MDPs [11]) stating that every MDP has an optimal policy which is stationary.

Next, in terms of space needed to record a winning strategy, the size of policies can be exponentially smaller than the size of policy trees, which can be useful when embedding a controller on-board an autonomous system having limited memory. More precisely, if R_π denotes the set of states reachable using π, policy π can be recorded as a table contains $|R_\pi|$ (s,c) pairs. On the other hand, let W be an equivalent winning strategy for $Q_N(M,G)$, that is a winning strategy inducing the same trajectories as π. Strategy W expressed as a policy tree may contain $|\mathbf{d}(U)|^{N/2}$ leaves, which is exponential in N, and which can be shown to be always greater than or equal to $|R_\pi|$.

A last remark concerns the semantics of the notion of goal. In QCSP, goal constraints are specified just after the rightmost quantifier in the quantification sequence. But there may exist winning strategies which never reach the goal: these strategies instead block the adversary at some step. In MGCSPs, the goal is guaranteed to be reached along every trajectory. Both notions of goal are however equivalent here due to the assumption of existence of a feasible decision in every non-terminal state, which ensures that no blocking can occur in $Q_N(M,G)$.

4   Algorithm

The algorithm proposed for solving reachability control problems over MGCSP is inspired by techniques for planning in non-deterministic domains [12]. One difference is the use of constraint programming to reason over the different relations.

General description. The algorithm is composed of three functions:

- **reachMGCSP**, responsible for exploring the different initial states,
- **exploreC**, responsible for exploring the different feasible controllable decisions $c \in \mathbf{d}(C)$ in a current s,
- **exploreU**, responsible to do the same for uncontrollable decisions $u \in \mathbf{d}(U)$.

Search behaves as an And/Or search in which Or nodes correspond to decisions in C and And nodes to decisions in U. The search space is explored in a depth-first manner, and only states which are reachable from initial states are considered.

During search, the algorithm maintains a current policy π. It also associates, with each state s, a mark $Mark(s)$ in $\{SOLVED, BAD, PROCESSING, NONE\}$. Mark $SOLVED$ means that state s has already been visited during search and there already exists in current policy π a recipe to reach the goal starting from s. Mark BAD means that there does not exist any solution policy starting from s. Mark $PROCESSING$ is associated with states on the trajectory currently explored. Mark $NONE$, which is not explicitly stored, is associated with all other states. In the implementation, state marks are recorded in a hash table, which is empty initially (all marks set to $NONE$).

A specificity of the algorithm concerns the handling of loops. A loop is a situation in which a state marked $PROCESSING$ is encountered again. When a loop is detected and the goal has not been reached yet, this means that the adversary has a way to generate an infinite loopy trajectory in which the goal is never reached. For example, assume that Figure 2 represents the set of feasible trajectories of a system. Trajectories $seq_1 : s_a \xrightarrow{c:0} s_b \xrightarrow{u:0} s_c \xrightarrow{c:0} s_d \xrightarrow{u:1} s_e \xrightarrow{c:0} s_b$ and $seq_2 : s_a \xrightarrow{c:0} s_b \xrightarrow{u:0} s_c \xrightarrow{c:0} s_d \xrightarrow{u:1} s_e \xrightarrow{c:1} s_d$ respectively loop over s_b and s_d. Therefore, trajectory $seq_3 : s_a \xrightarrow{c:0} s_b \xrightarrow{u:0} s_c \xrightarrow{c:0} s_d \xrightarrow{u:1} s_e$ cannot be extended to a solution. Set $J = \{s_b, s_d\}$ is called the *loop justification* of seq_3. It corresponds to the set of past states over which loops are detected when trying to reach the goal from seq_3. The mark of s_e, the last state of seq_3, cannot however be set to BAD because loops discovered depend on decisions made before s_e. For $seq_4 : s_a \xrightarrow{c:0} s_b \xrightarrow{u:0} s_c \xrightarrow{c:0} s_d$ and $seq_5 : s_a \xrightarrow{c:0} s_b \xrightarrow{u:0} s_c$, the loop justification is $\{s_b\}$. For $seq_6 : s_a \xrightarrow{c:0} s_b$, the loop justification is empty ($J = \varnothing$). This means that in seq_6, no state explored strictly before s_b is involved in the loops discovered after s_b. The mark of s_b can then be set to BAD. More generally, a state whose exploration does not succeed can be marked as BAD if the current loop justification is empty.

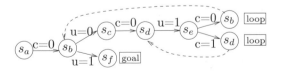

Fig. 2. Behavior of algorithm **reachMGCSP** in face of loops

Pseudo-code. Main function **reachMGCSP** takes as input a MGCSP M and a set of goal constraints G. It returns $(true, \pi)$ if M admits a solution policy π, $(false, \varnothing)$ otherwise. To do that, function **reachMGCSP** starts with an empty policy and analyzes every possible initial state s, i.e. every state s satisfying the initialization constraints in I (function *getSols* used in line 6 returns the set of solutions of a CSP). Every initial state s which does not satisfy the goal and whose mark differs from $SOLVED$ is then studied. If s is terminal or has mark BAD, then the control problem has no solution and $(false, \varnothing)$ is returned (line 8). Otherwise, s is explored further using a call to function **exploreC** (line 10).

---

1 Input: a MGCSP M and a set of goal constraints G
2 Output: a pair (b, π) with b a boolean and π a policy
3 **reachMGCSP**(M, G)
4 **begin**
5 $\quad$ $\pi \leftarrow \varnothing$
6 $\quad$ **foreach** $s \in getSols(I(S))$ **do**
7 $\quad\quad$ **if** $\neg G(s) \wedge (Mark(s) \neq SOLVED)$ **then**
8 $\quad\quad\quad$ **if** $E(s) \vee (Mark(s) = BAD)$ **then** **return** $(false, \varnothing)$
9 $\quad\quad\quad$ **else**
10 $\quad\quad\quad\quad$ $(covered, \pi, .) \leftarrow$ **exploreC**(s, π)
11 $\quad\quad\quad\quad$ **if** $\neg covered$ **then** **return** $(false, \varnothing)$
12 $\quad$ **return** $(true, \pi)$

Function **exploreC**(s, π) explores the possible decisions that can be made is state s. It returns a triple (b, π', J). b specifies whether policy π given in input can be extended so that the goal can always be reached starting from s. If $b = true$, π' is the extended policy covering s. If $b = false$, J is a set of states justifying the absence of solution starting from s. J corresponds to the loop justification described previously. The first part of **exploreC** (lines 5 to 10) determines all decisions c that are feasible in state s and all associated possible successor states s', by reasoning over CSP $F_c \wedge T_c \wedge (S = s)$. If some successor state s' obtained by applying c satisfies the goal or has mark $SOLVED$, then it suffices to set $\pi(s) = c$ to cover state s. The second part of function **exploreC** (line 11 to 27) traverses the set of successor states s' to be explored further. If s' has mark $SOLVED$, then a solution is found to cover state s (line 17). Otherwise, if s' has mark $PROCESSING$, the loop justification is extended (line 19). Otherwise, if s' has mark $NONE$, it is further explored via a call to function **exploreU** (line 22). If this call returns an extended solution policy, then the mark of s is set to $SOLVED$ and the new solution policy is returned (line 23). Otherwise, the loop justification is extended (line 24). If all successor states have been explored without finding a solution, then current state s is removed from the loop justification, its mark is set to BAD if the loop justification is empty, and an inconsistency result is returned (lines 25 to 27).

Function **exploreU** behaves similarly. The only differences are as follows. In the initial phase (lines 5 to 11), search can be pruned if there exists a successor

```
1  Input: a state s and a current policy π
2  Output: a triple (b, π′, J) with b a boolean, π′ a policy, and J a set of states
3  exploreC(s, π)
4  begin
5  │   toExplore ← ∅
6  │   foreach sol ∈ getSols(F_c(S, C) ∧ T_c(S, C, S′) ∧ (S = s)) do
7  │   │   (s, c, s′) ← (sol^{↓S}, sol^{↓C}, sol^{↓S′})
8  │   │   if G(s′) ∨ (Mark(s′) = SOLVED) then
9  │   │   │   setMark(s, SOLVED); return (true, π ∪ {(s, c)}, ∅)
10 │   │   └ else if ¬E(s′) then toExplore ← toExplore ∪ {(c, s′)}
11 │   π′ ← π
12 │   setMark(s, PROCESSING)
13 │   J ← ∅
14 │   while toExplore ≠ ∅ do
15 │   │   Choose (c, s′) ∈ toExplore; toExplore ← toExplore \ {(c, s′)}
16 │   │   if Mark(s′) = SOLVED then
17 │   │   │   setMark(s, SOLVED); return (true, π′ ∪ {(s, c)}, ∅)
18 │   │   else if Mark(s′) = PROCESSING then
19 │   │   │   J ← J ∪ {s′}
20 │   │   else if Mark(s′) = NONE then
21 │   │   │   π′ ← π′ ∪ {(s, c)}
22 │   │   │   (covered, π′, J′) ← exploreU(s′, π′)
23 │   │   │   if covered then setMark(s, SOLVED); return (true, π′, ∅)
24 │   │   └ else J ← J ∪ J′; π′ ← π′ \ {(s, c)}
25 │   J ← J \ {s}
26 │   if J = ∅ then setMark(s, BAD) else setMark(s, NONE)
27 └   return (false, π′, J)
```

state s' whose mark equals BAD, or such that s' is a terminal non-goal state. An inconsistency result is also directly returned if a loop is detected. For the second phase, in which the rest of the successor states are more finely studied, if the mark of one successor state s' equals BAD, then an inconsistency result is returned (line 17). Otherwise, a call to **exploreC** is invoked, in order to develop the different possible decisions that can be made in s' (line 19).

Proposition 2. *Algorithm* **reachMGCSP** *is sound and complete: it returns* $(true, \pi)$ *with* π *a solution policy if reachability control problem* (M, G) *admits a solution, and* $(false, \varnothing)$ *otherwise.*

Algorithmic improvements. The basic algorithm can be improved on several points. First, in **exploreC**, CSP $F_c(S, C) \wedge T_c(S, C, S') \wedge G(S')$ can be considered in order to faster determine whether there exists a controllable decision c allowing the goal to be directly satisfied, instead of enumerating all solutions of $F_c \wedge T_c$ and then checking whether one of them satisfies G. Similarly, it is possible to consider, in **exploreU**, CSP $F_u(S, U) \wedge T_u(S, U, S') \wedge E(S') \wedge \neg G(S')$ to search for adversary strategies which directly lead to a non-goal terminal state.

---

1 Input: a state s and a current policy π
2 Output: a triple (b, π', J) with b a boolean, π' a policy, and J a set of states
3 **exploreU**(s, π)
4 **begin**
5     $toExplore \leftarrow \varnothing$
6   **foreach** $sol \in getSols(F_u(S, U) \wedge T_u(S, U, S') \wedge (S = s))$ **do**
7        $s' \leftarrow sol^{\downarrow S'}$
8   **if** $(E(s') \wedge \neg G(s')) \vee (Mark(s') = BAD) \vee (s = s')$ **then**
9            $setMark(s, BAD)$; **return** $(false, \pi, \varnothing)$
10   **else if** $Mark(s') = PROCESSING$ **then** **return** $(false, \pi, \{s'\})$
11   **else if** $Mark(s') - NONE$ **then** $toExplore \leftarrow toExplore \cup \{s'\}$
12     $\pi' \leftarrow \pi$
13     $setMark(s, PROCESSING)$
14   **while** $toExplore \neq \varnothing$ **do**
15   Choose $s' \in toExplore$; $toExplore \leftarrow toExplore \setminus \{s'\}$
16   **if** $Mark(s') = BAD$ **then**
17           $setMark(s, BAD)$; **return** $(false, \pi', \varnothing)$
18   **else if** $Mark(s') = NONE$ **then**
19         $(covered, \pi', J) \leftarrow$ **exploreC**(s', π')
20   **if** $\neg covered$ **then**
21            $J \leftarrow J \setminus \{s\}$
22   **if** $J = \varnothing$ **then** $setMark(s, BAD)$ **else** $setMark(s, NONE)$
23   **return** $(false, \pi', J)$
24     $setMark(s, SOLVED)$; **return** $(true, \pi', \varnothing)$

In terms of space consumption, the algorithm records marks over reachable states only. But the set of such states may be large and recording marks may become expensive. To overcome this difficulty, some state marks could be forgotten during search: the algorithm then remains valid but may re-explore some parts of the search space. This option has not been used in the experiments.

Last, we consider in the MGCSP framework that the $\exists$-player begins to play. To handle situations in which the $\forall$-player begins, it suffices to replace the call to **exploreC** in function **reachMGCSP** by a call to **exploreU**.

5 Experiments

We ran our experiments on an Intel i5-520, 1.2GHz, 4GB RAM. Maximum computation time is set to one hour. Algorithm **reachMGCSP** is implemented in *Dyncode*, a tool developed on top of constraint programming library Gecode.[1] Any constraint available in Gecode can be used in Dyncode. Dyncode was initially introduced in [13] to handle control problems involving non-determinism and partial observability. Algorithms in [13] are less efficient than dedicated algorithm **reachMGCSP** over deterministic and completely observable problems.

---

[1] http://www.gecode.org/

For the experiments, we used min-domain for the variable choice heuristics and lexicographic ordering for the value choice.

We first compared Dyncode with Qecode[2], a QCSP+ solver based on Gecode. We performed experiments on three games already encoded in the Qecode distribution: NimFibo, Connect4, and MatrixGame. Figures 3(a) to 3(c) show that on these problems, Dyncode outperforms Qecode by several orders of magnitude.

For NimFibo (Figure 3(a)), Qecode can solve problems up to 40 matches, whereas Dyncode can solve instances involving several tens of thousands of matches. The time complexity observed with Dyncode is even linear in the number of matches, whereas there is an exponential blowup with Qecode. In other words, explicitly using the notion of state and recording good/bad states encountered during search breaks the problem complexity.

Connect4 is a two-player game over a six-row × seven-column board. At each step, a player puts a token in one column of the board. This token falls at the bottom of the column by the effect of gravity. A player wins if he manages to align four of his tokens horizontally, vertically, or diagonally. The game is null if there is no alignment and the board is full. As in the Qecode distribution, we consider here that the goal is to play without losing the game over a fixed number of steps. This variant is referred to as Connect4_Bounded. Figure 3(b) shows that Dyncode solves more instances than Qecode for this game. This time, there is an exponential blowup for both solvers, but the slope of the blowup is weaker for Dyncode. The first reason is again the explicit use of the notion of state, since in Connect4, several sequences of plays can lead to the same configuration. The second point is that Qecode initially creates many variables and constraints to encode the problem over a fixed horizon. In theory, it then performs so-called *cascade propagation* over the whole problem. On the opposite, Dyncode propagates constraints just over the current state and the next state. This may achieve less pruning, but this is performed much faster. We also realized experiments with random value choice heuristics and restarts, to see the effect of search diversification. We observed that randomization in Dyncode speeds search on some executions (e.g. Connect4_Bounded for game depth equal to 25 may be solved in about 30 minutes), but that it can lead to memory problems on other executions, due to the recording of state marks.

In MatrixGame, a 0/1 matrix of size 2^d is considered. At each turn, the ∃-player cuts the matrix horizontally and decides to keep the top or bottom part. The ∀-player then cuts the matrix vertically and keeps the left or right part. After d turns, the matrix is reduced to a single cell. The ∃-player wins if this cell contains a 1. Figure 3(c) shows that Dyncode performs better for this game, whose MGCSP encoding is such that the same state is never encountered twice. We believe that Dyncode is faster because it reasons over smaller CSPs.

Dyncode was also compared with Queso, a QCSP solver which was shown in [4] to outperform other QCSP solvers such as BlockSolve or QCSP-solve. We did not rerun Queso, which is not maintained anymore, but instead directly took the results provided in [4], obtained with a Pentium 4, 3.06GHz, 1GB RAM.

---

[2] http://www.univ-orleans.fr/lifo/software/qecode

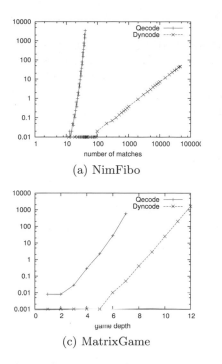

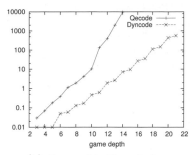

(a) NimFibo

(b) Connect4_Bounded

(c) MatrixGame

(d) Connect4_Full

Board size		CPU time (sec.)	
ncols	nrows	Queso	Dyncode
		3.06GHz,1GB RAM	1.2GHz,4GB RAM
4	4	1.05	0.44
4	5	9.13	1.47
5	4	63.57	6.44
5	5	1749.94	64.9
5	6	16012.50	1621.8

Fig. 3. Comparison of computation times obtained with Dyncode, Qecode (QCSP+ solver), and Queso (QCSP solver) on games (a) NimFibo, (b) Connect4_Bounded, (c) MatrixGame, (d) Connect4 Full; y-axis represents CPU time in seconds

Results are given in Figure 3(d) for Connect4, but this time with boards of size $N \times M$, and in which the goal for the ∃-player is to win the game. The results show that Dyncode outperforms Queso. Again, we believe that the notion of state is really useful here to avoid re-exploring several times the same part of the search space. Whereas Queso uses techniques called pure value rules and constraint propagation for reified disjunction constraints, the limited constraint propagation performed by Dyncode reduces computation times.

Dyncode could be compared against other tools: (a) tools for non-deterministic planning, e.g. MBP [12]; (b) tools for controller synthesis from the model checking community [14]; (c) tools for solving MDPs [11], by considering MGCSPs as MDPs with 0/1 probabilities. MDP algorithms exploring the whole state space, such as basic value/policy iteration, may not scale well for games. And/Or search algorithms exploring only reachable states may be more competitive, but their management of probabilities and Bellman backups may induce extra computation times. These comparisons are left for future work. An important aspect is the fact that these tools do not offer the flexibility of constraint-based models.

6   Conclusion

This paper showed that, at the moment, using QCSP/QCSP+ is not the best constraint-based way of solving control problems for dynamic systems satisfying the Markovian and complete observability assumptions. The strengths of quantified constraints are more appropriate for solving problems in which these assumptions are violated, or problems involving just a few alternations of quantifiers. In the future, we plan to extend MGCSPs to model control problems in which the number of uncontrollable transitions between two controllable steps is not fixed. Requirements more general than reachability could also be considered. This should be a step to cross-fertilize advances in constraint programming and work performed in the automata and model checking community.

References

1. Bordeaux, L., Monfroy, E.: Beyond NP: Arc-consistency for Quantified Constraints. In: Van Hentenryck, P. (ed.) CP 2002. LNCS, vol. 2470, pp. 371–386. Springer, Heidelberg (2002)
2. Mamoulis, N., Stergiou, K.: Algorithms for Quantified Constraint Satisfaction Problems. In: Wallace, M. (ed.) CP 2004. LNCS, vol. 3258, pp. 752–756. Springer, Heidelberg (2004)
3. Gent, I.P., Nightingale, P., Rowley, A.: Encoding Quantified CSPs as Quantified Boolean Formulae. In: Proc. of ECAI 2004, pp. 176–180 (2004)
4. Nightingale, P.: Non-binary Quantified CSP: Algorithms and Modelling. Constraints 14(4), 539–581 (2009)
5. Gent, I.P., Nightingale, P., Stergiou, K.: QCSP-Solve: A Solver for Quantified Constraint Satisfaction Problems. In: Proc. of IJCAI 2005, pp. 138–143 (2005)
6. Stergiou, K.: Repair-based Methods for Quantified CSPs. In: van Beek, P. (ed.) CP 2005. LNCS, vol. 3709, pp. 652–666. Springer, Heidelberg (2005)
7. Verger, G., Bessiere, C.: Blocksolve: a Bottom-up Approach for Solving Quantified CSPs. In: Benhamou, F. (ed.) CP 2006. LNCS, vol. 4204, pp. 635–649. Springer, Heidelberg (2006)
8. Benedetti, M., Lallouet, A., Vautard, J.: QCSP Made Practical by Virtue of Restricted Quantification. In: Proc. of IJCAI 2007, pp. 38–43 (2007)
9. Larson, R., Casti, J.: Principles of Dynamic Programming. M. Dekker Inc., New York (1978)
10. Bessiere, C., Verger, G.: Strategic Constraint Satisfaction Problems. In: Benhamou, F. (ed.) CP 2006. LNCS, vol. 4204, pp. 17–29. Springer, Heidelberg (2006)
11. Puterman, M.: Markov Decision Processes, Discrete Stochastic Dynamic Programming. John Wiley & Sons, Chichester (1994)
12. Bertoli, P., Cimatti, A., Roveri, M., Traverso, P.: Planning in Nondeterministic Domains under Partial Observability via Symbolic Model Checking. In: Proc. of IJCAI 2001, pp. 473–478 (2001)
13. Pralet, C., Verfaillie, G., Lemaître, M., Infantes, G.: Constraint-Based Controller Synthesis in Non-Deterministic and Partially Observable Domains. In: Proc. of ECAI 2010, pp. 681–686 (2010)
14. Piterman, N., Pnueli, A., Sa'ar, Y.: Synthesis of Reactive(1) Designs. In: Emerson, E.A., Namjoshi, K.S. (eds.) VMCAI 2006. LNCS, vol. 3855, pp. 364–380. Springer, Heidelberg (2005)

On Mini-Buckets and the Min-fill Elimination Ordering

Emma Rollon and Javier Larrosa

Departament de Llenguatges i Sistemes Informàtics
Universitat Politècnica de Catalunya, Spain

Abstract. *Mini-Bucket Elimination* (MBE) is a well-known approximation of *Bucket Elimination* (BE), deriving bounds on quantities of interest over *graphical models*. Both algorithms are based on the sequential transformation of the original problem by eliminating variables, one at a time. The order in which variables are eliminated is usually computed using the greedy min-fill heuristic. In the BE case, this heuristic has a clear intuition, because it faithfully represents the structure of the sequence of sub-problems that BE generates and orders the variables using a greedy criteria based on such structure. However, MBE produces a sequence of sub-problems with a different structure. Therefore, using the min-fill heuristic with MBE means that decisions are made using the structure of the sub-problems that BE would produce, which is clearly meaningless. In this paper we propose a modification of the min-fill ordering heuristic that takes into account this fact. Our experiments on a number of benchmarks over two important tasks (i.e., computing the probability of evidence and optimization) show that MBE using the new ordering is often far more accurate than using the standard one.

1 Introduction

The graphical model paradigm includes very important reasoning tasks such as solving and counting solutions of CSPs, finding optimal solutions of weighted CSPs, computing probability of evidences and finding the most probable explanation in Bayesian Networks. Mini-Bucket Elimination (MBE) [5] is a very popular algorithm deriving bounds on reasoning tasks over graphical models. The good performance of MBE in different contexts has been widely proved [5,7,11,12].

MBE is a relaxation of Bucket Elimination (BE) [2] and both algorithms work by eliminating the problem variables, one at a time. In BE, the order in which variables are eliminated is important because it determines the complexity of the algorithm. In MBE, the variable elimination order does not affect the complexity of the algorithm, which comes determined by a control parameter. However, as we show in this paper, such order greatly affects the accuracy of the bound.

The most common elimination order for both BE and MBE is the one given by the min-fill greedy heuristic [3]. This heuristic was originally designed for BE and it is there where it has a clear rationale: the greedy algorithm that computes the min-fill ordering takes into account the structure of the sequence of sub-problems that BE will subsequently produce. Thus, each time the algorithm decides the next variable to be eliminated it does so by considering the structure of the problem that BE will have at this point.

J. Lee (Ed.): CP 2011, LNCS 6876, pp. 759–773, 2011.

Using the same heuristic for MBE does not seem a good idea, because MBE produces a sequence of subproblems with a different structure. Thus, when MBE uses the min-fill heuristic it takes decisions based on a misleading information.

In this paper we show that a better elimination ordering for MBE may be computed by considering the real structure of its sequence of subproblems. To do that, we represent these subproblems by *induced z-bounded hyper-graphs* and compute the elimination ordering accordingly. We demonstrate that MBE using the new elimination ordering is often far more accurate than using the standard one on a number of benchmarks (i.e., *coding networks*, real-world *genetic linkage analysis*, real-world *noisy-OR* models, and *combinatorial auctions*) over two tasks (i.e., computing the probability of evidence, and finding the complete assignment with minimum cost in a WCSP).

2   Background

2.1   Graphical Models

A *graphical model* is a tuple $(\mathcal{X}, \mathcal{F})$, where $\mathcal{X} = (x_1, \ldots, x_n)$ is an ordered set of variables and $\mathcal{F} = \{f_1, \ldots, f_r\}$ is a set of functions. Variable x_i takes values from its finite domain $\mathcal{D}_i$. Each function $f_j : \mathcal{D}_{var(f_j)} \rightarrow A$ is defined over a subset of variables $var(f_j) \subseteq \mathcal{X}$ and returns values from a set A. For example, $\mathcal{X} = (x_1, x_2)$ with $\mathcal{D}_1 = \mathcal{D}_2 = \{0, 1\}$, and $\mathcal{F} = \{x_1 + x_2, x_1 * x_2\}$ is a graphical model. Abusing notation, the scope of a set of functions $\mathcal{F}$, noted $var(\mathcal{F})$, is the union of scopes of the functions it contains.

Given a graphical model, one can compute different *reasoning tasks*. A reasoning task is defined by two operations ($\bigotimes$ and $\Downarrow$) over functions. The *combination* of f and g, noted $f \bigotimes g$, is a new function h with scope $var(h) = var(f) \cup var(g)$, while the marginalization of a set of variables $\mathcal{W} \subseteq \mathcal{X}$ from function f, noted $f \Downarrow_{\mathcal{W}}$, is a new function h with scope $var(h) = var(f) - \mathcal{W}$. Computing the reasoning task means computing $(\bigotimes_{f \in \mathcal{F}} f) \Downarrow_{\mathcal{X}}$

The graphical model framework can be used to model a variety of important combinatorial problems. For example, if $\mathcal{F}$ is a set of cost functions (i.e, returning a non-negative value representing a cost) the graphical model is a weighted CSP. If we take the sum as combination and the minimum as marginalization, the reasoning task becomes $\min_{\mathcal{X}} \{\sum_{f \in \mathcal{F}} f)\}$, which is the minimum cost assignment of the weighted CSP. Alternatively, if $\mathcal{F}$ is a set of *conditional probability tables* we have a Bayesian Network. If we take the product as combination and the sum as marginalization, the reasoning task becomes $\sum_{\mathcal{X}} \{\prod_{f \in \mathcal{F}} f)\}$, which models the probability of the evidence. If $\mathcal{F}$ is a set of hard constraints (i.e, boolean functions) the graphical model is a classical CSP and the reasoning task $\sum_{\mathcal{X}} \{\prod_{f \in \mathcal{F}} f)\}$ counts its solutions.

2.2   Graph Concepts

The structure of a graphical model is represented by its associated *hyper-graph*.

Definition 1. *A hyper-graph H is a pair $H = (V, E)$ where V is a set of elements, called* nodes, *and E is a set of non-empty subsets of V, called* hyper-edges. *The width of hyper-graph H is the size of its largest edge.*

Definition 2. *Given a graphical model $P = (\mathcal{X}, \mathcal{F})$, its associated hyper-graph $H(P) = (V, E)$ is defined as $V = \{i \mid x_i \in \mathcal{X}\}$ and $E = \{var(f) \mid f \in \mathcal{F}\}$.*

The most fundamental structural property considered in the context of graphical models is *acyclicity*. Mainly, acyclicity is measured in terms of the *induced width*.

Definition 3. *Let $H = (V, E)$ be a hyper-graph, and let $o = \{x_1^o, \ldots, x_n^o\}$ be an ordering of the nodes in V where x_j^o is the jth element in the ordering. This induces a sequence of hyper-graphs $H_n, H_{n-1}, \ldots, H_1$ where $H = H_n$ and H_{j-1} is obtained from H_j as follows. All edges in H_j containing x_j^o are merged into one edge, called the induced hyper-edge, and then x_j^o is removed. Thus, the underlying vertices of H_{j-1} are $x_1^o, \ldots, x_{j-1}^o$. The induced width of H under o, noted $w^*(o)$, is the largest width among all hyper-graphs $H_n, \ldots, H_1$. The induced width of H, noted w^*, is the minimum induced width over all orderings o.*

Example 1. Consider a graphical model $P = (\mathcal{X}, \mathcal{F})$ where $\mathcal{X} = \{x_1, x_2, x_3, x_4\}$ and $\mathcal{F} = \{f_1(x_1, x_3), f_2(x_2, x_3), f_3(x_2, x_4), f_4(x_1, x_4)\}$. Its hyper-graph is $H(P) - (V, E)$, where $V = \{1, 2, 3, 4\}$ and $E = \{(1, 3), (2, 3), (2, 4), (1, 4)\}$. The lexicographical ordering $o = \{x_1, x_2, x_3, x_4\}$ induces the following sequence of hyper-graphs (where each hyper-graph is represented by its set of hyper-edges):

$$H_4(P) = \{(1, 3), (2, 3), (2, 4), (1, 4)\}$$
$$H_3(P) - \{(1, 3), (2, 3), (1, 2)\}$$
$$H_2(P) = \{(1, 2)\}$$
$$H_1(P) = \{(1)\}$$

The induced width of the problem is 2 - all edges in $H_4(P)$, $H_3(P)$ and $H_2(P)$ achieve this size.

2.3 Bucket Elimination

Bucket Elimination (BE) [2] (*non-serial dynamic programming* in [1] and *fusion algorithm* in [13]) is a general algorithm for the computation of reasoning tasks in graphical models. BE (Algorithm 1) works as a sequential elimination of variables. Given an arbitrary variable ordering $o = \{x_1^o, \ldots, x_n^o\}$ (line 1), the algorithm eliminates variables one by one, from last to first, according to o. The elimination of variable x_j^o is done as follows: $\mathcal{F}$ is the set of current functions. The algorithm computes the so called *bucket* of x_j^o, noted $\mathcal{B}_j$, which contains all cost functions in $\mathcal{F}$ having x_j^o in their scope (line 3). Next, BE computes a new function g_j by combining all functions in $\mathcal{B}_j$ and subsequently eliminating x_j^o (line 4). Then, $\mathcal{F}$ is updated by removing the functions in $\mathcal{B}_j$ and adding g_j (line 5). The new $\mathcal{F}$ does not contain x_j^o (all functions mentioning x_j^o were removed) but preserves the value of the result. The elimination of the last variable produces an empty-scope function (i.e., a constant) which is the result of the problem (line 7).

The correctness of the algorithm is guaranteed whenever the combination and marginalization operators satisfy the three *Shenoy-Shaffer axioms* [13]. The most important tasks over graphical models satisfy these axioms.

Algorithm 1. Bucket Elimination

> **Input** : A graphical model $P = (\mathcal{X}, \mathcal{F})$.
> **Output**: Evaluation of $(\bigotimes_{f \in \mathcal{F}} f) \Downarrow_{\mathcal{X}}$.

1 $\{x_1^o, \ldots, x_n^o\} \leftarrow \texttt{compute-order}(P)$;
2 **for** $j \leftarrow n$ **to** 1 **do**
3       $\mathcal{B}_j \leftarrow \{f \in \mathcal{F} \mid x_j^o \in var(f)\}$;
4       $g_j \leftarrow (\bigotimes_{f \in \mathcal{B}_j} f) \Downarrow_{x_j^o}$;
5       $\mathcal{F} \leftarrow (\mathcal{F} \cup \{g_j\}) - \mathcal{B}_j$;
6 **end**
7 **return** $\bigotimes_{f \in \mathcal{F}} f$;

Algorithm 2. Mini-Bucket Elimination

> **Input** : A graphical model $P = (\mathcal{X}, \mathcal{F})$; and the value of the control parameter z.
> **Output**: A bound of $(\bigotimes_{f \in \mathcal{F}} f) \Downarrow_{\mathcal{X}}$.

1 $\{x_1^o, \ldots, x_n^o\} \leftarrow \texttt{compute-order}(P)$;
2 **for** $j \leftarrow n$ **to** 1 **do**
3       $\mathcal{B}_j \leftarrow \{f \in \mathcal{F} \mid x_j^o \in var(f)\}$;
4       $\{Q_1, \ldots, Q_p\} \leftarrow \texttt{partition}(\mathcal{B}_j, z)$;
5   **for** $k \leftarrow 1$ **to** p **do**
6           $g_{j,k} \leftarrow (\bigotimes_{f \in Q_k} f) \Downarrow_{x_j^o}$;
7   **end**
8       $\mathcal{F} \leftarrow (\mathcal{F} \cup \{g_{j,1}, \ldots, g_{j,p}\}) - \mathcal{B}_j$;
9 **end**
10 **return** $\bigotimes_{f \in \mathcal{F}} f$;

Example 2. Consider the graphical model in Example 1. The trace of BE along lexico-graphical order is as follows.

Bucket	
$\mathcal{B}_4$	$f_4(x_1, x_4), f_3(x_2, x_4)$
$\mathcal{B}_3$	$f_1(x_1, x_3), f_2(x_2, x_3), g_4(x_1, x_2) = (f_4 \otimes f_3) \Downarrow_{x_4}$
$\mathcal{B}_2$	$g_3(x_1, x_2) = (f_1(x_1, x_3) \otimes f_2(x_2, x_3) \otimes g_4(x_1, x_2)) \Downarrow_{x_3}$
$\mathcal{B}_1$	$g_2(x_1) = g_3(x_1, x_2) \Downarrow_{x_2}$
Output	$g_1() = g_2(x_1) \Downarrow_{x_1}$

Since new functions have to be stored explicitly as tables, and their size is exponential on their arity, the time and space complexity of BE depends on the largest arity needed. This arity is captured by the structural parameter induced-width (see Section 3 for details).

Theorem 1. *Given a variable ordering o, the time and space complexity of BE is $O(exp(w^*(o) + 1))$ and $O(exp(w^*(o)))$, respectively.*

2.4   Mini-Bucket Elimination

All variable elimination algorithms are unsuitable for problems with high induced width due to its exponential time and space complexity. *Mini-bucket elimination* (MBE) [5] is an approximation of full bucket elimination that bounds the exact solution when the induced width is too large.

Given a bucket $B_j = \{f_1 \ldots, f_m\}$, MBE generates a partition $Q = \{Q_1, \ldots, Q_p\}$ of B_j, where each subset $Q_k \in Q$ is called *mini-bucket*. Given an integer control parameter z, MBE restricts the arity of each of its mini-buckets to $z + 1$. We say that Q is a z-*partition*. Then, each mini-bucket is processed independently. Algorithm 2 shows the pseudo-code of MBE.

Example 3. Consider our running example. The trace of MBE along lexicographical order and setting the value of the control parameter z to 1 is as follows.

Bucket	
B_4	$f_4(x_1, x_4)$, $f_3(x_2, x_4)$
B_3	$f_1(x_1, x_3)$, $f_2(x_2, x_3)$
B_2	$g_{42}(x_2) = f_3(x_2, x_4) \Downarrow_{x_4}$, $g_{32}(x_2) = f_2(x_2, x_3) \Downarrow_{x_3}$
B_1	$g_{41}(x_1) = f_4(x_1, x_4) \Downarrow_{x_4}$, $g_{31}(x_1) = f_1(x_1, x_3) \Downarrow_{x_3}$
Output	$g_1() = (g_{41}(x_1) \otimes g_{31}(x_1)) \Downarrow_{x_1}$, $g_2() = (g_{42}(x_2) \otimes g_{32}(x_2)) \Downarrow_{x_2}$

Note that since the final set of functions is $\{g_1(), g_2()\}$, the output valuation is $g_1() \otimes g_2()$.

The time and space complexity of MBE is $O(exp(z+1))$ and $O(exp(z))$, respectively. The parameter z allows trading time and space for accuracy. In general, higher values of z results in more accurate bounds. In the limit (e.g., when z is the number of variables of the problem) MBE behaves as BE and computes the exact result.

3   Variable Elimination Ordering

In this Section we show that the order in which variables are eliminated plays a very different role in bucket and mini-bucket elimination. In particular, the sequence of sub-problems generated by both algorithms is different. In spite of this key distinction, MBE uses the ordering procedure as designed for BE. We propose a modification of this pro-cedure in order to account for this fact.

3.1   Induced Hyper-Graphs and BE

There exists a close relation between the induced sequence of hyper-graphs and the elimination process of BE. The trace of BE in Example 2 showed how it is possible to compute the scopes of the functions that the algorithm will produce without actually ex-ecuting it. Since the hyper-graph precisely contains this information, we can easily show that the sequence of induced hyper-graphs is actually the sequence of hyper-graphs as-sociated with the sequence of subproblems produced by BE.

Algorithm 3. compute-order	Algorithm 4. compute-z-order
Input : A graphical model $(\mathcal{X}, \mathcal{F})$, and a variable selection heuristic h.	**Input** : A graphical model $(\mathcal{X}, \mathcal{F})$, and a variable selection heuristic h.
Output: A variable elimination ordering $\{x_1^o, \ldots, x_n^o\}$.	**Output**: A variable elimination ordering $\{x_1^o, \ldots, x_n^o\}$.
1 **for** $j \leftarrow n$ **to** 1 **do**	1 **for** $j \leftarrow n$ **to** 1 **do**
2 $\quad\mid\quad x_j^o \leftarrow \arg\min_{x_i \in \mathcal{X}}\{h(H(P_j), i)\}$;	2 $\quad\mid\quad x_j^o \leftarrow \arg\min_{x_i \in \mathcal{X}}\{h(H(\overline{P}_j), i)\}$;
3 **end**	3 **end**
4 **return** $\{x_1^o, \ldots, x_n^o\}$;	4 **return** $\{x_1^o, \ldots, x_n^o\}$;

Given a graphical model $P = (\mathcal{X}, \mathcal{F})$, let P_{j-1} be the subproblem produced by BE once variables $x_j^o, \ldots, x_n^o$ have been eliminated, where by definition $P_n = P$. P_{j-1} is obtained from P_j by computing a new function g_j with scope $var(\mathcal{B}_j) - \{x_j^o\}$, and removing the variable from the problem. Similarly, by definition $H_n = H(P)$, and induced hyper-graph H_{j-1} is obtained from H_j by merging all hyper-edges containing x_j^o and then removing x_j^o from the set of vertices. Note that the new hyper-edge is the scope of g_j, while the other hyper-edges are the scopes of the remaining functions in P_j. Therefore, H_{j-1} is the associated hyper-graph of P_{j-1} (i.e., $H_{j-1} = H(P_{j-1})$).

Example 4. Consider our running example and its BE trace in Example 2. Subproblems P_j are the following:

$$P_4 = \{f_1(x_1, x_3), f_2(x_2, x_3), f_3(x_2, x_4), f_4(x_1, x_4)\}$$
$$P_3 = \{f_1(x_1, x_3), f_2(x_2, x_3), g_4(x_1, x_2)\}$$
$$P_2 = \{g_4(x_1, x_2), g_3(x_1, x_2)\}$$
$$P_1 = \{g_2(x_1)\}$$

Note that the set of functions' scopes in each subproblem P_j corresponds to the edges in hyper-graph $H_j(P)$ in Example 1.

It is clear then that the induced width bounds the bucket's sizes generated during the elimination process and, as a consequence, the complexity of the algorithm. The size of the induced width varies with various variable orderings, leading to different performance guarantees. Finding the *best* ordering (i.e., the one with the smallest induced width) is NP-hard. Instead, useful variable selection heuristics as fill-in edges [3], and width of nodes [6] aim at finding *good* orderings.

Procedure compute-order (Algorithm 3) is a greedy search guided by the variable selection heuristic h defined on a hyper-graph $H = (V, E)$ and one node $i \in V$, noted $h(H, i)$. At iteration j, the algorithm selects the jth variable in the ordering (i.e., x_j^o) by ranking each node in subproblem P_j according to h and selecting the one minimizing it. Note that since the induced hyper-graph $H_j(P)$ represents subproblem P_j, the algorithm selects the best variable in the problem once variables $x_{j+1}^o, \ldots, x_n^o$ has been eliminated.

3.2 Induced z-Bounded Hyper-graphs and MBE

The sequence of induced hyper-graphs differ from the sequence of hyper-graphs associated with subproblems produced by MBE. The reason is that MBE partitions buckets whenever they have more than $z + 1$ different variables.

Given a graphical model $P = (\mathcal{X}, \mathcal{F})$, let $\overline{P}_{j-1}$ be the subproblem once MBE has eliminated variables $x_j^o, \ldots, x_n^o$ from P, where by definition $\overline{P}_n = P$. Consider that MBE does not partition buckets $\mathcal{B}_j, \ldots, \mathcal{B}_n$. Up to this point of the execution, MBE generates the same subproblems as BE (i.e., $P_j = \overline{P}_j, \ldots, P_n = \overline{P}_n$) and the induced hyper-graphs correspond to hyper-graphs associated with these subproblems (i.e., $H_j = H(\overline{P}_j), \ldots, H_n = H(\overline{P}_n)$). Now consider that bucket $\mathcal{B}_{j-1}$ has more than $z+1$ different variables. MBE will partition this bucket into mini-buckets. Namely, instead of computing a single function g_j over the bucket's scope, the algorithm will compute a set of functions g_{jk} over unions of scopes of bucket's functions. The hyper-graph associated with subproblem $\overline{P}_{j-1}$ would have one hyper-edge for each of the new functions' scope, while the induced hyper-graph H_{j-1} has only one hyper-edge over the scope of the bucket. Therefore, $H_{j-1} \neq H(\overline{P}_{j-1})$.

Example 5. Consider our running example and the trace of MBE in Example 3. Subproblems $\overline{P}_j$ are as follows:

$$\overline{P}_4 = \{f_1(x_1, x_3), f_2(x_2, x_3), f_3(x_2, x_4), f_4(x_1, x_4)\}$$
$$\overline{P}_3 = \{f_1(x_1, x_3), f_2(x_2, x_3), g_{41}(x_1), g_{42}(x_2)\}$$
$$\overline{P}_2 = \{g_{31}(x_1), g_{32}(x_2), g_{41}(x_1), g_{42}(x_2)\}$$
$$\overline{P}_1 = \{g_2(), g_{31}(x_1), g_{41}(x_1)\}$$

Note that induced hyper-graphs $H_3(P)$ and $H_2(P)$ in Example 1 are not associated with subproblems $\overline{P}_3$ and $\overline{P}_2$, respectively. The reason is that bucket $\mathcal{B}_4$ is partitioned into mini-buckets $\{f_4(x_1, x_4)\}$ and $\{f_3(x_2, x_4)\}$. The new computed functions are $g_{41}(x_1)$ and $g_{42}(x_2)$. None of the functions in $\overline{P}_3$ has scope $\{x_1, x_2\}$. However, the induced hyper-graph $H_3(P)$ has an hyper-edge on $\{x_1, x_2\}$.

Although this important difference, most previous investigations on MBE uses the elimination ordering as designed for BE. This does not seem a good decision because, as we have seen, the variable selection heuristic h ranks each node according to the given hyper-graph. Therefore, when computing the ordering for MBE, the heuristic selects the next variable to eliminate based on an *erroneous* structure.

We wish to compute the ordering over the hyper-graphs associated with each subproblem generated by MBE. Let us call z-*bounded hyper-graph*, the hyper-graph associated with subproblem $\overline{P}_j$ for any $j = 1 \ldots n$, and *induced z-bounded hyper-graphs*, the sequence of hyper-graphs associated with the sequence of subproblems $\overline{P}_1, \ldots, \overline{P}_n$.

Example 6. Consider the trace of MBE in Example 3. The sequence of associated induced z-bounded hyper-graphs (represented by their hyper-edges) is,

$$H(\overline{P}_4) = \{(1, 3), (2, 3), (2, 4), (1, 4)\}$$
$$H(\overline{P}_3) = \{(1, 3), (2, 3), (1), (2)\}$$

Iteration j	compute-order	compute-z-order
4	$H(P_4) = \{(1,3),(2,3),(2,4),(1,4)\}$	$H(\overline{P}_4) = \{(1,3),(2,3),(2,4),(1,4)\}$
	$h(\cdot,4) = 1$	$h(\cdot,4) = 1$
	$h(\cdot,3) = 1$	$h(\cdot,3) = 1$
	$h(\cdot,2) = 1$	$h(\cdot,2) = 1$
	$h(\cdot,1) = 1$	$h(\cdot,1) = 1$
	$x_j^o = 4$	$x_j^o = 4$
3	$H(P_3) = \{(1,3),(2,3),(1,2)\}$	$H(\overline{P}_3) = \{(1,3),(2,3),(1),(2)\}$
	$h(\ ,3) = 0$	$h(\ ,3) = 1$
	$h(\cdot,2) = 0$	$h(\cdot,2) = 0$
	$h(\cdot,1) = 0$	$h(\cdot,1) = 0$
	$x_j^o = 3$	$x_j^o = 2$
2	$H(P_2) = \{(1,2)\}$	$H(\overline{P}_2) = \{(1,3),(3),(1)\}$
	$h(\cdot,2) = 0$	$h(\cdot,3) = 0$
	$h(\cdot,1) = 0$	$h(\cdot,1) = 0$
	$x_j^o = 2$	$x_j^o = 3$
1	$H(P_1) = \{(1)\}$	$H(\overline{P}_1) = \{(1)\}$
	$h(\cdot,1) = 0$	$h(\cdot,1) = 0$
	$x_j^o = 1$	$x_j^o = 1$

Fig. 1. Trace of `compute-order` and `compute-z-order` using number of fill-in edges as variable selection heuristic h (ties are broken lexicographically). The value of z is 1.

$$H(\overline{P}_2) = \{(1),(2)\}$$
$$H(\overline{P}_1) = \{(1)\}$$

We propose to compute the elimination order according to the induced z-bounded hyper-graphs. We call this procedure `compute-z-order` (Algorithm 4). The main difference with respect to `compute-order` is that, at iteration j, the variable selection heuristic h will rank nodes in the z-bounded hyper-graph $H(\overline{P}_j)$ instead of ranking nodes in the hyper-graph $H(P_j)$ (line 2 in both algorithms). Note that in the limit (e.g., when z is the number of variables in the problem) both `compute-order` and `compute-z-order` are equivalent.

Example 7. Consider our running example. Let the variable selection heuristic h be number of fill-in edges, and let z be 1. In case of ties, the secondary variable selection heuristic is lexicographical order. Figure 1 shows the behavior of `compute-order` and `compute-z-order`. In summary, procedure `compute-order` outputs order $o = \{x_1, x_2, x_3, x_4\}$ while `compute-z-order` outputs order $o' = \{x_1, x_3, x_2, x_4\}$. Note that under o, MBE will split buckets $\mathcal{B}_4$ and $\mathcal{B}_3$ into two mini-buckets each. However, under o', MBE will split only bucket $\mathcal{B}_4$ into two mini-buckets and compute exactly the remaining buckets. As a consequence, the bound will provably be more accurate using o' (which is based on induced z-bounded hyper-graphs) than using o (which is based on induced hyper-graphs).

Since `compute-z-order` needs subproblems $\overline{P}_j$, computing the order as a preprocess could have the same complexity as MBE. However, it can be embedded in

---

Algorithm 5. Mini-Bucket Elimination with embedded compute-z-order

---

Input : A graphical model $P = (\mathcal{X}, \mathcal{F})$; and the value of the control parameter z.

Output: A bound of $(\bigotimes_{f \in \mathcal{F}} f) \Downarrow_{\mathcal{X}}$.

1 **for** $j \leftarrow n$ **to** 1 **do**
2      $x_j^o \leftarrow \arg\min_{x_i \in \mathcal{X}} \{h(H(\mathcal{X}, \mathcal{F}), i)\}$; // At each iteration $\overline{P}_j = (\mathcal{X}, \mathcal{F})$
3      $\mathcal{B}_j \leftarrow \{f \in \mathcal{F} \mid x_j^o \in var(f)\}$;
4      $\{Q_1, \ldots, Q_p\} \leftarrow \texttt{partition}(\mathcal{B}_j, z)$;
5   **for** $k \leftarrow 1$ **to** p **do**
6          $g_{j,k} \leftarrow (\bigotimes_{f \in Q_k} f) \Downarrow_{x_j^o}$;
7   **end**
8      $\mathcal{F} \leftarrow (\mathcal{F} \cup \{g_{j,1}, \ldots, g_{j,p}\}) - \mathcal{B}_j$;
9      $\mathcal{X} \leftarrow \mathcal{X} - \{x_j^o\}$;
10 **end**
11 **return** $\bigotimes_{f \in \mathcal{F}} f$;

MBE (Algorithm 5). Note that the time and space complexity of the new algorithm remains exponential on the control parameter z.

4 Empirical Evaluation

The good performance of mini-bucket elimination over different reasoning tasks has been already proved [5,7,11,12] . The purpose of these experiments is to evaluate the effectiveness of the new min-fill heuristic adapted to MBE over two important tasks: (i) computing the probability of evidence over Bayesian networks, and (ii) finding the minimum cost assignment of the weighted CSP.

We conduct our empirical evaluation on four benchmarks: coding networks, real-world linkage analysis models, real-world noisy-OR networks, and combinatorial auctions. The task on the first three benchmarks (all of them included in the UAI'08 evaluation[1]) is to compute the probability of evidence and MBE obtains upper bounds, while the task on the latter benchmark is optimization and MBE obtains lower bounds.

When computing the probability of evidence, we report the results using two different bucket partitioning policies as described in [12]: scope-based (SCP) and LMRE content-based heuristic. We use the number of fill-in edges as variable selection heuristic h with `compute-order` and `compute-z-order` (in the following called *BE fill-in* and *MBE fill-in*, respectively).

Unless otherwise indicated, we report the results in tables where the first column identifies the instance. Then, for each bucket partitioning heuristic we report the bound, relative error (RE), and cpu time in seconds using *BE fill-in* and *MBE fill-in*. For each instance, the relative error is computed as

$$RE = \frac{|bound - best\ bound|}{best\ bound}$$

Moreover, for each row we underline the best bound, and highlight in bold face the best bound wrt each bucket partitioning heuristic.

---

[1] http://graphmod.ics.uci.edu/uai08/Software

Table 1. Empirical results on coding networks. BN_126, ..., BN_134 instances

BN inst.'s number	SCP partition heuristic						LMRE partition heuristic					
	BE fill-in			MBE fill-in			BE fill-in			MBE fill-in		
	ub.	RE	Time	ub.	RE	Time	ub.	RE	Time	ub.	RE	Time
						$z = 20$						
126	1.31E-44	46.96	5.44	**2.72E-46**	0	6.7	2.49E-45	8.15	26.78	**1.15E-45**	3.23	24.87
127	**1.10E-49**	0	7.44	2.75E-46	2491.16	7.87	**1.73E-46**	1568.50	33.03	2.03E-46	1836.54	35.86
128	1.37E-41	127.18	7.17	**1.28E-42**	11.00	7.38	5.87E-41	547.40	34.54	**1.07E-43**	0	31.48
129	1.77E-46	333.65	6.2	**5.46E-47**	101.99	6.5	2.41E-44	45574.38	25.36	**5.30E-49**	0	27.84
130	8.22E-47	535.66	6.54	**1.53E-49**	0	6.45	1.03E-47	66.30	23.7	**8.44E-48**	54.11	24.59
131	5.03E-46	547.72	6.9	**9.16E-49**	0	5.41	2.28E-46	248.36	27.64	**1.96E-47**	20.36	25.94
132	1.29E-46	43.84	6.89	**1.04E-47**	2.61	6.44	1.05E-47	2.65	29.34	**2.88E-48**	0	24.66
133	**5.03E-46**	1.85	6.61	2.97E-45	15.82	7.28	2.70E-42	15296.10	24.93	**1.76E-46**	0	28.79
134	2.50E-44	8513.76	6.66	**2.94E-48**	0	6.69	**4.06E-45**	1381.71	29.69	5.49E-45	1866.70	29.45
						$z = 22$						
126	5.21E-43	3.98E+5	26.14	**5.72E-46**	437.12	25.15	9.70E-45	7422.72	107.16	**1.31E-48**	0	101.11
127	5.34E-48	0.68	28.17	**3.18E-48**	0	28.22	**2.26E-47**	6.11	108.68	2.76E-45	865.35	125.69
128	2.30E-44	1.23	25.58	**1.03E-44**	0	25.02	9.03E-42	872.98	130.68	**1.96E-43**	17.98	114.71
129	6.14E-45	5.19E+4	26.85	**1.18E-49**	0	26.04	3.65E-43	3.08E+6	89.18	**3.35E-47**	282.32	90.08
130	8.40E-47	1205.90	21.64	**1.61E-49**	1.31	24.1	2.49E-48	34.73	90.47	**6.96E-50**	0	77.76
131	**9.86E-48**	0.25	21.69	6.09E-47	6.72	24.59	2.71E-46	33.32	93.29	**7.88E-48**	0	81.37
132	1.46E-48	23.50	23.6	**5.96E-50**	0	20.52	1.49E-48	24.03	93.17	**5.44E-49**	8.13	90.88
133	8.50E-44	1327.32	23.05	**8.66E-45**	134.26	24.68	5.21E-45	80.37	99.4	**6.40E-47**	0	85.04
134	1.57E-46	5.32	26.5	**1.09E-46**	3.36	28.92	1.01E-46	3.07	105.31	**2.49E-47**	0	94.95

In all our experiments, we execute MBE in a Pentium IV running Linux with 4 Gb of memory and 3 GHz.

Coding networks. Our first domain is coding networks from the class of linear block codes [7]. All instances have 512 variables with domain size 2 and the induced width varies from 49 to 55. Table 1 shows the results for two different values of the control parameter $z = \{20, 22\}$.

The MBE fill-in computes the best upper bound on eight out of nine instances when $z = 20$, and on all instances when $z = 22$. Among these instances, the improvement over the best BE fill-in is usually of orders of magnitude for both values of z.

Using the SCP partitioning heuristic, the MBE fill-in outperforms the BE fill-in on seven instances when $z = 20$ and on eight instances when $z = 22$. The improvements are usually of orders of magnitude. The computation times of both orderings are very close. Using the LMRE partitioning heuristic, the MBE fill-in outperforms the BE fill-in on seven instances when $z = 20$, and on eight instances when $z = 22$. As for the previous partitioning heuristic, the improvements are in general of orders of magnitude, and the computation times are similar.

For space reasons, we do not report the number of mini-buckets processed in each run of MBE. However, we observed that when using MBE fill-in the algorithm processes less mini-buckets than when using the BE fill-in. Note that breaking a bucket into several mini-buckets is precisely what transforms the variable elimination scheme from exact (i.e, BE) to approximate (i.e., MBE). The less mini-buckets, the more similar to the exact algorithm and, as a consequence, the more accurate the bound.

Table 2. Empirical results on linkage analysis. Pedigree instances.

pedigree instance's number	SCP partition heuristic						LMRE partition heuristic					
	BE fill-in			MBE fill-in			BE fill-in			MBE fill-in		
	ub.	RE	Time	ub.	RE	Time	ub.	RE	Time	ub.	RE	Time
						$z = 17$						
7	1.34E-49	1.22E+4	4.29	**2.22E-51**	202.01	4.92	1.84E-53	0.68	8.54	**1.10E-53**	0	18.14
9	2.58E-66	136.76	1.76	**1.88E-68**	0	2.51	1.94E-67	9.32	2.72	**5.39E-68**	1.87	2.71
13	3.24E-15	9.43E+4	1.91	**1.39E-16**	4059.24	2.23	**3.43E-20**	0	2.54	1.42E-16	4129.41	3.00
18	4.15E-71	24.54	0.86	**3.47E-72**	1.13	0.95	2.08E-71	11.80	0.92	**1.63E-72**	0	0.98
20	3.82E-25	4.73	12.83	**6.66E-26**	0	15.57	**7.61E-26**	0.14	14.15	9.75E-26	0.46	23.16
25	1.57E-109	8.83	0.56	**1.99E-110**	0.24	0.65	3.33E-109	19.85	0.68	**1.60E-110**	0	0.65
30	4.57E-75	2418.39	1.46	**1.86E-77**	8.86	1.43	7.14E-76	376.82	1.65	**1.89E-78**	0	1.75
31	9.21E-51	1.17E+5	9.82	**6.67E-53**	849.54	11.5	**7.84E-56**	0	12.08	3.94E-52	5020.51	13.45
33	**1.70E-47**	17.05	3.53	5.33E-45	5645.31	5.3	**9.44E-49**	0	10.84	2.92E-46	308.02	8.50
34	2.97E-49	3.39E+4	32.81	**1.62E-51**	183.85	37.25	3.31E-53	2.79	49.75	**8.74E-54**	0	63.39
37	4.94E-109	7052.31	110.36	**3.19E-111**	44.45	131.21	8.86E-110	1263.00	243.17	**7.01E-113**	0.00	235.84
39	**2.58E-99**	0.09	1.25	7.35E-99	2.12	1.04	**2.35E-99**	0	1.28	6.76E-99	1.87	1.42
41	1.96E-61	19.36	69.22	**1.48E-62**	0.54	29.16	1.06E-61	9.98	90.5	**9.62E-63**	0	487.54
42	**1.22E-26**	0.00	15.84	1.69E-26	0.38	39	**1.50E-26**	0.23	25.7	3.71E-26	2.03	51.06
44	5.81E-55	131.49	1.99	**4.39E-57**	0	3.08	**4.10E-56**	8.35	3.58	8.08E-56	17.43	3.69
51	**1.74E-53**	862.93	3.09	9.76E-52	48484.18	3.53	**2.01E-56**	0	5.12	6.59E-56	2.27	4.43
						$z = 19$						
7	**1.35E-53**	814.96	24.52	1.63E-50	981031.51	29.49	6.20E-56	2.74	29.24	**1.65E-56**	0	65.00
9	7.37E-67	9869.66	6.27	**8.57E-70**	10.47	6.43	1.34E-68	177.77	11.01	**7.47E-71**	0	12.15
13	**2.01E-18**	45.03	6.51	1.24E-15	28356.80	8.44	**4.36E-20**	0	9.98	3.58E-17	821.45	12.60
18	**4.16E-76**	0	2.72	5.43E-76	0.31	2.78	2.92E-75	6.03	2.76	**1.58E-75**	2.81	2.81
20	2.24E-27	1.11	51.53	**1.52E-27**	0.43	43.69	1.12E-27	0.06	51.02	**1.05E-27**	0.00	87.88
25	4.87E-111	1.76	1.38	**4.50E-111**	1.55	1.94	**1.77E-111**	0	1.49	4.21E-111	1.38	1.94
30	**5.46E-80**	0	5.8	9.05E-80	0.66	5.29	1.03E-79	0.89	6.12	**8.02E-80**	0.47	5.40
31	**7.04E-56**	15.60	37.3	1.79E-55	41.28	48.23	**4.24E-57**	0	42.78	2.48E-56	4.86	60.05
33	**3.30E-46**	120.34	15.81	7.89E-46	289.04	17.38	**2.72E-48**	0	15.9	1.03E-46	36.70	24.13
34	**1.69E-51**	851.77	181.91	7.32E-51	3690.45	223.95	**1.98E-54**	0	331.9	1.71E-53	7.61	427.58
37	3.75E-113	0.11	206.35	**3.53E-113**	0.04	203.48	**3.39E-113**	0	368.57	5.99E-113	0.77	319.95
39	2.08E-100	2.07	8.85	**6.77E-101**	0	6.75	**1.35E-100**	0.99	8.88	1.89E-100	1.79	6.84
41	**3.00E-63**	309.19	266.96	1.14E-61	11784.67	311.98	1.82E-63	187.18	496.47	**9.68E-66**	0	612.99
42	2.01E-27	1.27	156.51	**1.37E-27**	0.55	203.89	1.14E-27	0.29	184.97	**8.84E-28**	0	198.82
44	6.39E-55	62.59	7.36	**5.63E-55**	55.05	10.34	**1.01E-56**	0	12.37	7.39E-55	72.60	13.57
51	1.10E-55	269.98	12.21	**4.07E-58**	0	13.66	**1.11E-55**	271.12	14.31	2.26E-55	554.91	14.53

Linkage analysis. Our second domain is real-world linkage analysis models. We used pedigree instances. They have 300 to 1000 variables with domain sizes from 1 (i.e., evidence variables) to 5, and induced widths of 20 up to 50. Table 2 shows the results.

The MBE fill-in computes the best upper bound on ten out of sixteen instances when $z = 17$, and on seven instances when $z = 19$. Among these instances, the improvement over the best BE fill-in is of orders of magnitude on eight out of ten (i.e., on 80% of) instances when $z = 17$, and on five out of seven (i.e., on 71%) when $z = 19$. Among instances where the BE fill-in computes the best upper bound, the improvement over the best MBE fill-in is of orders of magnitude on three out of six (i.e., on 50%) instances when $z = 17$, and on five out of nine (i.e., on 55%) when $z = 19$. In other words, when better, the MBE fill-in is usually orders of magnitude more accurate.

Using the SCP partitioning heuristic, the MBE fill-in outperforms the BE fill-in on twelve instances when $z = 17$, and on eight when $z = 19$. Among these instances, the improvement over the BE fill-in is always of orders of magnitude when $z = 17$, and from 6% up to orders of magnitude (on 37% of these instances) when $z = 19$. Using the LMRE partitioning heuristic, the MBE fill-in outperforms the BE fill-in on eight instances when $z = 17$, and on seven instances when $z = 19$. Among these instances,

Table 3. Empirical results on noisy-OR networks. Promedas instances.

or_chain numbers	Size	Mean RE				or_chain numbers	Size	Mean RE			
		SCP heuristic		LMRE heuristic				SCP heuristic		LMRE heuristic	
		BE fill-in	MBE fill-in	BE fill-in	MBE fill-in			BE fill-in	MBE fill-in	BE fill-in	MBE fill-in
1[0*]	12	916951	**165.80**	595.83	**9.85**	21*	10	97025.5	**365.01**	298.49	**1.03**
11*	10	163720	**1918.51**	8785.5	**13.05**	22*	10	4.98E+06	**20.77**	493.017	**6.34**
12*	9	343487	**80.44**	25293	**1.94**	23*	9	2.31E+09	**126119**	1.24E+06	**188.58**
13*	9	1.52E+07	**303.44**	10236.7	**5491.76**	24*	9	548805	**113.44**	4001.65	**23.55**
14*	10	54466.7	**135.01**	759.94	**1.79**	25*	4	510.92	**93.02**	**54.37**	93.62
15*	10	199.96	**17.95**	35.92	**9.86**	3*	10	1.00E+10	**3.02E+07**	4673.18	**0.11**
16*	10	8.64E+07	**58875.3**	468.50	**4.43**	4*	10	461584	**33.68**	2301.8	**1.30**
17*	9	1.23E+10	**9375.63**	311467	**13.66**	50*	9	1.64E+06	**1788.8**	71460.5	**7.69**
18*	9	5.50E+07	**204569**	19986.2	**2.13**	6*	10	1.06E+10	**1.15E+07**	2293.18	**10.81**
19*	9	1.17E+06	**2983.57**	208.47	**111.36**	7*	9	1.98E+10	**56410.1**	982912	**8.86**
2[0*]	10	3.59E+06	**126.63**	980.99	**42.66**	8*	9	207240	**4411.55**	90128.1	**19.75**

the improvement over the BE fill-in is of orders of magnitude on all of them when $z = 17$, while on six out of seven (i.e., on 87.5%) instances when $z = 19$.

Computation times show the same behavior as in the previous benchmark. Regarding the number of mini-buckets, a smaller number of mini-buckets is in general attached to a better accuracy. This suggests a heuristic strategy to select the ordering in a pre-processed way by selecting the order producing the smallest number of mini-buckets (or, equivalently, the smallest number of new induced hyper-edges).

Noisy-OR networks. Our third domain is real-world noisy-OR networks generated by the Promedas expert system for internal medicine [14]. The benchmark contains 238 instances having 23 up to 2133 variables (mean number is 1048) with binary domain sizes and induced width up to 60.

Table 3 summarizes the results for $z = 25$. We report the mean relative error among sets of instances. The first column identifies the instances included in each set as a regular expression. For example, the first row includes instances with names matching or_chain_1[0*] (e.g., or_chain_1, or_chain_10, or_chain_101, etc). The second column indicates the size of the set. As before, we underline the best relative error for each set of instances, and highlight in bold face the best relative error wrt each partition heuristic. We do not report cpu time because its behavior is the same as for the previous benchmarks.

The MBE fill-in outperforms the BE fill-in on all sets, with the exception of or_chain_25* (which only has 4 instances). The improvement among the best BE fill-in is always of orders of magnitude. Using the SCP partitioning heuristic, the MBE fill-in clearly outperforms the BE fill-in on all sets, while when using the LMRE partitioning heuristic, the MBE fill-in is superior to the BE fill-in on all sets but or_chain_25*.

Combinatorial auctions. Our last domain is combinatorial auctions (CA). They allow bidders to bid for indivisible subsets of goods. We have generated CA using the path model of the CATS generator [8]. We experiment on instances with 20 and 50 goods, varying the number of bids from 80 to 200. For each parameter configuration, we

Table 4. Empirical results on Combinatorial Auctions. Path distribution.

nb. bids	z	nb. goods = 20				nb. goods = 50			
		BE fill-in		MBE fill-in		BE fill-in		MBE fill-in	
		lb.	RE	lb.	RE	lb.	RE	lb.	RE
80	15	493	0.010	**498**	0	**424.9**	0	423.3	0.004
85	15	371.5	0.010	**375.3**	0	439.4	0.010	**443.8**	0
90	15	**463.4**	0.000	458.4	0.011	**400.7**	0.000	398.1	0.006
95	15	524.9	0.001	**525.3**	0	458.6	0.016	**466.1**	0
100	15	577.5	0.018	**588.1**	0	498.8	0.004	**500.9**	0
105	15	549.9	0.009	**555.1**	0	**550.1**	0	539.2	0.020
110	15	631.7	0.001	**632.1**	0	587.9	0.008	**592.7**	0
115	15	604	0.023	**618**	0	581.2	0.006	**585**	0
120	15	498.4	0.018	**507.7**	0	555.6	0.016	**564.9**	0
125	15	659.8	0.003	**662**	0	**566.2**	0	558.9	0.013
130	15	623.1	0.017	**633.9**	0	**550.6**	0	534.9	0.029
135	15	734.4	0.009	**740.7**	0	**562.2**	0	560.2	0.004
140	15	765.5	0.015	**776.8**	0	702.9	0.015	**713.9**	0
145	15	746.9	0.001	**748**	0	502.8	0.025	**515.8**	0
150	15	680.7	0.012	**689**	0	**697.5**	0.000	696.5	0.001
155	15	**671.4**	0	666	0.008	647	0.016	**657.6**	0
160	15	744.4	0.002	**745.8**	0	777.3	0.029	**800.9**	0
165	15	808.9	0.013	**819.2**	0	667.3	0.019	**680**	0
170	15	**707.6**	0	**707.6**	0	586.9	0.048	**616.2**	0
175	15	812.7	0.012	**822.6**	0	673.5	0.012	**682**	0
180	15	786	0.011	**794.4**	0	773.2	0.013	**783.1**	0
185	15	888.7	0.016	**902.9**	0	835.7	0.015	**848.7**	0
190	15	927.3	0.002	**929.1**	0	648	0.011	**655.3**	0
195	15	823.6	0.024	**844**	0	854.8	0.020	**872.6**	0
200	15	866.8	0.020	**884.9**	0	781.1	0.020	**797.1**	0
80	20	**513.2**	0	512.4	0.002	439.5	0.005	**441.8**	0
85	20	389.5	0.004	**390.9**	0	**471.8**	0	470.6	0.003
90	20	493.1	0.005	**495.6**	0	424.3	0.002	**425.2**	0
95	20	564.2	0.008	**568.8**	0	**488.8**	0	488.3	0.001
100	20	**620.3**	0	618	0.004	**526.7**	0	525	0.003
105	20	593.5	0.003	**595.3**	0	576.3	0.002	**577.5**	0
110	20	673.7	0.009	**679.5**	0	612.8	0.009	**618.4**	0
115	20	662.2	0.020	**675.5**	0	622.1	0.005	**625.1**	0
120	20	549.5	0.015	**557.9**	0	594.2	0.005	**597.2**	0
125	20	**719.9**	0	719.1	0.001	**615.8**	0	614.3	0.002
130	20	689.6	0.010	**696.8**	0	**587.4**	0	581.5	0.010
135	20	**802.1**	0	792.8	0.012	607.2	0.006	**610.7**	0
140	20	**838.7**	0	838	0.001	762.8	0.014	**773.7**	0
145	20	825.3	0.019	**841.3**	0	548.2	0.018	**558.2**	0
150	20	758.9	0.007	**764.6**	0	763.3	0.016	**775.7**	0
155	20	**749.8**	0	749.2	0.001	712.8	0.021	**727.9**	0
160	20	**841.6**	0	834.9	0.008	868	0.007	**873.7**	0
165	20	912.1	0.019	**929.8**	0	742.6	0.025	**761.4**	0
170	20	783.6	0.010	**791.9**	0	669.3	0.021	**684**	0
175	20	911.1	0.004	**914.5**	0	756.9	0.020	**772**	0
180	20	868	0.007	**873.8**	0	873.2	0.015	**886.4**	0
185	20	994	0.004	**998.2**	0	930.1	0.013	**942.7**	0
190	20	1045.6	0.006	**1051.4**	0	742.8	0.023	**760.3**	0
195	20	954.3	0.005	**958.8**	0	956.4	0.024	**980.2**	0
200	20	994.5	0.005	**999.7**	0	900.5	0.002	**902.4**	0

generate samples of size 10. Table 4 shows the results for $z = \{15, 20\}$. Recall that for optimization tasks, only the SCP heuristic is defined.

The behavior for both configurations is almost the same. For 20 goods, the MBE fill-in outperforms the BE fill-in on 23 out of the 25 configurations of different number of bids when $z = 15$, and on 18 when $z = 19$. For 50 goods, the MBE fill-in outperforms the BE fill-in on 18 configurations of bids when $z = 15$, and on 20 when $z = 19$.

It is important to observe that the improvement over the BE fill-in is not as significant as for previous benchmarks. One possible reason is the nature of the marginalization operator: when summing, the quality of all operands impacts on the quality of the result; while when minimizing, the quality of the minimum operand is the only one that determines the quality of the result. Indeed, further investigation is needed.

5   Related Work

There are two early approaches based on mini-bucket elimination which use a variable elimination ordering different to the one used by bucket elimination: *greedy SIP* [10] and *Approximate Decomposition* (AD) [9].

Greedy SIP solves the problem by iteratively applying bucket elimination over subsets of functions. At each iteration, all variables are eliminated from the current subset and its elimination ordering is the one with induced width bounded by the control parameter z. The order in which variables are eliminated can be different from one iteration to another.

AD solves the problem by iteratively eliminating the variables of the problem and maintaining the width of the new problems bounded by z. If the elimination of a variable causes the width of the new problem to be greater than z, the new function is approximated with a combination of simpler ones such that the width is maintained under z.

Our scheme resembles these two approaches on that none of them uses the variable elimination ordering as dictated by bucket elimination. However, the value of our work is on clearly showing why a variable elimination heuristic should fit the actual structure of problems generated after each variable elimination.

6   Conclusions

Bucket Elimination (BE) and Mini-Bucket Elimination (MBE) are based on the sequential transformation of the original problem by sequentially eliminating variables, one at a time. The result of eliminating one variable is a new subproblem. Under the same variable elimination ordering, they generate a different sequence of subproblems. Although this important difference, MBE uses the elimination order obtained by a procedure designed for BE. Since this procedure selects the next variable to eliminate according to the structure of subproblems produced by BE, it will select *erroneous* variables according to the structure of subproblems generated by MBE.

This paper investigates a modification on how to compute the elimination ordering for MBE. Our approach computes the ordering by considering the real structure of the sequence of subproblems produced by MBE thanks to induced z-bounded hypergraphs. We demonstrate the effectiveness of this new ordering on a number of benchmarks over two important tasks: computing the probability of the evidence and finding the minimum cost assignment of a weighted CSP. We observed that the higher improvements are obtained on the first task. The nature of the marginalization operator may explain this fact. We plan to further investigate this issue.

There are other approximation algorithms based on variable elimination orderings (e.g., Iterative Join Graph Propagation [4]). In our future work we want to study the impact of our approach on their accuracy.

Acknowledgement. This work was supported by project TIN2009-13591-C02-01.

References

1. Bertelè, U., Brioschi, F.: Nonserial Dynamic Programming. Academic Press, London (1972)
2. Dechter, R.: Bucket elimination: A unifying framework for reasoning. Artificial Intelligence 113, 41–85 (1999)
3. Dechter, R.: Constraint Processing. Morgan Kaufmann, San Francisco (2003)
4. Dechter, R., Kask, K., Mateescu, R.: Iterative join-graph propagation. In: Proceedings of the 18th Conference in UAI, Edmonton, Canada, pp. 128–136 (2002)
5. Dechter, R., Rish, I.: Mini-buckets: A general scheme for bounded inference. Journal of the ACM 50(2), 107–153 (2003)
6. Freuder, E.: A sufficient condition for backtrack-free search. Journal of the ACM 29, 24–32 (1982)
7. Kask, K., Dechter, R.: A general scheme for automatic generation of search heuristics from specification dependencies. Artificial Intelligence 129, 91–131 (2001)
8. Pearson, M., Leyton-Brown, K., Shoham, Y.: Towards a universal test suite for combinatorial auction algorithms. In: ACM E-Commerce, pp. 66–76 (2000)
9. Larkin, D.: Approximate decomposition: A method for bounding and estimating probabilistic and deterministic queries. In: Proceedings UAI, Acapulco, Mexico, pp. 346–353 (2003)
10. Larkin, D.: Semi-independent partitioning: A method for bounding the solution to cop's. In: Rossi, F. (ed.) CP 2003. LNCS, vol. 2833, pp. 894–898. Springer, Heidelberg (2003)
11. Park, J.D.: Using weighted max-sat engines to solve mpe. In: Proc. of the 18th AAAI, Edmonton, Alberta, Canada, pp. 682–687 (2002)
12. Rollon, E., Dechter, R.: New mini-bucket partitioning heuristics for bounding the probability of evidence. In: Proc. of the 24th AAAI, Atlanta, Georgia, USA (2010)
13. Shenoy, P.: Axioms for dynamic programming. In: Computational Learning and Probabilistic Reasoning, pp. 259–275 (1996)
14. Wemmenhove, B., Mooij, J.M., Wiegerinck, W., Leisink, M.A.R., Kappen, H.J., Neijt, J.P.: Inference in the promedas medical expert system. In: 11th Conference on Artificial Intelligence in Medicine, Amsterdam, The Netherlands, pp. 456–460 (2007)

Search Combinators

Tom Schrijvers[1], Guido Tack[2], Pieter Wuille[2],
Horst Samulowitz[3], and Peter J. Stuckey[4]

[1] Universiteit Gent, Belgium
tom.schrijvers@ugent.be
[2] Katholieke Universiteit Leuven, Belgium
{guido.tack,pieter.wuille}@cs.kuleuven.be
[3] IBM Research, New York, USA
samulowitz@us.ibm.com
[4] National ICT Australia (NICTA) and University of Melbourne, Victoria, Australia
pjs@cs.mu.oz.au

Abstract. The ability to model search in a constraint solver can be an essential asset for solving combinatorial problems. However, existing infrastructure for defining search heuristics is often inadequate. Either modeling capabilities are extremely limited or users are faced with a low-level programming language and modeling search becomes unwieldy. As a result, major improvements in performance may remain unexplored.

This paper introduces *search combinators*, a lightweight and solver-independent method that bridges the gap between a conceptually simple search language (high-level, functional and naturally compositional) and an efficient implementation (low-level, imperative and highly non-modular). Search combinators allow one to define application-tailored strategies from a small set of primitives, resulting in a rich search language for the user and a low implementation cost for the developer of a constraint solver. The paper discusses two modular implementation approaches and shows, by empirical evaluation, that search combinators can be implemented without overhead compared to a native, direct implementation in a constraint solver.

1 Introduction

Search heuristics often make all the difference between effectively solving a combinatorial problem and utter failure. Heuristics make a search algorithm efficient for a variety of reasons, e.g., incorporation of domain knowledge, or randomization to avoid heavy-tailed runtimes. Hence, the ability to swiftly design search heuristics that are tailored towards a problem domain is essential for performance. This paper introduces search combinators, an approach to modeling search that achieves exactly this.

In CP, much attention has been devoted to facilitating the modeling of combinatorial problems. A range of high-level modeling languages, such as Zinc [9], OPL [22] and Comet [20], enable quick development and exploration of problem models. However, we see very little support on the side of formulating accompanying search heuristics. Either the design of search is restricted to a small set of predefined heuristics (e.g., MiniZinc [10]), or it is based on a low-level general-purpose programming language

J. Lee (Ed.): CP 2011, LNCS 6876, pp. 774–788, 2011.

(e.g., Comet [20]). The former is clearly too confining, while the latter leaves much to be desired in terms of productivity, since implementing a search heuristic quickly becomes a non-negligible effort. This also explains why the set of available heuristics is typically small: it takes a lot of time for CP system developers to implement heuristics, too – time they would much rather spend otherwise improving their system.

In this paper we show how to resolve this stand-off between solver developers and users with respect to a high-level search language.

For the user, we provide a compositional approach for expressing complex search heuristics based on an (extensible) set of primitive combinators. Even if the users are only provided with a small set of combinators, they can already express a vast range of combinations. Moreover, using combinators to programm application-tailored search is vastly more productive than resorting to a low-level language.

For the system developer, we show how to design and implement modular combinators. Developers do not have to cater explicitly for all possible combinator combinations. Small implementation efforts result in providing the user with a lot of expressive power. Moreover, the cost of adding one more combinator is small, yet the return in terms of additional expressiveness can be quite large.

The tough technical challenge we face here does not lie in designing a high-level syntax; several proposals have already been made (e.g., [14]). Our contribution is to bridge the gap between a conceptually simple search language (high-level, functional and naturally compositional) and an efficient implementation (typically low-level, imperative and highly non-modular). This is where existing approaches fail; they restrict the expressiveness of their search specification language to face up to implementation limitations, or they raise errors when the user strays out of the implemented subset.

We overcome this challenge by implementing the primitives of our search language as *mixin* components. As in Aspect-Oriented Programming, mixin components neatly encapsulate the *cross-cutting behavior* of primitive search concepts, which are highly entangled in conventional approaches. Cross-cutting means that a mixin component can interfere with the behavior of its sub-components (in this case, sub-searches). The combination of encapsulation *and* cross-cutting behavior is essential for systematic reuse of search combinators. Without this degree of modularity, minor modifications require rewriting from scratch.

An added advantage of mixin components is extensibility. We can add new features to the language by adding more mixin components. The cost of adding such a new component is small, because it does not require changes to the existing ones. Moreover, experimental evaluation bears out that this modular approach has no significant overhead compared to the traditional monolithic approach. Finally, our approach is solver-independent and therefore makes search combinators a potential standard for designing search. For that purpose we have made our code available at
`http://users.ugent.be/~tschrijv/SearchCombinators/`.

2   High-Level Search Language

Before we tackle the modular implementation challenge in the next section, we first present the syntax of our high-level search language and illustrate its expressive power.

$$s ::= \text{prune}$$
    prunes the node
  | base_search(...)
    label
  | let(v,e,s)
    introduce new variable v with
    initial value e, then perform s
  | assign(v,e)
    assign e to variable v and succeed
  | post(c,s)
    post constraint c at every node during s

| if(c,s_1,s_2)
  perform s_1 until c is false, then perform s_2
| and($[s_1,s_2,\ldots,s_n]$)
  perform $s1$, on success $s2$ otherwise fail, ...
| or($[s_1,s_2,\ldots,s_n]$)
  perform $s1$, on termination start $s2$, ...
| portfolio($[s_1,s_2,\ldots,s_n]$)
  perform $s1$, if not exhaustive start $s2$, ...
| restart(c,s)
  restart s as long as c holds

Fig. 1. Catalog of primitive search heuristics and combinators

In this paper we use a concrete syntax for this language, in the form of nested terms, that is compatible with the *annotation* language of MiniZinc [10]. Other concrete syntax forms are easily supported (e.g., we support C++ and Haskell).

The *expression language* comprises the typical arithmetic and comparison operators and literals that require no further explanation. Notable though is the fact that it allows references to the constraint variables and parameters of the underlying model.

2.1 Primitive Search Heuristics

The search language is used to define a *search heuristic*, which a *search engine* applies to each node of the search tree. For each node, the heuristic determines whether to continue search by creating child nodes, or to prune the tree at that node.

The search language features a number of primitives, listed in the catalog of Fig. 1, in terms of which more complex heuristics can be defined. We emphasize that this catalog is open-ended; we will see that the language implementation explicitly supports adding new primitives. Primitive search heuristics consist of *basic* heuristics and *combinators*. The former define complete (albeit very basic) heuristics by themselves, while the latter alter the behavior of one or more other heuristics and combinators. The two basic search heuristics (base_search and prune) create child nodes in the search tree under the current node or prune the subtree starting from the current node, while combinators (all remaining items in Fig. 1) decide e.g. which of their sub-heuristics to apply or to restart search.

Note that the queuing strategy (such as depth-first traversal) is determined separately by the search engine, it is thus orthogonal to the search language.

Basic Heuristics. There are two basic heuristics:

– base_search(*vars*, *var-select*, *value-select*) specifies a systematic search. If any of the variables *vars* are still not fixed at the current node, it creates child nodes according to *var-select* and *value-select* as variable- and value-selection strategies respectively. We do not elaborate the different options; these have been extensively studied in the literature. For example we make use of MiniZinc [10] base searches.

– prune cuts the search tree below the current node, resulting in a non-exhaustive search (explained below).

Note that base_search is a CP-specific primitive; other kinds of solvers provide their own search primitives. The rest of the search language is essentially solver-independent. While the solver provides few basic heuristics, the search language adds great expressive power by allowing these to be combined arbitrarily using combinators.

Combinators. The expressive power of the search language relies on combinators, which combine search heuristics (which can be basic or themselves constructed using combinators) into more complex heuristics.

An example of a combinator from the literature is limited discrepancy search (LDS): lds(s) denotes a heuristic that performs LDS over an underlying heuristic s, which can in turn be an arbitrarily complex composition of *any* of the heuristics listed in Fig. 1.

Now that we have explained the parametrized notation, let us run down the combinators in the catalog:

– let(v, e, s): introduces a new variable v with initial value e and visible in the search s, then continues with s.
– assign(v, e): assigns the value e to variable v and succeeds. Technically, this is not a combinator, but we list it here as it is used in combination with let.
– if(c, s_1, s_2) evaluates condition c at every node. If c holds, then it proceeds with s_1. Otherwise, s_2 is used for the node and all its children.
– and($[s_1, \ldots, s_n]$): and-sequential composition runs s_1. At every success leaf of s_1, it runs and($[s_2, \ldots, s_n]$).
– or($[s_1, \ldots, s_n]$): or-sequential composition runs s_1. Upon fully exploring the tree of s_1, search is restarted with or($[s_2, \ldots, s_n]$) regardless of failure or success of s_1.
– portfolio($[s_1, \ldots, s_n]$), in contrast, also runs s_1 in full, but only if s_1 was not exhaustive, does it restart with portfolio($[s_2, \ldots, s_n]$) (see further details on the meaning of *exhaustiveness* in the next paragraph).
– restart(c, s): repeatedly runs s in full. If s was not exhaustive, it is restarted, until condition c no longer holds.
– post(c, s): provides access to the underlying constraint solver, posting a constraint c at every node during s. If s is omitted, it posts the constraint and immediately succeeds.

The attentive reader may have noticed that lds(s) is actually not listed among the primitive combinators. Indeed, Sect. 2.2 shows next that it is a composition of primitive combinators. Moreover, as we have already pointed out, the depth-first traversal that is commonly associated with lds is entirely orthogonal to the search language.

Exhaustiveness. When a search has fully explored the search (sub)tree, without purposefully skipping parts using the prune primitive, it is said to be *exhaustive*. This information is used to decide whether or not to revisit the same search node, as it happens in the portfolio and restart combinators. For instance, in case of lds($10, s$), if the search tree defined by s has been fully explored with 5 discrepancies, there is no use in restarting with higher discrepancy bounds as that would simply reexplore the same tree.

The prune primitive is the only source of non-exhaustiveness. Combinators propagate exhaustiveness in the obvious way. E.g., $\mathsf{and}([s_1, \ldots, s_n])$ is exhaustive if all s_i are, while $\mathsf{portfolio}([s_1, \ldots, s_n])$ is exhaustive if one s_i is.

Statistics. Several combinators are centered around a conditional expression c. In addition to the conventional syntax, such a condition may refer to one or more *statistics* variables. Such statistics are collected for the duration of a subsearch until the condition is met. For instance $\mathsf{if}(\mathsf{depth} < 10, s_1, s_2)$ maintains the search depth statistic during subsearch s_1. At depth 10, the if combinator switches to subsearch s_2.

We distinguish two forms of statistics: *Local statistics* such as depth and discrepancies express properties of individual nodes. *Global statistics* such as nodes, time, failures and solutions are computed for entire search trees.

It is worthwhile to mention that developers (and advanced users) can also define their own statistics, just like combinators, to complement any predefined ones. In fact, in the implementation, statistics are a *subtype* of combinators, that can be queried for the statistic's value.

2.2 Composite Search Heuristics

Our search language draws its expressive power from the combination of primitive heuristics using combinators. The user can create new combinators by effectively defining macros in terms of existing combinators. The following examples show how to construct complex search heuristics familiar from the literature.

Limit: The limiting combinator $\mathsf{limit}(c, s)$ performs s while c is satisfied. Then it fails:

$$\mathsf{limit}(c, s) \equiv \mathsf{if}(c, s, \mathsf{prune})$$

We can limit search using any of the statistics defined previously, or indeed create and modify a new let variable to define limits on search.

Once: The well-known $\mathsf{once}(s)$ combinator is a special case of the limiting combinator where the number of solutions is not greater than one. This is simply achieved by maintaining and accessing the solutions statistic:

$$\mathsf{once}(s) \equiv \mathsf{limit}(\mathsf{solutions} < 1, s)$$

In contrast to prune, $\mathsf{post}(\mathit{false})$ represents an *exhaustive* search without solutions. This is exploited in the exhaustive variant of once:

$$\mathsf{exh\_once}(s) \equiv \mathsf{if}(\mathsf{solutions} < 1, s, \mathsf{post}(\mathit{false}))$$

Branch-and-bound: A slightly more advanced example is the branch-and-bound optimization strategy:

$$\mathsf{bab}(obj, s) \equiv \mathsf{let}(best, \infty, \mathsf{post}(obj < best, \mathsf{and}([s, \mathsf{assign}(best, obj)])))$$

which introduces a variable $best$ that initially takes value ∞ (for minimization). In every node, it posts a constraint to bound the objective variable by $best$. Whenever a new solution is found, the bound is updated accordingly.

Restarting branch-and-bound: This is a twist on regular branch-and-bound that restarts whenever a solution is found.

$$\text{restart\_bab}(obj, s) \equiv \text{let}(best, \infty, \text{restart}(true, \text{and}([\text{post}(obj < best), \text{once}(s),$$
$$\text{assign}(best, obj)])))$$

For: The for loop construct ($v \in [l, u]$) can be defined as:

$$\text{for}(v, l, u, s) \equiv \text{let}(v, l, \text{restart}(v \le u,$$
$$\text{portfolio}([s, \text{and}([\text{assign}(v, v + 1), \text{prune}])])))$$

It simply runs the search s times, which of course is only sensible if s makes use of side effects or the loop variable v. Note that assign succeeds, so we need to call prune afterwards in order to propagate the non-exhaustiveness of s to the restart combinator.

Limited discrepancy search [6] with an upper limit of l discrepancies for an underlying search s.

$$\text{lds}(l, s) \equiv \text{for}(n, 0, l, \text{limit}(\text{discrepancies} \le n, s))$$

The for construct iterates the maximum number of discrepancies n from 0 to l, while limit executes s as long as the number of discrepancies is smaller than n. The search makes use of the discrepancies statistic that is maintained by the search infrastructure. The original LDS visits the nodes in a specific order. The search described here visits the same nodes in the same order of discrepancies, but possibly in a different individual order – as this is determined by the global queuing strategy.

The following is a combination of branch-and-bound and limited discrepancy search for solving job shop scheduling problems, as described in [6]. The heuristic searches the Boolean variables *prec*, which determine the order of all pairs of tasks on the same machine. As the order completely determines the schedule, we then fix the start times using exh_once.

$$\text{bab}(makespan, \text{lds}(\infty, \text{and}([\text{base\_search}(prec, \dots),$$
$$\text{exh\_once}(\text{base\_search}(start, \dots))])))$$

Fully expanded, this heuristic consists of 17 combinators and is 11 combinators deep.

Iterative deepening [7] for an underlying search s is a particular instance of the more general pattern of restarting with an updated bound.

$$\text{id}(s) \equiv \text{ir}(\text{depth}, 0, +, 1, \infty, s)$$
$$\text{ir}(p, l, \oplus, i, u, s) \equiv \text{let}(n, l, \text{restart}(n \le u, \text{and}([\text{assign}(n, n \oplus i),$$
$$\text{limit}(p \le n, s)])))$$

With let, bound n is initialized to l. Search s is pruned when statistic p exceeds n, but iteratively restarted by restart with n updated to $n \oplus i$. The repetition stops when n exceeds u or when s has been fully explored. The bound increases geometrically, if we supply $*$ for $\oplus$, as in the restart_flip heuristic:

$$\text{restart\_flip}(p, l, i, u, s_1, s_2) \equiv \text{let}(flip, 1, \text{ir}(p, l, *, i, u, \text{and}([\text{assign}(flip, 1 - flip),$$
$$\text{if}(flip = 1, s_1, s_2)])))$$

This alternates between two search heuristics s_1 and s_2. Using this as its default strategy in the *free search* category, the lazy clause generation solver *Chuffed* scored most points in the 2010 MiniZinc Challenge[1].

Hot start: First perform search heuristic s_1 while condition c holds to initialize global parameters for a second search s_2. This heuristic is for example used for initialization of the widely applied *Impact* heuristic [13]. Note that we assume here that the values to be initialized are maintained by the underlying solver and that we omit an explicit reference to it.

$$\mathsf{hotstart}(c, s_1, s_2) \equiv \mathsf{portfolio}([\mathsf{limit}(c, s_1), s_2])$$

Radiotherapy treatment planning: The following search heuristic can be used to solve radiotherapy treatment planning problems [1]. The heuristic minimizes a variable k using branch-and-bound (bab), first searching the variables N, and then verifying the solution by partitioning the problem along the row_i variables for each row i one at a time (expressed as a MiniZinc array comprehension). Failure on one row must be caused by the search on the variables in N, and consequently search never backtracks into other rows.

$$\begin{aligned} \mathsf{bab}(k, \mathsf{and}([\mathsf{base\_search}(N, \dots)] &+\!+ \\ [\mathsf{exh\_once}(\mathsf{base\_search}&(row_i, \dots)) \mid i \text{ in } 1..n])) \end{aligned}$$

Dichotomic search [17] solves an optimization problem by repeatedly partitioning the interval in which the possible optimal solution can lie. It can be implemented by restarting as long the lower bound has not met the upper bound (line 2), computing the middle (line 3), and then using an or combinator to try the lower half (line 5). If it succeeds, $obj - 1$ is the new upper bound, otherwise, the lower bound is increased (line 6).

$$\begin{aligned} \mathsf{dicho}(s, obj, lb, ub) \equiv &\mathsf{let}(l, lb, \mathsf{let}(u, ub, \mathsf{let}(h, 0, \\ &\mathsf{restart}(l < u, \\ &\mathsf{let}(h, l + \lceil (u - l)/2 \rceil, \\ &\mathsf{once}(\mathsf{or}([\\ &\mathsf{and}([\mathsf{post}(l \le obj \le h), s, \mathsf{assign}(u, obj - 1)]), \\ &\mathsf{and}([\mathsf{assign}(l, h + 1), \mathsf{prune}])])) \\ &))))) \end{aligned}$$

3 Modular Combinator Design

The previous section caters for the user's needs, presenting a high-level modular syntax for our combinator-based search language. To cater for the system developer's needs, this section goes beyond modularity of syntax, introducing modularity of *design*.

---

[1] http://www.g12.csse.unimelb.edu.au/minizinc/challenge2010/

Modularity of design is the one property that makes our approach practical. Each combinator corresponds to a separate module that has a meaning and an implementation independent of the other combinators. This enables us to actually realize the search specifications defined by modular syntax.

Modularity of design also enables growing a system from a small set of combinators (e.g., those listed in Fig. 1), gradually adding more as the need arises. Advanced users can complement the system's generic combinators with a few application-specific ones.

Solver independence is another notable property of our approach. While a few combinators access solver-specific functionality (e.g., base_search and post), the approach as such and most combinators listed in Fig. 1 are in fact generic (solver- and even CP-independent); their design and implementation is reusable.

The solver-independence of our approach is reflected in the minimal interface that solvers must implement. This interface consists of an abstract type State which represents a state of the solver (e.g., the variable domains and accumulated constraint propagators) which supports copying. Truly no more is needed for the approach or all of the primitive combinators in Fig. 1, except for base_search and post which require CP-aware operations for querying variable domains, the solver status and posting constraints. Note that there need not be a 1-to-1 correspondence between an implementation of the abstract State type and the solver's actual state representation; e.g., for solvers based on trailing, techniques such as [11] can be used. We have implementations of the interface based on both copying and trailing.

In the following we explain how modularity of design is obtained. We show how to isolate the cross-cutting behavior (Sect. 3.1) and state (Sect. 3.2) of each combinator in a separate module, and how to compose these modules to obtain the combined effect.

3.1   The Message Protocol

To obtain a modular design of search combinators we step away from the idea that the behavior of a search combinator, like the and combinator, forms an indivisible whole; this leaves no room for interaction. The key insight here is that we must identify finer-grained steps, defining how different combinators interact at each node in the search tree. Interleaving these finer-grained steps of different combinators in an appropriate manner yields the composite behavior of the overall search heuristic, where each combinator is able to cross-cut the others' behavior.

Considering the diversity of combinators and the fact that not all units of behavior are explicitly present in all of them, designing this protocol of interaction is non-trivial. It requires studying the intended behavior and interaction of combinators to isolate the fine-grained units of behavior and the manner of interaction. The contribution of this section is an elegant and conceptually uniform design that is powerful enough to express all the combinators presented in this paper.

We present this design in the form of a *message protocol*. The protocol specifies a set of messages (i.e., an interface with one procedure for each fine-grained step) that have to be implemented by all combinators. It further stipulates in what order the messages are sent among the combinators.

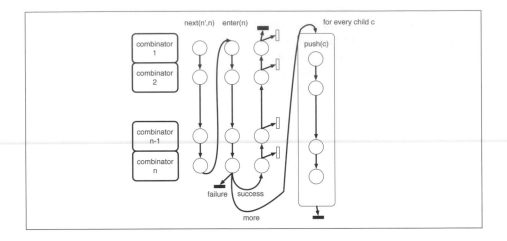

Fig. 2. The modular message protocol

General Setup. A node in the search tree consists of the corresponding solver State as well as the state information for the combinators. Search starts from the root node, which consists of a given initial solver State and state that is recursively initialized by the combinators that make up the search specification. Typically not all combinators are initialized from the start, e.g., $\text{and}([s_1, s_2])$ initializes s_1 from the start, but s_2 only when a success leaf of s_1 is reached.

From the root node, child nodes are derived and pushed onto an empty worklist. Then in the main loop, a node is popped from the worklist and processed, which may involve pushing new nodes on the worklist. Note that most systems will actually use a stack (implementing depth first search) for the worklist, but the protocol is orthogonal to the particular queuing strategy used.

Node Processing. Fig. 2 outlines the core combinator protocol. The diagram captures the order and direction of protocol messages between combinators for processing a single node of the search tree.

While in general a combinator composition is tree-shaped, the processing of any single search tree node n only involves a stack of combinators. For example, given $\text{or}([\text{and}([s_1, s_2]), \text{and}([s_3, s_4])])$, either s_1, s_2 or s_3, s_4 are *active* for n. The picture shows this stack of active combinators on the left. Every combinator in the stack has both a *super*-combinator above and a *sub*-combinator below, except for the *top* and the *bottom* combinators. The bottom is always a basic heuristic, typically a base_search.

The protocol is initiated by sending the enter(n) message (third column) to the top combinator, with the currently explored node n as an argument. The protocol ends whenever the combinator that last received a message decides not to pass the message on (depicted by an arrow to a small black rectangle; explained below).

The enter(*n*) message notifies all combinators of the new node *n* to be processed. Combinators may update their state, e.g., the node counter may increment its value. If the bottom is a base_search combinator, it checks the status of the node. If it has failed, the processing finishes. Otherwise, the base_search combinator checks whether there are children to be spawned from the current node (e.g., because some variables have not been instantiated yet). If there are none, the success message is sent. Otherwise, the children are created and one push(*c*) message is sent for each child *c*.

The success message is passed on bottom-up. Any combinator in between may decide to divert or drop the message. The former happens in the case of a sequential conjunction combinator and($[s_1, s_2]$): if s_1 has reached a successful leaf node in its search tree, a new search tree is spawned for s_2 rooted at the leaf of s_1.

The push(*c*) message proceeds top-down through each combinator. For instance, the number of discrepancies associated with the node *c* can be recorded. A base_search combinator records the constraint that is added to the solver state to create node *c*. Finally, *c* is pushed onto the search queue.

After processing of the current node *n* has finished, the search engine retrieves a new node n' from the search queue and re-initiates the protocol using the next(*n*, n') message. This message enables the combinators to determine whether *n* and n' are handled by exactly the same stack of combinators. That way, timing combinators can record time per subtree instead of per node, which leads to more accurate time measurements as timer resolution is usually too coarse to capture the processing of single nodes.

End of Processing. The black boxes in the figure indicate points where a combinator may decide to end processing the current node. These messages are propagated upwards from the originating combinator up to the root. One of the ancestor nodes may wish to react to such a message, in particular based on the following information.

Subsearch Termination and Exhaustiveness. A particular search combinator *s* is activated in a search tree node, then spreads to the children of that node and their descendants. When the last descendant node has been processed, *s* reverts back to the inactive status. This transition is important for several (mostly disjunctive) combinators. For instance, the portfolio($[s_1, s_2, \ldots]$) combinator activates s_{i+1} when s_i terminates. Whenever a combinator finishes processing a node (through success, failure or after spawning children) it communicates to its parent whether it is now terminated as a parameter of the message. In case of termination, it also communicates its exhaustiveness.

3.2 State Management

Most combinators are stateful in one way or another. For instance, the combinator if(nodes $< 1000, s_1, s_2$) maintains a node count, while and($[s_1, \ldots, s_n]$) maintains which of the sub-searches s_i is currently active.

We have found it useful to partition the state of search combinators in two classes, *global* and *local* state, which are implemented differently: *Global state* is shared among all nodes of an active combinator *s*. An update of the global state at one node is visible at all other nodes. The node count is an example of global state.

Local state is private to a single node of an active combinator *s*. An update to the local state at one node is not visible at another node. Local state is usually immutable and changes only through *inheritance*: child nodes derive their copy of local state from their parent's copy in a possibly modified form. For instance, node depth is a local state, where child nodes inherit the incremented depth of their parent. In and-sequential search, the index i of the currently active subsearch s_i is part of the local state.

4   Modular Combinator Implementation

The message-based combinator approach lends itself well to different implementation strategies. In the following we briefly discuss two diametrically opposed approaches we have explored: *dynamic composition* (interpretation) and *static composition* (compilation). Using these different approaches, combinators can be adapted to the implementation choices of existing solvers. Sect. 5 shows that both implementation approaches have competitive performance.

Dynamic composition. To support dynamic composition, we have implemented our combinators as C++ classes whose objects can be allocated and composed into a search specification at runtime. The protocol events correspond to virtual method calls between these objects. For the delegation mechanism from one object to another, we explicitly encode a form of dynamic inheritance called *open recursion* or *mixin inheritance* [2]. In contrast to the OOP inheritance built into C++ and Java, this mixin inheritance provides two essential abilities: 1) to determine the inheritance graph *at runtime* and 2) to use multiple copies of the same combinator class at different points in the inheritance graph. In contrast, C++'s built-in static inheritance provides neither.

The C++ library currently builds on top of the Gecode constraint solver[2]. However, the solver is accessed through a layer of abstraction that is easily adapted to other solvers (e.g., we have a prototype interface to the Gurobi MIP solver). The complete library weighs in at around 2500 lines of code, which is even less than Gecode's native search and branching components.

Static composition. In a second approach, also on top of Gecode, we statically compile a search specification to a tight C++ loop. Again, every combinator is a separate module independent of other combinator modules. A combinator module now does not directly implement the combinator's behavior. Instead it implements a code generator (in Haskell), which in turn produces the C++ code with the expected behavior.

Hence, our search language compiler parses a search specification, and composes (in mixin-style) the corresponding code generators. Then it runs the composite code generator according to the message protocol. The code generators produce appropriate C++ code fragments for the different messages, which are combined according to the protocol into the monolithic C++ loop. This C++ code is further post-processed by the C++ compiler to yield a highly optimized executable.

As for dynamic composition, the mixin approach is crucial, allowing us to add more combinators without touching the existing ones. At the same time we obtain with the press of a button several 1000 lines of custom low-level code for the composition of just a few combinators. In contrast, the development cost of hand crafted code is prohibitive.

---

[2] http://www.gecode.org/

A compromise between the above two approaches, itself static, is to employ the built-in mixin mechanism (also called *traits*) available in object-oriented languages such as Scala [4] to compose combinators. A dynamic alternative is to generate the combinator implementations using dynamic compilation techniques, for instance using the LLVM (Low Level Virtual Machine) framework. These options remain to be explored.

5   Experiments

This section evaluates the performance of our two implementations. It establishes that a search heuristic specified using combinators is competitive with a custom implementation of the same heuristic, exploring exactly the same tree.

Sect. 3.1 introduced a message protocol that defines the communication between the different combinators *for one node of the search tree*. Any overhead of a combinator-based implementation must therefore come from the processing of each node using this protocol. All combinators discussed earlier process each message of the protocol in constant time (except for the base_search combinators, of course). Hence, we expect at most a constant overhead per node compared to a native implementation of the heuristic.

In the following, two sets of experiments confirm this expectation. The first set consists of artificial benchmarks designed to expose the overhead per node. The second set consists of realistic combinatorial problems with complex search strategies.

The experiments were run on a 2.26 GHz Intel Core 2 Duo running Mac OS X. The results are the averages of 10 runs, with a coefficient of deviation less than 1.5%.

Stress Test. The first set of experiments measures the overhead of calling a single combinator during search. We ran a complete search of a tree generated by 7 variables with domain $\{0, \ldots, 6\}$ and *no* constraints (1 647 085 nodes). To measure the overhead, we constructed a basic search heuristic s and a stack of n combinators: portfolio([portfolio([... portfolio([s, prune]) ..., prune]), prune]), where n ranges from 0 to 20 (realistic combinator stacks, such as those from the examples in this paper, are usually not deeper than 10). The numbers in the following table report the runtime with respect to using the plain heuristic s, for both the static and the dynamic approach:

n	1	2	5	10	20
static %	106.6	107.7	112.0	148.3	157.5
dynamic %	107.3	117.6	145.2	192.6	260.9

A single combinator generates an overhead of around 7%, and 10 combinators add 50% for the static and 90% for the dynamic approach. In absolute runtime, however, this translates to an overhead of around 17 ms (70 ms) per million nodes and combinator for the static (dynamic) approach. Note that this is a worst-case experiment, since there is no constraint propagation and almost all the time is spent in the combinators.

Benchmarks. The second set of experiments shows that in practice, this overhead is dwarfed by the cost of constraint propagation and backtracking. Note that the experiments are not supposed to demonstrate the best possible search heuristics for the given problems, but that a search heuristic implemented using combinators is just as efficient as a native implementation.

	Compiled	Interpreted	Gecode
Golomb 10	0.61 s	101.8%	102.5%
Golomb 11	12.72 s	102.9%	101.8%
Golomb 12	125.40 s	100.6%	101.9%
Radiotherapy 1	71.13 s	105.9%	107.3%
Radiotherapy 2	11.78 s	108.3%	108.1%
Radiotherapy 3	69.89 s	108.1%	98.7%
Radiotherapy 4	106.04 s	109.2%	99.1%
Job-Shop G2	7.25 s	146.3%	101.2%
Job-Shop H5	20.88 s	153.2%	107.0%
Job-Shop H3	52.02 s	162.5%	102.8%
Job-Shop ABZ1-5	2319.00 s	103.7%	100.1%
Job-Shop mt10	2181.00 s	104.5%	99.9%

Fig. 3. Experimental results

Fig. 3 compares Gecode's optimization search engines with branch-and-bound implemented using combinators. On the well-known Golomb Rulers problem, both dynamic combinators and native Gecode are slightly slower than static combinators. Native Gecode uses dynamically combined search heuristics, but is much less expressive. That is why the static approach with its specialization yields better results.

On the radiotherapy problem (see Sect. 2.2), the dynamic combinators show an overhead of 6–9%. For native Gecode, exh_once must be implemented as a nested search, which performs similarly to the dynamic combinators. However, in instances 3 and 4, the compiled combinators lose their advantage over native Gecode. This is due to the processing of exh_once: As soon as it is finished, the combinator approach processes all nodes of the exh_once tree that are still in the search worklist, which are now pruned by exh_once. The native Gecode implementation simply discards the tree. We will investigate how to incorporate this optimization into the combinator approach.

The job-shop scheduling examples, using the combination of branch-and-bound and discrepancy limit discussed in Sect. 2.2, show similar behavior. In ABZ1-5 and mt10, the interpreted combinators show much less overhead than in the short-running instances. This is due to more expensive propagation and backtracking in these instances, reducing the relative overhead of executing the combinators.

In summary, the experiments show that the expressiveness and flexibility of a rich combinator-based search language can be achieved without any runtime overhead.

6   Related Work

This work directly extends our earlier work on **Monadic Constraint Programming** (MCP) [15]. MCP introduces stackable search transformers, which are a simple form of search combinators, but only provide a much more limited and low level form of search control. In trying to overcome its limitations we arrived at search combinators.

Constraint logic programming languages such as **ECLiPSe** [5] and **SICStus** Prolog [18] provide programmable search via the built-in search of the paradigm, allowing the user to define *goals* in terms of conjunctive or disjunctive sub-goals. The crucial difference to our combinator approach is that combinators can cross-cut the behavior of their sub-combinators, in the sense that a combinator higher up in the stack can interfere with a sub-combinator, while remaining fully compositional. This is not possible with Prolog goals, so apart from conjunction and disjunction, goal-based heuristics cannot be combined arbitrarily. ECLiPSe provides user programmable labeling as well as different strategies such as depth bounded, node bounded and limited discrepancy search. One can change the strategy, e.g., when the depth bound finishes. Users cannot define their own heuristics in the library, though they could be programmed from scratch.

The **Salsa** [8] language is an imperative domain-specific language for implementing search algorithms on top of constraint solvers. Its center of focus is a node in the search process. Programmers can write custom *Choice* strategies for generating next nodes from the current one; Salsa provides a regular-expression-like language for combining these Choices into more complex ones. In addition, Salsa can run custom procedures at the *exits* of each node, right after visiting it. We believe that Salsa's Choice construct is orthogonal to our approach and could be incorporated. Custom exit procedures show similarity to combinators, but no support is provided for arbitrary composition.

Oz [19] was the first language to truly separate the definition of the constraint model from the exploration strategy [16]. Computation spaces capture the solver state and the possible choices. Strategies such as DFS, BFS, LDS, Branch and Bound and Best First Search are implemented by a combination of *copying* and *recomputation* of computation spaces. The strategies are monolithic, there is no notion of search combinators.

IBM ILOG CP Optimizer [3] supports Prolog-style goals in C++ [12], and like Prolog goals, these do not support cross-cutting.

Comet [20] features fully programmable search [21], with a clean separation between search tree specification and exploration strategy. Search trees are specified using the non-deterministic primitives `try` and `tryall`, corresponding to our base_search heuristics. Exploration is delegated to a *search controller*, which, similar to our combinators, defines what to do when starting or ending a search, failing, or adding a new choice. Choices are represented as continuations. Complex hybrid heuristics can be constructed as custom controllers. The main difference to our approach is that controllers are not composable, but have to be implemented by inheritance or from scratch.

7 Conclusion

We have shown how combinators provide a powerful high-level language for modeling complex search heuristics. The modular implementation relieves system developers from a high implementation cost and yet imposes no runtime penalty.

For future work, the next step for us will be a full integration into MiniZinc. Furthermore, parallel search on multi-core hardware fits perfectly in our combinator framework. We have already performed a number of preliminary experiments and will further explore the benefits of search combinators in a parallel setting. We will also explore potential optimizations (such as the short-circuit of exh_once from Sect. 5) and different compilation strategies (e.g., combining the static and dynamic approaches from Sect. 4). Finally, combinators need not necessarily be heuristics that control the search. They may also monitor search, e.g., by gathering statistics or visualizing the search tree.

Acknowledgments. NICTA is funded by the Australian Government as represented by the Department of Broadband, Communications and the Digital Economy and the Australian Research Council. This work was partially supported by Asian Office of Aerospace Research and Development grant 10-4123.

References

1. Baatar, D., Boland, N., Brand, S., Stuckey, P.J.: CP and IP approaches to cancer radiotherapy delivery optimization. Constraints 16(2), 173–194 (2011)
2. Cook, W.R.: A denotational semantics of inheritance. Ph.D. thesis, Brown University (1989)
3. IBM ILOG CP Optimizer (2011), http://www-01.ibm.com/software/integration/optimization/cplex-cp-optimizer/
4. Cremet, V., Garillot, F., Lenglet, S., Odersky, M.: A core calculus for Scala type checking. In: Královič, R., Urzyczyn, P. (eds.) MFCS 2006. LNCS, vol. 4162, pp. 1–23. Springer, Heidelberg (2006)
5. ECLiPSe (2008), http://www.eclipse-clp.org/
6. Harvey, W.D., Ginsberg, M.L.: Limited discrepancy search. In: IJCAI, pp. 607–613 (1995)
7. Korf, R.E.: Depth-first iterative-deepening: an optimal admissible tree search. Artif. Intell. 27, 97–109 (1985)
8. Laburthe, F., Caseau, Y.: SALSA: A language for search algorithms. Constraints 7(3), 255–288 (2002)
9. Marriott, K., Nethercote, N., Rafeh, R., Stuckey, P., Garcia de la Banda, M., Wallace, M.: The design of the Zinc modelling language. Constraints 13(3), 229–267 (2008)
10. Nethercote, N., Stuckey, P.J., Becket, R., Brand, S., Duck, G.J., Tack, G.: MiniZinc: Towards a standard CP modelling language. In: Bessière, C. (ed.) CP 2007. LNCS, vol. 4741, pp. 529–543. Springer, Heidelberg (2007)
11. Perron, L.: Search procedures and parallelism in constraint programming. In: Jaffar, J. (ed.) CP 1999. LNCS, vol. 1713, pp. 346–361. Springer, Heidelberg (1999)
12. Puget, J.F.: A C++ implementation of CLP. In: Proceedings of the Second Singapore International Conference on Intelligent Systems (SPICIS). pp. B256–B261 (November 1994)
13. Refalo, P.: Impact-based search strategies for constraint programming. In: Wallace, M. (ed.) CP 2004. LNCS, vol. 3258, pp. 557–571. Springer, Heidelberg (2004)
14. Samulowitz, H., Tack, G., Fischer, J., Wallace, M., Stuckey, P.: Towards a lightweight standard search language. In: ModRef (2010)
15. Schrijvers, T., Stuckey, P.J., Wadler, P.: Monadic constraint programming. Journal of Functional Programming 19(6), 663–697 (2009)
16. Schulte, C.: Programming constraint inference engines. In: Smolka, G. (ed.) CP 1997. LNCS, vol. 1330, pp. 519–533. Springer, Heidelberg (1997)
17. Sellmann, M., Kadioglu, S.: Dichotomic search protocols for constrained optimization. In: Stuckey, P.J. (ed.) CP 2008. LNCS, vol. 5202, pp. 251–265. Springer, Heidelberg (2008)
18. SICStus Prolog (2008), http://www.sics.se/isl/sicstuswww/site/
19. Smolka, G.: The Oz programming model. In: van Leeuwen, J. (ed.) Computer Science Today. LNCS, vol. 1000, pp. 324–343. Springer, Heidelberg (1995)
20. Van Hentenryck, P., Michel, L.: Constraint-Based Local Search. MIT Press, Cambridge (2005)
21. Van Hentenryck, P., Michel, L.: Nondeterministic control for hybrid search. Constraints 11(4), 353–373 (2006)
22. Van Hentenryck, P., Perron, L., Puget, J.F.: Search and strategies in OPL. ACM TOCL 1(2), 285–315 (2000)

Variable Independence and Resolution Paths for Quantified Boolean Formulas

Allen Van Gelder

University of California, Santa Cruz
http://www.cse.ucsc.edu/~avg

Abstract. Variable independence in quantified boolean formulas (QBFs) informally means that the quantifier structure of the formula can be rearranged so that two variables reverse their outer-inner relationship without changing the value of the QBF. Samer and Szeider introduced the standard dependency scheme and the triangle dependency scheme to safely over-approximate the set of variable pairs for which an outer-inner reversal might be unsound (JAR 2009).

This paper introduces resolution paths and defines the resolution-path dependency relation. The resolution-path relation is shown to be the root (smallest) of a lattice of dependency relations that includes quadrangle dependencies, triangle dependencies, strict standard dependencies, and standard dependencies. Soundness is proved for resolution-path dependencies, thus proving soundness for all the descendants in the lattice.

It is shown that the biconnected components (BCCs) and block trees of a certain clause-literal graph provide the key to computing dependency pairs efficiently for quadrangle dependencies. Preliminary empirical results on the 568 QBFEVAL-10 benchmarks show that in the outermost two quantifier blocks quadrangle dependency relations are smaller than standard dependency relations by widely varying factors.

1 Introduction

Variable independence in quantified boolean formulas (QBFs) informally means that two variables that are adjacent in the quantifier structure can exchange places without changing the value of the QBF. The motivation for knowing such shifts are sound (i.e., cannot change the value of a closed QBF, which is *true* or *false*) is that QBF solvers have more flexibility in their choice of which variable to select for a solving operation. They are normally constrained to obey the quantifier order.

Samer and Szeider introduced dependency schemes to record dependency pairs (p, q) such that q is inner to p in the quantifier structure and any rearrangement that places q outer to p *might* be unsound. The absence of (p, q) ensures that there *is* some sound rearrangement that places q outer to p [6]. The idea is that the pairs in a dependency scheme can be computed with reasonable effort, and are a safe over-approximation of the exact relation that denotes unsound rearrangements of quantifier order. A smaller dependency scheme allows more

J. Lee (Ed.): CP 2011, LNCS 6876, pp. 789–803, 2011.

Fig. 1. Lattice of dependency relations

pairs to be treated as independent. They proposed two nontrivial schemes, the "standard" dependency scheme, which is easiest to compute, but coarse, and the "triangle" dependency scheme, which is more refined. Lonsing and Biere have reported favorable results on an implementation of the "standard" dependency scheme [5]. We are not aware of any implementation of triangle dependencies. Lonsing and Biere provide additional bibliography and discussion of other approaches for increasing solver flexibility.

This paper introduces **resolution paths** in Section 4 to define a dependency relation that is smaller than those proposed by Samer and Szeider. Resolution paths are certain paths in the resolution graph [7] associated with the quantifier-free part of the QBF. A hierarchy of new relations is introduced, called resolution-path dependencies (smallest), quadrangle dependencies, and strict standard dependencies. Quadrangle dependencies refine the triangle dependencies; strict standard dependencies refine standard dependencies. The resulting lattice is shown in Figure 1. Soundness is proved for resolution-path dependencies, thus proving soundness for all the descendants in the hierarchy. A slightly longer version of this paper contains some details omitted here, due to the page limit.[1]

The main obstacle is computing the dependency relation for anything more refined than standard dependencies or strict standard dependencies. Samer and Szeider sketched a polynomial-time algorithm, which enabled them to get interesting theoretical results involving triangle dependencies and back-door sets. It appears to be too inefficient for practical use on large QBF benchmarks and, to the best of our knowledge, it has not been implemented.

Samer and Szeider used a certain undirected graph, similar to what is called the clause-variable incidence graph in the literature, for their algorithm. This *clause-literal graph*, as we shall call it, is normally already represented in the data structures of a solver, as occurrence lists, and is practical to use for the standard dependency relation [5]. It is easy to see standard dependencies (and strict standard dependencies) are based on the connected components (CCs) of this graph. Strict standard dependencies, introduced in Definition 5.2, are essentially a cost-free improvement on standard dependencies, once this fact is recognized.

This paper shows in Section 6 that the **biconnected components** (BCCs) of the clause-literal graph provide the key to identifying dependency pairs for **quadrangle dependencies**, introduced in Definition 5.2. Like CCs, BCCs can

---

[1] Please see http://www.cse.ucsc.edu/~avg/QBFdeps/ for a more detailed version of this paper and a prototype program.

be computed in time linear in the graph size. Based on the BCC structure, the clause-literal graph can be abstracted into a **block tree**, so-called in the literature.

Quadrangle dependencies can be determined by paths in the block tree, which is normally much smaller than the clause-literal graph. Our algorithm could be modified to compute triangle dependencies, but this would cost the same as quadrangle dependencies, and produce less independence, so this modification has not been implemented. We avoid calling the quadrangle dependency relation a dependency *scheme* to avoid conflicting with the technical requirements stated by Samer and Szeider [6].

In a prototype `C++` implementation that builds dependency relations, computing BCCs was found to be as cheap as computing connected components (needed for any dependency relation), on the 568 QBFEVAL-10 benchmarks. Preliminary empirical results are given in Section 7, mainly consisting of statistics about the BCC structure and size of quadrangle dependency relations in these benchmarks.

The primary goal of this work to provide methods by which practical QBF solvers can soundly carry out a broader range of the operations they already perform. (Readers should be familiar with QBF solver operations to follow these paragraphs, or come back after reading Section 2.) The *universal reduction* operation is ubiquitous in QBF solvers. The standard requirement is that all existential literals must be independent of the universal literal u to be deleted in the *trivial* dependency relation. Theorem 4.9 shows that independence in the quadrangle relation is sufficient. Search-based QBF solvers make variable assignments as assumptions (the word "decision" is often used). Normally, an existential variable can be selected only if it is independent of *all* unassigned universal variables in the *trivial* dependency relation. Theorem 4.7 shows that independence in the quadrangle relation is sufficient.

2   Preliminaries

In general, *quantified boolean formulas* (QBFs) generalize propositional formulas by adding universal and existential quantification of boolean variables. See [3] for a thorough introduction and a review of any unfamiliar terminology. A *closed* QBF evaluates to either 0 (*false*) or 1 (*true*), as defined by induction on its principal operator.

1. $(\exists x\, \phi(x)) = 1$ iff $(\phi(0) = 1$ or $\phi(1) = 1)$.
2. $(\forall x\, \phi(x)) = 0$ iff $(\phi(0) = 0$ or $\phi(1) = 0)$.
3. Other operators have the same semantics as in propositional logic.

This definition emphasizes the connection of QBF to two-person games, in which player E (Existential) tries to set existential variables to make the QBF evaluate to 1, and player A (Universal) tries to set universal variables to make the QBF evaluate to 0 (see [4] for more details).

For this paper QBFs are in **_prenex conjunction normal form_** (**PCNF**), i.e., $\Psi = \overrightarrow{Q}.\mathcal{F}$ consists of prenex $\overrightarrow{Q}$ and clause matrix $\mathcal{F}$. Clauses may be written enclosed in square brackets (e.g., $[p, q, \overline{r}]$). Literals are variables or negated variables, with overbar denoting negation. Usually, letters e and others near the beginning of the alphabet denote existential literals, while letters u and others near the end of the alphabet denote universal literals. Letters like p, q, r denote literals of unspecified quantifier type. The variable underlying a literal p is denoted by $|p|$ where necessary.

The quantifier prefix is partitioned into _quantifier blocks_ of the same quantifier type. Each quantifier block has a unique _qdepth_, with the outermost block having qdepth $= 1$.

The proof system known as _Q-resolution_ consists of two operations, _resolution_ and _universal reduction_. Q-resolution is of central importance for QBFs because it is a sound and complete proof system [2]. Resolution is defined as usual, except that the clashing literal is always existential; universal reduction is special to QBF. Let α, β, and γ be possibly empty sets of literals.

$$\mathrm{res}_e(C_1, C_2) = \alpha \cup \beta \qquad \text{where } C_1 = [e, \alpha], \ C_2 = [\overline{e}, \beta] \qquad (1)$$

$$\mathrm{unrd}_u(C_3) = \gamma \qquad \text{where } C_3 = [C]_3 = [u, \gamma] \qquad (2)$$

Resolvents must be non-tautologous for Q-resolution. $\mathrm{unrd}_u(C_3)$ is defined only if u is **_tailing_** for γ, which means that the quantifier depth (qdepth) of u is greater than that of any existential literal in γ.

A **_Q-derivation_**, often denoted as π, is a directed acyclic graph (DAG) in which each node is either an input clause (a DAG leaf), or a proof operation (an internal node) with a specified clashing literal or reduction literal, and edge(s) to its operand(s). A _Q-refutation_ is a Q-derivation of the empty clause.

An **_assignment_** is a partial function from variables to truth values, and is usually represented as the set of literals that it maps to _true_. Assignments are denoted by ρ, σ, τ, etc. Applications of an assignment σ to a logical expression are denoted by $q\lceil_\sigma$, $C\lceil_\sigma$, $\mathcal{F}\lceil_\sigma$, etc. If σ assigns variables that are quantified in Ψ, those quantifiers are deleted in $\Psi\lceil_\sigma$, and their variables receive the assignment specified by σ.

3 Regular Q-Resolution

In analogy with regular resolution in propositional calculus, we define Q-resolution to be regular if no variable is resolved upon more than once on any path in the proof DAG. We need the following property for analyzing resolution paths.

Theorem 3.1. Regular Q-resolution and regular tree-like Q-resolution are complete for QBF.

Proof: The proof for regular Q-resolution is the same as in the paper that showed Q-resolution is complete for QBF [2]. It is routine to transform a regular Q-resolution derivation into a regular tree-like Q-resolution derivation of the same clause, by splitting nodes as needed, working from the leaves (original clauses) up. ∎

4   Resolution Paths

This section defines resolution paths and resolution-path dependencies, then states and proves the main results in Theorem 4.7 and subsequent theorems. Let a closed PCNF $\Psi = \vec{Q}.\mathcal{G}$ be given in which the quantifier block at qdepth $d+1$ is existential. Consider the *resolution graph* $G = (V, E)$ defined as follows [7]:

Definition 4.1. The *qdepth-limited resolution graph* $G = (V, E)$ at qdepth $d+1$ is the undirected graph in which:

1. V, the vertex set, consists of clauses in $\mathcal{G}$ containing some existential literal of qdepth at least $d+1$;
2. E, the undirected edge set, consists of edges between clauses C_i and C_j in V, where there is a unique literal q such that $q \in C_i$ and $\overline{q} \in C_j$, so that C_i and C_j have a non-tautologous resolvent. Further, q is required to be existential and its qdepth must be $d+1$ *or greater*. Each edge is annotated with the variable that qualifies it as an edge.

A ***resolution path of depth*** $d+1$ is a path in G such that no two *consecutive* edges are annotated with the same variable. (Nonconsecutive edges with the same variable label are permitted and variable labels with qdepths greater than $d+1$ are permitted.) ☐

Definition 4.2. We say that a literal p *presses on* an existential literal q in the graph G defined in Definition 4.1 if there is a resolution path of depth $d+1$ connecting a vertex that contains $\overline{p}$ with a vertex that contains q without using an edge annotated with $|q|$. Similarly, p *presses on* $\overline{q}$ if there is a resolution path of depth $d+1$ connecting a vertex that contains $\overline{p}$ with a vertex that contains $\overline{q}$ without using an edge annotated with $|q|$. ☐

One may think of "presses on" as a weak implication chain: if all the clauses involved are binary, it actually is an implication chain. An example is discussed later in Example 5.4 and Figure 3 after some other graph structures have been introduced. The intuition is that if literal p presses on literal q, then making p *true* makes it more likely that q will need to be *true* to make a satisfying assignment. Theorem 4.7 shows that transposing the variable order in the quantifier prefix is sound, even though many combinations of pressing are present. Only certain combinations are dangerous.

We say that a sequence S' is a ***subsequence*** of a sequence S if every element in S' is also in S, in the same order as S, but not necessarily contiguous in S.

The next theorem shows that Q-resolution cannot bring together variables unless there is a "presses on" relationship in the original clauses. This suggests that resolution paths are the natural form of connection for variable dependencies.

Theorem 4.3. Let $\Psi = \vec{Q}.\mathcal{G}$ be a closed PCNF. Let π be a regular tree-like Q-resolution derivation from Ψ. For all literals p and for all *existential* literals f, if there is a clause (input or derived) in π that contains both p and f, then the order of sibling subtrees of π may be swapped if necessary so that a resolution path from a clause with p to a clause with f appears as a subsequence of the leaves of π (not necessarily contiguous, but in order).

Proof: The proof is by induction on the subtree structure of π. The base case is that p and f are together in a clause of $\mathcal{G}$, say D_1, which is a leaf of π. Then D_1 constitutes a resolution path from p to f.

For any non-leaf subtree, say π_1, assume the theorem holds for all proper subtrees of π_1. That is, assume for all literals q and for all *existential* literals e, if there is a clause in a proper subtree of π_1, say π_2, that contains both q and e, then the subtrees of π_2 may be swapped so that a resolution path from a clause with q to a clause with e appears as a subsequence of the leaves of π_2.

Suppose that clause D_1, the root clause of π_1 contains both p and f. If p and f appear in a clause in a proper subtree of π_1, then the inductive hypothesis states that the needed resolution path can be obtained, so assume p and f do *not* appear together in any proper subtree of π_1.

Arrange the two principal subtrees of π_1 so that p is in the root clause of the left subtree and f is in the root clause of the right subtree (p and/or f might be in both subtrees). Let the clashing literal be g at the root of π_1. That is, g appears in the left operand and $\overline{g}$ appears in the right operand of the resolution whose resolvent is D_1.

By the inductive hypothesis, the left subtree has a resolution path P_L from a clause with p to a clause with g as a subsequence of its leaves. Also, the right subtree has a resolution path P_R from a clause with $\overline{g}$ to a clause with f as a subsequence of its leaves. Concatenate P_L and P_R (with the edge being labeled $|g|$) to give a resolution path from a clause with p to a clause with f. Since $|g|$ was a clashing literal at D_1, above the two subtrees, by regularity of the derivation, $|g|$ cannot appear as an edge label in either P_L or P_R, so the concatenation cannot have consecutive edges labeled with $|g|$. ∎

We now consider when transposing adjacent quantified variables of different quantifier types in the quantifier prefix does not change the value of the QBF.

Definition 4.4. Let a closed PCNF $\Psi = \overrightarrow{Q}.\mathcal{G}$ be given in which the universal literal u is at qdepth d and the existential literal e is at some qdepth greater than d. The pair (u, e) satisfies the **resolution-path independence criterion** if (at least) one of the following conditions hold in the depth-limited graph G defined in Definition 4.1:

(A) u *does not* press on $\overline{e}$ and $\overline{u}$ *does not* press on $\overline{e}$; or
(B) $\overline{u}$ *does not* press on e and $\overline{u}$ *does not* press on $\overline{e}$.

If u and e are variables, the pair (u, e) satisfies the **resolution-path independence criterion for variables** if any of (u, e) or $(u, \overline{e})$ or $(\overline{u}, e)$ or $(\overline{u}, \overline{e})$ satisfies the resolution-path independence criterion for literals. □

Definition 4.5. Let universal u and existential e be variables, as in Definition 4.4. We say the pair (u, e) is a **resolution-path dependency tuple** if and only if (at least) one of the following conditions holds in G:

(C) u presses on e and $\overline{u}$ presses on $\overline{e}$; or
(D) $\overline{u}$ presses on e and u presses on $\overline{e}$.

Lemma 4.6 states that either this definition or Definition 4.4, but not both, applies for pairs (u, e) of the correct types and qdepths.   □

Lemma 4.6. If u and e are universal and existential variables, respectively, then (u, e) satisfies the resolution-path independence criterion for variables if and only if e does *not* have a resolution-path dependency upon u.

    Proof: Apply DeMorgan's laws and distributive laws to the definitions.   ■

We are now ready to state the main theoretical results of the paper. We use *transpose* in its standard sense to mean interchange of two adjacent elements in a sequence.

Theorem 4.7. Let a closed PCNF $\Psi = \vec{Q}.\mathcal{G}$ be given in which the universal literal u is at qdepth d and is adjacent in the quantifier prefix to the existential literal e at qdepth $d + 1$. Let (u, e) satisfy the resolution-path independence criterion for literals (Definition 4.4). Then transposing $|u|$ and $|e|$ in the quantifier prefix does not change the value of Ψ.

    Proof: It suffices to show that transposing u to a later position does not cause Ψ to change in value from 1 to 0. We show this holds for all assignments σ to all variables outer to u in Ψ. That is, let $\vec{Q}_{rem}$ be the suffix of $\vec{Q}$ beginning immediately after $\forall u \exists e$, and define

$$\Phi = \forall u \exists e \, \vec{Q}_{rem}.\mathcal{F}, \quad \text{where } \mathcal{F} = \mathcal{G}\lceil_\sigma \tag{3}$$

$$\Phi' = \exists e \forall u \, \vec{Q}_{rem}.\mathcal{F}, \tag{4}$$

Note that if the hypotheses (A) and (B) in Definition 4.4 hold for Ψ, then they also hold for Φ. Throughout this proof "A" and "B" refer to these conditions. Suppose Φ' evaluates to 0. By Theorem 3.1 there is a regular tree-like Q-refutation π' of Φ'. Note that π' has no redundant clauses; they all contribute to the refutation. Let us attempt to use π' as a starter for π, which we want to be a Q-refutation of Φ. For notation, any primed symbol (such as D') in Φ' or π' represents the corresponding unprimed symbol (such as D) in Φ or π.

    What operation of π' can be incorrect for π? The only possibilities are a universal reduction involving a clause containing literals on both $|u|$ and $|e|$. In π', $|u|$ is tailing w.r.t. $|e|$, whereas in π it is not.

    The key observation is that a regular tree-like Q-refutation derivation from Φ' cannot produce certain clauses containing literals on both $|u|$ and $|e|$, due to Theorem 4.3. Any resolution path in Φ from u or $\overline{u}$ to e or $\overline{e}$ that is implied by applying Theorem 4.3 to π' cannot contain edges labeled with $|e|$, by regularity. So such a path is also a resolution path after the transposition of u and e in the quantifier prefix. Such a resolution path in Φ' or Φ is also a resolution path at the corresponding quantifier depth (i.e., $d + 1$) in Ψ. The theorem hypothesis that Definition 4.4 holds, together with Lemma 4.6, prohibits certain resolution paths that would imply that Definition 4.5 holds.

As stated, the only cases where the operation in π' might not be imitated in π are where the operation is a universal reduction on u or $\overline{u}$ in a clause D'. Let D in π correspond to D' in π'. Without loss of generality we assume that all universals *other than* u or $\overline{u}$ have already been reduced out of D'. There are several cases to examine, to show that the problematic operations in π' can always be transformed into correct operations in π that achieve a Q-refutation of Φ. It will follow that transposing u and e does not change the evaluation of Ψ.

If D' contains u, in π' let the clause $D'_2 = \mathsf{unrd}_u(D')$. D'_2 must contain e or $\overline{e}$ or the same reduction can apply to D.

If D' contains u and D'_2 contains e, we cannot have case (B), so consider case (A). The reduced clause D'_2 must resolve on e with some clause, say C', that contains $\overline{e}$. But C' cannot contain $\overline{u}$. Let π resolve D with C, giving D_2. D_2 must be non-tautologous and now u can be reduced out, constructing a Q-refutation of Φ.

If D' contains u and D'_2 contains $\overline{e}$, neither case (A) nor case (B) is possible.

If D' contains $\overline{u}$, in π' let the clause $D'_3 = \mathsf{unrd}_{\overline{u}}(D')$. D'_3 must contain e or $\overline{e}$ or the same reduction can apply to D.

If D' contains $\overline{u}$ and D'_3 contains e, D'_3 must resolve with some clause, say C'_3, that contains $\overline{e}$. C'_3 cannot contain u in either case (A) or (B). Let π resolve D with C_3, giving D_3. D_3 must be non-tautologous and now $\overline{u}$ can be reduced out, constructing a Q-refutation of Φ.

If D' contains $\overline{u}$ and D'_3 contains $\overline{e}$, we cannot have case (A), so consider case (B). The reduced clause D'_3 must resolve with some clause, say C'_4, that contains e. But C'_4 cannot contain u. Let π resolve D with C_4, giving D_4. D_4 must be non-tautologous and now $\overline{u}$ can be reduced out, constructing a Q-refutation of Φ. ∎

Corollary 4.8. If e is an existential pure literal in the matrix of a closed QBF Ψ, then e may be placed outermost in the quantifier prefix without changing the value of Ψ. If u is a universal pure literal in a closed QBF Ψ, then u may be placed innermost in the quantifier prefix without changing the value of Ψ. ∎

Next we consider cases in which u and e are separated by more than one qdepth. Although it might not be sound to revise the quantifier prefix, we still might be able to perform universal reduction and other operations soundly.

Theorem 4.9. Let a closed PCNF $\Psi = \vec{Q}.\mathcal{G}$ be given in which the universal literal u is at qdepth d and the existential literals $e_1, \ldots, e_k$ are at qdepths greater than d. Let $C_0 = [\alpha, u, e_1, \ldots, e_k]$ be clause in $\mathcal{G}$, where α (possibly empty) consists of existential literals with qdepths less than d and universal literals. For each $i \in \{1, \ldots, k\}$, let $(|u|, |e_i|)$ satisfy the resolution-path independence criterion for variables (Definition 4.4). Then deleting u from C_0 does not change the truth value of Ψ. That is, universal reduction on u in C_0 is sound.

Proof: The proof idea is similar to Theorem 4.7, but is more involved because Theorem 4.3 needs to be invoked on multiple subtrees. It suffices to show that deletion of u from C_0 does not cause Ψ to change from 1 to 0. We show this holds for all assignments σ to all variables outer to u in Ψ. That is, let $\vec{Q}_{rem}$ be the suffix of $\vec{Q}$ beginning immediately after $\forall u$, and define

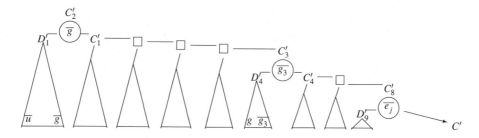

Fig. 2. Refutation π' exhibiting resolution path from $\overline{u}$ to $\overline{e_j}$ for proof of Theorem 4.9. Circles contain clashing literals of resolutions that derive clauses immediately above them.

$$\Phi = \forall u\, \overrightarrow{Q}_{rem}.\mathcal{F}, \quad \text{where } \mathcal{F} = \mathcal{G}\lceil_\sigma \tag{5}$$

$$\Phi' = \forall u\, \overrightarrow{Q}_{rem}.\mathcal{F}', \tag{6}$$

where $\mathcal{F}'$ is obtained from $\mathcal{F}$ by replacing clause $C = C_0\lceil_\sigma$ by $C' = C - \{u\}$. For notation, any primed symbol (such as D') in Φ' or π' represents the corresponding unprimed symbol (such as D) in Φ or π.

Suppose Φ' evaluates to 0. By Theorem 3.1 Φ' has a regular tree-like Q-refutation, say π', which we use as a starter for π. The only operation in π' that might be incorrect for π is a resolution involving a clause C_1 in π, where $u \in C_1$, u has been reduced out of C_1' in π', and the extra u causes the resolvent to be tautologous in π. Thus C_1 and C_1' contain at least one of the literals $e_1, \ldots, e_k$. Also C_1 and C_1' resolve with some clause $D_1 = D_1'$ that contains $\overline{u}$. We show this leads to a contradiction.

Figure 2 shows the proof ideas. Let the resolvent of C_1' and D_1' in π' be C_2' and let the clashing literal in D_1' be $\overline{g}$. By Theorem 4.3 there is a resolution path from $\overline{u}$ to $\overline{g}$ using (some of) the leaves of the subtree rooted at D_1'.

C provides a resolution-path from u to e_i in Φ, for each $i \in \{1, \ldots, k\}$ so to establish the contradiction, it suffices to show that there is a resolution path from $\overline{u}$ to $\overline{e_j}$, for *some* $j \in \{1, \ldots, k\}$. If g is equal to any of $e_1, \ldots, e_k$, we are done, so assume not.

Swap the order of sibling subtrees in π' as necessary to place C' on the rightmost branch, called the right spline. Find the *lowest* clause on this spline containing g. Call this clause C_3' and call its left child D_4'. D_4' contains g and the clashing literal used to derive C_3', say $\overline{g_3}$. If D_4' contains $\overline{e_j}$ for any $j \in \{1, \ldots, k\}$ rearrange its subtrees to exhibit a resolution path from g to $\overline{e_j}$ and we are done. Otherwise, rearrange its subtrees to exhibit a resolution path from g to $\overline{g_3}$, as suggested in the figure. Append this to the path from $\overline{u}$ to $\overline{g}$ (from the subtree deriving D_1'), giving a resolution path from $\overline{u}$ to $\overline{g_3}$.

Continue extending the path in this manner down the right spline. That is, let C_5' be the *lowest* clause on this spline containing g_3 and let its left child be D_6', etc. The figure does not show these details. Eventually, the left child of a spline clause contains some $\overline{e_j}$, shown as C_8' in the figure. (This must occur at some point because the first resolution above C' must use some $\overline{e_j}$ as the clashing literal.) When $\overline{e_j}$ is reached, a resolution path from $\overline{u}$ to $\overline{e_j}$ has been constructed, using the subtree that derives D_9' for the last segment.   ■

5   Clause-Literal Graphs

Let a closed QBF Ψ be given in which the quantifier block at qdepth $d+1$ is existential. We define qdepth-limited clause-literal graphs as follows:

Definition 5.1. The *qdepth limited clause literal graph* denoted as $G = ((V_0, V_1, V_2), E)$ at qdepth $d+1$ is the undirected tripartite graph in which: The vertex set V_0 consists of clauses containing some existential literal of qdepth at least $d+1$; The vertex set V_1 consists of existential positive literals of qdepth at least $d+1$ that occur in some clause in V_0. The vertex set V_2 consists of existential negative literals of qdepth at least $d+1$ that occur in some clause in V_0. The undirected edge set E consists of $(e_i, \overline{e_i})$, where $e_i \in V_1$, (e_i, C_j), where $e_i \in V_1$ and $C_j \in V_0$ and $e_i \in C_j$, and $(\overline{e_i}, C_j)$, where $\overline{e_i} \in V_2$ and $C_j \in V_0$ and $\overline{e_i} \in C_j$. See examples in Figure 3.   □

Several dependency relations can be specified in terms of paths in the depth-limited clause-literal graph G. Simple paths and simple cycles in G are defined as usual for undirected graphs.

Definition 5.2. Let u be a universal literal at qdepth d and let e be an existential literal at qdepth $d+1$. A dependency pair $(|u|, |e|)$ means $|e|$ depends on $|u|$.

1. *Standard* dependencies are based on connected components.
   stdDepA$(|u|, |e|)$ holds if any path in G connects a clause with universal literal u or $\overline{u}$ to a clause with existential literal e or $\overline{e}$.
2. *Strict standard* dependencies are based on connected components of G.
   ssDepA$(|u|, |e|)$ holds if some path in G connects a clause with universal literal u to a clause with existential literal e or $\overline{e}$, and some path in G connects a clause with $\overline{u}$ to a clause with e or $\overline{e}$.
3. *Quadrangle* dependencies are based on biconnected components and articulation points of G, because they involve paths that avoid a certain literal. (Definitions are reviewed at the beginning of Section 6.) Articulation points are the only vertices that *cannot* be avoided. quadDepA$(|u|, |e|)$ holds if; **(A)** Some path in G connects a clause with universal literal u to a clause with existential literal e and avoids vertex $\overline{e}$; *and* **(B)** some path in G connects a clause with universal literal $\overline{u}$ to a clause with existential literal $\overline{e}$ and avoids vertex e.
   Note that u and e can independently be chosen as positive or negative literals to satisfy the above conditions (A) and (B). The name "quadrangle" is chosen because all four literals on $|u|$ and $|e|$ are involved in the requirement.
4. *Triangle* dependencies are a relaxation of Quadrangle dependencies, also based on biconnected components and articulation points of G. Specifically, triDepA$(|u|, |e|)$ holds under the same conditions as quadDepA$(|u|, |e|)$, except in condition (B) the path may start at a clause with either u or $\overline{u}$.

Table 1. QBFs for Example 5.4

Ψ_1	$\forall u$	$\exists e$	$\forall t$	$\exists d$
C_1	u		t	$\bar{d}$
C_2	$\bar{u}$		$\bar{t}$	$\bar{d}$
C_3		e	t	d
C_4		$\bar{e}$	t	$\bar{d}$
C_5		e	$\bar{t}$	d
C_6		$\bar{e}$	$\bar{t}$	d

Ψ_2	$\forall u$	$\exists e$	$\forall t$	$\exists d$
C_1	u		t	$\bar{d}$
C_2	$\bar{u}$		$\bar{t}$	$\bar{d}$
C_3		e	t	d
C_4		$\bar{e}$	t	$\bar{d}$
C_7		$\bar{e}$	$\bar{t}$	d
C_6		$\bar{e}$	t	d

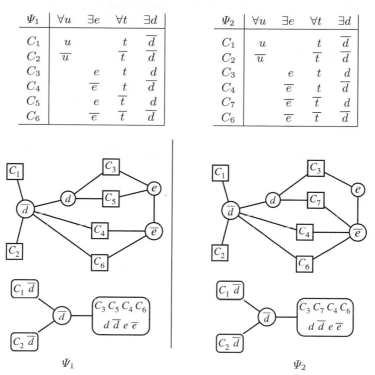

Ψ_1 Ψ_2

Fig. 3. (Above) Clause-literal graphs for Example 5.4. (Below) BCC-based block trees.

5. Paths for *resolution-path* dependencies, denoted by rpDepA($|u|, |e|$), are further restricted from those for quadrangle dependencies. Restrictions on paths are as follows: **(C)** If a path arrives at a literal node from a clause node, its next step must be to the complement literal. **(D)** If a path arrives at a literal node from its complement literal node, its next step must be to a clause node. If a path goes from C_1 to literal q, then to C_2, then both C_1 and C_2 contain q. This path is allowed for triangle and quadrangle dependencies, but not for resolution-path dependencies. □

Curiously, strict standard dependencies relax quadrangle dependencies in the opposite way from triangle dependencies. The motivation for strict standard dependencies is that they seem to be more efficient to compute than quadrangle dependencies, as discussed later.

Theorem 4.7 implies the following:

Corollary 5.3. With the preceding notation: **(1)** If the universal variable u at qdepth d has *no* tuple $(u, e) \in$ quadDepA such that the qdepth of e is less than $d + 2k$, where $k > 0$, then u can be placed at qdepth $d + 2k$ in the quantifier prefix without changing the value of Ψ. **(2)** If existential variable e at qdepth

$d + 1$ has *no* tuple $(u, e) \in$ quadDepA such that the qdepth of u is greater than $d - 2k$, where $k > 0$, then e can be placed at qdepth $d + 1 - 2k$ in the quantifier prefix without changing the value of Ψ.   ∎

Example 5.4. This example illustrates resolution-path dependencies, quadrangle dependencies, and their differences, with reference to various graph structures. Consider the closed QBFs Ψ_1 and Ψ_2, given in chart form in Table 1. In the following, the notation "$C_1(u)$" abbreviates the phrase "C_1, which contains the literal u," etc., and does not represent any operation on C_1.

In both formulas a quadrangle dependency quadDepA($|u|, |e|$) is established by the paths $C_1(u) \xrightarrow{|d|} C_4(\overline{e})$ and $C_2(\overline{u}) \xrightarrow{|d|} C_3(e)$. However, the first path is not a resolution path because d does not occur with opposite signs in C_1 and C_4. Indeed, in Ψ_1 neither u nor $\overline{u}$ presses on $\overline{e}$ by any resolution path, recalling that the universal t cannot be used for connection. Therefore e is independent of u based on rpDepA. It follows that u and e may be exchanged in the quantifier prefix without decreasing the value of Ψ_1 (and such a swap can never increase the value). Following this exchange, it is easy to see that u may be exchanged with t, then with d, and universally reduced out of all clauses.

Observe that Ψ_2 is the same as Ψ_1 except that it has C_7 instead of C_5. There is no obvious difference in the chart appearance, but now $C_1(u) \xrightarrow{|d|} C_7(\overline{e})$ is a resolution path and rpDepA($|u|, |e|$) holds in Ψ_2, so transposing u and e in the quantifier prefix is unsafe by this criterion.

The role of the block trees is explained in Section 6, in connection with biconnected components and articulation points of the clause-literal graph. The definitions are reviewed at the beginning of that section. Here we just note that the circular node is an articulation point and the rounded rectangular nodes are biconnected components.   □

6   Finding Dependency-Related Paths

Now we turn to the issue of computing quadDepA. Biconnected components play a central role. After reviewing the standard theory, this section describes how the specific information needed for quadrangle dependencies is extracted.

Recall that a subgraph, say B, of an undirected graph G is biconnected if and only if removing any one vertex and all edges incident upon that vertex does not disconnect the remaining subgraph. A **biconnected component (BCC)** of any undirected graph G is a *maximal* biconnected subgraph of G.

Each edge of G is in exactly one BCC. Also, two BCCs have at most one vertex in common. A vertex that is in more than one BCC is called an **articulation point (AP)**. Removal of an articulation point increases the number of connected components in G.

The BCCs and APs of the depth-limited clause-literal graph G can be found in time linear in its size. The code in [1, Fig. 7.26] avoids putting edges redundantly into the BCCs.

As a by-product, the BCC algorithm can determine simple connected components (CCs). An additional by-product of this algorithm is the creation of an acyclic undirected bipartite graph associated with each CC, called the **block tree**, in which the BCCs are collapsed to single vertices and are separated by the APs (see Figure 3). All universal literals incident upon each BCC can be collected, as well.

We continue with the terminology of Definition 5.1 for G, d, u, e, etc. It is easy to determine if there is a path in G between some clause containing u or $\overline{u}$ and a literal e in V_1: just check if one of those clauses is in the same CC as e. Since e and $\overline{e}$ are always in the same CC, the same clauses can reach $\overline{e}$. However, the triangle and quadrangle dependency relations require paths to e and $\overline{e}$ that avoid the complement literal. If neither e nor $\overline{e}$ is an AP of G, both of these paths must exist. In this case, the relevant universal literals for $|e|$ are just those that occur in some clause in the same CC as e. These sets of universal literals can be collected once, during the BCC algorithm.

Now suppose e or $\overline{e}$ or both are APs of G. The relevant universal literals for e can be found by starting a graph search of the block tree containing $|e|$, from e, and avoiding a visit of $\overline{e}$. The relevant universal literals for $\overline{e}$ can be found by starting a graph search of the block tree containing $|e|$, from $\overline{e}$, and avoiding a visit of e. As each BCC is visited, any universal literals at qdepth d can be collected. It appears that adapting this approach to compute triangle dependencies instead of quadrangle dependencies will not save much time. Details are omitted for lack of space, but are straightforward.

At this time, the question of whether resolution-path dependencies can be computed in polynomial time is open. We conjecture that it is possible, but the requirement that two consecutive edge labels in the resolution graph cannot be the same makes it difficult.

7   Empirical Data

A prototype program was implemented in C++ with the Standard Template Library to gauge the amount of variable independence that might be found by various dependency relations.[2] The program computes dependency-related quantities on QBF benchmarks. It was run on the 568 QBFEVAL-10 benchmarks. Two benchmarks had no universal variables, so the tables include data on 566 benchmarks. The platform was a 2.6 GHz 64-bit processor with 16 GB of RAM, Linux OS.

The computation was limited to the outermost universal block and the adjacent enclosed existential block. The number of "trivial dependencies" is simply the product of the sizes of these two blocks. The primary purpose of the program is to find out the relative sizes of the relations for standard dependencies, strict standard dependencies, and quadrangle dependencies. Only the outermost block pair is analyzed because this provides a direct comparison between standard

---

[2] Please see http://www.cse.ucsc.edu/~avg/QBFdeps/ for the prototype program.

Table 2. Eight largest QBFEVAL-10 benchmarks

Benchmark	Trivial (000,000)	CCs	Fraction of Trivial		
			Strict		
			Standard	Standard	Quadrangle
s3330_d10_u-shuffled	627	1	1	1	0.000076
s3330_d4_s-shuffled	68	1	1	1	0.000069
s499_d15_s-shuffled	15	1	1	1	0.000125
s510_d12_s-shuffled	16	1	1	1	0.000028
s510_d31_s-shuffled	122	1	1	1	0.000082
szymanski-24-s-shuffled	1293	1	1	1	0.001944
vonNeumann-rip...-13-c-	278	1	0.999999	0.999999	0.992812
vonNeumann-rip...-15-c-	627	1	0.999999	0.999999	0.993727

Table 3. Dependency fractions as unweighted ratios

Benchmark Group	Num. in Group	Average Trivial (000)	Avg. CCs	Avg. Fraction of Trivial		
				Strict		
				Standard	Standard	Quadrangle
Eight Largest	8	219363	1	1.0000	1.0000	0.2486
Str.Std. Helped	239	158	34.6	0.3722	0.3718	0.1928
Str.Std. No Help	319	359	9.8	1	1	0.7278

dependencies and quadrangle dependencies. Including multiple blocks would obscure the size relationships because standard dependencies use transitive closure when multiple blocks are involved, while quadrangle dependencies do not.

The benchmarks were partitioned into several groups to try to make the statistics more informative. Table 2 shows data for the eight largest benchmarks, as measured by the number of trivial dependencies. For six of these benchmarks, the Quadrangle relation is 3-5 orders of magnitude smaller than the Trivial, while the Strict Standard gives no reduction. On two others, no relation gives reduction.

Table 3 shows the eight largest as a group, and separate the remaining benchmarks according to whether Strict Standard Dependencies gave any reduction at all. Quadrangle dependencies give substantial additional reductions, beyond standard and strict standard dependencies. Although Strict Standard gave very little improvements in this test, they are essentially free, once the overhead of Standard has been incurred.

A serious question is whether the time needed to compute Quadrangle Dependencies pays back in more efficient solving. Experience with depqbf indicates tentatively that Standard Dependencies pay back in the long run [5]. For the 566 runs to get these statistics, the three longest runs took 75628, 2354, and 1561 seconds. The average of the remaining 563 runs was 9.40 seconds. Only finding the Strict Standard dependencies and the BCCs averaged 0.50 seconds on all 566 instances.

Concerning the three longest runs, two of these instances have never been solved by any solver, so in a sense, nothing has been lost. However, the third instance, `szymanski-24-s-shuffled`, is not considered exceptionally difficult. It took 75628 seconds to find the quadrangle dependencies, yet finding the BBCs took only three seconds, and computing the Standard Dependencies took only four additional seconds. We do not have an explanation for this outlier behavior.

8 Conclusion

This paper analyzes several new dependency relations for QBF solving, and shows they form a hierarchy, together with the standard and triangle relations proposed by Samer and Szeider. The root of the hierarchy and strongest for detecting variable *independence* is the resolution-path dependency relation. Its soundness is proved; soundness of supersets (more restrictive relations) is a corollary. Whether the resolution-path relation has an efficient implementation is an open question, so quadrangle dependencies, the next relation down in the lattice (Figure 1), were studied in more detail. Computational methods for quadrangle dependencies are described, using the theory of biconnected components, and a prototype was implemented to gauge the sizes of BCCs and related structures in benchmarks.

Future work includes a trial implementation of quadrangle dependencies in a QBF solver, but the publicly available solvers we looked at are not good candidates for such a retrofit by anyone except one of the original programmers, in most cases because the source code is *not* public. The few with public source code tend to lack documentation and contain numerous short-cuts to improve solver speed. Also, there are numerous ways to use dependencies, so one implementation experience will not be definitive.

Acknowledgment. We thank Florian Lonsing and Armin Biere for many helpful email discussions. We thank the anonymous reviewers for helpful comments.

References

1. Baase, S., Van Gelder, A.: Computer Algorithms: Introduction to Design and Analysis, 3rd edn. Addison-Wesley, Reading (2000)
2. Kleine Büning, H., Karpinski, M., Flögel, A.: Resolution for quantified boolean formulas. Information and Computation 117, 12–18 (1995)
3. Kleine Büning, H., Lettmann, T.: Propositional Logic: Deduction and Algorithms. Cambridge University Press, Cambridge (1999)
4. Klieber, W., Sapra, S., Gao, S., Clarke, E.: A non-prenex, non-clausal QBF solver with game-state learning. In: Strichman, O., Szeider, S. (eds.) SAT 2010. LNCS, vol. 6175, pp. 128–142. Springer, Heidelberg (2010)
5. Lonsing, F., Biere, A.: Integrating dependency schemes in search-based QBF solvers. In: Strichman, O., Szeider, S. (eds.) SAT 2010. LNCS, vol. 6175, pp. 158–171. Springer, Heidelberg (2010)
6. Samer, M., Szeider, S.: Backdoor sets of quantified boolean formulas. J. Automated Reasoning 42, 77–97 (2009)
7. Yates, R.A., Raphael, B., Hart, T.P.: Resolution graphs. Artificial Intelligence 1, 257–289 (1970)

Pruning Rules for Constrained Optimisation for Conditional Preferences

Nic Wilson and Walid Trabelsi

Cork Constraint Computation Centre,
Department of Computer Science,
University College Cork, Ireland
{n.wilson,w.trabelsi}@4c.ucc.ie

Abstract. A depth-first search algorithm can be used to find optimal solutions of a Constraint Satisfaction Problem (CSP) with respect to a set of conditional preferences statements (e.g., a CP-net). This involves checking at each leaf node if the corresponding solution of the CSP is dominated by any of the optimal solutions found so far; if not, then we add this solution to the set of optimal solutions. This kind of algorithm can clearly be computationally expensive if the number of solutions is large. At a node N of the search tree, with associated assignment b to a subset of the variables B, it may happen that, for some previously found solution α, either (a) α dominates all extensions of b; or (b) α does not dominate any extension of b. The algorithm can be significantly improved if we can find sufficient conditions for (a) and (b) that can be efficiently checked. In case (a), we can backtrack since we need not continue the search below N; in case (b), α does not need to be considered in any node below the current node N. We derive a sufficient condition for (b), and three sufficient conditions for (a). Our experimental testing indicates that this can make a major difference to the efficiency of constrained optimisation for conditional preference theories including CP-nets.

1 Introduction

Conditional preference languages, such as CP-nets and more general formalisms [4,9,6,15,2], can give a natural way for the user of a decision support system to express their preferences over multivariate options. A basic problem is: given a set of outcomes, determine which are the undominated ones, i.e., which are not considered worse than another outcome. For example, in a recommender system, one can use preference deduction techniques to infer, from the previous user inputs, which products may be preferred over others, and hence which are the undominated ones [11].

As shown in [5], one can use a depth-first search algorithm to find optimal solutions of a Constraint Satisfaction Problem (CSP) with respect to a set of conditional preferences statements (e.g., a CP-net). The algorithm in [5], as well as related algorithms in [14,15], involve using appropriate variable and value orderings so that solutions are generated in an order compatible with the conditional

J. Lee (Ed.): CP 2011, LNCS 6876, pp. 804–818, 2011.

preference statements. At each leaf node we check to see if the corresponding solution of the CSP is dominated by any of the optimal solutions found so far; if not, then we add this solution to the set of optimal solutions.

The standard dominance check for CP-nets and more general languages is computationally hard, as illustrated by the PSPACE-completeness result in [8]. In this paper we follow [14,16] in using a polynomial dominance relation, which is an upper approximation of the standard one; this enables much larger problems to be tackled (see [10] for experimental results regarding a recent implementation of the standard dominance queries).

Even so, this kind of constrained optimisation algorithm can clearly be computationally expensive if the number of solutions is large, since we have at least one dominance check (and possibly many) to make for each solution.

At a node N of the search tree, with associated assignment b to a subset of the variables B, it may happen that, for some previously found solution α, either (a) α dominates all extensions of b; or (b) α does not dominate any extension of b. The algorithm can be significantly improved if we can find sufficient conditions for (a) and (b) that can be efficiently checked (and that hold sufficiently often). In the positive case, (a), we can backtrack since we need not continue the search below N, hence pruning a possibly exponentially large part of the search tree. In the negative case, (b), α does not need to be considered in any node below the current node N, thus eliminating potentially exponentially many dominance checks involving α.

In this paper, we derive three polynomial sufficient conditions for (a), and one for (b). We have implemented and experimentally tested these in the context of a constrained optimisation algorithm, and they are seen to significantly improve the algorithm. Section 2 describes the background: the conditional preferences formalism in Section 2.1, and the polynomial notion of dominance in Section 2.2. The form of the constrained optimisation algorithm is described in Section 3. Section 4 describes the three polynomial sufficient conditions for the positive case (a), and Section 5 derives the polynomial sufficient conditions for the negative case, (b). Section 6 describes the experimental testing, and Section 7 discusses extensions.

2   Background Material

2.1   A Language of Conditional Preferences

Let V be a finite set of variables, and for each $X \in V$ let $\underline{X}$ be the set of possible values of X; we assume $\underline{X}$ has at least two elements. For subset of variables $U \subseteq V$ let $\underline{U} = \prod_{X \in U} \underline{X}$ be the set of possible assignments to set of variables U. The assignment to the empty set of variables is written $\top$. An *outcome* is an element of $\underline{V}$, i.e., an assignment to all the variables. For partial tuples $a \in \underline{A}$ and $u \in \underline{U}$, we say a *extends* u, if $A \supseteq U$ and $a(U) = u$, i.e., a projected to U gives u. More generally, we say that a *is compatible with* u if there exists outcome $\alpha \in \underline{V}$ extending both a and u, i.e., such that $\alpha(A) = a$ and $\alpha(U) = u$.

The language $\mathcal{L}$ consists of statements of the form $u : x > x' [W]$ where u is an assignment to set of variables $U \subseteq V$ (i.e., $u \in \underline{U}$), x, x' are different values of variable X, and $\{X\}$, U and W are pairwise disjoint. Let $T = V - (\{X\} \cup U \cup W)$. Such a conditional preference statement φ represents that given u and any assignment to T, x is preferred to x' irrespective of the values of W. If $W = \emptyset$ we sometimes write the statement just as $u : x > x'$.

The formal semantics is defined using total pre-orders[1] on the set $\underline{V}$ of outcomes. Formally, we say that total pre-order $\succcurlyeq$ *satisfies* $u : x > x' [W]$ if $tuxw \succcurlyeq tux'w'$ for all $t \in \underline{T}, w, w' \in \underline{W}$, since u is satisfied in both outcomes $tuxw$ and $tux'w'$, and variable X has the value x in the first, and x' in the second, and they differ at most on $\{X\} \cup W$.

If φ is the statement $u : x > x' [W]$, for $u \in \underline{U}$ and $x, x' \in \underline{X}$ then we define $u_\varphi = u$, $x_\varphi = x$, $x'_\varphi = x'$, $U_\varphi = U$, $X_\varphi = X$ and $W_\varphi = W$.

Subsets Γ of the language $\mathcal{L}$ are called *conditional preference theories (cp-theories)* [13]. For cp-theory Γ, and outcomes α and β we write $\alpha \succeq_\Gamma \beta$ when $\alpha \succcurlyeq \beta$ holds for all total pre-orders $\succcurlyeq$ satisfying each element of Γ (cf. Theorem 1 of [14]). CP-nets [3,4] can be represented by conditional preference theories that involve statements with empty W, and TCP-nets [6] with statements involving empty or singleton W [12].

2.2 Polynomial Dominance for Conditional Preferences

In this section we describe a polynomial dominance[2] relation for conditional preferences. This polynomial dominance relation is less conservative than the standard one, leading to fewer undominated solutions, which also can be advantageous. The definitions and results in this section come from [14] (and were generalised further in [16]).

A pre-ordered search tree (abbreviated to a *pos-tree*) is a rooted directed tree (which we imagine being drawn with the root at the top, and children below parents). Associated with each node r in the tree is a variable Y_r, which is instantiated with a different value in each of the node's children (if it has any), and also a total pre-order $\geqslant_r$ of the values of Y_r. A directed edge in the tree therefore corresponds to an instantiation of one of the variables to a particular value. Paths in the tree from the root down to a leaf node correspond to sequential instantiations of different variables. We also associate with each node r a set of variables A_r which is the set of all variables $Y_{r'}$ associated to nodes r' above r in the tree (i.e., on the path from the root to r), and an assignment a_r to A_r corresponding to the assignments made to these variables in the edges between the root and r. The root node r^* has $A_{r^*} = \emptyset$ and $a_{r^*} = \top$, the assignment to the empty set of variables. Hence r' is a child of r if and only if $A_{r'} = A_r \cup \{Y_r\}$ (where $A_r \not\ni Y_r$) and $a_{r'}$ extends a_r (with an assignment to Y_r).

---

[1] A total pre-order $\succcurlyeq$ is a binary relation that is reflexive ($\alpha \succcurlyeq \alpha$), transitive and complete (i.e., for all α and β, either $\alpha \succcurlyeq \beta$ or $\beta \succcurlyeq \alpha$). If both $\alpha \succcurlyeq \beta$ and $\beta \succcurlyeq \alpha$ then we say that α and β are $\succcurlyeq$-*equivalent*.

[2] The notion of dominance in this paper is quite different from the notion of dominance as in Symmetry Breaking via Dominance Detection [7] and related work.

Formally, define a node r to be a tuple $\langle A_r, a_r, Y_r, \geqslant_r \rangle$, where $A_r \subseteq V$ is a set of variables, $a_r \in \underline{A_r}$ is an assignment to those variables, $Y_r \in V - A_r$ is another variable, and $\geqslant_r$ is a total pre-order on the set $\underline{Y_r}$ of values of Y_r. We make two restrictions on the choice of this total pre-order: firstly, it is assumed not to be the trivial complete relation on $\underline{Y}$, i.e., there exists some $y, y' \in \underline{Y}$ with $y \not\geqslant_r y'$ (so not all y and y' are $\geqslant_r$-equivalent). We also assume that $\geqslant_r$ satisfies the following condition (which ensures that the associated ordering on outcomes is transitive): if there exists a child of node r associated with instantiation $Y_r = y$, then y is not $\geqslant_r$-equivalent to any other value of Y, so that $y \geqslant_r y' \geqslant_r y$ only if $y' = y$. In particular, $\geqslant_r$ totally orders the values (of Y_r) associated with the children of r.

For outcome α, define the *path to* α to be the path from the root which includes all nodes r such that α extends a_r. To generate this, for each node r we reach, starting from the root, we choose the child associated with the instantiation $Y_r = \alpha(Y_r)$ (there is at most one such child); the path finishes when there exists no such child. Node r is said to **decide** outcomes α *and* β if it is the deepest node (i.e., furthest from the root) that is both on the path to α and on the path to β. Hence α and β both extend the tuple a_r (but they may differ on variable Y_r). We compare α and β by using $\geqslant_r$, where r is the unique node that decides α and β. Each pre-ordered search tree σ has an associated total pre-order $\succcurlyeq_\sigma$ on outcomes which is defined as follows. Let $\alpha, \beta \in \underline{V}$ be outcomes. We define $\alpha \succcurlyeq_\sigma \beta$ to hold if and only if $\alpha(Y_r) \geqslant_r \beta(Y_r)$, where r is the node that decides α and β. We therefore then have that α and β are $\succcurlyeq_\sigma$-equivalent if and only if $\alpha(Y_r)$ and $\beta(Y_r)$ are $\geqslant_r$-equivalent. This ordering is similar to a lexicographic ordering in that two outcomes are compared on the first variable on which they differ.

Example of a pos-tree. Figure 1 shows an example pos-tree. The bottom left node in the diagram represents the pos-tree node $r = \langle \{X_1, X_3\}, x_1 x_3, X_2, x_2 \geqslant_r \overline{x}_2 \rangle$. The first component $A_r = \{X_1, X_3\}$ is the set of variables assigned above the node; the second component $a_r = x_1 x_3$ is the assignment to A_r made in the path from the root to r. The third component $Y_r = X_2$ is the variable that is ordered next, and the fourth component, $x_2 \geqslant_r \overline{x}_2$ is the local ordering on X_2. Note that the both the local (value) orderings and the variable (importance) orderings can differ in different branches of a pos-tree. Let α and β be the outcomes $x_1 \overline{x}_2 x_3$ and $x_1 x_2 \overline{x}_3$, respectively. The path to α includes the three nodes on the left hand of the figure. The path to β contains the root node and its left hand child, $r' = \langle \{X_1\}, x_1, X_3, x_3 \geqslant \overline{x}_3 \rangle$. Node r' therefore divides α and β. Since $Y_{r'} = X_3$, and $\alpha(X_3) \geqslant_{r'} \beta(X_3)$, we have $\alpha \succcurlyeq_\sigma \beta$. ∎

We say that pre-ordered search tree σ *satisfies* conditional preference theory Γ iff $\succcurlyeq_\sigma$ satisfies Γ (see Section 2.1). We give an alternative characterisation of this. Relation $\sqsupseteq_a^X$ on $\underline{X}$ is defined to be the transitive closure of the set of pairs (x, x') of values of X over all statements $u : x > x' [W]$ in Γ such that u is compatible with a.

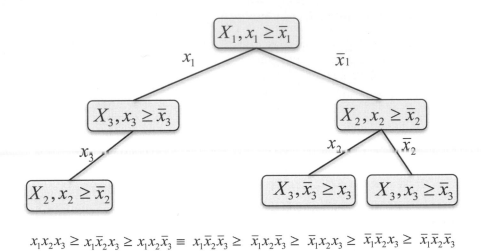

$$x_1 x_2 x_3 \geq x_1 \bar{x}_2 x_3 \geq x_1 x_2 \bar{x}_3 \equiv x_1 \bar{x}_2 \bar{x}_3 \geq \bar{x}_1 x_2 \bar{x}_3 \geq \bar{x}_1 x_2 x_3 \geq \bar{x}_1 \bar{x}_2 x_3 \geq \bar{x}_1 \bar{x}_2 \bar{x}_3$$

Fig. 1. An example pos-tree σ over binary variables $\{X_1, X_2, X_3\}$, and its associated total pre-order $\succcurlyeq_\sigma$ on outcomes. For each node r we only include its associated variable Y_r and the local ordering $\geqslant_r$.

Proposition 1 ([14]). *The following pair of conditions are necessary and sufficient for a pre-ordered search tree σ to satisfy the cp-theory Γ.*

(1) For any $\varphi \in \Gamma$ and outcome α extending u_φ: on the path to α, X_φ appears before every element of W_φ;
(2) for all nodes r in σ, $\geqslant_r \supseteq \sqsupset_{a_r}^{Y_r}$.

Condition (1) relates to the allowable variable orderings in a pre-ordered search tree satisfying Γ, and condition (2) restricts the value orderings.

For a given cp-theory Γ we define the relation $\unrhd_\Gamma$ (abbreviated to $\unrhd$) as follows: $\alpha \unrhd \beta$ holds if and only if $\alpha \succcurlyeq_\sigma \beta$ holds for all pos-trees σ satisfying Γ (i.e, all σ such that $\succcurlyeq_\sigma$ satisfies Γ). Proposition 1 of [14] shows that if $\alpha \succeq_\Gamma \beta$ then $\alpha \unrhd_\Gamma \beta$. Importantly, for any outcomes α and β it can be determined in polynomial time if $\alpha \unrhd_\Gamma \beta$: see Section 4.2 of [14].

3   Constrained Optimisation

In the constrained optimisation algorithms in [5,14,15] a search tree is used to find solutions of a CSP, where the search tree is chosen to be compatible with the cp-theory Γ, i.e., so that its associated total ordering on outcomes extends relations $\succ_\Gamma$ and $\unrhd_\Gamma$ (defined above in Sections 2.1 and 2.2, respectively). Methods for finding such search trees have been developed in [15], Sections 5 and 6. One can use a fixed variable ordering in the search tree if the cp-theory is fully acyclic—see [15], Section 5.1—i.e., there exists an ordering $X_1, \ldots, X_n$ of the variables such that for any statement $\varphi \in \Gamma$, if $X_i \in U_\varphi$ then $i < j$, where $X_\varphi = X_j$, and if $X_i \in W_\varphi$ then $i > j$.

3.1   Basic Constrained Optimisation Approach

We can make use of this compatible search tree as follows: when we find a new solution β we check if it is $\trianglerighteq$-undominated with respect to each of the current known set K of $\trianglerighteq$-undominated solutions (i.e., if it is *not* the case that there exists $\alpha \in K$ with $\alpha \trianglerighteq \beta$). If so, then β is an $\trianglerighteq$-undominated solution, since it cannot be $\trianglerighteq$-dominated by any solution found later. We add β to K, and continue the search. At the end, K will be the complete set of $\trianglerighteq$-undominated solutions (which is a subset of the set of $\succeq_r$-undominated solutions, since $\trianglerighteq \supseteq \succeq_r$).

Associated with each node of the search tree is a partial assignment b, which consists of the assignments to earlier variables B. We choose some uninstantiated variable $Y \notin B$, and assign values to Y in each child node. Also there is associated a current domain $\mathcal{D}(X)$ of each variable X. For $X \in B$, $\mathcal{D}(X) = \{b(X)\}$. For other variables X, $\mathcal{D}(X)$ is determined by constraint propagation [1], which may be done in a number of ways. The key property of $\mathcal{D}(X)$ is: for eliminated values x (i.e., $x \in \underline{X} - \mathcal{D}(X)$), there exists no solution β of the CSP extending b and such that $\beta(X) = x$. Backtracking occurs when any of the domains becomes empty, since there cannot then be any solution extending b. In the experiments described in Section 6 we enforce arc consistency to generate the current domains; however, other forms of consistency are possible, for example, global consistency where a value x is included in the domain of variable X if and only if there exists a solution β extending b and such that $\beta(X) = x$.

3.2   Incorporating Dominance and Non-dominance Conditions

At any node of a depth-first search algorithm for finding solutions of a CSP, we have an associated partial assignment b to the variables B that have already been instantiated, and we have the current domain $\mathcal{D}(X)$ of each variable X. We formalise this notion of a collection of domains as follows:

Definition 1. *A collection of domains is a function $\mathcal{D}$ on V such that $\mathcal{D}(X) \subseteq \underline{X}$, so that $\mathcal{D}(X)$ is a set of possible values of X. For outcome β, we say that β is of $\mathcal{D}$ if $\beta(X) \in \mathcal{D}(X)$ for all $X \in V$.*

We say that α dominates $\mathcal{D}$ if it dominates every β of $\mathcal{D}$, and α non-dominates $\mathcal{D}$ if it doesn't dominate any β of $\mathcal{D}$:

Definition 2. *Let α be an outcome and let $\mathcal{D}$ be a collection of domains. We define:*
— *α dominates $\mathcal{D}$ if $\alpha \trianglerighteq \beta$ for all β of $\mathcal{D}$.*
— *α non-dominates $\mathcal{D}$ if for all β of $\mathcal{D}$, $\alpha \ntrianglerighteq \beta$.*

Suppose that α is a solution we've already found, and that we are currently at a node of the search tree with associated partial assignment b and collection of domains $\mathcal{D}$. If we can determine that α dominates $\mathcal{D}$ then there is no need to explore nodes in the search tree extending partial assignment b, so we can backtrack at this node. If, on the other hand, we can determine that α non-dominates $\mathcal{D}$ then we can eliminate α from the set of current solutions for any node below the current node, because there is no need to check again that $\alpha \not\trianglerighteq \beta$, for solutions β extending b. In Section 4, we describe sufficient conditions for α dominating $\mathcal{D}$ that can be efficiently checked, and in Section 5, an efficient sufficient condition for α non-dominating $\mathcal{D}$.

4   Sufficient Conditions for Dominance

To show, given particular assumptions, that α dominates collection of domains $\mathcal{D}$, we need to show that there cannot exist a pos-tree σ satisfying Γ that strictly prefers some element β of $\mathcal{D}$ to α. (Because then $\alpha \succ_\sigma \beta$ for all σ satisfying Γ, and hence, $\alpha \trianglerighteq \beta$, for all β of $\mathcal{D}$.) The first rule gives conditions that imply non-existence of such a σ by just considering its root node; the second rule focuses on the node of σ that decides α and β.

4.1   The Root-Dominates Rule

We say that α root-dominates collection of domains $\mathcal{D}$ if: for all $Y \notin \bigcup_{\varphi \in \Gamma} W_\varphi$,
(i) $\alpha(Y) \sqsupset_\top^Y y$ for all $y \in \mathcal{D}(Y) - \{\alpha(Y)\}$;
(ii) if $\alpha(Y) \in \mathcal{D}(Y)$ then $\alpha(Y)$ and y are $\sqsupset_\top^Y$-equivalent for some $y \in \underline{Y} - \{\alpha(Y)\}$.
   The following result states the soundness of the root-dominates rule.

Proposition 2. *If α root-dominates $\mathcal{D}$ then α dominates $\mathcal{D}$, i.e., $\alpha \trianglerighteq \beta$ for all β of $\mathcal{D}$.*

Proof: Assume that α root-dominates $\mathcal{D}$, and consider any element β of $\mathcal{D}$, and any pos-tree σ satisfying Γ. Consider the root node r of σ with associated variable Y and local ordering $\geqslant$. Proposition 1, condition (1) implies that $Y \notin \bigcup_{\varphi \in \Gamma} W_\varphi$. If α and β differ on Y, then the root node decides α and β, and Proposition 1(2) and condition (i) imply $\alpha(Y) \geqslant \beta(Y)$, and hence $\alpha \succ_\sigma \beta$. If, on the other hand, $\alpha(Y) = \beta(Y)$, then condition (ii) implies, using Proposition 1(2), that $\alpha(Y)$ is $\geqslant$-equivalent to some other element of $\underline{Y}$, which implies, by the definition of a pos-tree, that the root node has no children. Hence the root node again decides α and β, and so $\alpha \succ_\sigma \beta$. Since σ was arbitrary, $\alpha \trianglerighteq \beta$, for all β of $\mathcal{D}$.   ∎

Example. Let V be the set of variables $\{X, Y, Z\}$ with initial domains as follows: $\underline{X} = \{x_1, x_2, x_3, x_4\}$, $\underline{Y} = \{y_1, y_2\}$ and $\underline{Z} = \{z_1, z_2\}$. Let cp-theory Γ consist of the five statements $\top : x_1 > x_3$, $\top : x_2 > x_3$, and $\top : x_2 > x_4 \; [\{Z\}]$, $x_1 : y_1 > y_2$, and $x_2 : y_2 > y_1$. Let α be the assignment $x_2 \, y_2 \, z_2$, and let $\mathcal{D}(X) = \{x_3, x_4\}$, $\mathcal{D}(Y) = \underline{Y}$ and $\mathcal{D}(Z) = \underline{Z}$. Then $\bigcup_{\varphi \in \Gamma} W_\varphi = \{Z\}$, and $\alpha(X) = x_2 \sqsupset_\top^X x_3$ and $\alpha(X) \sqsupset_\top^X x_4$. Also, $\alpha(Y) = y_2 \sqsupset_\top^Y y_1 \sqsupset_\top^Y y_2$, so $\alpha(Y)$ and y_1 are $\sqsupset_\top^Y$-equivalent. Hence, α root-dominates $\mathcal{D}$.   ∎

The first half of the definition of *root-dominates* is actually a necessary condition for dominance:

Proposition 3. *Suppose that α dominates collection of domains $\mathcal{D}$. Then $\alpha(Y)$ $\sqsupset_{\top}^{Y} y$ holds for all $Y \notin \bigcup_{\varphi \in \Gamma} W_\varphi$, and for all $y \in \mathcal{D}(Y) - \{\alpha(Y)\}$.*

Proof: Suppose there exists some $Y \notin \bigcup_{\varphi \in \Gamma} W_\varphi$ and $y \in \mathcal{D}(Y) - \{\alpha(Y)\}$ such that $\alpha(Y) \not\sqsupset_{\top}^{Y} y$. Then we can create a pos-tree σ with just a root node r, with associated variable $Y_r = Y$. We choose the local ordering $\geqslant_r$ so that $\geqslant_r$ contains $\sqsupset_{\top}^{Y}$ and is such that $\alpha(Y) \not\geqslant_r y$. (This is possible since $\alpha(Y) \not\sqsupset_{\top}^{Y} y$). By Proposition 1, σ satisfies Γ. Choose any β of $\mathcal{D}$ with $\beta(Y) = y$. Then, $\alpha \not\succ_\sigma \beta$, so $\alpha \not\trianglerighteq \beta$, and hence it is not the case that α dominates $\mathcal{D}$. ∎

When for all $Y \notin \bigcup_{\varphi \in \Gamma} W_\varphi$, domain $\mathcal{D}(Y)$ doesn't include $\alpha(Y)$, part (ii) of the definition of root-dominance holds vacuously, so Propositions 2 and 3 imply that root-dominance is a necessary and sufficient condition for dominance:

Proposition 4. *Suppose that $\mathcal{D}(Y) \not\ni \alpha(Y)$ for all $Y \notin \bigcup_{\varphi \in \Gamma} W_\varphi$. Then α root-dominates $\mathcal{D}$ if and only if α dominates $\mathcal{D}$.*

4.2   The Deciding-Node Dominance Rule

Let α be an outcome and let $\mathcal{D}$ be a collection of domains. Define S to be $\{Y \in V : \mathcal{D}(Y) \not\ni \alpha(Y)\}$. These are the variables that α and β differ on for all β of $\mathcal{D}$. Define Ψ to be the set of all $\varphi \in \Gamma$ such that $X_\varphi \in S$ and u_φ is compatible with $\alpha(V - S)$. (u_φ is compatible with $\alpha(V - S)$ if and only if for all $Y \in U_\varphi - S$, $\alpha(Y) = u_\varphi(Y)$.) Let $\alpha_* = \alpha(V - S)$. We will use the relation $\sqsupset_{\alpha_*}^{Y}$, defined in Section 2.2 as the transitive closure of all pairs (x_φ, x'_φ) such that $\varphi \in \Gamma$, $X_\varphi = Y$ and u_φ is compatible with α_*.

Definition 3. *Using the notation defined above, we say that α deciding-node-dominates $\mathcal{D}$ if $\alpha(Y) \sqsupset_{\alpha_*}^{Y} y$ for all $Y \notin \bigcup_{\varphi \in \Psi} W_\varphi$ and for all $y \in \mathcal{D}(Y) - \{\alpha(Y)\}$.*

The following proposition states the soundness of the deciding-node-dominates rule.

Proposition 5. *If α deciding-node-dominates $\mathcal{D}$ then α dominates $\mathcal{D}$.*

Proof: Consider any element β of $\mathcal{D}$, and any pos-tree σ satisfying Γ. Consider the node r of σ that decides α and β, with associated variable Y and tuple $a \in \underline{A}$. Firstly, $A \cap S = \emptyset$, since α and β agree on A but differ on each variable in S. If $\varphi \in \Psi$ then $X_\varphi \in S$, and so $X_\varphi \notin A$. This implies, using Proposition 1(1), that $Y \notin W_\varphi$, so we've shown that $Y \notin \bigcup_{\varphi \in \Psi} W_\varphi$. We have that $\alpha(V - S)$ extends a (since $A \subseteq V - S$ and α extends a), which immediately implies that $\sqsupset_a^{Y}$ contains $\sqsupset_{\alpha_*}^{Y}$. If α deciding-node-dominates $\mathcal{D}$ then $\alpha(Y) \sqsupset_{\alpha_*}^{Y} \beta(Y)$ or $\alpha(Y) = \beta(Y)$. Therefore, by Proposition 1(2), $\alpha(Y) \geqslant_r \beta(Y)$, showing that $\alpha \succ_\sigma \beta$, and hence $\alpha \trianglerighteq \beta$, as required. ∎

Example (continued). Consider again the example in Section 4.1. Then $S = \{X\}$, α_* equals the partial assignment $y_2 z_2$, and $\bigcup_{\varphi \in \Psi} W_\varphi = \{Z\}$. We have

$\alpha(X) = x_2 \sqsupset_{\alpha_*}^X x_3$, and $x_2 \sqsupset_{\alpha_*}^X x_4$, and $\alpha(Y) = y_2 \sqsupset_{\alpha_*}^Y y_1$, showing that α deciding-node-dominates $\mathcal{D}$, and hence, by Proposition 5, α dominates $\mathcal{D}$.

If we now remove statement $x_1 : y_1 > y_2$ from Γ we still have α deciding-node-dominates $\mathcal{D}$ but we no longer have α root-dominates $\mathcal{D}$.

In the following example, α does not deciding-node-dominate $\mathcal{D}$ but α root-dominates $\mathcal{D}$, and so α dominates $\mathcal{D}$. Let $\mathcal{D}(X) = \underline{X} = \{x_1, x_2\}$, let $\mathcal{D}(Y) = \underline{Y} = \{y_1, y_2\}$, and let $\mathcal{D}(Z) = \underline{Z} = \{z_1, z_2, z_3\}$. Let Γ consist of: $z_1 : x_1 > x_2$, $z_2 : x_2 > x_1$, $x_1 : y_1 > y_2$, $x_2 : y_2 > y_1$, $x_1 : z_1 > z_2$, $x_2 : z_2 > z_1$ and $x_1 y_2 : z_1 > z_3$. Let $\alpha = x_1 y_1 z_1$. Therefore, root-dominance and deciding-node-dominance are incomparable, and both are strictly stronger than dominance. ∎

When, for all variables Y, $\alpha(Y)$ is not in the current domain $\mathcal{D}(Y)$ of Y, we have $S = V$, $\alpha_* = \top$ and $\Psi = \Gamma$. The definition of *deciding-node-dominates* then becomes equivalent to part (i) of the definition of *root-dominates*, with part (ii) being vacuously satisfied. Using Proposition 4, we therefore have the following result showing that these dominance definitions are then equivalent.

Proposition 6. *Suppose that $\mathcal{D}(Y) \not\ni \alpha(Y)$ for all $Y \in V$. Then α deciding-node-dominates $\mathcal{D}$ iff α root-dominates $\mathcal{D}$ iff α dominates $\mathcal{D}$.*

4.3   Projection-Dominance Condition

Let b be an assignment to set of variables B, and let $\mathcal{D}$ be a collection of domains such that $\mathcal{D}(X) = \{b(X)\}$ for $X \in B$. It follows immediately that the condition $(*)$ below is a sufficient condition for: α dominates $\mathcal{D}$. (Recall, $\alpha(B)$ means α restricted/projected to B.)

$(*)$ $\gamma \trianglerighteq \beta$ for all outcomes $\gamma \in \underline{V}$ agreeing with α on B (i.e., $\gamma(B) = \alpha(B)$), and all $\beta \in \underline{V}$ extending b (i.e., $\beta(B) = b$).

In other words, if every outcome, whose projection to B is $\alpha(B)$, dominates every outcome whose projection to B is b. Condition $(*)$ can be determined directly using the polynomial algorithm in Section 5 of [16]. (In the notation of that paper we determine if $\Gamma^* \models_{\mathcal{Y}} \psi^*$, where $\mathcal{Y}$ is the set of singleton subsets of V, and ψ is the preference statement $\alpha(B) > b \parallel \emptyset$.) However, although this check is polynomial, it's a good deal more expensive than the root-dominates rule and the deciding-node-dominates rule.

5   A Sufficient Condition for Non-dominance

Let α be an outcome and let $\mathcal{D}$ be a collection of domains. We say that α *root non-dominates* $\mathcal{D}$ if there exists $Y \notin \bigcup_{\varphi \in \Gamma} W_\varphi$ such that $\mathcal{D}(Y) \not\ni \alpha(Y)$ and, for all $y \in \mathcal{D}(Y)$, $\alpha(Y) \not\sqsupset_\top^Y y$.

Proposition 7. *If α root non-dominates $\mathcal{D}$ then α non-dominates $\mathcal{D}$, i.e. for all β of $\mathcal{D}$, we have $\alpha \not\trianglerighteq \beta$.*

Proof: Consider any β of $\mathcal{D}$. Suppose α root non-dominates $\mathcal{D}$, so that there exists $Y \notin \bigcup_{\varphi \in \Gamma} W_\varphi$ such that $\mathcal{D}(Y) \not\ni \alpha(Y)$ and $\alpha(Y) \not\trianglerighteq_\top^Y \beta(Y)$. It follows, using Proposition 1, that we can define a pos-tree σ satisfying Γ with just a root node with associated variable Y and local ordering $\geqslant$ with $\alpha(Y) \not\geqslant \beta(Y)$. Then $\alpha \not\succcurlyeq_\sigma \beta$, which shows that $\alpha \not\trianglerighteq \beta$. ∎

Example (continued). Let Γ be as in the example in Section 4.1, let γ be the outcome $x_1 \, y_2 \, z_2$, and define $\mathcal{D}'$ by $\mathcal{D}'(X) = \{x_4\}$, $\mathcal{D}'(Y) = \underline{Y}$ and $\mathcal{D}'(Z) = \underline{Z}$. Then γ root non-dominates $\mathcal{D}'$, because $X \notin \bigcup_{\varphi \in \Gamma} W_\varphi = \{Z\}$, and $\mathcal{D}'(X) \not\ni \gamma(X) = x_1$, and $\gamma(X) \not\trianglerighteq_\top^X x_4$. ∎

6 Experimental Testing

6.1 Experimental Setup

We performed experiments with four families of cp-theories and several sets of binary CSP instances. The CSPs were generated using Christian Bessiere's random uniform CSP generator (www.lirmm.fr/~bessiere/generator.html). Experiments were run as a single thread on Dual Quad Core Xeon CPU, running Linux 2.6.25 x64, with overall 11.76 GB of RAM, and processor speed 2.66 GHz. We maintain arc consistency during the search algorithm, so that the current domains $\mathcal{D}(X)$ are generated from a partial assignment b by arc consistency [1]. The conditional preferences impose sometimes strong restrictions on the variable orderings that can be used in the search tree (corresponding to the condition (1) of Proposition 1), which much reduces the potential benefit of a dynamic variable ordering; for simplicity, we used a fixed variable ordering (which is possible since in the experiments we used only fully acyclic cp-theories [15], including acyclic CP-nets).

Random Generation of Preferences: We consider four families of cp-theories, CP-nets (*CPnet*), partial conditional lexicographic orders (*Lex*), a family with varying W component (*Rand-W*), and CP-nets with local total orderings (*CPn-to*). These are generated as follows. We order the variables V as $X_1, \ldots, X_n$. For each variable X_i we randomly choose the parents set U_i to be a subset of cardinality 0, 1 or 2 of $\{X_1, \ldots, X_{i-1}\}$. For the *CPnet* family we set $W_i = \emptyset$. For the *Lex* family we set $W_i = \{X_{i+1}, \ldots, X_n\}$. For random-$W$ (*Rand-W*) problems we define W_i to be a random subset of $\{X_{i+1}, \ldots, X_n\}$. Then, for each assignment u to U_i, we randomly choose an ordering $x^1, \ldots, x^m$ of the domain of X_i (so we'll usually have different orderings for different u). We then randomly choose a number of pairs (x^j, x^k) with $j < k$, except for the *CPn-to* family when we include all pairs (x^j, x^{j+1}), for $j = 1, \ldots, |\underline{X_i}| - 1$. For each of these pairs we include the corresponding statement $u : x^j > x^k \, [W_i]$ in the cp-theory Γ.

We consider ten versions of the algorithm. They differ according to whether they use root-dominance (labelled **r** in the tables), deciding node-dominance

Table 1. Mean number of optimal solutions for each preference family, and running times (ms), number of visited nodes and number of dominance checks at leaves for each preference family and each method. The CSPs were based on 10 four-valued variables, and averaged around 500 solutions.

	CP-nets			Rand-W			Lex			CPn-to		
# opt:	87.74			38.42			24.86			13.56		
Rules	*Time*	*#nd*	*chk*	*Time*	*#nd*	*chk*	*Time*	*#nd*	*chk*	*Time*	*#nd*	*chk*
Basic	7372	1173	22430	2097	1173	9181	1134	1173	5932	2263	1173	2248
r	10637	1172	22421	3312	971	8903	1609	647	4946	2706	1148	2227
d	4104	**536**	7956	677	209	1579	236	97	656	223	**148**	148
r+d	4156	**536**	7956	689	206	1578	234	97	656	226	**148**	148
p	32572	1173	89680	2705	291	10725	620	97	2950	11192	1173	12745
n	818	1173	979	675	1173	1817	560	1173	2031	908	1173	560
r+n	1438	1172	978	1896	971	1729	1628	647	1797	1501	1148	545
d+n	515	**536**	**288**	371	209	445	**205**	**97**	**323**	**124**	**148**	**12**
r+d+n	**514**	**536**	**288**	**363**	**206**	**444**	206	**97**	**323**	126	**148**	**12**
p+n	5150	1173	6136	1165	291	3099	386	**97**	1363	5325	1173	4170

(**d**), the projection-dominance condition (**p**), or the root non-dominance condition (**n**). These are compared against the basic algorithm (Section 3.1) which uses none of these additional pruning methods, and we also consider some combinations of the methods.

We performed two groups of experiments. The first group focused on comparing the different versions of the algorithm (see Tables 1 and 2). We used CSPs based on 10 four-valued variables. The second group (see Figure 2) considers how computation time—of two of the best plus the basic algorithm—varies with the number n of variables. The computation time clearly depends strongly on the number of solutions of the CSP. Because of this, we considered families of CSPs with approximately constant number of solutions, in order to obtain a clearer picture of the dependence on n. We used three-valued variables and CSPs where each constraint includes 7 of the 9 possible tuples. We then chose the number of constraints to be such that the expected number of solutions was around 1000, further filtering out CSPs differing from this by more than around 10%.

6.2   Discussion of Results

All figures in the tables and graphs are the mean over 50 random instances. The experimental results confirmed that no optimal solutions were lost by the additional pruning methods (as implied theoretically by Propositions 2, 5 and 7). Table 1 shows comparisons between all the methods for CSPs with around 500 solutions. Table 2 concerns CSPs with around 2000 solutions, and with around 10,000 solutions, where, for space reasons, we only include the results for the basic algorithm plus two of the best combinations, **r+d** and **r+d+n**.

Table 2. Mean number of optimal solutions for each preference family, and running times (ms) for each family and each method

	CPnet	Rand-W	Lex	CPn-to
10 vars, 4 values, Mean 1993 solutions				
# opt	221.2	73.0	39.5	16.4
Base	62608	14711	6496	13728
r+d	31998	3204	673	651
r+d+n	**2164**	**1557**	**509**	**445**
10 vars, 4 values, Mean 9910 solutions				
# opt	364.8	204.5	133.8	6.5
Base	564733	183710	110303	29285
r+d	278583	28666	8482	358
r+d+n	**18623**	**14595**	**5307**	**352**

The deciding-node-dominates rule (**d**) appears to be much the most effective of the three positive pruning schemes (i.e., **r**, **d** and **p**). With this rule the number of visited nodes and the number of dominance checks are reduced significantly in comparison with the basic algorithm. It seems that root-dominates can be slightly useful when used in conjunction with the deciding-node-dominates rule (**r+d**). The projection-dominates rule was not effective; although for the *Lex* and *Rand-W* families it pruned the search tree considerably, the costliness of the dominance test—which was applied at all nodes, not just leaf nodes—was detrimental, except for the *Lex* family (see Table 1). The root non-dominance condition can improve the performance of the algorithm considerably, especially for the *CPnet* and *CPn-to* families, since it can greatly reduce the number of dominance tests. An indication of how fast it is to check conditions **r**, **d** and **p** is given by considering the average time taken per node by their corresponding algorithms. In the experiments reported in Table 1, the version of the algorithm using **p** can be seen to take much more time per node than the **r** and **d** algorithms. For example, for the CP-nets family, algorithms **r**, **d** and **p** average around 9, 8 and 28 ms per node, respectively.

The results in Figure 2 indicate that the computation time does not increase very strongly with the number of variables. (By the way, it turns out that for each preference family, the mean number of optimal solutions does not vary greatly with n, being centred on around $160, 90, 60$ and 9 for the CPnet, Rand-W, Lex and CPn-to families, respectively.) For the Rand-W family, the new algorithms do not perform much (if at all) better than the basic algorithm. For the Lex family, the two new algorithms are mostly twice as fast as the basic one. For the CP-nets family, the **r+d** algorithm is only slightly better than the basic algorithm, but performs excellently on the CPn-to family with mostly an order of magnitude improvement, as does the **r+d+n** algorithm, which also shows more than an order of magnitude speed up for the CP-nets family.

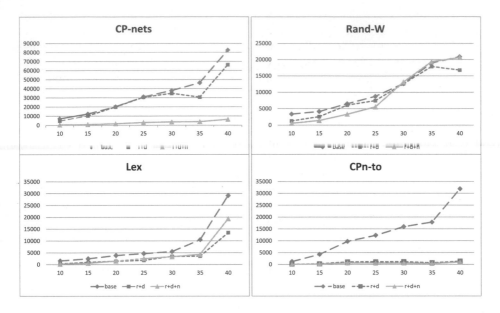

Fig. 2. Running time(ms) for each family of preferences for $n = 10, 15, \ldots, 40$ variables (having 3 values each). Each CSP has approximately 1000 solutions.

7   Discussion

The experimental results indicate that this approach to constrained optimisation for conditional preferences allows computation in a reasonable time even for problems of significant size (and problems of this kind, such as optimisation of configurable products, are not necessarily very large in practice). The additional methods developed in this paper can lead to a major improvement over the basic algorithm, often an order of magnitude improvement for the two CP-nets preference families. Interestingly, the non-dominance rule, which saves dominance checks when they are bound to fail below a node in the search tree, can be very effective, as well as one of the dominance rules. It could well be worth constructing and testing non-dominance rules in situations involving other forms of partially ordered preferences.

There are many ways of extending the approaches. For example, we could generalise to more expressive comparative preference languages (such as that defined in [16]); we could attempt to develop the positive dominance rules for propagation, i.e., for eliminating values in future domains; we could develop an approach that uses dynamic variable orderings, making use of the consistency conditions from Section 6 of [15]; we could try to amend the projection-dominance rule to take into account the reductions in the current domains $\mathcal{D}$; furthermore, unsound pruning rules can be used, in order to find a reasonable number of solutions very fast. It would also be interesting to try applying the pruning rule from [5], which could be effective when the domains are large.

The approach in this paper was based on a polynomial dominance relation $\trianglerighteq_\Gamma$, rather the standard one $\succeq_\Gamma$. However, the results of this paper are still very relevant if one is interested in finding optimal solutions with respect to the standard dominance relation, for example, for CP-nets. Let Ω be the set of solutions of the CSP. We are computing the set Ω' of solutions α of Ω such that there does not exist $\beta \neq \alpha$ with $\beta \trianglerighteq_\Gamma \alpha$. If one uses the standard dominance relation $\succeq_\Gamma$, then the set of optimal solutions Ω^o consists of all elements α of Ω such that there does not exist $\beta \neq \alpha$ with $\beta \succeq_\Gamma \alpha$. Because $\succeq_\Gamma$ is more conservative than $\trianglerighteq_\Gamma$ (i.e., $\alpha \succeq_\Gamma \beta$ implies $\alpha \trianglerighteq_\Gamma \beta$), Ω' is always a subset of Ω^o, so any solutions generated by the approach in this paper are also optimal with respect to the standard semantics—although they will not generally be all such optimal solutions. If one wants to generate the set Ω^o precisely, one can use the depth-first search algorithm again with the dominance checking at leaf nodes being done with $\succeq_\Gamma$ rather than with $\trianglerighteq_\Gamma$. The three dominance rules from Section 4 are no longer sound, but the non-dominance rule from Section 5 is still sound, and so can be used to reduce the number of dominance checks in the search.

We focused on the constrained optimisation algorithm when we can generate outcomes using a search tree in an order that is compatible with the conditional preferences. It is possible to apply our techniques also for the case where the order of outcomes generated is not necessarily compatible with the conditional preferences. (We'd need to do this, in particular, if Γ were inconsistent, i.e., if $\succeq_\Gamma$ were not acyclic, since then there'd be no compatible search tree.) Then, at a leaf node with associated complete assignment β, we need to check also if β dominates α, as well as if α dominates β, where α is an element of K, the current set of solutions. In contrast with the standard case, K is not monotonic increasing: it can lose elements as well as gain them. Nevertheless, the dominance rules developed in this paper can again be valuable in pruning the search.

We considered the case where the set Ω of outcomes is expressed as the solutions of a CSP. In other settings, the set of outcomes, representing a set of available products, for example, is listed explicitly. The new constrained optimisation algorithms developed in this paper apply also here. Again we define dynamic variable and value orderings that determine a search tree compatible with a set of conditional preferences; this search tree can be used to explore Ω (which is then implicitly being expressed as a decision tree), and find the optimal ones, using, as before, the positive and negative dominance rules to prune the search tree and reduce the dominance checks.

Acknowledgements. This material is based upon works supported by the Science Foundation Ireland under Grant No. 08/PI/I1912.

References

1. Bessiere, C.: Constraint propagation. In: Rossi, F., van Beek, P., Walsh, T. (eds.) Handbook of Constraint Programming. Elsevier, Amsterdam (2006)
2. Bienvenu, M., Lang, J., Wilson, N.: From preference logics to preference languages, and back. In: Proc. KR 2010 (2010)

3. Boutilier, C., Brafman, R., Hoos, H., Poole, D.: Reasoning with conditional ceteris paribus preference statements. In: Proceedings of UAI 1999, pp. 71–80 (1999)
4. Boutilier, C., Brafman, R.I., Domshlak, C., Hoos, H., Poole, D.: CP-nets: A tool for reasoning with conditional *ceteris paribus* preference statements. Journal of Artificial Intelligence Research 21, 135–191 (2004)
5. Boutilier, C., Brafman, R.I., Domshlak, C., Hoos, H., Poole, D.: Preference-based constrained optimization with CP-nets. Computational Intelligence 20(2), 137–157 (2004)
6. Brafman, R., Domshlak, C., Shimony, E.: On graphical modeling of preference and importance. Journal of Artificial Intelligence Research 25, 389–424 (2006)
7. Fahle, T., Schamberger, S., Sellmann, M.: Symmetry breaking. In: Walsh, T. (ed.) CP 2001. LNCS, vol. 2239, pp. 93–107. Springer, Heidelberg (2001)
8. Goldsmith, J., Lang, J., Truszczyński, M., Wilson, N.: The computational complexity of dominance and consistency in CP-nets. Journal of Artificial Intelligence Research 33, 403–432 (2008)
9. McGeachie, M., Doyle, J.: Utility functions for ceteris paribus preferences. Computational Intelligence 20(2), 158–217 (2004)
10. Santhanam, G., Basu, S., Honavar, V.: Dominance testing via model checking. In: Proc. AAAI 2010 (2010)
11. Trabelsi, W., Wilson, N., Bridge, D., Ricci, F.: Comparing approaches to preference dominance for conversational recommender systems. In: Proc. ICTAI, pp. 113–118 (2010)
12. Wilson, N.: Consistency and constrained optimisation for conditional preferences. In: Proceedings of ECAI 2004, pp. 888–892 (2004)
13. Wilson, N.: Extending CP-nets with stronger conditional preference statements. In: Proceedings of AAAI 2004, pp. 735–741 (2004)
14. Wilson, N.: An efficient upper approximation for conditional preference. In: Proceedings of ECAI 2006, pp. 472–476 (2006)
15. Wilson, N.: Computational techniques for a simple theory of conditional preferences. Artificial Intelligence (in press, 2011), doi:10.1016/j.artint.2010.11.018
16. Wilson, N.: Efficient inference for expressive comparative preference languages. In: Proceedings of IJCAI 2009, pp. 961–966 (2009)

Checking and Filtering Global Set Constraints

Justin Yip and Pascal Van Hentenryck

Brown University, Box 1910,
Providence, RI 02912, USA

Abstract. This paper considers feasibility checking and filtering of global constraints over set variables. It makes four main contributions. (1) It presents a feasibility checker for the global *alldisjoint* constraint. (2) It proposes primal filters for the combination of a global disjoint constraint and symmetry-breaking constraints. (3) It proposes dual filters for global intersection constraints. (4) It presents primal/dual filters for the combination of a global intersection constraint and symmetry-breaking constraints. All these contributions are independent of the underlying domain representation. Experimental results show that these proposals have complementary benefits, may improve efficiency significantly, and make it possible to solve larger instances of two standard benchmarks.

1 Introduction

Global set constraints have received very little attention primarily because of intractability results on both bound consistency and feasibility checking. However, they still offer significant opportunities for improving the performance of set solvers, since the alternative, i.e., not to prune the search space, seems even worse. Recent work explores two possible approaches to deal with these computational difficulties. On the one hand, one may relax the requirement for polynomial-time algorithms and settle for algorithms that may be exponential in the worst case but are reasonable in practice and prune substantial parts of the search tree. On the other hand, one may take the more conventional approach and relax completeness of the filtering algorithm.

This paper explores both approaches for several global intersection constraints. It has four main contributions, all of which are independent of the underlying representations of the set solver:

1. it introduces a feasibility checker for the global *alldisjoint* constraint for an explicit set domain representation;
2. it proposes a filter for the primal variables of the combination of a global *alldisjoint* constraint and symmetry-breaking constraints;
3. it presents a dual filter for the global *atmost-k* constraint that constrains the cardinalities of the dual variables;
4. it introduces primal/dual filters for the combination of a global *atmost-k* constraint and symmetry-breaking constraints.

J. Lee (Ed.): CP 2011, LNCS 6876, pp. 819–833, 2011.
© Springer-Verlag Berlin Heidelberg 2011

The dual and primal/dual filters for *atmost-k* constraint are particularly compelling. Their inference rules are completely different from the *alldisjoint* constraint (the special case where $k = 0$) since each element can be taken by multiple variables. They depend on the solutions of some combinatorial problems which are themselves set-CSPs. In turn, these CSPs can be solved by constraint programs using the dual filter, which again depends on the solution of some smaller combinatorial problems which are solved recursively by constraint programming. Experimental results show that these contributions are orthogonal and may substantially improve the performance of set solvers on two standard benchmarks, solving instances that could not be solved in reasonable time before and reducing CPU times by factors that exceed 1,000.

2   Set CSPs

A Set Constraint Satisfaction Problem (Set-CSP) consists of a set of set variables, whose domain values are *sets* of elements drawn from a universe $U(n) = \{1, ..., n\}$, and a set of constraints specifying relations between variables. The problem is to find a solution, i.e., an assignment of set variables to domain values satisfying all constraints. A set domain may represent a number of domain values exponential in the input size. Representations that either approximate the set domain or are as compact as possible have been investigated heavily. The subset-bound [1,2], length-lex [3], and some of their variations [4,5] are common approximate representations. An exact domain representation based on binary decision diagrams (BDDs) was proposed in [6]. The techniques presented in this paper are orthogonal to domain representations, although some representations are best positioned to exploit the inferences. The experimental results consider both length-lex and the subset-bound domains.

Many Set-CSPs uses dual modeling (e.g., [7]), the idea of jointly using several models of the same problem. In particular, Set-CSPs often contain a primal and a dual model. The primal model is a natural encoding of the problem, i.e., its (primal) variables represent the decisions one is interested in. The dual model associates a (dual) variable with each element in the universe and the value of a dual variable is a set of primal variables taking that value (Primal variables are often represented by their indices). In this paper, we use the term *primal filter* for a filtering algorithm on the primal variables and *dual filter* for a filtering algorithm on dual variables.

Many Set-CSPs exhibit *variable interchangeability*: given any solution, it is possible to generate another by swapping the assignment of two interchangeable variables. Ideally these symmetries should be eliminated to prevent the solver from visiting symmetric subtrees. Let X_1 and X_2 be two interchangeable set-variables. If $[X_1 = \{1, 2\}, X_2 = \{1, 3\}]$ is a solution, then the assignment $[X_1 = \{1, 3\}, X_2 = \{1, 2\}]$ is a symmetric solution. To eliminate such symmetric solutions, the model can post a static ordering constraint $X_1 \preceq X_2$. Models over set variables almost always impose such static lexicographic constraints to break variable symmetries. The choice of the ordering constraint $\preceq$ is arbitrary. Two common choices are the lexicographical [8] and length-lex [3] orderings which coincide when sets have the same length. This paper uses the lexicographical ordering for breaking symmetries but obviously the underlying domain representation can be based on the subset-bound, length-lex, or BDD domains. Adding static constraints to break symmetries was originally proposed in [9].

3   Contributions and Related Work

This section gives a broad perspectives on our research contributions and their relationships to prior work.

Exponential-Time Constraint Propagation. The complexity of global intersection constraints over sets has been investigated in depth in [13]. They showed that even feasibility checking is hard for global set constraints under some established domain representations. Our first contribution is to introduce a feasibility checker for the global *alldisjoint* constraint for an explicit set-domain representation, typically obtained during search from the solutions to a substructure of the problem. The feasibility checker takes exponential time in the worst case, since the feasibility of *alldisjoint* is NP-hard, but may bring significant improvements experimentally. This feasibility checker was motivated by the success of exponential-time algorithms to enforce bound consistency on unary intersection constraints [5]. *The experimental results provide further evidence that it may be valuable to shift the exponential behavior from the agnostic search to the constraints, where the semantics can be exploited.*

Dual Filters for Cardinalities. This paper presents a dual filter for the global *atmost-k* constraint which filters the cardinalities of the dual variables. It is a significant generalization of the *atmost-1* filter proposed in [14]. Indeed, if several variables in an *atmost-1* constraint shares an element, all their remaining elements must be disjoint, which simplifies reasoning considerably. In contrast, our *atmost-k* implementation solves a number of combinatorial counting problems to obtain lower and upper bounds on the cardinalities of dual variables and boost propagation. These counting problems are solved recursively as Set-CSPs using the results presented in the paper. *The experimental results shows that complex reasoning about the cardinalities of dual variables may bring significant benefits.*

Combining Set Constraints. The paper also illustrates the benefits of combining set constraints in two different ways. *First, it shows that inference rules combining primal and dual variables can bring significant pruning and deserve more systematic investigation. Second, it demonstrates the benefits of pushing symmetry-breaking constraints into global set constraints.* The idea of pushing symmetry-breaking constraints into other constraints has appeared in various papers. Hnich, Kiziltan, and Walsh [10] proposed a global constraint that combines symmetry breaking with a sum constraint. Katsirelos, Narodytska, and Walsh [11] proposed a generic framework for global constraint with symmetry-breaking constraints for vectors of variables. Yip and Van Hentenryck [12] proposed a generic framework for combining arbitrary binary length-lex propagators with ordering constraints and studied their benefits experimentally.

4   A Feasibility Checker for the AllDisjoint Constraint

This section presents a feasibility checker for the *alldisjoint* constraint.

Definition 1 (The AllDisjoint Constraint). *alldisjoint*$(X_1, ..., X_m)$ *holds if* $\bigwedge_{i<j} X_i \cap X_j = \emptyset$.

Definition 2 (The Feasibility Checker). *The (HasSolution) checker* $hs\langle\mathcal{C}\rangle(X_1, ..., X_m)$ *returns* $\exists x_1 \in D(X_1), ..., x_m \in D(X_m) : \mathcal{C}(x_1, ..., x_m)$, *where* $\mathcal{C}$ *is a constraint and* $D(X_i)$ *is the domain of* X_i *given as an explicit set of sets.*

If the set domains are given explicitly, checking feasibility is NP-hard. A similar result can also be given for the hybrid subset-bound/length-lex domain.

Theorem 1. $hs\langle alldisjoint\rangle(X_1, ..., X_m)$ *is NP-hard when* $D(X_i)$ *is specified as an explicit set of sets.*

Proof. A trivial reduction from the SETPACKING problem. Instance: a finite set S and a collection $\mathcal{S}$ of subset of S. Question: determine whether some m sets in $\mathcal{S}$ are pairwise disjoint. A solution to the problem is $\mathcal{S}' \subseteq \mathcal{S}$, where $|\mathcal{S}'| = m$ and sets in $\mathcal{S}'$ are pairwise disjoint.

We first assume all sets in $\mathcal{S}$ are not empty. Since otherwise, we can reduce the parameter m by the number of empty sets in $\mathcal{S}$. Given a SETPACKING instance, we construct a set-CSP such that it is feasible if and only if there exists m pairwise disjoint sets. In the CSP, there are m set variables with initial domain $\mathcal{S}$, and an *alldisjoint*$(X_1, ..., X_m)$ constraint. Intuitively, the variables correspond to the SETPACKING solution. The rewriting is obviously polynomial.

$\Rightarrow$ Given a solution to the SETPACKING problem, we construct a solution to the set-CSP. Let $\mathcal{S}' = \{s_1, ..., s_m\}$, we assign $X_i = s_i$. Since X_i has a initial domain of $\mathcal{S}$, s_i is a feasible domain value. The assignment also satisfies the *alldisjoint* constraint, since $\mathcal{S}'$ are pairwise disjoint.

$\Leftarrow$ Given a solution to the set-CSP, we construct a solution to the SETPACKING Problem. Consider a solution $[X_1 = s_1, ..., X_m = s_m]$, every pair of s_i are pairwise disjoint, and $s_i \in \mathcal{S}$. Moreover, as all s_i are non-empty sets, we have $s_i \neq s_j \; \forall i < j$ since they are disjoint. Therefore, $\mathcal{S}' = \{s_1, ..., s_m\}$ is a solution to the SETPACKING Problem.   □

The Feasibility Checker. Algorithm 1 is a feasibility checker for the *alldisjoint* constraint, assuming that the set variables take their elements in $\{1..n\}$. In the worst case, the checker takes exponential time but experimental results will demonstrate that it can bring substantial benefits in practice. The checker takes a set of set variables and returns a Boolean value indicating whether there are

Algorithm 1. $hs\langle alldisjoint\rangle(X_1, ..., X_m)$

```
1: for σ in {[v₁, ..., vₙ]|vₑ ∈ {1, ..., m} ∪ {⊥}} do
2:     [T₁, ..., Tₘ, T⊥] ← [D(X₁), ..., D(Xₘ), {{1..n}}]
3:     for e = 1 to n do
4:         T_σ(e) ← {t ∈ T_σ(e)|e ∈ t}
5:         for i in {1, 2, ..., σ(e) − 1, σ(e) + 1, ..., m} do
6:             Tᵢ ← {t ∈ Tᵢ|e ∉ t}
7:     if ⋀_{1≤i≤m} Tᵢ ≠ ∅ then
8:         return true
9: return false
```

solutions. Its key idea is to enumerate all the dual assignments (line 1) and to test whether they satisfy the domain constraints (lines 2–8). Since an element can be assigned to at most one set, a dual assignment assigns a variable index v_e to each element e (or $\perp$ if the element is not assigned to any set). To test whether a dual assignment is feasible, the checker maintains T_i to denote the feasible sets for variable X_i. Initially, T_i is initialized to $D(X_i)$. The dual assignment is then used to filter the T_i's. In particular, the checker considers each element e in turn (line 3) and removes from $T_{\sigma(e)}$ all the sets not containing e. In other words, $X_{\sigma(e)}$ is the variable e is assigned to and the checker prunes the domain of $X_{\sigma(e)}$ to ensure that they all contain e. It then prunes the domains of the other variables (lines 5–6) to make sure that they do not contain e. The checker returns true if no domain has become empty at the end of the computation (lines 7–8). If none of the dual permutations is a solution, the checker returns false (line 9). Observe that set $T_\perp$ is never pruned, since it contains the set of all elements initially. Line 4 can never remove its set and lines 5–6 never considers $T_\perp$.

Example 1. Consider the domains $D(X_1) = \{\{1,2\}, \{1,4\}, \{2,4,6\}\}$, $D(X_2) = \{\{1,2\}, \{2,5\}, \{2,6\}\}$, $D(X_3) = \{\{1,5\}, \{3\}, \{5\}\}$, and $\sigma = [1, 2, \perp, 1, 3, 2]$. The dual assignment assigns element 1 to variable 1. The algorithm removes domain values from $T_1, \ldots, T_3$, giving $T_1 = \{\{1,2\}, \{1,4\}\}$, $T_2 = \{\{2,5\}, \{2,6\}\}$, and $T_3 = \{\{3\}, \{5\}\}$. The same domain-reduction process is performed for all elements. At the end, $T_1 = \{\{1,4\}\}$, $T_2 = \{\{2,6\}\}$, and $T_3 = \{\{5\}\}$. Hence, the dual assignment is a solution. On the other hand, if the initial value of T_3 is $\{\{1,5\}, \{3\}\}$, it will become empty after processing element 3. In this case, the dual assignment is infeasible.   ∎

5   A Primal Filter for Symmetry-Breaking AllDisjoint

Pushing symmetry-breaking constraints into other constraints has been shown effective in prior work. This section discusses a primal filter for the combination of a global *alldisjoint* constraint and a chain of symmetry-breaking constraints.

Definition 3 (Symmetry-Breaking AllDisjoint). $alldisjoint_{\preceq}(X_1, ..., X_m)$ *holds if* $alldisjoint(X_1, ..., X_m) \wedge \left(\bigwedge_{i<j} X_i \preceq X_j \right)$.

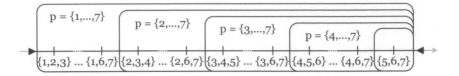

Fig. 1. How The Most Significant Set Element Determines the Possible Elements

Intuition. The key observation is that the most significant element of a variable X_i (i.e., the smallest value in X_i) determines an upper bound of the possible elements that can be taken by subsequent variables $X_j, \forall j > i$. Since the global *alldisjoint* constraint imposes that all variables take different elements, the total number of elements taken by all variables is known. If an element in X_i is such that there are not enough elements left for the variables $X_{i+1}, \ldots, X_m$, then it must be the case that X_i contains a smaller element.

Figure 1 depicts the idea and, in particular, the effect of the symmetry-breaking constraints on the possible values that variables can take. Consider a domain which contains all sets of cardinality 3 drawn from 1..7 and ordered lexicographically. The rectangles show how the most significant element determines the set of possible elements p for a set variable. If the most significant element of a variable X_i is 2, then its possible set is $\{2, ..., 7\}$. Moreover, if there is a lexicographic constraint between X_i and subsequent variables X_j $(j > i)$, then the set of possible elements for these subsequent variables is of cardinality at most 6, since their most significant element have to be at least 2.

Example 2. Consider a CSP with 3 variables X_1, X_2, X_3 of cardinality 3, taking their elements from 1..9, and a constraint $alldisjoint_{\preceq}(X_1, X_2, X_3)$. Assume that $X_1 \in \{\{1, 7, 8\}, \{1, 7, 9\}\}$, $X_2 \in \{\{2, 3, 4\}, ..., \{7, 8, 9\}\}$, and $X_3 \in \{\{3, 4, 5\}, ..., \{7, 8, 9\}\}$. The smallest element of X_2 cannot be 6, since this would leave only elements in $\{6, 7, 8, 9\}$ for filling X_2 and X_3 which need 6 distinct elements in total. It can be seen that the smallest element of X_2 can at most be 4, i.e., $X_2 \in \{\{2, 3, 4\}, ..., \{4, 8, 9\}\}$.

More propagation is possible when the required elements of earlier variables are considered. X_1 is taking elements 1 and 7, making it impossible for either X_2 or X_3 to take element 7. Suppose X_2 takes 4 as its most significant element, X_2 and X_3 pick elements from the set $\{4, 5, 6, 8, 9\}$, whose size is insufficient to fulfill the cardinality requirement. Hence, X_2 cannot start with element 4. ∎

A Reduction Rule. We present the primal filter for the symmetry-breaking *alldisjoint*. For simplicity, all set variables are assumed to be of cardinality c.

Rule 1 (Symmetry-Breaking AllDisjoint: Upper Bound)

$$\frac{1 \leq i \leq m \wedge \bigwedge_{i \leq j \leq m}(|X_j| = c) \wedge f = \max\{e | ave(i) \geq (m - i + 1)c\}}{alldisjoint_{\preceq}(X_1, ..., X_m) \longmapsto \min(X_i) \leq f \wedge alldisjoint_{\preceq}(X_1, ..., X_m)}$$

where $av_e(i) = (n - e + 1) - \sum_{j<i} |\{e' \in req(X_j) \mid e' \geq e\}|$, and $req(X_j)$ returns a set of required element in the domain of variable X_j.

The function $av_e(i)$ returns an upper-bound on the number of elements $X_i,...,X_m$ can take, assuming that X_i starts with element e. If the upper-bound is less than the total cardinality requirement (i.e., $(m - i + 1)c$), then the constraint is infeasible. The rule finds the largest element f such that the condition holds and imposes a constraint on the most significant element of X_i accordingly.

The primal filter is independent of the variable representation: it simply posts a constraint on the smallest element of variable X_i. If the length-lex representation for set variables is used, this update is particularly effective, since it directly updates the upper bound of the length-lex interval.

6 A Dual Filter for the Global Atmost-k Constraint

This section discusses the global *atmost-k* constraint which guarantees that every pair of set variables shares at most k elements. It is at least as difficult as the global disjoint constraint since the latter is a special case where $k = 0$.

Definition 4 (atmost-k). $atmost(k, X_1, ..., X_m)$ holds if $\bigwedge_{i<j} |X_i \cap X_j| \leq k$.

Early versions of the following theorem appeared in [13].

Theorem 2. $hs\langle atmost(k)\rangle(X_1, ..., X_m)$, where X_i are subset-bound, length-lex, or set variables with finite domains, is NP-hard.

We now present a dual filter for the global *atmost-k* constraint. For simplicity, we assume that all variables are of the same cardinality c. The basic idea underlying the dual filter is to state a redundant dual model reasoning on the cardinalities of the dual variables, knowing that their sum must be equal to mc. The dual model assumes the existence of a function $countAtmost(n,c,k)$ defined as follows.

Definition 5 (countAtmost). *Function* $countAtmost(n,c,k)$ *returns the maximum number of sets of cardinality c taking their values in $\{1..n\}$ and sharing at most k values.*

The dual filter is depicted in Figure 2. The first two lines define the dual model. Line (1) defines the dual variables: Y_e represents the indices of set variables which include element e. Line (2) defines the channeling constraints between the primal and dual variables. Line (3) is the core constraint: It ensures that the sum of the cardinalities is equal to $m \times c$, i.e., the number of variables multiplied by their cardinalities. To boost the pruning of this constraint, the key idea is to impose a lower and upper bound for the number of occurrences of each element e in the universe. The upper bound on $|Y_e|$ computes how many set variables can take an element e and is thus defined as $countAtmost(n-1, c-1, k-1)$ (Line (4)). Indeed, consider the set of variables taking element e, each of them has to take $c-1$ more elements from a universe of size $n-1$. To satisfy the intersection constraint, each

$$Y_e \subseteq \{1, ..., n\} \quad \forall 1 \leq e \leq m \tag{1}$$

$$e \in X_i \Leftrightarrow i \in Y_e \quad \forall 1 \leq i \leq n, 1 \leq e \leq m \tag{2}$$

$$\sum_{1 \leq e \leq m} |Y_e| = m\,c \tag{3}$$

$$|Y_e| \leq countAtmost(n-1, c-1, k-1) \quad \forall 1 \leq e \leq m \tag{4}$$

$$m - countAtmost(n-1, c, k) \leq |Y_e| \quad \forall 1 \leq e \leq m \tag{5}$$

Fig. 2. The Redundant Dual Filter for $atmost(k, X_1, ..., X_m)$.

---

pair can share at most $k - 1$ other elements since they are already sharing e. Hence, the maximum cardinality is bound by $countAtmost(n-1, c-1, k-1)$. The lower bound on $|Y_e|$ is obtained by computing how many set variables can exclude element e and is thus defined as $m - countAtmost(n-1, c, k)$ (Line (5)). Indeed, consider the set of variables not taking element e. These variables must draw elements from a universe of size $n - 1$, from which they have to pick c elements and each pair of variables can share at most k elements. The maximum number of variables not taking element e is therefore bound by $countAtmost(n-1, c, k)$ and element e has to occur in at least $m - countAtmost(n-1, c, k)$ variables. Observe that the dual filter is independent of the representation of set variables.

Implementation of countAtmost. We now discuss how to implement function $countAtmost$. There are at least three possibilities. (1) When available, it can be a lookup from a combinatorics table [15]; (2) It can be a constant-time approximation using extremal set theory [16]; (3) It can be implemented as an optimization problem! The first case is not a complete method since not all combinations of parameters are available. For the second case, let $s_1, ..., s_m$ be sets of cardinality c and n be their union size. If $\forall 1 \leq i < j \leq m, |s_i \cap s_j| \leq k$, then

$$n \geq \frac{c^2 m}{c + (m-1)k}.$$

This inequality can be used to obtain an upper bound on m. However, this bound is not tight. One can observe that m is not constrained when $c^2 - nk$ is negative.

Our implementation views the implementation of $countAtmost$ as an optimization problem which can be specified as

```
maximize m s.t.
```
$$|X_i \cap X_j| \leq k \quad \forall 1 \leq i < j \leq m$$
$$|X_i| = c \quad \forall 1 \leq i \leq m$$
$$X_i \subseteq \{1, ..., n\} \quad \forall 1 \leq i \leq m$$

This optimization problem can be solved by a sequence of feasibility problems using various values for m. As a result, $countAtmost$ itself can be implemented in terms of set-CSPs. Moreover, these set-CSPs also use a global $atmost$-k constraint

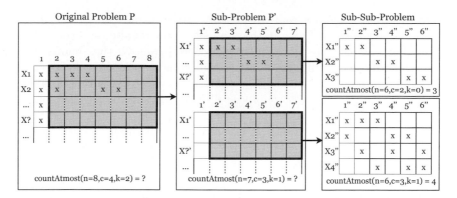

Fig. 3. How Many Set Variables Can Take an Element? ($n = 8, c = 4, k = 2$)

and hence they can use all the filters presented in this paper. In particular, our implementation posts the dual filter shown in Figure 2 which obviously depends on the values $countAtmost(n-1, c-1, k-1)$ and $countAtmost(n-1, c, k)$. These are computed recursively as two additional optimization problems. Since these recursive calls may involve the same sub-optimization problems, our implementation memoizes the result of each suboptimization and reuses them whenever appropriate in order to avoid solving the same suboptimizations repeatedly. The computation of these subproblems takes negligible time in our benchmarks and only takes place at the root of the tree. It is however interesting to see how the derivation of the dual filter requires the solving of set-CSPs which in turn uses the dual filter itself on smaller subproblems.

Example 3 (A Recursive Counting Procedure). Let $P = countAtmost(8, 4, 2)$, a problem with 8 set variables of cardinality 4 drawing their elements from a universe of size 8 and subject to a global *atmost-2* constraint. The dual filter associated with P needs to compute $countAtmost(7, 4, 2)$ and $countAtmost(7, 3, 1)$ in order to obtain the lower and upper bounds on $|Y_e|$. We only discuss the upper bound and the intuition is given in Figure 3. Each row corresponds to a variable and each column to an element. The symbol x on cell $(X_1, 1)$ denotes $1 \in X_1$.

The reasoning is illustrated on element 1 for simplicity but any element would do: They are undistinguishable. The upper bound on $|Y_1|$ is $countAtmost(7, 3, 1)$: Indeed, if variables $X_1, X_2, ..., X_?$ take element 1, the other elements taken by these variables (the shaded area on the left side of the figure) can share at most 1 element (since all of them are already sharing element 1 and they are all subject to a global *atmost-2* constraint). Hence, the shaded part can be seen as the subproblem $P' = countAtmost(7, 3, 1)$ (the middle part) where the universe size is reduced by 1, the cardinality is reduced by 1, and the intersection constraint parameter becomes $k = 1$.

The objective value of P' can be found by solving another set-CSP as specified on the previous page. To boost propagation, we also introduce dual filters for P' and the reasoning is illustrated on the abstract elements $1', ..., 7'$. We thus compute the upper bound $countAtmost(6, 2, 0)$ (top part on the right which corresponds to the shaded area in the top part in the middle) and $countAtmost$ $(6, 3, 1)$ (bottom part on the right which corresponds to the shaded area in the bottom part in the middle). The upper bound $countAtmost(6, 2, 0)$ is easy to compute since this is a *alldisjoint* constraint where every set variable has cardinality 2 and the universe is of size 6: There are at most 3 variables that can take value 1'. To obtain the lower bound, we exclude abstract element 1' and need to solve $countAtmost(6, 3, 1)$, since we have one fewer element in the universe. This value is also found by solving another set-CSP. The maximum number of sets excluding element 1' is 4. Hence element 1' occurs in *at least* $7 - 4 = 3$ variables in P'. Now that the lower and upper bounds are available for the dual filter, the set-CSP for P'. The optimal value is then found and used in the dual filter for P which is also solved as a set-CSP.   ∎

7   Primal/Dual Filters for Symmetry-Breaking Atmost-k

Section 5 presented a primal filter for the symmetry-breaking *alldisjoint*. It recognized that the most significant element determines the size of the possible sets for a variable and the lexicographically greater variables, enabling to achieve stronger propagation. Section 6 on the other hand presented a dual filter based on a dual model: It exploits the observation that an element cannot appear in, or be excluded from, too many variables, which imposes some strong cardinality constraint on dual variables. These ideas can be combined for the implementation of a global $atmost\text{-}k_{\preceq}$ constraint, which combines a global $atmost\text{-}k$ constraint and a chain of symmetry-breaking constraints.

Definition 6 (Symmetry-Breaking   Atmost-k). $atmost_{\preceq}(k, X_1, ..., X_m)$ *holds if* $atmost(k, X_1, ..., X_m) \wedge \bigwedge_{i<j} X_i \preceq X_j$.

Intuition. The primal/dual filter aims at answering the following questions which combines primal and dual aspects:

1. How many set variables must include the first e elements of the universe?
2. How many set variables must exclude the first e elements of the universe?

In general, variables that are greater lexicographically do not take small elements: These are taken by the lexicographically smaller variables. For the symmetry-breaking *alldisjoint* constraint, it was relatively easy to answer that question since every element can be taken by at most one variable. For the symmetry-breaking $atmost\text{-}k$ constraint, this situation is more complicated but we can reuse the function $countAtmost$ introduced for the dual filter.

Example 4 (Primal/Dual Exclusion). Consider 5 set variables $X_1, ..., X_5$ of cardinality 3 taking their values from a universe 1..7 and a global $atmost_{\leq}(1, X_1, ..., X_5)$. Since $countAtmost(6, 3, 1)$ returns 4, it follows that at most 4 variables can start with elements greater than or equal to 2. Due to the lexicographic constraint, X_1 must not start with element 2.   ∎

Example 5 (Primal/Dual Inclusion). Consider 5 variables $X_1, ..., X_5$ of cardinality 3 taking their values from $\{1..7\}$ and a global $atmost_{\preceq}(1, X_1, ..., X_5)$. There are at most 3 variables taking element 1 (see Figure 3). Hence, X_4 must start with element greater than 1 and we can post the constraint $\{2, 3, 4\} \preceq X_4$. ∎

Reduction Rules. We are now ready to present the two primal/dual reduction rules. The first rule reasons about the maximum number of variables that can exclude the first e elements and derives a constraint preventing early variables from starting with large values.

Rule 2 (Symmetry-Breaking Atmost-k: Exclusion)

$$\frac{1 \le e \le n - c \wedge \bigwedge_{i \le j \le m} |X_j| = c \wedge i = countAtmost(n - e, c, k) \wedge 1 \le i \le m}{atmost_{\preceq}(k, X_1, ..., X_m) \longmapsto \min(X_{m-i}) \le e \wedge atmost_{\preceq}(k, X_1, ..., X_m)}$$

When the length-lex representation is used for set variables, the derived constraint can be used to update the upper bound of the set variables: only the sets starting with an element no greater than e are left in the domain. The second rule reasons about the maximum variables that can take the first e elements and derives a constraint preventing late variables from taking the first e elements.

Rule 3 (Symmetry-Breaking Atmost-k: Inclusion)

$$\frac{1 \le e \le k \wedge \bigwedge_{i \le j \le m} |X_j| = c \wedge i = countAtmost(n - e, c - e, k - e) \wedge 0 \le i < m}{atmost_{\preceq}(k, X_1, ..., X_m) \longmapsto l \preceq X_{i+1} \wedge atmost_{\preceq}(k, X_1, ..., X_m)}$$

where $l = \{1, ..., e - 1\} \uplus \{e + 1, ..., c + 1\}$

When the length-lex representation is used for set variables, the derived constraint can be used to update the lower bound of the set variables which must become at least $l = \{1, ..., e-1\} \uplus \{e+1, ..., c+1\}$. Observe that the rule prevents X_{i+1} from taking *all* elements in $\{1, .., e\}$. The smallest set lexicographically not taking all elements in e starts with $\langle 1, ..., e-1 \rangle$, excludes e, and fills the remaining free slots with as small elements as possible, i.e., $\langle e + 1, e + 2, ..., c + 1 \rangle$.

8   Experimental Evaluation

This section evaluates the performance of all global set constraints. Two standard benchmark problems are used: the error correcting code and the social golfer problems. We assess the impact of the global constraint both on the length-lex domain, the subset-bound domain and, whenever possible, their hybridization. All models and algorithms are implemented in the COMET system. Our experiments are run on a Core2Duo 2.4GHz laptop with 4GB of memory. The symbol x indicates a timeout of 1800 seconds. Instances solved within 2% of the best time are bolded, and those with the smallest number of failures are also bolded.

Table 1. Error Correcting Code, Hamming Distance: The Length-Lex Domain

atmost-k (Fig. 2)						✔		✔	
atmost-k≺ (Rules 2&3)				✔				✔	
(l,d,w)	Opt	Time	Fails	Time	Fails	Time	Fails	Time	Fails
(9,4,4)	18	13.25	46003	3.61	14229	0.1	31	**0.09**	**23**
(9,4,5)	18	21.83	66527	0.76	1931	0.49	1003	**0.14**	**208**
(10,4,3)	13	1.96	12399	1.00	6869	**0.05**	**42**	**0.05**	**42**
(10,4,4)	30	149.76	227707	3.62	14301	0.15	39	**0.13**	**31**
(10,4,5)	36	x	x	7.83	22352	20.11	14211	**0.50**	**0425**
(10,4,6)	30	512.88	676025	5.81	10434	26.36	17460	**4.57**	**8067**
(10,4,7)	13	2.82	12680	0.58	2384	**0.08**	**32**	0.09	**25**
(11,4,3)	17	40.72	167518	12.48	64772	**0.09**	211	0.1	**211**

Table 2. Error Correcting Code, Hamming Distance: The Subset-Bound Domain

atmost-k						✔		✔	
atmost-k≺				✔				✔	
(l,d,w)	Opt	Time	Fails	Time	Fails	Time	Fails	Time	Fails
(9,4,4)	18	x	x	223.09	574188	0.48	279	**0.45**	**207**
(9,4,5)	18	x	x	43.74	100988	13.64	50552	**2.54**	**6749**
(10,4,3)	13	812.6	2218607	24.93	65568	0.3	244	**0.28**	**190**
(10,4,4)	30	x	x	235.6	591496	1.38	1360	**1.13**	**1072**
(10,4,5)	36	x	x	x	x	x	x	x	x
(10,4,6)	30	x	x	x	x	x	x	x	x
(10,4,7)	13	x	x	24.3	64158	0.57	1487	**0.39**	**517**
(11,4,3)	17	x	x	885.1	1952008	0.9	2137	**0.85**	**1661**

The Error Correcting Code Problem. The error correcting code problem is defined in terms of three parameters: (l, d, w). It is an optimization problem that finds the largest number of codewords satisfying the following constraints: a codeword is a 0/1-vector of length l, the sum of the vector is w, and every pair of codewords have a Hamming distance of at least d. The problem can be modelled using set variables whose characteristic function is the 0/1-vector. This has been used as a very challenging benchmark since the optimality proof requires an implicit enumeration of the whole search tree. Our basic model is based on [17]: it is solved as a feasibility problem, starting with an upper bound $ub = countAtmost(n - 1, c - 1, k - 1) + countAtmost(n - 1, c, k)$ and decreasing the bound by 1 each time until a solution is found.

Since the contributions of this paper apply to any domain representation, this section evaluates the global filtering techniques both on length-lex and subset-bound variables. The standard model [12] applies binary symmetry-breaking constraints and dual modeling for breaking value symmetries. The atmost-k constraint is posted as a collection of binary intersection constraints. The model is augmented with two sets of constraints. First, the dual filter imposes cardinality constraints on the dual variables (Section 6). Second, the primal/dual filter reasons jointly about the symmetry-breaking constraints and the atmost-k

Table 3. The Social Golfer Problem: The Length-Lex and Subset-Bound Domains

	Length-Lex				Subset-Bound			
alldisjoint (Alg.1)			✔				✔	
alldisjoint$_\prec$ (Rule 1)			✔				✔	
(g,s,w)	Time	Fails	Time	Fails	Time	Fails	Time	Fails
(5,3,7)	8.49	52008	**5.08**	**12211**	420.09	1726521	**19.13**	**40401**
(5,4,6)	59.43	303376	**39.39**	**120438**	297.09	1106954	**160.73**	**346424**
(6,5,6)	60.61	221033	**16.86**	**27545**	47.26	97991	**39.13**	**34773**
(6,6,4)	**602.83**	2049826	649.00	1890962	x	x	x	x
(7,3,9)	x	x	**1274.18**	**2837356**	x	x	x	x
(8,3,10)	150.67	668785	**47.51**	**88817**	1373.11	2091583	**273.07**	**204773**
(9,3,11)	15.57	61924	**1.99**	**2724**	744.94	760027	**5.83**	**3557**

constraints (Section 7). The dual and primal dual filters depend on the solutions to several optimization subproblems for the various calls to *countAtmost*. The experimental results report the *total CPU time* and the *total number of failures*, i.e., the sum of the CPU time and number of failures for all the sub-problems.

Table 1 and 2 present the results for length-lex variables and subset-bound variables respectively. On the length-lex domains, both the dual and primal/dual filters bring *substantial* improvements in performance when used independently and their benefits are almost always cumulative. Instance (10,4,5) is now in the reach of the length-lex representation and the times to solve (10,4,4) and (11,2,3) are reduced by factors of 1152 and 407. Similar benefits are observed on the subset-bound representation, although it is clearly inferior to the length-lex representation. Nevertheless, the results indicates the dual and primal dual filters provide significant benefits for both representations.

The Social Golfer Problem. The social golfer problem is defined by three parameters (g, s, w). The goal is to find a tournament schedule for $n = g \times s$ golfers for w weeks. In each week, golfers are allocated into g groups of size s. Every pair of golfers play in the same group at most once. We use the model and labeling strategy for hybrid length-lex/subset bound domain in [5].

The standard model uses the binary symmetry-breaking constraints in [12]. Two sets of constraints are added to the model. First, the *alldisjoint* global constraint expresses that all groups of the same week are disjoint. The *atmost1* unary constraint generates a list of domain values for every primal variable, and our *alldisjoint* feasibility checker uses such list (but is only applied if the domain size is no greater than 200). Such a *alldisjoint* constraint is posed for each week and is propagated at the end of every choice point. Second, the global constraint *alldisjoint$_\prec$* is applied to the first group of every week. These groups contains player 1, are mutually disjoint, and are in increasing order. Our model introduces a set of auxiliary variables sbx1[wi] which removes player 1 from sbx[wi,1] and posts the *alldisjoint$_\prec$*(sbx1[1], ..., sbx1[w]) constraint.

Table 4. The Social Golfer Problem: The Hybrid Length-Lex/Subset-Bound Domain

alldisjoint					✔		✔	
alldisjoint$_\preceq$			✔				✔	
(g,s,w)	Time	Fails	Time	Fails	Time	Fails	Time	Fails
(5,3,7)	10.2	30828	**5.39**	10909	13.78	27278	5.84	**9291**
(5,4,6)	58.85	118160	59.1	113802	**51.55**	82746	**52.06**	**79902**
(6,5,6)	39.66	59269	40.82	59269	**20.35**	19317	20.25	19317
(6,6,4)	**1184.88**	1799472	1233.69	1799472	1263.32	**1763316**	1310.54	**1763316**
(7,3,9)	1530.00	2212890	**1142.77**	1375063	1558.92	1726504	1146.88	1018831
(8,3,10)	62.71	65205	48.88	49955	51.31	43055	**46.08**	**31547**
(9,3,11)	5.07	3191	5.06	3191	**2.92**	**1169**	3.07	**1169**
(9,6,6)	44.73	34624	46.28	34624	**2.67**	**172**	2.74	**172**
(9,8,4)	28.31	29021	29.42	29021	**4.31**	**77**	4.38	**77**
(12,4,11)	31.12	10858	31.66	10858	**18.89**	3384	18.9	3384
(13,3,16)	x	x	3.98	1191	x	x	**3.36**	**47**
(13,5,10)	284.07	116615	298.78	116615	13.88	489	**13.93**	**489**
(13,6,8)	20.16	7067	20.07	7067	**3.56**	**153**	3.72	**153**
(13,8,6)	92.91	52326	99.53	52326	**71.88**	6670	70.69	6670
(13,9,5)	7.2	3016	7.32	3016	**4.38**	**530**	4.37	**530**

Table 3 first evaluates the *alldisjoint* constraint both on length-lex and subset-bound domains. Regardless of the domain representation, models using the *alldisjoint* checker and the symmetry-breaking filter obtain the best results in general. On instance $(9, 3, 11)$ for the subset-bound model, our contributions reduce the solving time by more than 120 times. Some previously out of reach instances, such as $(7, 3, 9)$, are now solved by the length-lex domain.

To evaluate the impact of each technical contributions independently and jointly, Table 4 reports the results for the various combinations of the contributions on the hybrid length-lex/subset-bound domain. Using *alldisjoint*$_\preceq$ allows the model to solve $(13, 3, 16)$ trivially, although it was out of scope for the hybrid length-lex/subset-bound representation so far. It also produces non-negligible improvements on several instances, including $(5, 3, 7)$, $(8, 3, 10)$, while incurring minimal overhead in general. The table also shows that the feasibility checker for *alldisjoint* has a huge impact: It reduces the number of failures and the CPU time tremendously on a substantial number of benchmarks. For instance, it reduces the CPU time on $(13, 5, 10)$ by a factor more than 20. In general, the model using both sets of global constraints is the most robust and improves the state of the art on most of the instances.

9   Conclusion

This paper studied feasibility checking and filtering for global constraints over set variables. It proposed an exponential-time feasibility checker for the *alldisjoint* constraint, by taking a dual perspective and enumerating all possible dual assignments. The paper also presented primal, dual, and primal/dual filters for the symmetry-breaking *alldisjoint*, the *atmost-k*, and the symmetry-breaking *atmost-k* constraints. The dual and primal/dual filters need to answer various counting problems (e.g., How many set variables must include/exclude the first e elements of the universe) which are viewed as optimization problems and solved using the filters recursively on smaller *atmost-k* constraints. Experimental results on two standard benchmark problems, the social golfer problem and the error correcting code, show that the feasibility checker and the filters are very effective and significantly improve state-of-the-art results on these problems. In particular, they are able to solve open instances for set representations and reduce CPU times by a factor greater than 1,000 on some instances.

References

1. Puget, J.F.: Pecos a high level constraint programming language. In: Proc. of Spicis (1992)
2. Gervet, C.: Interval propagation to reason about sets: Definition and implementation of a practical language. Constraints 1(3), 191–244 (1997)
3. Gervet, C., Hentenryck, P.V.: Length-lex ordering for set csps. In: AAAI. AAAI Press, Menlo Park (2006)
4. Azevedo, F.: Cardinal: A finite sets constraint solver. Constraints 12(1), 93–129 (2007)
5. Yip, J., Van Hentenryck, P.: Exponential propagation for set variables. In: Cohen, D. (ed.) CP 2010. LNCS, vol. 6308, pp. 499–513. Springer, Heidelberg (2010)
6. Hawkins, P., Lagoon, V., Stuckey, P.J.: Solving set constraint satisfaction problems using robdds. Journal of Artificial Intelligence Research 24, 109–156 (2005)
7. Cheng, B.M.W., Choi, K.M.F., Lee, J.H.M., Wu, J.C.K.: Increasing constraint propagation by redundant modeling: an experience report. Constraints 4(2), 167–192 (1999)
8. Frisch, A.M., Hnich, B., Kiziltan, Z., Miguel, I., Walsh, T.: Global constraints for lexicographic orderings. In: Van Hentenryck, P. (ed.) CP 2002. LNCS, vol. 2470, pp. 93–108. Springer, Heidelberg (2002)
9. Crawford, J.M., Ginsberg, M.L., Luks, E.M., Roy, A.: Symmetry-breaking predicates for search problems. In: KR, pp. 148–159 (1996)
10. Hnich, B., Kiziltan, Z., Walsh, T.: Combining symmetry breaking with other constraints: Lexicographic ordering with sums. In: AMAI (2004)
11. Katsirelos, G., Narodytska, N., Walsh, T.: Combining symmetry breaking and global constraints (2009)
12. Yip, J., Van Hentenryck, P.: Evaluation of length-lex set variables. In: Gent, I.P. (ed.) CP 2009. LNCS, vol. 5732, pp. 817–832. Springer, Heidelberg (2009)
13. Bessière, C., Hebrard, E., Hnich, B., Walsh, T.: Disjoint, partition and intersection constraints for set and multiset variables. In: Wallace, M. (ed.) CP 2004. LNCS, vol. 3258, pp. 138–152. Springer, Heidelberg (2004)
14. Sadler, A., Gervet, C.: Global reasoning on sets. In: Proceedings of Workshop on Modelling and Problem Formulation (FORMUL 2001), held Alongside CP 2001 (2001)
15. Colbourn, C.J., Dinitz, J.H., Ii, L.C., Jajcay, R., Magliveras, S.S.: The crc handbook of combinatorial designs (1995)
16. Jukna, S.: Extremal combinatorics (2001)
17. Sadler, A., Gervet, C.: Enhancing set constraint solvers with lexicographic bounds. J. Heuristics 14(1), 23–67 (2008)

Author Index

Printing: AZ Druck und Datentechnik GmbH, Berlin
Binding: Stein+Lehmann, Berlin